Springer Proceedings in Business and Economics

More information about this series at http://www.springer.com/series/11960

Rachid Benlamri • Michael Sparer
Editors

Leadership, Innovation and Entrepreneurship as Driving Forces of the Global Economy

Proceedings of the 2016 International Conference on Leadership, Innovation and Entrepreneurship (ICLIE)

 Springer

Editors
Rachid Benlamri
Lakehead University
Thunder Bay, ON, Canada

Michael Sparer
Mailman School of Public Health
Columbia University
New York, NY, USA

ISSN 2198-7246   ISSN 2198-7254   (electronic)
Springer Proceedings in Business and Economics
ISBN 978-3-319-82823-7   ISBN 978-3-319-43434-6   (eBook)
DOI 10.1007/978-3-319-43434-6

Printed on acid-free paper

This Springer imprint is published by Springer Nature
The registered company is Springer International Publishing AG
The registered company address is: Gewerbestrasse 11, 6330 Cham, Switzerland

Message from the Editors

It is our pleasure to welcome all participants to the *International Conference on Leadership Innovation and Entrepreneurship (ICLIE'16)* held at Atlantis, The Palm Dubai, United Arab Emirates, on April 20–22, 2016. ICLIE'16 is organized by the Canadian University Dubai and sponsored by Huawei, Air Canada, and our publishing partner Springer.

As His Highness Sheikh Mohammed bin Rashid Al Maktoum, vice-president and prime minister of the UAE and ruler of Dubai, has said, "The competitiveness race demands a constant flow of new ideas, as well as innovative leadership using different methods and tools to direct the change."

The 3-day conference will bring together researchers, practitioners, and policy makers to debate on the emerging challenges and long-term solutions to some of the key technological, innovative, and sustainability challenges arising in the globalized economy. World-renowned scholars and leaders in the field will address the UAE youth, government and industry representatives, and more than 150 expected delegates from around the globe. We are also engaging the UAE youth across the country to participate in this conference and sponsoring the top 10 entrants from UAE high schools in order for them to showcase their innovative projects to an international audience and as a way to foster and nurture the domestic youth entrepreneurial spirit in line with the vision and initiatives of HH Sheikh Mohammed bin Rashid Establishment for Young Business Leaders (YBL).

We are honored to welcome His Excellency Tun Dr. Mahathir Mohamad, former prime minister of Malaysia, who will share his insights on the role of leadership as a driving force for the global economy. On the subject of innovation, we will hear from Mr. David Wang, CEO of Huawei UAE, who will discuss the role of innovation in building a better connected tomorrow. The enterprise agenda will be addressed by Professor Benoit Montreuil of Georgia Tech Institute, and Dr. Margaret Dalziel of the University of Waterloo will discuss the challenges of logistics in a globalized business environment and the direction of entrepreneurship policy.

The call for papers of ICLIE'16 attracted 170 paper submissions from 36 countries all over the world. To ensure a high conference standard, each paper was sent to three reviewers. After a rigorous process based on the recommendations of the

TPC members, only 88 papers were accepted, of which 72 are published. The selected papers illustrate the state-of-the-art current discussions and development trends in the areas covered by the five tracks of the conference.

We are grateful to the Canadian University Dubai for hosting this conference. Also, we would like to express our thanks to the program committee, external reviewers, and the organizing committee for their wonderful work. We are grateful to Huawei and Air Canada for their sponsorship. Finally, we would like to thank all the participants of ICLIE'16.

Thunder Bay, ON, Canada   Rachid Benlamri
New York, NY, USA   Michael Sparer
April 2016

Contents

Part V   Islamic Banking and Finance

Contributors

Gasim Abdelrahman Department of Industrial Engineering and Engineering Management, University of Sharjah, Sharjah, United Arab Emirates

Salah Abunar College of Business Administration, University of Business and Technology, Jeddah, Saudi Arabia

Muhammad Hassan Bin Afzal Electrical and Electronic Engineering Department, Primeasia University, Dhaka, Bangladesh

Faculty of Business Studies (FBS), University of Dhaka (DU), Dhaka, Bangladesh

Udit Agrawal Indian Institute of Technology Delhi, Hauz Khas, New Delhi, India

Kamsuriah Ahmad Faculty of Information Science and Technology, Universiti Kebangsaan Malaysia, Bangi, Selangor, Malaysia

Norita Ahmad American University of Sharjah, Sharjah, United Arab Emirates

Shoaib Ahmed College of Business Administration, University of Business and Technology, Jeddah, Saudi Arabia

Mohammad Adnan Alakhras School of Engineering and Network Technology, Canadian University of Dubai, Dubai, United Arab Emirates

Abeer AlAli Department of Industrial Engineering and Engineering Management, University of Sharjah, Sharjah, United Arab Emirates

Hadi Ramadan Al-Ali Canadian University of Dubai, Dubai, United Arab Emirates

Mahmood Ali College of Business Administration, University of Business and Technology, Jeddah, Saudi Arabia

Saifeddin Alimamy University of Otago, Dunedin, New Zealand

Fatima Al-Mazrouee American University of Sharjah, Sharjah, United Arab Emirates

Ghassan Alnajjar Information Technology Department, Al Khawarizmi International College, Al Ain, United Arab Emirates

Mohammed Alaa H. Altemimi Management Information System Department, Faculty of Information Science and Technology, Universiti Kebangsaan Malaysia, Bangi, Selangor, Malaysia

Ola AlZawati Department of Industrial Engineering and Engineering Management, University of Sharjah, Sharjah, United Arab Emirates

Hayaa M. Azzam Kayiaseh American University of Sharjah, Sharjah, United Arab Emirates

Ali Abdulbaqi Ameen Faculty of Information Science and Technology, Universiti Kebangsaan Malaysia, Bangi, Selangor, Malaysia

Stuart Anderson ARTeFACT Business Transformation INC., Oakville, ON, Canada

D.F. Antiado College of Arts and Sciences, University of Modern Sciences, Dubai, United Arab Emirates

Alain April Department of Software Engineering, Universite du Quebec, Ecole de Technologie Superieure, Montreal, QC, Canada

Keetanjaly Arivayagan University Putra Malaysia, Serdang, Selangor, Malaysia

Said Baadel Canadian University of Dubai, Dubai, United Arab Emirates

University of Huddersfield, Huddersfield, UK

Mana Mohammed Al Bannai Canadian University of Dubai, Dubai, United Arab Emirates

Sabrine El Baroudi Canadian University of Dubai, Dubai, United Arab Emirates

Hanene Belhaj Department of Economics and Finance, School of Business Administration, Canadian University in Dubai, Dubai, UAE

Shukurat Moronke Bello Department of Business Administration and Entrepreneurship, Bayero University Kano, Kano, Nigeria

Rehan Bhana School of Computing and Digital Technology, Birmingham City University, Birmingham, UK

Rima M. Bizri, Ph.D. Management and Marketing Studies Department, College of Business Administration, Rafik Hariri University, Meshref, Lebanon

Christophe N. Bredillet Université du Québec à Trois-Rivières, Troi-Rivières, QC, Canada

F.G. Castillo Human Resource Management Program, School of Business Administration, Canadian University Dubai, Dubai, United Arab Emirates

May Chidiac Faculty of Humanities, Department of Media studies, Notre Dame University—Louaize, Zouk Mosbeh, Lebanon

Tina Comes Department of Information and Communication Technology, CIEM, University of Agder, Grimstad, Norway

Angelika C. Dankert Hochschule Aschaffenburg, Aschaffenburg, Germany

Kenneth R. Deans La Rochelle Business School, La Rochelle, France

Hamoud Dekkiche Canadian University of Dubai, Dubai, United Arab Emirates

Mohamed Djerdjouri School of Business and Economics, State University of New York at Plattsburgh, Plattsburgh, NY, USA

A. Donastorg Faculty of Science and Engineering, University of Wolverhampton, Wolverhampton, UK

Ravikiran Dwivedula Associate Professor, American College of Dubai, Al Garhoud, Dubai, UAE

Adjunct Professor, Université du Québec à Trois-Rivières, Troi-Rivières, QC, Canada

Elgilani Eltahir Elshareif Canadian University of Dubai, Dubai, United Arab Emirates

Chris I. Enyinda Department of Marketing and International Business, School of Business Administration, Canadian University Dubai, Dubai, UAE

Benno Feldmann International Business Department, University of Applied Sciences Worms, Worms, Germany

Rita Francese Dipartimento di Matematica e Informatica, Università degli Studi di Salerno, Fisciano, Italy

Amjad Gawanmeh Department of Electrical and Computer Engineering, Concordia University, Montreal, QC, Canada

Department of Electrical and Computer Engineering, Khalifa University, Abu Dhabi, UAE

Richard C. Geibel Fresenius University of Applied Sciences, Cologne, Germany

Juergen Gnoth University of Otago, Dunedin, New Zealand

Marko Grünhagen Eastern Illinois University, Charleston, IL, USA

Ankur Gupta Model Institute of Engineering and Technology, Jammu, Jammu and Kashmir, India

Nishtha Gupta Indian Institute of Technology Delhi, Hauz Khas, New Delhi, India

Ikhlaas Gurrib Canadian University of Dubai, School of Graduate Studies, Dubai, United Arab Emirates

Mireille Chidiac El Hajj Faculty of Economics and Business Administration, Department of Management, The Lebanese University, Beirut, Lebanon

Diana J. Haladay Canadian University of Dubai, Dubai, United Arab Emirates

Ali H. Halawi Lebanese International University, Beirut, Lebanon

Siti Suhaila Abdul Hamid Kolej Yayasan Pendidikan Cheras, Kuala Lumpur, Malaysia

Jamil Hammoud Rafic Hariri University, Mechref, Lebanon

Anwar Ul Haq Department of Computing, QA Higher Education, Birmingham, UK

Farooq Haq Canadian University of Dubai, Dubai, United Arab Emirates

Rosilah Hassan Faculty of Information Science and Technology, Universiti Kebangsaan Malaysia (UKM), Bangi, Malaysia

Pia Hautamäki Haaga-Helia University of Applied Sciences, Helsinki, Finland

University of Vaasa, Vaasa, Finland

Christina Herzog Institut de Recherche en Informatique de Toulouse, Université Paul Sabatier—Toulouse III, Toulouse, France

Mohd Nor Ismail Multi-Media University, Cyberjaya, Malaysia

Dian Indrayani Jambari Faculty of Information Science and Technology, Universiti Kebangsaan Malaysia, Bangi, Selangor, Malaysia

Ahmed K. Al Jarouf Canadian University of Dubai, Dubai, United Arab Emirates

Zahra Ladha Jiwani Canadian University of Dubai, Dubai, United Arab Emirates

Stefane Kabene Canadian University of Dubai, Dubai, United Arab Emirates

Muhammed Kabir Canadian University of Dubai, Dubai, United Arab Emirates

University of New Brunswick, Saint John, NB, Canada

Hanim Kamaruddin Faculty of Law, Universiti Kebangsaan Malaysia (UKM), Bangi, Selangor, Malaysia

Sakshi Kaushal University Institute of Engineering and Technology, Panjab University, Chandigarh, India

A. Khaled Faculty of Science and Engineering, University of Wolverhampton, Wolverhampton, UK

Svetlana N. Khapova VU University Amsterdam, Amsterdam, The Netherlands

Jalal Kiswani Solid-Soft Company, Amman, Jordan

Timo Korhonen Telecore Inc., Aalto University, Helsinki, Finland

Kulwant Kumar Chitkara University, Chandigarh, Punjab, India

Raj Kumari University Institute of Engineering and Technology, Panjab University, Chandigarh, India

Dorra Larbi University of Picardie Jules Verne, Amiens, France

Tiet Khanh Le International Business Department, University of Applied Sciences Worms, Worms, Germany

Dennis Lee American University of Dubai, Dubai, United Arab Emirates

Laurent Lefèvre INRIA-Lyon, ENS-Lyon, Lyon, France

Xiaoqi Ma Nottingham Trent University, Nottingham, UK

Fariedah Maarof Canadian University of Dubai, Dubai, United Arab Emirates

Asim Majeed School of Computing and Digital Technology, Birmingham City University, Birmingham, UK

Mohd Yunus Majid Universiti Tenaga Nasional, Bangi, Malaysia

Ahmed M. Makki University of Modern Sciences, Dubai, United Arab Emirates

Meghana Manickam Department of Management Science and Engineering, Stanford University, Stanford, CA, USA

Mohammed Al Mansoori Canadian University of Dubai, Dubai, United Arab Emirates

Anita Medhekar Central Queensland University, North Rockhampton, QLD, Australia

Abdelghani Mehailia School of Business Administration, Canadian University of Dubai, Dubai, UAE

Lloyd Miller Department of Economics and Business Administration Science, Cag University, Adana/Mersin, Turkey

Osman Mohamad Multimedia University, Cyberjaya, Selangor, Malaysia

Zulkifli Mohamad Pusat Citra Universiti, Universiti Kebangsaan Malaysia (UKM), Bangi, Selangor, Malaysia

Anastasiia Moldavska NTNU in Gjøvik, Gjøvik, Norway

Richard Abou Moussa Faculty of Economics and Business Administration, Department of Management, The Lebanese University, Beirut, Lebanon

Louis Jos Moyalan Canadian University of Dubai, Dubai, United Arab Emirates

Murad Mohammed Mujahed Canadian University of Dubai, Dubai, United Arab Emirates

Ralf Müller BI Norwegian Business School, Oslo, Norway

Sharefa Murad Department of Computer Information system, Middle East University, Beirut, Lebanon

Suzan Nooraddin Canadian University of Dubai, Dubai, United Arab Emirates

Vimala Nunavath Department of Information and Communication Technology, CIEM, University of Agder, Grimstad, Norway

Sarah Odofin Faculty of Engineering and Environment, Northumbria University Newcastle, Newcastle-Upon-Tyne, UK

Olga Ogorodnyk NTNU in Gjøvik, Gjøvik, Norway

Abdullah Abu Omar Department of Electrical and Computer Engineering, Khalifa University, Abu Dhabi, UAE

Abdussalam Ismail Onagun University of Modern Sciences, Dubai, UAE

Jade Opulencia Canadian University of Dubai, Dubai, United Arab Emirates

Norasmah Othman Faculty of Education, Universiti Kebangsaan Malaysia (UKM), Bangi, Selangor, Malaysia

Andri Ottesen Management Department, Business School, Australian College of Kuwait in Collaboration with Central Queensland University, Kuwait City, Kuwait

Stig Ottosson NTNU in Gjøvik, Gjøvik, Norway

Ignazio Passero Dipartimento di Matematica e Informatica, Università degli Studi di Salerno, Fisciano, Italy

Evtim Peytchev Nottingham Trent University, Nottingham, UK

Jean-Marc Pierson Institut de Recherche en Informatique de Toulouse, Université Paul Sabatier—Toulouse III, Toulouse, France

Zaidatol Akmaliah Lope Pihie University Putra Malaysia, Serdang, Selangor, Malaysia

Marc Poulin Canadian University of Dubai, Dubai, United Arab Emirates

Andreas Prinz Department of Information and Communication Technology, CIEM, University of Agder, Grimstad, Norway

Abdallah Qusef King Hussein Faculty of Computing Sciences, Princess Sumaya University for Technology, Amman, Jordan

Muhammad Sabbir Rahman International Islamic University, Kuala Lumpur, Selangor, Malaysia

Mariela Ranova-Fredrick American University of Sharjah, Sharjah, United Arab Emirates

Zaid O. Al Rayes American University of Sharjah, Sharjah, United Arab Emirates

S. Renukappa Faculty of Science and Engineering, University of Wolverhampton, Wolverhampton, UK

Roopali University Institute of Engineering and Technology, Panjab University, Chandigarh, India

A. Saeed Faculty of Science and Engineering, University of Wolverhampton, Wolverhampton, UK

Abdulrahman Salih Nottingham Trent University, Nottingham, UK

Ali Salman Lecturer at University of South Asia, Lahore, Pakistan

Rasha Abou Samra Higher Colleges of Technology, British University in Dubai, Dubai, UAE

Sahil Sawhney Model Institute of Engineering and Technology, Jammu, Jammu and Kashmir, India

Chitkara University, Chandigarh, Punjab, India

Rommel Pilapil Sergio Canadian University of Dubai, Dubai, United Arab Emirates

Khaled Shaalan British University in Dubai, University of Edinburgh, Edinburgh, UK

Hanifa Shah School of Computing and Digital Technology, Birmingham City University, Birmingham, UK

M. Silverio Faculty of Science and Engineering, University of Wolverhampton, Wolverhampton, UK

Monika Singla Indian Institute of Technology Delhi, Hauz Khas, New Delhi, India

Nadine Sinno Chair of the Hospitality and Tourism Department, Lebanese International University, Beirut, Lebanon

Torbjørn Skogsrød NTNU in Gjøvik, Gjøvik, Norway

Maria José Sousa CIEO, Algarve University, Faro, Portugal

Universidade Europeia, Lisboa, Portugal

Ayodeji Sowale Faculty of Engineering and Environment, Northumbria University Newcastle, Newcastle-Upon-Tyne, UK

Sarmila Md Sum Faculty of Social Sciences and Humanities, Universiti Kebangsaan Malaysia (UKM), Bangi, Selangor, Malaysia

S. Suresh Faculty of Science and Engineering, University of Wolverhampton, Wolverhampton, UK

Rizwan Tahir Business and Management Division, RIT Dubai, Dubai, United Arab Emirates

M.I. Tawadrous College of Arts and Sciences, University of Modern Sciences, Dubai, United Arab Emirates

Andrew Terry University of Sydney, Sydney, NSW, Australia

Faidon Theofanides Marketing Department, Business School, Australian College of Kuwait in Collaboration with Central Queensland University, Kuwait City, Kuwait

Andy Till Department of Business Administration, QA Higher Education, Birmingham, UK

Genoveffa Tortora Dipartimento di Matematica e Informatica, Università degli Studi di Salerno, Fisciano, Italy

Elissar Toufaily American University of Dubai, Dubai, United Arab Emirates

R. Venkatachalam Canadian University Dubai, Dubai, UAE

Mike-Lloyd Williams Department of Business Administration, QA Higher Education, Birmingham, UK

Mohamad Shanudin Zakaria Faculty of Information Science and Technology, Universiti Kebangsaan Malaysia, Bangi, Selangor, Malaysia

Hafizah Omar Zaki Multimedia University, Cyberjaya, Selangor, Malaysia

Wan Mimi Diyana Wan Zaki Faculty of Engineering and Built Environment, Universiti Kebangsaan Malaysia (UKM), Bangi, Malaysia

Tatiana Zalan American University of Dubai, Dubai, United Arab Emirates

Wael S. Zaraket American University of Science and Technology, Beirut, Lebanon

Zainal Abu Zarim Multimedia University, Cyberjaya, Selangor, Malaysia

Part I
Technology, Innovation, and Sustainability

Chapter 1
Modelling Technology Transfer in Green IT with Multi-agent System

Christina Herzog, Jean-Marc Pierson, and Laurent Lefèvre

Abstract While there is a tremendous increase in academic research and collaboration between academia, the results of exchange between industry and science are steady. To understand this complex situation and to propose an improvement for technology transfer between academia and industry, it is necessary to investigate the different partners involved. We present a multi-agent system to model this technology transfer of green IT in order to see the impact on the development of sustainability in our society. We define a sustainability indicator and we study its changes according to the parameters defined in the technology transfer.

Keywords Multi-agent system • Green IT • Technology transfer

Introduction

For the last 5–10 years, research on energy saving is getting more important for industry as well as for academia. Several studies conducted by environmental and international organisations warn about the steady increase of energy consumption in various fields as data centres and cloud computing. In some cases, the operating costs exceed the investment costs, and new methods are needed to reduce costs and environmental impact. New materials are developed by equipment manufacturers to reduce these costs. Only a few basic techniques are available to software and middleware levels.

C. Herzog (✉) • J.-M. Pierson
Institut de Recherche en Informatique de Toulouse, Université Paul Sabatier—Toulouse III, Toulouse, France
e-mail: herzog@irit.fr; pierson@irit.fr

L. Lefèvre
INRIA-Lyon, ENS-Lyon, Lyon, France
e-mail: laurent.lefevre@ens-lyon.fr

© Springer International Publishing Switzerland 2017
R. Benlamri, M. Sparer (eds.), *Leadership, Innovation and Entrepreneurship as Driving Forces of the Global Economy*, Springer Proceedings in Business and Economics, DOI 10.1007/978-3-319-43434-6_1

In laboratories, some techniques were developed and have promising results in energy savings. Unfortunately, the transfer (or even the creation of awareness of the possibilities in the usage of new technology) of these techniques to industries is limited to project partners, innovative companies or large private research centres.

In order to understand the reasons for problems in this technology transfer, we discuss a model of technology transfer. We define links between actors and their conversion in a multi-agent system. In this system each actor has objectives while interacting with other actors. The generic model is specialised in the field of green computing. Depending on the evolution of the system, the value of a sustainability indicator varies. Finally, this model allows to test several scenarios related to technology transfer and the impact on the participating actors and on the sustainability of the system.

The main contributions of this article are:

- A model of technology transfer between defined actors, their interactions with joint projects
- A formal concept of sustainability and its evolution
- A study of the impact of transfer settings on the evolution of the actors and the sustainability

The article is organised in the following way: firstly, the identification of the problem; secondly, the selection of actors and their links; and thirdly, a definition of sustainability. We present in section "Implementation of the Multi-agent System" the implementation of the model in a multi-agent system using NetLogo. Next, we present some simulation results in section "Experiments"; and finally, we present the state of the art in section "Related Work" with concluding remarks and ideas for future work given in section "Conclusion and Outlook".

Actors of Technology Transfer

In Herzog (2015) we have reviewed the literature and provided a detailed analysis of responses to a survey sent to colleagues in the field of green IT. Of these colleagues, we studied their motivations and their links with each other in the context of a transfer from academia to industry and vice versa. Our study identified the main players in this transfer, motivations (that turn into goals) and their modes of action. In this article, we devote ourselves to five major (researchers, research centres, enterprises, technology transfer offices and funding agencies) leaving to others future work (standardisation bodies, pressure groups, governments, angel investors). We now present the evidence we have gathered based on our choices for our model to transform these actors' agent in the multi-agent system. These choices allow us to highlight the critical aspects of transfer and are not intended to be exhaustive. Also, we have chosen to focus only on players in green IT and on their activity.

Researchers

At the heart of technology transfer, researchers produce knowledge through publications that they seek to increase in number (this will be their goal). Publications are related to the researchers' connections which are created at conferences and/or collaborative projects and to the financial budget of the researchers' research centre. More connections lead to more opportunities for publication. Researchers can be either permanent or non-permanent. Both are supervised by permanent research members of the university (whose number is limited) and have a limited duration contract (limited by duration of the project unless the link persists beyond the project).

Research Centres

Research centres bring together researchers. Often attached to a university, they try to contribute to the reputation of the universities and generate funding through participation in collaborative projects (having multiple partners) or direct collaborations (with companies). Research centres will have these targets in our model. Their reputation is based on a moving average of the number of publications and contracts in recent years, while the budget comes from contracts (which represent the majority of researchers' resources). The centres can encourage either more or fewer researchers by funding their research (favouring publications) and can either hire new researchers if resources permit or fire if resources are scarce.

Companies

Companies look to increase their profits by taking a competitive difference (it will be their goal). Participation in a collaborative project increases leadership if the project is successful, but requires human and financial investment that can be lost in the case of failure. They hire new employees to participate in contracts. They initiate direct collaborations with research centres and participate in collaborative projects. They dedicate a portion of their sales to research and development.

Technology Transfer Offices

Technology transfer offices (SATT in France, PSB in Austria) are structures associated with research centres, intended to facilitate and accelerate technology transfer. Their goal is to increase their own turnover (and therefore that of their public shareholders). This turnover is fixed (a percentage or a fixed amount) in the contract signed between research centres and partners. In return they provide names and contact details of potential partners. Due to this database, research centres and businesses can create contracts more easily.

Funding Agencies

Funding agencies will have a role as initiator of projects involving regular funds from which the research centres can start (with success in the particular open call) a collaborative project. Funds are limited, resulting in a selection of projects.

The Concept of Sustainability

Sustainability is a concept defined by the conjunction of three factors: environmental, social and economic. An actor of a system improves its durability if at least one of these factors improves. In the field of green computing, a more recently developed material often consumes less electricity (and therefore less environmental and economic impact), but at the same time the production, transport and purchase of new equipment and the recycling of old equipment have a negative impact on the environment, as well as negative social and economic impacts.

Our choice was to calculate the sustainability of each player and how to quantify the sustainability of the system as the mean of their sustainability. Thus we see how and by how much the objectives of each player contribute to the sustainability of the system.

Calculating a Sustainability Indicator

The sustainability indicator (SPI, sustainability performance indicator) has three factors, weighted at 33 % each. Each factor is itself dependent on several subfactors. We detail here below these subfactors along with their *relative* weights to its parent factor (W noted below).

The ecological factor is reflected by four values:

- Awareness: awareness of green IT solution. It increases with the number of publications and contracts and decreases as time passes. W = 10 %
- Reduce: the reduction of energy consumption. W = 30 %
- Reuse: reuse of materials. W = 30 %
- Recycling: recycling of materials into new products. W = 30 %

The 3Rs ("reduce", "reuse", "recycle") increase with the number of contracts by probabilities p1, p2, p3, respectively, where $p1 + p2 + p3 = 1$, indicating that a contract made progress in one of 3Rs in average. They decrease with an increasing number of employees, as each new employee causes more computers.

The social factor is tied with five values that show the role of an actor in society:

- Green-employment: employees recruited to work on green IT contracts. $W = 30\%$
- Awareness-consumption: knowledge of the consumption of IT in society. It increases with the number of publications and contracts (with more publications than contracts in proportion 80/20, because the society is more impacted by publications) and decreases with time. $W = 15\%$
- Rethink: the ability of an actor to rethink its green IT strategy. It increases with the number of contacts and researchers because it encourages brainstorming. It decreases as the number of contracts increases because researchers are then occupied for specific projects, with less freedom of thought. $W = 20\%$
- Image: the image of an actor in society. It increases with the number of publications, contracts and communication strategy and decreases with time. $W = 25\%$
- Standardisation influence: the influence of a player on the standardisation of organisations. It follows the number of employees and turnover and decreases with time. $W = 10\%$

The economic factor is reflected by three values:

- Economic impact: the economic impact of green solutions. It tracks the number of successful contracts. $W = 20\%$
- Turnover: turnover, which increases and decreases through contracts with investment and research funding. $W = 50\%$
- Attraction: represents the attractiveness of an actor for investors. It increases with the image of the actor and its turnover and decreases with time. $W = 30\%$

This particular model of composition has the advantage of connecting more elements of the system to a goal of sustainability. The weights above are not completely arbitrary but estimated through our field survey, interviews with colleagues and literature review.

Implementation of the Multi-agent System

Selecting the Framework

We implemented a multi-agent system with NetLogo 5.0.4.[1] It simulates the evolution and interaction of agents in complex worlds. NetLogo was created in 1999 by U. Wilensky and is regularly updated (Wilensky & Rand, 2015). It is used in many scientific fields: social science, economics, psychology, urban traffic, commercial distribution, biology, chemistry, modelling complex behaviours in a population, etc.

---

[1] http://ccl.northwestern.edu/netlogo/

In NetLogo, agents are *turtles*, *links*, *patches* or *observers*. Each agent operates independently in steps. The turtles represent the players in our world, the links are their connections. Observers collect the information of each agent in the simulation (they are used for statistics). We did not use patches.

Representation of the Actors and Their Evolution

Each agent has its own set of attributes, which change with interactions and time. Here we give the attributes for a researcher.

1	researchers-own [
2	permanent
3	my_contract_number
4	tt]

A researcher may be permanent or not (line 2, true or false). If it is not permanent, it is associated with a contract (line 3) and the length of his contract is given (line 4). This period may be extended in case of successful collaboration. The researchers are members of a research centre. This will be represented by a link between these two actors (see section "Representation of Links and their Evolution").

The main goal for a researcher is to publish and therefore should have an attribute reflecting this. However, this attribute is shared by others, so it is common to all the turtles, like other attributes given below:

1	turtles-own [
2	action_period
3	contract
4	newcontract
5	publication
6	newpublication
7	itr_cooling
8	its_virtual
9	itr_cloud]

Each turtle is active in the system at regular intervals (line 2). For example, a funding agency is active only every 6 months, or a company does a collaboration every 3 months on average. This random value is unique to each actor. Contracts and publications are stored (from the beginning, lines 3 and 5, and only the last iteration, lines 4 and 6). Lines 7–9 represent the interests of the player for three technologies having potential energy reduction in server rooms (and each actor will be different according to its interests).

Research centres have as attributes the amount dedicated to green research, their budget, their research results (the accumulation of publications of its researchers over time) and reputation (sliding value over 3 years accumulating publications and contracts). If a technology transfer office is attached to this research facility (which is not required), it will appear as a link (see section "Representation of Links and their Evolution").

The companies have a turnover and a R&D budget and a number of employees in R&D. Finally, funding agencies were modelled simply by regularly launching funds to create random amounts of projects between two agents.

Developments of all these actors over time are controlled by algorithms invoked every time step. In our model, a time step is equal to 1 day.

We now give the simplified algorithm of the evolution of researchers as agents. At each time step, if it is not a permanent, its ttl (time-to-life) is reduced. If it reaches zero, this researcher is removed from the system. Then, for each of its *regular* neighbours (definition in section "Representation of Links and their Evolution") and if the research centre of this researcher has sufficient funds dedicated to research (1000 in this case), then there is a probability of publishing with a neighbour (on average every 3 months with a probability of 20% acceptation). In this case, the research centre funds (1000) the publication. Each researcher updates its interests (itr_cooling, itr_virtual, itr_cloud) based on its regular neighbours and its research centre partners ("it is influenced"). Ties with neighbours can disappear (on average every 6 months), but also appear (every 3 months): the survey we conducted has shown that new contacts are 50% randomly created with other researchers and businesses, but favouring the compatibility of interests, 25% by the social network (the neighbours of its neighbours), 25% with the help of technology transfer offices (especially with companies).

The algorithm for a research centre is next. First, it updates its interests (average of those of its researchers), research results and its reputation. And if the budget is critical, it finishes the contract of a non-permanent, and then it updates its budget by paying the non-permanent. Depending on its action period, there is some change: if the budget is comfortable, hiring a non-permanent (for 1 year, to a maximum of 4 times more non-permanents than permanents) and dedicating an incentive as percentage of the budget to research (*incentive* is a parameter that will change in the experiments). Finally, if a funding agency launches a call, it tries to initiate a collaborative project. These are projects that will create technology transfer based on their success. The creation algorithm of such a project is too long to be included here, but it can be summarised by the following: a research centre seeks to form a consortium (between 3 and 6 partners) according to its own links, to the links of its researchers and those of its eventual technology transfer office. The other centres as well as companies can be partners if all their permanent researchers are not already in projects. If the project is accepted (20%) while research centres and companies receive a share of the funding (a fraction of which is taken as operating costs), research centres hire non-permanents on the project duration (between 24 and 48 months); companies invest what they receive. Finally, links (*project*, see section "Representation of Links and their Evolution") are created between all partners.

For a company, the algorithm of evolution is quite similar to that of a research centre except that it tries to create a direct partnership with a single research centre (links *partnership*).

Representation of Links and Their Evolution

In NetLogo links are also agents. We have defined several types of links:

- *Regular*: contacts between researchers (research centres and companies)
- *Project*: the relationship between a research centre and the project consortium
- *Partnership*: the relationship between a company and a research centre
- *Belong-to* and *tto-link*: the relationship between a research centre and its researchers and technology transfer office.

The *project* or *partnership* links refer to the characteristics of the collaboration (original investment for companies, strength of collaboration linked to the compatibility between the ends of the link, number of contracts and turnover generated by the link, lifetime of the link, number of researchers in research centre and business sides and finally contract number). For the other links, only the lifetime will have meaning.

Like all agents, links evolve step by step. For non-permanent links, the lifetime is reduced by one each time step. When the lifetime is zero:

- If it is a project, it is finished and each partner finds again its researchers available, but above all, as a function of conversion (conversion is success or failure of a project), he gains a profit up to four times the initial cumulative investment.
- If it is a partnership, the principle is the same except that only one company and one research centre are affected, and moreover the partnership will be extended if it was positive (favouring the efficient partnerships).
- Other links will disappear.

Integration of SPI in the Evolution of the System

There are two possibilities with respect to the SPI indicator: either the system observes its evolution passively or it is activated based on this value. To compare the two situations, we integrate the SPI in the behaviour of the actors:

- When a scientist creates a new contact, he uses the SPI rather than compatibility. Other researchers and companies with a higher value SPI will be promoted.
- When a research centre creates a new project, it prefers partners with a higher SPI value.
- When a company creates a new partnership, it prefers partners with a higher SPI value and invests more in R&D if it has a smaller relative value.
- When a TTO is queried to find partners, it will encourage those with the highest SPI value.

Experiments

Methodology and Objectives of Experiments

The proposed multi-agent system is complex (about 2000 lines of code) and has a large number of parameters to be tested. We looked at the behaviour of the system by varying its main parameters. We give here the results of a representative subset, the others can be found in (1) (a total of 4000 simulations were performed): maximum amount given by funding agencies, conversion rate, incentive rates. We compare the results of the objectives of each player and the SPI value based on these parameters.

The system studied has ten research centres (of which four have a TTO), 50 researchers and 20 companies. Larger experiments were conducted but did not provide more lessons while significantly increasing the simulation time (from 10 min to several hours for each experiment). Also, the studied area (green IT) is limited and larger simulations lose their reality. Regular links are randomly chosen at the beginning, and the social network is built scale-free. Other networks have been tested (random, small-world) but the differences are not significant because the initial network is quickly transformed by the evolution of the system.

Each experiment simulates 7280 days (20 years). We present average values for 50 runs with the same parameters.

Experiments Without Influence of SPI

Impact of the Maximum Amount Financed

Figure 1.1 shows the impact of funding on the average reputation of research centres. More important are the funds and reputation increases, which is logical since when more projects are launched, more researchers are employed and more publications are generated.

On the same case, the impact on total wealth of all the companies is not increased after funding more than 2.5M. Because even if the funding increases, companies do not have enough personnel to participate in the potential projects and in the end it does not benefit from more funding (leaving proportionally more funding to research centres). On publications of permanent researchers, the results show that the impact for them is zero: in fact, once the maximum size of their social network is reached (ten in our experiments), having more projects does not allow them to publish more. You can see by the way that the positive results on the reputation of the centres are largely due to non-permanents hired on projects. Finally, the value of the average SPI for research centres and companies is only slightly influenced positively (1 %).

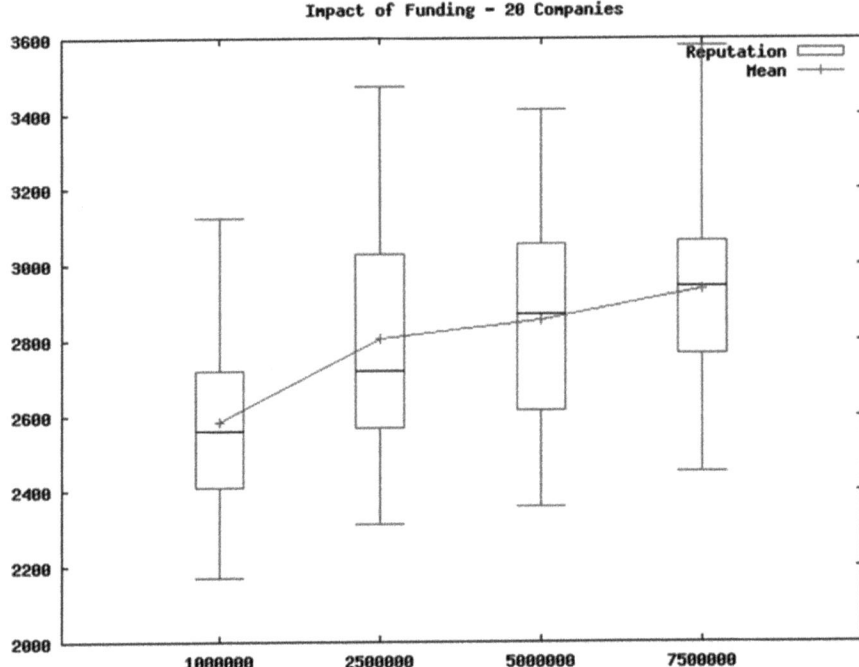

Fig. 1.1 Impact of funding on average reputation of research centres

Impact of the Conversion Rate

This section examines the impact of the conversion rate at the end of a project or partnership. Obviously, the higher it is, the more the profit is high and therefore the combined wealth of companies is high (Fig. 1.2).

This wealth in companies cause more collaborations, and thus research centres have more projects and are also wealthier, allowing them to hire non-permanents who allow to significantly increase the reputation and research results of these centres (+50 % between a rate of 10 and 90 %). For permanent researchers, there are no changes in terms of publication. Finally, the SPI sees its value increase by almost 40 %. Indeed, the calculation of the SPI is related to the number of researchers, either directly (*green-employment*) or indirectly (more people means more *standardisation influence*, more publications, etc.).

Impact of Incentive Rates

On average, every 6 months, research centres reallocate part of their budget to fund research (which has an impact on researchers' publications). This showed a positive effect with an increase of 5 % of the number of publications of permanent researchers between a rate of 10 % and a rate of 90 %. For research centres, this increase is not

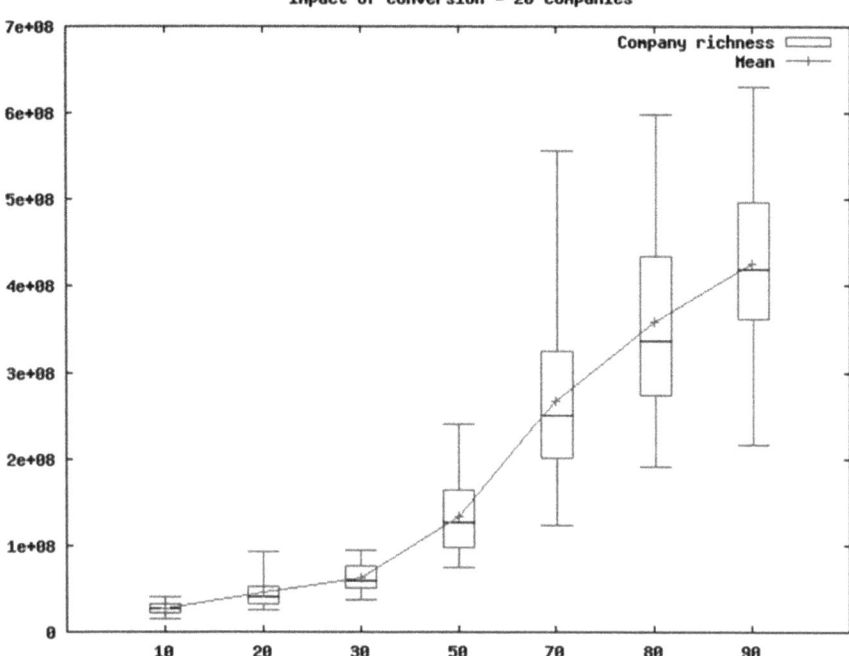

Fig. 1.2 Impact of conversion rate on companies' wealth

observed, and even there is a decrease: indeed, we calculated that these publications contribute around 40 % on research outcome generated in total. In parallel, research centres have fewer resources to hire non-permanents, which therefore generate fewer publications. This also has a negative impact on the SPI (−4 %) for the same reasons (but reversed) as the conversion rate.

Experiments with Influence of SPI

We now compare a situation where agents act, taking account of the value of SPI.

Impact of the Maximum Amount Financed

The first observation in Fig. 1.3 (normalised comparison) is that the situation without consideration of SPI is better than the new situation to corporate wealth when the amount of funding agencies is beyond 1M (up to 14 % more).

The second observation is that this wealth is more stable regardless of the amount of financing. This indicates that the introduction of this new behaviour has no negative effect and that companies are less sensitive to external financing.

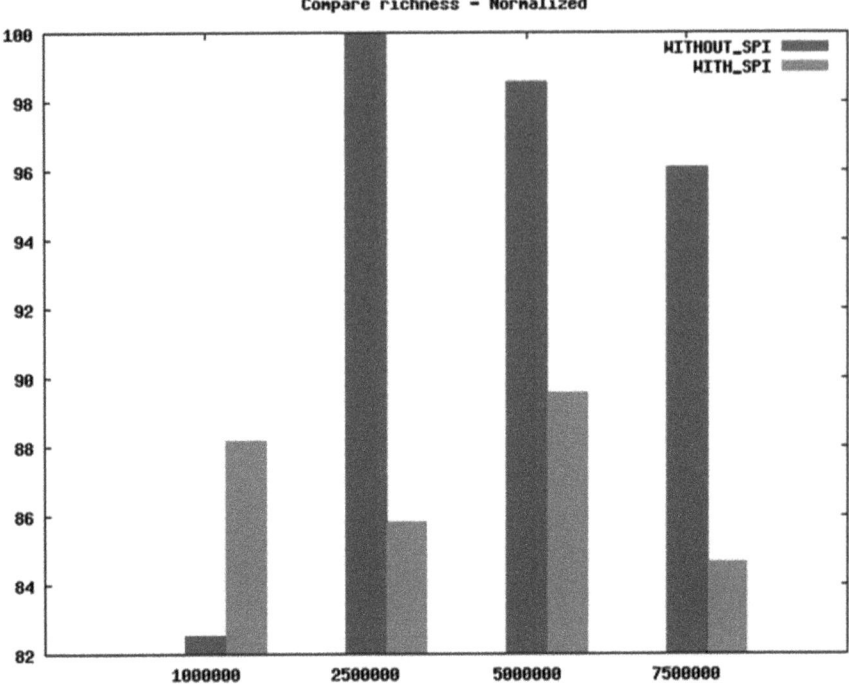

Fig. 1.3 Impact of funding on companies' wealth (*left*, without SPI; *right*, with SPI)

Similarly, publications (for researchers), the results of research and the reputation (for research centres) are not improved (−8 % for publications, −5 % for research results, −6 % for reputation). The difference between the two cases for SPI is only 2 %: the actors with low SPI at an early stage keep this low value (due to low activity), eventually degrading the average value, even if the others increase their value.

Impact of Conversion, Incentive

In almost all experiments, the goals achieved by the actors are very often below the case without SPI. We generally find that our agents do not change their behaviour enough to improve their SPI (and hence their sustainability) in the model. This will be the subject of future work: to change their behaviour or to change the calculation of the SPI.

Discussion

In this work, several simulation parameters were set a priori. Even if they were validated by previous sociological studies of selected players and correlated with a field survey, margin of error is considered in ongoing work.

Application model has been explained. Section "Simulation Model and Results Analysis" presents the simulation model and result analysis and finally section "Conclusion and Future Work" concludes the paper with future work.

Literature Search

This search presents overview of MCC and its architecture. It also focuses on review of work done in literature in areas of WBANs and different health monitoring systems.

Mobile Cloud Computing

The Fig. 2.1 shown below describes the architecture of MCC (Dinh et al., 2013). Mobile devices are connected to the mobile networks via base transceiver stations, access points, or satellites. The connectors (BTS, AP, or satellite) establish and control the connections and functional interfaces between the mobile networks and mobile devices. Request of the mobile users is broadcasted to the central servers. The servers check for authentication and authorization of the subscribers.

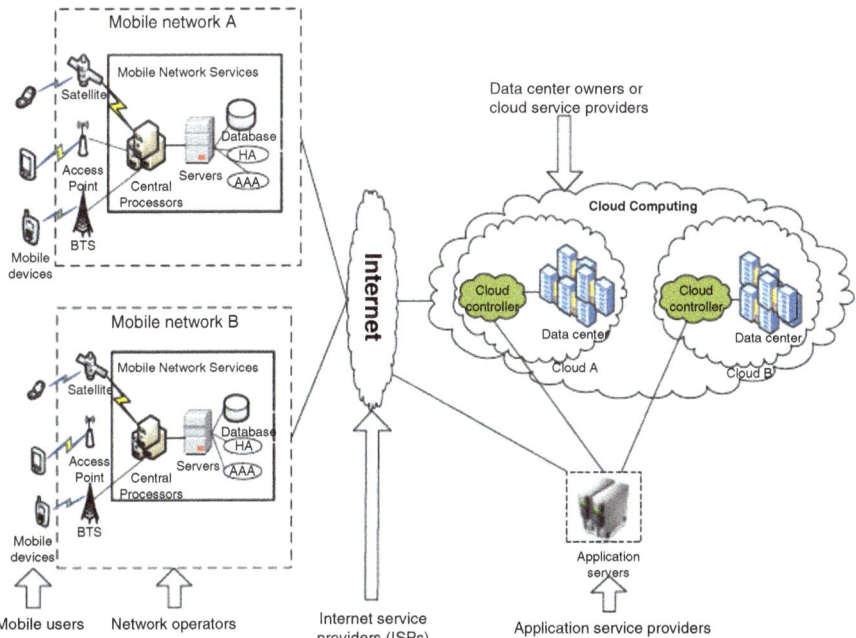

Fig. 2.1 Architecture of mobile cloud computing

After validating, the requests of the subscribers are delivered to cloud through the Internet. On the cloud, cloud controllers process the requests to provide mobile users with the corresponding cloud services.

MCC is an infrastructure where both the data storage and the data processing happen outside of the smart mobile device. Mobile cloud computing pursues the processing power and the data storage away from mobile phones into the cloud. This helps the smartphone users to utilize all the mobile applications without any hardware and storage constraints. MCC serves as bridge between the resource-intensive mobile devices and the resource-extensive cloud with several advantages such as enlarged battery lifetime, improved data storage capacity, enhanced processing power, upgraded reliability and availability, dynamic provisioning, and scalability (Dinh et al., 2013; Khan et al., 2014). The major applications of MCC are Mobile Commerce, Mobile Healthcare, M-learning, Mobile gaming, etc.

Related Work

A detailed survey of WBANs has been presented in literature (Zohreh et al., 2014). It also discusses the applications, inherent properties, topology, sensor nodes, and architecture of WBANs. This article provides insight into the basic architecture of WBANs. The relationship between the cloud and the WBANs is demonstrated (Lin et al., 2013). The performance of WBANs can be enhanced by using cloud computing. The data can be effectively offloaded to the cloud and easily accessed by the medical fraternity. Sensor-cloud infrastructure is described in Almashaqbeh et al. (2014). It explicates definition, architecture, and applications of the sensor networks and the cloud. A cloud computing-based energy-efficient mobile health-monitoring system, *namely*, HealthMon is proposed by Oberdan et al. (2010). The basic approach is to run some parts of the mobile application onto the cloud to save the battery lifetime of the smart mobile devices. Health monitoring based on the location of the patient is proposed in Khan et al. (2014). Data of non-hospitalized patients can be offloaded based on their physical location. Paper presents three different scenarios for home, hospital, and outdoor locations of the patients. The data on the cloud is accessed in accordance to the geographical location of the patient and the desired feedback is provided by the doctor. A CHMS model (Patino et al., 2013) is proposed for tracking the health status of non-hospitalized patients and provides high QoS and focus on connectivity between the data from the device to the cloud server. This paper presents the problem of traffic on the communication channel which can be solved by the dynamic frequency channel allocation to the users. Cavallari, Martelli, Rosini, Buratti, and Verdone (2014) emphasized on an issue that data is increasing at a huge amount in the communication channels, so the network operators need to offload the data to the cloud for better resource utilization of the communication link between the mobile devices and the remote end (cloud). Traffic on the cellular and WiFi channels needs to be controlled for effective utilization of resources. Through extensive literature review, it has been found that the eHealth Monitoring systems have issues like data transmission speed, delay, etc. In this paper, we have focused on remote health monitoring systems by transmitting data with and without aggregation on cloud.

Health Care Application Model

This section presents Health Care Application model. Health Care Application model is the outcome of distance health monitoring with the usage of sensor nodes and cloud computing. In this paper, we have proposed a HCA model to provide flexible, cost-effective, centralized, and real-time distance health monitoring system. eHealthCare is provided by HCA model that is composed of many sensor nodes. Each sensor node is attached to a single patient. It monitors the patient and collects the various physiological parameters. Figure 2.2 (Akrishnaan & Shridharan, 2014) shows the general architecture of HCA model, which has four basic modules sensor nodes, base transceiver station, real-time cloud, and the medical staff that works hand in hand. Sensor Nodes are the building blocks of the model (Oberdan et al., 2010; Zulqarnain et al., 2011). Sensor nodes monitor the patient and collect the vital biological signs. They are either connected to the communication network directly or are connected to the smart mobile device of the patient. HCA model connects the sensor nodes to the smart mobile device via communication technology such as Bluetooth, WiFi, or 2G. The smart mobile device processes the data with the help of a smart mobile application that calculates the desired physiological parameters. Mobile application on SMD classifies the data as critical and non-critical. The major HCA operation is the aggregation of non-critical data so that the overall transmission time and congestion over the network can be reduced. Critical and

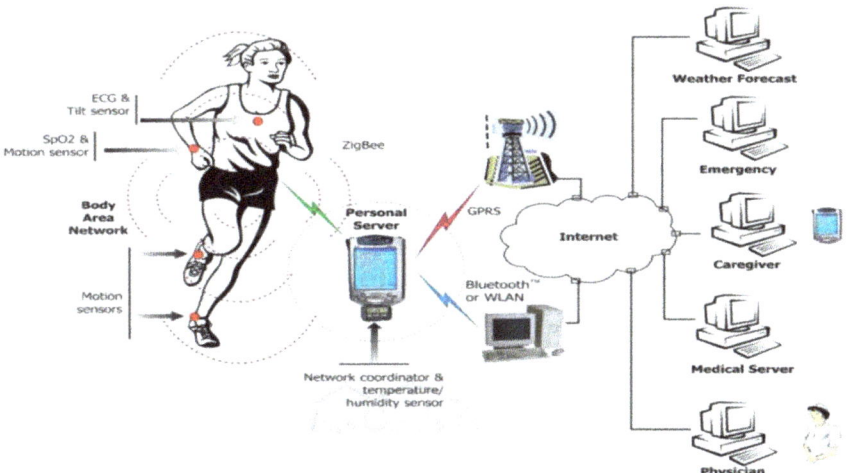

Fig. 2.2 Architecture of WBANs

super-critical data is transmitted without any delay. After the classification, data is transmitted to the simulated server. HCA model has used real-time cloud for data storage and processing. The data from the server is offloaded to the cloud. The healthcare database is maintained on the cloud. It records the patient data regarding the physiological parameters, patient profile, and patient history. Cloud provides efficient data accessing and processing. Medical Staff is the end user of the HCA model that accesses the patient data stored in the database on the cloud. This provides real-time feedback from the doctor. The medical fraternity can raise alarms for the patients or inform the family in case of emergency to avoid serious consequences.

Proposed Work

The HCA model is proposed to perform smart aggregation of the data received from the sensor nodes and then the data is offloaded to the cloud for further accessing. The patient data collected by the sensor nodes is transmitted to the smart mobile device of the patient. The smart mobile device computes the information regarding vital physiological parameters. We are considering ECG as a physiological parameter to be calculated. It is computed using a QRS Detect Algorithm. A smart mobile device application that uses QRS Detect Algorithm computes ECG. The data is then communicated to a simulated server. Upon receiving the data, smart mobile application classifies the data into normal, critical, and super-critical classes (Gholipour, 2015).

Table 2.1 shows the classification of data. HCA model aggregates the normal data. Normal data means non-critical data which does not require urgent attention from the medical fraternity. Critical or super critical data is not aggregated as it requires quick response from the doctor and is offloaded to the cloud with minimum delay. However, normal data is aggregated till it reaches to the threshold level of data size of application (assumed to be 50 sensor nodes). Thus, aggregation reduces and consumes less transmission time and reduces end-to-end delay.

The working of HCA model is based on three major functionalities, *namely*, data collection from sensor nodes which is the client end, data aggregation which is the intermediate performance of the model, and data offloading to the remote end for further accessibility. All the modules of the HCA model are explained below.

Table 2.1 Classification of heart beat rate

Heart beat rate (HBR)	Class
HBR >= 125 ‖ HBR < 50	Supercritical
HBR > 100 && HBR < 125 ‖ HBR >=50 && HBR < 60	Critical
HBR >= 60 ‖ HBR <= 100	Normal

A. Data Collection: The primary task of sensor nodes is to collect data from the human body. Sensor nodes generate a digital signal in correspondence to the collected data. The following algorithm explains the working of the sensor nodes and the smart mobile application.

Algorithm: GenSignal is a signal generation and data collection algorithm.

1. The sensor nodes sense the ECG signal from the human body.
2. The sensor nodes collect the information on the sampling rates of 256 or 512 bytes per second.
3. It rearranges and transmits the ECG signal to the smart phone device.
4. The smart phone loads the ECG signal.
5. The pre-embedded QRS detection algorithm in the smart-phones finds the QRS-peaks in the ECG signal.
6. The smart phone computes the heartbeat rate by calculating the number of QRS-peaks detected earlier.
7. The smart phone device then transmits the signal to the cloud healthcare network.

B. Aggregation: The major task of HCA is aggregation of the patient data before it is offloaded to the cloud. Aggregation is performed by the smart mobile application on SMD. The normal data of all the patients in a network is aggregated as per the threshold level of application data size. This reduces congestion on the network and makes transmission quicker. The critical and super-critical data is sent without delay. The following algorithm explains the working of the aggregator.

Algorithm: ToAggregate is an algorithm exists in SMA which deals with the data classification and aggregation.

1. The Smart mobile application receives the ECG signal from the smart phone.
2. The SMA evaluates the criticality level of the patient's heartbeat
3. All records classified as the super-critical and critical patient information are propagated to the server individually with higher priority for delivery.
4. All normal records are aggregated together and propagated to cloud-based healthcare network in the aggregated form.

C. Data Offloading: In HCA model, data is offloaded to a real-time cloud. The aggregated data is offloaded, whereas critical or super-critical data is offloaded as soon as possible with a minimum delay. The algorithm given below explains the data offloading procedure.

Algorithm: cloudHosting is an algorithm that shows how the offloaded data are stored on the real-time cloud database.

1. The aggregated data is forwarded to the cloud-based healthcare record management service.
2. The cloud healthcare server explodes the received array.
3. The server counts the records in the received information.
4. All of the records are saved in the database.

5. The critical alarm is raised according to the heart beat rate rules.
6. The concerned persons are informed about the critical status.

Simulation Model and Results Analysis

For simulation study, we have considered the three parameters, i.e., total transmission time, end-to-end delay, and aggregation time, on 2G and WiFi networks during peak hours and moderate hours as discussed below.

(a) Total Transmission Time: The foremost parameter used to test the efficiency of HCA is total transmission time. Total transmission time for HCA is calculated on two networks, *namely*, 2G and WiFi, during moderate and peak hours. Total transmission time is defined as the total time taken for offloading the ECG data onto the cloud, i.e., the time taken for data transmission from the generation of data on the sensor node to data offloading on the cloud. It is calculated as:

$$T_{time} = \sum_{k=1}^{n} t(k) + T_{aggregation} \qquad (2.1)$$

where n is the number of total sensor nodes

$T_{aggregation}$ is calculated from (2.4) as shown below.

(b) End-to-End Delay: Another prominent parameter to test the efficiency of the proposed system is end-to-end delay. The HCA calculates the end-to-end delay for 12, 25, and 50 number of sensor nodes on different networks such as 2G and WiFi during peak and moderate hours. Generally, it is defined as time taken to deliver a single packet data from the source to the destination. In this research, it is referred to as the difference between total time taken for delivering all the data packets from source to the destination and minimum time taken to deliver a packet from source to destination. The end-to-end delay must have minimum value to ensure early arrival of the packet at the destination.

$$T_{delay} = T_{time} - T_{min} \qquad (2.2)$$

where T_{min} is minimum time taken to deliver a packet from source to destination

$$T_{min} = f(Ttime, minimum) \qquad (2.3)$$

where T_{time} is actual time taken to deliver a packet from source to destination

(c) Aggregation Time: The third prominent parameter to test the efficiency of HCA is aggregation time which calculates the total time taken for aggregating the normal data in the network.

$$T_{aggregation} = \sum_{k=1}^{n} T(n) \qquad (2.4)$$

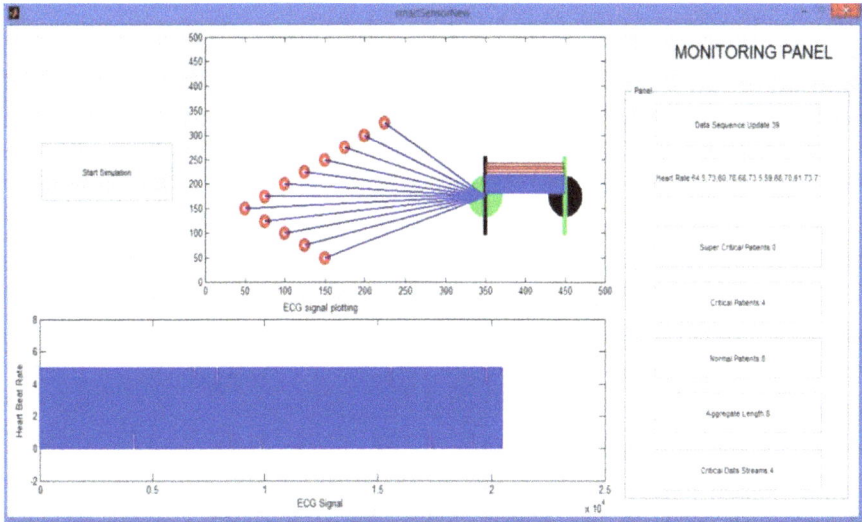

Fig. 2.3 Topology of HCA

where n is normal data

The HCA model is simulated using MATLAB and real-time cloud hosting on the server end. The patient data is saved on the cloud from where it is easily accessible by the medical staff. Real-time Cloud hosting is used in HCA model to create the patient database on the cloud. We have specified the URL address of the cloud where the data is to be sent. At that address, all the information regarding patient data is stored to be easily accessed by the doctor in future.

Implemented HCA model is dynamic and network-dependent. It is performed with 12 sensor nodes on both cellular and WiFi network and experiments are repeated 40 times so that maximum accuracy can be achieved. The number of normal, critical, and super-critical patients changes with each offloading iteration. The Fig. 2.3 shows the topology for HCA. The red, green, and black nodes are simulated as sensor nodes, SMA on mobile device and cloud, respectively. The blue lines show the connectivity between the components of the HCA model. The sensor nodes propagate the data and are processed by smart mobile application to the simulated server and simulated server offloads the data to the cloud. Smart mobile application aggregates the normal data and transmits the critical and super-critical data without aggregation.

HCA model is tested for effectiveness in terms of three parameters, which are total transmission time, end-to-end delay, and aggregation time. The performance of the HCA model is tested with 12, 25, and 50 sensor nodes in a WBAN and for total of 40 offloading iterations. The results shown by HCA (with aggregation) and existing health monitoring systems (without aggregation) are compared. The performance of the HCA and the existing health management systems is recorded and compared in four scenarios. The first is on 2G network during moderate hours,

Table 2.2 Total transmission time on 2G during moderate hours

	Without aggregation			With aggregation		
Sensor nodes	12	25	50	12	25	50
Total transmission time (seconds)	52.5342	62.0837	70.1882	21.5498	23.0691	30.6414

Table 2.3 Total transmission time on WiFi during moderate hours

	Without aggregation			With aggregation		
Sensor nodes	12	25	50	12	25	50
Total transmission time (seconds)	33.1627	40.9697	53.7481	12.313	16.5422	24.0082

Table 2.4 Total transmission time on WiFi duing peak hours

	Without aggregation			With aggregation		
Sensor nodes	12	25	50	12	25	50
Total transmission time (seconds)	38.0787	44.8449	61.77	14.5034	9.3238	27.755

Table 2.5 Total transmission time on 2G during peak hours

	Without aggregation			With aggregation		
Sensor nodes	12	25	50	12	25	50
Total transmission time (seconds)	60.877	68.157	78.098	34.583	43.042	63.1905

second on WiFi network during moderate hours, third on 2G network during peak hours, and fourth is on WiFi network during peak hours. The performance of HCA and existing health management systems is recorded and compared on these scenarios. The following tables show the result for the total transmission time, end-to-end delay, and aggregation time. They compare the values calculated while using HCA (with aggregation) and existing health management systems (without aggregation). The results are shown for 12, 25, and 50 number of sensor nodes in the network.

Tables 2.2, 2.3, 2.4, and 2.5 represent the total transmission time when data is offloaded to cloud. It can be seen that the total transmission time is reduced with data aggregation as compared to data transmission without aggregation by 58.9%, 62.8%, and 56.3% with 12, 25, and 50 sensor nodes, respectively, on 2G network during moderate hours. The total transmission time is reduced with data aggregation as compared to data transmission without aggregation reduced by 62.8%, 59.6%, and 55.3% with 12, 25, and 50 sensor nodes, respectively, on WiFi network during moderate hours. The total transmission time is reduced with data aggregation as compared to data transmission without aggregation reduced by 43.1%, 36.8%, and 19.1% with 12, 25, and 50 sensor nodes, respectively, on 2G network during peak hours. The total transmission time is reduced with data aggregation as compared to data transmission without aggregation reduced by 61.9%, 56.9%, and 55.0% with 12, 25, and 50 sensor nodes, respectively, on WiFi network during peak hours. The results show that the data consumes less transmission time with aggregation of normal data.

Table 2.6 End-to-end delay on 2G during moderate hours

	Without aggregation			With aggregation		
Sensor nodes	12	25	50	12	25	50
End-to-end delay (seconds)	0.914	1.119	1.341	0.1	0.108	0.11

Table 2.7 End-to-end delay on WiFi during moderate hours

	Without aggregation			With aggregation		
Sensor nodes	12	25	50	12	25	50
End-to-end delay (seconds)	0.657	0.737	1.056	0.048	0.153	0.367

Table 2.8 End-to-end delay on 2G during peak hours

	Without aggregation			With aggregation		
Sensor nodes	12	25	50	12	25	50
End-to-end delay (in seconds)	1.087	1.298	1.467	0.284	0.739	1.225

Table 2.9 End-to-end delay on WiFi during peak hours

	Without aggregation			With aggregation		
Sensor nodes	12	25	50	12	25	50
End-to-end delay (seconds)	0.695	0.851	1.278	0.104	0.162	0.387

Tables 2.6, 2.7, 2.8, and 2.9 show the end-to-end delay when data is offloaded to cloud. It can be seen that the end-to-end delay is reduced with data aggregation as compared to data transmission without aggregation reduced by 91.17%, 90.03%, and 89.05% with 12, 25, and 50 sensor nodes, respectively, on 2G network during moderate hours. The end-to-end delay is reduced with data aggregation as compared to data transmission without aggregation reduced by 92.60%, 79.24%, and 65.24% with 12, 25, and 50 sensor nodes, respectively, on WiFi network during moderate hours. The end-to-end delay is reduced with data aggregation as compared to data transmission without aggregation reduced by 85.03%, 80.96% and 69.71% with 12, 25, and 50 sensor nodes, respectively, on 2G network during peak hours. The end-to-end delay is reduced with data aggregation as compared to data transmission without aggregation reduced by 73.87%, 43.06%, and 16.40% with 12, 25, and 50 sensor nodes, respectively, on WiFi network during peak hours. The results show that the patient data has reduced end-to-end delay with aggregation of normal data.

Tables 2.10 and 2.11 compare the aggregation time and show that the HCA application takes same time to aggregate data when number of normal patients is same irrespective of the network, i.e., 2G or WiFi, because we are not considering any network characteristics like congestion, etc.

The above results show that the HCA model consumes less transmission time and end-to-end delay with data aggregation and hence could be helpful in eHealth monitoring systems.

Table 2.10 Aggregation time on 2G

	2G during moderate hours			2G during peak hours		
Sensor nodes	12	25	50	12	25	50
Aggregation time (seconds)	0.011	0.029	0.093	0.011	0.032	0.1

Table 2.11 Aggregation time on WiFi

	WiFi during moderate hours			WiFi during peak hours		
Sensor nodes	12	25	50	12	25	50
Aggregation time (seconds)	0.011	0.032	0.091	0.011	0.029	0.091

Conclusion and Future Work

The proposed HCA model enhances the distant health monitoring systems by classifying the collected ECG data of the patient as urgent or non-urgent and performing aggregation of the non-urgent data. Data aggregation reduces data transmission time and end-to-end delay. The HCA model also creates the patient database on the real-time cloud. The patient data is easily accessible to the medical fraternity that provides the real-time feedback. The results shown have proved the efficiency of the HCA model in terms of aggregation efficiency, end-to-end delay, and total transmission time.

Towards future, HCA model can be enhanced to add security of the patient data stored on the cloud and improving Quality of Service. Aggregation efficiency can be improved by taking into account the overhead of performing aggregation on the normal data as compared to existing aggregation models in WBANs.

References

Akrishnaan, K. S., & Shridharan, D. (2014, September). A review of reliable and secure communication in wireless body area networks. In *Proceedings of 13th IRF International Conference on* (pp. 32–44).

Almashaqbeh, G., Hayajneh, T., & Vasilakos, A. V. (2014, December). A cloud-based interference-aware remote health monitoring system for non-hospitalized patients. In *Global Communications Conference (GLOBECOM), 2014 IEEE* (pp. 2436–2441). IEEE.

Carlos Oberdan, R., Koch, F. L., Westphall, C. B., Werner, J., Fracalossi, A., & Salvador, G. S. (2010). A cloud computing solution for patient's data collection in health care institutions. In *Second International Conference on eHealth, Telemedicine, and Social Medicine, 2010, ETELEMED'10* (pp. 95–99). IEEE.

Cavallari, R., Martelli, F., Rosini, R., Buratti, C., & Verdone, R. (2014). A survey on wireless body area networks: Technologies and design challenges. *IEEE Communications Surveys & Tutorials, 16*(3), 1635–1657.

Dinh, H. T., Lee, C., Niyato, D., & Wang, P. (2013). A survey of mobile cloud computing: Architecture, applications, and approaches. *Wireless Communications and Mobile Computing, 13*(18), 1587–1611.

Gholipour, B. (2015). *Livescience*. Retrieved August 12, 2015, from http://www.livescience.com/42081-normal-heart-rate.html

Huasong, C., Leung, V., Chow, C., & Chan, H. (2009). Enabling technologies for wireless body area networks: A survey and outlook. *IEEE Communications Magazine, 47*(12), 84–93.

Khan, A. R., Othman, M., Madani, S. A., & Khan, S. U. (2014). A survey of mobile cloud computing application models. *IEEE Communications Surveys & Tutorials, 16*(1), 393–413.

Khan, N. A., Javaid, N., Khan, Z. A., Jaffar, M., Rafiq, U., & Bibi, A. (2012). Ubiquitous healthcare in wireless body area networks. In *2012 IEEE 11th International Conference on Trust, Security and Privacy in Computing and Communications (TrustCom)* (pp. 1960–1967). IEEE.

Lin, G., Iosifidis, G., Huang, J., & Tassiulas, L. (2013). Economics of mobile data offloading. In *2013 IEEE Conference on Computer Communications Workshops (INFOCOM WKSHPS)* (pp. 351–356). IEEE.

Miguel Angel Patino, G., Higashino, T., & Okada, M. (2013). Radio access considerations for data offloading with multipath tcp in cellular/WiFi networks. In *2013 International Conference on Information Networking (ICOIN)* (pp. 680–685). IEEE.

Van Daele, P., Moerman, I., & Demeester, Peter. (2014). Wireless body area networks: Status and opportunities. In *General Assembly and Scientific Symposium (URSI GASS), 2014 XXXIth URSI* (pp. 1–4). IEEE.

Zohreh, S., Abolfazli, S., Gani, A., & Buyya, R. (2014). Heterogeneity in mobile cloud computing: Taxonomy and open challenges. *IEEE Communications Surveys & Tutorials, 16*(1), 369–392.

Zulqarnain, R., Farooq, U., Jang, J. K., & Park, S. H. (2011). Cloud computing aware ubiquitous health care system. In *E-Health and Bioengineering Conference (EHB), 2011* (pp. 1–4). IEEE.

Chapter 3
Living Labs (LILA): An Innovative Paradigm for Community Development—Project of "XploR" Cane for the Blind

Asim Majeed, Rehan Bhana, Anwar Ul Haq, Hanifa Shah, Mike-Lloyd Williams, and Andy Till

Abstract The community development in different domains (business, education, welfare, etc.) has been the prime focus over the last decade due to the evolution of digital technologies and the shift in working patterns. However, many public and private investments have failed to produce sustaining and real value from them. The observed deficiencies which are causing the failure of community development projects ranged from initiation within the artificial and closed laboratory to open learning environments. The community development is entailed without understanding the real community needs, community's value chain, and potential problems with limited interactions. These shortcomings have resulted in failure to develop effective, prosperous, and world class communities, leveraging the new innovative and powerful approaches. An approach to developing collaborative systems, called Living Lab (LILA), is discussed in this paper and this approach has empowered and engaged the communities (students, lecturers, computer scientists, electronics engineers, visually impaired and blind people) to experiment and learn the innovative solutions of their real-world problems. The theme of this innovation-led approach is to embed community-driven solution within the communities.

This paper presents the actual framework for the establishment of a Living Lab using specific case study at Birmingham City University (BCU), along with its impact on community development. This research determines the key features that the visually impaired would find useful in a mobility cane called "XploR". The smart cane incorporates facial recognition technology to alert the user when

A. Majeed (✉) • R. Bhana • H. Shah
School of Computing and Digital Technology, Birmingham City University, Birmingham, UK
e-mail: Asim.Majeed@bcu.ac.uk; Rehan.Bhana@bcu.ac.uk; Hanifa.Shah@bcu.ac.uk

A.U. Haq
Department of Computing, QA Higher Education, Birmingham, UK
e-mail: Anwar.Haq@qa.com

M.-L. Williams • A. Till
Department of Business Administration, QA Higher Education, Birmingham, UK
e-mail: Mike-Lloyd.Williams@qa.com; Andy.Till@qa.com

© Springer International Publishing Switzerland 2017
R. Benlamri, M. Sparer (eds.), *Leadership, Innovation and Entrepreneurship as Driving Forces of the Global Economy*, Springer Proceedings in Business and Economics, DOI 10.1007/978-3-319-43434-6_3

they are approaching a relative or friend from up to 10 m away. This is a revolutionary 'smart' cane enabling blind people to instantly identify friends and family. The cane also features GPS functionality to aid navigation. This project is part of LILA, a European initiative encouraging entrepreneurship and fostering internationalisation.

Keywords Innovation • Living labs • Visually impaired • Facial recognition • Assistive technology

Introduction

The open real environment staged for experimenting, collaborating, and knowledge sharing is called Living Labs. The future directions of product developments are revealed through user experiences in Living Labs. The open-innovation model is drawn in many aspects and it gathers the interests of various action-based research active industries (Allee, 2008). The original concept of Living Lab became apparent when real-world projects were undertaken by the university students and the intention was to resolve those as part of their studies. The real purpose of concept LILA is to bring up the technological issues at home to the real-life context with the intention of prototyping, refining, and validating their solutions (Jackson, 2008). The international interests rose about integrating LILA approach within the community since 2006 when European Commission promoted a project of European innovative system requiring coordination and advancement. The users from the community would be involved by LILA in the process of co-creation of applications, services, and developments of new products (Kokkinakos et al., 2012). The LILA approach believes in furnishing a service or designing a product; the average user from the community is equipped well to do that. Therefore, LILA supports innovations creation and their validations within the real world of collaborative environments through Research and Development methodology.

The themed structure of LILA is to support innovations in all phases of the life-cycle and is based on diverse resources, actors, and activities. According to Welfens, Liedtke, and Nordmann (2010), LILA is a virtual reality or physical region partnerships of public–private people, which are formed by the stakeholders, universities, agencies, firms, and agencies collaborating with each other throughout the development lifecycle. The development lifecycle by LILA encompasses creation, prototyping, formation, validation of new products, services, and technologies within the context of real life environments, which helps in upscaling and commercialising the innovations rapidly within the global market (Schaffers, Guzman, Navarro, & Merz, 2010). This development approach also determines LILA as an open-innovation network, offering an innovative platform and research think-tank for various establishments associating the user-driven practices of innovations.

The user-led innovations are highly accredited by the organisations due to having a high commercial value minimising the risks involved when launching a service,

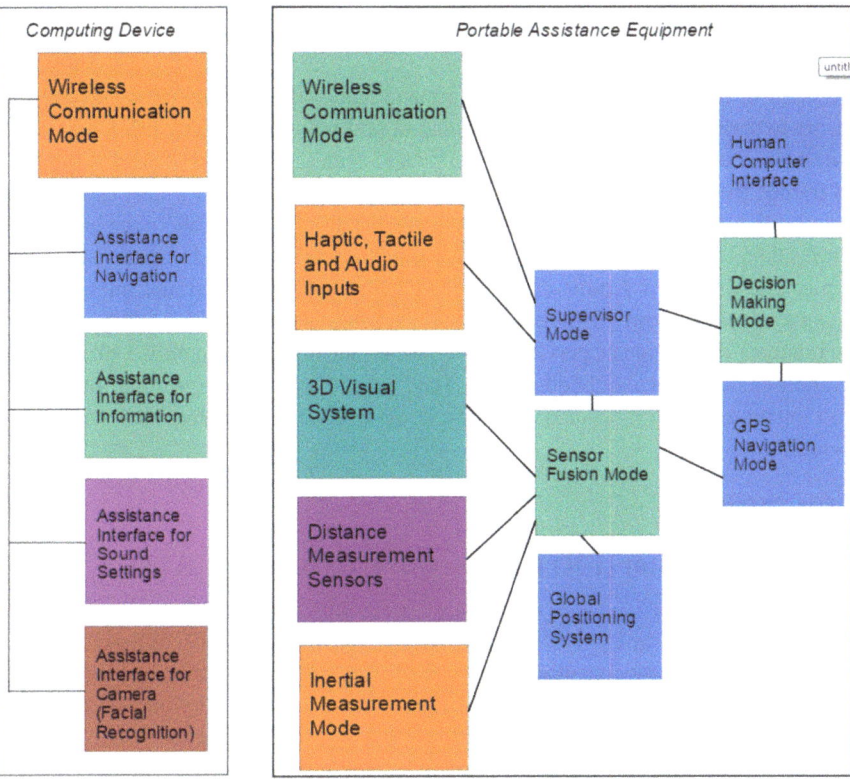

Fig. 3.2 Block diagram of the proposed system. *Adapted from*: Assistive technologies for visually impaired people (Liu et al., 2007)

information must be stored and correlated to the database of the environment. The obstacles can be detected by using Ultrasonic systems for measuring the distance. The GPS tracking uses movement sensors to locate the orientation of the person and trajectory tracking (Haraszy, Micut, Tiponut, & Slavic, 2011).

The absolute position of the visually impaired person can be obtained through a GPS system, but with errors of few meters due to slow sampling rate (Kramp et al., 2010). The GPS navigation embedded within "XploR" can be useful for outdoor journeys. The integration of quantisation noise and measurement helps to identify the location error to the inertial positioning system, which is encompassed by gyroscopes and accelerometers. To obtain superior results, magnetic compasses are used along with gyroscopes and accelerometers (Allee, 2008). The detection of obstacles and locations of people can be obtained through mobile robots integrated within the navigation. In the proposed model, various types of sensors are used to measure the location, and consequently, it requires complex computation processes (Lee et al., 2012). The sensor fusion module is responsible for communicating with the various types of sensors. In "XploR", the resolution of these problems is looked at carefully while embedding a Kalman Filter within the device (Tiponuţ et al.,2009).

Proposed System Design

The theme of this research work is to design and build a device, which uses ultrasonic sensors to sense the surrounding environment and incorporating a GPS navigation as well as a built-in camera to take pictures and scan them for the details of family and friends from information stored in the database. As soon as it finds obstacles, it sends feedback to the blind person wearing this device. The "XploR" cane has more features than the existing model of cane available for the blind and visually impaired people. The design of XploR differentiates itself from the traditional ones, which scans the obstacle from 10-m distance and alerts the user with four different types of vibrations. The design of previous devices scans the objects from only 4-m distance and there is no camera embedded in it. The "XploR" cane is embedding a camera, vibration motor, sensors to scan the obstacle, 10-m distance, and four different types of vibrations.

Facial Recognition (FR) and Assistive Technology (AT)

The Living Labs for this project have experimented with four different versions of facial recognition software called OpenCV and these are presented in the workshops. All previous versions have been classed and the prototype version 4B includes features such as built-in camera, facial recognition, GPS navigation, and Haptic touch. "XploR" cane has been designed in incubation hubs where students, computer scientists, entrepreneurs, and researchers met and discussed the project idea collaboratively. Birmingham City University and living lab collectively helped to exhibit the version 4B are the European BIC network.

A survey conducted by Liu, Baida, and Tan (2007) investigated the problems blind and visually impaired people faced when using the internet and identified four main problems to consider. Accessibility, the usability of assistive technology, content overview, and structure overview were identified as the main problems. This also leads to believe that there is a high percentage of unemployment within blind and visually impaired people due to the fact of being excessively demanding or extremely challenging for using office equipment. There are adverse opinions stated by employers about employing visually impaired people and rehabilitation counsellors have presented their views; which led them to focus on consumer abilities and then the employer needs (Patel & Vij, 2010).

Academic results of visually impaired and blind students varied considerably and depended on the assistive technology learning aid used. This disability restricts the blind people's learning and studying chances as compared to other normal students. Research conducted by Liu et al. (2007) finds that evidence from teachers of visually impaired students that there is a positive relationship between results and the use of assistive technology has enriched the quality of students' life and worked as a driving force to access the academic information. However, there was a lack of

Table 3.2 Insights of "XploR" functionality

Technical specifications	The "XploR" cane incorporates the following on its own board.
	• Bluetooth antenna
	• Bluetooth headset, Jabra
	• HD camera (facial recognition)
	• Power supply (via rechargeable battery)
	• ON/OFF button
	• Mowat sensor (vibrating motor)
	• Hardware rest button
	• Micro SD slot (SD/MMC)
	• USB_OTG
	• USB_HOST1
	• HDMI port
	• 4GB DDR3 SDRAM
	• EEPROM
	• Nottingham obstacle detector (NOD)
	• GPIO extension (1, 2, 3 and 4)
	• Recovery button
	• Hardware rest button
	• 32GB NAND flash
	• CHG_LED
	• PWR_LED
Ultrasound sensor module	There are other sensors available for detecting the objects and obstacles, but "XploR" has used Ultrasonic sensor due to being less affected by the colour and materials of obstacles. It also has the capability of detecting the objects up to 10-m range. This ultrasonic sensor is designed with a function of resisting the external disturbances, noise, and radiations. This sensor emits the sound rays every time, and as soon as these hit any object, they are reflected back to the source with the location and distance of the obstacle
Haptic touch (vibrators)	Mowat sensor is used in "XploR" which has five different analogue vibratory haptic pulses and these ranges could be set on the basis of the distance. In "XploR" cane case, the scanning area is up to 10-m and that is classified into five zones. The haptic touch would execute on the basis of where the object is located. All five zones have different level of haptic touches
Standard functionalities	The device "XploR" has following standard functions to help blind and visually impaired people for their mobility
	• Cane length could be increased or decreased by the user
	• Cane would come in two different, materials (Graphite and Aluminium)
	• Its weight would be light and easy to carry
	• Horizontal and vertical full spectrum IR camera and 270° viewing angle
	• Smartphone interface mount within the handle for navigation purposes
	• 24 h battery life
	• Vibrating device in handle to detect force feedback from camera detection
	• Handle can be detached from bottom part of cane
	• Panic button for assistance
	• Voice assistance/recognition

(continued)

Table 3.2 (continued)

Constraints	While developing "XploR" cane following constraints were raised:
	• Aluminium may not be durable enough and cane could be easily be broken
	• Weight of "XploR" cane would vary due to the specifications
	• Battery life issues
	• Camera would require to be adjusted by the user for viewing angle
	• Facial recognition depends on user's height
	• In "XploR" cane, we could not use Android OS due to the technical incompatibility issues of supporting camera, Mowat motor, and ultrasonic sensors

Conclusion

There is an enormous amount of assistive technologies available globally for the blind and visually impaired people, but their use is quite complex for them. Some of the assistive technologies are developed in various countries, but still unreachable by the blind and visually impaired people due to being expensive and lacking navigation features. The navigation support and facial recognition have always been a challenging problem for blind people along with finding the precise location of the obstacle. The already developed assistive technologies (e.g.; Eye Cane, White-Cane) did not have facial recognition features as well as no ability to sense the external environment through the auditory stimuli.

This paper presents "XploR" cane, a new innovation for blind people which is designed and developed at Birmingham City University (BCU) in co-operation with Living Labs (LILA). Although the integration of various assisted technologies within XploR was a great challenge, while developing it was ensured that all necessary aspects and features such as obstacle avoidance, facial recognition, route planning, GPS navigation, Bluetooth, haptic touch, and path sounder were embedded in it. This product concept was innovated with about 100 users across three NEW regions as part of LILA, and following the feedback from users and stakeholder, improvements were made in it, resulting in functionality of the "XploR" including face recognition and the ability to detect obstacles of up to 10-m radius.

Future Work

Although this device is developed keeping in view the various requirements of BVI people, it still requires future researchers to look into it through the following perspectives:

1. "XploR" can contain Braille keyboard, voice input unit, etc. Through this interface, different commands can be addressed to the computer.

Acknowledgment Authors wish to express sincere gratitude to Mr. Steve Adigbo (co-founder of Blindx) for rendering his help during this publication and LILA Interreg NWE project for its support to Blindx developers of XploR through the living labs model of transnational user groups.

References

Allee, V. (2008). Value network analysis and value conversion of tangible and intangible assets. *Journal of Intellectual Capital, 9*(1), 5–24. Retrieved from http://www.openvaluenetworks. com/Articles/Value_Conversion_JIC_online_version.pdf

Baida, Z., Rukanova, B., Liu, J., & Tan, Y. H. (2008). Preserving control in trade procedure redesign — The beer living lab. *Electronic Markets, 18*(1), 53–64.

Bowyer, K. W., Chang, K., & Flynn, P. (2006). A survey of approaches and challenges in 3D and multi-modal 3D + 2D face recognition. *Computer Vision and Image Understanding, 101*(1), 1–15.

Calamela, L., Defélixa, C., Picqd, T., & Retour, D. (2012). Inter-organisational projects in French innovation clusters: The construction of collaboration. *International Journal of Project Management, 30*(1), 48–59.

Chen, C., & Liu, L. Q. (2014). Pricing and quality decisions and financial incentives for sustainable product design with recycled material content under price leadership. *International Journal of Production Economics, 147*(3), 666–677.

Følstad, A. (2008, August). Living labs for innovation and development of information and communication technology: A literature review. *The Electronic Journal for Virtual Organisations and Networks, 10*. Special issue on Living Labs. Retrieved from http://iceconference.org/projects/264/Issues/eJOV%20Special%20Issue%20on%20Living%20Labs%202008/eJOV10_ SPILL7_Folstad_Living%20Labs%20for%20Innovation%20and%20De velopment.pdf

Haraszy, Z., Cristea, D. G., Tiponuţ, V., & Slavici, T. (2011). Improved head related transfer function generation and testing for acoustic virtual reality development. *Latest Trends on Systems, 2*, 411–417.

Haraszy, Z., Micut, S., Tiponut, V., & Slavic, T. (2011). Multi-subject head related transfer function generation using artificial neural networks. *Latest Trends on Systems, 1*, 399–405.

Helal, A., Moore, S., & Ramachandran, B. (2001). Drishti: An integrated navigation system for visually impaired and disabled. In *Proceedings of the 5th International Symposium on Wearable Computer, Zurich, Switzerland*.

Jackson, T. (2008). *Prosperity without growth?* London: Sustainable Development Commission.

Jayal, A., Badurdeen, F., Dillon, O., & Jawahir, I. (2010). Sustainable manufacturing: Modeling and optimization challenges at the product, process and system levels. *CIRP Journal of Manufacturing Science and Technology, 2*(3), 144–152.

Johnsen, T., Phillips, W., Caldwell, N., & Lewis, M. (2006). Centrality of customer and supplier interaction in innovation. *Journal of Business Research, 59*(6), 671–678.

Kokkinakos, P., Koussouris, S., Panopoulos, D., Askounis, D., Ramfos, A., Georgousopoulos, C., et al. (2012). Citizens collaboration and co-creation in public service delivery: The COCKPIT project. *International Journal of Electronic Government Research, 8*(3), 30.

Kramp, G., Nielsen, P., & Møller, A. S. (2010). Participatory interaction in therapeutical settings. Working paper. In *NordiCHI Conference*.

Lee, S. M., Olson, D. L., & Trimi, S. (2012). Co-innovation: Convergenomics, collaboration, and co-creation for organizational values. *Journal of Management History, Management Decision, 50*(5), 817–831.

Liu, J., Baida, Z., & Tan, Y. H. (2007). e-Customs control procedures redesign methodology: Model-based application. In *Proceedings of the 15th European Conference of Information Systems, St. Gallen, Switzerland*.

Patel, K. K., & Vij, S. K. (2010). Spatial navigation in virtual word. In *Advanced knowledge based systems: Model, Application and research* (Vol. 1, pp. 101–125).

Sakhardande, J., Pattanayak, P., & Bhowmick, M. (2012). Smart cane assisted mobility for the visually impaired. *World Academy of Science, Engineering and Technology, International Science Index 70, International Journal of Computer, Electrical, Automation, Control and Information Engineering, 6*(10), 1262–1265.

Schaffers, H., Guzman, J. G., Navarro, M., & Merz, C. (2010). *Living labs for rural development.* Madrid: TRAGSA. 249 pages. ISBN-13: 978-84-693-0040-4. Retrieved from www.c-rural.eu

Smit, D., Herselman, M., Eloff, J. H. P., Ngassam, E., Venter, E., Ntawanga, F., et al. (2011). Formalising living labs to achieve organisational objectives in emerging economies. In P. Cunningham & M. Cunningham (Eds.), *IST-Africa Conference Proceedings.* IIMC International Information Management Corporation, ISBN: 978-1-905824-24-3.

Thøgersen, J. (2007). Activation of social norms in social dilemmas: A review of the evidence and reflections on the implications for environmental behaviour. *Journal of Ecological Psychology, 28*(1), 93–112.

Tiponut, V., Ianchis, D., Bash, M., & Haraszy, Z. (2011). Work directions and new results in electronic travel aids for blind and visually impaired people. *Latest Trends on Systems, 2*, 347–353.

Tiponuț, V., Ianchis, D., & Haraszy, Z. (2009). Assisted movement of visually impaired in outdoor environments—Work directions and new results. In *Proceedings of the 13-th WSEAS Conference on SYSTEMS* (pp. 386–391). WSEAS Press.

Welfens, M. J., Liedtke, C., & Nordmann, J. (2010). *Sustainable consumption: Between unsustainable reality and peoples willingness to act* (Internal paper). Wuppertal: Wuppertal Institute for Climate, Environment and Energy.

Wong, M. E., & Cohen, L. (2012). *Assistive technology use amongst students with visual impairments and their teachers: Barriers and challenges in special education.* Singapore: National Institute of Education/Nanyang.

World Health Organization. (2016). *Global data on blindness. Facts sheet, key facts of the World Health Organization.*

Yu, W., Kuber, R., Murphy, E., Strain, P., & Mcallister, G. (2005). A novel multimodal interface for improving visually impaired people's web accessibility. *Virtual Reality, 9*(2), 133–148.

Zarandi, M. H. F., Mansour, S., Hosseinijou, S. A., & Avazbeigi, M. (2011). A material selection methodology and expert system for sustainable product design. *The International Journal of Advanced Manufacturing Technology, 57*(9), 885–903.

Chapter 4
Regenerator Losses in a Free Piston Stirling Engine

Ayodeji Sowale and Sarah Odofin

Abstract Due to the need for alternative means that can be used to generate power with high efficiency and less harm to the environment, the free piston Stirling engine has emerged and research has been carried out to prove its relevance. This study is carried out in the thermal energy conversion unit, using solar energy to generate power. This form of renewable energy can be employed for power production using the free piston Stirling engines which converts thermal energy into mechanical energy. The application is considered for micro-CHP applications in small-scale businesses and units. In this study the regenerator being the heart of the Stirling engine and its heat storage and recovery ability is analysed. The quasi-steady flow of the thermodynamic model of the free piston Stirling engine is developed, the thermal losses and effectiveness of the regenerator are considered and the effect on the output results generated during its operation is analysed and presented.

Keywords Free piston Stirling engine • Thermodynamic • Regenerator

Introduction

The free piston Stirling engine has been investigated in the past due to its external combustion, high efficiency and environmental friendly operation. The regenerator which is the major part of the engine which stores and releases heat to the working fluid in the engine during its backward and forward movement in the heat exchangers requires critical analysis for optimum performance. The thermal efficiency of the free piston Stirling engine is determined by the efficiency of the regenerator. The regenerator

A. Sowale (✉)
Faculty of Engineering and Environment, Northumbria University Newcastle,
A210 Ellison Building, Newcastle-Upon-Tyne NE1 8ST, UK
e-mail: ayodeji.sowale@Northumbria.ac.uk

S. Odofin
Faculty of Engineering and Environment, Northumbria University Newcastle,
E411 Ellison Building, Newcastle-Upon-Tyne NE1 8ST, UK
e-mail: sarah.odofin@Northumbria.ac.uk

© Springer International Publishing Switzerland 2017   47
R. Benlamri, M. Sparer (eds.), *Leadership, Innovation and Entrepreneurship as Driving Forces of the Global Economy*, Springer Proceedings in Business and Economics, DOI 10.1007/978-3-319-43434-6_4

consists of matrix layers to increase the effectiveness of its storage and release of heat absorbed from the working fluid. The porosity of each matrix determines the efficiency of the regenerator and has major impact of its performance. The porosity can be defined by the density of the mesh, void volume and the wire diameter. Therefore more consideration is required on the thermal losses that occur and also on the heat transfer and pressure drop of the oscillating flow of the working fluid in the regenerator.

Past Researches

Some investigations have been performed on the losses and effectiveness of regenerator in the Stirling engines. A research was performed by Abdulrahman on the engine regenerator as to design and carry out tests on the material to be used to make it effective (Abdulrahman, 2011). A numerical study was carried out on regenerator matrix design to improve the efficiency of a Stirling engine. A numerical model of the engine was developed, and a new regenerator design was optimized by dividing the regenerator matrix into three sections. The new design improved the overall temperature oscillations of the matrix and reduced the inflow effect on the matrix oscillations, thereby improving the efficiency of the engine (Andersen & Thomsen, 2006). A one-dimensional model was produced by de Boer (2009) for analysing Stirling engine regenerators. The model was developed from the simplified model considering the thermal and viscous losses. The output from the optimisation provided the optimal values of the piston phase angle and conductance of the regenerator to achieve maximum output power. A solution was obtained by Qvale and Smith (1968) on the thermal performance of a Stirling engine regenerator using the mass flow rate and sinusoidal pressure variation with phase angle between them. An observation by Popescu, Radcenco, Costea and Feidt (1996) states that the major reduction in the Stirling engine performance is by the nonadiabatic regenerator. The effects of the dead volumes and the efficiency of regenerator on the overall efficiency of the Stirling engine were carried out by Kongtragool and Wongwises (2006). The figure below shows the layout diagram of the gamma type free piston Stirling engine used in this study (Figs. 4.1 and 4.2).

Assumptions for the Mathematical Model

Certain assumptions were defined in order to obtain the mathematical model of the regenerator in the free piston Stirling engine.

1. The pressure drop in the regenerator is taken into account.
2. The internal, external and dissipation losses are taken into consideration.
3. The flow of the working gas is in one dimension and uniform.
4. The temperatures of the working gas in the heat exchangers are in thermal equilibrium with the surrounding walls.

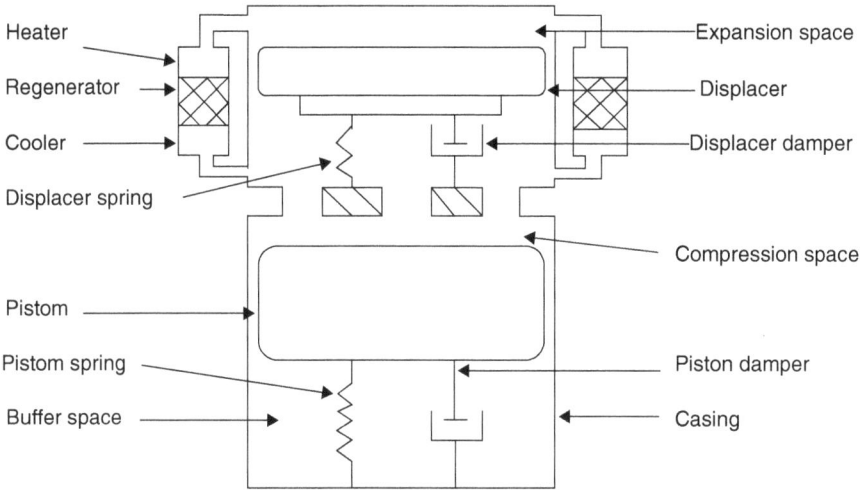

Fig. 4.1 Layout diagram of the free piston Stirling engine

Fig. 4.2 Top view
geometry of the
regenerator Formosa, 2013

5. The temperatures of the surrounding walls of the working gas volume changes with time.
6. The effect of gravitation is not considered in this analysis.
7. The working fluid is a perfect gas.
8. The regenerator temperature is required to be equal to the average of the cooler and heater temperature.

Methodology

In this study the second-order modelling of the quasi-steady flow model of free piston Stirling engine is developed using the fourth-order Runge-Kutta (rk4) method in MATLAB which solves second-order differential equations. The major focus was on the regenerator and its losses. The regenerator matrix was divided into ten parts in order to account for more accurate temperature difference and losses that occur in the regenerator during simulation. The temperature range between the heater and cooler was used to define the initial temperature of the working gas and the matrix in all regenerator parts. The input data for the engine geometry was defined. The pressure, pressure drops and heat transfers in the regenerator were calculated and the simulation was run over five cycles until convergence was achieved.

Equations for Regenerator Mathematical Model

The equations for determining the temperature, pressure drop and thermal losses are given below:

For the pressure in regenerator

$$P_r = P_k + \frac{\Delta P_k}{2} + (\Delta P_r)/2 \tag{4.1}$$

where P_k is the pressure in the cooler, ΔP_k is the pressure drop in the cooler and ΔP_r is the pressure drop in the regenerator.

For pressure drop in the regenerator, correlations were derived from the experimental analysis of the oscillating flow through regenerators. The evaluation of different correlations for determining the heat transfer coefficient and friction factor in regenerators was derived by Thomas and Pittman:

$$\Delta P = (2\,fr\,mu\,U\,V)/(A_{free}\,(dh^2)) \tag{4.2}$$

where fr is the Reynolds friction coefficient, mu is dynamic viscosity, U is fluid velocity, V is volume of the regenerator, A_{free} is the free flow area and dh is hydraulic diameter.

For the heat transfer in the regenerator

$$Qr = (V_r\,dP\,C_v)/R) - (C_p\,(T_k\,m_{kr}) - (T_h\,m_{rh})) \tag{4.3}$$

where dP is the pressure derivative in the engine, C_v is the specific heat capacity at constant volume, C_p is the specific heat capacity at constant pressure, T_k is the cooler temperature, m_{kr} is the mass flow from the cooler to the regenerator, T_h is the heater temperature and m_{rh} is the mass flow from the regenerator to heater.

For the regenerator temperature

$$T_r = P_r V_r /(Rm_r) \tag{4.4}$$

where P_r the pressure in the regenerator is, V_r is the regenerator volume, R is the universal gas constant and m_r is the mass flow in the regenerator.

Dissipation loss

$$Qr_{diss} = -\Delta P_r g_r Ac_r / (P_r / (RT_r))$$ (4.5)

where g_r is velocity multiplied by the density of working gas and Ac_r is the cross flow area from the cooler to regenerator.

Internal heat conduction loss

$$Qr_{lir} = k_r A_r (1 - poros) / l_r (T_{rr} - T_{kr})$$ (4.6)

where k_r is the thermal conductivity of regenerator matrix, A_r is the regenerator area, $poros$ is then porosity of regenerator matrix, l_r is length of regenerator, T_{rr} is the gas temperature of mass flow of regenerator part and is the gas temperature of mass flow from the compression space to regenerator.

External conduction loss

$$Qr_{ext} = (1 - \varepsilon) h_r Atep_r (T_m - T_r)$$ (4.7)

where ε (epsilon) the effectiveness of regenerator is, $Atep_r$ is surface area of regenerator and T_m is the temperature of regenerator matrix.

Tanaka, Yamashita and Chisaka (1990) defined the average heat transfer between the working gas and the matrix in the regenerator:

$$\overline{Nu} = 0.33\overline{Re}^{0.67}$$ (4.8)

$$NTU = 4\overline{Nu}H_D / Pr\,\overline{Re}d_h$$ (4.9)

$$\overline{h}_m = NTUC_p \dot{m} / A_{hm}$$ (4.10)

For (4.8)–(4.10), $\overline{Nu}$ is the mean Nusselt number, $\overline{Re}$ is the mean Reynolds number, NTU is the number of transfer units, H_D is the regenerator thickness, Pr is the Prandtl number, $\overline{h}_m$ is the mean heat transfer coefficient on matrix surface and A_{hm} is the area of heat transfer on the matrix.

To calculate the effectiveness of heat exchange in the regenerator

$$e_{eff} = \frac{NTU}{NTU + 2}$$ (4.11)

Input data for the design of the regenerator	
Length of regenerator	0.04 m
Outer diameter of regenerator	0.08 m
Inner diameter of regenerator	0.064 m
Wire diameter	0.0001 m
Porosity of regenerator	0.75

Input data for the design of the regenerator	
Mean pressure	70 bar
Expansion temperature	810 k
Compression temperature	320 k
Displacer stroke	0.0123 m

Numerical Results

In this present approach, the heat transfer coefficient, regenerator matrix, wire diameter and porosity of the regenerator are major factors that determine the efficiency of the regenerator. The losses that occur are taken into consideration, the outputs results are presented below and analysed.

Figure 4.3 shows the pressure drop in the regenerator parts, it can be observed that the pressure drop is constant in the ten regenerator parts. The major pressure drop in the engine is exhibited in the regenerator. Figure 4.4 shows the temperature variation in the topmost and the lowest part of the regenerator; the topmost part closest to the heater exhibits a higher temperature than the lowest part closest to the cooler and this shows the effects of the cooler and heater on the regenerator temperature.

In Fig. 4.5 the maximum heat loss due to external conduction in the regenerator parts is about 100 W; this is very significant as it determines the efficiency of the regenerator. Figure 4.6 shows the heat dissipation loss in the regenerator parts, the maximum heat loss due to dissipation is very low at about 0.4 W. This shows the regenerator matrix retains most part of the heat from the working fluid during the back and forth movement in the engine.

In Fig. 4.7 the maximum internal heat loss in the regenerator is about 200 W. In Fig. 4.8 the heat flow rate in the tenth part of the regenerator closer to the heater is about 6 kW, and the first part closer to the cooler exhibits about 0.3 kW; this shows

Fig. 4.3 Pressure drop in the regenerator

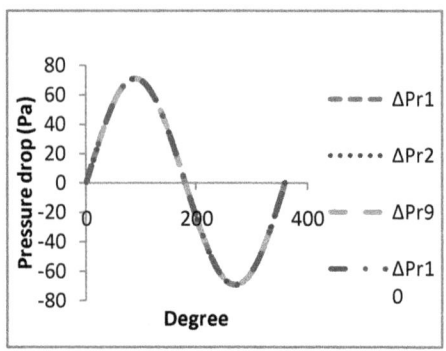

Fig. 4.4 Temperature variation in the first and tenth

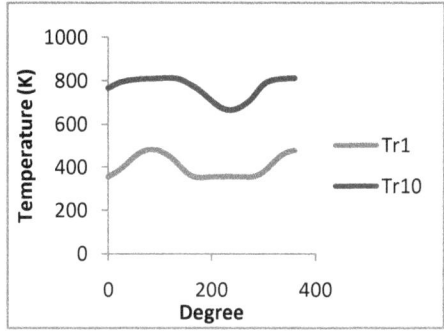

Fig. 4.5 The external heat loss in the regenerator

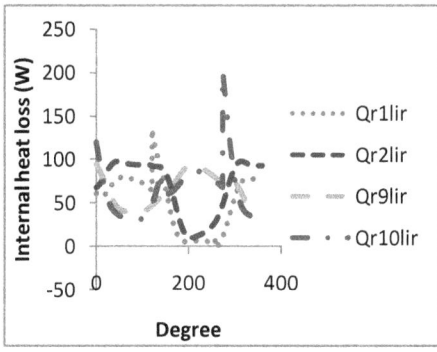

Fig. 4.6 Heat dissipation loss in regenerator

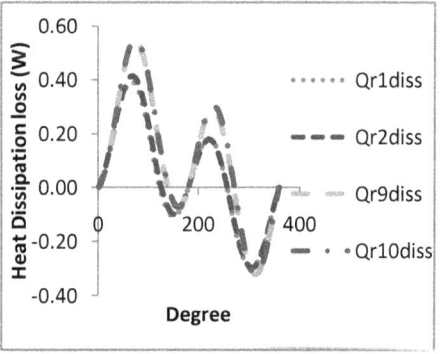

Fig. 4.7 Internal heat loss in the regenerator

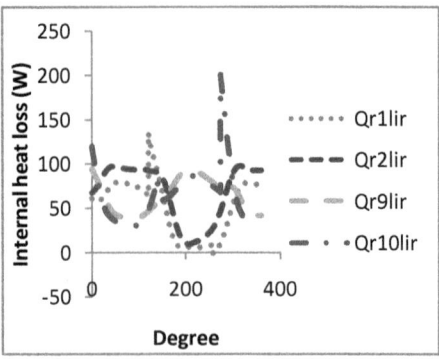

Fig. 4.8 Heat flow rate in regenerator

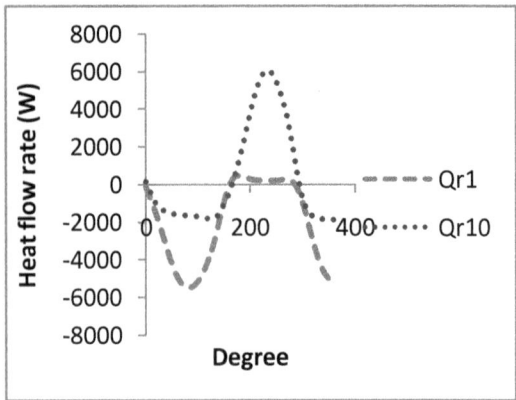

that there is more heat flow in one part of the regenerator than the other due to the decrease in the working gas temperature from the cooler to the regenerator while the parts closer to the heater exhibit a higher flow rate due to its proximity to the heater. This shows the engine performance depends on the regenerator effectiveness and its ability to accommodate high heat fluxes.

Conclusion and Future Work

The numerical solution and analysis of the regenerator in the free piston Stirling engine can be used to determine the heat transfer, temperature and thermal efficiency of the free piston Stirling engine. The output of the heat losses displayed a very significant effect in the regenerator performance. Careful consideration and measures should be taken to minimize the losses in the regenerator for a better engine performance and output power. Also, the higher the porosity of the regenerator the better the heat transfer. The engine exhibits a thermal efficiency of about 61 %. This method is very suitable for the regenerator analysis as it considers all the thermal losses, heat conduction loss and dissipation losses during the oscillatory movement of the working fluid back and forth through the heat exchangers. This analysis can be employed on the improvement and development of free piston Stirling engines for micro-CHP applications.

References

Abdulrahman, S. (2011). Selection and experimental evaluation of low-cost porous materials for regenerator applications in thermo acoustic engines. *Materials & Design, 32*(1), 217–228.

Andersen, S. K., & Thomsen, P. G. (2006). Numerical study on optimal Stirling engine regenerator matrix designs taking into account the effects of matrix temperature oscillations. *Energy Conversion and Management, 47*, 894–908.

de Boer, P. C. T. (2009). Optimal regenerator performance in Stirling engines. *International Journal of Energy Research, 33*, 813–832.

Kongtragool, B., & Wongwises, S. (2006). Thermodynamic analysis of a Stirling engine including dead volumes of hot space, cold space and regenerator. *Renewable Energy, 31*(3), 345–359.

Popescu, G., Radcenco, V., Costea, M., & Feidt, M. (1996). Optimisation thermodynamique en temps fini du moteur de Stirling endo- et exo-irréversible. *Revue Generale de Thermique, 35*(418–419), 656–661.

Qvale, E. B., & Smith, J. L. (1968). An approximate solution for thermal performance of Stirling engine regenerator. *Journal of Engineering for Power.*

Tanaka, M., Yamashita, I., & Chisaka, F. (1990). Flow and heat transfer characteristics of the Stirling engine regenerator in an oscillating flow. *JSME International Journal, Series 2, Fluid Engineering, Heat Transfer, Power, Combustion, Thermophysical Properties, 33*, 283–289.

Chapter 5
Adopting Business Analytics to Leverage Enterprise Data Assets

Mohamed Djerdjouri and Abdelghani Mehailia

Abstract In today's rapidly changing business environment, advances in information and communication technologies are happening at a very fast pace. As a result,
firms are under constant pressure to quickly adapt, be competitive, and identify new
business opportunities. Also, the amount of data collected by organizations today is
growing at an exponential rate and includes structured as well as new types of large
and real-time data across a broad range of industries such as streaming, geospatial,
social media, or sensor-generated data. Enterprise data have become an invaluable
strategic asset. Many organizations are using modern Business Analytics (BA) to
extract new insights and the maximum possible value from these data assets, which
will enable them to make timely and accurate decisions. In this paper, we briefly
describe business analytics and discuss how leading world class organizations are
adopting it and the technology environments that make it relatively easy and inex-
pensive and, the subsequent competitive benefits they have achieved. In addition,
we will report some findings from surveys of executives, managers, and professionals across industries about the use of analytics in their organizations, done recently
by IBM, SAS, MIT, and Gartner. Also, we will briefly address the organizational,
cultural, and technological challenges faced by organizations embracing business
analytics. Finally, we will discuss the unique obstacles and challenges encountered
by firms in developing countries with the goal of raising awareness of organizations
in the MENA region not only about these impediments but also about the benefits of
these technologies and the crucial role they play in the survival and competitiveness
of the firm in the complex and turbulent global market.

Keywords Business analytics • Big data • Datasets • Competitive advantage

M. Djerdjouri (✉)
School of Business and Economics, State University of New York at Plattsburgh,
Plattsburgh, NY, USA
e-mail: Djerdjm@Plattsburgh.edu

A. Mehailia
School of Business Administration, Canadian University of Dubai, Dubai, UAE
e-mail: ghani@cud.ac.ae

© Springer International Publishing Switzerland 2017   57
R. Benlamri, M. Sparer (eds.), *Leadership, Innovation and Entrepreneurship
as Driving Forces of the Global Economy*, Springer Proceedings in Business
and Economics, DOI 10.1007/978-3-319-43434-6_5

Introduction

Data is a strategic asset and business analytics provide the firm the tools to extract economic value from it. In today's business environment, massive amounts of data are being generated daily. According to the International Data Corporation (IDC), the world will generate an outstanding 35 Zettabytes of Data by 2020 (one Zettabyte = 1 trillion gigabytes), about 44 times more than 2009 (cf. Fig. 5.1). Also, Gartner reported that the growth of data volume between 2010 and 2015 reached 650 % (Gartner, 2016).

As of 2000, approximately 75 % of the data in the world was saved on analog media, film, or paper and only 25 % was digitized. Today, over 90 % of the world's data is digitized. In addition, these data include not only structured but also new types of unstructured and real time data generated through emails, text messages, social media sites, videos, and other means. Also, data can be generated by either people or machines. Data is becoming the new raw material of business and its economic input is almost equivalent to capital and labor (Zikopoulos et al. 2013). Also, as stated in the Gartner 2010, report information will be the twenty first century oil. However, research has also suggested that organizations are becoming overwhelmed by the amount of data collected and wrestle to understand how to use it to achieve business results. Data-driven companies treat their data as a strategic asset and try to leverage it for competitive advantage. According to a study by Gartner, business analytics is the top priority of chief information officers in the technology category and comprises a $12.2B market (Gartner, 2016). It is seen as a higher priority than such categories as mobile technology, cloud computing, and collaboration technology. In their CCF report, Koff and Gustafson (2011) state that we are witnessing both a data revolution and an evolution. There has been a steady evolution of computer

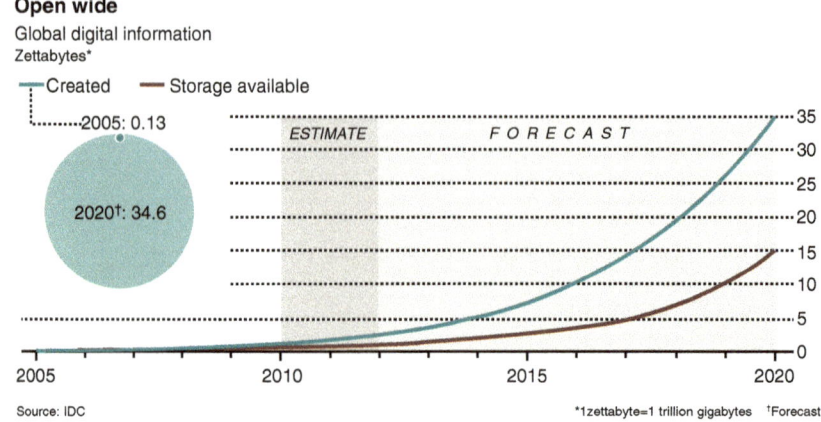

Fig. 5.1 Growth of data worldwide

and storage platforms, applications, architectures, and communication networks. And the revolution lies in the huge amounts of real time data organizations are collecting, the complexity and diversity of data, new rapid processing and storage methods, new linkages and the new analytics tools for gaining insights, and leveraging from the various datasets. The flood of large amounts of real time and various types of data is pressuring executives, managers, and professionals to make better and timelier decisions for their organizations. As a result, many companies are rushing to adopt business analytics and capitalize on these vast datasets of unstructured and real time data.

Evolution of Business Analytics

As a result of the pressure on organizations to leverage big data for competitive advantage and on managers and executives to make better decisions faster, there is a shift of paradigm towards using a more data-driven decision-making process to inform decisions at all levels of the organization and based on the use of business analytics (Evans and Linder (2012); Harvard Business Review Analytics Services (2012)). The institute for operations research and the management sciences (INFORMS) defines analytics as the scientific process of transforming data into insight for making better decisions. According to Davenport (2013), the field of business analytics was born in the mid-1950s. It followed a development of technological tools that can capture large amount of information and analytical tools and mathematical models that can help better analyze those data and recommend courses of action that were much better than what executives and decision makers could come up with using only their judgment and intuition. Analytics is in fact an evolution of quantitative analysis (operations research, statistics, and information systems), which has been in use for many decades already to assist executives and managers in making data-driven and better decisions. The difference today is the sheer volume of data collected and stored and the velocity at which it is being generated together with the advances made in information technology (Hopkins, 2010). Also, it has become more economically feasible to collect, store, process, and analyze unstructured data, such as web and network log data, or social media content. Moreover, more sophisticated algorithms and methods were developed to timely analyze these large datasets to reveal hidden patterns, provide insights, assess performance, track customer sentiment, and generate new business revenue-generating opportunities. Another development is that with the blending of visualization tools, analytics is much more compelling and easier to use, and as a result, more people in the organization can access the analytics tools and analyze all the data, and leveraging data from multiple sources. Even the name evolved from decision support systems to executive information systems, and then to online analytical processing, to business intelligence, and finally to analytics (Long & Brindley, 2013). The changes in the name appropriately reflect the evolution in the sophistication and reach within the organization; of the analytical tools to improve decision making at all levels. As stated by Koff and Gustafson (2011), the changes that took place in data and data analysis along the way include the volume of data that went from megabytes to terabytes and to petabytes and exabytes; the view that data represent an asset now and not just a fact; that we moved from just collecting data to connecting data and from analyzing only to predicting and uncovering insights within datasets. Also, we moved from only structured data to include more unstructured and timely data, from relational to non-relational, and from centralized to distributed parallel processing. Furthermore, there has been an evolution in the way data have been used over time. Davenport and Harris (2007) assert that analytics practitioners spent more than 95 % of their time reporting on the past and about 5 % on analysis of data. Also, if the firms use any analytics, it would be by a particular department or division of the firm and some of the time only to analyze a specific issue that arose. They also mentioned that the change in data analysis went from the activity of mainly reporting on what has happened in the business, to today's analytics which is explanatory and predictive. Modern analytics attempt to explain why things have happened and try to predict what might happen going forward. Today, we are witnessing the democratization and the spread of data analytics within the organization. Executives, managers, and professionals at all level of the firm demand more insights from the growing mass of real time, complex, and diverse data their firm collects. And they are getting the analytics tools to analyze the data themselves by building and manipulating more sophisticated models, in order to make timely and better decisions. Also, analytics professionals are becoming heavily relied upon when critical corporate decisions must be made. Consequently, the Burtch Works study (MIT Report, 2010) predicts that, analytics professionals are on the brink of taking more leadership positions in global corporations within the next 10–20 years. In short, the main driver of the evolution of analytics is the big data revolutionary change. The main characteristics of data are volume, variety velocity, and veracity. And velocity is considered the game changer because it is not just how fast data is produced or changed, but the speed at which it must be received, understood, and processed. Davenport (2013) contends that the evolution of analytics has gone through three phases so far. Analytics 1.0 is the era of business intelligence which started in 1950s and lasted until the mid-2000s where analytical tools were being used on mainly structured data to help managers take better courses of action. Then, Analytics 2.0 followed when companies like Google and Amazon started to collect and analyze large volumes of different types of data that was now not just internally but also externally sourced and unstructured. In this era, new and more powerful analytical tools were developed and companies hurried to upgrade their capabilities to substantially improve their fact-driven decision making and achieve competitive advantage. And in the last few years, he claims that we have entered the era of Analytics 3.0 when every firm in every industry realized that they too can get more insights from their data analysis, which can lead to lucrative new business opportunities. He called Analytics 3.0 the era of data-enriched offerings. Big data is changing the way analytics were commonly viewed, from data mining to advanced analytics.

Creating a Competitive Advantage

In today's complex business world, competitive companies are getting ahead by using lots of analytics to make the right decisions. The benefits achieved include improving processes, saving costs, and enhancing revenues (Hopkins et al., 2010). Studies show that organizations competing on analytics substantially outperform their peers. Pioneers such as UPS, Progressive, and Google are very aggressive about analytics; however, the majority of companies still have a long way to go in tying analytics to decision making throughout the organization. Every year, Gartner surveys almost 3000 CIOs to get insights into their strategies as well as digital businesses trends, opportunities, and threats. And for the fifth year in a row, analytics represents the top technology priorities in 2015 (Gartner, 2016). Also, IDC reports that the business analytics software market grew by 13.8 % during 2011 to $32B and predicts it to be at $50.7B in revenue by 2016 (Gartner, 2016). Nucleus Research finds a $10.66 payoff for every $1.00 spent on analytics applications (Clyde Holsapple, Lee-Post, & Pakath, 2014). There is a strong relationship of business analytics with profitability of businesses, their revenues, and the shareholders' returns (Watson (2011); Accenture Global Operations Megatrends Study (2014)). Moreover, business analytics enhances understanding of data, enables the creation of informative reports, and it is vital for businesses to remain competitive. In a survey of 3000 executive managers worldwide conducted by the MIT Sloan Management Review and the IBM Institute for Business Value (2012), findings revealed that top performing companies view analytics as a key differentiator that clearly separates them from the competition in the marketplace. The survey finds that top performers are three times more likely than lower performing companies to recognize that their heavy use of analytics within the organization gives them a substantial competitive advantage. Moreover, the managers mentioned that one of the key barriers to achieving the competitive advantage that big data can offer is their lack of understanding of how to use analytics to improve the business performance. In addition, the survey found that executive managers reported that their immediate plan for the next 2 years is to adopt emerging analytics tools within the organization, and these tools will supplement existing data reporting systems and uncover patterns and insights in the datasets and make them easy to understand and act upon. A Harvard Business Review Analytics Service global survey of 646 executives, managers, and professionals across all industries and geographies revealed that more than 70 % of the firms that had deployed analytics throughout their organizations reported improved financial performance, increased productivity, reduced risks, and faster decision making (The Burtch Works Study, 2015) (Fig. 5.2).

To understand how organizations could use business analytics to be more competitive, a survey of 4500 managers and executives from organizations in over 120 countries and 30 industries was conducted (Clyde Holsapple et al., 2014). The findings suggest two approaches to achieve competitive advantage through the adoption and use of analytics. In the first one, individual units within the organization use a wide range of analytical tools to make timely and better decisions autonomously.

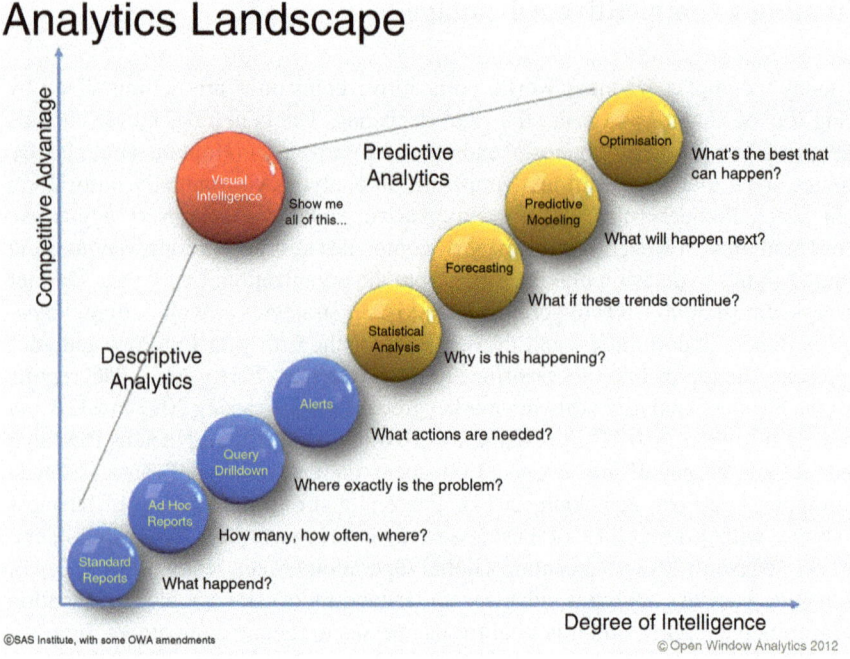

Fig. 5.2 Analytics and competitiveness

The second approach calls for a more collaborative effort where analytics are used broadly across all units. The collaborative approach is more likely to develop a somewhat level degree of expertise in analytics among all units of the organization, whereas the specialized or autonomous approach may lead to uneven levels of analytics sophistication among units and divisions. In a study conducted by The IBM Institute for Business Value and the Saïd Business School at the University of Oxford in mid-2012 with 1144 professionals from 95 countries across 26 industries, it was found that 63 % of companies reported that the use of analytics is creating a competitive advantage for their organizations (IBM Institute for Business Value, 2012). There were only 37 % with the same response in a similar study done 2 years before, a whopping 70 % increase in just 2 years. The study also made five key recommendations for a successful implementation of analytics in a firm and achieving rapid results and obtaining strategic value from data. The organization should commit initial efforts to customer-centric outcomes; develop an enterprise-wide big data blueprint; start with existing data to achieve near-term results; build analytics capabilities based on business priorities and; create a business case based on measurable outcomes. And the IBM-MIT Sloan Management Review and the IBM Institute for Business Value study identified information management, analytics tools and skills, and a data-oriented culture as the three essential competencies that enable organizations to build competitive advantage using analytics (Long & Brindley, 2013).

Analytics Implementation Challenges

It is very clear by now to many firms and organizations that data is a strategic asset and big data and business analytics offer them invaluable opportunities to improve decision making at all levels in their organizations and gain precious competitive advantage in the marketplace. However, it should also be made very clear to them that implementing analytics in an organization is a significant undertaking full of challenges and obstacles. And these impediments typically take a considerable amount of time to surmount. The implementation should be thoroughly thought out and carefully planned before being initiated. First and foremost, the firm must set a clear strategy with a clear investment plan in data processing and analytics tools. Old technology and servers are not designed to process, store, and manage real time and unstructured data. As a result, an investment in new information technology must be made, and at a minimum, new analytics and high computing servers and applications will be needed. The challenge here is to make others in the organization understand why the existing technology cannot be upgraded and adopted to handle the new type of data and analytics. Besides the challenges of storing and managing large amount of complex and varied data, a critical element is the quality of the data collected. Thus, it is imperative to clean up all data to remove incomplete, inaccurate, and duplicate data before storing it in data warehouses, because business analytics are as good as data itself. Moreover, data centers operations have to change from batch processing to allow managers and executives to run real time analytics. Another big challenge encountered when implementing analytics is the type and level of skills needed to take advantage of the opportunities analytics offer to the organization. Many companies initiating business analytics projects struggle to find qualified people to run analytics on their data sets. Many first turn to consultants in the beginning to help with the first projects and to train their employees. However, the everyday use of analytics requires managers and other professionals in the organization to have a good understanding of quantitative approaches, statistical methods, and mathematical modeling. As a result, the work of analytics professionals is being more valued and they are being now promoted to the position of trusted internal consultants. In fact, analytics professionals are poised to assume more managerial roles in the near future. Other challenges include securing commitment from all stakeholders, radically changing processes, and integrating new capabilities with people and setting their new roles. However, the most difficult challenge is to set off and lead the cultural and behavioral changes the organization must make to become data-driven. Also, distributed data analytics and decentralized data-based decision making can upset traditional power structure and relationships. The MIT Sloan management Review and the IBM Institute for Business Value study found a growing divide between organizations that have embraced and successfully implemented analytics and those that have not (Long & Brindley, 2013). This divide is more significant for companies operating in developing countries and their challenges are numerous and much more difficult to overcome. The most crippling challenge is the high cost and complexity of implementing data and analytics technology. Moreover, the majority of organizations do not have access to the latest technology. But no analytics models and data mining can be performed without data. Data is the quintessential ingredient of analytics. And a major problem in developing countries in general and the firms operating in those economies in particular is the lack of accurate and reliable data. In fact, in many cases no data or only minimum structured data are collected for specific projects. In a recent article, Shacklett (2014) reported that the majority of developing countries are not highly digitalized. Thus, generating and collecting data, structured and unstructured, that feeds into analytics is a major impediment. Moreover, for most business organizations, data on purchase orders, invoices, inventory, balance sheets, and information on consumer preferences is most likely to be found in spreadsheets, paper-based files and reports, and manually maintained ledgers. And the author indicates that none are readily convertible to digitized data that can be uploaded into analytics software. In addition, typically the management culture in these organizations is not suited yet to implementing big data and analytics. Companies have rigid hierarchical power structures and executives maintain a firm control of all decision making. Moreover, there is overreliance on managerial judgment such as intuition and instincts and never or rarely on data. However, the use of analytics requires first and foremost a move to a data-driven culture within the organization where data and analytics are distributed across the organization and decision making is more decentralized and more evidence-based. In fact, it requires a deep organizational behavior change and a paradigm shift in the business environment towards the importance of data collection and management and the use of analytics to improve performance and stay competitive in the global market place. Although the challenges listed seem insurmountable at first, it is conceivable for companies in the developing countries to close the big divide with organizations in developing countries by first realizing that data is a strategic asset for the company that can and must be leveraged to make fact-driven and better decisions and make the firm more competitive. In addition, governments should invest heavily in education in applied mathematics, statistics, and information systems and in providing better access to information and communications technologies. And companies must increase investment in information technology and analytics tools and in improving their mangers' analytical skills. In a recent paper, Long and Brindley (2013) warn managers and policy makers in the developing world about the importance of harnessing the velocity of data and analytics to be able to make decisions and adjustments in real time and be able to match these actions to the speed of the business opportunities. However, Lung et al. also caution about the importance of being able to collect, store, and use data that's collected. Moreover, to be good and useful, data needs to be clean, accurate, and transparent.

It also needs to be stored, analyzed, and properly shared within the organization. The question raised by Lung et al. is if the capabilities to do this exist in the developing countries. Big investments are needed in this area before businesses and other organizations in the developing economies can unlock the true value of data.

Discussion and Conclusion

Organizations are generating and storing very large amounts of data from social media, email, videos, presentations, and other nontraditional sources of information. These data comprehensively represent the aggregate experience of an organization with its customers, suppliers, and all other stakeholders. They are both structured as well as unstructured and are heterogeneous, real time, and complex. This drastic growth of data brings about challenging problems demanding new and innovative solutions. The challenges are twofold; first, how to store and manage the huge and diverse datasets, and second, how to effectively mine the datasets and analyze data using modeling, visualization, and forecasting techniques at different levels so as to unveil intrinsic properties and insights that will improve decision making at all levels of the organization. However, the benefits of this flood of data for the organizations far outweigh the challenges created in that it gives executives an unprecedented ability to better understand their customers and operations, anticipate challenges, and identify new business opportunities. And to fully exploit the opportunities and resolve the challenges, organizations are adopting business analytics.

Business Analytics is broadly defined as the scientific process of transforming large amount of data into insight for making better decisions using analytical tools. Descriptive analytics involve gathering and describing data; predictive analytics use past data to predict the future and, prescriptive analytics suggest a course of action. Gartner survey of 3000 CIOs revealed that business analytics represents their top technology priorities in 2015, the same result obtained in the five previous years. Also, the International Data Corporation (IDC) predicts that the business analytics software market will grow to $51 billion this year. In a study conducted by IBM and the MIT Sloan management Review, it is reported that high performing companies obtained a substantial competitive advantage in the marketplace through the heavy adoption and use of analytic throughout their firms. They also reported that they view analytics as a key differentiator that clearly separates them from their competitors. In addition, they agree that adopting analytics in the firm is a challenging endeavor and it takes time and patience before the firm can reap the benefits. All over the world, we are witnessing an exponential growth of data, a large amount of which are typically unstructured that need more real time analysis. And many for profit as well as not-for-profit companies and government agencies are becoming interested in the high potential of effectively processing and analyzing these big datasets. As a result, many of them are announcing major plans to accelerate the adoption of business analytics within their organizations. Moreover, more and more executives, managers, and professionals are cultivating their quantitative skills to be able to take full advantage of the business analytics tools within their organization in order to understand what data is important to them and how to dive deeper into it and extract key patterns and insights that will help them better test their assumptions and make better decisions at their level. Although a handful of companies in the emerging markets and the developing world have implemented some analytics in few departments or divisions, by and large many are not aware of the new data revolution or do not clearly understand how analytics-driven management creates value for the organization and gives it a competitive advantage in the global market. In addition to the regular challenges faced by companies operating in advanced economies, the ones in developing countries face many more difficult obstacles such as the high implementation cost of data analytics, the lack of access to the latest technology, the lack of accurate and reliable data, the hierarchical company structure, and overreliance on executive who maintain a firm control of all decisions. A required change in culture and organizational behavior and a resolute move to a data-driven culture must be initiated before any successful analytics endeavor can be embraced.

The use of business analytics continues to grow. Investments in data and analytics technologies to improve decision making are steadily increasing and, these investments are being made by organizations in business, government, law, non-profits organizations, and education. However, the big data and analytics movement is still at an early stage in its development. Many executives and managers companies are still struggling to figure out how to implement and use analytics in their companies. And, understanding the capabilities and techniques of analytics is crucial to managing in today's business environment. Finally, as an extension of this introductory paper, the authors will conduct a study of companies in the Middle East and North Africa (MENA) region to assess the level of awareness of executives, managers, and professionals about the data revolution taking place in the world today and their understanding of how analytics-driven management can create value for the organization. The study will also investigate which companies are already using or have short-term plans to use analytics in their everyday decision making and the level of sophistication of their analytics tools.

References

Accenture Global Operations Megatrends Study. (2014). *Big data analytics in supply chain: Hype or here to stay?* Accenture report. Retrieved from www.accenture.com/megatrends

Clyde Holsapple, C., Lee-Post, A., & Pakath, R. (2014). A unified foundation for business analytics. *Decision Support Systems, 64*, 130–141.

Davenport, T. (2013, December). Analytics 3.0. *Harvard Business Review*.

Davenport, T. H., & Harris, J. G. (2007). *Competing on analytics*. Boston: Harvard Business School Press.

Evans, J., & Linder, C. (2012). Business analytics: The next frontier for decision sciences. *Decision Line, 43*(2), 4–7.

Gartner. (2016). *Building the digital platform: Insights from the 2016 Gartner CIO agenda report.* Gartner Executive Programs, Gartner Corporate Headquarters. Retrieved from www.gartner.com

Harvard Business Review Analytics Services. (2012). *The evolution of decision making: How leading organizations are adopting a data-driven culture*. Harvard Business Review analytics services report, 2012. Harvard Business School.

Hopkins, M. S. (2010). Are you ready to reengineer your decision making? *MIT Sloan Management Review, 52*(1), 1–7.

Hopkins, M. S., LaValle, S., Balboni, F., Kruschwitz, N., & Shockley, R. (2010). 10 data points: Information and analytics at work. *MIT Sloan Management Review, 52*(1), 27–31.

IBM Institute for Business Value. (2012). *Analytics: The real-world use of big data—How innovative enterprises extract value from uncertain data.* The IBM Institute for Business Value report. Retrieved from www.ibm.com/iibv

Koff, W., & Gustafson, B. (2011). *Data rEvolution.* Leading Edge Forum, Computer Sciences Corporation.

Long, J., & Brindley, W. (2013). *The role of big data and analytics in the developing world.* Chapter 3, Accenture. Retrieved from www.accenture.com/technologyindevelopment

MIT Report. (2010). Retrieved from http://sloanreview.mit.edu/article/are-you-ready-to-reengineer-your-decision-making/

Shacklett, M. (2014). Starting with small data in emerging markets to get to bid data analytics. *TechRepublic.* Retrieved from http://www.techrepublic.com/article/start-with-small-data-in-emerging-markets-to-get-to-big-data-analytics/

The Burtch Works Study. (2015). *Burtch Works LLC report.*

Watson, H. (2011). Business analytics insight: Hype or here to stay? *Business Intelligence Journal, 16*(1), 4–8.

Zikopoulos, P. C., Deroos, D., Parasuraman, K., Deutsch, T., Corrigan, D., & Giles, J. (2013). *Harness the power of big data—The IBM big data platform.* New York, NY: McGraw Hill.

Chapter 6
Enterprise Architecture for Innovation Realization and Sustainability

Stuart Anderson

Abstract We live in a world of changing business environments, competition, mergers, acquisitions, and evolving economic climates. Innovation for the sustainability of global enterprise is a must. There is no shortage of ideas; IBM launched ten new IBM businesses, following an online collaboration of 150,000 global participants (IBM Innovation Jam® 2006). Innovative organizations can still fail at implementation. Lack of business capability, process maturity, vision, and leadership plays a significant part in innovation failure. This paper describes a model for successful innovation realization, leveraging The Open Group's Enterprise Architecture framework (TOGAF® v9.1). A framework through which an enterprise can mature, develop its innovation capabilities and support innovation sustainability.

Keywords Innovation • Sustainability • Framework • ADM • TOGAF • Governance • Capability • Global • Enterprise • Maturity • Risk • Collaboration • Ideas • Creativity • Culture • Leadership • Vision

Introduction

The ever changing environment of competition, mergers, acquisitions and evolving economic climates, places increased significance on innovation for the sustainability of global enterprise. It's a matter of survival! Innovation, innovation, and innovation.

Even with the innovation mantra and widespread understanding that innovation is a must, there are still many failures, e.g., Blockbuster, Sony, and Sun Microsystems. Innovation presents many challenges: organizational, cultural, and societal. It's not a lack of ideas; the idea pipeline can be readily filled. Consider IBM's online idea collaboration events. IBM brought together more than 150,000 people from 104 countries and 67 companies. Ten new IBM businesses were launched as a result

S. Anderson, BSc (Hons), CEng MBCS CITP, MCQI CQP, ITIL®, TOGAF® (✉)
ARTeFACT Business Transformation INC., Oakville, ON, Canada
e-mail: art_e_fact@outlook.com

© Springer International Publishing Switzerland 2017   69
R. Benlamri, M. Sparer (eds.), *Leadership, Innovation and Entrepreneurship as Driving Forces of the Global Economy*, Springer Proceedings in Business and Economics, DOI 10.1007/978-3-319-43434-6_6

(IBM Innovation Jam®, 2006). IBM conducted a 52-h "Business of Things Jam." The online event had 1900 registrants in 70 countries, generating over 1100 discussion threads (IBM Innovation Jam®, 2015).

The big challenge is how an enterprise selects the idea to champion and its capability to innovate through to realization. Is it organization culture, silo thinking and/or inability to implement? The difference between thinkers and doers, you need both. The reality is the complexity of today's global innovation environment requires a multidisciplinary, cross-functional approach that takes account of the current enterprise maturity (capabilities, competencies, processes, technology, commitment, leadership and vision).

This paper will focus on describing a model for innovation realization and sustainability, leveraging The Open Group Enterprise Architecture Framework (TOGAF® v9.1). We have the idea bucket; let's select the best ideas aligned to the enterprise strategic vision and implement on an ongoing, sustainable manner.

Innovation Success Factors

It is important to have an innovation realization model that accommodates iteration cycles to fine tune the new or enhanced product or service. Briones (2012) states "To develop disruptive innovations, one round of 'voice of the customer' is not enough…."

A framework that accommodates learning, experimentation, and discovery is required. The innovation journey can result in different paths and outcomes. Christensen (1997) states "The Stage-Gate system assumes that the proposed strategy is the right strategy; the problem is that except in the case of incremental innovations, the right strategy cannot be completely known in advance."

There are many attributes to be considered for innovation delivery success. Little (2013) describes a number of critical success factors within the "Growth Accelerator Framework":

- **Growth Roadmaps**: A vision of each innovation increment and end state.
- **Pilot Solutions**: To learn, test, and adjust your ideas.
- **Organization and Processes**: The impact to your organization, supply chain and partners.
- **Culture and Change Leadership**: Setting the scene that this is not a one-off event but a continuous journey and it's okay to fail.
- **Capabilities and Tools**: Enterprise growth requires new capabilities to execute the innovation agenda and new capabilities to deliver and support the innovation solutions. The end result is about increasing business capability.

The Open Group Architecture Framework (TOGAF®)

The Open Group Architecture Forum, comprised of more than 200 enterprises, develops and maintains the TOGAF standard (TOGAF® v9.1). TOGAF is the de facto global standard for Enterprise Architecture, a framework for enabling business change

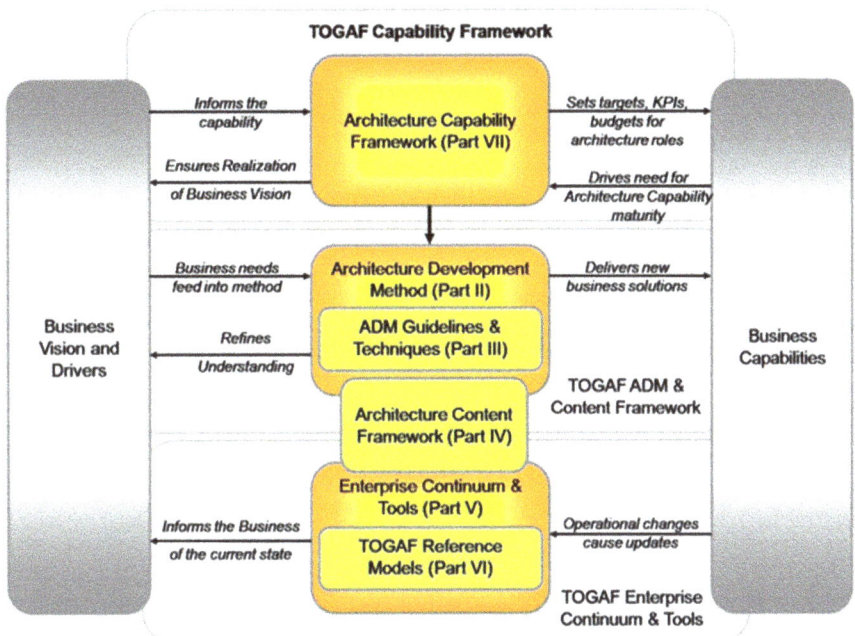

Fig. 6.1   TOGAF Capability Framework © The Open Group

through *Boundaryless Information Flow*™. The Open Group is a vendor and customer neutral body of like-minded contributors to global enterprise standards. Figure 6.1 describes the relationship between business vision and resultant business capability, realized through application of the TOGAF framework (TOGAF® v9.1).

Innovation Vision

Innovation requires a vision of the future state: the product, service and business model. Leadership is necessary to ensure the right decisions at the right time, to manage disruptive impacts and willingness to change course. Over the past 10 years' enterprises have deployed growth strategies through mergers and acquisitions, innovation through global expansion, creating supply chain efficiencies and standardizing and/or leveraging acquired enabling technologies.

An innovation vision is required, an ability to describe the journey, timeframe, focus of change, innovation value and outcome. The innovation vision may be strategic (focused on breadth, a 3-year horizon, to break into new markets or complete a global expansion) or tactical (short-time span of 6–12 months, focused on a specific capability, e.g., enhanced mobile cloud services or segment line of business); see Fig. 6.2.

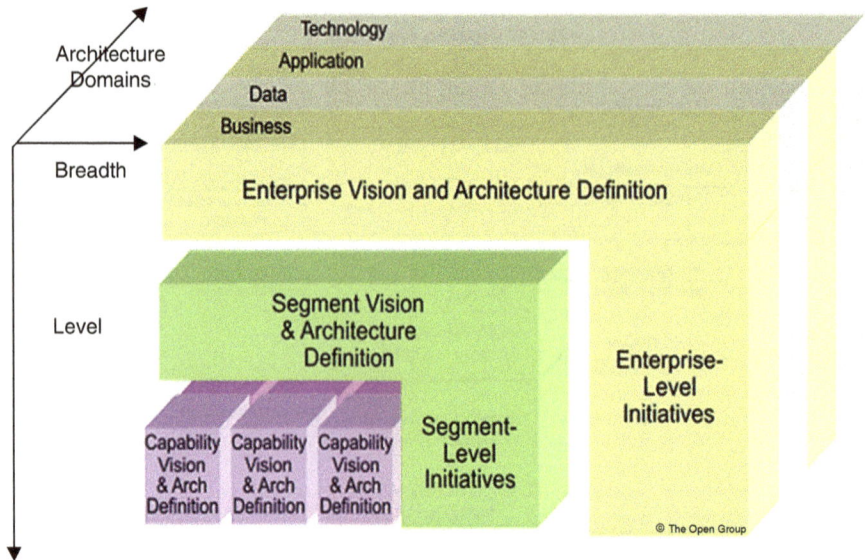

Fig. 6.2 Innovation Increment Coverage © The Open Group

Architecture Development Method

The ADM is the core of the TOGAF® framework (see Fig. 6.1). This section describes the ADM Phases at a high level and how it can be applied to innovation realization. If you replace the labels "architecture" with "innovation," e.g., *innovation development* iteration, it will help with the ADM process assimilation:

– **Preliminary**: Define the context for the innovation event, standards, principles, tools, resources and innovation maturity target (an opportunity to increase the enterprise's innovation capability). External standards can be leveraged to assess, for example, IT governance maturity COBIT® (Anderson, 2013) or benchmark, baseline and/or establish innovation opportunities. An assessment of the enterprise innovation readiness is a prerequisite to manage innovation risk. The Canadian Government Business Transformation Enablement Program (BTEP 2004) provides tools for assessing transformation readiness and risks, equally relevant to assessing the enterprise's innovation readiness.

– **Phase A Innovation Vision**: The innovation ideas' long list is examined by the leadership team and an innovation focus is established, aligned to the enterprise business strategy. The innovation vision, desired outcome (enterprise product or service to be realized), is defined at a conceptual level. The ADM iteration model is also defined in phase A (see Fig. 6.3). Perhaps a full ADM cycle at a high-level

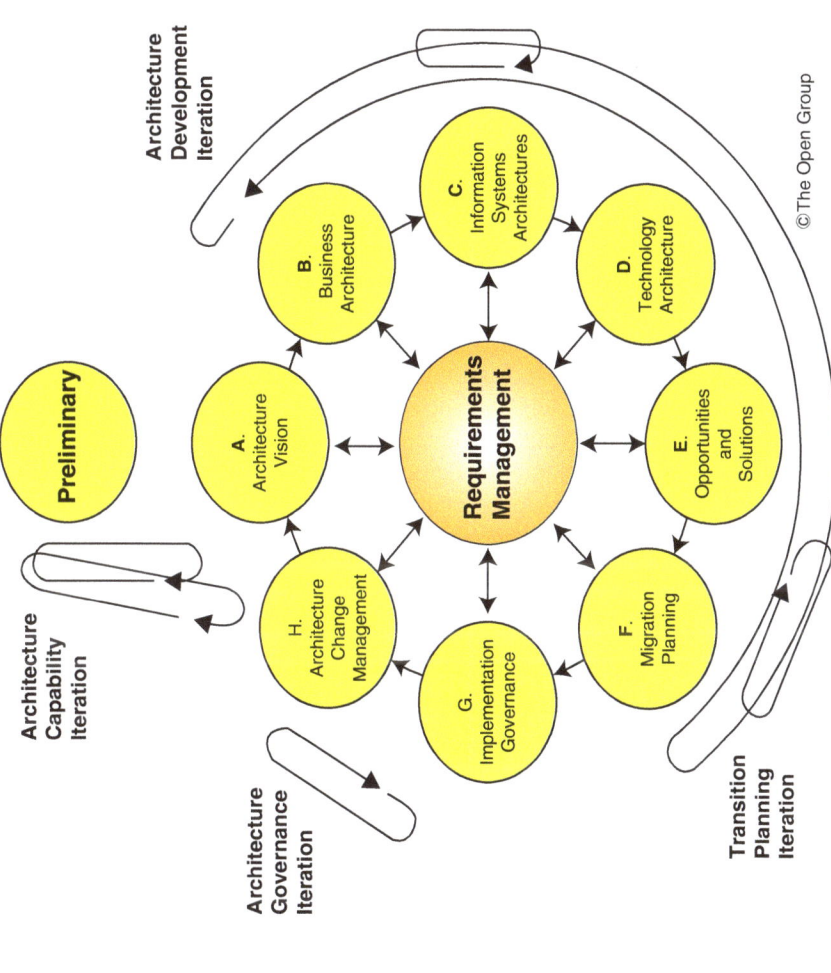

Fig. 6.3 Architecture Development Method (ADM) © The Open Group

or specific phase iteration at a more detailed level is required to realize the innovation vision.

- **Phase B Business Innovation**: An assessment of the business change impact (services, organization structure, people impacts, etc.) is made in phase B. A merger will have significant impacts in this area as a result of service consolidation and rationalization, e.g., changes to supply chains and customer support channels.
- **Phase C Information Systems Innovation**: Defining the enterprise data and application portfolio change impacts. Perhaps the innovation opportunity is to leverage the strength of the mobile application of one enterprise with that of the information centric, highly mature business intelligent strength of the other enterprise.
- **Phase D Technology Innovation**: The change impacts associated with the IT infrastructure are defined. Perhaps a change in IT service model is required to support the new mobile application and business intelligence platform. A move away from "on premise" to the cloud "as a service," on demand model leveraging, e.g., a mobile platform and security services.
- **Phase E Opportunities and Solutions**: The change impacts, identified through the gap analysis activities in phases B, C and D, are analyzed collectively and potential solutions defined. Perhaps a solution that leverages cloud services and niche outsourcing services, such as a data analytics platform, will support the innovation realization. Consolidation of gap analysis outputs is a complex activity, as Fig. 6.4 shows pictorially. An enterprise-wide, cross-functional team will work together to define solution options, considering everything from design, build and test, deployment, support and maintenance. The enterprise capability readiness assessment is revisited. How big is the change impact, relative to

Fig. 6.4 Complexity of technology innovation

proposed solutions? What are the organization impacts to be addressed? An initial innovation *Transition Roadmap* is developed.

- **Phase F Migration Planning**: The initial roadmap is reviewed and built upon, in the context of the broader innovation project portfolio; business cases, success criteria and metrics are developed, including an implementation risk assessment.
- **Phase G Implementation Governance**: The governance framework to ensure adherence to the originating innovation principles, standards, innovation scope and vision established in phase A. The goal is to ensure business benefit realization and risk management toward achieving the innovation outcomes.
- **Phase H Innovation Change Management**: Focused on managing the overall enterprise innovation framework, maintaining the ideas' pipeline and initiating innovation iterations through the ADM. Ensuring that the capability of the innovation team (skills, knowledge, competencies, tools, methods, techniques, etc.) are matched with the increased enterprise capability, introduced through successive innovation initiatives.
- **Requirements Management**: Focused on managing the stream and changes to innovation requirements, developed from the gap analysis performed in phases A, B, C and D; and subsequently reviewed, consolidated, and prioritized through the remaining ADM phases.

Table 6.1 describes where the critical "Innovation Success Factors" are addressed within the TOGAF® Architecture Development Method (ADM).

Table 6.1 Innovation success factors and ADM

Innovation success factors	TOGAF® ADM
Growth roadmaps	Established in the Vision Phase. Defined in Migration Phase G (portfolio level) and maintained in Change Management Phase H
Pilot solutions and iteration	Accommodates great flexibility and user-defined iteration model, supporting pilots, enterprise learning, exploration and experimentation, measurement, monitoring and control
Organization and processes	Business Innovation Phase B focuses on the organization and business process impacts through a formal gap analysis, current Vs future state. Phase E focus includes organization and process solution optioning
Culture and change leadership	Considered in the Preliminary Phase, Vision Phase A, Solutions Phase E, Governance Phase G, and Innovation Change Management Phase H
Capabilities and tools	Enterprise capabilities, readiness and maturity to deliver innovation initiatives are defined in the Preliminary and Vision Phases. Capability management for ongoing innovation delivery and management, performed in Innovation Change Management Phase H
Enterprise reference standards	Applicable reference standards (cross-border, country, legal, policy, industry), solution reuse collateral, etc., considered in Preliminary Phase

Conclusion

This paper provides a high-level summary of the TOGAF® Architecture Development Method (ADM) and its applicability to innovation realization. Critical success factors are addressed comparatively with some key criterion from industry innovation sources. Innovation delivery is a complex endeavor, requiring skill, knowledge, leadership commitment and capability. An innovation framework that accommodates an enterprise capability maturity model is a prerequisite. The TOGAF® v9.1 framework can be applied to achieve innovation realization, given it is closely aligned to the *innovation criteria for success* stipulated by a number of researchers and innovation specialists (Briones, 2012; Christensen, 1997; Little, 2013).

The Open Group's Enterprise Architecture Framework (TOGAF®) has evolved to reach version 9.1 in 2011, since its originating first edition in 1995. It has many contributors and learnings from global practitioners, making it a reliable and proven framework for application across many industry sectors.

Innovation realization requires leadership, strong governance and risk management. An enterprise's maturity, both to accept and manage the change necessary to be innovative, and its capability maturity to deliver the innovation are critical success factors. A framework through which an enterprise can mature, develop its innovation capabilities, provides the means for innovation realization and sustainability.

References

Anderson, S. (2013). COBIT IT governance case study. Financial services IT transformation. In *British Computer Society (BCS) International IT Conference, Abu Dhabi, UAE*.

Briones, J. (2012). *New approach to manage disruptive innovation in an environment of high uncertainty*. Retrieved March 22, 2016, from http://www.innovationmanagement.se/author/jose-briones/

Christensen, C. M. (1997). *The innovator's dilemma: When new technologies cause great firms to fail*. Boston, MA: Harvard Business Review Press.

IBM Innovation Jam®. (2006). *A global innovation jam*. Retrieved March 22, 2016, from http://www-03.ibm.com/ibm/history/ibm100/us/en/icons/innovationjam/

IBM Innovation Jam®. (2015). *The business of things. Designing business models*. Retrieved March 22, 2016, from http://www-935.ibm.com/services/us/gbs/thoughtleadership/businessofthings/

ISACA. *Control Objectives for Information & Related Technology (COBIT®)*. Retrieved from March 22, 2016, from http://www.isaca.org/COBIT/Pages/default.aspx

Little, A. D. (2013). *The growth accelerator managing innovation based growth*. Retrieved from March 22, 2016, from http://www.adlittle.com/downloads/tx_adlreports/The_Growth_Accelerator.pdf

The Open Group Architecture Forum. *TOGAF architecture framework (TOGAF® v9.1)*. Retrieved March 22, 2016, from http://www.opengroup.org/subjectareas/enterprise/architecture

Treasury Board of Canada Secretariat. (2004). *Business transformation enablement program. A template for transformation readiness review*. Retrieved March 22, 2016, from www.tbs-sct.gc.ca/btep-pto/index_e.asp

Chapter 7
Developing Medical Record for Follow-Up of Wet Age-Related Macular Degeneration

Timo Korhonen

Abstract In this paper we consider development of a user-friendly medical record to follow-up treatment of wet AMD (age-related macular degeneration) with VEGF (vascular endothelial growth factor) inhibitors. A systematic user-centered design process is described that is realized together with ICT—experts and doctors. We will underline especially ways to solve challenges relating to multidisciplinary communication of all parties involved. The developed application tracks macula condition and medical treatments and can display them in a user-friendly fashion. Data searches can be done for a dedicated patient or overall patient histories. Modern ICT offers also several ways to process and represent the collected big data such that significant sickness development trends are easier to recognize and follow. Usability feedback mechanisms for health-care personnel are also discussed in the various application development phases that should be used to ensure user application quality and the continuous quality development of the respective caretaking practicalities.

Keywords Age-related Macular Degeneration • Big data • Healthcare

Background

Macular degeneration is a leading cause of vision loss in Americans 60 years of age and older. As many as 11 million people in the United States have some form of age-related macular degeneration. Also, in general, advanced age-related macular degeneration is a leading cause of irreversible blindness and visual impairment in the world. Age-related macular degeneration can be responsible of irreversible destruction of the macula, which leads first to loss of the sharp, fine-detail vision and later potentially to total blindness.

The macular degeneration is divided to dry and wet—types which of the wet-type is currently much easier to treat and is in the focus of this paper. In the wet macular degeneration (wet AMD), abnormal blood vessels (choroidal neovascularization,

T. Korhonen (✉)
Telecore Inc., Aalto University, Helsinki, Finland
e-mail: timo2228@gmail.com

© Springer International Publishing Switzerland 2017
R. Benlamri, M. Sparer (eds.), *Leadership, Innovation and Entrepreneurship as Driving Forces of the Global Economy*, Springer Proceedings in Business and Economics, DOI 10.1007/978-3-319-43434-6_7

77

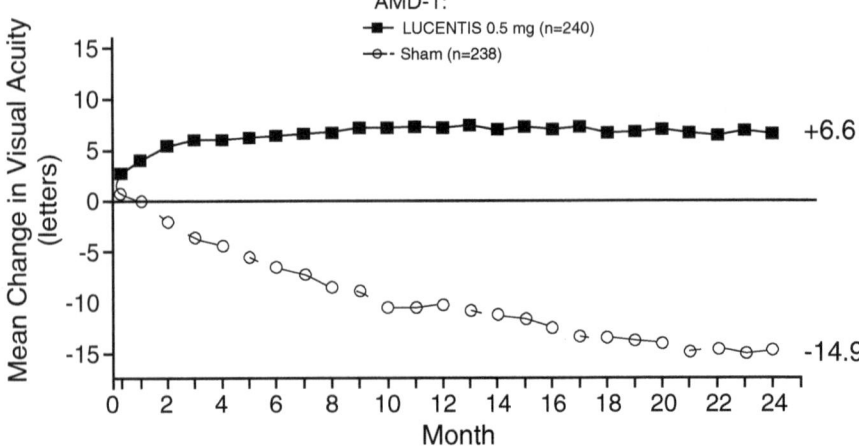

Fig. 7.1 Change of visual acuity in 24 months treatment with and without Lucentis VEGF—for wet AMD (http://www.rxlist.com/lucentis-drug/clinical-pharmacology.htm)

CNV) grow under the retina and macula resulting in bleeding and fluid leaking causing the macula to bulge or lift up. This can distort or finally destroy macular vision.

First ways to treat wet AMD were to seal retinal leaking vessels with a laser. The earliest treatment was laser photocoagulation that was followed by photodynamic therapy (PDT) where a light-activated drug is injected intravenously. The PDT does not cure the sickness but just hinders its worsening by patching the leaking vessels. Later a protein was located in the eye which accelerates development of blood vessels called "vascular endothelial growth factor" (VEGF). Then drugs were developed to inhibit VEGF operation. Three common types of VEGF inhibitors are in use: Eylea, Lucentis, and Avastin. All of these are given by intraocular injection. Generally, it is estimated that more than 30 VEGF inhibitors have been identified and tested in more than 2000 clinical trials.[1] Figure 7.1 summarizes the treatment effect with Lucentis VEGF inhibitor. We can see that the Lucentis injections can help to maintain visual acuity over the 24-month treatment period very well compared to the case where no treatment is given (Sham curve of Fig. 7.1).

Information and Communication Technology in Health-Care Applications

Amount of medical data is exploding in written and image form. An elementary question is how to effectively access, visualize, and understand the data. This framework is currently commonly addressed as the big data, challenge, and especially in

[1] https://www2.mdanderson.org/depts/oncolog/articles/12/6-jun/6-12-3.html

medical treatments the applicable answers relate to personal health and treatment costs that both are very important societal issues also. It is important that medical practices should be uniform. Therefore treatment cases should be efficiently classified and respective treatment practices carefully constructed. This is not possible if the information gathered during the treatment is not systematically analyzed and displayed for the doctors and nurses in charge of the care. This means that the medical personnel should be able to store and access the clinical data in efficient ways. An important role of the caretaking organization of its own is to practice high-quality research to process and publish new findings that would thus be available also to the worldwide medical community. This is often hampered by modest holistic information storage, processing, and visualization tools available in hospitals that don't support integrated ways to understand and manipulate the large amount of information available from various sources in current treatment chains.

Development of the wet AMD treatment follow-up tool for our target organization, Helsinki University Central Hospital, Department of Ophthalmology, started from the following research questions:

- Doctors and nurses giving wet AMD treatments experienced that it was difficult to get coherent and easy to grasp overall picture of the treatment progress both in individual and group levels over the treatment time periods.
- In practical wet AMD treatment time/patient is highly restricted, and the number of patients to be treated is large compared to the resources available. Hence, the follow-up application tools should be not only easy to use but also rich in information and data visualizations. User interface needs to be hierarchical such that seldom used features don't distract attention when not needed.
- Patient privacy issues should be clearly solved; still the application should be cloud based for scalability and easy maintenance.

Challenges of Clinical Cooperation for ICT Experts and Clinicians

Various medical application areas have specific ICT requirements. Objectives of creating and upkeeping medical records need to be carefully considered jointly with all the relevant experts. One should note that truly useful medical records are more than just repositories or data storages. Functional medical record solutions help to understand and jointly analyze the stored data. Also, data connections to practical treatment work need to be clearly applied in database user interfaces such that the database access application is easy to use both by doctors and nurses. Connection to personal health records can also be supported that can enable patient-specific feedbacks. Mutual understanding of ICT experts and medical professionals requires careful management of the respective user-centered design methods when the user application is designed and updated. The relating application design process is demanding due to its highly iterative, recursive, and multidisciplinary nature.

Applying User-Centric Design in Medical ICT User Application Design

A key question in truly functional medical record development is how to enable constructive interference between doctors, patients, and ICT experts while the user application service model is developed and elaborated. Technological persons have ideas of technical solutions, but they don't necessarily easily understand the relating medical processes and treatment targets. On the other hand, doctors know the medical goals and details but are only seldom clearly aware of ICT realization options and challenges of service or user interface designs. Both ICT experts and doctors can easily lack motivation in user application design if the mutual benefits are not continuously clarified for all parties. This can be realized by brainstorming practical benefits potentially to be achieved and by using design demos and prototypes in various stages of the design process to keep the proposed design details in some practical level that are easy to understand, discuss, and share by all parties. When the caretaking practices can be improved by better understanding the treatment processes, more efficient and user-friendly caretaking policies can be developed. High-quality medical records can provide a quick overview of treatments as well as to match, support, and develop current medical care practices of the clinic.

Generally speaking, context of use is a very important framework for medical record quality inspections. Hence we need to consider technical, physical, social, and organizational environment for particular users, tasks, and equipment. A summarizing illustration of some appropriate quality grading template is given in Bevan (1995), Table 1. For a holistic discussion of user-centered design connection to product development, see for instance Korhonen and Ainamo (2003).

Figure 7.2a shows the applied user-centered design process. The context of use and application requirements are first discussed with medical experts where after a service mock-up (Usability Net) is constructed reflecting both medical and ICT requirements. In the next meeting, the mock-up is reviewed and modification options

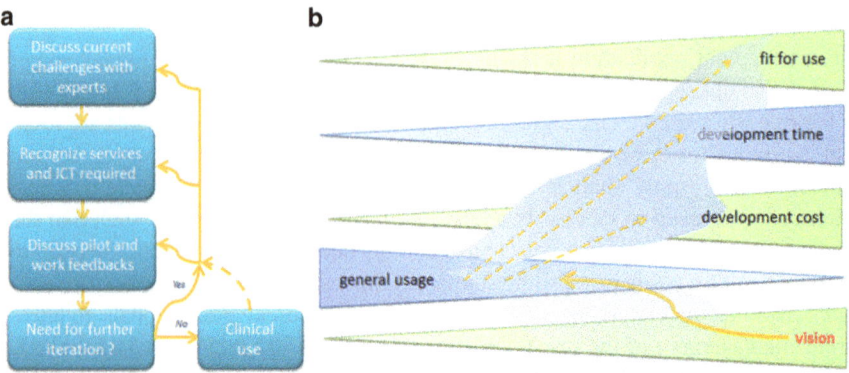

Fig. 7.2 (**a**) Applied user-centered design process, (**b**) trade-offs in clinical ICT development

discussed. These meetings are then continued until mutual satisfaction is reached. Thereafter application is taken into use in parallel of present tools that enables their safe comparison in clinical settings. Results of these clinical tests are then summarized and further jointly discussed. For a longer run, user feedback gathering and related gathered data processing practicalities are then agreed in order to maintain and further develop the wet AMD medical record application.

Figure 7.2b depicts some important general trade-offs of clinical ICT application development. First, there needs to be fit for usage. This means that the developed user application (e.g., user service) needs to be usable and truly useful for all user groups. Especially, the application should not increase workload by offering no clear improvements for care. Often, for instance, multiple feedings of a great number of similar data to different applications can be especially frustrating and time consuming. Application development time and cost go hand in hand. We generally expect that the longer the application development time is the more development costs will accumulate but also some better fitness of use should be obtained. Also, if the application is longer time developed, all parties involved should be able to increase their vision of the problems faced. In practice, however the development time and money is highly constrained that underlines importance of practical vision and development methodology of the developers to maximize general usage of the application. For instance, it is very common that medical or ICT experts can suggest some fancy service features that are not necessarily important for fitness of use. Therefore, efficient research conflict resolution methodology is required. In practice, this can be realized by parallel mock-ups that demonstrate the application with the various suggested features. When these alternatives are discussed in expert groups, a common understanding of applicable development pathways can be better realized.

Case study

Overview of the developed tool is shown in Fig. 7.3a. The application consists of two basic modules: *The User Module* consisting of Graphical User Interface, Access Management, Treatment Plan, Special Conditions, Search/data Export, and Help. *The Network (cloud) Module* consists of Secured Network Access, Patient Database, and Image Repository.

The system application is realized by Google App Engine. The Fig. 7.3b shows an overview of the developed application. The application main screen describes wet AMD development during the treatment period in terms of visual acuity (ETDRS letters) and retinal thickness (average in micrometers) for each clinic visit. The main user interface provides access to treatment plan details and enables to inspect various diagnostic images of retina. These include especially ANG angiography overall condition of retinal blood vessels and OCT retinal tomography images (abbreviations in caps refer to retinal images of Fig. 7.3b). The help feature is realized by task-tailored video clips that show in detail how each of the tasks relating to

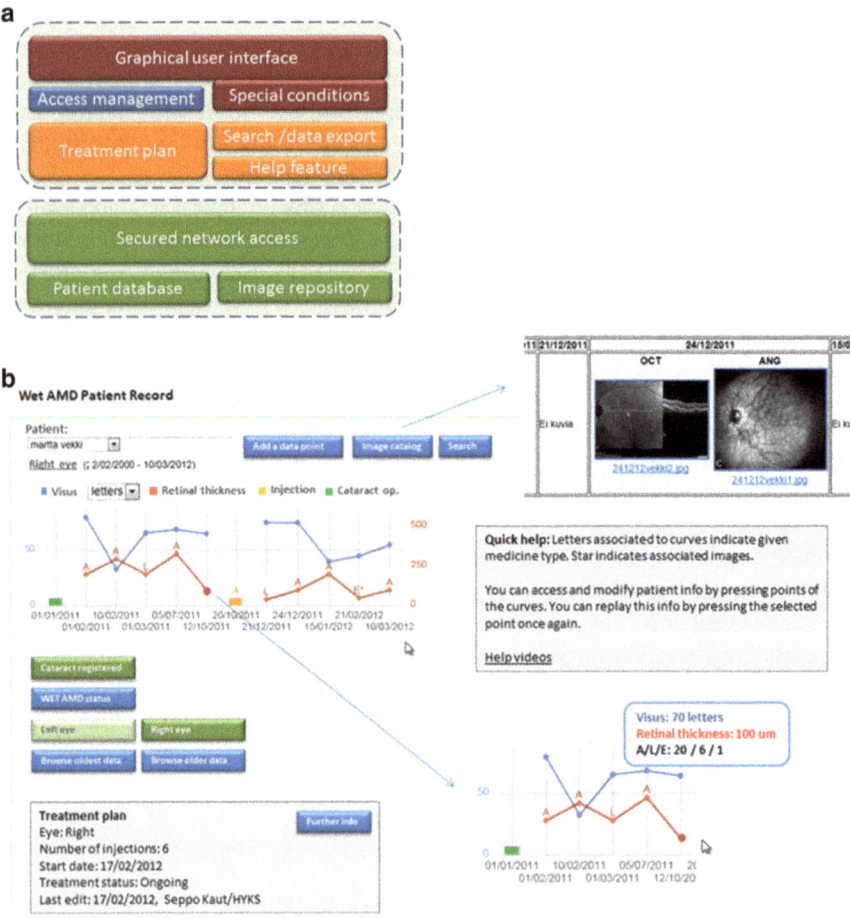

Fig. 7.3 Realization—wet AMD follow-up tool: (**a**) *upper figure*, system modules; (**b**) *lower figure*, outline of the main screen functionalities with treatment curves and retina—figures (A/L/E refers to Avastin, Lucentis, and Eylea intraocular injections)

the treatment plan is realized in the application. The secured patient access is realized by https protocol and users are protected by personalized passwords.

Applications and Future Perspectives

Present wet AMD caretaking challenge includes especially better treatment practice individualization matching to patients' genome and external factors. Identification of valid biomarkers (Schmidt-Erfurth & Waldstein, 2016) relevant for visual function, disease activity, and prognosis can provide some more solid guidance for individual- and population-based therapeutic management. If patients could be classified early enough, improved treatment efficiency with lesser contraindications could result. Generally, an integrated analysis of the relevant functional and structural features of the care can thus be developed involving reliable automated algorithms and computational data analysis. For this application one can use, for instance, variance or regression analysis, linear/nonlinear models/regression, and multivariate/cluster analysis addressing various retinal and treatment parameters. This poses a significant big data visualization and analysis challenge due to a large number of patients and parameters characterizing each patient with wet AMD condition. We have investigated so far neural networks for recognizing of patient categories and nonlinear parametric retinal characteristic models to track treatment efficiency that will be reviewed in our presentation.

Summary

We have discussed in this paper process and challenges of developing a user-friendly wet AMD follow-up tool. Due to large degree of multidisciplinary context of use and user-/task-related factors, the wet AMD medical record development is a very demanding task. The ICT experts should apply discussions and repeated user-tested iteration loops with jointly agreed quality indicators while compressing ideas to truly usable designs. The ICT experts should be flexible to consider ideas openly. Medical professionals describe their problem frameworks from multiple angles using medical terms that need to be clarified. Building demos and/or quick prototypes and using them in the development discussions can be highly efficient in illustrating practical realizations and in clarifying design options. Analysis of relating patient data provides a big data challenge whose successful solutions can improve quality of care and reduce contraindications.

Acknowledgments This work has been financially supported by Helsinki University Central Hospital, Department of Ophthalmology, Finland, and Aalto University, Finland. The Author worked for this study with Telecore Inc. and is currently affiliated to Aalto University via Adj. Prof. (Docent) nomination.

References

Bevan, N. (1995). Measuring usability as quality of use. *Software Quality Journal, 4*, 115–150.
Google App Engine. Retrieved from https://cloud.google.com/appengine/
Korhonen, T., & Ainamo, A. (2003). *Handbook of product and service development in communication and information technology*. Boston: Kluwer Academic Press.
Schmidt-Erfurth, U., & Waldstein, S. M. (2016). A paradigm shift in imaging biomarkers in neovascular age-related macular degeneration. *Progress in Retinal and Eye Research, 50*, 1–24.
Usability Net. Retrieved from http://www.usabilitynet.org/home.htm

Chapter 8
Mobile Computing in the Construction Industry: Main Challenges and Solutions

M. Silverio, S. Renukappa, S. Suresh, and A. Donastorg

Abstract Cloud computing (CC) enables users to access application remotely, providing mobility and ubiquitous data access; this would be an advantage in construction management. In addition, mobile cloud computing (MCC) enables mobile devices to augment constrained resources such as processing, storage, and battery autonomy by using the cloud infrastructure. This paper is aimed at proposing solutions to some of the main challenges of the construction sector by adopting mobile cloud services. A literature review was performed highlighting the potential benefits and risks in the implementation of CC, infrastructure and execution of MCC, and main challenges in the construction industry. The main benefits of adopting cloud-based resources are cost reduction, system mobility, system flexibility, and system maintenance. While the main risks are information security, privileged user access, regulatory compliance, data location, availability, and disaster recovery. In terms of execution, cloud-based mobile applications present mostly benefits since they enable users to execute ubiquitously high-performance operations in mobile devices. The review of the literature provided enough information for this paper to suggest solutions to some of the main challenges in the construction sector, namely: design, materials, finance, management, and knowledge. The solutions are mainly based on providing mobility, ubiquitous data access, and improved cross-functional communication.

Keywords Sustainability • Mobile cloud computing • Construction industry • AEC sector • Mobile computing

M. Silverio • S. Renukappa (✉) • S. Suresh • A. Donastorg
Faculty of Science and Engineering, University of Wolverhampton, Wulfurna Street, City Campus, WV11LY, Wolverhampton, UK
e-mail: m.a.silveriofernandez@wlv.ac.uk; suresh.renukappa@wlv.ac.uk; s.subashini@wlv.ac.uk; A.Donastorg@wlv.ac.uk

© Springer International Publishing Switzerland 2017
R. Benlamri, M. Sparer (eds.), *Leadership, Innovation and Entrepreneurship as Driving Forces of the Global Economy*, Springer Proceedings in Business and Economics, DOI 10.1007/978-3-319-43434-6_8

Introduction

The concept of CC was first introduced in 2004 (Vouk, 2008). It has been defined by practitioners in commercial and academic spheres in different perspectives and visions. More than 20 definitions have been found by Vaquero et al. (2009) about CC. The most widely recognized definition of CC is provided by the National Institute of Standards and Technology (NIST). According to NIST definition of CC:

> Cloud computing is a model enabling ubiquitous, convenient, on-demand network access to a shared pool of configurable computing resources (e.g. networks, servers, storages, applications and services) that can be rapidly provisioned and released with minimal management effort or service provider interaction.

CC makes applications available remotely and would be an advantage in construction management. This would allow the staff to work from any place without being tied to any specific location (Rountree & Castrillo, 2013). Cloud computing also provides a healthy working environment and contributes to energy sustainability by cutting down the use of multiple servers and computers by using virtual computing technology. This would reduce the carbon footprint and also cut down the floor space needed for multiple server racks (Menken, 2012). In addition to these positive features, there is a set of potential risks in implementing CC. Such risks include but are not limited to data security, integration with legacy systems, and inability to restore and backup data (Jansen & Hooks, 2011). Any industry attempting to implement CC should consider both benefits and risk in its implementation.

The construction sector is a fragmented industry, where many stakeholders and parties need to work together to deliver a project successfully. This industry has always had challenges like finance, reputation, and productivity; current trends in the industry attempt to embed sustainability into projects and implement relative new technologies like BIM, which transforms the typical building design cycle. Furthermore, new management tools and techniques have been developed which enhance productivity and cross-communication. Considering the fragmented nature of information in construction explained by Box (2014) and all the new technologies currently being implemented in construction projects, it seems necessary to redefine the main challenges facing the industry. Subsequently, forefront technologies should be proposed as solutions for the industry since this might provide new insight to legacy and brand new challenges in the construction sector.

This paper aims contribute to a broader research about the implementation of mobile devices in the construction sector, by establishing how one of the technologies found in mobile devices (in this case mobile cloud computing) can be used to solve some of the main challenges found in construction projects. It is the interest of this paper to discuss the solutions offered by MCC in the construction industry.

MCC comes from the integration of CC in handheld devices which provides mobility and ubiquitous data access as main features. According to Abolfazli, Sanaei, Ahmed, Gani, and Buyya (2014), the infrastructure of MCC suggests an objective and subjective perspective for addressing an MCC environment, which in terms of execution of cloud-based mobile applications present mostly benefits since they enable users to execute ubiquitously high-performance operations in mobile devices.

Research Methodology

This paper is aimed at exploring potential benefits and risks in the implementation of CC, infrastructure and execution of MCC, and main challenges in the construction sector. Finally, this paper proposes potential solutions to some of these challenges by adopting MCC.

This paper follows a systematic approach for reviewing compendium of literature in order to explore the current research in this field. The search for peer-reviewed journal articles has been done via databases, and subsequently, this allowed to perform a literature review. A literature review is a systematic and reproducible method for identifying and synthesizing the existing body of recorded work generated by researchers or scholars (Fink, 1998). It provides a summary of themes and issues in a specific research field. Due to the ever increasing number of academic papers (journals, books, conferences, and workshops), literature reviews have become an indispensable method for synthesizing a specific research field (Teuteberg & Wittstruck, 2010).

This study first identifies the current definition for CC and the main features found in the cloud computing model. The different types of cloud models are defined as well as the different service models. Sections "Potential Benefits of Implementing Cloud Computing in Construction Management" and "Potential Risks in the Adoption of Cloud Computing" details the potential benefits and risks related to the implementation of cloud services in a company. Section "Mobile Cloud Computing" goes a step further and describes the infrastructure and execution of MCC. The main challenges in the construction industry found in the literature are presented in section "Main Challenges in the Construction Industry". After providing with an understanding of the current challenges in the construction sector, section "Mobile Cloud Computing as a Solution for Challenges in Sustainable Construction" presents solutions for some of these challenges, based on the benefits offered by MCC. Finally, conclusions were drawn, summarizing how the infrastructure and execution of MCC can be integrated into construction projects and help with some of the main challenges of the industry.

Results

Classification and Service Models of Cloud Computing

According to NIST, the cloud computing model comprises five essential characteristics, three service models, and four deployment models (Mell & Grance, 2010).

The characteristics found in the cloud computing model are on-demand self-service, resource pooling, broad network access, measured service, and rapid elasticity (Mell & Grance, 2010). On-demand service denotes the unilateral provisioning of resources without human interaction with the provider while resource pooling refers to the aggregation of resources such as storage, bandwidth, etc. Broad network access denotes services being delivered over a network. Measured service is the automatic control and optimization of resources through pay-per-use metering capabilities. Finally rapid elasticity accounts for resources being dynamically scaled up and down with demand (Brender & Markov, 2013).

There are different types of clouds, each with its own advantages and disadvantages. According to NIST in terms of deployments, there are private clouds, public clouds, community clouds, and hybrid clouds (Mell & Grance, 2010). In public clouds service providers offer their resources as services to the general public. On the other hand in private clouds, the cloud infrastructure is provided only for the use of a single organization, thus giving the organization more control over security and transparency. Community clouds provide cloud infrastructure to several organizations with similar security concerns and compliance requirements (Carroll, Van Der Merwe, & Kotze, 2011). Hybrid clouds are a combination of several cloud types, such as public, private, or community (Brender & Markov, 2013).

When migrating to a cloud computing system, organizations can choose the right combination of CC service models according to their needs. The three CC service models are Software as a Service (SaaS), Platform as a Service (PaaS), and Infrastructure as a Service (IaaS). Figure 8.1 shows a current example of services offered within each model (Zhang, Cheng, & Boutaba, 2010).

IaaS refers to the on-demand provisioning of infrastructural resources, such as processing, storage, and networks. Examples of this type of cloud solution include Amazon's Elastic Compute Cloud (EC2), Joyent, and GoGrid (Sultan, 2011). PaaS refers to providing platform layer resources such as operating system support and software development frameworks, thus offering an operating platform that enables the disposition of existing applications that use programming tools from the provider. Products in this group include Microsoft Azure, Google App Engine, and Amazon Web services (Sultan, 2011). PaaS provider can run its cloud on top of an IaaS provider's cloud; however, according to Zhang et al. (2010) in current practice, IaaS and PaaS providers are often parts of the same organization (e.g., Salesforce

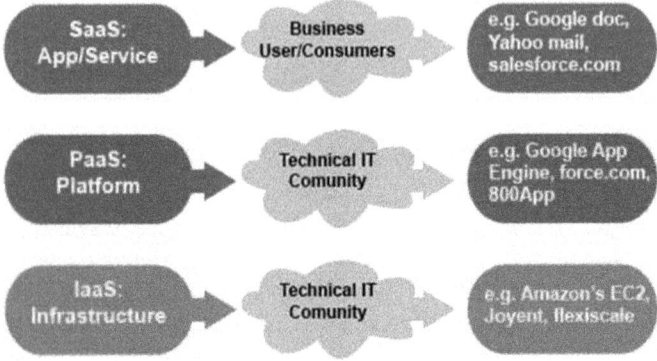

Fig. 8.1 Service models in cloud computing

Fig. 8.2 Service models diagram according to Zhang et al. (2010)

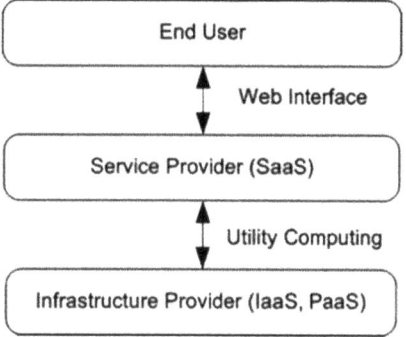

and Google). For this reason, the term "infrastructure providers" is utilized when referring to PaaS and IaaS providers (see Fig. 8.2).

On top of PaaS and IaaS, there is SaaS, which runs on cloud infrastructure and provides a range of applications, such as spreadsheets, word processing, HR management, customer relationship management (CRM), enterprise resource planning (ERP) systems, etc. With a limited control over the applications' configuration settings, SaaS has the lowest degree of customization; nevertheless, users can also customize the products by developing specific components based on application program interfaces (APIs) made available by cloud providers (Sultan, 2010).

Potential Benefits of Implementing Cloud Computing in Construction Management

Cheng and Kumar (2012) reviewed previous studies regarding the perceived benefits of the cloud computing model according to the IT Cloud Services Survey conducted by the International Data Corporation. Subsequently, the nature of the construction industry and the cloud computing model was reviewed, suggesting four major benefits of CC for construction collaboration and management. Such improvements are in cost, mobility, flexibility, and maintenance and updating.

- *Cost reduction*

The conventional way of IT delivery presents a major difference with cloud computing model mainly because of the utility-based pricing model of such model. Most AEC companies are SMEs with small employees and little budget; these features are a crucial barrier of IT adoption in the AEC industry. CC presents itself as a solution that seems to address this vital issue for the construction industry (Cheng & Kumar, 2012).

Currently, cloud computer users pay the service providers based on a month or annual subscription, also depending on the amount of IT resources and time that are used. Traditionally, companies make payment at the time when they purchase software and hardware systems. The initial investment is redeemed, eventually depending on the designated usage duration of the systems. Enabling cloud users to pay monthly or for their usage allows them to switch to cheaper options whenever available or required. The user can also terminate the contract earlier with the cloud service providers if the project finishes in a shorter timeframe (Cheng & Kumar, 2012).

- *System mobility*

In a cloud computing environment, systems and programs operate on the clouds. That means end users can access the same information from different locations and run computationally demanding applications such as structural analysis only by using a web-enabled device, e.g., desktop computers or smart phones.

- *System flexibility*

The level of IT that a project needs varies throughout its lifecycle, hence the convenience of cloud-based resources. These can be flexibly deployed and terminated, as well as scaled up and down. Consequently, IT cost changes to a variable cost rather than a fixed cost.

- *System maintenance*

IaaS and PaaS providers continuously maintain their systems and deliver IT resources such as CPUs, memory, and operating systems as individual services. As a result, this avoids the disposal of companies' obsolete computers and continuous installation of patches for operating systems.

Potential Risks in the Adoption of Cloud Computing

CC presents significant risks and challenges. According to a survey of nearly 1800 US businesses and IT professionals by the Information Systems Audit and Control Association (2010), 45 % consider the risks of CC as outweighing the benefits. Brender and Markov (2013) establish the main topics of concern regarding the adoption of CC from a management point of view as follows: information security, privileged user access, regulatory compliance and data location, investigative support, availability and disaster recovery, and provider lock-in and long-term viability.

- *Information security*

Information security is one of the major concerns regarding the adoption of cloud services; the technology's presence on the Internet and the substantial concentration of data present an attractive target for hackers (ENISA, 2009). According to Carroll et al. (2011), information security is rated as a top threat in interviews with South African participants. In addition, Sultan (2011) cites a survey carried out by the International Data Corporation (IDC) where around 75 % of respondents said they were concerned about security.

- *Privileged user access*

Another important risk is privileged user access; this denotes the existing risk of a malicious insider who may cause brand damage and financial and productivity losses to a cloud customer (Hubbard and Sutton, 2010). For a better understanding, it is necessary to remember that the processing of sensitive data outside the premises of a company bypasses the security controls that an in-house IT department employs. Hence a good practice for customers is to procure information on the hiring and oversight of privileged cloud administrators (Heiser & Nicolett, 2008). A solution established for this concern is the use of the least privilege principle, which proposes granting to individuals or processes the minimum privileges and resources for the minimum period of time required to complete a task (CSA, 2011).

- *Regulatory compliance*

Regulatory audit compliance is an important concern among cloud subcontractors. According to Heiser and Nicolett (2008), traditional cloud providers have to submit to security certifications and external audit and provide customers with information about the security controls that have been evaluated. With regard to the privacy regulations in different jurisdictions, data location is a big concern among companies subcontracting cloud services. One example is the data held in US-based data centers, which may be accessed by the US government as provided by the Patriot Act.

- *Data location*

EU governments have privacy regulations that prohibit the release of certain data outside of the EU. Consequently, companies like Amazon and Microsoft allow their customers to choose the physical location of the data (e.g., EU or the USA).

- *Availability and disaster recovery*

Availability of cloud services is an important point of concern for businesses, especially for critical business processes. Heiser and Nicolett (2008) suggest that any enterprise procuring outsourcing critical business processes to the cloud should establish, together with the provider, a service-level agreement (SLA) for the availability of service for critical business processes. A similar issue is disaster recovery. According to Carroll et al. (2011), it is considered as an area of critical importance and ranks second after information security by 66.7 % of the votes. In addition Prakash (2011) establishes the importance for a business to require information on what happens to their data in case of disaster and how long the recovery process could last.

- *Additional risks and challenges*

After analyzing a study conducted by consulting firm Cambridge Technology Partners about Swiss businesses' engagement in CC, Brender and Markov (2013) obtained several legal, technical, and operational risks or threats in migrating to a cloud service. The original study submitted five reports analyzing the risks and challenges and proposing mitigation practices in the adoption of public cloud services by five companies based in Switzerland. Two of these companies can be considered as small and medium enterprises (SMEs) and the other three as economically significant enterprises.

The risks summarized by Brender and Markov (2013) are teething problems, application performance on the cloud, loss of governance, determination of the competent authorities in case of conflict, cost, economic denial of service, data segregation, data destruction, data traceability, security during data transportation, security of financial transactions, and physical security and natural disasters.

Mobile Cloud Computing

MCC employs both the storage services and application processing services of computational clouds to enable off-device storage and compute-intensive applications on mobile devices (Ahmed, Gani, Sookhak, Ab Hamid, & Xia, 2015). According to Abolfazli et al. (2014), MCC focuses on alleviating resource limitations in mobile devices by implementing a variety of augmentation strategies, such as storage augmentation, screen augmentation, application processing augmentation, and energy augmentation. Ahmed et al. (2015) establish MCC as a computing model which reduces the development and execution cost of mobile applications while at the same time extends the widespread services and resources of computational clouds for mitigating resource limitations in mobile devices, hence enabling the mobile user to acquire new technology conveniently on demand basis.

- *Infrastructure and management of mobile cloud computing*

The augmentation of computing resources of mobile devices is possible thanks to MCC. Several infrastructures need to work in the same environment in order to enable MCC, namely, wireless infrastructure, backhaul, backbone, provider infrastructure, and cloud infrastructure (Marotta et al., 2015). This infrastructure can be better appreciated in Fig. 8.3.

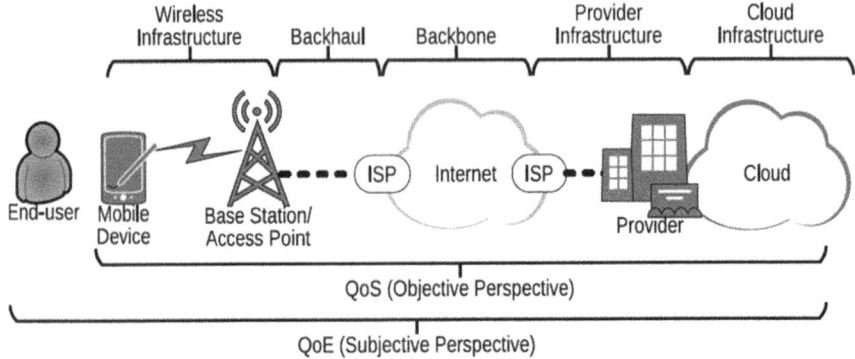

Fig. 8.3 Mobile cloud computing environment (Marotta et al., 2015)

The end user establishes communication with a base station or access point though a mobile device, requesting a resource augmentation from the cloud. After reaching the base station, the request is forwarded through the backhaul to an Internet service provider (ISP). The backbone routes the request along one or several ISPs. Once the request reaches the destination ISP, it accesses the provider infrastructure, where the target cloud receives the request and allocates resources inside the cloud infrastructure. Inside the cloud infrastructure, virtual nodes communicate with one another through virtual links; such links are an abstraction of the real network links with specific features, such as routing protocol, capacity, and virtual node endpoints. Finally, the cloud provides the requested resources, replying to the mobile device across the five infrastructures (Marotta et al., 2015).

The Quality of Service (QoS) provides an objective view about the quality of network, considering parameters like throughput, delay, and jitter; QoS encompasses every element of the MCC infrastructure with the exception of the end user (Abolfazli et al., 2014). On the other hand, the Quality of Experience (QoE) provides a subjective view about the quality of network, with parameters like satisfaction level with application navigation, cloud ubiquity, and response time (Rengaraju, Lung, Yu, & Srinivasan, 2012). Both QoS and QoE parameters are important for a MCC service. Usually, administrators focus their attention on QoS parameters, whereas end users pay more attention to QoE parameters.

In terms of management, Marotta et al. (2015) mapped five functional areas into key requirements for any MCC management systems, namely, fault, configuration, performance, accounting, and security. These requirements are better explained in Table 8.1.

Marotta et al. (2015) establish two management entities in the network management research field, namely, agents and managers. The agent is a software module placed inside an infrastructure component and is responsible for monitoring local

Table 8.1 MCC management requirements (Marotta et al., 2015)

Requirement	MCC environment
Fault	The management system must be aware of the five infrastructure faults to avoid QoS and QoE degradation
Configuration	The management system must reconfigure the five infrastructures to achieve correctness and autonomy based on QoS and QoE
Accounting	The management system must monitor and measure the usage of the five infrastructure through QoS and QoE for billing correctness and auditing purposes
Performance	The management system must support a large number of mobile services performing asynchronous communications to avoid compromising the proper operation of the MCC environment
Security	The management system must authenticate, authorize, and account (AAA) end users' actions inside the MCC environment, avoiding impersonation attacks as well as providing a stronger auditing

parameters, such as maximum transmission unit and available memory. The manager, on the other hand, is a role assumed by a network node, e.g., routers or computers, and is responsible for retrieving information from agents and managing a network slice or domain.

- *Execution of cloud-based mobile applications*

Cloud-based mobile applications run both on the cloud and mobile devices, consisting of two types of components: transferable and nontransferable. Transferable components are compute-intensive tasks and do not interact with the mobile hardware. Instead, they are transferred to the cloud. Nontransferable components are implemented in the mobile devices and are designed for especial functionalities, such as user interface and hardware access (Cuervo et al., 2010).

In MCC Ahmed et al. (2015) define three states for cloud-based application, such as running state, paused state, and terminated state. The execution of a mobile application starts as soon as the user taps the application icon. After this, the application enters into the running state where different tasks can be performed. When the migration into the cloud is required, the application enters into paused state, and all the running states are saved and migrated to the cloud server where the application is resumed and reconfigured using the saved states. Finally, after finishing the execution on the cloud server, the results are pushed back to the mobile device, where the application resumes its execution, where on completion the application stops and enters into the terminated state.

In context of optimal application execution, various metrics are defined by Ahmed et al. (2015) for optimal application migration of mobile applications. These metrics can be classified into five different areas, namely, network, application type, mobile device, and cost and user preferences.

Network-related parameters are wireless link quality, latency, security, available bandwidth, network latency, and network cost. In order to attain the optimal execution of mobile cloud applications, it is recommended to select a network with low latency, available bandwidth, and better wireless link quality, thus reducing execution time.

The application type plays an important role in the adoption of a cloud integration. The characteristics of mobile applications vary from application to application. According to Zhang and Figueiredo (2006), mobile applications can be classified as CPU-intensive, memory-intensive, and input/output-intensive. In addition, Nazir, Ma, and Seneviratne (2009), Cano and Domenech-Asensi (2011), and Ballagas et al. (2007) classify mobile applications as delay sensitive, security intensive, and network intensive, respectively. When considering off-loading the processing tasks of an application to the cloud, the best candidates are memory and CPU-intensive applications; whereas input, network, and security-intensive application will show more constraints to run in a remote cloud.

Important metrics to consider related to mobile devices are CPU speed, memory, storage, battery, wireless access technologies, and number of interfaces. These parameters are used to build the processing load, which is used to determine if an application process may not have a sufficient number of CPU cycles for its execution. Subsequently, such application requires migration to a remote cloud server for smooth execution Lenders, Wagner, and May (2006).

The parameters related to cost are mainly the monetary cost of wireless networks and the cloud. Usually users can use WiFi for application off-loading; nevertheless whenever WiFi is not available, a mobile user can switch to the Internet service provided by the network.

In terms of user preferences, there are three parameters to consider for running an application in dynamics wireless environment with a variety of access technologies, namely, Quality of Services, cost, and security.

Main Challenges in the Construction Industry

Proverbs et al. (2000) established the main challenges and problems facing the UK construction industry at the time. These problems were also classified by relevance according to interviews and surveys to construction company directors.

There are 18 challenges grouped in nine categories: (1) public perception, (2) tendering problems, (3) procurement problems, (4) design challenges, (5) finance, (6) human resources, (7) productivity, and (8) material and (9) technological challenges.

A posterior trending research in sustainability revealed a whole set of challenges regarding sustainability in construction. Ayarkwa, Agyekum, and Adinyira (2011) highlighted the following barriers for the successful implementation of lean construction in the Ghanaian construction industry: finance, politics, management, technical, sociocultural, and knowledge. Häkkinen and Belloni (2011) studied the following barriers for sustainable building on the basis of literature and interviews carried out in Finland: steering and regulation, demand and the role of clients, procurement and tendering processes, process phases and scheduling of tasks, cooperation and networking, knowledge and common language, availability of integrated methods, and innovation.

The barriers found by Häkkinen and Belloni (2011), Ayarkwa et al. (2011), and Proverbs et al. (2000) can all be embedded into a list of challenges in the construction industry which encompasses the latest trending research in sustainability; such challenges are public perception, design, human resources, materials, tendering and procurement, finance, management, knowledge, sociocultural barriers, and political challenges.

There is a sustainability aspect inherent in each one of these challenges. In terms of sustainability, all the challenges are intertwined, as a consequence by offering a solution to one of the challenges others might be benefited. From simple inspection and analysis, six challenges show potential for improvement by the implementation of MCC technologies. Those challenges are (1) design problems, (2) materials, (3) finance, (4) technology, (5) management, and (6) knowledge. The remaining barriers will be indirectly affected by the enhancement of the selected group.

Mobile Cloud Computing as a Solution for Challenges in Sustainable Construction

MCC carries all the benefits and risks of cloud computing into a mobile device, thus providing to the user with mobility. This section addresses how MCC can support the construction industry in regards of the challenges of sustainable construction. The challenges addressed are (1) design, (2) materials, (3) finance, (4) management, and (5) knowledge. These challenges/barriers (selected from section "Main Challenges in the Construction Industry") were obtained from analyzing prior literature and combining the typical challenges in construction with new sustainability issues and concepts.

- *Solutions for design challenges*

According to Proverbs et al. (2000), over-specification is one of the main issues related to design; some buildings have been found to have an unnecessary number of features and areas due to over-specification. Nevertheless, nowadays, there are more technologies related to the design field of construction (e.g., BIM and CAD), which provide designers with a much faster design cycle. With technologies like BIM and CAD being implemented in the current industry, there is a lot of design iterations and changes being made during a construction project, and this is one of the main causes of design-related errors. BIM brings the idea of converging all the models into one model where every party of the design team (electrical, architectural, etc.) can load their designs and see how it affects the other party.

For successfully implementing BIM in a project, it is necessary to use CC for collaboration and communication between different design teams. This enables BIM users to load and access the BIM model from the cloud. By adding MCC users are also able to perform design queries and access real-time information regarding the BIM model.

- *Solutions for material-related challenges*

The main material-related issues in the construction sector are a lack of environmentally sustainable materials and waste management. These barriers have a direct impact on the success of implementation of sustainable construction principles. The main solution for these barriers is providing digital control of the entire material lifecycle, from fabrication and shipment to inspection and disposal. Currently, mobile devices like tablets can provide a ubiquitous solution which eliminates paper-based material management processes (e.g., Jovix). MCC is a key element for making this kind of solution ubiquitous and totally eliminating the use of paper, consequently decreasing errors related to materials management.

- *Solutions for financial challenges*

Financial barriers have always been an issue in the construction industry, but lately with new sustainability practices, there is a fear of higher investment costs and long payback periods. According to Ayarkwa et al. (2011), the additional cost of providing measures to improve the sustainability of construction works is a major barrier to the realization of sustainable construction concept. From a financial point of view, CC can help to reduce costs in a construction project due to its flexibility to expand according to the project's requirements; however, these cost reductions contribute against the classic financial barrier in a construction project and not against the sustainability-related financial aspects.

- *Solutions for management challenges*

Project management encompasses many aspects of construction projects such as productivity, scheduling of tasks, and process phases. Shehu and Akintoye (2010) identified the major challenges to the successful practice of program management in the UK construction industry; some of the top challenges are late delivery of projects, lack of knowledge to evaluate risks, lack of cross-functional communication, etc. MCC enables management tools to be used on site; consequently, managers can embed these features into their project management strategy. By embedding mobility and ubiquitous data access into their strategy, managers can enhance their productivity and cross-functional communication; thus, MCC should positively benefit a project's punctual delivery and scheduling of tasks.

- *Solutions for knowledge challenges*

The knowledge-related barriers found in the construction sector are mainly related to a lack of the required skill set or technical knowledge for a specific task in a project. Häkkinen and Belloni (2011) discuss the lack of knowledge and information in a sustainable building project, highlighting the integration of sustainability into building design. According to Ayarkwa et al. (2011), some of the barriers related to knowledge and awareness in a sustainable construction environment are a lack of professional knowledge, lack of awareness of clients, lack of awareness of benefits, ignorance/misunderstanding about sustainability, lack of education, and lack of knowledge in sustainable design.

CC can be a solution in terms of providing a common terminology between every construction project party. By uploading all the technical information in the cloud and giving access to the project's management workforce, a common terminology can be established, and cross-communication can be improved. MCC has the potential to enable mobile devices to access any kind of technical information, thus giving access to the management workforce on a daily basis to obtain any relevant technical data from any location. Nevertheless, this solution should be used as a consultation bank and not as a replacement for staff training.

Conclusions

CC presents itself as a technology with mobility, flexibility, and ease of maintenance. MCC alleviates resource limitations in mobile devices by augmenting storage, energy, and application processing. In contrast, information security is one of the major challenges and concerns when adopting cloud services. According to Carroll et al. (2011), information security is rated as a top threat. With major technology companies like Google, Amazon, and Apple acting as cloud service providers, we can expect an enormous and constant effort from these companies in increasing information security.

By analyzing the benefits and risks of MCC, this paper offered solutions for some of the main challenges in the construction industry, such as design, materials, finance, management, and knowledge. The main proposition of value made by MCC is providing the users with mobility and the ability to perform queries and access real-time information ubiquitously. Based on this premise, the industry can create and incorporate a new set of tools for optimizing different aspects of a construction projects' life cycle. Consequently, the information decentralization in the construction industry highlighted by Box (2014) could be reduced if such tools are implemented.

References

Abolfazli, S., Sanaei, Z., Ahmed, E., Gani, A., & Buyya, R. (2014). Cloud-based augmentation for mobile devices: Motivation, taxonomies, and open challenges. *IEEE Communications Surveys & Tutorials, 16*(1), 337–368.

Ahmed, E., Gani, A., Sookhak, M., Ab Hamid, S. H., & Xia, F. (2015). Application optimization in mobile cloud computing: Motivation, taxonomies, and open challenges. *Journal of Network and Computer Applications, 52*, 52–68.

CSA (2011). Security guidance for critical areas of focus in cloud computing v3. 0. *Cloud Security Alliance.*

Ayarkwa, J., Agyekum, K., & Adinyira, E. (2011). *Barriers to sustainable implementation of lean construction in the Ghanaian building industry* (p. 67). Paper presented at the Sixth Built Environment Conference Johannesburg South Africa July 31–August 2, 2011.

Ballagas, R. A., Kratz, S. G., Borchers, J., Yu, E., Walz, S. P., Fuhr, C. O., et al. (2007). *REXplorer: A mobile, pervasive spell-casting game for tourists* (pp. 1929–1934). Paper presented at the CHI'07 Extended Abstracts on Human Factors in Computing Systems.

Box. (2014). *The information economy: A study of five industries.* Available: https://www.box.com/blog/mapping-the-information-economy-a-tale-offive-industries/.

Brender, N., & Markov, I. (2013). Risk perception and risk management in cloud computing: Results from a case study of Swiss companies. *International Journal of Information Management, 33*(5), 726–733.

Cano, M., & Domenech-Asensi, G. (2011). A secure energy-efficient m-banking application for mobile devices. *Journal of Systems and Software, 84*(11), 1899–1909.

Carroll, M., Van Der Merwe, A., & Kotze, P. (2011). *Secure cloud computing: Benefits, risks and controls* (pp. 1–9). Paper presented at the Information Security South Africa (ISSA), 2011.

Cheng, J. C., & Kumar, B. (2012). Cloud computing support for construction collaboration. In *Mobile and pervasive computing in construction* (pp. 237–254).

Cuervo, E., Balasubramanian, A., Cho, D., Wolman, A., Saroiu, S., Chandra, R., et al. (2010). *MAUI: Making smartphones last longer with code offload* (pp. 49–62). Paper presented at the Proceedings of the 8th International Conference on Mobile Systems, Applications, and Services.

European Network and Information Security Agency. (2009). *Cloud computing: Benefits, risks and recommendations for information security.* ENISA.

Fink, A. (1998). *Conducting research literature reviews: From paper to the internet.* 1st ed. Los Angeles, United States: Thousand Oaks : Sage Publications.

Häkkinen, T., & Belloni, K. (2011). Barriers and drivers for sustainable building. *Building Research & Information, 39*(3), 239–255.

Heiser, J., & Nicolett, M. (2008). *Assessing the security risks of cloud computing. Gartner report.*

Hubbard, D., & Sutton, M. (2010). Top threats to cloud computing v1. 0. *Cloud Security Alliance.*

ISACA, U. (2010). *ISACA US IT risk/reward barometer survey.* The Information Systems Audit and Control Association [Online]. Retrieved December 12, 2014, from http://www.Isaca.org/About-ISACA/Press-room/News-Releases/2010/Pages/ISACA-US-IT-Risk-Reward--Barometer-Survey.Aspx

Jansen, W., & Hooks, C. (2011) *Security and privacy issues in cloud computing system sciences (HICSS).* Paper presented at the 2011 44th Hawaii International Conference on.

Lenders, V., Wagner, J., & May, M. (2006). *Analyzing the impact of mobility in ad hoc networks* (pp. 39–46). Paper presented at the Proceedings of the 2nd International Workshop on Multi-Hop Ad Hoc Networks: From Theory to Reality.

Marotta, M. A., Faganello, L. R., Schimuneck, M. A. K., Granville, L. Z., Rochol, J., & Both, C. B. (2015). Managing mobile cloud computing considering objective and subjective perspectives. *Computer Networks.*

Mell, P., & Grance, T. (2010). *The NIST definition of cloud computing.* New York: Assoc Computing Machinery.

Menken, I. (2012). *An introduction to Cloud Computing.* Emereo Publishing.

Nazir, F., Ma, J., & Seneviratne, A. (2009). *Time critical content delivery using predictable patterns in mobile social networks* (Vol. 4, pp. 1066–1073). Paper presented at the International Conference on Computational Science and Engineering, 2009, CSE'09.

Prakash, S. (2011). Risk management: Cloud computing considerations. *Canadian Management Accounting.*

Proverbs, D.G., Holt, G.D. and Cheok, H.Y., 2000. Construction industry problems: the views of UK construction Directors, 16th Annual ARCOM Conference 2000, pp. 73–81.

Rengaraju, P., Lung, C., Yu, F. R., & Srinivasan, A. (2012). On QoE monitoring and E2E service assurance in 4G wireless networks. *IEEE Wireless Communications, 19*(4), 89–96.

Rountree, D. and Castrillo, I., 2013. The basics of cloud computing: Understanding the fundamentals of cloud computing in theory and practice. Newnes.

Shehu, Z., & Akintoye, A. (2010). Major challenges to the successful implementation and practice of programme management in the construction environment: A critical analysis. *International Journal of Project Management, 28*(1), 26–39.

Sultan, N. (2010). Cloud computing for education: A new dawn? *International Journal of Information Management, 30*(2), 109–116.

Sultan, N. A. (2011). Reaching for the "cloud": How SMEs can manage. *International Journal of Information Management, 31*(3), 272–278.

Teuteberg, F., & Wittstruck, D. (2010). A systematic review of sustainable supply chain management. *Multikonferenz Wirtschaftsinformatik, 2010*, 203.

Vaquero, L.M., Rodero-Merino, L., Caceres, J. and Lindner, M., 2009. A Break in the Clouds: Towards a Cloud Definition. New York: Assoc Computing Machinery.

Vouk, M.A., 2008. Cloud computing - Issues, research and implementations, 2008, IEEE, pp. 31–40.

Zhang, Q., Cheng, L., & Boutaba, R. (2010). Cloud computing: State-of-the-art and research challenges. *Journal of Internet Services and Applications, 1*(1), 7–18.

Zhang, J., & Figueiredo, R. J. (2006). *Application classification through monitoring and learning of resource consumption patterns* (10 pp). Paper presented at the 20th International Parallel and Distributed Processing Symposium, 2006, IPDPS 2006.

Chapter 9
Mapping Business-Aligned IT Perspective Patterns: A Practice in Public Service Organization

Dian Indrayani Jambari and Siti Suhaila Abdul Hamid

Abstract The articulation of business-IT strategic alignment includes its representation as strategic knowledge for organization to shape the best strategic plan. Although the complexity affects generally any organization, special concern is paramount on the business-IT strategic alignment in public service organization as efficiency of its business is fundamental to serve the best to the public. The efficiency is achievable through a well-aligned IT to business strategy. Hence, this study investigates the articulation of the alignment patterns through mapping the business-aligned IT according to public service organization's strategic domains. The motivation is to identify and analyze the business-IT strategic alignment patterns as a significant factor to support strategic alignment evaluation. The alignment perspective patterns are mapped on a matrix developed from concepts in strategic alignment model. The established perspective patterns are valuable as an influential aspect in the re-strategy effort to increase the effectiveness of the public service performance.

Keywords Business-aligned IT • Alignment mapping • Alignment pattern • Public service

D.I. Jambari (✉)
Faculty of Information Science and Technology, Universiti Kebangsaan Malaysia, Bangi, Selangor, Malaysia
e-mail: dian@ukm.edu.my

S.S.A. Hamid
Kolej Yayasan Pendidikan Cheras, Kuala Lumpur, Malaysia
e-mail: siti_suhaila@yahoo.com

© Springer International Publishing Switzerland 2017   101
R. Benlamri, M. Sparer (eds.), *Leadership, Innovation and Entrepreneurship as Driving Forces of the Global Economy*, Springer Proceedings in Business and Economics, DOI 10.1007/978-3-319-43434-6_9

Introduction

Complexity in business and IT alignment in an organization is heavily influenced by changes in business environment and rapid advancement of IT innovations as business enabler (Chan & Reich, 2007). The importance to address the complexity is echoed in business and IT strategic alignment studies from multiple perspectives (Baker & Niederman, 2014; Belfo, 2013; Cuenca, Boza, & Ortiz, 2011; Luftman & Derksen, 2012; Schobel & Denford, 2013; Shanks, Bekmamedova, & Willcocks, 2013; Ullah & Lai, 2011) and is relevant in different business domains and organizational sizes (Gutierrez, Orozco, & Serrano, 2009). This indicates the holistic environment of the business and IT alignment in an organization. However, the state of misalignment between business and IT strategies still exists and continuously identified as hindering factor to the organization's effort toward efficiency and effectiveness (Kappelman, McLean, Johnson, & Gerhart, 2014). Hence it motivates the ongoing effort on assessing the state of alignment to reduce misalignment.

Misalignment imposes negative risks to organization's profitability and performance level. Specifically in nonprofit organization such as public service agencies, strategic alignment is pertinent as evident in government initiative study focusing on the impact of IT as its business service enabler and value creator (Gil-Garcia, Helbig, & Ojo, 2014). The interest to gain IT value that maximizes benefit to the organization demands the mechanism to analyze business and IT strategic alignment (Yetton, Henningsson, & Bjørn-Andersen, 2013). However, the analysis is complicated when analyzing existing strategic alignment established after a period of time as it requires the evaluation of its alignment current state. The evaluation is the initial step in the entire business and IT strategic alignment analysis to enable organization to gauge the fitness of its alignment in order to strategize potential IT value gains (Luftman, 2004). The alignment current state is the condition of the business and IT alignment represented by the alignment patterns and strengths. Failure to diagnose the correct current state will tamper the correctness of further analysis on the alignment and resulted in unsuccessful strategy for gaining IT values to the business (Avison, Jones, Powell, & Wilson, 2004). Although current studies on alignment evaluation acknowledges the criticality of analyzing the current state of alignment, minimum focus has been given on investigating the mechanism to analyze it.

The classic model widely applied and the main reference in business and IT alignment is strategic alignment model (SAM) (Avison et al., 2004; Gerow, Grover, Thatcher, & Roth, 2014; Gutierrez & Serrano, 2007; Khan, Qureshi, & Zaheer, 2012). SAM specification of the four quadrants representing business and IT aspect position in the organization is the fundamental view for the multiple perspectives that exists in modern organization (Henderson & Venkatraman, 1999). The practicality of SAM has been critically challenged (Avison et al., 2004; Ward, 2011) and demanded in business and IT management practices (Alaeddini & Salekfard, 2013). Practical approaches to analyze the state of the alignment have been proposed (Khaiata & Zualkernan, 2009; Luftman, 2003). However, evidence on the success of the approaches is minimal (Kaidalova & Seigerroth, 2012).

The alignment framework described by Avison et al. (2004) motivates this study in analyzing the state of business and IT alignment through the articulation of its patterns. However, further work associated to the original work has been focusing on developing alternative mechanisms or as supporting context for investigation on strategic alignment (Al-Debei & Avison, 2010; Bleistein, Cox, Verner, & Phalp, 2006). No evidence was found of attempts to implement Avison et al.'s (2004) proposed framework in public service organizations to address the call for more various implementations of the framework for comparative study. Therefore, we attempt to adapt the framework for analyzing the business and IT strategic alignment patterns in a public service organization.

A case study in a municipal council as representative of a public service organization is applied in the investigation of this study. The council administers the entire municipality in six districts. 56.16 % of its spending budget has been allocated for services and resources related to the management of IT to support the business functions toward ensuring effective and efficient services to its constituents. However, preliminary investigation has discovered that assessment on the relationship of the IT with the council business strategy has not been performed since 2009, and the council lacks proper articulation of its business and IT linkages (Pelan Strategik, 2009). Its IT position in the business is unclearly represented and defined due to the unsystematic analysis of its alignment to the business.

Analysis to identify and articulate the strategic alignment patterns is important to verify the alignment established and supports the assessment process of the alignment (Bergeron, Raymond, & Rivard, 2004). The knowledge of the alignment perspective patterns allows organization to be aware of inefficiencies in its alignment (Silva, Figueroa, & Gonzãlez-Reinhart, 2007). The finding from the pattern analysis enables the public service organization to re-strategize its business effectiveness and efficiency.

Mapping Business-Aligned IT Perspective Patterns

Mapping the business-aligned IT perspective patterns consist of three phases: (1) first is input identification that extracts the information in the IT landscape of the council. The information is analyzed and its linkages with the business strategies are established for the pattern-mapping process. (2) Next is mapping process, carried out by mapping the business-aligned IT in a matrix. (3) Last is pattern identification, where the mapping process outcome is referred to the Perspective Pattern Analysis Table to articulate the alignment patterns established. Figure 9.1 illustrates the details of the mapping process.

Data is collected qualitatively from relevant information at different phases of the research. Observation is performed and logged in the initial phase through the engagement with the council. The data collection process also involves gathering and selecting relevant official documentations. To corroborate the information articulated from the documents, semi-structured interview sessions are carried out to collect supporting

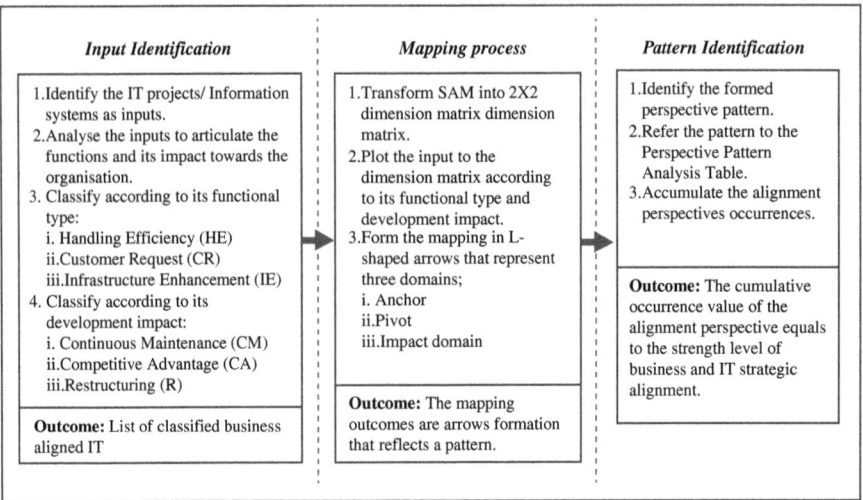

Fig. 9.1 Business-aligned IT perspective pattern-mapping process

information on the business and IT landscape in the council. A set of council personnel including seven head departments, two business executives, and three IT officers have been involved for the interviews to minimize bias and also to capture the holistic perspectives of the alignment. The observations also articulate the council's existing approach in managing its business and IT alignment.

Content analysis technique on the documentations has been carried out to extract the required information for mapping the alignment. Similar method is performed to the interview manuscripts to obtain information that enhances the articulation from the documentations. The analysis then implements the alignment mapping to produce a pattern map. The map is then validated through a round table session with key decision makers in the council. Structured round table discussion is used to gain consensus agreement on the existing business direction of the IT landscape of the council.

Input identification is the initial process of extracting information on the IT components from the IT landscape documentations. The IT components consist of the existing active IT projects and information systems (IS) being used in the council. Identified IT components are then analyzed to establish its alignment to the business strategies through dual classifications that linked it to its corresponding business strategies in the following sequence: (1) the IT functional type and (2) its development impact to the business. HE is defined as the business strategy category for IT components that promote efficiency to the organization's administration and management. CR is the IT components that promote the fulfillment of the customer request. IE is the IT components that promote improvements toward the quality of the current infrastructure. In the second classification, CM is the business strategy classification for IT components that requires constant maintenance for its business functional importance. CA is for IT components that increase the advantages as a competitive business within its market, and R is for IT components that lead restructuring efforts to shift the business strategic direction.

Concepts in SAM are adapted as the alignment mapping grounds by transforming it into a 2×2 matrix representation to cluster the business landscape, IT landscape, and the two organizational level, strategic and operational level. The matrix consists of four domains as defined in Henderson and Venkatraman (1999). The business-aligned IT components established as input are mapped into the domain clusters of the matrix. The positioning of the input in the mapping is rationalized and determined by the organization decision makers. The positioning is then represented into L-shaped arrow formations on the matrix as alignment patterns. The mapping process produces an overall alignment pattern map of the organization business-aligned IT landscape. The L-shaped arrow formations denote the anchor, pivot, and effected domains as the three influential domains in the business-aligned IT. The anchor domain leads the business and IT linkages. The pivot domain then navigates the direction of the linkages, while the effected domain is the effect from the anchor.

The final phase identifies the strength of alignment patterns of the business and IT components in the council. The identification process is performed by referencing the L-shaped arrows in the alignment map against Perspective Pattern Analysis Table by Coleman and Papp (2006) and consulted with the council decision makers. The pattern type reflects the position of each IT components in the business landscape (Bergeron et al., 2004). The perspectives in the L-shaped arrows are differentiated according to its different configurations. The number of similar perspectives identified represents its strength in the council's alignment. Pattern with the strongest strength indicates the primary alignment pattern in the council as the influential perspectives that impacts the business and IT alignment.

Results and Discussion

The council IT strategy has clustered its IT components into information systems (IS), electronic services (eS), and IT infrastructures (ITinfra). Each component comprises of subcomponents such as applications, systems, tools, and technical skills that reflects the IT operations. The classification of the IT clusters with the business strategies according to its functional type and development impact resulted in a set of eight pairings of business-aligned IT. The classification performed in the council shows that the IT components within the IS cluster are aligned to promote efficiency in the business, impacting its maintenance plan (IS{HE/CM}), competitiveness (IS{HE/CA}), and restructuring plan (IS{HE/R}). While, eS cluster is aligned to support the customer needs and impacting the council's competitiveness (eS{CR/CA}) and maintenance plan (eS{CR/CM}). ITinfra cluster is aligned to support the enhancement of the infrastructure, which impacts the maintenance (ITinfra{IE/CM}), competitiveness (ITinfra{IE/CA}), and restructuring plan (ITinfra{IE/R}). The eight business-aligned ITs are then formed into L-shaped arrows mapped in the matrix and resulted in the emergence of four patterns visually represented in Fig. 9.2.

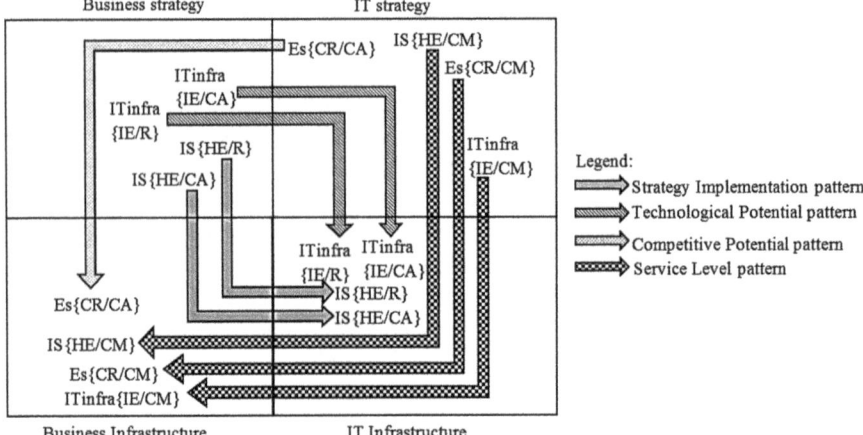

Fig. 9.2 Business-aligned IT perspective pattern map

In the council, service level pattern reigned as the primary pattern based on its occurrence in the mapping. It shows that the IT components impact the council main business offering, which is providing business services efficiently to its constituents. The second strongest pattern emerged is the strategy implementation pattern and technological potential pattern. The former indicates that the IT components have influence toward the business strategy implementation. The latter pattern indicates the potentials of its existing IT components to gain more business values for the council. The weakest pattern formed is the competitive potential pattern indicating that the business and IT components in the council are less focused on making financial profits in its competing business market.

The primary pattern serves as the most prominent indicator to the state of the strategic business and IT alignment in the council. However, the remaining three patterns are not dismissed. They are influential factors to complement the primary pattern and provide holistic indicators to the business and IT alignment. The information can be referred to support decision making in re-strategizing the business and IT strategic level.

Conclusion

The implementation of the pattern-mapping framework has successfully derived the patterns for the business-aligned IT components in the municipal council. The systematic mapping process enables the articulation of the prominent pattern that reflects the current alignment state between the business and IT strategies in the council. The research finding initiates the change in the practice of analyzing the alignment state in public service organization, which can assist in strategizing efforts of future strategic plans for performance improvements and innovations in its service offerings.

However, this study is limited as it is carried out in one instance of the public service organization. The single instance posed a constraint in claims for generalization from the research findings. From the study, it has been observed that there is a social and cultural aspects involved that influences the state of the alignment. This is due to the involvement of highly intense cultural and social values derived from stakeholders in the organization's working environment (Elias, 2012). These values can be an influential resource that impacts the business and IT alignment in an organization (Gregor, Hart, & Martin, 2007; Lee, Kim, Paulson, & Park, 2008; Reich & Benbasat, 2000).

The significance of cultural values in relation to IT in public service organization is acknowledged and gaining interest in research (Welch & Feeney, 2014). Therefore, it is beneficial to explore the impact or influence of the social and cultural perspectives toward the business-IT strategic alignment. Principles in organizational semiotics in describing organization as an information system have the potential as the foundation for establishing and measuring business and IT strategic alignment in public service organization (Liu, Sun, Jambari, Michell, & Chong, 2011; Sun, Liu, Jambari, & Michell, 2016).

Acknowledgment This research was supported by the Young Researchers Grant (*Geran Galakan Penyelidik Muda*) in Universiti Kebangsaan Malaysia (GGPM-2014-044).

References

Alaeddini, M., & Salekfard, S. (2013). Investigating the role of an enterprise architecture project in the business-IT alignment in Iran. *Information Systems Frontiers, 15*(1), 67–88.

Al-Debei, M. M., & Avison, D. (2010). Developing a unified framework of the business model concept. *European Journal of Information Systems, 19*(3), 359–376.

Avison, D., Jones, J., Powell, P., & Wilson, D. (2004). Using and validating the strategic alignment model. *The Journal of Strategic Information Systems, 13*(3), 223–246.

Baker, E. W., & Niederman, F. (2014). Integrating the IS functions after mergers and acquisitions: Analyzing business-IT alignment. *The Journal of Strategic Information Systems, 23*(2), 112–127. doi:10.1016/j.jsis.2013.08.002.

Belfo, F. (2013). A framework to enhance business and information technology alignment through incentive policy. *International Journal of Information Systems in the Service Sector, 5*(2), 1–16.

Bergeron, F. O., Raymond, L., & Rivard, S. (2004). Ideal patterns of strategic alignment and business performance. *Information & Management, 41*(8), 1003–1020.

Bleistein, S. J., Cox, K., Verner, J., & Phalp, K. T. (2006). B-SCP: A requirements analysis framework for validating strategic alignment of organizational IT based on strategy, context, and process. *Information and Software Technology, 48*(9), 846–868.

Chan, Y. E., & Reich, B. H. (2007). IT alignment: What have we learned? *Journal of Information Technology, 22*, 297–315.

Coleman, P., & Papp, R. (2006). *Strategic alignment: Analysis of perspectives*. Paper presented at the Proceedings of the 2006 Southern Association for Information Systems Conference, Florida, USA.

Cuenca, L., Boza, A., & Ortiz, A. (2011). An enterprise engineering approach for the alignment of business and information technology strategy. *International Journal of Computer Integrated Manufacturing, 24*(11), 974–992. doi:10.1080/0951192x.2011.579172.

Elias, N. F. (2012). The impact of information systems from the perspective of IS stakeholders in Malaysia. *International Journal on Advanced Science, Engineering and Information Technology, 2*(6), 1–5.

Gerow, J. E., Grover, V., Thatcher, J., & Roth, P. L. (2014). Looking toward the future of IT-business strategic alignment through the past: A meta-analysis. *MIS Quarterly, 38*(4), 1059–1085.

Gil-Garcia, J. R., Helbig, N., & Ojo, A. (2014). Being smart: Emerging technologies and innovation in the public sector. *Government Information Quarterly, 31*(Suppl 1), I1–I8.

Gregor, S., Hart, D., & Martin, N. (2007). Enterprise architectures: Enablers of business strategy and IS/IT alignment in government. *Information Technology & People, 20*(2), 96–120.

Gutierrez, A., Orozco, J., & Serrano, A. (2009). Factors affecting IT and business alignment: A comparative study in SMEs and large organisations. *Journal of Enterprise Information Management, 22*(1/2), 197–211.

Gutierrez, A., & Serrano, A. (2007). Assessing strategic, tactical and operational alignment factors for SMEs: Alignment across the organisation's value chain. *International Journal of Value Chain Management, 2*(1), 33–56.

Henderson, J. C., & Venkatraman, N. (1999). Strategic alignment: Leveraging information technology for transforming organizations. *IBM Systems Journal, 38*(2–3), 472–484.

Kaidalova, J., & Seigerroth, U. (2012). *Business information systems workshops: An inventory of the business and IT alignment research field* (pp. 116–126). Berlin: Springer.

Kappelman, L., McLean, E., Johnson, V., & Gerhart, N. (2014). The 2014 SIM IT key issues and trends study. *MIS Quarterly Executive, 13*(4), 237–263.

Khaiata, M., & Zualkernan, I. A. (2009). A simple instrument to measure IT-business alignment maturity. *Information Systems Management, 26*(2), 138–152.

Khan, S. A., Qureshi, S. A., & Zaheer, A. (2012). Extending the IS strategic alignment model: A study from the perspective of service industries. *Actual Problems of Economics, 2*(4), 252–258.

Lee, S. M., Kim, K., Paulson, P., & Park, H. (2008). Developing a socio-technical framework for business-IT alignment. *Industrial Management & Data Systems, 108*(9), 1167–1181.

Liu, K., Sun, L., Jambari, D., Michell, V., & Chong, S. (2011). *Advanced information systems engineering: A design of business-technology alignment consulting framework* (pp. 422–435). Berlin: Springer.

Luftman, J. (2003). Assessing IT/business alignment. *Information Systems Management, 20*(4), 9–15.

Luftman, J. (2004). Assessing business-IT alignment maturity. *Strategies for Information Technology Governance, 4*, 99.

Luftman, J., & Derksen, B. (2012). Key issues for IT executives 2012: Doing more with less. *MIS Quarterly Executive, 11*(4), 207–218.

Pelan Strategik 2009-2013. (2009). Retrieved from http://www.mpkj.gov.my/sgr_mpj-theme/pdf/Pelan_Strategik_MPKj.pdf

Reich, B. H., & Benbasat, I. (2000). Factors that influence the social dimension of alignment between business and information technology objectives. *MIS Quarterly, 24*(1), 81–113.

Schobel, K., & Denford, J. S. (2013). The chief information officer and chief financial officer dyad in the public sector: How an effective relationship impacts individual effectiveness and strategic alignment. *Journal of Information Systems, 27*(1), 261–281.

Shanks, G., Bekmamedova, N., & Willcocks, L. (2013). Using business analytics for strategic alignment and organisational transformation. *International Journal of Business Intelligence Research, 4*(3), 1–15.

Silva, L., Figueroa, B. E., & González-Reinhart, J. (2007). Interpreting IS alignment: A multiple case study in professional organizations. *Information and Organization, 17*(4), 232–265.

Sun, L., Liu, K., Jambari, D. I., & Michell, V. (2016). Evaluating business value of IT towards optimisation of the application portfolio. *Enterprise Information Systems, 10*(4), 378–399.

Ullah, A., & Lai, R. (2011). Modeling business goal for business/IT alignment using requirements engineering. *Journal of Computer Information Systems, 51*(3), 21–28.

Ward, K. (2011). Examining changes in the strategic alignment model's alignment factors over time: A case study. *Review of Business Information Systems, 15*(4), 31–38.

Welch, E. W., & Feeney, M. K. (2014). Technology in government: How organizational culture mediates information and communication technology outcomes. *Government Information Quarterly, 31*(4), 506–512.

Yetton, P., Henningsson, S., & Bjørn-Andersen, N. (2013). "Ready to acquire": The IT resources required for a growth-by-acquisition business strategy. *MIS Quarterly Executive, 12*(1), 19–35.

Chapter 10
An Approach Towards Assessing Effective IT Governance Setting: Malaysia Public Sector Case Study

Mohammed Alaa H. Altemimi and Mohamad Shanudin Zakaria

Abstract Great strides have been made in IT governance in the past decade. Today's organizations need a flexible, complementary, and collaborative IT governance setting to prosper in a turbulent environment that would enable organizations to sustain realizing value from IT instead of restraining its contribution by emphasizing control. The review of existing literature to identify and determine best practices had been studied by previous researchers in order to construct the factors within each category. The aim of this paper is to identify the domain of IT governance and provide insights practice with each domain that was detected through literature.

Keywords IT governance • IT governance mechanism • IT decision-making

Introduction

IT governance (ITG) has been raised in priority and contributes to higher returns on assets at a time while business increasingly invests money on technology. Several definitions have been consensus on the definition of IT governance and the need for good IT governance with the underlying principle being to create framework to direct, manage, and control the use of IT. IT governance is the integrated part of corporate governance that is focused on IT-related investment decisions driven by corporate and business unit needs (Brisebois, Boyd, & Shadid, 2007). Also, IT governance is a shared decision-making process used by corporate executives and

M.A.H. Altemimi (✉)
Management Information System Department, Faculty of Information Science and Technology, Universiti Kebangsaan Malaysia, Bangi, Selangor 43600, Malaysia
e-mail: mohd.altemimi@yahoo.com

M.S. Zakaria
Faculty of Information Science and Technology, Universiti Kebangsaan Malaysia, Bangi, Selangor 43600, Malaysia
e-mail: msz@ukm.my

© Springer International Publishing Switzerland 2017   111
R. Benlamri, M. Sparer (eds.), *Leadership, Innovation and Entrepreneurship as Driving Forces of the Global Economy*, Springer Proceedings in Business and Economics, DOI 10.1007/978-3-319-43434-6_10

focused specifically on ensuring that investments into information systems generate business value (Brisebois et al., 2007; Winniford, Conger, & Erickson-Harris, 2009).

Today's IT business environment requires good IT governance mechanisms. Role of IT governance mechanisms has been heightened since the corporate collapse of Enron and WorldCom and the subsequent passing of governance legislation in the form of the Sarbanes-Oxley Act in the USA in 2002 (Brown & Grant, 2005). Organizations need to employ well-designed, well-understood, and transparent governance mechanisms to deliver stakeholder value to intensify the role on boards and executives to ensure effective oversight of IT, making IT governance integral to overall corporate governance in order to achieve effective IT governance (Weill & Ross, 2004).

However, Information Technology Governance Institute (2009) stated, in spite of the adoption of IT governance structures, processes, and mechanisms by large companies, others have yet to even begin to start their IT governance programs. And in addition to this, many top-management executives have little understanding of the structures and mechanisms needed to ensure adequate IT governance.

An Overview of Information Technology Governance (ITG)

ITG is a term that has been evolving rapidly over the last few years, especially in practitioners' communities. The IT Governance Institute is taking a leading role in the debate. Today's organizations need a flexible, complementary, and collaborative IT governance to prosper in a turbulent environment. And that would enable organizations to sustain realizing value from IT instead of restraining its contribution by emphasizing control.

Peterson (2004) indicates that well-known academics (Weill and Ross; Van Grembergen; Zmud and Sambamurthy; and Peterson) all started their IT framework development by defining the term IT governance. According to them, good IT governance is a subset of good corporate governance, and at its core, a good IT governance framework will cause the organization to use specific structures and mechanisms to align its enterprise IT strategy with its business performance goals. In order that ITG is recognized as an extension of corporate governance, the IT Governance Institute (Information Technology Governance Institute, 2008) indicates that corporate governance is the "Methodology by which a corporation is directed, administered and controlled, whereas IT governance supports achieving corporate objectives, strategy, direction, administration and control, using appropriate IT investment and resource management." It consists of the leadership, organizational structures, and processes that ensure that the enterprise's IT sustains and extends the organization's strategies and objectives (Information Technology Governance Institute, 2008). In other words, IT governance is the mechanism to ensure that organizational strategic processes in place sustains and extends the organizations' goals and objectives.

Weill and Ross (2004) emphasized the significance of IT governance when IT is integrated within the organization. Weill and Ross (2004) define IT governance as 'specifying the decisions, rights, and accountability framework to encourage desirable behavior in the use of IT'. Zmud and Sambamurthy (1999) describe IT governance as a measure of organizational authority for IT activities. Peterson (2004) adds that 'IT governance describes the distribution of IT decision-making rights and responsibilities among different stakeholders in the enterprise, and defines the procedures and mechanisms for making and monitoring strategic IT decisions'. However, Patel (2002) declared that IT governance serves to address the design and development of effective organizations through IT, structures, and processes. Chin, Brown, and Hu (2004) concluded from their review of the literature that IT governance is affected by the corporate governance structure, stressing the integration of IT with the organization. They noted that IT governance is affected by the organization's culture and IT competence. Moreover, they mention that how enterprise embraces the usage of IT will determine the benefits received from that usage. In same way, Schwartz (2007) defined IT governance as 'an organizational body or group focused on aligning the strategy of the IT department with organizational goals and strategies'. And therefore, IT governance people implement mechanisms to measure the performance of the IT department.

Weill and Ross (2004) conducted a survey of 256 IT organizations; they declared that IT decision makings were led by management, business unit leaders, and IT specialists in each of the respective areas:

- IT principles. IT and top management or business unit leaders.
- IT architecture. IT specialists and top management or business unit leaders.
- IT infrastructure. IT specialists and top management or business unit leaders.
- Business application need. Corporate and business units, with or without IT.
- IT investment. IT and top management or business unit leaders.

Weill and Ross (2004) outlined in their survey of best practitioner of effective IT governance performance that 45 % or more managers in leadership positions could accurately describe their IT governance, while in below-performing enterprises, only few in leadership positions could describe their governance process. In addition, two principles emerged from the best performing cases of IT governance including:

1. Business and IT professionals collaborate on business-oriented IT decisions (investment, principles, and business application needs).
2. The best arrangement of decision rights for technical decisions (IT architecture and IT infrastructure) depends on such factors as the synergies between business units, the current IT portfolio, strategic goals, industry differences, and so on.

Organizations' ability to develop important policies, such as privacy, security, and business continuity; to implement important IT decisions; and to coordinate IT personnel activities effectively have major effect to enhance IT performance. Anyway, good IT governance is about how effectively IT used to grow and develop the business. This meant the steering committees of decision making have to ensure that organization uses IT resources effectively and efficiently. Similarly, IT governance is the process by which firms align IT actions with their performance goals and assign accountability for those actions and their outcomes. They focused on the implementation of structures and processes in an IT system.

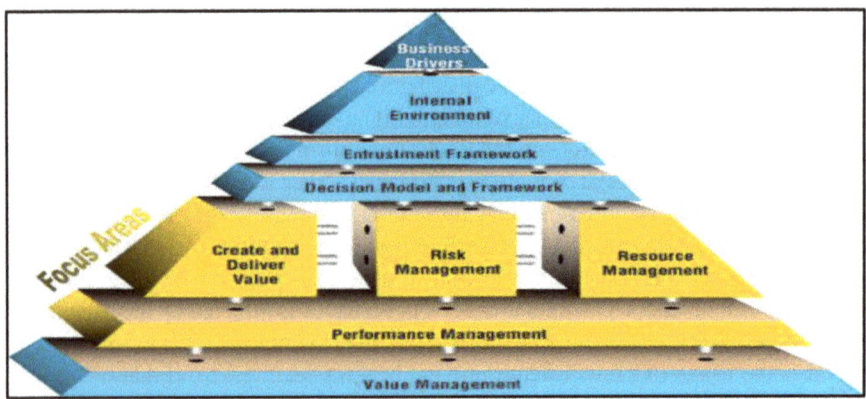

Fig. 10.1 IT governance focus area

Many researchers deliberated in the contexts of ITG, IT performance, and investment. Peterson (2002) and Ribbers, Peterson, and Parker (2002) stated that effective IT governance structure and process lead to high IT performance. Bowen, Cheung, and Rohde (2007) suggest that IT governance effectiveness influences IT governance and IT implementation success. Linking practice with strategy, the framework proposed here adopts the balanced scorecard framework for monitoring corporate performance as the impact of IT governance effectiveness. Although Ortiz (2003) points out solid relationship between IT governance implementation and organizational performance, there is no direct influence of IT governance on IT investment performance in the USA and Canada (Gu, Xue, & Ray, 2008). However, IT governance was found to moderate the relationship between IT capital and IT investments.

Recently, there have been attempts to think about IT governance holistically. As the two main IT control and implementation frameworks, ITIL and COBIT have begun to mature; there have been attempts to map frameworks to each other (Information Technology Governance Institute, 2008). Robinson (2007) attempted to look at IT governance holistically by crafting IT governance architecture by providing robust model that encompasses all aspect of IT governance structure, processes, and mechanisms, as shown in Fig. 10.1. This is a very new area of research in IT governance in which further refinement will benefit both academics and practitioners alike.

Robinson (2007) developed his IT governance architecture as a multilayered model, with the business drivers of the organization at the top of the pyramid, working down through layers that include the internal environment, "accountability and authority" framework (entrustment framework), and models for policy and procedure decisions. Moving further down his IT governance architectural pyramid, he goes on to illustrate the importance of creating and delivering value and performing risk and resource management. Finally, providing the foundation to all IT governance activities are the functions of performance management and value management.

However, this literature shows that proper IT governance provides significant value to the organization in terms of strategic competitive advantage, increased value of IT investments to the firm, and ensuring strict compliance with corporate governance regulations, such as SOX. Yet a large portion of the literature also showed that ensuring a firm's structures, processes, and mechanisms are optimized for good IT governance remains a multifaceted and complex task.

IT Governance Mechanism

IT governance is complex and dynamic in nature; a typical IT governance framework is used to describe the structures, processes, and mechanisms related to IT key decisions in an enterprise (Information Technology Governance Institute, 2003; Van Grembergen, De Haes, & Guldentops, 2004; Weill & Ross, 2004) as shown in Fig. 10.2. Several researchers have depicted that at least 20 % higher returns on assets result in those organizations that adopted proper IT governance mechanisms than those with weaker governance (Weill & Ross, 2004).

IT governance consists of a set of interdependent subsystems using a mix of structures, processes, and relational mechanisms that work together as a whole in order to assist the proper deployment of ITG using (Grant, Brown, Uruthirapathy, & McKnight, 2007; Patel, 2004; Peterson, 2004; Van Grembergen & de Haes, 2005, 2009; Van Grembergen et al., 2004; Weill & Ross, 2004; Zmud & Sambamurthy, 1999).

However, Van Grembergen and De Haes (2009) have identified 33 practices for IT governance and classified them in three categories of structure, processes, and relational mechanism.

Examples of ITG dimensions: structures, processes, and relational mechanisms, include:

- Structures. CIO on Board, executive management committees, IT strategy committee, IT leadership committees, and IT steering committee(s).
- Processes. Strategic information systems planning, balanced (IT) scorecards, information economics, service level agreements, control objectives for information and related technologies and the ITIL, IT portfolio, and demand management.
- Relational mechanisms. Active participation and collaboration between principal stakeholders, partnership rewards and incentives, business/IT co-location, cross-functional business/IT training, and rotation.

Fig. 10.2 Elements of an ITG framework

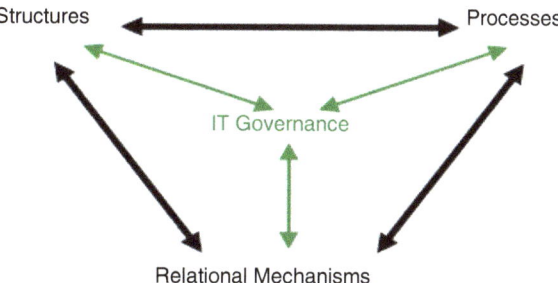

IT Governance Constraints

There are many constraints that face organizations that are trying to implement an effective IT governance structure and process when there are significant IT investments involved. Without effective governance to deal with these constraints, IT projects will have a higher risk of failure. Each organization faces its own unique challenges as their individual environmental, political, geographical, economic, and social issues differ.

It would never be able to list all concern relating to IT governance, but following are common to most organizations. The IT Governance Institute (ITGI) suggests that the organizations' challenges and concerns include the following five points:

– Aligning IT strategy with the business strategy;
– Cascading strategy and goals down into the enterprise;
– Providing organizational structures that facilitate the implementation of strategy and goals;
– Insisting that an IT control framework be adopted and implemented;
– Measuring IT performance.

Anyway, any one of these issues can present obstacles to providing effective governance.

– Senior Management not engaging IT.
– Poor Strategic Alignment
– Lack of Project Ownership
– Poor Risk Management
– Ineffective Resource Management

IT Governance Dimension

Structure - Oriented

Structure describes the way IT function is carried out and how the organizational structure can organize the IT division in the organization (Rau, 2004). IT governance structure scope covers a range of issues that would include most, if not all, of the possible IT issues in a particular setting (i.e., procurement, standards, architecture, policies, business-IT alignment).

The literature of term of structure refers for two aspects: (1) Authority and Membership (2) Coordination of mechanism.

1. The *authority* indicates how power, rights, roles, and responsibilities are distributed between and among levels and/or even devices for making IT decisions between management-business and IT committee cooperation (Van Grembergen, 2003; Weill & Ross, 2004) (e.g. steering committees).

Weill and Ross (2004) mentioned that the most effective IT decision-making structures include CIOs on various executive steering committees, executive management committees, IT leadership committees, and business/IT relationship managers (e.g. steering committee, office of IT architecture, service level agreements), the establishment of various technology and business councils, and 'architecture, engineering, and infrastructure' boards that develop, implement, and enforce IT policies, procedures, and standards throughout the organization. The minimal effective IT decision-making structures were the capital approval committee and the architectural committee. On the other hand, Grant et al. (2007) detail the governance structure on how many committee levels or layers there are and outline each of their primary roles; for example, through designating responsibility to an IT executive and relevant IT committees (Van Grembergen & de Haes, 2005). Also, Ward and Peppard (2002) presented IT governance structures as a hierarchy of business and IT steering groups, starting at the top with the executive steering groups and moving down the hierarchy through separate business strategy and IT steering groups to lower-level groups that control decisions of application management, service management, and technical management. In addition, the IT function itself requires structure as well as deciding where the IT decision-making authority is located within the organization (Van Grembergen et al., 2004).

However, an effective IT governance structure ensures that all stakeholder concerns and interests are considered including measures of both project performance and IT sustainment performance. In the same way, Schwartz (2007) stated ITG structure should answer key performance questions, such as is the investment in IT worth the return, does the IT department management measure their performance, and is the IT department functioning well overall.

2. The *coordination of mechanism* refers to the actual distribution of authority among level of decision-making. Weill and Ross (2004) viewed structure as 'a rational set of arrangements and mechanisms'.

Anderson (2004) mentioned the effective implementation of an IT governance structure requires an understanding of how IT and the business should work together. Also, Luftman (2002) pointed out the relational mechanisms between IT governance structures, business functions, and IT processes and communications are critical to preventing IT alignment failure. Chin et al. (2004) emphasized the importance of integrating the IT governance structure into the overall organizational governance to provide strategic advantage, to achieve business objectives, and to optimize the value received from information technology. Similarly, Patel (2002) emphasized the importance of aligning IT strategy with business strategy, suggesting that IT governance should be rooted in business logic. Luftman and Brier (1999) examined the IT/business alignment and found that the most important enablers of this alignment included senior executive support for IT, IT being involved in business strategy development.

Ward and Peppard (2002) stated that IT governance decision is "strong links to and from" through the executive steering groups and the lower-level groups, to ensure that the decisions made at the various levels of the other steering groups are coordinated and acted upon. As an example, the IT strategy committee reviews and approves IT strategy which provides high-level direction and control over IT to deliver value and manage risks, while the IT council committee considers different levels of policies and investments (Van Grembergen et al., 2004). In practice, different committees encompass different memberships and authority and are subject to organizational culture. However, Weill and Ross (2004) suggest that the number of governance mechanisms be limited.

Weill and Ross (2005) identify three IT governance structures for organizations as:

1. Centralized,
2. Decentralized or
3. Federal IT governance structures.

According to Luftman (2003), the IT governance structural choice impacts the IT strategic alignment process. In a Centralized IT governance structure, the organization's corporate IT unit has complete authority and decision-making power for all IT decisions, while in a Decentralized IT governance structure, it distributes all authority and decision-making power to individual business and functional unit within the organization for their IT architecture, standards, and applications (Peterson, 2002). While in a Federal IT governance structure, authority over decision making is distributed between a central body and individual organizational units (or a state level CIO and state agency CIOs) over corporate IT architecture. In other words, the Federal structure is a combination of the Centralized and Decentralized structures.

In addition, by studying the nature of IT governance, Chin et al. (2004) compared the impact of centralized versus decentralized controls and structures. They found that centralized control of IT allowed for board oversight, consistent strategic approach, and economies of scale. The authors also noted that though centralized control may result in sacrificing specific needs of individual subunits, decentralized control of IT to enable the addressing of those specific needs also had its disadvantages. They found that organizations that had decentralized control experienced increased costs and reduced integration. A hybrid approach used by some firms in their study enabled central control of IT infrastructure and specific deployments at divisional levels. Weill and Ross (2004) also considered the issue of centralized versus decentralized governance and found that organizations that were top performers as measured by profit tended to have centralized IT governance, which resulted in standardized approaches, lower costs, and formalized assessments of IT-related endeavors. Even with a degree of decentralization to enable flexibility, Weill and Ross concluded that a hybrid approach would have merit, rather than giving total control of IT governance to the divisional level.

Process - Oriented

Henderson, Venkatraman, and Oldach (1996) define process in terms of the IT infrastructure such as systems development and operations infrastructure. More recently, the emphasis of IT governance is to implement processes that ensure strategic alignment between IT and business. Strategic alignment ensures that IT projects are aligned with strategic business objectives, and consequently are funded and prioritized. Van Grembergen (2003) refers to the process of 'formalization of strategic IT decision making' and that appropriate IT monitoring procedures are required to achieve improvements and sustain positive outcomes including key performance indicators through service level agreements, IT demand management, IT portfolio management, and chargeback systems (Symons, 2005) (e.g. IT balanced scorecard). Weill and Ross (2005) also identify that the most effective alignment processes were tracking IT projects and resources consumed. The least effective were charge back mechanisms and tracking the business value of IT investments.

Besides IT balanced scorecards, project tracking systems enable the IT strategy committee to detect and correct any deviations and alter strategy when required (Information Technology Governance Institute, 2003). Furthermore, Van Grembergen and de Haes (2005) suggest organizations need to find a good balance of measures between output and performance, comprising technical measures and business measures. Technical measures evaluate technical-related issues such as IT downtime and access failure (an internal perspective), while business measures evaluate business-related issues such as customer satisfaction (an external perspective).

While the IT governance process can take on various forms within different companies, depending upon whether IT management is a centralized organization, decentralized, or a hybrid of both within the corporate entity, Selig (2008) presented hierarchical model of 'IT/business steering and governance boards, committees, and roles'. The top management team consists of "executive and small business unit," while steering committees are responsible to review IT/business alignment plans, IT investment portfolios, set portfolio priorities, and select, approve, and fund major IT projects. In other words, the corporate boards are responsible for working in "different areas of focus" like 'program, technology, architecture, infrastructure, and operations management' to ensure the business and IT goals of the organization are optimized.

Rational - Oriented

Relational mechanisms—this term describes how to manage the ITG framework for attaining and sustaining business/IT alignment that cover advocates, channels, and educational efforts that overspread IT governance principles, policies, and outcomes of IT decision-making processes (Information Technology Governance Institute, 2003; Weill & Ross, 2004).

As stated by the IT Governance Institute, IT governance requires leadership to ensure that IT activity is sustained and extended to achieve the organization's goals. The emphasis on leadership is confirmed by Weill (2004) who found that the factor that most separates top-performing organizations from substandard-performing organizations is the quality of senior leadership in making IT decisions. Leadership should be proactive and strategic (Broadbent, 2003), which requires commitment from the top and supportive behavior that leads to effective resource allocation to IT (Weill & Ross, 2004).

Weill and Ross (2004) stated that leadership requires commitment from the top and supportive behavior that leads to effective resource allocation to IT. Van Grembergen (2000) adds that organization capacity is the key success factor for IT governance exercised by the board, executive management, and IT management. As defined by Henderson et al. (1996), organizational capacity refers to the human skills and capabilities required to support and shape the business. Meanwhile, Weill and Ross (2004) declared the need to educate the organization on how governance decisions are made in order to reduce the mystery of IT and encourage lower level managers to accept responsibility for effective IT use. Moreover, Weill and Ross (2004) confirmed that implementation of IT governance requires organizations to rethink their governance structure and individuals to re-learn their roles and relationships. An important emphasis of well-defined identification of all involved parties from board of directors to low level managers will have big impact to clear IT governance and unambiguous roles and responsibilities (Van Grembergen et al., 2004). Information Technology Governance Institute (2009) indicates the board of directors committees have to play an active role to ensure that IT goals and objectives are aligned with the business' goals and objectives.

Finally, are about 'the active participation of and collaborative relationship among corporate executives, IT management & business management' (Van Grembergen, 2003) (e.g. training) as shown in Table 10.1.

Setting of Effective ITG Elements

An understanding of the IT governance concept is essential for organizations to gain a better perspective on the governance activity and provides focus for management attention. The review of existing literature is to identify and determine best practices that had been studied by previous researchers in order to construct the factors within each category. In order to identify settings practices, those had been studied by previous researchers or were identified in professional publications or pioneer organizations; an understanding of the IT governance concept is essential to achieve higher efficiency and effectiveness within IT governance functions. However, the role of IT in transforming government has grown due to the performance rankings, budget crises, and technology changes.

Conceptualizing IT governance is not easy. Definitions, whether academic or practical, commonly refer to IT governance as a set of decision-making structures, roles, responsibilities, and practices geared toward achieving desired objectives (Weill & Ross, 2004). In other words, IT governance implementation requires defining structure (roles and responsibilities), processes, and relational mechanisms at each of the operational, management, and strategic levels within organizations. Furthermore, where IT governance is concerned, the key issues are how strong and well-articulated corporate governance is, how it translates into IT governance, how

Table 10.1 IT governance dimensions

Category	Driver	Authors
Structure-oriented	● Authority and membership	Grant et al. (2007), Van Grembergen (2003), Van Grembergen and de Haes (2005), Van Grembergen et al. (2004), and Weill and Ross (2004)
	● Coordination of mechanism	Anderson (2004), Chin et al. (2004), Luftman (2002), Weill and Ross 2004, and Weill and Ross (2005)
Process-oriented	● Key business/IT alignment process	Henderson et al. (1996) and Van Grembergen (2003)
	● Regulatory and environmental process	COBIT, ISACA (2015)
	● Resources utilization and operation management process	COBIT, ISACA (2015)
	● Risk, compliance, and security process	ISACA (2015), COBIT, ITIL
	● Performance monitoring	Information Technology Governance Institute (2003) and Symons (2005)
Rational mechanisms-oriented	● Leadership and management style	Information Technology Governance Institute (2003) and Weill and Ross (2004)
	● Commitment, supportive, and awareness	Van Grembergen et al. (2004) and Weill and Ross (2004)
	● Skills and knowledge (organ capacity)	Van Grembergen (2000) and Weill and Ross (2004)
	● Collaborative and communication	Van Grembergen (2003) and Van Grembergen and De Haes (2009)

both are deployed over the whole organization, and whether it knows how to use IT governance to support innovation.

The process of IT governance starts with setting clear objectives for the organizations IT in order to provide the initial directions. This is followed by strategic planning and execution of the IT objectives. The implementation of the IT governance strategy, policy, and action plan will ensure that IT governance is managed more effectively. A continuous loop is then established for measuring performance, comparing it to objectives, leading to redirection of activities and changed objectives where appropriate. In other words, ITG adjustment is the business-IT objective as the first process to provide direction through IT activities, measuring performance, comparing objectives, and getting outcome in the re-direction processes which require changing in proper time to adjust and signify the objectives acceptably. Due to establishing direction, IT module must concern benefits by developing automation, cutting costs, and controlling risks. According to our definition to IT governance in section "Overview of Information Technology Governance (ITGov)", we classify IT governance elements to such domains, then we define practice with each category, as shown in Table 10.2.

Table 10.2 Effective IT governance settings (drivers and practices)

Category	Driver	Practices
Structure-oriented	• *Authority*	• Ensure CIO play a major role in implementing ITG
		• Verify CIO as member of the IT strategy committee and has voting rights on IT strategy committee
		• Designating responsibility to an IT executive and relevant IT committees
		• Deciding where the IT decision-making authority is located
	• *Coordination mechanism*	• Maintain a good understanding of and knowledge about IT governance framework, responsibilities, task, and how IT and the business should work together
		• The IT council committee considers different levels of policies and investments
		• Ensure IT strategy committee at the level of executive officers reviews and approves IT strategy and policy decisions in order to provide high-level direction, control over IT to deliver value, and manage risks in appropriately planning perspective
		• Maintain IT Architecture Steering Committee being part of the successful ITG model to provide guidance and advise on IT architecture and standards
		• Maintain IT Project Steering Committee focusing on prioritizing and managing IT projects
		• Maintain IT Audit Committee for IT audit activates
		• Maintain Data Protection and Privacy Advisor Committee being part of the successful ITG model
Process-oriented	• *Key business/IT alignment*	• Formalization of strategic IT decision making
		• Ensure ITG framework be related to core value of public sector mission and vision
		• Ensure that IT projects are aligned with strategic business objectives, and consequently are funded and prioritized
		• Ensure the clarity of IT budget control
	• *Regulatory and environmental*	• Passing of government legislation
		• Support in developing regulatory policy and strategy
		• Support in reviewing and managing relationships with other licensees and access agreements
		• Knowledge of competition law equivalent to public sector environment (e.g., telecom environment with ministry of telecom and agency related)

	• Resources utilization and operation management	• Dealing with new process, process efficiency, change to value, structural change enhancement, infrastructure, information, or people to be optimized
	• Compliance, risk, and security	• Enforce and investigate breach of established policies and procedures to ensure complete compliance to legal and corporate policies
		• Compliance related reports covering KPI reporting
	• Performance monitoring	• Ensure Performance Measurement detect and correct any deviations for achieve improvements in order to focus in achieving business objective to ensure IT deliver value to business
Relational mechanisms-oriented	• Leadership and management style	• Require quality of senior leadership in making IT decisions
		• Ensure to educate the organization on how governance decisions are made in order to reduce mystery of IT
		• Encourage lower level managers to accept responsibility for effective IT use
	• Commitment, support, and awareness	• Ensure commitment and supportive behaviour towards ITG from executive staff to ensure complete understanding of concept which leads to effective resource allocation of IT
		• Ensure clear and unambiguous roles and responsibilities for the board of directors
		• Require individuals to re-learn their roles and relationships
	• Knowledge and skills (organ capacity)	• Ensure Human skills, and Capabilities to support & shape the business
	• Collaborative and communication	• Ensure Active participation and formal relationship among corporate executives, IT management, and business management (e.g., training)

Methodology of Effective IT Governance

This paper describes the case of an IT governance implementation in a Malaysia Public Sector service. Case research is particularly appropriate for research within the IT area because researchers in this field often lag behind practitioners in discovering and explaining new methods and techniques (Benbasat, Goldstein, & Mead, 1987). As already mentioned, IT governance is now on the agenda of many executives, and consultants are dispersing the concept. Like Benbasat et al. (1987), we believe "that the case research strategy is well-suited to capturing the knowledge of practitioners and developing theories from it". The role of the researchers was purely the role of observers who were interested in investigating how the IT governance practices were applied by practitioners and how the experience and knowledge of practitioners could help to improve their proposed IT governance framework. In this case research, data was gathered by conducting several face-to-face in-depth interviews with IT and business representatives: the CIO, project managers of the IT governance project, a member of the Board of Directors who is also the member of the Executive Committee, and the director of 'organization'.

Assessing Effective IT Governance Setting at Case 'X'

This section reports and interprets the results of the extreme case analysis. To create effective IT governance benchmark, Malaysian public sector services organizations were invited to participate in the research, leveraging the channels of existing CIO networks. From this request, organization 'X' committed to participate under the condition that anonymity was guaranteed. In this organization 'X', interviews took place to assess the effective IT governance setting practices used (see "Appendix"), on a scale from 1 to 3 (1—Low, 2—Medium, 3—High). During each face to face interview, it was ensured that at least one senior representative from the business and one senior representative from IT were present who had a view on how IT governance was addressed in their environment to get a full view of the IT governance practices.

When comparing the averages of IT governance practices maturity per domain of structures, processes, and relational mechanisms, it again appears that in general the highly aligned organizations have clearly more effective IT governance structures and processes, as shown in Fig. 10.3. This figure also shows that practices, on average, were bit less compared to structures, indicating that it is probably more difficult to implement achieved processes compared to structures. This finding is also supported by the personal experiences of the researchers in running an IT governance practices.

A possible explanation might be that the structures and processes applied in organization X, which had already been working on IT governance for more than 6 years, were already thoroughly embedded in day-to-day practice and became part of the organization's culture. This could explain that there was less need to manage the relational aspects of IT governance (Fig. 10.4).

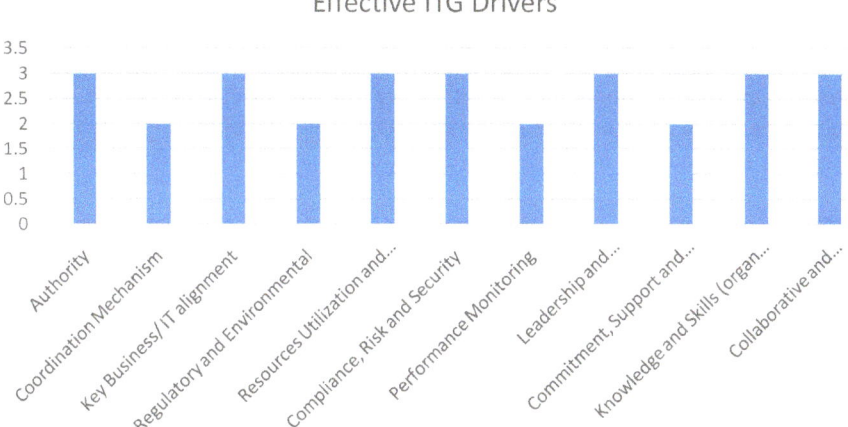

Fig. 10.3 Average elements of ITG

Fig. 10.4 Average ITG category

Conclusion

In summary, IT has been playing a more important role for organizations in achieving their goals. ITGov is an integral part of corporate governance. IT governance ensures that IT goals are met and IT risks are mitigated such that IT delivers value to sustain and grow the organization. Thus, it's crucial for organization to establish good governance in IT to obtain more effective use of IT. IT governance should be highly practical and relevant to practical organizations. The aim of this paper is to identify the domain of IT governance and provide insights practice with each domains which were detected through literature. This paper wants to contribute to that part of the IT governance body of knowledge, by describing how an organization can implement IT governance, using a mixture of processes, structures, and relational mechanisms, and by analyzing how these practices are used at a Malaysian public sector agency. This paper will therefore be the start for a new area of research within the rich field of ITG and may hopefully be a basis for new insights to come.

Appendix

Please fill the assessment in the Scale columns based on the format below.

1. Low importance
2. Medium Importance
3. High Importance

Table 10.3 Scale practices of effective IT governance

Effective IT governance subsystems			
Category	Indicator	*Measures*	*Scale*
Structure-oriented	● Authority	How well an effective empower and clear roles and responsibilities be assigned for board of directors, an executive and relevant IT committee	
	● Coordination of mechanism	How well an effective excellent coordination could be established and maintained to improve organizational performance	
Process-oriented	● Key business/IT alignment	How well an effective strategic objective aligned to IT projects and delivery to improve organizational performance	
	● Regulatory and environmental process	How well an effective regulatory and policy be developed, adjusted, controlled or directed according to particular rules, principles or specifications	
	● Resources utilization and operation management	How well an effective utilization of IT resources (process, infrastructure, information, and people) and management of operation be done	
	● Compliance, risk, and security	How well an effective complies with standard defined, policies, and procedures to ensure complete compliance to legal and corporate policies	
	● Performance monitoring process	How well an effective focus in achieving critical business objective to ensure IT deliver value to business	

(continued)

Table 10.3 (continued)

Effective IT governance subsystems			
Category	Indicator	*Measures*	*Scale*
Rational mechanisms-oriented	● Knowledge and skills	How well effective skills and capabilities to support and shape the business	
	● Leadership and management style	How well the process of decision-making being managed to improve organizational performance	
	● Commitment, supportive, and awareness	How well an effective commitment, supportive behavior and awareness lead to effective resource allocation of IT, value, and beneficial	
	● Collaborative and communication	How well an effective teamwork and communication within organization to improve organizational performance	

References

Benbasat, I., Goldstein, D., & Mead, M. (1987). The case research strategy in studies of information systems. *MIS Quarterly, 11*(3), 368–386.

Bowen, P. L., Cheung, M. Y. D., & Rohde, F. H. (2007). Enhancing IT governance practices: A model and case study of an organization's efforts". *International Journal of Accounting Information Systems, 8*(3), 191–221.

Brisebois, R., Boyd, G., & Shadid, Z. (2007, August). Canada—What is IT governance? And why is it important for the IS auditor? into IT. *The INTOSAI IT Journal, 25*, 30–35. Retrieved from http://www.intosaiitaudit.org/intoit_articles/25_p30top35.pdf

Broadbent, M. (2003). *The right combination*. Retrieved April 11, 2003, from www.cio.com

Brown, A. E., & Grant, G. G. (2005). Framing the frameworks: A review of IT governance research. *Communications of the Association for Information Systems, 15*, 696–712.

Chin, P. O., Brown, G. A., & Hu, Q. (2004). The impact of mergers and acquisitions on IT governance structures: A case study. *Journal of Global Information Management, 12*(4), 50–74.

Grant, G. G., Brown, A., Uruthirapathy, A., & McKnight, S. (2007). An extended model of IT governance: A conceptual proposal. In *Proceedings of the 13th Americas Conference of the Information Systems, Keystone, CO*.

Gu, B., Xue, L., & Ray, G. (2008). IT governance and IT investment performance: An empirical analysis. In *Proceedings of the Twenty-Ninth International Conference on Information Systems, Paris* (pp. 1–17).

Henderson, J. C., Venkatraman, N., & Oldach, S. (1996). Aligning business and IT strategies. In J. N. Luftman (Ed.), *Competing in the information age: Strategic alignment in practice*. Oxford: Oxford University Press.

Information Technology Governance Institute. (2003). *Board briefing on IT governance*. Retrieved July 7, 2008, from www.itgi.org/Template_ITGI.cfm?Section¼Recent_Publications&CONTE NTID¼39652&TEMPLATE¼/ContentManagement/ContentDisplay.cfm

Information Technology Governance Institute. (2008). *Aligning COBIT®4.1, ITIL® V3 and ISO/ IEC 27002 for business benefit*. Retrieved November 10, 2010, from http://www.isaca.org/ Knowledge-Center/Research/ResearchDeliverables/Pages/Aligning-COBIT-4-1-ITIL-V3-and-ISO-IEC-27002-for-BusinessBenefit.aspx

Information Technology Governance Institute. (2009). *An executive view of IT governance*. Rolling Meadows, IL: Author.

Luftman, J. N. (2002). Assessing IT-business alignment maturity. *Communications of AIS, 4*(14).

Luftman, J. N. (2003). Assessing IT-business alignment. *Information Systems Management, 20*(4), 9–15.

Luftman, J. N., & Brier, T. (1999). Achieving and sustaining business-IT alignment. *California Management Review, 42*(1), 109–122.

Ortiz, S. A. (2003). *Testing a model of the relationships among organisational performance, IT-business alignment and IT governance* (Unpublished PhD thesis, University of North Texas, Denton, TX).

Patel, N. (2002). Emergent forms of IT governance to support global e-business models. *Journal of Information Technology Theory and Application, 4*(2), 33–48.

Patel, N. (2004). An emerging strategy for e-business IT governance. In W. Van Grembergen (Ed.), *Strategies for information technology governance*. Hershey, PA: Idea Group.

Peterson, R. R. (2002). *Information technology governance processes under environmental dynamism: Investigating competing theories of decision making and knowledge sharing*. Retrieved June 8, 2009, from http://latienda.ie.edu/working_papers_economia/WP02-31.pdf

Peterson, R. (2004). Integration strategies and tactics for information technology governance. In W. Van Grembergen (Ed.), *Strategies for information technology governance* (pp. 37–74). Hershey, PA: IGI.

Rau, K. G. (2004). Effective governance of IT: Design objectives, roles and relationships. *Information Systems Management, 21*(4), 35–42.

Ribbers, P. M. A., Peterson, R. R., & Parker, M. M. (2002). Designing information technology governance processes: Diagnosing contemporary practices and competing theories. In *Proceedings of the 35th Hawaii International Conference on System Sciences, Big Island, HI* (pp. 1–12).

Robinson, N. (2007). The many faces of IT governance: Crafting an IT governance architecture. *Information Systems Control Journal, 1*, 1–4.

Schwartz, K. D. (2007, May). *IT governance definition and solutions. IT governance topics covering definition, objectives, systems, and solutions*. CIO. Retrieved from http://www.cio.com/article/111700/IT_Governance_Definition_and_Solutions#what

Selig, G. (2008). *Implementing IT governance: A practical guide to global best practices in IT management*. Zaltbommel, The Netherlands: Van Haren.

Symons, C. (2005). *IT governance framework: Structures, processes and communication*. Retrieved December 10, 2008, from www.cba.co.nz/download/Forr051103656300.pdf

Van Grembergen, W. (2000). The balanced scorecard and IT governance. *Information Systems Control Journal, 2*, 40–3.

Van Grembergen, W. (Ed.). (2003). *Strategies for Information Technology Governance,* . Hershey, PA: Idea Group.

Van Grembergen, W., & de Haes, S. (2005). Measuring and improving IT governance through the Balanced Scorecard. *ISACA Journal, 2*.

Van Grembergen, W., & De Haes, S. (2009). *Enterprise governance of information technology: Achieving strategic alignment and value*. New York, NY: Springer.

Van Grembergen, W., De Haes, S., & Guldentops, E. (2004). Structures, processes, and relational mechanisms for IT governance. In W. Van Grembergen (Ed.), *Strategies for information technology governance* (pp. 1–36). Hershey, PA: IGI.

Ward, J., & Peppard, J. (2002). *Strategic planning for information systems*. Chichester: Wiley.

Weill, P. (2004). Don't just lead govern: How top-performing firms govern IT. *MIS Quarterly Executive, 3*(1), 1–17.

Weill, P., & Ross, J. W. (2004). *IT governance: How top performers manage IT decision rights for superior result*. Boston, MA: Harvard Business School Press.

Weill, P., & Ross, J. (2005). A matrixed approach to designing IT governance. *MIT Sloan Management Review, 46*(2), 26.

Weiss, J., & Anderson, D. (2004). *Aligning Technology and Business Strategy: Issues & Frameworks, A Field Study of 15 Companies*, In Proceedings of the 37th Hawaii International Conference on System Sciences, (Jan) 2004.

Winniford, M., Conger, S., & Erickson-Harris, L. (2009). Confusion in the ranks: IT service management practice and terminology. *Information Systems Management, 26*(2), 153–163. doi:10.1080/10580530902797532.

Zmud, R., & Sambamurthy, V. (1999). Arrangements for information technology governance: A theory of multiple contingencies. *MIS Quarterly, 23*(2), 261–290.

Mohammed Alaa H. Altemimi is a Ph.D. candidate in the Management Information System Dept. faculty of Information Science and Technology, Universiti Kebangsaan Malaysia (UKM), Malaysia. He holds a Master degree in MIS from the UKM with distinguished honors, plus BCS. He worked previously as an IT Projects consultant and lecture in both of Management / IT dept. His current research interests focuses on IT Governance and Management, Alignment, IT services and economic issues, Enterprise Architecture in the area of Public organizations as well as new teaching approaches for those fields. His email address is mohd.altemimi@yahoo.com.

Mohamad Shanudin Zakaria is an associate professor at Faculty of Information Science and Technology, Universiti Kebangsaan Malaysia. Currently, he is the Director of Information Technology Centre. His current research interests are in Business and IT Alignment, IT Service Management, the application of systems thinking in organizations, and Service Science. His email address is msz@ukm.edu.my.

Chapter 11
Implementing a Mass Customization Business Model in the Health Industry

Marc Poulin

Abstract The healthcare industry is undergoing many challenges due to rising costs, lower governmental support, and ineffectiveness of many treatments. One popular approach to address these issues is the P4 vision where prevention and patient participation is paramount. To implement these newer approaches, there are business process challenges in order to control costs and offer the new personalized approach. The mass customization business model has been successful in offering various levels of personalization with costs and delivery delays similar to mass production. Although it has been researched and implemented for the manufacturing industry, research has shown potential in the service industry.

This article presents a business model founded on mass customization to address certain challenges in the health industry. The article discusses the issues and presents an approach to remedy the problems. The business model is demonstrated through an actual global health company head quartered in Dubai.

Keywords Business model • Healthcare industry • Mass customization • IT • B2C

Introduction

In many parts of the world, it is no secret that the health systems are becoming more costly and not effective. Their current medical system encourages doctors to increase treatment through drugs and medical procedures rather than on healing patients. Doctors are paid when patients are sick. There is a recent trend in the last decade toward an integrated healthcare system focusing, predicting, and preventing disease rather than treatment. According to renown Steven Trobianic, M.D., Yale Board Certified Neurologist, we are standing at the brink of a consumer-driven healthcare revolution that will forever change how we view the process of aging, the medical care we receive, and the medications we use. A recent approach toward this change

M. Poulin (✉)
Canadian University Dubai, Dubai, United Arab Emirates
e-mail: marc@cud.ac.ae

© Springer International Publishing Switzerland 2017
R. Benlamri, M. Sparer (eds.), *Leadership, Innovation and Entrepreneurship as Driving Forces of the Global Economy*, Springer Proceedings in Business and Economics, DOI 10.1007/978-3-319-43434-6_11

is the popular P4 medicine: personalized, predictive, preventive, and participatory. This research will be illustrated through a new health organization that seeks to address this problem in the health industry.

This holistic approach to health involves a new context for providing healthcare. First, due to the personalization component, there are many more potential treatments to address the variety of personal health problems among patients. There are fewer "once one-solution-fits-all" policies but rather a multitude of factors that when combined together can confuse a practitioner in providing the best service. Secondly, in many parts of the world, healthcare budgets are being compressed especially in the public sector. Consequently, it makes it challenging for doctors to demand higher prices for personalized services, especially when not guaranteeing results. Lastly, patients are becoming more educated through accessible online information and health technologies that can provide vital measurements such as heart beat and blood pressure at a very low cost.

This challenge in the health industry is similar to firms following a mass production model, which mainly focuses on high volume for each product it offers, a limited variety of products to offer, and low prices. Since the 1990s, many such firms have turned to the mass customization business model to offer variety at low prices. The hypothesis of this article claims that the mass customization model can be transferred in the health industry, which would help support the new health trends.

The article presents an innovative business model to support a new offer in the health industry. The proposed business model incorporates key success factors from mass customization. The research is exploratory in nature while the model is being implemented in an actual global health company. The article will present the model, the challenges, and learnings thus far.

Literature Review

Current business models in the healthcare industry are struggling with issues such as rising costs through inefficient use of resources and being reactive to patient healthcare problems. Many services are offered by both the public and private sector, which present further challenges in providing a seamless service to patients, instead of the current situation of spreading services and patient data in separated systems. Chawla and Davis (2013) demonstrate the potential of using the available healthcare-related data through data mining to personalize the assessment of your health.

Mass customization (MC) was first coined by Davis (1987) where he defined MC as a paradoxical concept that refers to a firm offering a relatively wide range of product variety but with price and delivery delay closely resembling those of mass producers. Among the various definitions, it is not exactly clear where MC begins or ends with regard to product variety and price. He states that with MC, price premiums associated to customization of a product should still make the final product accessible to the mass market. In terms of delivery delay, Franke and Piller (2004) suggest that customers are willing to wait about 10 % longer for personalized products, but this can vary by industry. In previous research, "personalization offers" via an eight-level personalization offer model, Poulin, Montreuil, and Martel (2006) expand the standard MC definition. The model claims that firms can mass produce personalized products with a much wider range of price and delivery delay. Complexity of offers depends on the customer penetration point in the supply chain and in the number of offers existing simultaneously.

MC and personalization has frequently been identified as an important business strategy to compete in today's global economy (Lampel & Mintzberg, 1996; Pine, 2008). The literature indicates that key success factors that arose were modularization, standardization, postponement, configurators, and customer interaction (Duray, 2004; Hvam, Mortensen, & Riis, 2008; Piller & Tseng, 2003).

Many models were developed to represent ways to mass customize. In an attempt to provide managers with a framework to develop the type of mass customization they should pursue, Gilmore and Pine (1997) identified four distinct approaches: collaborative, adaptive, cosmetic, and transparent. Collaborative customizers conduct a dialogue with individual customers to help the customers define their needs, to identify what product/service mix would precisely meet those needs, and hence to design individualized products/services accordingly. On the other hand, adaptive customizers offer one standard, but customizable, product that is designed in such a way that users may alter it themselves. Cosmetic customizers present a standard product differently to different customers by packaging it differently for each customer (e.g., communicating the product benefits differently or engraving the customer's name on the product). Finally, transparent customizers provide individualized customers with unique product offerings but without letting them know explicitly that the product offering has been customized for them. Gilmore and Pine (1997) state that companies may combine two or more of the approaches so as to meet the precise needs of their customer.

In the service industry, such as with healthcare, the concept of mass customization is different since there is an inherent customization process during the creation and delivery of the service. The customer involvement at various stages of the service can create challenges but also opportunities to satisfy their customer, which is highly impacted on the decisional freedom given to employees (Kaplan & Haenlein, 2006). As with products customization, the customer involvement is a key issue that needs to be controlled. With products, product platforms are created where a set of rules will control the personalization outcome, but for services, these "platforms" are less rigid and difficult to implement especially when there is a high level of personalization. Gwinner, Bitner, Brown, and Kumar (2005) claim that the ability for employees to adapt and live up to customer needs is a strength that enables customization after the service has begun and cannot be preconfigured. A negative impact would be to have costly customized services with poor quality since the employee was given too much latitude. Furthermore, relative to product mass customization, Heim and Sinha (2001) claim that service customization could be much more complex in variety, and it is difficult to predetermine all the possibilities. An important element is to carefully assess the customer needs during the configuration process. The concept of personas is sometimes used to represent a customer segment that require a number of service components, or "customer operating segments" (Frei, 2008), similar to modules in a product platform.

Research Methodology

Problem Description

The firm from the research study wanted to find a way to make a serious change, but they knew traditional business models in the health industry would not work. The follow requirements needed to be met:

1. The healthcare services should not only be reactive and focus only on sick patients but should also be preventive or proactive to reduce the number of patients becoming sick.
2. The approach needed to be personalized, not a "one-size-fits-all" approach such as when prescribing medicine, in order to have the most effectiveness.
3. Services needed to be affordable, not necessarily dependent on insurance or government support.
4. Mobile technology, health devices, and software should be adopted and linked together for monitoring quickly and effectively.
5. The service should use a holistic view of the client's health and not only on traditional westernized view of healthcare treatment.

Problem Statement

What business model can enable a firm to offer personalized and effective health services and controllable cost and quick delivery time?
   Subproblems that result from the main problem are:

– How is the personalization done effectively and quickly?
– How are the services provided quickly and at reasonable cost?
– How can the model incorporate new technologies easily?

Research Approach

Since the problem addressed is new and primary data is available, an exploratory and descriptive research approach was adopted. The approach was to take notice of all key issues and note how industry and research solutions could address the principal challenges. Key variables and parameters were identified for future research.
   Information was collected by participatory approaches of the author and by interviews with upper management in the firm. Open-ended questions were used to iden-

tify the constraints, objectives, and possible solutions. With this analysis, business model was created by referring to literature and industry experts. The research is currently ongoing but many findings can be shared.

To assure the validity and reliability of the information, interviews were conducted with all upper management and at various points in time. Although there were some changes in answers due to fluctuations within the environment, the answers were consistent.

Proposed Model

The Service Offer

The proposed model is founded on the key success factors of mass customization: product platforms, postponement of differentiation, configuration tool kits, customer involvement, and use of technology.

The first step for mass customization models is to identify the potential solution space and the product platforms that will need to be created to address the solution space. The solution space is limited by costs, time, accessibility, and technology available. The firm's vision is laid on the founding physician's view on healthcare as being holistic and preventative. The approach was to consider any biomarker or key information of the client to monitor his current state and risk of developing health issues. Their MMM model was based on the process of **m**easuring, **m**entoring, and **m**onitoring a patient. Hence, the business model needed to include technologies and processes that would support these three steps and being able to scale at low cost. The solution space is currently vague as it will be limited by price, technologies, and regulations in each market.

One of the most important steps was to create the product platform. In mass customization, this consists of a certain number of modules and components that can be joined together by following a set of rules, in order to produce a product for the end client. For instance, in the car industry, VW has created a product platform that is used to produce various cars (VW golf, WV Tiguan, Audi A3, Audi A4, etc.) by sharing the same car frame, and components like the 2 L turbo motor, but some luxury components are only reserved to some products (Audi). The increase in standard parts and modules allows for savings while offering variety. In the service industry such as healthcare, there are supplementary challenges in creating a platform since there are many sources of variability, and it is difficult to create comprehensive rules that can address any condition.

In healthcare, the "product" is actually a combination of physical products and services to produce the end service for a customer. The first building blocks of the platform are processes and resources required to measure the patient's condition. The first elements in the platform can be shown by part A in Fig. 11.1, which shows the overview of the service offer. Various equipment and processes are used to obtain data and information, and a particular attention was made to adopt standards

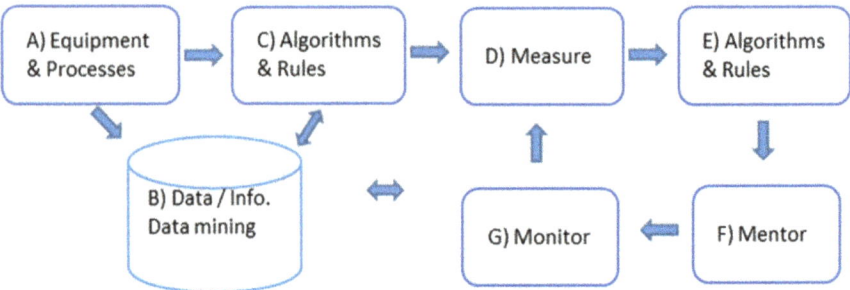

Fig. 11.1 Service model for customized preventive healthcare

and flexible equipment, that can be mixed and matched to do a wide variety of tests. Equipment and processes (such as taking blood) could provide pure data that needs to be processed, or some equipment will process the data and provide value-added information (B in Fig. 11.1). The algorithms and rules will use the data and information to provide a report (D in Fig. 11.1) that includes some of the raw data and some risk factors calculated from functions in C. The report in D is meant to observe the condition of the patient or client but not to prescribe any products, actions, or mentoring. It is actually in step E where other algorithms analyze the data from the measurement step and then proposes actions for the physician. Some actions are straightforward, but for many categories, the algorithm will narrow down the potentially good propositions for the patients. It is up to the physician to make the final decision in the mentoring (F) step. Once the client has been recommended products and actions, he will be monitored at a distance by the physician and other health professionals in the network. This is accomplished with an app provided by the firm and medical devices/accessories that captures key measurements and transmits to the app. A popular device is the Fitbit watch or band that can measure heart rate or steps in real time. The physician will have another version of this app that enables him to have visibility on all his patients and thus monitor in real time. The physician is now in a mode to monitor key biomarkers and make adjustments before the patients have serious health issues. An example of this could be prediabetic patients with high blood pressure. Depending on the feedback from the monitoring step, the physician might again go to step D and redo measurements that can only be done at the clinic or a hospital. Several studies such as by Acheampong and Vimarlund (2016) have shown how this type of collaboration between the health professionals and patients can help detect many potential health risks.

Another key component to this model is the constant improvement in the algorithms. During the complete process, patient data is kept in a central data base (B) where analysis and data mining will be done to see the effectiveness of the algorithms. Over time, algorithms will be modified in functions of learnings made over the large volume of data. Since the company is deploying on a global scale, data volume will grow rather quickly.

Implementing Mass Customization Principles

In order to provide this personalized health model, it is clear there will be a wide range of final "products," almost an infinite amount of "solutions." It is clearly not a one-size-fits-all approach or even putting patients in predetermined "profiles" that correspond to preset recipes for healthcare. When the company combines the potential tests, devices, food, and lifestyle recommendations, the solutions space is almost unlimited. In order to provide this service at an affordable cost, the following mass customization principles were adopted.

Product Platform

The company carefully selected components of their solution that could be easily mixed and matched to create variety. For instance, a blood test for blood sugar was chosen so it can be used for all types of patients. Similarly, to the creation of a product platform form products, the firm designed a platform for all services rather than the traditional approach of designing for one or few services at a time.

In order to make the components of the platform function properly, a set of rules and algorithms were developed to indicate how they all work together. These will include constraints and setting of parameters when components are matched together for a service.

Postponement

An important concept to adopt for cost reduction is the postponement of differentiation between services. The firm tried to make the early processes such as measuring, as similar as possible, between services in order to minimize the variety of resources and thus reduction of setups.

Configurators

Configurators are vital in mass-customized offers as they enable the match between customer needs and the endless combination of services that the firm could provide. Customers do not want to be confused by all the variety but want their needs met. The firm has not presently finished the customer interface of its configurator, but they have created a first version of the algorithms to match customer needs with a service. Although it's left to the end, the customer interface is very important in the buy-in of the customer and understanding the service.

	Product Mass Customization	Mixed Mass Customization
Product platform	Components, modules, rules, identified solution space	Service: tests, mentoring (profiles) Product: nutraceuticals, compound pharmacy Modules: groups of tests for multiple offers Expert rules to narrow solution space
Postponement	Standardized components and fixtures	Standardized services during measurement
Customer involvement	Customer input at various production phase	Customer involved at all stages
Configurator	Matches offering to customer needs Use of online configuration tools	Questionnaire and interview supported by software with algorithms Data mining improves personalization of service

Fig. 11.2 Mass customization vs. mixed customization

Customer Involvement

Customer involvement is quite natural in the customization of services in comparison to the products. From the initial stage of measuring, the customer is involved in the customization of his solution. The firm was careful in minimizing the number of processes during this interaction and in making the process simple throughout all the complexity. For instance, in a basic program, there are about 225 biomarkers recorded as data to generate reports and recommendations. Most of this data is not initially seen by the customers since they are captured by medical instruments.

Conclusion

The article attempted to present an innovative business model inspired by mass customization models in order to address new challenges in the health industry. The firm in the case study is in its early stages of business but has seen the benefits of the suggested model. The author will be closely involved in the ongoing business development in order to conduct more studies on several components of the model, the success and failures, and hopefully generalize approaches for other similar industries. Personalization of services is constantly increasing and is still a challenge for companies wanting to fill that need.

References

Acheampong, F., & Vimarlund, V. (2016). Innovative healthcare through remote monitoring: Effects and business model. *International Journal of Information System Modeling and Design, 7*(1), 1–66.

Chawla, N., & Davis, D. (2013). Bringing big data to personalized healthcare: A patient-centered framework. *Journal of General Internal Medicine, 3*(28), 660–665.

Davis, S. (1987). *Future perfect*. Reading, MA: Addison-Wesley.

Duray, R. (2004). Mass customizer's use of inventory, planning techniques and channel management. *Production Planning & Control, 15*(4), 412–421.

Franke, N., & Piller, F. (2004). Value creation by toolkits for user innovation and design: The case of the watch market. *Journal of Product Innovation Management, 21*(6), 401–415.

Frei, F. X. (2008, April). The four things a service business must get right. *Harvard Business Review, 2008*, 70–80.

Gilmore, J. H., & Pine, J. (1997). The four faces of mass customization. *Harvard Business Review, 75*(1), 91–101.

Gwinner, K. P., Bitner, M. J., Brown, S. W., & Kumar, A. (2005). Service customization through employee adaptiveness. *Journal of Service Research, 8*(2), 131–148.

Heim, G. R., & Sinha, K. K. (2001). A product-process matrix for electronic B2C operations: Implications for the delivery of customer value. *Journal of Service Research, 3*(4), 286–302.

Hvam, L., Mortensen, N., & Riis, J. (2008). *Product customization*. Berlin: Springer.

Kaplan, A. M., & Haenlein, M. (2006). Toward a parsimonious definition of traditional and electronic mass customization. *Journal of Product Innovation Management, 23*(2), 168–182.

Lampel, J., & Mintzberg, H. (1996). Customizing, customization. *Sloan Management Review, 38*(1), 21–30.

Piller, F., & Tseng, M. (2003). New directions for mass customization—Setting an agenda for future research and practice in mass customization, personalization, and customer integration. In M. Tseng & F. Piller (Eds.), *The customer centric enterprise: Advances in mass customization and personalization* (pp. 519–535). Berlin: Springer.

Pine II, B. (2008). From mass to smart customization. In *The MIT Smart Customization Seminar, Cambridge*.

Poulin, M., Montreuil, B., & Martel, A. (2006). Implications of personalization offers on demand and supply network design: A case from the golf club industry. *European Journal of Operations Research, 169*, 996–1009.

Chapter 12
Genetic Algorithm Systems for Wind Turbine Management

Sarah Odofin and Ayodeji Sowale

Abstract In this paper, the importance of wind turbine renewable energy management is important. Wind turbine is sophisticated, expensive and complicated in nature. Fault diagnosis is vital for wind turbine healthy operational state for reliability that is of high priority prognostic for effective management system. A novel algorithm is proposed to optimise the observer monitoring system performance to support practical operation. Reducing unplanned maintenance costs for uninterrupted healthy reliable operations will aid the online monitoring of the turbine behaviour.

Keywords Wind turbine • Genetic algorithm • Optimisation • Observation

Introduction

Wind turbine as a kind of clean renewable energy resource has contributed greatly to the world's power production which has several benefits amongst other sources of energy supply and is still rapidly expanding in terms of market, installation and deployment (Bertling & Ribrant, 2006). Operations, maintenance and reliability of wind turbines have received much attention over the years due to the rapid expansion of wind farms (Odofin, Gao & Sun, 2015). The trends of how to reduce operational and maintenance (O&M) cost are researchers' concerns to guarantee low

S. Odofin (✉)
Faculty of Engineering and Environment, Northumbria University Newcastle,
E411 Ellison Building, Newcastle-Upon-Tyne NE1 8ST, UK
e-mail: sarah.odofin@Northumbria.ac.uk

A. Sowale
Faculty of Engineering and Environment, Northumbria University Newcastle,
A210 Ellison Building, Newcastle-Upon-Tyne NE1 8ST, UK
e-mail: ayodeji.sowale@Northumbria.ac.uk

© Springer International Publishing Switzerland 2017
R. Benlamri, M. Sparer (eds.), *Leadership, Innovation and Entrepreneurship as Driving Forces of the Global Economy*, Springer Proceedings in Business and Economics, DOI 10.1007/978-3-319-43434-6_12

repairs, higher availability period, more reliability, safety and minimise the costs of maintenance as well as repair. To keep power production cost minimal, the modern strategy supports large-scale form to be placed offshore where wind speeds are much higher. Though, availability may fall below 60 % of offshore wind turbine systems, leading to a substantial interruption due to the high occurrence of components failure (Nelson, 2009).

These are costly tasks as, for example, the cost of replacing the gearbox accounts for about ten percent of the wind turbine construction and installation cost, which eventually results in an increase of the energy production cost. There is a continuing increase of growth in the yearly wind turbine installed in a global size, thereby making it to have a prospect in the nearest future as seen in Fig. 12.1 (Tchakoua et al., 2014). The cumulative demand of energy is of acute significance for the world economic growth and environmental protection. Plant operator's key importance is close observation for unexpected faults normally during practical operation which could eventually sense some form of false alarms which are critical for reliable operation. The assured action is taken with regard to warning power downtime or preventing the turbine from shutting down in order to escape severe or risky failure happening.

Condition monitoring (CM) and fault diagnosis are of high priority to wind turbine due to complexity, expenses and prone to faults which sustains the system performance. This motivates monitoring the behaviour of the system to give timely response to the human operator or controller.

The prospective unexpected changes in component could affect the repair cost, unplanned maintenance, hazards and less tolerance system performance of the component failure that could lead to key economic problem. Availability is focused on Kusiak and Li (2011) that revealed about 75 % of the yearly interruption is triggered by about 15 % of the failures, the average failure rate and average downtime per component in WTs.

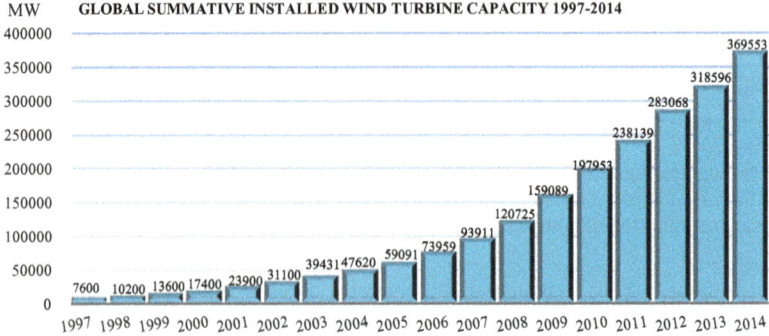

Fig. 12.1 The annual global chain installed wind power capacity from 1997 to 2014 (Tchakoua et al., 2014)

Fault Diagnosis for Wind Turbine Management

There have been various types of conventional monitoring turbine system like supervisory control and data acquisition (SCADA) which can only predict some specific faults with a reasonable amount of 60 min precision before they happen; according to Engelbrecht (2007), this could lead to some missed signals. Other monitoring devices like observer (filter) approach have been employed for monitoring and diagnosing wind turbine system for consistent reliability check.

In practical wind farm operations, uncertainties like disturbances and modelling errors are really inevitable. This has motivated the need for a profound effective real monitoring system such that the fault diagnosis tool will be more robust against any uncertainties during normal operations. Many approaches have been proposed to challenge this uncertainty concern, like the unknown input observer and the optimisation approach like evolutionary, eigenstructure assignment. Though, the study has been progressing to achieve a reliable method. Environment degradation could often have direct or indirect effects on practical systems; this has driven the need to improve the solution reliability. A healthy real monitoring system can be used to detect and diagnose the exact situation and the extent of unexpected changes in the system. There is a need for innovative intelligent approach to advance a reliable operation and reduce the maintenance cost for continuous sustainable approach towards renewable energy production that would be beneficial to industries and end-user consumers.

GA Optimisation-Based Approach

Genetic algorithm (GA) is a stochastic optimisation method for solving constrained and unconstrained problems based on natural selection process to perform a biological evolution. Algorithm is known as a precise procedure of guidelines on how to execute an uncertainty task/a highly effective method for problem-solving. GA is a developed soft computing approach for searching natural selection and genetics and evolutionary stochastic optimisation motivated by the evolutionary biological methods of survival of the fittest mainly for optimising models. This universal philosophy is employed to solve the robustness concern in model-based FD. GA is an artificial intelligence (*AI*) for solving extensive collection of everyday problems naturally based on searching rule to exhibit robust quality anticipated search set which guides the design process (Odofin, Ghassemlooy, Kai, & Gao, 2014). AI is a useful tool that is capable of solving large engineering complex problems which are apparently difficult to be solved using other traditional techniques. This problem-solving tool is better at diagnosis state and enhancing wind turbine system performance. GA has proven to be able to handle rapidly most complex uncertainty challenges than just other artificial intelligence algorithms that are slower and will not cope when applied to other situations (Fig. 12.2).

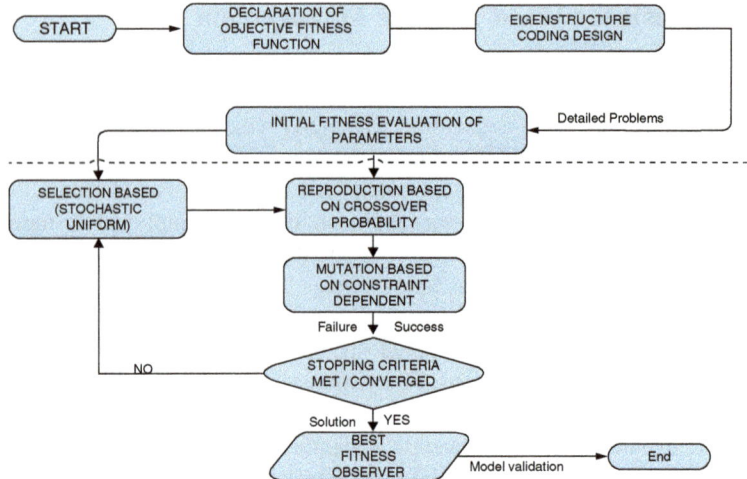

Fig. 12.2 Computational structure of GA optimisation

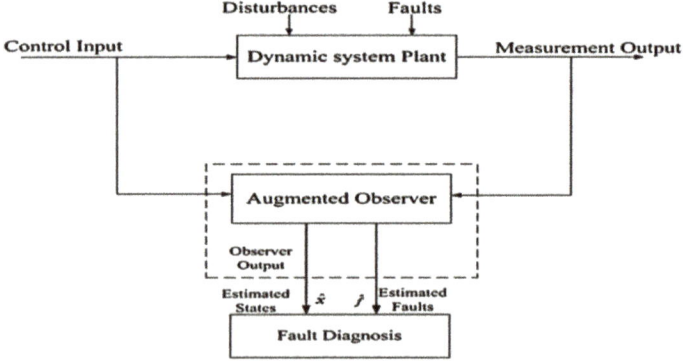

Fig. 12.3 Diagram of augmented observer

Monitoring design goal is to propose an improved observer real-time monitoring and fault diagnosis system. The better observer is a combination of GA, eigenstructure assignment and augmented system concepts presenting an improved optimised monitoring system performance according to Kai, Gao and Odofin (2015) and Zhu and Gao (2014) (Fig. 12.3).

The observer gain matrix $\left(\bar{K}\right)$ is proposed to reduce the effect of uncertainties in the estimation error. This permits an operative monitoring system to tolerate a sustainable performance adaptations providing enough time to planned turnaround maintenance process for effective turbine management.

The parameter designed matrix whose elements can be chosen freely is as follows:

$$W = \left[w_1 \cdots w_{n_r} \ w_{1,re} \cdots w_{n_c,re} \ w_{1,im} \cdots w_{n_c,im} \right] \in R^{p \times \bar{n}}$$

$$V = \left[v_1 \cdots v_{n_r}\; v_{1,re} \cdots v_{n_c,re}\; v_{1,im} \cdots v_{n_c,im} \right] \in R^{\bar{n} \times \bar{n}}$$

Therefore, the parametric representation of the observer gain $\bar{K}$ is given by

$$\bar{K} = \left[WV^{-1} \right]^{T}$$

The evolutional final optimal process can be displayed below (Fig. 12.4).

The optimal GA-based observer gain matrix fault is calculated and verified as

$$
\bar{K} =
\begin{bmatrix}
-0.0037 & -0.0053 & 0.0071 & 0.0001 \\
-17.3390 & -26.8135 & -31.3327 & 0.3679 \\
-26.3733 & -32.7155 & -64.0829 & 0.2484 \\
-0.0283 & -0.0487 & -0.0720 & 0.0007 \\
-3.0730 & -6.5951 & -16.9141 & -60.2632 \\
39.6491 & 247.8310 & 146.4340 & -5.1615 \\
1.8789 & -0.8540 & -3.6742 & 0.0015 \\
-1.4823 & 3.1287 & -2.8359 & -0.0005 \\
3.1459 & 1.5077 & 8.3643 & -0.0040 \\
3.0748 & -0.4325 & -1.7292 & 0.0004 \\
25.3790 & 36.4629 & 62.3357 & -0.2486 \\
2.2416 & 1.1250 & 7.5367 & -0.0018
\end{bmatrix}
$$

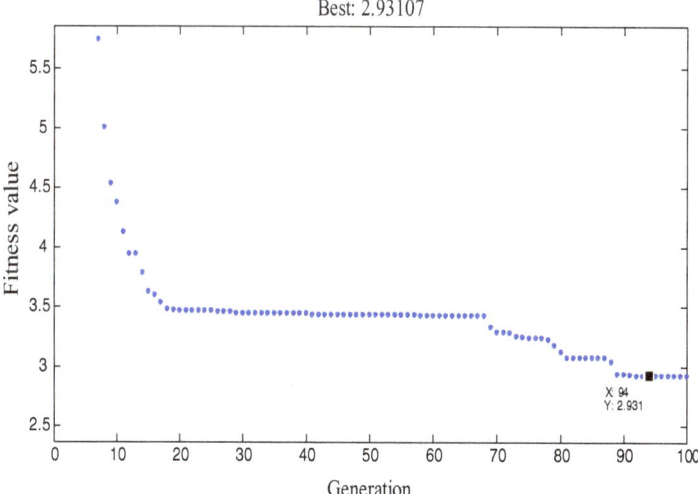

Fig. 12.4 The final optimal evolutional process for wind turbine

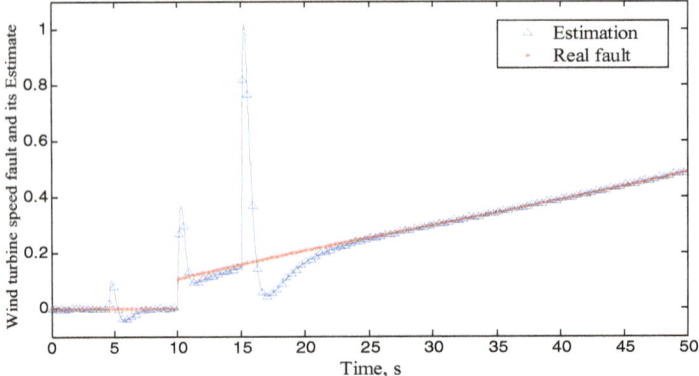

Fig. 12.5 The drifting wind turbine speed fault and its estimation

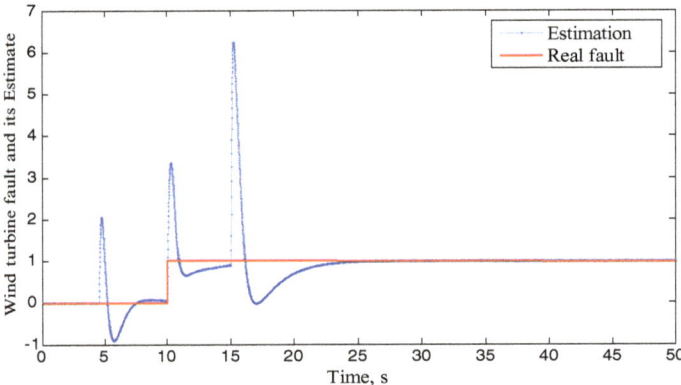

Fig. 12.6 The abrupt wind turbine speed fault and its estimate

The trajectory monitoring path is excellent, and tracing the actual wind turbine speed fault signal signifies as the "red line", and the "blue line" shows observer system tracking the real signal. The system performance and robustness properties are as desired for wind turbine dynamic system (Figs. 12.5 and 12.6).

The global optimised observer solution would improve the system performance and has proven to reduce the concerns of the practical applicability with the aid of the hybridised GA technique.

Conclusion and Future Work

The proposed monitoring and fault diagnosis system sustained the main concern of wind turbine. The main contribution is the momentary innovative hybrid monitoring system that will enhance an effective management system in wind energy industry.

GA has proven the competency employed to find the optimal solution to the observer that aids adequate management tool. The robustness and performance key property of the control system have been greatly optimised. The computation cost has been reduced in the system performance. The proposed designed techniques will reliably sustain the improved monitoring system strategy. Other additional investigations would be developed considering other artificial intelligence systems.

Acknowledgement   The authors would like to thank Naijapals for their financial support towards this study and the supervisory team for their support.

References

Bertling, L., & Ribrant, J. (2006). Survey of failure systems with focus on Swedish wind power plants during 1997–2005. *IEEE Transactions on Energy Conversion, 22*(1), 167–173.

Engelbrecht, A. P. (2007). *Computational intelligence.* Chichester, West Sussex: Wiley.

Kai, S., Gao, Z., & Odofin, S. O. (2015). Robust sensor fault estimation for induction motors via augmented observer and GA optimisation technique. In *International Conference on Mechatronics and Automation, August 2–5* (pp. 1727–1732).

Kusiak, A., & Li, W. (2011). The prediction and diagnosis of wind turbine faults. *Renewable Energy, 36,* 16–23. Elsevier Ltd.

Nelson, V. (2009). *Wind energy: Renewable energy and the environment.* CRC Press/ Global Wind Statistics (GWEC) 2014. Global Wind Energy Council. Retrieved February 25, 2015, from http://www.gwec.net/global-figures/graphs/

Odofin, S., Gao, Z., & Sun, K. (2015). Robust fault diagnosis for wind turbine systems subjected to multi-faults. *International Journal of Electrical, Computer, Energetic, Electronic and Communication Engineering WASET, 9*(2).

Odofin, S. O., Ghassemlooy, Z., Kai, S., & Gao, Z. (2014). Simulation study of fault detection and diagnosis for wind turbine system. PGNet. In *15th Annual Postgraduate Symposium on the Convergence of Telecommunications, Network and Broadcasting, Liverpool, UK, June 2014.*

Tchakoua, P., Wamkeue, R., Ouhrouche, M., Slaoui-Hasnaoui, F., Tameghe, T. A., & Ekemb, G. (2014). Wind turbine condition monitoring: State-of-the-art review, new trends, and future challenges. *Energies, 7*(4), 2595–2630.

Zhu, Y., & Gao, Z. (2014). Robust observer-based fault detection via evolutionary Optimization with applications to wind turbine systems. In *Proc. IEEE 9th Conference on Industrial Electronics and Applications, Hangzhou* (pp. 1627–1632).

Chapter 13
Qualitative and Quantitative Study on Videotaped Data for Fire Emergency Response

Vimala Nunavath, Andreas Prinz, and Tina Comes

Abstract During search and rescue (SAR) operations, information plays a significant role in empowering the emergency response personnel at various levels. But, understanding the information which is being shared between/among emergency personnel is necessary to improve current coordination systems. However, such systems can help the first responders to gain/increase their situational awareness and coordination. Moreover, there is still the lack of automatic and intelligent tools that can contribute to structure, categorize, and visualize the communicated content that occur during SAR operations. Therefore, in this paper, we present the concept of such analysis by using the qualitative methodology and current findings from an indoor fire game. The result shows first responders' communicated content and their corresponding content categories. This approach, therefore, provides a better way to learn about exchanged information and relevant information categories from videotaped data.

Keywords Indoor fire emergency management • Qualitative data analysis • Videotaped data • Serious game • Information sharing

Introduction

A complex network of different Emergency Response Organizations (EROs) such as fire, police, and health care personnel get involved in responding to any emergencies. During the response, these responders need to coordinate and share the quality information with each other to ensure that they have a shared understanding of the situation to align their actions. By interviewing different EROs who are involved in the emergency management, they all also agree that to accomplish the

V. Nunavath (✉) • A. Prinz • T. Comes
Department of Information and Communication Technology, CIEM, University of Agder,
Jon Lillethuns Vei 9, Grimstad, Norway
e-mail: vimala.nunavath@uia.no; andreas.prinz@uia.no; tina.comes@uia.no

© Springer International Publishing Switzerland 2017
R. Benlamri, M. Sparer (eds.), *Leadership, Innovation and Entrepreneurship as Driving Forces of the Global Economy*, Springer Proceedings in Business and Economics, DOI 10.1007/978-3-319-43434-6_13

goals and tasks, all first responders are mostly scattered geographically at the emergency scene and share a lot of information between or among these first response teams. Furthermore, these EROs also said that just sharing data does not help them in gaining situational awareness and coordination. They should have access to accurate, quality, and needed information (Nunavath, Radianti, Comes, & Prinz, 2015).

On the other hand, having access to the quality information in a chaotic situation, however, is also a challenging task as it involves uncertainties and highly volatile information sharing. So, the goal of the information sharing is to provide the right information to the right person at the right time. Whereas, Situational Awareness refers to the dynamic understanding of an emergency situation that a responder has, i.e., "what is going on" (Endsley, 1995; Nunavath et al., 2015). Therefore, the research questions which we try to get answers in this paper are "*What kind of information is being shared, how much quality present in the shared information and how this information will lead first responders in gaining situational awareness, coordination.*" The answers to these questions will help the EROs to change their future response behavior as well as to learn about their failures.

However, there has been a lot of research done on applying qualitative methodology for analyzing data in many domains, e.g., psychology (Smith, 2015), sociology (Marvasti, 2003), education (Jacobs, Kawanaka, & Stigler, 1999), political science (Van Evera, 1997), and public health (Baum, 1995). But, as per our knowledge, in emergency management, not many looked into generating information content categories from the collected videotaped data (consists: shared information) by using qualitative methodology. So, the method used for analyzing the content categories from communicated data thus in fact considered as the main contributions of this paper.

Augmented reality serious games are excellent instruments to use in disaster management exercises (Meesters & van de Walle, 2013). These experiments can help to understand the communicated content and find out the corresponding information content category. Especially for emergencies, only very mature systems can be tested in reality because if errors occur, it can result in harmful consequences. Furthermore, experiments are vital to helping researchers and practitioners to understand better the exchanged information and related information content categories which emerge within and across emergency response teams (Kurapati, Kolfschoten, Verbraeck, Corsi, & Brazier, 2013; Nunavath et al., 2015). In this paper, a game was designed to allow the research team to report qualitative and quantitative analysis made on the collected communicated data from a search and rescue game experiment.

We present our results for analyzing exchanged information with their corresponding information content. The analysis was done only after the game play. The purpose of this kind of analysis is to make the researchers, as well as the EROs, learn by highlighting the particular aspects of the response behavior such as coordination, situational awareness, information sharing, and information quality. We anticipate that EROs can be benefited by this kind of analysis for training and exercise purposes to improve their response behavior as well as shorten the response time.

This paper begins by describing the description of the developed emergency scenario, which was used to collect the data. The paper then explains the research
method that we used for analyzing the collected videotaped data. The result part
shows the analyzed content and corresponding information content categories. The
conclusion section summarizes the lessons learned from this research and discusses
directions for future work.

Developing a Serious Game and Scenarios

For collecting data, a serious indoor fire game was designed and played with a total
duration of 30 min at the University of Agder (UiA) with 23 voluntary participants
and 11 observers (i.e., four firefighters and rest UiA staff) to test a developed
smartphone application called SmartRescue. This app is an Android-based application which allows both first responders as well as victims to send and receive
emergency-related data such as the location of the fire and the victims with the help
of embedded sensors of the smartphone such as accelerometer, gyroscope, GPS,
humidity, thermometer, and so on.

In this game, two scenarios were designed. In the first scenario, only first
responders were given the smartphones with installed Zello application (Zellowalkie-
talkieapp) that used as information sharing tool. In the second scenario, both the
players and victims were given with SmartRescue application and walkie-talkies
(WT). These WTs were used as information sharing tool. The detailed description
of the tools and the first responder groups division for both scenarios can be seen in
the previous research (Nunavath, Radianti, Comes, & Prinz, 2016).

No, we actually divided the 23 members into 3 teams (each team includes 3 other
members (total 9 members)) and one CM (1) and one MCU (1). The total will be 11
(acted as emergency responders). Each team consists of three members: one as
smoke diver leader (SDL) and other two as smoke diver members (SDs) and the rest
as victims. The participants were briefed about their goals and tasks before the game
start. The design of the game and division of the teams were done according to the
obtained knowledge from the interviews with the real firefighters and also from the
provided documents (beredskap, 2003a, 2003b).

From the interviews and guidelines from the documents, we got to know that
only SDs enter into the burning building in pairs to start search and rescue process
to evacuate the victims from the affected area. However, SDL does not enter into the
affected building. He stays near the entrance to the building to obtain the big picture
of the situation. He is also responsible for guiding his team members (SDs) by providing the needed information. SDL reports to the CM and receives orders and
information from him. If any of the SDs is injured, SDL will inform to the CM and
replaces his role with SD role. Crew Manager is in charge of his crew safety. He
orders and shares/provides the needed information with SDLs. However, Medical
Care Unit is responsible for noting down the brought victims (either injured or
found or dead or conscious or unconscious) and informing to the CM (Sarshar,
Radianti, & Gonzalez, 2015).

Research Methodology

Videotaped Data Collection

During the game, we have used four video recorders to record the entire game. These video recorders placed in all corners of one of the floors in a building where the fire game was conducted. Moreover, we gave smart glasses and GoPros to the participants to record entire SAR operation of both scenarios. The reason for using video recorders for data collection was that it can provide the researchers a unique opportunity to revise the tapes again and again.

Moreover, videos can be played, replayed, speedup, allowed or paused, discussed, analyzed, and reanalyzed. Thus, provides the videos provide the insight of the communication content with the action (Morse & Pooler, 2008). Furthermore, after the game, the research team had a chance to discuss the key points with the players and with the observers. And then the players were given the opportunity to make any further comments on their experience and difficulties during game experiment if they felt to discuss. The discussion lasted approximately 30 min for both scenarios.

Videotaped Data Analysis

The verbal content of the emergency communication messages was analyzed through the thematic analysis which is a basic method for qualitative analysis method. Thematic analysis is a method for identifying, analyzing, and reporting patterns (themes or categories) of the data (Braun & Clarke, 2006). The analysis was inductive with themes driven from the data collected. So, after the game, the research team extracted the recorded videos and uploaded to our personal computer to analyze them. After uploading, we have played the videos, again and again, to extract and transcribe the communicated messages in excel sheets for both scenarios and the obtained data was separated into two columns and now ready for coding. The first column is with the timeline of the communication and the second column is with the communicated content.

Coding is one of the several methods of working with and building knowledge about data. A Code is an abstract representation of an object or phenomenon or a way of identifying themes in a text. Coding the text for qualitative analysis is a way of tagging or indexing it to facilitate later retrieval and allows you to recontextualize the data (Pat Bazeley, 2013). Before coding, transcripts were first read, and the content familiarized. Coding was done in NVivo 10.0 (QSR International) and codes that summarized the meaning of text segments were used. Coded sections of the transcripts were then organized into preliminary categories.

As we code, Nvivo tool indexes (adding or tagging flags to) the text or videos by storing the references to the document at the node. In this tagging process, Nvivo is not making a copy of the text at the node, but connecting the concepts or categories with the data. The data that have been coded will be accessible from the nodes. In

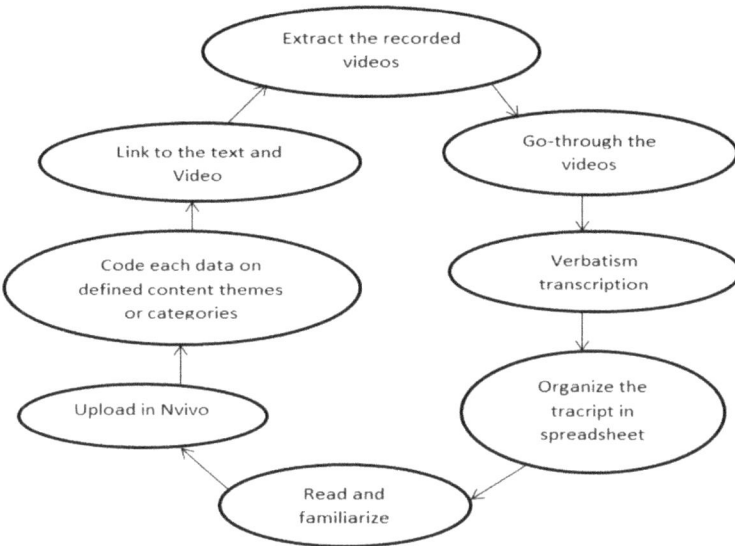

Fig. 13.1 Coding style

coding process, transcripts were reread and double coded and discussed with other researchers to maximize the reliability. If the communicated messages double coded, i.e., fall into different categories, it can be tagged more than once at any node. So, this text at the node is not doubled (Pat Bazeley, 2013). From Fig. 13.1, the process of coding style that we have used can be seen.

Results

In this section, the result of the qualitative analysis of the videotaped data is presented for both scenarios. As the game was designed for 30 min, for the first scenario, the total messages that were communicated during the game were 75 and for the second scenario, it was 68.

Qualitative and Quantitative Analysis

After the final coding, four information content categories (also called as nodes) emerged from the data: *Situational Awareness, Information Sharing, Coordination, and Information Quality*. These categories were similar for both scenarios. Primary information categories and subcategories are described later.

Situational Awareness

As described earlier, the category which was emerged from the communicated data was "Situational Awareness." This information category was further divided into subcategories, i.e., Reporting, Rescuing, and Assessment. During search and rescue operation, first responders need to get awareness of the situation to accomplish their missions and goals. The awareness of the situation can be achieved only when they have proper access to the quality information. From the communicated data, for reporting, first responders had followed both top-down and bottom-up approach. That means SDs and SDLs report information to their respective leaders. The reported information helped the first responders to assess the situation and to perform tasks and achieve their goals such as rescuing. The excerpt of the communicated content for situational awareness can be seen in Table 13.1.

As you can see from Fig. 13.2, in scenario one, the communication content about *Situational Awareness (SA)* was shared 50 out of 75 messages. Whereas, in the second scenario, the communicated content about SA was 83 times out of 68. The reason for this result must be because of several messages can be coded several times at different nodes. Moreover, in the second scenario, the players, both first responders and victims were given with SmartRescue application which helped them to get access to the information such as the location of the fire and the victims through embedded sensors. This available information must have been shared and made the first responders gain the Situational Awareness.

Information Sharing

Another node (category) which was derived from the analysis was Information Sharing. This category was further subdivided into Irrelevant Information Shared and Delay. While responding to emergency, information sharing plays a vital role in which first responders collectively utilize their available informational resources. But, the information which is being shared might consist of irrelevant information and with delays. From the game and communicated content, we extracted communicated data with irrelevant information and with delay. Table 13.1 presents the excerpt of such information.

From Fig. 13.2, for the first scenario, Irrelevant and Delay Information have been shared 29 times out of 75 messages. But, in the second scenario, only 5 times out of 68, Irrelevant and Delay Information have been shared. The reason might be because of not having supporting tools in the first scenario and having access to relevant information in the second scenario.

Coordination

The third category which was emerged from the qualitative analysis was Coordination. This category also further parted into two subcategories, i.e., coordination success and coordination failure. Coordination is done based on the available information.

Table 13.1 Extracted categories and subcategories and examples by using qualitative analysis

Categories	Sub-categories	Description	Example of communicated content
Information sharing (exchange of information within or among teams)	Irrelevant information	Irrelevant information occurred when needed (shared)	Requested: "we need wheel-chair"
			Responded: "At the east, fire starting in the middle"
	Delay	When information is requested, it was replied with time delay	Required: "at 00:10:01, any fire in the north"
			Replied: "at 00:20:05, yes, north corridor is on fire"
Situational awareness (to know what is happening in the vicinity)	Reporting	Reporting to corresponding leaders and fellow emergency personnel	"Room clear"
	Rescuing	Actions/messages that lead or involve saving the victims	"A victim hiding in the media room. Can you please help them to get him out" (From MCU to CM and from CM to SDL and from SDL to SDs)
	Assessment	Process of achieving, acquiring or maintaining situational awareness	"Go to other directions to see if you can find any victims going nearest fire"
Coordination (aligning one's actions with other members to achieve a shared goal)	Coordination success	Messages that were performed results in coordination success	"Can you check room 23?"
			"Yes checked"
	Coordination failure	Messages that were not performed results in coordination failure	"Please see rooms 60, 61, 62"
Information quality (information that meets the needs of teams)	Timeliness	Messages that shared and received in time and up-to-date	"In the east, 67 room, the fire is started"
	Completeness	Messages that shared and received were with complete information	"Please come back and see room 55 an 56"

When SDs perform and confirm the actions based on the orders that have been got from their respective leaders, then that message confirms the coordination Success. Whereas, when SDs fail to perform the actions of the given orders of their leaders, that kind of messages proves coordination failure. The excerpt of such kind of messages is given in Table 13.1.

For both scenarios the communication content that shared for *Coordination (C)* was almost same. Even though having and not having SmartRescue application did not make much difference in sharing coordination-related messages. The difference can be seen in Fig. 13.2.

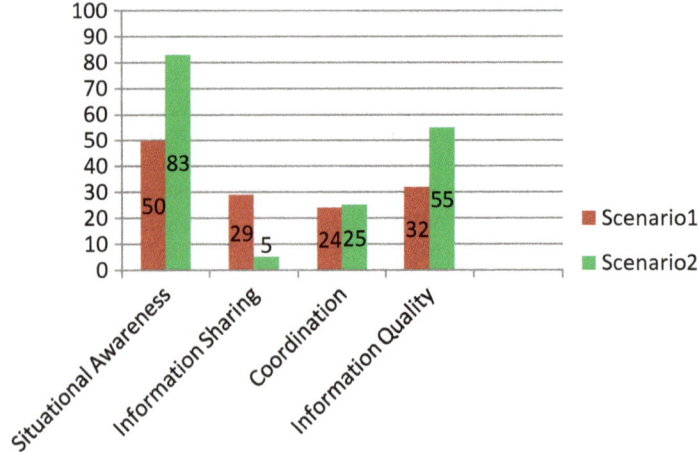

Fig. 13.2 Quantitative analysis for scenario comparison based on the information categories

Information Quality

The last category that was obtained from the qualitative analysis was information quality (IQ). During SAR operation, information has to meet the needs of first responders to accomplish their goals. However, information quality, unfortunately, is difficult to observe, capture, or measure. So, to measure the IQ, quality dimensions are the way. Based on the literature (Singh, Singh, Park, Lee, & Rao, 2009) and qualitative analysis, we have subdivided this category into two subcategories, i.e., Timeliness and Completeness.

From the communicated data, Timeliness and Completeness related communicated content shared 32 times out of 75 messages in scenario 1. While in second scenario 55 shared messages were with timeliness and completeness. The reason for sharing more quality information in second scenario was about having access to accurate and quality information. It was possible because of the SmartRescue supporting tool.

Discussion

Throughout this paper, we have analyzed the videotaped data which was collected from an emergency indoor fire game both qualitative and quantitatively to understand the first responders' situational awareness, coordination, and information quality through shared information in both scenarios. However, it is seen from the communicated information that in both scenarios, the first responders shared similar kind of information but with different volume. As a result, the situational awareness, information sharing, coordination, and information quality for both scenarios are distinct.

However, the methodology that we have used is extremely well suited to analyzing the complicated and functional data. An advantage of this method is that large volumes of textual data and different textual sources can be dealt with and used with proven evidence. Especially, in emergency management, qualitative analysis can be used as an important way of analyzing the communicated data to understand the response behavior and to learn the categories of the exchanged information.

The visualized data in Fig. 13.2 confirms that there is a significant difference between scenario 1 to scenario 2 on situational awareness, information sharing, and information quality. Exchanged information has an effect on this significant difference. Whereas, communication content for coordination category was almost same. Hence, visualization is a good way of communicating the data in an efficient way to create a mental picture by looking at the figures (Nunavath et al., 2015).

When communicated content gets analyzed, we envision that EROs get an idea of a lot of things, i.e., what and how much information was being used to get situational awareness and coordination, how much quality information was shared, and so on. The results presented in this paper are based on the small dataset. But in real emergency situations, large datasets are observed and communicated. To analyze such large sets of emergency data after any emergency, this kind of approach is a suitable way.

Conclusion and Future Work

Improving situational awareness, coordination, information quality, and information sharing in any emergency situations through automatic methods requires an understanding of the information communicated by those who are responding to the event. Our analysis of videotaped data during an indoor fire drill with two scenarios identifies categories of situational awareness, information sharing, and coordination and information quality of information through exchanged information during search and rescue operation. Furthermore, based on the results of our study, our potential future research directions will be to run the same experiment with a large number of real firefighters analyze the generated communicated content with the same methodology. The results which we get from the future study will be compared with the present study to check the validity of the results.

Moreover, another future direction will be to develop a working framework to inform the design and implementation of software systems that employ information sharing strategies. The expectation is that such systems to be used by first responders to help them for improving situational awareness, coordination, and information sharing and information quality during fire emergency events.

Acknowledgments This study is carried out in collaboration with the SmartRescue project led by Prof. Ole-Christoffer Granmo and cofunded by Aust-Agder utviklings-og-kompetansefond (AAUKF, projectnr. 2011–2006). We would like to owe our gratitude to the Grimstad fire station personnel who supported us during the development of different stages of the experiment, to the students that took part in the game execution, and finally to Mehdi Lazreg Ben, Jaziar Radianti for their constant support in the data analysis process. Finally, we thank the observers who provided their valuable suggestions after the game.

References

Baum, F. (1995). Researching public health: Behind the qualitative-quantitative methodological debate. *Social Science & Medicine, 40*(4), 459–468.

beredskap, D. f. s. o. (2003a). *Veiledning om røyk og kjemikaliedykking.*

beredskap, D. f. s. o. (2003b). *Veiledning til forskrift om organisering og dimensjonering av brannvesen.* Retrieved from http://www.dsb.no/Global/Publikasjoner/2003/Veiledning/veilorgdimensavbrannv2003.pdf

Braun, V., & Clarke, V. (2006). Using thematic analysis in psychology. *Qualitative Research in Psychology, 3*(2), 77–101. doi:10.1191/1478088706qp063oa.

Endsley, M. R. (1995). Measurement of situation awareness in dynamic systems. *Human Factors: The Journal of the Human Factors and Ergonomics Society, 37*(1), 65–84.

Jacobs, J. K., Kawanaka, T., & Stigler, J. W. (1999). Integrating qualitative and quantitative approaches to the analysis of video data on classroom teaching. *International Journal of Educational Research, 31*(8), 717–724.

Kurapati, S., Kolfschoten, G., Verbraeck, A., Corsi, T. M., & Brazier, F. (2013). *Exploring shared situational awareness in supply chain disruptions.* Paper presented at the ISCRAM 2013: Proceedings of the 10th International Conference on Information Systems for Crisis Response and Management, Baden-Baden, Germany, May 12–15, 2013.

Marvasti, A. (2003). *Qualitative research in sociology.* London: Sage.

Meesters, K., & van de Walle, B. (2013). *Disaster in my backyard: A serious game introduction to disaster information management.* Paper presented at the Proceedings of the 10th International ISCRAM Conference.

Morse, J. M., & Pooler, C. (2008). Analysis of videotaped data: Methodological considerations. *International Journal of Qualitative Methods, 1*(4), 62–67.

Nunavath, V., Radianti, J., Comes, M., & Prinz, A. (2015, May). Visualization of information flows and exchanged information: Evidence from an indoor fire game. In *The Proceedings of 12th International Conference on Information Systems for Crisis Management and Response (ISCRAM).*

Nunavath, V., Radianti, J., Comes, T., & Prinz, A. (2016). The impacts of ICT support on information distribution, task assignment for gaining teams' situational awareness in search and rescue operations. In S. M. Thampi, S. Bandyopadhyay, S. Krishnan, K.-C. Li, S. Mosin, & M. Ma (Eds.), *Advances in signal processing and intelligent recognition systems* (Vol. 425, pp. 443–456). Berlin: Springer.

Pat Bazeley, K. J. (2013). *Qualitative data analysis with Nvivo* (pp. 1–305).

Sarshar, P., Radianti, J., & Gonzalez, J. J. (2015). On the impacts of utilizing smartphones on organizing rescue teams and evacuation procedures. In *Proceedings of the ISCRAM 2015 Conference, ISCRAM 2015.*

Singh, P., Singh, P., Park, I., Lee, J., & Rao, H. R. (2009). Information sharing: A study of information attributes and their relative significance during catastrophic events. In K. J. Knapp (Ed.), *Cyber-security and global information assurance: Threat analysis and response solutions.* Hershey, PA: IGI.

Smith, J. A. (2015). *Qualitative psychology: A practical guide to research methods.* London: Sage.

Van Evera, S. (1997). *Guide to methods for students of political science.* Ithaca, NY: Cornell University Press.

Zellowalkie-talkieapp. Zello walkie-talkie software application. *Zello walkie-talkie software application.* Retrieved from http://zello.com/app

Chapter 14
AIbot: Do Virtual Worlds Strengthen the Credibility of Artificially Intelligent Bots?

Sharefa Murad, Ignazio Passero, Rita Francese, and Genoveffa Tortora

Abstract This paper presents AIbot, an assistant system for helping the exploration and fruition of distance didactic activities in Virtual Worlds. The proposed automatic assistant aims at reaching a natural appearance and a usual interaction style: it concretizes in an avatar, the typical character that habitually represents users during their Virtual World experiences. The utilization of an AIML engine lets AIbot to interact with users in a quasi natural manner and using the ordinary text chat channels. Aiming at evaluating how the Virtual World environment influences user perceptions of artificial intelligence, a controlled experiment has been performed as a modified Turing test: the users randomly interact with a human controlled avatar and with AIbot aiming at understanding the nature of the interlocutor intelligence between human or programmed. Results are really positive and provide interesting suggestions on the adoption of automatic user assistant systems in Virtual Worlds.

Keywords Virtual worlds • e-Learning • Artificial intelligence • Bot • Automatic aiding systems • Turing test

Introduction

In this paper, we present AIbot (Fig. 14.1), an automatic system adopted as a permanent e-learning assistant for Virtual World remote students in their didactic and exploring actions. The system integrates several technologies for conversation and virtual character control. The Research also introduces an Artificial Intelligence

S. Murad (✉)
Department of Computer Information system, Middle East University,
Sabtieh, Beirut, Lebanon
e-mail: smurad@meu.edu.jo

I. Passero • R. Francese • G. Tortora
Dipartimento di Matematica e Informatica, Università degli Studi di Salerno, Fisciano, Italy
e-mail: ipassero@unisa.it; francese@unisa.it; tortora@unisa.it

© Springer International Publishing Switzerland 2017
R. Benlamri, M. Sparer (eds.), *Leadership, Innovation and Entrepreneurship as Driving Forces of the Global Economy*, Springer Proceedings in Business and Economics, DOI 10.1007/978-3-319-43434-6_14

159

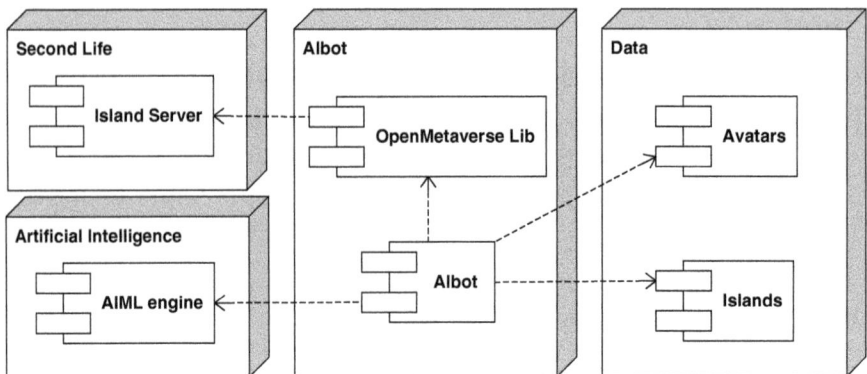

Fig. 14.1 The AIbot system organization

Test specific for evaluating the AIbot system aiming at complementing the users' impressions collected with a questionnaire.

Chabots (chatterbots, or chat bots) are computer programs designed to simulate an intelligent conversation with one or more human users via auditory or textual methods. Traditionally, the aim of such simulations is to fool the user into thinking that the programs output has been produced by a human (The Turing Test) (Chatterbot).

Chatbots come in form of auto answering machines or even in 2D or 3D web interfaces with an interpreter program that interacts with users. Pandorabots (Pandora Bots), Alice Artificial intelligence Foundation (Alice Bot), Elizabeth (Elizabeth Bot) and program-O (Program-O) are examples of chat bot interpreter programs based on AIML. Chatbots took several roles varying between: Entertainment, Commerce and industry service, Gaming (Blue Mars) and Education (Ramachandran, Movva, Li, Anantharam, & Graves, 2007). When hosted in 3D Virtual Worlds, these programs are often in the form of automatically controlled objects or characters (the avatars). Second Life (SL) is an interactive virtual world in which players create their own avatar that represents themselves in the interaction with the simulated world and with the alter egos of other people (Second Life). Exploring SL drives users in a mixture of worlds ranging from extreme realism to very fantastic, sometimes bizarre, places.

Many academic institutions adopt Virtual Worlds for didactic settings (Bifrost & University of Southern Denmark; De Lucia, Francese, Passero, & Tortora, 2009a; EDTEC Virtual Campus & San Diego State University) or for fostering distance collaboration (De Lucia, Francese, Passero, & Tortora, 2008, 2009b; Erra & Scanniello, 2010). Also commercial enterprises (AMD Developer Central; IBM Italia Region) are involving themselves in SL activities with a broad band of interests ranging from the simple need to occupy new spaces and experiment new forms of communication, to the interest towards a very big user community. Distance learning (De Lucia et al., 2009a), scientific (Cochrane, 2006) or commercial simulations are some examples of the power of SL technology in satisfying user interests. SL also has the possibility of developing and controlling your own characters using the OpenMetaverse library (LibOpenMetaverse); more details of its use will be explained in the later sections of this paper focused on the system implementation. 3D interface bots come in SL in two forms: Prim-bots connected by LSL script (AA (Artificial Avatars); Linden Scripting Language; XD Fusion) and Avatar bots connected in variety of ways (J&M Creations-Scripts; SLBot; Toys Bot) with their intelligence engines. The Turing Test (TT) was first introduced by Turing (1950) and it is a test on machine's ability to demonstrate intelligence. It is also presented as an imitation game in which the machine mimics human behaviour. A human judge engages in a natural language conversation with one human and one machine, each of which tries to appear human and whose real nature is unknown to him. If the judge cannot reliably distinguish the machine from the human, the machine is said to have passed the test.

Numerous versions of the TT have been mooted through the years (The Turing Test Page), using it to test the intelligence of their programs or modifying it according to the context in which the intelligence has to be verified. The Ultimate TT introduced by Barberi (1992) is a virtual TT with a comprehensive environment of sight, sound and body, allowing the judge to base his decision not only on written words, but on spoken speech, non-verbal cues and body movement. The test still holds to the spirit of the original TT. There is still a human judge that uses his intelligence and savvy to test the subject. Like the original test, the judge has no way of knowing if the subject is human or not before interacting with it. Like the original test, the goal is to create a simulation of human actions so realistic that not even other humans can tell the difference. Neumann, Reichenberger, and Ziegler (2009) suggested variations of the (standard interpretation of) the TT for the challenges arising from new technologies such as internet and virtual reality systems. Hingston (2009) described a new design for a TT for game bots. He tries to reach a more natural evaluation method, where the judges are simply game players and judging is an inherent part of the game.

The rest of paper is organized as follows: section "The Proposed System" describes the proposed system. The evaluation of the experience is discussed in section "Evaluation", while section "Results" gives more details on the results. Finally, section "Conclusion" concludes.

The Proposed System

The proposed system is an automatic assistant and is adopted for providing information on SL e-learning activities and settings. AIbot welcomes distance learners on Unisa Computer Science Island in SL and aims at reaching a natural interaction style: it appears as an avatar and adopts the usual communication channels and behaviours. Because of its representation and conduct, when in the virtual setting, users perceive it just as another user, naturally ask information to it and seem more available to interact with AIbot respect to other forms of assistant (scripted objects or panels).

Figure 14.1 shows the main components of the system and their interactions. In particular, the central node depicts the AIbot core component that adopts the

OpenMetaverse library (LibOpenMetaverse) for communicating with the SL server (represented by the top leftmost component of the diagram). Two separate nodes host the data broker (the rightmost part of the image in Fig. 14.1) and the AIML (Wallace, 2003) engine adopted for the AI.

The AIML Engine

AIbot is capable of autonomously answer to user phrases listened on the text chat channel. At this aim, an artificial intelligence engine has been embedded and controls the conversation. The Artificial Intelligent Markup Language (AIML) is a XML dialect for creating natural language software agents (AIML) and is used for interpreting user phrases and generating the AIbot natural human answers. AIML specifies pairs composed by a pattern and a template. When an utterance from a user matches a pattern in the pairs, the agent returns the associated template phrase.

AIML was originally adapted from a non-XML grammar also called AIML and formed the basis for the first Alicebot, A.L.I.C.E., the Artificial Linguistic Internet Computer Entity (Alice Bot). In particular, to obtain the most natural and human-like conversation, we adopt the open source cross platform Rebecca AIML (Rebecca AIML), also known for being embedded in the ALICE software (Alice Bot), the famous original chat robot, three-time winner of the Loebner prize for the "most human computer" (Loebner Prize). Rebecca AIML also comes with a set of administrative tools and supports C# (Microsoft C#) language which we adopted to develop AIbot. Table 14.1 reports some extracts from automatic chat conversation between our AIbot and a human controlled avatar. How is it possible to see, the credibility of AIbot conversation varies according to the spoken subject.

The AIbot Blind Controller

The AIbot controller is a C# program that uses Second Life OpenMetaverse library to connect to SL, controlling its avatar and, in particular, the conversations with other users. The program listens to the chat channel, invokes the AIML engine service to generate the answer and sends it back to SL, following the usual chatting interaction metaphors. In particular, when the engine is parsing the chat and producing the answer, the automatically controlled avatar appears digitizing the chat messages on an imaginary keyboard, following the expected behaviour of SL characters, which users are accustomed to see. As Fig. 14.2 depicts, the program interface is organized in three main areas aggregating similar commands: *The Simulation Controls, The Avatar Movement* and *The Chat Area.*

The AIbot controller interface exposes only the main control commands provided by the OpenMetaverse library. In addition, we designed the AIbot application without providing users with a complete view on the SL environment, so that we

Table 14.1 Samples of chatbot conversations

The human	The program
Do you like art	Yes I enjoy art very much, especially painting
What kind of paintings	I can't decide. You choose
How about abstracts	What is it to you
....	....
I prefer using Google	Have you tried a web search? Does it find what you are looking for?
Usually, doesn't it find what you are looking for?	I think there might be a few exceptions
Interesting comparison, like what exceptions. what does that have to do with exceptions	"Interesting comparison"? What does it have to do with exceptions?
....	....
Not sure	You're not sure of what?
I don't know	I am as good as it gets
Your as good as it gets in what?	Is that a fact
....	....
Do you like logic	I use it as often as possible
That's nice	Me either
Just a bit actually	Not much, eh?
Do you like television	Yes I love TV
What is your favourite show	My favourite show is STAR TREK VOYAGER
Nice	Are you getting bored?
I like your style	You like my style
Yes	Alright then

developed a blind SL client: AIbot is fundamentally an AI manager and needs just a reduced interface for controlling the actions.

The *Simulation Controls* area, as shown in Fig. 14.3, groups commands for connecting and disconnecting from the SL environment and changing the SL avatar used. Acting on this interface, it is possible to retrieve the avatar position and to display its status with respect to the logging operations. Other simple avatar behaviours, like following an avatar, sitting or flying and changing the character status (i.e. present or away) are controlled in the *Movement* area shown in Fig. 14.3. Also basic avatar movements may be requested acting on the four buttons towards N, E, S and W directions and walking the distance selected in a numeric text box.

As an answer to what listened on the common chat channel, the *Chat Area* is updated with the text generated by the AIML engine. This area has a twofold utility: it allows the human AIbot controller to access the text and send it to SL with a random delay as a normal conversation answer. The first benefit is in the correct control of answers (AIbot human controller can change or modify the answer), but the user intervention is useful also to simulate a thinking time delay in the AIbot–users interaction.

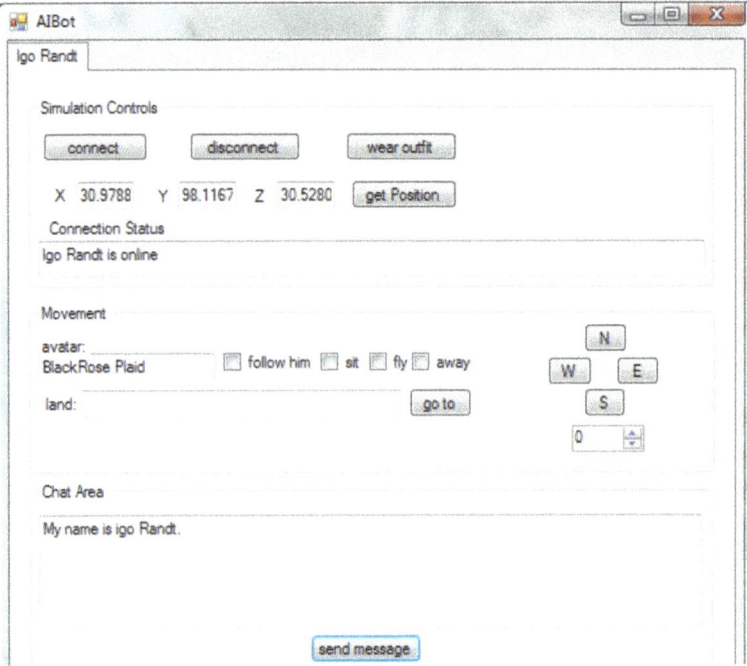

Fig. 14.2 The AIbot controller interface

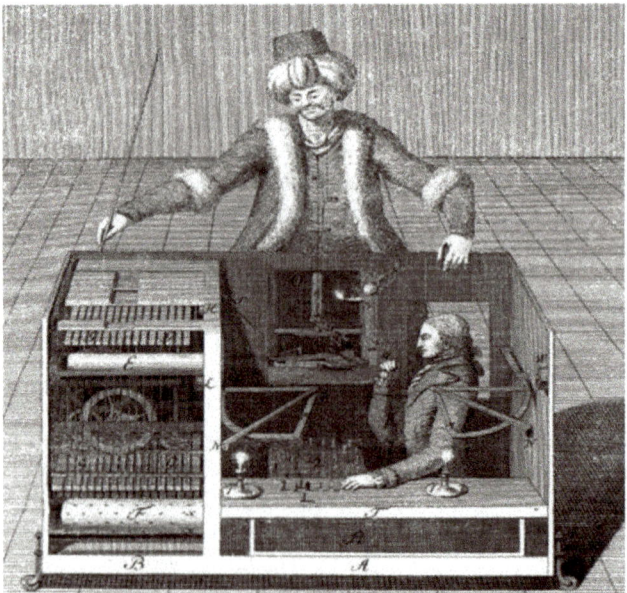

Fig. 14.3 The fake chess-playing machine

Evaluation

The proposed work aims at evaluating if Virtual Worlds influence users' perceptions and let them feel stronger reality sensations with respect to a traditional chat setting (mainly due to involvement, realism, etc.) when interacting with an automatic answer machine, because of the surrounding environment and of the adopted communication metaphors. Our idea is experimenting if the AI behind a SL automatic character and immersed in a Virtual World may appear more effective and more human-like. In order to accomplish this, we designed a controlled experiment as an empirical evaluation inspired by the classic TT.

The Modified Turing Test

For the evaluation of the AIbot system, and in particular of the support provided by Virtual Worlds to the credibility of automatic answering avatars, we adopted a modified version of the TT. In general, the purpose of the TT is not specifically to determine whether a computer is able to fool an interrogator to exchange a machine for a human, but rather whether a programmed intelligence could imitate a human.

The main difference between the classic TT and the variation we propose is that we exploit the Turing idea for organizing a comparison between in-world and out-world observers. In our design, with respect to the classical TT, we added the judge actors that passively and from outside SL observe the conversation aiming at guessing the nature of participants.

This change in the test mechanism adds a new challenge to the experience, in view of the fact that the environment ability to strengthen the naturalness of the bot is tested by a direct performance comparison. If it is possible to observe any statistical difference between in-world and out-world AI recognizing performances, we can argue that SL, and Virtual Worlds in general, impact on user credibility of AIML chat bots.

Where Is the Hidden Dwarf?

One of the prerequisites of the proposed modified TT is in the possibility of hiding a human interlocutor and an automatic one behind a SL avatar. The Chat Area controls have this specific goal. According to the proposed TT, the AIbot human controller schedules the response times and intervenes in the discussion only when needed. This mechanism enables to recreate the fake chess-playing machine (The Fake Chess-Playing Machine) of the end of last century. The system was playing chess with human users simulating a robot automatic behaviour, but its intelligence was due to a person hidden inside the machine. According to this metaphor, the intervening AIbot human controller, is the hidden dwarf who is not obliged to be closed in a dark and narrow box, as depicted in Fig. 14.3. However, our metaphor slightly differs: users know that both human and automatic intelligence are involved, but their goal is to understand which the SL avatar that hides the AIML controller is.

The Experiment

The tasks to accomplish were easy, just requiring the SL text chat; however, all subjects were trained on basic SL commands and communication channels in a collective session performed before the experiment start. Overall, 24 students of the first level degree in Computer Science of the University of Salerno offered themselves as subjects and voluntarily took part in the experiment. In particular, the experiment was organized in 12 comparison sessions and each one lasted less than half hour involving the following actors:

- The *AIbot avatar*, that automatically answers to the chat messages using the AIML engine, leaded by a human controller, whose goal is simply avoiding answers that can clearly reveal the speaker as a program (i.e. answers such as, "I am a (ro)bot", "I am an automatic answering machine", "I have no human feelings", etc.).
- The *SL avatar* connected and controlled in SL by a human.
- The *Subject avatar* that performs a conversation chatting with both AIbot and the SL avatars inside the SL environment.
- The external *judges* that evaluate, from outside the SL environment, the two chat conversations generated by the Subject avatar with the SL and with the AIbot avatars.

The subject sample was equally partitioned in the SL avatar and Judge sets and the experiment has been singularly performed by each couple of subjects (SL avatar and Judge) in the SE4eL (Software Engineering for e-Learning) laboratory of our University.

Figure 14.4 depicts the experiment organization with the actors involved in the empirical evaluation. As shown, the chat is at the core of the communication accessed from inside SL by SL subjects and observed from outside by the Judges. In particular, the experiment proposes two subtasks to the subjects in a random order:

1. *Conversation with AIbot avatar*

   A human speaker controls the AIbot and limits to filtering out direct self-nature answers that can suggest the nature of interlocutor to subjects

2. *Conversation with the SL avatar*

   A human speaker controls a regular SL avatar acting on the standard SL client and chats with the subject.

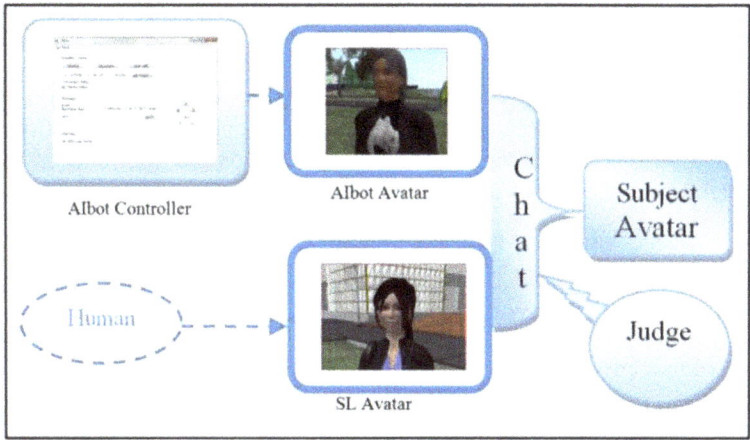

Fig. 14.4 The experiment organization

Both conversations continue also when the subject is sure about the nature of his interlocutor but the SL avatar signals to the experiment conductor he is ready to take a decision: the number of exchanged messages is then adopted as a performance metric on which basing the comparison test. The judges simply observe, from outside SL, the track of conversations message by message and evaluate the nature of the interlocutors without being influenced by the environment. Also their AI recognizing performances are evaluated in terms of number of read messages (remember that the SL conversation does not interrupt as the SL avatar has a sure answer about the nature of his interlocutor).

After the experiment, both subjects, the participating human and the external judge, answer to the question:

1. *What of the two conversations you had was with a human?*

This question has only a control nature, since until now, AIML bots have always been recognized and we do not hope to alter users' perception so much to change this. The subjects are also asked to answer to the following questions aiming at understanding the degree of credibility, perceived:

2. *How sure was your judgement?*

This question aims at quantifying how the subject is sure of his decision.

3. *How quick was your judgement?*

This question aims at quantifying the perceived quickness in taking the final decision.

The last two questions of the proposed questionnaire are reserved to participants in the SL avatar role:

4. *How SL Avatars represent human being?*

5. *Even if synthetic, do you think SL makes the bot more credible?*

All the questions are evaluated on the five-point Likert scale (Oppenheim, 1992) ranging from 1 (for nothing) to 5 (very much).

At the end, we obtained a subjective evaluation by analysing the questionnaire answers and an objective assessment was performed on the performance metric values establishing the statistical plausibility of the following hypotheses:

H_0: A 3D virtual environment does not affect AI credibility when perceived via the textual chat and from a speaking avatar.

Against the alternate one:

H_1: A 3D virtual environment improves AI credibility when perceived via the textual chat and from a speaking avatar.

Results

The experiment provided both subjective (questionnaire) and objective (performance metric) evaluations. Figure 14.5 reports the box plots describing the scores obtained by each question of the questionnaire. The boxes are aggregated with respect to the subjects the related question is directed to: on each box, the central mark is the median, the edges of the box are the 25th and 75th percentiles, the whiskers extend to the most extreme not outliers data points while the outliers are plotted individually as crosses.

The left-hand side of Fig. 14.5 reports results for the questions 2 and 3, the right-hand side of the picture aggregates questions 4 and 5. As it is possible to see in Fig. 14.5, with respect to questions 2 and 3, the SL environment gives user a higher

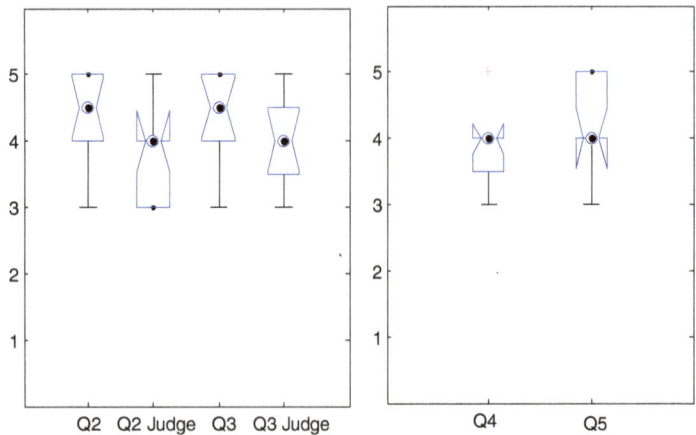

Fig. 14.5 The questionnaire results

sureness in recognizing the interlocutor nature (Subject avatar) and a relative quickness perception with respect to outside SL (Judge). Indeed, by deeply analysing the experiment chat records, we noticed as defect of the AIbot prototype the absence of knowledge on the surrounding environment and events. However, this issue affected only two sessions and, even if it reduces the perception of realism, it will be partially overcome by the fully working AIbot. Indeed, the working system will be devoted to automatic assisting users and the AIML patterns will be strongly localization customized for explicitly matching questions about the Unisa Computer Science Island (Unisa Computer Science) and hosted activities.

The score obtained by questions 4 and 5 states that SL avatar are perceived to be well representing humans ($\mu = 3.92$) and that, once found the AIbot program, it appears to be well integrated (or hidden) in the environment and similar, in terms of behaviour, to the other users ($\mu = 4.25$).

Figure 14.6 reports the objective performance metric defined as *the number of exchanged messages the user needs before being able to understand if he is interacting with a human or an automatic entity*. The boxes are organized with respect to the target of recognition process: *AIbot* and *AIbot J.* ones refer to the recognition of AIML speaker, respectively, from inside and outside SL, while *SL avatar* and *SL avatar J.* are the plots depicting human intelligence recognition performances. As it is possible to see, also for objective metric the SL environment seems to improve the performances. The AIbot and AIbot J. boxes of Fig. 14.6 (i.e. respectively, the performances for recognizing AI by Subject avatar and by the Judges as external observers) reveal a little difference and the second appears to require less messages to take a decision on the interlocutor nature.

Basing on AIbot and AIbot J. values, it is possible to confute, via a Mann–Whitney test (Gibbons, 1976), the null hypothesis reported in the previous section. This test has been chosen as non-parametric hypothesis verification because of the

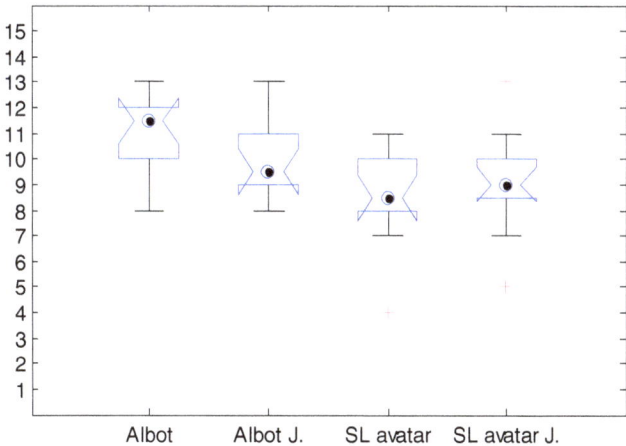

Fig. 14.6 The performance metric: number of messages required for understanding the interlocutor nature

low cardinality of compared samples that does not support the normality requirement of other parametric tests. With $W = 179.5$ and $p = 0.047$, at a significance level $\alpha = 0.05$ there is not enough statistical evidence to conclude that AIbot does not improve AI credibility (i.e. AIbot requires more messages with respect to AIbot judged). Indeed, it is also possible to quantify at 90 % confidence that the true difference between AIbot and AIbot J. is between 0.036 and 1.963.

The opposite trend is shown by the performance metric measuring the number of messages in the case of a human interlocutor. Figure 14.6 shows, on the rightmost side, the box plots depicting the recognition performances of a human in SL (SL avatar) and from outside the environment (SL avatar J.). The first observation on these data is that the recognition happens quickly than in the case of AIML conversation. In addition, the 3D environment seems to negatively influence the performances: an average value of 8.58 messages is required for recognizing human intelligence in SL while an external observer needs, on average, 9.17 messages. As a post-experiment discussion with subjects revealed, this phenomenon has been due to the movements of human-controlled avatars that appear different from AIbot ones. Indeed, during the experiment, the human movements were providing important clues to the subjects. Resuming, SL enhances AIbot performances providing a setting that requires more messages to let users discover the programmatic nature of AIML conversations while for human interlocutors the contrary happens.

Conclusion

This paper presents end evaluates AIbot, an AIML chatting assistant system for helping the e-learning community that meets on Unisa Computer Science Island, in Second Life. AIbot appears as an avatar, the typical character that usually represents users during their Virtual World experiences. The utilization of an AIML engine lets AIbot to be able to interact with other users in a natural manner and on the ordinary text chat channels.

An evaluation of the system has been organized as a controlled experiment to establish if the Virtual World environment influences user perceptions of artificial intelligence. In particular, we performed a modified Turing test: the users randomly interact with a human-controlled avatar and with AIbot aiming at understanding if the nature of the interlocutor intelligence is human or programmed. With the same aim, a second set of subjects, the judges observes, message by message, the chat record. Results obtained analysing subjective opinions and objective performances are good and suggest improving the AIbot intelligence by adding more knowledge about localization and activities.

References

AA (Artificial Avatars). Retrieved January 2016, from http://slurl.com/secondlife/Bay%20City%20-%20Docklands/198/143/25
AIML. Retrieved April 2011, form http://en.wikipedia.org/wiki/AIML

Alice Bot. Retrieved April 2011, from http://www.alicebot.org/aiml.html

AMD Developer Central. Retrieved January 2016, from http://maps.secondlife.com/secondlife/AMD%20Dev%20Central/124/84/49

Barberi, D. (1992). *The ultimate Turing test.* Retrieved April 2011, from http://david.barberi.com/papers/ultimate.turing.test/

Bifrost Island, University of Southern Denmark. Retrieved April 2011, from http://slurl.com/secondlife/bifrost/101/74/23/

Blue Mars. Retrieved April 2011, from http://create.bluemars.com/wiki/index.php/Chatbot_Technology_Comparison

Chatterbot. Retrieved April 2011, from http://en.wikipedia.org/wiki/Chatterbot

Cochrane, K. (2006). Case study: International spaceflight museum. In *The Proceedings of the Second Life Community Convention, San Francisco, USA August 20, 2006* (pp. 2–5).

De Lucia, A., Francese, R., Passero, I., & Tortora, G. (2008). Supporting Jigsaw-based collaborative learning in Second Life. In *Proceedings of the 8th IEEE International Conference on Advanced Learning Technologies, ICALT 2008*

De Lucia, A., Francese, R., Passero, I., & Tortora, G. (2009a). Development and evaluation of a virtual campus on Second Life: The case of SecondDMI. *Computers & Education, 52*(1), 220–233.

De Lucia, A., Francese, R., Passero, I., & Tortora, G. (2009b). Development and evaluation of a system enhancing Second Life to support synchronous role-based collaborative learning. *Software: Practice and Experience, 39*(12), 1025–1054.

EDTEC Virtual Campus, San Diego State University. Retrieved April 2011, from http://slurl.com/secondlife/Meadowbrook/220/82/23/

Elizabeth Bot. Retrieved April 2011, from http://www.philocomp.net/ai/elizabeth

Erra, U., & Scanniello, G. (2010). Assessing communication media richness in requirements negotiation. In *IET Software (previously published as IEE Proceedings Software)*.

Gibbons, J. D. (1976). *Nonparametric methods for quantitative analysis.* New York: Holt, Rhinehart, and Winston.

Hingston, P. (2009, September). A Turing test for computer game bots. *IEEE Transactions on Computational Intelligence and AI in Games, 1*(3), 169–186.

IBM Italia Region. Retrieved April 2011, from http://maps.secondlife.com/secondlife/IBM%20Italia/124/138/50

J&M Creations-Scripts. Retrieved April 2011, from http://slurl.com/secondlife/Nebo/126/94/23

LibOpenMetaverse. Retrieved April 2011, from http://www.openmetaverse.org/

Linden Scripting Language. Retrieved April 2011, from http://wiki.secondlife.com/wiki/LSL_Portal

Loebner Prize. Retrieved April 2011, from http://www.loebner.net/Prizef/loebner-prize.html

Microsoft C#. Retrieved April 2011, from http://msdn.microsoft.com/en-us/vcsharp/aa336809

Neumann, F., Reichenberger, A., & Ziegler, M. (2009). *Variations of the Turing test in the age of internet and virtual reality* (pp. 355–362). Berlin: Springer.

Oppenheim, N. (1992). *Questionnaire design, interviewing and attitude measurement.* London: Pinter.

Pandora Bots. Retrieved April 2011, from http://www.pandorabots.com/

Program-O. Retrieved April 2011, from http://www.program-o.com

Ramachandran, R., Movva, S., Li, X., Anantharam, P., & Graves, S. (2007). *Wxguru: An ontology driven chatbot prototype for atmospheric science outreach and education.* Retrieved April 2011, from http://gsa.confex.com/gsa/2007GE/finalprogram/abstract_122101.htm

Rebecca AIML. Retrieved April 2011 from http://rebecca-aiml.sourceforge.net/

Second Life. Retrieved April 2011, from http://secondlife.com

SLBot. Retrieved April 2011, from http://www.niondir.de/slbot/index.php

The Fake Chess-Playing Machine. Retrieved April 2011, from http://en.wikipedia.org/wiki/The_Turk

The Turing Test Page. Retrieved April 2011, from http://www.fil.ion.ucl.ac.uk/~asaygin/tt/ttest.html

Toys Bot. Retrieved April 2011, from http://slbot.thoys.nl/
Turing, A. M. (1950). Computing machinery and intelligence. *Mind, 59*(236), 433–460.
Unisa Computer Science. Retrieved April 2015, from http://slurl.com/secondlife/Unisa%20
     Computer%20Science/76/89/32
Wallace, R. (2003). *The elements of AIML style*. ALICE A. I. Foundation.
XD Fusion. Retrieved April 2011, from http://slurl.com/secondlife/Schell/212/178/91

Chapter 15
Implementation of Hybrid Artificial Intelligence Technique to Detect Covert Channels Attack in New Generation Internet Protocol IPv6

Abdulrahman Salih, Xiaoqi Ma, and Evtim Peytchev

Abstract Intrusion detection systems offer monolithic way to detect attacks through monitoring, searching for abnormal characteristics, and malicious behavior in network communications. Cyber-attack is performed through using covert channel which currently is one of the most sophisticated challenges facing network security systems. Covert channel is used to ex/infiltrate classified information from legitimate targets; consequently, this manipulation violates network security policy and privacy. The New Generation Internet Protocol version 6 (IPv6) has certain security vulnerabilities and need to be addressed using further advanced techniques. Fuzzy rule is implemented to classify different network attacks as an advanced machine learning technique, meanwhile, Genetic algorithm is considered as an optimization technique to obtain the ideal fuzzy rule. This paper suggests a novel hybrid covert channel detection system implementing two Artificial Intelligence (AI) techniques, Fuzzy Logic and Genetic Algorithm (FLGA), to gain sufficient and optimal detection rule against covert channel. Our approach counters sophisticated network unknown attacks through an advanced analysis of deep packet inspection. Results of our suggested system offer high detection rate of 97.7 % and a better performance in comparison to previous tested techniques.

Keywords Cyber-attack • Covert channel • ICMPv6 • IPv6 • Fuzzy genetic algorithm (FGA) • AI

A. Salih (✉) • X. Ma • E. Peytchev
Nottingham Trent University, Nottingham, UK
e-mail: FB104480@ntu.ac.uk; xiaoqi.ma@ntu.ac.uk; evtim.peytchev@ntu.ac.uk

© Springer International Publishing Switzerland 2017
R. Benlamri, M. Sparer (eds.), *Leadership, Innovation and Entrepreneurship as Driving Forces of the Global Economy*, Springer Proceedings in Business and Economics, DOI 10.1007/978-3-319-43434-6_15

Introduction

The growth of dependability on the Internet in every day services made people susceptible to all kinds of cyber-attacks such as fraud, spam, phishing, and all types of unauthorized access through ID theft. Despite the fact that the security issues in IPv6 were addressed and improved, other issues are still need to be investigated due to the inherited design vulnerability and the incomplete implementation process of this protocol in all operating systems (Zander, Armitage, & Branch, 2006). The protocol itself is already over a decade old; however, its approvals in early stages reaching 12.25 % according to latest statistics performed (Salih, Ma, & Peytchev, 2015a, 2015b).

The low and inevitable acceptance of IPv6 results in an insufficient understanding of its security properties (Martin & Dunn, 2007; Supriyanto, Hasbullah, Murugesan, & Ramadass, 2013). IPv6 had no cryptographic protection when deployed and even the successful deployment of Internet Protocol Security (IPsec) within IPv6 cannot give any guarantee or additional security against hidden channel attacks (Supriyanto et al., 2013; Zander et al., 2006).

The protocol dimension representing the removed, changed, and new values in the header fields according to its suggested new design by the Interned Assigned Numbers Authority (IANA) and Request For Comments (RFC 2460) (Martin & Dunn, 2007; Zander et al., 2006). IPv6 header fields as given in Table 15.1 have potential to carry anomaly attacks depending on the modified value of each field in the packet transmission over the net (Choudhary, 2009; Supriyanto et al., 2013; Wendzel, Zander, Fechner, & Herdin, 2015).

There are two main types of Intrusion Detection System (IDS) techniques that can perform security analysis: the anomaly detection method and the misuse detection (signature-based) method. Anomaly detection depends on the conventional profile in order to identify any abnormality in the traffic, whereas signature-based detection uses signature identification technique to detect attacks (Gomez & Dasgupta, 2002; Liu & Lai, 2009). Interestingly, three important techniques are used by misused detection approach:

1. Signature-based approaches.
2. Rule-based approaches or also called expert systems.
3. Genetic Algorithms (GA).

Table 15.1 Extracted IPv6 header fields and their correspoud format values

ID	Field	Covert channel	Bandwidth
1	Traffic class	False traffic class	8 bits/packet
2	Flow label	False flow label	20 bits/packet
3	Payload length	Increase value to insert extra data	Various
4	Next header	Set a valid value to add an extra extension header	Various
5	Hop limit	Increase/decrease value	$\approx$1 bit/packet
6	Source address	False source address	16 bytes/packet

Internet Control Message Protocol version 6 (ICMPv6) is a vital component and an integral part of IPv6 and should be fully implemented by every IPv6 node according to RFC (4443); however, this particular aspect obviously means hidden channels (Martin & Dunn, 2007). ICMPv6 reports errors encountered in processing packets (Choudhary, 2009) and it does other Internet-layer functions such as diagnostics. It produces two types of messages: Information Notification and Error Notification. It uses Type and Code fields to differentiate services, in which both are vulnerable to be misused by bad guys to perform different attacks, i.e., denial of Service (DoS), Man-in-the-Middle (MITM), and spoofing attacks (Choudhary, 2009; Martin & Dunn, 2007; Supriyanto et al., 2013).

In this paper, we suggest a new hybrid approach using fuzzy logic and genetic algorithm to detect network storage covert channels in IPv6. The process analyses the IPv6 and ICMPv6 header fields values and explains the viability of holding strange values which consequently indicating an abnormal behavior and possible covert channel existence.

The rest of the paper is organized as follow: section "Related Work" describes briefly some related works; section "Proposed Framework" discusses the proposed research methodology, the theory, and techniques implemented; section "Experiment and Result Discussion" discusses the experiments and initial results obtained from the testing phases, and finally section "Conclusion and Future Work" discusses Conclusions and Future work.

Our proposed security system offers a better performance in high accuracy and prediction of the future unknown attacks against legitimate targets.

Related Work

Previous researchers in network anomaly detection focused on IPv4 (Sohn, Seo, & Moon, 2003; Vivek & Kalimuthu, 2014; Zander et al., 2006); however, fewer researchers were concerned about security vulnerabilities of the new generation protocol IPv6 due to its incomplete implementation. Hidden information could be transferred very easy in the data section of the packet due to the large size and it is relatively unstructured in comparison to headers.

Salih et al. (2015a, 2015b) argue that covert channels could be encoded in the unused or reserved bits in the packet header frame, these unused header fields are designed for future protocol improvements, as they will be dismissed by IDS and Firewalls (Liu & Lai, 2009; Supriyanto et al., 2013; Zander et al., 2006); furthermore, this exception caused by the presence of specific values in protocol standards (Martin & Dunn, 2007; Zander et al., 2006). Different machine learning techniques have been used in IDS in a revolutionary status since 1990s. Genetic algorithm started to be used in IDS since 1995 when Crosbie and Spafford (Jongsuebsuk, Wattanapongsakorn, & Charnsripinyo, 2013) applied a hybrid approach of a multiple agent and Genetic Programming (GP) to detect network anomalies. GA is used in many proposed approaches in intrusion detection techniques due to its intensive capabilities.

Sohn et al. (2003) mentioned the Support Vector Machine in passive warden to detect TCP anomaly within the IP ID and TCP ISN. This method was not preferable for well understood and explicit features in his proposed IP IDs and ISNs steganography hidden communication channels; furthermore, SVM can only identify simple aspects as it could unlikely detect complex structure deployed in TCP/IPv6 fields and their interdependencies.

Gomez and Dasgupta (2002) suggested fuzzy and genetic algorithm to detect and classify behavioral intrusion suing a benchmark data KDD99 dataset. They used evolutionary techniques and genetic algorithm which managed to classify four attack classes and one normal class.

Salih et al. (2015a, 2015b) proposed new Intelligent Heuristic Algorithm (IHA) with an enhanced machine learning technique; Nave Bayes classifier to detect covert channels in IPv6. The authors used enhanced decision trees C4.5 and Information Gain to improve the detection rate. Accuracy in this approach was 94 % with very low false negative rate.

Proposed Framework

Different approaches exist for anomaly detection, i.e., signature, behavior, and protocol-based detection. Infrequent researchers use machine learning technique to tackle anomaly attacks in IPv6 and ICMPv6 due to its incomplete implementation and design complexity (Zander et al., 2006). Our approach uses pattern behavior of the header value to determine the identified data that has been transferred stealthily by the attacker using covert channels without affecting the normal communication.

Fuzzy Genetic Algorithm (FGA)

Genetic Algorithm is an evolutionary Artificial Intelligence (AI) optimization technique based on some synthetic keys such as natural selection and genetics (Chen, Jakeman, & Norton, 2008). Fries (2008) verified that John Holland with his academic colleagues at the University of Michigan has invented GA in the 1960s and the 1970s and explained the mechanism behind it. GA is based on Darwinians biological principle of evolution: The survival of the fittest. It uses three dominant functions: selection, crossover, and mutation when optimizing a population of candidate solution and to predefine fitness. This algorithm has been successfully implemented (Hoque, Mukit, Bikas, & Naser, 2012; Jongsuebsuk et al., 2013) to solve significant collection of complex optimization problems when search area is too broad. We propose an enhanced version of (Fries, 2008) rule-based algorithm with new and different attacks, i.e., covert channels in the new generation network protocols IPv6/ICMPv6. The framework uses new simulated primary data and NSL-KDD99 benchmark data to verify the results. The suggested Fuzzy Genetic

Fig. 15.1 Suggested
genetic algorithm process
to tackle covert channel
attacks

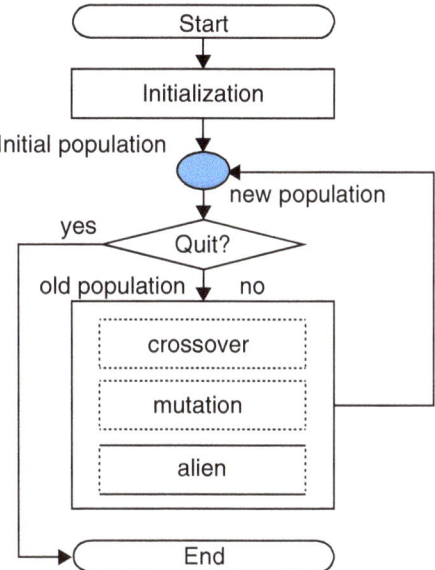

Algorithm (FGA) as shown in Fig. 15.1 can perform classification process of two classes: normal and anomaly with an improved high detection rate.

The following steps are the main modules in the framework. An overview of the algorithms example is given in Algorithm 1, Algorithm 2, and Algorithm 3.

1. Data Capture: Jpcap library packet sniffer is a Java API used to capture simulated packets for 2 min and dissection process is done to extract the targeted IPv6 and ICMPv6 header fields as given in Table 15.2.
2. Packet Analysis: In this stage the input pcap data after field selection process will go through the following subprocesses:

   (a) Transform and normalize every attribute of the header to some sort of a real number giving the range of 0.0–7.0, which means the minimum and the maximum subset values of the attribute from the training data will set in a range of 0.0 and 7.0.
   (b) After transformation and normalization processes of the attributes and convert them to numerical formats, detection rules will be suggested as given in Tables 15.3 and 15.4 for all records. The output of the detection rule will be the probability of each packet and will count for true positive and true negative. The algorithm randomly will create a rule in the initial stage. Then an evolutionary concept is used from GA to improve the rule in the training state.
   (c) We need to extract the records according to the rules, processing the fitness function in equation 1 to calculate the fitness value of each detection rule. Occasionally save the highest fitness value which indicates the best rule.
3. Process the evolutionary GA approaches: crossover, mutation, and alien to extract the next rules.

Table 15.2 Covert channels data format and values

ID	Header format	Value type	Class
1	Traffic_Class	Numeric	Normal or covert
2	Flow_Label	Numeric	Normal or covert
3	Hop_Limit	High, low, moderate	Normal or covert
4	Payload_Length	Increased, decreased, low	Normal or covert
5	Source_Address	Numeric	Normal or covert
6	Next_Header	Numeric	Normal or covert
7	ICMPv6_Type	Numeric	Normal or covert
8	ICMPv6_Code	Numeric	Normal or covert
9	Reserve_Bit	Numeric	Normal or covert
10	ICMPv6_Payload	Numeric	Normal or covert

Table 15.3 Fuzzy logic detailed for each data record

Data type	Value											
Fuzzy logic	0	1	0	0	1	1	1	0	0	1	0	1
Symbol		a			b			c			d	
Numeric	2			3			4			5		

Fuzzy Algorithm (FA)

In this stage, we encode a fuzzy logic for each attribute and then normalize the sub-set value in a range of 0.0–7.0 as mentioned earlier. The encoded fuzzy logic rule is explained in Algorithm 1. So every single rule will involve ten blocks of feature values as given in Table 15.2 including the class type at the end of the string and then each rule will be mapped to its corresponding record as shown in Fig. 15.2.

Once we run the rule over a record trying to match each attribute with one block of the rule. The probability measurement whether it is an attack or not will be performed by the parameter of each block using the Fuzzy rules as shown in Algorithm 1. An assessment of the probability for each block will be done to predict the likelihood if the record is an attack class or a normal class, and this is done through taking into account the average of the probability against the threshold mean value.

Then we compare the predicted output against the actual result as in Fries (2008); furthermore, we will calculate the rule measurement performance through maximization of the fitness function using equation (1) as its embedded in Algorithm 2.

$$fitness\ function = \frac{a}{A} - \frac{\beta}{B} \qquad (1)$$

Table 15.4 Suggested fuzzy logic encoding for each attribute

010	011	100	101		
a = 2	b = 3	c = 4	d = 5		
Attribute 1					

010	011	101	111		
a = 2	b = 3	c = 5	d = 7		
Attribute 2					

010	011	100	101		
a = 2	b = 3	c = 4	d = 5		
Attribute 3					

101	011	100	101	Covert
a	b	c	d	Class
Attribute 10				

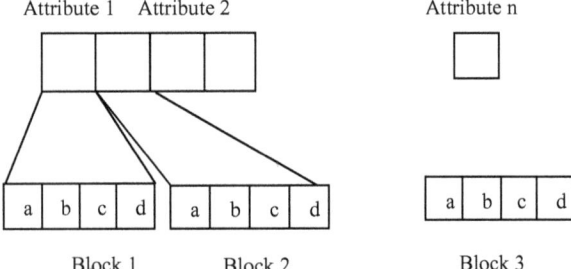

Fig. 15.2 Explained string encoding

Genetic Algorithm

Principally, not all attacks against legitimate targets have static patterns; however, fuzzy logic will detect both types: normal and abnormal. The suggested fuzzy logic as given in Table 15.3 is encoded into four parameters; a, b, c, and d where

$$a \leq b \leq c \leq d$$

According to a trapezoidal shape (Fries, 2008) it is very likely to be capable using the parameters to measure the likelihood of the attack through each attribute as described in Algorithm 3.

Algorithm 1
Fuzzy logic based on Jongsuebsuk et al. (2013) with some modifications and corrections

```
If (value >a) && (value <b) {
specificity = (value - a) / (b-a)
}
else if ( value ≥ b and value ≤ c) {
specificity = 1.0;
}
else if (value > c and value < d) {
specificity = (d - value) / (d-c)
}
else {
specificity =0.0
}
```

Table 15.5 Sample of simulated attacks using covert channels in IPv6

Attack test case	Performed commands

Payload fields covert channels	`-send(IPv6(dst=`
	`"FFe2::3") /IPv6DestOpt(options=`
	`[PadN(optdata=("22222222")`
	`)]+[PadN(optdata=`
	`("3333333333333333"))]) /`
	`ICMPv6EchoRequest(id=1))`

Covert channel using PadN option	`-IPv6DestOpt(type=02data= "YYYYY")/icmpechorequest`

Preprocessing Simulation Data

We performed two experiment tests on our suggested model; first, we used our simulated attack tool built and written in Python programming language (Scapy) to simulate attacks in a controlled LAN network lab environment. A sample of the covert channel's attack is given in Table 15.5 and then we captured packets in pcap format using Wireshark. The attribute instances from the header values have preprocessed into transformation, discretization (Wendzel et al., 2015), and normalization as mentioned in packet analysis section. According to previous research performed by Salih et al. (2015a, 2015b) a new limited generation of covert channels primary data will be created including instances of different possible attacks in IPv6 and ICMPv6. The primary data consists of 600,000 records which contain more than ten attack instances. The objective tested attacks are Covert channels, Denial of Service (DoS), Probing, and R2L.

Evaluation Criteria Parameters

To evaluate the performance of the algorithm, we used the following three metrics:

- False positive rate (FPR): ratio of normal packets will be classified as attacks out of the total normal packets accounts.
- False negative rate (FNR): ratio of attacks that misclassified as normal from total numbers, but it is attack.
- True Positive & True Negative (Detection rate): is the total normal and attacks that have been correctly classified out of the whole testing data (Fig. 15.3).

Algorithm 2
Fuzzy Genetic Algorithm is based on algorithm in Fries (2008) with few corrections.

Fig. 15.3 A fuzzy logic
trapezoidal represented
four parameters based on
Fries (2008); A ≤ B ≤ C ≤ D

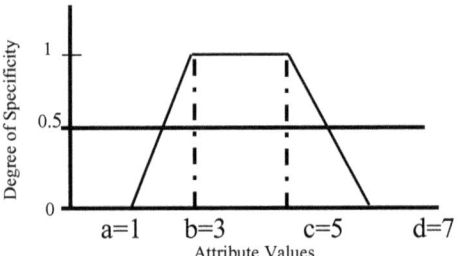

```
 Initial rules ();
while {
       For each packet {
    for each rule {
                     for each attribute {
specificity = fuzzy ();    // Algorithm 1
total= total +specificity;
}
         If (totalprob > threshold)
      class is attack;
    else
   class is normal;
  }
 compare the predicted result with actual result
find A, B, α, and β,
}
calculate fitness        // create next generation
preserve_best ()
crossover ()
mutation ()
alien ()
}
// A is total number of attack records. B is total number of normal
records. α is total number of attack records correctly identified
as attack β is total number of normal records incorrectly classi-
fied as attack (false positive).
```

Experiments and Results Discussion

In the first step of the proposed framework, we designed and configured a separate
IPv6 LAN topology network as shown in Fig. 15.4 according to the network system
environment requirements. A Security tool was created along with THC in Hauser
(2013) to simulate different attacks in both protocols: IPv6 and ICMPv6 (Martin &
Dunn, 2007; Supriyanto et al., 2013).

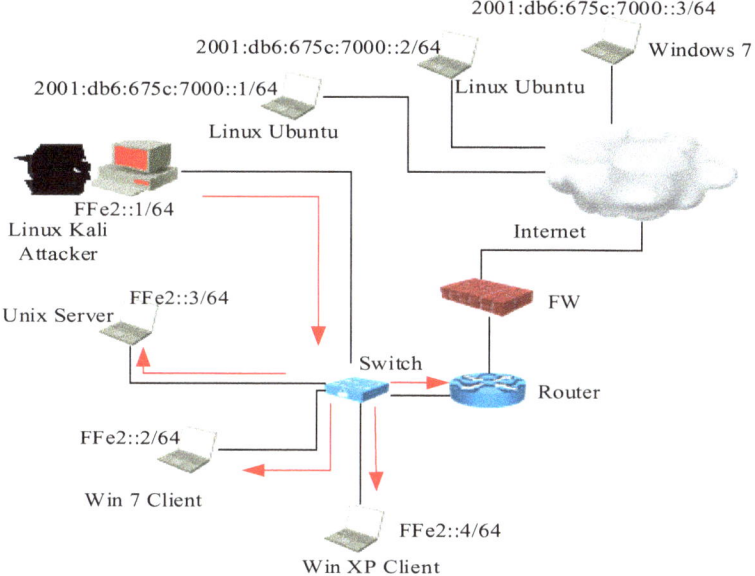

Fig. 15.4 Configured IPv6 LAN network topology to perform attack simulation

We implemented the system using Weka 3.7 database system built with java programming Language and performed on personal computer with 3.1 GHz Inter core i5 CPU 3450 and 8 GB RAM. With regards to the GA implementation, we focused on ten sizes of the population for each generation; however, each individual will present a possible detection rule, and we chose two best individuals or rules, in which should have the highest fitness value from the present generation. We used uniform random as a selection method to select the parent in crossover process, this is to identify the members of the new generation, finally applying the single-point crossover in which will give the implemented rate of 20 % for alien and 30 % for mutation.

The training dataset contained 11 attributes or features including the one target value or labeled class either normal or attack (covert) as given in Table 15.6. We performed two experiments: first test was for the known attacks simulated from rules using Fuzzy Genetic Algorithm depicting two main attacks DoS and Probe using the primary dataset as a test data. In the second test, we evaluated our approach on a benchmark data such as Network Simulation Language Knowledge Data Discovery (NSL-KDD'99) choosing 20 % of the dataset for testing phase in order to detect known and unknown attacks (Tavallaee, Bagheri, Lu, & Ghorbani, 2009).

Algorithm 3
The Fuzzy logic to identify three known attacks.

Table 15.6 Analysis output format of covert channel characteristics

R #	TC	FL	HL	PL	NH	SA	Type	Code	RB	PYL	Class
1	0	0	High	Increased	0	0	0	1	0	1	Covert
2	1	1	Low	Unchanged	1	1	1	0	1	1	Covert
3	1	1	Moderate	Decreased	1	1	0	0	0	0	Normal
4	1	1	Moderate	Decreased	1	1	0	1	0	0	Normal
5	1	1	Low	Unchanged	1	1	1	0	1	1	Covert
6	1	1	Moderate	Decreased	1	1	0	0	0	0	Normal
7	0	1	Moderate	Unchanged	1	1	1	0	1	1	Covert
8	1	1	Low	Unchanged	1	1	0	0	1	1	Covert
9	0	1	Low	Unchanged	1	1	1	1	0	0	Covert
10	1	1	Low	Unchanged	1	1	1	0	1	1	Covert

```
If (dos_rule =1 || probe_rule=1 || R2L=1)
It is attack;
else if
If (dos_rule = 0 || probe_rule= 0 || R2L= 0)

it is normal;
end if
}
```

- **Experiment 1**: The size of the primary dataset was not suitable to be used as testing data, so we chose 10 % for a training dataset in the first attempt consisted of 60,000 instances, although the process focused on detecting the following attacks instances:

  - Probe
  - Denial of Service (DoS)
  - Root to Local (R2L).

The first experiment results given in Table 15.7 and the graph in Fig. 15.4, we observe significant accuracy rates of the suggested approach detecting DoS training dataset by 95.3 %, the Probe attack detection by 96.8 %, and R2L accuracy detection by 97.7 % with a false positive rate by 3.7 %. However when we performed the testing phase overall of the attack types the results have increased to 97.7 % and the false positive decreased to 1.7 % which shows a better performance and high accuracy improved by using the suggested FG Algorithm.

- **Experiment 2**: In order to extend the proficiency of the proposed model and to validate it, we used the NSL-KDD99 dataset (Tavallaee et al., 2009). This dataset was collected at the Massachusetts Institute of Technology (MIT) in Lincoln Lab to evaluate intrusion detection systems; however, it lacks instances of IPv6 attack types except the ICMPv4, and IP ID covert channels (Zander et al., 2006) which have similar principle techniques manipulating such attacks. McHugh and Mahoney in Mahoney and Chan (2003) criticized the DARPA dataset for not containing some background noise, i.e., packet storms, strange packets, etc.

Table 15.7 Results of primary data using FGA to detect different attacks

Attack name	Attack type	Total packets	Test data	TPR %	FPR %	DR %
Smurf	DoS	27,500	10,000	94.8	5.2	**95.3**
Pod	DoS			95.8	4.2	
Teardrop	DoS			97.8	2.2	
Covert channels	DoS			94.6	5.4	
Ipsweep	Prob	17,800	8000	96.8	3.2	**96.8**
Portsweep	Prob			94.8	5.2	
Spy	R2L	14,700	5000	97.8	2.2	**97.7**
Stan	R2L			95.9	4.1	
Multihop	R2L			97.7	2.3	
Normal	Normal	30,000	30,000	99.6	0.4	99.6
Total testing rate				**97.7**	**1.7**	

We trained the fuzzy genetic algorithm on testing dataset in which 20 % of the NSL-KDD data was taken for this purpose. Each connection record consists of 41 features and labeled in order sequences such as 1, 2, 3, 4, 5, 6, 7, ... 41 in addition to the 42nd attribute which is the assigned class: normal or anomaly. These attributes fall into four main categories as in Mahoney and Chan (2003) and Tavallaee et al. (2009). We chose six types of DoS instances, four attack types of Probe instances, and four types of R2L attack instances from the training dataset performing five test Cases C1, C2, C3, .., C5 for each category as given in Table 15.8. We have tested 14 attack types as well as the normal connections. Considerably, we chose 4 types of the attacks as unknown attacks in the testing dataset in order to test our Fuzzy Genetic Algorithm (FGA). The attack types are Neptune, Xmas Tree, Multihop, and Spy. Finally, we tested each type of attacks separately to examine and investigate the accuracy and to observe the performance of the detection method. See Table 15.8 for details of the testing cases results.

Discussion

The results of both experiments confirm the initial hypothesis of our suggested Fuzzy Genetic Algorithm (FGA). The performance of the process was impressive with regards to the significant accuracy to each test experiments phases so far. In Table 15.7 and Fig. 15.5, we observe the distinguished correctness and low false positive of the suggested mechanism.

The test was carried out using our primary data which were generated from two security tools: our security tool written in Python and (THC) tool which was written in C (Hauser, 2013). The testing dataset was taken from the overall training dataset to perform the detection; moreover, the accuracy is competitive with an average of

Table 15.8 Suggested five test cases to detect attacks using hidden channels

#	Data type	Category	C1	C2	C3	C4	C5
1	Smurf	DoS	x		x		
2	Pod	DoS	x			x	
3	Teardrop	DoS	x				
4	Jping	DoS		x			
5	UDP flood	DoS			x		x
6	neptune	DoS		x			x
7	Ipsweep	Prob				x	
8	Portsweep	Prob		x			x
9	Hostscan	Prob				x	
10	Xmas tree	Prob		x		x	
11	Spy	R2L			x		
12	Satan	R2L			x		
13	ftp_write	R2L		x		x	
14	Multihop	R2L			x		
15	Normal status	Normal	x	x	x	x	x

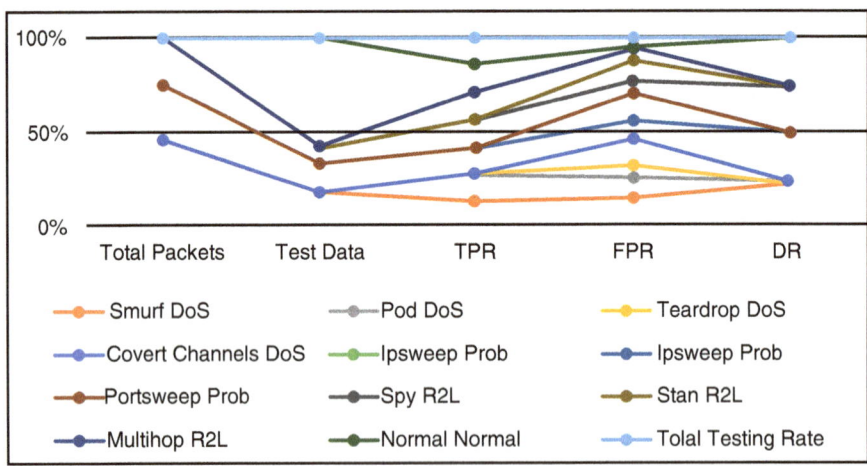

Fig. 15.5 Results of suggested FGA framework to detect covert channels

97.7 % of the total testing data and with 96.6 % for the training dataset. To validate the efficiency of the suggested technique, we performed the second experiment with another classification algorithm: Naïve Bayes classifier. Obviously, this step gave us an indication of potential improvement of our suggested approach.

To analyze the results given in Table 15.9 and the Graph in Fig. 15.6, we compared the outcome (DR) of the Test Cases observing that only one test case (TC4), which we used Naive Bayes classifier was better than FGA. However, in test cases

Table 15.9 Results of suggested fuzzy genetic algorithm (FGA) results using five test cases

TC	Data type	Naive Bayes DR (%)	Av (%)	FGA DR(%)	Av (%)
1	Neptune	92.4	91.15	97.8	**96.37**
	Xmas tree	91.7		96.1	
	Multihop	90.7		93.1	
	Spy	89.8		98.5	
2	Jping	88.6	61.9	98.4	**95.6**
	UDP flood	28.6		94.8	
	Pod	68.5		93.6	
3	Ipsweep	55.3	64.46	94.6	**94.03**
	Portsweep	93.6		92.4	
	Hostscan	44.5		95.1	
4	Smurf	95.6	91.75	90.5	**90.3**
	Satan	87.9		90.1	
5	Teardrop	67.3	72.3	89.9	**91.65**
	ftp_write	77.3		93.4	

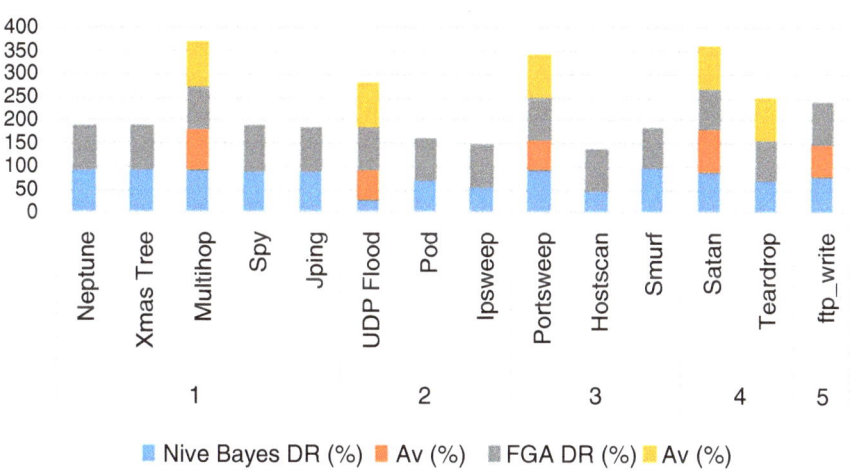

Fig. 15.6 Results of unknown attack detection testing NSL-KDD dataset using suggested FGA framework

TC1, TC2, TC3, and TC5, FGA was improved exclusively and depicted the unknown attacks with the highest accuracy detection rate (DR) by 96.37%, meanwhile Naive Bayes algorithm obtained an average of detection rate of 91.15% in test case 1 with differences of 5.22%, then in test case 2 Naive Bayes obtained 61.9% accuracy in detection rate, while the FGA accuracy detection rate was 95.6% with over 33.7% differences in DR.

Significantly, Naive Bayesian Algorithm gave a low detection rate in test case 3 with the difference of 29.84 % obtaining 64.46 % accuracy, but FGA obtained in the same test case over 94.03 %. Fuzzy Genetic Algorithm has an overall detection rate with 93.59 % running on NSL-KDD'99 dataset in the second experiment, while getting 97.7 % in the first experiment using our primary generated attack data types.

Conclusion and Future Work

Similar to what Fries (2008) and Jongsuebsuk et al. (2013) suggested for TCP/IPv4 attacks, new attempts required to detect storage covert channels and anomaly attacks in TCP/IPv6 using Artificial Intelligence Techniques in respond to the novel vulnerabilities in this protocol. Potentially, this approach should act as a countermeasure restrain to sophisticated attack tools used by hackers. Using Fuzzy Genetic Algorithm to tackle such network threats in IPv6 and ICMPv6 protocols will add a new route of cutting-edge solutions for security systems in the real world. We have answered the project question about the possibility to detect and mitigate unknown and new attacks through covert channels manipulation using Artificial Intelligence techniques. However, approaches in Supriyanto et al. (2013); Salih et al. (2015a, 2015b); Liu and Lai (2009); Saad, Manickam, and Ramadass (2013); and Bahaman, Anton Satria, and Mas'ud (2011) dealing with IPv6 security sophisticated threats have some concerned issues as mentioned in Salih et al. (2015a, 2015b).

In this paper, we applied an enhanced Fuzzy Genetic Algorithm (FGA) approach to suggest a novel IDS for IPv6/ICMPv6. We implemented a hybrid Genetic and Fuzzy rules due to the fast, flexible, and high performance given to detect unknown attacks (Hoque et al., 2012) and covert channels in IPv6. Furthermore, we proposed ten characteristics of different attack instances against this New Generation Internet Protocol. This proposed approach in FGA heterogeneously reduces the probabilistic stimulation, which leads to higher accuracy in detection and classification process, because the Fuzzy Genetic Algorithm is a rule based, consequently leads to less computation time, lower false negative rate (FNR), and higher true positive rate (TPR) in comparison to other tested MLA techniques.

Future work will focus on the MITM attack detection to examine the certainty and specificity of the features selected in the primary dataset. Aiming to use an enhanced Support Vector Machine (SVM) in a supervised learning approach and compare it against our current approach to see the efficiency and the performance of both methodologies. However, an SVM can only identify simple features (Sohn et al., 2003), it is unlikely to detect complex values in IPv6 header fields and the embedded (Wendzel et al., 2015) interdependencies without other advanced techniques. This will reduce and eliminate partially the unauthorized access and its side effects on classified data communication using IPv6.

References

Bahaman, N., Anton Satria, P., & Mas'ud, Z. (2011). Implementation of IPv6 network testbed: Intrusion detection system on transition mechanism. *Journal of Applied Sciences, 11*(1), 118–124.

Chen, S. H., Jakeman, A. J., & Norton, J. P. (2008). Artificial intelligence techniques: An introduction to their use for modelling environmental systems. *Mathematics and Computers in Simulation, 78*(2), 379–400.

Choudhary, A. R. (2009, November). In-depth analysis of IPv6 security posture. In *2009 5th International Conference on Collaborative Computing: Networking, Applications and Worksharing*.

Fries, T. P. (2008, July). A fuzzy-genetic approach to network intrusion detection. In *Proceedings of the 10th Annual Conference Companion on Genetic and Evolutionary Computation* (pp. 2141–2146). ACM.

Gomez, J., & Dasgupta, D. (2002, June). Evolving fuzzy classifiers for intrusion detection. In *Proceedings of the 2002 IEEE Workshop on Information Assurance* (Vol. 6, No. 3, pp. 321–323). New York: IEEE Computer Press.

Hauser, M. (2013). *IPv6 security vulnerabilities*. Retrieved February 10, 2016, from https://www.thc.org/thc-ipv6

Hoque, M. S., Mukit, M., Bikas, M., & Naser, A. (2012). *An implementation of intrusion detection system using genetic algorithm*. ArXiv preprint arXiv: 1204.1336.

Jongsuebsuk, P., Wattanapongsakorn, N., & Charnsripinyo, C. (2013, January). Network intrusion detection with Fuzzy Genetic Algorithm for unknown attacks. In *2013 International Conference on Information Networking (ICOIN)* (pp. 1–5). IEEE.

Liu, Z., & Lai, Y. (2009). A data mining framework for building intrusion detection models based on IPv6. In *Advances in information security and assurance* (pp. 608–618). Berlin: Springer.

Mahoney, M. V., & Chan, P. K. (2003, September). An analysis of the 1999 DARPA/Lincoln Laboratory evaluation data for network anomaly detection. In *Recent advances in intrusion detection* (pp. 220–237). Berlin: Springer.

Martin, C. E., & Dunn, J. H. (2007, October). Internet Protocol version 6 (IPv6) protocol security assessment. In *Military Communications Conference, 2007, MILCOM 2007, IEEE* (pp. 1–7). IEEE.

Saad, R. M. A., Manickam, S., & Ramadass, S. (2013) Intrusion detection system in IPv6 network based on data mining techniques—Survey. In *Proceedings of 2nd International Conference on Advances in Computer and Information Technology ACIT 2013, Malaysia*.

Salih, A., Ma, X., & Peytchev, E. (2015a). Detection and classification of covert channels in IPv6 using enhanced machine learning. In *Proceedings of the International Conference on Computer Technology and Information Systems, (ICCTIS) N & N Global Technology DUBAI, UAE*.

Salih, A., Ma, X., & Peytchev, E. (2015b). New intelligent heuristic algorithm to mitigate security vulnerabilities in IPv6. *International Journal for Information Security (IJIS), 4*. doi: 04. IJIS.2015.1.3.

Sohn, T., Seo, J., & Moon, J. (2003, October). A study on the covert channel detection of TCP/IP header using support vector machine. In *ICICS* (pp. 313–324).

Supriyanto, Hasbullah, I. H., Murugesan, R. K., & Ramadass, S. (2013). Survey of internet protocol version 6 link local communication security vulnerability and mitigation methods. *IETE Technical Review, 30*(1), 64–71.

Tavallaee, M., Bagheri, E., Lu, W., & Ghorbani, A. A. (2009). A detailed analysis of the KDD CUP 99 data set. In *Proceedings of the Second IEEE Symposium on Computational Intelligence for Security and Defense Applications 2009*.

Vivek, T. K., & Kalimuthu, M. (2014, March). Improving intrusion detection method for covert channel in TCP/IP network. *International Journal of Computer Science Trends and Technology (IJCST), 2*(2).

Wendzel, S., Zander, S., Fechner, B., & Herdin, C. (2015). Pattern-based survey and categorization of network covert channel techniques. *ACM Computing Surveys (CSUR), 47*(3), 50.

Zander, S., Armitage, G., & Branch, P. (2006, December). Covert channels in the IP time to live field. In *Proceedings of Australian Telecommunication Networks and Applications Conference (ATNAC)*.

Abdulrahman Salih is a Ph.D. candidate at Nottingham Trent University. He received his M.Sc. with Distinction in IT Security from University of Westminster, London in 2010, and his B.Sc. (Horns) Software Engineering from Nottingham Trent University in 2007. He worked as a Network Security Engineer for Planet Solutions in London before rejoining NTU. He is the founder and CEO of KNCIS in Sweden-UK, specializing in Cyber Security Analysis. FB104480@ntu.ac.uk

Xiaoqi Ma is a Senior lecturer and a leader of many modules; Security Technologies, Computer Security and Advanced Security Technologies in the School of Science and Technology at Nottingham Trent University. He is a member of the Intelligent Simulation, Modelling and Networking Research Group (ISMN). He obtained PhD from Reading University in 2007 in Cryptographic Network Protocols. He contributed in more than 20 publications in International Journals, conferences, and book chapters, xiaoqi.ma@ntu.ac.uk

Evtim Peytchev is a Reader in Wireless, Mobile and Pervasive Computing in the school of Science and Technology at Nottingham Trent University, UK. He is leading the Intelligent Simulation, Modelling and Networking Research Group, which consists of five lecturers, three Research Fellows, and six research students. He is the Module Leader for Systems Software; and Wireless and Mobile Communications. He also teaches on the modules Software Design and Implementation; Mobile Networking; Enterprise Computing; and Computer Architecture, evtim. peytchev@ntu.ac.uk

Chapter 16
What Is and How to Develop Sustainable Innovation?

Stig Ottosson, Anastasiia Moldavska, Olga Ogorodnyk,
and Torbjørn Skogsrød

Abstract Today the terms sustainable development and sustainable innovation are often used. But what is meant by these terms, other than that they in some ways are connected to the terms 'green' and 'ecological' seen in a long-term perspective? How, in turn, are sustainable innovations developed? Studying the literature on the topic leads to the conclusion that there is no precise or established definition of sustainable innovation, sustainability and sustainable development.

A conclusion in the paper is that we now need to focus on how to develop new sustainable innovations, and for these, product development is the most important element. It has been found that Dynamic Product Development (DPD™) is a model that satisfies the different definitions on sustainability that have been proposed.

The result of a product development project is based on the product developer's knowledge, experience and ability. The leadership of an entrepreneur (or intrapreneur) is also important for the level of sustainability of an innovation that is achieved. Therefore, the product developers and entrepreneurs need to be educated in a broader perspective than is common in the technical field today. The product developers must also be monitored in the actual work situation to ensure that new products that are not sustainable are not being marketed. This, in turn, calls for a similar, broader perspective in management education.

To describe **what** a sustainable innovation is and **how** it is developed, the following definitions are proposed: **a sustainable solution** is a solution that has been developed to be a long-lasting, environmentally responsible solution for the provider (the business), the society and also the users; **an innovation** is a new solution that has been 'sold' and is used by more than one user or that is used in at least one-use situation; **the innovation process**, done as **an innovation project**, contains all of the stages from idea generation, development (R&D) and commercialization to an implemented solution on the market.

S. Ottosson (✉) • A. Moldavska • O. Ogorodnyk • T. Skogsrød
NTNU in Gjøvik, Gjøvik, Norway
e-mail: stig.ottosson@ntnu.no; anastasiia.moldavska@ntnu.no;
olga.ogorodnyk@stud.ntnu.no; torbjorn.skogsrod@ntnu.no

© Springer International Publishing Switzerland 2017   191
R. Benlamri, M. Sparer (eds.), *Leadership, Innovation and Entrepreneurship as Driving Forces of the Global Economy*, Springer Proceedings in Business and Economics, DOI 10.1007/978-3-319-43434-6_16

Keywords Innovation • Innovation process • Innovation project • Sustainability • Sustainable innovation

Introduction

The terms 'sustainability', 'sustainable development', 'sustainable solutions' and 'sustainable innovations' are frequently used, for example, in marketing and sales situations. These terms usually represent positive characteristics.

This paper discusses the background of the terms 'sustainable' and 'innovation'. The focus is mainly on how to develop new products and services from the point of view of their environmental impact 'from the cradle to the grave'.

Theory

Today, 'sustainable innovation' includes two terms that are popular, but rather unclear. Here, they will be discussed individually, leading to solutions for carrying out sustainable product development.

History of 'Sustainability'

The popularity of the term 'sustainable' started with the report, 'Our Common Future', which was released in 1987 by the World Commission on Environment and Development (WCED). The commission was chaired by Mrs. Gro Harlem Brundtland, who served previously as the prime minister of Norway for three periods. The Brundtland Report stated that development only is sustainable if it 'meets the needs of the present without compromising the ability of future generations to meet their own needs' (World Commission on Environment Development, 1987). A popular simplifying picture, based on the Brundtland Report, is shown in Fig. 16.1. Note that there is no focus on how to develop sustainable solutions, but only depicts what is wanted from the solutions.

In the years following the release of the Brundtland Report, many discussions arose on what sustainable development is and how it can be applied in practice. For example, between 1995 and 2000, sustainable development was actively debated, and attempts were made to change the definition from the initial report. The key issue was that the term 'sustainable development' is not merely ambiguous, but essentially contested (Jacobs, 1995). In other words, the term was not regarded to be clearly defined in a sense that it did not include several internal concepts and was also not interpreted in the same way by different individuals. Further, in 1999,

Fig. 16.1 The three pillars of sustainability (Figure from 'The Three Pillars of Sustainability')

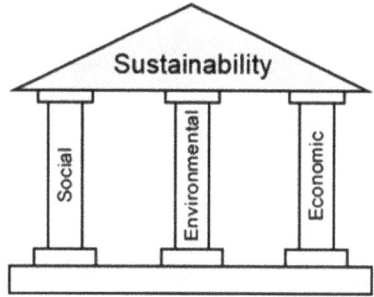

according to a definition proposed by Elliott (1999), 'sustainable development' was stated as being 'fundamentally about reconciling the development and the environmental resources on which society depends'.

In 1989, the non-profit organization, The Natural Step, was launched (http://www.thenaturalstep.org). It proposed four sustainability principles, based on the principles that in a sustainable society, nature shall not be subject to the systematic increase of:

1. Concentrations of substances from the earth's crust (such as fossil CO2 and heavy metals)
2. Concentrations of substances produced by society (such as antibiotics and endocrine disruptors)
3. Degradation by physical means (such as deforestation and draining of groundwater tables)
4. Structural obstacles to people's health, influence, competence, impartiality and meaning

The Natural Step also proposed a four-step procedure (A, B, C and D) to accomplish sustainable development (see Fig. 16.2). Note that the model presents a strict business viewpoint and that there is no guidance on how to develop sustainable products and solutions.

Since 1995, the concept of Dynamic Product Development (DPD™) has been and is being developed (Ottosson, 1996). The ™ mark is only used to prevent the term to be misused and its principles distorted. The term 'sustainable' was not used in the early work in the development of DPD™, but the focus was on how to develop new products in a responsible and efficient way, which can be seen as satisfying the value 'D' in Fig. 16.2. The core was a user-centred design taking society's demands as well as business' demands into account in an integrated way—which was a bit controversial because the focus at that time was on 'design for the manufacture and assembly' of products. In DPD™, the three outer demands for the product developers were (are) established as satisfy 'performance', 'cost' and 'development time' set for each development project (see Fig. 16.3).

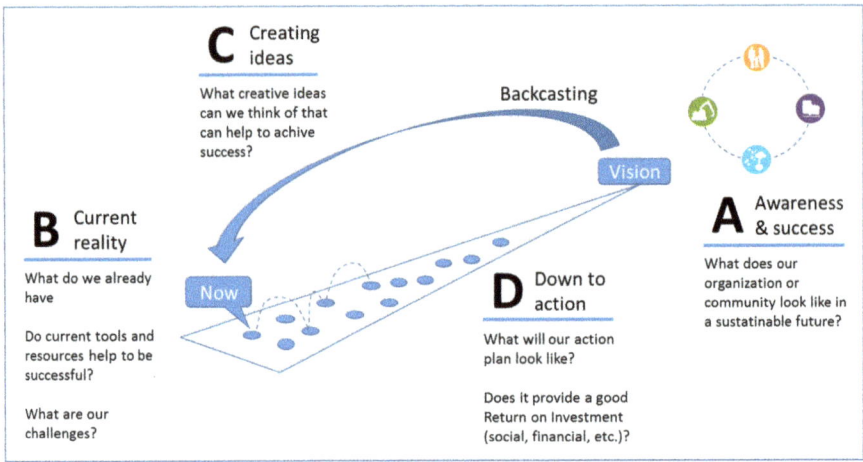

Fig. 16.2 The ABCD process of The Natural Step as a guideline (Based on The Natural Step)

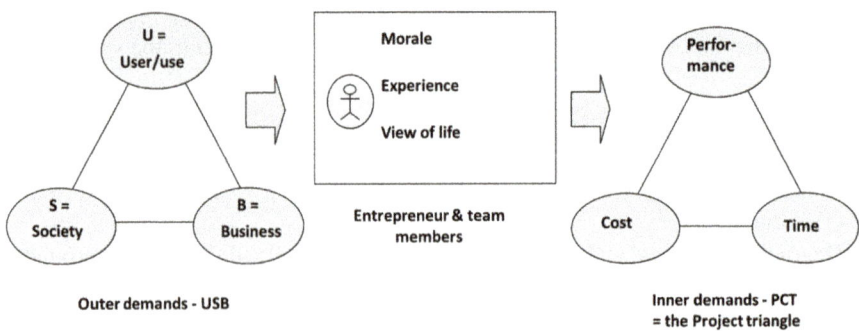

Fig. 16.3 The DPD™ view of satisfying different demands in the development process (Ottosson, 2009)

In 1999, the concept of 'sustainable development' was articulated in other scientific papers as 'a discourse of ethics, which specifies human conduct with regard to good and evil' (Acselrad, 1999). Haughton (1999) summarized the ideas of sustainable development in 'five principles based on equity: futurity—inter-generational equity; social justice—intra-generational equity; transfrontier responsibility—geographical equity; procedural equity—people treated openly and fairly; and interspecies equity—importance of biodiversity' (Haughton, 1999; Hopwood, Mellor, & O'Brien, 2005). These discussions led to the conclusion that 'the conceptual basis of sustainable development has been weak from the start' (Fischer & Hajer, 1999).

In 2000, the state of the art of the sustainable development process was summed up as 'three elements to be sustained (Nature, Life Support, and Community) and three elements to be developed (People, Economy and Society)' (Valentin & Spangenberg, 2000).

In 2001, 'one of the few agreements within the sustainable development debate was that there is no clear agreement on what the term means' (Chatterton & Style, 2001). Research continued as the sustainability question became more and more important because of global warming and calculations of fossil fuel reserves. Workshops were organized, but it was concluded that sustainability is 'laden with so many definitions that it risks plunging into meaninglessness, at best, and becoming a catchphrase for demagogy, at worst' (Workshop on Urban Sustainability ds a Comprehensive Geographical Perspective on Urban Sustainability. NJ: Rutgers University, 2001).

In 2002, the issue was to find a definition, not for the whole countries or companies but for each citizen of the earth individually: 'after all, its [sustainable development's] main message is that in thinking about environment and development issues, just as in thinking about one's own life, one must figure out how to live off interest and not capital' (Holliday, Schmidheiny, & Watts, 2002). Even though this attempted to clarify the message, it did not explain how to apply it to everyday life and which new laws to follow. As a result Luke (2005) claimed that 'the sustainable development project is neither 'sustainable' nor 'developmental''. Such a position is easy to understand, because if a concept cannot be clearly defined, how can it bring any kind of sustainability or development to the world?

As a result, thoughts about the pluralism of the term started to appear. The UK Government, for example, in its sustainable development strategy, defines sustainable development as 'the simple idea of ensuring a better quality of life for everyone, now and for generations to come' (Defra, 2005). At the same time, attempts to make the concept universal continued: 'sustainable development is a human-centred view of the inter-relations between environmental and socio-economic issues' (Hopwood et al., 2005). Figure 16.4 shows how social, environmental and economic dimensions in 2005 were seen to be related to each other.

In 2007, one view was that 'rather than focus on searching for a definitive meaning of "sustainable development" … it is necessary to recognize the multiplicity of sustainabilities' (Rocha, Searcy, & Karapetrovic, 2007). To some extent, this was happening because the majority of definitions were far from being the same.

Fig. 16.4 Key dimensions of measuring sustainable development based on Stevens (2005) (The illustration is from 'The Three Pillars of Sustainability')

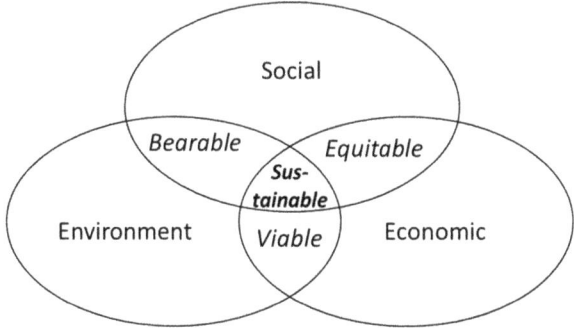

For example, Harding (2006) had stated that 'the triple bottom line refers to satisfaction of not just the long recognized bottom line of meeting economic goals (profits) but also the need to meet environmental and social goals (or bottom lines) simultaneously in carrying out business'. At the same time, Gibson (2006) had summarized general requirements of sustainable development as 'social and ecological integrity; opportunity; equity; efficiency and throughput reduction; democracy and civility; precaution and adaptation; and immediate and long-term integration' (Gibson, 2006; Rocha et al., 2007). As is seen from the last definition, some of the attempts to explain the term brought even more confusion than clarity to the concept of 'sustainable development'.

In addition, some scientists, instead of simplifying the problem and dividing it into manageable parts, were adding new questions.

'Analytically, the debates over the meaning of the term can be seen as revolving around three general questions: is sustainable development about integrating environmental considerations into the economic development process or is it about a development process of a different quality; is sustainable development fundamentally a political, legal, economic or an environmental/ecological concept; is the concept inherently conflicting and what is the nature of the contradiction?' (Jensen, 2007).

Others were solving the problem with a rather simple answer—'sustainable development does not consume resources. It uses and re-uses them, endlessly' (Orecchini, 2007). From such a point of view, it is possible to conclude that the (only) aim of sustainable development is to increase the use of renewable energy sources and to have a strong recycling and reusing policy.

In 2008, Skowroński (2008) wrote that 'what the sustainable development concept has to offer is a qualitatively new form of aware and responsible life at the level of the individual and of society'. Jabareen (2008) commented on that 'On one hand, 'sustainability' is seen as a characteristic of a process or state that can be maintained indefinitely. On the other hand, however, development is environmental modification, which requires deep intervention in nature and exhausts natural resources'.

In 2008, Mark (2008) proposed that 'Sustainable development includes all business and community planning and operating decisions with due consideration for: (1) people—employees, customers, shareholders, community residents, or anyone that is involved or affected; (2) planet—material and energy resource management that does not hurt the environment; and (3) profits—or economics or prosperity. Sustainable development takes a different, more caring look at how people interact with themselves and how their activities affect the planet and the general well-being of life for sustained economic growth'.

In 2010, modern technology, as a major factor for making the world more sustainable, was highlighted as 'Preserving resources by minimizing their environmental impact, improving energy efficiency, reducing waste, and adopting new environmentally friendly technology will be the trends in the future for robot manufacturers' (Heinberg, 2012).

However, at the end of 2010, many questions about sustainable development remained. 'Does it [sustainable development] refer to climate change and the environment; or is it [sustainable development] more than that?' (Walters, 2010).

In 2011, Baumgartner (2011) stated that sustainable development 'is about enhancing the possibilities for improvement in the quality of life for all people on the planet and it is about respecting and living within the limits of ecosystems'. Such a definition describes the core of the concept well, but does not answer the hardest question—how can this be achieved? At the same time, formulations of clear goals of the term were appearing: 'the fundamental objective of sustainable development is to meet human needs…economic growth is required in areas where the basic needs are not met…development should not endanger natural systems that sustain life on the earth: the atmosphere, water, soil and living beings' (Koho, Torvinen, & Romiguer, 2011). Further confirmation of such ideas was once again described through the old paradigm of the triple bottom line: 'sustainable development generally refers to achieving a balance among the environmental, economic, and social pillars of sustainability' (Murphy, 2012) (c.f. Fig. 16.1).

Later, a change to the triple bottom line idea was proposed, using other categories that are more applicable to different countries or societies. 'The three pillars of sustainability are replaced by four categories, comprising the environment, state, capital and labour' (Deutz, 2014). The extension, however, did not cover all of the pillars of sustainability, and furthermore, it still did not explain means of achieving the above-mentioned sustainable development goals.

In Germany, the government wanted to promote the computerization of manufacturing, as a contribution to 'green manufacturing'. The term 'Industry 4.0', meaning the fourth industrial revolution, was/is used, which is a collective term embracing a number of contemporary automation, data exchange and manufacturing technologies. Industry 4.0 also facilitates the vision and execution of a 'smart factory'. On 8 April 2013, at the Hanover Fair, the final report of the Working Group Industry 4.0 was presented.

Nowadays, it is becoming more and more accepted that sustainable development cannot be defined once and forever. It is a term that can be perceived differently, depending on the area of its application and goals of those applying it. 'Sustainable development has always been a "flexible" concept interpreted in many different ways' (Kambites, 2014). Another useful 'assumption is that sustainable development is based not on economic, social, ecological, or institutional dimensions, but rather on their *system* seen as an *integrated whole*' (Ciegis, Ramanauskiene, & Martinkus, 2015).

There is still no agreement on a definition of the term 'sustainable development'. There are two main views—one of them is to specify the term and make it universal, while the second claims that this cannot be done because of the flexibility and pluralism of the question. More important than a discussion of the meaning of the term is to discuss how to develop sustainable products and services and how to get managers and product developers to acquire appropriate knowledge and experience to prevent the development, production and marketing of non-sustainable products.

Sustainable Product Development

There are many factors affecting the development of new products. Figure 16.5 shows some background issues and considerations to explore when starting the development of a new product.

Many new product development (NPD) models exist, but so far only one— Dynamic Product Development (DPD™)—seems to include more than one or two of the outer demands (USB) in Fig. 16.2 in the development process.

The entrepreneur/project leader and the product development team (c.f. Fig. 16.3) will strongly influence the environmental impact during the whole product life cycle of the product and the supplementary products that the primary product may need to function as intended. Figure 16.6 shows the recommended actions to develop a sustainable product solution. The numbers in the figure refer to:

1. Based on the intended user and the use of the product, seek to enhance safety and quality of life from the use of the product
2. Decrease the resource utilization and the costs throughout the whole PLC depending on the initial quality and price of the product and its variants
3. Minimize the negative impact on the environment throughout the PLC

Fig. 16.5 Some background issues and considerations to explore when starting the development of a new product (Ottosson, 2009)

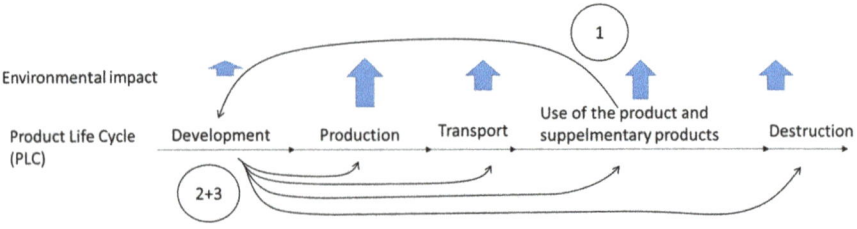

Fig. 16.6 Actions to develop a sustainable product solution

The decision-making tasks in the product development process in Fig. 16.6 (e.g. the choice of solution principles or the specification of materials and geometry) are often difficult to determine because the basic objectives (such as cost, function and quality) are interdependent. This is the reason why the approach/concept of 'Design for X (DfX)' was proposed in the early 1990s (Hubka, 1995). At that time, DfX was defined as 'all endeavors towards making the right decisions in the product development process on basis of a sufficient and universally applicable knowledge basis' (Huang, 1996). Because there are both objectives that support each other and others that compete against each other in the development process, DfX provided 'a systematic guidance for making decisions in product development related to products, processes and plants' (Bauer & Meerkamm, 2007). Step by step, the family of DfX has grown so that, today, there is a large number of Xs mentioned and used in engineering design, which can be pictured as a family tree (Bauer, 2003).

With many Xs to take into consideration in the development process, product developers have to select and weight different DfX criteria (Bauer & Meerkamm, 2007). However, the order in which the different DfXs should be carried out in order to achieve an optimal result, when it comes to satisfying demands of the project triangle (cost, time and properties), has not been adequately discussed. Probably this is mainly because each development process is unique and complex and thereby difficult to handle in a scientific way. However, coming back to the discussions on sustainability, it seems to be reasonable to pursue a user-centred design.

Initially, the focus of product development was on satisfying the needs of business/profit. Thus, Design for Manufacturing and Assembly (DfMA or DFMA) was primarily interested in these goals in the development process. Generally, the practice of applying DfMA is to identify, quantify and eliminate waste or inefficiency in a product design. Therefore DfMA can be seen as a component of lean manufacturing, for example (Holweg, 2007). DfMA is also used as a benchmarking tool to study competitors' products and as a cost tool to assist in supplier negotiations (Boothroyd, Dewhurst, & Knight, 2010).

In the middle of the 1990s, user-centred design (UCD) and Design for Usability (DfU), as well as Design for Ergonomics (DfEr), began to be broadly used, for example (Jordan, 1998). From about 2005, Design for the Environment (DfE) and sustainable design also gained increased interest in product development.

Step by step new DfX has been added to the DfX family, while the order in which to satisfy them has become an issue in itself although not much discussed. Logically, the priority order when developing a new product should be to satisfy the users/use, the society and the business. The simple reason is that without pleased users, there will be no (economically) sustainable business. Without satisfying society demands on sustainable (green) products, there will also be no sustainable businesses. Thus, satisfying user demands in the development process is of prime interest, followed by satisfying the sustainable demands on the product life cycle (PLC) chain from 'the cradle to the grave' of the product.

Seen from a user's point of view, a product can have at least six important product values, which can overlap each other (Ottosson, 2009):

- *Functional values* are dependent on the technical solutions, mostly hidden inside the product. The function can be as simple as just filling out the space (e.g. the gas in a balloon or the concrete in walls). It can also be advanced, encompassing all degrees between simple and advanced (e.g. an engine in a car has simple as well as advanced parts and systems).
- *Perception/sensorial values* are based on what we experience with our five basic senses (see/hear/taste/touch/smell) from outside and/or in contact with a product. The product semantics are important parts of these values.
- *Image values* are based on the image we get of the product and what we think of it, for example, when we close our eyes. Brand names, patents, the image given on web pages, stories and the expressed experiences of the product by other users will influence and develop the image we have of the product. The product semantics can influence these values.
- *Emotional values* are the passion/feelings we have for a product. The product semantics can influence these values.
- *Sustainability values* are long-lasting, environmentally responsible values for the users, the society and the providers (the businesses).

The different values of a product solution can be satisfied by using the different 'Design for X' possibilities, as shown in Table 16.1.

Good functional values and usability are interrelated. According to ISO (1998), usability is 'the effectiveness, efficiency and satisfaction with which specific users can achieve specified/particular goals in particular environments'. On a deeper level, these three terms have the following meanings:

- *Effectiveness*—Is the proposed product effective for reaching the goal? Is it possible to implement the findings in real user environments? What is required to

Table 16.1 Some design methods to use to achieve different values in product solutions

Product values	DfX etc.	Abbreviations for
Functional values	DfU	Design for usability
Emotional values	DfEr	Design for ergonomics
	DfSe	Design for service
Sensorial values	DfAe	Aesthetical design (industrial design)
Image value		
Emotional values		
Sustainability values	DfEn	Design for environment
	DfMA	Design for manufacturing and assembly
	DfQ	Design for quality
	DfL	Design for logistics
	LCA	Life cycle analyses
	FTA	Failure tree analyses

make that happen (e.g. educational needs, training needs, expert needs, acquisition of tools, organizational change)?

- *Efficiency*—Is the proposed product efficient to use? Is it tricky to use? Is it time/resource intensive?
- *Satisfaction*—Will the users find the use of the product more pleasant to use than what they experienced before the implementation? Will the users feel that the outcome is more efficient? Will the use of the new product contribute to a better economical result for the individual, or will it reduce failure risks in any aspect?

Still another aspect of the usability of a product is that it should contribute to a barrier-free world for any user. This is called universal design, for which seven principles have been proposed (Story, Mueller, & Mace, 1998):

1. Equitable use
2. Flexible in use
3. Simple and intuitive
4. Perceptible information
5. Tolerance for error
6. Low physical effort
7. Size and space for approach and use

To find a functional design that takes into consideration the different usability aspects, the systematics of BAD, PAD, MAD and CAD has been shown to produce good results. Brain Aided Design (BAD) means thinking of a different abstract solution. Pencil Aided Design (PAD) means sketching. MAD means making a model in as simple a way as possible. PAD, MAD and CAD were terms that were used in the early 1990s in the architecture department of Chalmers University of Technology in Sweden (Branzell, 1995). At that time, creative methods, such as brainstorming, were much discussed to solve problems. In order to include individual creativity, BAD was proposed as an addition to the PAD-MAD-CAD chain (Ottosson, 1995).

Figure 16.7 explains the abbreviations, as well as the recommendation to start the work at an abstract and wholeness level and then to proceed to the detailed and concrete level. The order in which the different activities are carried out is dependent on the products to be developed, the newness desired, time limits and other issues. The end result is a model, and with additional information, it can be called a product concept.

If the optimal order of the priorities when developing a new product is to satisfy the users/use, the society and the business, DfU must be addressed first, after which the other DfXs can be integrated step by step. Figure 16.8 shows an illustration of the steps to be taken for the development of a mechanical product. As shown in the figure, new development must always be checked against DfU so that the usability is not hampered.

In contrast to what is generally taught—that all demands must be set before commencing with the creation of a concept—we have found in industrial and student projects that a faster and less risky way is to start only with one primary and

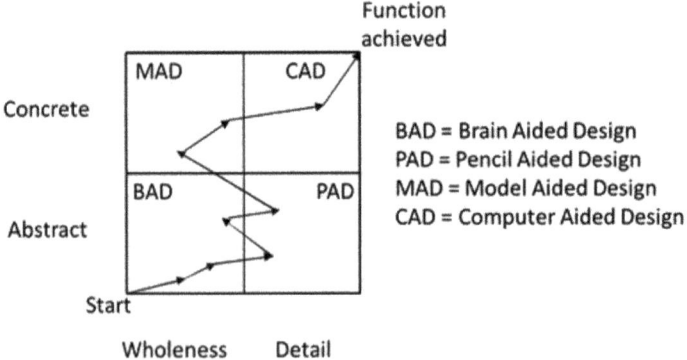

Fig. 16.7 To find a functional solution from a wish, different steps are needed (Ottosson, 2009)

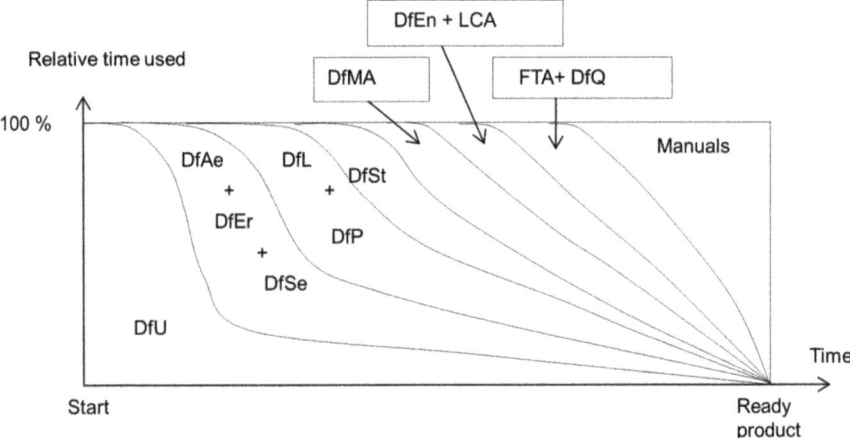

Fig. 16.8 An example of the order in which a new mechanical product can be developed to obtain an optimal result that satisfies many different demands (Ottosson, 2009)

two or three secondary demands and then proceed with creating concepts and solutions to satisfy them (Ottosson, 2004). When one or more of the concepts and solutions have been found, more demands can then be added for each of them. These demands can result in the necessity to find new solutions. If a solution does not hold in the test and evaluation phase, it is stopped from further development, and documentation is made of the findings and experiences. We have found that using this principle in practical work, which is shown in Fig. 16.9, the work can go ahead at a high speed, resulting in a final concept and a solution that are both well documented.

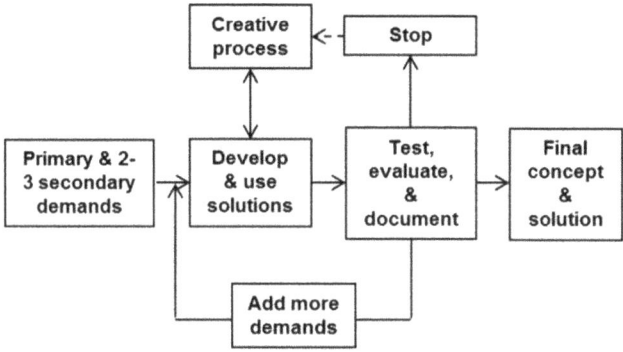

Fig. 16.9 The concept development is an iterative process in DPD™ (Ottosson, 2009)

Innovation Theory

The term 'innovation' is apparently derived from the Latin 'novus', which means new or young or novel. Unfortunately, there is no single, accepted definition of the term 'innovation'. Historically, innovation was defined as the introduction of new elements or a new combination of old elements in industrial organizations (Schumpeter, 1934). Thus, his focus was on the actual new ideas or inventions but not on the realization of them. Later Kanter (1983) defined innovation as the process of bringing any new, problem-solving idea into use.

In our times, the terms 'innovation' and 'sustainability' have both become buzz-words, with no single definition. In general, 'innovation' is a positively loaded term that brings hope in difficult times for actors in the private sector, the public sector and the idealistic (non-profit) sector, as well as for the whole economies. However, it is seldom explained in terms of how to create successful innovation. Even more unclear is how to develop 'sustainable innovations' although we might have an intuitive feeling that the expression refers to the development of something good.

According to conventional understanding, 'innovations' (independent of a definition of the term) are only done in the private sector (Mulgan, 2007). However, in reality, they have often been and are being developed in the public sector or in the idealistic (non-commercial) sector. For example, from the public sector, we have gained the Internet (CERN), the World Wide Web (DARPA) and the new teeth and prostheses made with titanium (Gothenburg University). In the idealistic sector, different open-source solutions have been and are being developed frequently. When the new solutions in these sectors mature, they often 'migrate' into the private sector to become commercial products. This might be why we perceive innovations as something emerging from the private sector.

Thus, innovations are and must be created and developed in all three sectors, although the aims of the work differ. For the private sector, the main aim is to create a sustainable profit. For the public sector, the main aim is to give better service to the

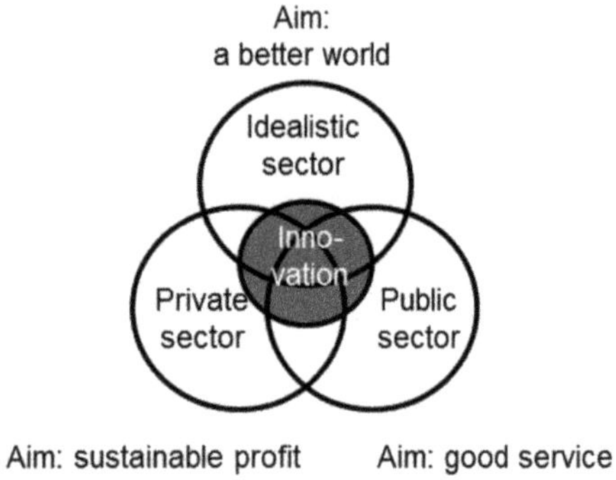

Fig. 16.10 Innovative work in different sectors has different aims (Ottosson, 2009)

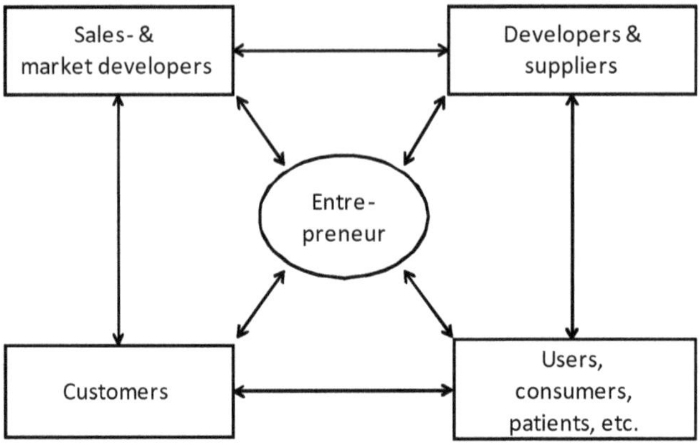

Fig. 16.11 Innovation development takes place in a complex adaptive social system (Ottosson, 2009)

people in the society. For the non-commercial sector, the goal is often a better world. All of these activities may encompass a local or global scale. Figure 16.10 shows these aims for the three sectors, which are strongly connected to USB in Fig. 16.3.

If we think of 'innovation' as a substantive—the end result of a long development project—the mission of an 'innovation project' is to carry out all its activities on a micro level in an organization in order to develop, market and sell a new product and/or service with the aim that it will be used or consumed. Today, the selling price is often zero, especially in the non-profit sector. An 'innovation process' includes the work done following this system, led by the innovation project team of an entrepreneur.

Simply stated, the entrepreneur is like the spider in the innovation process web, in which the sales personnel and market developers must be closely related to the potential customers, while the product developers—and supply chain developers—must be closely related to the users and consumers of the products being developed (see Fig. 16.11). Thus, an innovation project is an example of a complex, adaptive social system, encompassing a number of interrelations.

In general, projects are set up to make something unique. Performance demands, cost limits and completion dates are normally set before the project begins. Innovation projects differ from other projects in that they often determine the demands from trial and error, they have no clear finishing dates or rolling cost limits, and they can receive income from the sales of the new products.

A short definition of an innovation covering all sectors of the society might be (Ottosson, 2013):

> Innovations are new products and/or services that have been "sold" and taken in use in a local geographical market.

A more comprehensive definition of an innovation, based on the short definition, is that it is a new product (i.e. goods, services and/or information) that has been bought or adopted and has been taken in use. Thus, a new product that has not been bought or adopted is not a new innovation. A new product that has only been acquired but has not been used is also not a product innovation. Note, however, that 'acquiring' should be understood here in a wider perspective than just an immediate payment of money. For products/services that are given away free of charge, these products/services are often meant to generate other benefits sooner or later, such as revenue, contacts, membership, publicity or information.

'Adoption', in the definition, means that the product is stored, used or used up/consumed (see Fig. 16.12). Although it may sound strange, end users can be (human) users or consumers, animals or machines, among others. To make sure the products under development become 'good enough' in terms of hard and soft values, the product developers need to collect relevant information about their use, both before and during the entire development process.

A buyer's/customer's decision to acquire a product is dependent on many things, such as which buyer category the customer belongs to, the customer's present and/or future need of the product, the solution(s) offered by the product, the customer's emotional value of the product, the total price of the product during the time it is in the customer's possession and use, the financial situation of the customer,

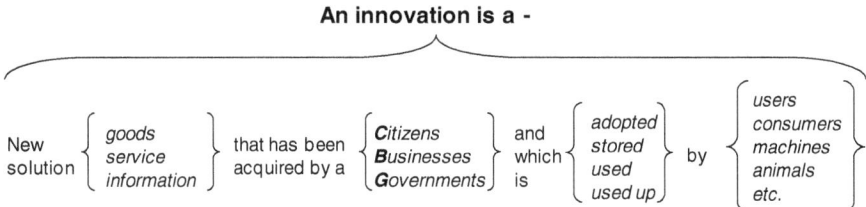

Fig. 16.12 A wider definition of demands on an innovation (Ottosson, 2009)

the estimated further sales price or the positive or negative value of it at the time of its disposal. The marketers, as well as the sales people, can 'educate' the customers and users to buy/use sustainable products.

Reflections

The Brundtland Report and all the various papers and articles that have been written on the subject of sustainability seem to have had the goal of defining the term. The Natural Step has carried the focus forward to 'down to action'. Therefore, a question is if Dynamic Product Development (DPD™) can satisfy the different views of sustainable product development.

As each innovation is unique, each innovation project needs a unique business idea or a unique set of ideas to be sustainable at different levels. Figure 16.13 shows how different views on sustainability can be used as inputs in DPD™, in order to guide product developers to develop sustainable products. The time component is then integrated into the term performance-cost-time (PCT), setting the boundaries of most development projects. Thus, DPD™ seems to be a useful match between different views on what sustainable innovation is and how to develop them.

Neither 'sustainable development' nor 'innovation' is a well-defined term. To describe *what* 'sustainable innovation' is and *how* it is developed, the following definitions are proposed. *A sustainable solution* is a solution that has been developed to be a long-lasting, environmentally responsible solution for the provider (the business), the society and the users. *An innovation* is a new solution that has been 'sold' and is used by more than one user or that is used in at least one-use situation. *The innovation process*, carried out as *an innovation project*, contains all stages from idea generation, development (R&D) and commercialization to an implemented solution on the market.

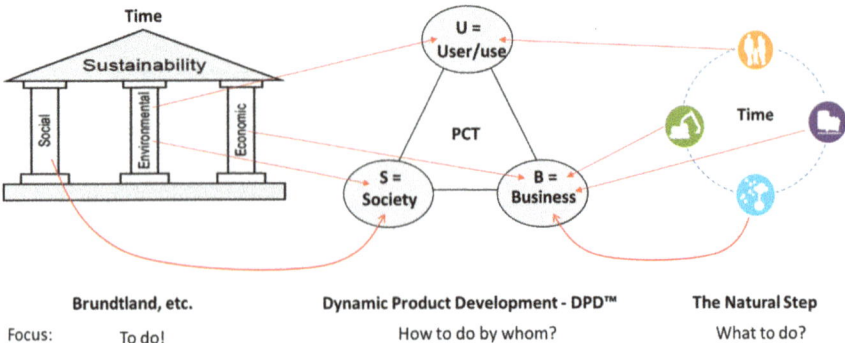

Fig. 16.13 The DPD™ principles are well positioned for the actual development of sustainable new products, forming the base of new innovations

Conclusions

We now need to focus on *how* to develop new sustainable innovations, for which the product development is the most important aspect. It has been found that Dynamic Product Development (DPD™) is a model that satisfies the various definitions of sustainability that have been proposed.

The result of a product development project is based on the product developer's knowledge, experience and ability. The leadership of an entrepreneur (or intrapreneur) is vitally important to the level of sustainability of an innovation. Therefore, product developers and entrepreneurs need to be educated in a broader perspective than that which is common in the technical field today. Product developers must also be monitored in their actual work situation in order to prevent the marketing of new products that are not sustainable. This, in turn, calls for a similar broader perspective in management education.

References

Acselrad, H. (1999). *Sustainability and territory: Meaningful practices and material transformations* (pp. 37–57). London, UK: ZED Books.

Bauer, S. (2003). *Design for X–Ansätze zur Definition und Strukturierung.* Paper presented at the DFX 2003: Proceedings of the 14th Symposium on Design for X, Neukirchen/Erlangen, Germany, October 13–14, 2003.

Bauer, S., & Meerkamm, H. (2007). *Decision making with interdependent objectives in design for X.* Paper presented at the Proc. of the 16th.

Baumgartner, R. J. (2011). Critical perspectives of sustainable development research and practice. *Journal of Cleaner Production, 19*(8), 783–786.

Boothroyd, G., Dewhurst, P., & Knight, W. A. (2010). *Product design for manufacture and assembly.* Boca Raton, FL: CRC Press.

Branzell, A. (1995). *Något om...: liten skissbok om det upplevda rummet* (in Swedish). Gothenburg, Sweden: Department for Architecture, Chalmers Technical University.

Chatterton, P., & Style, S. (2001). Putting sustainable development into practice? The role of local policy partnership networks. *Local Environment, 6*(4), 439–452.

Ciegis, R., Ramanauskiene, J., & Martinkus, B. (2015). The concept of sustainable development and its use for sustainability scenarios. *Engineering Economics, 62*(2).

Defra, U. (2005). *Securing the future: UK government sustainable development strategy* (p. 40). United Kingdom Department of the Environment, Food and Rural Affairs.

Deutz, P. (2014). A class-based analysis of sustainable development: Developing a radical perspective on environmental justice. *Sustainable Development, 22*(4), 243–252.

Elliott, J. (1999). *An introduction to sustainable development* (2nd ed.). Routledge: London.

Fischer, F., & Hajer, M. (1999). *Living with nature: Environmental politics as cultural discourse* (pp. 58–80). Oxford: Oxford University Press.

Gibson, R. B. (2006). Sustainability assessment: Basic components of a practical approach. *Impact Assessment and Project Appraisal, 24*(3), 170–182.

Harding, R. (2006). Ecologically sustainable development: Origins, implementation and challenges. *Desalination, 187*(1), 229–239.

Haughton, G. (1999). Environmental justice and the sustainable city. *Journal of Planning Education and Research, 18*(3), 233–243.

Heinberg, R. (2012). *What is sustainability?* Santa Rosa, CA: Post Carbon Institute.

Holliday, C. O., Schmidheiny, S., & Watts, P. (2002). *Walking the talk: The business case for sustainable development*. San Francisco: Berrett-Koehler.

Holweg, M. (2007). The genealogy of lean production. *Journal of Operations Management, 25*(2), 420–437.

Hopwood, B., Mellor, M., & O'Brien, G. (2005). Sustainable development: Mapping different approaches. *Sustainable Development, 13*(1), 38–52.

Huang, G. (1996). *Design for X: Concurrent engineering imperatives*. London: Chapman and Hall.

Hubka, V. (1995). *DESIGN FOR—DF. Fertigungsgerechtes Konstruieren*. Paper presented at the Beiträge zum 6. Symposium.

ISO. (1998). *ISO 9241-11. Ergonomic requirements for office work with visual display terminals (VDTs)—Part 11: Guidance on usability*.

Jabareen, Y. (2008). A new conceptual framework for sustainable development. *Environment, Development and Sustainability, 10*(2), 179–192.

Jacobs, M. (1995). *Reflections on the discourse and politics of sustainable development: Part I— Faultlines of contestation and the radical model*. Lancaster: Centre for the Study of Environmental Change, University of Lancaster.

Jensen, H. B. (2007). From economic to sustainable development: Unfolding the concept of law. *Systems Research and Behavioral Science, 24*(5), 505–513.

Jordan, P. W. (1998). *An introduction to usability*. Boca Raton: CRC Press.

Kambites, C. J. (2014). 'Sustainable development': The 'unsustainable' development of a concept in political discourse. *Sustainable Development, 22*(5), 336–348.

Kanter, R. M. (1983). *The change masters: Innovation and entrepreneurship in the American corporation*. New York: Touchstone Book.

Koho, M., Torvinen, S., & Romiguer, A. T. (2011). *Objectives, enablers and challenges of sustainable development and sustainable manufacturing: Views and opinions of Spanish companies*. Paper presented at the International Symposium on Assembly and Manufacturing (ISAM).

Luke, T. W. (2005). Neither sustainable nor development: Reconsidering sustainability in development. *Sustainable Development, 13*(4), 228–238.

Mark, A. P. (2008). Sustainable development. In *Encyclopedia of energy engineering and technology* (Vol. null, pp. 1406–1411). Taylor & Francis.

Mulgan, G. (2007). *Ready or not? Taking innovation in the public sector seriously*. London. Retrieved from http://www.nesta.org.uk/sites/default/files/ready_or_not.pdf

Murphy, K. (2012). The social pillar of sustainable development: A literature review and framework for policy analysis. *Sustainability: Science, Practice, & Policy, 8*(1), 15–29.

Orecchini, F. (2007). A "measurable" definition of sustainable development based on closed cycles of resources and its application to energy systems. *Sustainability Science, 2*(2), 245–252.

Ottosson, S. (1995). *Boosting creativity in technical development*. Paper presented at the Proceedings of the Workshop in Engineering Design and Creativity, Pilsen, Hungary, November.

Ottosson, S. (1996). Dynamic product development: Findings from participating action research in a fast new product development process. *Journal of Engineering Design, 7*(2), 151–169.

Ottosson, S. (2004). *Verification of product development methods*. Paper presented at the Proceedings of the TMCE Conference, Lausanne, Switzerland, April 13–17.

Ottosson, S. (2009). *Frontline innovation management*. Göteborg, Sweden: Tervix. ISBN 978-91-977947-7-0.

Ottosson, S. (2013). *Practical innovation theory*. Göteborg, Sweden: Tervix. ISBN 978-91-977947-7-0.

Rocha, M., Searcy, C., & Karapetrovic, S. (2007). Integrating sustainable development into existing management systems. *Total Quality Management & Business Excellence, 18*(1–2), 83–92. doi:10.1080/14783360601051594.

Schumpeter, J. A. (1934). *The theory of economic development: An inquiry into profits, capital, credit, interest, and the business cycle*. New Brunswick, NJ: Transaction Books.

Skowroński, A. (2008). A civilization based on sustainable development: Its limits and prospects. *Sustainable Development, 16*(2), 117–125. doi:10.1002/sd.341.

Stevens, C. (2005). *Measuring sustainable development*. Retrieved from http://www.oecd.org/std/35407580.pdf

Story, M. F., Mueller, J. L., & Mace, R. L. (1998). *The universal design file: Designing for people of all ages and abilities*. Raleigh, NC: North Carolina State University, Center for Universal Design.

The Natural Step. Retrieved from http://www.thenaturalstep.org/our-approach/

The Three Pillars of Sustainability. Retrieved from http://www.thwink.org/sustain/glossary/ThreePillarsOfSustainability.htm

Valentin, A., & Spangenberg, J. H. (2000). A guide to community sustainability indicators. *Environmental Impact Assessment Review, 20*(3), 381–392. Retrieved from http://dx.doi.org/10.1016/S0195-9255(00)00049-4

Walters, S. (2010). 'The planet will not survive if it's not a learning planet': Sustainable development within learning through life. *International Journal of Lifelong Education, 29*(4), 427–436. doi:10.1080/02601370.2010.488807.

Workshop on Urban Sustainability (National Science Foundation). (2001). *Towards a comprehensive geographical perspective on urban sustainability*. New Brunswick, NJ: Rutgers University.

World Commission on Environment Development. (1987). *Our common future*. Oxford: Oxford University Press.

Chapter 17
A Conceptual Model of the Relationship Between Aligned Innovations and Sustainable Development for Project-Based Organizations

Rasha Abou Samra and Khaled Shaalan

Abstract This paper is a critical review of the conceptual models that are developed in the area of finding motivators behind different parties' alignment to implement innovation and to develop more sustainable projects. Different parties always have diversified interests. The alignment of those parties has to have drivers, but at the same time it has also challenges. Investigations of drivers and challenges will facilitate better achievement of sustainable development goals. Alignment of organizational projects creates new opportunities in the market for those projects. The second part of this research paper presents a conceptual model architecture. This model is explaining inhibitors and reinforcements for having innovative projects. The model shows that innovative projects have certain characteristics. The purpose of innovative projects in this research is alignment and resources optimization for better sustainability. The main goal of the research is providing an approach for best practice of achieving sustainability among innovative projects.

Keywords Innovation • Sustainable • Development • Alignment

Introduction

Innovations are the short-term monopoly providers. The best exit the company can take to escape the sever competition is the innovation exit gate. The organization is dominating its channels of distribution, new segments of customers, and patents for a certain period of time that is enough to make a good profit. The market share is the

R.A. Samra (✉)
Higher Colleges of Technology, British University in Dubai, Dubai, UAE
e-mail: Rasha.abousamra@hct.ac.ae

K. Shaalan
British University in Dubai, University of Edinburgh, Edinburgh, UK
e-mail: Khaled.shaalan@buid.ac.ae

© Springer International Publishing Switzerland 2017
R. Benlamri, M. Sparer (eds.), *Leadership, Innovation and Entrepreneurship as Driving Forces of the Global Economy*, Springer Proceedings in Business and Economics, DOI 10.1007/978-3-319-43434-6_17

goat of the fox in the market. Monopoly is having all the market profits for a certain period of time. Repeating this monopoly is made by repeated successful commercialized innovations. This study attempts to investigate the challenges and drivers behind aligned innovations and how these innovations can serve the sustainable development targets of the society. Many factors are interacting with each other to achieve a successful aligned innovation. The manager, team, culture, level of trust, and commitment to the new alignment are all important factors. The failure of the innovation is commonly not because of the scarcity in ideas. It is usually because of the mismanagement of those ideas. The environmental influences may represent a barrier in front of the successful achievement. The more sub-ideas are involved in the innovation, the more successful it will become. Capabilities are dynamic not static. More dependency is on organic organizational structures rather than on mechanistic structures for better innovations. High connectivity and knowledge sharing are key factors for sustainable development innovations.

Innovation from a Project Management Perspective

Innovation is taking something new (Tidd, 2001) and living and breathing outside the box (Nicholls & Branson, 1998). Innovation is the sign of competitiveness (Bessant & Tidd, 2011), continuous improvement (Dulaimi & Kumaraswamy, 2000), and seeking differentiation (Harrison, Rouse, and Amabile 2014). In the Romanian context, Tomescu, Bucurean, Abrudan, and Rosca (2004) found that the organizational capacity to innovate depends on the quality of its human resources, having a proactive management style, openness toward innovation by the management team, a reward and recognition system, research infrastructure availability, and the financial resources allocated for innovation. The customer is always of greater value (Cardwell, 2013). The innovation's ability to provide a higher value to its customer is its price (Mayer, 2006). The goal of the innovation may suffer from incompatibility (Dulaimi et al., 2005) which may cause a failure during the innovation project management (Mayle, 2006). New projects in the market are made to gain profits (Smith & Yousuf, 2012). The idea is that those projects' originality of innovations may lead to short-term monopoly in the marketplace. The expected profit that may come to the organization before other competitors are able to imitate its innovations is a case of market short-term monopoly. There is a link between the innovation's monopoly on one side and the need to the project, the problem this project can solve, and the opportunities available in the market for this project on the other side. Furthermore, the innovative organization is learning and searching for new ideas (Dulaimi & Ang, 2009); the customer also is learning, searching, and comparing among competitors (Jamali & Sidani, 2008). The organizational internal role in tracking comparisons from the customer's point of view is a rich source of innovative ideas (Armstrong & Foley, 2003). Having customers play a role in launching new innovations is important especially if those customers are representing different market segments. This enables the innovative organization to have its honest market ambassadors (Dulaimi et al., 2010). Having the highest quality, being very fast, and being very cheap is a mixture that has inputs from internal customers and external customers as well (Besterfields et al., 2011). Even if the mixture is radically changing, assuring that it is the customer who is willing to buy motivates the multifunctional team to maintain competitiveness. Even if this innovation requires a radical change such that significant parts of the organization have to change, the decision will be taken for better marketing positioning and for better marketing differentiation (McCaffer & Edum-Fotwe, 2000). Scientists of innovation are tracking the types of changes that happen in the market (Freeman & Capper, 2000). One example on those radical changes due to innovation is the innovation made by Nokia. The company is changed dramatically in order to stay competitive. It started in forest-cutting business and moved to paper, then to a "paperless office" of IT, and finally to mobile phones (Dulaimi et al., 2010). New knowledge, new technology, and competitors' strategies are reasons for innovation discontinuity. The speed of innovation is an important factor for facing those challenges (Mayle, 2006). Innovations always grow from something else that exists (Cardwell, 2013). This is related to the available knowledge assets (Weir, Huggins, Schiuma, & Lerro, 2003). Originality of innovation is mainly the problem to be solved. It is where we have to create new knowledge. In many cases the innovative solution of a certain problem is only a change in the way of using something that already exists in the market. Many innovations need supplementary sub-innovations to succeed. A new idea will not grow unless new supplementary modifications are innovated to support its success. Supplementary modifications come from stakeholders of the innovation project, or they may come from thinkers who belong to different analogies (Freeman & Capper, 2000). This interprets the fact that 60 % of R&D innovations are market failures (Dulaimi et al., 2010). Innovations are shifting the multifunctional team from the comfort zone to a new discomfort zone but not necessarily to more complexity. New knowledge may lead to higher levels of simplicity (Smith & Yousuf, 2012). The innovation may take the form of replacing complexity by simplicity if it is desired by the customer (Handy, 1999). The manager of the project has to move the innovation through a quick gradual process of reducing the uncertainty and increasing the commerciality by supporting the innovation with more sub-innovations (Hargadon & Sutton, 2000), facilitations, feedback loops, and knowledge sharing (Arumugam, Antony, & Kumar, 2013). This way of thinking will balance the relationship between progressing with the risk of failure and stopping with the risk of missing the opportunity (Dulaimi et al., 2010). The multifunctional team's job at gradual stages will be represented in providing different rephrasing of the problems (Hofseted & Hofstede, 2004), solutions (Kotler & Schlesinger, 1979), and the "know how" (Smith & Yousuf, 2012). This represents a process of new knowledge creation. The alignment between the multifunctional team and the smart customers will increase the commerciality of the product innovation (Andreeva & Kianto, 2011). This is opposing the findings of Goldenberg in 1999 that showed that newness to the firm is correlated with failure rather than success. Knowledge sharing with customers plays a great role in avoiding failure sharing (Grey, 2014). Project managers play the role of project champions when they take the decision to actively promote the progress of the innovation through its critical stages (Lane & Lubatkin, 1998). Nam and Tatum in 1992 found that the ideas are available, but the decision and the environmental influences are the controlling variables. The influence of the project manager on the important players in his/her project is a strategic goal that enables the PM to succeed (McKenna, 2012). Innovations provide the organization with the reputation of pioneers and the early learning curve benefits (Brix & Lauridsen, 2012). The innovators can create barriers to the entry of new competitors like design, patents, and standards (Cardwell, 2013). The innovators can dominate the new supply and distribution networks (Dulaimi et al., 2010). The conclusion is that there is a need to study the challenges and driving forces for having innovative projects. It is also important that those projects work on innovations continuously without harming environmental resources. The resources optimization as well as better market opportunities can be better achieved by projects' alignment. The drivers and the challenges of alligned innovative projects are discussed in the following lines.

Drivers and Challenges of Projects Alignment

This study assumes that one of the important drivers behind project alignment is the buyer-seller relationship. Boeck and Fosso Wamba (2008) found that cooperation in the supply chain is defined by the desire to make shared supply chain projects. The relationship between the organization and its supplier must not be a win-lose relationship (Ergano et al., 2001). Both must work together cooperatively in a win-win relationship style to fulfill the needs of the end user (Patterson et al., 2009). Even if they want to innovate and introduce a new product to the end user, they must cooperate to teach the end user the new need and to make sure that the needed supplies for introducing this new innovation are available and under control (Schein, 2010). A win-lose alignment will minimize the level of trust that represents one of the alignment drivers (Stelling et al., 2006). Even the length of the relationship among aligned projects will be negatively affected by having a win-lose type of relationships. If parties of alignment believe that the competitive position they have before alignment will be improved after alignment, this will lead to synergy among them and will enhance the success of this alignment. The researchers assume that the creation of technological bridges among organizational projects will reinforce the optimization of the benefits of organizational flows. This assumption matches with the findings of Boeck and Fosso Wamba (2008). They mentioned that the digital economy links will lead to a more competitive performance. As a conclusion researchers think that performance competitiveness may represent one of the main criteria for measuring the efficiency of project alignment. Each partner in the relationship wants to make sure that the other partner will uphold obligations and will act in the best interest of the other partner(s). This kind of relationship is known as the level of trust among partners as found by Palmatier, Dant, Grewal, and Evans (2006). The level of trust is a driver if it is high enough among partners to go for the alignment choice. Researchers assume that the organizational culture plays a great role in creating higher levels of trust among partners. Another factor is the interaction between the level of trust and the expectations of partners of the aligned projects. Projects are built to fulfill a need, to solve a problem, or to make use of an opportunity. The cooperation variable was defined by Palmatier et al. (2006) by the willingness to undertake complementary actions to achieve mutual goals. Fulfillment of needs is an example of projects' goals. If the alignment took place among projects that have homogeneous segments of customers' needs, it will facilitate creating mutual trust among aligned parties. In order to be able to reach that point, the aligned parties will need an effective flow of information among parties. Loops of information sending and receiving are one of the basic needs in achieving a mutual understanding of the alignment. Building the aligned project structure will last as long as all parties are cooperating to fulfill the customer's needs. We always perform the marketing job in order to build long strong relationships with customers; hence, we expect that the alignment will not be able to build a long relationship with customers unless the alignment itself is built for a long-term commitment among parties. However, there are some projects that have short-term goals in certain markets as a marketing strategy. We would say that the length of the relationship will largely depend on the type of strategy used by the aligned projects. The mutual trust and benefits are positives of the alignment. On the contrary Walter, Helfert, and Müller (2000) found that there are mutual sacrifices regarding all aspects of the relationship. Each party will compare between the trade-off benefits and sacrifices of the alignment. If benefits are expected to be larger than the expected alignment sacrifices, then the party will take the alignment choice for a better competitive position. The researcher expects that this will greatly depend on the power structure among parties. The interdependence and the power imbalance play an important role in one party's ability to influence the other party to do or accept something it normally would not accept or do (Anderson & Weitz, 1989). As such the criteria of the alignment success will depend on the expectations of the dominant party in the first place (Gratton, 2007). Another factor here is that the dominant culture of the new aligned projects will be more affected by the party that has the higher level of power in the relationship. It is expected that the party with less power will have more behavioral and organizational modifications to meet the needs of the other party (Brennan, Turnbull, & Wilson, 2003). If the difference in the level of power between aligned parties is too big or too small, then it will be expected to have dysfunctional conflicts in the aligned projects. Keeping moderate levels of power difference will increase the functional conflict rather than the dysfunctional one (Abousamra, 2002; Palmatier et al., 2006). Another driver for alignment is that having new ideas from other specializations may lead to a higher degree of novelty in the innovation which leads to better monopoly dominance in the market at the beginning of launching the innovation. Remember the case of thinking of producing artificial arms and legs for people who had lost their arms or legs. The idea of having a new specialization that mixes between medicine and engineering in what we call medical engineering specialization is a good example on novelty of the innovation. The idea is that we have to get out of the "specialization" box and merge our box with other "specializations" boxes in order to find an innovation with a high degree of novelty. Co-creation of ideas will lead to economies of scope (Møller, 2008) by using similar processes to deliver a set of innovations. The critical factor in the co-creation strategy is the matching relationships between customers and suppliers. An important challenge is finding the alignment partner that has the acceptable level of trust between top managers, relatedness of partner businesses, complementary resources, access to links with major common buyers, reputation, sharing of financial risk, and access to a distribution channel. If those aspects are available, then they may be transformed into drivers. The past experience with the partner and the access to labor common culture are also challenges. A good, strong driver is knowledge sharing through technological tools. The firm size of the partner also is a challenge. Hot spots also are drivers behind successful alignment (they mean cooperative mindset × boundary spanning × igniting purpose × productive capacity) (Dulaimi et al., 2010; Hammuda & Dulaimi, 1996; 1997). An intellectual capital, emotional capital, and social capital are engaged in a reinforcing cycle for alignments. Alignments between organizations and their projects are affected by both the clarity of roles and responsibilities of the participating organizations and the governmental cross-boundary information sharing. The first factor is affected by three variables: exercise of authority, diversity of participating organizations and their goals, and past experiences. Scope management, cost management, and human resources management are challenges that hinder the success of the project alignment.

Market Opportunities Created by Aligned Innovations

The marketing department is one of the drivers behind launching new innovations. The literature revealed that the marketing department has soft tactics and hard tactics for influencing the development of new products (Gima & Li, 2000). Soft tactics may be represented in the information exchange with decision makers, providing recommendations, requests, or taking the support from other departments by forming coalitions. Hard tactics may include a legalistic plea, upward appeal, and persistent pressure on the decision maker to start developing the innovation. The influence of the marketing department was found to be moderately high (Tidd & Bessant, 2013), and the use of soft tactics is more effective than the use of hard tactics. It is obvious that the marketing department itself may need to make an alignment with other departments to get the needed support (Ulrich & Eppinger, 2011). A previous research in the Chinese context found that there is interdependence between the marketing department and the R&D department in new product development projects (Gima & Li, 2000). Innovations are related to higher market shares and better profitability. It is also linked to retaining talented staff. Innovation is leaving the comfort zones to other new uncertain zones (Microsoft and Apple on TVs). To motivate the project staff to leave their comfort zones and to shift to the uncertain ones, there has to be some dynamic capabilities (Güttel & Konlechner, 2007). Guttel and Konlechner from Vienna found that dynamics are needed to govern the ratio between exploration (e.g., R&D and product development) and exploitation (reengineering and replication). They found that there must be some cultural and structural mechanisms to enable simultaneous exploration and exploitation. All these aspects lead the researchers to consider the internal innovators as internal customers for each other in a certain structure. This structure includes customers of ideas and semi-finalized innovations. The customer-supplier internal relationships enhance the feeling of self-worth and reinforce the innovation climate.

Contribution of Innovation in Achieving Sustainable Development Goals

Sustainable development ("SD") is about "making individual well-being rise over time" (Dulaimi et al., 2010). The innovative ideas may be affected by the social categorization within the innovation team. This categorization affects the use of knowledge diversity within the team (Paletz & Schunn, 2010). In the Tehran Oil Refinery Company, it was found that organizational trust affects the organizational product innovativeness, process innovativeness, behavioral innovativeness, and strategic innovativeness (Golipour, Jandaghi, Mirzaei, & Arbatan, 2011). Sustainable development values are the same, but the conditions needed to achieve it are not the same. Sustainable development is related to the ability to compete globally (Abu Dhabi Executive Council Policy 2007–2008). Transparency, accountability, more efficiency, more excellence, and competition for talents are all drivers for engagement in sustainability innovations. Meeting the present needs without negatively affecting the future needs is an equation that explains the importance of the engagement in the SD innovations as soon as possible.

> Sustainability management is the integrated and systematic management of economic, environmental and social performance in a way that maximizes benefits for both the business and stakeholders. (Dulaimi et al., 2010)

Innovations need knowledge, and SD needs a knowledge-based economy. The governmental effort to reach a knowledge-sharing system is a chance to enable innovations to achieve SD. Innovating new methods of resources optimization is a form of SD. Mayle (2006) found that innovations are either customer driven or crises driven. This means that in both cases there are better life objectives coming through the new project development (Iman Assalama, 2009).

Conceptual Model for Achieving Sustainability Innovations

Based on the literature review and critical analysis in the first part of this research, researchers designed the following conceptual model for sustainability innovations (Fig. 17.1).

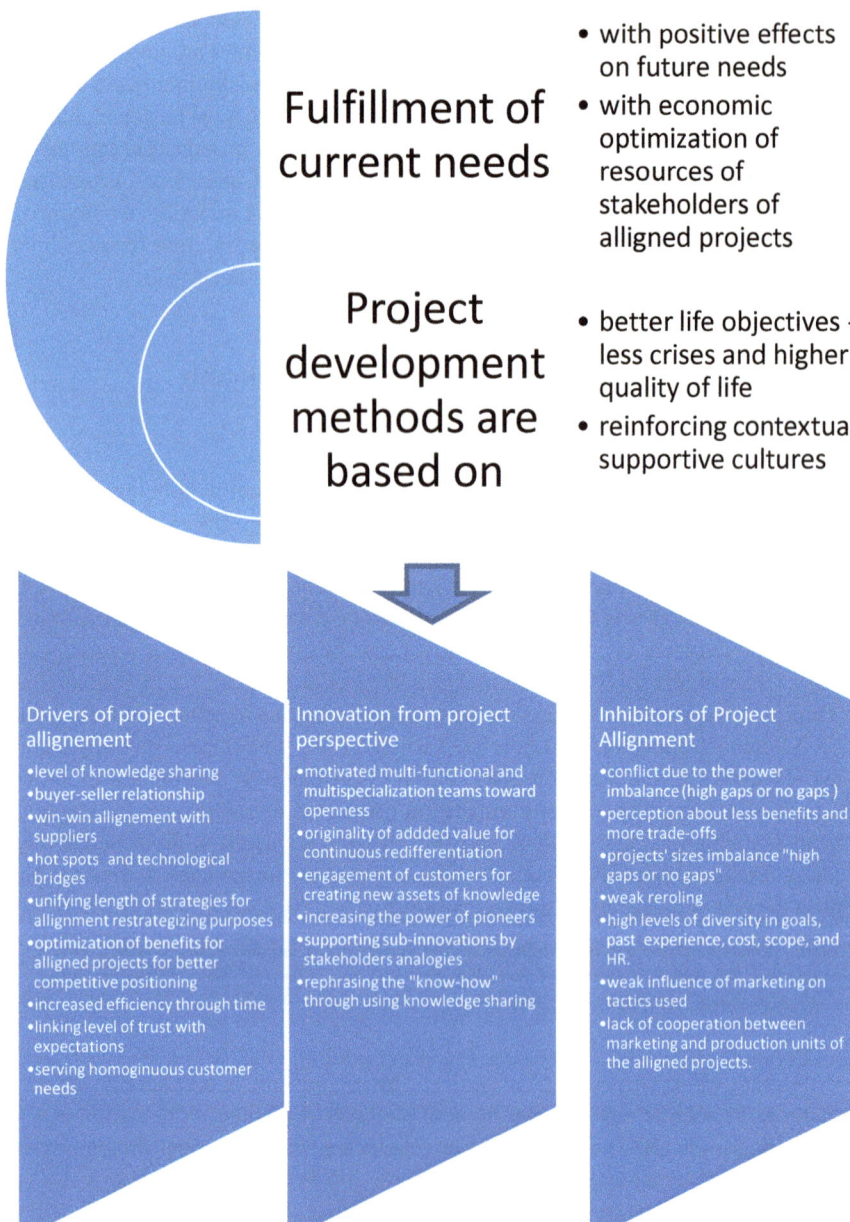

Fig. 17.1 Conceptual model of achieving sustainability innovations

In this figure researchers show how innovation from project perspective is positioned among a group of factors. Some of those factors are drivers for alignment and others are inhibitors. Then the figure shows how aligned innovations can lead sustainability innovations. Sustainability innovations include having fulfilled needs without harming the fulfillment of future needs. It also includes developing new methods to build the needed contextual culture and to achieve a better life for future generations.

Conclusion

This paper conducted a critical review of the drivers and challenges of innovation projects' alignments. A challenge for having sustainable development-aligned innovations is needed. This challenge may be the benchmark, the customer problems, or a crisis. The driver for having a sustainable development-aligned innovation is also needed. The driver may be represented by the availability of capabilities, an innovation champion, an innovative climate, or a high-connectivity technology. The support of the top management and the government is essential for success. Managers of projects must put the innovation as the sixth condition of the SMART goal. The innovation is the green card to rapid profits' achievement. Training on creative thinking and building the human skills of innovation must be continuous and must lead to a competitive advantage for the organization. Achieving this competitive advantage on the level of the whole world must become the target of the organization that wants to achieve sustainability and to survival. Researchers initiated a conceptual model for their understanding of reinforcing and inhibiting factors affecting the innovative alignment among project based-organizations.

We recommend that the sustainable development projects start with the alignment between the needs and the problems of customers. The kind of problem the customer has determines the kind of needs she/he will feel. The alignment projects between suppliers and their organizations and between those organizations and their customers are great sources of sustainable development innovations. Furthermore we recommend to take the common criteria that determine the drivers and challenges of alignment within the UAE and to measure their existence percentages in different contexts of the country. This kind of research will facilitate removing the barriers among different contexts in the future and establishing more successful alignment innovations.

References

Abousamra, R. (2002) *The relationship between the characteristics of intra-group conflict and the levels of organizational conflict—Applied research on the Egyptian constructions sector* (Unpublished Master Thesis, Ein Shams Library).

Anderson, E., & Weitz, B. (1989). Determinants of continuity in conventional industrial channel dyads. *Marketing Science, 8*(4), 310–323.

Andreeva, T., & Kianto, A. (2011). Knowledge processes, knowledge-intensity and innovation: A moderated mediation analysis. *Journal of Knowledge Management, 15*(6), 1016–1034.

Armstrong, A., & Foley, P. (2003). Foundations for a learning organization: Organization learning mechanisms. *The Learning Organization, 10*(2), 74–82. Emerald Group Publishing Ltd.

Arumugam, V., Antony, J., & Kumar, M. (2013). Production economics linking learning and knowledge creation to project success in Six Sigma projects: An empirical investigation. *International Journal of Production Economics, 141*(1), 388–402. Retrieved from http://doi.org/10.1016/j.ijpe.2012.09.003.

Barnaba, V., Paroli, M., & Piconese, S. (2012). The ambiguity in immunology. *Frontiers in Immunology, 3*. 10.3389/fimmu.2012.00018.

Bessant, J., & Tidd, J. (2011). *Innovation and entrepreneurship* (2nd ed.). Chichester: Wiley.

Besterfield, D. H., Besterfield-Michna, C., & Besterfield-Sacre, M. (2011). *Total quality management* (3rd ed.). Delhi: Pearson Education India.

Boeck, H., & Fosso Wamba, S. (2008). RFID and buyer-seller relationships in the retail supply chain. *International Journal of Retail & Distribution Management, 36*(6), 433–460. 10.1108/09590550810873929.

Brennan, D. R., Turnbull, P. W., & Wilson, D. T. (2003). Dyadic adaptation in business-to-business markets. *European Journal of Marketing, 37*(11/12), 1636–1665.

Brix, J., & Lauridsen, K. M. (2012). Learning styles and organizational development in practice: An exploratory study of how learning styles and individual learning strategies can facilitate organizational development. *International Journal of Innovation and Leaning, 12*(2), 181.

Cardwell, D. (2013, January 22). LEDS emerge as popular green lights. *New York Times*. Retrieved from www.nytimes.com/2013/01/22/business/leds-emerge-as-a-popular-green-lighting.html?nl=todaysheadlines&emc=edit_th_20130122&_r=1&

Chen, W. W., & Deo, R. S. (2006). The variance ratio statistic at large horizons. *Econometric Theory, 22*(2). 10.1017/s0266466606060099.

Dulaimi, M. F., Alhashemi, M., Ling, F. Y. Y., & Kumaraswamy, M. (2010). The execution of public–private partnership projects in the UAE. *Construction Management and Economics, 28*(4), 393–402. 10.1080/01446191003702492.

Dulaimi, M., & Ang, A. F. (2009). Elements of learning organisations in Singapore's construction industry. *Emirates Journal for Engineering Research, 14*(1), 83–92.

Dulaimi, M., & Kumaraswamy, M. (2000). Procuring for innovation: The integrating role of innovation in construction procurement. In *Proceedings of the Association of Researchers in Construction Management, Glasgow, UK*.

Dulaimi, M., Nepal, M., & Park, M. (2005). A hierarchical structural model of assessing innovation and project performance. *Construction Management and Economics, 23*(6), 565–577.

Ergano, K., Duncan, A., Adie, A., Tedla, A., Woldewahid, G., Ayele, Z., et al. (2001). *Implementation challenges of innovation systems perspective in Fodder production in Ethiopia*. Addis Ababa, Ethiopia: International Livestock Research Institute.

Freeman, M. A., & Capper, J. M. (2000). Obstacles and opportunities for technological innovation in business teaching and learning. *International Journal of Management Education, 1*, 37–47.

Gima, K., & Li, H. (2000). Marketing's influence tactics in new product development: A study of high technology firms in China. *Journal of Product Innovation Management, 17*, 451–470.

Golipour, R., Jandaghi, G., Mirzaei, T., & Arbatan, R. (2011). The impact of organizational trust on innovativeness at the Tehran oil refinery company. *African Journal of Business Management, 5*(7), 2660–2667.

Gratton, L. (2007). *Hot spots*. Harlow: Pearson Education.

Grey, S. (2014, July). *Unknown unknowns*. Published under Enterprise risk management and ISO 31000, Project risk management and IEC 62198, Risk assessment. Retrieved July 2014, from http://broadleaf.com.au/resource-material/unknown-unknowns/

Güttel, W., & Konlechner, S. W. (2007). *Dynamic capabilities and competence obsolescence: Empirical data from research-intensive firms*. Learning Fusion. p. 357.

Hammuda, I., & Dulaimi, M. (1996). Empowering the organization: A comparative study of different approaches to empowerment. In *CIB Beijing International Conference, China, 21–24 October*.

Hammuda, I., & Dulaimi, M. (1997). The theory and application of empowerment: A comparative study of the different approaches to empowerment in construction, service, and manufacturing industries. *International Journal of Project Management, 5*(5), 289–296.

Handy, C. (1999). *Understanding organizations* (4th ed.). Oxford: Oxford University Press.

Hargadon, A., & Sutton, R. (2000, May/June). Building an innovation factory. *HBR*, pp. 157–166.

Harrison, S., Rouse, E. D., & Amabile, T. M. (2014). Flipping the script: Creativity as an antecedent. *Academy of Management Proceedings, 2014*(1), 10457–10457. 10.5465/ambpp.2014. 10457symposium.

Hofseted, G., & Hofstede, G. (2004). *Cultures and organizations: Software of the mind*. New York: McGraw Hill.

Jamali, D., & Sidani, Y. (2008). Learning organizations: Diagnosis and measurement in a developing country context. *The Learning Organization, 15*(1), 58–74.

Lane, P. J., & Lubatkin, M. (1998). Relative absorptive capacity and inter-organizational learning. *Strategic Management Journal, 19*, 461–477.

Mayer, M. (2006, May 17). *License to pursue dreams*. Stanford Technology Ventures Program/ Stanford School of Engineering. Retrieved June 20, 2012, from http://ecorner.stanford.edu/ author/marissa_mayer

Mayle, D. (2006). Innovation in practice. In J. Henry & D. Mayle (Eds.), *Creativity, innovation and change media book* (pp. 33–38). Milton Keynes: Open University.

McCaffer, R., & Edum-Fotwe, F. T. (2000). Engineering and the future of construction. Industry: Realities and emerging possibilities. In: *Proceedings, 4th Asia-Pacific Structural Engineering and Construction Conference (APSEC 2000), September 13–16, 2000, Kuala Lumpur* (pp. 33–40).

McKenna, E. (2012). *Business psychology and organizational behavior: A student handbook* (5th ed.). Hove, England: Psychology Press.

Møller, A. P. (2008). Interactions between interactions. *Annals of the New York Academy of Sciences, 1133*(1), 180–186. 10.1196/annals.1438.007.

Nicholls, R. J., & Branson, J. (1998). Coastal resilience and planning for an uncertain future: An introduction. *The Geographical Journal, 164*(3), 255. 10.2307/3060614.

Paletz, S. B. F., & Schunn, C. D. (2010). A social-cognitive framework of multidisciplinary team innovation. *Topics in Cognitive Science, 2*(1), 73–95. 10.1111/j.1756-8765.2009.01029.x.

Palmatier, R. W., Dant, R. P., Grewal, D., & Evans, K. R. (2006). Factors influencing the effectiveness of relationship marketing: A meta-analysis. *Journal of Marketing, 70*(4), 136–153.

Patterson, F., Kerrin, M., Gatto-Roissard, G., & Coan, P. (2009). *Everyday innovation: How to enhance innovative working in employees and organisations*. London, UK: NESTA.

Schein, E. (2010). *Organizational culture and leadership* (4th ed.). San Francisco: Wiley.

Smith, A., & Yousuf, H. (2012, January 19). Kodak files for bankrupcy. *CNNMoney*. Retrieved July 20, 2012, from http://money.cnn.com/2012/01/19/news/companies/kodak_bankruptcy/ index.htm?Iid=EL

Stelling, A., Millar, J., Phengsavanh, P., & Stur, W. (2006). Establishing learning alliances between extension organizations: Key learnings from Laos. *Extension Farming Systems Journal, 5*(1), 221–234.

Tidd, J. (2001). Innovation management in context: Environment, organization and performance. *International Journal of Management Reviews, 3*(3), 169–183. 10.1111/1468-2370.00062.

Tidd, J., & Bessant, J. (2013). *Managing innovation: Integrating technological, market and organisational change* (5th ed.). West Sussex, England: Wiley.

Tomescu, M., Bucurean, M., Abrudan, M., & Rosca, R. (2004). *Ten key concepts and the success of Romanian organizations* (p. 120). Bucharest: University of Oradea CODECS Publishing House.

Ulrich, K. T., & Eppinger, S. D. (2011). *Product design and development* (5th ed.). Boston: McGraw Hill.

Walter, A., Helfert, G., & Müller, T. A. (2000). *The impact of satisfaction, trust, and relationship value on commitment: Theoretical considerations and empirical results*. Paper presented at the 16th IMP Conference, Bath.

Weir, M., Huggins, R., Schiuma, G., & Lerro, A. (2003). Valuing knowledge assets in renewable energy SMEs: Some early evidence. *Electronic Journal of Knowledge Management, 8*(2), 225–234.

Chapter 18
Project Manager Roles in Software Information Systems: Case Studies from Jordan

Abdallah Qusef and Jalal Kiswani

Abstract In the traditional software development life cycle (SDLC), the project management theory assumes the involvement of project manager in every phase of the project with all parties. However, this will not be always possible because of the variation of software projects based on the project size (small, medium, and enterprise), which affects the project constraints of cost, time, and scope. In this paper, we take real-life case studies of successful projects in Jordan to be classified based on many factors, and then, we define the responsibilities of the project managers in every class based on those case studies.

Keywords Software project management • Software development life cycle

Introduction

Many people and organizations today have a new interest in project management. Until the 1980s, project management primarily focused on providing schedule and resource data to top management in the military, computer, and construction industries. Project managers must strive not only to meet specific scope, time, cost, and quality goals of projects, but must also facilitate the entire process to meet the needs and expectations of people involved in project activities or affected by them.

Many of the theories and concepts of project management are not difficult to understand. What is difficult is implementing them in various environments. Project managers must consider many different issues when managing projects. In this short

A. Qusef (✉)
King Hussein Faculty of Computing Sciences, Princess Sumaya University
for Technology, Amman, Jordan
e-mail: a.qusef@psut.edu.jo

J. Kiswani
Solid-Soft Company, Amman, Jordan
e-mail: Jalal.kiswani@solid-soft.net

© Springer International Publishing Switzerland 2017
R. Benlamri, M. Sparer (eds.), *Leadership, Innovation and Entrepreneurship as Driving Forces of the Global Economy*, Springer Proceedings in Business and Economics, DOI 10.1007/978-3-319-43434-6_18

paper, we work on classifying software projects based on a proposed taxonomy, which is more discussed in the following section. Every class was then character-ized, its main constraints that affect the success of such class were identified, and an appropriate case study for successful projects that matches the same level of the project was selected. The next step was to study the selected case in terms of the best approach of managing the project and how the responsibilities were set to project managers to achieve the project goals. The rest of paper is organized as follows: section "Proposed Classification of Software Projects" presents the proposed clas-sification of software projects, while sections "Small-Size Projects", "Medium-Size Projects", and "Enterprise-Size Projects" discuss the different project management roles depending on proposed classification. Finally, section "Conclusion and Future Work" summarizes our conclusions and future work.

Proposed Classification of Software Projects

Unlike projects in many other industries, IT projects can be very diverse. Some involve a small number of people installing off-the-shelf hardware and associated software. Others involve hundreds of people analyzing several organizations' busi-ness processes and then developing new software in a collaborative effort with users to meet business needs. Because of the diversity of IT projects and the newness of the field, it is important to develop and follow best practices in managing these varied projects. That way, IT project managers will have a common starting point and method to follow with every project (Mellisa & McGreogr, 2000); the authors defined what makes a software project small based on four factors; the develop-ment, organization's size, quality attributes, and personnel interactions. Building on this, Table 18.1 shows classification of software projects was based on: project complexity, development organization size, quality attributes, personnel interac-tion, and SDLC process, estimated lines of code, and project duration. In project complexity, the main focus is on the complexity of the domain knowledge required. For example, a project is said to be small when it does not require a domain special-ist in the business analysis phase of the project. Rather, the analysis is conducted through a traditional process with stakeholders or through a simple research.

Small-Size Projects

Based on the taxonomy in Table 18.1, the main characteristics of small-sized proj-ects are the low need of domain knowledge, along with relatively short period of project, and where the client budget is very limited. For this size of projects, we select three case studies developed in Solid-Soft Company[1], named Smart-UMS, Smart-Sharia Audit, and Smart-Lottery. The scope of Smart-UMS is to integrate

---

[1] http://www.solidsoft.jo/LTR/products.xhtml

Table 18.1 Proposed taxonomy of software projects

Criteria	Small	Medium	Enterprise
Project complexity	Simple domain knowledge required	Partial domain knowledge required	Complex domain knowledge required
Quality attributes	Less need and involvement of quality attributes (such as reliability, security, and performance)	Not all quality attributes are always implemented	Mandatory need of all quality attributes
Personnel interactions	Informal communication and shallow management structure		Formal communication and hierarchical organization structure
SDLC process	Informal and not full		Formal and supported with management methodologies for the development organization
Duration	2–5 months	6–12 months	More than 1–3 years
Design and software architecture	Simple		Complex

Smart-UMS with the legacy registration system of Hiteen College (HC) in Amman-Jordan to be able to produce all the required reporting ad data from the legacy system and UMS through unified system. Smart-UMS was developed, implemented on time and within the budget, and is running in production since March 2008. The Smart-Sharia Audit is a web-based application that automates all the audit processes to ensure that all the internal processes are complaint with the Islamic sharia rules governed by the central banks of the countries applying sharia-audit rules. This project has been designed and implemented in Jordan Dubai Islamic bank. The last project (i.e., Smart-Lottery) is a prize draw management system that automates the process of draws from the basic configurations to the detailed dynamic configurations of official draws mainly for the banking industry. Smart-Lottery is currently implemented in Oman Arab bank.

The main constraints for all above projects were budget and time and implementation issues. In particular, implementing the above systems using a full SDLC cycle was impractical because it will increase the cost and duration. Thus, the solution was to assign the project to a full-stack-developer, a technical person with extensive experience in delivering full software solutions with minimal supervision from top management and support from other senior team members. The full stack developer is able to act in every phase of SDLC; however, the SLDC in such case was informal and implemented only as required (e.g., the analysis phase was only about 20 % without any official documentation of SRS or any other scope documents).

In this type of projects, the PM responsibilities almost based on project coordination between the full-stack developer and the client, including visits and arrangements, and there was no formal PM deliverables like project charters, project plans, status reports …ctc. The coordination of the different phases through the project management cycle ensures that all areas of the project come together to deliver the project to a successful conclusion. Based on these responsibilities of PM, this kind of projects doesn't require long-expertise in PM, and Junior PM can do the job with minimal super-vision from the management.

Medium-Size Projects

The main characteristic of such projects is complex scope, where most likely this type of clients does not have exact requirements or scope of work, which creates gap during the project execution. For this type of projects, we selected ETHIX-Net,[2] which is E-Banking system owned by ITS (International Turnkey Solutions), a company based in Kuwait with more than 1500 employees distributed on many countries. In 2014, ITS decided to revamp the project to apply the latest standards based on Java EE technologies; the main objective of the revamp projects is to be fancy graphical user interface, with highly dynamic configuration and parameterization along with unified development API's and framework.

The main issues of ETHIX-Net project are requirements and architecture. The lack of clear and detailed requirements and requirements gap will lead to expensive cost of time and resources to recover the changes. The architecture is very critical in ETHIX-Net project; it starts by choosing the right technology, architecture, and design of the project; since the main issues with such project types are requirements and architecture, the solution was to allocate an experienced functional consultant in the project domain who was able to provide all the required details regarding the scope, and the second action was to outsource an experienced architect to handle the architecture, design complexity of the system, and to be the first adviser for the technical team during the project development. Since this project was involving many resources with different seniority levels with relatively medium duration for project delivery (10 months), this project required a dedicated senior project manager who was working with the teams on daily basis and was able to communicate effectively with the other related departments, top management. Communication is used to inform and educate the project stakeholders about the project objectives, risks, assumptions, and constraints. Project managers in the role of communicators take two functions: to gather information from project staff and other people involved with the project; and distribute the information to stakeholders.

Enterprise-Size Projects

The main characteristics of this type of projects are time, huge team, and the complexity of the application in terms of number of components and subsystems that shall be integrated with each other in an effective way. For this type, the best to

---

[2] http://www.its.ws/EnUniversalBanking.cms

approach is a countrywide solution, so we selected PS-ECC.[3] PS-ECC is the first of kind country-wide image-based check-clearing solution that is currently implemented in seven countries. ECC has been developed by Progress-Soft Company, which is a Jordanian company that has been established since 1989 with focusing on the image-based solutions for the banking industry.

The main issues of ECC were the working hierarchy and the work coordination between different involved parties, along with creating unified working structure for all the project components, with keeping the deliverables matching the scope which may change in any time since this domain is highly coupled with the regulations of high-level councils or boards. The development company has been able to address these issues by creating a clear job-hierarchy and organization chart. In particular, Progress-Soft established many departments like: design and architecture department, quality assurance department, dedicated teams for the core development, and dedicated team for the integration projects. In addition, the company implemented a working mythology based on classical SDLC and agile processes and insured the centralization of the project critical decisions by technical-lead architect and lead project manager.

The role of lead project manager was to coordinate all the managerial activities between all parties along with taking the critical decisions and the tough communications with the external parties to be able to achieve the project objectives. In particular, project manager transmits the information to the external environment, such as the general public to gain support to the project.

Conclusion and Future Work

This paper explores an actual case study from Jordan in order to help the development-organizations to select the best process and required resources to achieve project goals. However, more case studies are needed to support the proposed classification and more guidelines can be used as an input for modifying the current standard processes in developing organizations.

Acknowledgment   The authors would like to thank Dr. Muhanna Muhanna for his help and valuable ideas.

Reference

Mellisa, L. R., & McGreogr, J. D. (2000). A software development process for small projects. *IEEE Software, 17*(5), 96–101.

---

[3] http://www.progressoft.com/?option=com_products&prodId=3

Chapter 19
Divided We Fall: A Case Study of ERP Implementation Failure in a Middle Eastern Country

Mahmood Ali, Lloyd Miller, Shoaib Ahmed, and Salah Abunar

Abstract ERP system implementation allows organisations to integrate different departments working in silos, while allowing them to have real-time business visibility and access to centralised information. ERP implementation is fraught with challenges and requires substantial resources and effort with no guarantee of success. The study of ERP implementation is limited mostly to developed countries, but the need for ERP implementation in developing countries is growing. However, many organisations are reluctant to adopt ERP systems, due to lack of implementation experience and fear of a failed implementation. To improve our understanding of what may lead to implementation failure in developing countries, this study adopts a case study research methodology to investigate a failed ERP implementation in a Middle Eastern country, and the critical success factors (CSFs) which contribute towards failure. The findings identify factors, including country and organisational culture, lack of change management strategies, system choice, customisation, and internal politics as contributing towards implementation failure. This study provides insights into the role of CSFs in ERP implementation failure in developing countries. The critical factors identified, appear to be correlated, meaning changes in one factor, will have an impact on another. The study provides organisational guidance for planning implementation strategy, based on the role of CSFs during implementation. Further, by drawing on the findings, we relate how an organisation can better utilise and prioritise CSFs to avoid a failed implementation.

Keywords ERP systems • ERP implementation • Middle East • ERP failure • Critical factors

M. Ali (✉) • S. Ahmed • S. Abunar
College of Business Administration, University of Business and Technology,
Jeddah, Saudi Arabia
e-mail: m.ali@ubt.edu.sa; shoaib@ubt.edu.sa; salah@ubt.edu.sa

L. Miller
Department of Economics and Business Administration Science,
Cag University, Adana/Mersin, Turkey
e-mail: lloydmiller01@hotmail.com

© Springer International Publishing Switzerland 2017   229
R. Benlamri, M. Sparer (eds.), *Leadership, Innovation and Entrepreneurship as Driving Forces of the Global Economy*, Springer Proceedings in Business and Economics, DOI 10.1007/978-3-319-43434-6_19

Introduction

Enterprise resource planning (ERP) systems, integrate different operational processes across an organisation, providing centralised information sharing, which could lead to increased productivity and profitability. ERP systems have arguably become essential for companies in order to gain competitive advantages, such as cost reductions, integration of operations and departments, business process improvements, and increased effectiveness and competitiveness (Vlachos, 2006). These changes may provide an organisation with valuable competitive advantages, particularly where the competition has not adopted an ERP system (Yusuf, Gunasekaran, & Abthorpe, 2004). Despite the benefits of ERP systems, implementation is known for its complexities and frequent failures.

ERP systems have changed the way many organisations function. They are developed around best business practices, and require organisations to realign their business processes around the new ERP system, which often proves challenging. These challenges are such, the literature reports that 66–70 % of ERP implementation projects in developed countries failed to achieve all of their implementation goals (Carlo, 2002; Ehie & Madsen, 2005; Lewis, 2001; Shores, 2005; Ward, Hemingway, & Daniel, 2005; Zabjek, 2009). The literature reviewed points to lack of research in the area of ERP implementation failure in developed countries generally (Akkerman & Helden, 2002; Barker & Frolick, 2003; Gargeya & Brady, 2005; Scott & Vessey, 2000). However, research on ERP implementation in developing countries, in the Middle East in particular, is severely lacking. Several factors make the Middle East a unique environment to study, the most important being Baker, Al-Gahtani, and Hubona (2007) suggestion that findings from IT implementation (such as ERP systems) in developed countries are not necessarily applicable to developing countries. Following this suggestion, this study examines a failed ERP implementation in a Middle Eastern country, in the context of the role of critical success factors. Besides addressing the gap in knowledge, this research aims to identify and analyse factors, which require consideration and careful planning to achieve successful ERP implementations.

This paper is organised as follows. First, a review of the literature on critical success factors is carried out in section "Critical Success Factors", followed by the organisation's background in section "Organisational Case Study". The decision to implement ERP system is discussed in section "ERP System Selection". ERP system implementation and challenges are presented in section "Oracle Implementation Teams". It is followed by a review of major critical factors contributing to failure in section "Implementation Failure and Lessons Learned", and explaining failure and lessons learned in section "Conclusion". Finally, some concluding thoughts are offered.

Critical Success Factors

According to Rockhart (1979), critical success factors (CSFs) are those key areas in which favourable results are absolutely necessary for a business to successfully compete. The process of identifying CSFs help to ensure those factors receive the

Table 19.1 Somers and Nelson (2001) list of CSFs

1.	Top management support	12. Dedicated resources
2.	Project team competence	13. Use of steering committee
3.	Interdepartmental cooperation	14. User training on software
4.	Clear goals and objectives	15. Education on new business processes
5.	Project management	16. BPR
6.	Interdepartmental communication	17. Minimal customisation
7.	Management of expectation	18. Architecture choices
8.	Project champion	19. Change management
9.	Vendors support	20. Partnership with vendors
10.	Careful package selection	21. Use of vendors' tool
11.	Data analysis and conversion	22. Use of consultant

necessary attention required. Bradley (2008) states that in terms of ERP implementation, CSFs are those conditions that must be met in order for the implementation process to occur successfully.

The Literature suggests that significant research in the areas of CSFs for ERP implementation is required. Indeed, Bancroft, Seip, and Sprengel (1998) identify CSFs for successful implementation as top management support, the presence of a champion, good communications with stakeholders, effective project planning, re-engineering business processes, and including a business analyst on the project team. Similarly, Bingi, Sharma, and Godla (1999) identify CSFs they consider must be understood to ensure implementation success, including top management commitment, business process reengineering, integration, ERP consultant, implementation time and cost, ERP vendors, selecting right employees, and employee morale. Following an extensive review of the literature and practitioners recommendations, Somers and Nelson (2001) present a comprehensive taxonomy of CSFs for ERP implementation (Table 19.1). Additionally, Nah, Lau, and Kuang (2001) and Delgado (2006) classify CSFs according to each implementation phase and their temporal importance across different stages of implementation. Adopting a holistic approach, Umble, Haft, and Umble (2003) identified not only CSFs, but implementation procedures critical to successful implementations.

The literature on CSFs for ERP implementation is extensive. Due to the broad nature of ERP, researchers have focussed on the different aspects of implementation. Despite the variation in the focus of researchers, there are certain CSFs that are considered common and critical; irrespective of the implementation or implementation strategies. For the purpose of this research, we have adopt Somers and Nelson (2001) list of CSFs as a reference for observing the role CSFs play in the implementation process. Although it is understandable that not all 21 CSFs will play a significant role, a comprehensive list will cover the wider spectrum of implementation, considering the lack of research in the area. While doing so, we hope to identify additional unique CSFs, according to local culture and work ethics, which may assist our further understanding of ERP implementation in developing countries.

Organisational Case Study

Alpha Corporation (Alpha Corp) is a state-owned corporation situated in the oil-rich Middle East. Established in the 1980s, Alpha Corp has diverse business interests, encompassing all aspects of the hydrocarbon industry, from onshore and offshore upstream exploration, through to production and refining, marketing, retailing, petrochemicals, and marine transportation. Alpha Corp has eight major subsidiaries and employs more than 18,000 employees. Beta Corp, a major subsidiary of Alpha Corp, is responsible for oil refining and gas liquefaction, and the marketing of petroleum products nationally through a chain of 119 filling stations. It also operates three major refineries situated across the country.

ERP System Selection

Since its inception, Beta Corp has sought to expand its core operations. Being solely responsible for the country's national petroleum sector, Beta Corp demonstrates its understanding of the need to stay abreast of new technology by constantly upgrading refinery operations. This was critical since more than two million barrels of petroleum is refined daily, involving a significant number of workers, and constant maintenance of refineries. This was achieved by the installation and implementation of a variety of stand-alone IT hardware and software information systems. However, these systems, working in silos, were unable to cope with the increasing organisational demand. As a result, the need for an advanced integrated centralised information system, capable of assimilating and coordinating diverse operations taking place at different locations soon became apparent. To overcome the absence of a decentralised information system and lack of coordination, Beta Corp undertook a review of ERP systems available on the market. Systems reviewed, included Oracle, SAP, JD Edwards, and Baan. The review identified Oracle system version 11i, as most suitable for the organisation.

Oracle is the world's second largest ERP system developer with more than 65,000 customers. It offers applications of various sizes for several industries. Oracle's core applications include customer relationship management (CRM), enterprise resource planning (ERP), financial management, human capital management, supply chain management, and transportation management. Oracle also has several enterprise software product lines, which include Oracle Fusion Applications, Oracle E-Business Suite, Peoplesoft Enterprise, and JD Edward Enterprise One.

In the next section, the Oracle implementation team is discussed. It is followed by the Oracle implementation methodology, Oracle implementation, and finally, the factors contributing to implementation failure.

Oracle Implementation Teams

Once Beta Corp management had decided on Oracle system, it engaged a well-known and respected United Kingdom (UK) consultancy firm as Project Management Office (PMO). The UK PMO team consisted of one project manager and five members with diverse implementation skills and experience to oversee the implementation. Following consultation with Beta Corp management, the (PMO) decided to implement the ERP system in three phases. Phase one, Oracle Financial Module with an HR backbone for payroll and HR administration would be implemented immediately. However, phase two, Oracle Process Manufacturing (OPM), and phase three, Oracle Time and Labour (OTL) modules implementation would follow at a later date.

Shortly after appointing the UK PMO team, Beta Corp, without consultation or explanation, appointed a second PMO team called Sigma Corp to manage the overall project, including the UK PMO. This immediately caused conflict within Beta Corp's existing IT department, which felt the decision undermined its authority, as it was responsible for new IT Implementation. The general feeling among Beta Corp's IT staff was that Sigma Corp was set up to pacify certain individuals within the organisation and to create direct competition to Beta Corp IT department. It was further observed that some staff members within Beta Corp's steering committee were unhappy with a particular member of the Sigma Corp PMO team, who whilst influential, was considered unapproachable and difficult to deal with.

As Sigma Corp had no ERP project management implementation skills or experience, in consultation with the UK PMO, it engaged the services of external consultancy firm, 'A', giving it responsibility for implementation. Because of the scope and size of the project, firm 'A' hired the services of consultancy firm 'B' to aid the implementation (Fig. 19.1).

Oracle Implementation Methodology

Oracle system uses the Oracle Application Implementation Methodology (AIM) consisting of the following seven-step procedure (Liu, Chen, & Romanowski, 2009):

1. Definition: set up the scope, target, and terminology of the project and plan the information infrastructure and technique for reaching the target.
2. Operation analysis: provide training about standard system functions for key users, analyse the demand and status quo of each division, and clarify the information flows between business operations and application systems in order to develop solution architecture.
3. Solution design: complete operation models to fulfil the organisation's demand, including business requirement mapping, gap analysis reports, start-up planning for

Fig. 19.1 Organisation
hierarchy for
implementation process

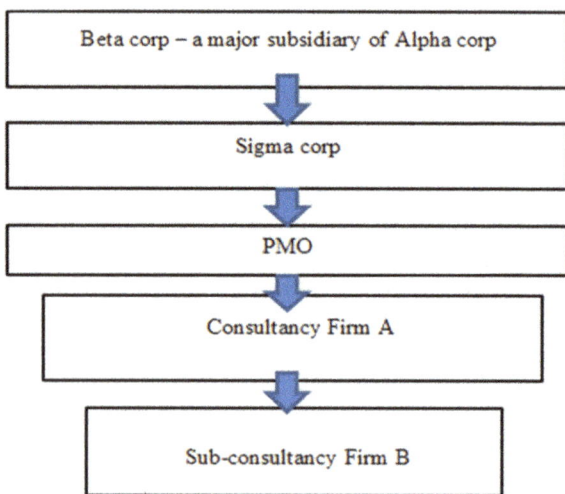

the application system, and operation process schedules; decide on interfaces for demand processing, data conversion, scope of customisation, and scheduling.

4. Build: construct test environments for checking each function and build interfaces for demand processing, data conversion, and customised modules.

5. Documentation: produce reference manuals such as system configuration setup documentation, system operation procedure manuals, and end user operation manuals to support practical applications.

6. Transit: provide end users with training, operational tests, data preparation, and system conversion in order to assist the organisation and to familiarise users with the new working environment.

7. Production: convert to use of new systems; track the performance of the new systems; initiate the follow-up programme.

Oracle Implementation

Working in conjunction with each other, consultancy firm 'A' and 'B' commenced phase one of the ERP implementation project, the Oracle Financial Module. However, due to lack of pre-planning, several major issues quickly immerged. The first relating to the development of more than 120 new integration interfaces for the new system. The high number due to integrating different systems with an older distribution and control system (DCS) for refineries. In addition, issues resulting from the number of processes to be implemented and quality of users arose. Users lacked confidence even after undergoing several training sessions. However, despite the delays caused by these issues, the Financial Module was successfully implemented.

Phase two of implementation saw firm 'A' and 'B' commence implementation of the Oracle Payroll and Oracle Process Management (OPM) modules. Implementation complexities were encountered immediately. Oracle Payroll is a complex module with several business processes, such as overtime calculations, rewards, benefits, compensation, and conditions of employment, etc. which complicated implementation. This complexity was further compounded as the consultants lacked the skills, understanding, and experience required to implement a complex system such as Oracle. In addition, as in the first phase, implementation encountered user resistance, as there was a general feeling that users did not want the system to be implemented.

Despite the known and unresolved implementation flaws in the new ERP system, the consultants, as is normal practice during any implementation, initially conducted several internal tests, which unsurprisingly, failed. Despite knowledge of this unresolved failure, the consultants invited end users to a full system testing, which was disastrous. This severely dented trust and confidence in the consultants and organisational trust in the Oracle Payroll implementation.

After several additional failed testings, and pressure from Sigma Corp, the UK PMO advised consultant firms 'A' and 'B' to find and resolve all outstanding implementation technical issues and perform rigorous inside testing before inviting users back for final testing.

Following the PMO instructions to carry out additional test runs, consultants firm 'A' and 'B' called Beta Corp managers and users to a final test run. This test run highlighted several major flaws within the system, such as system instability, absolute failure to give results, and lack of integration between different organisational functions. To overcome these issues, the consultants suggested a parallel test run. This suggestion was totally rejected by Beta Corp, who insisted on no further changes to the planned cut-off date. After several more test runs and technical changes, the consultancy firms persuaded Beta Corp to approve the system in the current form. Once the PMOs started the cut over (shut down the old system, and start to use the new system) and the payroll run, the ERP system completely failed to produce any results. As a result of the total ERP system failure, the UK PMO project manager was dismissed, and the consultants threatened with legal action.

The implementation failure negatively impacted the implementation of the next OPM module. Due to the unsavoury experience with the Payroll module, Beta Corp end users were hesitant to get involved with the implementation. They reluctantly agreed to participate in the testing, however, even though the PMO offered a smooth cut over, they totally rejected the system. The system was consequently shelved and never implemented by Beta Corp. The performance of the project consultants, and the project delays also impacted negatively on the PMO's image, as they failed to manage and complete the project as efficiently as their contracts required them to do.

In the following section, we dissect the implementation process and analyse the factors contributing towards failure.

Critical Factors Contributing to Implementation Failure

1. Organisational politics

   Organisational politics played a critical role in implementation failure. Although there was an existing IT department responsible for IT implementation, a new PMO was engaged (Sigma Corp) to manage the implementation. This undermined the role of Beta Corp's existing IT department and created animosity, with users not wholeheartedly accepting the existence of Sigma Corp. In addition, there were personality clashes between Beta Corp and Sigma Corp employees. It was also rumoured that Sigma Corp was trying to take over the IT department and wanted implementation success under its name. All these factors further complicated the implementation process.

2. Work inefficiencies

   The implementation lacked interdepartment planning and coordination. The scope of implementation required a well-planned strategy; however, no strategy was put in place. The business blueprints developed by the consultants for implementation were insufficient for the needs of a complex project. There were gaps in the implementation process, which laid the foundation for future implementation complications. Furthermore, end users had not been sufficiently involved in the project, and therefore not educated about the benefits of the new system, resulting in a lack of user motivation. Moreover, users were generally observed working to cover their backs and save their job, and not interested in the bigger goal of achieving implementation objectives.

3. Number of Interfaces

   The interface is the languages and codes the applications use to communicate with each other and the hardware. The number of interfaces can vary depending on the nature of the new and existing systems. The scope of implementation, and the presence of the other systems, including the DSC, contributed towards a higher number of interface requirement during the implementation. This created a dual impact on the implementation. First, extra resources were diverted to develop the interfaces causing severe project delays, and second, the interfaces between the different systems produced a series of difficult to resolve integration issues.

4. Lack of user's cooperation and involvement

   Due to the undefined roles of departments, user's involvement and cooperation became difficult to secure. There was a total lack of team effort. Instead, users were generally concerned with individual performance. In addition, the lack of a user education strategy contributed significantly towards user's lack of empathy towards the new system. During the system testing phase, users were initially reluctant to participate in the testing, and reluctant to offer opinions and feedback about system performance. In fact, it was observed that users were attempting to avoid using the system where possible.

5. System Selection

Implementation team members interviewed for this study expressed a complete lack of confidence in Oracle systems. According to one IT specialists, in terms of reliability and response time, Oracle is not a stable system in comparison to the other major ERP systems available on the market. Also, the Oracle methodology is weak in terms of change management, which may be the reason the implementation resulted in total chaos during implementation.

6. Lack of Change Management Strategy

Interestingly, the change management aspect of implementation was completely overlooked. No single team was responsible for the creation and implementation of a change management strategy, although this was the responsibility of Sigma Corp, as PMO. However, Sigma Corp failed to appreciate the importance of having a strategy in place, and attempted to resolve implementation issues, as they aroused. In addition, there were no provisions to retrain, motivate, recognise, and appreciate employees' efforts.

7. Business process reengineering

The common issue faced during any ERP enterprise system implementation is the incompatibility of ERP processes with organisational businesses processes. In order to fully benefit from a new system, it is essential that organisations restructure their business processes. In this case study, the implementation team failed to develop a proper and adequate realignment strategy, which led to system complexities and the need to customise the new system.

8. Customisation

ERP systems come with standard business processes derived from best business practices. It is therefore always advisable to implement ERP system in its vanilla form or with minimal customisation. There are numerous examples in the literature of failed implementations due to excessive customisation. In the case of Beta Corp, the lack of business process reengineering meant that a significant percentage of the new system had to be customised. Not only did this cause time and cost overruns, but it also undermined the basic purpose of ERP incorporating best business practices. This created further complexities for the implementation team, which also contributed towards implementation failure.

9. Selection of Consultants

The procedures for the selection of consultancy firm A and B are unclear. There appears to have been little research into the ERP implementation track record of consultancy firm A, which lacked staff with direct hands on experience in Oracle implementation, which should have been a prerequisite of the contract. The consultant's lack of implementation experience in a complex Oracle system, including testing and gaining system approval, resulted in total failure of Payroll module implementation which contributed significantly to overall project failure.

10. Project management

Interestingly, two PMOs were engaged to carry out the Oracle implementation project. A UK PMO was initially hired to oversee and manage the implementation. Later, Sigma Corp was established to act as overall PMO for implementation. Beta Corp had its own existing IT department, with responsibility for implementing new IT solutions, and whose employees did not welcome the new PMO team, as they felt it encroached on their existing IT role. This situation was further aggravated by the head of Sigma Corp, who Beta Corp's IT department considered unapproachable, autocratic, and who always wanted things to be done his way. This created circumstances where the UK PMO struggled to effectively perform its role as project manager. In addition, the UK PMO was constantly forced by Sigma Corp to get work done, using any means necessary, and was constantly scrutinised and criticised. When things went wrong, Sigma Corp would put the entire blame for failure on the contractors, despite the UK PMO only carrying out the instructions given to it by Sigma Corp. The breakdown in the relationship between Beta Corp and the UK PMO resulted in the termination of the UK PMO project manager's contract.

11. Culture

Local culture played an important role in the project failure. In the Middle East, organisations tend to be centralised, and workers tend to be individualists, with little concept of teamwork, and being able to see the bigger picture. The head of Sigma Corp was an influential person, who kept all decision-making firmly under his control. He wanted to take the credit for implementation success, but in order to do so, needed to either take control of Beta Corp IT department, or bypass it. A continuous power struggle between departments and individuals had developed, with little consideration of the impact of this on implementation.

A discussion explaining the ERP failure and lessons that could be learned is presented in the net section. While doing so, we refer to Somers and Nelson's (2001) CSFs, specifically those which are observed during the implementation and will explain them in the context of this implementation with a supporting literature review.

Implementation Failure and Lessons Learned

The Oracle ERP implementation reviewed in this study can be classified as a failure. The primary reason for ERP implementation is to take organisational efficiency to the next level, unlike the fiasco observed at Beta Corp. Whilst the major critical factors are identified in the previous section proved fatal at Beta Corp, they can be a source of guidance for future successful implementations.

1. Organisational politics

Organisational politics had a significant impact on the Oracle implementation outcome at Beta Corp. Organisational politics involves intentional acts of influence to enhance or protect the self-interest of individuals or groups (Allen,

Madison, Porter, Renwick, & Mayes, 1979; Kacmar & Ferris, 1993; Salin, 2003). Mintzberg (1985) classify organisational politics as informal, parochial, and illegitimate behaviour, which is intended to displace legitimate behaviour.

This suggests that individual's behaviour can be manipulative, subversive, and an abuse of legitimate power. The implementation process discussed above reveals such characteristics from individuals during the implementation. There are several possible negative outcomes associated with organisational politics, such as reduced organisational citizenship behaviour (Randall, Cropanzano, Bormann, & Birjulin, 1999), reduced individual and organisational performance (Vigoda, 2000), poor employee attitudes (Vigoda, 2000; Witt, Andrews, & Kacmar, 2000), negligent and aggressive behaviour (Vigoda, 2000), withdrawal behaviour (Poon, 2003; Vigoda, 2000), negative psychological states (anxiety and job stress) (Poon, 2003).

Janssens, Sels, and Van den Brande (2003) suggest that presence of organisational politics is a breach of contract, as it fails to provide the employee with a workplace climate where individuals are treated with respect, dignity, and equality. To overcome this, managers should provide employee support, not only work related but also moral. Socioeconomics rewards could also play a critical role. It is essential that employees feel that their interests are taken care of, and that they work in an environment which believes in equal opportunity without any coercion.

2. Work inefficiency

Work inefficiency could relate to the general approach to the implementation process, problem-solving, strategy formation, planning, and control. Any implementation requires extensive preparations and involves the selection of an implementation process. Since implementation in itself is complicated and costly, lack of efficient planning could further complicate the implementation process and push it over budget. In this case study, work efficiency was a by-product of several factors such as lack of understanding of business processes, inexperienced consultants, conflict of interest, lack of sense of ownership, lack of coordination, and teamwork. These factors resulted in lower morale, individualism, bottlenecks, and a lack of sense of purpose among team members which directly impact the work efficiency.

3. Developing Interfaces

Interface development is a normal but critical part of ERP implementation. An efficient way to implement ERP systems is to keep the process simple. A good implementation attempts to keep the number of interfaces to a minimum. However, due to the scope of implementation at Beta Corp, an extensive number of interfaces were required to interact with the vast IT system, resulting in major complexities. The process of developing many interfaces can be time consuming and divert financial and human resources away from other essential processes. At Beta Corp, this situation could have been substantially reduced by departments and individuals working together to develop a business processes blueprint, and based on it, attempt to create the minimal number of interfaces.

4. Lack of user's cooperation and involvement

An essential attribute for the success of any implementation requires an organisational culture which stresses the value of shared common goals and values of trust between the parties involved (Stefanou, 1999). Therefore, since ERP systems are cross-functional, the involvement and cooperation of all stakeholders is critical for success (Robinson & Dilts, 1999). If for any reason there are no shared goals during the implementation process, steps should be taken by senior management to motivate employee involvement and cooperation. This could have been achieved by educating users about the organisational and person benefits of the new systems. Users can also be encouraged by rewards and recognition.

5. System selection

System selection is one of the most critical decisions made in the planning phase. It could have far and wide repercussion and, therefore, should be made with utmost care and with complete knowledge. Janson and Subramanian (1996) suggest that choosing the right ERP system to satisfy organisational information needs is essential, as this will ensure minimal modification, and successful implementation and use. Selecting the wrong system could have dire consequences including failed implementation as discussed in this case study.

6. Change management strategy

One critical part of a change management strategy is to promote user acceptance and positive attitudes towards implementation while managing the changes brought in by a new system. Nah et al. (2001) stress the need of formally preparing a change management programme by the implementation team. This could have been achieved at Beta Corp through getting users onboard and explaining the need for the ERP system, its benefits, and how it would make their work life more efficient (Bajwa et al., 2004; Somers & Nelson, 2001). Research shows a direct correlation between an effective change management strategy and a successful implementation (Grover, Jeong, Kettinger, & Teng, 1995). The lack of a change management strategy can lead to implementation chaos, as was the case at Beta Corp. Without an appropriate change management strategy, organisations can face critical issues and may not even be able to adopt the new system.

7. Business process reengineering

Bingi et al. (1999) suggest that for an ERP system to be effective, it is essential that organisations restructure their business processes. This strategy is the critical factor behind every successful ERP implementation (Willcocks & Sykes, 2000). Lack of business process reengineering (BPR) or an alignment strategy is a commonly cited CSF for ERP implementation. Beta Corp lacked this critical success factor, which resulted in an incomplete description of how the business will operate after the package had been implemented (Bingi et al., 1999; Nah et al., 2001).

8. Customisation

The customisation aspect of ERP implementation is a widely debated issue. It refers to the customisation of a new ERP system around current business processes, instead of realigning business processes around the new system. Janson and Subramanian (1996) suggest that since customisation can lead to increased information system costs, longer implementation times, and more importantly, an inability to benefit from original systems upgrades, customisation should only be performed when it is absolutely critical. Implementing an ERP system with minimal customisation requires the support of several factors, most important of which, is primarily streamlining the operations, and reengineering the business, which will assist the organisation to operate more smoothly (Gargeya & Brady, 2005).

9. Consultants

The experience of the consultants in any implementation is a critical factor. Beta Corp failed to adequately check the experience of its contracted consultants. Welti (1999) concluded that the success of the project depends strongly on the capabilities of the consultants. They should be involved in all stages of the implementation process, such as pre-planning, planning, testing, and the performance evaluation phase. It is critical that the consultants have the knowledge and implementation experience, must work closely with users, and be willing to transfer knowledge to them. In the case of the organisation under study here, the consultants had neither the skills nor experience to undertake the project, and the project was further besieged by infighting between the project leaders and existing IT department.

10. Project Management

An efficient project management team is the backbone of a successful IT implementation. Ryan (1999) suggests the presence of hardware and software; coupled with organisational, human, and political issues, make ERP projects complex, requiring new project management skills. An individual or group of people should be given responsibility to drive success in project management (Rosario, 2000). Part of effective project management can be Scope development, establishing milestones (Holland, Light, & Gibson, 1999), establishing timeliness (Rosario, 2000), meeting deadlines (Wee, 2000), and establishing training programmes (Falkowski, Pedigo, Smith, & Swanson, 1998). Beta Corp's lack of project management vetting contributed to the project failure as it failed to ensure its projects managers had the necessary skills and experience to successfully manage the project to completion.

11. Culture

Culture refers to both country and organisational culture. Hofstede (1991) describes culture as the collective programming of minds, which distinguishes members of one human group from another, through a set of shared beliefs. Organisational culture, on the other hand, is a set of shared assumptions and understandings about organisational functioning (Deshpande & Webster, 1989). Organisational culture plays a significant role in ERP implementation success (Boersma & Kingma, 2005). Boersma and Kingma (2005) suggest that organisational culture can shape ERP technology, and in turn, this technology influences organisational culture. Similarly, several studies have highlighted the impact of country culture on ERP implementation such as in Iran (Dezdar, 2012), China and Finland (Yizi, 2007), Jordan (Hawari & Heeks, 2010), and Saudi Arabia (Saleh, Abbad, & Al-Shehri, 2013).

Conclusion

ERP implementation is a highly complex issue, requiring equally complex planning from start to finish. Although companies have been implementing ERP systems across businesses in developed countries for the last two decades, implementation is still a complex undertaking, which requires extensive planning. The results from studies on ERP implementation in developed countries have provided us with important clues about what factors can make an implementation successful or unsuccessful in those countries. The literature is, however, scant when it comes to studies on implementation in developing countries, particularly in the area of failed ERP implementations. Baker et al. (2007) does however; suggest that findings from IT implementation (such as ERP systems) in developed countries are not necessarily applicable to developing countries. This study presents a case study of a failed implementation in a Middle Eastern country.

The case study, being a government-owned organisation, had significant resources at its disposal for expenditure on the project implementation. However, lack of project, and understanding of local and organisational culture led to the project ending in total implementation failure. Other factors contributing to implementation failure include lack of a change management strategy, poor system selection, and lack of project team competencies. Critically, process realignment and culture played a major role in the failed implementation. Contrary to Baker et al. (2007) suggestion, this study identifies that factors, which contribute towards implementation failure in developing countries, are similar to factors found in developed countries.

The finding from the study could be beneficial for organisations planning to implement ERP system in both developed and developing countries. It offers guidance to factors that should be given special attention during implementation. Further, it suggests that CSFs are interrelated, such that organisational inefficiency can impact realignment strategy, which could have a negative impact on project management. Lastly, organisational culture can influence every aspect of implementation.

There are limitations to this study. First, the study focuses on a single implementation; therefore, generalisation should be drawn with caution. Second, findings from the study may not be applicable in a developed country since the availability of resources and experience of the team may widely vary. Despite these limitations, the study contributes to knowledge by providing an essential understanding of the role of critical factors during implementation in developing country and how they can influence the outcome. This study should enable practitioners to better understand how to achieve a successful implementation.

References

Akkermans, H.A. and van Helden, K. (2002) 'Vicious and virtuous cycles in ERP implementation: a case study of interrelations between critical success factors', European Journal of Information Systems, 11, 35–46.

Allen, R. W., Madison, D. L., Porter, L. W., Renwick, P. A., & Mayes, B. T. (1979). Organizational politics: Tactics and characteristics of its actors. *California Management Review, 22*(1), 77–83. Retrieved from http://dx.doi.org/10.2307/41164852.

Bajwa, D.S., Garcia, J.E. and Mooney, T. (2004) 'An integrative framework for assimilation of enterprise resources planning systems; phases, antecedents, and outcome', Journal of Computer Information Systems, 44, 81–90.

Baker, E. W., Al-Gahtani, S. S., & Hubona, G. S. (2007). The effect of gender and age on new technology implementation in a developing country: Testing the theory of planned behaviour (TPB). *Information Technology & People, 20*(4), 352–375. Retrieved from http://dx.doi.org/10.1108/09593840710839798.

Bancroft, N., Seip, H., & Sprengel, A. (1998). *Implementing SAP R/3'* (2nd ed.). Greenwich, UK: Manning Publications.

Barker, T., & Frolick, M. (2003). ERP implementation failure: A case study. *Information Systems Management, 1*, 44–49. Retrieved from http://dx.doi.org/10.1201/1078/43647.20.4.20030901/77292.7.

Bingi, P., Sharma, M. K., & Godla, J. K. (1999). Critical issues effecting an ERP implementation. *Information Systems Management, 16*(3), 7–14. Retrieved from http://dx.doi.org/10.1201/1078/43197.16.3.19990601/31310.2.

Boersma, K., & Kingma, S. (2005). Developing a cultural perspective on ERP. *Business Process Management Journal, 11*(2), 123–136. Retrieved from http://dx.doi.org/10.1108/14637150510591138.

Bradley, J. (2008). Management based critical success factors in the implementation of Enterprise Resource Planning systems. *International Journal of Accounting Information Systems, 9*, 175–200. Retrieved from http://dx.doi.org/10.1016/j.accinf.2008.04.001.

Carlo, M. (2002). Enterprise software has to fit like a good suit. *Advanced Manufacturing*. Retrieved from http://www.automationmag.com/erp-software.html

Deshpande, R., & Webster, F. E. (1989). Organizational culture and marketing—Defining the research agenda. *Journal of Marketing, 53*(1), 3–15. Retrieved from http://dx.doi.org/10.2307/1251521.

Dezdar, S. (2012). Strategic and tactical factors for successful ERP projects: Insights from an Asian country. *Management Research Review, 35*(11), 1070–1087. Retrieved from http://dx.doi.org/10.1108/01409171211276945.

Ehie, I. C., & Madsen, M. (2005). Identifying critical issues in ERP implementation. *Computer in Industry, 56*, 545–557. Retrieved from http://dx.doi.org/10.1016/j.compind.2005.02.006.

Falkowski, G., Pedigo, P., Smith, B., & Swanson, D. (1998). A recipe for ERP success. *Beyond Computing*, 44–45.

Gargeya, V., & Brady, C. (2005). Success and failure factors of adopting SAP in ERP system implementation. *Business Process Management, 11*(5), 501–516. Retrieved from http://dx.doi.org/10.1108/14637150510619858.

Grover, V., Jeong, S., Kettinger, W., & Teng, J. T. (1995). The implementation of business process reengineering. *Journal of Management Information Systems, 12*(1), 109–144. Retrieved from http://dx.doi.org/10.1080/07421222.1995.11518072.

Hawari, A., & Heeks, R. (2010). Explaining ERP failure in a developing country: A Jordanian case study. *Journal of Enterprise Information Management, 23*(2), 135–160. Retrieved from http://dx.doi.org/10.1108/17410391011019741.

Hofstede, G. (1991). *Cultures and organisations: Software of mind*. London: McGraw.

Holland, P., Light, B., & Gibson, N. (1999). A critical success factors model for enterprise resource planning implementation. In *Proceedings of the 7th European Conference on Information System* (Vol. 1, pp. 273–297).

Janson, M. A., & Subramanian, A. (1996). Packaged software: Selection and implementation policies. *INFOR, 34*(2), 133–151.

Janssens, M., Sels, L., & Van den Brande, I. (2003). Multiple types of psychological contracts: A six-cluster solution. *Human Relations, 56*(11), 1349–1378. Retrieved from http://dx.doi.org/10.1177/00187267035611004.

Kacmar, M. L., & Ferris, G. R. (1993). Politics at work: Sharpening the focus of political behavior in organizations. *Business Horizons, 36*(4), 70–74. Retrieved from http://dx.doi.org/10.1016/s0007-6813(05)80123-5.

Ladebo, O. J. (2006). Perception of organisational politics: Examination of situational antecedents and consequence among Nigeria's extension personnel. *Applied Psychology: An International Review, 55*(2), 255–281. Retrieved from http://dx.doi.org/10.1111/j.1464-0597.2006.00230.x.

Lewis, B. (2001). The 70-percent failure. *InfoWorld.* Retrieved from http://www.infoworld.com/articles/op/xml/01/10/29/011029opsurvival.html

Liu, C., Chen, L., & Romanowski, R. (2009). A electronic material flow control system for improving production efficiency in integrated-circuit assembly industry. *International Journal for Advanced Manufacturing Technologies, 42,* 348–362. Retrieved from http://dx.doi.org/10.1007/s00170-008-1603-5.

Mintzberg, H. (1985). The organization as political arena. *Journal of Management Studies, 22*(2), 133–154. Retrieved from http://dx.doi.org/10.1111/j.1467-6486.1985.tb00069.x.

Nah, G. F. H., Lau, J. L. S., & Kuang, J. (2001). Critical factors for successful integration of enterprise resource planning. *Business Process Management Journal, 7*(3), 285–296. Retrieved from http://dx.doi.org/10.1108/14637150110392782.

Nah, F.F.H. and Delgado, S. (2006) 'Critical success factors for Successful implementation of Enterprise Resources Planning Implementation and upgrade', Journal of Computer Information Systems, 47, 99–113.

Poon, J. M. L. (2003). Situational antecedents and outcomes of organizational politics perceptions. *Journal of Managerial Psychology, 18*(2), 138–155. Retrieved from http://dx.doi.org/10.1108/02683940310465036.

Randall, M. L., Cropanzano, R., Bormann, C. A., & Birjulin, A. (1999). Organizational politics and organizational support as predictors of work attitudes, job performance, and organizational citizenship behavior. *Journal of Organizational Behavior, 20*(2), 159–174. Retrieved from http://dx.doi.org/10.1002/(sici)1099-1379(199903)20:2%3C159::aid-job881%3E3.0.co;2-7.

Robinson, A. G., & Dilts, D. (1999). OR & ERP: A match for the new millennium? *OR/MS Today, 26*(3), 30–35.

Rockart, John F. (1979) 'Chief Executives Define Their Own Data Needs.' Harvard Business Review, 81–92.

Rosario, J. G. (2000). *On the leading edge: Critical success factors in ERP implementation projects.* Philippines: Business World.

Ryan, H. W. (1999). Managing development in the era of large complex systems. *Information Systems Management, 16*(2), 89–91. Retrieved from http://dx.doi.org/10.1201/1078/43188.16.2.19990301/31182.14.

Saleh, M., Abbad, M., & Al-Shehri, M. (2013). ERP implementation success factors in Saudi Arabia. *International Journal of Computer Science and Security, 7*(1), 15–30.

Salin, D. (2003). Bullying and organisational politics in competitive environment and rapidly changing work environment. *International Journal of Management and Decision, 4*(1), 35–46. Retrieved from http://dx.doi.org/10.1504/ijmdm.2003.002487.

Scott, J., & Vessey, I. (2000). Implementing enterprise resource planning system; The role of learning from failure. *Information Systems Frontiers, 2*(2), 213–232. http://dx.doi.org/10.1017/cbo9780511815072.011.

Shores, B. (2005). Failure rates in global ITS projects and the leadership challenges. *Journal of Global Information Management, 8*(3), 1–6. Retrieved from http://dx.doi.org/10.1080/1097198x.2005.10856399.

Somers, T. M., & Nelson, K. (2001). The impact of critical success factors across the stages of enterprise resource planning implementation. In *Proceeding of the 34th Annual Hawaii International Conference on System Sciences, Maui, HI*. Retrieved from http://dx.doi.org/10.1109/hicss.2001.927129

Stefanou, C. (1999). Supply chain management and organizational key factors for successful implementation of Enterprise Resource Planning (ERP) systems. In *Proceeding of the Americas Conference on Information Systems, Milwaukee, WI* (pp. 800–802).

Umble, E. J., Haft, R. R., & Umble, M. M. (2003). Enterprise resources planning implementation procedure and critical success factors. *European Journal of Operational Research, 146*(2), 241–257. Retrieved from http://dx.doi.org/10.1016/s0377-2217(02)00547-7.

Vigoda, E. (2000). Organizational politics, job attitudes, and work outcomes: Exploration and implications for the public sector. *Journal of Vocational Behavior, 57*, 326–347. Retrieved from http://dx.doi.org/10.1006/jvbe.1999.1742.

Vlachos, N. (2006). Key aspects for a successful ERP implementation Greece. In *3rd International Conference on Enterprise Systems and Accounting, Santorini Island, Greece*.

Ward, J., Hemingway, C., & Daniel, E. (2005). The framework for addressing the organisational issues of enterprise systems implementation. *Journal of Strategic Information Systems, 14*(2), 97–119. Retrieved from http://dx.doi.org/10.1016/j.jsis.2005.04.005.

Wee, S. (2000, February). Juggling toward ERP success: Keep key success factors high. *ERP News*. Retrieved from http://www.erpnews.com/erpnews/erp904/02get.html

Welti, N. (1999). *Successful SAP R/3 implementation: Practical management of ERP projects*. Harlow, England: Addison-Wesley.

Willcocks, L.P. and Sykes, R. (2000) 'The role of the CIO and IT function in ERP', Communication of the ACM, 43, 32–38.

Witt, L. A., Andrews, M. C., & Kacmar, M. (2000). The role of participation in decision-making in the organizational politics—job satisfaction relationship. *Human Relations, 53*, 341–358. Retrieved from http://dx.doi.org/10.1177/0018726700533003.

Yizi. H. (2007) 'A comparative study of critical success Factors for ERP system implementation in China and Finland.' Swedish School of Economics and Business Administration.

Yusuf, Y., Gunasekaran, A., & Abthorpe, M. S. (2004). Enterprise information systems project implementation: A case study of ERP in Rolls-Royce. *International Journal of Production Economics, 87*, 251–266.

Zabjeck, D., Kovacic, A. and Stemberger, M.I. (2009) 'The influence of business process management and some other CSFs on successful ERP implementation', Business Process Management Journal, 15(4), 588–608.

Chapter 20
Embracing Off-Grid Communities in Rural Bangladesh to Promote Sustainable Living

Muhammad Hassan Bin Afzal

Abstract The term "off-grid community" specifically defines certain clusters of people, and their main electrical supply line is not connected with any available national grid line for electricity needs in everyday life. Rather, these people fulfill their electricity needs from a small to medium-scale, self-sustained off-grid energy system (OGES). This choice of embracing OGES can be out of extreme necessity or voluntary. This paper primarily focuses on the feasibility of implementing off-grid energy system to support the rural communities in Bangladesh. It also focuses on the cost-benefit analysis in embracing the off-grid energy system in the longer run. A dedicated section highlights the SWOT analysis and STP analysis of installing and implementing self-sustained OGES. Finally, this paper recommends different yet appropriate types of OGES for various remote rural locations in Bangladesh for sustainable and environment-friendly electricity generation and supply.

Keywords Off-Grid communities • Sustainable living

Introduction

The term "off-grid community" specifically defines certain clusters of people, and their main electrical supply line is not connected with any available national grid line for electricity needs in everyday life. This choice can be voluntary or may be measured. For example, in the case of two most populous countries in the world such as India and China, still good amount of rural people are not connected to national grid electricity line due to remoteness and other relevant issues. So their source of light is candles and/or kerosene hurricane lanterns. On the other hand, a group of people may be decided to live off the grid and design their own resources to obtain electricity. The best example can be the off-grid communities in Canada;

M.H.B. Afzal (✉)
Electrical and Electronic Engineering Department, Primeasia University, Dhaka, Bangladesh

Faculty of Business Studies (FBS), University of Dhaka (DU), Dhaka, Bangladesh
e-mail: hasssans@ieee.org

© Springer International Publishing Switzerland 2017
R. Benlamri, M. Sparer (eds.), *Leadership, Innovation and Entrepreneurship as Driving Forces of the Global Economy*, Springer Proceedings in Business and Economics, DOI 10.1007/978-3-319-43434-6_20

these communities are not connected to any sort of national grid line and draw their electrical needs by using mostly diesel generators (Rezaei, 2015). Apart from diesel generators, there are three types of off-grid power supplies such as individual off- grid system, battery based off-grid system, and battery-less off-grid systems.

There are both substantial advantages and disadvantages of living in off-grid communities. If it is by choice then there is huge cost associated with this preferred lifestyle, such as buying lands near to water source, electricity production, food, and maintenance. In contrast, the poor and disadvantaged rural people in remote places, uses alternate resources due to inaccessibility of electricity. Also the Amish people in Pennsylvania do not use any electrical resources at all, and it is their choice (Afzal et al., 2014a; Scott, 2012). In modern day off-grid communities, most of them use diesel generator and solar power energy to fulfill their energy needs. Both of these choices are very expensive. Whereas diesel-powered generator leaves an utterly undesirable negative impact on the surrounding environment, transportation of diesel into remote off-grid communities is another major concern because of possible spillage which would badly affect the local vicinity.

This paper primarily focuses on the feasibility of implementing off-grid energy system to support the rural communities in Bangladesh. It also focuses on the cost-benefit analysis in embracing the off-grid energy system (OGES) in the longer run. A dedicated section highlights the SWOT analysis and STP analysis of installing and implementing self-sustained OGES. Finally, this paper recommends different yet appropriate types of OGES for various remote rural locations in Bangladesh for sustainable and environment-friendly electricity generation and supply.

Off-Grid Energy and Bangladesh

Bangladesh is one of the most populous countries in the world with such small total area. The economy of Bangladesh largely depends on agriculture, and most of the rural people are directly involved in harvesting various seasonal crops. Unfortunately large segments of these rural disadvantaged farmers are deprived of national grid electricity supply. This causes enormous challenges in the process of obtaining economic growth in the longer run. Although, the local government and authority took several effective steps to appropriately distribute electricity among the rural people and communities in Bangladesh, still the source and produced electricity deemed insufficient to serve the mass rural community in Bangladesh. Basically there are three key options to provide electricity to remote and rural places in Bangladesh. These options are:

1. Extending the national grid line
2. Creating alternative grid line
3. Provide diesel generators

According to the present available data, almost 62 % of the total population of Bangladesh is currently connected to electricity line, and more than 80 % of this

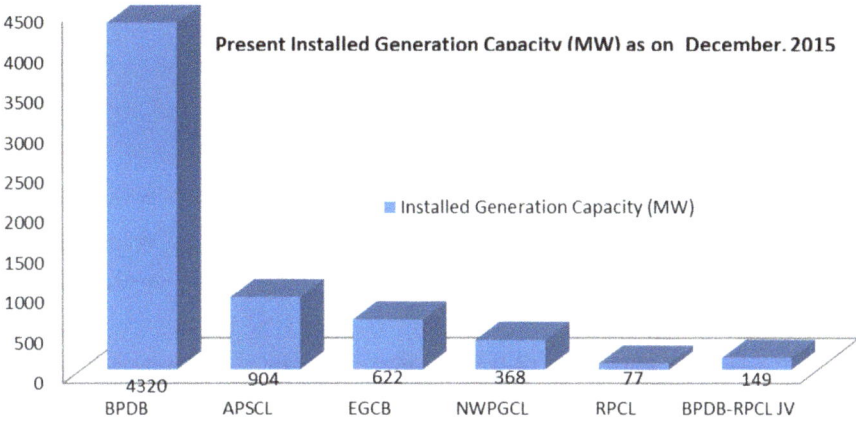

Fig. 20.1 Generated electricity in Bangladesh (public sector), Dec 2015

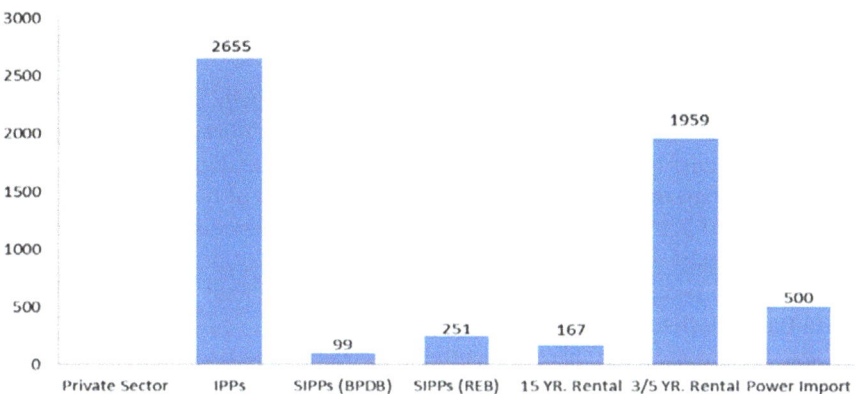

Fig. 20.2 Generated electricity in Bangladesh (private sector), Dec 2015

population is urban users. This statistics so vividly represents the inequality in distributing electricity among both rural and urban population of Bangladesh. In order to solve this problem with a sustainable approach, this is the high time to adopt the innovative approach such as developing an off-grid mini grid in remote places and provide electricity to rural communities in Bangladesh.

In Fig. 20.1 it can be clearly observed that currently the public sector in Bangladesh produces approximately 54 % total electricity for the total population. This data is taken from the data available in BPDB year-end report (Bangladesh Power Development Board, 2016). Furthermore, the rest of the MW of electricity is acquired from the private sector. Figure 20.2 shows the sources of the produced electricity from private sector, which is around 46 % of total produced electricity in Bangladesh.

According to a recent study conducted by Alliance for Rural Electrification, to extend the national grid in remote and rural places in Bangladesh is quite

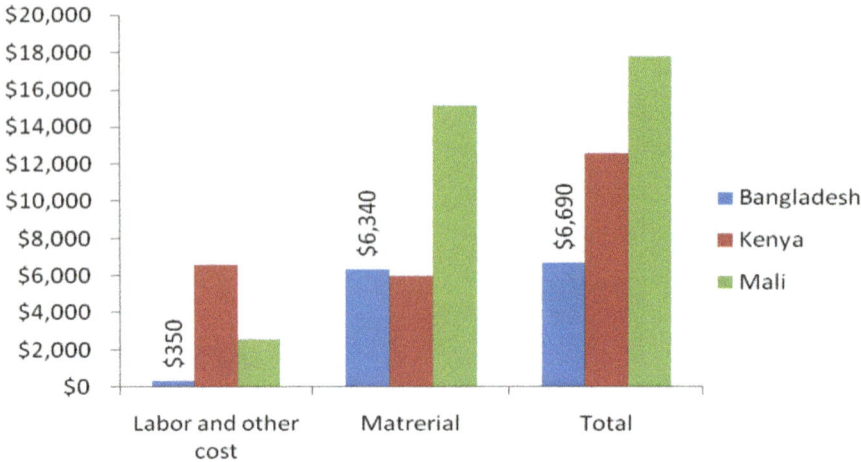

Fig. 20.3 Comparative cost analysis of extending national grid

cheap compared to some developing countries located both in South Asia and Africa (Bangladesh Power Development Board, 2016). The following diagram aptly represents the cost-benefit analysis of extending the national grid in Bangladesh compared to some developing countries in different parts of the world.

From Fig. 20.3 it is clearly demonstrated that cost of extending national grid in Bangladesh is quite affordable due to low labor cost and relevant material availability. Still, due to certain unavoidable reasons, it is fairly difficult to extend national grid in Bangladesh to support the rural population in obtaining electricity.

These reasons are stated here sequentially, such as:

1. Impractical promises made by political leaders
2. Sheer difficulty in obtaining grant funding from both local and international donors
3. Unable to create appropriate awareness among rural population to build mini grids
4. Inadequate resources study to build and operate a grid energy system

Living in Off-Grid Community: Challenges and Opportunities

There are both substantial advantages and disadvantages of living in off-grid communities. If it is by choice, then there is huge cost associated with this preferred lifestyle, such as buying lands near to water source, electricity production, food, and maintenance. In contrast, the poor and disadvantaged rural people in remote places use alternate resources due to inaccessibility of electricity. Also the Amish

Fig. 20.4 SWOT analysis of living in off-grid communities

people in Pennsylvania do not use any electrical resources at all, and it is their choice (Afzal et al., 2014a; Bangladesh Power Development Board, 2016; Kraybill, 2003; Scott, 2012).

In modern day off-grid communities, most of them use diesel generator and solar power energy to fulfill their energy needs. Both of these choices are very expensive. Whereas diesel-powered generator leaves utterly undesirable negative impact on the surrounding environment, transportation of diesel into remote off-grid communities is another major concern because of possible spillage which would badly affect the local vicinity.

Based on the Fig. 20.4 SWOT analysis, it is clearly visible that although off-grid communities seem more interesting and environmental friendly, still there are important issues to be taken care of before adopting it in full fledge. One of the major concerns is initial installation cost which is extremely high. Normal people would rather choose to use national grid electricity rather than adopting off-grid technology. The second concern is high consumption of fuels, specifically diesel, which results not only bad environmental effects but also creates huge scarcity of diesel for future generation. Adopting wind, water, and solar energy is much more environmental friendly, but the initial installation cost is abruptly high and requires a huge location. Also by transforming occupied available natural water resources into hydropower might result in water shortage for a local community.

Scope and Opportunities of Implementing Off-Grid Energy Systems in Bangladesh

Most of the rural population in Bangladesh is involved in farming activities as a main source of income, which is why biogas-based, off-grid mini-energy grid is the most suitable option for producing and distributing electricity. Basically both rice straw and rice husk. Both of these crop-waste elements are abundantly available in rural and remote areas of Bangladesh due to huge cultivation of rice. Albeit, both of these rice-waste products are currently used in various other purposes such as animal food and generating fire for cooking and other various purposes. The specific target is to produce off-grid, sustainable, and cost-effective energy-producing plant in remote places in Bangladesh to produce and provide electricity to rural people in Bangladesh. In order to achieve such target, application of clean energy as input in biogas plant is extremely essential, this also ensures not to impact both the environment and surrounding in any negative manner. In order to assess the importance of using clean energy to produce electricity in remote and rural areas in Bangladesh, a detailed action plan is being conducted.

Table 20.1 depicts few basic pointers on embracing sustainable off-grid communities for the future generation. One thing is certain; to build a sustainable off-grid community for the future, finding a clean, alternative, and natural energy source is highly anticipated. Because it is still in the sophomoric stage, which definitely requires further thorough research to find a better and cost-effective solution in producing electricity from natural resources without affecting the environment, both western and eastern societies are contemplating with the idea of adopting off-grid community concept to conserve energy, and this could be hugely beneficial for the future generation. But it is highly obligatory to make sure that further research, policy implementation, and specific set of rules and regulation have already been introduced while adopting the off-grid community, so that it will not cause any sort of negative impact on the surroundings but rather makes a sustainable and healthy living lifestyle choice for humanity (Gunaratne, 2002; Khandker et al., 2014; Ullah, Hoque, & Hasib, 2012). Both government agencies and policy makers are required to work together to ensure a globalized energy sustainability and healthy off-grid community access for human beings.

Table 20.1 Actions to take and/or actions to avoid in adopting off-grid community system

Immediate action required	Highly suggested for better outcome	Things to avoid completely
To find an alternative and sustainable renewable energy option to replace diesel generator	Appropriate fund management in reducing the high initial installation cost for off-grid community	Diesel-based generators results in carbon emission, leakage, spillage, and causes negative environmental effects
Identify suitable locations in earth which is geographically more appropriate and suitable to produce off-grid energy (such as wind, water, solar)	To ensure availability and accessibility to these off-grid communities for common people	Mismanagement of unused remaining energy

Table 20.2 Comparative analysis of rice-waste usage in generating electricity

	Transition ratio from 1 ton (970.18 kg) rice paddy	
Type of resources	Rice straw	Rice husk
Quantity	290 kg	220 kg
Moisture content	Negligible	5–12%
Possibility of generating power	100 kWh of power	93–129 kWh of power

Result and Analysis

Based on extensive amount of agricultural activities being taken in rural places in Bangladesh, both rice straws and rice husk are best options as clean energy resources to produce electricity in remote places in Bangladesh. Now, the next steps are to conduct the feasibility study into those places (Afzal et al., 2014b; Zafar, 2015). Possible electricity can be produced using both rice straws and rice husks as shown in Table 20.2.

Based on the findings above, it is clearly demonstrated that rice husk got the high potential to produce electricity compared to rice straw. The western and modernized countries already applied this technique to produce electricity from the rice industry wastage. Unfortunately the developing countries are still lacking in taking effective steps to utilize appropriately the rice wastage to produce electricity. But Bangladesh still got the huge potential to utilize both rice straws and rice husk to produce electricity and serve the rural and remote population located in various locations. In order to achieve this target, three effective steps are urgently required. These steps are:

- **Segmentation**—Locate, identify, and pinpoint the remote areas without electricity.
- **Targeting**—Appropriately target the donor/funding party to develop a sustainable hybrid clean energy-based technology to generate electricity and serve the people.
- **Positioning**—Strategic locations to be identified and finalized to implement a hybrid power plant to serve the rural community without electricity.

Conclusions

This study specifically focuses on the imminent problem of not having electricity in remote places in Bangladesh which negatively affects the further effective progress of Bangladesh. An in-depth feasibility should be immediately conducted with the approval of government authority to address this problem, and further action plans should be taken to integrate foreign donors and grant teams to support the rural electrification project. As discussed before, it would be quite illogical to extend the national grid to certain locations in Bangladesh due to various practical reasons. Instead, if it is possible to adopt off-grid energy system which can serve the surrounding communities in a sustainable way, then it would create a much more positive impact on the development on the remote and rural community development. Further extensive investigative research should immediately take place to find feasible and sustainable solutions to adopt the clean energy off-grid energy system which can serve the people without creating any adverse impact on the surrounding environment.

References

Afzal, M. H. B., & Bhuiyan, M. (2014a). *Sustainable trend analysis of annual divisional rainfall in Bangladesh*. In ISFRAM 2014 (pp. 257–270). doi:10.1007/978-981-287-365-1_21

Afzal, M. H. B. (2014b). Large scale IT projects: Study and analysis of failures and winning factors. *IETE Technical Review, 31*(3), 214–219. doi:10.1080/02564602.2014.906862

Bangladesh Power Development Board. (2016). *Key statistics*. Dhaka: Bangladesh Power Development Board. Retrieved January 3, 2016.

Gunaratne, L. (2002, May). *Rural energy services best practices* (Revised). United States Agency for International Development Under South Asia Regional Initiative for Energy.

Khandker, S. R., Samad, H. A., Sadeque, Z. K. M., Asaduzzaman, M., Yunus, M., & Haque, A. K. E. (2014). Surge in solar-powered homes experience in off-grid rural Bangladesh. In *2014 International Bank for Reconstruction and Development/The World Bank 1818 H Street NW, Washington DC 20433*.

Kraybill, D. B. (2003). *Who are the Anabaptist? Amish, Brethren, Hutterites and Mennonites*. Scottdale: Herald Press.

Rezaei, M. (2015). Off-grid: Community energy and the pursuit of self-sufficiency in British Columbia's remote and First Nations communities. *Local Environment*.

Scott, S. E. (2012). The Amish way of life in modern American Society. *Senri Ethnological Studies, 79*, 33–48.

Ullah, M. H., Hoque, T., & Hasib, M. M. (2012). Current status of renewable energy sector in Bangladesh and a proposed grid connected hybrid renewable energy system. *International Journal of Advanced Renewable Energy Research, 1*(11), 618–627.

Zafar, S. (2015, November 25). Biomass resources from rice industry. *Bioenergy Consult*.

Chapter 21
The Role of Organisational Commitment, Leadership Style, Strategic Human Resources Practices and Job Satisfaction Towards Sustainable Tourism Industry: Comparative Study in the UAE and Malaysia

Zainal Abu Zarim, Osman Mohamad, Muhammad Sabbir Rahman, Hafizah Omar Zaki, Rommel Pilapil Sergio, and Diana J. Haladay

Abstract The role of organisational commitment, leadership and strategic human resources practices towards developing a sustainable tourism industry has received limited attention under multi-country perspective. The aim of this research project is to concentrate on testing hypothesis derived from theories presented by leading scholars regarding the potential impact of organisational commitment, leadership style, strategic human resources practices and job satisfaction towards developing sustainable tourism industry, using cross-sectional data from the UAE and Malaysia. The research is empirically motivated where the survey is to be conducted among managers and employees from different tourism service providers in the UAE and Malaysia. Convenience sampling and a survey of questionnaires have been utilised in both countries. Although several assumptions and judgements have been tested regarding the foundation of sustainable tourism, there were still very few empirical research gaps on the comparative study with regard to strategic human resources aspects in preparing a sustainable tourism industry. The research findings showed that there is a positive and significant relationship between the independent variables, such as organisational commitment, leadership style, strategic human resources practices and job satisfaction with the dependent variable, sustainable tourism in both countries. The findings also revealed the antecedents of creating

Z.A. Zarim (✉) • O. Mohamad • H.O. Zaki
Multimedia University, Cyberjaya, Selangor, Malaysia
e-mail: azzainal@mmu.edu.my

M.S. Rahman
International Islamic University, Kuala Lumpur, Selangor, Malaysia

R.P. Sergio • D.J. Haladay
Canadian University of Dubai, Dubai, United Arab Emirates

© Springer International Publishing Switzerland 2017
R. Benlamri, M. Sparer (eds.), *Leadership, Innovation and Entrepreneurship as Driving Forces of the Global Economy*, Springer Proceedings in Business and Economics, DOI 10.1007/978-3-319-43434-6_21

255

sustainable tourism industry by concentrating on human resources practices which is deemed to contribute to the UAE and Malaysian tourism industry. This explains the necessity for intra-country cooperation (between the UAE and Malaysia) for the preparation of a favourable environment and mobilisation of strategic human resources for sustainable tourism growth.

Keywords Organisational commitment • Leadership style • Strategic human resources practices • Job satisfaction and sustainable tourism industry

Introduction

The wave of globalisation is significantly affecting the interrelated concerned parties of hospitality, travel and tourism. Globally, tourism is regarded to be the fastest growing industry (WTO, 2003). In the 1960s, the UAE described as 'barren coastlands largely populated by nomadic tribes where the only occupations are fishing and pearling' (Henderson, 2006). Dubai was that time treated as unitary of the least developed nation in the world (Sharpley, 2008). Under the leadership of Sheikh Rashid Bin Saeed Al Maktoum transformed Dubai from a 'barren coastland' into the 'dream world of conspicuous consumption' (Sharpley, 2008). The government of the UAE puts tourism at the core of its economic prosperity by diversifying and strengthening its economy, while reducing its dependency on oil (Sharpley, 2008). The policy of developing sustainable tourism industry is ideally suited because of its strategic location at the 'confluence of the Middle East, Asia, Western Africa, and Central/Eastern Europe' (Balakrishnan, 2009). For this consequence, tourism is identified as a feasible economic development alternative, and Sheikh Mohammed Bin Rashid Al Maktoum sets a strategic vision for the emirate: 'tourism would act as a catalyst for foreign direct investment and wider business development, rather than just establishing a tourism industry' (Sharpley, 2008).

On the other hand, in Malaysia, the momentum for tourism development began in the 1970s, after the 1972 Conference of the Pacific Areas Travel Association (PATA) in Kuala Lumpur. Following that event, the government granted more recognition to the tourism industry by creating the Tourism Development Corporation (TDC) in 1972 and continued with the completion of the National Tourism Master Plan in 1975 (Sirat, 1993). Marzuki, Jantan, and Mohamed (2008), argued that to expand and diversify the Malaysian economy, tourism can play an important role which ultimately reduces the country's dependency on a narrow range of activities and markets. The Eighth Malaysia Plan (2001–2005) was formed for strategies and policies of tourism development aimed to achieve sustainable growth of this sector by balancing between environment, economy, social and cultural issues in all tourism activities, and planning where priority is also given to improve human resource development and developing strategic alliances and international cooperation. Subsequently, the Ninth Malaysia Plan (2006–2010) also stressed the significance of sustainable tourism development. The plan actually more focused on tourism services development and human resources improvement. Grounded on the above discussion, we can explain that the tourism industry in both countries requires a drive force with an evolving hospitality skills set that conforms to international demand associated with high-end leisure products in order to safeguard its competitiveness.

As a consequence, the number of researchers focusing on human resources in the context of the sustainable hospitality, travel and tourism industry increases (Gannon & Johnson, 1997). Obviously, wide ranges of human resource scope (organisational commitment, leadership style, human resources practices and job satisfaction) are significantly at present to hospitality, travel and tourism organisations. Keep and Mayhew (1999) highlighted the issues of HRM in the tourism industry, which suggested a number of issues, including low wages, inadequate or nonexistent career structures, lack of evidence of good HRM practices, high degrees of labour turnover, difficulties in recruitment and retention of employees. Understanding this reality of underprivileged employment practices, Riley and Love (2000) believed that macroeconomics factors are the central deciding factor for HRM practices in tourism and hospitality. Further, scarcity exists in the texts published to date that compare the mainstream of human resource theory and its practices with the context of hospitality, travel and tourism between the UAE and Malaysia. It is obvious that to offer high-quality services to the tourists' managers of tourism industry face real challenges in recruiting, training and sustaining a committed, competent and well-motivated workforce. This inquiry tries to address some of the central strategic human resource (HR) issues that may act as a significant part in order to achieve sustainable tourism. To act thus this research will critically look back some of the antecedents which lead to sustainable tourism in both countries' perspectives (the UAE and Malaysia). In performing so, good practices of each state will be chewed over so that the benchmark can easily be managed by other counterparts. This inquiry is particularly important because we believe that organisational commitment, leadership style, strategic human resources practices and job satisfaction play a significant function in the growth and endurance of the tourism industry.

Above all the comparison functions to spotlight the differences characterising in overall organisational behavioural and human resources issues in the tourism sector between the two countries (the UAE and Malaysia). Although the geographical spaces in between these two countries are far, yet though the findings obviously display some similarity and significant differences in HRM practices in the tourism sector. These disputes are currently poorly understood and under researched; this inquiry is thus significant for its supply of new empirical data, especially with reference to organisational commitment, leadership style, strategic human resources and job satisfaction.

Literature Review

Wright and McMahan (1992) define strategic human resource management (SHRM) as the process of planned human resource deployment and activities that aims to enable the enterprise to reach its end. Wright (1998) also implies that SHRM is a procedure where the deployment of human resources provides a firm to acquire competitive advantage. The characteristics of SHRM can be described into two categories, namely horizontal fit and vertical fit. Horizontal fit involves practising human resources through an appropriate alignment with one another's activity, for instance, employees, recruitment, selection and training, while vertical fit is concerned about the alignment between a company's HRM practice and its business strategy (Delery, 1998; Schuler & Jackson, 1987). The nature of the sector is changing with different demands of tourism segments with demanding various information on destinations and new merchandise. These challenges claim for a new approach to be taken by the managers in their human resources management. This could be categorised into three central ideas: (1) continuous change and invention, (2) continuous enrichment of the human capital, and (3) development of multidisciplinary teams (Costa, 2004).

Hall and Jenkins (2004) outline a range of human resources practices which is identified as important elements to develop organisational strategies aimed at securing high-tone services. These are recruitment and selection, retention, teamwork, training and development, appraisal, rewarding, job security, employee involvement and employee relations. To satisfy the employees, the major challenges of a manager are to retain the employees which will finally raise the organisational capabilities to back up its competitiveness in the market (Barney, 1991; Sinangil, 2004; Stonich, 1998). That is why firms need to merge with the leadership styles and cultures within an organisation human resource practices (Lok & Crawford, 1999; Sheridan, 1992).

According to Porter, Steers, Mowday, and Boulian (1974), commitment is accepting and realising the organisational aims and the willingness to lick with the commitment being an organisational member. Researchers have already found a firm link between organisational commitment and strategic human resources practices which will ultimately enhance individual skills, motivation and empowerment attitudes towards the organisation (D'Cruz & Noronha, 2011). In fact, several scholars also agreed that organisational commitment and strategic human resource practices are a source of sustainability of an organisation (Becker & Gerhart, 1996; Pfeffer, 1994).

In addition, De Cieri and Kramar (2008) initiate the measurement of human resources practices, for instance, job analysis or design, recruitment and selection, training and development, operation management, pay structure, incentive, benefits, employee retention and employee relations. Job satisfaction refers to 'the attitudes and impressions people have about their work' (Armstrong, 2003). Greenberg and Baron (1995) discuss that job satisfaction is an individual's cognitive, emotive and evaluative approach to the business. Together with Locke (1976), they contend that job satisfaction is predominantly linked to the organisational capacity of achieving its demands. So far, previous empirical research supported that the strategic human resource practices directly influence on the job satisfaction of employees (Ogilvie, 1986; Wimalasiri, 1995). Furthermore, the link between commitment and job satisfaction has also been proven by previous researchers (Achoui & Mansour, 2007; Becker & Billings, 1993; Williams & Hazer, 1986).

The character of leadership has become critical in the carrying out of strategic human resource practices, especially in an environment that is continually changing (Cope & Waddell, 2001). Withal, the attitudes and expectations of leaders may impact on the enthusiasm of the workers (Lok & Crawford, 1999). On the other hand, Robbins and Coulter (2008) identify the function of cultural norms which defined as a circle of shared beliefs between members of an organisation may dominate in between leadership style and strategic human resource practices (Kerr & Slocum, 2005; Kopelman, Brief, & Guzzo, 1990; Scott-Findlay & Estabrooks, 2006).

Conceptual Framework

The research begins by developing theoretical framework that establishes the link between organisational commitment, leadership style, strategic human resources practices and job satisfaction towards building sustainable tourism industry. The conceptual framework of the study as shown in Fig. 21.1 emphasises the variables—organisational commitment, leadership style, strategic human resources practices, job satisfaction and sustainable tourism. By assumption, the variables, for instance, organisational commitment, leadership style, strategic human resources practices and job satisfaction, are positively linked to sustainable tourism.

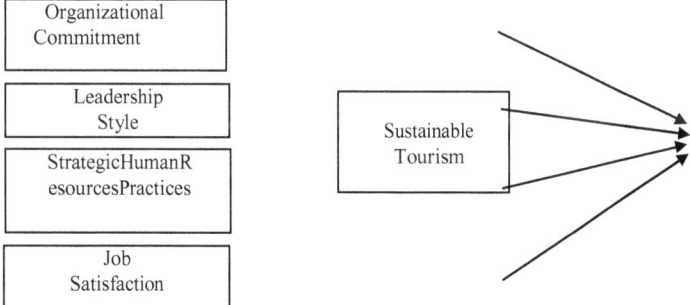

Fig. 21.1 Conceptual framework of the study

Research Question and Objectives

Based on the conceptual framework, the research questions are as follows:

(a) How will organisational commitment, leadership style, strategic human resources practices and job satisfaction impact on the development of sustainable tourism industry?
(b) Is there any significant difference between organisational commitment, leadership style, strategic human resources practices and job satisfaction with sustainable tourism between the UAE and Malaysia?

This research also looks at the following objectives:

(a) To determine to what extent of impact exist among organisation commitment, leadership style, strategic human resources and job satisfaction towards building sustainable tourism industry.
(b) To explore the direct impact and effects of all variables on tourism industry for both countries, the UAE and Malaysia.

There are five hypotheses that have been identified and tested in this study:

H1: Organisational commitment is significantly correlated to sustainable tourism.
H2: The leadership style is significantly correlated to sustainable tourism.
H3: Strategic human resources practices are significantly correlated to sustainable tourism.
H4: Job satisfaction is significantly correlated to sustainable tourism.
H5: Sustainable tourism is significantly correlated to organisational commitment, leadership style, strategic human resource practices and job satisfaction.

Methodology

The study has targeted a total of 600 samples for data collection purposes. Questionnaires were used as a medium/tool for data collection and have been distributed to employees at the tourism industries in the UAE and Malaysia. Each country was, respectively, given 300 samples for distribution. The study is an application-based study which runs on a quantitative method of research. In this sense, data collection derived from primary data which is the questionnaire and from all secondary sources such as websites, articles and reports. The convenience-sampling method was used for the questionnaires distribution to the employees who are currently working in various tourist organisations in Malaysia and the UAE.

Information are gathered using the firms intercept procedure. Specifically, the questionnaire for this discipline answered a number of functions by translating research objectives into a series of motions. Firstly, the motions and response formats have been standardised where all respondents faced the same stimuli. The questionnaire has been planned in a manner to provide comprehensible questions to prompt respondents to corporate and complete accurately all the questions asked. It is also to facilitate and simplify the analysis of the data as most of the questions are precoded or have used a standardised response format. The queries are going to be taken in such a manner as to make responses easy to drop a line and allow clear statistical assessment to be done. Secondly, the sampling process of this research required a pick of a sufficient number of constituents from the population at least 300, and based on the information gathered from a subset, an inference of the characteristics of the entire population could be drawn.

In this inquiry, the Likert scales are used in the questionnaire. Indeed respondents completing the questionnaires in this research are allowed to put their answer anywhere on the Likert scale. More importantly, five-point Likert scale with all points labelled are used for the collection of most of the data as this type of scale is widely applied by marketing and management researchers which allow for a stage of intensity and feelings to be conveyed. In brief, care will be required in constructing measurement and scaling routines for the questionnaire design process in this inquiry.

The data analysis part has been conducted through the use of SPSS. All the independent variables and dependent variable were used as the main predictors in the analysis of descriptive statistics, correlation matrix, Kaiser-Meyer-Olkin (KMO) and Bartlett's test, communalities, as well as coefficient and regression. The output has highlighted the relationships and the significant acceptance of variable used in the study.

Findings and Discussion

Demographic Analysis

The study has been initiated by engaging several demographic elements such as age, gender, qualification, experience, position, status and nationality. Quantitatively, the frequencies of these data (demographic data) from both countries, Malaysia and the UAE, are valid as there is no missing data from the total sample of 300 distributed questionnaires.

About 30% of the respondents in Malaysia are aged 30–34, 13 % aged 20–24 and 9 % aged above 40, while others from ages 25–29 to 35–39 remain constant at 24 %. This has somehow indicated that (refer to Fig. 21.2) much of the employees working for a tourism industry are those of the generation Y age ranging from 25 to 34. Whereas in the UAE, those age ranging from 30 to 34 at 30 % and 35–39 at 29 %

Fig. 21.2 Pie chart depicting age of the respondents in Malaysia and the UAE (Dubai) tourism industry

Age	Malaysia (%)	Dubai (%)
20 – 24	13	19
25 – 29	24	13
30 – 34	30	30
35 – 39	24	29
> 40	9	9

Gender	Malaysia (%)	Dubai (%)
Male	49	68
Female	51	32

Fig. 21.3 Pie chart depicting gender of the respondents in Malaysia and the UAE (Dubai) tourism industry

Table 21.1 Demographic frequencies of respondents from Malaysia and the UAE

Malaysia		UAE (Dubai)
Qualification	Most are bachelor degree holders	Most are diploma holders
Experience	Most has served for 1–2 and 7–8 years	Most has served more than 10 years
Position	Most are administrator and tour guide	Most are administrator and others
Marital status	Most are married and single	Most are married
Nationality	100 % are Malaysian	Most of them are locals and internationals

were seemed as the highest age range working for the tourism industry. Hence, this has indicated that the tourism industry in the UAE employs more of the later stage of the generation Y. Although this is part of the study, differences in ageing do not affect the sustainability of the tourism industry in both countries.

Consistently in Fig. 21.3, gender has played an important role to this study. In Malaysia itself, the respondents between male and female do not differ much. 51 % of the respondents are female, and 49 % are male. This has resulted in almost balance work acceptance. The study can conclude that in Malaysia's tourism industry there is no gender bias or discrimination. While in the UAE, only 32 % of the female respondents are female, and 68 % more are male. This had indicated that the tourism industry in the UAE welcomes more male rather than female employees. However, these results cannot be made into a direct or final judgement of a tourism industry's sustainability. It might be the cause of culture and diversity differences (Table 21.1).

With regards to qualification, the respondents from Malaysia are mostly degree holders at 47 % with a small group of masters' degree holders at 2.3 %. While in the UAE, most of the respondents are those with diploma at 56 % and with the least of 1 % of degree holder. The huge gap of qualification of respondents in both countries might be due to the level of work requirements and other needs. In line with this, experience is taken into great importance. In Malaysia, most of the respondents working for or in the tourism industry have more or less 1–8 years of working experiences. Whereas in the UAE, the respondents have more than 10 years of working experience.

In this light, 68 % of the respondents working in various tourism companies in Malaysia are administrators and tour guides. Hence in the UAE, tour guide constitutes 6.3 % where 47 % falls into others or random work task in the tourism company. Much of the respondents from Malaysia are both male and female where male constitutes 51 % and female 49 %. In the UAE, most of the respondents are male with 68 % and female with 32 %. The study has ended the demographic part with question on nationality deriving from both countries. The respondents from Malaysia are 100 % Malaysian citizens. While in the UAE, about 10.3 % respondents are Malaysian, and 82.7 % are inclusive of local Arabs and internationals.

Research Findings

Looking at the mean in Table 21.2, it can be seen that job satisfaction has the highest mean followed by leadership style with 3.76. Therefore, it can be concluded that job satisfaction and leadership style are the most important variables that can influence the sustainability of a tourism industry in Malaysia.

While in the UAE, it can be seen that leadership style with 4.42 and strategic human resource practices with 4.41 have the highest mean. Therefore, it can be concluded that leadership style and strategic human resource practices are the most important variables that can influence the sustainability of a tourism industry in Dubai.

For Malaysia and the UAE, the correlation coefficient output has the same result. Table 21.3 shows that there is a correlation between all the variables, organisational commitment, leadership style, strategic human resource practices, job satisfaction and sustainability, which can be identified through the correlation coefficient of 1.0. Other than that, all variables have also more than 0.21 level of correlation coefficient which can be deemed as statistically significant with each other.

The KMO measures the sampling adequacy which should be greater than 0.5 for a satisfactory analysis to proceed. Kaiser (1974) recommend 0.5 as minimum values between 0.7 and 0.8 as acceptable and values above 0.9 as superb. Therefore, based

Table 21.2 Descriptive statistics

Malaysia	Mean	Std. deviation	N
Organisational commitment	3.73	.45	300
Leadership style	3.76	.50	300
Human resource	3.71	.44	300
Job satisfaction	3.78	.48	300
Sustainable tourism	3.63	.53	300
United Arab Emirates (Dubai)	Mean	Std. deviation	N
Organisational commitment	4.36	.60	300
Leadership style	4.42	.66	300
Strategic human resource practices	4.41	.65	300
Job satisfaction	4.19	.70	300
Sustainable tourism	4.07	.80	300

Table 21.3 The correlation matrix

Malaysia	OC	LS	SHR	JS	ST
Organisational commitment (OC)	1.00				
Leadership style (LS)	.54	1.00			
Strategic HR practices (SHR)	.53	.64	1.00		
Job satisfaction (JS)	.82	.65	.55	1.00	
Sustainable tourism (ST)	.78	.52	.61	.56	1.00
United Arab Emirates (Dubai)	OC	LS	HR	JS	ST
Organisational commitment (OC)	1.000				
Leadership style (LS)	.804	1.000			
Strategic HR practices (SHR)	.709	.883	1.000		
Job satisfaction (JS)	.690	.657	.597	1.000	
Sustainable tourism (ST)	.591	.646	.510	.701	1.000

Table 21.4 Kaiser-Meyer-Olkin (KMO) and Bartlett's test

Malaysia		
Kaiser-Meyer-Olkin measure of sampling adequacy		.713
Approx. chi-square		1031.683
Bartlett's test of sphericity	df	10
	Sig.	.000
United Arab Emirates (Dubai)		
Kaiser-Meyer-Olkin measure of sampling adequacy		.786
Approx. chi-square		1218.777
Bartlett's test of sphericity	df	10
	Sig.	.00

on Table 21.4, the KMO measure in Malaysia is 0.713. While in the UAE, the KMO measure is 0.786. With this, it showed that sampling adequacy for Malaysia and the UAE is acceptable for this study.

Consistently looking at the Bartlett's test, the study has identified the strength of the relationship among variables. In the table above, it can be seen that the Bartlett's test of sphericity for both countries is significant. That is, its associated probability is .000 which is less than 0.05.

Communalities functions by showing how much of the variance in the variables has been accounted for by the extracted factors. In Table 21.5, in Malaysia, it is evidenced that over 78 % of the variance in organisational commitment is accounted for while 74 % of the variance in job satisfaction is accounted for. This can mean that Malaysian employees working in the tourism industries are prone to organisational commitment and being satisfied with their work. Whereas in the UAE, over 86 % of the variance in leadership style is accounted for while 78 % of the variance in organisational commitment is accounted for by the extracted factors. This can mean that employees in the tourism industries in the UAE prefer leadership style and committing to their work.

Table 21.5 Communalities

Malaysia	Initial	Extraction
Organisational commitment	1.000	.788
Leadership style	1.000	.634
Strategic human resource practices	1.000	.623
Job satisfaction	1.000	.746
Sustainable tourism	1.000	.695
United Arab Emirates (Dubai)	*Initial*	*Extraction*
Organisational commitment	1.000	.781
Leadership style	1.000	.866
Strategic human resource practices	1.000	.746
Job satisfaction	1.000	.707
Sustainable tourism	1.000	.625

Table 21.6 Regression for Malaysia

Model summary

Model	R	R Square	Adjusted R square	Std. error of the estimate
1	.837[a]	.700	.696	.29492

[a]Predictors: (constant), JS, SHR, LS, OC

		ANOVA[a]				
Model		Sum of squares	df	Mean square	F	Sig.
	Regression	59.962	4	14.991	172.35	.000[b]
1	Residual	25.659	295	.087		
	Total	85.621	299			

[a]Dependent variable: ST
[b]Predictors: (constant), JS, SHR, LS, OC

Coefficients[a]

Model		Unstandardized coefficients		Standardized coefficients	t	Sig.
		B	Std. error	Beta		
	(Constant)	−.325	.164		−1.976	.049
	OC	1.028	.066	.883	15.612	.000
1	LS	.106	.050	.099	2.111	.036
	SHR	.356	.052	.294	6.798	.000
	JS	−.425	.068	−.385	−6.261	.000

[a]Dependent variable: ST

The multiple regression analyses were conducted to examine the relationship between dependent and independent variables in the study. In Table 21.6, the multiple regression model with all four predictors produced $R^2 = .700$, $F(4,295) = 172.35$, $p < .001$. As can be seen in the table, the organisational commitment (OC), leadership

Table 21.7 Regression for United Arab Emirates (Dubai)

Model summary

Model	R	R square	Adjusted R square	Std. error of the estimate
1	.757[a]	.574	.568	.5301

[a]Predictors: (constant), JS, HR, OC, LS

Model		ANOVA[a]				
		Sum of squares	df	Mean square	F	Sig.
	Regression	111.593	4	27.898	99.29	.000[b]
1	Residual	82.890	295	.281		
	Total	194.483	299			

[a]Dependent variable: ST
[b]Predictors: (constant), JS, HR, OC, LS

Coefficients[a]

Model		Unstandardized coefficients		Standardized coefficients		
		B	Std. error	Beta	t	Sig.
	(Constant)	.233	.238		.982	.327
	OC	−.038	.092	−.029	−.416	.678
1	LS	.742	.117	.615	6.363	.000
	HR	−.388	.100	−.314	−3.880	.000
	JS	.580	.062	.504	9.312	.000

[a]Dependent variable: ST

style (LO) and strategic human resource practices (SHR) have positive regression weights, indicating that these predictors will not affect the tourism industry in Malaysia and were expected to contribute to the sustainability of the country's tourism industry. The job satisfaction (JS) has a significant negative weight (opposite in sign from its correlation with the criterion), indicating that job satisfaction has lower impact to the sustainability of the country's tourism industry (a suppressor effect). Therefore, job satisfaction did not contribute to the multiple regression model.

The multiple regression analyses were conducted to examine the relationship between dependent and independent variables in the study. The multiple regression model with all four predictors produced $R^2 = .574$, $F(4,295) = 99.29$, $p < .001$. As can be seen in Table 21.7, the leadership style (LS) and job satisfaction (JS) have positive regression weights, indicating that these predictors will not affect the tourism industry in the UAE and were expected to contribute to the sustainability of the country's tourism industry. On the other hand, the organisational commitment (OC) and strategic human resource practices (SHR) have a significant negative weight (opposite in sign from its correlation with the criterion), indicating that organisational commitment and job satisfaction have lower impact to the sustainability of the country's tourism industry. Therefore, organisational commitment and job satisfaction did not contribute to the multiple regression model.

Conclusion

This study showed a positive output where much of the hypothesis tested were correlated with each other and is significant with the dependent variable. Based on the findings, it is understood that both countries have a slight difference in the final output; thus, it is not much of a differences. In a developing country like Malaysia where cultural activities and historical places are rampant, the respondents are more into giving their commitment to their company and respecting their bosses as leaders. They are also prone to strategic human resource practices, while job satisfaction gives a secondary effect to their work. These predictors are assumed to be a significant contributor to the sustainability of the Malaysian tourism industry as a whole.

As for a country with modern setting such as the UAE or preferably known as Dubai, the respondents are prone to follow orders of their leaders by respecting their bosses' leadership style. They seek satisfaction from their daily job. Predictors such as organisational commitment and strategic human resource practices were among the less attention paid to among the respondents. This might occur due to the various background and nationality of the international respondents. In this sense, diversity is the main consideration in analysing such ground.

Hypothetically, there is a positive and significant relationship between the independent variables such as organisational commitment, leadership style, strategic human resources practices and job satisfaction with the dependent variable sustainable tourism and vice versa. In conclusion, all the five hypotheses are well accepted and can be expanded into another research and managerial study in the future.

References

Achoui, M., & Mansour, M. (2007). Employee turnover and retention strategies: Evidence from Saudi companies. *International Review of Business Research Papers, 3*(3), 1–16.

Armstrong, M. (2003). *Human resource practices*. London: Kogan Page.

Balakrishnan, M. S. (2009). Strategic branding of destinations: A framework. *European Journal of Marketing, 43*(5–6), 611–629.

Barney, J. (1991). Firm resources and sustained competitive advantage. *Journal of Management, 17*(1), 99–120.

Becker, T. E., & Billings, R. S. (1993). Profiles of commitment: An empirical test. *Journal of Organizational Behavior, 14*(2), 177–190.

Becker, B., & Gerhart, B. (1996). The impact of human resource management on organizational performance: Progress and prospects. *Academy of Management Journal, 39*(4), 779–801.

Cope, O., & Waddell, D. (2001). An audit of leadership styles in e-commerce. *Managerial Auditing Journal, 16*(9), 523–529.

Costa, J. (2004). The Portuguese tourism sector: Key challenges for human resources management. *International Journal of Contemporary Hospitality Management, 16*(7), 402–407.

D'Cruz, P., & Noronha, E. (2011). The limits to workplace friendship: Managerialist HRM and bystander behaviour in the context of workplace bullying. *Employee Relations, 33*(3), 269–288.

De Cieri, H., & Kramar, R. (2008). *Human resource management in Australia: Strategy people performance* (3rd ed.). Sydney: McGraw Hill Australia Pty Limited.

Delery, J. E. (1998). Issues of fit in strategic human resource management: Implications for research. *Human Resource Management Review, 8*(3), 289–309.

Gannon, J., & Johnson, K. (1997). Socialization control and market entry modes in the international hotel industry. *International Journal of Contemporary Hospitality Management, 9*(5/6), 193–198.

Greenberg, J., & Baron, R. J. (1995). *Behavior in organization: Understanding and managing the human side of work.* Upper Saddle River, NJ: Prentice Hall.

Hall, C. M., & Jenkins, J. (2004). Tourism and public policy. In A. A. Lew, C. M. Hall, & A. M. Williams (Eds.), *A companion to tourism* (pp. 525–540). Oxford: Blackwell.

Henderson, J. M. (2006). Recognition and attention guidance during contextual cueing in real-world scenes: Evidence from eye movements. *The Quarterly Journal of Experimental Psychology, 59*(7), 1177–1187.

Kaiser, H. F. (1974). An index of factorial simplicity. *Psychometrika, 399*, 31–36.

Keep, E., & Mayhew, K. (1999). *The leisure sector.*

Kerr, J., & Slocum, J. W. (2005). Managing corporate culture through reward systems. *The Academy of Management Executive, 19*(4), 130–138.

Kopelman, R. E., Brief, A. P., & Guzzo, R. A. (1990). The role of climate and culture in productivity. *Organizational Climate and Culture, 282*, 318.

Locke, E. A. (1976). The nature and causes of job satisfaction. *Handbook of Industrial and Organizational Psychology, 1*, 1297–1343.

Lok, P., & Crawford, J. (1999). The relationship between commitment and organizational culture, subculture, leadership style and job satisfaction in organizational change and development. *Leadership & Organization Development Journal, 20*(7), 365–374.

Marzuki, A., Jantan, M., & Mohamed, B. (2008). Analysing impacts from tourism development: A framework method. In *Proceedings of National Symposium on Tourism Research* (p. 49).

Ogilvie, J. R. (1986). The role of human resource management practices in predicting organizational commitment. *Group & Organization Management, 11*(4), 335–359.

Pfeffer, J. (1994). Competitive advantage through people. *California Management Review, 36*(2), 9.

Porter, L., Steers, R., Mowday, R., & Boulian, P. (1974). Organizational commitment, job satisfaction, and turnover among psychiatric technicians. *Journal of Applied Psychology, 59*, 603–609.

Riley, R. W., & Love, L. L. (2000). The state of qualitative tourism research. *Annals of Tourism Research, 27*(1), 164–187.

Robbins, S. P., & Coulter, M. (2008). *Management.* Upper Saddle River, NJ: Pearson Prentice Hall.

Schuler, R. S., & Jackson, S. E. (1987). Linking competitive strategies with human resource management practices. *The Academy of Management Executive, 1*(3), 207–219.

Scott-Findlay, S., & Estabrooks, C. A. (2006). Mapping the organizational culture research in nursing: A literature review. *Journal of Advanced Nursing, 56*(5), 498–513.

Sharpley, R. (2008). Consuming dark tourism: A thanatological perspective. *Annals of Tourism Research, 35*(2), 574–595.

Sheridan, J. E. (1992). Organizational culture and employee retention. *Academy of Management Journal, 35*(5), 1036–1056.

Sinangil, H. K. (2004). Globalisation and managing organisational culture change: The case of Turkey. *Psychology & Developing Societies, 16*(1), 27–40.

Sirat, J. A. (1993). U.S. Patent No. 5,218,646. Washington, DC: U.S. Patent and Trademark Office.

Stonich, S. C. (1998). Political ecology of tourism. *Annals of Tourism Research, 25*(1), 25–54.

Williams, L. J., & Hazer, J. T. (1986). Antecedents and consequences of satisfaction and commitment in turnover models: A reanalysis using latent variable structural equation methods. *Journal of Applied Psychology, 71*(2), 219.

Wimalasiri, J. S. (1995). An examination of the influence of human resource practices, organisational commitment and job satisfaction on work performance. *International Journal of Management, 12*, 352–352.

World Trade Organization. (2003). *Annual report WTO 2003.* ISSN 1020-4997 Printed in France.

Wright, A. H. (1998). The simple genetic algorithm and the Walsh transform: Part II, the inverse. *Evolutionary Computation, 6*(3), 275–289.

Wright, P. M., & McMahan, G. C. (1992). Theoretical perspectives for strategic human resource management. *Journal of Management, 18*(2), 295–320.

Chapter 22
The Role of Leaders on Creating Creative Climate That Stimulates Creativity and Innovation in the Workplace (Ongoing Research)

Gasim Abdelrahman and Ola ALZawati

Abstract The purpose of this study is to investigate the role of leaders on creating creative climate that supports innovation, change, and creativity in the organization. It will mainly answer how can leaders create a creative climate that stimulates creativity and innovation in the workplace? An organizational model named leadership-creative-climate model has been developed in order to examine this role. Moreover, an assessment survey will be developed and validated. A sample was selected from a local organization in UAE. It was grouped into three categories—highly innovative, moderately innovative, and low innovative—based on an electronic suggestion system results. The selected sample involves more than 350 respondents. Surveys will be distributed electronically to the respondents. Structured Interviews will be conducted with the key seniors and employees. Results of the surveys and structured interviews will be analyzed statistically and discussed critically. Then, conclusions regarding the role of leaders on creating creative climate that stimulates creativity and innovation in the organization will be derived, and the influences of leaders on each of the nine creative climate dimensions will be addressed. Finally, the model will be enhanced and verified based on the empirical data of the conducted case study and combined methodological framework that involves leadership-creative-climate model, and the assessment survey will be developed.

Keywords Innovation leadership • Creative climate • Creative climate dimensions • Innovation

G. Abdelrahman (✉) • O. ALZawati
Department of Industrial Engineering and Engineering Management, University of Sharjah, Sharjah, United Arab Emirates
e-mail: gasim.hawarii@gmail.com; olakzawati@gmail.com

© Springer International Publishing Switzerland 2017
R. Benlamri, M. Sparer (eds.), *Leadership, Innovation and Entrepreneurship as Driving Forces of the Global Economy*, Springer Proceedings in Business and Economics, DOI 10.1007/978-3-319-43434-6_22

Introduction

In recent scholarly and managerial literature, there is considerable evidence that innovation is essential to achieve the long-term success of a company in modern competitive markets. Due to the rapidly changing economy, innovation is becoming more and more critical for the success and survival of many organizations. Although several factors shaping innovation (e.g., strategy, climate, etc.) have been examined in the literature, the leadership of innovation has received relatively less attention (Byrne, Mumford, Barrett, & Vessey, 2009). One of the major factors repeatedly suggested to affect innovation is leadership. Leaders can create and manage an organizational culture that promotes innovation, can be product champions or heroic innovators who support innovation throughout the process of its implementation, and can create organizational structure needed to support innovativeness.

In the processes of innovation, where innovation is consequence of the company's strategy and not a one-time accidental incident, leaders make people aware of the goal, communicate, and justify the reasons for taken action and related benefits. They also show the direction of the action and tips related to searching innovative solutions. One of the most important roles that leaders play within organizational setting is to create the climate for innovation (cited by Tidd & Bessant, 2013). The purpose of this study is to examine the role of leaders on creating creative climate that stimulates innovation and creativity in the organization.

Problem Formulation

The creation of an innovation-friendly culture requires that leaders acquire new leadership skills to engage and lead staff. Despite contributions and increasing volumes of research data, the research base on innovation leadership remains fragmented and discipline specific and seldom brought to the levels of integration needed for practical design and implementation of leadership development interventions. At least one critical question remains unanswered, namely, what it is that innovation leaders do that brings about success in innovation (cited by Vlok, 2012)? Although the innovation literature base is extensive, the research in this area is rather restricted (Katerzyna, 2012). Hence, there is a significant need to examine the role of leaders on creating creative climate that stimulates creativity and innovation in the workplace. This study answers two questions: (1) How can innovative leaders create a creative climate that stimulates creativity and innovation in the workplace? What are the influences of innovative leaders on each of the nine dimensions of creative climate?

Innovation Leadership and Creative Climate

While innovation and leadership have both been featuring extensively in scholarly and general management literature for decades, the combination appears to be relatively new and growing fast (Vlok, 2012). Innovation leadership appears to be a new branch of study dealing with new complexities in value realization and the role of innovation in dealing with these. The first scholarly use of the term is uncertain, but one such reference originates from a study by Carmeli who examined the importance of innovation leadership in cultivating the strategic fit of the organization with its environment and enhancing various economic, relationship, and product performance outcomes. The results suggest that innovation leadership significantly enhanced firm performance (cited by Vlok, 2012).

Despite the traditional view of leadership behavior, concern for task, and concern for people, innovation leadership suggests a third factor, concern for change. Innovation leadership involves two components: (1) an innovative approach to leadership, which involves bringing new thinking and different actions to how leaders lead, manage, and go about their work and think differently about their roles and the challenges the organization face and (2) leadership for innovation through which leaders must learn how to create an organizational climate where others apply innovative thinking to solve problems and develop new products and services and growing culture of innovation not just hiring a few creative outliers (David & Dan, 2014). Leaders should pay great attention to both components; however, this study focuses on the second component of innovation leadership "leadership for innovation."

Climate is the observed and recurring patterns of behavior, attitudes, and feelings that characterize life in the organization. It is distinct from culture in that it is more observable at the surface level within the organization and more amenable to change and improvement efforts (Tidd & Bessant, 2013). Creative climate is characterized by nine dimensions which have been discussed frequently in the literature. The Situational Outlook Questionnaire (SOQ) has been in use for many years as an assessment of the climate that supports change, innovation, and creativity (Isaksen, 2007). The Situational Outlook Questionnaire has defined the nine dimensions of creative climate as presented by Isaksen (2007). Isaksen and Akkermans (2011) has conducted a study using the Situational Outlook Questionnaire (SOQ) of the nine dimensions of creative climate. Organizational climate as an intervening variable between leadership behavior and innovation was confirmed through partial correlation and mediation analysis. The results of the study confirmed that leadership behavior does, in fact, play a very important role in creating an organizational climate that supports innovation. de Jong and Den Hartog (2007) identified 13 leader behaviors that encouraged both idea generation and application of those ideas in producing innovation. Some examples include stimulating knowledge diffusion, providing vision, showing support for innovation, and providing resources. All the leader behaviors they identified included an implicit link to the leader's role in creating a climate for creativity and organizational innovation.

Fig. 22.1 Leadership-creative-climate model

In this paper a model named leadership-creative-climate model is proposed in order to examine the role of leaders on creating creative climate that stimulates creativity and innovation in the workplace. It is suggested that leaders can create and support climate for creativity through three channels: (1) organizational policies, strategies, and rules; (2) organizational systems and processes; and (3) leadership behavior. Each component can be developed, utilized, and continuously enhanced in order to create and support climate for creativity in the workplace. Each component will support the nine dimensions of the creative climate. Figure presents the leadership-creative-climate model (Fig. 22.1).

Methodology

An organizational model named leadership-creative-climate model has been developed in order to examine the role of leaders on creating and supporting creative climate. An assessment survey will be developed and validated in order to (1) determine how can leaders create and support creative climate through leadership-creative-climate model and (2) assess to what extent leaders are supporting climate for creativity in the organization. A sample was selected from a local organization in UAE. It was grouped into three categories—highly innovative, moderately innovative, and low innovative—based on an electronic suggestion system results.

The selected sample involves more than 350 respondents. Surveys will be distributed electronically to the respondents. Structured Interviews will be conducted with the key seniors and employees. Results of the surveys and structured interviews will be analyzed statistically and discussed critically. Then, conclusions regarding the role of leaders on creating creative climate that stimulates creativity and innovation in the organization will be derived, and the influences of innovative leaders on each of the nine creative climate dimensions will be addressed. Finally, the model will be enhanced and verified based on the empirical data of the conducted case study and combined methodological framework that involves creative-leadership-creative-climate model, and the assessment survey/tool will be developed.

References

Byrne, C. L., Mumford, M. D., Barrett, J. D., & Vessey, W. B. (2009). Examining the leaders of creative efforts: *What do they do, and what do they think about? Creativity and Innovation Management, 18*, 256–268.

David, H., & Dan, B. (2014). *Innovation leadership how to use innovation to lead effectively, work collaboratively, and drive results*. Center for Creative Leadership.

de Jong, J. P., & Den Hartog, D. N. (2007). How leaders influence employees' innovative behaviour. *European Journal of Innovation Management, 10*(1), 41–64.

Isaksen, S. G. (2007). The Situational Outlook Questionnaire: Assessing the context for change. *Psychological Reports, 100*(2), 455–466.

Isaksen, S. G., & Akkermans, H. J. (2011). Creative climate: A leadership lever for innovation. *The Journal of Creative Behavior, 45*(3), 161–187.

Tidd, J., & Bessant, J. R. (2013). *Managing innovation: Integrating technological, market and organizational change*. Chichester: Wiley.

Vlok, A. (2012). A leadership competency profile for innovation leaders in a science-based research and innovation organization in South Africa. *Procedia—Social and Behavioral Sciences, 41*, 209–226.

Chapter 23
Building the Responsible Leader in Universities: An Integrated Model

Mireille Chidiac El Hajj, Richard Abou Moussa, and May Chidiac

Abstract Inclusive leadership qualities are needed to assume responsibility for and meet complex global challenges. This study is a thorough search of published literature. It includes observations, scholarly work, and reports of studies. New insights are generated based on the grounded theory and dialectic between data collection and analysis. The objective of this study is to produce a framework for the responsible leader based on a set of integrated conceptual models. The outline of the "responsible leader" is organized around an innovative, socially responsible citizen who supports business ethics and comprehends sustainable governance.

Keywords Inclusive leadership • Responsible leader • Global changes • Grounded theory • Responsible citizen • Socially responsible • Sustainable governance • Ethically responsible • Responsibly innovative • Influence • Education

Introduction

With more importance given to social and environmental problems and their implication on daily life, the role of companies and their leaders has come into question. For some time, there has been a decline in the notions of responsibility and ethics in organizations and among individuals due to the overzealous support of capitalism and "the pursuit of profit beyond the limit set by the needs" (Weber, 1904/2008, p. 29). It is time to rethink tools to combat and limit the damage.

M.C. El Hajj, Ph.D. (✉) • R.A. Moussa, Ph.D.
Faculty of Economics and Business Administration, Department of Management, The Lebanese University, Beirut, Lebanon
e-mail: mireillehajj@hotmail.com; ramoussa@gmail.com

M. Chidiac, Ph.D.
Faculty of Humanities, Department of Media studies, Notre Dame University—Louaize, Zouk Mosbeh, Lebanon
e-mail: mchidiac@ndu.edu.lb

© Springer International Publishing Switzerland 2017   275
R. Benlamri, M. Sparer (eds.), *Leadership, Innovation and Entrepreneurship as Driving Forces of the Global Economy*, Springer Proceedings in Business and Economics, DOI 10.1007/978-3-319-43434-6_23

Faced with the deregulation phenomena, financial scandals (Biais, 2008), and human and environmental disasters, the need to reformulate ethical reflection and responsible education has resurfaced to the point of becoming the backbone of daily concerns. It is in this context that the Organisation for Economic Co-operation and Development (OECD, 2009) appealed to values such as transparency, objectivity, reliability, honesty, prudence, and the now lost confidence. It pointed to the importance of the role of education in universities, as well as the notion of how "education has a key role to play" (Morin, 1999).

To meet the new complex global challenges—such as water and energy security, climate change, and environmental degradation—we need "a clear vision, focus, and inclusive leadership qualities. These skills should be part of the development of future business leaders, and therefore, they should be part of the curricula and research programs of business schools and departments of universities" (European Commission, 2008). The objective of education, according to Durkheim (1968–2013), does not amount only to the mere acquisition of knowledge but also to the training of citizens. It is up to educational institutions which "have always had the tripartite mission to instruct, cultivate and converse, to transmit factual knowledge and also the values and principles which are deemed necessary to the rules of social life" (Audigier, 1991). Hence, education must be forward looking and built around contemporary issues, and the results of evolutions of culture, societies, and environments, in order to prepare the present and future responsible members of society, since "Education is the force of the future" (Morin, 1999).

Evidently, in all countries, a major challenge of education for sustainable development has risen. And that it is "the duty of Higher Education to help people to understand and adapt to a pace of change which is, as yet, 'unnatural' to all cultures" (UNESCO, 1997). Through reassessment of education based on the contemporary conduct of men and women, UNESCO has strived to reorient education toward sustainable development. Within the context of education for a sustainable future, Morin (1999) exposed the central problems needed to teach in the modern age and offered seven pointers, two of which are teaching the human condition and teaching the ethics of humanity. The question is to articulate a way of thinking, to overhaul the teaching methods while reforming attitudes, and to encourage ethical behavior.

It is noteworthy that current teaching methods are used in attempts to cultivate responsible students. However, there seems to be a gap: traditional educational methods such as lectures do not correlate well with the development of the new concept of *responsible leadership*. Therefore, there is a need for more interactive learning approaches, where the teacher can play the role of a moderator rather than of a lecturer. Developing new frontiers is essential in building socially responsible abilities.

Given the fact that sustainability education requires fundamental changes in the basic concepts—or a paradigm shift—as described by Michener et al. (2001), students can be educated in alternative ways (Kurland et al., 2010). This study sheds the light on how to build the "responsible leader," by going beyond the traditional methods and the currently used tools in universities.

To propose a new model of leadership, key issues had to be addressed: it was necessary to depict the current state of teaching social responsibility and sustainability in higher education and analyze qualitative information related to existing strategies. It was observed that the demand for a socially responsible leader is increasing, but this demand cannot be met due to the shortage of tools and strategies for this new type of leadership. So far, the literature reviewed had been treating related topics separately. There was no evidence of combining the different levels of responsibility effectively or shaping them systematically in an integrated approach. Grounded theory helps in engineering such novel approaches.

A New Mission for Universities: Making Leaders Out of Students

"Preparation for working life should become one of the major axes of the educational project of any higher education institution" (Attali, 1998). In his text, Attali discussed the role of higher education in improving society and inducing sustainable development. The role of universities would be twofold. On one hand, universities must anticipate needs and contribute to changes and developments in economic, technological, and labor sectors. On the other, they should be subject to changes and should "give students the opportunity to fully develop their own abilities with a sense of social responsibility, and teach them to become active full members of democratic society and cultivate members of society that promote equity and justice" (World Declaration on Higher Education—UNESCO, 1998).

Christensen, Peirce, Hartman, Hoffman, and Carrier's (2007) article on the inclusion and coverage of ethical issues, social responsibility, and sustainability of the top 50 global MBA programs revealed the following: (1) the majority of schools require one or more of the abovementioned subjects in their MBA program, and a third of the schools require covering at least three subjects; (2) there is a tendency toward including courses related to sustainable development; (3) the students' interest in these topics is high; and (4) several schools teach these topics through technical learning and experiential immersion.

Another report of UNESCO (2015) maintains that education and teaching are expected to increase emphasis on values and attitudes. In a globalized world, it is necessary to enable learners of any age to "acquire the values, knowledge and skills which are based on, and promote respect for human rights, social justice, diversity, gender equality and environmental sustainability, and empowers them to become responsible global citizens." For the next 8 years (UNESCO, 2013), the universities in their tripartite dimension of teaching, research, and civic engagement should therefore be heavily involved in this new discourse. "The goal is to train responsible global citizens" (UNESCO, 2013).

Hahn's (1998) comparative study—conducted in countries like Germany, Denmark, Great Britain, and the USA—concludes that there is a strong correlation between individual participation in civic life and institutes that encourage their students not only to participate and discuss issues of public interest but also to act accordingly. Other studies have also shown that corporate social responsibility (CSR) education in Europe has come a long way. Programs and optional modules of sustainability at the masters level are increasingly taught in different European regions or groups of European countries. Data analysis and research on CSR, sustainability, and partnership governance has become more entrenched in European universities. In general, these issues have become mature fields of study and are not to be overlooked. This maturity is reflected in the increase in the adoption of European case studies, and the decrease in the use of speakers, as teaching tools in CSR education (Orlitzky & Moon, 2008). The launch of a global network of over 130 companies and academic institutions under the name of the Academy of Business in Society (ABIS),[1] in 2001, had helped to promote sustainable business practices through partnership, learning, and research. It allowed companies to benefit from academic knowledge through research, to focus on strategic priorities and sustainable development programs, and to integrate research in business school education. Internet research, particularly of the Web pages of the Leiden, Delft, and Rotterdam universities, revealed that those universities joined their efforts in partnership to teach students innovation and problem solving related to sustainability, social responsibility, and responsible governance.

In the USA, there is emphasis on ethics education. For example, a "task force" was created, the EETF (Ethics Education Task Force), to strengthen the requirement of teaching ethics in MBA programs, to gain accreditation for business schools, and to highlight the importance of ethics education (Phillips, 2004). In addition, exercises are employed with students to increase their moral reasoning abilities, to reflect on ethical decisions based on their own experiences, to analyze situations using multiple perspectives, to clarify complex ethical dilemmas of the business world, and to prepare and educate them to consider the various ethical issues in business (Phillips, 2004). The investigation by Matten and Moon (2004)[2] questions whether business schools "are no more than brainwashing institutions, educating their graduates only in a relatively narrow shareholder value ideology, which has been raised by numerous commentators in the aftermath of recent corporate scandals in America." However, their study showed that practitioners and the industry are keenly interested in the issues of CSR and sustainability. The futuristic vision for educators in business schools is rather optimistic regarding the apprehension of the role of ethics in business.

---

[1] According to Web search: "ABIS (formerly known as EABIS) was founded in 2001 and launched at INSEAD in 2002 with the support of the leading Business Schools in Europe (INSEAD, IMD, London, ESADE, IESE, Copenhagen, Warwick, Vlerick, Ashridge, Cranfield, Bocconi) in partnership with IBM, Microsoft, Johnson and Johnson, Unilever and Shell."

[2] Following the American companies' scandals, Matten and Moon's study came in response to the various criticisms that have been raised by many commentators in the business press such as academicians.

In fact, universities, such as Stony Brook University[3] in New York, are offering majors in sustainability, BS in Coastal Environmental Studies, BA in Sustainability Studies, BA in Ecosystems and Human Impact, BA in Environmental Humanities, and BA in Environmental Design, Policy, and Planning, in order to prepare students for important environmental careers of the future. In this context, European and American universities such as Edinburgh University in the UK, University of Oldenburg in Germany, and MIT and Harvard University in the USA are mainly working on bringing support and guidance to students and procuring funds to purchase new equipment to support sustainable labs. "People who decide to take a course on environmental issues therefore need to go beyond the simplistic environmental arguments […] and take first step in examining issues that are of current concern, such as the operationalisation of sustainability" (Simon, 2002).

Efforts however remain insufficient. In his article in the *Wall Street Journal*, "How Business Schools Have Failed Business: Why Not More Education on the Responsibility of Boards?," Jacobs (2009) points the finger at universities. According to him, business schools have failed to teach responsibility and good governance to business leaders and policy makers. Convinced that there is a bias in teaching business ethics and governance, he wondered: "Could we have avoided most of the economic problems we now face if we had a generation of business leaders who were trained in designing compensation systems that promote long-term value?"

Lebanon provides the context for the practical side of this research. It is therefore important to note that in Lebanon, the Lebanese University is a model for private universities that tend to emphasize autonomy (UNESCO, PNUD, 1996). However, the law that governs the Lebanese University is 40 years old (1967). It is a law that rifts between the legislation and its application in the field and between the law and the requirements of a modern administration. The coexistence of public higher education through the Lebanese University and private higher education through all the other universities could have been more valuable had it not been a proliferation of

---

[3] A Web search showed that the "interdisciplinary field of Sustainability Studies was developed in response to the growing need for environmental literacy and awareness as a solution to unsustainable human behavior and environmental degradation. Sustainability means long-lasting health, integrity, diversity, and vitality for all living systems — including individual, community, ecosystem, and biome. Stony Brook's Sustainability Studies' academic programs include interdisciplinary and trans-disciplinary instruction in sustainable development, urban and suburban planning, landscape architecture, environmental policy, environmental humanities (including literature, media, film and cultural studies), etc. The program curriculum includes extensive collaborative and interactive learning, problem solving, and direct hands-on engagement. Graduates from the Sustainability Studies Program are prepared to enter a variety of careers and graduate programs including education, law, politics, policy and planning, journalism, business, landscape and architectural design, renewable energy, conservation, marine sciences, forestry, environmental health, food studies, and the arts, among others. 'Green Job' growth is steadily rising and is outpacing most other employment areas. The study of sustainability teaches students to be proactive, critical and creative thinkers who seek and find solutions to environmental problems. Sustainability Studies at Stony Brook offers five majors, six minors and a graduate certificate in GIS, as well as a Fast-track BA-MBA."
Retrieved from: http://www.stonybrook.edu/commcms/sustainability/what_is_sustainability.html

institutions of higher education of highly uncertain quality, which do not always meet the needs of Lebanon (UNESCO, PNUD, 1996).

Despite several efforts, it is clear that higher education in Lebanon has to some extent failed to accompany the globalized labor market, form a competitive workforce, or form sound citizenship. As mentioned by the Lebanese Association for Educational Studies (LAES, 2006), the problems are numerous, some related to low practical training and undeveloped programs of partnership and affiliation in certain specializations with companies and other educational institutions. Our preliminary observations indicated that some efforts have been recently made in order to implement new units, labs, curricula, and even green campuses in some universities, especially in those that are accredited or seeking accreditation. The purpose is to install incremental changes that can help in molding the student, who is supposed to become responsible, and preparing him/her to work for a more just and sustainable society.

Methodology

While the literature tends to present a relatively limited view by pointing to concepts separately, this study will try to mold, order, and position specific scattered elements in one shape: the shape of the "responsible leader." By referring to the grounded theory, the researchers aim to develop the new concept that is connected to the new reality. As Glaser and Strauss (1967) described it, the grounded theory is willing to "Identify a phenomenon, object, event or setting of interest."

The literature study is a thorough search of published literature. Similar to grounded theory, it includes different kinds of data (Glaser & Strauss, 1967). In addition to academic texts, reference is made to journals, along with newspaper articles, that can provide a main source of information for an in-depth literature search and to Internet research. In order to broaden the understanding of the new concept, existing theories, critical opinions, and identified current models were reviewed.

The study also includes 35 university professors and administrators from different prominent universities[4] in Lebanon, whose assignment was to assist in a reflection paper in which they describe the different traits of the leader we need in our societies. The discourse of 16 different guest speakers[5]—coming from different backgrounds

---

[4]Namely: the American University of Beirut, Balamand University, Beirut Arab University, Lebanese American University, Lebanese University, Sagesse University, Université Saint-Esprit—Kaslik, Université Saint-Joseph, Antonine University, and Notre Dame University—Louaize.

[5]We met the people we interviewed at the Women on the Frontlines conference (WOFL), held in March 1 in Beirut. The panels covered topics such as women in international affairs, women in entrepreneurship and in the business world, and others. Whether diplomatic, talk-show interviewers, entrepreneurs, or in art and culture, all interviewers, who have inspired leadership and change, agreed that a new type of leadership is needed, especially between women, requiring youth engagement and focusing on human rights, development, citizenship, and civic engagement. Their different ideas inspired us on how being a responsible youth participating in decision making can make a difference.

and discussing and exploring the new traits of the leader our society is seeking—is explored. The dialectic between the data collection and analysis process enabled the researchers to develop a new theoretical approach. This powerful theory that "grounds itself in reality through systematically generated research" (Olson & Raffanti, 2004) helped "plant the seeds" of a new leadership model that improves organizational and educational practices, providing tools for implementation and assessment of the implications of the concepts that fit the new environment imperatives.

According to the World Commission on Environment and Development, "Sustainable development is development that meets the needs of the present without compromising the ability of future generations to meet their own needs." Sustainability development does not have limits, but it is rather recognized as a set of notions and definitions of development that evolve in relation to changing requirements and possibilities (UNESCO, 1997). To solve its challenges, a strong leadership is needed, an "abstract of time, place and people". And that is someone who has the ability to understand complex challenges, to respond to them, and to create value from team players. Applied to education, power in the classrooms should therefore be "democratically shared" (Brookfield, 1999; Olson & Raffanti, 2004): everyone, including teachers, is to be equally engaged in shared education and learning and also in discovery, relevance, and creative concepts. The implication is grounded learning based on pushing students toward critical thinking, empowering them, listening to them, and accepting their answers (not underestimating them). This moves teaching to a higher, more theoretical, level of comprehension (Olson & Raffanti, 2004). To address such a paradigm shift, this research links fundamental concepts in order to capture the pillars that "characterize the central phenomenon" (Strauss, 1987, p. 7). Theoretical codes are drawn from existing theories and diverse reliable interviews to assist the theoretical integration. In this process, this study extracts the traits of the responsible leader, who can shape our communities and organizations: a responsible person, molded not only through the eyes of scholars and authors but also of the community and educators.

Interviews with People in Charge

This research deployed different types of interviews: structured, semi-structured, and informal. The purpose was to learn how people in charge of education, who by virtue of their position and authority, are able to inspire others, lead them, and offer them a role model to follow. Their influence confirms the notion that, "instead of trying to change or eradicate misappropriate leadership concepts and values at a later age, it is much better to care for their good formation and foundation as earlier as possible, during [head]teacher initial formation [at university level]" (Argyropoulou, 2015).

In order to establish if there is differentiation between current students and students that the community aspires to have, the interviewees were asked to describe the present student and compare that description with the needed student for the future. The interviews addressed the characteristics of future students; how they can

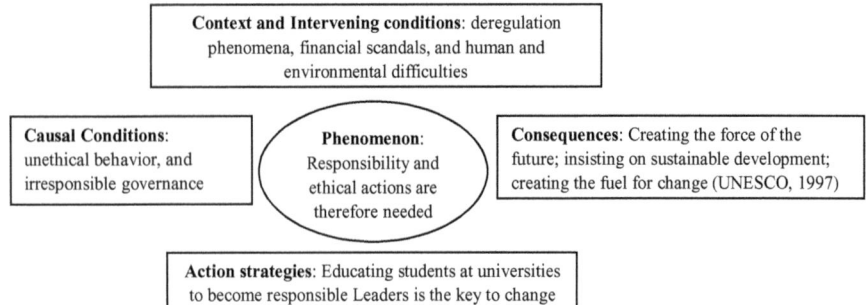

Fig. 23.1 Coding paradigm for the type of wanted leadership taken from Strauss and Corbin (1990, p. 98)

become critical thinkers and effective leaders who are able to solve problems logically, ethically, and innovatively; and how they can be transformed into enthusiastic and integrated leaders who can communicate clearly and who will not be afraid to challenge conventions using proper tools and means.

As described by Glaser and Strauss (1967), when referring to the open coding codes, data was collected and divided into similar groupings, to establish preliminary categories of information concerning the sought traits of a leader, which represents our field of investigation. In this context, memos were written and sorted, and the results were weighted to clarify the concepts (Bohm, 2004). The researchers identified a new type of leadership that needs to be built at a university level. However, this new type of leadership needs new types of tools that are different from those usually used in universities. Then, the preliminary categories were thematically divided in order to form the axial coding. This step refined the concept, locating it at the center (cf. Fig. 23.1).

Under this particular set of conditions, an action strategy is to be adopted: educating university students to make responsible leaders out of them. The sequences emerged as follows: it is imperative to teach, firstly, civic engagement and, secondly, ethics and sustainable governance, while encouraging innovation by stimulating thinking and encouraging better ideas.

A Complex World Seeking Framework for a "Responsible Leader" and for Tools to Build the Paradigm

The definition of leadership as designated by Harvard is adopted: it is the "capacity to guide and sustainably mobilize a group of individuals towards achieving specific goals." Leadership approaches are different: they are diverse but converge on some issues. From the traits theory that focuses on personal characteristics (related to intelligence, knowledge, integrity, expertise, and others) to the behavioral theory, the attribution theory, the Fiedler contingencies, the path-goal theory, the situational theory, and the transformational leadership in all its variations such as ethical leadership, etc., most agree that leaders can provide real targets and share knowledge with their group.

However, the role of today's leader has surpassed this context. The reasons are many: disconnection between the world of finance and the real economy, detachment between the leader and his followers, division between governance and the voiceless in our systems, failure of current governance, and excessive and irresponsible use and management of ecological and social resources. It must be said that all these factors respond on one hand to the voice of the market, profit and shareholder, largely ignoring the needs at the base of the socioeconomic pyramid, while on the other hand, they respond to the voice of old academic programs. It is time to change practices, to innovate pedagogical postures, and to break the standardized methods (Argyropoulou, 2015; European Commission, 2013; MIT Sloan School of Management, 2015; Starratt, 2004; University of Edinburgh, 2015).

The complex world is looking for a leader who could make the shift from *sensus privatus* to Aristotle's *sensus communis*: the "I" to "we," the "ego" to "eco" (Otto & Kaufer, 2013), and "self-centeredness" to "straight centrism" (De Menthon, 2011). It seeks a leader who can engage in a subject as vast as the social, environmental, and ecological fields. Isn't leadership "doing the right thing" (Drucker, 2006)? In the light of all these facts, meeting the challenges of today requires deep changes in our consciousness, our views, our values, and our cultural paradigms. Therefore, these changes demand a new framework, some new tools, and some "highly cultural products" (AIZ, 2013), to help the emergence of new qualities and shapes of a new leadership.

What are the appropriate teaching tools to increase student engagement and enhance learning? David Kolb's model (1999), entitled "experiential learning theory," presents a cycle consisting of four sequential stages: concrete experience, observation and reflection, formation of abstract concepts and generalizations leading up to the creation of assumptions regarding the implications of abstract concepts in new situations, and ultimately the verification of these concepts in real situations. The knowledge gained through concrete experience—effective, immediate, and intuitive—will be named apprehension. The one acquired from the abstract conceptualization—cognitive, rational, and understanding—will be named symbolic.

In their article "Cross-Cultural Training Effectiveness: A Theoretical Review and a Framework for Future Research," Black and Mendenhall (1989) draw attention to the difference between currently used theories and cognitive behaviors. The first explains how individuals learn and use their knowledge through the mind via the processing of information. The second argues that learning is determined by behaviors and experience. Hands-on training methods are based on simulations, field studies, "role plays," and others, which have been proven to be much more effective than traditional conferences and videotapes.

As for Starratt (2004), he stressed that the world in which educational leaders operate is changing. Therefore, schools must prepare their students "to participate as active citizens of the global community, rather than as spectators or tourists. Schools need to target their curriculum toward preparing youngsters with the desperately needed understandings, perspectives, and skills this global transition will demand. A different kind of school leader will be required—a multidimensional leader that understands the various dimensions of the learning tasks which schools must cultivate. In turn, these leaders must have a moral vision of what is required of them and of the whole community. A moral vision of taking proactive responsibility for making this kind of learning a reality is required."

The New Approach: The Future Responsible Leader Should Be a Committed Citizen

Defining citizenship: Baylis and Smith (2001) identified citizenship as only the "status that gives the right to participate and be represented in politics." However, according to Marshall (1950), citizenship was not only comprised of political rights and obligations. In his essay entitled *Citizenship and Social Class*, published in 1950, Marshall added civil and social rights along with the political ones. Alongside the political dimension which implies the right to participate in the exercise of political power, including the right to vote and the right to be elected, the civil element assumes the necessary rights of individual freedom, such as freedom of expression, human, religion, property, and others. There are also social rights which cover the right to well-being, access to culture, etc.

"Facing the radically new situation of humanity," the Charter of Human Responsibilities (2001) created next to the UN Charter and the Universal Declaration of Human Rights a set of new rules and established new regulatory standards. It recommended that companies should agree on a "common ethicality to manage our entire planet." The charter is intended as a frame of reference for both personal conduits for political life, institutional and jurisdictional, which point to ethics and accountability, the twin leitmotifs of any human interaction.

Besides the legal status and social roles, new values were tied to citizenship, defined by civility, citizenship, and solidarity. Civility is the mutual recognition and tolerance between individuals, out of respect for the dignity of the human person. Citizenship is linked to the active behavior of the citizen in everyday and public life, to act on behalf of the general interest. Solidarity is to help the less fortunate, directly or through public policies (Documentation Française, 2015).

Referring to our interviewees, being a citizen is therefore primarily being responsible. According to them, the contemporary citizen is expected to turn into a "player" of society, concerned not only in the financial and material but also in the human and social. This context brings us back to Kerr (2004), who attributed the success of civic education in schools and universities to a series of factors in three different levels. On the managerial level, success is mainly due to leaders, coordinators, and allocation of resources. On the institutional level, the success factors are mainly attributed to clear and consistent understanding of the meaning of civic education, the training and development of teachers and educational institutions, and the evolution of education of young students' citizenship skills and experiences. In terms of education, the positive relationship between schools and universities on one hand and the community on the other would favor students the opportunity to engage in society.

What tools? This context implies a dedicated and enthusiastic staff and participation and commitment from students in decisions that affect their education and development. It mainly involves the maintenance of active forms of engagement, including debate, dialogue, and reflection, to help students to think, reflect, and take action. To move away from current approaches, scholars are recommending "design thinking," to educate responsible citizenship. Design thinking is an approach to learning that focuses on developing students' creative confidence through hands-on projects that encourage action and foster active problem solving (Kwek, 2011). It refers to a set of cognitive activities one engages in during a design process, to come up with more innovative solutions to problems, by referring to "critical thinking" and "divergent thinking" (Meredith, 2015).

The Future Responsible Leader Should Be Socially Responsible

The definition of the Green Paper (2001) on social responsibility recognizes that it is a "voluntary integration of social and environmental concerns in business operations and in relations with all internal and external stakeholders…" (Green Paper, 2001). Being socially responsible means not only having rights but also obligations toward the society, the environment, and the world around us, to "meet the needs of the present without compromising the ability of future generations to meet their own needs" (WCED, 1987). As for our interviewees, being a socially responsible leader is risky, especially as interest and social responsibility practices do not always align with the business world, which comes in parallel with Porter and Kramer (2006)[6] and appeals to sustainable development that aligns with the concept of social responsibility. The real challenge of both themes being to combine three dimensions: the environmental (natural resource consumption, land use, etc.), the economic (economic performance, respecting the principles of business ethics and stakeholders, etc.), and the social one (working conditions, training, respect for human rights, diversity, etc.).

"We are all responsible!" (De Menthon, 2011), and we cannot ignore our duties. This is the reason why, according to De Menthon (2011), we have to employ "the emergency logic" and the implementation of short-term solutions over longer-term evaluation that must be reflected in commitments and actions. However, such acts require a close collaboration between universities and companies to help operate

---

[6] Porter and Kramer (2006) state: "Many companies have already done much to improve the social and environmental consequences of their activities, yet these efforts have not been nearly as productive as they could be—for two reasons. First, they pit business against society, when clearly the two are interdependent. Second, they pressure companies to think of corporate social responsibility in generic ways instead of in the way most appropriate to each firm's strategy. The fact is, the prevailing approaches to CSR are so fragmented and so disconnected from business and strategy as to obscure many of the greatest opportunities for companies to benefit society. If, instead, corporations were to analyze their prospects for social responsibility using the same frameworks that guide their core business choices, they would discover that CSR can be much more than a cost, a constraint, or a charitable deed—it can be a source of opportunity, innovation, and competitive advantage."

social responsibility and sustainability concepts, theoretically and practically. "Some pioneering curricula and institutions are beginning to adopt this type of approach (reinvention of knowledge) by conducting in-depth work with the teachers. They design programs combining solidarity, efficiency and creativity that stir cultures and disciplines, while developing new forms of experiential learning, and approaching not only companies, but also NGOs and the voluntary sector. The objective of these new forms of education is to prepare the younger generation to be tomorrow's responsible managers" (L'herminier, 2015).

What tools? To this end, L'herminier (2015) offers five rules to adopt: (1) faculty mentors should be armed with competencies; (2) a transdisciplinary and interdisciplinary approach in education should be applied to break down barriers between skills and knowledge; (3) "outdoor education" should be exercised through active teaching, based on the "learning by doing" methodology; (4) collaboration between academia and business should be promoted; and (5) the basics of managerial ethics should be taught. The training is centered on case studies, compliance with regulations and international standards, knowledge of tools developed in organizations, etc.

The Future Responsible Leader Should Be Responsibly Innovative

Transformation cannot derive from routines. The majority of our interviewees agreed that a responsible leader needs to develop innovative actions and to think outside the box. To meet the challenge of a rapidly changing world in an information-intensive age and to achieve the goals of quality education, there is a great need to develop a broadened vision of educational goals (Zhao, 2005). Because of its advantages of flexibility, diversity, and availability, "learning to do" is one of the four main pillars of learning that implies bringing newly acquired knowledge into practice. This pillar is a shift from skill to competence. It is the "ability to communicate effectively with others; aptitude toward team work; social skills in building meaningful interpersonal relations; adaptability to change in the world of work and in social life; competency in transforming knowledge into innovations and job-creation; and a readiness to take risks and resolve or manage conflicts."

Responsible innovation is beneficial in three ways: to business, to society, and to students. The universities of Leiden, Delft, and Rotterdam have already contributed in teaching responsible innovation. To help students think about people, the planet, and profit, students were divided into groups, to teach them how to become societally conscious and understand dilemmas in responsible innovation, to forge their entrepreneurial spirit, to become open-minded with a flexible and proactive attitude, and to make them value-driven to contribute to financial, ecological, and social sustainability. "Key to this is giving students more opportunities to leave their institutions with the knowledge, skills and attributes required to critically challenge the world around them, and a desire and willingness to tackle social, economic and environmental issues and inequalities" (University of Edinburgh, 2015).

What tools? According to the European Commission (2013), some universities such as Leiden, Delft, and Rotterdam[7] are adopting the modern approach to industrial design, through a process of identifying the problem, analyzing the problem (through brainstorming and other analyses), defining problems (with data visualization), designing solutions (through S-curve, risk-cost-benefit analysis), implementing solutions (through change management), and evaluating solutions (through multicriteria analysis, performance management, cause and effect diagram, critical path, risk matrix, etc.). Other institutions are adopting the intellectual entrepreneurship approach that moves the mission of institutions of higher learning from "advancing the frontiers of knowledge" and "preparing tomorrow's leaders" to "serving as engines of economic and social development" (European Commission, 2013).

The Future Responsible Leader Should Be Willing to Support Ethical Conduct

Given the complexity of the business world and the advent of the new dimension of globalization, CSR is a concept that is evoked during the perspective of what drives the company's performance. This is a three-dimensional voluntary integration, environmental, social, and economic, that uses four levels according to Carroll (1991). Carroll's pyramid (1991) offers the mixture of two components: ethics and responsibility. Carroll's ethical responsibility consists of what is generally expected by society beyond the economic and legal.

In the context of ethics in business, some authors argue that ethical behavior is a personal attribute and cannot be taught as a single course. Certainly the history of a person, his values and previous experience, has an impact on his view of ethics. However, students can learn about ethical behavior by being exposed and engaged in ethical dilemmas, as mentioned by the interviewers. "Making them critical minds and teachers, able to assess the school democracy, equality and equity; to avoid the traditional teaching method and to propose a modern combination of traditional and open learning method and material, can motivate students" (Argyropoulou, 2015). Experiences can develop their ability to use their knowledge (Prosser, 1995).

In his book *Teaching Business Ethics for Effective Learning*, Sims (2002) explains that traditional teaching methods and the passive attitude of a teacher who addresses topics such as the ethics of business can only harm the education material and will ultimately fall short in preparing students to world affairs, for ethics is "the set of personal standards of conduct generally accepted and respected by every member of a society" that "determines the emergence of the social community and the political community to a global one" (Sekiou, 2001). In this extension, the

---

[7] Leiden University, TU Delft, and Erasmus University Rotterdam work together in numerous areas in education, research, and valorization. In their strategic alliance, established in 2012, they built "The Centre for Sustainability" that provides research-based knowledge and solutions on resource efficiency, by connecting universities, companies, and governments.

OECD (2009) had defined a new set of codes of ethics and professional morality in demanding business conduct, to better build the new international financial system and to restore a "greener" growth.

What tools? It is through active teaching that learning can become more effective. It is in this context that Sims (2002, p. 82) defines the experiential training of the teaching of business ethics as follows: "Teaching Business Ethics is a series of learning experiences that encourages active, experiential learning and uses a variety of teaching activities to meet the diverse needs of students." The main goal is to cultivate in students the analytical skills necessary to solve the issues of business ethics, expose them to the complexity of ethical decision making, and increase awareness in their ethical, legal, and social business decisions (Gandz & Hayes, 1988; LeClair, 1999; McDonald & Donleavy, 1995). Personal integrity, professional ethics, and strategic thinking can be learned only through active teaching (Emerson & Smutko, 2011), based on field studies (Pfeffer, 1993) to learn more about the company (Rousseau & Mccarthy, 2007). The *Code Soleil*, a reference book for teachers, phrases this well: Teaching should show dynamism and a kind of communicative heat. It should be a reflection of the soul that penetrates the entire class. In this context, "the instructor must instill in his students the behaviors that society requires, a constant education, that is adapted to the needs of the environment where they live" (Code Soleil, 1952).

The Future Responsible Leader in the Context of a Sustainable Governance

The alignment of all mentioned topics indicates a need for the reconsideration of the concept of governance. ISO 26000, which refers to societal responsibility, outlines that "the main characteristic of social responsibility is reflected in the willingness of an organization to take responsibility for the impacts of its activities and its decisions on society and the environment and to account in a behavior that is transparent and ethical."

Scholars such as Wade (1994); Ostrom, Gardner, and Walker (1994); and Baland and Platteau (1996) classify most natural resource systems as common pool resources. They generate finite quantities of resources, and many actors can appropriate them for consumption and exchange. Divided into nonrenewable and renewable resources, they can be overused and destroyed. They are the reason why many organizations are increasingly interested in conducting their activities while becoming more concerned about the three Es: environment, economics, and equity.

Our interactive discussions with people in charge from different backgrounds showed that the sustainable governance model works toward sustainability through learning by doing and doing by learning to solve problems related to energy, mobility, agriculture, water management, health care, education, construction, and industry. Thus dealing with all these persistent societal problems requires "raising awareness, cooperation and strategic capabilities at the level of the innovations, a structured process of social experimentation and learning" (Loorbach, 2010). According to Loorbach, developing this new mode of governance can establish "the balance between structure and spontaneity, between management and self-organization, between long-term ideals and short-term action and between theory and practice."

What tools? Otto and Kaufer (2013) introduced a tool called the "simulation game." In their book, *Leading from the Emerging Future: From Ego-System to Eco-System Economies*, Otto and Kauffer describe the work of Professor John Sterman, who divided a group of students into teams, each team representing a group of key countries at the United Nations. As head of the ongoing negotiations on carbon emissions, the team had to work on a simulation model using real climate data. The various teams were responsible for calculating the likely outcomes of climate change, to present the devastating and destabilizing impact of their collective decisions about the world and to finally reflect on the lessons and learn. The challenge was to simulate a system of eco-economy in order to learn to act collectively, intentionally, effectively, and collaboratively and to recognize that the world needs a sustainable governance to ensure the sustainability of the planet.

"The Pantheon of the Responsible Leader"

The selective coding organized and integrated categories and themes in a coherent way that helped the understanding of the new phenomenon. As a starting point, memos, notes, and networks were coded and then compared with reality. Then, after increasing the comprehensiveness of the final product and approaching to saturation, it was found that the classical method of education is no longer sufficient: it has become evident that responsible leaders cannot emerge with the use of traditional tools. As the world attempts to adapt to the escalating changes in society and environment over the past decades, the need for a "responsible leader" has become increasingly obvious. Responsible leadership is one of the keys to future survival. We want to participate in a world that takes into account social impact, promotes discipline, and gives meaning to the sustainable interdependent world. All the links we have forged between the different themes led us to construct the model that can qualify the new "responsible leader," a leader who is able to ensure sustainability, the welfare of society, and equitable access to resources for today and tomorrow.

The current approach of today's leader is striving to work in an acceptable formula. Still different forms of critiques have arisen similar to those described by Jacobs (2009). A dichotomy has been created between the ways that current leaders are evolving in practice and the ideal model everyone is seeking for. Current leaders are ahead on an unstable summit in a world that is demanding a "wider-ranging political and moral responsibilities" (UN, 2015). Most of them are achieving success. Yet achieving success in a risky environment is one thing, and setting back in a safer, more sustainable world is another. To bridge the gap, the new responsible leader should be more engaged. Some essential elements are to be implemented: responsibility, sustainability, and solidarity. To strike the balance between the leadership that we know and the new leadership role, an increase in responsibility, in commitment, in sustainability, and in equity should be observed, which leads us to our pantheon-shaped model which illustrates the responsible leader.

The pantheon model has one strong base: the responsible citizen. Four different pillars emerge from the base. The first one is socially responsible, the second innovatively responsible, the third governing sustainably, and the fourth ethically responsible. All four surfaces are equally important and when practiced will lead to one entity: the "responsible leader." In other words, a "responsible leader" emerges from the four inherent components and the one strong base. If one surface is weak or inexistent, the "structure" weakens. If more than one surface is weak or inexistent, the pantheon cannot survive for long and will ultimately crumble, taking down with it the figure of the responsibly engaged citizen. Figure 23.2 illustrates the pantheon of tomorrow's "responsible leader."

By definition, leadership is an influence relationship with the capacity to guide followers toward desired goals. If we read the model inversely, the responsible leader thusly influences and guides his/her group members to follow the four precepts of social responsibility, sustainability concerns, ethical responsibility, and innovative approaches, in order to instill and realize the general desired vision of socially engaged citizenship.

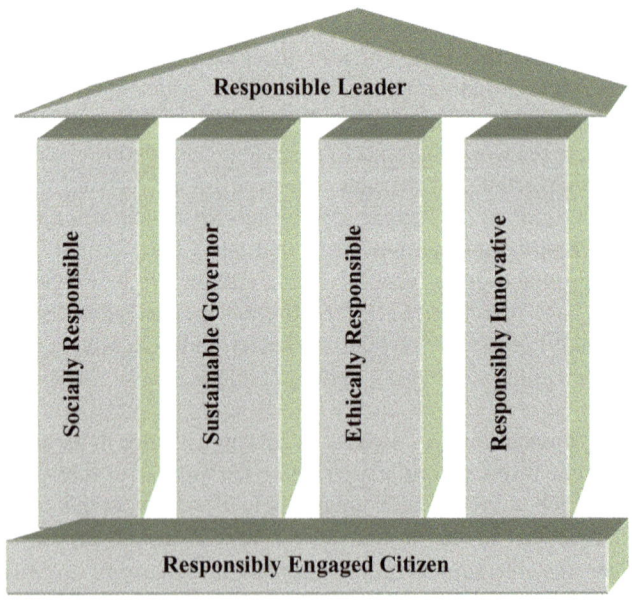

Fig. 23.2 Illustrating the pantheon of the "responsible leader"

Some Limitations of the New Concept

We distanced ourselves from existing theories to allow our model of the new responsible leader to grow out of the data. We reached saturation by gathering all data and statements from the field and through our observations; however, some gaps still exist and can provide topics for further research to refine the model. In examining the model, the tools, and the implications of this study, several points need to be addressed:

First, this paper presents observations, readings, literature, and Web site searches that follow the Straussian approach. We believe that the theory fits and is readily applicable (Glaser & Strauss, 1967). It guides us on how to build the new "responsible leader" with all the tools needed to create a solid foundation, for if we invest in improper tools, we will end up with a poor, unsustainable structure. Still, it would be interesting to uncover if all these successful tools and materials already applied in the West are also as effective in the Middle Eastern universities. Resick, Hanges, Dickenson, and Mitchelson's (2006) study revealed an interesting finding. It suggested that there is a "universal endorsement for the importance of the components of ethical Leadership; however, societies differ in the degree of endorsement." According to the study, (1) Middle Eastern societies tend to endorse character/integrity, altruism, collective motivation, and endorsement dimensions to a lesser extent than other societies; (2) power distance is a highly valued aspect of culture in Middle Eastern societies; (3) protecting one's reputation and saving face are extremely important and tremendous challenges for the individual can be observed if the leader's reputation is tarnished; and (4) ethical leadership takes on additional components that address upholding predominantly Islamic values. Since such dimensions were not observed in our study, tools must be appropriately used respecting the Arab values that are upheld in the Middle Eastern context.

Second, the ethical behavior of the teachers can be questioned: what if the teachers are not ethical themselves? If it is the case, would the mentioned tools remain sufficient and relevant? In addition to educational tools, ethical behavior is to be integrated into university policies to ensure a supportive environment for overall ethical behavior. Diligent follow-up of the implementation of those policies is required. The objective is to educate both students and teachers to become more ethical. Although we cannot change an educator's ethical orientation overnight, we hope that university administrators will work on selecting only fit educators, whose curriculum vitae are amply studied. Moreover, educators need to incorporate, in their ethics education and ethical behavior, value orientation and virtue in a materialistic world (Tang & Chen, 2008). Besides laws and the legal system, a change of ethical community-system building (McCabe, Butterfield, & Treviño, 2006) is to be observed.

Third, the evolution of society does not occur in a stable or linear environment but rather in a dynamic one. To meet the current challenges of human and social vulnerability, universities are inclined to build the "leader of tomorrow" through formal education. However, leaders are not only made out of education. Several other factors, environmental and personal, can influence the decision maker's choice of ethical or unethical behavior (Bommer, Gratto, Gravander, & Tuttle, 1987).

On the environmental level, teaching students how to make more adequate decisions that can better correspond to humanistic, religious, cultural, and societal values of society at large can be applicable only if social values apply to professional decisions (Pavlovic, 1980). Following formal codes of ethics and stated policies can affect the peer environment and can surely have a continuing influence on moral actions (Bommer et al., 1987). On the individual level, Kohlberg's (1963–2008) theory of moral development argues that most individuals are in the conventional stage and are thus not 100 % ethical. It demonstrates that the context plays a big role in determining ethical behavior. But it also postulates that in the conventional stage, individuals tend to follow the values, rules, and regulations. They do what others believe to be right. They respect authority and uphold laws, believing that this will maintain social order and protect and sustain society.

The presented responsible leadership model is believed to be important for making leaders out of university students, by using appropriate tools and materials. However, the study also showed in contrast that the tools cannot fit if they are not integrated within a context of policies and regulations that are implemented at different levels: in the universities, in the professional environment, and in the larger society.

References

AIZ. (2013). *Leadership for global responsibility*. Retrieved August 13, 2015, from https://www.giz.de/…/giz2013-de-aiz-toolbox-leadership-development

Argyropoulou, E. (2015). The challenge of ethical leadership university courses: Preparing leaders for an uncertain, turbulent and divert future. *Revista Lusófona De Educação, 30*(30), 15–41.

Attali, J. (1998). *Pour un modèle européen d'enseignement supérieur*. Paris: Stock.

Audigier, F. (1991). Enseigner la société, transmettre des valeurs: La formation civique et l'éducation aux droits de l'homme: Une mission ancienne, des problèmes permanents, un projet toujours actuel. *Revue française de pédagogie, 94*, 37–48.

Baland, J.-M., & Platteau, J.-P. (1996). *Halting degradation of natural resources: Is there a role for rural communities?* Oxford: Clarendon.

Baylis, J., & Smith, S. (2001). *The globalisation of world politics. An introduction to international relations*. Oxford: Oxford University Press.

Biais, B. (2008, May). Les scandales financiers: Aléa moral ou problème éthique? *Esprit, 2008*, 200–203.

Black, J. S., & Mendenhall, M. (1989). A practical but theory-based framework for selecting cross-cultural training methods. *Human Resources Management, 28*(4), 511–539.

Bohm, A. (2004). Theoretical coding: Text analysis in grounded theory. In U. Flick, E. Kardoff, & I. Steinke (Eds.), *A comparison to qualitative research*. London: Sage.

Bommer, M., Gratto, C., Gravander, J., & Tuttle, M. (1987). A behavioral moral of ethical and unethical decision making. *Journal of Business Ethics, 6*(4), 265–280.

Brookfield, S. D. (1999). *Discussion as a way of teaching: Tools and techniques for democratic classrooms*. San Francisco: Jossey-Bass.

Carroll, A. B. (1991). The pyramid of corporate social responsibility: Toward the moral management of organizational stakeholders. *Business Horizons, 34*, 39–48.

Charter of Human Responsibilities. (2001). Retrieved September 20, 2015, from http://www.charter-human-responsibilities.net

Christensen, L. J., Peirce, E., Hartman, L. P., Hoffman, W. M., & Carrier, J. (2007). Ethics, CSR, and sustainability education in the "Financial Times" top 50 global business schools: Baseline data and future research directions. *Journal of Business Ethics, 73*(4), 347–368.

Code Soleil. (1952). *Le livre des instituteurs*. Paris: SUDEL.

De Menthon, S. (2011). *La responsabilité sociétale des entreprises*. Rapport RSE, Ministère du travail, de l'emploi et de la santé. Retrieved August 20, 2015, from http:// travail-emploi.gouv. fr/IMG/…/Rapport final RSE.pd

Documentation Française. (2015). Retrieved September 4, 2015, from http://www.alliance21. org/2003/rubrique290.html

Drucker, P. (2006). *The effective executive: The definitive guide to getting the right things*. London: HarperCollins.

Durkheim, É. (2013). *Éducation et sociologie*. Paris: PUF. (Original work published 1968)

Emerson, K., & Smutko, L. S. (2011). *UNCG guide to collaborative competencies*. Portland, OR: Policy Consensus Initiative and University Network for Collaborative Governance.

European Commission. (2008). *Entrepreneurship in higher education, especially within non-business studies*. Final report of the expert group. Retrieved September 20, 2015, from http:// ec.europa.eu/enterprise/policies/sme/documents/education-training-entrepreneurship/

European Commission. (2013). *Improving the quality of teaching and learning in Europe's higher education institutions*. High Level Group on the Modernization of Higher Education. Retrieved September 20, 2015, from http://wwwec.europa.eu/education/library/reports/modernisation_en.pd

Gandz, J., & Hayes, N. (1988). Teaching business ethics. *Journal of Business Ethics, 7*, 657–669.

Glaser, B., & Strauss, A. (1967). *The discovery of grounded theory: Strategies for qualitative research*. Mill Valley, CA: Sociology Press.

Green Paper. (2001, July). *Promoting a European framework for corporate social responsibility*. Brussels: European Commission.

Hahn, C. (1998). *Becoming political: Comparative perspectives on citizenship education*. Albany, NY: SUNY Press.

Jacobs, M. (2009). How business schools have failed business. *The Wall Street Journal*. Retrieved August 20, 2015, from http://www.wsj.com/articles/SB124052874488350333

Kerr, D. (2004). Citizenship education in the curriculum: An international review. *The School Field, 10*(3/4), 91–110.

Kohlberg, L. (2008). The development of children's orientations toward a moral order sequence in the development of moral thought. *Human Development, 51*, 8–20.

Kurland, N. B., Michaud, K. E. H., Best, M., Wohldmann, E., Cox, H., Pontikis, K., et al. (2010). Overcoming silos: The role of an interdisciplinary course in shaping a sustainability network. *Academy of Management Learning and Education, 9*(3), 457–476.

Kwek, S. H. (2011). *Innovation in the classroom: Design thinking for 21st century learning*. Retrieved September 20, 2015, from http://www.stanford.edu/group/redlab/cgibin/publica-tions_resources.php

L'herminier, S. (2015). *Tu seras un manager responsable mon fils! Intégrer la RSE dans l'enseignement supérieur*. Gap, France: Ed Yves Michel.

Lebanese Association for Educational Studies (LAES). (2006). *National Education Strategy in Lebanon*. Retrieved September 4, 2015, from http://www.laes.org/…/Vision%20Document%20 French%20

LeClair, D. T. (1999). The use of a behavioral simulation to teach business ethics. *Teaching Business Ethics, 3*, 283–296.

Loorbach, D. A. (2010). Transition management: New mode of governance for sustainable development. *Governance, 23*, 161–183.

Marshall, T. H. (1950). *Citizenship and social class: And other essays*. Cambridge: University Press.

Matten, D., & Moon, J. (2004). "Implicit" and "explicit" CSR: A conceptual framework for understanding CSR in Europe. In A. Habisch, J. Jonker, M. Wegner, & R. Schmidpeter (Eds.), *CSR across Europe*. Berlin: Springer.

McCabe, D. L., Butterfield, K. D., & Trevinõ, L. K. (2006). Academic dishonesty in graduate business programs: Prevalence, causes, and proposed action. *Academy of Management Learning and Education, 5*(3), 294–305.

McDonald, G. M., & Donleavy, G. D. (1995). Objections to the teaching of business ethics. *Journal of Business Ethics, 10*, 829–835.

Meredith, J. (2015). Design thinking and the internal: A case study. In R. V. Zande, E. Bohemia, & I. Digranes (Eds.), *Proceedings of the 3rd International Conference for Design Education Researchers*. Portland, OR: PSU Library.

Michener, W. K., Baerwald, T. J., Firth, P., Palmer, M. A., Rosenberger, J. L., Sandlin, E. A., et al. (2001). Defining and unraveling biocomplexity. *BioScience, 51*(12), 1018–1023.

MIT Sloan School of Management. (2015). *Sustainability initiative MIT sustainability summit 2015*. Retrieved September 4, 2015, from http://mitsloan.mit.edu/sustainability

Morin, E. (1999). *Seven complex lessons in education for the future* [Les sept savoirs nécessaires à l'éducation du futur] (N. Poller, Trans.). UNESCO, EDP-99/W.

OECD. (2009). Principes directeurs de l'OCDE à l'intention des firmes Multinationales. Pouvoir des consommateurs. *L'éthique des affaires et les principes de l'OCDE : que faire pour éviter une nouvelle crise?* Paris: OCDE.

Olson, M., & Raffanti, M. A. (2004). *Grounded learning: An application of grounded theory in educational practice*. Paper presented at the Grounded Theory Symposium, Alexandria, VA. Retrieved September 10, 2015, from http://home.mindspring.com/~tagregory/sitebuilder-content/sitebuilderfiles/RO.pdf

Orlitzky, M., & Moon, J. (2008). *Second European survey on corporate social responsibility research, education, and other initiatives in business schools and universities* (Draft Report to EABiS). Retrieved September 10, 2015, from https://www.nottingham.ac.uk/business/ICCSR/research.php?action...id

Ostrom, E., Gardner, R., & Walker, J. (1994). *Rules, games, and common-pool resources*. Ann Arbor: Univ. Mich. Press.

Otto, S., & Kaufer, K. (2013). *Leading from the emerging future: From ego-system to eco-system economies: Applying theory U to transforming business, society, and self*. San Francisco: Berrett-Koehler.

Pavlovic, K. R. (1980). Autonomy and obligations: Is there an engineering ethics? In A. Flores (Ed.), *Ethical problems in engineering: Readings* (2nd ed.). Troy, NY: Renssealer Polytechnique Institute.

Pfeffer, J. (1993). Barriers to the advance of organizational science: Paradigm development as a dependent variable. *The Academy of Management Review, 18*(4), 599–620.

Phillips, S. M. (Chair). (2004). *Ethics education in business schools*. Report of the Ethics Education Task Force to AACSB International Board of Directors, St. Louis, Missouri. Retrieved September 20, 2015, from: http://gfmc.org/issues/pdfs/Ethicseducation.pdf

Porter, M., & Kramer, M. (2006). *Strategy and society: The link between competitive advantage and corporate social responsibility* (Harvard Business Review). Boston, MA: Harvard Business School Press.

Prosser, A. (1995). *Teaching and learning social responsibility* (HERDSA Gold Guide No.3). Canberra: HERDSA.

Resick, C., Hanges, P., Dickenson, M., & Mitchelson, J. (2006). A cross-cultural examination of the endorsement of ethical leadership. *Journal of Business Ethics, 63*, 345–359.

Rousseau, M., & Mccarthy, S. (2007). Educating managers from an evidence-based perspective. *Academy of Management Learning and Education, 6*, 84–101.

Sekiou, L. (2001). *Gestion des Ressources Humaines*. Brussels: Ed. De Boeck.

Simon, S. (2002). Participatory online environmental education at the Open University UK. In W. Leal Filho (Ed.), *Teaching sustainability in universities*. Frankfurt: Peter Lang.

Sims, R. (2002). *Teaching business ethics for effective learning*. West Port, CT: Praeger.

Starratt, R. (2004). *Ethical leadership*. San Francisco: Jossey-Bass.

Strauss, A. (1987). *Qualitative analysis for social scientists*. New York: Cambridge University Press.

Strauss, A. L., & Corbin, J. M. (1990). *Basics of qualitative research: Grounded theory procedures and techniques*. Newbury Park, CA: Sage.

Tang, T. L.-P., & Chen, Y.-J. (2008). Intelligence vs. wisdom: The love of money, machiavellianism, and unethical behavior across college major and gender. *Journal of Business Ethics, 82*, 1–26.

UNESCO, PNUD. (1996). *Le système d'enseignement supérieur et l'université Libanaise-Eléments de diagnostic*. Retrieved September 16, 2016, from http://unesdoc.unesco.org/images/0013/001358/135878fo.pdf

United Nations. (2015). *Paris climate summit must balance leadership role of developed countries, responsibility of developing ones, says secretary-general at G20 meeting*. Retrieved August 10, 2015, from http://www.un.org/press/en/2015/sgsm17327.doc.htm

United Nations Educational, Scientific and Cultural Organization (UNESCO). (1997). *Educating for sustainable future: A transdisciplinary vision for concerted action*. Retrieved August 20, 2015, from http://www.unesco.org/education/tlsf/mods/theme_a/.../mod01t05s01.html

United Nations Educational, Scientific and Cultural Organization (UNESCO). (1998). *World declaration on higher education for the twenty-first century: Vision and action and framework for priority action for change and development in higher education*. Retrieved August 20, 2015, from http://www.unesco.org/education/educprog/wche/declaration_eng.htm

United Nations Educational, Scientific and Cultural Organization (UNESCO). (2013). *Global citizenship education: Preparing learners to the challenges of the 21st century*. Retrieved August 10, 2015, from http://www.unesco.org/new/en/global-citizenship-education/

United Nations Educational, Scientific and Cultural Organization (UNESCO). (2015, October). Forum Mondial sur les politiques de jeunesse. *Transformations sociales et Dialogue interculturel*. Retrieved August 10, 2015, from http://fr.unesco.org/events/forum-mondial-politiques-jeunesse

University of Edinburgh. (2015). Social responsibility and sustainability. *University and EUSA win NUS sustainability and social responsibility awards*. Retrieved August 20, 2015, from http://www.ed.ac.uk/about/.../news/university-and-eusa-win-nus-srs-awards

Wade, R. (1994). *Village republics: Economic conditions for collective action in South India*. Oakland: ICS Press.

WCED. (1987). *Our common future: Report of the world*. Retrieved September 12, 2015, from http://www.un-documents.net/our-common-future.pdf

Weber, M. (2008). *The protestant ethic and the spirit of capitalism* (R. Swedberg, Ed.). New York: W. W. Norton and Company. (Original work published 1904)

Zhao, Z. N. (2005). *Four 'Pillars of Learning' for the reorientation and reorganization of curriculum: Reflection and discussion*. Asia-Pacific Programme of Educational Innovation for Development (APEID)/UNESCO Asia Pacific Regional Bureau for Education.

Chapter 24
On the Analysis of Cyber Physical Systems

Abdullah Abu Omar, Amjad Gawanmeh, and Alain April

Abstract CPS uses recent computing, communication, and control methods to monitor and control geographically dispersed field sites in order provide and maintain a high level of confidence about their operation and, hence, plays an important role in several sustainable systems and has extraordinary significance for the future of several industrial domains. The complexity of these systems requires that adequate attention is paid to their design process, since any failure in detecting errors in safety critical systems can lead to catastrophic situations. This work shows how different methods can be used for the analysis of CPS at different levels of abstraction. The method is demonstrated on an industrial case study of a four-tank process that illustrates several challenging features in the design and implementation of CPS.

Keywords Cyber physical systems • CPS • Performance analysis • Four-tank process

Introduction

The new paradigms and tremendous advances in computing, communications, and control have provided and supported wide range of applications in all domains of live, in particular, bridging the physical components and the cyberspace leading to the Cyber Physical Systems (CPS) (Rawat, Rodrigues, & Stojmenovic, 2015).

A.A. Omar (✉)
Department of Electrical and Computer Engineering, Khalifa University, Abu Dhabi, UAE
e-mail: 100038694@kustar.ac.ae

A. Gawanmeh
Department of Electrical and Computer Engineering, Concordia University,
Montreal, QC, Canada

Department of Electrical and Computer Engineering, Khalifa University, Abu Dhabi, UAE
e-mail: amjad.gawanmeh@kustar.ac.ae

A. April
Department of Software Engineering, Universite du Quebec, Ecole de Technologie
Superieure, Montreal, QC, Canada
e-mail: alain.april@etsmtl.ca

© Springer International Publishing Switzerland 2017
R. Benlamri, M. Sparer (eds.), *Leadership, Innovation and Entrepreneurship as Driving Forces of the Global Economy*, Springer Proceedings in Business and Economics, DOI 10.1007/978-3-319-43434-6_24

The notion of CPS is to use recent computing, communication, and control methods to design and operate intelligent and autonomous systems that can provide using cutting edge technologies. This requires the use of computing resources for sensing, processing, analysis, predicting, understanding of data, and then communication resources for interaction, intervene, and interface management. In addition, it provides control for systems so that they can interoperate, evolve, and run in a stable evidence-based environment. CPS plays an important role in several sustainable systems and has extraordinary significance for the future of several industrial domains, and hence, it is expected that the complexity of CPS will continue to increase due to the continuous integration of cyber components with physical and industrial systems.

This paper presents a practical method for using three different techniques for the analysis of CPS systems. In the first, we use Matlab in order to provide an exact solution under specific initial conditions for the system. In the second, we provide an approximated model and use simulation in order to validate design requirement. Finally, we present a system formal model at high level of abstraction and use formal analysis (Abrial, 2009) to verify design properties. We illustrated the proposed method on the four-tank problem, which is a multivariable control process that demonstrates several challenging problems.

Proposed CPS Analysis Methodology

Practically, the design of the system is conducted based on proper rigorous methods, by first providing exact model using a set of differential equations and then using analytical methods to find solutions for the given set of equations that is achieved under certain assumptions. For instance, the controller is designed by providing a solution for the set of equations under certain initial conditions. While this assumption is practical, it only guarantees the stability of the system under the assumed initial conditions only. Hence, it is recommended that a complex system such as CPS should go through different types of analysis in order to provide high level of assurance about its reliability, which in turn reduces the chance of errors in its operation. Figure 24.1 illustrates our proposed novel method for the analysis of CPS systems, where the behavior of the given system is usually described using an exact model with a set of differential equations.

We first intend to find the solution of the problem based on Okpanachi (2010) by solving the system of equations and implement it using Matlab. Next, we intend to apply linear approximation on the model of the process under analysis, which is a common practice in the design of several control systems. The approximated model is implemented using high level language and then simulated based on high level control strategies that we defined. A set of design requirement to be met by the system are then identified. For instance, stability is one of the fundamental requirements that a control process must satisfy. Based on this, it can be shown that the behavior of the approximated model is analogous to the behavior of the original

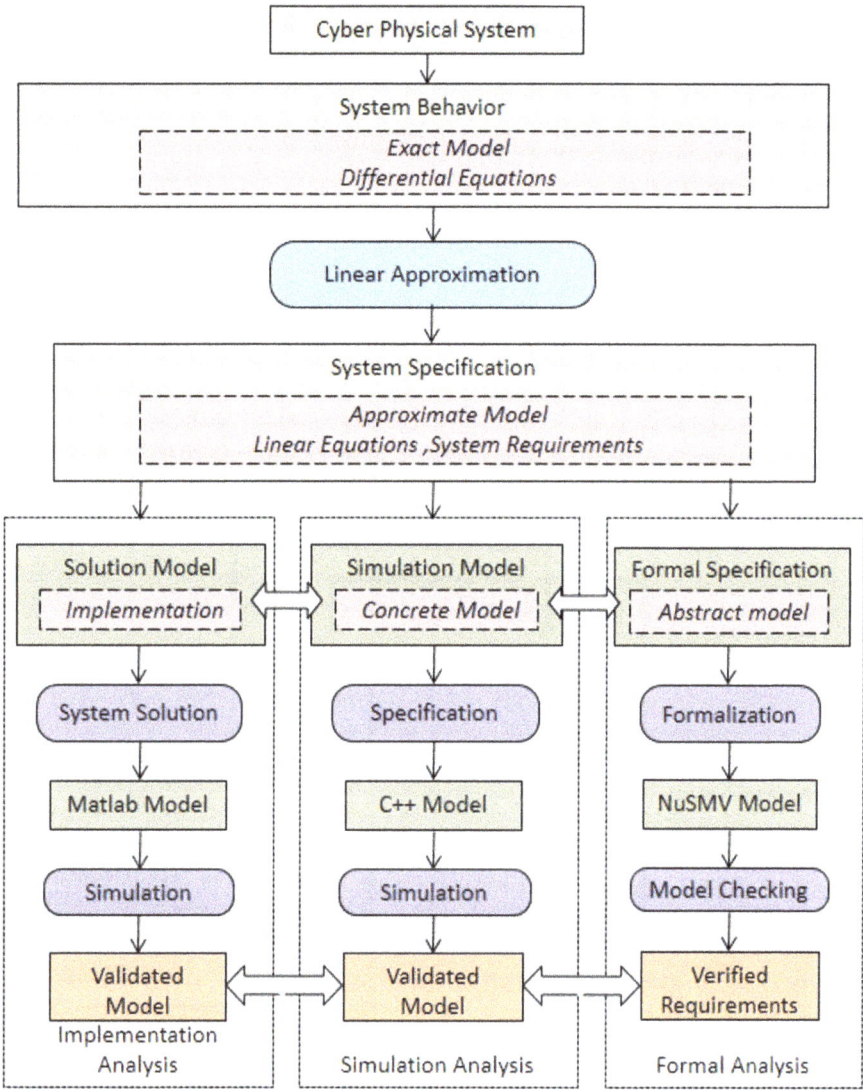

Fig. 24.1 Proposed CPS analysis methodology

model. Then, we intend to use formal specifications in order to derive an abstract model for the given system, which is then implemented using the underlying verification tool. The set of requirement are then formally verified for this model. For instance, when model checking (Baier & Katoen, 2008) is used, the system must be represented as a state-based model, and requirement are represented as properties. In the next section, we present a practical case study that was previously implemented in a CPS system. The example chosen contains different aspects of a complex CPS system and outlines several challenges in the design, operation, analysis and verification of CPS systems.

Case Study: Four-Tank Control System

We demonstrate the proposed analysis methodology on the four-tank process, which was originally proposed in Johansson (2000) as a multivariable control process. The problem has been implemented using different control strategies (Okpanachi, 2010), and also it was implemented within SCADA environment (Anseth et al., 2010). We follow the specifications and the mathematical model of the system as it was deduced in (Okpanachi, 2010). Figure 24.2 below illustrate a diagrammatic representation of the quadruple-tank process which consists of four interconnected water tanks and two pumps. There are two sensors that provide water level for the two main tanks. As illustrated in Fig. 24.2, pump01 extracts water from the bottom reservoir and feeds into tank 1 and tank 4 via a three-way valve (valve 1), while pump 2 feeds tank 2 and tank 3 via another three-way valve (valve 2). The voltages to the two valves are manipulated such that they determine the proportion of the flow that

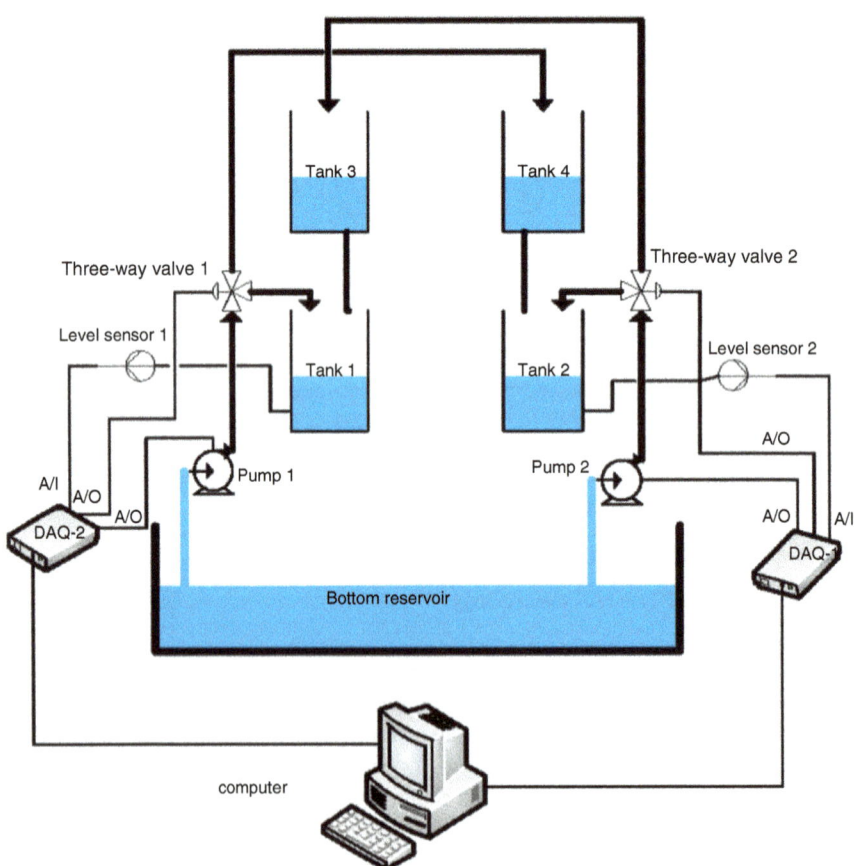

Fig. 24.2 The four-tank process

goes into the tanks associated with each. Based on the process controller implemented in (Anseth et al., 2010), the regulation of this process is designed using different types of controllers; however, it has been concluded based on several researches that the splitting of water flow from the pump into all the four tanks causes process interactions and control loop interactions (Okpanachi, 2010).

The linearized model of the quadruple-tank process has a multivariable zero, which can be located in either the left or the right half-plane by simply changing a valve. Both the location and the direction of a multivariable zero are important for control design. They have direct physical interpretations for the quadruple-tank process, which make the process suitable to use in control education. The mathematical model for the four-tank process was derived by applying the mass balance and Bernoulli theorem to each tank and can be described using nonlinear differential equations, shown below for all tanks (Johansson, 2000).

$$\frac{dh_1}{dt} = \frac{a_1}{A_1}\sqrt{2gh_1} + \frac{a_3}{A_1}\sqrt{2gh_3} + \frac{\gamma_1 k_1}{A_1}v_1 \qquad (24.1)$$

$$\frac{dh_2}{dt} = \frac{a_2}{A_2}\sqrt{2gh_2} + \frac{a_4}{A_2}\sqrt{2gh_4} + \frac{\gamma_2 k_2}{A_2}v_2 \qquad (24.2)$$

$$\frac{dh_3}{dt} = \frac{a_3}{A_3}\sqrt{2gh_3} + \frac{(1-\gamma_2)k_2}{A_3}v_2 \qquad (24.3)$$

$$\frac{dh_4}{dt} = \frac{a_4}{A_4}\sqrt{2gh_4} + \frac{(1-\gamma_1)k_1}{A_4}v_1 \qquad (24.4)$$

where the parameters used above include A_i for cross-sectional area of tank i, a_i is for cross-sectional area of the outlet of the tank, h_i is for the water level in tank i, v_i is for the voltage applied to pump i, k_i is the flow from pump i, and g is the acceleration due to gravity. The nonlinear model of equations was linearized around the chosen working point given by the level in the tanks; hence, in our analysis, we will follow a similar approach, where an approximate model will be provided around the working point of the tank level with an accepted margin of error (Anseth et al., 2010; Johansson, 2000; Okpanachi, 2010). A proposed solution for the system differential equations was provided by Okpanachi (2010); hence, we intend to use Matlab analysis based on the above solution. The system mode of above equations is approximated by using simple linear approximations and working around a relatively small delta around the chosen working point given by the level in the tanks. We intend to run simulations for different types of settings for initial value of water level in the tanks and also for pumps and valves. For instance, the initial values for pump voltages can be considered as v1=4 V, v2=1.5 V, where the pump operates on a voltage of scale between 0 and 5 V. While the valve initial values can be set to $\gamma_1=0.4$, and $\gamma_2=0.4$, then the simulation can be run for different cases of initial value for the four tanks.

Conclusion and Future Work

This paper proposed a novel reliability analysis approach for CPS systems based on a combination of techniques including linear approximation, abstraction, simulation, and model checking. We use simulation in order to validate the set of control strategists applied on the linearized model can lead into a stable system under given set of initial conditions. Next, we intend to implement the solution of the problem using Matlab and use formal specifications in order to derive an abstract model for the given system, which is then implemented using model checking to verify high level properties about the behavior of the system, which can be used efficiently to validate design requirements, for instance, *starting from the initial state, the water level in tanks 1 and 2 must always reach the level between the two threshold defined in the setup*. To the best of our knowledge, there is no work in literature that addressed reliability analysis of CPS at different levels of abstraction. As a future work, we intent to implement this method and demonstrate it on the four-tank process system.

References

Abrial, J. R. (2009). Faultless systems: Yes we can! *IEEE Computer Journal, 42*(9), 30–36.

Anseth, R., Manjula, E. V., Obada, S. S., Okpanachi, A. D., Raghunath, B., & Utake E. O. (2010). *Design of scada system used on a four-tank laboratory process*. Technical Report SCE4006. Norway: Telemark University College.

Baier, C., & Katoen, J.-P. (2008). *Principles of model checking*. Cambridge, USA: MIT Press.

Johansson, K. H. (2000). The quadruple-tank process: A multivariable laboratory process with an adjustable zero. *IEEE Transactions on Control Systems Technology, 8*(3), 456–465.

Okpanachi, A. V. (2010). *Developing advanced control strategies for a 4-tank laboratory process*. Master's Thesis report.

Rawat, D. B., Rodrigues, J. J. P. C., & Stojmenovic, I. (2015). *Cyber-physical systems: From theory to practice*. Boca Raton, FL: CRC Press.

Chapter 25
Innovative Marketing in the Health Industry

Zahra Ladha Jiwani and Marc Poulin

Abstract The health care industry continues to face the challenges of being able to provide high quality services at an acceptable cost. One of the challenges being faced is the reactive versus proactive mode of health professionals and patients, in dealing with health issues. This is due in part to the incongruent incentive structures in place for the B2B stakeholders, as well as the need to create greater awareness of preventive care and its benefit over reactive care.

While some stakeholders are now increasing their focus on preventive health care initiatives in order to be more effective and efficient, the health care industry still faces the ultimate marketing challenge of changing health care providers to shift towards a more proactive versus reactive approach to health care.

This article explores the literature and industry best practices in marketing for companies focusing on preventive health care. The article discusses a variety of ideas and critically analyzes their potential in the context of a company's innovative business model on the global market.

Keywords Innovation • Health industry • Marketing • B2B • Preventive • Social marketing

Introduction: Shifts in Healthcare

There is growing evidence of increasing preventive health care practices in order to decrease the costs of healthcare, as well as increase the overall well-being of patients. Innovative companies are attempting to create new business models to make this transition but a key objective is an effective marketing strategy. Since the business model adopted by the firm in our case study will influence the selection of marketing techniques, we will present the basic principles of their model in our

Z.L. Jiwani (✉) • M. Poulin
Canadian University of Dubai, Dubai, United Arab Emirates
e-mail: Zahra.jiwani@cud.ac.ae; marc@cud.ac.ae

© Springer International Publishing Switzerland 2017   303
R. Benlamri, M. Sparer (eds.), *Leadership, Innovation and Entrepreneurship as Driving Forces of the Global Economy*, Springer Proceedings in Business and Economics, DOI 10.1007/978-3-319-43434-6_25

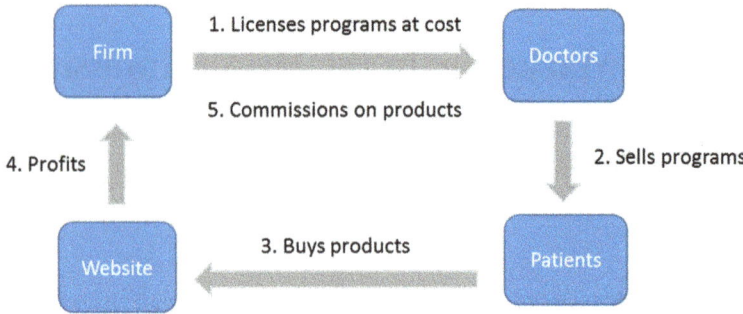

Fig. 25.1 Firm's revenue model

introduction. It is clear that creating awareness of the benefits and solutions to all stakeholders will be the major challenge.

The firm in our case study was quite conscious of the resistance health professionals and institutions would have by increasing a focus on preventive health care, where effectiveness is more long term, difficult to prove, and that revenues are reduced due to preventive solutions that are less expensive. In fact, the physician who founded the firm had himself made the transition from traditional health care models to preventive. He was part of private clinics and hospitals where actions were driven by short term revenues in a reactive system.

The strategy of the firm was to develop a model where the doctors would have an insignificant cost to make the transition, be more effective, have support, and gradually replace their source of revenues. The firm created innovative and holistic programs that consist of procedures and medical equipment used to measure, mentor, and monitor patients. As depicted in the firm's revenue model in Fig. 25.1, it licenses these programs to doctors while making no profit. This approach eases the doctor's adoption of the new approach. The firm then supports the doctors in treating their patients effectively. The firm created an app and monitoring software where clients are followed in real time in order to capture personal health data. The data is used to make adjustments to the programs and coach the patient more frequently, hence be in preventive health care mode. The firm offers very attractive products at wholesale prices to patients such as healthy organic food, medical accessories and devices, nutraceuticals, and pharmaceuticals, and all of these products are only made available if they support the patients' health. In this model, the firm obtains its profit from the products and not the programs. The doctors obtain a commission from all of their patients' purchases on the firm's e-commerce website. Gradually over time, the doctors would obtain a growing recurring income that would replace revenues from a reactive system. Although the firm is selling programs to doctors (B2B), the success of their model stems from doctors promoting the effectiveness and efficiency of the firm's products. Hence, if the patients or the general public are not open or aware to the effectiveness of preventive health care, then this model will face major obstacles to succeed.

According to the American Board of Medical Specialties (ABMS), preventive medicine aims to protect, promote, and maintain health and well-being and to prevent disease, disability, and death (ACPM, 2016). While this may seem logical and understood, it remains to be comprehended by the vast majority of health care providers in the industry, and for those who do have a basic or more thorough understanding of it, they still may not see the value in adopting this preventive versus reactive approach in their practices. The industry is starting to see some derived demand from patients, who are making an effort to make lifestyle changes in their health before they reach a point of diagnosis, resulting in a decrease quality of life, and increased costs to insurance companies overall. An important challenge remains how to show precise value of the preventive approach.

Globally, it is evident that the healthcare industry is continually challenged with the task of being able to provide high quality services at costs that fit within the strict public budgets. While health professionals as well as patients have always taken a reactive approach to healthcare, we are starting to see a shift as many stakeholders see the importance of preventative health care, and how this can lead to more effective and efficient healthcare outcomes. To date, most doctors have been trained and are paid for treating patients, making reactive measures more enticing than preventative measures. Patients are also not incentivized to live a preventative life and seek advice from health professionals beforehand, as their medical coverage reimburses them for treatments after diagnosis of issues and illnesses. The fact that drugs and medical treatments required to treat reactive diagnosis could substantially be decreased if preventative healthcare was put in place makes this an issue worth exploring. Dr. Michael E. Porter states that the "only way to truly contain costs in health care is to improve outcomes. Achieving and maintaining good health is much less expensive than the consequences of poor health." He believes that nations will require movement towards universal insurance coverage as well as restructuring the care delivery system. When many people lack access to primary and preventive care, high-value care can be a challenge, explaining why countries that have implemented universal insurance have lower health care spending than the USA (Porter, 2009). A study conducted by Bertucci et al. analyzed three preventive approaches: school-based programs, dietary restrictions, and increased exercise. Their results showed that prevention would extend quality years of life to more Americans at a lower cost than when primarily implementing reactive care (Bertucci & Miller, 2010).

The second challenge facing innovative companies in this industry is the ability to market their services to these healthcare providers (B2B) that would be open to increase their preventive health care efforts. Many healthcare providers, given their current incentive and pay structures, are not incentivised to practice preventive care with their patients since they bill and get paid for reactive solutions. For some health care providers, it is a lack of understanding of preventive care in general, and for others it's a lack of access to the required equipment and instruments to aid in the delivery of such a practice, and for others, it is also the need for more education to demonstrate this seems to be a worthwhile manner in which to practice, both from a payment perspective and a results perspective. As shown in Fig. 25.1, the firm needs to market the new revenue stream of reoccurring revenues from different products.

The paper will discuss how healthcare providers can benefit within a business model proposed by the firm. They can not only benefit from patients who currently ask about a preventive approach to their health, but also from those who do not ask for various reasons such as lack of understanding, awareness, or simply lack of interest and conviction. The paper will discuss how the more traditional marketing vehicles are not sufficient on their own, and the methods such as social marketing, loyalty and advocacy, as well as consumer decision-making models are all conducive to effective marketing towards B2B in the healthcare industry. Finally, the authors will recommend an innovative marketing model that combines effective decision-making steps with the need to develop the health providers into advocates. Strategies for the integration of social marketing and sales will also be integrated for each step of the process from awareness to purchase.

Literature Review

The first part of the literature review will give a brief understanding of preventive care and its importance today. It will present support for various benefits of preventive health care such as cost reduction and greater effectiveness. The aim of the literature review is also to discuss the need for the healthcare industry to intervene and contribute to creating and building awareness of preventive medicine as a whole, to the B2B sector. Finally, it will cover how social marketing, loyalty programs, and consumer behavior decision-making models all play a vital role in marketing to healthcare providers and how it has led to success in changing health related behaviors.

As mentioned in the introduction, the objective of preventive medicine is to protect, promote, and maintain health and well-being and to prevent disease, disability, and death (ACPM, 2016). Woolf defines two types of prevention. Primary prevention can prevent the disease process in its earliest stages by promoting healthier lifestyles or immunizing against infectious disease. Secondary prevention can reduce subsequent morbidity or mortality, by detecting and treating asymptomatic risk factor (Woolf & Atkins, 2001). Preventive medicine physicians are "uniquely trained in both clinical medicine and public health. They have the skills needed to understand and reduce the risks of disease, disability, and death in individuals and in population groups" (Hull, 2008). Surprisingly, preventive medicine is not a new field. In fact, it has been a recognized specialty in the USA since 1954, making us wonder why experts in this field are not fully being utilized, especially nowadays when it is needed more than ever before (Hull, 2008). With modern IT technology that allows us to monitor vital signs and key biomarkers, combined with the medical research on causes of diseases, preventive healthcare is becoming more viable.

Globally, we are seeing a rise in severe illnesses. In the USA, for instance, we are seeing rising levels of obesity and the associated chronic diseases, increasing the number of patients being diagnosed with cardiovascular disease, diabetes, and cancer (Hull, 2008). Bertucci et al. also state that although the majority of government and public attention is given to reactive healthcare, the best way for America to solve its growing health concerns such as obesity is to improve awareness and policy for preventive measures (Bertucci & Miller, 2010).

It is believed that disease prevention/health promotion approaches are the solution to slowing the rise in health care spending (Thorpe, 2005). By changing lifestyles, it is possible to prevent a disease, thereby avoiding the expensive and rising medical and pharmaceutical treatments that are associated with the diagnosis, making it more evident that we need to focus on overall health and wellness proactively, instead of reactively (Griffiths, 2014). Chronic diseases, such as heart disease, cancer, and diabetes, are responsible for seven of every ten deaths among Americans each year and account for 75 % of the nation's health spending (Prevention, 2013).

With regard to the role of the B2B sector in healthcare, the clinician plays a pivotal role in both primary and secondary prevention. It is this segment in healthcare that administers vaccinations, screens for risk factors such as high blood pressure and high cholesterol, gives patients advice about smoking, provides screening tests for early detection of cancer and other chronic conditions, and advises patients about the benefits and risks of preventive therapies (Woolf & Atkins, 2001).

Research shows that many physicians still do not know about preventive care and its benefits in comparison to reactive care, and how to implement it. Research conducted by Christian et al. studied 500 doctors to test their awareness of prevention guidelines for cardiovascular disease in the USA. Their results concluded that while awareness of the different guideline was high, the efforts to promote their utilization were still needed. They believe that targeted education and support for prevention of CVD is required to help these physicians (Christian & Mills, 2006). According to the Australian Medical Association (AMA), the effectiveness of preventative care is dependent on doctors having the most up-to-date information and best-practice guidelines (AMA, 2007).

According to Woolf and Atkins (2001), some of the challenges facing physicians in implementing preventive care may be:

1. Conflicting recommendations from different organizations
2. The advocacy positions that some of the physicians hold
3. Time pressures that these clinicians face may have them question the value of some routine preventive interventions
4. Although the public has access to more information regarding prevention, this may be seen as commercial self-interest (Woolf & Atkins, 2001)

There are several marketing approaches that can be used to produce innovative marketing strategies in the health care industry. Jiwani (2014) has investigated consumer behavior, which include the hierarchy of effects model, the consumer decision-making model, the Fishbein attitude model, and several others. The Fishbein model, for example, could be used if we are interested in understanding consumer attitudes towards cars. We would create a list of attributes such as style, acceleration, price, etc. The consumers are then asked to give each brand of interest a specific rating. From this, we would know whether or not the consumer feels that the chosen brands possess each of the selected attributes and to what level (Jiwani, 2014).

This model, although relevant in understanding consumer behavior, does not allow us to understand their thought process in selecting these brands prior to rating the brands. Another influential model is the hierarchy of effects model. This model was developed by Lavidge and Steiner (1961). According to the hierarchy of effects model, a consumer goes through several steps before making a purchase decision. They include awareness, knowledge, liking, preference, conviction, and the actual purchase (Lavidge and Steiner 1961).

The hierarchy of effects model begins with the state where a consumer has no awareness about the brand. Then, awareness is created as a result of external stimuli such as advertising or word of mouth. By obtaining and absorbing more information related to the product, the consumer gains more knowledge. This information generally causes either a like or dislike feeling in an individual, which then has the potential to lead to brand preference. Once an individual likes the brand, they need to be convinced to actually make a purchase (Lavidge and Steiner 1961).

Another widely used model is the consumer decision-making model, which was first introduced by John Dewey in 1909 (Granbois, 1979). This model states that individuals go through five stages when making purchase decisions. First, they recognize a problem or need for something. Then they gather information, evaluate alternatives, make a purchase, and, finally, do a post-purchase evaluation.

One component that seems to be a key in marketing to B2B but is not part of the thus far mentioned models is the idea of building loyalty during the process and especially once purchase is made. McKinsey Consulting has done extensive research on this and uses it in several of their models both in B2B and B2C marketing. One in particular is the Loyalty Loop Model (Court & Elzinga, 2009). The company developed this model after conducting research on the purchase decisions of nearly 20,000 consumers across five industries and three continents. Their results determined three key findings. First, due to the increase in media and products, marketers need to find new ways to have their brands enter the consumer's mind at the start of the decision-making process. In addition, they need to determine methods for two-way communication with their consumers. Finally, the comfirmation that there is a need for loyalty programs, in order to build relationships with customers (Court & Elzinga, 2009).

From the literature related to marketing for healthcare, emerges the idea of social marketing. Many innovative companies today are exploring social marketing as a vehicle to connect with health practitioners. As in traditional marketing, the development and implementation of social marketing programs is based on the four Ps: product, price, place, and promotion, but in addition it incorporates the partnership and participation of stakeholders to enhance public health and engage policy makers (Suarez-Almazor, 2011). Andreasen A. defines social marketing as "the application of proven concepts and techniques drawn from the commercial sector to promote changes in diverse socially important behaviors such as drug use, and smoking" (Evans, 2006). It has been used to influence health behavior in a very positive way (Evans, 2006). Its role in preventive care will be discussed, linking it to the results that preventive care aims to prove. Social marketing is defined as using marketing principles to influence the acceptability of social ideas (Lefebvre, 2011). It was used early on in developing countries to foster the use of various health-related products and services. In addition, it has been used in the developed world to reduce behavioral risk factors for diseases (Lefebvre, 2011).

Results from a study conducted by (Stead & Gordon, 2007) found that social marketing can form an effective framework for behavior change interventions and can provide a useful "toolkit" for organizations that are trying to change health behaviors (Stead & Gordon, 2007). Evan uses the example of then changing health behaviours of Hispanics. He believes that social marketers use such factors to construct conceptual frameworks that model complex pathways from messages to changes in behavior (Evans, 2006).

While decision-making models, loyalty programs, and social marketing have proven to be effective in the B2B segment of healthcare, it must be noted that traditional vehicles to advertising must not be ignored. Traditional marketing techniques have always been used to communicate the four Ps: product, promotion, price, and place. The objective of traditional marketing is to increase sales. Strategies have included advertising, Sales Promotion, sponsorships, Marketing literature, Public relations, Personal Selling, and Direct Marketing. According to Paramount MD Digital Marketing, B2B in healthcare still requires traditional forms of advertising because key decision-makers at companies still see value in being able to present printed materials to others involved in the process, during board meetings (Paramount MD Digital Marketing, 2011). In addition, personal selling methods whereby a company representative meets face to face with the prospective buyer is a key to building long term relationships with them (Michael Solomon, 2013). Customers expect a sales representative to be extremely knowledgeable about their business and perhaps even their own individual profile (Lingqvist & Plotkin, 2015). Lingqvist et al.'s research showed that a B2B customer will regularly use six different interaction channels throughout the decision journey, and that the traditional sales model that follows steps from lead to purchase is no longer successful on its own. Instead, B2B companies across industries are moving towards journey-based sales strategies (Lingqvist & Plotkin, 2015).

Research Methodology

Problem Description

The firm faces two key challenges in the area of marketing.

1. Despite physicians and other B2B customers only having established incentive structures for reactive measures, they should adopt a more preventive approach to healthcare, knowing that this will be conducive to minimizing the risks of patients becoming sick at a later stage. The firm needs to create awareness and educate the B2B segment on the benefits involved in adopting this approach.
2. The firm needs to determine what marketing strategies to adopt in order to successfully target these B2B customers.

Problem Statement

What marketing strategies can the firm employ in order to encourage the B2B sector to move towards a more preventive versus reactive approach to practicing medicine?
Subproblems that result from the main problem are:

1. What marketing strategies can be used to create awareness among healthcare providers who lack any knowledge or experience with preventive versus reactive medicine?
2. For those physicians who have awareness and interest in preventive care, what marketing strategies can be used to show that the firm's solutions are an appropriate and feasible solution?
3. What are the ways in which this company can incentivize this B2B segment to adopt the firm's solutions throughout the purchase process?

Research Approach

The research approach was exploratory and descriptive in nature due to the novelty of the business model and the recent changes in the health sector. The authors conducted several interviews with the firm's stakeholders using open ended questions. The authors also interacted with the firm since the initial stages of establishing the business model in order to understand the key issues, challenges, and possible solutions.

A challenge with this research approach is to validate and have reliable information. The authors had constant interaction and repeated questions to various levels of management. This research approach is may be difficult to rely on when drawing conclusions but it is quite appropriate to identify many issues and understand the challenges.

Proposed Marketing Strategy and Marketing Model

Based on the barriers in the literature review, and the learning opportunities, the marketing framework below is being proposed as part of the marketing strategy that a company facing this problem can use to achieve its goals. Sufficient information is available to make sound proposals to the firm in addressing its two key marketing challenges. With regard to the first issue of how to address the B2B segment in adopting the preventive versus reactive attitude towards healthcare, the firm in our case study needs to create awareness and educate both the B2B on the importance of preventive versus reactive approaches to healthcare, giving them evidence based reasons to embrace this method. In addition, once awareness has been created, we can address the second issue of educating health professionals and providing solutions to implement services, through use of technology and equipment that will help them in the process of practicing preventive care. Moreover, strategies will be discussed for how the company can sell the incentives that the B2B segment will obtain through implementation of this practice.

Given all of the marketing models discussed in the literature review, there is missing a key component—loyalty, the McKinsey Loyalty loop model (Lingqvist & Plotkin, 2015) will be incorporated to better fit this industry and the firm in question. As discussed in the literature review, loyalty plays a significant role in retaining customers and building long term relationships. So the basics of the framework will come from traditional decision-making models that include the steps of awareness, familiarity, consideration, purchase, and loyalty. The model will be geared towards a more B2B perspective. The authors believe that in order to grow a business further, advocacy is a key component in such a model and therefore it has been added at the end of the decision journey. Advocacy from the physicians who have already converted to preventive care successfully can help the company encourage other health care providers to adopt the same methods, by acting as a key opinion leader for the preventive care practice. In the model, advocacy is shown to loop back to awareness, familiarity, consideration, purchase, and loyalty because through advocacy of the programs, the physicians become instrumental in creating greater awareness among their peers in the industry. Furthermore, the advocate can also be instrumental in influencing physicians going through each of the other steps in the process. In addition to the model, social marketing and sales steps will be integrated for each of the model. As we saw in the literature review, traditional marketing methods are still relevant and applicable in B2B healthcare, but not on their own. As a result, some of the strategies discussed in the model include personal selling, sponsorships, and printed materials like brochures, but knowing the importance of using a decision journey as well, it is clear that the marketing strategies should be integrated into the decision-making journey, while also keeping in mind the importance of creating advocates at the end of the journey to further help create awareness in preventive care. In order to successfully execute the above strategies and for a company to know how and when to discuss the incentives physicians will gain through preventive medicine, this framework should be utilized to ensure that at each phase of the process, it is clear what the objective is, and what the social marketing and sales strategies are (Fig. 25.2).

The model has six steps including awareness, familiarity, consideration, purchase, loyalty, and advocate. The first step in the model is to create awareness with the physicians. The objective is to ensure that doctors see preventive care as relevant to them and their patients. The social marketing and sales strategies that will fulfill this objective is to introduce the importance of preventive care and how it differs from reactive clinical evidence that is available on preventive versus reactive care and any physician and patient testimonials that are available. The next step is to create familiarity and the objective is twofold. First, to understand what preventive care is, what it entails, and what the service offering would be to the patient. Second, to understand how it compares to practicing reactive medicine. In order to satisfy this objective, use of marketing materials with the Business Value Proposition and Customer Value Propositions for reactive care is mandatory. In addition, sponsored conferences with other physicians in the field should be part of this step. Moreover, marketing materials with the Business Value Proposition and Customer Value Propositions for reactive care should be used here to allow the physician to gain

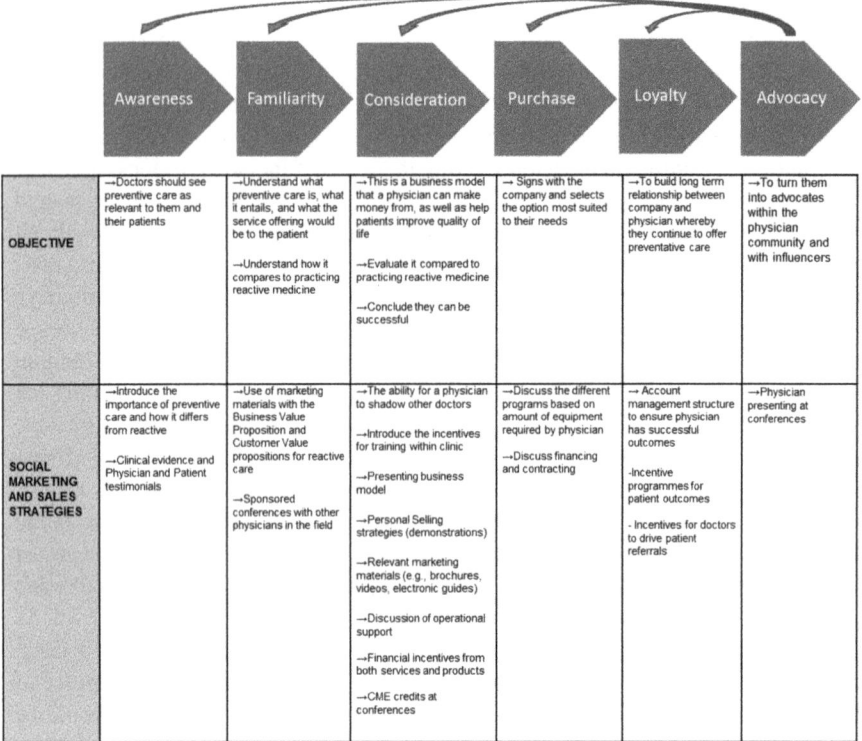

Fig. 25.2 Preventive care integrated advocacy path model

more knowledge on the preventive care approach. The third step is consideration. The objective is to show the physician that they can make significant profit from the new business model, as well as help patients improve quality of life. Physicians should be able to evaluate it compared to only practicing reactive medicine, and conclude that they can be successful using this approach. Moreover, personal selling strategies are the key and can be done by demonstration of the equipment in each program and how the results can be measured. Also, the physician should be made aware that they would receive operational support including equipment installation, managing consumer files, and creating reports by patient. Furthermore, the physician would be made aware of the financial potential gain from this business model, including multiple patient visits for services provided, as well as commission on online products purchased by the patient. Also, relevant marketing materials (e.g., brochures, videos, and electronic guides) can be useful at this stage to build their confidence towards the next step which is purchase. The objective at this step is to have the physician sign with the company and select the program most suited to their needs. The social marketing steps include discussing the different programs based on amount of equipment required by the physician and discussing financing and contracting. The next step is loyalty. The objective here is to build long term relationship between the company and physician whereby they continue to offer preventative care. This can be accomplished through an account management structure to ensure that the physician has successful outcomes. In addition, incentives can be offered to drive patient referrals to other patients, as well as incentives to reward physicians for positive patient outcomes. In order to move towards the final step of advocacy, the physicians could present at conferences, and become key opinion leaders to help create awareness among other physicians who have not yet switched to preventive care methods. Also, the physician advocate could be influential to other physicians going through each and every stage of the process, which is why the arrows go from advocate to each of the other five steps.

Conclusion

The challenge of converting B2B clients to move towards adopting a more preventive practice versus a more reactive one is not an easy task. The article's purpose was to address the issues related to this which include educating the segment on the need and benefits of B2B not only for themselves as physicians but also for their patients. The second issue was what marketing strategies to follow to successfully target the B2B segment given the constantly changing marketing environment and the overall challenges of dealing with the more complex nature of the B2B market. Finally, the issue of how to incentivize this B2B segment to actually practice this, given their existing payment structure of reactive practices, was mentioned as a challenge.

The literature review pointed to key points about marketing models that work to take the B2B segment through a journey from the first point of creating awareness to the last point of getting the purchase. What we saw in those models was the lack of focus on loyalty being a key component. The McKinsey decision journey model was discussed to highlight the important role that loyalty plays in this market. In addition, given the importance of developing advocates in order to grow a business, advocacy was added as a step in the process, demonstrating how it would loop back to creating greater awareness in the community. Moreover, social marketing emerged as an important strategy for working with healthcare and an opportunity was realized for using social marketing in trying to sell the idea of preventive care. As a result, the authors proposed a hybrid model, using the traditional decision journey marketing model (Court & Elzinga, 2009), adding the loyalty component from the McKinsey model, and integrating advocacy and social marketing as well. A framework was presented with steps of the process to be followed. Moreover, each category was discussed in terms of the objective, and the corresponding and needed social marketing and sales strategies were recommended for each step. It is believed that through this model, a firm can take physicians and other B2B healthcare providers through the journey of adopting a more preventive versus reactive approach to medicine by starting with awareness, ending at purchase, while at the same time building a long term relationship with them. The proposed model differs from others in that it is recommended specifically for spreading the awareness of preventive care to physicians in the B2B segment, and as mentioned, most models to date do not incorporate the three components of the traditional consumer decision journey model, the aspect of advocacy, and the integration of social marketing and sales strategies along each step of the consumer decision journey process, specifically for preventive care in the B2B market.

We believe this exploratory research will lead to further research on several topics such as comparing various marketing strategies in this context, modifying the strategy by geographic region given that the firm is global, and generalizing the strategy to other industries that require similar market shifts. Within marketing, research could be done on branding and sales within the firm's model. Consumer surveys could surely provide feedback on the effectiveness of the firm's initial strategy.

References

ACPM. (2016). *ACPM*. Retrieved from American College of Preventive Medicine. http://www.acpm.org/?page=whatispm.

AMA. (2007). *Doctors and preventative care—2010*. Retrieved from Australian Medical Association. https://ama.com.au/position-statement/doctors-and-preventative-care-2010.

Bertucci, M., & Miller, A. (2010). Cutting the fat on healthcare: An investigation of preventive healthcare and the fight on obesity. *Undergraduate Research Journal for the Human Sciences, 9*(1).

Christian, A. H., & Mills, T. (2006). Quality of cardiovascular disease preventive care and physician/practice characteristics. *Journal of General Internal Medicine, 21*(3), 231–237.

Court, D., & Elzinga. D. (2009). *McKinsey Quarterly*. Retrieved from http://www.mckinsey.com/business-functions/marketing-and-sales/our-insights/the-consumer-decision-journey.

Evans, W. D. (2006). How social marketing works in health care. *British Medical Journal, 332*(7551), 1207–1210.

Granbois, D. (1979). Consumer decision making—Fact or fiction? *Journal of Consumer Research, 7*, 331–333.

Griffiths, J. (2014). Health care cost savings—Proactive prevention or reactive treatment. 20–22.

Hull, S. K. (2008). A larger role for preventive medicine. *AMA Journal of Ethics, 10*(11), 724–729.

Jiwani, Z. (2014). *Generation Y's purchasing path to customer decision making & satisfaction*. Doctoral Thesis, International School of Management.

Lavidge, R. C., & Steiner, G. A. (1961). A model for predictive measurements of advertising effectiveness. *Journal of Marketing, 25*(11), 59–62.

Lefebvre, C. (2011). An integrative model for social marketing. *Journal of Social Marketing, 1*(1), 54–72.

Lingqvist, O., & Plotkin, C. L. (2015). Do you really understand how your business customers buy? *McKinsey Quarterly*, 1–11.

Michael Solomon, A. H. (2013). Personal selling: The personal touch of the marketing communications. In A. H. Michael Solomon (Ed.), *Marketing: Real people, real choices* (pp. 409–410). Pearson: Upper Saddle River, NJ.

Paramount MD Digital Marketing (2011). Retrieved from http://www.paramountmd.com/print-vs-online-advertising-what-works-in-healthcare/.

Porter, M. E. (2009). A strategy for health care reform—Toward a value-based system. *New England Journal of Medicine, 361*(2), 109–112.

Prevention, C. F. (2013). Retrieved from http://www.cdc.gov/healthcommunication/toolstemplates/entertainmented/tips/preventivehealth.html.

Stead, M., & Gordon, R. (2007). A systematic review of social marketing effectiveness. *Health Education, 107*(2), 126–191.

Suarez-Almazor, M. E. (2011). Changing health behaviors with social marketing. *Osteoporosis International, 22*, 461–463.

Thorpe, K. E. (2005). The rise in health care spending and what to do about it. *Health Affairs, 24*(6), 1436–1445.

Woolf, S. H., & Atkins, D. (2001). The evolving role of prevention in health care. *The American Journal of Preventive Medicine, 20*, 13–20.

Chapter 26
Effect of Power Saving Techniques on the Quality of VoIP

Mohammad Adnan Alakhras

Abstract Power saving techniques in wireless networks have an effect on the quality of VoIP applications. These techniques are used to reduce the consumption of power when mobile terminals are used for VoIP. This paper will introduce a study on the effect of different techniques (used to reduce power consumption at various layers of the wireless network) on voice quality of service (QoS). The study will concentrate on jitter and delay of voice packets. Current standards for power saving techniques, at each network layers, will be discussed, and their effectiveness will be analyzed. WLAN is used in this study to fully analyze the effect of these power saving techniques on the voice packets jitter and delay. Simulation results are presented to demonstrate the analysis.

Keywords Power saving • VoIP • Jitter • WLAN • QoS

Introduction

The energy required to keep wireless devices connected to the network over longer period of time needs to be looked at carefully. Power saving schemes have been developed in order to address this problem. Solutions at different layer of the network stack have been proposed, and each of them promises to provide energy savings.

VoIP over WLAN communication is rapidly gaining acceptance over other techniques, but each technology has issues that must be addressed in order to ensure a successful deployment. Figure 26.1 illustrates a typical VoIP deployment.

Delay and jitter are the most important for VoIP as a real-time streaming application. Packets containing voice data must be delivered in a timely manner in order to ensure user satisfaction.

M.A. Alakhras (✉)
School of Engineering and Network Technology, Canadian University of Dubai,
Dubai, United Arab Emirates
e-mail: malakhrasl@cud.ac.ae

© Springer International Publishing Switzerland 2017   317
R. Benlamri, M. Sparer (eds.), *Leadership, Innovation and Entrepreneurship
as Driving Forces of the Global Economy*, Springer Proceedings in Business
and Economics, DOI 10.1007/978-3-319-43434-6_26

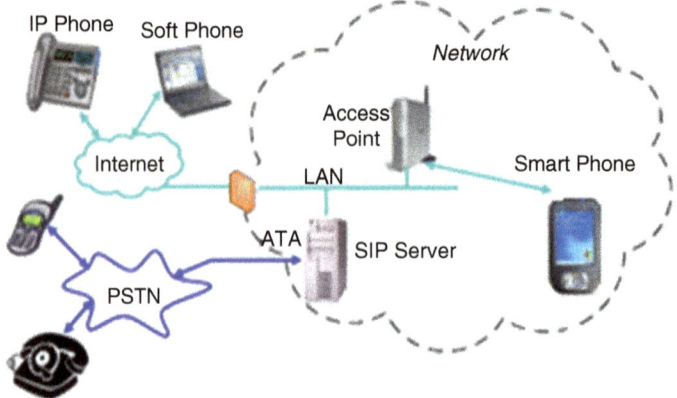

Fig. 26.1 A typical VoIP deployment

The larger the delay, the lower the perceived quality of voice for the persons who are communicating. Jitter (delay variation) influences quality if it exceeds a maximum value.

Standards have been developed for wireless network related to the managing of power consumed by individual nodes in each of these networks. Performing power saving is important for wireless networks, so this paper focuses primarily on the power saving schemes used by WLANs.

This paper is organized as follows: section "Wireless LANs" provides a brief overview of WLANs, including a discussion of how the network performs power saving. Section "Power Saving Techniques" follows with an introduction to the different power saving techniques used within the various network protocol layers. It talks about the recent advances that have been made in the field of power saving. Section "Effect of 802.11 Power Saving Mechanisms on the Quality of Voice" talks about the effect the power saving techniques have on the QoS of the VoIP over WLAN. Section "Simulation Results" provides a summary of what is planned to be done related to the QoS, delay, and jitter in VoIPoWLAN and shows the results obtained and proposed enhancements.

Wireless LANs

Most of the wireless LANs are based on the IEEE 802.11 standard. It provides functionality for wireless devices to communicate in a way similar to the traditional wired LAN. Devices in these networks normally operate at a higher data rate. They are usually made to communicate over longer distances as well. Because of this higher data rate and longer range (higher transmission power), they consume more power. To reduce the power consumed, a power saving scheme known as PSM (Power Save Mode) is built into the 802.11 standard.

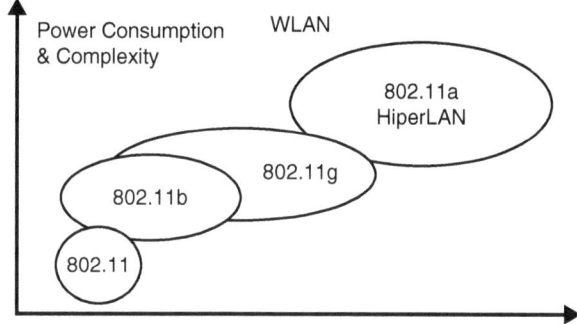

Fig. 26.2 Power consumption in IEEE 802.11 networks

Many variations of the 802.11 standard have emerged, each with its own set of enhancements over the original 802.11 standard. Some of these improvements are for enhanced quality of service (QoS) (802.11e), security (802.11i), throughput (802.11n), as well as dynamic frequency selection and transmission power control (802.11h). Of all the variations, however, only 802.11h deals with improving the power saving capabilities of 802.11. Transmission power control is a method of controlling the topology of a network by reducing the power at which certain nodes in the network are allowed to transmit. However, the 802.11h enhancement standard provides the facility to define a policy for implementing a transmission power control. Figure 26.2 shows how these different types of networks compare in terms of data rate and power consumption.

Power Saving Techniques

Many power saving techniques used by the standards to reduce the power consumed in the network are introduced. These techniques exist for all the layers of the network protocol stack.

Application Layer

Many techniques can be used to reduce the power consumed by a wireless device at this layer, such as load partitioning which lets power intensive computation to be done at the base station rather than the device (Jones, Sivalingam, Agrawal, & Chen, 2001). Another technique uses proxies to inform an application of the changes in battery power in order to limit the functionality and provide the needed ones (Karl, 2003).

Transport Layer

By reducing the number of retransmissions due to lost packets, it conserves energy at the transport layer (Karl, 2003). Also, in a wireless network, losses should not be interpreted as congestion. These techniques are not used when dealing with VoIP over wireless as the transport protocol used is UDP.

Network Layer

Power saving at this layer is related to performing power efficient routing through a multi-hop network (Zheng, Hou, & Sha, 2003; van Dam & Langendoen, 2003; Simunic, 2005). They are typically a backbone based, topology control based, or a hybrid of both. Where in the backbone based protocol, backbone nodes remain active at all times, while others sleep periodically. The backbone nodes establish a path between all source and destination nodes in the network. Any node in the network must therefore be within one hop of at least one backbone node, including backbone nodes themselves (Alghamdi, Xie, & Qin, 2005).

Energy saving is achieved by allowing non-backbone nodes to sleep periodically, as well as by periodically changing which nodes make up the backbone.

Figure 26.3 shows how packets would be routed, where black nodes are the backbone nodes, while numbered nodes are the non-backbone nodes. Solid lines indicate paths which a packet may travel, while dashed ones show paths that are sleeping.

Topology based routing protocols achieve energy savings by reducing the transmission power of all nodes in a network such that the network remains connected, but all nodes operate with the lowest transmission power possible.

Location based topology control protocols use the topology of the network to provide the most energy efficient communication path. In some cases, the path may take a larger number of hops in the network than would be taken when transmitting directly from one node to another. This can be done if the energy consumed in transmitting to a far node is significantly greater than the energy consumed when transmitting using a large number of nodes that are within closer range of one another (Zheng et al., 2003).

Fig. 26.3 Backbone based
routing protocol

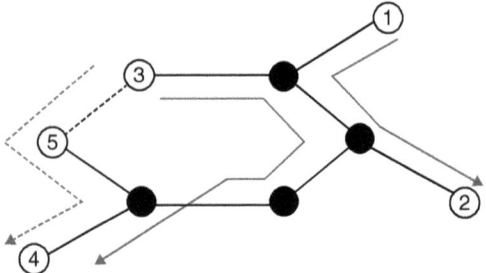

Data Link Layer

The most common techniques used to save energy at the link layer are concerned with reducing the transmission overhead during the Automatic Repeat Request (ARQ) and Forward Error Correction (FEC) schemes. These schemes are used to reduce the number of packet errors at the receiving node.

Results have shown that it is more energy efficient to transmit at a lower transmission power and have to send multiple ARQs than to send at a high transmission power and achieve better throughput. Other power saving techniques are based on packet scheduling protocol (Anastasi, Conti, Gregori, & Passarella, 2004). By scheduling multiple packet transmission to occur back to back, it may be possible to reduce the overhead associated with sending each packet individually. By reducing the number of retransmissions, the power consumption is reduced.

MAC Layer

At the MAC layer, the power saving is done by sleep scheduling protocols. Lots of power is wasted listening on the radio channel, while there is nothing to receive. The radio wakes up whenever it needs to transmit or receive packets and then goes back to sleep.

Sleep scheduling protocols can be broken up into two methods: (a) senders and receivers know when each other should be on and send to one another during those time periods. They go to sleep otherwise. (b) Nodes can send and receive packets according to the preamble bytes sent by a packet in order to synchronize the starting point of the incoming data packet between the transmitter and receiver. Once the receiver wakes up, it synchronizes to these preamble bytes and remains on until it receives the packet.

Physical Layer

A technique known as Remote Access Switch (RAS) can be used to wake up a receiver only when it has data to receive. A low power radio circuit is run to detect activity on the channel. When this activity is detected, the circuit wakes up the rest of the system for reception of a packet. A transmitter has to know what type of activity needs to be sent on the channel to wake up each of its receivers.

Effect of 802.11 Power Saving Mechanisms on the Quality of Voice

A typical VoIP involves a constant flow of the VoIP frames, from the handset (HS) to the voice gateway and vice versa. Since the station generally knows in advance the frame arrival rate, delay, and bandwidth requirements of the voice application, it can reserve resources and set up power saving mechanism for its flows. An HS may remain in active mode, always ready for the voice transmission. In this case, the AP transmits voice frames as they arrive according to the CSMA/CA rules. However, if power saving is desired, the HS can employ the power save building blocks to wake up, exchange the VoIP frame with its AP, and go back to sleep.

The HS can use information such as the arrival time between voice frames, along with a power save mechanism, to get itself to sleep between consecutive voice frames. The power saving techniques for allowing the HS to sleep between voice frames using the CSMA/CA access mechanism during a VoIP call is explained below. The effect of these techniques will be studied to explore their effect on the quality of voice in terms of delay and jitter. The time taken to put the HS to sleep and then activate is expected to have significant effect on delay as well as jitter.

Power Save Mode Technique

The PS bit in the data frame is used to initiate the change of the power state. When there is a data to transmit, the HS moves from sleep mode to active mode, then it sets the PS bit to active in the voice frame, to announce the change of its power state. Since the voice coders at both sides share the same frame duration, the HS stays in active mode after transmission, to allow a frame buffered at the AP to be received. So the AP sends buffered frames to the HS only after it has completed the reception of the frame from the SHShhHS. The AP sets the "more data" bit to FALSE in its last frame, to announce the end of its transmission. Then, the HS needs to complete a successful initiation frame sequence (with the PS bit set to sleep) to move back to the sleep mode. Null frame is normally sent if there is no data frame to transmit, in this case the PS bit is set to sleep.

PS-Poll Based Technique

In this technique, the HS will ask for the AP frames using the PS-Poll frame. This is done so that the HS needs to wait for the AP to deliver transmission; instead, the PS-Poll frame is used to get the buffered frame at the AP. But when the HS needs to transmit frames, it moves first to the active mode and then transmits its data. If there is any buffered frame at AP to transmit, the AP sets the "more data" bit to TRUE in the acknowledgment message to announce the presence of this frame. When the HS sees that the "more data" bit is set to TRUE, it will continue to send a PS-Poll frame to retrieve the buffered AP frame.

Power Saving Effect on VoIP Quality

The 802.11 WLAN power saving techniques have some issues on the VoIP quality and operation, mainly in terms of delay and jitter.

In the first technique, the PS-bit based mechanism, it offers one way for the HS to go to sleep mode, through initiating a frame exchange sequence while the PS bit is set to sleep. So, an extra HS initiated frame exchange is required for every voice frame transfer, in order for the HS to indicate the power state changes. Since the voice frame payload is in the order of 20 ms for voice application, the header of the extra frames can introduce more delay that needs to be studied.

In the second technique, PS-Poll based, the priority of the buffered AP frame is not known to the HS, hence these frame will not be sent until the PS-Poll frame is sent and at the best effort access category. So the best effort priority is used to retrieve the buffered AP voice frame, even though they are set to the highest priority. The best effort retrieval is initiated by the frame exchange sequence of the PS-Poll frame. When the data and voice traffic are available at the AP point, the best effort priority will deal with both frames in the same way and at the same level of priority, even though the voice frames should be granted the highest priority. The reason is that the voice packets should be initiated by the PS-Poll frame. The effect of the PS-Poll frame on the voice packet delay and jitter will be demonstrated in the simulation results.

Simulation Results

The effect of the power saving standards in the 802.11 WLAN on the QoS of the VoIP in terms of the delay and jitter will be introduced using simulation. The setup of the simulation will be as shown in Fig. 26.4. The way the simulation has been carried out is by turning off the power saving options and running the system using different number of calls. The results were recorded in terms of the delay, jitter, and the active period. The same simulation is repeated using the PS-Poll mechanism (power saving is turned on). We used WinEyeQ (a real-time software based monitor and protocol analyzer) to observe, diagnose, and evaluate VoIP performance. A call generator and SIP signaling that comply with the standards were also used. Using the above setup, we measured the throughput, delay, and jitter. The relationship between calls and throughput is shown in Fig. 26.5, the relationship between calls

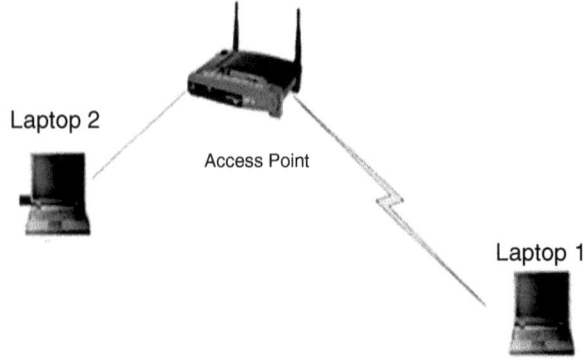

Fig. 26.4 Simulation system setup

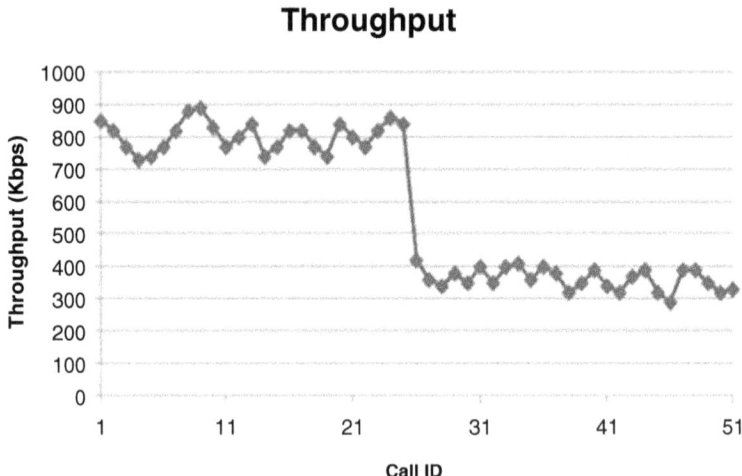

Fig. 26.5 Effect of power saving on throughput

and jitter is shown in Fig. 26.6, and the relationship between calls and delay is shown in Fig. 26.7. As seen in the figures, the system was running initially without activating the power saving and the throughput was around 800 Kbps. The effect of activating the power saving is shown in the second half of the figure where the throughput has dropped to around 360 Kbps. As noticed, the throughput has been reduced by an order of half. The same argument applies to Fig. 26.6 where the jitter was around 15 ms before the power saving is turned on, and then it jumps to around 45 ms once the power saving is turned on. The delay in the first part of Fig. 26.7 was around 105 ms before the power saving is turned on, and then it jumps to around 185 ms once the power saving is turned on.

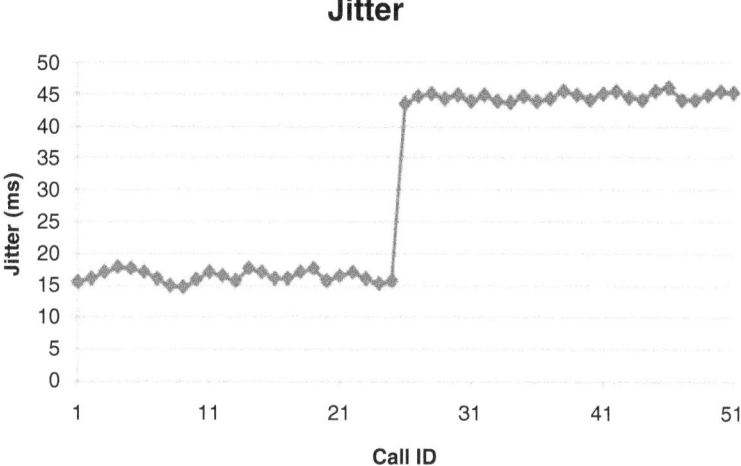

Fig. 26.6 Effect of power saving on jitter

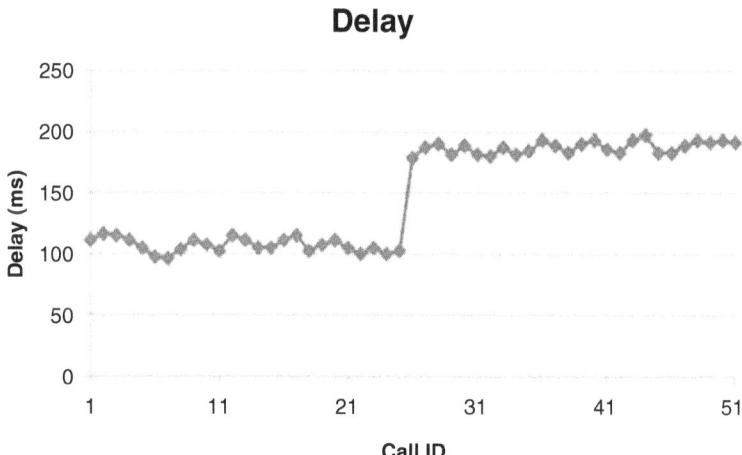

Fig. 26.7 Effect of power saving on delay

Conclusion and Future Work

The quality of VoIP over wireless LAN is affected by power saving techniques used to reduce power consumption. This paper demonstrates the effect of existing power saving techniques on voice packets specifically on delay and jitter. It was noticed, through simulation, that the jitter and delay are highly affected when the power saving is turned on. So different power saving techniques need to be explored to reduce the power consumption, while the effect on jitter and delay is minimized.

References

Agarwal, Y., Schurgers, C., & Gupta, R. (2005). Dynamic power management using on demand paging for networked embedded systems. In *Proceedings of the 2005 Conference on Asia South Pacific Design Automation* (pp. 755–759). New York, NY: ACM Press.

Alghamdi, M. I., Xie, T., & Qin, X. (2005). PARM: A power-aware message scheduling algorithm for real-time wireless networks. In *Proceedings of the 1st ACM Workshop on Wireless Multimedia Networking and Performance Modeling* (pp. 86–92).

Anastasi, G., Conti, M., Gregori, E., & Passarella, A. (2004). A performance study of power-saving polices for Wi-Fi hotspots. *Computer Networks: The International Journal of Computer and Telecommunications Networking, 45*(3), 295–318.

Chen, H., & Huang, C.-W. (2004). Power management modeling and optimal policy for IEEE 802.11 WLAN systems. In *IEEE Vehicular Technology Conference*.

Chen, Y., Smavatkul, N., & Emeott, S. (2004). Power management for VoIP over IEEE 802.11WLAN. In *IEEE Vehicular Technology Conference*.

Jones, C. E., Sivalingam, K. M., Agrawal, P., & Chen, J. C. (2001). A survey of energy efficient network protocols for wireless networks. *Wireless Networks, 7*(4), 343–358.

Karl, H. (2003). An overview of energy-efficiency techniques for mobile communication systems. TKN Technical Reports Series. Technische Universitaet Berlin.

Simunic, T. (2005). Power saving techniques for wireless LANs. In *Proceedings of the Conference on Design, Automation and Test in Europe—Volume 3* (pp. 96–97).

van Dam, T., & Langendoen, K. (2003). Energy-efficient MAC: An adaptive energy-efficient MAC protocol for wireless sensor networks. In *Proceedings of the 1st International Conference on Embedded Networked Sensor Systems* (pp. 171–180).

Zheng, R., Hou, J. C., & Sha, L. (2003). Resource management: Asynchronous wakeup for ad hoc networks. In *Proceedings of the 4th ACM International Symposium on Mobile Ad Hoc Networking & Computing* (pp. 35–45).

Chapter 27
Cultural Business Intelligence in Management

Nadine Sinno

Abstract This research reveals the concept of intelligence in modern management, particularly the management of Lebanese tourism organizations.

In this world of continuous change and development, organizations should be competitive to be able to face the challenges of globalization. To attain a high level of competences and therefore competitiveness, it is necessary for organizations to deepen their professional and cultural knowledge in the focus of offering to consumers the best products and services and to build a relationship of loyalty–fidelity between the organization and the market.

This study focuses on the role of the cultural intelligence as the capability to function effectively in a variety of cultural context. In fact, cultural intelligence provides insights about individual capabilities to cope with multicultural situations, engage in cross-cultural interactions, and perform in culturally diverse work groups.

The success of tour operators through intelligent management and cultural intelligence will benefit the tourism sector with economic and competitive advantages.

We identified the topic in all its complexity to a set that will converge into the world of culture in its general concept, and into the inter-culture as relational concept.

Keywords Business intelligence • Competitiveness • Customer service • Culture • Intelligence • Cultural intelligence • Tourism • Globalization • Tourists • Cross-culture

Introduction

The world continues relentlessly to write about the consequences of the globalization of markets, the internationalization of products, and the free movement of goods. We are now living in a "Global Village" and subsequently, the globalization is affecting all phases of design, development, production, distribution, and consumption of goods and services.

N. Sinno (✉)
Chair of the Hospitality and Tourism Department, Lebanese International University,
Beirut, Lebanon
e-mail: nadine.sinno@liu.edu.lb

© Springer International Publishing Switzerland 2017   327
R. Benlamri, M. Sparer (eds.), *Leadership, Innovation and Entrepreneurship as Driving Forces of the Global Economy*, Springer Proceedings in Business and Economics, DOI 10.1007/978-3-319-43434-6_27

Thus, due to this new economic dimension, firms are facing an increased complexity in the market conditions and unexpected, hardly conceivable, situations. The firms are now obliged to adapt to a completely different working concept, jostling violently, the traditional habits of management and trade relations. Therefore, firms should consider to introduce a new dimension in the market rivalry and to enter into a total new level of unbeatable competition.

What does this upheaval of the way of work brings to the enterprise and to individuals in their daily lives? The simple and logic answer would be: the radical change of the way of thinking, working, and even living. The phenomenon of change is accompanied by an adaptation that will be constant, continuous, progressive, and inevitable. The train is running!

At the Business Management level, the influence of this unexpected upheaval generated a critical market situation: adapt, adopt, or die! Companies should adopt changes in the thinking strategy, in the working process, and in the market approach methodologies.

The company should accept the changes underway and adapt to a new vision of the operational environment. The company must have the skills or at least develop the minimum resources to be able to adapt and then change. However, change requires accepting to give up comfortable and safe habits while accepting uncertainty about the future and facing risks (economic, adaptation, social tolerance, etc.). Nevertheless, the change must go for the better without causing any regression. This implies that a change in the managerial thinking does not only follow the changes adopted by the operating environment but also to anticipate future tracks.

The first step for modern management practices is to measure the competence of each individual. Afterwards, the management has to measure the collective ability of the groups in analyzing situations. Finally, it has to identify knowledge improvement areas to develop individual skills and overall performance. The employee in the learning enterprise is an actor of progress and it is enormously important to develop his/her skills.

An important feature of the learning organization is the sharing of knowledge between employees, at all levels. This division involves ongoing communication between members of a single organization to ensure a constant knowledge transfer.

The company must develop a kind of a learning culture and must also rethink the knowledge management strategy to transform the cultural life of the company into a learning life.

At this stage, the company will be considered *intelligent*!

Literature Review

Intelligent Management

An intelligent organization manifests collectively specific learning skills, innovation, and flexibility. This type of organization is particularly suited to deal with the unexpected and permanent changes in its environment, in a world more than ever complex.

Comparing between the intelligent enterprise and the conventional enterprise, the first management style uses the knowledge and experience of the individual and makes them accessible and usable within the entire company (Landier & Thesmar, 2010). While the latter one preserves jealously conservative structures that prevents the company from fully adhering to the changes facing the business world today (Khadige, 2011).

The intelligent enterprise collects, categorizes, manages, and disseminates the knowledge gained from various sources such as marketing research, individual and cultural experience in its academic and vocational sense.

The general objectives of the intelligent enterprise are: increased national and global market share, diversified activities, project profitability, profits, etc.

Additionally, the intelligent enterprise must consider another important capital: the fact that each individual/employee has one or more forms of intelligence, which the employee can use at work. Furthermore, the company must consider the fact that these forms of intelligence are often unusable when faced by the work routine or the pyramidal structure of the company. In this case, the employee's intelligence is measured only by the fact of obeying to the top management and finalizing tasks before deadline.

At this stage, the intelligent manager must identify the existing skills and measure the human resources performance. At the same time, he must develop the principle of collective intelligence in the business for well transmitted ideas and knowledge to achieve a high degree of cooperation and reflection.

But how can individuals and employees cooperate when each comes from a different background? Is the collective intelligence[1] sufficient for creating harmony and resolving interpersonal conflict among employees or between groups of workers?

Cultural Intelligence in Business Management

As previously mentioned, in a global village, corporate visions and objectives are no longer limited to the local market, but the company's success is determined by creating an international identity.

Therefore, the company is obliged to have:

1. Agents abroad, that will represent its products or services,
2. Affiliations, that are to say to associate with other economic entities to ensure a presence and an international economic activity, and
3. Mergers with other international companies to take advantage of the existing markets.

---

[1] Collective intelligence is shared or group intelligence that emerges from the collaboration, collective efforts, and competition of many individuals and appears in consensus decision making (Wikipedia).

In these cases, contact between different cultures will be done in different ways, and culture tends to influence the way of thinking and working. It is therefore crucial to decrypt the operating software of the different cultures and to use a form of analytical intelligence represented by Cultural Intelligence (CQ).

Different approaches have been proposed for the cultural intelligence. Gardner (1997) popularized the idea that intelligence is more than a cognitive capacity. In fact, human potential cannot be limited to cognitive intelligence, the way it is described and defined in society. People with this particular intelligence have the ability to steer their way through unfamiliar cultural interactions.

Cultural intelligence is the ability to negotiate effectively with people from different cultural backgrounds using four components: cognitive factors, metacognitive factors, motivational factors, and behavioral elements (Early & Ang, 2003).

1. The Head/Cognitive. Learning by heart the beliefs, habits, and taboos of foreign cultures.
2. The Body/Physical. Showing recognition of the other culture; actions and demeanor must prove that the individual, to some extent, entered their world.
3. The Heart/Emotional/Motivation. The interest vis-à-vis staff of different cultures. Adapting to a new culture involves overcoming obstacles. People can do that only if they believe in their own effectiveness.

It is no longer enough to learn and understand different cultures but it is primordial to have the ability to develop and accept different attitudes, to understand the world with unknown behaviors, and to be able to act adequately in actual situations.

When an organization has the need to collaborate with partners in other countries, it is essential to prevent misunderstandings and conflicts. The intelligent manager will therefore ensure that the key people have understood the strategic context of intercultural work, and that they have the motivation and the right attitude needed to understand and act when confronting culturally different individuals.

These key people must know how to establish good communication based on mutual understanding. The goal is to understand what is happening internally and externally facing people with different ways of thinking and acting. Cultural intelligence provides a framework, a language to understand and enjoy the differences rather than tolerate or ignore them.

This definition emphasizes the idea that cultural encounters success is not a question of opposition or contradiction but a complementarity. Understanding the "other" culture, paying attention to its standards, and developing techniques and skills to bridge differences.

Therefore, cultural intelligence involves a combination of three dimensions (Plum, 2007):

The Intercultural Commitment
Intercultural Communication
The Cultural Understanding

It can be deduced that the primary function of cultural intelligence refers to the intercultural commitment and deals with the driving forces of the situation.

It includes the emotions and attitudes towards cultural differences, the ability to control emotions and give a true image of the company in a cross-cultural interaction; this marks the primordial point of action.

The second dimension, intercultural communication, is a dimension of action. This part needs to have a mastery of communication. It brings an intercultural commitment, deeper understanding, and acceptance of differences.

The third dimension, cultural understanding, is the ability to become integrated into a different culture.

Concisely, cultural intelligence is the ability to recognize the shared beliefs, values, attitudes, and behaviors of members of a group and, more importantly, the ability to effectively apply this knowledge to the realization of a specific project or a range of activities. It is often seen as a synonym of cultural knowledge. However, cultural intelligence is more than mere knowledge of another culture.

Intercultural problem is at the heart of many professional practices, and any citizen's engagement in the context of globalization. With the explosion of this problem, how will individuals, social groups, and States react?

A large number of studies have been conducted on this for 40 years with international staff, resulting in a sort of consensus around six specific criteria of intercultural effectiveness: empathy, respect, interest for the local culture, flexibility, tolerance, and technical competence.

In an attempt to highlight the role of cultural intelligence in intercultural relations in the workplace, a study centered on the Lebanese tour operators was conducted. The choice of this case study is linked to the cross-cultural nature of the tourism industry and the need for cultural understanding in inter-employee relations and customer–employee relations. This research suggests the application of cultural intelligence in modern management as a tool for the development of the tourism enterprises.

From this point, several questions arise. Does cultural intelligence exist in the Lebanese tourism enterprises? How is the cultural intelligence used as a tool for having a competitive advantage in the tourism sector?

Research and Analysis

Culture Intelligence in Tourism Management

Applying cultural intelligence in tourism is a call to action to all stakeholders (tourists and locals) to develop a controlled-friendly tourism. Cultural intelligence promotes intercultural dialogue while allowing to provide sustainable solutions to local community development needs.

Furthermore, cultural intelligence plays an increasingly central role in planning a tourist package by tour operators. The tourism market is structured around powerful tour operators, the oldest of which dates back from the late nineteenth century. Meanwhile, a large number of small and medium enterprises (SMTEs) have specialized in tourism, in particular by proposing new forms of stays.

Intercultural interactions are essential and extremely intense in the tourism sector. To be able to study the Lebanese tourism service providers, we have done the following fieldwork:

First of all, we conducted several focus groups; these groups were divided into three categories:

1. Cultural intelligence of the employees of Lebanese tourism enterprises
2. Cultural intelligence and preferences of tourists traveling for leisure
3. Cultural intelligence and preferences of tourists traveling for business purpose

The questions solicited included:

- Why do tourists travel?
- According to which criteria do they chose their tourism service provider?
- How do they act in intercultural situations?
- What is the relation between their culture and their preferences?

We have analyzed the qualitative data collected using a thematic, descriptive approach that looks across all the data and identifies the common, recurrent main themes and we have summarized all the collected views.

Eventually, the findings of the study showed that the Lebanese tourism enterprises work on the basis of intuition and improvisation, and crisis management.

In general, management relies on previous experiences and practicalities not academic theories and practices. In fact, Lebanese tourism enterprises are not aware of their role as intercultural agents and they are not using culture as an integral element of their competitive advantage.

On the other side, leisure tourists are very interested in knowing different cultures. In fact, Lebanese tourists adapt to different cultures easily because they research about the destination before traveling. Tourists confirmed that there is a strong relation between their preferences and their culture and that the culture of a destination is an important factor for choosing a destination.

As for the businessmen, they travel to prefixed destinations, usually by their enterprises. They look for comfort and high quality of service and they require fast professional service.

Most of the businessmen visited more than six countries and they are well aware of cultural differences in destinations and they take it into consideration. Mainly when they want to travel with families, they chose places that were known and previously explored to avoid any irregularities.

This study showed that the concept of culture plays a vital role in the choice of the destination of the tourist.

Culture holds a great impact on the perception of the client and his degree of satisfaction. Tourism service providers should respond to the cultural needs of the clients to be able to penetrate the international tourist market. Also, the employees should be culturally intelligent to serve their client base.

Undoubtedly, the tourism industry and culture are interrelated. Seeking the culture of the other is an inherent part of the client's motivation in choosing the trip. Leader tour operators mentioned that to satisfy the tourists and to meet their expectations it is necessary, if not imperative, to have a "cultural knowledge" and know how while planning packages.

Therefore, an intelligent tour operator should:

1. Understand the needs and expectations of customers to create services and suitable packages. For example, the tour operator may divide the services according to customers "cultural segments."
2. Know the most important characteristics of different cultures: values, attitudes, language, and customs for providing excellent quality of service and to obtain customer's loyalty. In fact, the quality of service is generally perceived subjectively and is directly related to the client's culture.

Therefore, to provide the best quality in tourism services, a framework that takes into account the different dimensions of national culture of tourists must be established. In this case, the Hofstede model can be used to distinguish between cultures.

Hofstede and Hofstede (2005) established a theory on the cultural dimensions that offers a systematic framework for evaluating differences between nations and cultures. Every culture works according to its own values and its members behave according to the rules that are appropriate in a given situation.

Hofstede explained two kinds of culture:

"Culture 1": knowledge, art, and literature.
"Culture 2" is defined as the collective programming of the mind which distinguishes the members of a group or class of people over another. It includes all the simple and ordinary life activities: Greet, Eat, Express, Hide feelings, Keep a certain physical distance with others, Follow the rules of hygiene, Fear, Anger, Love, Joy, and sadness, and The ability to observe the environment and to talk with others.

Intelligent tour operators should analyze and compare the cultures of destinations based on pre-established guidelines such as Hofstede's dimensions. This approach can be used to explain to the client the culture of the visited destination and, secondly, if there are employees of different nationalities or cultures, this approach resolves the issues of international management from the perspective of the "cultural distance."

Conclusion and Recommendations

In conclusion, this research highlighted the need for an intelligent style of management in businesses, considering the cultural intelligence as a company's performance enhancement tool. Sales force must increasingly adapt to the culture of the clients while promoting their services. The staff of the company should be able to communicate effectively with each other and with the customers. In addition, the enterprises must literally go beyond the traditional promotional pitch and develop cultural knowledge of the customer, in terms of expectations and desires. Cultural intelligence is a holistic concept. This concept covers all aspects of our social and intercultural life since ancient times until today. Living together in a global village cannot be successful without openness to others and understanding the others.

The tourism sector employees must have the ability to work in a multicultural environment. It is possible to develop cultural intelligence employees through the below suggested actions:

1. Assessing the cultural intelligence of employees, and from their strengths and weaknesses, establish a development plan.
2. Developing and training intercultural competence for the employees. The training should aim to strengthen intercultural competences and not only to communicate across cultures.

The courses that will strengthen intercultural competences are:

- Information sessions and awareness data to all staff;
- Coaching, in small groups or individually;
- Customized training, structured and interactive in two or three modules of half a day;
- Public meetings to information and training;
- E-learning;
- Lectures, video; and
- Case studies, discussion groups.

The development of intercultural competence is an investment rather than a cost. The company must devote the necessary time to ensure the impact of its actions and return on investment. It is important to address the subject deeply using training and individual coaching. It is essential to consider training as an ongoing and dynamic process. Also, companies should stimulate employees' motivation with simple activities that increase their comfort with different cultures. In the context of diversity, the company will strive to develop social activities that will allow staff to mingle, share, and build relationships.

References

Early, C., & Ang, S. (2003). *Cultural intelligence: Individual interactions across cultures*. Stanford, CA: Stanford University Press.

Gardner, H. (1997). *Les formes de l'intelligence*. Paris: Editions Odile JACOB.

Hofstede, G., & Hofstede, J. (2005). *Cultures and organizations: Software of the mind* (2nd ed.). New York, NY: McGraw-Hill.

Khadige, C. (2011). Réflexions sur l'entreprise intelligente. http://cgcjmk.blogspot.com/view/sidebar/2011/01/reflexions-sur-lentreprise-intelligente.html.

Khadige, C. Intelligence, entrepreneuriat et résilience d'entreprise. found in http://www.fgm.usj.edu.lb/files/a122009.pdf. last retrieved, 14 August 2016

N.D. (2001). L'organisation apprenante. fiche technique numéro 16. lettre du cedip. p. 4 http://www.needocs.com/document/management-divers-rh-l-organisation-apprenante,6642.

Plum, E. (2007). Cultural intelligence: A concept for bridging and benefiting from cultural differences. http://www.athenas.dk/elisabeth-plum-artikel-et.htm.

Landier, A., & Thesmar, D. (2010). Intelligence Collective et Action Publique, Revue commentaire. Automne 2010. Volume 33/Numéro 13.

Chapter 28
Is the Avalanche of E-learning Coming to the UAE?

Dennis Lee, Elissar Toufaily, and Tatiana Zalan

Abstract The higher education system worldwide is on the cusp of disruptive change due to innovative education providers such as digital platforms and universities offering fully online or blended programs. While the e-learning industry in the UAE is projected to grow significantly, the level of adoption of e-learning has not been high. The overall purpose of our multistage research project is to understand the barriers to the adoption of e-learning in the UAE despite the benefits of online education, such as lower costs and pedagogical benefits. We propose a preliminary conceptual framework explaining the students' attitudes and intention to adopt e-learning. In our future research, we will refine and test the conceptual framework and provide guidelines for higher education institutions and policymakers on institutional change to support e-learning initiatives.

Keywords Higher education • E-learning • Students' perceptions • Barriers to adoption • The UAE

Introduction

The title of the paper alludes to the widely cited report by Barber, Donnely, and Rizvi (2013) *An Avalanche is Coming* on the potentially disruptive change facing the global higher education system. Specifically, a new phase of competition is emerging, as the very notion of the traditional university is coming under pressure from innovative "disruptors" such as digital platforms (e.g., Coursera, edX, and Udacity) and universities offering low cost fully online or blended programs (Weise & Christensen, 2014; Barber et al., 2013). For example, the growth of applications to online MBAs has outstripped some traditional formats of the degree (Murray, 2016). These changes are driven by escalating costs and tuition fees in traditional universities, learners' desire for flexibility, and advances in ICT. These developments go

D. Lee (✉) • E. Toufaily • T. Zalan
American University of Dubai, Dubai, United Arab Emirates
e-mail: dlee@aud.edu; etoufaily@aud.edu; tzalan@aud.edu

© Springer International Publishing Switzerland 2017   335
R. Benlamri, M. Sparer (eds.), *Leadership, Innovation and Entrepreneurship as Driving Forces of the Global Economy*, Springer Proceedings in Business and Economics, DOI 10.1007/978-3-319-43434-6_28

hand in hand with the globalization of the higher education industry and improvements in e-learning pedagogy enabling a fusion of modularization and mastery-based learning (Bowen, 2012; Christensen & Eyring, 2011; Weise & Christensen, 2014). For the purposes of this research, we define *e-learning as web-based learning which utilizes web-based communication, collaboration, multimedia, knowledge transfer, and training to support learners' active learning without the time and space barriers* (Lee, Yoon, & Lee, 2009).

The e-learning market in the Middle East is projected to grow to US$560M in 2016, at an annual growth rate of 8.2% (Docebo, 2014). While the UAE (and the region) scores well on e-readiness (i.e., adoption of digital technologies) (UNESCO, 2013), the adoption of e-learning has not been as widespread: currently, the UAE boasts only one fully online university (Hamdan Bin Mohammed Smart University). In line with the global trend, the costs of higher education in the UAE have been rising. On the other hand, e-learning provides many opportunities for media-based, student-centered, and interactive learning environments that support active learning and critical thinking (Huffaker & Calvert, 2003), skills that are perceived to be largely missing yet critical for the UAE students to be able to participate in the knowledge economy, locally, and globally (Hvidt, 2015). As reputable institutions enter the UAE market with fully online or blended deliveries in increasing numbers, the future of traditional local universities may be in serious jeopardy.

The overall purpose of our multistage research project is to understand the barriers to the adoption of e-learning in the UAE despite the benefits of online education, such as lower costs (reflected in the prices paid by students) and pedagogical benefits. More specifically, the objectives are to:

1. Propose a preliminary conceptual framework explaining the students' attitudes and intention to adopt e-learning;
2. Refine and test the conceptual framework from students' perspective; and
3. Provide guidelines for higher education institutions and policymakers on institutional change and support for e-learning initiatives.

The paper proceeds as follows. We start with the section "Literature Review" which has informed our preliminary conceptual model (section "Preliminary Conceptual Framework"). Our research design is explained in the section "Research Design," and references are provided in the last section of the paper.

Literature Review

As stated in the introductory part of the paper, barriers to e-learning in the UAE, a country with high level of ICT penetration, and an extensive offering of online courses are of great concern to educational institutions and policymakers. A large number of studies investigated the learner's acceptance of e-learning, the instructor's acceptance of e-learning, and organizational and strategic factors that affect the adoption and delivery of e-learning. Prior literature has identified several factors as barriers to, and drivers of, e-learning from a student perspective. For example, Law,

Lee, and Yu (2010) find that extrinsic motivational factors such as social pressures and competition have a considerable impact on student learning, and that both intrinsic (such as individual's attitude and expectation) and extrinsic motivators (such as rewards and recognition) significantly influence students' self-efficacy. Hernandez, Montaner, Sese, and Urquizu (2011) propose the use of extrinsic motivators (i.e., doing an activity for specific reasons) in order to improve the learning outcomes and experiences of online learners. Students can be motivated if they are able to gain recognition from their instructors. This will improve the students' attitude to learning because a positive attitude enables learners to use more ICT interactive tools to prove to the instructor that they deserve high grades. When students adopt online learning components, Smart and Cappel (2006) found that the senior students have more technological experience than the freshman and junior students. This is because these fourth year students are better independent learners than the younger students.

Instructor performance also impacts the e-learner satisfaction. According to Bolliger and Martindale (2004), online learners will find satisfaction when they can easily access technology. This satisfaction has positive correlation with the performance of online instructors: the online instructors must be perceived as available at all time, be a motivator to the student, and communicate with students on a regular basis (Sun, Tsai, Finger, Chen, & Yeh, 2008). However, the absence of interaction based on a face-to-face context is a major concern in online teaching and learning (So & Brush, 2008). Students are often in isolation and unsupported during the learning process (Cereijo, 2006); moreover, they are expected to be motivated and self-disciplined to work as independent learners without getting much assistance from instructors. Students who are more confident in their ability to use e-learning on their own are more likely to become good users of e-learning (Abbad, Morris, & De Nahlik, 2009).

Another stream of research has demonstrated that the Internet and technology quality affect satisfaction with e-learning (e.g., Piccoli, Ahmad, & Ives, 2001) and that e-learning course quality has a large positive effect on e-learners' satisfaction (Sun et al., 2008). In order to ensure the delivery of high quality e-learning courses at universities, Ehlers (2009) recommends that a set of standards be adopted to evaluate learning content and processes, and certifying and accrediting programs and institutions. A combination of factors like retention rate, academic outcomes, and success in online student and faculty support are considered as important to make a quality online course (Shelton & Saltsman, 2004). To influence students' learning performance, there should be well-designed courses, curricula, and learning materials, which will facilitate meaningful educational experiences. Institutions who offer e-learning courses must therefore attain curriculum quality certification from accreditation sources to enhance and improve teaching excellence (Bhuasiri, Xaymoungkhoun, Zo, Rho, & Ciganek, 2012).

A number of studies have investigated the benefits of e-learning to students and instructors, such as the flexibility of the online delivery format (Chakraborty & Nafukho, 2015). E-learning allows students to study in a self-paced mode as compared to traditional classroom learning. Students consider online learning as both place- and time-independent, permitting them to continue their conversations with instructors without any interruptions (Arbaugh, 2002). This model of delivery is of particular benefit to students who want to balance their studies, family, and work-related activities if they take an online course (Sun et al., 2008). Likewise, Maki, Maki, Patterson, and Whittaker (2000) find that students perceive the convenience of the online course as a benefit and enjoy the flexibility of the online learning environment. The online classroom setting encourages more student participation, and provides students with a better chance to reflect and research before discussing the issues in classes (Ni, 2013).

Contextual factors have been found to influence e-learning. Specifically, culture appears to have a major impact on learning preferences and information processing capacity of individuals (Samovar, Porter, & McDaniel, 2009). The cultures of the Middle Eastern cluster of countries have high preferences for avoiding uncertainty (House et al., 1999; Ronen & Shenkar, 1985). According to Hofstede (2011), people in these cultures feel threatened when faced with ambiguous or unknown situations. states that the introduction of e-learning will pose a considerable challenge to Arab students. A study by the World Bank in 2007 stated that students in this region are passive learners and do not apply their learning through critical thinking (Galal, 2007). Many of these students are highly dependable on their teachers when they want to acquire new knowledge (Lansari, Tubaishat, & Al-Rawi, 2010). A recent report by the Dubai School of Government's Governance and Innovation Program reveals that many students who are enrolled in universities are still lacking problem-solving, critical thinking, and communication skills (Salem, Mourtada, & Alshaer, 2013). This lack of skills will thus be a big obstacle in the e-learning environment for the young Arab students who are more accustomed to rote learning during their early schooling. Clearly, if online learning is integrated with face-to-face learning, the sociocultural environment may affect students' perceptions (Alebaikan & Troudi, 2010). Alebaikan and Troudi (2010) state that students in Saudi universities are finding the new way of learning confronting, as they have been used to the traditional classroom-based lecture. Yet in another study by Al-Jarf (2005), freshman students were not taking online classes seriously because they were not used by existing instructors at the college. Further, the low public esteem for online learning in the workplace is another important reason to reject e-learning by many universities, academics, and students (Mirza & Al-Abdulkareem, 2011). According to Dirani and Yoon (2009), the online degree is seen to give access to fewer job opportunities and is not perceived as comparable to traditional degrees. Additionally, the learner's attitude and lack of prior knowledge of IT use are major factors that affect the acceptance of e-learning by students (Selim, 2007; Ozkan & Koseler, 2009). Finally, language is a barrier to adoption as online repositories that contain educational material in the Arabic language are lacking (Al-Khalifa, 2008).

Preliminary Conceptual Framework

Based on the literature review, a preliminary conceptual framework (Fig. 28.1) is proposed. This conceptual model identifies three major categories—offer characteristics, individual and psychological characteristics, and sociocultural factors—that influence learner' attitudes, which in turn will affect his/her intention to adopt e-learning.

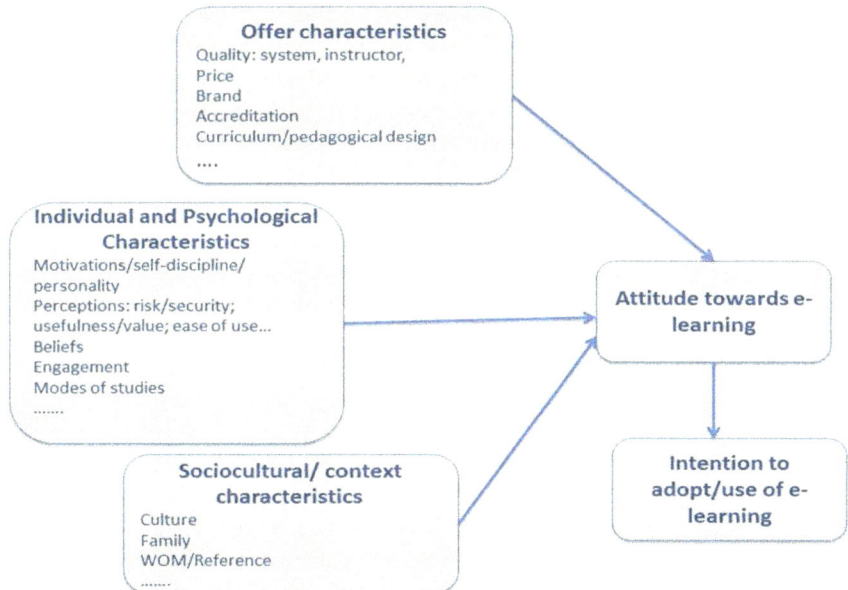

Fig. 28.1 Preliminary conceptual framework

Research Design

In order to understand the issues associated with the perceptions of e-learning and barriers to adoption in the UAE context, a mixed-method design will be used comprising two stages. A qualitative approach will be used in stage 1 with the purpose to capture the different barriers to the adoption of e-learning by the UAE students. Stage 1 will result in a clearer understanding of the UAE context-specific constructs that will emerge from respondents' answers. The outcome will be a refined theoretical framework (with added and/or removed constructs) based on the findings in stage 1, which will provide richness and a thorough understanding of the topic. A series of in-depth interviews will be conducted with university students who did not complete an online course offered by a higher education institution in the UAE or abroad. According to the Ministry of Higher Education and Scientific Research, in 2014 the offering of online courses and e-learning program is extensive, with 105 online foreign universities have been accredited by the UAE. Of those universities, 46 are in the United Kingdom, 34 in the USA, and five in New Zealand (The National, 2014)

The number of interviews is not fixed in advance. Sample size should generally follow the principle of saturation (Glaser & Strauss, 1967), whereby data collection stops when new data do not shed any further light on the issue under investigation. Following Miles and Huberman (1994), a purposeful sampling technique will be used to identify and target the specific individuals representing the spectrum of knowledge and experience relevant to this study.

Stage 2 will focus on the quantitative data collection via an online structured questionnaire that includes the constructs identified through the literature review and refined in stage 1. Data will be collected from a sample of BA and MBA students in the UAE. Questionnaires will be revised by experts (mainly academics) with significant understanding of e-learning to evaluate the length and appropriateness of the questions. Then, a quantitative pretest to ensure the reliability and the validity of the measurement instruments will be conducted on a pilot sample of 30 students with no prior e-learning experience. After refining the scales, an online survey instrument (via Survey Monkey) will be administered. An email invitation will be sent to students from universities across the UAE to participate in the study including the site link. We have identified four universities through professional networks, with academic colleagues showing interest in assisting with the data collection. Moreover, to secure a high response rate, the questionnaire will also be administered to students face to face by visiting classes and asking students to complete the questionnaire. The criterion to qualify a respondent for the surveys is that the student has never been enrolled in an online course or program before. We aim at a sample size of at least 500 students, as it is recommended for studies with descriptive and explanatory purposes (Malhotra, 2010).

For consistency, measures will be adopted or derived from previous studies on online education and student perceptions. A seven-point Likert scale ranging from 1 (strongly disagree) to 7 as (strongly agree) will be used.

Descriptive statistics using SPSS software will be used to describe the profile of the sample as well as the constructs of the study. Then, confirmatory factor analysis will be conducted to evaluate the adequacy of the model using EQS 6.1. Convergent and discriminant validity of the scales will be assessed consistent with the Fornell and Larcker (1981) guidelines. Finally, structural equation modeling will be performed. The hypothesized relationships in the proposed research model will simultaneously be tested via path analysis. The results of the structural equation model will be interpreted and guidelines for higher education institutions and policymakers will be proposed.

Conclusion

The research project will result in a conceptually grounded and empirically verified model of e-learning adoption, which will contribute to a detailed understanding of the barriers and enablers of e-learning adoption in the UAE context, which is currently lacking.

The expected results will help decision markers in higher education institutions to face these barriers, strengthen the implementation of e-learning, and build strategies to improve the learner satisfaction. The results may provide an opportunity to better understand the media-based, leaner-centered, and interactive environments that support active learning and critical thinking. Additionally, results will help practitioners and especially students and managers with full-time jobs to continue pursuing education and degrees with more flexibility and satisfaction. Furthermore, by understanding the e-learning environment, its drivers, and barriers, system administrators will be able to ensure all system functionalities and system performance for a better learning. When assessing learners' perceptions of the quality and enthusiasm of instructors, school administrators will have guidelines in selecting and training instructors for e-learning courses. Higher education institutions will be provided by guidelines on institutional change and support for e-learning initiatives.

References

Abbad, M. M., Morris, D., & De Nahlik, C. (2009). Looking under the bonnet: Factors affecting student adoption of e-learning systems in Jordan. *The International Review of Research in Open and Distributed Learning, 10*(2).

Alebaikan, R., & Troudi, S. (2010). Blended learning in Saudi universities: Challenges and perspectives. *Research in Learning Technology, 18*(1).

Al-Jarf, R. S. (2005). The effects of online grammar instruction on low proficiency EFL college students' achievement. *Asian EFL Journal, 7*(4), 166–190.

Al-Khalifa, H. (2008). Building an Arabic learning object repository with an ad hoc recommendation engine. In *Proceedings of iiWAS2008*, November 24–26, 2008, Linz, Austria, pp. 390–394.

Arbaugh, J. B. (2002). Managing the on-line classroom: A study of technological and behavioral characteristics of web-based MBA courses. *The Journal of High Technology Management Research, 13*(2), 203–223.

Barber, M., Donnely, K., & Rizvi, S. (2013). *The avalanche is coming*. London: Institute for Public Policy Research.

Bhuasiri, W., Xaymoungkhoun, O., Zo, H., Rho, J. J., & Ciganek, A. P. (2012). Critical success factors for e-learning in developing countries: A comparative analysis between ICT experts and faculty. *Computers & Education, 58*(2), 843–855.

Bolliger, D. U., & Martindale, T. (2004). Key factors for determining student satisfaction in online courses. *International Journal on E-learning, 3*(1), 61–67.

Bowen, W. C. (2012). *The 'cost disease' in higher education: Is technology the answer?* The Tanner Lectures, Stanford University, October. http://ithaka.org/sites/default/files/files/ITHAKA-TheCostDiseaseinHigherEducation.pdf. Accessed 20 January 2012.

Cereijo, P. M. V. (2006). Attitude as predictor of success in online training. *International Journal on E-Learning, 5*(4), 623–663.

Chakraborty, M., & Nafukho, F. M. (2015). Strategies for virtual learning environments: Focusing on teaching presence and teaching immediacy. *Internet Learning, 4*(1), 2.

Christensen, C., & Eyring, H. (2011). *The innovative university: Changing the DNA of higher education from the inside out*. San Francisco, CA: Jossey-Bass.

Dirani, K. M., & Yoon, S. W. (2009). Exploring open distance learning at a Jordanian university: A case study. *The International Review of Research in Open and Distributed Learning, 10*(2).

Docebo. (2014). *e-Learning market trends and forecast 2014—2016*. https://www.docebo.com/whitepaper-elearning-market-trends-and-forecast-2014-2016/?CP. Accessed 10 January 2016.

Ehlers, U. D. (2009). Web 2.0-e-learning 2.0-quality 2.0? Quality for new learning cultures. *Quality Assurance in Education, 17*(3), 296–314.

Fornell, C., & Larcker, D. F. (1981). Evaluating structural equation models with unobservable variables and measurement error. *Journal of Marketing Research, 18*(1), 39–50.

Galal, A. (2007). *The road not traveled: Education reform in the MENA region*. Washington, DC: World Bank.

Glaser, B., & Strauss, A. (1967). *The discovery of grounded theory*. London: Weidenfeld and Nicolson.

Hernandez, B., Montaner, T., Sese, F. J., & Urquizu, P. (2011). The role of social motivations in e-learning: How do they affect usage and success of ICT interactive tools? *Computers in Human Behavior, 27*(6), 2224–2232.

Hofstede, G. (2011). Dimensionalizing cultures: The Hofstede model in context. *Online Readings in Psychology and Culture, 2*(1), 8.

House, R. J., Hanges, P. J., Ruiz-Quintanilla, S. A., Dorfman, P. W., Javidan, M., Dickson, M., et al. (1999). Cultural influences on leadership and organizations: Project GLOBE. *Advances in Global Leadership, 1*(2), 171–233.

Huffaker, D. A., & Calvert, S. L. (2003). The new science of learning: Active learning, metacognition, and transfer of knowledge in e-learning applications. *Journal of Educational Computing Research, 29*(3), 325–334.

Hvidt, M. (2015). *Transformation of the Arab Gulf economies into knowledge economies: Motivational issues related to the tertiary educational sector*. Doha: Arab Center for Research and Policy Studies.

Lansari, A., Tubaishat, A., & Al-Rawi, A. (2010). Using a learning management system to foster independent learning in an outcome-based university: A Gulf perspective. *Issues in Informing Science & Information Technology, 7*, 7387.

Law, K. M., Lee, V. C., & Yu, Y. T. (2010). Learning motivation in e-learning facilitated computer programming courses. *Computers & Education, 55*(1), 218–228.

Lee, B. C., Yoon, J. O., & Lee, I. (2009). Learners' acceptance of e-learning in South Korea: Theories and results. *Computers & Education, 53*(4), 1320–1329.

Maki, R. H., Maki, W. S., Patterson, M., & Whittaker, P. D. (2000). Evaluation of a web-based introductory psychology course: I. Learning and satisfaction in on-line versus lecture courses. *Behavior Research Methods, Instruments, & Computers, 32*(2), 230–239.

Malhotra, N. K. (2010). *Marketing research: An applied orientation*. London: Pearson.

Miles, M. B., & Huberman, A. M. (1994). *Qualitative data analysis: An expanded sourcebook*. London: Sage.

Mirza, A. A., & Al-Abdulkareem, M. (2011). Models of e-learning adopted in the Middle East. *Applied Computing and Informatics, 9*(2), 83–93.

Murray, S. (2016). EdTech: Mooc platforms force b-schools to embrace blended online/campus learning, *Business Because*, 20 January, http://www.businessbecause.com/news/mba-distance-learning/3729/mooc-platforms-force-bschools-to-innovate. Accessed 25 January 2016.

Ni, A. Y. (2013). Comparing the effectiveness of classroom and online learning: Teaching research methods. *Journal of Public Affairs Education, 19*(2), 199–215.

Ozkan, S., & Koseler, R. (2009). Multi-dimensional students' evaluation of e-learning systems in the higher education context: An empirical investigation. *Computers & Education, 53*, 1285–1296.

Piccoli, G., Ahmad, R., & Ives, B. (2001). Web-based virtual learning environments: A research framework and a preliminary assessment of effectiveness in basic IT skills training. *MIS Quarterly, 25*(4), 401–426.

Ronen, S., & Shenkar, O. (1985). Clustering countries on attitudinal dimensions: A review and synthesis. *Academy of Management Review, 10*(3), 435–454.

Salem, F., Mourtada, R., & Alshaer, S. (2013). Transforming education in the Arab world: Breaking barriers in the age of social learning. *Arab Social Media Report, Dubai School of Government–DSG*.

Samovar, L., Porter, R., & McDaniel, E. (2009). *Communication between cultures*. Boston, MA: Cengage Learning.

Selim, H. M. (2007). Critical success factors for e-learning acceptance: Confirmatory factor models. *Computers & Education, 49*(2), 396–413.

Shelton, K., & Saltsman, G. (2004). The dotcom bust: A postmortem lesson for online education. *Distance Learning, 1*(1), 19–24.

Smart, K., & Cappel, J. (2006). Students' perceptions of online learning: A comparative study. *Journal of Information Technology Education: Research, 5*(1), 201–219.

So, H. J., & Brush, T. A. (2008). Student perceptions of collaborative learning, social presence and satisfaction in a blended learning environment: Relationships and critical factors. *Computers & Education, 51*(1), 318–336.

Sun, P. C., Tsai, R. J., Finger, G., Chen, Y. Y., & Yeh, D. (2008). What drives a successful e-Learning? An empirical investigation of the critical factors influencing learner satisfaction. *Computers & education, 50*(4), 1183–1202.

The National. (2014). UAE releases list of accredited foreign online universities. http://www.the-national.ae/uae/education/uae-releases-list-of-accredited-foreign-online-universities. Accessed 10 January 2016.

UNESCO. (2013). *Information and communication technology (ICT) in education in five Arab States*. Montreal: UNESCO Institute for Statistics. http://www.uis.unesco.org/Communication/Documents/ICT-arab-states-en.pdf. Accessed 20 December 2015.

Weise, M., & Christensen, C. (2014). *Hire education*. Redwood City, CA: The Clayton Christensen Institute for Disruptive Innovation.

Chapter 29
Facilitating Conditions and Cost in Determining M-Commerce Acceptance in Jordan: Initial Findings

Ghassan Alnajjar

Abstract The technology acceptance model (TAM) is practically explaining behavioral intention (BI). However, extensions are needed to further examine BI toward mobile commerce (m-commerce) acceptance due to the insufficient power of just two constructs perceived usefulness (PU) and perceived ease of use (PEOU) to explain BI. Therefore, limitations of TAM lead this research to extended TAM in two ways. First, facilitating conditions (FC) factor is not considered in TAM. In fact, Davis assumed that everyone is in control of the resources regarding adopting a new system. Second, cost is one of the obstacles in adopting m-commerce. High cost can decrease the acceptance rate of m-commerce. M-commerce services involve fees (connections fees, subscription fees, or roaming fees). TAM does not explain cost factor, because TAM was applied mostly in an organizational context that does not involve cost by the end-users in workplace. This research intends to address the above limitations by augmenting facilitating conditions and cost.

Keywords TAM • M-commerce • Jordan • Facilitating conditions • Cost

Introduction

The m-commerce acceptance literature revealed that numerous studies were conducted in developed countries and some Eastern Asian countries. There is a lack of research in the Arab world including Jordan concerning m-commerce acceptance. As far as the researcher knowledge, very few studies address m-commerce acceptance in the Arab countries including Jordan. Filling the gap in the academic literature is one of the motivations for conducting this research in Jordan with a different culture.

G. Alnajjar (✉)
Information Technology Department, Al Khawarizmi International College,
Al Ain, United Arab Emirates
e-mail: Ghassan.najjar@khawarizmi.com

© Springer International Publishing Switzerland 2017   345
R. Benlamri, M. Sparer (eds.), *Leadership, Innovation and Entrepreneurship as Driving Forces of the Global Economy*, Springer Proceedings in Business and Economics, DOI 10.1007/978-3-319-43434-6_29

In addition, broadly speaking, there is a high contradiction between the penetration rate of mobile phones and the lack of the adoption rate of m-commerce in Jordan. In 2009, Jordan reached 101 % penetration of mobile subscribers (The-Jordan-Times, 2009). On the other hand, the low rate of m-commerce acceptance is noticeable in the country. In other terms, the affordability and the availability of mobile phones do not guide us to predict the adoption rate of m-commerce in Jordan.

The researcher motivated to study the factors that influencing users and potential adopters for ICT technologies in the Arab world due to the growth of ICT in the region. Recent reports have shown a stellar upsurge in the internet users with 600 % increases from 2002 to 2007, which is the largest in the world (Dutta & Mia, 2009), also a remarkable growth in mobile penetration in the region as well. M-commerce refers to direct or indirect transactions over wireless telecommunication by using mobile devices such as mobile phones or personal digital assistants.

M-commerce acceptance rate varies in different cultures. Arab countries and Jordan in specific are a collectivist culture. Social norms score higher in collectivist cultures and these social norms can play a major role in adopting or rejecting a new technology (Ramayah, Rouibah, Gopi, & Rangel, 2009).

The purpose of this paper is to augment and examine facilitating conditions and cost. The rest of the paper is structured as follows: The literature review provides brief review of the litarature in the research field. Then, the Framework and hypothesis section describes the proposed framework and related hypotheses. We then discuss data collection process and finally, we conclude with the discussion of the results..

Literature Review

Most of the theories of technology acceptance have been developed in countries such as the USA. Additionally, many of the technology acceptance theories have not been broadly investigated outside of developed countries such as in the Arab countries (Almutairi, 2007), while findings have been inconsistent where these theories have been tested in developing countries (AbuShanab, Pearson, & Setterstrom, 2010; Bandyopadhyay & Fraccastoro, 2007). A number of authors have suggested that this inconsistent in predictive power could be associated with the differences in the cultures within the particular nations (AbuShanab et al., 2010; Bandyopadhyay & Fraccastoro, 2007). Several studies compared developing countries to the USA (where technology adoption theories have been developed) and concluded that culture influenced behavioral intention and they argued that end-users in different cultures respond differently. Predicting individuals' intention to adopt m-commerce in a collectivist culture, low individualism, and high uncertainty avoidance comparing to western society is worthy of investigating with regard to FC and cost factors.

Facilitating conditions are defined as external environments of serving individuals to remove (overcome) barriers and difficulties to use a new technology (Gu, Lee, & Suh, 2009; Venkatesh, Morris, Davis, & Davis, 2003). FC factor is a "core construct" in UTAUT that effecting use behavior (Venkatesh et al., 2003). FC factor consists of two dimensions: resource factors (time and money), and technology factors (technology supports) relating to compatibility issues that contain the usage (Lu, Liu, Yu, & Wang, 2008; Lu, Yu, Liu, & Yao, 2003). According to Venkatesh, Brown, Maruping, and Bala (2008), behavioral intention is a reflection of the users or potential users' internal representation of beliefs. TAM does not support the external factors that can affect the performance of an adoption (behavior). In other words, the role of external factors (facilitating conditions) that can potentially facilitate or hold back the performance of a behavior is not captured by TAM.

Cost is defined as the degree to which users perceive that using m-commerce is expensive (costly) (Wei, Marthandan, Chong, Ooi, & Arumugam, 2009). Cost factor is a "core construct" in TAM3 that effecting use behavior (Venkatesh & Bala, 2008). Individuals may decide not to use the m-commerce services due to price considerations. Prices, costs, or fees (e.g., additional expenses, equipment costs, access cost, and transaction fees) are important components that make m-commerce use more costly than the traditional e-commerce (Wu & Wang, 2005). A number of studies argue that cost could be a main barrier for the acceptance of m-commerce. For example, in a study investigating behavioral intention to use mobile banking in Taiwan, the researchers found that perceived financial cost is negatively effecting the behavioral adoption towards the usage of m-banking. In a study by Shin (2011), the researcher argued that cost of using 4G including the initial investment in devices, subscription initiation, charges, and monthly payments are negatively influencing intention.

Framework and Hypotheses

Figure 29.1 illustrates the research model for the study. TAM presents the theoretical framework for this research. The extension is derived from UTAUT and TAM3. While the paper focuses on the effects of facilitating conditions on attitude, PU, PEOU, BI, and cost on BI and attitude, the original TAM factors are not tested in this paper. In this study, we propose six hypotheses over the model.

Fig. 29.1 Research model (*blue boxes* are the original TAM factors)

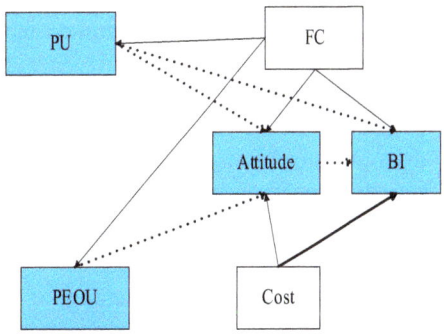

Facilitating conditions are viewed as an external control in the environment (Gu et al., 2009). Usage (behavior) could not take place if the external control in the environment does not exist. FC factor consists of two dimensions: resource factors (time and money), and technology factors (technology supports) relating to compatibility issues that contain the usage (Lu et al., 2003; 2008). It has been viewed that IT usage will be less likely if less money, less time, and less technological support exist. Prior studies have pointed out the significance of facilitating conditions on attitude and behavioral intention (Crabbe, Standing, Standing, & Karjaluoto, 2009; Saeed, 2011; Van Biljon & Kotzé, 2008). In addition, when individuals feel the availability of resources, the availability of knowledge and the presence of facilitating conditions, it could develop a positive attitude and it is expected to increase the intention. In the view of the above arguments, the following hypotheses are proposed:

H1: FC positively influences BI
H2: FC positively influences attitude

In the case of PU and PEOU, in this study the researcher believes that individuals perceive m-commerce to be easy to use and useful when the external environment conditions assisting them in learning how to use m-commerce despite the ability to use it skillfully (Gu et al., 2009) and discovering the advantages of m-commerce. Studies empirically investigated the relationships and found that facilitating conditions were significantly influenced by perceived usefulness (Lu et al., 2008) and by perceived ease of use (Gu et al., 2009). Therefore, the following hypotheses are proposed:

H3: FC positively influences PU
H4: FC positively influences PEOU

Cost referred to as "the extent to which the individual perceives using m-commerce is costly" (Wei et al., 2009, p. 375). Cost, price, or the financial factor considered one of the most issues in m-commerce adoption from a consumer's perspective (Wu & Wang, 2005). According to Raleting and Nel (2011), cost was not considered as one of the determinants of TAM model. Since TAM was developed for an organizational context, the actual end-users are different from who is paying for the technology (Raleting & Nel, 2011).

However, from the individuals' context perspective, when m-commerce consumers are paying for the services, cost becomes a critical factor that may affect the consumers' behavior. According to Kuo and Yen (2009), we found that perceived fee negatively influenced the user's attitude and behavioral intention toward 3G service adoption. Another study (Wei et al., 2009) found that perceived cost was negatively related to the acceptance of m-commerce. They stated that high prices of subscription and communication fees would lead to the decrease of m-commerce adoption. Considering the above arguments, the increase of prices for access, transaction fees, subscription fee, roaming fees, and connection fees will have a negative impact on attitude and behavioral intention. Therefore, the following hypotheses are proposed:

H5: Cost negatively influences BI
H6: Cost negatively influences attitude

Data Collection

A survey questionnaire was employed to gather data using 7-point Likert scale. The scale ranges from (1) "strong disagree" to (7) "strong agree" with (4) as "neutral." The questionnaire contains two parts. The first part is primarily the demographics information. The second part contains the main questionnaire. The participants were university students selected randomly from public and private universities in Jordan. A total of 448 responses were obtained from 500 questionnaires. From the 448, 36 were discarded due to missing or incomplete data. The collected data was analyzed using the SPSS 17 software.

Results

The age distribution of the participants is predominantly between 18 and 26 (92.5%). The gender distributions of the participants are (60.4%) males and (39.6%) females. Most of the participants are undergraduate students (88%). Majority of participants (86.9%) are using prepaid scheme. About 92.5% of the participants are internet users more than 1 year. Although 73.1% of the participants are aware of m-commerce, only 20.1% are m-commerce users.

Table 29.1 shows the descriptive statistics for the constructs, number of items, and Cronbach Alphas. All Cronbach Alphas values are greater than 0.60, which indicates that the instrument has internal consistency. The research hypotheses were tested by linear and multiple regression analysis. All hypotheses were supported. Table 29.2 shows the results of hypotheses testing.

Table 29.1 Descriptive statistics and reliability

Construct	Mean	SD	Number of items	Cronbach's alpha
Attitude	4.66	1.186	3	0.773
FC	4.58	1.159	2	0.614
Cost	3.24	1.324	3	0.879

Table 29.2 Research hypotheses results

	Research hypothesis	St. coefficients beta	Sig. level	Support
H1	FC→BI	0.399	0.000	Yes
H2	FC→Attitude	0.291	0.000	Yes
H3	FC→PU	0.182	0.024	Yes
H4	FC→PEOU	0.242	0.002	Yes
H5	Cost→BI	−0.132	0.005	Yes
H6	Cost→Attitude	−0.119	0.014	Yes

Discussion of Research Hypotheses

Results from this research model explain the constructs that are influencing PU, PEOU, attitude, and BI to predict m-commerce adoption in Jordan. The following conclusions were drawn from the model.

The findings support the research hypothesis (H1: FC→BI). The empirical result from this study indicated a significant and positive relationship between facilitating conditions and behavioral intention. Hence, the hypothesis H1 is supported. This result is consistent with other previous studies (Crabbe et al., 2009; Saeed, 2011; Van Biljon & Kotzé, 2008).

The hypotheses (H2: FC→Attitude), (H3: FC→PU), and (H4: FC→PEOU) are supported by the results of this research. The empirical findings from this study indicated that the facilitating conditions construct is an important factor to predict aattitude, PU, and PEOU in Jordan towards adopting m-commerce. This finding reveals the aspects of facilitating conditions are significantly recognized by the participants in Jordan. This result is consistent with the findings of other studies (Lu et al., 2008; Raleting & Nel, 2011). According to Lu et al. (2008), facilitating conditions have been recognized as more influential than other factors on acceptance and infusion of IT/IS innovations.

The findings support the research hypothesis (H5: Cost→BI). Cost in this current study has a significant and a negative effect on individual's behavioral intention towards the use of m-commerce in Jordan; hence, the hypothesis H5 is supported. In other words, cost is one of the barriers that prevents Jordanians from adopting m-commerce. The hypothesis (H6: Cost→Attitude) is supported in this research and shows the relationship between cost and attitude is significantly negative. Therefore, hypothesis H6 is supported. This result indicated cost is an important predictor of attitude in Jordan and one of the antecedents of attitude.

Conclusion

The main objective of this research is to address the limitations by augmenting facilitating conditions and cost in TAM. Evidently, the study found that facilitating conditions can predict BI, Attitude, PU, and PEOU in Jordan. Moreover, cost can predict BI and Attitude. This study tested the connection between the antecedents to adopt m-commerce in Jordan, rather than the usages of m-commerce. Future study should use a longitudinal point of view.

References

AbuShanab, E., Pearson, J. M., & Setterstrom, A. J. (2010). Internet banking and customers' acceptance in Jordan: The unified model's perspective. *Communications of the Association for Information Systems, 26*(1), 23.

Almutairi, H. (2007). Is the "technology acceptance model" universally applicable? The case of the Kuwaiti Ministries. *Journal of Global Information Technology Management, 10*(2), 57–80.

Bandyopadhyay, K., & Fraccastoro, K. A. (2007). The effect of culture on user acceptance of information technology. *Communications of AIS, 2007*(19), 522–543.

Crabbe, M., Standing, C., Standing, S., & Karjaluoto, H. (2009). An adoption model for mobile banking in Ghana. *International Journal of Mobile Communications, 7*(5), 515–543.

Dutta, S., & Mia, I. (2009). The Global Information Technology Report 2008–2009, Mobility in a Networked World, Technical report of the World Economic Forum & INSEAD, Published by World Economic Forum under ISBN-13:978-92-95044-19-7.

Gu, J.-C., Lee, S.-C., & Suh, Y.-H. (2009). Determinants of behavioral intention to mobile banking. *Expert Systems with Applications, 36*(9), 11605–11616.

Kuo, Y.-F., & Yen, S.-N. (2009). Towards an understanding of the behavioral intention to use 3G mobile value-added services. *Computers in Human Behavior, 25*(1), 103–110.

Lu, J., Liu, C., Yu, C. S., & Wang, K. (2008). Determinants of accepting wireless mobile data services in China. *Information & Management, 45*(1), 52–64.

Lu, J., Yu, C. S., Liu, C., & Yao, J. E. (2003). Technology acceptance model for wireless Internet. *Internet Research, 13*(3), 206–222.

Raleting, T., & Nel, J. (2011). Determinants of low-income non-users' attitude towards WIG mobile phone banking: Evidence from South Africa. *African Journal of Business Management, 5*(1), 212–223.

Ramayah, T., Rouibah, K., Gopi, M., & Rangel, G. J. (2009). A decomposed theory of reasoned action to explain intention to use internet stock trading among Malaysian investors. *Computers in Human Behavior, 25*(6), 1222–1230.

Saeed, K. (2011). *Understanding the adoption of mobile banking services: An empirical assessment.* Paper presented at the AMCIS 2011 Proceedings—All Submissions, Detroit, Michigan.

Shin, D. H. (2011). The influence of perceived characteristics of innovating on 4G mobile adoption. *International Journal of Mobile Communications, 9*(3), 261–279.

The-Jordan-Times. (2009). Internet users reach 28 per cent in first three quarters. Retrieved February 7, 2010, from http://www.jordantimes.com/?news=21795&searchFor=mobile%20phones

Van Biljon, J., & Kotzé, P. (2008). Cultural factors in a mobile phone adoption and usage model. *Journal of Universal Computer Science, 14*(16), 2650–2679.

Venkatesh, V., & Bala, H. (2008). Technology acceptance model 3 and a research agenda on interventions. *Decision Sciences, 39*(2), 273–315.

Venkatesh, V., Brown, S. A., Maruping, L. M., & Bala, H. (2008). Predicting different conceptualizations of system use: The competing roles of behavioral intention, facilitating conditions, and behavioral expectation. *MIS Quarterly, 32*(3), 483–502.

Venkatesh, V., Morris, M. G., Davis, G. B., & Davis, F. D. (2003). User acceptance of information technology: Toward a unified view. *MIS Quarterly, 27*(3), 425–478.

Wei, T. T., Marthandan, G., Chong, A. Y. L., Ooi, K. B., & Arumugam, S. (2009). What drives Malaysian m-commerce adoption? An empirical analysis. *Industrial Management & Data Systems, 109*(3), 370–388.

Wu, J.-H., & Wang, S.-C. (2005). What drives mobile commerce? An empirical evaluation of the revised technology acceptance model. *Information & Management, 42*(5), 719–729.

Chapter 30
Auditing and Comparing Innovation Management Capability in the Municipal Field: A Case Study

Ola AlZawati, Abeer AlAli, and Gasim Abdelrahman

Abstract The purpose of this paper is to audit and compare innovation management capability of two organizations using an auditing tool proposed by Tidd and Bessant (*Managing Innovation: Integrating Technological, Market and Organizational Change*, 5th ed. Wiley, West Essex, 2014) which constitutes of five dimensions: Strategy, Innovation Process, Learning, Innovative Organization, and Linkages. Both organizations were selected from the municipal field, a municipality in UAE and a municipality in Jordan. A sample was selected from each organization from High Suggestion Department (HSD) and Low Suggestion Departments (LSD). The auditing tool was distributed to respondents. Results have been obtained and discussed. A comparison has been conducted between both organizations in terms of their innovation management capabilities. Moreover, a comparison has been conducted between the HSD and LSD within each organization. The results of the study revealed that the municipality in UAE obtained higher scores in all auditing dimensions; hence, it is concluded that the municipality in UAE has higher innovation management capability than the municipality in Jordan. Moreover, each organization shall take care of the different components of innovation management with balance in order to maintain it.

Keywords Innovation auditing • Innovation management capability • Innovation auditing tool • Innovation auditing dimensions

O. AlZawati (✉) • A. AlAli • G. Abdelrahman
Department of Industrial Engineering and Engineering Management, University of Sharjah,
Sharjah, United Arab Emirates
e-mail: U15105721@sharjah.ac.ae; U15100767@sharjah.ac.ae; U00045808@sharjah.ac.ae

© Springer International Publishing Switzerland 2017   353
R. Benlamri, M. Sparer (eds.), *Leadership, Innovation and Entrepreneurship
as Driving Forces of the Global Economy*, Springer Proceedings in Business
and Economics, DOI 10.1007/978-3-319-43434-6_30

Introduction

Innovation audits review current institution practices to advise on alternative and additional measure and techniques that companies can adopt to improve and maximize their innovation capabilities (Mobbs, 2011). One of the main benefits of conducting an innovation audit in the organization is to address its innovation management capability's weaknesses and strengths. Management innovation involves the introduction of novelty in an established organization, and as such it represents a particular form of organizational change (Birkinshaw, et al. 2008). This will help in determining opportunities for improvements in the innovation management process in the organization and in ensuring continuous improvement of innovation management capability. Innovation auditing also helps in benchmarking between organizations through comparing auditing reports. The purpose of this study is auditing and comparing innovation management capabilities of two organizations working in the same field, the municipal work, a municipality in UAE and a municipality in Jordan. It will mainly answer the question of: How well does each organization manages its innovation?

Innovation Auditing

Innovation is to really innovate within your domain, and expand your reach (Burnett 2011). Innovation audit is defined as a tool that can be used to reflect on how the innovation is managed in a firm and is a significant breakthrough in the area of technological innovation management (Cited by Abdel-Razek and Alsanad, 2014). Literature existed have examined the different types of innovation auditing, and discussed some of the benefits of doing innovation audits in organizations. There are many auditing tools and frameworks presented in the literature for measuring and auditing innovation in organizations. Radnor and Noke (2006) developed an auditing tool named "innovation compass," which was formulated through research and aims to understand innovation process within organizations. Tidd and Bessant (2014) have presented an auditing tool which looks at the organization from five factors that affect innovation management capability. These factors which were characterized as dimensions in the auditing tool are: Learning, Strategy, Linkages, Innovative Organization, and Innovation Process. It utilizes a questionnaire composed of 40 questions. Each dimension is represented by six questions in the survey. In this paper, Tidd and Bessant (2014) auditing tool was selected for the study.

Methodology

The methodology of the research is summarized in Fig. 30.1. It starts by selecting the auditing tool to be used in the study, and then the targeted samples in the selected organizations are determined, then conducting the auditing study by distributing auditing surveys to the respondents, then results and analysis, and finally conclusions.

Fig. 30.1 Methodology of
the study

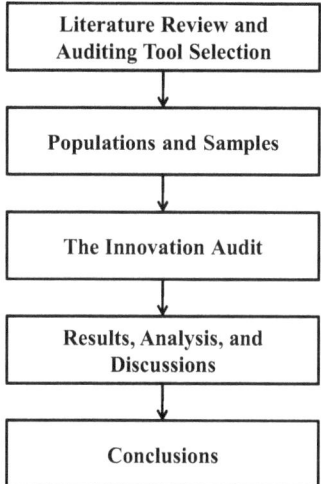

The study was conducted on two municipal organizations one in UAE and the other in Jordan. The municipality in UAE has launched an innovation policy and strategy and innovation lab, and more than 140 million dirhams have been spent on rewards of innovation, trainings, researches, etc. The municipality of Jordan recently launched an award (named King Abdullah bin AlHussien Award for Innovation) to encourage and support innovation climate in Jordan.

Populations and Samples

Based on the statistics received from both organizations, the researchers decided to select technical core business departments (CBD) for the study as they form 58 % and 38 % of the municipalities in UAE and Jordan, respectively. The departments of the highest percentage of suggestions (most innovative) and the ones with the lowest percentage of suggestions (least innovative) were selected for the study. Table 30.1 presents the selected departments and their contribution percentages.

Conducting the Innovation Audit in Both Organizations

Tidd and Bessant (2014) innovation auditing tool was implemented in both organizations through distributing the innovation auditing surveys to all targeted respondents. The percentages of categories of participants who participated in the auditing are presented in Tables 30.2 and 30.3.

Table 30.1 Selected departments (samples) for the study

Institution	Selected CBD of UAE		Selected CBD of Jordan	
Departments	Customer services	Public parks and agriculture	Planning of areas	Roads maintenance
Number of suggestions	586	363	4	2
Total number of employees (sample)	110	2324	7	366
% of contribution in suggestions	530	15.6	57.14	0.54

Table 30.2 Summary of the municipality in UAE respondents

Category	Segmentation	No. of respondents	% of participation
Ranking	Leaders	8	10.96
	Employees	65	89.04
	Total	73	100
Educational qualifications	Ph.D./Master degree	7	9.59
	High diploma	7	9.59
	Bachelor	28	38.36
	Secondary school	31	42.46
	Total	73	100
Job titles	Engineers	9	12.33
	Technicians	5	6.85
	Administrators	59	80.82
	Total	73	100
Gender	Male	28	38.36
	Female	45	61.64
	Total	73	100

Results, Analysis, and Discussions

The results of the innovation auditing study in both organizations are shown in the innovation auditing radar in Fig. 30.2.

A comparison between both organizations has been conducted in order to compare the innovation management capability of the organizations operating in the municipal field but located in the different countries such as UAE and Jordan taking into account that both countries are developing countries. The results show that the municipality in UAE is managing its innovation better than the municipality in Jordan in all auditing dimensions. The least difference between both organizations was in the learning dimension, followed by linkages, innovation process, innovative organization, and strategy. The average scores and percentages of differences of the auditing dimensions for both organizations are shown in Table 30.4.

Table 30.3 Summary of the municipality in Jordan respondents

Category	Segmentation	No. of respondents	% of participation
Ranking	Leaders	32	36
	Employees	56	64
	Total	88	100
Educational qualifications	Ph.D./Master degree	2	2
	High diploma	15	17
	Bachelor	40	46
	Secondary school	31	35
	Total	88	100
Job titles	Engineers	23	26
	Technicians	11	13
	Administrators	54	61
	Total	88	100
Gender	Male	71	81
	Female	17	19
	Total	88	100

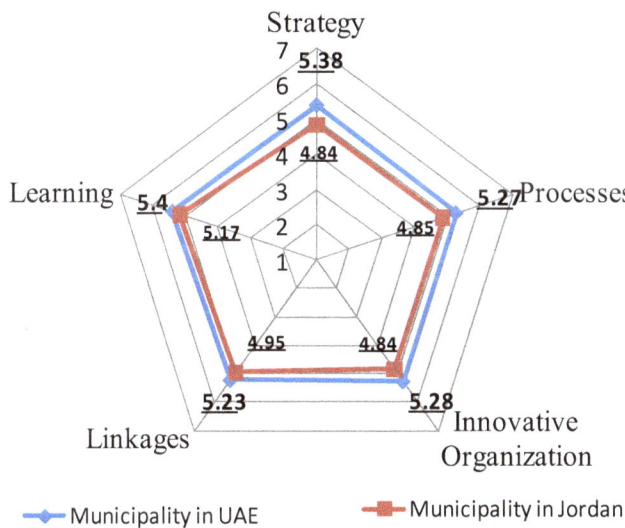

Fig. 30.2 Innovation auditing radar for both organizations

As shown in Table 30.4, the differences between both organizations are small and they range from 3.21 to 7.7 %. However, this presents an indication that both organizations are to a limited extent close in terms of their innovation management capabilities. Nevertheless, the municipality in UAE received higher scores in all dimensions which reveals that its innovation management capability is higher than the municipality in Jordan.

Table 30.4 Average scores and percentages of difference between both organizations

Dimension	Municipality in UAE	Municipality in Jordan	% of difference
Strategy	5.38	4.84	7.70
Processes	5.27	4.85	5.96
Innovative organization	5.28	4.84	6.29
Linkages	5.23	4.95	4.05
Learning	5.4	5.17	3.21

Table 30.5 Most and least innovative departments' results for the municipality in UAE

Dimension	Most innovative (HSD) department	Least innovative (LSD) department	% of difference
Strategy	5.77	5.04	10
Innovation process	5.6	4.98	9
Innovative organization	5.66	4.95	10
Linkages	5.68	4.83	12
Learning	5.8	5.05	11

A comparison was also made between high innovative departments, high Suggestion Departments (HSD) with the least innovative department, low Suggestion Department (LSD) within each organization. Table 30.5 presents the results of the municipality in UAE departments.

Comparing the average scores of HSD and LSD (av. score 5.7 and 4.97, respectively), and analyzing the HSD and LSD individual scores, it is clear that the HSD received higher scores in terms of their innovation management which motivates them to participate in the suggestion system, while the LSD received less scores in terms of innovation auditing dimensions. Taking a deeper look at the scores of the municipality in UAE, HSD and LSD both agreed that the municipality in UAE is managing learning and strategy very well, with almost similar scores. HSD lowest scores showed that the municipality in UAE needs to work more on processes through working on mechanisms to run projects on time and within budget, while the LSD thinks that the municipality in UAE needs to pay attention to the linkages and partnerships especially the cooperation with universities and other research centers. Moreover, the results reveal that the difference between both departments is somehow small ranging from 9 to 12%.

Similarly, the most innovative department and least innovative department of the municipality in Jordan were audited and compared. Table 30.6 presents the results of the municipality in Jordan departments.

The HSD and LSD in Jordan agreed that the municipality is managing learning very well, although with different scores, 6.75 and 5, respectively. Both agreed that the municipality needs to work more on fostering a systematic comparison of its products and services with other firms.

The HSD lowest average score of 6.4 was given to innovative organization which indicated that more focus is needed on the organizational level and especially on areas of communication between departments and the support of teams. The LSD

Table 30.6 Most and least innovative departments' results for the municipality in Jordan

Dimension	Most innovative (HSD) department	Least innovative (LSD) department	% of difference
Strategy	6.63	4.75	27
Innovation process	6.63	4.63	29
Innovative organization	6.38	4.75	23
Linkages	6.63	4.88	25
Learning	6.75	5	25

lowest average score of 4.63 was given to process. LSD respondents believe that the municipality has mechanisms in place to search for new innovations, launching new ideas, and managing them but they also indicate that the municipality in Jordan needs to give special focus on the process of selection of innovation projects, allowing fast track process of small projects, and early involvement of all employees in developing new products.

Comparing the average scores of HSD and LSD (av. score 6.6 and 4.8, respectively), and comparing the individual scores of each dimension of the audit of each department, as shown in Table 30.6, the employees at HSD believe that the municipality manages its innovations better than the employees of the LSD. The HSD focused on the innovation organization dimension as an area for improvement, while the LSD lowest score was given to the innovation process. HSD were satisfied in general with the management of innovation. Their audits resulted with higher score than the LSD. On the other hand, the LSD auditing scores were less than the HSD in all dimensions.

Conclusions

The objective of this study was to conduct an innovation audit in two organizations from the municipal field operating in two different countries.

The least difference between the organizations was in the learning dimension (3.21 %) and the most difference was in the strategy dimension (7.7 %). According to GII report 2015, UAE and Jordan improved in the institution and learning aspects as inputs. Supported by facts from both organizations, the municipality in UAE has developed and started the implementation of a 3-year strategy, while the municipality in Jordan has only a methodology of suggestions.

According to respondents' perception and based on the municipality in UAE available innovation policies and strategies, the municipality in UAE needs to communicate this strategy well according to certain procedures. The municipality in UAE also is paying attention to the learning dimension and specially to learn from employees' own mistakes but needs to work more on linkages. On the other hand, according to respondents' perception and based on the municipality of Jordan available policies, it is focusing more on the operational level including processes and learning. It needs to pay more attention on the strategic level of innovation, developing an innovation strategy and fostering the different fields of an innovative organization especially a motivating rewarding system and awareness of the importance of innovation to compete.

Moreover, the two organizations shared different gaps in the results and mainly in the strategy and learning dimensions, including sharing with networks and universities, and ability to learn from innovations to compete.

References

Abdel-Razek, R. H., & Alsanad, D. (2014). Auditing and comparing innovation management in organizations. *Global Journal of Business Research, 8(49)*

Birkinshaw, J., Hamel, G., & Mol, M. J. (2008). *Management innovation.* London Business School, University of Reading. Retrieved from http://faculty.london.edu/jbirkinshaw/assets/documents/5034421969.pdf.

Burnett, M. (2011). *Measuring innovation sustaining competitive advantage by turning ideas into value. BearingPoint.* Retrieved from http://www.bearingpoint.com/ecomaXL/files/Innovation_High_Res.pdf.

Mobbs, C. W. (2011). *What are innovation audits?* Innovation for Growth Limited, UK. Retrieved from http://www.innovationforgrowth.co.uk/What%20are%20innovation%20audits.pdf.

Radnor, Z. J., & Noke, H. (2006). Development of an audit tool for product innovation: The innovation compass. *International Journal of Innovation Management, 10*(1), 1–18.

Tidd, J., & Bessant, J. (2014). *Managing innovation: Integrating technological, market and organizational change* (5th ed.). West Essex: Wiley.

Chapter 31
Sustainable Development of Rural Communities in Bangladesh by Integrating Mobile Internet and Agent Banking Technology

Muhammad Hassan Bin Afzal

Abstract Bangladesh is one of the most populous countries in the world and mass people are still unbanked and still not included under central financial banking service. This causes huge setbacks in progressing the financial status of Bangladesh. In order to avoid such problematic scenario, the central bank of Bangladesh, Bangladesh bank decided to adopt and promote agent banking service in rural areas of Bangladesh to include the mass rural population under central financial enclosure. As of current situation, mobile operators can play a vital role to promote and educate and motivate the rural people of Bangladesh to be registered and use the service of agent banking to perform their daily financial tasks. Furthermore, mobile operators along with top banking software farms and banks can work together to build a unified platform to provide effective agent banking service in real time to the rural people of Bangladesh. This paper specifically discusses about mobile learning system for the rural people in order to educate them about the advantages and various useful services of banking system of Bangladesh. Furthermore, this paper also promotes a unified system based on mobile platform which can benefit both banking industry as well as their customers to get quick and risk-free financial services. This will result a better economical situation in Bangladesh and the rural people will be benefited from better, secure and quick financial services from Bangladeshi banks.

Keywords Mobile platform development for agent banking • Mobile learning system for rural people • Unified mobile platform for real-time banking • Banking service for rural people

M.H.B. Afzal (✉)
Electrical and Electronic Engineering Department, Primeasia University, Dhaka, Bangladesh

Faculty of Business Studies (FBS), University of Dhaka (DU), Dhaka, Bangladesh
e-mail: hasssans@ieee.org

© Springer International Publishing Switzerland 2017   361
R. Benlamri, M. Sparer (eds.), *Leadership, Innovation and Entrepreneurship as Driving Forces of the Global Economy*, Springer Proceedings in Business and Economics, DOI 10.1007/978-3-319-43434-6_31

Introduction

From end to end acclimatizing the new-fangled form of banking services such as online banking and mobile banking, Bangladeshi banks at present seized the golden opportunities towards progressive steps en route for modern banking features. Nevertheless, with the purpose of serving the enormous unbanked predominantly countryside individuals, who are lacking suitable enlightenment, access to internet and branch banking facility, the agent banking is the proper solution for them. The way up-to-the-minute technologies and facilities are developed and fulfilled every day to aid the bank customers, it is the high time to embrace and broadcast the agent banking method among countryside and inaccessible places in Bangladesh in order to bring in more clienteles and deliver them excellent support with least possible concern. Along these lines, agent banking can be a leading way out to serve the large unbanked rural populaces in Bangladesh and they can be fostered by providing a personalized bank account, sheltered money transfer and a complete financial inclusion.

Bangladesh bank by this time procured advanced phases to bring around and encourage the banking sector towards success by obtaining the total financial inclusion. Bangladesh bank also released committed guideline and list procedures as how to apply for agent banking. It's up to the banking authorities, how they act in response on this and become accustomed with this new exciting banking prospect (Bangladesh Bank, 2013).

As of current situation, mobile operators can play a vital role to promote and educate and motivate the rural people of Bangladesh to be registered and use the service of agent banking to perform their daily financial tasks. Furthermore, mobile operators along with top banking software farms and banks can work together to build a unified platform to provide effective agent banking service in real time to the rural people of Bangladesh. This paper specifically discusses about mobile learning system for the rural people in order to educate them about the advantages and various useful services of banking system of Bangladesh. Furthermore, this paper also promotes a unified system based on mobile platform which can benefit both banking industry as well as their customers to get quick and risk-free financial services. This will result a better economical situation in Bangladesh and the rural people will be benefited from better, secure and quick financial services from Bangladeshi banks (The current state of the financial sector of Bangladesh: An analysis, 2011).

Objective of This Research Study

Originally, the objective was to study, investigate, explore and analyse the current developments in banking industry to find some feasible options to offer a total financial inclusion which specifically highlights and includes the mass unbanked rural population of Bangladesh. In order to find some probable solutions, Bangladesh bank came up with the idea and implementation of agent banking among the mass unbanked population and to highlight the branchless banking. In order to deliver effective quality agent banking service among rural, unbanked and disadvantaged population in Bangladesh, both mobile internet network and mobile application developments play significant roles. The comprehensive objective of this research study is detailed below sequentially:

- Study and research the comparative analysis of mobile banking vs. agent banking
- Scope of improvements in current running model of mobile banking software
- Deliver least criterions and supplies for agent banking setups
- Heighten economic enclosure for Bangladeshi unbanked rural people
- Deliver for agent banking as a distribution network for posing banking facilities
- To emphasize the importance of mobile internet in promoting agent banking

The Method of Completing This Study

The procedure of completing this study encompassed thorough surveillance, adamant discussion with workforces, in-depth research study and communicating with successful agent banking services. Further observations are pointed out below:

- To fully realize and understand the needs and requirements of unbanked people
- In organizing this report both primary and secondary resources of material have been applied
- The study necessitates a methodical technique from choice of the subject to concluding report
- To achieve the concluding report and prediction, the data foundations are to be acknowledged and composed, categorized, evaluated and deduced in a logical approach.

Categorizing the Data Resources

The necessary data foundations were collected from various sources and both primary and secondary data resources are extensively identified. Then, it was decided in a meeting which segments are essential to complete the study effectively. Both primary and secondary sources of data were equally important to carry out this study effectively and successfully.

The Primary Resource of Data/Information

- In person exchange of information of potential unbanked rural population
- In person exchange of information with the respective bank officials
- Everyday deskwork report study

The Secondary Resource of Data/Information

- Bangladesh bank press release, guideline and annual reports
- In-depth investigative study of various global successful agents banking enterprises
- Gather knowledge about the successful agent banking network and their working principle
- Research findings and articles acquired from different archives and from internet online databases

Importance of Agent Banking in Bangladesh

As stated by Bangladesh bank in the provided guideline for agent banking for all the Bangladeshi banks, it clearly illustrated the following statement, "Agent banking means providing limited scale banking and financial services to the underserved population through engaged agents under a valid agency agreement, rather than a teller/cashier. It is the owner of an outlet who conducts banking transactions on behalf of a bank. Globally these retailers are being increasingly utilized as important distribution channels for financial inclusion. Bangladesh Bank has also decided to promote this complimentary channel to reach to the poor segment of the society as well as existing bank customer with a range of financial services especially to geographically dispersed locations. With a view to ensuring the safety, security and soundness of the proposed delivery channel Agent Banking Guidelines have been framed by the Bangladesh Bank to permit banks to be engaged in agent banking." It is undoubtedly noticeable from above cited announcement that Bangladesh bank is very much concerned to endorse the agent banking component in the midst of all the banks for an overall monetary enclosure for the Bangladeshi population unambiguously emphasizing that the countryside individuals who are in broad spectrum are not contained within any sort of banking service (Atandi, 2013).

Agent banking supports on condition that banking facilities to those bank customers channel through the associated agents under a legal agency agreement, compared to any standard means of teller/cashier/ATM booth service. The designated and lawfully associated agent of a government approved bank, who is also the proprietor of an outlet, basically carries out all the banking activities on behalf that bank. There are specific set of guidelines, rules and regulations and agent selection criteria in order to open an agent banking outlet. The categories of banking services may vary from country to country but there are certain levels of services that agents are not allowed to perform (Panamax Mobifin, n.d.). Only a branch bank can authorize and perform those tasks. However, agents can collect all the required information and hand them over to the bank for further official process.

Here, Fig. 31.1 portrays the difference between national banking system and agent banking system in Kenya, where leading bank providers have additional 748 banking agents in comparison to national bank. Additionally, the figure also represents vari-

Focus On Agency Banking In Kenya

While the national sample did not have a significant portion of bank agents in it, an additional sample of 748 banking agents was conducted for leading bank providers. The next three slides compare the two leading bank networks to the two leading telecom networks.

Metric	Comparison of Bank vs. MNO Agents in Kenya
Location	FSP Maps shows 83% of bank agents and 76% of MNO agents are rural in Kenya, while only 30% of Tanzanian and 44% of Ugandan MNO agents are rural.
Demographics	Both models have similar metrics for agent gender, dedication,, and exclusivity, but bank agents are more educated than MNO agents.
Transactions	MNO agents do more transactions per day, but data indicates that bank agents might do larger sized transactions.
Liquidity	Both models locate close to rebalancing points, and rebalance at similar costs and frequencies.
Support	Both models extend high quality levels of support to agents, visiting often and regularly.
Maturity	While the MNO networks of agents have been around longer, both models heavily recruit new agents and therefore are dominated by agents lacking operational experience.

Fig. 31.1 Comparison of bank and MNO agents in Kenya (*Source*: Helix Institute website)

ous important factors while deciding the locations to spread the agent banking module in a specific location. While branch banks require a high building cost and human resources management, the agent banking does not require huge human resources, but it does require close supervision and guidance in order to provide transparent and sincere customer support and customer transactions (Liang & Reichert, 2012).

Just like Fig. 31.1, where both the similarities and dissimilarities of agent banking and branch banking were discussed in detail for Kenyan Banking industry, Fig. 31.2 describes the close relationships between mobile banking and agent banking.

There are a number of resemblances between mobile banking and agent banking, including agency demographics and metrics of support. To a certain extent, both mobile network based money transfer system and agent banking offer similar financial services to their customers, but agent banking offers more wide ranges of service and it is not totally device/USSD network dependent service. Agent banking offers the similar branch bank like services to their customers, while the customers does not require to visit the banks which saves them a lot of hassle, time and related cost.

Differences Between Mobile Banking and Agent Banking (Bangladesh Bank Guideline)

According to Bangladesh Bank Guideline, there are certain differences in access options and activities. Mobile banking is designed to allow uninterrupted access between the individual customer and the designated bank.

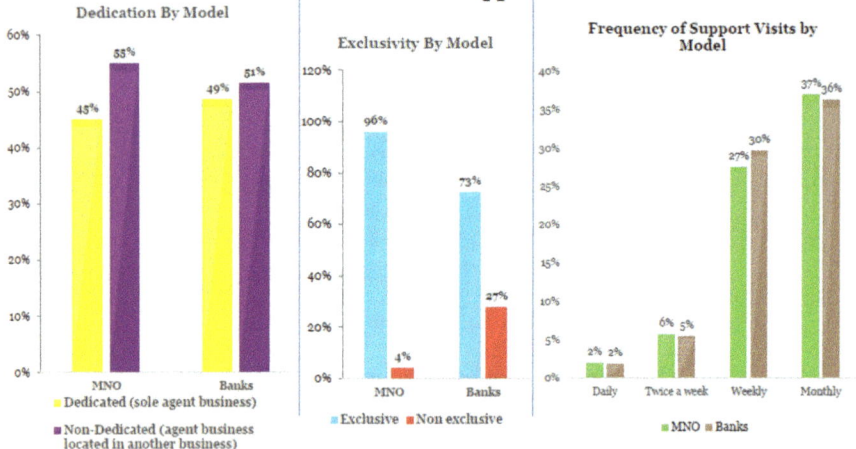

Fig. 31.2 Similarities between mobile money and agent banking in Kenya (*Source*: Helix Institute of Digital Finance website)

Whereas, the agent works as an intermediary between the bank and the localized customers to provide them support. Few basic differences are stated in Table 31.1. in detail. Based on this information, it is clearly evident that what are the significant advantages and disadvantages for real-time operating the agent banking in Bangladesh (Hartmann, Evensen, Görg, Farjami, & Long, 1999).

Advantages and Disadvantages of Agent Banking

After a thorough research and investigative study, it has been found out that it is quite cost saving and cheaper option to adopt agent based banking technology to serve the unbanked people in Bangladesh rather than opening and setting up a branch bank in remote locations to serve the unbanked population. It costs only 2–4% when a bank decides to spread outgent based banking technology in a specific location rather than opening up branch banking. Figure 31.3 clearly depicts the comparative benefits of operating gent based banking technology compared to branch based banking options.

Based on Fig. 31.3, it is clearly stated that it is most expensive while operating the branch banking compared to both agent banking and mobile-based banking. While agent banking can offer same level of customer satisfaction as branch banking, it also reduces the operational cost for the respective banks. But it definitely requires close monitoring and regular maintenance and cash management service. If these matters are well handled, then Bangladeshi banks can be huge benefited from

Table 31.1 Differences between mobile banking and agent banking according to Bangladesh Bank Guideline

Mobile banking	Agent banking
No such requirements	Should be assigned with a localized branch
Requires either network operator/mobile internet to validate mobile login/password	Able to support host validation for PIN/password/biometrics authentication
No such requirements	Banks should publish list as well as addresses of cash points/agents/partners in their website
In opening of mobile account, the bank is required to follow KYC (know your customer) guideline set by the central bank. No transaction would be allowed before verifying and approving the KYC form	Although KYC not required, still requires to follow the selection process detailed in section 12
Discouraging OTC and encouraging P2P and Partial OTC	Acts on behalf of bank and able to provide services to the customers
Mobile banking is a personalized access to client's bank account and allows to perform balance check, balance transfer and even request for loans and withdraw money in real time	Agent banking is working on behalf of a localized branch of a bank to facilitate the bank customers in local vicinity

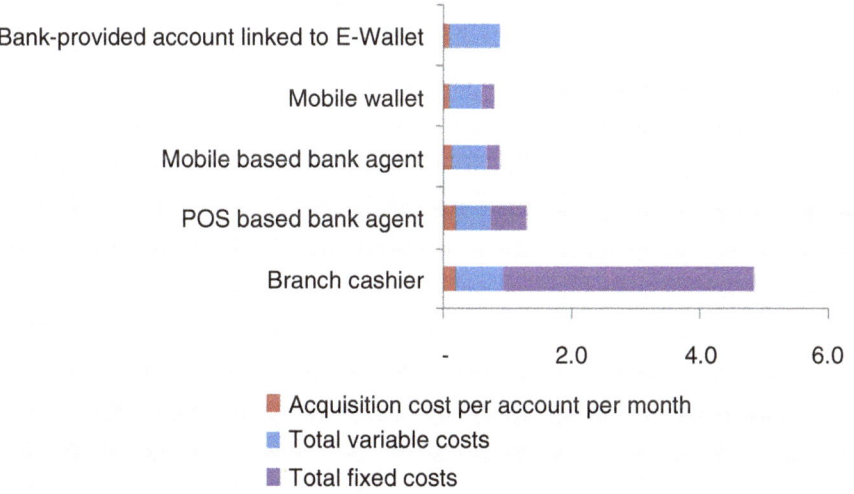

Fig. 31.3 A comparative study for operating mobile banking vs. agent banking vs. branch banking (*Source*: Helix Institute of Digital Finance website)

promoting and adopting agency banking in serving the mass unbanked population (Agent banking in Latin America, 2012).

Role of Mobile Internet and Mobile App. in Agent Banking Expansion

In order to successfully implement the agent banking method in rural and unbanked areas of Bangladesh, the primary concern is the availability of internet coverage. Couple of Bangladeshi mobile operators is currently providing total inclusion of mobile networks all over Bangladesh. The same cannot be said about high-speed mobile internet. Furthermore, appropriate mobile application and/or software support required to be developed to support the real-time transaction for agent banking customers (Siddiquie, 2014).

With the intention of achieving total financial inclusion in Bangladesh, the concerned government authorities can take effective steps in promoting agent banking. The initial step can be started with providing intensive training program for the interested parties so that these future banking agents are aware of ins and outs of standard banking guideline in Bangladesh as well as how to operate the agent banking in unbanked areas as well as how to deliver real-time customer service. This sort of strategies and framework can be proved immensely beneficial in the longer run in order to achieve total financial inclusion in Bangladesh by delivering the agent banking in rural and unbanked areas effectively.

In recent times, current water resources department of Bangladesh are working together with new ICT platforms to deliver the Bangladeshi citizens more effective services (Afzal Hossain & Afzal, 2013). Similarly, Bangladesh bank also needs to utilize the available ICT resources to achieve the total financial inclusion in future times. A certain ICT approach was initially discussed in order to distribute the rainfall data information among poor and disadvantaged rural population to help them plan accordingly for their irrigation management around the year using the social media platform as well as ICT technologies (Afzal & Bhuiyan, 2015). In order to make this agent banking approach successful among the rural areas of Bangladesh as well as to obtain the total financial inclusion by including all these rural people under centralized banking service, certain well-planned ICT service is urgently required, where mobile network and mobile internet play the most important role to make the banking service feasible and available among the rural people of Bangladesh (Afzal, 2014).

According to the latest The 2015 Brookings Financial and Digital Inclusion Project Report (Villasenor, West, & Lewis, 2015), the latest step of promoting agent banking in Bangladesh could result in better financial inclusion specifically serving the rural population of this country as well as helping the country's overall financial condition in the future.

Conclusion

Through adapting the newer form of banking services such as online banking and mobile banking, Bangladeshi banks already took progressive steps towards modern banking attributes. But, in order to serve the large unbanked mainly rural people, who are deficient of appropriate education, access to internet and branch banking service, the agent banking is the appropriate solution for them. The way latest technologies and services are invented and implemented every day to serve the bank customers, it is the high time to adopt and disseminate the agent banking method among rural and remote places in Bangladesh in order to bring in more customers and provide them excellent support with minimum fuss. In this way, agent banking can be a prime solution to serve the large unbanked rural people in Bangladesh and they can be benefitted by obtaining a personalized bank account, secure money transfer and a complete financial solution. It will also help to grow the banking industry of Bangladesh in a more positive and progressive way.

Current Challenges and Future Works

Based on in-depth research analysis and studying the current trends of Bangladeshi banking industries, it is quite evident that acceptance of agent banking platform in Bangladesh could result in significant progress towards positive trend of the country's economic situation compared to branch banking. This case is much stronger when huge chunk of bank financial transactions occur in high-volume operation, low-balance accounts that are common among underprivileged rural consumers. Despite the fact that banking agents inflate the set of fruitful clienteles, the viability boundary can be hard-pressed even extra with mobile-based advanced networking and well-qualified agent team. Nevertheless, numerous aspects still require further closer attention in order to improve the profitability of agent banking in Bangladesh. These are stated below sequentially:

- Agent banking cannot perform general marketing and pull-off promotional campaign to increase the customer base. In order to do that, respective banks require deploying dedicated marketing team in order to inspire, motivate and attract the large unbanked population towards agent banking.
- The core banking software is quite expensive, complex and requires a certain level of mastery and academic qualification to operate smoothly and serve the bank consumers. While, in order to promote the agent banking, banks require adopting a minimal featured technology which is quite easy to operate but must include the basic banking financial transaction features to support the consumers.

First and foremost important matter is to improve the internet network in rural areas of Bangladesh, so that the agent booths can perform their consumer banking tasks in real time and also provide extra layer of financial security. All the recruited agents are required to be well trained and able to operate and handle daily tasks in that dedicated software. A good and effecting mandatory training session is highly required. Also the nearest branch bank required to have dedicated team of technical support as well cash liquidity support. Create proper awareness among rural people that agent banking is as secure as branch banking and their wealth is quite safe and secure. Periodical checking on agent booths is also essential in order to avoid any sort of discrepancies and financial maladministration and mishandling.

References

Afzal, M. H. B. (2014). Large scale IT projects: Study and analysis of failures and winning factors. *IETE Technical Review, 31*(3), 214–219. Web: 28 Apr 2015.

Afzal, M. H. B., & Bhuiyan, M. (2015). Sustainable trend analysis of annual divisional rainfall in Bangladesh. *ISFRAM, 2014*, 257–270. Web: 28 Apr 2015.

Afzal Hossain, A. F. M., & Afzal M. H. B. (2013). Management of irrigation and drainage systems using mathematical modelling. *Journal of Applied Water Engineering and Research, 1*(2), 129–136. Web: 28 Apr 2015.

Agent banking in Latin America. (2012). Alliance for Financial Inclusion, 1–20.

Atandi, F. (2013). Challenges of agent banking experiences in Kenya. *International Journal of Academic Research in Business and Social Sciences, 3*(8), 397–412.

Bangladesh Bank. (2013). *Guidelines on agent banking for the banks*. Retrieved March 10, 2015, from http://www.bangladesh-bank.org/aboutus/regulationguideline/psd/agentbanking_banks_v13.pdf

The current state of the financial sector of Bangladesh: An analysis. (2011). *AIUB Bus Econ Working Paper Series* (AIUB-BUS-ECON-2011-03).

Hartmann, J., Evensen, R., Görg, C., Farjami, P., & Long, H. (1999). Agent-based banking transactions and information retrieval—What about performance issues? http://citeseerx.ist.psu.edu/viewdoc/download?doi=10.1.1.40.802&rep=rep1&type=pdf

Liang, H., & Reichert, A. K. (2012).The impact of banks and non-bank financial institutions on economic growth. *Service Industries Journal*. doi:10.1080/02642069.2010.529437.

Panamax Mobifin. (n.d.). Retrieved March 7, 2015, from http://www.panamaxmobifin.com/agency.php

Siddiquie, M. (2014). Scopes and threats of mobile financial services in Bangladesh. *IOSR Journal of Economics and Finance (IOSR-JEF), 4*(4), 36–39.

Villasenor, J., West, D., & Lewis, R. (2015). The 2015 Brookings Financial and Digital Inclusion Project Report.

Part II
Contemporary Leadership and Management

Chapter 32
Clustering Countries According to Their Cultural Proximity and Similarity

Angelika C. Dankert, Hamoud Dekkiche, Said Baadel, and Stefane Kabene

Abstract Clustering countries mathematically according to Geert Hofstede's cultural proximity and similarity factors is one way of classifying regional communities into well-defined cultural categories. Trying to test this statement mathematically shows that classifying countries or cultures remains complex. The approach shows a lack of an overall scheme and even when common variables exist, it seems that random and coincidental similarity weighs strongly on most variables used in the model. The results emphasize the need for more research in order to support the model.

Keywords Wheel of cultural clusters • Cultural proximity • Cultural dimensions • Geert Hofstede • Robert J. House

Introduction

The twenty-first century is a century of full globalization in which people, companies, and countries are closely interlinked. Cross-cultural management, intercultural exchange, and cultural proximity concern not only huge MNCs, but happen on a personal level due to increased demographic changes like migration, expatriate work-placement, student-study-abroad possibilities, and social media opening the doors to foreign cultures, traditions and people just a click-away.

A.C. Dankert (✉)
Hochschule Aschaffenburg, Aschaffenburg, Germany
e-mail: angelika_dankert@yahoo.de

H. Dekkiche • S. Kabene
Canadian University of Dubai, Dubai, United Arab Emirates
e-mail: angelika_dankert@yahoo.de

S. Baadel
Canadian University of Dubai, Dubai, United Arab Emirates

University of Huddersfield, Huddersfield, UK

© Springer International Publishing Switzerland 2017
R. Benlamri, M. Sparer (eds.), *Leadership, Innovation and Entrepreneurship as Driving Forces of the Global Economy*, Springer Proceedings in Business and Economics, DOI 10.1007/978-3-319-43434-6_32

373

The field and science of "Cultural Studies" is relatively new: Geert Hofstede was the first one to "unpack culture", changing the biased way of thinking about culture being too complex to be split in its single variables. Business-driven, more research was undertaken when companies started aiming for worthy capital spending and foreign direct investments and therefore needed more information about countries and their citizens to understand the domestic culture. Robert J. House is the man behind the Global Leadership and Organizational Behavior Effectiveness Study (GLOBE Study): including the findings of previous investigators a "Wheel of Cultural Clusters" was published constituting countries representing a similar culture within one cluster. The meaningful statement is that countries accumulated to one cluster not directly next to each other but opposite are the most contrasting ones regarding cultural values, norms and beliefs and vice versa, the summarized countries within cultural clusters directly next to each other show the greatest similarities. Trying to prove this statement mathematically, it gets obvious that "21st century culture unpacked" is still complex, manifold and basically multifaceted due to its diversity based on many variables.

Theoretical Framework

An increased level of globalization characterizes today's world. It is defined as the process of international market integration aiming for an interdependent world. The movement caused cross-border linkages and resulted in a strong degree of transnational integration in the field of economy, finance, trade, communication and people (Lethaus, 2009). Globalization is characterized by a continuous integration resulting in complex relations between countries, companies and people around the globe (Andruseac, 2015).

Born and raised in a certain culture, influenced by the immediate environment and shaped according to norms, values and beliefs of this certain group characterizes every individual around the globe. The purpose of this study is to prove mathematically the statement of House's "Wheel of Cultural Clusters" by applying Hofstede's Cultural Dimension Theory on the countries Robert J. House did research on. The Wheel's Statement is that clusters directly next to each other show a greater resemblance in cultural norms, values and beliefs (including economic and socio-demographic data) and vice versa cultural clusters directly opposite each other show the least similarity, meaning the two cultural clusters opposite each other represent countries with contrasting characteristics. The paper aims to prove House's Wheel mathematically by comparing scores of clusters and its countries while searching for matching results using different variables being correlated with the examined dimension.

Etymologically, the term "culture" refers to the Latin word *cultura* (cultivating the spirit), *colere* (to inhabit, worship) and *cultus* (dominantly religion oriented) (Wahrig, 1986). The anthropological concept of "culture" combines knowledge, belief, art, morals and values as well as law and habit acquired by man as a member of society (Tylor, 1974). Therefore, culture is the shared way of life of a particular group of people at a certain time with focus on general customs and beliefs (Cambridge English Dictionary, 2015). It is about the behavioral patterns shown by a particular group or society (Hopkins, 2009).

Searching for cultural dimensions to analyze and systematically classify cultures is the major focus in the field of "intercultural research" aiming to facilitate the understanding of cultural differences. The scientific field of study deals with the impact of culture on the individual and the society. According to Hofstede, culture is defined as "[…] the collective programming of the mind that distinguishes the members of one group or category of people from others". The heart of a culture is the sum of all moral concepts and values formed over a long time. Hofstede's "programming of the mind" refers to the process of socialization, which every individual experiences without being aware of the procedure to be programmed in conformity with a particular culture. The invisible "programming" is collective rather than individual (Slavik, 2004) and the programming determinants are influenced by the close social environment (Vieregg, 2009).

In 1991, Robert J. House published the "Global Leadership and Organizational Behavior Effectiveness Study" (Acronym: GLOBE Study) based on the evaluation of 17,300 middle managers in 951 companies around the globe (Hoppe, 2007). Building on the findings of e.g. Hofstede, House developed nine cultural dimensions to portray similarities and differences in culture, values, beliefs and practices. Six out of the nine dimensions have their origin in Hofstede's previous developments (House, 2004). From the anthropological background, the developed dimensions were applied in 62 "societal cultures" and grouped in 10 "societal clusters" containing the total number of societies belonging to the respective cluster.

Societies belonging to one cluster are more alike regarding values and norms than societies from different clusters. House's "Wheel of Cultural Clusters" identified that clusters being directly opposite each other (e.g. Middle East vs. Anglo) are most unrelated to each other, whereas clusters directly next to each other (e.g. Southern Asia and Confucian Asia) have most substantial similarities regarding values, behavior and norms (Hoppe & Eckert, 2014) (Fig. 32.1).

The study on Leadership and Organizational Behavior Effectiveness can be summarized with the result that a leader's effectiveness is always contextual, meaning it is embedded in the societal and organizational norms, values and beliefs. The GLOBE Study managed to empirically investigate the relationship between culture and leader behavior in societies using both quantitative and qualitative methods.

However House's Development of a Wheel of Cultural Clusters has precursors: In a paper published by Ronen and Shenkar in 1985, the authors developed an "Eight Cluster Study for Cross-Cultural Comparison" focused on the released intercultural research data up to this time. The paper was developed to prove that the cultural environment influences employee's attitude and behavior and that it is the reason for intercultural individual differences. The authors treated cultures as entities and used nations to establish clusters of countries with similarities according to the organizational variables. As national boundaries limit legal, political, and social environments of people's operations, clusters were formed by nations (Ronen & Shenkar, 1985).

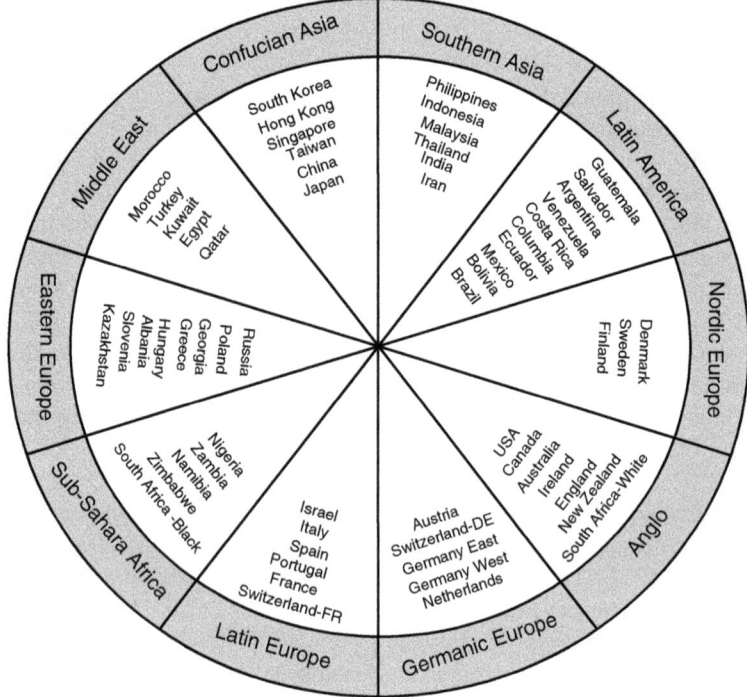

Fig. 32.1 House's wheel of cultural clusters (House, 2004)

Ronen and Shenkar developed a scheme, later on published as the first Wheel of Cultural Clusters, where countries are geographically clustered because geography, language (linguistic family) and religion are closely related to each other, but also the impact of immigration and colonialization had been taken into account.

Methodology

House's Wheel of Cultural Clusters contains 61 countries from all around the globe, categorized by similarities into 10 clusters after extensive research:

- Southern Asia (Cluster 1, Letter A)
- Latin America (Cluster 2, Letter B)
- Nordic Europe (Cluster 3, Letter C)
- Anglo (Cluster 4, Letter D)
- Germanic Europe (Cluster 5, Letter E)
- Latin Europe (Cluster 6, Letter F)
- Sub-Sahara Africa (Cluster 7, Letter G)

 − Eastern Europe (Cluster 8, Letter H)
 − Middle East (Cluster 9, Letter I)
 − Confucian Asia (Cluster 10, Letter J)

Each country within a cluster was given an updated score for the six dimensions of Hofstede to facilitate a comparison on a scale from 0 to 100:

 − Power Distance Index (PDI) (Dimension 1)
 − Individualism vs. Collectivism (IDV) (Dimension 2)
 − Masculinity vs. Feminity (MAS) (Dimension 3)
 − Uncertainty Avoidance Index (UAI) (Dimension 4)
 − Long-term vs. Short-term Orientation (LTO) (Dimension 5)
 − Indulgence vs. Restraint (IND) (Dimension 6)

The arithmetic mean for the sum of all countries within a cluster was calculated for each of Hofstede's dimensions. The final six scores for the above mentioned dimensions gave an overall look of one cultural cluster by showing mathematically the gap between Hofstede's 0–100 (low–high) scale for comparison. Using Hofstede's words, the results exposed how the societies behind a cluster were "programmed" according to values, norms and beliefs.

House's Wheel of Cultural Clusters was created to show that clusters directly next to each other are most alike and clusters directly opposite each other contain countries showing the least resemblance. To prove this statement with regard to the cultural dimensions as a score for each country, a mathematic formula was created where A–J represent cultural clusters while letters are rotating clockwise in House's existing Wheel of Cultural Clusters:

$$A(\text{Dimension 1}) - B(\text{Dimension 1}) < A(\text{Dimension 1}) - F(\text{Dimension 1})$$

Figure 32.2 is a facilitated version of House's Wheel with the abbreviations A–J used in the formula. After calculation of Dimension 1, the formula is used again to calculate the results for Dimensions 2–6 using the same scheme as described above. Letters opposite each other are most antithetic regarding values, beliefs and norms and vice versa letters directly next to each other are most alike. It is to prove that after the calculation the difference in scores as a result will be the lowest by subtracting the arithmetic means of two closely neighbored clusters within the same dimension. Vice versa the result by subtracting scores within the same dimension will be the highest when subtracting two cultural clusters that are opposite each other, explaining the huge difference in norms, values and beliefs portrayed in Hofstede's Dimensions on the scale for comparison and House's Wheel including its precursors.

The end-results with the calculated scores might be + or −, but the negative sign is irrelevant for the mathematical proof. Anytime a lower score in e.g. PDI is subtracted by a higher score in PDI, the negative sign will appear but the number as result is just about the difference in number itself, meaning the larger the difference, the more diverse and unequal the two cultural clusters, the smaller the difference, disregarding any algebraic sign, the closer the two cultural clusters.

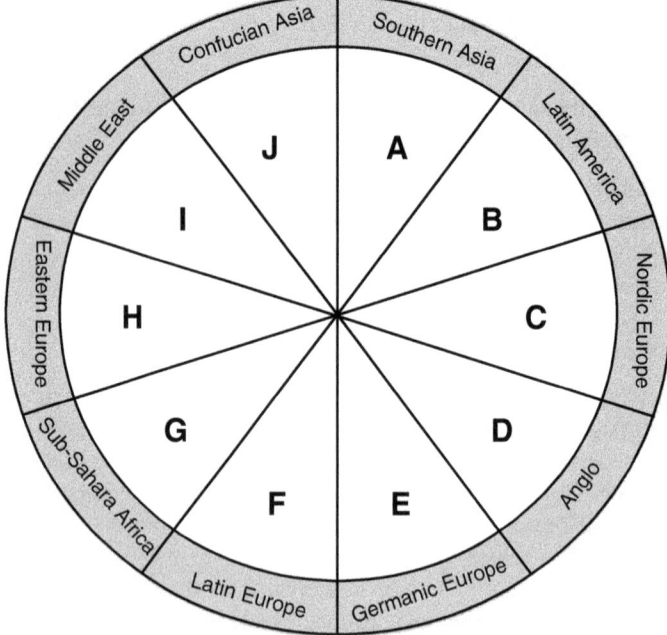

Fig. 32.2 House's wheel simplified (House, 2004 facilitated by Dankert, 2016)

Discussion

It was expected that the results from subtracting scores from cultural clusters neighboring each other (meaning cultural values, norms and beliefs are *very much* or *more* alike) are lower than the results from subtracting scores from opposite cultural clusters. In this case, the score difference was expected to be *the highest* or *higher*. Green highlighted scores represent a positive outcome for proving House and red highlighted scores signify that the mathematical proof of cultural proximity indicated by the Wheel of Cultural Clusters is negative, as the result of subtracting two scores from directly opposite located cultural clusters is lower than the one of two directly neighboring cultural clusters.

In Tables 32.1, 32.2, 32.3, 32.4, 32.5, 32.6, 32.7, 32.8, 32.9, and 32.10, Hofstede's six Dimensions are abbreviated according to the officially used acronyms, starting the calculation with D1, etc. Other used units in 4.1–4.6 are described below.

Table 32.1 Results for Southern Asia

A(D1)—B(D1)<						A(D1)—F(D1)					
13.50	9.39	−3.61	−34.39	15.00	−40.33	31.00	−27.67	−1.67	−32.33	−14.17	−2.87
PDI	IDV	MAS	UAI	LTO	IND	PDI	IDV	MAS	UAI	LTO	IND

Table 32.2 Results for Latin America

B(D1)—C(D1)<						B(D1)—G(D1)					
37.67	−48.56	36.78	45.89	−19.17	13.33	1,50	−19.22	1.69	33.14	−5.17	18.67
PDI	IDV	MAS	UAI	LTO	IND	PDI	IDV	MAS	UAI	LTO	IND

Table 32.3 Results for Nordic Europe

C(D1)—D(D1)<						C(D1)—H(D1)					
−8.24	−11.24	−45.76	−7.71	9.86	−0.10	−44.00	25.83	−41.67	−51.00	−13.33	36.17
PDI	IDV	MAS	UAI	LTO	IND	PDI	IDV	MAS	UAI	LTO	IND

Table 32.4 Results for Anglo

D(D1)—E(D1)<						D(D1)—I(D1)					
4.97	13.17	2.43	−17.49	−41.26	13.03	−38.43	47.32	15.68	−33.54	9.81	42.43
PDI	IDV	MAS	UAI	LTO	IND	PDI	IDV	MAS	UAI	LTO	IND

Table 32.5 Results for Germanic Europe

E(D1)—F(D1)<						E(D1)—J(D1)					
−16.90	9.57	8.50	−18.63	21.40	11.20	−35.07	43.07	0.67	10.03	−10.10	20.90
PDI	IDV	MAS	UAI	LTO	IND	PDI	IDV	MAS	UAI	LTO	IND

Table 32.6 Results for Latin Europe

F(D1)—G(D1)<						F(D1)—A(D1)					
−16.00	17.83	−0.25	31.08	24.00	−18.80	−31.00	27.67	1.67	32.33	14.17	2.87
PDI	IDV	MAS	UAI	LTO	IND	PDI	IDV	MAS	UAI	LTO	IND

Table 32.7 Results for Sub-Sahara Africa

G(D1)—H(D1)<						G(D1)—B(D1)					
−7.83	−3.50	−6.58	−38.25	−27.33	30.83	−1.50	19.22	−1.69	−33.14	5.17	−18.67
PDI	IDV	MAS	UAI	LTO	IND	PDI	IDV	MAS	UAI	LTO	IND

Table 32.8 Results for Eastern Europe

H(D1)—I(D1)<						H(D1)—C(D1)					
−2.67	10.25	11.58	9.75	33.00	6.17	44.00	−25.83	41.67	51.00	13.33	−36.17
PDI	IDV	MAS	UAI	LTO	IND	PDI	IDV	MAS	UAI	LTO	IND

Table 32.9 Results for Middle East

I(D1)—J(D1)<						I(D1)—D(D1)					
8.33	8.92	−12.58	26.08	−61.17	−8.50	38.43	−47.32	−15.68	33.54	−9.81	−42.43
PDI	IDV	MAS	UAI	LTO	IND	PDI	IDV	MAS	UAI	LTO	IND

Table 32.10 Results for Confucian Asia

J(D1)—A(D1)<						J(D1)—E(D1)					
−12.83	−5.83	9.50	3.67	45.67	−6.83	35.07	−43.07	−0.67	−10.03	10.10	−20.90
PDI	IDV	MAS	UAI	LTO	IND	PDI	IDV	MAS	UAI	LTO	IND

Table 32.11 Overview of the examination outcome for proving House

8	9	4	5	1	6
2	1	6	5	9	4
PDI	IDV	MAS	UAI	LTO	IND

Corruption Rate	0–100 (Highly Corrupt–Very Clean)
Global Competitiveness Index	1–7 (Low–High Degree of Competitiveness)
Happy Planet Index	Depending on Life Expectancy, experienced Well-Being, Ecological Footprint. The higher the score, the higher the HPI
Hofstede Score	0–100 (Low–High in the respective Dimension)
Peace Index	5–1 (Very High–Very Low); 0 = Not included

By evaluating the data it gets obvious that only the two dimensions *PDI* (8:2) and *IDV* (9:1) score as expected. The scores for *MAS* (4:6) and in particular *LTO* (1:9) do not fit in the estimated range at all. Although *UAI* ranks just medium (5:5), *IND* scores almost the same (6:4) which was not anticipated. Table 32.11 is a summary of all dimensions and the outcome for proving House.

The result leads to the assumption that other variables might be the reason for this research result. Therefore different variables are examined to explain this phenomenon, e.g. Peace Index, Global Competitiveness Index (GCI), Corruption Rate, Governmental Debt, GDP per Capita, and GDP Growth (GDP Grw.) as well as the Unemployment Rate for the respective countries. Moreover the Happy Planet Index (HPI) consisting of Life Expectancy, experienced Well-Being, and Ecological Footprint is studied. The Life Satisfaction Index (LSI) is also investigated and compared, however not available for all countries listed in House's Wheel of Cultural Clusters.

Power Distance Index

Scores used: Corruption Rate (CR), Peace Index (PI), GCI, HPI, Life Expectancy (LE) and LSI.

Note: Following the idea that opposite located cultural clusters show the least/ lower resemblance and cultural clusters next to each other show the highest/higher resemblance, the scores of the respective Hofstede Dimension in direct comparison of two opposite clusters have to be seen as "Black-or-White," meaning either "high hierarchical ordered" or "low hierarchical ordered."

The investigation is about finding a scheme behind the results by comparing different variables matching the respective dimension in a tabular comparison of high/low rating cultural clusters. It is to prove that the result by subtracting scores of clusters directly opposite each other shows a higher difference in numbers than by subtracting scores of clusters neighboring each other using the formula:

$$A\left(\text{Dimension1}\right) - B\left(\text{Dimension1}\right) < A\left(\text{Dimension1}\right) - F\left(\text{Dimension1}\right).$$

The PDI is a dimension of Hofstede referring to the degree of acceptance and expectation that power is distributed unequally within a society. Cultural clusters rating high identify a strong hierarchical order where every individual has to know their place. In contrast, societal clusters with a low PDI are described as the sum of countries demanding justification for power and flat hierarchy pressuring equality (Hofstede Center, 2015).

Despite the slight difference in the subtracted, accumulated scores of Sub-Sahara Africa (63.50) and Latin America (65.00), the PDI can be taken as a proof of House's Wheel with a total score of 8:2, meaning in eight out of ten cases the result of subtracting the scores of cultural clusters next to each other is lower than the result by subtracting scores from opposite clusters (Table 32.12).

Sub-Sahara Africa (63.50) and *Latin America* (65.00) are direct counterparts but nevertheless score similar and can therefore in an overall view be categorized as more hierarchical oriented, as both are above average as well as *Confucian Asia* (65.67). In addition to the above mentioned, *Southern Asia* (78.50), *Middle East* (74.00) and *Eastern Europe* (71.33) are high PDI societies scoring 60 and above.

Table 32.12 Cluster accumulated PDI indices for direct counterparts [scale: 0–100 (low–high)]

Confucian Asia	65.67	← →	Germanic Europe	30.60
Eastern Europe	71.33	← →	Nordic Europe	27.33
Latin Europe	47.50	← →	Southern Asia	78.50
Anglo	35.57	← →	Middle East	74.00
Sub-Sahara Africa	63.50	← →	Latin America	65.00

These societal clusters can be described as slightly corrupt in comparison to the other clusters, where the Peace Index is medium. The GCI and the LSI rate below the low scoring PDI clusters (all apart from Confucian Asia). The Life Expectancy is below and on average of 74. With regard to the lowest scoring cultural clusters in the dimension of PDI, *Nordic Europe* (27.33), *Germanic Europe* (30.60), *Anglo* (35.57) and *Latin Europe* (47.50) all show a very low level of corruption (apart from Latin Europe scoring the same as Confucian Asia, but Confucian Asia rates higher in PDI) and a high level of security indicated by a very high/highest score in Peace Index (apart from Confucian Asia). The Life Expectancy is one of the highest above average as well as the LSI rating is hugely above average (apart from Latin America).

It can certainly be said that a high PDI is closely related to a higher level of corruption within a societal cluster, leading to less stability resulting in a lower Peace Index and a slightly lower GCI. To some extent, societal clusters of high Power Distance Indices score lower in Life Expectancy and Life Satisfaction (apart from Latin America and the fact that there is no data available for Southern Asia and Sub-Sahara Africa). The scores from the PDI dimension of Hofstede and the applied formula in House's Wheel of Cultural Cluster to calculate the difference in scores prove the lower score result in neighboring clusters and the higher score result in directly opposite located clusters, leading to the result that House's Wheel can be mathematically proven (Table 32.13).

Individualism vs. Collectivism

Scores used: Corruption Rate (CR), Peace Index (PI), GCI, HPI, Life Expectancy (LE) and LSI.

Note: Following the idea that opposite located cultural clusters show the least/lower resemblance and cultural clusters next to each other show the highest/higher resemblance, the scores of the respective Hofstede Dimension in direct comparison of two opposite clusters have to be seen as "Black-or-White," meaning either "individualistic" or "collectivistic."

The investigation is about finding a scheme behind the results by comparing different variables matching the respective dimension in a tabular comparison of high/low rating cultural clusters. It is to prove that the result by subtracting scores of clusters directly opposite each other shows a higher difference in numbers than by subtracting scores of clusters neighboring each other using the formula:

$$A(\text{Dimension1}) - B(\text{Dimension1}) < A(\text{Dimension1}) - F(\text{Dimension1}).$$

The Dimension of IDV is defined as the "I" versus "We" orientation in societies. Individualistic societies focus on caring for themselves and their immediate families and the achievement of the individual is paramount. Collectivistic societies are

Table 32.13 Cluster accumulated scores for different variables

Cluster name	PDI	CR	PI	GCI	HPI	LE	LSI
Southern Asia	78.50	37.83	3.00	4.52	49.08	71	–
Latin America	65.00	36.10	3.30	3.98	55.15	74	7.55
Nordic Europe	27.33	89.33	5.00	5.40	41.83	81	9.53
Anglo	35.57	74.57	4.29	5.17	41.86	77	7.40
Germanic Europe	30.60	80.00	5.00	5.48	46.93	81	8.83
Latin Europe	47.50	63.50	4.17	4.92	46.87	82	6.30
Sub-Sahara Africa	63.50	35.80	3.00	3.86	34.74	54	–
Eastern Europe	71.33	44.63	3.63	4.25	41.25	75	2.46
Middle East	74.00	46.80	3.60	4.44	37.48	74	3.00
Confucian Asia	65.67	64.33	4.17	5.32	42.66	80	4.20

Outcome for the PDI Index: 8:2

Table 32.14 Cluster accumulated IDV indices for direct counterparts [scale: 0–100 (low–high)]

Confucian Asia	24.33	← →	Germanic Europe	67.40
Eastern Europe	43.50	← →	Nordic Europe	69.33
Latin Europe	57.83	← →	Southern Asia	30.17
Anglo	80.57	← →	Middle East	33.25
Sub-Sahara Africa	40.00	← →	Latin America	20.78

Table 32.15 Cluster accumulated scores for different variables

Cluster name	IDV	CR	PI	GCI	HPI	LE	LSI
Southern Asia	30.17	37.83	3.00	4.52	49.08	71	–
Latin America	20.78	36.10	3.30	3.98	55.15	74	7.55
Nordic Europe	69.33	89.33	5.00	5.40	41.83	81	9.53
Anglo	80.57	74.57	4.29	5.17	41.86	77	7.40
Germanic Europe	67.40	80.00	5.00	5.48	46.93	81	8.83
Latin Europe	57.83	63.50	4.17	4.92	46.87	82	6.30
Sub-Sahara Africa	40.00	35.80	3.00	3.86	34.74	54	–
Eastern Europe	43.50	44.63	3.63	4.25	41.25	75	2.46
Middle East	33.25	46.80	3.60	4.44	37.48	74	3.00
Confucian Asia	24.33	64.33	4.17	5.32	42.66	80	4.20

Outcome for the IDV Index: 9:1

about the collective, business and relation is closely related to each other and unquestionable loyalty within even the extended family is given (Hofstede Center, 2015) (Table 32.14).

Regarding societal clusters opposite each other, Table 32.15 demonstrates a high difference in scores for all cultural clusters, leading to the assumption that opposite located clusters in the IDV Dimension are indeed dissimilar, proving House's statement about opposite cultural clusters.

Calculating the accumulated scores against each other there is only one exception in which a score does not meet the requirements to fit in the scheme: The difference in scores between the neighboring clusters of Latin America and Nordic Europe is higher, as *Latin America* (20.78) is highly collectivistic oriented and *Nordic Europe* (69.33) represents a strong individualistic society, than the subtracted opposite cluster scores of Latin America and *Sub-Sahara Africa* (40.00), leading to a mathematical relationship of 9:1.

Collectivistic societies like *Latin America* (20.78), *Confucian Asia* (24.33), *Southern Asia* (30.17), *Middle East* (33.25), *Sub-Sahara Africa* (40.00) and *Eastern Europe* (43.50) score higher in corruption and lower in stability resulting in a lower Peace Index compared to individualistic societies. The score for Global Competitiveness is slightly below IDV high rating clusters, as well as the average Life Expectancy of 74 (all apart from Confucian Asia) and the LSI (apart from Latin America).

It can be summarized that the higher the score in individualism, the lower the corruption rate leading to more stability and a higher level of peace within countries of that respective cluster. Clusters of accumulated individualistic countries score above average in Life Expectancy and are happier with their life (apart from Southern Asia and Latin America). To conclude: the happier a society, the longer the life expectancy of its people, the higher the competition including a high level of stability and peace and low corruption rate.

Masculinity vs. Feminity Index

Scores used: GDP per Capita, GDP Grw., Corruption Rate (CR), Peace Index (PI), GCI, HPI, Life Expectancy (LE), LSI and Ecological Footprint (EF).

Note: Following the idea that opposite located cultural clusters show the least/lower resemblance and cultural clusters next to each other show the highest/higher resemblance, the scores of the respective Hofstede Dimension in direct comparison of two opposite clusters have to be seen as "Black-or-White," meaning either "masculine" or "feminine."

The investigation is about finding a scheme behind the results by comparing different variables matching the respective dimension in a tabular comparison of high/low rating cultural clusters. It is to prove that the result by subtracting scores of clusters directly opposite each other shows a higher difference in numbers than by subtracting scores of clusters neighboring each other using the formula:

$$A(\text{Dimension1}) - B(\text{Dimension1}) < A(\text{Dimension1}) - F(\text{Dimension1}).$$

The MAS Index refers to attributes most valued in certain societies. In masculine societies, assertiveness, achievement and any form of material reward is prevailing; however, in feminine societies, caring for each other, cooperation and quality of life are paramount (Hofstede Center, 2015).

Table 32.16 Cluster accumulated MAS indices for direct counterparts [scale: 0–100 (low–high)]

Confucian Asia	58.33	← →	Germanic Europe	59.00
Eastern Europe	57.33	← →	Nordic Europe	15.67
Latin Europe	50.50	← →	Southern Asia	48.83
Anglo	61.43	← →	Middle East	45.75
Sub-Sahara Africa	50.75	← →	Latin America	52.44

In only four out of ten cases, the counterparts directly opposite each other shown in Table 32.16 can be described as least resembling: *Eastern Europe* (57.33)—*Nordic Europe* (15.67) and *Anglo* (61.43)—*Middle East* (45.75). The remaining six cultural clusters do not significantly differ in scores that could lead to a declaration of showing the least resemblance as extreme counterparts.

As masculine societies refer to the so-called "male attributes" including elbow mentality, assertiveness and aggressiveness, it might be assumed that the GDP (and GDP Grw.) is higher compared to female societies, valuing caring and consensus-finding. Moreover the rate of corruption and the ecological footprint should be higher in these tough, masculine societies, where it is about success, rewards, or failure mirrored in a high score for the GCI. In contrast, feminine societies are considered "well-being countries," where attributes like harmony, quality of life and finding a good work–life balance prevail. These attributes might therefore lead to a higher Peace Index, higher HPI and longer Life Expectancy. The level of Life Satisfaction should theoretically be higher in a feminine society as well.

The evaluated data allows to conclude that cultural clusters considered as masculine societies are *Anglo* (61.43), *Germanic Europe* (59.00), *Confucian Asia* (58.33), and *Eastern Europe* (57.33). Especially for the Anglo and the Germanic Europe Cluster, a high GDP per Capita and a very low level of corruption can be proven. The GDP Grw. is stable but not as high as in the cultural clusters covering developing countries. Eastern Europe's GDP is far below the average of these masculine societal clusters, finding its explanation in the economic and (communistic) political history, leading to further debates, which are not part of this paper. Confucian Asia rates as a masculine society, the level of corruption is slightly above medium. Its GDP Grw. is the third highest in comparison to all ten societal clusters but not surprising as Confucian Asia includes China, recording an economic growth of 7% for almost the last 30 years. Checking the Ecological Footprint it can be proven that Anglo and Germanic Europe as well as Confucian Asia have high Ecological Footprints, but again Eastern Europe does not fit in the row with an average score of 3.66 in this category (Table 32.17).

It can be proven to a certain extent that masculine societies have a lower level of corruption, a higher GDP per Capita and a stable GDP Grw. leading to a high Ecological Footprint. The Peace Index is high as well compared to all societal clusters and with an average Life Expectancy of 74 years, masculine societies are above medium life expectancy.

Whereby *Latin Europe* (50.50) and *Sub-Sahara Africa* (50.75) are considered as average societal clusters, *Northern Europe* (15.67), *Middle East* (45.75) and *Southern Asia* (48.83) are defined as feminine societies. The GDP is the lowest for

Table 32.17 Cluster accumulated scores for different variables

Cluster name	GDP per Capita	GDP Grw.	CR	PI	GCI	HPI	LE	LSI	EF
Southern Asia	5,112.22	4.98	37.83	3.00	4.52	49.08	71	–	2.00
Latin America	8,257.34	2.23	36.10	3.30	3.98	55.15	74	7.55	2.50
Nordic Europe	56,489.90	1.00	89.33	5.00	5.40	41.83	81	9.53	6.70
Anglo	44,553.79	2.77	74.57	4.29	5.17	41.86	77	7.40	5.24
Germanic Europe	59,194.80	1.23	80.00	5.00	5.48	46.93	81	8.83	5.30
Latin Europe	42,057.17	1.10	63.50	4.17	4.92	46.87	82	6.30	4.53
Sub-Sahara Africa	3,549.42	4.80	35.80	3.00	3.86	34.74	54	–	1.60
Eastern Europe	12,916.64	2.84	44.63	3.63	4.25	41.25	75	2.46	3.66
Middle East	31,446.02	1.98	46.80	3.60	4.44	37.48	74	3.00	5.48
Confucian Asia	35,059.63	3.15	64.33	4.17	5.32	42.66	80	4.20	4.56

Outcome for the MAS Index: 4:6

the two average rated clusters; nevertheless, the feminine rated Southern Asia Cluster is also one of the lowest with regard to GDP per Capita. As expected, the GDP Grw. in the developing country clusters like Southern Asia, Sub-Sahara Africa and Confucian Asia is the highest; Nordic Europe gives an exception for high GDP per Capita, low GDP Grw., lowest Corruption rate and highest score in Peace Index in comparison to all clusters as well as one of the highest scores in Life Expectancy.

To a certain extent, a similarity within clusters of pure masculine and of pure feminine societies can be proven, but again too many exceptions mislead and indicate that there is no sum of variables that might increase the likeliness of certain patterns within a culture.

Uncertainty Avoidance Index

Scores used: Peace Index (PI), Corruption Rate (CR), Life Expectancy (LE) and LSI.

Note: Following the idea that opposite located cultural clusters show the least/ lower resemblance and cultural clusters next to each other show the highest/higher resemblance, the scores of the respective Hofstede Dimension in direct comparison of two opposite clusters have to be seen as "Black-or-White," meaning either "unsecure" or "more relaxed" about future unknown events.

The investigation is about finding a scheme behind the results by comparing different variables matching the respective dimension in a tabular comparison of high/ low rating cultural clusters. It is to prove that the result by subtracting scores of clusters directly opposite each other shows a higher difference in numbers than by subtracting scores of clusters neighboring each other using the formula:

$$A(\text{Dimension1}) - B(\text{Dimension1}) < A(\text{Dimension1}) - F(\text{Dimension1}).$$

Table 32.18 Cluster accumulated UAI indices for direct counterparts [scale: 0–100 (low–high)]

Eastern Europe	88.00	← →	Nordic Europe	37.00
Latin America	82.89	← →	Sub-Sahara Africa	49.75
Latin Europe	80.83	← →	Southern Asia	48.50
Middle East	78.25	← →	Anglo	44.71
Germanic Europe	62.20	← →	Confucian Asia	52.17

The UAI refers to the degree in which a society feels uncomfortable with uncertainty and ambiguity. The question is how to deal with the unknown future: "laissez-faire" or developing control mechanisms. Scoring high in the UAI refers to a collective of anxious individuals trying to prevent the "unknown" by putting rules and rigid codes of behavior resulting in intolerance for the so-called "adventurous" ideas. In contrast, societies scoring low in the UAI remain more relaxed about the future and do not need a variety of codes to prevent the potential unknown (Hofstede Center, 2015).

Countries of opposite located clusters show less or least similarities according to House's Wheel of Cultural Clusters. The contradictory result of culturalities in the respective dimension leads to scores of high vs. low with the exception of Confucian Asia and Germanic Europe. These two cultural clusters show a difference in scores, but not necessarily an extreme polarized score result as the compared clusters fitting in the scheme (Table 32.18).

It is surprising that cultural clusters directly next to each other do not show a certain similarity as expected in House's Wheel, as they ought to have the greatest resemblance. Regarding the scores, there is a huge gap between *Latin Europe* to *Sub-Sahara Africa* and *Eastern Europe* (80.83—49.75—88.00) and also by precisely examining the scores for *Southern Asia*, *Latin America*, and *Nordic Europe* (48.50—82.89—37.00) there should be a more smooth transition in respect of their position in the wheel.

Clusters rating high in the UAI are: *Eastern Europe* (88.00), *Latin America* (82.89), *Latin Europe* (80.83), *Middle East* (78.25) and *Germanic Europe* (62.20). Mostly clusters rating high in the UAI score high as well in the Corruption Rating like Middle East, Eastern Europe and Latin America. Clusters with a rating of "very high" and "high" in the Peace Index also have a very low/low corruption rate as both indicators are closely related to each other and as it shows the level of peacefulness, influencing stability and reliability of the state's system and the authorities, including the degree of security within the society and the extent of domestic and international conflicts as well as the degree of militarization.

Nevertheless no specific relationship can be found regarding the degree of Uncertainty Avoidance and the scores for Peace Index and Corruption Rate. As both Latin Europe and Germanic Europe are examples for clusters rating high in the UAI, both score high in the Peace Index and low in Corruption. However the Anglo and Confucian Asia Cluster both score low in UAI referring to a more laissez-faire

Table 32.19 Cluster accumulated scores for different variables

Cluster name	UAI	PI	CR	LE	LSI
Southern Asia	48.50	3.00	37.83	71	–
Latin America	82.89	3.30	36.10	74	7.55
Nordic Europe	37.00	5.00	89.33	81	9.53
Anglo	44.71	4.29	74.57	77	7.40
Germanic Europe	62.20	5.00	80.00	81	8.83
Latin Europe	80.83	4.17	63.50	82	6.30
Sub-Sahara Africa	49.75	3.00	35.80	54	–
Eastern Europe	88.00	3.63	44.63	75	2.46
Middle East	78.25	3.60	46.80	74	3.00
Confucian Asia	52.17	4.17	64.33	80	4.20

Outcome for the UAI Index: 5:5

attitude with regard to unknown future events, but their level of Peace is high and the rate of Corruption is low as well. Including additional variables like Life Expectancy and examining the LSI, it can be concluded that again no specific relationship can be established for the societal perception of unknown future events, neither for the ones being more relaxed nor the ones being unsecure about it.

In five out of ten clusters, House's wheel can be mathematically proven, but in the remaining five cultural clusters the difference in scores of neighboring clusters is higher than the subtracted opposite cluster scores, leading to a non-proof with a balanced result of 5:5 (Table 32.19).

Long-Term vs. Short-Term Orientation

Scores used: Peace Index (PI), Corruption Rate (CR), HPI, Life Expectancy (LE) and LSI.

Note: Following the idea that opposite located cultural clusters show the least/lower resemblance and cultural clusters next to each other show the highest/higher resemblance, the scores of the respective Hofstede Dimension in direct comparison of two opposite clusters have to be seen as "Black-or-White," meaning either "long-term" or "short-term" oriented.

The investigation is about finding a scheme behind the results by comparing different variables matching the respective dimension in a tabular comparison of high/low rating cultural clusters. It is to prove that the result by subtracting scores of clusters directly opposite each other shows a higher difference in numbers than by subtracting scores of clusters neighboring each other using the formula:

$$A(\text{Dimension1}) - B(\text{Dimension1}) < A(\text{Dimension1}) - F(\text{Dimension1}).$$

Table 32.20 Cluster accumulated LTO indices for direct counterparts [scale: 0–100 (low–high)]

Confucian Asia	83.50	← →	Germanic Europe	73.40
Eastern Europe	55.33	← →	Nordic Europe	42.00
Latin Europe	52.00	← →	Southern Asia	37.83
Anglo	32.14	← →	Middle East	22.33
Sub-Sahara Africa	28.00	← →	Latin America	22.83

The "Long-Term vs. Short-Term Orientation" is about societies and their focus and/or embracement of the future. Societies scoring high are more long-term oriented, keen on ways to prepare for the future, e.g. investment in education. Societies scoring low here view societal changes with suspicion and value traditions. This Hofstede Dimension deals with future and past as variables seen and treated differently (challenges or benefits) in conflicting societies (Hofstede Center, 2015).

As Germanic Europe (73.40) and Confucian Asia (83.50) both score high in LTO, identifying their long-term orientation, the majority of the remaining eight cultural clusters scores below 50 or on average, which can be seen in Table 32.20.

The probability to think positively of the future and to embrace future events without anxiety should theoretically be increased with a higher level of stability within the country, security and therefore easily abbreviated possibilities for the individual and the collective to self-realize projects without hesitation due to trembling of future events. Interestingly, scoring high in the Peace Index does not necessarily lead to a high score in LTO (Nordic Europe scoring 5 out of 5 in the Peace Index but only 42.0 in LTO), although peace might be closely related to stability and consistency. The same issue can be found with the Corruption Rate, again Germanic Europe showing a low level of corruption, but Nordic Europe and Anglo as well and Confucian Asia are slightly above medium, but nevertheless the LTO Indices indicate that only for Germanic Europe and Confucian Asia a positive correlation between low level of corruption, high level of peace, and long-term orientation can be proven.

Cultural clusters being more long-term oriented identify a higher Life Expectancy (apart from Nordic Europe and Anglo) and a medium/above medium rate for the HPI (Latin America and Southern Asia Cluster rating higher). However no relationship can be found between the long-term orientation and the degree of Life Satisfaction as too many exceptions prevent from stating that short-term oriented societies are more satisfied with their lives (Latin America, Nordic Europe, and Anglo), as Germanic Europe and Latin Europe Cluster also rate high in LSI but are highly long-term oriented and for the Cluster of Confucian Asia rating the highest in LTO, the societies are just the third least happiest with their life.

To a certain extent, it can be summarized that scoring high in LTO refers to a high score in the Peace Index combined with low corruption rate and a medium rate for happiness. The Life Expectancy is higher in long-term oriented societies but no final abbreviation can be made for the degree of Life Satisfaction in a short- or long-term oriented societal cluster. Nevertheless only in one out of ten societal clusters

Table 32.21 Cluster accumulated scores for different variables

Cluster name	LTO	PI	CR	HPI	LE	LSI
Southern Asia	37.83	3.00	37.83	49.08	71	–
Latin America	22.83	3.30	36.10	55.15	74	7.55
Nordic Europe	42.00	5.00	89.33	41.83	81	9.53
Anglo	32.14	4.29	74.57	41.86	77	7.40
Germanic Europe	73.40	5.00	80.00	46.93	81	8.83
Latin Europe	52.00	4.17	63.50	46.87	82	6.30
Sub-Sahara Africa	28.00	3.00	35.80	34.74	54	–
Eastern Europe	55.33	3.63	44.63	41.25	75	2.46
Middle East	22.33	3.60	46.80	37.48	74	3.00
Confucian Asia	83.50	4.17	64.33	42.66	80	4.20

Outcome for the LTO Index: 1:9

the subtracted score from neighboring societal clusters is lower than the result of directly opposite located cultural clusters, leading to a 1:9 relationship against the prediction of the Wheel of Cultural Clusters (Table 32.21).

Indulgence vs. Restraint

Scores used: HPI, LSI, GDP per Capita, GDP Grw. and GCI.

Note: Following the idea that opposite located cultural clusters show the least/lower resemblance and cultural clusters next to each other show the highest/higher resemblance, the scores of the respective Hofstede Dimension in direct comparison of two opposite clusters have to be seen as "Black-or-White," meaning the society is either "indulgent" or "restraint."

The investigation is about finding a scheme behind the results by comparing different variables matching the respective dimension in a tabular comparison of high/low rating cultural clusters. It is to prove that the result by subtracting scores of clusters directly opposite each other shows a higher difference in numbers than by subtracting scores of clusters neighboring each other using the formula:

$$A(\text{Dimension1}) - B(\text{Dimension1}) < A(\text{Dimension1}) - F(\text{Dimension1}).$$

The IND Index is defined as the degree to which a society allows and supports enjoying life and having fun aiming for a work–life balance (indulgent society), whereas restraint societies attach value on strict norms the individuals have to follow. Human needs are suppressed and regulated, leading to a society in which people "live to work" (Hofstede Center, 2015).

Table 32.22 Cluster accumulated IND indices for direct counterparts [scale: 0–100 (low–high)]

Sub-Sahara Africa	63.00	← →	Latin America	81.67
Southern Asia	41.33	← →	Latin Europe	44.20
Confucian Asia	34.50	← →	Germanic Europe	55.40
Eastern Europe	32.17	← →	Nordic Europe	68.33
Middle East	26.00	← →	Anglo	68.43

Table 32.23 Cluster accumulated scores for different variables

Cluster name	IND	HPI	LSI	GDP per Capita	GDPG	GCI
Southern Asia	41.33	49.08	–	5,112.22	4.98	4.52
Latin America	81.67	55.15	7.55	8,257.34	2.23	3.98
Nordic Europe	68.33	41.83	9.53	56,489.90	1.00	5.40
Anglo	68.43	41.86	7.40	44,553.79	2.77	5.17
Germanic Europe	55.40	46.93	8.83	59,194.80	1.23	5.48
Latin Europe	44.20	46.87	6.30	42,057.17	1.10	4.92
Sub-Sahara Africa	63.00	34.74	–	3,549.42	4.80	3.86
Eastern Europe	32.17	41.25	2.46	12,916.64	2.84	4.25
Middle East	26.00	37.48	3.00	31,446.02	1.98	4.44
Confucian Asia	34.50	42.66	4.20	35,059.63	3.15	5.32

Outcome for the IND Index: 6:4

Table 32.22 shows the more indulgent countries on the left side and the more restraint countries on the right site according to the idea that cultural clusters opposite each other should have the least resemblance resulting in a total score that is higher than subtracting the accumulated scores of each two clusters directly next to each other. Comparing opposite counterparts, one cluster has to be more indulgent as both show the least resemblance, so the one with the (compared) higher score is measured as more restraint.

Table 32.23 shows the accumulated scores for different indices that are of importance for the investigation in this dimension. Societies like *Latin America* (81.67), *Anglo* (68.43), *Nordic Europe* (68.33), *Sub-Sahara Africa* (63.00) and *Germanic Europe* (55.40) are called indulgent societies scoring high in both, IND and LSI. Their GDP per Capita is above average (excluding Sub-Sahara Africa and Latin America). Otherwise the height of GDP per Capita does not have an influence on the HPI (Latin America and Southern Asia) and also the GDP Grw. is not related to the degree of Global Competitiveness (Nordic Europe, Germanic Europe and Anglo).

Again too many exceptions prove that no certain assumption can be made. IND does not for sure have an influence on GDP per Capita as only three out of the five highest scoring IND clusters can refer to a very high GDP, but due to different reasons which are not part of this paper. The score of LSI might be related to the degree of indulgence as well as the HPI. In total, the subtraction of scores proves a 6:4 favoring the statement of House's Wheel. Nevertheless in four cases the subtracted scores of opposite located clusters resulted in lower differences than the neighboring cluster score results.

Conclusion and Future Work

During the research and examination of societal clusters aiming to prove the statement of House's Wheel of Cultural Clusters by applying Hofstede's Dimension Scores for House's listed countries within a cluster, Hofstede's quotation can be used to mark the complexity and multifaceted angles that have to be considered by investigating in this broad field: "Culture is only meaningful by comparison."

Hofstede did an immense improvement in the field of intercultural studies by defining dimensions to make a comparison of cultures possible as the diversity and complexity even within a culture including the subcultures is huge. The development and publication of the Wheel of Cultural Clusters is even more simplifying the understanding of the world's numerous cultures. Accumulating the individual scores for every societal cluster, followed by subtracting the final scores from directly opposite located cultural clusters versus the realized result by subtracting scores from neighboring clusters should ideally lead to the relationship:

$$A(\text{Dimension1}) - B(\text{Dimension1}) < A(\text{Dimension1}) - F(\text{Dimension1}).$$

Theoretically the results would prove House's Wheel, but the equation is not always resulting in a low difference of neighboring clusters and a high difference in scores of opposite located clusters. Therefore it can be summarized that although there are common variables leading to a certain scheme, enough exceptions reinforce a non-existence of an overall scheme. Common variables can definitely be found, but again in some dimensions the exceptions occur in such a gravity portraying the lack of an overall archetype, which leads to the assumption that a potential similarity is more random and coincidental. The results emphasize the need for more research in order to support the model aiming to find an overall scheme.

Clustering countries mathematically according to Geert Hofstede's cultural proximity and similarity factors is one way of classifying regional communities into well-defined cultural categories. Trying to test this statement mathematically shows that classifying countries or cultures still remains complex. Even if common variables exist, it seems that the random similarity weighs strongly on most variables as explained before.

Trying to "unpack" culture in the twenty-first century à la Hofstede is still a challenge, as many variables and sub-variables determine the broad research area. More and more research is undertaken in the field of Intercultural Science; however, the term "culture" remains highly multifaceted. The quotation of Ralph Waldo Emerson summarizes the multilayered background behind the term "culture" in the style of the Iceberg Model best: "Culture is one thing and varnish is another."

References

Andruseac, G. (2015). Economic security—New approaches in the context of globalization. CES Working Papers.

Cambridge English Dictionary. (2015). Meaning of "culture". http://dictionary.cambridge.org/dictionary/english/culture?a=british. Accessed 14 Jan 2016.

Hofstede Center. (2015). http://geert-hofstede.com/national-culture.html. Accessed 19 Jan 2016.

Hopkins, B. (2009). *Cultural differences and improving performance, how values and beliefs influence organizational performance*. Surrey: Gower.

Hoppe, M. (2007). Culture and leader effectiveness: The GLOBE study. http://www.inspireimagineinnovate.com/pdf/globesummary-by-michael-h-hoppe.pdf. Accessed 11 January 2016.

Hoppe, M., & Eckert, R. (2014). Leader effectiveness and culture: The GLOBE study. http://www.ccl.org/leadership/pdf/assessments/globestudy.pdf. Accessed 12 Jan 2016.

House, R. J. (2004). *Culture, leadership and organizations; the globe study of 62 societies*. Thousand Oaks, CA: Sage.

Lethaus, P. (2009). *Die wirtschaftliche Globalisierung in der sozialen Diskussion* (1st ed.). Germany: Norderstedt.

Ronen, S., & Shenkar, O. (1985). Clustering countries on attitudinal dimensions: A review and synthesis. *Academy of Management Review, 10*(3), 435–454.

Slavik, H. (2004). *Intercultural communication and diplomacy*. Geneva: DiploFoundation.

Tylor, E. B. (1974). *Primitive culture: Researches into the development of mythology, philosophy, religion, art, and custom*. New York: Gordon Press.

Vieregg, S. (2009). Entscheidungs- und Organisationstheorie. In E. Kahle (Ed.), *Kulturelle Faktoren in der internationalen Geschäftsentwicklung*. Germany: Wiesbade.

Wahrig, G. (1986). *Deutsches Wörterbuch*. Gütersloh/München: Bertelsmann Verlag GmbH.

Chapter 33
Human Resources Management Skills Needed by Organizations

Maria José Sousa

Abstract This article analyses the concept of skills and also investigates the skills needed by organizations in Human Resources as a strategic area. The relevance of \ purpose is to identify the skills to be developed in Human Resources Courses in Higher Education. The skills needed by the organizations were identified through document analysis based on prospective studies developed in industry between 2011 and 2014. The research problem considered the analytical dimension of skills development in organizations anchored to the following research questions: What are the skills needed to be developed in Higher Education Courses to transform the Human Resources function strategic for organizations? This study is centred on the research of more relevant skills which can contribute to transform the Human Resources function strategic for organizations contributing for the improvement of their performance and competitiveness in the market.

Keywords Skills • Organizations • Higher education • Human resources management • Human resources development

Introduction

The main goal of this research is to identify the skills needed by organizations and make recommendations for the higher education human resources courses.

The identification and development of skills are challenging tasks, either internally within organizations or externally by the universities. In this article the focus will be the identification of human resources management skills and the suggestion of their development in higher education courses.

These are skills that need to be integrated into the human resources management courses in higher education context and this research tries to analyse if the skills

M.J. Sousa (✉)
CIEO, Algarve University, Faro, Portugal

Universidade Europeia, Lisboa, Portugal
e-mail: maria-jose.sousa@universidadeeuropeia.pt

© Springer International Publishing Switzerland 2017   395
R. Benlamri, M. Sparer (eds.), *Leadership, Innovation and Entrepreneurship as Driving Forces of the Global Economy*, Springer Proceedings in Business and Economics, DOI 10.1007/978-3-319-43434-6_33

identified by the organizations as fundamental for their competitiveness are being developed by the universities.

This article briefly explores the concept of skills, followed by the presentation of the methodology that was used as the basis for the skills identification in the organizations and also in the university human resources management courses context and concludes with the research findings.

Literature Overview

In the 1980s the concept of skills started to have a big importance due to technological, organizational, and economic factors. It begins to be considered as a resource — of individual and organizational nature—which would allow competitiveness and productivity advantages to companies.

Historically, the word skills has been used to refer individual characteristics. However, in the concept of Prochno (2001), although the skills always refer to the individual, all of them have two dimensions, the individual and the collective (organizational). In this way, the concept of skills assumes a rather large scope which makes it complex and makes its comprehension/understanding and concept delimitation difficult.

The concept has been studied by several authors such as Mulder (2000, 2001) and previously by Norris (1991) and Ellström (1997). Skills development prevails as a research issue in higher education dominion because it is the main goal to be achieved by the students. Skills development is perceived as a strategic management tool to cope with the current business environment (Nyhan, 1998), mainly because the market has changed from one of mass production to one of customization where quality, price and speed of delivery are stressed.

This change has brought about new circumstances in which many organizations struggle to cope: new and emerging customer segments, cultural diversity in a global marketplace, market volatility, raised customer expectations about quality of products and services, and the impact of internet on an organization's core business (Markowitsch et al., 2001). In the job market there has been a growth in higher-level jobs such as managerial and professional positions that require flexibility and problem-solving skills.

In this context, the complexity and the uncertainty, partly due to the globalization and accelerated rhythm of technological change, demand human resources with skills that help the organizations to overcome the appearing challenges.

Research Questions

The following research questions have guided the present study:

RQ 1   What were the Human Resources Management skills identified in the prospective studies?

RQ 2   What were the levels of skills development in the high education Human Resources Management courses?

RQ 3   What were the relationships between the perceived HRM skills development and various factors such as gender, employed/unemployed, type of organization and job variables?

Methodology

In this study, two sources of data were collected as follows: (1) document analysis and (2) online survey.

1. The main technique used was content analysis from the document analysis of prospective studies in industry about Human Resources Management skills needed by the organizations. This methodology was used to analyse the skills identified by the organizations which participated in the study.
2. The second technique to collect data was an online survey applied to 250 students and were obtained 117 valid questionnaires equivalent to 46.8 % response rate. The statistical analyses Cronbach's alpha Coefficient, Chi-square Tests, and Mann–Whitney Tests, conclusions point to generally positive perceptions for organizational development and for student's development.

In total the questionnaire consisted of 30 questions covering the following areas:

- Students background information (Question 1–4)
- List of skills development during high education human resources management courses (Question 5–30).

Content Analysis

In order to answer the research question (RQ 1) What were the Human Resources Management skills identified in the prospective studies? it was developed a content analysis from the literature review of prospective studies on Human Resources Management skills. This methodology was used to analyse the presence of skills associated with the following dimensions: "human resources management (HRM)", "leadership" and "human resources development (HRD)", and the period considered was between 2011 and 2014. A list of skills were made organized in the following structure:

Human Resources Management (skills needed by human resources managers and technicians):

- skills at the level of the definition of human resources management strategies integrated into the business strategies;
- skills related to the human resources management practices and techniques: employees administrative processes,

- capacity to manage strategic deals and alliances within the organization in order to implement HRM strategic practices, to give response to the company strategy;
- capacity to diversify the business area, identifying new business opportunities, i.e. HRM consultancy to the other departments of the organization to maximize the capacities and competencies of the employees;
- social and relational skills, in what concerns the capacity of communication, leadership and interpersonal relationships.

Leadership (skills needed by all managers)

- skills related to the employees performance development;
- skills associated with the development of new opportunities for the employees through techniques such as coaching and mentoring.
- Skills associated with the motivation techniques in order to potentiate the employees performance;
- skills associated with the technique to improve employees satisfaction, specially through recognition instruments
- skills related to the corporate governance;
- communication skills in order to improve the commitment of the employees;
- skills related to the management of employees expectations about their development in the organization;
- skills associated with the management of the cultural differences among employees.

Human Resources Development (skills needed by all managers and all technicians)

- skills associated with the new forms of work organization, in what regards the methods of teamwork, flexibility to adapt to changes in the working processes (as a response to a high rhythm of innovation);
- knowledge about different types of technologies;
- skills regarding a bigger initiative, decision taking and responsibility assuming;
- skills on innovation and creativity in order to develop new products and services;
- skills associated with the analysis of information related to productivity, in what concerns manpower optimization of costs;
- capacity to adapt to organizational change;
- capacity of developing social and relational knowledge which allows the coordination of working teams, taking advantage of all the potential of its elements.

Survey Analysis

Regarding the survey, the respondents were presented with 24 items representing HRM skills, leadership skills and HRD skills which emerged from the content analysis from the prospective studies in industry.

Table 33.5 shows the dimensions of the questionnaire:

The first dimension of the questionnaire integrates the HRM skills needed by the organizations: HRM strategies, HRM practices and techniques, Management of strategic deals and alliances, Diversify the business as a HRM consultancy service to other departments within the organization, Social and relational skills, People management, and Communication.

The second dimension of the questionnaire integrates the leadership skills: Employees performance, Development opportunities, Motivation of employees, Satisfaction of employee, Corporate governance, Communication, Managing expectations, and Integrating cultural differences.

Finally the third dimension integrates the HRD skills on: new forms and models of work organization, new technologies, organizational change, initiative, decision taking and responsibility, creativity and innovation.

Respondents were asked to rate the skills on a 5-point Likert scale ranging from 1 = no development; 2 = weak development; 3 = moderate development; 4 = considerable development; 5 = strong development.

Results from the Survey

Respondents were primarily from male gender ($n = 64$) and secondarily from female gender ($n = 53$), please see Table 33.1.

Most part of the respondents were employed ($n = 97$) and unemployed a minor part ($n = 20$), please see Table 33.2.

The types of respondent organizations were primarily education ($n = 18$), public sector ($n = 18$), health and social work ($n = 13$), commercial services ($n = 12$), manufacturing non-food ($n = 16$), transportation, communication ($n = 11$), financial services ($n = 14$) and other ($n = 15$), please see Table 33.3.

Respondents characterized their jobs as top management ($n = 12$), middle management ($n = 18$), executive level ($n = 20$), technical specialist ($n = 21$) and support staff ($n = 13$), please see Table 33.4.

RQ 2 What were the levels of skills development in the high education human resources management courses?

According to the perceived skills development the resulting mean scores varied for human resources management skills between 2.5 and 3.2, for leadership skills between 2.9 and 3.27, and human resources development skills between 2.3 and 3.4, as outlined in Table 33.5. Therefore all the skills identified by the prospective studies had a moderate development in the high education human resources management courses.

RQ 3 What were the relationships between the perceived HRM skills development and various factors such as gender, employed/unemployed, type of organization and job variables?

Cronbach's alpha (α) for all 117 respondents' HRM skills items was calculated and a value of 0.1 was obtained, which allows for the creation of a new variable by

Table 33.1 Background information on students who participated in the study—gender

	N	%
Male	64	54.7
Female	53	45.2
Total	117	100.0

Table 33.2 Background information on students who participated in the study—employee or unemployed

	N	%
Employee	97	82.9
Unemployed	20	17.1
Total	117	100.0

Table 33.3 Background information on students who participated in the study—type of organization

Type of organization ($n = 117$)	n	%
Education	18	15.4
Public sector	18	15.4
Commercial services	12	10.3
Health and social work	13	11.1
Manufacturing non-food	16	13.7
Transportation, communication	11	9.4
Financial services	14	12.0
Other	15	12.8
	117	100.0

Table 33.4 Background information on students who participated in the study—job

Job characterization of respondents ($n = 117$)	n	%
Top management	12	10.3
Middle management/line manager	18	15.4
Executive level	30	25.6
Technical specialist/engineer/quality control	21	17.9
Staff/carry out primary work process	12	10.3
Support staff	13	11.1
Other	11	9.4
	117	100.0

combining the 7 items. Similar calculations were made for the 10 leadership skills items and the 7 HRD skills items to achieve scores of 0.78 and 0.80, respectively.

The differences between various factors of interest and these three new key variables were assessed using Mann–Whitney U Test (gender, employment situation, job organization and type of organization). The results showed significant relationships between perceived HRM skills development and job ($X2 = 180.81$; df. = 47; Sig. = 0.00); perceived leadership skills development ($X2 = 175.33$; df. = 51; Sig. = 0.00) and perceived HRD skills development ($X2 = 170.25$; df. = 40; Sig. = 0.00). No significant differences were found between the three skills variables and type of organization, gender, and employed/unemployed variables.

Table 33.5 Perceived development of skills by the students (1 = no development; 2 = weak development; 3 = moderate development; 4 = considerable development; 5 = strong development) — [Cronbach's alpha (number of items) Mean (1–5) (SD)]

Rank	Skills	Cronbach's alpha	Mean	S.D.
Human resources management skills		0.71 (*n* = 7)		
1	HRM strategies		3.10	1.23
2	HRM practices and techniques		3.10	1.22
3	Management of strategic deals and alliances		3.10	1.18
4	Diversify the business as a HRM consultancy service		2.50	1.23
5	Social and relational skills		3.20	1.18
6	People management		3.20	1.16
7	Communication		3.20	1.16
Leadership skills		0.78 (*n* = 10)		
1	Employees performance		3.27	1.19
2	Development opportunities		3.22	1.25
3	Motivation of employees		3.15	1.23
4	Satisfaction of employee		3.12	1.26
5	Corporate governance		3.12	1.25
6	Communication		3.07	1.25
7	Managing expectations		3.07	1.21
10	Integrating cultural differences		2.97	1.22
Human resources development skills		0.80 (*n* = 7)		
1	New forms and models of work organization		3.10	1.22
2	New technologies		3.40	1.24
3	Organizational change		3.25	1.25
4	Initiative, decision taking and responsibility		2.30	1.20
5	Creativity and Innovation		3.20	1.26
6	Analysis of information		3.19	1.23
7	Social and relational knowledge		3.19	1.22

Conclusion

The motivation for this research has its roots in a lack of a systematic development approach about universities and industry. There was little or no support for connecting these two dimensions, which have made it a very interesting challenge to embrace.

In this context two approaches to skills development can certainly be identified: the organizational development approach and the universities development approach, which can be complementary, approaching the industry to the university context.

This research identified three types of skills through document analysis of prospective studies in industry — human resources management, leadership and human resources development, and tries to analyse the perception of the students from higher education human resources management courses about the level of development of those skills.

According to the students, the skills identified had a moderate development in the high education human resources management courses. This conclusion leads us to rethink the pedagogical model of these courses that are taught at higher education level.

It's also possible to conclude that there are significant relationships between perceived human resources management skills development and the student's job, but no significant differences were found between the three skills dimensions—human resources management, leadership, and human resources development—and the type of organization, gender, and employed/unemployed variables.

This study will help universities and industry to be more integrated and to rethink their strategies according to skills development in order to respond to the challenges of the market.

References

Ellström, P. E. (1997). The many meanings of occupational competence and qualification. *Journal of European Industrial Training, 21*(6/7), 266–273.

Markowitsch, J., Kollinger, I., Warmerdam, J., Moerel, H., Konrad, J., Burell, C., & Guile, D. (2001). *Competence and human resource development in multinational companies in three European Union Member States: A comparative analysis between Austria, the Netherlands and the U.K.* [online]. Thessaloniki: CEDEFOP. Available from http://eric.ed.gov/ERICDocs/data/ericdocs2/content_storage_01/0000000b/80/0d/ef/e0.pdf (9 December 2015).

Mulder, M. (2000). *Creating competence: Perspectives and practices in organizations.* Paper presented at AERA, New Orleans. Enschede: Faculty of Educational Science and Technology, University of Twente.

Mulder, M. (2001). Competence development—some background thoughts. *Journal of Agricultural Education and Extension, 7*(4), 147–159. ISSN: 1389-224X.

Norris, N. (1991). The trouble with competence. *Cambridge Journal of Education, 21*(3), 331–341.

Nyhan, B. (1998). Competence development as a key organisational strategy experiences of European companies. *Industrial and Commercial Training, 30*(7), 267–273.

Prochno, P. (2001). *Relationships between innovation and organizational competences.* Paris: INSEAD.

Chapter 34
A Case for Strategic Management in Higher Education in India

Sahil Sawhney, Ankur Gupta, and Kulwant Kumar

Abstract Higher Education in India remains heavily critiqued for not meeting stakeholder expectations. Enhancing overall quality and effectiveness remain the priority areas for institutions which battle existential concerns and student disconnect in a rapidly changing and competitive landscape. Strategic management has been employed by a variety of industries to articulate a future vision and outline specific short-term and long-term goals with a view to drive competitive advantage. Higher education institutions globally and especially in the USA have led the adoption of formal strategic management frameworks with a high degree of success. This paper reviews the evolution of strategic management in higher education worldwide. The Indian higher education space is specifically examined for application of the strategic management practice. Finally, a strong case is made for institutionalizing the use of strategic management in India to cope with the prevailing challenge.

Keywords Strategic management • Indian Higher Education

Introduction

The last two decades have witnessed unprecedented growth of the Indian Higher Education (IHE) sector. As per the Deloitte Report on Indian Higher Education Sector (Deloitte, 2012) IHE has emerged as the largest in the world in terms of

S. Sawhney (✉)
Model Institute of Engineering and Technology, Jammu, Jammu and Kashmir, India

Chitkara University, Chandigarh, Punjab, India
e-mail: Sahil.adm@mietjammu.in

A. Gupta
Model Institute of Engineering and Technology, Jammu, Jammu and Kashmir, India
e-mail: ankurgupta@mietjammu.in

K. Kumar
Chitkara University, Chandigarh, Punjab, India
e-mail: Kulwant.kumar@chitkara.edu.in

© Springer International Publishing Switzerland 2017   403
R. Benlamri, M. Sparer (eds.), *Leadership, Innovation and Entrepreneurship as Driving Forces of the Global Economy*, Springer Proceedings in Business and Economics, DOI 10.1007/978-3-319-43434-6_34

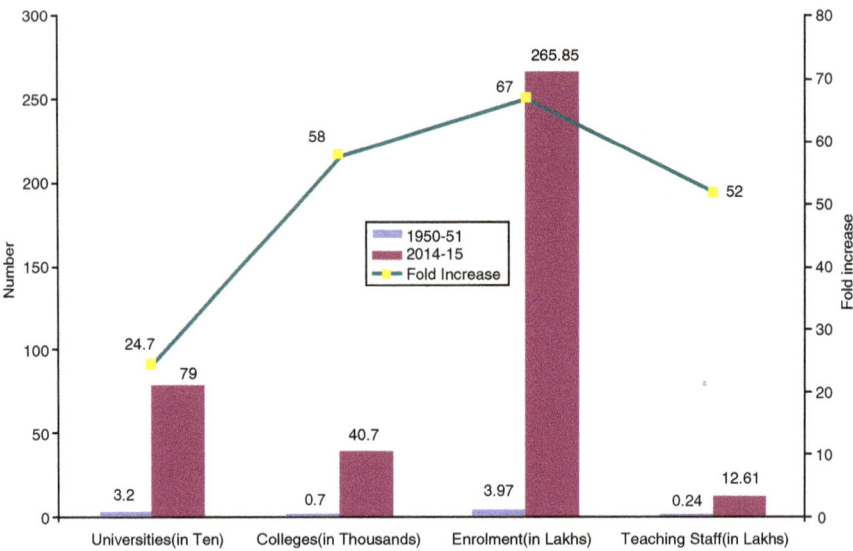

Fig. 34.1 Growth of Indian Higher Education during 1950–2015 (UGC, 2014)

number of institutions. Figure 34.1 highlights the growth in higher education since Independence in terms of institutions, universities, colleges and faculty members.

Despite its size and scope, the Gross Enrolment Ratio (GER) in IHE continues to be far below the global average of 30 % whereas China has already surpassed the figure by mid-2014. As per the prediction made by National Knowledge Commission, India would need an investment of $190 Billion to achieve the desired target GER of 30 % (Deloitte, 2012).

The rapid growth witnessed in the higher education sector has generated numerous challenges with the key ones being ensuring quality, increasing employability of graduates, improving quality of research and achieving global standards. As per the Times Higher Education World University Ranking 2015–2016 India has only 4 universities among the top 400 with the highest ranked Indian Institute of Science (IISc) falling in the range of 251–300. China with 11, South Korea with 9, Japan with 6 and Singapore with 2 fares much better than India in the Asian context when the relative sizes of these countries and GDP growth are factored in. Therefore, there is an urgent need to reassess Indian policy on higher education while devising strategic frameworks for continuous and comprehensive quality improvement. This paper makes a strong case for the institutionalization of strategic management at the level of individual institutions of Higher Education in India with a special focus on institutions in the private sector. It traces the evolution of strategic management in higher education worldwide establishing a strong correlation between strategic management and sustained institutional excellence. The challenges in implementing strategic management in IHE at large are also discussed and finally some ideas for its successful adoption are presented.

Strategic Management in Higher Education: Global Evolution

> Strategy is the determination of the basic long-term goals of an enterprise, and the adoption of courses of action and the allocation of resources necessary for carrying out these goals (Chandler, 1962).

The discipline of Strategic Management originated in the business sector in late 1950s when many business organizations rapidly started adopting strategic management to plan, develop and execute processes for competitive advantage. The importance of Strategic Management by public and non-profit organizations was felt in early 1980s in the USA when the Higher Education system faced challenges like reduced financial support, lower enrolments and resource mobilization. As mentioned by Bryson (*Strategic Planning for Profit and Non-Profit Organizations* 2011), Harvard Business School through its Harvard Policy model had developed the most renowned and successful models of strategic planning for profit and non-profit organizations. The idea and thought process of applying strategic management and planning in the academic set-up was first brought by George Keller, in his book, *Academic Strategy: The Management Revolution* (1983). Before that, there were only discussions of the applicability of strategic planning to higher education.

As per Keller (1997) that effective strategic planning is what separates the average from the above average, and makes planning institutions emerge as leading institutions. Hunt, Oostiing, Stevens, and Loudon (n.d.) state several reasons for implementing strategic planning in private higher education system, including:

1. To improve performance toward meeting the mission statement;
2. To improve performance toward increasing the academic standing;
3. To increase accomplishments with the same or lower level of resources;
4. To clarify the future direction of the institution;
5. To meet the requirements of accreditation or of a government agency;
6. To solve major problems (threats) or address significant opportunities.

Table 34.1 presents an overview of global strategic management adoption.

According to Watson (*Managing Strategy* 2000) managing strategy is vital for a university, as it provides the realization of its core activities.

Table 34.1 Global adoption of strategic management and outcomes

Year of inception	Country	Current state of strategic management	No. in top 400
1980	USA	Strategic Planning has become a well-adopted management practice in higher education. All the institutions have detailed strategic plans available on their website for transparency and public view. It's mandatory for all institutions to have strategic plans for university accreditation	100
1984–1989	UK	All the institutions were instructed by government to come up with strategic plan	46

(continued)

Table 34.1 (continued)

Year of inception	Country	Current state of strategic management	No. in top 400
1986	Europe	The Centre for Strategic Management of European Universities was created in 1986 with a vision to promote strategic management practice in academic set-up. In its recent Europe 2020 strategy there was a strong need to put emphasis on increasing the performance by modernizing their governance and train their leaders. Project "MODERN" is a consortium of 10 crore and 31 associate partners to prepare the higher education to work under external threats (Benneworth, 2011)	47
1990	China	China government laid strong emphasis on enhancing the international competitiveness of its higher education in the early 1990s in the form of two major projects—211 and 985 under which institutions were directed to come up with strategic plans (Council, 2013)	11
1987–1988	Australia	The federal government in 1988 brought new reforms under which it was made mandatory for the institutions to have strategic plans	22
1995	Singapore	The Institutions and the government of Singapore devised strategic plans aimed at promoting the internationalization of their education system and programmes	2

Indian Higher Education Scenario

Due to globalization and India's aim of becoming a knowledge power-house, providing quality education to sustain its growth has become one of key focus areas of government policies. IHE has thus witnessed a number of reforms, policies, regulatory bills unfolding since Independence with a view to achieve its aggressive goals of equity, excellence and access. Unfortunately, successive policies have missed out on strategic planning for IHE as a whole and also not envisioned the adoption of strategic management by individual institutions for overall quality improvement. Even the accreditation processes in India make no mention of adoption of strategic management while evaluating institutional governance and leadership.

   "… *Our university system is, in many parts, in a state of disrepair…almost two-third of our universities and 90 per cent of our colleges are rated as below average on quality parameters…*" Former Prime Minister of India Dr. Manmohan Singh (*PM's address at University of Mumbai* 2007). From being classified as a perennial sunrise industry, the Indian Higher Education Sector is in a state of deep recession. The All India Council for Technical Education (AICTE) has disclosed that out of the nearly 16 lakh seats in engineering available across India, nearly 8 lakh seats remained vacant in 2015 leading to closure of several hundred institutions (Sahasrabudhe, 2015). The state of this sector is counter-intuitive to the healthy state of the Indian Economy and an underperforming education sector can have long-term negative repercussions on the future projections for the Indian economy (Gupta, 2005). Table 34.2 summarizes the challenges facing IHE.

Table 34.2 Challenges in IHE

Challenges	Manifested issues
Policy paralysis	• Pace of educational reforms inconsistent • Funds deployed for capacity expansion and not capability development • Regulatory framework stifling autonomy
Lack of curriculum reforms and Pedagogy innovation	• Institutes cannot undertake curriculum revision • Courses not designed to inculcate industry-relevant skills, research, innovation or entrepreneurship • Outdated teaching pedagogy and low ICT-usage
Lack of manpower planning	• Oversupply of seats in some courses and undersupply in others • Industry-needs not considered while opening new institutions/courses or for intake planning
Faculty crunch	• Low quality faculty • Low quality PhD programmes • 30–40% of senior faculty positions are unfilled across premier institutions and universities (Verma, 2015)
Gaps in the accreditation process	• Only 25% institutions accredited • Flawed process not continuous or comprehensive • Bill on Mandatory Accreditation languishing in Indian Parliament for approval
Lack of industry linkages and poor employability	• Insufficient industry participation in curriculum development, joint research and faculty development • Report by NASSCOM indicates 80% of engineering and 90% of the management graduates not directly employable by industry (Jaipuria, 2014)
Low quality research and innovation	• No Indian university top 100 of the world as research output and impact form major chunk of the weightage criteria • The India's relative citation index is half that of world's average (Young, n.d.)
Governance and leadership	• Leadership vacuum • Heads of institutions have little experience of modern management principles

Strategic Management Adoption in Higher Education

The adoption of formal strategic management by institutions of Higher Education in India is in a nascent state. A survey of the top institutions of national importance indicates the stark absence of strategic management. Barring two Indian Institutes of Technology IIT Madras and IIT Bombay none of the other institutions have their strategic plans published on their websites. Even when strategic plans are available, it is not clear whether strategic management has been adopted both in processes or practices. The scenario is even bleaker in the private sector, which alone accounts for over 75% of all enrollments in the higher education sector.

Very few researchers in India (Pingle & Kaul, 2011; Raghunandhan & Sequeria, 2013; Raghunandhan, 2009) have focused on strategic management. The sheer absence of studies and literature pertaining to implementation of strategic management highlights the lack of awareness and emphasis on strategic management in IHE as compared to institutions in developed and developing countries which were quick to adopt Strategic Planning for safeguarding their interests in a globally competitive environment. The future success of the IHE will depend on how quickly institutions adapt to this changed scenario and create strategic plans to build new capacities and capabilities to thrive. Adopting strategic management by institutions in India seems to be a logical, yet challenging due to the following reasons:

1. The current leadership is not equipped with the skill set to envisage and implement strategic planning in a vast majority of the institutions.
2. Decision-making processes in institutions have a long life-cycle being participative and consensus-based, preventing agile responsiveness.
3. IT-adoption and skills remain poor across a vast majority of institutions. Even when adopted, its success remains limited.
4. Institutions are caught up in regulatory hurdles and lack the autonomy needed to chart their own course.
5. Institutions have a very narrow understanding of strategic management, limited to devising the vision, mission and providing broad directions for institutional growth. Detailed mechanisms for tracking, monitoring and designing corrective or strategic interventions are missing.

The Road Ahead

Given the huge challenges that confront IHE, some ideas towards effective and successful implementation of strategic management at individual institutions are presented below:

1. Intensive training for the leadership teams at institutions on strategic management and modern management practices should be conducted on priority.
2. IT-adoption in the areas of learning management, student engagement, analytics and performance management to be fast-tracked.
3. Create financial outlays to support strategic management and invest in faculty development, research and innovation and unique student experiences.
4. Corporatize select functional areas. Create a pool of professional managers with specialized positions such as strategic managers to drive strategy adoption and implementation.
5. Identify mentor institutions and seek help in developing core competencies in strategic management.
6. Create strong incentives for stakeholders in achieving strategic objectives.

At the Government/policy/regulatory levels the following initiatives can be considered:

1. Formulate and articulate a National Strategic Management Framework for IHE with a buy-in from all State Governments for effective implementation.

2. Reduce regulatory obstacles for high-performance institutions rewarding them with autonomy. Let the free-market regulate.
3. Adopt IT analytics framework to create transparency, objectivity and effectively determine institutional output and outcomes. Gupta (2013) presents a cloud-based analytics framework for managing institutional quality.
4. Create centers of excellence in strategic management in institutions of national importance which extend help to other institutions backed by solid research and demonstrated best-practices.
5. Make adoption of strategic management a core element of the accreditation process.
6. Introduce higher degree programs, certifications and world-class training pro-grammes on strategic management for institutions.

Conclusion

Research, business case studies and empirical evidence establish a strong correlation between strategic management and organizational excellence. Internationally, institutions of higher education have strongly ingrained strategic management practices and processes. This has resulted in these universities obtaining consistently high ranks across several international rankings. We strongly advocate the adoption of strategic management by the Indian Higher Education sector to overcome the critical challenges facing it today. We believe that the survival of the sector and its ability to meet and exceed global standards in the next two decades shall depend inexorably on effective strategic planning and execution.

References

Benneworth, P. (2011). *Towards a strategic management agenda for University Knowledge Exchange*. European Centre for Strategic Management. Brussels.

Bryson, J. (2011). *Strategic planning for profit and non-profit organizations*. Wiley, U.S.A.

Chandler, A. D. (1962). *Strategy and structures*. Cambridge: MIT Press.

Council, B. (2013). *A brief overview of Chinese higher education system*. British Council, India.

Deloitte. (2012). *Indian higher education sector-opportunities aplenty, growth aplenty*. Deloitte, India.

Gupta, A. (2013). Performance insight 360: A cloud-based quality management framework for educational institutions in India. *15th IEEE Conference on Business Informatics*, IEEE, USA.

Gupta, A. (2005). Securing the future of the Indian it industry: A case for educational innovation; challenges and the road ahead. *International Journal of Industry and Higher Education, 19*(6), 423–431.

Hunt, C. M., Oostiing, K. W., Stevens, R., & Loudon, D. (n.d.). *Strategic planning for private higher education*. New York: Haworth Press.

Jaipuria, S. (2014). Retrieved from Times of India: http://timesofindia.indiatimes.com/home/education/news/Higher-Education-in-India-An-introspection/articleshow/38776482.cms.

Keller, G. (1983). *Academic strategy: The management revolution in American higher education.* Baltimore, MD: Hopkins University Press.

Keller, G. (1997). Examining what works in strategic planning. In M. Peterson, D. Dill, L. Mets & Associates (Eds.), Planning and managing for a changing environment: A handbook on redesigning postsecondary institutions. San Francisco: Jossey-Bass.

Pingle, S., & Kaul, N. (2011). Performance management in institutes of higher education through balance scorecard: A conceptual study. *GFJMR, 2,* 1–21.

Raghunandhan, T. (2009). Strategy: A pedagogy for efficient, accountable and socially responsive higher education. *Global Business and Management Research, 1*(1),36–49.

Raghunandhan, T., & Sequeria, A. H. (2013). Strategic management in centrally funded technical institutions in India. *International Journal of Management Research and Business Strategy,* 2(1),15–31.

Sahasrabudhe, A. D. (2015). Retrieved from Deccan Chronicle: http://www.deccanchronicle.com/150801/nation-current-affairs/article/2015-50-cent-engineering-seats-go-vacant-across-country.

Singh, M. (2007). *PM's address at the 150th anniversary function of University of Mumbai.* Retrieved from Internet Archive wayback machine: https://web.archive.org/web/20120112072640/http://pmindia.nic.in/speech/content.asp?id=555.

Times Higher Education. (2016). Retrieved from Times Higher Education World university ranking: https://www.timeshighereducation.com/world-university-rankings/2016/world-ranking/page/3/length/25.

UGC. (2014). *UGC annual report 2014.* New Delhi: UGC.

Verma, P. (2015). Retrieved from Economic Times: http://economictimes.indiatimes.com/jobs/iits-facing-faculty-shortage-by-up-to-40-beefing-up-compensation-packages-to-attract-talents/articleshow/47636795.cms.

Watson, D. (2000). *Managing strategy.* Buckingham: Open University Press.

Young, E. A. (n.d.). Retrieved from Ernst and Young: http://www.ey.com/IN/en/Industries/India-sectors/Education/Higher-Education-in-India--Twelfth-Five-Year-Plan--2012-2017--and-beyond.

Chapter 35
The Effect of International Accounting Standards on Management Behavior: A Study on Earnings Management Behavior in Countries with High Investor Protection

Benno Feldmann and Tiet Khanh Le

Abstract The objective of this study is to examine the effect of the international financial reporting standards (IFRS) implementation on earnings management behavior in countries with high investor protection and strong legal enforcement. It does this by looking at a sample of 199 public listed companies from seven selected countries over a period of 15 years (before and after IFRS adoption). The results of this study suggest that in high investor protection countries, earnings management in general and accrual-based earnings management (AEM) in particular are more implemented during the IFRS application period than during the national generally accepted accounting principles (GAAP) application period. The study also suggests that earnings reports are more manipulated when firms face financial distress. However, it does not have enough evidence to conclude that real earnings management (REM) is more or less practiced after the transition to IFRS and whether there is a substitutional relationship between REM and AEM.

Keywords International accounting standards • Earnings management • Investor protection • Management behavior

Introduction

With the objective to develop a single set of high quality, understandable, enforceable, and globally accepted financial standards based upon clearly articulated principles, the international financial reporting standards (IFRS) of the International Accounting Standards Board (IASB) have become a common language of accountants, investors, regulators, and business leaders. Since 2001, almost 120 countries have required or

B. Feldmann (✉) • T.K. Le
International Business Department, University of Applied Sciences Worms,
Erenburger Str. 19, 67549 Worms, Germany
e-mail: feldmann@hs-worms.de

© Springer International Publishing Switzerland 2017
R. Benlamri, M. Sparer (eds.), *Leadership, Innovation and Entrepreneurship as Driving Forces of the Global Economy*, Springer Proceedings in Business and Economics, DOI 10.1007/978-3-319-43434-6_35

permitted the use of IFRS (IASB, 2015). Due to the differences between IFRS and national generally accepted accounting principles (GAAP), the adoption of IFRS may have impacts not only on accounting and financial reporting systems, but also on other areas of an organization including people, process, and technology, for example, information technology systems, tax reporting requirements, internal reporting, key performance metrics, and the tracking of stock-based compensation. This paper focuses only on the impacts of IFRS on the behavior of the company management in countries with high investor protection and strong legal enforcement.

According to McKee (2005), a company management has a vital interest in how earnings are reported and the executives need to understand the effect of their accounting choices so that they can make the best possible decisions for the company. The notion that investor's reliance on accounting information to value stocks can provide managers incentives to manipulate earnings in order to influence short term share price performance or to show more stable financial figures is illustrated in previous studies (Dye, 1988; Healy & Wahlen, 1999). Moreover, prior research also documented that the executive compensation structures can lead to earnings management (EM) (e.g., Bergstresser & Philippon, 2006; Peng & Roell, 2008; Oberholzer-Gee & Wulf, 2012). Taken together, EM appears to be a universal phenomenon and deserves the attention of regulators, auditors, accountants, business professionals, accounting researchers, and investors and given the fact that earnings manipulation practice of the company management has affected the accounting quality of financial statements, EM behavior is chosen as a proxy for management behavior in this research. In this paper, EM is categorized into accrual-based earnings management (AEM) and real earnings management (REM).

Roychowdhury (2006, p. 336) defined REM as "management actions that deviate from normal business practices, undertaken with the primary objective to mislead certain stakeholders into believing that earnings benchmarks have been met in the normal course of operation." On the other hand AEM refers to *managers' opportunistic use of the flexibility allowed under accepted accounting standards* (e.g. *GAAP, IAS, IFRS*) *to change reported earnings without changing the underlying cash flows.* (Adapted from Zeyun, 2009)

Recent research suggests that high investor protection and strong legal enforcement systems are the necessary determinants of high quality financial statement numbers (e.g., Nabar & Boonlert-U-Thai, 2007; Francis & Wang, 2008; Houqe, Van Zijl, Dunstan, & Karim, 2011). Investor protection is defined as *the power to prevent managers from expropriating minority shareholders and creditors within the constraints imposed by law* (La Porta, Lopez-de-Silanes, Sheiler, & Vishny, 2002; Leuz, Nanda, & Wysocki, 2003; Enomoto, Kimura, & Yamaguchi, 2015). In the literature, investor protection has been considered as one of the important factors affecting the EM behavior of managers. Therefore, the research chose samples in selected countries with high investor protection rankings according to World Bank Group (2014) ratings 2014 and high legal enforcement scores (with updated data from 2000 to 2014) used in the study of La Porta et al. (1998), namely: Canada, Denmark, France, Hong Kong, Ireland, Norway, and United Kingdom. These seven selected countries had to meet other additional requirements, such as experiencing no hyper-inflation during the period of 2000–2014, adopting full IFRS, and making no modifications to IFRS. The purpose of this selection is an attempt to mitigate or decrease the potential effects of the country-specific factors on the consistency of the results of the research.

The aim of this paper is to give an answer to the question whether in countries with high investor protection, adopting IFRS will promote, deter, or not affect the degree of EM. Once the EM behavior is clarified, the answer will contribute to strengthen or weaken the prevailing opinion that adopting IFRS improves the quality of financial information and promotes comparability with global accounting practices. There are four hypotheses tested in the research to study the behavior of management regarding EM including AEM and REM.

Hypothesis Development and Methodology

Prior research provides mixed evidence and conflicting results on the effect of IFRS on EM behaviors. As mentioned previously, strong investor protection laws are fundamental conditions for high quality accounting since strong protection limits managers' ability to acquire private control benefits, and reduces their incentives to mask firm performance. For example, Leuz et al. (2003) suggested that investor protection played an important role in influencing international differences in corporate EM. The weak legal environment might also facilitate opportunistic EM resulting in lower earnings quality (Ball, Kothari, & Robin, 2000; Leuz et al., 2003; Siegel, 2005). Hence, it may be argued that the increase or decrease in EM may be affected by investor protection rather than IAS only. The existing literature points to the need for the investigation of the effects of IAS on EM behavior in countries with high or low investor protection. This research will re-examine the notions that whether IAS increase, decrease, or not affect the manipulation of EM without the noise of investor protection and legal enforcement factors by choosing the samples in countries with high investor protection rankings and high legal enforcement scores. The paper did not compare the degree of EM between two groups: low and high investor protection but chose a sample of high investor protection countries to observe the degree of EM whether it is maintained, decreased, or increased before and after the adoption of IFRS. In a nutshell, there are two directions which the literature points out: either the implementation of IFRS will decrease or increase EM. Based more on the latter direction, the first hypothesis is developed:

Hypothesis 1   In high investor protection countries, earnings management during the IFRS application period was more implemented than during the national GAAP application period.

The value of aggregate EM has a (−) direction: the higher the value, the lower the degree of EM. Therefore, the symbol "<" stated in the alternative hypothesis stands for more implementation of EM and the symbol "≥" in the null hypothesis indicates less or equal degree of EM implementation.

Furthermore, firms can use multiple EM strategies, e.g., AEM and REM to manage their earnings (e.g., Cohen & Zarowin, 2010; Dechow, Ge, & Schrand, 2010; Badetscher, 2011; Kothari, Mizik, & Roychowdhury, 2016). Burgstahler and Eames (2006) documented in detail that both AEM and REM were managed upwards to avoid reporting earnings lower than analyst forecasts. As a consequence, Hypotheses 2 and 3 for AEM and REM are developed:

Hypothesis 2 In high investor protection countries, accrual-based earnings management during the IFRS application period was more implemented than during the national GAAP application period.

Hypothesis 3 In high investor protection countries, real earnings management during the IFRS application period was more often implemented than during the national GAAP application period.

The values of AEM and REM have also a (–) direction: the higher value represents lower degree of AEM and REM, respectively. Therefore, the symbol "<" in alternative hypothesis stands for more implementation of AEM/REM and the symbol "≥" in null hypothesis indicates a less or equal degree of AEM/REM implementation.

However, the managers tend to trade off using AEM and REM to achieve their objectives and they consider the two strategies as substitutes (Zang, 2007, p. 676). Prior research have also documented that managers prefer REM to AEM (e.g., Graham, Harvey, & Rajgopal, 2006; Roychowdhury, 2006; Cohen et al., 2010; Enomoto et al., 2015). Based on these arguments, it is expected that the companies might use both AEM and REM to edit reported earnings and that in high investor protection countries, it is predicted that the managers tend to avoid accrual-based earnings manipulations and to take advantages of REM techniques. Thus, the fourth hypothesis is developed in this research to test the relationship between AEM and REM. A negative correlation suggests substitutability between AEM and REM. It also suggests that managers tend to substitute AEM for REM.

Hypothesis 4 In high investor protection countries, during the IFRS application period accrual-based earnings management was negatively correlated with real earnings management.

To understand the effects of IAS on EM behaviors, several steps were taken. Firstly, patterns of aggregate earnings management (including aggregate EM, aggregate AEM, and aggregate REM) activities over the period of 14 years (2001–2014)[1] were plotted on charts to examine the effects of IFRS adoption on EM. Secondly, this study tested hypotheses to determine if different types of EM are maintained, increased, or decreased after adopting IFRS. Particularly, it focused on the comparison of AEM and

---

[1] A period of 15 years (2000–2014) was observed. However, the calculations in the measurements of this study were based on lagged values, depending on how the formulas are structured; the observed period could be reduced to 14 years (2001–2014 for AEM measurements) or 13 years (2002–2014 for REM measurements).

REM during the IFRS application period and during the national GAAP application period. Lastly, it tested the hypothesis pertaining to the relationship of AEM and REM in countries with high investor protection, in a period of IFRS application. The measures of both AEM and REM were adapted from the methodology developed by Leuz et al. (2003), adopted by Cai (2008), and recently employed and further developed by Enomoto et al. (2015). The following subsection presents the explanations of measuring AEM and REM and their aggregate values.

For the purpose of plotting, the changes in patterns of EM activities on charts and of testing hypotheses, the aggregate AEM, aggregate REM, and aggregate EM are calculated as follows:

$$Aggregate\ AEM = AEM1 + AEM2 + AEM3 * (-1)$$
$$Aggregate\ REM = REM1 + REM2$$
$$Aggregate\ EM = Aggregate\ AEM + Aggregate\ REM$$

Aggregate AEM is the total of AEM1 (smoothing reported earnings by using accruals), AEM2 (correlation between the changes in accruals and changes in operating cash flow), and AEM3 (magnitude of accruals). Aggregate REM is the total of REM1 (sales and production manipulation) and REM2 (discretionary expenditure manipulation). Aggregate EM is the total of aggregate AEM and aggregate REM.

High value of aggregate AEM, aggregate REM, and aggregate EM suggests a low level of earnings manipulation. In aggregate AEM, the direction of AEM3 is reversed by multiplying with (−1) because it has an opposite direction as compared to other variables: the higher value of AEM3 suggests a higher value of earnings smoothing.

Empirical Results

To have an overview of EM behavior in high investor countries, the aggregate EM, aggregate AEM, and aggregate REM of sample countries, excluding Canada due to its difference of IFRS adoption timeline, were calculated and plotted in Chart 35.1. Chart 35.1 indicates that as compared to the period before adopting IFRS, the aggregate levels of AEM after adopting IFRS are higher through years and the aggregate levels of REM after adopting IFRS are lower through years. This is inconsistent with the statement of Enomoto et al. (2015) that REM should be more constrained and that AEM should be less implemented in countries with strong investor protection. From the chart, it is of note that there are several points of time where the levels of aggregate EM and AEM changed significantly.

Firstly, in 2005, both AEM and REM increased significantly as compared to previous years. This may be explained by the fact that 2005 is the year of mandatory adoption of IFRS in six selected sample countries (excluding Canada) where all of their selected sample firms changed from national GAAP to IFRS. There are two explanations that may be interpreted: either IFRS's increased financial reporting flexibility may provide more EM opportunities for firms or the change to new accounting standards may affect the levels of EM in short term, known as transition effects.

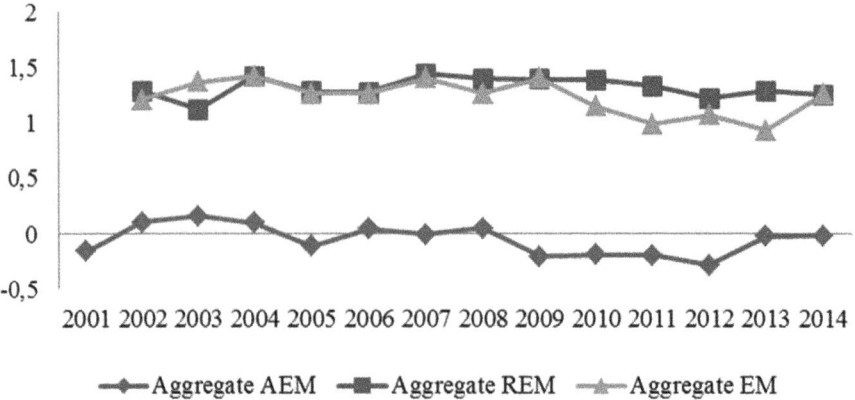

Chart 35.1 General trend of accrual-based earnings management (AEM), real earnings management (REM), and EM during 2001–2014

Secondly, AEM started to increase in 2008 and stayed at high level till 2012 and EM started to increase in 2009 and also stayed at high level till 2014. This trend might come from the effects of global financial crisis of which impact was felt broadly across the globe in 2008/2009. The 2008 financial crisis is considered by many economists to have been the worst financial crisis since the Great Depression of the 1930s.[2] This financial crisis may create or magnify incentives to manage earnings because during the crises, firms often experience a systematic decline in incomes. The reduced earnings might be attributed to macroeconomic shocks rather than to the poor performance by managers. Empirical evidence suggests that firms engage in aggressive EM during periods of financial crisis (Chia, Lapsley, & Lee, 2007; Johl, Jubb, & Houghton, 2007; Molik, Mir, & Khokan, 2013). Molik et al. (2013) also found that managers tend to time their earnings announcement (with earnings shocks) to occur soon after their industry peers' warnings to minimize their apparent responsibility for earnings shortfalls.

Independent Samples t-Test for Hypothesis 1

An independent test was run on the data as well as 95 % confidence intervals for the mean difference. It was found that the degree of EM in the IFRS using period (1.211 ± 0.374) was significantly more than (the lower the value, the higher the degree of EM) the degree of EM in the national GAAP using period (1.445 ± 0.424), $t_{(89)} = -2.618$, $p = 0.010$. The null hypothesis $H1_0 = \text{EM-IFRS} \geq \text{EM-GAAP}$ is rejected. The alternative hypothesis $H1_1 = \text{EM-IFRS} < \text{EM-GAAP}$ is accepted.

---

[2] Reuters, Three top economists agree 2009 worst financial crisis since Great Depression; Risks increase if right steps are not taken. Available from: http://www.reuters.com/article/2009/02/27/idUS193520+27-Feb-2009+BW20090227 (27 Feb 2009).

Table 35.1 Independent samples *t*-test results for Hypothesis 1

		t-test for equality of means						
							95% confidence interval of the difference	
				Sig.	Mean	Std. error		
		t	df	(2-tailed)	difference	difference	Lower	Upper
EM	Equal variances assumed	−2.618	89	0.010	−0.234	0.089	−0.411	−0.056
	Equal variances not assumed	−2.489	43,986	0.017	−0.234	0.094	−0.423	−0.044

As a result of this test, it can be concluded that in high investor protection countries, EM during the IFRS application period is more implemented than during the national GAAP application period (Table 35.1).

Independent Samples t-Test for Hypothesis 2

An independent *t*-test was conducted on the data as well as 95% confidence intervals for the mean difference. It was found that the degree of AEM in the IFRS using period (-0.101 ± 0.295) was significantly higher than (a lower value represents a higher degree of EM) the degree of AEM in the national GAAP using period (0.159 ± 0.385), $t_{(89)} = -3.506$, $p = 0.001$. It means that the null hypothesis $H2_0 = $ AEM-IFRS $\geq$ AEM-GAAP is rejected. The alternative hypothesis $H2_1 = $ AEM-IFRS $<$ AEM-GAAP is accepted. As a result of this test, it can be concluded that in high investor protection countries, AEM during the IFRS application period is more implemented than during the national GAAP application period (Table 35.2).

Independent Samples t-Test for Hypothesis 3

An independent samples *t*-test was performed on the data as well as 95% confidence intervals for the mean difference. It was found that the degree of REM in the IFRS using period (1.297 ± 0.242) was insignificantly more than (a lower value represents for a higher degree of EM) the degree of REM in the national GAAP using period (1.321 ± 0.221), $t_{(89)} = -0.443$, $p = 0.659$. Hence, there is not enough evidence to reject the null hypothesis: $H3_0 = $ REM-IFRS $\geq$ REM-GAAP (Table 35.3).

On the one hand, the independent samples *t*-tests provided significant results to conclude that in high investor protection countries, EM in general and AEM in particular are more implemented during the IFRS using periods than during the national GAAP using period. Since higher EM indicates lower quality of financial reporting, it may be interpreted that in high investor protection countries, IFRS have not provided better quality of financial reporting. This may be because the increased financial reporting flexibility under IFRS provides more EM opportunities for managers.

Table 35.2 Independent samples *t*-test results for Hypothesis 2

		t-test for equality of means						
							95 % confidence interval of the difference	
		t	df	Sig. (2-tailed)	Mean difference	Std. error difference	Lower	Upper
AEM	Equal variances assumed	−3.506	89	0.001	−0.261	0.074	−0.408	−0.113
	Equal variances not assumed	−3.146	39,419	0.003	−0.261	0.083	−0.428	−0.093

Table 35.3 Independent samples *t*-test results for Hypothesis 3

		t-test for equality of means						
							95 % confidence interval of the difference	
		t	df	Sig. (2-tailed)	Mean difference	Std. error difference	Lower	Upper
REM	Equal variances assumed	−0.443	89	0.659	−0.024	0.054	−0.131	0.084
	Equal variances not assumed	−0.460	53,280	0.648	−0.024	0.052	−0.129	0.081

The higher flexibility under IFRS is reflected in choosing alternative accounting methods and permits measurements such as fair value accounting. Moreover, a principle-based accounting standard is embedded with lower specificity and more judgement from managers, which may result in higher opportunities for EM. On the other hand, the test failed to reveal a significant difference between the two groups of REM. It also means that in high investor protection countries, the degree of REM during the IFRS application period and during the national GAAP application period was quite similar. This behavior may be explained by the disadvantages of using REM. As explained, using REM may affect the future economic performance of the firm negatively and the firm may bear more costs as compared to AEM. Therefore, REM was maintained at stable levels in these countries between 2002 and 2014.

Testing Bivariate Correlation Between AEM and REM for Hypothesis 4

Before testing the bivariate correlation between AEM and REM, the auto-correlation between these two variables was calculated because the data are time-series data collected over 14 years. The Durbin–Watson test was performed and had a D–W

Table 35.4 Correlation between aggregate AEM and REM

		Aggregate AEM	Aggregate REM
Aggregate AEM	Pearson correlation	1	−0.106
	Sig. (2-tailed)		0.403
	N	64	64
Aggregate REM	Pearson correlation	−0.106	1
	Sig. (2-tailed)	0.403	
	N	64	64

value of 2.226. If the D–W value is close to 0 or 4, it indicates a strong or negative correlation amongst residuals. For data has strong auto-correlation, the bivariate correlation will be insignificant. In that case, the auto-regression should be run instead of bivariate correlation. The result is close to 2, meaning there is no serial correlation between variables.

Table 35.4 reports the Pearson correlation between the pooled aggregate AEM and aggregate REM. Consistent with Hypothesis 4, aggregate AEM is negatively correlated with aggregate REM (−0.106). However, the test is insignificant at $p=0.403>0.050$. Hence, there is not enough evidence from the data to conclude that in high investor protection countries, in the period of IFRS application, AEM is negatively correlated with REM.

The bivariate correlation between AEM and REM was also tested in each single country, and there was only one case, namely France showing a significant negative relationship between the two variables: $p=−0.599$, Sig. $=0.031$ (2-tailed). A negative correlation suggests substitutability between AEM and REM. The result suggests that in France managers tend to substitute AEM for REM. However, there is not enough evidence to state that in high investor protection countries (groups of selected sample countries) the correlation between AEM and REM is negative. It may be interpreted that REM may not be chosen as a substitute for AEM because its relative costs are higher than the costs of AEM. For example, it may be more expensive to depart from normal business practices for firms that are under pressure of high competition within the industry since it would reduce their competitive advantage relative to their industry peers which face less competition. Another explanation is that using REM results in higher levels of taxable income (Zang, 2012).

Conclusions

This paper studied the effects of IAS on management behavior of 199 public listed companies, particularly in countries with high investor protection and strong legal enforcement, namely: Canada, Denmark, France, Hong Kong, Ireland, Norway, and United Kingdom. Since EM was chosen as a proxy for the behavior of managers, it examined whether firms in high investor protection countries engage in EM, AEM, and REM more often during the IFRS using period than under the local

GAAP using periods. This research is in line with many researchers identifying that EM increased after IFRS adoption (e.g., Lin & Paananen, 2006; Christensen, Lee, Walker, & Zeng, 2015; Ahmed, Neel, & Wang, 2012; Capkun, Collins, & Jeanjean, 2012; Salewski, Teuteberg, & Zülch, 2014). Furthermore, the study also tested the bivariate correlation between aggregate AEM and aggregate REM in the selected sample countries to examine whether firms trade off AEM and REM as substitute.

The results of this study show that in high investor protection countries, the degree of EM in general and AEM in particular increased after changing from national GAAP to using IFRS. This was mainly through greater use of discretionary accruals. Consequently, it can be concluded that in high investor protection countries, IFRS has not provided a better quality of financial reporting and that managers tend to take the opportunities of higher flexibility which this principle-based accounting standards have to engage in earnings manipulation to achieve a specific reported earnings objective. This paper will, hence, increase the investor's awareness regarding high quality of financial reporting of IFRS because this study shows evidence that even in high investor protection and high legal enforcement countries, EM under IFRS has been practiced more than under national GAAP.

The research suggests that in high investor protection countries, the degrees of REM during these two periods were rather similar. The independent samples *t*-test did not reveal a significant difference between REM under IFRS and local GAAP. This may give spaces for future research on the behavior of REM in low investor protection countries to see how different the pattern of REM between low and high investor protection groups of countries is. Furthermore, except for the case of France, this study failed to find a substitutive relation between REM and AEM in samples of high investor protection countries. According to Bae, Tan, and Welker (2008) and Cai, Rahman, and Courtenay (2008), France has the highest score of difference between local GAAP and IFRS as compared to other countries in the samples. France gets 12 score, while others get lower scores, for example, United Kingdom gets 1, Hong Kong gets 3, and Canada gets 5. Difference between national GAAP and IFRS is the summary score of how domestic GAAP differs from IAS on 21 key accounting dimensions. Higher value represents more discrepancies between national GAAP and IFRS. This does point out the need for additional studies which should take the difference between national GAAP and IFRS as a control variable of choosing samples or examine the relationship between the behaviors of EM and differences between IFRS and domestic GAAP.

Furthermore, the statistical tests in this study were run only with a limited number of 2883 firm year observations as in Leuz et al. (2003), Enomoto et al. (2015), or in similar studies. However, limitation is unavoidable because of the high requirements for sampling sets in this research and the long time periods examined (15 year time series). Future research could extend this sample sizes to produce a more robust statistical result.

References

Ahmed, A. S., Neel, M. J., & Wang, D. (2012). Does mandatory adoption of IFRS improve accounting quality? Preliminary evidence. *Contemporary Accounting Research, 30*(4), 1344–1372.

Badetscher, B. A. (2011). Overvaluation and choice of alternative earnings management mechanisms. *The Accounting Review, 86*(5), 1491–1518.

Bae, K.-H., Tan, H., & Welker, M. (2008). International GAAP differences: The impacts on foreign analyst. *The Accounting Review, 83*(3), 593–628.

Ball, R., Kothari, S., & Robin, A. (2000). The effect of international institutional factors on properties of accounting earnings. *Journal of Accounting and Economics, 29*(1), 1–51.

Bergstresser, D., & Philippon, T. (2006). CEO incentives and earnings management. *Journal of Financial Economics, 80*(3), 511–529.

Burgstahler, D., & Eames, M. (2006). Management of earnings and analysts' forecasts to achieve zero and small positive earnings surprises. *Journal of Business Finance and Accounting, 33*(5–6), 633–652.

Cai, L., Rahman, A. R., & Courtenay, S. M. (2008). The effect of IFRS and its enforcement on earnings management: An international comparison. http://ssrn.com/abstract=1473571. Accessed 16 Sept 2009.

Capkun, V., Collins, D. W., & Jeanjean, T. (2012). *Does adoption of IAS/IFRS deter earnings management?* Ph.D thesis, University of Iowa.

Chia, Y. M., Lapsley, I., & Lee, H. W. (2007). Choice of auditors and earnings management during the Asian financial crisis. *Managerial Auditing Journal, 22*(2), 177–196.

Christensen, H. B., Lee, E., Walker, M., & Zeng, C. (2015). Incentives or standards: What determines accounting quality changes around IFRS adoption? *European Accounting Review*, Forthcoming.

Cohen, D. A., & Zarowin, P. (2010). Accrual-based and real earnings management activities around seasoned equity offerings. *Journal of Accounting and Finance, 50*(1), 2–19.

Dechow, P., Ge, W., & Schrand, C. (2010). Understanding earnings quality: A review of the proxies, their determinants and their consequences. *Journal of Accounting and Economics, 50*(2), 344–401.

Dye, R. (1988). Earnings management in an overlapping generation's model. *Journal of Accounting Research, 26*(2), 195–235.

Enomoto, M., Kimura, F., & Yamaguchi, T. (2015). Accrual-based and real earnings management: An international comparison for investor protection. *Journal of Contemporary Accounting and Economics*, Forthcoming.

Francis, J., & Wang, D. (2008). The joint effect of investor protection and big 4 audits on earnings quality around the world. *Contemporary Accounting Research, 25*(1), 157–191.

Graham, J. R., Harvey, C. R., & Rajgopal, S. (2006). Value destruction and financial reporting decisions. http://ssrn.com/abstract=871215. Accessed 6 Sept 2006.

Healy, M. P., & Wahlen, M. J. (1999). A review of the earnings management literature and its implications for standard setting. *Accounting Horizons, 13*(4), 365–383.

IASB. (2015). *International financial reporting standards IFRS® (Red Book)*. London: IFRS Foundation.

Johl, S., Jubb, C. A., & Houghton, K. A. (2007). Earnings management and the audit opinion: Evidence from Malaysia. *Managerial Auditing Journal, 22*(7), 688–715.

Kothari, S. P., Mizik, N., & Roychowdhury, S. (2016) Managing for the moment: The role of real activity versus accruals earnings management in SEO valuation. The Accounting Review: March 2016, Vol. 91, No. 2, pp. 559–586.

La Porta, R., Lopez-de-Silanes, F., Sheiler, A., & Vishny, R. (2002). Investor protection and corporate valuation. *Journal of Finance, 75*(3), 1147–1170.

Leuz, C., Nanda, D., & Wysocki, P. (2003). Earning management and investor protection: An international comparison. *Journal of Financial Economics, 69*(3), 505–527.

Lin, H., & Paananen, M. (2006). *The effect of financial systems on earnings management among firms reporting under IFRS*. Business School Working Papers UHBS 2006-2.

McKee, T. E. (2005). *Earnings management: An executive perspective*. Mason, OH: Thomson.

Molik, T. A., Mir, M., & Khokan, B. R. M. M. (2013). Earnings management during the Global Financial Crisis: Evidence from Australia. *Proceedings of International Business and Social Sciences and Research Conference 16–17 December 2013*, Cancun, Mexico.

Nabar, S., & Boonlert-U-Thai, K. K. (2007). Earnings management, investor protection, and natural culture. *Journal of International Accounting Research, 6*(2), 35–54.

Houqe, M. N., Van Zijl, T., Dunstan, K., & Karim, A. W. (2011). The effect of IFRS adoption and investor protection on earnings quality around the world. *The International Journal of Accounting, 47*(3), 333–355.

Oberholzer-Gee, F., & Wulf, J. (2012). *Earnings management from the bottom up: An analysis of managerial incentive below the CEO*. Harvard Business School Strategy Uni Working Paper No. 12-056.

Peng, L., & Roell, A. (2008). Executive pay and shareholder litigation. *Review of Finance, 12*(1), 141–184.

Roychowdhury, S. (2006). Earnings management through real activities manipulation. *Journal of Accounting and Economics, 42*(3), 335–370.

Salewski, M., Teuteberg, T., & Zülch, H. (2014). Short-term and long-term effects of IFRS adoption on disclosure quality and earnings management. http://ssrn.com/abstract=2398305. Accessed 19 Feb 2014.

Siegel, J. (2005). Can foreign firms bond themselves effectively by renting U.S. securities laws? *Journal of Financial Economics, 75*(2), 319–359.

World Bank Group (2014). Doing business. Protecting minority investor. http://www.doingbusiness.org/data/exploretopics/protecting-minority-investors.

Zang, A. Y. (2012). Evidence on the trade-off between real activities manipulation and accrual-based earnings management. *The Accounting Review, 87*(2), 675–703.

Zeyun, C. (2009). *The choice between real and accounting earnings management*. Ph.D thesis, University of Houston.

Chapter 36
Intercultural Competencies for Career Advancement: A Comparative Study of Managerial Competencies in United Arab Emirates and Malaysia

Diana J. Haladay, Rommel Pilapil Sergio, Ahmed M. Makki, Zainal Abu Zarim, and Mohd Nor Ismail

Abstract This research paper examines competencies and career advancement of 338 managers in two different countries: the United Arab Emirates and Malaysia. The descriptive-correlational survey method has been utilized. Research findings show that managerial competencies are similar across the two countries. It also reveals that managerial competencies are also a strong predictor of career advancement. There is limited research on the impact of culture on competencies and career advancement in non-Western countries. Thus, this research study benchmarks the similarities and differences of the impact of culture and competencies in career advancement at the managerial level in these two non-Western countries.

Keywords Intercultural competencies • Career advancement • Managerial competencies • United Arab Emirates • Malaysia

Introduction

Globalization is no longer a dream of the future, but is the predominant reality of the business environment in the twenty-first century. This means that the majority of business enterprises have business interests in more than one country, creating a complex employment market where multinational organizations compete with local

D.J. Haladay (✉) • R.P. Sergio
Canadian University of Dubai, Dubai, United Arab Emirates
e-mail: diana@cud.ac.ae; rommel@cud.ac.ae

A.M. Makki
University of Modern Sciences, Dubai, United Arab Emirates

Z.A. Zarim • M.N. Ismail
Multimedia University, Cyberjaya, Selangor, Malaysia

© Springer International Publishing Switzerland 2017   423
R. Benlamri, M. Sparer (eds.), *Leadership, Innovation and Entrepreneurship as Driving Forces of the Global Economy*, Springer Proceedings in Business and Economics, DOI 10.1007/978-3-319-43434-6_36

and regional enterprises for a global workforce comprised of both local and expats from around the world.

Thus, the challenge of operating successfully globally is compounded by the necessity to understand the interface between the management practices of the parent company and the cultural and management practices of the local country, in addition to the cultural and management expectations of the expat workforce employed in the local market.

Hofstede (1980), Schein (2010), and Bolman and Deal (2011) believe that the effectiveness or ineffectiveness of management practices and their associated competencies are culturally determined. Major consulting companies such as The Hay Group and Development Dimensions International have played a significant role in the globalization of business. Thus, other researchers believe that even though managerial competencies were developed in the USA, and reflect Western values, they are being applied globally with the unquestioned belief that these management practices and competencies are universally valid (House, 1998; Triandis, 2004).

This study examines managerial competencies required for performance and career advancement in two different countries: the UAE and Malaysia. Specifically it seeks to identify competencies that differentiate one cultural group from another, identify shared competencies, and the reasons for these differences and similarities. Private and public sector management practice has been examined separately due to the differences in the competencies required of each. This study builds on a previously done comparative study of managerial competencies between the UK and Singapore (Chong, 2013).

Review of the Related Literature

Managerial Competency

It was Boyatzis (1982; *The Competent Manager*) who popularized the usage of competencies for business purposes as a means for organizations to identify high-performing employees and improve organizational performance (Ulrich, 2013). Lawler (1994) suggests that competencies are a far more appropriate measurement and predictor of employee performance than job-based assessment systems. This is due to the instability of the global competitive business environment and the need for continuous organizational change and learning on the part of the employee—issues which are not addressed in the traditional job-based assessment system. Thus, using competencies, rather than job-based systems, "facilitates organizations developing organizational capabilities that provide competitive advantage." (Lawler, 1994, p. 6)

A review of the literature on competencies reveals a wide-ranging definition of competencies so that there is no single agreed-upon definition (Strebler, 1997; Jubb & Robotham, 1997). Some authors, such as Boyatzis (1982), Burgoyne (1993), and Sternberg and Kolligian (1990), focus on competencies as traits and behaviors of employees. Catano, Fitzgerald, Hackett, Wiesner, and Methot (2009) see competencies as the "group of behaviors involving the knowledge, skills, and the ability to perform a task or role."

Other authors focus on competencies as the effectiveness of job-specific performance. In line with this, Hoffmann (1999) and Hager, Gonczi, and Athanasou (1994) define competencies as "the standard or quality of the outcome of the person's performance." Cheng, Dainty, and Moore (2005) extend the definition of competencies and argue that managerial effectiveness is dependent upon a "role" of social interactions and the ability to perceive and manage the expectations of employees. In this way, organizational (task-specific) and personal (managerial) competencies are related to the extent that managerial competencies are derived from the values and core competencies of the organization.

In this study, the term "competencies" is used interchangeably to refer to personal, managerial, organizational task-specific, and social interaction performance. Managerial competency profiles are based upon individual characteristics, job tasks, and roles required for acceptable and outstanding performance. These performance-based competencies are evaluated through observed behaviors. In line with this practice, this study examines the supervisor's assessment of their managers' competencies and compares them with the managers' career progressions. The link between job competencies and career advancement will help to identify competencies that differentiate faster progressing managers from their peers.

National Culture, Ethnicity, and Managerial Competencies

To be effective in global business environment, organizations must identify the skills and competencies that are most important for their managers. Managers need to understand what is needed to succeed in their organizations so that they can successfully execute their current roles and responsibilities and be well-positioned for future promotions (Kraut, Pedigo, McKenna, & Dunnette, 1989). Given the rapid acceleration of globalization and the resulting increased global competition, it becomes imperative that organizations understand the impact of culture on manager's performance. Accordingly, the question becomes to what extent do national cultural values impact managerial performance? In other words, are there universal managerial competencies or do national cultures require separate and distinct managerial competencies?

Early authors focused on the differentiating nature of culture. Triandis (1982) and Schein (2010) define culture as a group's shared reaction to an external environment that, over time, shapes the history, language, and perceptions of the group members. Thus, culture represents the shared understanding of a collective that differentiates it from other collectives (House, Javidan, Hanges, & Dorfman, 2002). House and Aditya (1997) claim that cultural differences are deeply ingrained and do not change over time.

In contrast, through their GLOBE studies, House (1998) found that there were both cultural-specific dimensions (emic qualities) and universal dimensions (itic qualities). The Big Five Inventory (BFI) has been shown to apply across many cultures (Aziz & Jackson, 2001; Denissen, Geenen, Van Aken, Gosling, & Potter, 2008). Hay/McBer (Whitfield, 1995) found that there were three "universal competencies" (leadership, communication, and adaptability) required by international managers. Dulewicz (1989) identified four "supra-competency" clusters: conceptualizing, aligning, interacting, and creating success, which correlated with high performance, while Woodruffe (1993) identified generic management competencies, which he called "universal" competencies. Tung (1981) proposes that there is a universal competence of "communicative ability" which crossed all job types.

There is an emerging trend among authors suggesting that national cultures are converging due to the impact of globalization and corporate cultures are being replaced by a universal organizational identity (Lorbiecki & Jack, 2000). Managerial competencies are more often shaped by the value systems of the West, rather than national value systems. In line with this reasoning, Bouteiller and Gilbert (2005) argue that managerial competencies must converge due to the internationalization of businesses combined with the need for a standardized approach to management practices. Finally, as Jordan and Cartwright (1998) observe, the difficulty of specifying national competencies for each geographical region of the global makes it impossible to not rely on core competencies.

In summary, a review of the literature indicates that despite cultural differences, there are commonly held human values that transcend culture. Managerial competencies are based upon those behaviors that are associated with the common innate human values which are embedded within cultural dimensions. As a result, it is expected that there will be broad similarities in the selection of managerial competencies required for the job performance of manager working in different cultural environments. These similarities ought to appear in empirically determined competency clusters or categories.

H_o1: There are no significant differences in the job competency of the respondents when grouped according to the demographic variables of national culture.

H_o2: Job competencies are not predictors of career advancement.

Objectives of the Study

This study aims to: (1) examine the significant differences in job competencies and demographic variables in terms of nationality; and (2) determine the significant relationship between job competencies and career advancement among respondents.

Methodology

This research paper utilized descriptive-quantitative method through structured survey with 338 managers in Malaysia and the UAE. These respondents were selected through accessibility sampling technique from private and government organizations possessing at least 5 years of experience.

The Demographic Profile Sheet (DPS), Job Competency Survey (JCA), and Career Advancement Profile (CAP) were the research instruments used to gather demographic characteristics, managerial competencies, and career advancement, respectively. The DPS includes items such as nature of company, gender, nationality, education, and age. The adopted JCA measures five areas of managerial competencies such as intellectual information handling, communication, management, interpersonal, and personal dimensions which are the most significant competencies related to career advancement. On another hand, the CAP is reflected in five different levels such as very high, high, average, low, and very low to be able to relate it to managerial competencies.

Descriptive statistics were employed to provide quantitative descriptions of the respondents' demographic characteristics such as frequency and percentages distribution. The *t*-test for independent groups, one-way ANOVA, and regression analysis were used to test the three null hypotheses on the difference and significant relationship among variables.

Results

The Demographic Profile of the Respondents

As can be seen from Table 36.1, 70.1 % of the respondents represent the United Arab Emirates compared to the Malaysian samples with 29.1 %.

The Significant Differences in Job Competencies and Demographic Variables

Table 36.2 shows the significant differences in job competencies variables in terms of nationality.

On nationality data, it can be noted that it does not impact all the areas (intellectual handling, communication, management, interpersonal, and personal) of managerial job competencies. This supports the idea that regardless of the nationality of the respondents coming from the United Arab Emirates and Malaysia, managerial competencies on the job do not actually vary. Thus, the null hypothesis that there are no significant differences in job competencies and demographic variable in terms of nationality is accepted.

Table 36.1 Sample characteristics

National demographic variables nationality	f	%
UAE	237	70.1
Malaysian	101	29.9

Table 36.2 The significant differences in job competencies and demographic variables

Nationality				
Intellectual information handling	−1.075	0.283	Accept	Not significant
Communication	−1.784	0.075	Accept	Not significant
Management	−0.500	0.617	Accept	Not significant
Interpersonal	−0.901	0.368	Accept	Not significant
Personal	−0.856	0.393	Accept	Not significant

Table 36.3 Correlation between job competencies and career advancement

Job competencies	b	t	Sig.	Decision of Ho	Inference
Intellectual information handling	0.239	4.517	0.000	Reject	Significant
Communication	0.192	3.596	0.000	Reject	Significant
Management	0.212	3.986	0.000	Reject	Significant
Interpersonal	0.245	4.638	0.000	Reject	Significant
Personal	0.151	2.800	0.005	Reject	Significant

The Significant Relationship Between Job Competencies and Career Advancement

Table 36.3 below exhibits the correlational data between job competencies and career advancement.

It can be assessed that all areas of managerial job competencies significantly relate to career advancement. This implies that the more competent the managers are in all aspects of their job, the higher their career advancement will be or vice versa. For example, the higher the rate of risk taking, business sense, and problem-solving skills managers have, the more exposure to promotion there will be. Thus, the null hypothesis that there is no significant relationship between job competencies and career advancement is rejected.

Discussion

A comparison between managerial job competencies and demographic variables between managers in the United Arab Emirates and Malaysia reveals little differences between the two groups. In both groups, there are five broad managerial competencies required for managers: intellectual information handling, communication, interpersonal, and personal. This similarity in the broad managerial competencies required in both countries supports the view that there are common managerial competencies between different cultures (House et al., 2002; Triandis, 2004). This empirical evidence that there is a broad common set of similar managerial competencies in two non-Western countries is an important finding supporting the conclusions of other researchers who maintain that national cultures are converging due the impact of globalization and, consequently, management competencies are becoming universally valid (Aziz & Jackson, 2001; Whitfield, 1995; Woodruffe, 1993; Tung, 1981; Lorbiecki & Jack, 2000). As the business environment of the twenty-first century continues to become more global and globally dispersed, this concept of universal competencies as indicators of required managerial performance is a critical and noteworthy topic for additional research.

Finally, career advancement is linked to performance, which is reflected in the organization's required managerial competencies. This link between managerial competencies and career advancement was found to be valid in both the career paths of United Arab Emirates and Malaysian managers. This finding supports the view that competencies are generally used to evaluate the performance and quality of output of managers, as well as to identify high-performing managers and improve organizational performance (Hager et al., 1994; Boyatzis, 1982; Ulrich, 2013). It also suggests that the use of managerial competencies, rather than the traditional job-based system, enables organizations to facilitate the continuous organizational change and learning needed to maintain a competitive advantage (Lawler, 1994).

Conclusion

This study can be viewed as part of a theoretical and empirical effort aimed at understanding the relationship between national culture, managerial competencies, and career advancement. Given the limited empirical research on the intersect of these three components, this study contributes significantly to the body of knowledge in this area. Moreover, it is the first study that looks at the issues in the context of two differing non-Western cultures and two differing non-Western countries: the United Arab Emirates and Malaysia.

As globalization is a predominant reality of business in the twenty-first century, answers to these inquiries are critically important to enable organizations to effectively work across global locations and markets. Both managers and organizations need to be clear on what competencies are required for success globally and to what extent national cultures, demographic variables, and nature of the company impact their choice of required managerial competencies. This understanding will enable organizations to better evaluate and promote high-performing individuals. Thus, this study has practical implications at both the individual managerial levels.

References

Aziz, S., & Jackson, C. J. (2001). A comparison between three and five factor models of Pakistani personality data. *Personality and Individual Differences, 31*(8), 1311–1319.

Bolman, L. G., & Deal, T. E. (2011). *Leading with soul: An uncommon journey of spirit* (Vol. 381). San Francisco, CA: Wiley.

Bouteiller, D., & Gilbert, P. (2005). Intersecting reflections on competency management in France and in North America. *Relations Industrielles/Industrial Relations, 60*(1), 3–28.

Boyatzis, R. (1982). *The competent manager: A model for effective performance*. New York, NY: Wiley.

Boyatzis, R. E. (2008). Competencies in the 21st century. *Journal of management development, 27*(1), 5–12.

Burgoyne, J. G. (1993). The competence movement: Issues, stakeholders and prospects. *Personnel Review, 22*(6), 6–13.

Catano, V. M., Fitzgerald, C., Hackett, R., Wiesner, W., & Methot, L. (2009). *Recruitment and selection in Canada*. Boston, MA: Cengage Learning.

Cheng, M. I., Dainty, A. R., & Moore, D. R. (2005). Towards a multidimensional competency-based managerial performance framework: A hybrid approach. *Journal of Managerial Psychology, 20*(5), 380–396.

Chong, E. (2013). Managerial competencies and career advancement: A comparative study of managers in two countries. *Journal of Business Research, 66*(3), 345–353.

Denissen, J. J., Geenen, R., Van Aken, M. A., Gosling, S. D., & Potter, J. (2008). Development and validation of a Dutch translation of the Big Five Inventory (BFI). *Journal of Personality Assessment, 90*(2), 152–157.

Dulewicz, V. (1989). Assessment centres as the route to competence. *Personnel Management, 21*(11), 56–59.

Hager, P., Gonczi, A., & Athanasou, J. (1994). General issues about assessment of competence. *Assessment and Evaluation in Higher Education, 19*(1), 3–16.

Hoffmann, T. (1999). The meanings of competency. *Journal of European Industrial Training, 23*(6), 275–286.

Hofstede, G. (1980). Motivation, leadership, and organization: Do American theories apply abroad? *Organizational Dynamics, 9*(1), 42–63.

House, R. J. (1998). A brief history of GLOBE. *Journal of Managerial Psychology, 13*(3/4), 230–240.

House, R. J., & Aditya, R. N. (1997). The social scientific study of leadership: Quo vadis? *Journal of Management, 23*(3), 409–473.

House, R., Javidan, M., Hanges, P., & Dorfman, P. (2002). Understanding cultures and implicit leadership theories across the globe: An introduction to project GLOBE. *Journal of World Business, 37*(1), 3–10.

Jordan, J., & Cartwright, S. (1998). Selecting expatriate managers: Key traits and competencies. *Leadership and Organization Development Journal, 19*(2), 89–96.

Jubb, R., & Robotham, D. (1997). Competences in management development: Challenging the myths. *Journal of European Industrial Training, 21*(5), 171–175.

Kraut, A. I., Pedigo, P. R., McKenna, D. D., & Dunnette, M. D. (1989). The role of the manager: What's really important in different management jobs. *The Academy of Management Executive, 3*(4), 286–293.

Lawler, E. E. (1994). From job-based to competency-based organizations. *Journal of Organizational Behavior, 15*(1), 3–15.

Lorbiecki, A., & Jack, G. (2000). Critical turns in the evolution of diversity management. *British Journal of Management, 11*(s1), S17–S31.

Schein, E. H. (2010). *Organizational culture and leadership* (Vol. 2). San Francisco, CA: Wiley.

Sternberg, R. J., & Kolligian, J. E., Jr. (1990). *Competence considered*. New Haven, CT: Yale University Press.

Strebler, M. (1997). *Getting the best out of your competencies*. Grantham: Grantham Book Services.

Triandis, H. C. (1982). Dimensions of cultural variation as parameters of organizational theories. *International Studies of Management and Organization, 12*(4), 139–169.

Triandis, H. C. (2004). The many dimensions of culture. *The Academy of Management Executive, 18*(1), 88–93.

Tung, R. L. (1981). Selection and training of personnel for overseas assignments. *Columbia Journal of World Business, 16*(1), 68–78.

Ulrich, D. (2013). *Human resource champions: The next agenda for adding value and delivering results*. Boston, MA: Harvard Business Press.

Whitfield, M. (1995). High-flyer hazards. *People Management, 1*(24), 9.

Woodruffe, C. (1993). What is meant by a competency? *Leadership and Organization Development Journal, 14*(1), 29–36.

Chapter 37
Managerial Recruitment Issues in China: The Expatriate Factor

Stefane Kabene, Said Baadel, and Angelika C. Dankert

Abstract With China becoming the world's largest economy, it must somehow manage the existing human capital. The problem lies in the lack of managerial talent currently located in China. This paper attempts to look how China is currently recruiting managers and examines the factors hindering the recruitment of Chinese-born and expatriate managers. China is recruiting managers using the same methods as the Western world. However, a strong emphasis is put on a factor known as guanxi. The shortage of Chinese-born managers can be attributed to financial reasons and the lack of education and government commitment. China's culture is a major factor hindering the success of expatriates as well as the organizational structure in China because of the socialist culture. These issues must be addressed to attract managers into China to successfully compete in a globalized economy.

Keywords Hofstede cultural dimensions • Red guards • Guanxi

Introduction

Many experts tout that this century will belong to China. Indeed, it is difficult to argue against the idea. The Chinese market comprises one-fifth of the world's population, and its economy is expected to surpass that of the USA in the next decade, making it the largest. With the sudden economic upturn that China has experienced, many human resource issues have surfaced, particularly in the areas of recruitment and retention. Despite the increasing number of Chinese attending higher education, China is experiencing a shortage of qualified managers to lead organizations. Many

S. Kabene (✉)
Canadian University of Dubai, Dubai, United Arab Emirates
e-mail: stefane@cud.ac.ae

S. Baadel
Canadian University of Dubai, Dubai, United Arab Emirates

University of Huddersfield, Huddersfield, UK

A.C. Dankert
Hochschule Aschaffenburg, Aschaffenburg, Germany

© Springer International Publishing Switzerland 2017   431
R. Benlamri, M. Sparer (eds.), *Leadership, Innovation and Entrepreneurship as Driving Forces of the Global Economy*, Springer Proceedings in Business and Economics, DOI 10.1007/978-3-319-43434-6_37

experts agree that this may be the central roadblock to China's ability to grow successfully in the foreseeable future.

There are many pressing issues for the field of human resources in China, yet the priority of this list of concerns is the lack of managers. Illuminating this shortage is China's future. It is headed towards a more globalized economy and as more foreign investors are lured into the Chinese economy, more information will be demanded in the field of human resources (Melvin & Sylvester, 1997). Foreign firms invest about one billion each week in China (Ahmad, 2005). Part of this investment goes towards the expatriate managers recruited there. Therefore companies are increasingly interested in knowing the qualities of a manager that would fit in with the corporation and adapt with the culture of China.

In addition, many recruiters have discussed the relative difficulty of hiring managers in comparison with other countries. China's dilemma when it comes to hiring managers is to choose between bureaucratic or entrepreneurial ones. While the bureaucratic ones are more respectful of administration rules, they are however slower in decision making than the entrepreneurial ones, who on the other hand can be quite unpredictable (Perkowski, 2005). And because government-owned businesses are still a significant value to the market, there is an assumption that national politics can influence recruitment methods as well.

Demography of China

China has had a turbulent history. A prominent memory in the minds of many Chinese is the Cultural Revolution. Taking place in 1966, it was a revolt against the Chinese Communist Party (CCP) (Ebrey, 2004). Whatever traditions were considered 'old', along with concepts of capitalism, were denounced. To fight for the revolution, Mao Zedong, the leader of the revolt, chose teenagers and university students to form what was known as the Red Guards. At this time, many schools had stopped teaching because it was considered a method of learning 'tradition' (Ebrey, 2004). Thus, many of the Red Guards, now in their prime working years, are left with uncompleted education, which complicates recruitment of skilled labor.

Another demographic context to consider is the one-child policy. Since the 1980s the government has placed a regulation on the number of births each family is allowed (Ebrey, 2004). This generation is now reaching the age of entering into the working market. Though many of them have favorable resumes, and English skills, recruiters have reported that it is relatively difficult to find natural team-players to recruit (Ahmad, 2005).

Factors Hindering Recruitment of Expatriate Managers

Some scholars have recently argued that China could benefit from the learning opportunities provided by the employment of expatriate managers. Unfortunately, there are considerable roadblocks to recruiting individuals who are willing and able to participate in international assignments. Even more important than expatriate recruitment are the measures taken to retain these international professionals.

Many expatriate managers experience difficulties adjusting to a new cultural environment. In a study of the Beijing hotel industry it was discovered that as many as 40% of all expatriate managers end their foreign assignments early because of poor performance and an inability to adapt to Chinese culture. For those managers that stayed, 50% asserted that they performed at a low level of effectiveness. In the USA, failure rates are quite high, as premature returns occur in 30% of overseas assignments. These failure rates represent significant costs to the parent company, as the average cost per failure is estimated to lie between $65,000 and $300,000 (Hutchings, 2003).

According to Nish (1996), most failures were attributed to the expatriate's ineffectiveness in a number of essential areas. In order of highest to lowest frequency, the following is a list of the most common causes of expatriate manager failure:

1. Spouse's inability to adjust to foreign environment
2. Manager's inability to adjust to foreign environment
3. Other family-related problems
4. Manager's personality or emotional immaturity
5. Manager's lack of technical competence
6. Manager's lack of motivation to work overseas

Of these causes, cultural aspects of the foreign environment are causing the expatriate to perform poorly. Unfamiliarity with Chinese organizational structure, leadership requirements, *guanxi*[1] and other cultural intricacies affect the ability of expatriates to cope. These struggles, in turn, can lead to poor emotional states, provide the impression of technical incompetence and reduce overall motivation.

The typical organizational structure of Chinese businesses is a significant cultural hurdle for visiting managers. Ambler and Witzel (2000) explain that, historically, most organizations in China are hierarchal, with a few powerful leaders in the highest ranks. This high level of power distance was observed in Hofstede's international comparison of cultural dimensions (Table 37.1).

A comparison of cultural dimensions between China and the west, mainly United States of America and Canada show a striking difference.

Interestingly, Hofstede found that Chinese low score of 20 on individualism. This means that in-group considerations are high and people tend to hire or promote within their in-groups in exchange for loyalty. While this is not surprising for a col-

Table 37.1 Hofstede comparison of cultural dimensions (Schafer, 2005)

Region	Power distance	Individualism	Uncertainty avoidance
United States	Low	High	Low
Canada	Low	High	Low
China	High	Low	Moderate

[1] Knowing someone who knows someone who is qualified for the job.

lectivist nation, it also means that Chinese employees expect much guidance and leadership from their managers in the process.

One senior HR manager of a multinational enterprise in China commented on this mentality, which can still trouble HR managers today:

> Workers from state-owned enterprises still think that the factory boss should be their uncle; responsible for any and every personal problem they have …If the boss does not appear helpful and supportive, the workers will complain to their boss's superior—and this can cause problems (Ahlstrom, Foley, Young, & Chan, 2005).

China is a dynamically changing society. The effectiveness of visiting managers is greatly affected by the perception of their presence. Many younger, educated Chinese see western policy as a good replacement for old-fashioned methods (Ambler & Witzel, 2000). Others prefer to stick with Confucius ideals. Expatriates tend to have an easier time adjusting when their presence is welcomed, as those who perceive to be adjusting poorly will tend to perform similarly. In a study of expatriate perceptions, only 11 % felt they were successful in their management role (Selmer, 2004). Negative perceptions were attributed mainly to feelings of alienation and frustration consistent with culture shock. Interestingly, while most interviewees believed that their adjustment and effectiveness on both work and non-work levels would have been increased by having received some prior cultural training, only 27 % of expatriates claim to have received training prior to arriving, or during their assignment, in China (Hutchings, 2003).

Discussion and Analysis

There is such a vast difference between Chinese and Western cultures. This difference in culture and lifestyle is a major complication facing expatriate managers, particularly with regard to their success in international assignments. For example, there is a considerable difference in the power distance as shown in Fig. 37.1 above. China has a score of 80 which is considered in the high end compared to USA and Canada. This score indicates that the Chinese society in general accepts the inequality amongst people such that there is hardly any defense against superiors abusing their powers. Employees in this kind of society also tend to not have aspirations beyond their rank. A key aspect of this problem is that it is intrinsic. The problem cannot be resolved through external means such as compensation. The solution lies in rectifying the lack of cultural understanding which sends many expatriates home prematurely.

The added responsibility of responding effectively to cultural differences and performing the leadership role expected of them in the Chinese workplace causes undue stress which is also a big turnoff for expatriates. The ability to understand cultural concepts is important for expatriate managers to successfully adjust to the foreign environment. It is also important if expatriates want to be effective leaders.

According to Hofstede's model of cultural dimensions, Chinese employees expect a large amount of guidance and instruction from their managers. They also expect the manager to support them on a personal level. Due to the fact that China is a collectivist society, the employees expect a certain amount of security as well.

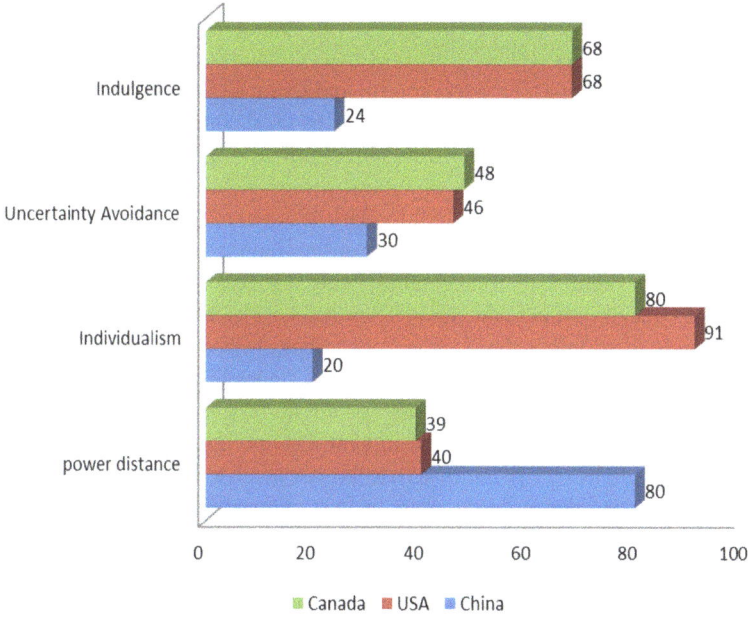

Fig. 37.1 Hofstede comparison of cultural dimensions (The Hofstede Center, 2016)

Expatriates must realize that their management style must drastically change to suit the needs of the organizational and Chinese culture.

With respect to quality, expatriate managers must weigh professional skills and technical competence against their ability to adapt to China's environment. The ability to adapt to local cultures is a crucial factor, involving not only the manager but also his or her partner and family. Sufficient numbers of programs are not in place for an expatriate and his or her family to educate them on cultural issues and appropriate management techniques.

Another key aspect we see is the low Indulgence score of 24 compared to the two North American countries. A low score in this regard indicates that China is a restrained society where employees are not putting much emphasis on leisure time and that their actions are somehow restrained by social norms. This is a major consideration for expatriates coming from the western world.

Conclusion and Recommendations

High numbers of expatriate assignments end prematurely. Reasons for failure include many of the following:

- Psychological issues regarding change
- Differing management styles in China and the West

- Drastically different cultural environments
- Lack of cultural training and adaptability skills

Improving the ability to effectively recruit and retain Chinese-born and expatriate managers is a vital task that organizations in China must address. Without the appropriate remedies to these problems, China will continue to encounter great difficulty in managing the growing number of organizations located in China thus being unable to compete in the increasingly boundary-less world.

Finally, improving the conditions for expatriate managers would help to recruit and retain more of them. Expatriates, while being a source of managerial talent, are also a good source of indirect education. They can lead by example if conditions are ideal. Expatriate recruitment should be a joint process between the international firm and the target country. By involving both parties, managers identified for international assignments will have the adequate professional and technical expertise, as well as being recognized for their environmental adaptiveness. This puts emphasis on creating opportunities for potential expatriates to receive the cultural training they require before starting their assignments. In fact, cultural training programs should be mandatory for any managers who wish to practice in China. With the high costs associated with failure, neither China, nor firms operating there can ignore the importance of adequately preparing expatriates and their families for the experience.

References

Ahlstrom, D., Foley, S., Young, M. N., & Chan, E. (2005). Human resource strategies in post-WTO China. *Thunderbird International Business Review, 47*(3), 263–285.

Ahmad, S. (2005). Executive dialogue: The China syndrome. *The Economist Business Review*. Retrieved February 18, 2016, from http://www.economist.com/business/globalexecutive/dialogue/displaystory.cfm?story_id=4312272

Ambler, T., & Witzel, M. (2000). *Doing business in China*. New York, NY: Routledge.

Ebrey, B. (2004). *The Cambridge illustrated history: China*. Cambridge: Cambridge University Press.

Hutchings, K. (2003). Cross-cultural preparation of Australian expatriates in organizations in china: The need for greater attention to training. *Asia Pacific Journal of Management, 20*, 375–396.

Melvin, S., & Sylvester, K. (1997). Shipping out. *China's Business Review, 24*(3), 30–34.

Nish, I. (Ed.). (1996). *Work and society: Labour and human resources in East Asia*. Hong Kong: Hong Kong University Press.

Perkowski, J. (2005). Mind China's management gap. *Far Eastern Economic Review, 168*(5), 38–42.

Schafer, S. (2005). China: Help wanted; the nation faces a critical shortage of top managers, a situation that could threaten its economic boom. *Newsweek, 146*(18), 36.

Selmer, J. (2004). Psychological barriers to adjustment and how they affect coping strategies: Western business expatriates in China. *International Journal of Human Resources Management, 12*(2), 151–165.

The Hofstede Center. (2016). Retrieved February 20, 2016, from http://geert-hofstede.com/

Chapter 38
Human Resource Management Practices: A Case of Telecommunication Company in the United Arab Emirates

Rommel Pilapil Sergio, Louis Jos Moyalan, Hadi Ramadan Al-Ali, and Mana Mohammed Al Bannai

Abstract Human resource management (HRM) plays a critical role in any organization. It attributes to the fact that human resources are the most important asset an organization has. Employees are mandated to transform company strategies and goals into tangible outcome and for this reason, they provide a source of competitive advantage to an organization. The study utilized case study method by describing the HR practices that includes career and development programs, employee performance and evaluation system, and staffing functions of a telecommunication company in the UAE through an interview with the HR manager. The purposively selected telecommunication company has claimed to have achieved tremendous success due to its strong leadership and commitment to quality. Although the company has made strides in its HR practices, there is a need to improve to maximize the potential of its workforce.

Keywords Human resource management practices • Telecommunication company • United Arab Emirates

Introduction

Indeed, human resource management (HRM) entails the integrated use of policies, procedures, and practices that provide a wide range of function needed to plan, train, and support the workforce (Caliskan, 2010). HRM normally focuses on people, how they fit into an organization, and ways of using them effectively.

R.P. Sergio (✉) • L.J. Moyalan • H.R. Al-Ali • M.M. Al Bannai
Canadian University of Dubai, Dubai, United Arab Emirates
e-mail: rommel@cud.ac.ae; email@rommelsergio.com

© Springer International Publishing Switzerland 2017   437
R. Benlamri, M. Sparer (eds.), *Leadership, Innovation and Entrepreneurship as Driving Forces of the Global Economy*, Springer Proceedings in Business and Economics, DOI 10.1007/978-3-319-43434-6_38

The HRM framework indicates support across organizational functions. Such framework mirrors the practices ideal of any organization to reflect in their set of rules and regulations. In today's world, many HR practitioners adhere to the fact that there are similarities in the HR practices and that there are universal set of expected series of tasks in conjunction with the policies and procedures of the company.

Moreover, HR is one of the most important assets of an organization and it is the chief factor in achieving a competitive advantage in the market. Managing human resources in an effective way is the deciding factor in the success or failure of the organization, and it is very challenging as compared to managing technology or capital and for its effective management, organization requires effective HRM system. HRM system should be backed up by sound HRM practices. HRM practices refer to organizational activities directed at managing the pool of human resources and ensuring that the resources are employed towards the fulfillment of organizational goals. These HR practices can easily get distorted by external or internal factors and must always be maintained and regulated in the organization.

Sound HR practices can serve as a backbone of any firm's recognition and goodwill in the market and can serve to attract fresh blood into the company by serving as a nonmonetary incentive. They can also help curve down the turnover ratio of employees if implemented effectively.

Review of the Related Literature

Several studies have indicated that effective HR-based programs enhance HR practices. In the study of Haladay, Sergio, Opulencia, and Antiado (2015), the key findings revealed that the rapidly changing nature of business in the UAE, HR managers are not able to fully implement "talent management" as a strategic tool but rather are working on transitioning to this practice in the future. In such study, the primary challenges faced by HR managers surveyed include: (1) high turnover and low retention, (2) regional cultural practices impacting HR policies and procedures, (3) insufficient or nonexistent succession planning, and (4) operating in various economic zones within the UAE (Haladay et al., 2015).

Another related study with resemblance to this current research has been conducted by Gernal, Sergio, and Al Shuali (2013), and they have examined the cultural orientations of Omani employees by linking them to their preferences of HRM policies and practices in a telecommunication setting. The study reveals that the Omanization policies are introduced to tap HRM development programs in various areas in both public and private sectors.

Specifically, on compensation and benefits, one of the HR practices is the administration of bonuses that are often given based on one's accomplishments. These reward programs normally reward people to encourage them to generate more profits. Profit sharing entails creating money disbursed to staff by taking a given percentage of company profits. Profit sharing rewards programs aim to reward employees for assisting the company to achieve its profit goals. Above all, stock options have become increasingly widespread in large companies to reward upper and middle level managers. These programs give the workforce to right to invest and purchase company shares at a given price for a given amount of time. The Board of Directors normally authorizes stock options and approved by the shareholders. Similar to profit sharing plans, these stock options aim to reward staff for serving the company for a long period. It is worth noting that many employees are motivated by monetary rewards at least for some time. However, the motivational power of money decreases and employees get used to the compensation they receive (Pasaoglu & Tonus, 2014). For this reason, money is not the only factor that determines job performance. Perhaps, what comes out clearly is that employees are often motivated by the work along with the environment they work as opposed to the amount of compensation they receive. Therefore, the amount of compensation needs to include both nonmonetary and monetary ideas. Successful companies ensure to have established compensation and reward systems that aim to cultivate employee commitment to their jobs and the organization and ultimately improve their satisfaction. Compensation and employee reward system describe programs established by organizations to reward high-performing employees and motivate others to improve their productivity. Reward systems are often considered separate from salary systems (Pasaoglu & Tonus, 2014). Reward programs include variable pay, bonuses, profit sharing, and stock options. Variable pay describes a compensation program where a portion of an employee's salary is at risk. It ties to the performance of an individual or company performance.

In terms of career development and education programs, the HR department is mandated to ensure that it allows employees to advance in their careers. By definition, career development entails the lifelong process of learning and work to ensure that employees reach their potential. It also aims to ensure that the organization has the necessary skills to succeed now and in the future (Pasaoglu & Tonus, 2014).

Another practice the HR department is mandated is to conduct a performance evaluation of its staff. It provides an opportunity to evaluate or assess the performance of employees and to adjust accordingly. The primary objectives of performance evaluation system incline on providing an equitable measurement of employee contribution and accurate documentation (Singh, Sharma, & Khattra, 2011).

The HRM department has an immense responsibility of planning and managing a diverse workforce. Companies that succeed often are those that hire staff who have diverse skills and competencies (Gilani, Zadeh, & Saderi, 2012). With the current globalization, people are no longer required to work in certain places, but they can work even in foreign countries. Thus, the HRM department is obligated to seek for these talented and skilled workers to meet the mission and vision of the company. An accepted diversity entails acknowledging, accepting, understanding, and celebrating differences among people with gender, sexual orientation, ethnicity, age, and intellectual abilities.

Another area of consideration is the immense responsibility of planning and managing a diverse workforce. Companies that succeed often are those that hire staff who have diverse skills and competencies (Gilani et al., 2012). With the current globalization, people are no longer required to work in certain places, but they can work even in foreign countries. Thus, the HRM department is obligated to seek for these talented and skilled workers to meet the mission and vision of the company.

An accepted diversity entails acknowledging, accepting, understanding, and celebrating differences among people with gender, sexual orientation, ethnicity, age, and intellectual abilities.

Lastly, the practice on staffing clearly indicates that the workforce plan entails the process of analyzing firm's likely future needs for staff in terms of skills, numbers, and locations (Louch, 2014). Workforce planning is a systematic process that examines what an organization needs to accomplish due to the business goals and strategies (Gilani et al., 2012). It then compares current workforce data and external workforce segment and creates a gap analysis, which highlights critical talent segments, general workforce needs, and needs to be required. Workforce planning allows an organization to plan on how it would meet its needs through employee recruitment and training. It is vital that companies plan and regularly hire more staff to address its needs.

Objectives of the Study

This study intends to: (1) describe the different functional areas of HRM and (2) recommend relevant insights in line with the HR practices of the telecommunication company involved in the study.

Methodology

This research describes the large-scale telecommunication company's HRM practices in the UAE. The HR manager heading the human resource department was interviewed in order to get data on the nature of their HRM programs. Data gathered were taken from programs that were validated through in-depth interviews with the respondent. Moreover, this qualitative-descriptive research utilized the case study method.

Results

The results and discussion point to the research findings in terms of the five different distinct HR practices.

Compensation and Benefits

A wide range of compensation and reward system for the employees with the intent of motivating them increase their productivity. The HR department employs stock options to allow the managerial staff to invest in the company and grow in their financial wealth. This reward system allows the management and other employees to feel a sense of ownership and ultimately ensure that they remain committed to the organization. Another commonly used reward system is bonuses. The company gives bonuses to employees who show exemplary performance with the intent of motivating them to perform even much higher. These reward systems have increased customer satisfaction because employees provide quality services.

Career and Development Programs

A good HR department is mandated to introduce educational programs to allow employees to acquire skills and reach their potential. The company under study is committed to improving its workforce by providing them with the necessary educational programs and career development. The company recently unveiled its third 5-year plan aimed at recruiting Emirati nationals to fill up supervisory and technical engineering posts. So far, the company has appointed about 3258 UAE nationals who now account for about 36 % of the workforce in the UAE.

To achieve the goals of Emiratization, the HR launched its first plan in 1999 followed by another in 1996, and the third plan in 2006. The HR department has created a comprehensive strategy to hire the best talent. It has made it clear that UAE nationals will fill key positions including engineering and technical departments. The company follows Emiratization policies in hiring people for key leadership positions. Currently, the company has over 85 % of its top executive management occupied by UAE nationals, which ideally reflects the successful implementation of UAE Emiratization policy. The HR department provides the all-inclusive training activities which support Emiratization in the UAE. The intent of this training is to develop productive and high-performing individuals. As a direct initiative of the HR department, the company has established an Academy, which is ranked as the leading training center for leadership skills, business, telecommunication, governmental development, and information technology.

For newly recruited staff, the HR department provides them with two training programs. One of its training programs caters for UAE nationals. A career in the company largely means a lifelong opportunity for employees to explore their potential and continuous growth. The company provides the best opportunity for employees to build their career. To support career development, the company caters for tuition fees for employees who want to advance in their career. The company has partnered with numerous local colleges and universities to provide training to its staff. The organization believes that people are the most important asset and has created several developmental projects that target a wide range of careers right from when joins the company to the executive level. The core objective of its Career Development Section centers on building the next generation of corporate personalities in the company.

Employee Performance and Evaluation System

A performance evaluation system not only aims to assess employee performance, but it allows for employee development along with organizational improvement. It also helps an organization to identify high-performing staff, reduce employee turnover, and identify areas for improvement. With its important role, the HR department is mandated to ensure that it conducts an objective performance evaluation to improve employee performance and organizational success. The company has implemented a performance evaluation system, which aims to assess the performance of employees. The company conducts regular performance reviews through which it determines employees to promote. It often conveys feedback to employees through formal communication and meetings.

Diversity Management

The company under study is an equal opportunity employer and remains committed to supporting diversity. The HRM believes that diversity enriches company performance, its services, its employees, and the communities in which it operates. The company has established a diversity department that remains committed to ensuring that it meets its diversity objectives. The company has committed itself to promoting diversity of culture and languages in its services and workforce. While the HR department remains committed to developing a diverse organization, evidence reveals that the company is yet to achieve true diversity.

Staffing

In the company, the planning process occurs continuously throughout the year. The company often makes quarterly reviews in the months of May, August, and November to allow for adjusting levels and allow recruitment if needed. The company often allows an adequate amount of time and flexibility to meet its demand needs or staff and ensure that it meets strategic objectives. The HR department regularly advertises vacancies both internally and externally. Perhaps the use of this strategy centers on its commitment to developing emirates talent by allowing employees to ascend in their career ladder and provide jobs for fresh graduates from UAE colleges. Through its annual appraisal scheme, employees can apply for higher positions.

Conclusion

The company under study is a leading telecommunication company headquartered in the UAE. Similar to any organization, the company depends on its workforce or human resource to transform strategic goals into the desired results. Due to its massive operations, the HR department is tasked with ensuring proper management of human resources to achieve set goals and objectives. As revelead in this paper, the HR department perfoms different functions including rewarding employees, providing career development programs HR, evaluating employee performance, and staffing.

The company has made a substantial investment in education programs as exemplified by its educational institution under the company. It supports and provides career advancement opportunities to its employees. The company recently unveiled its third 5-year plan aimed at recruiting Emirati nationals to fill up supervisory and technical engineering posts. It has also adopted a remarkable compensation system to keep employees motivated in their work and to the organization. Staffing with emphasis on workforce planning process occurs continuously throughout the year to allow for adjustment levels and recruitment if needed.

Recommendation

The link between organizational performance and HR practices has been clearly established in the reviewed literature. It suggests that HR practices play a critical role in driving organizational effectiveness.

The HR department must develop a more effective compensation system and reward system. It needs to ensure that the objective and philosophy of the system are well specified. Perhaps, some of the objectives that may work for the company include fair and competitive compensation and attracting talent to achieve the organization's objectives (Hollon, 2011). The HR department can also state clearly that the compensation system aims to retain employees largely by instilling a sense of ownership and long-term commitment. The company should not rely only on financial rewards. The HR department also needs to establish nonfinancial reward programs to drive employee performance.

The company needs to develop high-level workforce planning capabilities (Carter & Carmichael, 2011). High-performing companies incorporate sophisticated workforce and forecasting analytics into their HR processes. By so doing, they transform company-wide talent, external workforce segment, and business data into workable insights, which they use and can share with other leaders. The insights inform both short-term and long-term decisions about the talent an organization has ways to develop it, the talent it needs and way of attracting it.

The company should improve diversity, ensuring the effective recruitment and hiring, and by implementing diversity policies (Hollon, 2011). The company needs to review its HR practices and policies to identify barriers, as well as opportunities for success. It needs to broaden its recruitment effort and reduce biases in the selection process. More attention should go to recruiting talented candidates. However, recruitment and selection is not enough to ensure diversity. The company should develop sound diversity policies and ensure their effective implementation. This will ensure that all employees are given a fair chance in promotions to top leadership positions. As part of developing a culture of diversity, the HR team should begin training employees on diversity to ensure that they understand and appreciate the differences in the workplace. Above all, the HR department must try to improve its career development programs to ensure that it provides every person with an equal opportunity to reach his or her potential. It is particularly important because the number of women and minorities in top executive position is very low.

The HR function and roles should not be viewed as independent of each other rather they should be approached in a holistic manner because they are interconnected. For instance, proper HR and workforce planning would influence the efficacy of educational programs or performance evaluations. For this reason, the policies, processes, and procedures need to be integrated to ensure that the HR department achieves its strategic goals.

References

Caliskan, E. E. (2010). The impact of strategic human resource management on organizational performance. *Journal of Management, 6*(2), 100–116.

Carter, L., & Carmichael, P. (2011). *The best of best practices: Critical success factors for identifying and measuring industry leading management solutions.* Retrieved from https://www.td.org/Publications/Magazines/TD/TD-Archive/2011/08/The-Best-of-Best-Practices-Critical-Success-Factors-for-Identifying-and-Measuring-Industry-Leading-M

Gernal, L. M., Sergio, R. P., & Al Shuali, M. (2013). Looking ahead: Scanning change management and its implications to human resource management practices. *IAMURE International Journal of Business and Management, 7*, 1.

Gilani, M. H., Zadeh, S. M., & Saderi, R. H. (2012). The role of strategic human resource management in creation of competitive advantages. *International Journal of Business and Social Science, 3*(16), 225–240.

Haladay, D., Sergio, R., Opulencia, M. J., & Antiado, D. (2015). Moving towards strategic advantage: Transitioning from traditional human resource practices to talent management.

Hollon, J. (2011, January 27). *New study: The top10 best practices of high impact HR organization.* Talent Management and HR. Retrieved from http://www.eremedia.com/tlnt/new-study-the-top-10-best-practices-of-high-impact-hr-organizations/

Louch, P. (2014, March 10). *Workforce planning is essential to high performing organizations.* Society for Human Resource Management. Retrieved from http://www.shrm.org/hrdisciplines/technology/articles/pages/louch-workforce-planning.aspx

Pasaoglu, D., & Tonus, Z. (2014). Strategic importance of human resource practices on job satisfaction in private hospitals. *Social and Behavioral Sciences, 150*(15), 394–403.

Singh, S., Sharma, G., & Khattra, N. (2011). Impact of human resource management on the organization. *Social Science Research Network.*

Chapter 39
Knowledge Management Practices in Saudi Arabian Public Sector Organisations: A Case of the Ministry of Justice

A. Khaled, S. Renukappa, S. Suresh, and A. Saeed

Abstract In the early part of the twenty-first century, public and private sector organisations are under pressure due to population growth, financial constraints, resource scarcity, social justice and climate change. These challenges are felt by public and private sector organisations alike in some form and need to be addressed. To meet the challenges and take the available opportunities, government must actively pursue initiatives to adopt Knowledge Management (KM) tools, techniques and philosophies. There is, however, a paucity of empirical research on the key KM practices that have been implemented in the Ministry of Justice (MOJ) of the Kingdom of Saudi Arabia (KSA)—which is the core rationale for this paper. This paper is based on a thorough review of the empirical literature, exploring the importance of KM, the structure of the MOJ and the key drivers of and challenges to implementing KM strategies within KSA public sector organisations. It is concluded that managing knowledge is a complex process because it is usually linked to long-term time horizons, a high level of uncertainty and impacts that are often difficult to quantify. If public sector organisations do not fully comprehend what drives the need for managing knowledge, they may fall into the trap of creating inefficient strategies and operational plans.

Keywords Ministry of Justice • Knowledge management • Saudi Arabia • Communities of practices

Introduction

There is a need to examine the particular context of the public sector regarding the need for Knowledge Management (KM) practices especially in the context of the Ministry of Justice (MOJ) of the Kingdom of Saudi Arabia (KSA).

A. Khaled • S. Renukappa (✉) • S. Suresh • A. Saeed
Faculty of Science and Engineering, University of Wolverhampton, Wulfurna Street, City Campus, WV11LY, Wolverhampton, UK
e-mail: k.m.a2@wlv.ac.uk; suresh.renukappa@wlv.ac.uk; s.subashini@wlv.ac.uk; s.alnabt@wlv.ac.uk

© Springer International Publishing Switzerland 2017
R. Benlamri, M. Sparer (eds.), *Leadership, Innovation and Entrepreneurship as Driving Forces of the Global Economy*, Springer Proceedings in Business and Economics, DOI 10.1007/978-3-319-43434-6_39

445

Therefore, various related aspects have been covered and this also includes theoretical and practical examples by using authentic and contemporary sources. With the upsurge in digital connectivity, government agencies all around the world are utilising information and communication technology (ICT) in order to enhance productivity, increase transparency, improve accountability and facilitate reforms of the public sector (Tambyrajah & Al-Shawabkeh, 2009). Because government agencies are knowledge-based organisations, developing KM is crucial for governmental organisations in KSA at the local, regional or national level. KM has also become one of the ingenuities within most countries' e-Government Plans (Yahya & Farah, 2009). This research paper presents a synopsis of KM initiatives and developments in the public sector predominantly from developing countries. The main advantage of KM is to maximise productivity in the public sector while augmenting delivery of public service. More specifically, the objectives for KM initiatives, according to Jain and Jeppesen (2013) and Stricker (2014) include:

1. Maximising competencies across all public services by linking silos of information across different levels of government and across borders.
2. Consolidating outdated or developing new systems to improve overall performance and capitalise on a more integrated, broader and more easily reached knowledge base.
3. Improving liability and accountability and justifying risk through the establishment of informed decisions and also resolving issues more quickly, reinforced by access to transparent and integrated information across all managerial boundaries.
4. Delivering improved and more cost effective fundamental services such as increasing partnerships with and awareness among the public.

All of the above-mentioned objectives lead to the sharing of knowledge which is consistent with the survey finding and provides access to expertise and knowledge. As a result, most KM activities establish the retention of lessons learnt and best practices. These activities can be applied to both practices within engagement with citizens as well as with the government agencies.

Government organisations are encouraged to explain and publish all of their non-sensitive public policies online. As the public expects to receive more transparent, open and responsive services from government organisations, they have to recover their ability to engage with the public effectively. Public discussion and public consultation are considered to be the appropriate processes for looking at the ideas, views, concerns and feedback of all stakeholders in establishing, developing and executing public policies and programmes (Chaudhary, 2014). In a large number of developed countries, it is apparent that a central government portal with feedback forums has been introduced, allowing them to engage fully with both citizens and organisational employees. This has usually been one of the first KM activities.

Why KM for Ministry of Justice in the Kingdom of Saudi Arabia

Salwa (2010) stated that KSA is one of those countries that are striving to establish a knowledge-based society and this provides a strong reason why the MOJ has been chosen for the formulation and implementation of KM. In addition, to this, there are several functional, operational and management related generic issues that provide the impetus for the implementation of KM in the public sector. These were identified by Ahmed (2011) using the Delphi technique, speaking to 14 extremely eminent Saudi experts in KM. Collectively, their answers classified key obstacles to KM. Ahmed (2011) research leads to the classification of the following obstacles:

- Organisation barriers
- Leadership barriers
- Technology barriers
- Learning barriers

An increasingly well-informed population needs the public sector to have the best freshly generated knowledge, simply because their knowledge is growing swiftly and they have increasing numbers of notable players in the sector. KM relies on the idea that the most treasured asset of an organisation is the knowledge contained by its employees (Ahmed, 2011); an emphasis enforced by the increasing rate of change presently occurring in the corporate sector and in society in general.

According to Cardoso, Meireles, and Ferreira Peralta (2012), KM has detected that 'knowledge work' is involved in almost all types of employment. Therefore, it has been recommended that staff should be 'knowledge workers'. This is a move away from the traditional reliance on the manual skills of the worker towards a situation in which the worker is valued for the knowledge they have. Thus, in any institute or corporation, the most significant interests and endeavours of any worker comprise utilisation of information, designing and contribution. In this age of advancement, the efficiency and value of government can be enhanced and fortified by utilising KM. On the one hand the public sector and NGOs encounter these contests, while on the other hand they also take good advantage of these changes which are proposed by the knowledge-based economy, globalisation and new development of ICT (De Angelis, 2013).

Four pillars of the Knowledge Economy (KE) framework suggested by Krstić and Stanišić (2013) are as follows:

- An economic and institutional regime. It delivers criteria, inducements and better economic plans and these further encourage the effective deployment as well as the sharing of resources. Creativity and incentives are also encouraged in order to use current knowledge, creation and dissemination.
- An educated and skilled population. This type of population has the capability to continuously modify, exalt and adjust their abilities so as to proficiently develop, reveal and utilise data.

- An effective revolution system of organisations, universities, consultants and research institutes. All of these organisations and institutes make people aware regarding rebellion of information. The stock of global knowledge is not only exploited by different people but they also adjust and integrate it according to local requirements.
- A dynamic and modern information infrastructure. Efficient transmission, propagation as well as handling of data can be expedited through modern infrastructure (Krstić & Stanišić, 2013).

These four pillars of KE assist the establishment of the sharing and exploitation of data. Consequently, KSA has developed and adopted a specific set group of initiatives by following these four pillars. Additionally, these pillars can also enhance the worth that is included in provisions, properties and the level of Saudi economic development (UNDP, 2010).

Methodology

Considering the nature of this research study in which the KM prospects of a public sector organisation are under inspection, it was vital to engage in the extraction of precise and relevant information from an adequate sample of the population with the help of appropriate research methods. There are various methods of research available which represent certain sets of benefits and certain sets of limitations; i.e. qualitative and quantitative research approaches are two popular methods in this regard. However, in this research context, the use of a mixed method approach has been selected which is also known as the pragmatic research method because it entails mixed use of qualitative and quantitative techniques (Gill & Johnson, 2010). Therefore, it was proposed that both qualitative and quantitative approaches would be used in this study. A questionnaire tool and interview methods were used for the data collection process; i.e. a questionnaire was used to gather data from employees and managers, whereas the interview method was applied for collecting data from executives and heads of different departments in the ministry. This helped with collecting rich data by covering all of the required and relevant aspects related to the research area.

Outlook of Ministry of Justice

The future of KSA as a structural state and the position of the MOJ within that state is a very interesting study. For the MOJ to continue to be viable demands the application of KM to ensure their better functioning. First of all, the existence of 25 different departments within the MOJ reflects the comprehensive nature of this ministry and the broad functioning of this ministry within the country. Financial management, arbitration management, budget management, the planning department, statistics management and general department of information technology are

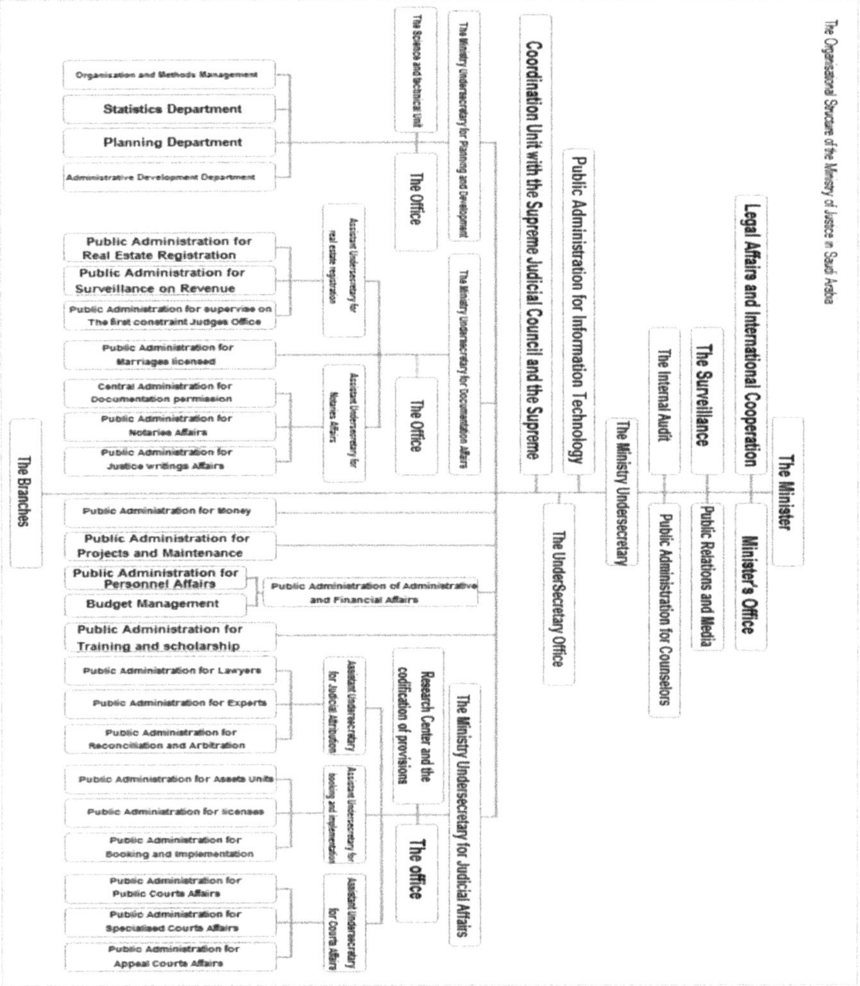

Fig. 39.1 The hierarchy of the Ministry of Justice (MOJ). *Source*: Ministry of Justice (2016b)

just some of the wide range of departments contained within the MOJ (Ministry of Justice, 2016a). This structure of the MOJ in KSA reflects how a flow of information and knowledge sharing is an essential ingredient that can make or break the adequate functioning and decision-making of the ministry, as the functions of this ministry are sensitive and require careful attention. Figure 39.1 gives the official structure of the ministry and this is taken directly from their official website:

KM techniques and tools are vital in the context of this ministry because the frequent cooperation and interaction of these departments are essential for the smooth functioning of this ministry which naturally demands the implementation of KM approaches to enable its staff and executives to display sustainable performance over a longer period of time. This point can be emphasised as the KSA consists of

Fig. 39.2 The provinces of the Kingdom of Saudi Arabia (KSA). *Source*: Saudi Embassy (2016b)

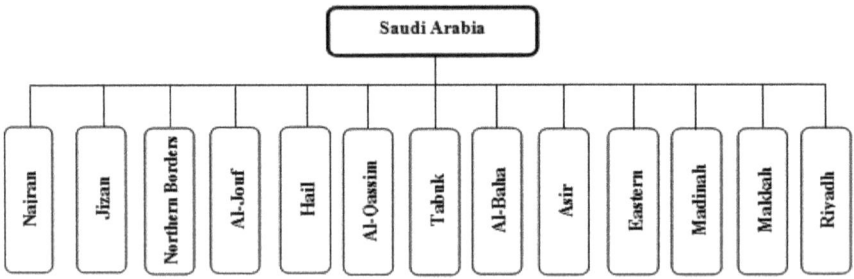

Fig. 39.3 The provincial capitals. *Source*: Saudi Embassy (2016a)

13 provinces (Saudi Embassy, 2016a). Below in Fig. 39.2 is given the map of KSA showing the 13 provinces (their capital cities are listed in Fig. 39.3).

The MOJ has to deal with the operations and issues pertaining to all 13 provinces which ultimately increases the demand to implement KM techniques across the ministry which will also extract the best out of individuals working in the ministry. Moreover, the MOJ also possesses a media centre that operates frequently to issue press releases and news related to the ministry. Therefore, the outlook for the MOJ makes it clear that KM is needed by this ministry.

Sharia courts are the building blocks of the court system in KSA (Al-Farsy, 2009). This structure of the MOJ simplifies the ways for the people of KSA to choose regarding their cases. The department of General Directorate of Training and Scholarship is another vital element of the MOJ's structure because it develops the individuals working in the MOJ. Within the MOJ structure, the Budgetary department is another key component which has been a centre of controversy in recent years. The Control department is another component operating under the

MOJ; i.e. the agency documentation affairs is a core component of the MOJ within which the control department works as a sub-component (i.e. as a control management agency). This department comes under the provision and authority of the Public Administration for Notaries Affairs. This sub-department is also referred to as the Deputy Ministry for Documentation which signifies the importance of this component for the MOJ. This sub-department has also been connected with the General Administration of inquiries and studies. A range of tasks are performed by this department such as follow-up attendance through a request of daily or monthly leave and attendance data; i.e. virtue notaries in writing (Ministry of Justice, 2016c). This sub-department also prepares and studies essential reports related to these activities. The necessary reports are then prepared after investigation with notaries (Ministry of Justice, 2016c).

Public Administration for Research is one of the 25 departments that function within the MOJ. This department tends to draw the established principles by the Court of Cassation (COC) in its principles or judgments developed by the Supreme Judicial Council. This department also prepares specific provisions of the publishing groups along with research preparation and they do this on the formal request of the Department of Justice.

Another task that this department performs is giving responses and answers to the judges' inquiries (Ministry of Justice, 2016d). The Department of Attorney is another important component of the MOJ which performs diverse activities on a regular basis. Working on the development and follow-up of the profession is one prime task that this department performs along with managing the lawyers' disciplinary committee. This department also gathers recruit advisers which are formal requests from outside the kingdom. An important role performed by this department is the maintenance of close ties with international, regional and local organisations pertaining to the legal profession. The studies conducted by this department tend to initiate amendments and regulations pertaining to the legal system and profession (Ministry of Justice, 2016e).

Challenges for KM in the Public Sector

KM is increasingly significant for the government as they deal with upcoming challenges faced by the KM economy. These challenges are addressed in the following phases (OECD, 2003):

1. Knowledge has become a basic determinant of intensity and competitiveness in the public sector. Administration conveyance and policymaking are the fundamental errands for government. In an information economy, governments are progressively confronting competition in these areas at both the national and international level. For example, at the global level, non-government organisations and government organisations are in competition with remote organisations conveying comparable administration (OECD, 2003). Exploration establishments compete to draw in the best researchers and subsidies, while universities are progressively in rivalry to attract the most investment from abroad, the best students,

the best professors and the best educators. At the national level, rivalry among public bodies has been additionally expanded after the decentralisation forms. In the public sector, products and capital are not as paramount as in the private sector but knowledge seems to be. Knowledge is a vital component of rivalry and is a focal asset of the administration. Successful working of government rests on viable procurement and the spread of knowledge.

2. Private organisations manufacture goods and offer services that increasingly provide intangible capital, competing directly with the public sector in order to deliver the goods and provision of services such as security, science, education and knowledge. For example, as stated by the OECD (2002), through coaching and distance learning of courses and information on the internet, private organisations are enhancing the influence of training for common citizens and are enhancing public education as well; a service which was conventionally offered by the public sector. Because knowledge-oriented private organisations are meeting more customer demands and receiving more customisation, these organisations would also expect comparable advantages from the public sector.

3. Retirement of civil servants and successive exchange of knowledge specialists across government divisions additionally present difficulties for the maintenance of information and safeguarding of institutional memory and the preparation of new staff. There is likewise increasing competition for talent with a capacity to impart learning.

KM Challenges for the Ministry of Justice in the Kingdom of Saudi Arabia

The Saudi MOJ is in charge of the operation of 154 notary public offices, 272 courts and 13 regulatory branches. Approximately 1600 judges are among the total staff of 23,000 and handle around 1.3 million cases in 1000 listening rooms yearly. The ministry has generally confronted difficulties in transforming huge quantities of cases rapidly, alongside issues such as checking IDs and providing administration in remote areas. These issues were exacerbated by non-existent or outdated system links in a few areas. Server centres had a tendency to serve only in regional or provincial business offices, hampering institutionalised administration conveyance. Finally, the ministry confronted operational expenses connected with utilising diverse innovations as a part of distinct areas (Cisco, 2013).

Cultural Issues

Dehghani and Ramsin (2015) reflected that successful execution of KM in organisations poses the biggest challenge of cultural differences and compatibility. How individuals relate with each other and the dynamics of the MOJ culture as an organisation can be a serious challenge for the MOJ while implementing KM because KM requires the presence of a positive and shared culture.

To ensure that KM fits comfortably with the national cultural ideals, it needs to be emphasised that KM involves all parties; it is representative of collectivism, not individualism and as such should be fully acceptable to the citizens of KSA.

Other cultural considerations associated with KM in the MOJ could be connected to attitudes to overseas workers and to women but these must be resolved internally in a way that does not offend Sharia law or the constitution and emphasises that knowledge held by *any* individual is of value to the MOJ and must be utilised to its best extent, using a Knowledge Map (KMap) of the MOJ as a starting point.

Communication Issues

Effective KM results can be achieved by introducing, improving and increasing two-way communication, which is essential in organisations (Tıngoy & Kurt, 2009). Therefore, developing and maintaining effective communication throughout the MOJ at all levels can be a serious challenge for the MOJ. This has so far not been fully addressed by the MOJ, although it is an on-going project. It is essential for the development of KM because knowledge held but not shared or used is knowledge wasted (Taylor, 2013). Awareness of the importance of each individual's knowledge is growing (Girard & McIntyre, 2010) and as it does, sharing and disseminating that knowledge is increasing in importance (Hau, Kim, Lee, & Kim, 2013). As shown above, the MOJ has its own department responsible for the training and advancement of members of the MOJ staff (the General Directorate of Training and Scholarship) and this directorate needs to ensure that 'effective communication' is a core subject for trainees.

Lack of Competencies

Proper implementation of KM requires the organisation to possess an aware and skilled workforce who can fit into the KM culture and in this regard managerial competency is of the utmost importance (Dewhurst, Hancock, & Ellsworth, 2013). Therefore, the MOJ can face a shortage of effective and competent managers who are capable of handling and managing KM activities within the MOJ. This is another area in which the training directorate needs to take direct action. The directorate can ensure that every member of staff at the MOJ has at least a basic grounding in the required competencies and that managers are not appointed unless they are competent in every aspect. This is an area the MOJ needs to follow the practices of the private sector and learn from the major companies that already utilise KM effectively and efficiently.

Lack of Leadership for KM

Effective KM cannot be ensured on a long-term basis in organisations if leadership support and participative leadership is unavailable for organisations (Chandrasegaran et al., 2013). Therefore, for the MOJ a lack of effective and proactive leadership can also appear as a challenge in the long-run. Leadership training is an essential key to effective KM (Hmshari, 2013) because unless the management display KM characteristics, the rest of the staff will not do so. If any organisation, public or private, has a shortage of effective and successful leaders, it will not be prosperous or worthwhile. Cultivating leadership in management trainees must be a core element of the programme for the training directorate in the same way that it is regarded as essential in the private sector.

Lack of Employee Engagement and Commitment

A positive and high level of employee engagement and commitment tends to enhance the extent of benefits that organisations can derive from KM activities (Chandrasegaran et al., 2013). A lack of engaged and committed individuals can be a serious matter of concern for the MOJ in Saudi organisational culture. In fact, this is yet another area in which the training directorate needs to take action to ensure that the staff members are valued as Knowledge Workers (KW) (Chu, Krishna Kumar, & Khosla, 2010). This is also closely related to staff retention; not necessarily a problem for the MOJ but nevertheless, the more valued a member of staff feels, the more likely they are to remain in the employment of the ministry.

Lack of Awareness of Knowledge Assets

Where KM should reside holds crucial importance for longevity and effectiveness (Groff & Jones, 2012). For the MOJ, it will be a major challenge for deciding and knowing where KM should reside because this will directly affect the KM initiative within the MOJ.

This is the main reason that it is essential to carry out a knowledge audit and draw up a KMap. The KMap is an essential tool for the knowledge manager because it allows the manager to categorically know what knowledge is where. This allows the manager to utilise retiring staff to pass on their specific knowledge to the new intake so that their knowledge is not permanently lost when they reach retirement (Hau et al., 2013).

Keeping Up with Technology Changes

The awareness, presence and utilisation of technology tools are another major challenge that organisations face during KM activities (Lopez, Peon, & Ordás, 2009). This is because both effectiveness and rapidness are required in KM initiatives and it will be difficult for the MOJ to identify quick and responsive KM technology-based tools for enhancing the end results of KM for the MOJ.

In addition, the MOJ must carefully choose the best technology for their specific needs (Kingston, 2010). There are several different approaches to sharing knowledge and each requires different technological hardware. Thus it is essential to plan both aspects when trying to keep up with technology; it is also necessary for the courts to ensure that any new systems remain compatible with the existing or legacy IT systems in order to preserve older records and knowledge.

Business Needs

Since 1970, the MOJ in KSA has been in charge of enhancing the organisation of a boundless arrangement of courts and judges in a country the size of Western Europe (Library of Congress, 2006). Innovation is presently assuming an expanding part in institutionalising the business procedures of legitimate organisations and enhancing the business discernment, business information (BI) data accessible to judges and legal officials. Modernisation of the organisation of the courts and legal framework had the full support of King Abdullah and will continue under the rule of King Salman. His administration has distributed US$1.9 billion (Sar7 billion) to a reconstructing and updating project covering 478 legal offices (Stensile, 2012).

The undertaking involves making an IT framework at all court structures and public accountant offices in the kingdom. According to the Chief Information Officer at the MOJ, Mr. Majid Ibrahim Al-Adwan, they are working towards updating 400 new courthouses and public accountant offices. The objective is to modernise work reforms. An expanding number of the courts in the kingdom are currently joined with online services and brought together in the framework so that they can be checked and monitored through it (Microsoft, 2012; Wienroth, Morling, & Williams, 2014).

The courts' organisation framework in KSA in recent years has created a system utilising Oracle running on physical servers. Reacting to the administration's approaches to the modernisation of business courses of action, the MOJ needed to further create and modernise its administrations through a heterogeneous environment including an alternate major vendor. In particular, it is expected to create a BI framework for courts and other legitimate administrations with open access for more substantial openness and a collaborative environment for public accountants. It additionally expects to redesign the IT infrastructure, including working frameworks and informing arrangements (Microsoft, 2012; Wienroth et al., 2014).

Driving Factors in the Public Sector

Driving factors in the public sector note that the sharing of knowledge is not a natural phenomenon in the corporate sector. It requires a psychological model transformation. A culture of knowledge sharing has to be formed to transform the behaviours and attitudes of individuals working in the organisation as well as to cut down barriers (Bolisani & Handzic, 2014). The suggested structure recommends the following to generate the required transformation:

1. Increase awareness of the advantages of KM. Staff and managers are supposed to be well informed about the changes and benefits that KM can offer them as well as their organisation. Although they feel and acknowledge the power of knowledge, they have to believe in the power of sharing knowledge (Bolisani & Handzic, 2014).
2. Increase the trend of knowledge sharing by building an environment of trust because when people know one another they are more inclined to share knowledge. More knowledge is shared by people if they are more trusting.
3. As an ideal, a leader should encourage knowledge sharing. A champion is required for KM implementation.

The MOJ should establish a formal system for rewards and recognition to foster knowledge sharing. Workers have to be formally rewarded and recognised, not just for knowledge sharing with others but also for their willingness to utilise the knowledge shared by others (Kim, Lee, Chun, & Benbasat, 2014).

It is very important for organisations to create and foster communities of practice (COPs). COPs are organisational centres of knowledge in which individual groups having similar job-related duties but do not participate in an officially established work team generating, disseminating and practising knowledge (Bi & Jiang, 2012). COPs can have a wider significance than simply sharing implied knowledge. These can be productive in the activities of the public sector, either on a specific or generic basis. Organisations need to foster COPs by ensuring the availability of resources and also through permitting members the chance to participate in order to develop and sustain COPs (Bi & Jiang, 2012).

Conclusion

When researching KM and its application within the MOJ in KSA, the importance of this relatively new approach has been clearly demonstrated. There are several key points that have been concluded from the above discussion such as the importance of cultural, technological and communication challenges for effective KM; i.e. both in the specific context of the MOJ and public sector organisations in general. Currently, government as well as non-government organisations throughout the world are facing a delay due to which some hurdles arise in KM. Exploitation of knowledge in services can be enhanced through KM which is integrated with their national systems, dogmas, rulings and strategies. However, hurdles and trials in KM agendas differ according to the situation of the respective country. Some factors can influence and enhance the working environment of a country. The educational and cultural levels of any society, telecommunications infrastructure, technology, research and development, science and technology strategies are some of these key factors that can influence the working environment at large. It is concluded that managing knowledge is a complex process because as they are usually linked to long-term time horizons, a high level of uncertainty, and impacts that are often difficult to quantify. If public sector organisations do not fully comprehend what drives the need for managing knowledge, they may fall into the trap of creating an inefficient strategy and operational plans. It should be noted that for some public sector organisations the key drivers may vary.

To gain sustainable competitive advantage, it is necessary for decision makers to recognise and use a blend of ICT (Information and Communications Technology) and non-ICT based KM techniques and technologies. It is advisable to use conventional, simple, low cost and easy to use with minimum training needs KM techniques and technologies.

References

Ahmed, Z. (2011). *Barriers to knowledge management in Saudi Arabia*. Dissertation, The Faculty of The School of Engineering and Applied Science, The George Washington University.

Al-Farsy, F. (2009). *Modernity and tradition: The Saudi equation*. New York: Routledge and Taylor & Francis.

Bi, P., & Jiang, W. (2012). Research on application of knowledge management in public sectors. *Information engineering and applications* (pp. 506–513), Lecture Notes in Electrical Engineering, Vol. 154.

Bolisani, E., & Handzic, M. (2014). *Advances in knowledge management: Celebrating twenty years of research*. London: Springer.

Cardoso, L., Meireles, A., & Ferreira Peralta, C. (2012). Knowledge management and its critical factors in social economy organizations. *Journal of Knowledge Management, 16*(2), 267–284.

Chandrasegaran, S. K., Ramani, K., Sriram, R. D., Horváth, I., Bernard, A., Harik, R. F., et al. (2013). The evolution, challenges, and future of knowledge representation in product design systems. *Computer-Aided Design, 45*(2), 204–228.

Chaudhary, S. (2014). Leveraging personal networks to support knowledge management in a public sector organisation in Kuwait. *Libri, 64*(4), 341–349.

Chu, M.-T., Krishna Kumar, P., & Khosla, R. (2010). Profiling knowledge workers for communities of practice: A strategic alternative perspective. *The International Conference on Data and Knowledge Engineering*.

Cisco. (2013). Saudi MOJ: Ministry of Justice Modernizes Customer Technology Platform [Online]. http://www.cisco.com/c/dam/en/us/solutions/collateral/data-center-virtualization/saudi_moj_v5cs.pdf. Accessed 27 Jan 2016.

De Angelis, C. T. (2013). A knowledge management and organizational intelligence model for public administration. *International Journal of Public Administration, 36*(11), 807–819.

Dehghani, R., & Ramsin, R. (2015). Methodologies for developing knowledge management systems: An evaluation framework. *Journal of Knowledge Management, 19*(4), 682–710.

Dewhurst, M., Hancock, B., & Ellsworth, D. (2013). *Redesigning knowledge work*. Brighton, MA: Harvard Business School Publishing.

Gill, J., & Johnson, P. (2010). *Research methods for managers* (4th ed.). London: Paul Chapman Publishing.

Girard, J., & McIntyre, S. (2010). Knowledge management modelling in public sector organisations: A case study. *International Journal of Public Sector Management, 23*(1), 71–77.

Groff, T. R., & Jones, T. P. (2012). *Introduction to knowledge management.* Amsterdam: Butterworth Heinemann.

Hau, Y. S., Kim, B., Lee, H., & Kim, Y. G. (2013). The effects of individual motivations and social capital on employees' tacit and explicit knowledge sharing intentions. *International Journal of Information Management, 33*(2), 356–366.

Hmshari, A. O. (2013). *Knowledge management the way to excellence and leadership.* Amman: Dar Al Safa for Publishing and Distribution.

Jain, A. K., & Jeppesen, H. J. (2013). Knowledge management practices in a public sector organisation: The role of leaders' cognitive styles. *Journal of Knowledge Management, 17*(3), 347–362.

Kim, T. H., Lee, J. N., Chun, J. U., & Benbasat, I. (2014). Understanding the effect of knowledge management strategies on knowledge management performance: A contingency perspective. *Information and Management, 51*(4), 398–416.

Kingston, J. (2010). Choosing a knowledge dissemination approach. *Knowledge and Management Process, 16*(3), 167–170.

Krstić, B., & Stanišić, T. (2013). The influence of knowledge economy development on competitiveness of southeastern Europe countries. *Industrija, 41*(2), 151–167.

Library of Congress (2006). Profile: Saudi Arabia [Online]. http://lcweb2.loc.gov/frd/cs/profiles/Saudi_Arabia.pdf. Accessed 27 Jan 2016.

Lopez, P., Peon, P., & Ordás, C. (2009). *Information technology as an enabler of knowledge management: An empirical analysis.* New York, NY: Springer Science Business Media, LLC.

Microsoft. (2012). Saudi Ministry Modernizes Administration with Data Warehouse Solution [Online]. https://customers.microsoft.com/Pages/CustomerStory.aspx?recid=15435. Accessed 27 Jan 2016.

Ministry of Justice. (2016a). Home [Online]. https://www.moj.gov.sa/ar/Ministry/Departments/Pages/default.aspx. Accessed 27 Jan 2016.

Ministry of Justice. (2016b). Organisational structure [Online]. https://www.moj.gov.sa/ar/Ministry/Pages/OrganizationalStructure.aspx. Accessed 27 Jan 2016.

Ministry of Justice. (2016c). Control department [Online]. https://www.moj.gov.sa/ar/Ministry/Notary/Pages/default.aspx. Accessed 27 Jan 2016.

Ministry of Justice. (2016d). Public Administration Research [Online]. https://www.moj.gov.sa/ar/Ministry/Departments/Pages/ReserchDept.aspx. Accessed 27 Jan 2016.

Ministry of Justice (2016e). Attorneys [Online]. https://www.moj.gov.sa/ar/Ministry/Departments/Mohammah/Pages/default.aspx. Accessed 27 Jan 2016.

OECD. (2002). Knowledge Management Project [Online]. http://www.oecd.org/denmark/2756535.pdf. Accessed 27 Jan 2016.

OECD. (2003). Knowledge Management in government [Online]. http://www.oecd.org/gov/budgeting/43495554.pdf. Accessed 27 Jan 2016.

Salwa, A. (2010). *Strategic knowledge management system in public sector in Saudi Arabia: An adaptation of the Balanced Scorecard.* PhD thesis, University of Portsmouth.

Saudi Embassy. (2016a). Provincial System [Online]. https://www.saudiembassy.net/about/country-information/government/provincial_system.aspx. Accessed 27 Jan 2016.

Saudi Embassy. (2016b). Map of provinces [Online]. http://www.saudiembassy.net/about/country-information/map_of_provinces.aspx. Accessed 27 Jan 2016.

Stensile, S. (2012). *Regime stability in Saudi Arabia: The challenge of succession.* New York: Routledge.

Stricker, U. (2014). *Knowledge management practice in organisations: The view from inside.* Hershey, PA: IGI Global.

Tambyrajah, A., & Al-Shawabkeh, A. (2009). Developing performance indicators for knowledge management. *Proceeding of the Eighth European Conference on Knowledge Management*, Barcelona, pp. 972–981.

Taylor, G. (2013). Implementing and maintaining a knowledge sharing culture via knowledge management teams: A shared leadership approach. *Journal of Organisational Culture Communications & Conflict, 17*(1), 69–91.

Tıngoy, O., & Kurt, E. (2009). Communication in knowledge management practices: A survey from Turkey. *Problems and Perspectives in Management, 7*(2), 46–50.

UNDP. (2010). Saudi Arabia [Online]. Available at: http://web.undp.org/evaluation/documents/thematic/cd/Saudi-Arabia.pdf. Accessed 27 Jan 2016.

Wienroth, M., Morling, N., & Williams, R. (2014). Technological innovations in forensic genetics: Social, legal and ethical aspects. *Recent Advances in DNA & Gene Sequences (Formerly Recent Patents on DNA & Gene Sequences), 8*(2), 98–103.

Yahya, K., & Farah, S. (2009). *Management in public sector: Global and regional comparison.* The Institute of Public Administration Conference for Administrative Development, Riyadh.

Chapter 40
Leadership Types in the Middle Eastern Context

Wael S. Zaraket and Ali H. Halawi

Abstract Leadership has undergone enormous development over the past 30 years. Effective leadership carries direct emphasis on productivity, loyalty, and talent management. This study depicts the notion of the current leadership practices in the Arab world, and what solutions should exist to such practices. This study will delineate the relation between Middle East culture and the leadership style practices. In addition, this study will represent the personality types/leadership styles depicted in the pictures of animals.

Keywords Leadership • Transformational leadership • Transitional leadership • Authentic leadership • Path-goal leadership • Personality types/leadership

Introduction

Despite the abundance of publications on leadership from the human and business perspectives, the understanding of leadership has undergone enormous development over the past 30 years. In turbulent economic and political environments accentuated by corporate scandals, economic recessions, and Arab national coup d'états, people feel apprehensive about and demanding for genuine political, social, and business leadership.

In corporate environments, managers and employees have become captivated by the idea of leadership. Interest in leadership can be considered a framework of voluminous studies and research by scholars and practitioners. Therefore, corporations continually seek to recruit, hire, and train new employees with leadership aptitudes because of their ability to enrich their organizations and help others in the organization attain their professional and personal goals.

W.S. Zaraket (✉)
American University of Science and Technology, P.O. Box 16-6452, Beirut, Lebanon
e-mail: wzaraket@aust.edu.lb

A.H. Halawi
Lebanese International University, P.O. Box 146404, Beirut, Lebanon
e-mail: ali.halawi@liu.edu.lb

© Springer International Publishing Switzerland 2017   461
R. Benlamri, M. Sparer (eds.), *Leadership, Innovation and Entrepreneurship as Driving Forces of the Global Economy*, Springer Proceedings in Business and Economics, DOI 10.1007/978-3-319-43434-6_40

Scholars and practitioners of the business environment now recognize the word "Leadership" as jargon that can have different meanings for different people; these meanings are interrelated to managerial theorists. Leadership is defined as a process whereby one person influences a group of individuals to achieve a common goal (Northouse, 2007). This definition and many others covering the notion of leadership indicate that leadership is a process that seeks to influence others within a group for the sake of attaining a goal. Leadership is therefore described as a process whereby the leader affects and is affected by followers. Thus, the focal point of such a definition is that the reciprocal relation between leaders and followers can be either beneficial or detrimental.

As a result, leadership is concerned with the explicit perception of common goals in groups, and accentuates the idea that leaders and followers have a mutual purpose (Rost, 1991). Moreover, Jago (1982) has inferred that leadership is a process of interaction between leaders and followers and, therefore, can be learned.

Literature Review

Leadership and Management

Effective leadership and management are critical requirements for the prosperity of a corporation, where they have a combined influence on subordinates and on accomplishing corporate goals. According to Kotter (1990), the function of management is to impose order and consistency in the organization, whereas the duty of leadership is to bring about change to achieve goals. The study of management emerged at the dawn of the twentieth century with the materialization of our industrialized economy, and was intended to curtail chaos in organizations in order to make them more efficient and effective, while leadership produced constructive change.

Although there exist clear differences between management and leadership, the two terms are interrelated. When managers are playing their role in influencing subordinates to meet their goals, then they are also involved in leadership. On the other hand, when leaders use the functions of management, then they are involved in management. In any corporation, therefore, the two roles can collide under the same title, task, or duty (Zaleznik, 1977).

An organization imposing a pattern of management that excludes leadership collaboration will foster a classical bureaucracy, a situation that will lead to organizational decadence. Hence, the degree of innovation in an organization depends on the reciprocal blending of leadership, which is concerned with the process of developing mutual purposes and management, which is directed towards coordinating activities in order to get the job done (Rost, 1991).

Leadership in the Arab World

During the past 30 years, the corporate sector across the Arab world (Middle East and North Africa: *MENA*) has enjoyed enormous development. A large number of retailing conglomerates in the Arab world have attained regional and global expansion, but few of them are ever interested in strategic human resource management and strong leadership. The reluctance to focus on managerial and leadership issues and the failure to affiliate the corporation's strategic goals with the two burgeoning human resource and leadership majors is a dilemma to most Arab organizations.

This paper will focus on leadership approach and employee productivity for corporate Arab employees, and discuss how the duties of Arab CEOs and managers are so critical that they should implement their leadership skills to enhance their employees' organizational commitment and devotion to their institution (Harshbarger, 1989). Over the past 30 years, the corporate sector in the Arab world has experienced massive growth and market penetration; nevertheless, a dilemma emerged on the surface: Are the employees sufficiently committed to productivity in the organizations they work in?

Firms confirm that employees are their major asset and should be considered an endowment from the labor market to the firm. The prosperity of an organization depends on having a solid and secure talented workforce, which can add value to the organization's operations and structure. To conquer these priorities, therefore, Western organizations have redefined the role of an effective human resource management strategy. Human resource management functions in the business operations have ebbed and flowed during the 1960s and 1970s, when the personnel departments in organizations were often viewed as the "health and happiness" crews (Decenzo & Robbins, 2010) specialized in planning picnics, scheduling vacations, enrolling workers for health care coverage, and planning retirement parties. The human resource strategy today is to attract, train, develop, and retain employees who are suited to a business environment that aims to achieve productivity, labor proficiency, job satisfaction, and job commitment.

Western and Arab business sectors operating in different fields share common interests such as retail marketing, finance, and accounting. Nevertheless, the Western practices in human resource have expanded and advanced, while the Arab management practices are stagnant in their infant stages. To elaborate on this point, we will explore developments in the most powerful economies in the MENA region—the Gulf Council Countries (GCC). The population of the GCC has increased more than ninefold during the past 60 years—from 4 million in 1950 to 46 million in 2011 (GCC, 2011)—which constitutes one of the highest population growths in the world. This growth has been caused not by natural escalation of the indigenous people of the Arab gulf states, but by the influx of expatriates. More than 12 million foreign workers are found in the GCC, and in UAE alone, 90 % of the workforce in 2006 was foreign (IMF, 2011). The difference between workforce management decisions in the Arab states and Western Europe is that in the Arab gulf states, foreign workers are hired both in high-status jobs as professional employees and in low-status jobs, while in Western Europe, foreign workers are acquired mainly for low-status jobs (Chart 40.1).

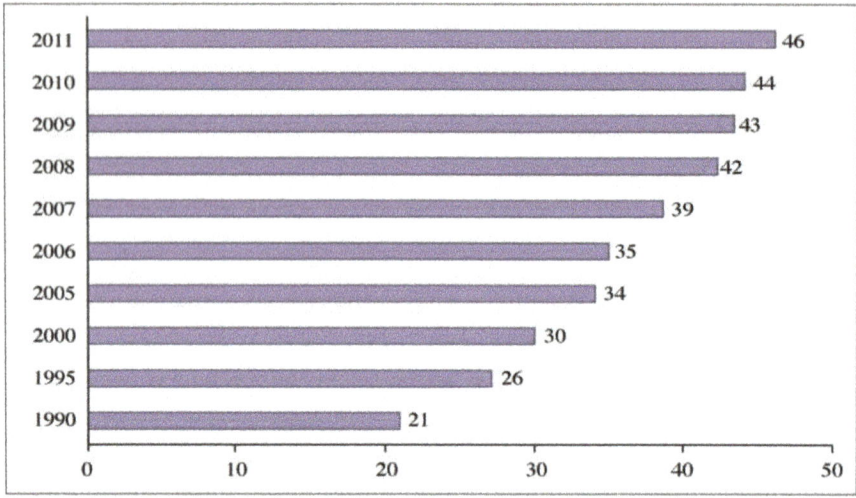

Source: Statistical Gulf Council Countries Data Base

Chart 40.1 GCC population. *Source*: Statistical Gulf Council Countries Data Base

The Arab leaders working in the GCC should realize that this proliferation of expatriates in their countries can be used as competitive advantage for GCC econo-mies. Treating expatriates as purely labor and enacting laws to minimize the num-ber of expatriate employees such as Saudization and Emartization will lead to declining expatriate productivity and efficiency. The reason expatriates will lose interest and become inefficient workers is that they feel their job security is under threat and believe that they will hit the glass ceiling and never hold leadership titles, which are reserved for nationals and protected by government legislation. Expatriates working in the Arab gulf will also feel demotivated by fear of losing their jobs and their pensions.

The Arab human resource operation's threshold should be to mitigate the loss of human assets, whether the employees are nationals or expatriates. The goal of Arab business leaders is to sustain the employees' commitment and loyalty to the organi-zation, and to achieve this, they need to enrich their employees' thorough motiva-tion and career development plans.

Enhancing the Leadership Skills

Managers with viable prerogative do not always become the leader in a particular setting, and in fact, managers with limited knowledge preclude the success of stra-tegic goals. Consequently, there is a demand for managers who promise emergent leadership and who urge others to believe in the organization's strategic goals and trust the manager's ability to achieve such goals (Fisher, 1974). What is missing in the Arab corporations, therefore, is the capacity of CEOs and human resource managers to disseminate the transformational leadership concept with their employees; such a process needs to be preserved through applying interpersonal skills and creating cooperate relationships with others.

Organizational hierarchy shows that two prevalent forms of authority exist inside corporations: position power and personal power. The inevitable influence of having higher status than others is known as position power, which is widely practiced in Arab countries; it is explicit for the corporations' employees' low future orientation and uncertainty avoidance. Arab managers and employees have the same dilemma of preserving status and directive leadership style (Northouse, 2013).

Conversely, Kotter (1990) abridged the notion of personal power as the leader-influential capacity seen by followers as likable, knowledgeable, and a role model. Hence, the perception of personal power supporting the leadership style can foster organizational success. This type of organized leadership and managerial structure is not practiced in Arab corporations, because of the prevalence of family-owned businesses with few key decision-makers and limited opportunity for organizational transparency, global market penetration, and employee engagement.

This is illustrated by Herfy, for example, the fast-food burger chain in Saudi Arabia. Established in 1981 (Herfy, 2010), the company employs more than 2000 employees in more than 190 locations across Saudi Arabia, and is supported by great consumer demand for fast food. However, Herfy's assertiveness in repudiating the unassailable opportunity of the Arab region demand for fast food is strongly recommended by middle-level managers in order to expand and start operating regionally based on the managers' market awareness and consumers' taste. Moreover, Herfy's lack of transparency in organizational strategic goals and the top decision process damages employees' motivation and organizational commitment. Herfy is an example of an Arab corporation where only directive leadership is implemented and where managerial two-way communication process with followers is neglected.

A supportive leadership style does not work well with coercive leadership. Managers who influence others to act against their will and are interested in their own goals rather than in a common goal show symptom of coercive leadership. Arab business leaders and executives should strive to build organizational goals and commitment doctrine inside the company; the new generation of corporate Arab leaders must foster charismatic leadership (Bass, 1990) and transformational leadership to avoid losing employees or being diverted from achieving organizational goals. The Arab corporate sector needs the aforementioned leadership styles so as to implement change and make employees believe in the organizational long-term and short-term strategic goals.

The aim of Arab organizations to enhance team leadership has not been fully realized. Quality teams and continuous improvement should foster a culture of learning and the sharing of knowledge. Arab companies should therefore embrace a learning culture of prevalent team leadership. This managerial process, urging Arab managers with prerogative duties, should be nurtured by top management in order to ensure group effectiveness and the meeting of organizational goals. Hence, team leaders as the middle managers need to master effective communication skills and adapt a mental model of the situation in which the managers can assess both the environmental surroundings of the company and the current contagious issue.

Arab executives and decision-makers should encourage human resource managers and employees to act as agents of continual transformation. The role of the human resource professionals has evolved into developing organizational strategic plans. Arab human resource professionals and consultants should apply Western human resource policies to change many of their obsolete practices and policies so that they become more successful with the goals and challenges facing their organizations. Managers of Arab corporations should therefore adapt a strategy through which they can monitor group dynamics and take actions to ensure team effectiveness.

Arab companies must maintain a strategy to implement a transformational leadership plan rather than the classical transactional leadership strategy. The pervasive transactional leadership style focuses on a reciprocal exchange between the leader and the follower, such as incentives and promotion for outstanding performance. Nevertheless, Arab corporations should recognize the concept of transformational leadership, which emphasizes how followers reach their fullest potential affiliated with organizational strategic goals. In summary, MENA managers should delineate effective Strategic Human Resource Managers (SHRM) to allay obsolete leadership practices in order to initiate organizational development based on team leadership, learning, knowledgeable workers, and committed and motivated employees.

Taking Action

The focal point is to inaugurate, train, and find transformational leaders who can groom employees to understand the importance and value of organizational goals. Subordinates set their career goals from the early stages of joining a company. Thus, as transformational leaders, Arab managers should use their motivation and intellectual stimulation to synergize the employees' own self-interest with organizational goals.

A study by the American Society for Training and Development of more than 500 US based companies found that those that invested the most in training and development, such as in leadership, had a shareholder return that was 86 % higher than that of companies in the bottom half (Noe, 2010). Arab firms must allay the fears of their expatriate and local middle-level managers, and strongly encourage their development. High managerial positions within a firm must realize that employees need to be actively engaged in order to achieve success Organizational Citizenship Behavior (OCB), and all activities should be influenced by human resource management practices. Hence, Arab human resource practitioners must attract, retain, develop, and motivate their skilled mid-level managers, who can be groomed for leadership positions within the strategic decision hierarchy.

Mid-level managers and well-performing bottom-of-the-line employees are an indispensable source of information on market trends and consumers taste; therefore, the performance of these employees must be merited by the top management through employee engagement. Leadership training for precedence positions can create a learning culture where the experience of these employees can be communicated to others.

There are many pitfalls on the road to success; theorists and books attest that in today's business environment the only constant is change, which can be seen in products, organization development, and much more. Therefore, Arab companies should adapt to a changing environment where all bottom-line employees—such as sales representatives, middle line managers—as well as executives embrace a culture of learning, embarking on a pattern of a path-goal theory (House, 1996). With this imposed pattern, it is clear that Arab organizations can embrace a culture of lifelong learning, requiring all employees to continually acquire and share knowledge through path-goal leadership (House, 1971).

The inevitable question is why Arab companies should disseminate a culture of learning in a labor market where most of the employees are expatriates. To answer this question, we have to accentuate the concept of knowledge worker and talent management. Arab companies should place emphasis on attracting, developing, and retaining knowledge workers to ensure that the company succeeds. Therefore, the business environment requires knowledge workers who can contribute to the company and their colleagues through their knowledge and work experience. Hence, the duty of management is to enhance the sharing of knowledge, with no place for an individual or team to hoard information and knowledge.

Both management and knowledge workers share responsibility in creating an environment where the company can be a place to develop managerial talent with leadership skills. The purpose of such managerial philosophy is to support the employees through training, continuous learning, talent management, and employee engagement. Consequently, the company can leverage intangible assets, as the company's competitive advantage is hard to duplicate or imitate.

Arab corporations should be grooming leaders who can lead with integrity and invest their competency in the organization. The new era of Arab corporate leaders should motivate employees to offer superior customer service and ensure long-term value for stakeholders. Consequently, the previous discussion reflects the idiosyncrasies of an authentic leader (Gardner & Avolio, 2005), who nurture the enlargement of authentic qualities in their followers. In consequence, Source: Statistical Gulf Council Countries Data Base these national and expatriate followers' authenticity will be reflected in their performance and in their commitment to organizational goals.

Leaders can play a critical role in sharing their life story and career path of success with their followers. To be recognized as an authentic leader with a symbolic figure takes shrewdness and versatility from the managers and leaders to sustain their image in the eyes of their followers and achieve their mutual goal (Shamir & Eilam, 2005).

Middle East Globe's Cluster

House et al. delineate the strongest study in the area of culture and leadership. Published in 800 pages, the GLOBE study, named for the Global Leadership and Organizational Behavior Effectiveness and covering 63 societies, offers a direct description of the relation between culture and leader. The principal objective of the GLOBE project is to disseminate the influence of culture on leadership behavior, using quantitative methods of research covering 17,000 managers in more than 950 organizations around the world.

GLOBE output studies described nine cultural dimensions: power distance, institutional collectivism, in-group collectivism, uncertainty avoidance, assertiveness, future orientation, performance orientation, human orientation, and gender egalitarianism. The 62 countries studied by GLOBE researchers have been divided into ten regional clusters based on geography, religion, and historical background (Fig. 40.1); one of these clusters is the Middle East cluster, which will be discussed in this paper.

Through the GLOBE studies, Table 40.1 sensitizes the characteristics of each regional cluster and how each cluster matches each of the nine cultural dimensions. As we see from Table 40.1 that the Middle East region consisting of Morocco,

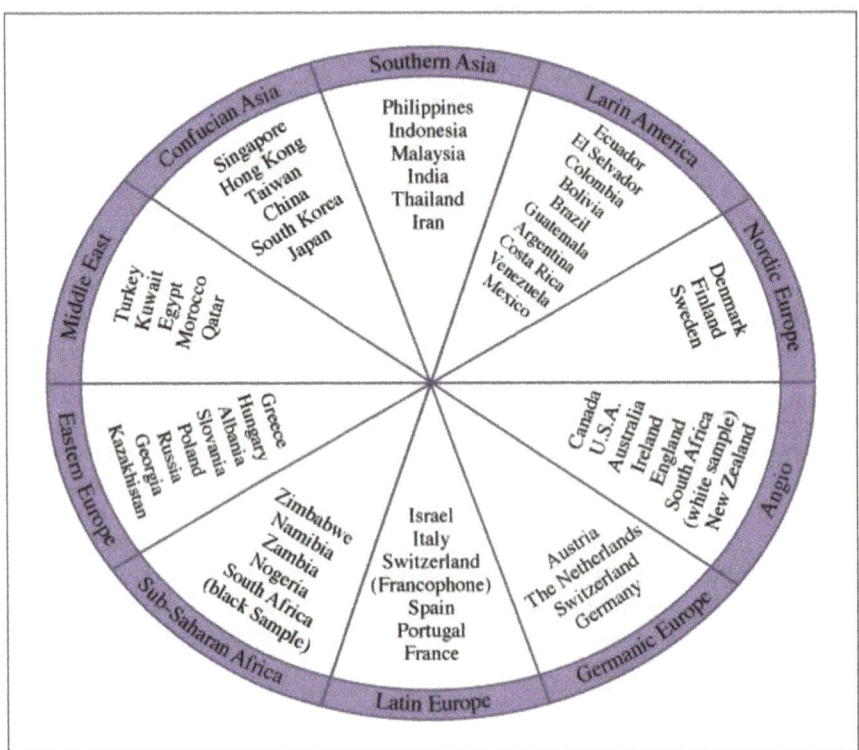

Source: Adapted from House et al. Culture, Leadership, and Organization: The Globe Study of 62 Societies

Fig. 40.1 Country clusters according to the Global Leadership and Organizational Behavior Effectiveness (GLOBE). *Source*: Adapted from House et al. Culture, Leadership, and Organization: The GLOBE Study of 62 Societies

Table 40.1   Cultural clusters classified on cultural dimension

Cultural dimension	High-score clusters	Low-score clusters
Assertiveness orientation	Eastern Europe	Nordic Europe
	Germanic Europe	
Future orientation	Germanic Europe	Eastern Europe
	Nordic Europe	Latin America
		Middle East
Gender egalitarianism	Eastern Europe	Middle East
	Nordic Europe	
Humane orientation	Southern Asia	Germanic Europe
	Sub-Saharan Africa	Latin Europe
In-group collectivism	Confucian Asia	Anglo
	Eastern Europe	Germanic Europe
	Latin America	Nordic Europe
	Middle East	
	Southern Asia	
Institutional collectivism	Nordic Europe	Germanic Europe
	Confucian Asia	Latin America
		Latin Europe
Performance orientation	Anglo	Eastern Europe
	Confucian Asia	Latin America
	Germanic Europe	
Power distance	No clusters	Nordic Europe
Uncertainty avoidance	Germanic Europe	Eastern Europe
	Nordic Europe	Latin America
		Middle East

Source: Adapted from House et al. Culture, Leadership, and Organization: The GLOBE Study of 62 Societies

Qatar, Egypt, Turkey, and Kuwait scored high in group collectivism and low in future orientation, gender egalitarianism, and uncertainty avoidance. This indicates that people in these countries or regions tend to be family-oriented and are proud of their families, tribes, and organizations. It is clear that the people of the Middle East region are not consistence and like to stress current issues rather than to focus on future-oriented objectives (House, Hanges, Javidan, Dorfman, & Gupta, 2004).

Hitherto, Arab corporations did not know how to cultivate the massive effort of their businesses' local growth in order to build a real conglomerate sprawling regionally or around the globe. Arab corporations managed by the current leaders carry parochial management decisions for local and regional development only. With such a managerial perspective, it is clear that the management style of leading the business, from training, staffing, career development, and strategic planning, will fall into the same dilemma of limitation. Having a vision for where the company will stand 20 or 30 years from now should be carried by a future-oriented culture. Arab management that is a reflection of the society and the culture they exist in lack long-term oriented planning and will only preside over well-established corporations operating only to the local market, where there are limitations in lack of diversification and other external factor that might influence negatively the business locally.

Personality Type/Leadership

In this paper, we will be introducing for future research the personality type/leadership depicted in animals. There are four main types of animals to keep in mind: Lion, Elephant, Hyena, and Rooster. Most people should fall in one of these four personality/leadership types but still many can fall in more than one animal type subject to the situation and the circumstances. The Lion characterized by laissez-faire leadership style, delegation, charismatic, and focus on strategic observation. The Elephant, characterized to be team oriented, group sympathetic, warm, and reflect the path-goal leadership approach. The Hyena, portrayed as ultimate team oriented, well organized, agenda plan oriented, thorough tactics with his/her team members. Last, the Rooster, depicted as solo leader/management style, enjoys control and discipline, protective, and likes the show to run at his own discretion.

All of the aforementioned personality types/leadership represented in animal figures set to be under further research in a study covering sample population of top management and middle management positions in the Middle East region. The focal reason for this approach is to distinguish the Middle Eastern region with all its idiosyncrasies from the Western Context and the common leadership and managerial theories.

Conclusion

To clarify the foregoing information, we need to express the nexus between the Middle East cluster and their leadership behavior. Figure 40.2 shows Middle East leadership practices in the business field: Arab leadership style emphasizes the safety and security of the leader and the group (Self-Protective Leadership), and in addition, Arab leaders should be passionate, generous, and sensitive towards their followers (Human-Oriented Leadership). Arab leaders also prefer to be independent, autonomous, and portrayed as a unique symbol (Autonomous Leadership). Conversely, they find the other three leadership behaviors as less influential for an effective leadership behavior (House et al., 2004).

Protecting the manager's position when it stems from the self-protective leadership may indicate a deficiency in a performance appraisal system. According to human resource strategy, recruitment, training, performance appraisal, and other human resource activities should be synchronized to achieve the strategic goals stated by both the vision and the mission statement. Nevertheless, the detrimental

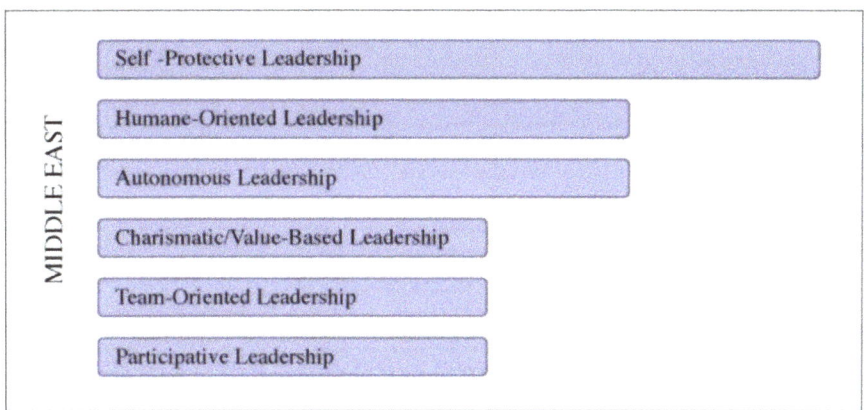

Source: Adapted from House et al. Culture, Leadership, and Organization: The Globe
Study of 62 Societies

Fig. 40.2   Middle East leadership behavior. *Source*: Adapted from House et al. Culture, Leadership, and Organization: The GLOBE Study of 62 Societies

factor arises, for example, when after being hired, the chosen candidate is working in the company according to the promised career development pathway, but the managers/leaders refuse to give up their positions. This interferes with the whole structured performance appraisal system, where employees must be groomed to hold higher managerial positions.

If there exists a glass ceiling that precludes employees from their earned career pathway, then we see disenchanted employees who start neglecting their duty of aligning their effort with the organization's goals.

Finally, we need to recognize the major steps top management and human resource practitioners can pursue in order to build a well-structured managerial structure and achieve long-term strategic goals. We need to reassess the training programs offered, which should entail innovative and leadership skill training programs rather than such barren training programs as time management and communication skills. Managers should also initiate employee career assessment and employee performance appraisals for every employee in each department, because evaluations are important for development and productivity.

In addition, Arab organizations should rejuvenate their organizational culture by eliminating the employees' seclusion and reinventing employee engagement. Employee incentives are not the only motivator of satisfactory performance. Nevertheless, workplace incentives can ignite employees' exuberance, examples of incentives being employee engagement, job rotation, and training programs. Companies must remain dedicated to recruiting, hiring, and training knowledgeable workers with special aptitudes that meet the organization's culture of knowledge sharing and learning.

References

Bass, B. M. (1990). *Bass and Stogdill's handbook of leadership: A survey of theory and research.* New York, NY: Free Press.
Decenzo, D., & Robbins, S. (2010). *Human resource management.* Hoboken, NJ: Wiley.
Fisher, B. A. (1974). *Small group decision-making: Communication and the group process.* New York, NY: McGraw-Hill.
Gardner, W. L., & Avolio, B. J. (2005). Authentic leadership development: Getting to the root of positive forms of leadership. *The Leadership Quarterly, 16*(3), 313–338.
Gulf Council Countries. (2011). Statistical Gulf Council Countries Data Base. http://sites.gcc-sg.org/Statistics/. Accessed 25 Oct 2013.
Harshbarger, B. (1989). Faculty commitment to the university: Influence and issue. *The Review of Higher Education, 13*(1), 29–45.
Herfy. (2010). Over three decades of success. http://www.herfy.com/index.php?option=com_content&view=article&id=64&Itemid=72&lang=en. Accessed 12 Aug 2013.
House, R. J. (1971). The path-goal theory of leader effectiveness. *Administrative Science Quarterly, 16*(3), 321–339.
House, R. J. (1996). Path-goal theory of leadership: Lessons, legacy, and a reformulated theory. *The Leadership Quarterly, 7*(3), 323–352.
House, R. J., Hanges, P. J., Javidan, M., Dorfman, P. W., & Gupta, V. (Eds.). (2004). *Culture, leadership, and organizations: The GLOBE study of 62 societies.* Thousand Oaks, CA: Sage.
IMF. (2011). Gulf Cooperation Council Countries (GCC): Enhancing economic outcomes in an uncertain global economy. http://www.imf.org/external/pubs/ft/dp/2011/1101mcd.pdf. Accessed 25 Oct 2013.
Jago, A. G. (1982). Leadership: Perspectives in theory and research. *Management Science, 28*(3), 315–336.
Kotter, J. P. (1990). *A force for change: How leadership differs from management.* New York, NY: Free Press.
Noe, R. A. (2010). *Employee training and development* (5th ed.). Burr Ridge, IL: McGraw-Hill.
Northouse, P. (2013). *Leadership: Theory and practice.* Thousand Oaks, CA: Sage.
Northouse, P. G. (2007). *Leadership: Theory and practice* (4th ed.). Thousand Oaks, CA: Sage.
Rost, J. C. (1991). *Leadership for the twenty-first century.* New York, NY: Praeger.
Shamir, B., & Eilam, G. (2005). What's your story? A life-stories approach to authentic leadership development. *The Leadership Quarterly, 16*(3), 395–417.
Zaleznik, A. (1977). Managers and leaders: Are they different? *Harvard Business Review, 55*(3), 67–78.

Chapter 41
Women on Corporate Boards: The New Zealand Perspective

Rizwan Tahir

Abstract The purpose of this paper is to analyse the issue of gender diversity on corporate boards in New Zealand companies. Despite the increased interest in diversity on corporate boards, very few studies have focused specifically on the issue of gender diversity in the corporate boards. This benchmark study contributes to the literature of corporate governance by analysing the presence of women on corporate boards in New Zealand. The research results indicate that women are severely underrepresented. The situation becomes more serious when we observe that in New Zealand more than 90 % of the companies listed on the New Zealand stock exchange lack any female voice on their board. The figures depicting female directors as a proportion of total directorship spotlight the need for New Zealand government and companies to develop effective strategies to increase the representation of females on corporate boards.

Keywords Gender diversity • Corporate governance • Corporate boards • New Zealand

Introduction

The structure of the corporate boards is often viewed as one of the more important issues in evaluating the effectiveness of this specialized governance structure. The purpose of a corporate board is to help management develop business strategies and to set policy objectives. Boards are often responsible for the selection of Chief Executive Officers (CEOs) and, through their regular meetings, ensure effective strategic planning for the company. In addition, they oversee adherence to regulatory requirements and monitor financial performance (Arfken, Bellar, & Helms, 2004). Most effective corporate boards are composed of members who bring skills, diversity and experience to a company to complement other directors.

R. Tahir (✉)
Business and Management Division, RIT Dubai, P.O. Box 341055, Techno Point Building, Dubai Silicon Oasis, Dubai, United Arab Emirates
e-mail: rxtcad@rit.edu

© Springer International Publishing Switzerland 2017 473
R. Benlamri, M. Sparer (eds.), *Leadership, Innovation and Entrepreneurship as Driving Forces of the Global Economy*, Springer Proceedings in Business and Economics, DOI 10.1007/978-3-319-43434-6_41

According to Burton and Ryall (1995), the concept of diversity goes beyond that of active representation in that it seeks not representatives of particular, identified interests, but people with certain characteristics arising out of various experiences which might effectively come to bear on a policy issue but which have not been used in the past. So Burton highlights, in effect, a "skill" versus "representation" argument for diversity. More precisely diversity in age, gender, ethnicity and ideas can offer companies a number of advantages including new ideas, better product development and positioning, different opinions and even additional accountability. For women, board membership provides an opportunity to test ideas and to support a corporation's view on public policy (Arfken et al., 2004).

The recent corporate ethical and financial scandals have forced changes in the composition and functioning of board of directors. Public initiatives for board reforms are not just on issues of compliance and legislating for tougher regulations of publicly held corporations, but increasingly involve how the boards work (van der Walt & Ingley, 2003). These pressures, as well as the waves of mergers and acquisitions and a recent economic recession have changed corporate governance climate.

The purpose of this paper is to analyse the issue of gender diversity on corporate boards in New Zealand companies. Despite the increased interest in diversity on corporate boards, very few studies (e.g. Arfken et al., 2004) have focused specifically on the issue of gender diversity in the corporate boards. This benchmark study also contributes to the literature of corporate governance by analysing the presence of women on the corporate boards of the companies based in New Zealand, a small industrialized country where domestic conditions are different from those of the multinationals from the USA, Europe and Japan that have dominated the past research attention.

The Financial Crisis: Changing Role of Corporate Board

As companies now grapple with financial crisis of a magnitude that few have experienced before, their corporate boards should begin by questioning their fundamental strategic beliefs: Is our view of the products and markets realistic? Does our financial planning and strategy take into account the uncertain new conditions? Can we exploit the current glut of ideas and skills? How can we learn from the problems that our competitors are experiencing?

Most board members will believe that radical change is unnecessary and that "normal situation" will soon resume. Their experiences during less severe crises — such as those in 1997, or 2008 — will drive them into a false sense of complacency and very few will adjust their strategies and policies sufficiently. This action is the result of a clinically observed human trait of being overly influenced by past experiences and judgments. Researchers in the area of decision-making term it *anchoring*. The problem is made worse by the natural rhythms that tend to reinforce rather than challenge anchored thinking. It is important that in the coming months board chairs need to challenge their board members to think things through afresh.

Mobilizing the board to tackle this financial crisis requires a complete overhaul of how its members interact. The only way is to force change. The chair needs to underline the gravity and urgency of the situation by summoning the board to extraordinary "credit crunch" meetings, "survival" meetings, "does our plan still make sense" meetings and "how can we turn this pain into an opportunity" meetings. Without disrupting the rhythm, anchored thinking will continue to dominate (Campbell & Sinclair, 2009).

Diversity Defined

Diversity is defined as differences in the most literal form of the word but the term according to Arfken et al. (2004) has been transformed to a purposeful strategic direction where differences are valued. Differences can be associated with age, gender, religion, physical appearances, culture, job function or experience, disability, ethnicity and personal style. Empirical research has shown that diversity generally increases group-level outcomes like creativity and the quality of decision-making (Bantel & Jackson, 1989; Magjuka & Baldwin, 1991; Jehn, Northcraft, & Neale, 1999). Diversity may affect either the quantity and quality of information used by the group or improve group processes and may produce significant value on teams (Morrison, 1992).

Diverse teams tend to consider more perspectives, which may arise from the minority group members who consistently voice alternative hypotheses and analyses (McLeod & Lobel, 1992; Watson, Kumar, & Michaelson, 1993). The cognitive conflict between the majority and minority groups may also improve the quality of the arguments, causing group members to more carefully reason and support their suggestions. In an early model of how group composition and other variables affect group outcomes, Gladstein (1984) proposed that group performance depends on six key group processes: open communication, supportiveness, conflict, effective discussion of strategy, weighting of inputs and boundary management. Campion, Medsker, and Higgs (1993) connected group effectiveness to group processes including potency perceptions, social interactions, communication and coordination. In their model, diversity improves outcomes if it increases potency, social interaction, communication and coordination. This research suggests that gender diversity on teams results in better group outcomes in many business and group settings.

However, diversity in groups may create significant costs and impair group-level outcomes in other settings (Campion et al., 1996; William & O'Rielly, 1998). There is evidence that diversity negatively affects individual identification with the group, as well as job satisfaction, causing lower group commitment and higher turnover for minority group members (Tsui & O'Reilly, 1989; Pfeffer, 1983). At the same time, diverse group members may have difficulty communicating with each other, causing an increase in coordination costs (Lang, 1986; Zenger & Lawrence, 1989). There is also an evidence that net gains from diversity depends largely on whether new group norms have developed to mitigate its negative consequences (Chatman & Flynn, 2001). Overall previous research has shown that diversity can both enhance and degrade group outcomes.

Fister (2003) argued that one major benefit of diverse groups is that they provide superior information for decision-making. In practice, this means that women can bring unique and valuable information, developed through past experiences that men either do not or cannot have. Information is often heterogeneously distributed by gender, such as having single-gender groups results in less than perfect information and inefficient decision-making. A heterogeneous distribution of information suggests a social network with structural holes, in which some information is contained solely within one social group that is largely disconnected from other social groups (Burt, 1997). In this structural hole model, any person who bridges the gap between the disconnected social groups can distribute the information across the boundaries. If the minority group provides a unique piece of information to the majority group, which is superior and accepted by the group, then the group outcome will be positive and strong. The uniqueness of information arises from this particular type of social network with pockets of disconnected groups (Fister, 2003). Using this line of reasoning, some researchers (Morrison, 1992; Fernandez, 1993; Burke, 1993) have proposed that companies serving diverse a customer population should reflect that diversity in their line and staff positions to ensure a match between customer needs and company capabilities, although the empirical evidence provides mixed results (Leonard & Levine, 2002).

Gender and Diversity

A major demographic shift since the 1960s has seen increasing gender diversity on American board of directors. In 1969, there were fewer than 50 women serving on large American boards of directors (Catalyst, 2004). In 2008, women held 15.2 % of directorships at Fortune 500 companies; this number was 14.8 % in 2007 (Catalyst, 2009). Over the past 30 years, female representation on the boards has increased at an 11 % compound annual rate, and the percentage of corporate director seats held by women doubled from 5 % in 1987 to 11 % in the late 1990s (Catalyst, 2000; Daily et al., 2000). Women now hold between 5 and 15 % of director positions in English speaking industrialized economies: 5 % in Great Britain (FTSE 100), 6 % in Canada (FP500), 10 % in Australia, 11 % in the USA (S&P 500) and 14 % in New Zealand (Catalyst, 1998, 1999).

There is some evidence that gender diversity can be an important characteristic of corporate boards that has the potential to add value to the businesses. Previous research (Bilimoria & Piderit, 1994; Kesner, 1988) has indicated that men and women differ in board committee service and attitudes about board services (Talmud & Izraeli, 1999; Hillman, Cannella, & Paetzold, 2000). Managers also differ in their opinion towards gender diversity on boards. At one extreme, almost three out of four managers surveyed in 1993 indicated that recruiting a female director was a top priority, and almost nine in ten managers expressed that increasing female representation on boards is an important general principle (Mattis, 2000). At the other extreme, the CEO of Cypress Semiconductor wrote in a letter explaining his company board composition, "Bluntly stated, a "woman's view" on how to run our semiconductor company does not help us, unless that woman has an advanced technical degree and experience as a CEO" (Pfeffer & O'Reilly, 2002). Clearly, it is evident that the shift to hiring more female directors has not affected all companies.

Theoretical Perspective

Two main theoretical perspectives in the management and corporate governance literature underlie the rationale for board diversity. The first is agency theory that can be briefly summarized as the board's monitoring role (in its stewardship capacity) in protecting shareholder interests from the self-interests (the agency costs) of management. The second perspective relating to arguments in favour of diversity is the resource dependence view that regards the corporate board as an essential link between the organization and the key resources necessary to maximize it performance. These theoretical underpinnings clearly highlight the role of the corporate board in carrying out its governance function (van der Walt & Ingley, 2003).

Agency theory is the theoretical framework most often used by the researchers in finance and economics to understand the link between board characteristics and firm value. Fama and Jensen (1983) propose a very important role for the board as a mechanism to control and monitor managers. The role of the board in an agency framework is to resolve agency problems between managers and shareholders by setting compensation and replacing managers who do not create value for the shareholders (Carter, Simkins, & Simpson, 2003). One of the key elements of an agency view of the corporate board is that the heterogeneous board members will not collude with each other to subvert shareholder interest because board members have incentives to build reputation as expert monitors. Board diversity is critical for the board to function in the best interest of the shareholders.

It can be argued that diversity increases board independence because female board directors might ask question that would not come from male directors with more traditional backgrounds. The Australian Report of the Industry Task Force on Leadership and Management (Burton & Ryall, 1995) suggested that women directors are economically advantageous to a company. The report claimed that well-balanced boards that include women directors reduce the likelihood of corporate failures. Homogeneous groups tend to have homogenous ways of solving company problems: "group think" errors would less likely to occur with a heterogeneous board (Burgess & Tharenou, 2000).

Taking the resource dependence view, the board is seen as a potentially important strategic resource for the organization, especially in linking the firm to external resources, such as providing a linkage to a nation's business elite, access to capital, connections to competitors, or market and industry intelligence (Ingley & Van Der Walt, 2003). Diversity in this context argues for a broader range of backgrounds among directors in providing this resource.

The Case of New Zealand

New Zealand's small corporate sector is a microcosm of western business thought and practice (Hawarden & Stablein, 2008). In 2004, there were some 160,000 for profit corporate enterprises operating in New Zealand. These enterprises had over 1.1 million employees (Goh, 2005). New Zealand is predominantly a nation of small business enterprises (SMEs). In February 2006, 96.4% of enterprises employed 19 or fewer people (Fabling 2007). A much smaller corporate sector consists of 1600 companies with approximately more than 100 employees. Many of these larger firms are foreign-owned. Approximately 200 of these companies are listed on the New Zealand Stock Exchange (www.nzx.com).

New Zealand's liberal, tolerant and diversity focused political climate, combined with its advanced equal opportunity philosophies and first world technology and business practices, encourages the success of women in the public arena. Despite this, NZ is far from being a pioneer in promoting women to boards of directors in the corporate sector (Hawarden & Stablein, 2008). In this sector, "glacier progress" towards gender equity (McGregor & Fountaine, 2006) persists despite increasing participation by women in the workforce at lower levels (Murray, 2006).

Women are gradually entering senior management levels, but very few are being appointed as CEOs. While the pipeline to the board table appears to be correspondingly limited (Rotherham, 2007). A lack of suitably experienced and qualified women has been frequently touted locally and internationally as a major reason for the low representation of women at board level (Singh & Vinnicombe, 2004; van der Walt & Ingley, 2003), the ease with which women of calibre were found to populate the state sector boards in New Zealand has highlighted the fatuous nature of this argument.

The small and close-knit nature of the New Zealand business community and pool of directors has been well documented over the years (Stablein, Cleland, Mackie, & Reid, 2004). A group of experienced directors who sit on multiple boards together is noticeable and constitutes an easily identifiable "old boys network", with a sprinkling of women directors, the so-called "Queen Bees" (Dalton, 2007). These New Zealand women in the corporate boards tend not to be proactive in recommending other women for board appointments or mentoring other aspiring women for positions on corporate boards. The prevailing attitude among female directors is that they have achieved success through their own merits and others should be capable of similar success without extra assistance. An element of denial of discrimination pervades this group despite the statistics indicating otherwise (Rotherham, 2007).

New Zealand Exchange (NZX) comprises of three securities markets—the New Zealand Stock Market (NZSX), the New Zealand Debt market (NZDX) and the New Zealand Alternative Market (NZAX). The NZSX includes most of the corner stone New Zealand companies. The NZDX sells a range of investment securities that include corporate bonds and fixed income securities; and the NZAX aims for the developing companies and companies with non-traditional structures.

New Zealand Stock Market

According to the 2008 census by the Human Rights Commission, women hold 8.65 % of board directorship of companies listed on the NZSX. This figure is derived from the top 100 companies by market capitalization and compromises 54 female directorships held by 45 women out of the total of 624 directorships. The figures compare with 7.13 % recorded in 2006.

Pumpkin Patch Limited and Kingfish Limited came out as top 100 companies that have gender equality on their board. Almost ten top 100 companies have at least two or more female directors on their board. One of the top ten companies is Vector Limited and the other nine are Westpac Banking Corporation, AMP Limited, Michael Hill International Limited, Delegat's Group Limited, EBOS Group Limited, Telstra Corporation Limited, Abano Healthcare Group Limited, NZ Windfarms Limited and Rachina Pacific Limited. Only 40 of the top 100 NZSX listed companies have any female directors, an increase of only three from the 2006 census report. One woman holds three directorships of top 100 companies and seven others hold two directorships (Human Rights Commission Census, 2008).

Vector Limited is the only NZSX listed company that has added two women to its corporate board since the previous census in 2006. The five other companies that have added one woman since 2006 are Michael Hill International Limited, EBOS Group Limited, The Warehouse Group Limited, Kiwi Income Property Trust and Wakefield Health Limited. Three companies—PGG Wrightson Limited and Australian 20 Leaders Fund have dropped female board directors and now have no female directors, while Telecom Corporation of NZ Limited currently has only one female director.

New Zealand Debt Market

It is reported in the 2008 census that women hold 5.73 % of directorships in the 53 NZDX listed companies with only 13 companies having female directors. Three companies had two women, and the other ten had just one female director each.

New Zealand Alternative Market

Human Rights Commission Census (2008) concluded that women hold 5.07 % of directorships in 28 NZAX listed companies. Interestingly, the total number of directors on the NZAX has increased to 138 from 122 in 2006; the total number of seven female directors remains unchanged between the two census reports. Oyster Bay Marlborough Vineyards Limited is the only company on the NZAX that has two women on its corporate board and five other companies have one woman each.

Only six of the 28 companies have any female board directors. The New Zealand Wine Company has not had a female director on its board since 2005. The NZAX listed companies have dramatically decreased their proportion of women corporate directors over three census reports from 16.39 % in 2004 to 5.74 % in 2006, reaching to a new low of 5.07 % in 2008 (Human Rights Commission Census, 2008).

Discussions and Implications

Women are almost nonexistent on the corporate boards of New Zealand private sector companies. It is reported that women hold 8.65 % of board directorships of listed companies on NZSX, 5.73 % of directorships in the 53 NZDX listed companies and 5.07 % of directorships in 28 NZAX listed companies. The situation becomes more serious when we look into the number of New Zealand companies without any female board representation. In New Zealand, more than 90 % of the listed companies are without any female voice on their board. Compared to the 18 % of Fortune 500 firms with no women director on their corporate board (Arfken et al., 2004), New Zealand companies lag significantly in their incorporation of women. The figures depicting female directors as a proportion of total directorship spotlight the need for women and New Zealand companies to develop effective strategies to increase their gender representation.

In the New Zealand corporate sector, getting that first substantive corporate board appointment is competitive for men and women directors alike. The small number of women on private sector boards demonstrates that clearly there are some odds and that they are heavily stacked against women, stopping women from achieving this crucial first appointment. Aspiring corporate board members, particularly women with high ambitions, are in difficult position to accept high risk appointments and set themselves up for failure. Once entry to the elite group of experienced corporate directors is achieved, such directors have the luxury of refusing corporate appointments and can cherry pick the more high profile and less risky appointments (Hawarden & Stablein, 2008).

In New Zealand, more needs to be done to tackle the lack of opportunities for talented women in corporate boards. Benchmarking studies can be undertaken annually, and chairmen, chief executives and women directors can be invited to work with the responsible policymakers to develop a gender-equitable pool of talent for leadership. Given the nature and composition of corporate boards, government and major shareholders such as banks should be encouraged to identify women directors in the public sector organizations who could be suitable for the corporate boards of private sector companies.

The examples of change efforts underway around the world basically take two approaches. One is the cognitive dissonance approach that is about pushing change. This approach assumes that changed behaviour will result in changed attitudes. By requiring companies to add women to their boards, as in Scandinavia and Israel, the hope is that companies will then see the benefits, and consequently, the attitude that causes barriers will change (Adam & Flynn, 2005). The other approach involves facilitative, collaborative change management, characterized by Meyerson (2001) as the tempered radical approach. This is accomplished by fostering and promoting the option of tapping current underutilized resources of qualified women and by lending a helping hand in a pull fashion.

In New Zealand, a combination of push and pull strategies may well prove successful. Women in the corporate sector can argue that the consolidation of power, privilege and wealth in the private hands will only entrench the existing male elites. At the same time, gender parity will require the stronger medicine of legislated quotas, as is happening in other countries. On the other hand, the politicians in New Zealand would hope that the increasing pool of experienced female board directors would trickle through to the boards of the private sector (Hawarden & Stablein, 2008). However, it is my belief that in order to achieve this, a group that is an active and vocal both in political and in commercial sectors is needed to drive the process forward. The lesson from New Zealand is that equality in gender is hard earned, has to be promoted vigilantly and needs an undermining political will in addition to its supportive social philosophies.

Finally, it is important that solutions are found that allow the women to play a more equal role in corporate boards. Not all the Kiwi women will want to become directors, nor are they all likely to have the right aptitudes and competences for such positions. But it is essential for a small country like New Zealand to utilize the whole of its talent pool in its business, not just half of it.

References

Adam, S., & Flynn, P. (2005). Local knowledge advances women's access to corporate boards. *Corporate Governance: International Review, 13*(6), 836–846.

Arfken, D. E., Bellar, S. L., & Helms, M. M. (2004). The ultimate glass ceiling revisited: The presence of women on corporate boards. *Journal of Business Ethics, 50*, 177–186.

Bantel, K. A., & Jackson, S. E. (1989). Top management and innovations in banking: Does the composition of the top team make a difference. *Strategic Management Journal, 10*, 107–124.

Bilimoria, D., & Piderit, S. (1994). Board committee membership: Effects of sex-based bias. *Academy of Management Journal, 37*, 1453–1477.

Burton, C., & Ryall, C. (1995). "Managing for diversity", in industry task force on leadership and management skills. In *Enterprising nation: Renewing Australia's managers to meet the challenges of the Asia-Pacific century* (Research Report), Vol. 2, pp. 765–814. Canberra: Australian Government Publishing Service.

Burgess, Z., & Tharenou, P. (2000). What distinguishes women non-executive directors from executive directors? In R. J. Burke & M. C. Mattis (Eds.), *Women in management: International challenges and opportunities* (pp. 111–127). Dordrecht: Kluwer.

Burke, R. (1993). Women on corporate boards of directors. *Equal Opportunities International, 12*, 6.

Burt, R. (1997). The contingent value of social capital. *Administrative Science Quarterly, 42*, 339–365.

Campbell, A., & Sinclair, S. (2009). The crisis: Mobilizing boards for change. *McKinsey Quarterly*. http://www.mckinseyquarterly.com/Governance/Boards/the_crisis_Mobilizing_boards_for_change_2300.

Campion, M., Medsker, G., & Higgs, A. (1993). Relationship between work group characteristics and effectiveness: Implication for designing effective work groups. *Personnel Psychology, 46*, 823–850.

Carter, D., Simkins, B., & Simpson, W. (2003). Corporate governance, board diversity, and firm value. *The Financial Review, 38*(1), 33.

Catalyst. (1998). The 1998 catalyst census of women board of directors of the Fortune 500. http://www.catalyst.org/publication/168/1998-catalyst-census-of-women-board-directors-of-the-fortune-500.

Catalyst. (1999). The 1999 catalyst census of women board of directors of the Fortune 1000. http://www.catalyst.org/publication/167/1999-catalyst-census-of-women-board-directors-of-the-fortune-1000.

Catalyst. (2000). The 2000 catalyst census of women corporate officers and top earner. http://www.catalyst.org/publication/175/2000-catalyst-census-of-women-corporate-officers-and-top-earners.

Catalyst. (2004). Study of 353 Fortune 500 companies connects corporate performance and gender diversity. http://www.catalyst.org/publication/82/the-bottom-line-connecting-corporate-performance-and-gender-diversity.

Catalyst. (2009). The promise of future leadership: A research on highly talented employees in the pipeline. http://www.catalyst.org/file/340/pipeline's_broken_promise_final_021710.pdf.

Chatman, J., & Flynn, F. (2001). The influence of demographic composition on the emergence and consequences of cooperative norms in groups. *Academy of Management Journal, 44*(5), 956–974.

Daily, C., Dalton, D., & Cannella, A. (2003). Corporate governance: Decades of dialogue and data. *Academy of Management Review, 28*, 371–382.

Dalton, C. (2007). Queen bees: All sting, no honey. *Business Horizon, 50*(2), 3349–3352.

Fama, E., & Jensen, M. (1983). Separation of ownership and control. *Journal of Law and Economics, 26*, 301–325.

Fernandez, J. (1993). *The diversity advantage: How American business can outperform Japanese and European companies in global marketplace*. New York: Lexington Books.

Fister, T. W. (2003). *Causes and consequences of board composition*. Doctoral Dissertation, University of Illinois at Urbana-Champaign.

Goh, K. (2005). Development in the New Zealand corporate sector. *The Reserve Bank of New Zealand, 68*(2), 11–14.

Gladstein, D. L. (1984). Groups in context: A model of task group effectiveness. *Administrative Science Quarterly, 29*, 499–517.

Hawarden, R., & Stablein, R. (2008). New Zealand women directors: Many aspire but few succeed. In S. Vinnicombe, V. Singh, R. Burke, D. Bilimoria, & M. Huse (Eds.), *Women on corporate boards of directors* (Vol. 1, pp. 57–66). Cheltenham: Edward Elgar Publishing Limited.

Hillman, A., Cannella, A., & Paetzold, R. (2000). The resource dependence role of corporate directors: Strategic adaptation of board composition in response to environmental change. *Journal of Management Studies, 37*, 235–255.

Human Rights Commission Census. (2008). *New Zealand census of women participation*. Human Rights Commission, Wellington, New Zealand. http://www.hrc.co.nz/hrc_new/hrc/cms/files/documents/28-Mar-2008_12-59-39_2008_Census_of_Womens_Participation.pdf.

Ingley, C., & Van Der Walt, N. (2003). Board configuration: Building better boards. *Corporate Governance, 3*(4), 5–17.

Jehn, K., Northcraft, G., & Neale, M. (1999). What differences make a difference: A field study in diversity, conflict and performance in workgroups. *Administrative Science Quarterly, 44*, 741–763.

Kesner, I. (1988). Directors characteristics and committee membership: An investigation of type, occupation, tenure and gender. *Academy of Management Journal, 31*, 66–84.

Lang, K. (1986). A language theory of discrimination. *Quarterly Journal of Economics, 101*, 363–382.

Leonard, J., & Levine, D. (2002). *Diversity, discrimination and performance*. Working paper. University of Vaasa, Finland.

Magjuka, M., & Baldwin, T. (1991). Team based employee involvement programs: Effects of design and administration. *Personnel Psychology, 44*, 793–812.

Mattis, M. (2000). Women corporate directors in the United States. In R. J. Burke & M. Mattis (Eds.), *Women on corporate boards of directors*. Dordrecht: Kluwer.

McGregor, J., & Fountaine, S. (2006). *New Zealand census of women's participation*. Human Rights Commission and New Zealand Centre for Women Leadership, Massey University, Wellington.

Meyerson, D. E. (2001). Radical change the quiet way. *Harvard Business Review, 79*, 92–100.

Morrison, A. (1992). *The new leaders: Guidelines on leadership diversity in America*. San Francisco, CA: Jossey-Bass.

Murray, G. (2006). *Capitalist networks and social power in Australia and New Zealand*. Aldershot: Ashgate Publishing Ltd.

Pfeffer, J. (1983). Organizational demography. In L. L. Cunnings & B. M. Shaw (Eds.), *Research in organizational behaviour* (Vol. 5, pp. 299–357). Greenwich, CT: JAI Press.

Pfeffer, J., & O'Reilly, C. (2002). *Hidden value: How great companies achieve extraordinary results with ordinary people*. Cambridge: Harvard Business School Press.

Rotherham, F. (2007). Women in business special report. *Unlimited Magazine*, September. http://unlimited.co.nz/unlimited.nsf/default/B2AB3FB13A94DB7ECC25733800791DD8.

Singh, V., & Vinnicombe, S. (2004). Why so few women directors in top UK board-rooms? Evidence and theoretical explanations. *Corporate Governance: An International Review, 12*(4), 479–488.

Talmud, I., & Izraeli, D. (1999). The relationship between gender and performance issues of concern to directors: Correlates or institution? *Journal of Organizational Behaviour, 20*, 459–474.

Tsui, A., & O'Reilly, C. (1989). Beyond simple demographic effects: The importance of relational demography in superior-subordinate dyads. *Academy of Management Journal, 32*, 402–423.

van der Walt, N., & Ingley, C. (2003). Board dynamics and the influence of professional background, gender and ethnic diversity of directors. *Corporate Governance, 11*(3), 218–226.

Watson, W., Kumar, K., & Michaelson, L. (1993). Cultural diversity's impact on interaction processes and performance: Comparing heterogeneous and diverse task groups. *Academy of Management Journal, 36*, 590–602.

William, K., & O'Rielly, C. (1998). Forty years of diversity research: A review. In M. Neale, E. Mannix, & D. Gruenfeld (Eds.), *Research on managing groups and teams*. Greenwich, CT: JAI Press.

Zenger, T., & Lawrence, B. (1989). Organizational demography: The differential effects of age and tenure distributions on technical communication. *Academy of Management Journal, 32*, 353–376.

Chapter 42
The Effects of Age on Job Crafting: Exploring the Motivations and Behavior of Younger and Older Employees in Job Crafting

Sabrine El Baroudi and Svetlana N. Khapova

Abstract *Purpose:* This paper contributes to the job-crafting theory of Wrzesniewski and Dutton (The Academy of Management Review 26(2):179–201, 2001) by exploring the effects of age on job-crafting behaviors (i.e., task crafting, relational crafting, and cognitive crafting) and on job-crafting motivations (i.e., the need for personal control, the desire to create and sustain a positive self-image, and the need for human connection).

Design/methodology/approach: Semi-structured interviews were conducted with 16 younger and 15 older employees ($n=31$) at a socially responsible non-profit organization in the Netherlands. The qualitative data were analyzed in two major steps: (1) identifying job-crafting motivations and behaviors in older and younger employees and (2) identifying and comparing the differences in the job-crafting motivations and behaviors between older employees and younger employees.

Findings: We found that both older and younger employees are likely to engage in job-crafting behavior to assert control over their jobs and to create a positive self-image. However, younger employees may have two different motivations (personal control and positive self-image) for engaging in such job-crafting behavior. Whereas both younger and older employees engage the most in task crafting, younger employees are more likely to engage in all three types of job-crafting behavior; additionally, we found that the three different forms of job-crafting behavior of younger employees occur in conjunction with one another.

Research limitations/implications: This study contributes to the original job-crafting model of Wrzesniewski and Dutton (The Academy of Management Review 26(2):179–201, 2001) by including the effect of age in the model, and by

S. El Baroudi (✉)
Canadian University of Dubai, Dubai, United Arab Emirates
e-mail: sabrine.elbaroudi@cud.ac.ae

S.N. Khapova
VU University Amsterdam, Amsterdam, The Netherlands

© Springer International Publishing Switzerland 2017
R. Benlamri, M. Sparer (eds.), *Leadership, Innovation and Entrepreneurship as Driving Forces of the Global Economy*, Springer Proceedings in Business and Economics, DOI 10.1007/978-3-319-43434-6_42

485

demonstrating the importance of studying the three original main job-crafting motivations and behaviors separately from one another.

Practical implications: This paper addresses the multigenerational challenges of the contemporary workforce. It demonstrates that managers may play a pivotal role in stimulating older employees to engage in job-crafting behaviors by informing them about job-crafting strategies and providing them with more opportunities to engage in job crafting.

Originality/value: This paper is original in that it re-examines, refines, and enriches the job-crafting model of Wrzesniewski and Dutton (The Academy of Management Review 26(2):179–201, 2001), which is receiving a growing interest among researchers and business practitioners.

Keywords Job crafting • Age • Older employees • Younger employees • Motivations

Introduction

The concept of job crafting, which is defined as "the physical and cognitive changes that individuals proactively make in the task and relational boundaries of their work" (Wrzesniewski & Dutton, 2001, p. 179), has received much interest from both researchers and practitioners (Bakker, 2010; Tims, Bakker, & Derks, 2013). However, perhaps because they were inspired by the concept's agentic perspective on employees, few authors have engaged in re-examining, refining, and/or enriching the original job-crafting model. Instead, most emerging papers have consisted of tests of the Wrzesniewski and Dutton (2001) model in various populations and work contexts (e.g., Berg, Dutton, & Wrzesniewski, 2008; Leana, Appelbaum, & Shevchuk, 2009). To our knowledge, only the study by Berg, Wrzesniewski, and Dutton (2010) examines the original job-crafting model. Their study concludes that the process of job crafting is much more complicated than as suggested by Wrzesniewski and Dutton (2001). For example, whereas the original model treats perceived opportunities to craft as fixed limits, Berg et al. (2010) found that perceived challenges limit the opportunities that employees see for job crafting.

   In this paper, we propose that the influence of age on job crafting is another important aspect of job crafting that received scant attention from Wrzesniewski and Dutton (2001) in their original work. To illustrate, life-span theorists propose that individuals go through different trajectories of development across their lifetimes. These experiences (work and non-work) influence the development of skills and work beliefs and may, in turn, contribute to work motivations across life spans (Kanfer & Ackerman, 2004, p. 442). This finding suggests that the *job-crafting motivations* of older and younger employees might be different and that *actual job-crafting behaviors* could also be different. How older and younger employees engage in job crafting and what their job-crafting motivations are remain unknown in research on job crafting. In addition to its theoretical contributions, this study also has important implications for practice. Given the aging workforce (Avery, McKay, & Wilson, 2007), addressing this issue is timely and may help managers better understand how their older and younger employees engage in this form of proactive behavior.

The purpose of this article is to enrich the job-crafting model of Wrzesniewski and Dutton (2001) by including the effects of age in the model. We explored the different job-crafting behaviors of older and younger employees and the motivations that shape these behaviors. To accomplish our goal, we undertook a qualitative study in 2010 and conducted 31 interviews with employees at a socially responsible non-profit organization in the Netherlands. Before presenting our eventual findings, we present a brief theoretical review of the effects of age on job crafting.

Job-Crafting Model: A Brief Review

Wrzesniewski and Dutton (2001) define job crafting as "the physical and cognitive changes that individuals proactively make in the task and relational boundaries of their work" (p. 179). In doing so, employees engage in three forms of job-crafting behavior. The first form, *task crafting*, involves changing the job's task boundaries by changing the number, scope, or type of job tasks performed at work. The second form, *relational crafting*, entails changing the relational boundaries of the job, which involves changing either the quality and/or the amount of interaction with others at work. Employees can decide how frequently they wish to interact with others on the job and can also determine the quality of those interactions. The third form, *cognitive crafting*, occurs when employees change the cognitive task boundaries of their jobs, which may take many different forms, according to Wrzesniewski and Dutton (2001); one way involves altering how one sees the job (either as a set of discrete work tasks or as an integrated whole). This form of job-crafting behavior often stimulates employees to change how they approach their jobs.

The motivation for job crafting arises from three individual needs. Job crafting will often result from situations in which employees believe that their needs are not being met in their job as it is currently designed (Wrzesniewski & Dutton, 2001, p. 183). The first motivation is the need for personal control. Wrzesniewski and Dutton (2001) argue that having or taking control over job tasks or the overall purpose of work constitutes a basic human need for individuals because it will help them avoid alienation from work (Rogers, 1995; Wrzesniewski & Dutton, 2001, p. 179/181). The second motivation concerns the desire to create and sustain a positive sense of self in one's own eyes (Steele, 1988; Wrzesniewski & Dutton, 2001, p. 183) and in the eyes of others (Baumeister, 1982; Erez & Earley, 1993; Wrzesniewski & Dutton, 2001, p. 183). This motivation arises when employees have jobs that make the positive construction of the self difficult. Employees will change the tasks and relationships that comprise their jobs to enable a more positive sense of self to be expressed and confirmed by others. The third motivation concerns a need for human connection and arises because individuals are motivated to forge connections with others as a means of introducing meaning into their lives (Baumeister & Leary, 1995; Wrzesniewski & Dutton, 2001, p. 183).

Age and Motivations for Job Crafting

Several theories implicitly or explicitly suggest that work motivations change as individuals become older. For example, the life-span developmental theory proposes that individuals experience shifts in the availability of internal and external resources throughout their life span. Whereas younger adults are typically on a trajectory of growth or gains in resources, older adults are faced with growing loss (Baltes & Smith, 2003; Freund, 2006). According to Freund (2006), this finding implies that younger adults are more likely to be motivated to achieve higher levels of performance than to counteract losses. Conversely, older adults are likely to show greater motivation to counteract losses than to optimize their level of performance. Thus, the life-span developmental theory suggests that the job-crafting motivations of both younger and older employees arise because of a need for personal control. However, for younger employees, this motivation is expressed as a need to control their performances, whereas for older employees, it is expressed as a need to control losses.

Research by McAdams, St. Aubin, and Logan (1993) suggests that generativity motives — the tendency to care for others and help the broader society and future generations — increase with age. Kanfer and Ackerman (2004) argue that employees who are driven by generativity motives will focus their attention on the process and collaborative nature of goal accomplishments at work. Compared with younger employees, older employees will be more likely to seek human connections. Therefore, we expect significant differences in individual motivations for job crafting among younger and older employees. Although existing theories concerned with age differences speculate about what the possible differences might be, research exploring employee motivations for job crafting is needed to clarify these differences.

Age and Job-Crafting Behaviors

De Lange et al. (2009) suggest that, due to their accumulated work experience, older employees have led careers that better fit their self-concept than their younger colleagues. In addition, Edwards, Cable, Williamson, Schurer Lambert, and Shipp (2006) argue that older employees typically have occupations with more job control than their younger colleagues. Because two individual needs (personal control and positive self-image) are expected to be more fulfilled by older employees, we assume that older employees will engage less in job crafting than their younger peers. We continue by relating existing theory about age to the three types of job-crafting behaviors.

Age and Task Crafting

Older and younger employees are likely to engage differently in task crafting, which may be explained by the differences in the work style ascribed to both groups. A person's work style refers to his/her approach to problems and outlook on work-related issues (Williams, Parker, & Turner, 2007). Older employees have been found to have a more routinized work style than their younger peers (Maurer, 2001). In particular, Yeatts, Folts, and Knapp (2000) have shown that older employees invest more time and energy in the traditional or routinized approach to performing job tasks. This in contrast to younger employees who have gained their experience in a work environment in which flexibility is the norm (Yeatts & Hyten, 1998; Yeatts et al., 2000). In a similar vein, Furunes and Mykletun (2005) found that older employees approach job tasks differently and have a professionalism related to the job routine that younger employees do not have.

Additionally, it has been argued that older employees will not accept a different work style than their own (Garg, 1991). Consistent with this argument, older employees were found to be less receptive to new ideas, less adaptable, and more rigid than younger employees (Maurer, 2001). In light of these theories, we expect older employees to be less motivated (than younger employees) to craft their tasks.

Age and Relational Crafting

We further suggest that older and younger employees craft their relational boundaries at work differently. Several theories and related streams of literature support this suggestion. One example is *the relational demography theory*. Relational demography refers to an individual's demographic characteristics that are relative to a referent group (Goldberg, 2005; Armstrong-Stassen & Lee, 2009). Relational age denotes how an individual's age compares with the actual or perceived age distribution within the organization, work group, or supervisor–subordinate dyad (Armstrong-Stassen & Lee, 2009). In her study, Lawrence (1990) found that higher proportions of younger peers in work groups are likely to lead older employees to have less trust in their group members; involving a greater number of older peers would stabilize the work group and lead to better relationships (Finkelstein, Burke, & Raju, 1995). The effect of perceived relative age is particularly salient for older employees (Cleveland & Shore, 1992).

The socio-emotional selectivity life-span theory from Carstensen, Pasupathi, Mayr, and Nesselroade (2000) offers another explanation, which suggests that individuals select goals in accordance with their perceptions of the future as being limited or open-ended (Lang & Carstensen, 2002), and this selection in turn affects how they craft their social interactions. For example, younger generations perceive time as open-ended (holding a "time since birth" perspective) and are likely to be motivated by growth- or knowledge-related goals that can be useful in the more distant future, which includes acquisition of new information and new contacts. By contrast, older generations perceive time as a constraint (holding a "time till death" perspective) and are more motivated by achieving short-term emotion-related goals, such as deepening one's existing relations (De Lange et al., 2009).

In light of these streams of literature, we expect that both older and younger employees will be likely to engage in relational job crafting—with certain significant differences, however. In particular, we expect the following: older employees are likely to be more motivated to improve the quality of their relationships and increase the amount of interaction they have with their fellow peers. By contrast, we expect that younger employees are likely to be more motivated to increase the amount of interaction they have by forming new relationships.

Age and Cognitive Crafting

As opposed to older employees, younger employees are described in the literature as individuals who continuously want to learn (Lang & Carstensen, 2002) and acquire new information (De Lange et al., 2009). Moreover, there are more possibilities to gain knowledge for younger employees compared to older employees. For example, the literature on older employees suggests that similarly situated older employees may be treated less favorably than younger employees with respect to access to training (Maurer, 2001) and that older employees have less access to employer-funded and employer-provided training than younger employees have (Armstrong-Stassen & Lee, 2009). Younger employees can use the acquired new knowledge to think of different and more efficient ways of performing tasks, whereas older employees are less able to do so. In turn, younger employees are more likely to change the way they think about their work than older employees and to change the way they approach their jobs, which is a consequence of cognitive crafting (Wrzesniewski & Dutton, 2001). Based on this literature, we expect that younger employees are likely to be more motivated to engage in cognitive crafting.

If older employees engage in this form of job crafting, we suggest that this behavior arises because of their interpersonal relationships at work. As has been previously argued, older employees will be more motivated to deepen their existing relationships at work (De Lange et al., 2009, p. 5). Nahapiet and Ghoshal (1998) found that such relationships provide a direction for knowledge sharing. We therefore assume that older employees might change the way they think about job performances because of the experiences of their colleagues. Job meaning results from the influential information offered by other employees about their experience of the tasks that embody work (Wrzesniewski, Dutton, & Debebe, 2003).

Although the literature allows us to make different assumptions about the effects of age on job-crafting motivations and behaviors, it says nothing about the actual motivations and behaviors of older and younger employees. We seek to address this shortcoming by including the effect of age in the original job-crafting model of Wrzesniewski and Dutton (2001).

Method

Context and Sample

Our aim was to elaborate our theory around the forms of job crafting as defined by Wrzesniewski and Dutton (2001) by exploring the effects of age on job-crafting motivations and behaviors. Although the authors previously have applied themselves to distinguish main job-crafting motivations and behaviors, no scholars have yet studied how and why older employees engage in these behaviors compared to younger employees. Thus, this study fits the criteria of using a qualitative study design. Strauss and Corbin (1990, p. 19) noted: "Qualitative methods can be used to uncover and understand what lies behind any phenomenon about which little is yet known. It can be used to gain novel and fresh slants on things about which quite a bit is already known."

We searched for an age diverse sample that would allow us to divide participants into groups of older employees (aged 45+) and younger employees (aged 44 and younger) to compare their job-crafting motivations and behaviors. Kooij, de Lange, Jansen, and Dikkers (2009) found that researchers who examine older employees in organizations often put the threshold at 40 or 45, while other authors have described older employees as aged 45+ (Ilmarinen, 2001; Furunes & Mykletun, 2005). Applying this criterion, we conducted this research in a socially responsible non-profit organization that aims at providing care and assistance to homeless and socially vulnerable citizens. This organization is located in the Netherlands with approximately 202 employees (and a number of volunteers and trainees). Employees in the sample occupy managerial positions (positions that require higher educational levels) and operational positions (positions that require lower educational levels). For the most part, employees work with little direct supervision and have a high degree of decision latitude in their jobs.

Our sample was selected based on two criteria. First, because we sought to compare different job-crafting motivations and behaviors of older and younger employees, the sample had to consist of a group of 15 older and a group of 15 younger employees. Second, the sample had to be selected by making use of theoretical sampling techniques, which are supposed to decrease the prevalence of biases in samples and increase their representativeness (Saunders, Lewis, & Thornhill, 2007, p. 218). To meet this last criterion, all employees were divided into two groups: one group of older employees (aged 45+) and one group of younger employees (aged 44 and younger). Older and younger employees were randomly selected from both groups and invited by email to participate in the study. Our final sample consists of 16 younger employees who all occupy operational positions and 15 older employees. Out of these 15 older employees, four occupy managerial positions, and the others occupy operational positions.

Data Collection

The primary method of data collection involved semi-structured interviews ($n=31$). We used the interview protocol of Berg et al. (2010), whose interview protocol explored how employees describe their perceptions of and experiences with job crafting. In each interview, questions were posed about the following. First, we asked about the three different job-crafting behaviors in the Wrzesniewski and Dutton (2001) model. We sought to pose these questions in a general way such that participants were encouraged to describe their own beliefs and assumptions. According to

Saunders et al. (2007, p. 318), this approach is a good way of overcoming interviewer bias (where interviewers create a bias in responses). If participants did not understand a specific question, general examples of job crafting were given. Second, we asked about the job-crafting motivations behind such behavior. Third, and finally, we asked about desired job-crafting behavior. Because certain jobs and tasks tend to provide more opportunities for job-crafting behavior than others (Lyons, 2008), this last question was asked to explore the desired job-crafting behavior of participants who occupy jobs that provide fewer opportunities for job crafting.

The interviews were performed at the workplace of the participants. The interviews were tape recorded and transcribed by utilizing data sampling, which restricts transcribing to the sections of interviews that are pertinent to specific research questions (Saunders et al., 2007, p. 475). In this study, the only interview sections transcribed were those in which participants mentioned a proactive behavior that they had previously undertaken or wanted to undertake and that fits in the three different job-crafting behaviors of the Wrzesniewski and Dutton (2001) model. Additionally, their job-crafting motivations were also transcribed.

Data Analysis

In an iterative fashion, we analyzed the qualitative data by traveling back and forth among the data. This analysis utilized two major steps.

Step 1: Identifying the job-crafting motivations and behaviors of older and younger employees. We began by employing three coding schemes for each individual job-crafting behavior. The categories of the coding schemes were derived from the Wrzesniewski and Dutton (2001) model, which meant that we used a *directed approach* in our qualitative content analysis (Hsieh & Shannon, 2005). According to Saunders et al. (2007, p. 479), this approach is a good way of creating meaningful categories for classifying data. The first coding scheme was employed to analyze how participants engaged in task crafting. According to Wrzesniewski and Dutton (2001), employees engage in task crafting by altering the form or number of activities they engage in while doing a job. We used these two activities as the categories for the first coding scheme. The second coding scheme was employed to analyze how participants engaged in relational crafting. Because this practice involves changing either the quality or amount (or both) of interaction with others at work (Wrzesniewski & Dutton, 2001), we used these two activities as the categories for this coding scheme. The last coding scheme was employed to analyze how the participants engaged in cognitive crafting. According to Wrzesniewski and Dutton (2001), this activity refers to altering how one sees a job. We used this activity as the category for this last coding scheme. Finally, to analyze the job-crafting motivations of participants, a *motivations* category was added to all coding schemes with three subcategories: (1) *personal control*, (2) *positive self-image*, and (3) *human need for connection to others*.

Because the transcripts consist only of proactive behaviors that fit into the three individual job-crafting behaviors and job-crafting motivations of the Wrzesniewski and Dutton (2001) model, we were able to assign quotes to the right coding schemes.

The data of the older and younger employees were coded separately. After having coded the data of all participants according to the coding schemes, the transcripts were read again to make sure that no relevant data were missing.

Step 2: Comparing and identifying the differences between the job-crafting motivations and behaviors of older and younger employees. In this phase, we integrated all three coding schemes into one. We used the coding schemes from the first phase to note how often participants mentioned engaging or wanting to engage in the three different job-crafting behaviors and how often they mentioned the three different job-crafting motivations. These data were coded separately for both groups, which allowed us to compare the data from both groups. Next, we offer a brief overview of our findings, followed by a discussion of how our findings elaborate the job-crafting theory. Finally, we conclude with a discussion of the implications of our study for job-crafting theory.

Findings

In this section, we present our findings and use them to describe how older and younger employees engaged in the three job-crafting behaviors and what their job-crafting motivations are. We also include a table with examples of job-crafting behaviors and motivations that were given by several participants.

Task Crafting: Altering the Form of Activities

Older Employees

Most of the older employees described making proactive changes to the form of their assigned job activities by changing the way they performed their tasks. Consistent with Wrzesniewski and Dutton (2001), asserting more control over their jobs and creating a positive self-image were among their key motivations. The main motivator, which is the desire to assert more control over their jobs, arose from the need for work efficiency. The need to create and sustain a positive self-image arose when employees were not satisfied with the content of their jobs and when they had the belief that their colleagues were not satisfied with their job performances.

Additionally, we found that the key motivators also occurred in conjunction with one another. One of the home assistants explained how he made his job more challenging (positive self-image) and how this change could help him perform his work better (personal control):

> I felt that my job was actually more appropriate for lower-skilled employees, because I was only busy with practical things. For example, serving food to clients. I wanted more of a challenge… so I started to talk with clients about their personal problems. That was really interesting, and I learned more about my clients, which is useful for the performance of my work. (participant 18, home assistant)

Younger Employees

Younger employees also engaged in this activity by changing the way they performed their tasks to work more efficiently. Unlike older employees, younger employees were thus only motivated to assert control over their work. Several younger employees also mentioned changing how they performed their tasks because they noticed that their colleagues worked more efficiently. In these cases, a cognitive change with respect to tasks occurred and triggered task crafting (Wrzesniewski & Dutton, 2001). For example, a facility manager explained changing her thoughts about how to do archival work because of a colleague, which forced her to change how she performed this task. To illustrate:

> I am not really good at archival work, but I need to do this work anyway. I have a colleague who can do it a lot better and faster than me. So whenever he does the archival work, I try to observe what he is really doing. He brings structure to his work and I am now trying to do that as well. Otherwise this archival work will remain a never-ending task. (participant 3, facility manager)

Task Crafting: Altering the Number of Activities

Older Employees

Almost all older employees described altering the number of their assigned job activities by increasing the number. Employees occupying higher positions discussed engaging in this behavior to assert control over their job performance. Other employees had the desire to create and sustain a positive self-image by feeling that they had the ability and expertise to do more tasks or other tasks than they were formally assigned to do. In a few cases, we again found that such job-crafting motivations occurred in conjunction with one another.

The following example of a receptionist illustrates how he is motivated to create a positive self-image:

> I heard that we will expand soon; hopefully, I will then get a leading role in the mailroom. I mean, I know I am old, and I think my younger coworkers have a greater chance of getting that position. But I have gained relevant experience in my life to hold such a responsibility. You know, even if I am old, I still would like to develop myself and get a higher position. Besides that, I feel that I can do a lot more than what I do now. (participant 9, receptionist)

Younger Employees

Younger participants also engaged in this behavior mostly by increasing the number of their activities at work; a few mentioned decreasing their activities. The main motivation behind their behavior was to create a positive self-image. However, unlike older employees, younger employees sought to do this by creating a positive sense of themselves *in the eyes of others* (Baumeister, 1982; Erez & Earley, 1993; Wrzesniewski & Dutton, 2001, p. 183). Their additional motivation was to assert control over their work to conduct their jobs more efficiently. The following example describes an employee who engaged in task alteration so that his clients had a positive image about him:

> Some of our clients have the responsibility to deliver our mail to institutions located throughout the city. This usually happens once a week, and they are allowed to borrow a bicycle from the organization to do this. But, one of my clients wanted to work more, which is a good thing, so I gave him permission to borrow a bicycle twice a week. This is actually against our policy, but I think that my client has good intentions, and I feel that supporting him is the right thing to do. (participant 31, personal assistant)

Finally, these findings—concerning the task-crafting behavior of younger employees—reveal that this form of job-crafting behavior triggers cognitive job-crafting behavior. One of the younger employees mentioned that he noticed that he had to change his attitude toward colleagues to improve their collaboration, because of his additional team manager tasks.

Relational Crafting: Altering the Quality of Interaction

Older Employees

All older employees were engaged in this behavior to assert control over their jobs. They discussed engaging in this behavior to control conflicts at work and improve their work performance. For example, the service manager indicated that she adjusted the quality of her interactions to improve the atmosphere in the store and the work performances of her colleagues:

> How I interact with colleagues depends on where I am at that moment. When I work in one of my stores, I have informal conversations with my employees, because I feel that this leads to a better atmosphere and the employees perform better. (participant 10, service manager)

Younger Employees

Almost all younger employees described altering the quality of their interactions by changing the topics of conversations. Their main motivation was to control their jobs by trying to improve the execution of their work.

A further motivator was fulfilling a basic human need to connect with others. Participants discussed wanting to communicate with certain colleagues about topics other than work. Their aim was to introduce meaning into their lives (Baumeister & Leary, 1995) because they wanted to learn from the life experiences of others:

> I also like to talk about topics other than work with colleagues who have the same age as me. I can get along with them much better, maybe that is because we are at the same stage of our lives and we face the same problems. It is nice then to hear each other's solutions and ideas and to learn from this. (participant 14, home assistant)

Finally, we found that cognitive crafting could trigger relational crafting. For example, the employee of the policy department mentioned changing her perception about the employees of the organization. She explained that during the past 2 years, some of her colleagues worked for a short period in the organization and left quickly. Therefore, she decided not to invest much time in relationships with colleagues and interacted with them only about work-related issues. She altered her thoughts about what her job is *relationally*, which—according to Wrzesniewski and Dutton (2001)—is an aspect of cognitive crafting. By contrast, we found that task crafting might also trigger cognitive crafting, which in turn might foster relational-crafting behavior. The care coordinator noticed (because of his additional team manager tasks) that his colleagues did not appreciate his dominant attitude. He therefore decided to change the way he communicated with them.

Relational Crafting: Altering the Amount of Interaction

Older Employees

Most of the older employees described participating in this form of job crafting by either decreasing or increasing the amount of interaction with specific colleagues. They were mainly motivated to assert control over their jobs because they mentioned doing so for the purpose of their work performance or to avoid workplace conflict. Only a few mentioned wanting to fulfill a basic human need to connect with others by forming friendly relationships. For example, a team manager discussed forming a friendly relationship with a colleague because he finds sociability at work important. The following example illustrates the control motivation and shows how cognitive crafting might foster relational-crafting behavior:

> I noticed how well a colleague communicated with her clients. You know, our clients don't always listen to us, they are hard to deal with. But this colleague had good conversations with her clients. So I started to talk with her a lot to ask her how she was able to make them listen to her. Her advice was useful, and now I try to improve how I communicate with clients. (participant 18, home assistant)

Younger Employees

Most participants described engaging in this behavior by decreasing the amount of their interaction with others at work. They mentioned changing the amount of their interactions for the purpose of their work performance (control motivation). For example, a personal assistant indicated that she increased the amount of interaction with a specific colleague to learn from him and improve her work performance. Consistent with Wrzesniewski and Dutton (2001), this finding reveals that relational crafting triggered cognitive crafting, which in turn fostered task-crafting behavior. The employee described changing the way she thought about how to conduct her work, and she finally changed her work style.

A further motivator was creating and sustaining a positive self-image. Participants discussed decreasing the amount of their interactions because their relationships affected the positive images that colleagues had about them:

> I could collaborate very well with one colleague, but once, she attacked me verbally about work in front of everyone. Honestly, I did not do anything wrong, and now other colleagues will think I don't work well. I think it was totally unfair of her to attack me like that, even if I did something wrong we can talk about that in private. Now, I avoid talking to her. (participant 20, personal assistant)

Cognitive Crafting: Changing the Cognitive Task Boundaries

Older Employees

Older employees engaged the least in this third form of job-crafting behavior. Unlike task and relational crafting, participants did not indicate that they wanted to engage in this behavior. However, the cognitive changes in their work occurred because of their accumulated work experience. In turn, this accumulated work experience triggered behavioral changes in the way they performed their jobs (Wrzesniewski & Dutton, 2001). In most cases, older employees reacted to this change by trying to assert control over their work. For example, a service manager explained how she unexpectedly noticed that the motivation level was low at her workplace. Therefore, she had to change her own behavior and began motivating employees to avoid dealing with a lack of staff.

Several employees mentioned reacting to the cognitive change by creating and sustaining a positive self-image in their own eyes:

> When I had just started, I worked together with social workers. They seemed to be well qualified, and I got a bit insecure about my own skills. I needed a lot of time for certain tasks, because I was afraid I would not perform as well as they did. But later on, I realized that their knowledge of work was quite limited. So, I gained more self-confidence, and I picked up requests easily. (participant 18, home assistant)

Younger Employees

Younger employees also discussed engaging in this behavior because of their accumulated work experience. This change triggered a behavioral change in the way they did their jobs (Wrzesniewski & Dutton, 2001). Most participants reacted to this change by trying to assert control over their work performance. A few participants indicated that they wanted to create a positive self-image in the eyes of others. For example, a personal assistant described how she noticed that certain clients were not well-groomed. Therefore, she began advising clients about their appearance during counseling conversations. However, she explained that she stopped giving such advice when she perceived that her clients and colleagues did not appreciate it (participant 13). Table 42.1 illustrates other examples of job-crafting behaviors.

Table 42.1 Evidence of differences in job-crafting behaviors of older and younger employees

Forms of job crafting	Older employees	Younger employees
Task crafting		
Altering the form of activities	Dinner and lunch should be prepared on time every day for our clients. I noticed just recently that my colleagues had problems with meeting the deadline. Now, I figured out how we could work faster, and I came up with the idea to order smarter. Now, I order sliced vegetables instead of whole pieces in order to save time. (personal control) (team manager)	Last year, I started doing the administration of the bills of our residents. But I couldn't find the information I needed. The administration was a real mess, so I thought of introducing a new, better-organized system. (personal control) (financial administrative employee)
		Our clients are stubborn and don't always listen to us. But I noticed that my colleague jokes a lot with her clients when she wants them to do something. For example, once she asked a client to clean up his room and he refused. When she made a couple of fun jokes, he surprisingly started cleaning his room. Now, I use jokes as well and it really helps. (personal control) (personal assistant)
Altering the number of activities	I would like to do more HRM tasks, because I often deal with HRM issues during my current job. But honestly, I want to do more, because I know I am able to do more (positive self-image) (prevention officer)	Other than my main tasks, I do additional team manager tasks as well. Also, if there is some work left that is undone, I finish this. My effort is really necessary, and I want my organization to achieve good results. Besides, my colleagues will know that I contribute to achieving good organizational results and that I deserve to work here (positive self-image) (care coordinator)
	Doing interviews with volunteers is not a formal task of mine, but I started doing the interviews a while ago. I don't think that any of my other colleagues have the required expertise to do the interviews. So I do it now because we need to recruit the best volunteers in our team in order to reduce our high workload a bit (personal control) (service manager)	I would like to manage more projects. Now, this is something sector managers do, but they seem to have a busy schedule. So I can do a lot of their work, because I have the expertise and experience to do this. I will discuss this with them soon, I am sure that they will appreciate me doing this. (positive self-image) (policy employee)
Relational crafting		
Altering the quality of interaction	I have had a couple of intense conflicts with one colleague, because he is a person who acts out of emotion. Unfortunately, we have to collaborate often for work. So I only communicate with him for work purposes and I try to do this in a professional way. For example, I don't laugh when I talk and I certainly don't make any jokes. It's a pity that I have to do this, but I need to make sure that we'll not have another conflict; otherwise, it will affect our work. (personal control) (home assistant)	I try to deepen my relationship with colleagues by talking to them about personal issues instead of only work. I think we need to get to know each other better, because then we know what we can and cannot say to each other. This is useful for giving feedback. You know how to do this better when you know the person better. If this works out well, we will give each other easier feedback and we'll improve our collaboration and performances. (personal control) (home assistant)

Altering the amount of interaction	*I need the contribution of some colleagues for the implementation of my own work. I form and adjust my relationships based on the work I have to do. For example, now I communicate a lot with a colleague from another department, because we work together on a project. When we finish the project, I am sure I'll contact him less often. (personal control) (prevention officer)*	*When I had just started working here, I talked a lot with one specific colleague. But he started to have feelings for me and he obviously wanted more in our relationship. So I decided to talk less often to him. I don't want such a relationship at work, because this will affect our collaboration. (personal control) (personal assistant, participant 11)*
Cognitive crafting	*Before I started working here, I was told that I would do administrative tasks as well. I was happy to hear this, because it meant that I could do more than just answering phone calls. But in practice, this turned out not to be true, which I find very disappointing. Unfortunately, my work is now too boring for me. (positive self-image) (receptionist)* *The longer I worked here, the more I felt that the organization started to require more from the staff. A lot of employees couldn't handle this and got fired or left the organization voluntarily. To make sure I wouldn't lose my job, I did my best and worked harder to adjust to these new requirements. (personal control) (personal assistant)*	*When I had just started working here, I obviously underestimated the empowerment of employees. I have to do more work than I expected to be doing, and I still have to adjust myself to this workload. For example, if there is coffee on the ground people send a request to the facility service and ask for a cleaner. I don't understand why they can't get a napkin and clean the coffee themselves. (personal control) (facility manager)* *In the beginning, we didn't work with computers, and now we do. I never expected that I would need a computer for my tasks, and honestly, I am not really good at working with computers. So I looked for a colleague who knows a lot about computers and who was willing to help me out with this. Luckily, I found one, and now I can do my computer tasks a lot faster. (personal control) (personal assistant)*

Discussion

We began our article by discussing why the influence of age should have been included in the original job-crafting model of Wrzesniewski and Dutton (2001). Here we continue this discussion by relating our findings to the previous literature.

We found that both older and younger employees engaged the most in task crafting. However, younger employees participated more in all three forms of job-crafting behavior. This finding supports the assumption of De Lange et al. (2009) who suggested that older employees would engage less in job crafting because they had achieved careers that better fit their self-concept and occupations with more job control (Edwards et al., 2006). Building on the research of Berg et al. (2010), who found that the three different forms of job-crafting behavior are interrelated and can trigger or be triggered by one another, we found that this interrelationship occurs more often with the job-crafting behavior of younger employees. Whereas Berg et al. (2010) did not directly find that task and relational crafting give rise to cognitive crafting, we found that this might be the case for relational crafting.

Additionally, Wrzesniewski and Dutton (2001) argued that job-crafting motivations arise from three individual needs: *asserting personal control*, *creating a positive self-image*, and *a need for human connection to others*. In our study, we found that motivations for cognitive crafting do not arise from individual needs but from accumulated work experience. Finally, to our knowledge, both older and younger employees motivated to engage in job crafting to assert control over their work. Their additional motivation is to create and sustain a positive self-image *in their own eyes* (older employees) *and in the eyes of others* (younger employees). Moreover, we found that the different job-crafting motivations (particularly of younger employees) occur in conjunction with one another.

Theoretical Implications

We sought to relate existing theory about older and younger employees to different job-crafting behaviors. Here, we return to those behaviors and discuss how our study builds or extends the job-crafting theory of Wrzesniewski and Dutton (2001).

Task Crafting We began this paper by arguing that older employees would be less motivated to craft their tasks because the literature suggests that older employees are less flexible in adjusting their work style (Garg, 1991). However, in our study, both older and younger employees engaged in this behavior for the same purpose. Employees changed the way they performed their tasks or wanted to conduct their jobs differently because they were motivated to find more efficient ways of working (*personal control motivation*). However, younger employees engaged much more in this type of behavior. Given this finding, we propose that older employees are indeed less flexible in adjusting their work style than their younger peers. Throughout their accumulated work experience, older employees had learned how to work efficiently; thus, there is no need to change their work style.

Furthermore, we also found that most of the older and younger employees engaged in this type of behavior by increasing the number of their activities. Whereas most of the older employees were motivated to assert a certain control over their jobs, younger employees were more motivated to create a positive self-image *in the eyes of others*. Although previous research suggests that older employees (compared to younger employees) are motivated to substantially reduce the levels of effort in their work tasks (Kanfer & Ackerman, 2004, p. 453), our research shows that older employees are willing to increase their levels of effort if that will help them to assert more control over their work. Conversely, younger employees will increase their levels of effort to convince colleagues that they are motivated and able to deliver good results. This finding supports the assumption of Kooij et al. (2009), who argued that older employees tend to adjust their personal preferences to meet the demands of their current work situation, whereas younger employees tend to adjust the current work situation to achieve or maintain the desired developmental outcomes.

Relational Crafting Based on Carstensen's socio-emotional selectivity life-span theory (Carstensen et al., 2000) and *the relational demography theory*, we expected that older employees would be more motivated (than younger employees) to improve the quality of their interactions and to increase the amount of interactions with their fellow peers. However, we found that both older and younger employees only changed the topics of their conversations. Whereas all older employees engaged in this behavior to assert control over their jobs, younger employees also wanted to fulfill a basic human need for connection to others. Although this finding does not speak directly to the social context, it is plausible that the social context has formed the behavior of older employees. If the social context of these older employees consists only of younger colleagues, then we predict that older employees might encounter difficulty in deepening their relationships. Previous studies have shown that younger generations are particularly motivated to continuously engage in new social interactions (De Lange et al., 2009). When studying such job-crafting behavior in older employees, further research should include the social context to validate our prediction. In this case, the effect of perceived relative age is particularly significant for older employees (Cleveland & Shore, 1992).

Furthermore, we expected younger employees to be more motivated to increase the amount of their interactions to acquire new information for purposes of their work. We found that: (1) both older and younger employees discussed decreasing or increasing the amount of their interactions with colleagues in executing their work (personal control motivation) and (2) younger employees engaged more in this behavior than older employees. However, contrary to our expectations, whether younger employees increase (form new social interactions) or decrease the amount of their interaction depends on the execution of their work.

Cognitive Crafting We discussed that we expected older employees to engage in this type of behavior because of their interpersonal relationships with their peers. Because we expected older employees to deepen their existing relationships at work (De Lange et al., 2009), we expected them to share work-related knowledge in their relationships (Nahapiet & Ghoshal, 1998) and change the way they think about how to conduct their jobs (because of the accumulated work experience of their colleagues)

(Wrzesniewski et al., 2003). Our research shows that older employees engage the least in this job-crafting behavior. As previously discussed, we also found that older employees did not deepen their existing relationships, and we predict that this fact is the reason for their cognitive crafting behavior. However, future research must study whether cognitive crafting arises because of such deep relationships to validate our prediction.

With respect to the behavior of younger employees, we argued that younger employees would be more motivated to engage in job-crafting behavior because they aim at continuously acquiring new knowledge (Lang & Carstensen, 2002). Therefore, younger employees can change the way they think about their work more often than older employees. Consistent with our previous expectations, we found that: (1) younger employees engaged much more in this form of job-crafting behavior and (2) that several younger employees deliberately changed the way they performed their tasks because they noticed that one of their colleagues performed tasks more efficiently.

Limitations and Future Research

Sample As with all attempts to build and elaborate theory from a limited sample, caution is warranted when generalizing these findings to other organizations. For example, Lyons (2008) found that context may influence the likelihood of employees engaging in job-crafting activities. Different organizations are supposed to offer opportunities, invitations, and (perhaps) incentives to employees to modify their jobs. We also believe that changes in organizational cultures may influence job-crafting activities.

Research Opportunities As noted in the introduction, our work focuses on exploring the job-crafting motivations and behaviors of older and younger employees. Wrzesniewski and Dutton (2001) argued that the activity has both individual and organizational effects. Future researchers may wish to more explicitly compare the individual and organizational effects of the job-crafting behaviors of older and younger employees. Another future research opportunity is to study the collaborative job-crafting behaviors of older employees. Leana et al. (2009) refer to collaborative job crafting as an activity that is conducted by informal groups of employees, who together determine how to alter the work to meet shared objectives. We believe that older employees will engage more in such activities because they focus their attention more on the process and collaborative nature of goal accomplishments at work (Kanfer & Ackerman, 2004). Finally, we recommend future researchers to draw further on the research of Berg et al. (2010) and focus on studying how older employees from different organizational levels engage in job-crafting behavior. We found in our study that older employees from lower organizational levels were more motivated to craft their tasks (than older employees at higher organizational levels) because they were not satisfied with their current job tasks. However, because of a lack of time, we could not pay much attention to this effect.

Context   Finally, we must also be careful about the unique nature of our setting. We previously argued that perceived age dissimilarity (in the social context at work) might influence the relational and cognitive job-crafting behavior of older employees. However, we have not examined whether older employees perceived age dissimilarity in their social context. Therefore, we were not able to make any assumptions about this effect, and we recommend that future researchers address this question further.

Conclusion and Implications for Organizational Practice

Job Crafting Matters to Organizations and Their Employees   Prior studies have demonstrated that job crafting should receive more attention at work because of its positive effects on well-being (Tims, Bakker & Derks, 2013), work behavior, and performance outcomes (Lyons, 2008). Furthermore, job crafting is supposed to help employees meet personal and organizational goals (Berg et al., 2010). Our study reveals that older employees are less motivated to engage in job-crafting behaviors than younger employees. Thus, one implication of our study is that managers should stimulate the job-crafting behaviors of older employees to enable them to contribute more to organizational goals. For example, managers might inform older employees about job-crafting strategies and explain to them the positive individual and organizational consequences, because job crafting may lead to higher levels of work engagement and work performance (Gruman & Saks, 2011). Additionally, managers might stimulate older employees with lower job positions to take the initiative in making their work more challenging, or they could provide them with more opportunities to engage in job crafting (Wrzesniewski & Dutton, 2001). Our findings show that these employees may have job-crafting desires that they are not able to fulfill themselves.

Finally, because we found that not all types of job-crafting behaviors may be beneficial for work collaborations and organizations in general (e.g., blocking off communication with colleagues and making decisions that are against organizational policies), we recommend that managers communicate work responsibilities in a clear manner to all employees. Managers should be aware of their employees' job-crafting behaviors and, when required, assist them with job crafting to align it with organizational goals (Tims, Bakker, Derks, & van Rhenen, 2013).

References

Armstrong-Stassen, M., & Lee, S. H. (2009). The effect of relational age on older Canadian employees' perceptions of human resource practices and sense of worth to their organization. *The International Journal of Human Resource Management, 20*(8), 1753–1769.

Avery, D. R., McKay, P. F., & Wilson, D. C. (2007). Engaging the aging workforce: The relationship between perceived age similarity, satisfaction with coworkers, and employee engagement. *Journal of Applied Psychology, 92*(6), 1542–1556.

Bakker, A. B. (2010). Engagement and "job crafting": Engaged employees create their own great place to work. In S. L. Albrecht (Ed.), *Handbook of employee engagement: Perspectives, issues, research and practice* (pp. 229–244). Cheltenham: Edward Elgar.

Baltes, P. B., & Smith, J. (2003). New frontiers in the future of aging: From successful aging of the young old to the dilemmas of the fourth age. *Gerontology, 49*, 123–135.

Baumeister, R. F. (1982). A self-presentational view of social phenomena. *Psychological Bulletin, 91*, 3–26.

Baumeister, R. F., & Leary, M. R. (1995). The need to belong: Desire for interpersonal attachments as a fundamental human motivation. *Psychological Bulletin, 117*, 497–529.

Berg, J. M., Wrzesniewski, A., & Dutton, J. E. (2010). Perceiving and responding to challenges in job crafting at different ranks: When proactivity requires adaptivity. *Journal of Organizational Behavior, 31*, 1–50.

Berg, J. M., Dutton, J. E., & Wrzesniewski, A. (2008). What is job crafting and why does it matter. *Retrieved form the website of Positive Organizational Scholarship on April, 15*, 2011.

Carstensen, L. L., Pasupathi, M., Mayr, U., & Nesselroade, J. R. (2000). Emotional experience in everyday life across the adult life span. *Journal of Personality and Social Psychology, 79*, 644–655.

Cleveland, J. N., & Shore, L. M. (1992). Self- and supervisory perspectives on age and work attitudes and performance. *Journal of Applied Psychology, 77*, 469–484.

De Lange, A. H., Taris, T. W., Jansen, P., Kompier, M. A. J., Houtman, I. L. D., & Bongers, P. M. (2009). On the relationships among work characteristics and learning-related behavior: Does age matter? *Journal of Organizational Behavior, 31*, 1–26.

Edwards, J. R., Cable, D. M., Williamson, I. O., Schurer Lambert, L., & Shipp, A. J. (2006). The phenomenology of fit: Linking the person and environment to the subjective experience of person environment fit. *Journal of Applied Psychology, 91*, 802–827.

Erez, M., & Earley, C. (1993). *Culture, self-identity and work.* New York: Oxford University Press.

Gruman, J. A., & Saks, A. M. (2011). Performance management and employee engagement. *Human Resource Management Review, 21*, 123–136.

Finkelstein, L., Burke, M., & Raju, N. (1995). Age discrimination in simulated employment contexts: An integrative analysis. *Journal of Applied Psychology, 80*, 652–663.

Freund, A. M. (2006). Age-differential motivational consequences of optimization versus compensation focus in younger and older adults. *Psychology and Aging, 21*(2), 240–252.

Furunes, T., & Mykletun, R. J. (2005). Age management in Norwegian hospitality businesses. *Scandinavian Journal of Hospitality and Tourism, 5*, 116–134.

Garg, A. (1991). Ergonomics and the older worker: An overview. *Experimental Aging Research, 17*(3), 143–155.

Goldberg, B. (2005). How to become employer of choice for the working retired. In P. T. Beatty & R. M. S. Visser (Eds.), *Thriving on an aging workforce: Strategies for organizational and systemic change* (pp. 170–178). New York: Krieger Publishing Company.

Hsieh, H. F., & Shannon, S. E. (2005). Three approaches to qualitative content analysis. *Qualitative Health Research, 15*(9), 1277.

Ilmarinen, J. (2001). Aging workers. *Occupational and Environmental Medicine, 58*, 546–552.

Kanfer, R., & Ackerman, P. L. (2004). Aging, adult development, and work motivation. *The Academy of Management Review, 29*(3), 440–458.

Kooij, D., de Lange, A., Jansen, P., & Dikkers, J. (2009). Older workers' motivation to continue to work: Five meanings of age. A conceptual review. *Journal of Managerial Psychology, 23*(4), 364–394.

Lang, F. R., & Carstensen, L. (2002). Time counts: Future time perspective, goals and social relationships. *Psychology and Aging, 17*, 125–139.

Lawrence, B. (1990). At the crossroads: A multiple-level explanation of individual attainment. *Organization Science, 1*, 65–85.

Leana, C., Appelbaum, E., & Shevchuk, I. (2009). Work process and quality of care in early childhood education: The role of job crafting. *Academy of Management, 52*, 1–56.

Lyons, P. (2008). The crafting of jobs and individual differences. *Journal of Business and Psychology, 23*, 25–36.

McAdams, D. P., St. Aubin, E. D., & Logan, R. L. (1993). Generativity among young, midlife, and older adults. *Psychology and Aging, 8*(2), 221–230.

Maurer, T. J. (2001). Career—relevant learning and development, worker age, and beliefs about self-efficacy for development. *Journal of Management, 27*, 123–140.

Nahapiet, J., & Ghoshal, S. (1998). Social capital, intellectual capital, and the organizational advantage. *Academy of Management Review, 23*, 242–266.

Rogers, J. K. (1995). Just a temp: Experience and structure of alienation in temporary employment. *Work and Occupations, 22*, 137–166.

Saunders, M., Lewis, P., & Thornhill, A. (2007). *Research methods for business students* (5th ed.). Harlow: Prentice Hall.

Steele, C. M. (1988). The psychology of self-affirmation: Sustaining the integrity of the self. In L. Berkowitz (Ed.), *Advances in experimental social psychology* (Social psychological studies of the self: Perspectives and programs, Vol. 21, pp. 261–302). San Diego: Academic.

Strauss, A., & Corbin, J. (1990). *Basics of qualitative research: Grounded theory procedures and techniques*. Newbury Park, CA: Sage.

Tims, M., Bakker, A. B., & Derks, D. (2013). The impact of job crafting on job demands, job resources and well-being. *Journal of Occupational Health Psychology, 18*(2), 230–240.

Tims, M., Bakker, A. B., Derks, D., & van Rhenen, W. (2013). Job crafting at the team and individual level: Implications for work engagement and performance. *Group and Organization Management, 38*, 427–454.

Williams, H. M., Parker, S. K., & Turner, N. (2007). Perceived dissimilarity and perspective taking within work teams. *Group Organization Management, 32*, 569–597.

Wrzesniewski, A., & Dutton, J. E. (2001). Revisioning employees as active crafters of their work. *The Academy of Management Review, 26*(2), 179–201.

Wrzesniewski, A., Dutton, J. E., & Debebe, G. (2003). Interpersonal sensemaking and the meaning of work. *Research in Organizational Behavior, 25*, 93–125.

Yeatts, D. E., & Hyten, C. (1998). *High-performing self-managed work teams: A comparison of theory to practice*. Newbury, CA: Sage.

Yeatts, D. E., Folts, W. E., & Knapp, J. (2000). Older workers' adaptation to a changing workplace: Employment issues for the 21st century. *Educational Gerontology, 26*, 565–582.

Chapter 43
A Simulative Comparison of Output Commercial Value, Employment, and Pollution Levels Between a Chemical Cluster and a Standalone Aluminum Smelting Plant

Andri Ottesen and Faidon Theofanides

Abstract Scholars and business practitioners have provided valuable insights into the clustering phenomenon and its impact on firms' performance. Nonetheless, supporting evidence from the chemical industry remains underreported. Chemical enterprises undertake collaborative forms to overcome the weaknesses faced by individual organizations in an attempt to tackle production efficiency and operational risks. This paper provides a simulative comparison of output commercial value, employment, and pollution levels between a chemical cluster (consisting of five medium-sized chemical plants) and a standalone aluminum smelting plant, using the case study approach. The research objectives are related in identifying which option: (a) provides more total value of commercial products (production output multiplied by market prices) per megawatt (MW) of electricity, (b) creates more jobs per megawatt, and (c) has lower level of pollutants. The research approach combines quantitative secondary data and a set of in-depth interviews among managers of the chemical plants and other knowledgeable persons or field experts. Consequently, the study makes a relevant contribution to the cluster literature and proposes some useful recommendations for policy-makers and individual chemical firms. The empirical findings of the simulative comparative case study are not sufficient for making generalizations about any kind of cluster or industrial sector.

Keywords Chemical cluster • Green chemical plant

A. Ottesen (✉)
Management Department, Business School, Australian College of Kuwait in collaboration with Central Queensland University, Kuwait City, Kuwait
e-mail: andri.ottesen@ack.edu.kw

F. Theofanides
Marketing Department, Business School, Australian College of Kuwait in collaboration with Central Queensland University, Kuwait City, Kuwait
e-mail: f.theofanidis@ack.edu.kw

© Springer International Publishing Switzerland 2017
R. Benlamri, M. Sparer (eds.), *Leadership, Innovation and Entrepreneurship as Driving Forces of the Global Economy*, Springer Proceedings in Business and Economics, DOI 10.1007/978-3-319-43434-6_43

Introduction

Clusters are defined by Porter (1998) as: "geographic agglomerations of companies, suppliers, service providers, and associated institutions in a particular field." Nowadays, a prevailing term for clusters is "synergic formations." During the past 15 years, we have witnessed clusters being adopted as a form of policy business panacea. The rise and importance of such cluster policies is well recognized in many developed countries globally. On the other hand, there has also been significant critique around the theoretical and empirical basis underlying the explosion of policies to support clusters.

This paper provides empirical evidence about the benefits of chemical clusters, using the case study approach. More specifically, it presents a comparison simulative case study. The comparison is between a proposed chemical park of five interconnected chemical plants and an aluminum smelting plant. Case study data were collected from a variety of primary and secondary sources to enhance the credibility of the case study findings, such as Environmental Impact Assessments (EIAs), the London Metal Exchange, the Innovation Center of Iceland, a set of in-depth interviews among managers of the chemical plants and other knowledgeable persons/experts.

Literature Review and Research Hypothesis

Clusters designed to develop and support networking among groups of co-located companies and other economic agents are very popular among economically developed countries. Cluster development measures and the resulting business clusters have been repeatedly evaluated in the framework of wider policy areas such as SME development, innovation policy, and regional development (Theofanides, 2007). In many countries, there are programs set up specifically to promote cluster development. Such programs can be carried out by existing actors (for example, a government agency), or new actors can be set up to run them. Often, one of the purposes of such programs is to help initiate cluster organizations; that is, the program provides financing or otherwise promotes the formation of cluster-specific organizations, typically in some form of public–private partnership (Theofanides, 2007). A country can have many (even hundreds) of such cluster-level organizations in operation.

The rise of such cluster policies has corresponded both with the emergence of systemic concepts of business innovation (Freeman, 1987; Lundvall, 1992; Nelson, 1993 etc.) and with the establishment and growing popularity of the "cluster" concept itself (Porter, 1990, 1998, 2003; Schmitz, 1995). On the other hand, there has also been significant critique around the theoretical and empirical basis underlying the explosion of policies to support clusters (Belussi, 2006; Benneworth & Charles, 2001; Duranton, Martin, Mayer, & Mayneris, 2010; Lorenzen, 2005; Martin & Sunley, 2003 etc.). According to Aragon, Aranguren, Diez, Iturrioz, and Wilson (2014), it is difficult to rigorously show whether or not clusters in fact have positive effects on economic development processes. As Perry (2005) argues, "it has been possible to pick and mix research evidence too freely." In many occasions, clusters are being adopted as a form of policy business panacea, without considering the local conditions. Synthesizing the cluster literature, the most important advantages of chemical clusters are: reduced costs and risks, accessible resources, synergies in energy and matter utilization, shared services for utilities, access to transportation and logistical capabilities, share best practices in health, safety, and the environment.

According to Ketels (2007), companies can achieve higher levels of productivity, because they have close access to specialized suppliers and service providers and can rapidly learn from the best practices of close competitors. The same author proposes that cluster initiatives need to take a role in improving the overall competitiveness of a region, even beyond the boundaries of their cluster. Productivity, as measured in terms of the rate of output per unit of input, can be associated with the commercial value when we incorporate into the analysis the real market prices for all units of output. So the commercial value of chemical products can be computed by multiplying the units of output with their respective market prices.

Based on the above analysis, the paper proposes the following hypothesis:

Hypothesis 1 The chemical cluster provides more total value of commercial products (production output multiplied by market prices) per megawatt (MW) of electricity compared to the standalone aluminum smelting plant.

There are some studies which seek to explore the degree to which industrial clusters are associated with employment levels. An emphasis on linking economic development with workforce development has grown (Simon & Hoffman, 2004; Markusen, 2004; Harper-Anderson, 2008). As it can be easily understood, for the capital-intensive industries allocated to the chemical cluster category the focus on jobs can be particularly problematic. Fowler and Kleit (2014) found out that the presence of industrial clusters is associated with lower poverty rates. Joblessness is an important cause of poverty; therefore, it is meaningful to assert that industrial clusters reduce poverty rates, because they increase the level of employment within a specific geographical region. Moreover, the same authors stated that "regions with a higher share of employment in clusters, and with that employment dispersed across many industries within the same cluster, fare even better, than those where employment is concentrated in a single industry". There is a growing recognition that cluster development and employment growth need to go hand in hand, therefore it makes sense to hypothesize that:

Hypothesis 2 The chemical cluster creates more jobs per megawatt, compared to the standalone aluminum smelting plant.

There is no doubt that the economic boom has led to a general decline in environmental quality. Chemical plants need constantly to find ways to improve energy efficiency and moderate the consumption of natural resources (Shao, Tang, Zhang, & Li, 2006). Any cluster form needs to balance between economic development and environmental health. The main research question is: do clusters cause major environmental problems compared to standalone plants? A rational way to approach this question is to identify the amount of waste produced by the two options. Another important element that needs to be taken into consideration is the secondary unintended result of the production process (defined as by-product); if the by-product can be used as an input into the production process of another plant (that is the case of a cluster) and not considered as waste, then environmental problems might reduce (less waste).

Based on the above analysis, the paper proposes the following hypothesis:

Hypothesis 3 The chemical cluster has lower level of pollutants compared to the standalone aluminum smelting plant.

Methodology and Limitations

The methodological approach used is a simulation case study, which aims to compare a proposed chemical cluster of five interconnected chemical plants and an aluminum smelting plant, of which the owners have expressed interest in building plants in Helguvík, Iceland in 2012. Simulation is the imitation of the operation of a real-world process or system (Banks, Carson, Nelson, & Nicol, 2001). In our case, the model is the chemical cluster and the aluminum smelting plant, whereas the simulation represents the hypothetical operation of the system, based on real production data. The production data have been collected from EIAs. In general, case study data were collected from a variety of sources to enhance the credibility of the case study findings. Apart from the quantitative secondary data collected from the EIAs, a set of in-depth interviews among managers of the chemical plants and other knowledgeable persons or field experts have been conducted.

More specifically, facts and figures are based on public records from EIAs from: (a) the aluminum company—Nordural ehf. (2007), (b) the silicon metal company—United Silicon Iceland Ltd. (2012), and (c) the glycol company—Atlantic Green Chemicals Ltd. (2011). The figures for the CO_2 recycling plant—Carbon Recycling International (CRI, 2008)—are derived from the EIA for their plant at Svartsengi. Figures for the pulp bleaching plant—Kemira (2011)—are derived from EIA at Bakki in the northern part of Iceland. Finally, input/output analysis for the biodiesel company Lífdísill (2012) is derived from a report from the National Research Laboratory/Innovation Center of Iceland. The outputs of these chemical plants have also been scaled up proportionally from the EIA figures (Innovation Center of Iceland, 2012) in relation to input in order to optimize use of hydrogen, methanol, and steam (Chlorine Plant 2x, Biodiesel 6,5x, and Glycol Plant 1,6x, and CO Recycling Plant 5x). Data about job creation were verified by interviews with Icelandic Investment Agency and Federation of Industries (Skúladóttir, 2013; Haflidason, 2013).

The unit market prices, used to calculate the commercial value of the output of the chemical cluster, were taken from the London Metal Exchange (2016). Finally, the unit market prices, used to calculate the commercial value of the output of the aluminum smelting plant, were collected by interviewing the managing director of the Godavari Bio-refinery in Holland (Rangarjan, 2016).

Regarding the research limitations, we need to address the following: simulation concerns the manipulation of a number of variables and conditions of a model representing a real system. However, manipulation of a single variable or condition (for optimization purposes) often means that the reality of the system as a whole can be lost. As a matter of fact, the selection of the chemical cluster (five plants) was based on input–output optimization, which might be difficult to be found in real-life business scenarios. Skeptics believe that a simulation model is a simplified representation of a real-life situation, therefore it provides limited knowledge. Furthermore, the case study approach continues to be criticized for its lack of generalizability. The word "generalizability" is defined as the degree to which the findings can be generalized from the study sample to the entire population (Polit & Hungler, 1991). Taking into consideration the research limitations, the authors argue that the problems related to simulation and generalization have little relevance to the goals of the study, which are more to explore rather than describe and generalize.

Case Study Discussion

This paper presents a comparison simulative case study. The comparison is between a proposed chemical park of five interconnected chemical plants and an aluminum smelting plant. In 2012, the aluminum company—Nordurál, the silica metal company—United Silicon Iceland (USI), and the glycol company—Atlantic Green Chemicals (AGC) had all completed EIAs as a prerequisite for operational permit and had been allocated a designated lot within the industrial area of Helguvík harbor. CRI had signed Memorandum of Understanding (MoU) with the municipality governing the area about participating in the formation of a green chemical cluster (Reykjanes Municipality Homepage, 2012). The pulp bleach company Kemira had made an EIA and has been allocated a lot in Bakki, north of Iceland. Efforts were being made to provoke their interest to relocate to the area. The biodiesel company, Lifdisill, was operating a small company and expressed interest in building a large biodiesel company.

The combined use of electricity of the cluster is projected to be 253 MWe (megawatt electric) compared to 435 MWe for the aluminum plant. In 2012, there was not enough electricity available for both projects at the same time frame. Furthermore, CO_2 emission quotas restriction under the Kyoto agreement did not allow for both projects. Thus, criteria were made to evaluate the two options in terms of: (a) the commercial value of products per MWe, (b) job creation per megawatt, and (c) total emission to the air of CO_2 and other Green House Gas (GHG) emissions.

Figure 43.1 shows the input and the output of the chemical cluster. The silicon dioxide smelting plant produces silicon metal, but releases CO_2 and steam. The pulp bleaching plant produces chlorate to bleach paper, but releases hydrogen as a by-product. The carbon recycling plant uses CO_2, steam, and hydrogen from the pulp bleaching plant as an input to produce methanol. The biodiesel plant uses water, steam, waste (cooking oil and animal fat), and rapeseed oil and turns that into biodiesel with the use of methanol,

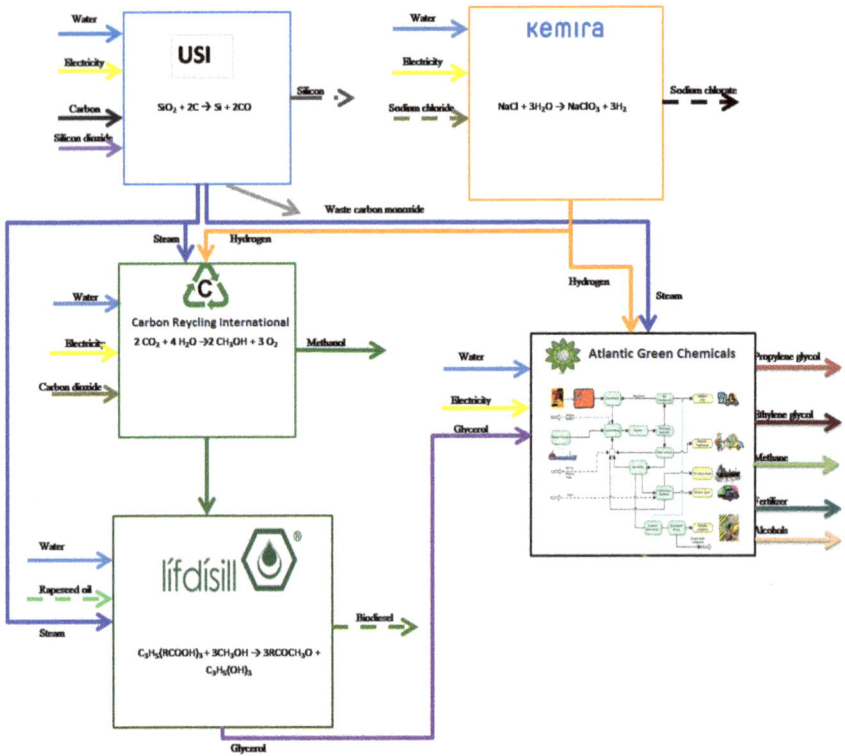

Source: author's collection/archive

Fig. 43.1 Input–output process of the simulative chemical. *Source*: Author's collection/archive

releasing glycerin as a by-product. Finally, the glycol company takes the glycerin from the biodiesel production and converts it into deicing material for airplanes, using hydrogen and steam from the other plants.

As seen in Tables 43.1 and 43.2, the absolute number of job placements is higher for the chemical cluster (378 jobs) compared to the aluminum plant (350 jobs). Furthermore, the aluminum plant uses almost twice as much energy (435 MW) compared to the chemical cluster (253 MW). When energy is the highest cost factor and the limited resource, such findings become significant. Table 43.3 uses the updated market prices (February 2016) and the output level of both options (aluminum plant vs chemical cluster) indicated in the EIAs in order to calculate the net commercial value of the products. The results of this analysis are: the value of commercial products is (in rounded numbers): (a) 411 million USD from the aluminum smelting plant and (b) 620 million USD from the chemical cluster. Furthermore, when the commercial value is divided by units of megawatt of electricity, then the difference becomes even more apparent: (a) 944,827 USD per 1 MW for the aluminum smelting plant and (b) 2,450,592 USD per 1 MW for the chemical cluster or

Table 43.1 Input–output analysis of the chemical cluster in Helguvík, Iceland

Silica smelting plant — United Silicon Iceland			CO₂ recycling plant — Carbon Recycling International			Chlorine/Bleach plant — Kemira			Biodiesel plant — Lifdisell			Glycol plant — Atlantic Green Chemicals		
	Quantity	Units		Quantity	Units		Quantity	Units		Quantity	Units		Quantity	Units
Input			*Input*			*Input*			*Inputs*			*Input*		
Quartz	234	kt/year	CO₂	48	kt/year	NaCl	108	kt/year	Methanol	40	ML/year	Glycerol	211.2	kt/year
Carbon	216	kt/year	Hydrogen	7.2	kt/year				Rapeseed	334.1	ML/year	Hydrogen	4	kt/year
			Steam	98	kt/year				Steam	780	kt/year	Steam	796.8	kt/year
Electricity	130	MW	Electricity	1	MW	Electricity	120	MW	Electricity	1	MW	Electricity	1	MW
Water	97,200	kt/year	Water	0.03	kt/year	Water	100	kt/year	Water	3159	kt/year	Water	531.2	kt/year
Output—main product			*Output—main product* Renewable			*Output—main products*			*Output—main products*			*Output—main products*		
Silicon	90	kt/year	Methanol	40	ML/year	NaClO	200	kt/year	Biodiesel	287.6	kt/year	Pro. Glycol	165.1	kt/year
By-products						*By-products*			*By-products*			Ethyl Glycol	21.1	kt/year
Steam	1620	kt/year				Hydrogen	11.2	kt/year	Glycerol	35.1	kt/year	Alcohols	6.4	kt/year
CO₂	218	kt/year										Fertilizer	3.2	kt/year
Job creation	160		*Job creation*	35		*Job creation*	91		*Job creation*	56		*Job creation*	36	

Sources: Environmental Impact Analysis and Innovation Center of Iceland/National Research Laboratory

Table 43.2 Input–output analysis on aluminum smelter in Helguvik, Iceland

Aluminum plant						
Nordurál/Century Aluminum						
	Quantity	Units		Quantity	Units	
Input			*Output—main product*			
Aluminum						
Oxide	480	Kt/year	Aluminum	250	Kt/year	
Carbon	130	Kt/year	*By-product*			
Electricity	435	MW	CO_2	365	Kt/year	
			Job creation			350

Source: Environmental Impact Assessment for Aluminum Plant in Helguvik, Iceland

Table 43.3 Net commercial value of the products of the aluminum smelting plant and the chemical cluster

Aluminum plant				Chemical park			
Commercial production	Quantity Kt/year	Price in USD/KT	Value M USD	Net commercial	Quantity Kt/year	Price in USD/KT	Value M USD
Aluminum	250	**1643**	**410.8**	Silica metal	90	2506	225.5
				Pulp bleach	200	450	90.0
				Biodiesel	288	647	186.2
				Propylene glycols	165	630	104.0
				Ethylene glycols	21	520	10.9
				Industrial alcohols	6	450	2.7
				Fertilizer	3	100	0.3
				Total			619.7

Source: Unit prices: London Metal Exchange, ICIS Chemical Business 3.2.2016, and interview with Godavari Bio-refinery in Holland

2.59 times more commercial value for every MWe in favor of the chemical park. Therefore, *hypothesis 1* is supported.

Job creation is also a factor that was measured and again the numbers are in favor of the chemical cluster with 378 jobs created for the chemical cluster and 350 jobs created for the aluminum smelting plant. Furthermore, when the number of jobs is divided by units of megawatt of electricity, we get these numbers: (a) 0.8 jobs per 1 MW for the aluminum smelting plant and (b) 1.49 jobs for the chemical cluster per 1 MW, so 0.69 times more jobs for every MWe in favor of the chemical park. Therefore, *hypothesis 2* is supported (Table 43.4).

Finally, pollution is an important factor. Case study data indicate that the pollution through emissions released into the air from the aluminum smelting plant is 365 kt/CO_2 per annum, while the relative figure for the chemical cluster is 170.

Table 43.4 Commercial value of products and job creation per MW

Aluminum smelter					Chemical park					
Value in M. USD	MWe	Value M. USD per MWe	Job creation	CO_2 Net CO_2 emission Kt/year	Value in M. USD	MWe	Value M. USD per MWe	Jobs creation	CO_2 Net CO_2 emission Kt/year
411	435	0.9	350	365	619.7	253	2.4	378	170
			0.8/MWe					1.5/MWe	

Source: Calculated values from EIAs and Innovation Center of Iceland

As some of the CO_2 from the silica plant is reused, the net emission of CO_2 emission to the air is 170 kt/CO_2 which is less than half of the emissions of the proposed aluminum plant. Therefore, *hypothesis 3* also is supported.

Managerial Implications and Future Research Proposals

The paper provides evidence that chemical clusters can be more competitive compared to standalone chemical plants. Global economic crisis and its consequential effects on the global chemical industry indicate that individual chemical organizations should undertake collaborative forms to overcome production efficiency problems, increase synergies, and become more competitive. Chemical plants will have a greater chance of survival if they become members of a cluster system because the commercial value of their output will be higher compared to choosing to produce independently. Furthermore, the empirical findings of the simulative case study clearly demonstrate that chemical clustering policies can also reduce unemployment and pollution levels at a given geographical location.

The attempt in this paper however is to take the cluster theory beyond bare economics and competitive advantage, "The Cluster Theory 2.0," by adding a physics (natural) dimension. That is, respect and utilization for matter and energy in any form or shape is at the heart of this theory. Within the chemical industries, factories are called "Plants" as each factory operates similar to a botanical plant which transforms CO_2 to breathable air through a process called *Photosynthesis*. Chemical clusters create a garden or a (chemical) park (cluster) of plants, which each uses spare energy and effluence output as an input to the next plant, thus mimicking nature itself, creating an eco-system of chemical plants.

In terms of managerial implications, an important issue to take into consideration is that investors have started to prefer the Middle East, China, India, and Asia for investments on the chemical industry. Even though, the case study simulation was conducted in Iceland, the application of a similar chemical cluster could be proposed for the Middle East, mainly the GCC states (Saudi Arabia, Kuwait, the United Arab Emirates, Qatar, Bahrain, and Oman). These counties face three economic, social, and environmental problems: (a) according to the IMF, these countries have the least diversified industries in the world, as the oil industries are predominant in the region, (b) in the light of very low oil prices, there is a rather sizable budget deficit in every country as the sales of oil is the main source of state income, and (c) the GCC countries carbon foot print is about 4 times larger than the average European country. The topic for further study (and partial solution to these three problems the region faces) would be to explore the option building chemical clusters as the natural extensions of oil refineries since most of all the chemicals are based on hydrocarbon source mostly known as oil and gas. Chemical parks in GCC countries could create more (commercially) valuable products than oil exports and provide industry diversification at a very environmental manner.

Conclusion

The aim of this paper was to compare a proposed chemical cluster of five interconnected chemical plants and an aluminum smelting plant in order to explore which option: (a) provides more total value of commercial products per megawatt, (b) creates more jobs per megawatt, and (c) has lower level of pollutants. Overall the simulative case study analysis suggests that the proposed chemical cluster in Helguvik (Iceland) produces significantly more commercial value and creates slightly more jobs per megawatt electric than the proposed aluminum smelting plant. Furthermore, the chemical cluster yields less pollution. Judging from these empirical findings (everything else being equal), the proposed chemical cluster is categorized as a more utilitarian option.

References

Aragon, C., Aranguren, M., Diez, M., Iturrioz, C., & Wilson, R. (2014). Participatory evaluation: A useful tool for contextualizing cluster policy? *Policy Studies, 35*(1), 1–21.

Atlantic Green Chemical Ltd. (2011). *Bioalcohol- and glycol plant at Helguvik Harbor—Environmental impact assessment, Icelandic National Planning Agency, Reykjavik.* http://www.agc.is/wp-content/uploads/2011/09/L%C3%ADfalk%C3%B3h%C3%B3l-og-Gl%C3%BDk%C3%B3lverksmi%C3%B0ja-Frummatssk%C3%BDrsla.pdf. Accessed February 1, 2016.

Banks, J., Carson, J., Nelson, B., & Nicol, D. (2001). *Discrete-event system simulation* (p. 3). Prentice Hall. ISBN: 0-13-088702-1.

Belussi, F. (2006). In search of a useful theory of spatial clustering. In B. T. Asheim, P. Cooke, & R. Martin (Eds.), *Clusters and regional development* (pp. 69–89). London: Routledge.

Benneworth, P., & Charles, D. (2001). Bridging cluster theory and practice: Learning from the cluster policy cycle. In P. Den Hertog, E. Bergman, & D. R. Charles (Eds.), *Innovative clusters: Drivers of national innovation systems* (pp. 389–403). Paris: OECD.

Carbon Recycling International. (2008). *CO_2 recycling from Svartsengi Power Plant—Environmental impact assessment, Reykjavik.* http://www.skipulag.is/media/attachments/Umhverfismat/203/2008060100.pdf. Accessed February 1, 2016.

Duranton, G., Martin, P., Mayer, T., & Mayneris, F. (2010). *The economics of clusters: Lessons from the French experience.* Oxford: Oxford University Press.

Fowler, C. S., & Kleit, R. G. (2014). The effects of industrial clusters on the poverty rate. *Economic Geography, 90*(2), 129–154.

Freeman, C. (1987). Networks of innovators: A synthesis of research issues. *Research Policy, 20*(5), 499–514. doi:10.1016/0048-7333(91)90072-X.

Haflidason, K. (2013). Project Manager for Chemical Project at Invest Iceland, Personal Interview on 19 October 2013, Reykjavik, Iceland.

Harper-Anderson, E. (2008). Measuring the connection between workforce development and economic development: Examining the role of sectors for local outcomes. *Economic Development Quarterly, 22*, 119–135.

Innovation Center of Iceland. (2012). *Input–output analysis of Grundartangi Industrial Park—Study file: 8HK12091, Reykjavik.* http://www.ssv.is/Files/Skra_0057238.pdf. Accessed February 1, 2016.

Kemira. (2011). *Iceland National Planing Agency, Natrium Cloride Plant Kemira at Bakki in Husavik, North East of Iceland, Reykjavik.* http://www.skipulag.is/media/attachments/Umhverfismat/867/201105053.pdf. Accessed February 1, 2016.

Ketels, C. (2007). *The role of clusters in the chemical industry*. European Petrochemical Association (EPCA).

Lífdísill. (2012). *Input/output analysis for bio-diesel, National Research Laboratory/Innovation Center of Iceland*. London Metal Exchange, ICIS Chemical Business, 3.2.2016.

Lorenzen, M. (2005). Editorial: Why do clusters change. *European Urban and Regional Studies, 12*(3), 203–208. doi:10.1177/0969776405059046.

Lundvall, B. (1992). *National systems of innovation. Towards a theory of innovation and interactive learning*. London: Pinter.

Markusen, A. (2004). Targeting occupations in regional and community economic development. *Journal of the American Planning Association, 70*, 253–268.

Martin, R., & Sunley, P. (2003). Deconstructing clusters: Chaotic concept or policy panacea? *Journal of Economic Geography, 3*(1), 5–35. doi:10.1093/jeg/3.1.5.

Nelson, R. (1993). *National innovation systems: A comparative analysis*. Oxford: Oxford University Press.

Nordurál. (2007). *Aluminum smelter in Helguvik with annual production up to 250.000t Álver í Helguvík. Environmental impact assessment*. Reykjavik: Icelandic National Planning Agency. http://www.skipulagsstofnun.is/media/attachments/Umhverfismat/587/Matsskýrsla_2007-08-31_low%20res.pdf. Accessed February 1, 2016.

Perry, M. (2005). Clustering small enterprise: Lessons from policy experience in New Zealand. *Environment and Planning C: Government and Policy, 23*(6), 833–850. doi:10.1068/c0504.

Polit, D., & Hungler, B. (1991). *Nursing research: Principles and methods*. New York: JB Lippincott.

Porter, M. E. (1990). *The competitive advantage of nations*. New York: Free Press.

Porter, M. E. (1998). Clusters and the new economics of competition. *Harvard Business Review, 76*, 77–91. http://hbr.org/1998/11/clusters-and-the-new-economics-of-competition/ar/1.

Porter, M. E. (2003). The performance of regions. *Regional Studies, 37*(6/7), 549–578. doi:10.108 0/0034340032000108688.

Rangarjan, R. (2016). Managing Director at Godavari Biorefinary Holland, phone inerview on 3.2.2016.

Reykjanes Municipality Homepage. (2012). http://www.reykjanesbaer.is/upplysingatorg/frettir-og-tilkynningar/samningur-um-throun-efnavinnslugards-i-helguvik/18815/18.   Accessed October 2012.

Schmitz, H. (1995). Collective efficiency: Growth path for small scale industry. *Journal of Development Studies, 31*(4), 529–566. doi:10.1080/00220389508422377.

Shao, M., Tang, X., Zhang, Y., & Li, W. (2006). City clusters in China: Air and surface water pollution. *Frontiers in Ecology and the Environment, 4*(7), 353–361.

Simon, M., & Hoffman, L. (2004). *Final report: The next generation of workforce development project: A six-state policy academy to enhance connections between workforce and economic development policy*. Available online: http://wdr.doleta.gov/research/FullText_Documents/2005_05_final_dol_workforce_academy.pdf

Skúladóttir, B. (2013). Director for Environmental Affairs at Federation of Industries, Personal Interview on 19 October 2013, Reykjavik, Iceland.

Theofanides, F. (2007). *Europe INNOVA cluster mapping project-country report: Greece*. Norway: Oxford Research AS.

United Silicon Iceland Ltd. (2012). *Environmental impact assessment on up to 100.000t of silica smelting*.

Chapter 44
Is Spiritual Tourism an Innovation in Tourism for India and Pakistan?

Farooq Haq and Anita Medhekar

Abstract This conceptual paper attempts to build on the argument that innovation in tourism is a less focused topic in business and academic research. The growing interest in the practice and business of spiritual tourism cannot be ignored. This interest motivates the research aiming to present spiritual tourism as an innovation in tourism, specifically in India and Pakistan. In this unique study, the innovation in tourism is appreciated and analyzed from dimensions of product, process, and people, falling under the umbrella of architectural and revolutionary innovation. Hence the three elements of the tourism product: people, places, and events are adapted to align with the spiritual tourism as a tourism innovation. India and Pakistan are selected as the two countries since both carry the status of multifaith-purpose spiritual tourism destinations. This original research emphasizes on recognizing spiritual tourism as an innovation in tourism based on its products and services illustrating architectural and revolutionary innovation. The paper concludes with a matrix mapping elements of spiritual tourism with the dimensions of tourism innovation, hence filling a gap in the literature on tourism innovation and spiritual tourism. A relevant empirical study of travelers visiting India and Pakistan for spiritual tourism is a palpable future study.

Keywords Spiritual tourism • Revolutionary innovation • Tourism marketing • Architectural innovation • India and Pakistan

Introduction

Innovation is not a buzz word, as many consider in the marketing world, but it is an architect of competitive advantage of a company (Randhawa et al., 2016). Innovation reflects upon the goal and ambition of an organization. This ambition

F. Haq (✉)
Canadian University of Dubai, Dubai, United Arab Emirates
e-mail: Farooq@cud.ac.ae

A. Medhekar
Central Queensland University, North Rockhampton, QLD, Australia

© Springer International Publishing Switzerland 2017
R. Benlamri, M. Sparer (eds.), *Leadership, Innovation and Entrepreneurship as Driving Forces of the Global Economy*, Springer Proceedings in Business and Economics, DOI 10.1007/978-3-319-43434-6_44

can be achieved through innovation presented by its products and services. In tourism, innovation is considered pivotal, but it is also known as the least studied area of tourism (Randhawa et al., 2016; Santos, Burghausen, & Balmer, 2016; Moscardo, 2008). Generally, the debate on innovation focuses on new products and technologies; all innovation is based on confronting existing assumptions and channels of thinking. Moscardo (2008) argues that one approach to redesign innovation in tourism is to ignore the recognized and almost cliché goal of sustainable tourism. An efficient approach to knowledge management systems or tourism processes is required to achieve innovation in tourism (Hall & Williams, 2008; Moscardo, 2008).

Since the events of September 9–11 and the subsequent wars, people around the world have been observed to be more inclined towards spirituality for various personal and social reasons; people are pursuing spiritual answers for the questions rising from the failure of materialistic lifestyles (Blomfield, 2009; Kraft, 2007; Mitroff, 2003). The emerging awareness and attention to spirituality had a significant impact on many businesses around the world (Brownstein, 2008; Fernando & Jackson, 2006; Lewis & Geroy, 2000). The tourism industry is one of the industries which experienced a very explicit effect of this spiritual refocus of international business (Finney, Orwig, & Spake, 2009; Geary, 2008; Tilson, 2005; Cohen, 1992). This influence of spirituality on tourism industry gave birth to spiritual tourism as an innovation stimulating new products, people, processes, marketing, and organizations linked with tourism people, places, and events. Every state has something to offer to the global tourist; even the poorest nations can present their heritage, traditional beliefs related sites, culture, and natural places to tourists searching for the "new" (Haq & Medhekar, 2015), hence triggering an innovative spiritual tourism product or service or experience.

Tourism around the world received around 332 million international tourists from January to April 2015, which is 14 million more than the same period last year, an increase of 4% (WTO, 2015). Tourism has shown worldwide growth with an increase of 4.3% in 2014 associating with the upwards trend of international tourism in recent years, which averages more than 4.5% international tourist per year since 2010 (WTO, 2015). According to World Tourism Organization (WTO, 2009), 689 million people traveled to foreign countries in 2000, out of which nearly 40 million people traveled for spiritual purposes from Christian, Muslim, and Hindu families. By the year 2020, UNWTO (2008) has projected that international tourist arrivals are expected to reach 1.6 billion.

Spiritual tourism as an academic and commercial concept is a new type of tourism that has risen from the combination of special interest and cultural tourism and views religious tourism and pilgrimage as subsets of spiritual tourism while conceptually overlapping with each other. It is agreed that spiritual tourism requires a strong multifaith sociocultural background rather than big roads, bridges, and hotels, etc. That is why India and Pakistan embraced spiritual tourism as an innovative way to internationalize their businesses and had reasonable success as discussed further in the upcoming sections of this paper. This conceptual paper starts with a literature review on various aspects of tourism innovation and spiritual tourism, pinpointing towards the research problem and objectives for this study. Findings and discussion of this study present the people, places, and events associated with spiritual tourism mapped with various dimensions of tourism innovation.

Literature Review

Innovation

The literature on innovation presents service and product innovations as separate disciplines since services engage customers more closely in an innovation process (Randhawa et al., 2016; Decelle, 2006). With respect to innovation in tourism, products and services need to be considered as the same, since tourism innovation is a new or significantly improved offering for tourists. This paper will consider tourism products and services as one and the argument regarding their similarities and differences is beyond the scope of this study.

Innovation can be defined in several ways, depending on the buyers and sellers for a particular product in a specific market (Haq, 2013). The pioneer of the innovation theory, Joseph Schumpeter (1883–1950), observed that innovation is always about a new product, new production process, new markets, new leaders, or new organizations, and moving towards new combinations of these (Schumpeter, 1934). All these factors of new products, processes, people, and markets can be applied for innovation in tourism (Ali, Ryu, & Hussain, 2016; Chubchuwong & Speece, 2016; Decelle, 2006; Weiermair, 2006). It can be further argued that since tourists seek experience rather than destination, it can be offered by innovation of the tourism product as experience rather than offering singular tourism elements (Weiermair, 2006). Hjalager (2010) also suggested that destination acts as a stage where various tourism agents are actors and only continuous learning from customers can help to make the tourism experience more innovative. This is where the spiritual tourism product or experience can be presented as an innovation in tourism (Haq, 2013). A spiritual tourist will be seeking and experiencing spiritual development at the same place where someone else will be studying culture, history, or heritage (Haq & Medhekar, 2013).

The concepts of innovations presented by Abernathy and Clark (1985) have been further classified as tourism innovation types by Hjalager (2002), which highlights the significance of customer orientation in innovation. Hjalager (2002) derived four types of tourism innovations: regular innovations, niche innovations, revolutionary innovations, and architectural innovations. This research study analyzes these types and concludes that spiritual tourism has connections with regular innovations and niche innovations; however, the role of revolutionary innovations and architectural innovations seems more dominating to recognize spiritual tourism as an innovation in tourism. The revolutionary innovations demand introduction of new methods to shift staffing structures, and association with similar markets with new methods, hence product and people innovations are covered (Chubchuwong & Speece, 2016; Weiermair, 2006; Decelle, 2006; Hjalager, 2002). While architectural innovations demand creation of new events and redefining the physical infrastructure, hence process innovations are covered (Weiermair, 2006; Decelle, 2006; Hjalager, 2002).

Spiritual Tourism

It has been observed that spiritual tourism is thought of as a new impression in travel and tourism. The fact is that faith and religious matters have been the primary reasons for traveling in human history (Haq & Jackson, 2009; Hall, 2006). As an example, if food or gastronomic tourism or cooking TV programs are new trends, then it does not imply that people did not eat before, as it is a basic human need. The only commercial issue is that human needs have to be defined as a marketing product or service and nourished under the umbrella of an international brand. Hence, applying the theory of revolutionary innovation, it can be implied that new methods need to be approached for the same markets.

People traveling as spiritual tourists have defined themselves in a variety of means: as "travelers," "seekers," "pilgrims," "devotees," "event attendants," and "adventurers," etc. "Interestingly, many spiritual tourists have been classified by academic researchers as practicing pilgrimage, religious, special interest, cultural or experiential tourists" (Haq & Jackson, 2009, p. 142). These tourists can be attracted towards spiritual tourism if innovation is applied effectively. A considerable amount of research has been published on the six million spiritual tourists who travel annually to Lourdes in France, the millions of people visiting Jerusalem or Mecca for Hajj every year, and the visits to Indian Ashrams (Finney et al., 2009; Sharpley & Sundaram, 2005).

The knowledge base provided by the discussion in this section of the paper provides a firm foundation for the conceptualization of spiritual tourism. Adapting the definition of cultural tourists, a spiritual tourist could be described as someone who visits a place out of his/her usual environment, with the intention of spiritual growth (in relation to God or the Divine), regardless of the main reason for traveling (McKercher, 2002). A recently established definition of a spiritual tourist will be adopted in this study to underpin the South Asian business of spiritual tourism as: "someone who visits a specific place out of his/her usual environment, with the intention of spiritual meaning and/or growth, without overt religious compulsion, which could be religious, nonreligious, sacred or experiential in nature, but within a Divine context, regardless of the main reason for traveling" (Haq & Jackson, 2009, p. 145).

Spiritual tourism could be viewed as a broad concept that involves tangible and intangible products and services. In this research, tangible items will include churches, mosques, temples, shrines, and other spiritual centers which indicate architectural innovation in tourism. Meanwhile, intangible products and services will include organized spiritual events, seminars, festivals, and gatherings with spiritual motives which confirm revolutionary innovation in tourism.

Research Problem and Objectives

The overarching research problem of this paper is to prove that spiritual tourism can be considered as a tourism innovation in India and Pakistan. This research studies the spiritual tourism in India and Pakistan to observe innovation in tourism policies and practices. The research problem is addressed in this paper by setting the objective of analyzing various tourism places, people, and events in both countries linked with architectural and revolutionary innovation. The effective goal of this study is to present a link between various spiritual tourism social and business practices that lead towards presenting spiritual tourism as a tourism innovation.

Findings

The previous sections of this paper presented a structure of this research by defining spiritual tourism and tourism innovation. After recognizing the Indian and Pakistani traveling practices and activities for spiritual purpose, a detailed study of the tourism material and information was conducted to highlight each country's potential linked with spiritual tourism. Findings of the research conducted in both countries with respect to their spiritual tourism and its links with architectural and revolutionary innovation are explained below.

India

World Tourism Organization (WTO, 2015) reported that international tourist inflow in India is expected to grow at 6.5 % CAGR per annum. In 2010, the foreign tourist arrivals were 2.5 million in 2008, to 6.0 million in 2010 and expected to grow to 10 million by 2020. This is due to the success of Incredible India Campaign and tourism trade fairs organized by the government in partnership with the industry. Hence business opportunities in many niche new products such as farm and village tourism, ecotourism, heritage tourism, cultural tourism, and spiritual tourism can be cultivated to reap sustainable economic benefits. The Indian government has strategically developed spiritual tourism circuits such as in the footsteps of Buddha circuit and likewise other circuits have been suggested by Haq and Medhekar (2015) to promote spiritual tourism.

Religious or spiritual tourism in India accounts for 90 % of domestic tourism (Haq & Medhekar, 2015; Shinde, 2007). Shinde (2007) explores the movement of Indian tourists as pilgrims from an informal to an organized and formal industry of religious tourism in Vrindavan, Mathura near Agra. He argues that spiritual/religious tourism is moving into a new form of business opportunity as an innovation for the entrepreneurship and management (Shinde, 2010).

There are numerous Hindu, Islamic, and Sikh religious places, rives, mountains, temples, and Mosques of historical importance in all the States of India, from Kashmir in the Himalayas to Kanyakumari in the Southern tip of India, and Gujarat in the West to Bengal in the East, that it is not possible to mention all (Bandyopadhyay, Morais, & Chick, 2008). The key Hindu religious sites are Vaishno Devi in Kashmir, Allahabad where the three holy rivers meet coming from the Himalayas, Banaras–Kashi, Nasik, Amritsar Sikh Golden Temple, and numerous Hindu temples in South India. Similarly there are numerous famous Islamic Mosques some 700 years old in ruins and many still in use from the fourteenth century Delhi Sultanate and mainly from the Mughal period (Gupta, 1999). Moreover, Buddhism originated in India and spread worldwide, leaving many sacred sites for Buddhists that have earlier been ignored as spiritual tourism treasures (Haq & Medhekar, 2015).

Only recently, the Buddhist Circuit—in the footsteps of Buddha Trial by Indian Ministry of Tourism, in collaboration with Indian Railways, indicates the innovative steps taken by the government. Sharpley and Sundaram (2005) in their exploratory research studied the visits to Sri Aurobindo Ashram by the western tourists in South East India. They found that some were permanent spiritual tourists and others were temporarily visitors to the Ashram to experience spirituality in India, and concluded that "there is a continuum of Spirituality inherent in tourism, though this is related to tourists' experience rather than initial motivation" (p. 161). Sen (2005) also stresses upon religious plurality of India based on a large and prominent Sikh population, and a substantial number of Christians, whose settlements go back at least to the fourth century, and practitioners of Jainism and Buddhism, which had been for a long period the official religion of many Indian rulers. These places signify the rich Indian multifaith and multicultural, spiritual heritage, emphasizing upon the potential for architectural tourism innovation in India.

Pakistan

The cultural and social infrastructure of Pakistan is strongly embedded in different spiritual and religious traditions. Several destinations in Pakistan are revered by spiritual tourists belonging to religions of Islam, Hindu, Buddhist, and Sikh. For Muslim or Islamic tourists, Pakistan presents a wide spectrum of old and modern Mosques, Madrassas, and shrines of revered Sufi Saints (Haq & Wong, 2011). The annual "Ijtima" or gathering of Muslims from around the world in Raiwind attracts more than two million Islamic tourists to teach and learn Islamic spiritual theory and practice (Haq & Wong, 2011). A good example of a progressive message on spiritual tourism in Pakistan can be found in an article in The Economist, "Of saints and sinners," which reflected upon Sufism, music, and Pakistan's Sufi shrines (The Economist, 2008).

Pakistan is home to numerous spiritual places belonging to religions other than Islam; these religions include Buddhism, Hinduism, Christianity, and Sikhism (Haq & Medhekar, 2015; Wannell & Hasan, 2008; Singh & Narang, 2004). There are some churches and Christian monasteries in Pakistan that were built some hundred years ago during the British Empire of the Indian subcontinent. Similarly, there are several historical and modern temples and religious centers associated with other religions as discussed in the previous section. Pakistan accommodates hundreds of Sufi shrines, for example, Al-Hajveri (referred to as Daata Ji by the devotees) in Lahore, Shah Abdul Latif Bhitai in Sind, and Baha-ud-Din Zakariya in Multan. Pakistan also offers historical places built and established by the past Muslim rulers since the eighth century, which attract many Muslim tourists from all over the Islamic world (Haq & Medhekar, 2010).

In practice, tableegh trips are very common among Muslim countries of South Asia, which motivates men to travel in groups to various Mosques and stay, pray, and eat there (Haq & Wong, 2011). These groups generally consist of educated Muslim men of all ages who visit and stay in various mosques, meet with the local Muslims, meet with non-Muslims, teach and learn Islamic theory and practice, with the sole purpose of reviving Islam (Sikand, 2006). A typical tableegh group entails of one or two vehicles for transport and their food is cooked in the mosques where they sleep on the floors in their sleeping bags while they continue their own and others' spiritual development. This spiritual exercise has its origins in the early twentieth century India (Sikand, 2006).

Discussion

The previous section illustrated highlights of spiritual tourism business and social practices in India and Pakistan. The spiritual tourism people, places, and events in both countries need to be projected as an innovation to achieve sustainable success. The earlier sections discussed various dimensions of innovation in tourism, which will be studied and adapted in this section.

The example of Mahabodhi Temple complex in Bodhgaya, India being declared as a World Heritage site by UNESCO in 2002 supports the discussion of this paper. Moreover, the Bihar State Tourism Department projected Bodhgaya as a spiritual tourism destination by Brand Buddhism to international tourists and also developed five-star golf course and hotels (Geary, 2008). If this was left to the Central Government, then innovations will be ignored and the condition of Bodhgaya would be similar to many other historical and spiritual places in India and Pakistan which are neglected, not restored, and vandalized. Vukonic (2015) has argued by providing theoretical and empirical support that economic impact of the special area of religious tourism or spiritual tourism should be exploited by developing countries to create opportunities. This is the discussion here in this paper, suggesting that this new overhauling of spiritual tourism in both countries could be done under the umbrella of revolutionary and architectural innovation.

Since this study has recognized that spiritual tourism as an innovation in tourism can be more related to "revolutionary" and "architectural" types of innovation. It has also been observed that both these types of innovation encompass product and process innovation in practice (Weiermair, 2006; Decelle, 2006). Based on the

Table 44.1 Spiritual tourism places, people, and events as tourism innovation

Countries	Architectural innovation		Revolutionary innovation
	Products/places	Events	People
India	Historical and holy places: temples/sites for Hindus and Buddhists, Mosques, Colonial Churches, and Ashrams	Anniversaries of Sufis, Gurus and various religious leaders and Hindu gods, annual sacred gatherings	Religious leaders and spiritual gurus, Missionaries like Mother Teresa, Hindu gods
Pakistan	Mosques, Sufi Shrines, Churches, and Monasteries, Hindu, Sikh, and Buddhism historical and holy sites	Anniversaries of Sufis, Tableegh Ijtimas, multifaith seminars, annual holy gatherings	Sufis of the past and present, Islamic Leaders

Source: Based on this study

details of spiritual tourism products and services being offered, or not offered, in India and Pakistan, this research emphasizes on applying revolutionary and architectural innovation. The specific people, places, and events associated with spiritual tourism in both countries can be mapped with revolutionary and architectural innovation as illustrated in Table 44.1.

Conclusions and Future Research

This study that was based on analyzing spiritual tourism in India and Pakistan regarding tourism places, people, and events, and attempted to map with dimensions of tourism innovation. The paper has analyzed innovation in tourism from dimensions of product, process, and people, falling under the blanket of architectural and revolutionary innovation. The three elements of the tourism product: people, places, and events were examined to align with the spiritual tourism as a tourism innovation. India and Pakistan were selected as the two countries since both carry the reputation and image of multicultural and multifaith spiritual tourism destinations. This research concludes with the suggestion to accept spiritual tourism as an innovation in tourism based on its products and services illustrating architectural and revolutionary innovation. This paper delivers a different concept based on service and tourism related innovation and maps it with spiritual tourism that is not a new product, but needs to be launched as an innovation cemented in architectural and revolutionary dimensions.

An empirical study to confirm findings of this research is an obvious future research direction. In order to test and confirm the reliability and validity of conceptual findings of this research presenting spiritual tourism as a tourism innovation, further qualitative and quantitative study is recommended. The quantification of findings related to spiritual tourism in India and Pakistan based on behavior and attitude of tourists needs to be undertaken in order to reach evidence based tourism marketing strategies. An empirical study on the behavior of travelers and visitors who qualify as spiritual tourists, regardless of their religion and nationality, is an imperative future study. Similarly, more new and useful segments of spiritual tourists visiting India and Pakistan could be identified by an empirical research based on tourist's regional, religious, ethnic, and sectarian backgrounds. A quantitative research would provide better marketing information on tourists' tastes and preferences for tourism marketers in India and Pakistan. Meanwhile, a qualitative study could be conducted with management and organizers of places, people, and events linked to spiritual tourism in South Asia, which will provide in-depth details regarding the innovation in tourism businesses.

References

Abernathy, W., & Clark, K. (1985). Innovation: Mapping the winds of creative destruction. *Research Policy, 14*(1), 3–22.

Ali, F., Ryu, K., & Hussain, K. (2016). Influence of experiences on memories, satisfaction and behavioral intentions: A study of creative tourism. *Journal of Travel & Tourism Marketing, 33*(1), 85–100.

Bandyopadhyay, R., Morais, D. B., & Chick, G. (2008). Religion and identity in India's heritage tourism. *Annals of Tourism Research, 35*(3), 790–808.

Blomfield, B. (2009). Markers of the heart: Finding spirituality in a bus marked tourist. *Journal of Management, Spirituality & Religion, 6*(2), 91–106.

Brownstein, B. (2008). Profitability and spiritual wisdom: A tale of two companies. *Business Renaissance Quarterly, 3*(3), 137–143.

Chubchuwong, M., & Speece, M. W. (2016). The "people" aspect of destination attachment in international tourism. *Journal of Travel & Tourism Marketing, 33*(3), 348–361.

Cohen, E. (1992). Pilgrimage centre: Concentric and eccentric. *Annals of Tourism Research, 18*(1), 33–50.

Decelle, X. (2006). A dynamic conceptual approach to innovation in tourism. In OECD (Ed.), *Innovation and tourism policy* (pp. 85–105). Paris: OECD.

The Economist. (2008). *Of saints and sinners: The Islam of the Taliban is far removed from the popular Sufism practiced by most South Asian Muslims.* Retrieved December 22, 2008, from http://www.economist.com/world/asia/displaystory.cfm?story_id=12792544#top.

Fernando, M., & Jackson, B. (2006). The influence of religion-based workplace spirituality on business leaders' decision-making: An inter-faith study. *Journal of Management & Organization, 12*(1), 23–39.

Finney, R. Z., Orwig, R. A., & Spake, D. F. (2009). Lotus-eaters, pilgrims, seekers, and accidental tourists: How different travellers consume the sacred and the profane. *Services Marketing Quarterly, 30*(2), 148–173.

Geary, D. (2008). Destination enlightenment: Branding Buddhism and spiritual tourism in Bodhgaya, Bihar. *Anthropology Today, 24*(3), 11–14.

Gupta, V. (1999). Sustainable tourism: Learning from Indian religious traditions. *International Journal of Contemporary Hospitality Management, 11*(2/3), 91–95.

Hall, C. M. (2006). Buddhism, tourism and the middle way. In D. J. Timothy & D. Olsen (Eds.), *Tourism religion and spiritual journeys* (pp. 172–185). London: Routledge.

Hall, M. C., & Williams, A. M. (2008). *Tourism and innovation.* New York, NY: Routledge.

Haq, F. (2013). Islamic spiritual tourism: An innovative marketing framework. *International Journal of Social Entrepreneurship and Innovation, 2*(5), 438–447.

Haq, F., & Jackson, J. (2009). Spiritual journey to Hajj: Australian and Pakistani experience and expectations. *Journal of Management, Spirituality & Religion, 6*(2), 141–156.

Haq, F., & Medhekar, A. (2010). Spiritual tourism business rising between India and Pakistan amidst the political crisis: A conceptual framework. *Journal of Business and Technology, 2*(2), 78–87.

Haq, F., & Medhekar, A. (2013). Branding spiritual tourism as an innovation for peace between India and Pakistan. *International Journal of Social Entrepreneurship and Innovation, 2*(5), 404–414.

Haq, F., & Medhekar, A. (2015). Spiritual tourism between India and Pakistan: A framework for business opportunities and threats. *World Journal of Social Sciences, 5*(2), 190–200.

Haq, F., & Wong, H. (2011). Exploring marketing strategies for Islamic spiritual tourism. In O. Sandikci & G. Rice (Eds.), *Handbook of Islamic marketing* (pp. 319–337). Northampton, MA: Edward Elgar.

Hjalager, A. M. (2002). Repairing innovation defectiveness in tourism. *Tourism Management, 23*(1), 465–474.

Hjalager, A. M. (2010). A review of innovation research in tourism. *Tourism Management, 31*(1), 1–12.

Kraft, S. E. (2007). Religion and spirituality in Lonely Planet's India. *Religion, 37*(3), 230–242.

Lewis, J. S., & Geroy, G. D. (2000). Employee spirituality in the workplace: A cross-cultural view for the management of spiritual employees. *Journal of Management Education, 24*(5), 682–694.

McKercher, B. (2002). Towards a classification of cultural tourists. *International Journal of Tourism Research, 4*(1), 29–38.

Mitroff, I. (2003). Do not promote religion under the guise of spirituality. *Organization, 10*(2), 375–380.

Moscardo, C. (2008). Sustainable tourism innovation: Challenging basic assumptions. *Tourism and Hospitality Research, 8*(1), 4–13.

Randhawa, P., Kim, M., Voorhees, C. M., Cichy, R. F., Koenigsfeld, J. P., & Perdue, J. (2016). Hospitality service innovations in private clubs. *Cornell Hospitality Quarterly, 57*(1), 93–110.

Santos, F. P., Burghausen, M., & Balmer, J. M. T. (2016). Heritage branding orientation: The case of Ach. Brito and the dynamics between corporate and product heritage brands. *Journal of Brand Management, 23*(1), 67–88.

Schumpeter, J. (1934). *The theory of economic development.* Boston, MA: Harvard University Press.

Sen, A. (2005). *The argumentative Indian: Writings on Indian history, culture and identity.* London: Penguin.

Sharpley, R., & Sundaram, P. (2005). Tourism: A sacred journey? The case of Ashram tourism, India. *International Journal of Tourism Research, 7*(3), 161–171.

Shinde, K. A. (2007). Visiting scared sites in India: Religious tourism or pilgrimage? In R. Raj & N. D. Morpeth (Eds.), *Religious tourism and pilgrimage management: An international perspective* (pp. 170–183). Wallingford: CAB International.

Shinde, K. A. (2010). Entrepreneurship and indigenous entrepreneurs in religious tourism in India. *International Journal of Tourism Research, 12,* 523–535.

Sikand, Y. (2006). The Tablighi Jama'at and politics: A critical re-appraisal. *Muslim World, 96*(1), 175–195.

Singh, S. P., & Narang, S. S. (2004). *Guru Granth Sahib: Repository of universal truths, India perspectives.* Retrieved August 2, 2007, from http://mea.gov.in/indiaperspective/2004/122004.pdf

Tilson, D. J. (2005). Religious-spiritual tourism and promotional campaiging: A church-state partnership for St. James and Spain. *Journal of Hospitality & Leisure Marketing, 12*(1–2), 9–40.

United Nations World Tourism Organization, UNWTO. (2008). *Tourism highlights* (2008th ed.). Madrid: UNWTO.

Vukonic, B. (2015). Religion, tourism and economics: A convenient symbiosis. *Tourism Recreation Research, 27*(2), 59–64. doi:10.1080/02508281.2002.1108122.

Wannell, B., & Hasan, S. K. (2008). Historical forts in Pakistan. *Journal of the Royal Asiatic Society, 18*(4), 534–537.

Weiermair, K. (2006). Product improvement or innovation: What is the key to success in tourism? In OECD (Ed.), *Innovation and growth in tourism* (pp. 53–67). Paris: OECD.

World Tourism Organization (WTO). (2009). *Facts and figures.* UNWTO World Tourism Barometer. Retrieved May 5, 2009, from http://unwto.org/facts/eng/barometer.htm

WTO. (2015). World Tourism Organization, South Asia. Retrieved August 10, 2015, from www.worldtourism.org/regional/south_asia/asia

Chapter 45
Business-to-Business Buyer–Seller Interactions: Personality and Transformational Leadership Theories' Perspective

Pia Hautamäki

Abstract The literature has observed that business-to-business (B2B) selling is transitioning to relational partnerships with customers and long-term collaborations with suppliers to achieve a competitive advantage and reduce costs. Studies have made it clear that personal similarities between the initial salesperson and buyer can improve cooperation in buyer–seller interactions, and this interactional aspect offers value to customers. According to recent studies, the way salespeople initiate a partnership with their contact people is an important part of relational value formation. Nevertheless, this subject is rarely discussed in the literature. This study addresses this gap by adding personality theory and the theory of transformational leadership to illustrate how different customers with different personality types want to be treated by salespeople before and during buyer–seller interactions. This study recommends using these theories in buyer–seller interactions to meet the customers' relational, interactional and behavioural needs.

Keywords Business to business • Initiating relationship • Myers–Briggs Type Personality Indicator • MBTI • Transformational leadership • Selling

Introduction

For a leader to meet the appropriate situational requirements of followers, it is essential to understand the aspects of the leader's own personality and the follower's personality type (Routamaa & Ponto, 1994; Routamaa, Honkonen, Asikainen, & Pollari, 1997). This study applies leadership and personality theories to buyer–seller interactions from an individual perspective between the salesperson and the

P. Hautamäki (✉)
Haaga-Helia University of Applied Sciences, Helsinki, Finland

University of Vaasa, Vaasa, Finland
e-mail: pia.hautamaki@gmail.com

© Springer International Publishing Switzerland 2017
R. Benlamri, M. Sparer (eds.), *Leadership, Innovation and Entrepreneurship as Driving Forces of the Global Economy*, Springer Proceedings in Business and Economics, DOI 10.1007/978-3-319-43434-6_45

customer, where the customer's relational, interactional and behavioural needs have to be met individually (Baumann & Le Meunier-FitzHugh, 2014; Biong & Selnes, 1995; Guenzi, Pardo, & Georges, 2007; Hohenschwert & Geiger, 2015).

Today more than ever, salespeople and their managers are dealing with new challenges such as increasingly complex environments, the transition from products to services or bundles of products and services, changing technologies and increasing customer expectations (Ingram, Laforge, Locander, Mackenzie, & Podsakoff, 2005). Business-to-business (B2B) customers can find information on the Internet and buy tangibles from online stores. B2B customers still need salespeople to buyer-seller encounters for advice and collaboration when buying intangibles and services. The literature has noticed this change and now defines B2B sales as a human-driven interaction (Dixon & Tanner, 2012), recognizing that interactional elements provide value in buyer–seller interactions (Echeverri & Skalen, 2011; Geiger & Guenzi, 2009; Hohenschwert & Geiger, 2015; Hohenschwert, 2012; Salomonson, Åberg, & Allwood, 2012). Nevertheless, there are only few studies from buyers' side (Crosby, Evans, & Cowles, 1990).

If the buying process has changed, B2B selling also has changed from promotional aspects towards relational and interactional cooperation with customers with common aims to build long-term partnerships. Recent changes in buying and the business environment require changes in the B2B sellers' work on an individual level with their customers. Often the salesperson is the only link between the sales organization and the customer. The traditional method of sales in which the focus was on adding value by communicating product information to customers is now totally changed (Rackham & De Vincentis, 1998). Relational and interactional elements are important to forming value with the customer (Echeverri & Skalen, 2011; Ford, 1980; Grönroos & Voima, 2013; Haas, Snehota, & Corsaro, 2012; Hohenschwert & Geiger, 2015) and personality types have been recognized as an element of forming value in buyer–seller interactions (Dion, Easterling, & Miller, 1995). In buyer–seller interactions, the salesperson can adjust his or her relational behaviours to match customer needs.

Literature have explored management and leadership as a dyadic phenomenon for decades. As Avolio and Bass (1995) put it, the leader's behaviour depends on defining the individual need of his followers. Elevating and developing followers is the way to realize their full potential and achieve high performance. Most leadership studies are from the leader's side and although some studies have addressed the follower's point of view (Hautala, 2005, 2006, 2007, 2008; Routamaa et al., 1997). Additionally, studies illustrate that often the appraisal of leaders shows the typical personality behavioural expectations of the followers' types (Hautala, 2005; Routamaa et al., 1997).

As addressed earlier, the role of a salesperson in B2B as a relationship builder between sales organizations and customer organizations is central (Schwepker, 2003). However, the actual relational behaviours required for both leading activities and selling lack an accepted interpretation of relational selling behaviours (Biong & Selnes, 1995; Ford, 1980).

This study explores how customers with different personality types want to be treated and led in buyer–seller interactions from a relational perspective (see Fig. 45.1). Sales organizations need these answers to satisfy customers' relational, interactional and behavioural needs in the buyer–seller interactions and provide value to their customers.

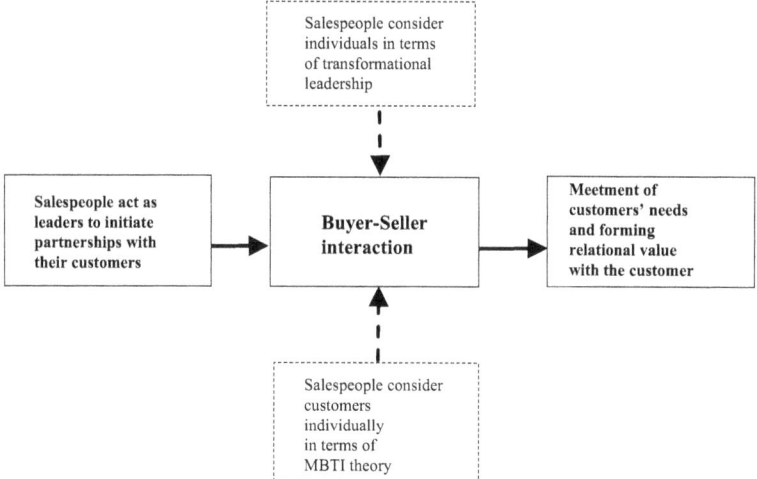

Fig. 45.1 Theoretical framework of the study

Relational Selling in the Field of B2B Sales

While there are more studies on the phases during and after sales meetings, this study addresses the first interactional encounters with customers when the salesperson's main task is to initiate a partnership with the customer. Biong and Selnes (1995) have described that in relational selling the salesperson's task is to initiate partnership and to create long-term commitment with the customer. This study includes the interactional and behavioural skills necessary for the relational aspect of selling.

Research shows that selling today has more relational aspects and takes place on a personal level in buyer–seller interactions (Dixon & Tanner, 2012; Echeverri & Skalen, 2011; Hohenschwert & Geiger, 2015; Vargo & Lusch, 2004). Dixon and Tanner (2012) defined selling as a 'human-driven interaction', transforming the traditional interpretation of sales, which is no longer adequate (Moncrief & Marshall, 2005). Today, customers look for long-term relationships and their demands come from a more comprehensive perspective and skill set than ever before (Haas et al., 2012).

Traditionally, sales studies have focused on outcome measures such as sales revenue or profit. According to earlier studies of relational selling, often the approach has concentrated on interactional competences or quality (Biong & Selnes, 1995; Crosby et al., 1990; Jones, Brown, Zoltners, & Weitz, 2005) or on competencies that build trust, gain commitment and develop satisfactory relationships (Doney & Cannon, 1997; Dwyer, Schurr, & Oh, 1987; Jolson, 1997). In business today, the activities that salespeople take an on individual level with the customer before and during a meeting are more important than ever. Recent sales research has acknowledged that initiating new relationships requires the capability to understand human perspectives to draw out customers' latent needs and motives (Haas et al., 2012).

Salespeople as a Leader in Interactions

According to leadership studies, followers favour leaders whose daily work appears to be honest, competent, credible and inspiring (Bass, 1985). This study sees the salesperson as a leader to the customer, but in a natural capacity and without any authority. Customers have the power in buyer–seller interactions because they have choose if, when and where to buy. However, this study sees buyers and sellers as equal in their relationship because mutual commitment brings competitive advantage to both parties. As Bass (1997, p. 20) put it, both the salesperson and the leader have the same role in influencing the perceptions, cognitions and decisions of the customer or follower to be successful. While before, salespeople might have had numerous potential customers in a portfolio, nowadays they follow more of a leadership model, as leaders may have from 3 to 20 immediate followers (cf. Bass, 1997).

In 1978, Burns developed the transformational leadership (TF-leadership) model and many researchers have since defined the concept further Bass (1985). This study contributes to the literature by using the TF-leadership model and its components: charismatic, inspirational, intellectual stimulation and individual consideration. Charismatic leadership refers to sharing a vision and having a strong influence on followers by providing a sense of mission. Inspirational leadership articulates high expectations to followers and communicates the importance of purpose and commitment. Intellectual stimulation encourages using new approaches to solve problems and change the old ways of thinking. Individual consideration means all followers are treated individually, considering their personal growth and individual development.

The TF-leadership model has been shown to positively relate to individual follower performance and is strongly related to contextual performance, instead of task performance (Wang, Oh, Courtright, & Colbert, 2011). Additionally, the model of TF-leadership has been largely studied outside the sales area and these studies have found many positive outcomes (Felfe & Schyns, 2010; Hautala, 2005; Hautala, 2006; Wang et al., 2011; Sparks & Shenk, 2001; Uusi-Kakkuri & Brandt, 2015). Dubinsky, Yammarino, Jolson, and Spangler (1995) earlier suggested that transactional leadership would better address salespeople than TF-leadership. If today the sales manager's role is seen primarily as a problem solver, there is a need to change towards role of a system designer or an architect (Ingram et al., 2005). This same change is suggested also by Dixon and Tanner (2012) when they claim that salespeople need the skills to act as an architect of change. It may be seen that in sales studies, selling is seen to be consistent with task-oriented activities, while selling and buying might be seen contextually, where TF-leadership has been found to increase performance (Wang et al., 2011).

Thus selling characterizes relational aspects with a long-term perspective (Biong & Selnes, 1995; Dixon & Tanner, 2012; Haas et al., 2012; Verbeke, Dietz, & Verwaal, 2011) and value formation relationally is seen as crucial with customers (Echeverri & Skalen, 2011; Hohenschwert & Geiger, 2015; Salomonson et al., 2012). The Bass (1985) theory seeks to combine some of the earlier studies on customer-favoured relational activities in buyer–seller interactions (see Fig. 45.2). The relational selling approach strongly focuses on quality, building trust, commitment and satisfactory relationships (Biong & Selnes, 1995; Crosby et al., 1990;

Transformational Leadership Components of	Different Sales Approaches in Buyer-Seller Interaction	Different Sales Approaches in Research	Contribution of This Study to the Relational Selling Approach
Charismatic Leadership	Aims for long-term partnerships	Biong et al., 1995; Ingram et al., 2002; Williams et al., 2007	Sense of mission: vision and mission need to be shared
Inspirational Leadership	Salesperson as a change architect	Dixon et al., 2012	Communicate the importance of the discussed context rather than product information
Intellectual Stimulation	Challenging the customer	Rapp et al., 2014; Storbacka et al., 1994	Encourage the customer to alter the way of thinking and provide alternatives
Individual Consideration	Forming interactional value with the customer	Echeverri et al., 2011; Dixon et al., 2012; Haas et al., 2012; Hohenschwert et al., 2015	Treat the customer as another human being, handle concerns and worries, give advice to lead the internal buying process

Fig. 45.2 Comparing components of TF-leadership to different sales studies

Doney & Cannon, 1997; Dwyer et al., 1987; Jolson, 1997; Jones et al., 2005). These studies however did not acknowledge the shared vision and mission that lead to long-term partnerships and context-based information sharing that are more indicative of a change architect.

In TF-leadership theory, encouraging followers to alter their ways of thinking can be related to sales, in which a salesperson may be seen as an expert—a role that is important in today's buyer–seller interactions. Since the seller and buyer roles are equal, both parties bring their best understanding of a situation to reach a common goal. Individual consideration means that the salesperson treats the customer as another human being who has concerns and worries about the future, and needs to be interacted with on an individual level. As several people can influence a customer's buying decision (Ingram, 2004), salespeople need to advise the customer, lead the internal buying process and resolve other decision maker's worries.

The immediate aim in TF-leadership is to motivate followers to see the importance and value of favoured outcomes, motivating followers to transform their own self-interest to that of the organization and increase the followers' needs to head for the common future (Bass, 1985). Translating this to sales, a salesperson can motivate the customer to commit to a long-term partnership to meet common goals (the mission) before or during the first buyer–seller interaction. When salespeople use the TF-leadership approach in buyer–seller interactions, this approach can increase the salesperson's performance and commitment to organization and foster customer satisfaction, performance and commitment to the sales organization in buyer–seller interactions (Dubinsky et al., 1995; Ingram et al., 2005).

Different Personality Types in Interactions

Leadership studies have noted that both the supervisors' and followers' personalities are important to satisfaction and performance (Hautala, 2005). Hence, individual consideration is included in this study also by using the Myers–Briggs Type

Indicator (MBTI). This is because relationship between personality and TF-leadership has been documented in several studies (Brandt & Laiho, 2013; Carroll, 2010; Hautala, 2005; Uusi-Kakkuri & Brandt, 2015).

The MBTI is a commonly used tool in research, especially on organizations, leadership and relationship studies (Dion et al., 1995; Routamaa & Debnath, 2011; Routamaa & Edinger, 2013; Routamaa, Hautala, & Mohsin, 2007, 2009; Routamaa, 2014; Routamaa & Ponto, 1994; Routamaa & Rautiainen, 2002). Avolio and Howell (1992) found that the personality of a leader and a follower can predict satisfaction with the leader and unit performance. Felfe and Schyns (2010) found that followers who share a similar personality type with their leaders are more likely to develop a strong commitment to their leader. When these results are compared to buyer–seller interactions, salespeople using both TF-leadership behaviours and individual consideration in terms of personality may meet customer needs in buyer–seller interactions (Dion et al., 1995; Felfe & Schyns, 2010; Routamaa & Ponto, 1994; Routamaa et al., 1997).

The Myers–Briggs theory is based on Jung's work on psychological types. It consists of eight different preferences illustrating a person's orientation of energy (E for Extravert or I for Introvert), the need for information and the way of gathering it (S for Sensing or N for Intuition), the preferred way of making decisions (T for Thinking or F for Feeling) and the way of living (J for Judging or P for Perceiving). Each person has one preference that is stronger than another and these four strongest preferences identify the person's personality type (Myers & Myers, 1993, 1992; Myers & McCaulley, 1992).

According to MBTI, customers also differ, for example, in how they prefer to be approached, how much information they need and how they make decisions (Myers et al., 1992). As a result, salespeople must have a deep understanding of their own personality types and those of their customers to be able to initiate new partnerships effectively. When MBTI is used to address customers, Extravert (E) customers derive energy from the outside world, while the Introvert (I) customers desire to be alone with their own thoughts. Customers who are Sensing (S) gather information with their five senses and concentrate on small things, while Intuitive (N) customers use their imagination and are able to see the big picture. Thinking (T) customers speak directly and use logic to make decisions (they may appear to be impersonal). Feeling (F) customers take other persons' feelings into account when they make decisions and communicate. Customers who are Judging (J) types favour order and closure in their own lives and strictly schedule meetings, while Perceiving (P) customers are flexible and tend to go with the flow (Myers et al., 1992). If the salesperson is aware of these personality types, they can more effectively build relationships by speaking to the customer and dealing with them in a manner that will make them feel comfortable.

Studies have shown that the most common personality types of B2B customers are ESTJ (Extravert, Sensing, Thinking, Judging) and ISTJ (Introvert, Sensing, Thinking, Judging) (Dion et al., 1995; Macdaid, McCaulley, & Kainz, 1995), and the most common cognitive style, therefore, is ST. The ST person favours facts and is practical, task-oriented and knows quantitative measures (see Fig. 45.3). The NT MBTI cognitive style prefers actions and information on the future possibilities on a conceptual level, and is ready to make decisions if receives this required information. The SF type prefers information on the current situation and prefers making decisions as part of a group, while the NF type prefers information on current pos-

Salesperson Should	Example
Keep to the facts	For ST customers presenting the facts is the way to be professional
Stay on a practical level	Present facts but talk in practice what it means
Keep it short and task-oriented	Try to keep the talk short and talk only about the tasks
Use fewer personal expressions	ST customers want to have a relationship on a professional level, so keep expressions clear and simple
Give direction	for ST customers, it is important to go make the case step-by-step
Prepare to be tested	Only speak of known facts and come back later if the facts are not known with certainty

Fig. 45.3 Meeting the needs of the most common cognitive styles of B2B buyers. Adapted and reworked from Brock (1994)

sibilities and makes decisions by mutual agreement. The most common cognitive style of buyers is ST, and these people work most favourably with others who have the same ST cognitive style. Compared to other styles, NT, SF and NF personalities prefer to work with opposite cognitive styles (NT with SF, SF with NT and NF with ST). Additionally, the ST person concentrates on cost-benefit analysis only (Walck, 1996; Myers & Myers, 1993).

The study by Dion et al. (1995) revealed that if the customer perceives a connection with the salesperson, sales performance increases and the customer feels positive about the sales relationship. Clack et al. (2004) found in their study from the medical sector that patients' complaints about doctors were concerned largely with communication rather than clinical competence. The authors claimed that poor communication may be due to personality type differences across the S-N dimension. Similarly, it was found that sellers' communication skills are significant when determining a buyer's perceived quality of the relationship during the buying process (Parsons, 2002). Based on these results, buyers seem willing to choose long-term relationships with sellers who meet the buyers' needs.

In multiple leadership studies, the most common personality types for Finnish leaders were ENTJ, ESTJ and ISTJ (Järlström, 2000; Routamaa, 2010, 2011; Routamaa & Ou, 2012a, 2012b; Routamaa et al., 2012). Although ST is the most common managerial type in China and Finland and the most common B2B buyer type in Finland and the USA (Dion et al., 1995; Hautamäki & Routamaa, 2016; Macdaid et al., 1995), NT is a more frequent managerial type in the USA and Sweden (Routamaa, Yang, & Ou, 2010; Routamaa & Ou, 2012a, 2012b). Interestingly, SF and NF are common managerial types in the retail sector (Routamaa & Hautala, 2009; Schaubhut & Thompson, 2008). In addition, Hautamäki and Routamaa (2016) found that B2B purchasing department managers were also I and IS types. Compared to earlier personality studies on buyer–seller interactions, it should be noted that the personality types of manager professions are almost the same as in purchasing professions. This may be because purchasers have often worked as supervisors (cf. Dion et al., 1995).

Note that when the customer is a J type, as addressed earlier, clearly set goals and early decision-making are important to interactions, while P customers will make a decision only after they have all the facts and will postpone decision-making until they do. Hence, in buyer–seller interactions, it is crucial to give enough time and information to P customers and be organized and systematic when dealing with J customers (Hautala, 2008; Myers & Myers, 1993).

Often, a customer acts as a director or manager. These may be NT persons. Unlike the ST customer, the NT customer tends to focus on the big picture and how this generalization can create logical options (Myers et al., 1992). Due to the relational aspects of buyer–seller interactions nowadays, the different cognitive processes, personalities and needs of each party may affect the outcome (cf. Myers et al., 1992). Hence, personality aspects are important to consider when preparing for any buyer–seller encounter.

Conclusion and Future Work

Recent changes in the B2B environment challenge salespeople to form relational value with their customers when initiating long-term partnerships, but the literature has not defined a concrete model of forming value with the customer. This study uses TF-leadership and MBTI personality theory perspectives to address this research gap on buyer–seller interactions. As the complexity of customer needs increases in the future, forming relational value with the customer when initiating a partnership will increase in importance. The theory of TF-leadership brings new knowledge of charismatic, inspirational, intellectual and individual leadership to buyer–seller interactions and relationships. Because the business challenges are complex, TF-leadership theory explains creating a common vision and mission with the customer (charismatic leadership) so that the customer has a sense of mission and cooperation from the beginning, as long-term partnerships are important nowadays (Biong & Selnes, 1995; Ingram, LaForge, & Leigh, 2002; Williams & Plouffe, 2007) and sharing a common future can help salespeople to engage the customer in meeting common goals.

Additionally, in TF-leadership, the inspirational leadership approach communicates the importance of the context to customers. This contributes to the relational selling approach and buyer–seller interaction so salespeople can provide information according to what individual customers want to know within a situational context. Intellectual stimulation enables salespeople to challenge the customer and encourage new ways of doing business. Individual consideration enables salespeople to understand and address customers' context, concerns and worries.

It is crucial for salespeople to define the buyer's preferred way of working when initiating relationships and to adjust their behaviour according to the customer's personality. Salespeople also need to take into account a customer's Judging preference. Customers with J preference prefer clearly set goals and systematic proceedings to the promised goals. This should been considered when making promises to customers when initiating new relationships.

This study shows that relational value formation with the customer may be defined as relational, interactional and behavioural to meet customer personality needs using the TF-leadership behaviour model. It is recommended in buyer–seller interactions to take into account the most common cognitive style of buyers (ST) and their preferred method of interaction. Applying the TF-leadership and MBTI studies from the follower's side (Hautala, 2008) to a buyer–seller setting, it is recommended that salespeople assimilate TF-leadership theories and methodologies into buyer–seller interactions while initiating relational and long-term partnerships with customers.

For future studies, it would be beneficial to empirically assess customer need fulfillment after salespeople have used individual consideration and TF-leadership methods. Sales managers should find this study beneficial, as the study of similar personality types brings perceived quality to relationships and helps to build up a positive connection with customers. It is important to recruit different personality types to work as salespeople, so a complementary personality type can be assigned to each particular buyer. Working in teams could also improve the relational value formation with customers because there would most surely be at least one salesperson with the proper personality type to understand a customer's needs and form an effective relationship.

References

Agndal, H. (2006). The purchasing market entry process—A study of 10 Swedish industrial small and medium-sized enterprises. *Journal of Purchasing and Supply Management, 12*, 182–196. doi:10.1016/j.pursup.2006.10.004.

Ahearne, M., Jelinek, R., & Jones, E. (2007). Examining the effect of salesperson service behavior in a competitive context. *Journal of the Academy of Marketing Science, 35*(4), 603–616. doi:10.1007/s11747-006-0013-1.

Avolio, B. J., & Bass, B. M. (1995). Individual consideration viewed at multiple levels of analysis: A multi-level framework for examining the diffusion of transformational leadership. *Leadership Quarterly, 6*(2), 1048–9843.

Avolio, B. J., & Howell, J. M. (1992). The impact of leader behavior and leader-follower personality match on satisfaction and unit performance. In K. E. Clark (Ed.), *Impact of leadership*. Greensboro, NC: Center for Creative Leadership.

Bass, B. M. (1985). *Leadership and performance beyond expectations*. New York: Free Press.

Bass, B. M. (1997). Personal selling and transactional/transformational leadership with effective leadership. *Journal of Personal Selling and Sales Management, 17*(3), 19–28.

Baumann, J., & Le Meunier-FitzHugh, K. (2014). Trust as a facilitator of co-creation in customer-salesperson interaction: An imperative for the realization of episodic and relational value? *Academy of Marketing Science Review, 4*(1/2), 5–20. doi:10.1007/s13162-013-0039-8.

Biong, H., & Selnes, F. (1995). Relational selling behavior and skills in long-term industrial buyer-seller relationships. *International Business Review, 4*(4), 483–498. doi:10.1016/0969-5931(95)00028-3.

Brandt, T., & Laiho, M. (2013). Gender, personality and transformational leadership: An examination of leader and subordinate perspectives. *Leadership & Organization Development Journal, 34*, 44–66.

Brock, S. A. (1994). *Introduction to Type® and selling*. Mountain View, CA: CCP.

Carroll, G. K. (2010). An examination of the relationship between personality type, self perception accuracy and transformational leadership practices of female hospital leaders. Dissertation, Graduate College of Bowling Green State University, Bowling Green, OH.

Clack, G. B., Allen, J., Cooper, D., & Head, J. O. (2004). Attitudes personality differences between doctors and their patients: Implications for the teaching of communication skills. *Medical Education Medical Education J1-Medical Education, 38*, 177–186. doi:10.1046/j.1365-2923.2004.01752.x.

Crosby, L. A., Evans, K. R., & Cowles, D. (1990). Relationship quality in services selling: An interpersonal influence perspective. *Journal of Marketing, 54*(July), 68–81.

Dion, P., Easterling, D., & Miller, S. J. (1995). What is really necessary in successful buyer/seller relationships? *Industrial Marketing Management, 24*(1), 1–9. doi:10.1016/0019-8501(94)00025-R.

Dixon, A. L., & Tanner, J. J. F. (2012). Transforming selling: Why it is time to think differently about sales. *Research, XXXII*(1), 9–13. doi:10.2753/PSS0885-3134320102.

Doney, P. M., & Cannon, J. P. (1997). An examination of the nature of trust in buyer-seller relationships. *Journal of Marketing, 61*(April), 35–51. doi:10.2307/1251829.

Dubinsky, A. J., Yammarino, F. J., Jolson, M. A., & Spangler, W. D. (1995). Transformational leadership: An initial investigation in sales management. Journal of Personal Selling and Sales Management. doi:10.1080/08853134.1995.10754018.

Dwyer, F. R., Schurr, P. H., & Oh, S. (1987). Developing buyer-seller relationships. *Journal of Marketing, 51*(2), 11–27. doi:10.2307/1251126.

Echeverri, P., & Skalen, P. (2011). Co-creation and co-destruction: A practice-theory based study of interactive value formation. *Marketing Theory, 11*(3), 351–373. doi:10.1177/1470593111408181.

Felfe, J., & Schyns, B. (2010). Followers' personality and the perception of transformational leadership: Further evidence for the similarity hypothesis. *British Journal of Management, 21*(2), 393–410. doi:10.1111/j.1467-8551.2009.00649.x.

Ford, D. (1980). The development of buyer-seller relationships in industrial markets. *European Journal of Marketing, 14*(5/6), 339–353.

Geiger, S., & Guenzi, P. (2009). The sales function in the twenty-first century: Where are we and where do we go from here? *European Journal of Marketing, 43*, 873–889. doi:10.1108/03090560910961434.

Grönroos, C., & Voima, P. (2013). Critical service logic: Making sense of value creation and co-creation. *Journal of the Academy of Marketing Science, 41*(2), 133–150. doi:10.1007/s11747-012-0308-3.

Guenzi, P., Pardo, C., & Georges, L. (2007). Relational selling strategy and key account managers' relational behaviors: An exploratory study. *Industrial Marketing Management, 36*(1), 121–133. doi:10.1016/j.indmarman.2005.03.014.

Haas, A., Snehota, I., & Corsaro, D. (2012). Industrial marketing management creating value in business relationships: The role of sales. *Industrial Marketing Management, 41*(1), 94–105. doi:10.1016/j.indmarman.2011.11.004.

Hautala, T. (2005). The effects of subordinates' personality on appraisals of transformational leadership. *Journal of Leadership & Organizational Studies, 11*(4), 84–92. doi:10.1177/107179190501100407.

Hautala, T. (2008). TJ leaders as transformational leaders: Followers' and leaders' appraisals. *Journal of Psychological Type, 68*(9), 78–88.

Hautala, T. M. (2006). The relationship between personality and transformational leadership. *Journal of Management Development, 25*(8), 777–794. doi:10.1108/02621710610684259.

Hautala, T. M. (2007). Impact of followers' type on their expectations of leaders: An individual consideration in transformational leadership. *Journal of Psychological Type, 67*(4), 30–37.

Hautala, T. M., & Routamaa, V. (2008). Linking type and archetypes. In *Proceedings of Sixth Psychological Type and Culture—East and West: A Multicultural Research Symposium*, Honolulu, HI.

Hautamäki, P., & Routamaa, V. (2016). Personality types in buyer-seller interactions. In *Proceedings of the 14th International Conference of the Society for Global Business & Economic Development*.

Hohenschwert, L. (2012). Salespeople's value creation roles in customer interaction: An empirical study. *Journal of Customer Behaviour, 11*(2), 145–166. doi:10.1362/1475392 12X13420906144679.

Hohenschwert, L., & Geiger, S. (2015). Interpersonal influence strategies in complex B2B sales and the socio-cognitive construction of relationship value. *Industrial Marketing Management, 49*, 139–150. doi:10.1016/j.indmarman.2015.05.027.

Ingram, T. N. (2004). Future themes in sales and sales management: Complexity, collaboration, and accountability. *Journal of Marketing Theory and Practice, 12*, 18–28.

Ingram, T. N., Laforge, R. W., Locander, W. B., Mackenzie, S. B., & Podsakoff, P. M. (2005). New directions in sales leadership research. *Journal of Personal Selling & Sales Management, 25*(2), 137–154. doi:10.1080/08853134.2005.10749055.

Ingram, T. N., LaForge, R. W., & Leigh, T. W. (2002). Selling in the new millennium: A joint agenda. *Industrial Marketing Management, 31*(7), 559–567. doi:10.1016/S0019-8501(02)00175-X.

Järlström, M. (2000). Personality preferences and career expectations of Finnish business students. *Career Development International, 5*(3), 144–154. doi:10.1108/13620430010371919.

Jolson, M. A. (1997). Broadening the scope of relationship selling. *Journal of Personal Selling & Sales Management, XVII*(4), 75–88. doi:10.1080/08853134.1997.10754112.

Jones, E., Brown, S. P., Zoltners, A. A., & Weitz, B. A. (2005). The changing environment of selling and sales management. *Journal of Personal Selling & Sales Management, XXV*(2), 105–111.

Jung, C. (1921). *Psychological Types. The Collected Works of C. G. Jung*. Princeton, NJ: Princeton University Press.

Kouzes, J. M., & Posner, B. Z. (1998). *The leadership challenge. How to make extraordinary things happen in organizations*. San Francisco CA: Jossey-Bass, Wiley Print.

Liang, N., & Parkhe, A. (1997). Importer behavior: The neglected counterpart of international exchange. *Journal of International Business Studies, 28*(3), 495–530. 36p.

Macdaid, G., McCaulley, M. H., & Kainz, R. I. (1995). *Myers-Briggs type indicator: Atlas of type tables*. Gainesville, FL: Center for Applications of Psychological Type.

Moncrief, W. C., & Marshall, G. W. (2005). The evolution of the seven steps of selling. *Industrial Marketing Management, 34*(1), 13–22. doi:10.1016/j.indmarman.2004.06.001.

Myers, I. (1992). *Introduction to type. A description of the theory and applications of the Myers-Briggs type indicator*. Palo Alto, CA: Consulting Psychologist Press.

Myers, I., & McCaulley, M. (1992). *Manual: A guide to the development and use of the Myers-Briggs type indicator*. Palo Alto, CA: Consulting Psychologist Press.

Myers, I., & Myers, P. (1993). *Gifts differing. Understanding personality type*. Palo Alto, CA: Consulting Psychologist Press.

Myers, I. B., & Myers, P. B. (1995). *Gifts differing: Understanding personality type*. Palo Alto, CA: Consulting Psychologist Press.

Overby, J. W., & Servais, P. (2005). Small and medium-sized firms' import behavior: The case of Danish industrial purchasers. *Industrial Marketing Management, 34*(1), 71–83. doi:10.1016/j.indmarman.2004.08.001.

Parsons, A. L. (2002). What determines buyer-seller relationship quality? An investigation from the buyer's perspective. *Journal of Supply Chain Management, 38*(2), 4–12. doi:10.1111/j.1745-493X.2002.tb00124.x.

Rackham, N., & De Vincentis, J. (1998). *Rethinking the sales force: Refining selling to create and capture customer value*. New York: McGraw Hill.

Routamaa, V. (2010). Building innovative teams. Electronic In *Proceedings: SGBED 3rd Research Symposium*, EADA, June 17–18, Barcelona, Spain.

Routamaa, V. (2011). Personality types and entrepreneurial orientation. In J. Glassman (Ed.), *Enterprise management in a transitional economy and post financial crisis*. Nanjing: Nanjing University.

Routamaa, V. (2014). Building innovative teams on diverse creativity. In R. Subramanian, M. Rahe, V. Nagadevara, & C. Jayachandran (Eds.), *Rethinking innovation: Global perspectives*. Routledge and Taylor & Francis. ISBNA10: 0415748186.

Routamaa, V., & Edinger, P. (2013). Relationship of cognitive styles and team roles. *International Journal on Applied Management Sciences & Global Developments, 1*, 2.

Routamaa, V., & Debnath, N. (2011). Singapore relationships between culture and values: A comparative study between Finland and India. In *Proceedings of the Twelfth International Conference of the Society for Global Business & Economic Development*, July 21–23, 2011, pp. 358–365.

Routamaa, V., & Hautala, T. M. (2008). Understanding cultural differences: The values in a cross-cultural context. *International Review of Business Research Papers, 4*(5), 129–137.

Routamaa, V., & Hautala, T. (2009). Katse naamion taa—Itsetuntemuksesta voimaa (A Look behind the Mask—Powered by Self-Knowledge). Vaasa: Leadec-Kustannus.

Routamaa, V., Hautala T. M., & Mohsin M. (2007). Managing cultural differences: Values and work goals in culture and personality contexts. In *Proceedings of the 10th International Conference Creativity & Innovation: Imperatives for Global Business and Development*, August 8–11, Kyoto, Japan.

Routamaa, V., Hautala, T. M., & Tsuzuki, J. (2009). Values and cultures in integrating business: A comparison of Bulgaria, Finland and Japan. *World Journal of Management, 1*(1), 13–22.

Routamaa, V., Honkonen, M., Asikainen, V., & Pollari, A.-M. (1997). Psychological type and leadership styles—Subordinates' point of view. In *Proceedings of the Leadership and the Myers-Briggs Type Indicator, Second International Conference*, Washington, DC, USA.

Routamaa, V., & Ou, J. (2012a). Cultures and managers' type structures: A comparison of China, Finland and South Africa. In *Proceedings of the 16th International Business Research Conference*, April 2012, Dubai.

Routamaa, V., & Ou, J. (2012b). Managers' recruitment—the companies' most strategic decision: China, USA and Sweden compared. In *Proceedings of the 2nd Annual International Conference on Human Resource Management and Professional Development for the Digital Age (HRM & PD 2012)*, September, Indonesia.

Routamaa, V., & Ponto, V. (1994). Situational leadership and the MBTI types of certain Finnish managers. In *Proceedings of the Myers-Briggs Types Indicator and Leadership: An International Research Conference*. National Leadership Institute, Maryland, USA.

Routamaa, V., & Rautiainen, L. (2002). Type and expatriate adjustment in a new culture. In *Proceedings of the Conference Working Creatively with Type and Temperament*, September 19–22, Sydney, Australia.

Routamaa, V., Yang, H., & Ou, J. (2010). Managers' type distributions in three continent—Do cultures matter. In *Proceedings of the Seventh Psychological Type and Culture—East and West: A Multicultural Research Symposium*, January, Honolulu, HI.

Routamaa, V., & Ou, J. (2012). Managers' recruitment—The companies' most strategic decision China, USA and Sweden compared. In *2nd Annual International Conference on Human Resource Management and Professional Development for the Digital Age* (pp. 142–143). Singapore: Global Science and Technology Forum. doi:10.5176/2251-2449_HRM&PD12.17.

Salomonson, N., Åberg, A., & Allwood, J. (2012). Industrial marketing management communicative skills that support value creation: A study of B2B interactions between customers and customer service representatives. *Industrial Marketing Management, 41*(1), 145–155. doi:10.1016/j.indmarman.2011.11.021.

Schaubhut, N. A., & Thompson, R. C. (2008). *MBTI® type tables for occupations* (2nd ed.). Mountain View, CA: CPP.

Schwepker, C. H., Jr. (2003). Customer-oriented selling: A review, extension, and directions for future research. *Journal of Personal Selling & Sales Management, 23*(2), 151–171. doi:10.1002/mar.20011.

Stiakakis, E., & Georgiadis, C. K. (2009). E-service quality: Comparing the perceptions of providers and customers. *Managing Service Quality, 19*(4), 410–430. doi:10.1108/09604520910971539.

Tichy, N., & Devanna, M. (1986). *The transformational leader*. San Francisco, CA: Wiley.

Uusi-Kakkuri, P., & Brandt, T. (2015). Preferred leadership behaviours by different personalities. *International Journal of Business and Globalisation, 15*(4). doi:10.1504/IJBG.2015.072518.

Vargo, S., & Lusch, R. (2004). Evolving to a new dominant logic for marketing. *Journal of Marketing*.

Verbeke, W., Dietz, B., & Verwaal, E. (2011). Drivers of sales performance: A contemporary meta-analysis. Have salespeople become knowledge brokers? *Journal of the Academy of Marketing Science, 39*(3), 407–428. doi:10.1007/s11747-010-0211-8.

Walck, C. L. (1996). Management and leadership. In Hammer (Ed.), *MBTI applications. A decade of research on the Myers-Briggs Type Indicator®*. Palo Alto, CA: Consulting Psychologist Press.

Wang, G., Oh, I.-S., Courtright, S. H., & Colbert, A. E. (2011). Transformational leadership and performance across criteria and levels: A meta-analytic review of 25 years of research. *Group & Organization Management, 36*(2), 223–270. doi:10.1177/1059601111401017.

Williams, B. C., & Plouffe, C. R. (2007). Assessing the evolution of sales knowledge: A 20-year content analysis. *Industrial Marketing Management, 36*, 408–419. doi:10.1016/j.indmarman.2005.11.003.

Chapter 46
Educational Tourism in Dubai: The Global Higher Education Hub Across Culture

D.F. Antiado, F.G. Castillo, and M.I. Tawadrous

Abstract Tourism in Dubai is an integral part of the Dubai government's strategy for a sustainable future. Dubai being the most populous among the seven Emirates of United Arab Emirates serves as a gateway for tourism, business, investment, and education. Educational tourism is becoming a popular destination in major key cities around the world and Dubai, United Arab Emirates, is one of the leading destinations in that aspect. Dubai's reputation in the tourism industry is remarkable as it offers better infrastructure, quality of life, and most of all a very safe place for education, tourism, and more. Educational tourism in Dubai plays significant role in knowledge management across society. This research study examines the suitability of Dubai as the frontrunner as education hub in United Arab Emirates and in the GCC region. Understanding the diversity makes it a multicultural educational hub for education and tourism.

Keywords Educational tourism • Knowledge management • Multicultural diversity • UAE

Introduction

Tourism in Dubai is an integral part of the Dubai government's strategy for a sustainable future. Dubai being the most populous among the seven Emirates of United Arab Emirates serves as a gateway for tourism, business, investment, and education. Educational tourism is becoming a popular destination in major key cities around

D.F. Antiado (✉) • M.I. Tawadrous
College of Arts and Sciences, University of Modern Sciences, Dubai, United Arab Emirates
e-mail: arizdjonde@yahoo.com; drmaher310@yahoo.co

F.G. Castillo
Human Resource Management Program, School of Business Administration,
Canadian University Dubai, Dubai, United Arab Emirates
e-mail: fermin.castillo@cud.ac.ae

© Springer International Publishing Switzerland 2017
R. Benlamri, M. Sparer (eds.), *Leadership, Innovation and Entrepreneurship as Driving Forces of the Global Economy*, Springer Proceedings in Business and Economics, DOI 10.1007/978-3-319-43434-6_46

the world and Dubai, United Arab Emirates, is one of the leading destinations in that aspect. Dubai's reputation in the tourism industry is remarkable as it offers better infrastructure, quality of life, and most of all a very safe place for education, tourism, and more. Educational tourism in Dubai plays significant role in knowledge management across society.

Tourism when combined with education forms a formidable combination that attracts both tourism and education as competitive option in deciding which course to study. There are many factors to be considered in selecting which institution to pursue higher education studies as Dubai offers many relevant opportunities and choice of careers to undertake. Dubai among the seven Emirates is home to many local and international colleges and universities. There are universities from different curricula like American, Australian, British, Canadian, and more. The diversity that those curriculum and instruction provide is the mixture of best standards and practice that can be applied in United Arab Emirates. Many countries in the Middle East started to have international students as part of their admission, because we have seen movement of workforce diversity and student across culture is part of it. The Dubai's Strategic Plan aims to maintain double economic growth: to achieve a Gross Domestic Product (GDP) of more than 120 billion USD in year 2017. Currently Dubai already diversified their economy in major sectors like manufacturing, services, aviation, education, and tourism.

Combining education and tourism will provide better opportunities for growth and progress across sectors of the economy. The diversity in Dubai is perhaps one of the most important aspects of its success in obtaining foreign students across continents. Many consider Dubai as the best place to enjoy both education and tourism, as the city can offer many great experiences including great cosmopolitan. The strategic location and favorable social infrastructure are among the key elements of deciding place of studies. The cost of living also plays important factor in the decision aside from the fact that students want a learning environment that is safe and order. A piece of mind for students is always the most important aspect of their learning journey, because it gives them the opportunity to show their knowledge, skills, and abilities in a different level.

The mixture of culture across region helps Dubai and United Arab Emirates to be a competitive place for educational tourism. More than rich heritage of United Arab Emirates, the people residing can exercise their faith with respect to other religion. The kind of respect given among people is the most important aspect of the living and choosing the place of studies. Dubai opens its door for opportunities across culture to show its intellectual beings. Creation of agencies that will handle local and international colleges and universities are value added to their certificates and documentation. This ensures that the degrees obtained are mark of quality and standards as a practice among leading colleges and universities worldwide. The learning environment in Dubai and United Arab Emirates provides a better and competitive journey of educational tourism that opens its door for opportunities across culture and regions. This makes educational tourism in Dubai to be one of the most ideal locations for learning and discovering oneself.

Literature Review

Dubai has a diverse and a well established economy that can be compared to their known cities in the world. Dubai is famously known as the "shopping capital of the Middle East." The city became known and this is because of many shopping centers and malls across the Emirates of Dubai. Fashion and glamor are among the distinct things they can offer the world wherein travelers, tourist, and backpackers across Asia, Europe, Africa, North and South America draw attention to Dubai. Those spotlights still hold the city because of its unique and sound environment for shopping and a lot more. Boutiques, electronic shops, department stores, and supermarket are accessible across Dubai which makes the place more convenient to both travelers and tourists. Aside from that, cars, clothing, jewelry, furniture, and sports equipment are within reach.

More than education, foreign students are looking forward to explore other things which they feel that will enhance their search for knowledge. Student exchange programs are a common practice in many colleges and universities across the globe. Dubai is home to many foreign colleges and universities in different levels. The creation of KHDA (Knowledge and Human Development Authority – Dubai) oversees many aspects of education aside from quality. The agency takes a look and assesses the suitability of institution to conduct such.

Many countries and cities around the world started to capitalize in various means in dealing with their culture and heritage. As a matter of fact, it gives them opportunities for cultural tourism, ecotourism, agritourism, and other information centric tourism that will increase tourism and visitors. Wells (1986) and many others identified the myriad benefits of narrative to education and Gretzel and Fesenmaier (2002) have done the same for tourism. In educational tourism view, Lanegran (2005) concluded that a high-quality educational tour is the one in which a cohesive story is woven while traveling through the landscape. Many students around the world are always looking for a city and country where they can explore educational opportunities and at the same time enjoy touring and exploring. We have seen students who are becoming more into an explorer than learner, because they look for opportunities which include employment. Due to taxes and cost of living overseas, many students are becoming more into a working professional where they can combine both. That lifestyle really fits Dubai and United Arab Emirates as the best option for foreign and local students.

Aside from tourism, there are many other aspect and purpose of traveling which can be considered as a subgroup of tourists around the world wherein a portion according to Niemela (2010) includes educational tourism, cultural tourism, special interest tourism, heritage tourism, and niche tourism. Educational tourism is a "tourist activity undertaken by those who are undertaking an overnight vacation and those who are undertaking an excursion for whom education and learning is a primary or secondary part of their trip." That definition started to evolve due to many factors that affect decision-making and choice of schools. Educational tourism can be defined as travel and tourism combined with education. It can be further labeled as exploring tourism while educating the hunger for knowledge and well-being. It's not only about knowledge but what opportunities that are waiting for you.

In recent years, United Arab Emirates has emerged as popular hub for educational tourism in the GCC region but also globally. The country is a perfect blend and mixture of local Emirati and international culture in one place. It is very much visible today if we are talking about food, arts, structure and engineering, and more. Since then the educational opportunities in the Dubai and United Arab Emirates started to blossom, as they show the world that they can offer many things. Today, Dubai and United Arab Emirates offer comprehensive education for both males and females. Other countries nearby have on tourists, which makes the United Arab Emirates the best option and best place in exploring educational tourism.

A business degree is remaining to be the top choice of course among students in Dubai. In fact, in a study conducted by Knowledge and Human Development Authority (KHDA 2014) there are around 52,586 students attending higher education institution in Dubai and 22,890 about (44 %) are studying business. This proves that studying business reflects the business environment that is happening in Dubai.

The statistics below shows the distribution of higher educational institution across United Arab Emirates (Table 46.1). Dubai was the top among the seven Emirates and the number is growing as many foreign institutions are planning to establish educational center/branches in Dubai. This creates a very positive image for Dubai as the best destination for educational tourism with more value for their money.

Dubai being the largest among the seven Emirates strongly depicted that it has big potential to be the hub of higher education. There are public government institutions like Zayed University and Higher Colleges of Technology that offer scholarship which attracts many deserving students. In 2015, there is an increase of 9.4 % for new enrollees, while the graduates for the coming years started to boost. Emirati students accounted to 43.2 % (22,694) of the total higher education population. It has an increase of 10 % from 2013 statistics. Indian students are the second most enrolled with 16 and 14 % Arab students. The remaining accounts to students outside GCC region/rest of the world. There are more than 150 different nationalities that are currently studying in Dubai which makes it a sound choice for international students.

There are 56 % males and 44 % females in the higher education institutes. The gender balance and equality in United Arab Emirates in the higher education provides a better ratio for both genders. A study conducted by Dubai International

Table 46.1 List of higher educational institutions across United Arab Emirates combined MOHESR-CAA and KHDA approved institution. Some offers branches across UAE. Please check MOHESR-CAA and KHDA for the latest

	Emirates	No. of higher education Institutions
1	Abu Dhabi	22
2	*Dubai*	*66*
3	Sharjah	9
4	Ajman	5
5	Umm al-Quwain, Ras al-Khaimah, and Fujairah	12

Academic City (DIAC), in conjunction with Deloitte (2013), shows that globally United Arab Emirates ranks number 4 as the leading education hub among emerging economies. The USA is rank number 1 followed by United Kingdom (no. 2) and Canada (no. 3). Aside from that, United Arab Emirates is seen as the fourth most attracted education destination in the world for students seeking to pursue their studies abroad. The survey of over 2400 students and a cross section of companies were carried out to provide DIAC and Deloitte (2013) with the region's most comprehensive, independent study regarding workforce skill gaps that currently exist within emerging markets. Deciding where to study is a major decision that families need to take; as a matter of fact, we have seen many foreign expats as residents across United Arab Emirates. Many of them were more than 30 years on continuous stay in UAE making it as one of the best places for education and tourism.

The Travel and Tourism Competitiveness Report of 2015 ranked the United Arab Emirates as the top in the Middle East and North African region; globally ranked 24th place, over ten million recorded tourists in 2013; ranked 3rd with its world-renowned air transport infrastructure serving as a gateway for Europeans to Africa, the Middle East, and Asia; ranked 1st for its effective branding campaigns enabling business environment for the industry's development; and ranked 30th in its effort to facilitate travel and ease visa requirements. With these developments, Dubai ranked as one of the top five dynamic city destinations among 132 important cities in the world (Global Destination Index, 2009–2015). Further, Dubai evolved as the world champion having 4.9 visitors per resident in 2009 to 5.7 in 2015. Comparing 450 cities across the world, Dubai which ranks 75th worldwide continues to rank highest for quality of living across Africa and the Middle East. Tourism contributes significantly to Dubai's economy supporting its large retail industry and hospitality sector. Since Dubai had become one of the popular destinations in major key cities of the world, educational tourism (one of the forms of tourism) would most likely be a significant source of revenue. This research study examines the suitability of Dubai as the frontrunner as education hub in United Arab Emirates and in the GCC region. Understanding the diversity makes it a multicultural educational hub for education and tourism.

Global Trends in Educational Tourism

A growing trend in global tourism is the increasing rate of youth, student, and educational travel. As market trends indicate (http://www.student-market.com/youth-travel), students traveling abroad to pursue higher education continue as a high revenue generator. The rapidly rising middle class from current two billion to five billion in 2030 as projected, increased access to more disposable income, increased appetite for more international experiences, more affordable transportation prices and ease of travel, fewer political and cultural barriers, and most importantly as a result of globalization, businesses seeking employees with international experience have been cited as the drivers influencing the increasing trend of the youth, student, and educational travel market. As cited, the 1990 trends of youth, student, and educational travel represented 15 % of the tourism market, increasing by 20 % in the last decade, and which is expected to increase in the near future by 25 %.

Regional Hubs Attracting a Greater Share of the Global Student Population

The UNESCO Institute for Statistics (UIS) report (UNESCO, 2016) indicates that the number of students pursuing their higher education abroad continues to increase; however, it was observed that students have shifted to regional destinations that offer more affordable and culturally relevant programmes of study. Although the USA and the United Kingdom remain the strongest destination for students seeking quality education, the regional hubs have become a favored destination due to lower travel costs and its appeal of cultural familiarity. In the Arab States, Saudi Arabia and Dubai (United Arab Emirates) have outpaced the United Kingdom in attracting students coming from the Arab region increasing from 12 to 30% from 1999 to 2013.

Issues, Challenges, and Discussions

Apart from success, there are always issues and challenges that surround the educational tourism being faced by Dubai and United Arab Emirates in general. Perhaps the cost of living and future tax that will be introduced maybe a great challenge in sustaining their competitive advantage. Dubai positioned to be the leading hub across culture because of its unique overall educational superiority. That multicultural environment poses a challenge, as each culture has its unique taste and preferences that you can find only in Dubai.

Challenges to Higher Education in Dubai and United Arab Emirates

- Intense competition among colleges and universities (local and international)
- Cost and fees (tuition and other fees involved)
- Social infrastructures and facilities
- Local and international accreditation
- Flexibility, adaptability, and sustaining their operations
- Attracting and retaining qualified faculty, administrator, and staffs
- Collaborate and partnership with industry/private sectors, government, and others

– Investment on ICT (information, communications, and technology)
– Linking academic experience that will lead to employment
– Knowledge management society that leads to lifelong learning

There are many issues and challenges that educational tourism in Dubai is facing which makes it more competitive than other key cities in the world. Those identified challenges serve as opportunities for them to work in partnership and collaboration with other sectors of the economy. To constantly improve and ensure better access to higher education remains to be one of the priority projects of Government of Dubai. Business management courses remain to be the top choice among courses offered across Dubai and UAE. This simply means that business is open 24/7 per day and all night long. The competitive advantage of educational institution across Dubai can be attributed to the mixture of faculty members, staffs, and administrator. The similarities and differences across culture are its main strength where people valued respect and confidence.

Creation of educational hub department or agency that is under KHDA or MOHESR can be a good strategy in order to sustain and keep their strengths as educational providers and planners.

Educational Tourism Opportunities in Dubai and United Arab Emirates

There are many indicators aside from quantitative stats that support Dubai as the forefront of educational hub in the world today. The stats is just one of the aspects of plate and has more to dig into that. Based from our interviews of many international students, they have mentioned that strategic location of academic institution is one of the factors to decide. The accreditation, both local and international, is also a main factor in deciding to join an institution, and more importantly the fees involved is their main concern.

Students employable are one of the main reasons why foreign students decided to study in Dubai and United Arab Emirates. Even undergraduate is acceptable in many industries as long as the language and skills are within the acceptable range. This practice cannot be found in other countries, as they have minimum job specification set for the work/job. Here in Dubai and United Arab Emirates, the job opportunities are very much fluid and this is because of favorable economic climate of the country.

Despite rumors that taxes may be enforced in the near future, still Dubai can be a competitive place for higher education. It is not only the cost but the opportunities that they are giving which cannot be found in another city or country. Being the host for the 2020 Expo gives Dubai and United Arab Emirates that boost in the education sector and tourism.

Conclusions and Recommendation

Dubai remains to be the forefront of education hub in the United Arab Emirates and the world. To be among the top five is a great accomplishment; however, sustaining the rank is something they want to keep if not exceeding in the near future.

Education tourism can become a major source of engine of economic growth and/increasing source of revenue if Dubai is able to sustain its position as the educational hub for higher education in the GCC region and globally. Emerging as a popular hub for educational tourism, Dubai has competitive advantage among other regions which can be attributed to the following: earning recognition as one of the key cities or the top tourist destination in the world offering many great experiences (great cosmopolitan); strategic location and favorable social infrastructure; has a diverse and established economy; is a home to many colleges and universities across the globe offering curriculum and instruction combining best standards and practice; and ensures a safe learning environment.

It is in this light that combining education and tourism will provide better opportunities for growth and progress across sectors of Dubai's economy. The Government of Dubai through the Ministry of Higher Education-CAA, KHDA, and Ministry of Tourism should collaborate its efforts to create policies that will enhance international educational tourism. The collaborative initiatives may include provision of lower cost of living, affordability, and accessibility of education and travel programs compared with other educational tourist destinations, provide experiences and quality services adapted to the needs and expectations of the international students pursuing higher education market or sector, and introduce competitive initiatives to attract international students using diverse marketing strategies.

References

Deloitte & DIAC. (2013). [Online]. Available from http://me-newswire.net/news/uae-seen-as-one-of-the-worldrsquos-top-five-education-destinations/en
Global Destination Index. (2015). *Global Destination Index, 2009–2015* [Online]. Available from http://gulfnews.com/news/uae/education/business-degree-is-still-number-one-choice-among-dubai-students-1.1312942
Gretzel, U., & Fesenmaier, D. R. (2002). The new realities of destination, networks and communities into DMO strategies. *Proceedings of the Annual Conference, Travel and Tourism Research Association*, Edmonton Alberta, Canada.
IIE. (2015). [Online]. Available from http://www.iie.org/Who-We-Are/News-and-Events/Press-Center/Press-Releases/2015/2015-11-16-Open-Doors-Data and http://www.iie.org/Research-and-Publications/Open-Doors/Data/Economic-Impact-of-International-Students
Lanegran, D. A. (2005). Enhancing and using a sense of place within urban areas: A role for applied cultural geography. *Professional Geographer, 38*(3), 224–228.
Niemela, T. (2010). *Motivation factors in dark tourism: Case House of Terror at Lahti. Nature and Soft Adventure Tourism*. CABI.
Ritchie, B., Carr, N., & Cooper, C. (2003). *Managing educational tourism*. Available from http://books.google.lv/books

UAE News. (2014). Dubai emerging as global higher education hub. *UAE Government News* [Online]. Available from http://search.proquest.com/docview/1565485763?accountid=145382

UNESCO. (2016). [Online]. Available from http://www.uis.unesco.org/Education/Pages/international-student-flow-viz.aspx (January 21, 2016).

Wells, G. (1986, 1999). *Dialogic inquiry: Towards a sociocultural practice and theory of education*. Cambridge: Cambridge University Press.

Chapter 47
Principals' Creative Leadership Practices and School Effectiveness

Keetanjaly Arivayagan and Zaidatol Akmaliah Lope Pihie

Abstract Using a quantitative approach, this study was aimed at determining teacher's perceptions of principals' creative leadership practices for enhancing the effectiveness of secondary schools in Klang District in Malaysia. Premised on the Generativity Theory, the eight main core skills of challenges, broadening, capturing, manages teams, models core competencies of creativity expression, provides resources, provides work environment, and positive feedback and recognition, were examined to explore the concept of creativity in leaders. The model of High Performing School (HPS) was used to measure the School Effectiveness. A total of 250 teachers from these ten schools participated in the survey. The data was collected and analyzed. The findings revealed a moderate correlation between school principals' creative leadership practice and school effectiveness, followed by multiple regressions' analysis indicated creative leadership practices dimension; Encourage Capturing received the strongest weight in the prediction. This study offers a dynamic perspective for school principals to practice creative leadership as the key factor for transforming school into an effective school.

Keywords Creative leadership • Generativity Theory • High performing school • School effectiveness

Introduction

In today's world, education which is known as the heart of human progress has been rapidly transformed at an unprecedented rate (Cisco, 2011). The fundamental role played by school leaders in sprouting high performing schools has been recognized by researchers, policymakers, and practitioners (Darling-Hammond, LaPointe, Meyerson, Orr, & Cohen, 2007). The rapid evolution in school leadership research has brought an extraordinary transformation in the twenty-first century education. In this context,

K. Arivayagan (✉) • Z.A.L. Pihie
University Putra Malaysia, Serdang, Selangor, Malaysia
e-mail: keetanjaly@gmail.com; zalp@upm.edu.my

© Springer International Publishing Switzerland 2017
R. Benlamri, M. Sparer (eds.), *Leadership, Innovation and Entrepreneurship as Driving Forces of the Global Economy*, Springer Proceedings in Business and Economics, DOI 10.1007/978-3-319-43434-6_47

leadership is seen as the linchpin of an effective school (Shannon & Bylsma, 2007). Much research has been conducted to identify the most appropriate leadership style. Recently, research in creative leadership has ballooned to encompass the essential qualities in organizational leaders (Petrie, 2014). Many studies are emphasizing on the momentous of leadership in mobilizing creativity (Epstein, Kaminaka, Phan, & Uda, 2013; Botha, 2013; Puccio, Murdock, & Mance, 2011; Stoll & Temperley, 2009). This fact can be supported through this study that there is a growing demand to apply creative leadership skills in educational institutions.

The Research Problem

Malaysia intends to transform its educational system, in line with the 2020 Vision. Many educational policy reforms have taken place which imposed high demand on principals' to increase the outcome of their teachers and students towards achieving high performing school (HPS) (Ismail, 2012). From the occurrence above, the pressure is more likely to be felt by the school leaders, who stand as the mediator between the school, students, parents, and communities as well as the Ministry of Education. Prior research has been undertaken on the issues and challenges faced by the management of eefctive schools in Malaysia (Kamaruddin, 2006). The findings revealed that although effective schools have been commenced in 1995 but the development and realization towards them is still in the infancy stage. Nevertheless, lacking adequate skills to adapt the changes and stress related to their jobs, school administrators and teachers often experience frustration and exhaustion, which may led them to leave the field of education (Ruzanna, 2014).

However, researchers have encounter creativity as an important tool of a leader's mind in directing changes towards an effective school in this challenging reform environment (Thomson, 2011; Kuan Chen Tsai, 2012; Botha, 2013). A study by Ubben, Hughes and Norris (2004) on creative leadership and effective school revealed that school leaders must be prepared and equipped with the knowledge and skills of problem solving in a practical way to enhance the development and professional growth of teachers. Turnbull (2012) in his study indicated that creative leadership seen as important aspect to enhance students learning. This noteworthy role is important as principals who learnt how to handle and direct changes effectively have succeeded compared to schools that are still mediocre (Azam & Hamidon, 2013).

A preliminary literature review revealed several research gaps on the extent to which school leaders need to incorporate creativity skill, as it is the most essential leadership quality in the twenty-first century (Botha, 2013; Turnbull, 2012; Puccio et al., 2011). Eventhough creative leadership skills are practiced more in corporate organizations (Kuan Chen Tsai, 2012), it is therefore essential to practice in school organization to overcome the unmanageable issues as stated above as well as to enhance school effectiveness.

Objectives of the Study

This research had two objectives:

(1) To determine the relationship between principals' creative leadership practices and school effectiveness through teacher's perceptions.
(2) To identify creative leadership factors that contribute towards school effectiveness.

Literature Reviews

School Effectiveness

In the past decade, school effectiveness has drawn attention to numerous studies, which had been conducted in both western and eastern countries (Lazaridou & Iordanides, 2011). School effectiveness or also known as High Performing School (HPS) has been defined as an organization that shares common characteristics, such as effectual instructional leadership, efficient student assessment, conducive atmosphere, proper guideline and well disciplined, class size, and stakeholders' relationship (Kamaruddin, 2006). It can also be defined as the ability of the school to reform and increase student achievement (Teddlie & Reynolds, 2000).

For the purpose of this research, school effectiveness is defined as an educational reform tool for long and short term process based on the nine key factors: (1) Vision, (2) Standard and Expectation, (3) Effective Leadership, (4) Collaboration and Communication, (5) Aligned with standards, (6) Monitoring of teaching and learning, (7) Professional Development, (8) Learning Environment and (9) Community and Parents involvement (Shannon & Bylsma, 2007).

The High Performing School model (Shannon & Bylsma) was adopted as the preferred model for this research. The HPS model is useful for analyzing school effectiveness as it has been examined and scrutinized in more than 20 schools to study school effectiveness (Lazaridou & Iordanides, 2011). Scott, Parsley, & Fantz (2014) examined teacher perceptions on school effectiveness and student outcomes. Their findings revealed that the nine characteristics of HPS model are correlated to each other. This finding also has been supported by Ndiritu, Gikonyo, & Kimani (2015), Oei Siok Fei, (2015) and Lazaridou & Iordanides, (2011) findings. Similarly, they indentified that Shannon and Bylsma's HPS model comprise the gist of leadership, which is seen as the subset that represses the rest of the characteristics of school effectiveness as shown in Fig. 47.1.

The literature revealed that HPS characteristics have also been adopted by Jamaica's Ministry of Education as a landmark education blueprint with the aim of transforming Jamaican schools into effective schools (Ministry of Education Jamaica, 2014). Shannon and Blysma's HPS, indicate a logical approach in improving all rounded

Fig. 47.1 Shannon and Bylsma's High Performing School model. (*Source*: Adapted from Shannon & Bylsma, 2007)

education and incorporate school leaders to move advance, collectively as well coherently. Viewed in this context, this research will reflect a new dimension in improving the current characteristics of effective schools, specifically school leadership.

Creative Leadership

Researchers have been trying to pin down what are the essential qualities or skills to be an outstanding school leader in ushering students, teachers, and communities into a world-class education (Darling-Hammond et al., 2007). Subsequently, in order to be an effective school leader, in this twenty-first century, a whole different set of tools and thinking skills are required. The development of the twenty-first century leadership skills which include creativity, critical thinking, foster collaboration and communication, generating novel ideas, problem-solving, information literacy, and digital leader is required by school leaders in order to survive in such tumultuous times (Harris, 2009; Petrie, 2014). Nevertheless, these qualities are bonded with creative leadership compared to other leadership traits (Ubben, Hughes, & Norris, 2004; Kuan, 2012; Zacher & Johnson, 2014).

Researchers also have encountered creativity as an important tool of a leader's mind in directing changes (Thomson, 2011; Kuan, 2012; Botha, 2013). The juxtaposition of these three leadership traits which are instructional leadership, transformational leadership and entrepreneurial leadership creates very interesting challenges and opportunities - accentuate on the instructional learning, engaging with reform and taking expansion opportunities in creating a prepossessing educational landscape. The existing literature indicated that creative leadership is a well rounded and distilled mixture which consists of a set of overlapping of instructional leadership, transformational leadership, and entrepreneurial leadership (West-Burnham, 2008; Petrie, 2014; Sohmen, 2015).

The concept of creativity in leaders was explored using Generativity Theory also known as the Creativity Theory (Epstein, 1999). Based on the Generativity Theory, Epstein and his research team had developed eight types of skills and abilities for school leaders and manager and these are: (1) challenges, (2) broadening, (3) capturing, (4) manages teams, (5) models core competencies of creativity expression, (6) provides resources, (7) provides work environment, and (8) positive feedback and recognition that were derived from Generativity Theory to boost leaders competencies in creativity (Epstein et al., 2013). Generativity Theory provide an appropriate strategy for recognizing the necessary competency of a leader by assessing the current competency levels of the leader to increase productivity as well as to develop competencies for multi-tasking (Chance, 1999; Epstein, 1999).

Viewed from this perspective, the Generativity Theory was considered to be most appropriate for this research to examine creative ledaership practices.

School Effectiveness and Creative Leadership

According to Lezotte (1991), the quality of education in school strongly related to effective leadership and school performances. In this context, Stoll and Temperley (2009) believed that creative leadership focuses on seeing and doing things differently to improve student performances and directing the school to a better prospect. Thus, leadership is considered as a significant element in its relationship with school effectiveness, as leadership acts as an important buffer to form school effectiveness (Shannon & Bylsma, 2007; Azam & Hamidon, 2013). Even though the studies that are directly related to creative leadership practices with school effectiveness are very limited but studies involving creativity skill in leadership are quite a number (Basadur, 2004; Petrie, 2014). A few of the important studies relating to creative leadership practices with school effectiveness were conducted by Ubben et al. (2004), Turnbull (2012), Azam and Hamidon (2013), Ashley and Reiter-Palmon (2009), and Sohmen (2015). A study by Ubben et al. (2004) on creative leadership and effective school revealed that school leaders must be prepared and equipped with knowledge and problem-solving skill in a practical way to enhance the development and professional growth of teachers. Turnbull (2012) in his study indicated that creative leadership is seen as important aspect to enhance students' learning. This noteworthy role is important as principals will learn how to handle and direct changes effectively (Azam & Hamidon, 2013). Ashley and Reiter-Palmon (2009) also acknowledged that creativity in leadership will fabricate a creative climate. Besides that, Sohmen (2015, p. 1) opined that creative leadership plays an important element in school, as it *"fuels vision, spawns novel ideas, crafts diverse methods, and produces innovative output."*

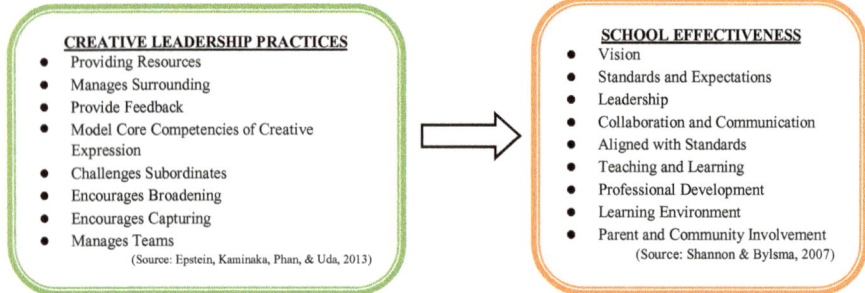

Fig. 47.2 The Conceptual Framework. (*Source*: Developed for this research)

Basadur (2004) and Petrie (2014) reviews wrapped up that creativity in leadership is essential to initiate and sustain school improvement. According to Harris (2009), the prime mover of school effectiveness based on the literature repeatedly refers to the necessity for a critical thinking leader.

Therefore, there is a need to focus on creativity skills in school leadership (Chan, 2009). Turnbull (2012) opined that the hallmark of creative leadership serves as catalyst in resolving the problems by executing the outcomes. Hence, creative leadership will be viewed as of great importance in the school educational transformation. On that note, schools need creative leaders in supporting their school to achieve HPS. This research conceptual framework as showed in Fig. 47.2 is built from the understanding of Generativity Theory (Epstein, 1999; Epstein et al., 2013) and model of HPS (Shannon & Bylsma, 2007) with an objective to illustrate the relationship between creative leadership practices and school effectiveness based on the literature review.

Methodology

Design and Sampling

In this study, a quantitative-correlational design was used. This study was conducted at Klang District, Selangor. The sample size consists of 250 teachers who were selected from ten (10) normal secondary schools out of 29 schools using cluster random sampling.

Instrument

School effectiveness questionnaires were obtained from Shannon and Bylsma's (2007) HPS model with a total of 60 items which consisted of nine dimensions. Meanwhile, creative leadership instrument was based on Epstein Creativity

Competencies Inventory for Managers (*ECCI-m*) which was developed by Epstein et al. (2013). The instrument consists of 48 items with eight dimensions. The questionnaires were adapted with permission from the authors. For each item, the response was modified by researcher into five-point Likert scale range from strongly disagree (1) to strongly agree (5).

Validity and Reliability

The instruments indicated overall good Cronbach alpha value for school effectiveness dimensions ($\alpha=0.957$) and creative leadership dimensions ($\alpha=0.801$) as supported by the George and Mallery (2001, p. 127) rule of thumb; therefore, the instruments are accepted for consideration in this study. Teachers' participation was voluntary. Out of 400 teachers who were surveyed, 270 respondents returned their questionnaires. From this total, 20 questionnaires were not complete, leaving a total of 250 responses for data analysis from a total of 400 questionnaires, thus a valid response rate of 62.5%. Hence, a response rate between 60 and 70% is considered good and sufficient to report a study as well as in performing analysis (Babbie, 1998).

Data Analyses

In this study, the inferential statistic methods such as correlation analysis (Pearson correlation) and multiple regressions are used. Pearson correlation is utilized to determine the relationship between the independent variable (creative leadership practices) and dependent variable (school effectiveness). The rule of thumb based on Hinkle et al. (1979) is used to interpret the size or magnitude or strength of correlation or relationship in this research. Lastly, multiple regressions are used to explore the influence of creative leadership practices on school effectiveness. All collected data are analyzed by using the Statistical Package for Social Science (SPSS) Version 21.0.

Findings and Discussion

Research Question 1: What Is the Relationship Between Creative Leadership Practices and School Effectiveness?

The heart analysis of this study is to determine the relationship between principals' creative leadership practices and school effectiveness based on teacher's perceptions in selected normal secondary schools in Klang District. The findings from this study indicated that the relationship of creative leadership practices by school

Table 47.1 Correlation between school principals' creative leadership practices and school effectiveness

Variables		Practices	School effectiveness
Practices of creative leadership by school principals	Pearson correlation	1	0.617[a]
School effectiveness	Pearson correlation	0.617[a]	1

[a]Correlation is significant at the 0.1 level (2-tailed)
Source: Developed for this research

Table 47.2 Pearson product–moment correlation coefficients among the creative leadership dimensions and school effectiveness variables $n=250$

	Y	X_1	X_1	X_3	X_4	X_5	X_6	X_7	X_8
Y	1								
X_1	0.439[a]	1							
X_2	0.413[a]	0.623[a]	1						
X_3	0.545[a]	0.644[a]	0.641[a]	1					
X_4	0.577[a]	0.504[a]	0.582[a]	0.575[a]	1				
X_5	0.451[a]	0.564[a]	0.659[a]	0.618[a]	0.687[a]	1			
X_6	0.563[a]	0.598[a]	0.550[a]	0.585[a]	0.675[a]	0.598[a]	1		
X_7	0.604[a]	0.501[a]	0.616[a]	0.656[a]	0.680[a]	0.645[a]	0.501[a]	1	
X_8	0.482[a]	0.586[a]	0.534[a]	0.603[a]	0.681[a]	0.695[a]	0.583[a]	0.533[a]	1

[a]Correlation is significant at the 0.05 level (2-tailed)
Where
Y=School effectiveness
X_1=Provides resources
X_2=Manages surrounding
X_3=Provides feedback and recognition
X_4=Models core competencies of creative expression
X_5=Challenges subordinates
X_6=Encourages broadening
X_7=Encourages capturing
X_8=Manages teams
Source: Developed for this research

principals towards school effectiveness as perceived by the teachers showed moderate significant correlation $r = 0.617, p < 0.01$ as illustrated in Table 47.1. This result indicates that there is a lacking of creativity skill applied in school leadership towards school effectiveness. However, the finding was in line with Botha (2013) review that there is a substantial relationship between creative leadership and school improvement.

The correlation matrix between dependent variable (school effectiveness) and independent variable (creative leadership) is exhibited in Table 47.2. Findings also indicated statistically significant correlation among all the eight dimensions of creative leadership practices with school effectiveness. On the whole, at 5% of significance level, there are enough evidences to indicate that there is a substantial relationship between creative leadership practices and school effectiveness, respectively.

It is seen that the school principals have not clearly cultivated and navigated their teachers and school staff in providing adequate resources and managing surroundings. In Murillo and Roman's (2011) findings, it is found that school resources provide a significant contribution towards students' outcome with the basic availability of teaching materials such as board, globe, calculators, etc. Epstein et al. (2013) identified that with appropriate school resources, it will be able to stimulate teacher's creativity and high order thinking skills. This statement is supported by Puccio et al. (2011) and Papa (2011) as today's school leader need a process formula and adequate tools to make the formula work towards transforming the school into a digital era.

However, school leaders are still lacking in expressing creativity competencies, providing feedback, and recognition. OECD (2009) conducted a study on school evaluation, teacher appraisal, and feedback and found out that there is a positive correlation between principals' feedback and teacher's appraisal. Ololube (2006) also indicated in his study that the responsibility of school leader lies primarily in offering sufficient and constructive feedback as well providing recognition based on their performance. This statement was supported by Epstein et al. (2013) studies which pointed out that school leaders interact and offer incentives to staff by encouraging them to think creatively in developing new ideas in teaching and learning.

The findings from this study indicated that school leaders have deficiency in challenging their teachers and school staffs to stimulate creative thinking as well as school leaders are insufficient in encouraging broadening and capturing among teachers. The concept of teaching creatively has been accentuated numerous times by the Ministry of Education (The Malaysia Education Blueprint 2013–2025, 2012). It is very essential for teachers to be stimulated at workplace to work creatively by involving a divergent pattern to challenge ideas and embrace creativity as a part of learning (Brown, 2006; Puccio et al., 2011; Epstein et al., 2013).

When school leaders are able to broaden teachers knowledge and skills outside of their expertise, this will create a smooth pathway for teachers to preserve new ideas in their instructional practices (Hare, 2010; Adams, 2013). Janson and McQueen (2007) also stated that it is important for school leaders to encourage capturing and broadening in teachers to ensure proper adaption to the complexity and context of teaching and learning. Moreover, the findings from this also indicated that school leaders have less skill in managing teams. This indicated that school leaders must have a joint effort with teachers and school staffs to increase student learning by optimizing creativity output (Epstein et al., 2013).

The findings from this study revealed that teachers do feel that principals should imply creative leadership practices, as this will help to enhance school effectiveness. The more school principals' put efforts to encourage and guide creative thinking, the more it will help teachers, school staffs as well as students and parents to work together to generate novel ideas. Nonetheless, this study was not designed to determine whether an increase in a variable causes an increase in the other variables. However, it is more apt to pursue the school effectiveness when school principals practice creative leadership.

Research Question 2: What Are the Creative Leadership Factors that Contribute Towards School Effectiveness?

The findings from this study further clarify that the domain Encourage Capturing in the creative leadership practices received the strongest weight in the prediction (Standardized $\beta=0.383$, $p < 0.05$) followed by Model Core Competencies of Creative Expression (Standardized $\beta=0.278$, $p < 0.05$), and Encourage Broadening (Standardized $\beta=0.191$, $p < 0.05$) as portrayed in Table 47.3. These three variables showed significant relationship in making an unique contribution to the prediction of school effectiveness. It can be concluded that 43 % of the variance in school effectiveness can be explained by creative leadership practices. However, there are still 56.6 % variation of school effectiveness that can be explicated by other variables which is not carried out in this research. The regression analysis showed that creative leadership practice was partially related to school effectiveness. If we take a closer look in this dimension, it is evidently showed that there is a connection. The ultimate aim of principal in Encourage Capturing is to preserve new ideas by providing appropriate supplies or software which allows teachers' to reflect and create innovative teaching methods and thus, implementing those innovations in teaching and learning (Gulamhussein, 2013; Epstein et al., 2013). This demonstrates that the school leaders are in favor of creative solutions, fresh ideas, and exploring innovative ways to equip students and teachers towards school improvement and school effectiveness.

More broadly, these findings highlighted that the importance of practicing creative leadership as the twenty-first century leadership skills to facilitate schools

Table 47.3 Estimates of coefficients for school effectiveness

Dimensions	Unstandardized coefficients		Standardized coefficients			Collinearity statistics	
	B	Std. error	Beta	t	p-value	Tolerance	VIF
Constant	2.468	0.130					
Provides resources	0.110	0.048	0.184	2.291	0.023	0.354	2.822
Manages surrounding	0.010	0.045	0.016	0.216	0.829	0.423	2.364
Provides feedback and recognition	0.077	0.042	0.151	1.832	0.068	0.335	2.988
Models core competencies of creative expressions	0.179	0.063	0.278	2.832	0.005	0.237	4.226
Challenges subordinates	0.034	0.048	0.056	0.704	0.482	0.360	2.782
Encourages broadening	0.117	0.045	0.191	2.616	0.009	0.426	2.347
Encourages capturing	0.211	0.049	0.383	4.296*	0.000	0.287	3.487
Manages teams	0.026	0.060	0.035	0.439	0.661	0.358	2.795

*$p<0.05$
$R=0.67$, $R^2=0.45$, Adj. $R^2=0.43$; $F=24.83$, $p=0.00$
Source: Developed for this research

towards HPS. This requires the leaders to have new mindsets and master the critical thinking skills by unlocking the creativity practices (Zacko-Smith, Puccio, & Mance, 2010). From this finding, it shows that teachers are aware of the importance of school principals practicing creative leadership in leading school towards effective school. Most importantly, school leaders must have the eager to discover creative leadership approaches and keep innovating in how they lead successful. Clearly, these findings are consistent with the reviews of previous research (e.g., Ubben, 2000; Turnbull, 2012; Azam & Hamidon, 2013; Ashley & Reiter-Palmon, 2009; Sohmen, 2015) as noted in the literature review of this study.

Conclusion and Future Work

In a nutshell, there is a moderate significant relationship between principals' creative leadership practices and school effectiveness through teachers' perceptions. This study implies that school leaders should heavily facilitate and employ "Encourage Broadening" in leading school towards HPS, as it received the strongest weight in the prediction. The idea of creative leadership is the stark departure from a conventional role of a principal as an administrative leader to imaginative and resourceful leadership (Thomson, 2011). Creative leadership is seen as an ability to solve problems and develop creative solutions to increase productivity, engage teachers in problem-solving, and encourage teacher's professional growth (Botha, 2013). Creative leaders have the capacity to come up with new ideas to solve problems and exploiting opportunities (Petrie, 2014). The leaders must be a part and parcel of a school organization that has the capability in producing the conditions that enable students, teachers, and communities to work together to generate ideas. These ideas will help the organization to move forward towards the transformation. Schools are aware that they need to adapt to the rapidly changing times. This will be an essential dimension for the twenty-first century school principals, as they will counterpart worldwide and increasingly expected to lead in inspired ways, to keep up with the new challenges, expectations, and demands of modern-day society.

Implication of the Study

This study provides a new evidence of practicing creative leadership towards school effectiveness. The findings of this study will help school administrators to recognize, describe, and appreciate the importance of school leaders to practice creative leadership towards achieving school effectiveness. Besides that, school administrators can learn how to generate sufficient ideas before making any decisions. In this study, it shows that it is essential for school leaders to become skillful at exercising creative leadership dimensions in improvising school effectiveness. This study implies that school leaders should heavily facilitate and employ Encourage Broadening in leading school towards HPS. In this case, it will help to motivate school leaders and teachers as well as to bring out new ideas and methods in teaching and learning. This study also indicates that there is a moderate relationship between creative leadership practices and school effectiveness, which concludes that there is a need for leaders to be creative to improve school performance. The results of this study can also be used to enhance and support school organization efforts in addressing creative culture, transformation of creative workforce, or to initiate any creative changes in school management.

Recommendation for Practice and Future Research

By practicing creative leadership:

- It enables school leaders to open up new ways of solving daily school problems.
- School principal will be able to stimulate creativity and encourage implementation of idea.
- It helps to increase employees' (teachers and school staff) ability in offering new insights to innovation environment (Puccio et al., 2011). If these are true, it suggests that training on brain techniques and stimulating creative thinking will help school leaders to unlock their brain power and generate novel ideas.
- It is recommended that school leaders and teachers should be more open, positive, consistent, and constructive to give feedback in order to achieve effective communication.
- Principals should improve their role, as it is essential for the twenty-first century school leadership in leading school towards school effectiveness.

Acknowledgments The authors would like to take this opportunity to thank Emeritus Professor Dr Robert Epstein for granting permission to use his survey tool (*ECCI-m*) as well as to Shannon and Bylsma's High Performing School questionnaires. Thanks to Malaysia Ministry of Education, Selangor Education Department, and Klang Districts Education for allowing the authors to conduct this research. Authors would also like to express their gratitude to the ten selected normal secondary school principals for permitting authors to conduct the research at their school and teachers for their willingness to participate in this survey as well as family and friends for their support.

References

Adams, J. W. (2013). *A case study: Using lesson study to understand factors that affect teaching creative and critical thinking in the elementary classroom*. Doctor of Education Educational Leadership and Management, Drexel University, Philadelphia, PA. Retrieved April 27, 2015, from https://idea.library.drexel.edu/islandora/object/idea%3A4131

Ashley, G. C., & Reiter-Palmon, R. (2009). Review of creative leadership: Skills that drive change. *Psychology Faculty Publications Paper 53, 3*(2), 124–125. Retrieved May 28, 2015, from http://digitalcommons.unomaha.edu/psychfacpub/53/.

Azam, O., & Hamidon, R. (2013). Innovative leadership: Learning from change management among Malaysian secondary school principals. *World Applied Sciences Journal, 23*(2), 167–177.

Babbie, E. (1998). Survey Research Methods (2nd ed.). Belmont: Wadsworth.

Basadur, M. (2004). Leading others to think innovatively together: Creative leadership. *Leadership Quarterly, 15*, 103–121.

Botha, R. J. (2013). The need for creative leadership in South African schools. *African Studies, 72*(2), 307–320. doi:10.1080/00020184.2013.812876.

Brown, J. S. (2006). New learning environments for the 21st century: Exploring the edge. *Change, 38*, 18–24. Retrieved from http://www.johnseelybrown.com/Change%20article.pdf.

Chan, Y. F. (2009). Leadership characteristics of an excellent principal in Malaysia. *International Education Studies, 2*(4), 106–116.

Chance, P. (1999). Where Does Behavior Come From? A Review of Epstein's Cognition, Creativity, and Behavior. The Behavior Analyst, 22(2), 161–163. Retrieved from http://www.ncbi.nlm.nih.gov/pmc/articles/PMC2731348/.

Cisco. (2011). *Transforming education, transforming lives: A path toward next generation teaching and learning.* USA: Cisco and/or its affiliates. Retrieved March 20, 2015, from www.cisco.com/go/education

Darling-Hammond, L., LaPointe, M., Meyerson, D., Orr, M. T., & Cohen, C. (2007). *Preparing school leaders for a changing world: Lessons from exemplary leadership development programs.* Stanford: The Wallace Foundation. Retrieved March 6, 2015, from http://www.wallacefoundation.org/knowledge-center/school-leadership/key-research/Documents/Preparing-School-Leaders.pdf.

Epstein, R. (1999). Generativity theory. *Encyclopedia of Creativity, 1*, 759–766.

Epstein, R., Kaminaka, K., Phan, V., & Uda, R. (2013). How is creativity best managed? Some empirical and theoretical guidelines. *Creativity and Innovation Management, 22*(4), 359–374.

George, D., & Mallery, P. (2001). *SPSS for windows step by step: A simple guide and reference 10.0 update* (3rd ed.). Needham Heights, MA: Allyn & Bacon.

Gulamhussein, A. (2013). *Teaching the teachers: Effective professional development in an era of high stakes accountability.* Alexandria, VA: The Center for Public Education.

Gumusluoglu, L., & Ilsev, A. (2009). Transformational leadership, creativity, and organizational innovation. *Journal of Business Research, 62*, 461–473.

Harding, T. (2010). Fostering creativity for leadership and leading change. *Arts Education Policy Review, 111*(2), 51–53.

Hare, J. (2010). *Holistic education: An interpretation for teachers in the IB programmes.* Cardiff: International Baccalaureate Organization. Retrieved October 24, 2015, from http://www.godolphinandlatymer.com/_files/IB/5814BF78BFFF6064F25D143FBB622152.pdf.

Harris, A. (2009). Creative leadership: Developing future leadership. *Management in Education, 23*(1), 9–11.

Hinkle, D. E., Wiersma, W., & Jurs, S. G. (2003). Applied statistics for the behavioral sciences. Boston: MA: Houghton Mifflin.

Ismail, M. R. (2012). *Dissertation: Teachers' perceptions of principal leadership style and how they impact on teacher job satisfaction.* Degree of doctoral dissertation, Colorado State University, Fort Collins, CO. Retrieved March 28, 2015, from http://digitool.library.colostate.edu///exlibris/dtl/d3_1/apache_media/L2V4bGlicmlzL2R0bC9kM18xL2FwYWNoZV9t ZWRpYS8xNjkzNjk=.pdf

Janson, A., & McQueen, R. J. (2007). Capturing leadership tacit knowledge in conversations with leaders. *Leadership and Organization Development Journal, 28*(7), 646–663.

Kamaruddin, K. (2006). *Management of effective schools in Malaysia: Issues and challenges.* Retrieved October 25, 2014, from http://www.jgbm.org/page/21%20%20Kamaruddin.pdf

Kuan, C. T. (2012). Creative leadership for directing changes. *Business Management and Strategy, 3*(2), 76–84.

Lazaridou, A., & Iordanides, G. (2011). The principal's role in achieving school effectiveness. *International Studies in Educational Administration, 39*(3), 3–19.

Lezotte, L. (1991). *Correlates of effective schools: The first and second generation.* Okemos, MI: Effective Schools Products, Ltd.

Ministry of Education Jamaica. (2014). *School effectiveness toolkit.* Jamaica: Inter-American Development.

Murillo, F. O., & Roman, M. (2011). School infrastructure and resource do matter: Analysis of the incidence of school resource on the performance of Latin American students. *Effectiveness and School Improvement: International Journal of Research Policy and Practice, 22*(1), 29–50.

Ndiritu, A., Gikonyo, N., & Kimani, G. (2015). Preaching and drinking wine: A necessity for transformational leaders in effective schools. *International Journal of Education and Research, 2*(3), 1–10.

OECD (2009). *Creating effective teaching and learning environments: First results from TALIS.* Paris: International Teaching and Learning Survey (TALIS). Retrieved October 12, 2015, from http://www.oecd.org/dataoecd/17/51/43023606.pdf

Oei, S. F. (2015). The role of school principal in transforming an Indonesian. *International Journal of Research Studies in Management, 4*(1), 15–35.

Ololube, N. P. (2006). *Teachers job satisfaction and motivation for school effectiveness: An assessment.* Finland: Essays in Education (EIE). Retrieved October 12, 2015, from http://www.usca.edu/essays/vol182006/ololube.pdf.

Papa, R. (2011). *Technology leadership for school improvement.* Thousand Oaks, CA: SAGE Publications, Inc.

Petrie, N. (2014). *Future trends in leadership development.* UK: Center for Creative Leadership.

Philip, H. (2009). *Leadership for 21st century schools: From instructional leadership to leadership for learning.* Hong Kong: The Hong Kong Institute of Education.

Puccio, G. J., Murdock, M. C., & Mance, M. (2011). *Creative leadership: Skills that drive change* (2nd ed.). London: Sage.

Ruzanna, M. N. (2014). *Hubungan antara Beban Tugas dan Kemudahan Sumber dengan Kepusaan Kerja dalam Kalangan Guru Teknikal di Sekolah Menengah Pendidikan Khas Vokasional (SMPKV).* Selangor: University Putra Malaysia.

Scott, C., Parsley, D., & Fantz, T. (2014). *Connections between teacher perceptions of school effectiveness and student outcomes in Idaho's low-achieving schools.* Institute of Education Sciences (IES), U.S. Department of Education. Washington, DC: The National Center for Education Evaluation and Regional Assistance (NCEE). Retrieved from http://ies.ed.gov/ncee/edlabs

Shannon, G. S., & Bylsma, P. (2007). *Nine characteristics of high-performing schools: A research-based resource for schools and districts to assist with improving student learning. OSPI* (pp. 1–146). Washington, DC: Superintendent of Public Instruction.

Sohmen, V. S. (2015). Reflections on creative leadership. *International Journal of Global Business, 8*(1), 1–14. Retrieved June 18, 2015, from http://www.gsmi-ijgb.com/Documents/IJGB%20V8%20N1%20P01%20Victor%20Sohmen%20%E2%80%93Reflections%20on%20Creative%20Leadership.pdf.

Stoll, L., & Temperley, J. (2009). Creative leadership: A challenge of our times. *School Leadership and Management, 29*(1), 65–78.

The Malaysia Education Blueprint 2013–2025 (2012). *Malaysia: Ministry of Education.*

Thomson, P. (2011). Creative leadership: A new category or more of the same? *Journal of Educational Administration and History, 43*(3), 249–272.

Turnbull, J. (2012). *Creative educational leadership: A practical guide to leadership as creativity.* London: Bloomsbury Academic.

Ubben, G. C., Hughes, L. W., & Norris, C. J. (2004). *The principal: Creative leadership for excellence in schools* (5th ed.). UK: Pearson/A and B.

West-Burnham, J. (2008). *Creative leadership.* Paper presented at the International Symposium on the Art of Creative Leadership, Bali.

Zacher, H., & Johnson, E. (2014). Leadership and creativity in higher education. Studies in Higher Education, 1–15. doi: http://dx.doi.org/10.1080/03075079.2014.881340.

Zacko-Smith, J. D., Puccio, G. J., & Mance, M. (2010). Creative leadership: Welcome to the 21st century. *Academic Exchange Quarterly, 14*(4), 133–138.

Keetanjaly Arivayagan Keetanjaly Arivayagan always has a growing desire to contribute towards the education world. This has stimulated her to explore the ideal quality of school leadership with the integration of creativity and problem-solving skills. Her passion and strong determination has encouraged her to persuade her studies in Master of Education specializing Educational Administration in University Putra Malaysia (UPM) which is one of the top public universities in Malaysia. She has recently completed a research titled Teacher's Perceptions Related to School Principals' Creative Leadership practices towards School Effectiveness. The findings of this study would be very useful in civilizing and sustaining the quality of school leadership and school management towards the twenty-first century education as well as help school leaders to realize their potential.

Zaidatol Akmaliah Lope Pihie Professor Dr. Zaidatol Akmaliah Lope Pihie is a professor at the Faculty of Educational Studies, Universiti Putra Malaysia. She has served in UPM since 1981. She graduated from Southern Illinois University—Carbondale, USA. She completed her Ph.D. degree in 1992, and was promoted to Associate Professor in 1997 and subsequently to full professor in 2003. From April 2001 to November 2002 she was appointed as the head of education department, as Deputy Dean of Faculty of Education from November 2002 to November 2005, and as Deputy Dean (Research and Graduate Studies) from September 2010 to September 2012. She was also a Senate member in April 2005 to March 2008, and July 2011 to June 2014. Her areas of specializations are in entrepreneurship education, leadership, and educational management as well as teaching methodology. She has presented and published a number of academic papers overseas and locally within her area of interest. She supervises 30 Ph.D. students and 18 had graduated. She is actively involved in research activities. Her researches are mostly related to her area of expertise. She had received three gold medals, six silver medals, and nine bronze medals from UPM through her research effort.

Part III
International Entrepreneurship and Small Business

Chapter 48
Family Entrepreneurial Teams Under the TPB Lens

Rima M. Bizri

Abstract In recognition of the synergies gained from the formation of family entrepreneurial teams, FETs have lately come under extensive examination. This chapter investigates the antecedents of FET formation from the perspective of the theory of planned behavior. Results confirm the significant influence of positive attitude, perceived behavioral control, and, to a lesser extent, subjective norms. Further investigation of the influence of subjective norms on FET formation revealed interesting conclusions.

Keywords Family entrepreneurial teams • Theory of planned behavior • Antecedents

Introduction and Theoretical Framework

Much has been written about the importance of entrepreneurship in stimulating economic growth in developing countries. Among the recent trends in entrepreneurial research is the exploration of family members' tendencies to start entrepreneurial ventures as family teams. Family entrepreneurial teams or FETs (Discua Cruz, Howorth, & Hamilton, 2013) enjoy not only the synergies that come with teams, but more specifically those that come with "family" teams. In recognizing their potential benefits, this chapter seeks to investigate the factors that lead to FET formation. The results of such investigation would serve to help policy makers promote FETs by influencing the factors that may lead to their formation, and, in doing so, facilitate family entrepreneurship.

In the study of entrepreneurship, researchers need to examine a variety of factors that potentially play a role in starting new ventures. If they focus only on the firm level, they will not be able to detect other lines of entrepreneurial behavior

R.M. Bizri, Ph.D. (✉)
Management and Marketing Studies Department, College of Business Administration,
Rafik Hariri University, Meshref, Lebanon
e-mail: bizrirm@rhu.edu.lb

© Springer International Publishing Switzerland 2017 571
R. Benlamri, M. Sparer (eds.), *Leadership, Innovation and Entrepreneurship as Driving Forces of the Global Economy*, Springer Proceedings in Business and Economics, DOI 10.1007/978-3-319-43434-6_48

(Davidsson & Wiklund, 2001) including the formation of FETs, all the more reason to suggest shifting the analysis to the family team level (Scott & Rosa, 2002).

One of the most important aspects of FETs is their formation. If researchers can better understand the antecedents of FETs, they might perhaps be able to suggest ways to positively influence those factors to facilitate and accelerate FET formation. There have been a few valuable studies (e.g., Ensley & Pearson, 2005; Schjoedt, Monsen, Pearson, Barnett, & Chrisman, 2013; Pearson, Carr, & Shaw, 2008; Ucbasaran, Lockett, Wright, & Westhead, 2003) on the various dynamics of FETs including an entire special issue (Schjoedt et al., 2013) which investigated FET formation, composition, behaviors, and performance, thereby confirming the importance of FETs as a topic for research separate from entrepreneurship as a generic process. However, aside from those, "little work has been done regarding the composition of family entrepreneurial teams and even less concentrates on family firms outside of the United States or Western Europe" (Schjoedt et al., 2013, p. 5).

With the cognitive model having gained much support in recent years, it is argued that understanding how entrepreneurs think would help explain and predict entrepreneurial intention and consequently behavior (Krueger, Reilly, & Carsrud, 2000). To the author's knowledge, no previous studies on FET formation have been found that operationalize the theory of planned behavior, let alone in a non-Western context, despite its consistent ability to explain the entrepreneurial process. In addition, most studies on FET formation focus on Western culture and very few, if any, tackle FET formation in non-Western cultures despite the wealth and complexity these aspects may bring into the discussion.

This study seeks to explore the antecedents of FET formation from the cognitive perspective, using Ajzen's theory of planned behavior (Ajzen, 1991). Identifying the cognitive variables that may influence the entrepreneur's intention to start an FET will likely help in augmenting our understanding of the process, leading educators, practitioners, and policy makers to better manage and facilitate that process.

The theory of planned behavior suggests that an individual's positive attitude toward entrepreneurship, subjective norms that support it, and perceived behavioral control are likely to be strong predictors of entrepreneurial intention, and thereby behavior (Ajzen, 1991). The current study operationalizes Ajzen's model of planned behavior to predict individuals' intent to start FETs. It suggests that an individual's positive attitude toward starting FETs, and subjective norms that support FET formation, together with a heightened perceived behavioral control on part of the individual, is likely to have a significant influence on FET formation. However, it is cautioned that the TPB model elements and the variance explained by the model will differ by country as foreseen by Ajzen (Engle et al., 2010). This is where the current study will hopefully add value.

The main research question of this study is the following: "What are the antecedents of FET formation from the perspective of the theory of planned behavior?" Answering this question would help policy makers influence those antecedents in order to promote the formation of FETs. Consequently, the hypotheses of the study are as follows:

H_1: The family members' attitudes toward FETs influence their decision to start an FET.

H_2: The family members' perceptions of social norms influence their decision to start an FET.

H_3: The family members' perceived behavioral control influences their decision to start an FET.

Context and Methodology

The study was performed in Lebanon, a small Middle Eastern nation on the eastern coast of the Mediterranean. This country enjoys a deep cultural heritage and powerful social units where family ties play a significant role in shaping individual behavior. The influence of family opinion is clearly visible in most decisions made by its members due to the intimate relationships that exist between them and that have been nurtured with time and continuous interaction.

This study borrowed the previously developed and validated scales of Liñán and Chen (2009) which were designed to measure entrepreneurial intention as a function of attitude, subjective norms, and perceived behavioral control. In this study however, those scales were slightly adjusted to reflect the entrepreneurial intention to form an *FET*, as opposed to the intention to start a new venture. Therefore, four items were selected to test respondents' personal attitudes toward starting an FET, three items to test subjective norms, five items to test respondents' PBC, and four items to test their intention to start an FET. Two additional PBC items were added to reflect the understanding of PBC in the Lebanese context.

A test of scale reliability shows that the multi-item measures have alpha-coefficients ranging between .702 and .854, which satisfies the reliability criterion suggested by Nunnally (1978). Six questions in the demographic section asked about the respondent's age, gender, education, experience, and if one's family owned and operated a family business. Data gathered from this section would shed light on the profile of the respondents and whether any of those variables might influence their decision to form an FET.

The questionnaires were distributed among Lebanese graduate students pursuing their MBAs and senior business students about to graduate. The rationale behind targeting this category of respondents is that these young people are backed by the theoretical knowhow and practical wisdom of the faculty who taught them and the academic institutions they attended, and are therefore more likely to be driven toward entrepreneurial action. The data collection process generated 286 usable questionnaires and numerous statistical analyses were done using SPSS, the most important of which were factor analysis and regression analysis. Then, to investigate one of the outcomes of the study, a focus group technique was used in which three focus groups were conducted on separate occasions.

Findings and Discussion

The factor analysis that was performed on the data generated four factors designated as the dependent variable "entrepreneurial intention," and three independent variables of this study, namely "positive attitude," "subjective norms," and "perceived behavioral control," explaining 65.78 % of the variance in entrepreneurial intention, as shown in Table 48.1.

These factors were then used in a regression analysis which showed that the three elements of TPB explained a good portion of the decision to start FETs (adjusted $R^2 = .546$) with a statistically significant F change (Sig. = .000), as shown in Table 48.2.

The results of the regression analysis showed that all three elements of TPB were statistically significant, with the largest standardized beta coefficient belonging to the attitude variable ($B = .657$), followed by perceived behavioral control ($B = .319$), and lastly subjective norms ($B = .132$). Thus all three hypotheses were supported, as shown in Table 48.3. The findings of this study suggest that the elements of TPB, namely positive attitude, subjective norms, and perceived behavioral control, have a significant influence on family members' intentions to start an FET.

Table 48.1 Total variance explained

Component	Rotation sums of squared loadings		
	Total	% of variance	Cumulative %
1	4.388	24.380	24.380
2	3.353	18.628	43.008
3	2.367	13.149	56.157
4	1.732	9.623	65.780

Extraction method: Principal component analysis

Table 48.2 Model summary

Model	R	R^2	Adjusted R^2	Std. error of the estimate
1	.742[a]	.551	.546	.67389798

[a]Predictors: (Constant), SN_Factor, Attitude_Factor, PBC_Factor

Table 48.3 Regression analysis—the coefficient table

Coefficients[a]

Model		Unstandardized coefficients		Standardized coefficients		
		B	Std. error	Beta	t	Sig.
1	(Constant)	−2.369E-16	.040		.000	1.000
	PBC_Factor	.319	.040	.319	8.000	.000
	Attitude_Factor	.657	.040	.657	16.450	.000
	SN_Factor	.132	.040	.132	3.309	.001

[a]Dependent variable: Zscore: Intention to form an FET

The results of this study confirm the influence of attitudes, perceived behavioral control, and subjective norms on the entrepreneur's intention to start an FET, thus extending the scope of the TPB to reach FET formation and not merely individual entrepreneurial ventures.

In Middle Eastern culture, family values are extremely powerful and young adults are brought up to cherish and value family ties. Therefore, those potential entrepreneurs grow up with a strong positive attitude toward family engagements such as FETs. These potential entrepreneurs are also raised to be internally motivated, and to feel that they can perform the entrepreneurial behavior with ease, especially when they attempt it with the backing of kin. Therefore, the results of this study suggest that having strong feelings of ease in forming an FET is likely to encourage individuals to form FETs.

The last variable, subjective norms, also had a statistically significant positive effect, albeit a low beta coefficient ($B = .132$). This was a bit surprising given the collective context in which the study was performed. The results showed that the respondents perceived subjective norms as having a weaker effect than the other two variables, something that went against the predictions of the researcher. Previous studies showed that individuals are likely to undertake behaviors that are encouraged by significant members of their social circle (Kristiansen & Indarti, 2004). Knowing Middle Eastern culture, there is no stronger influence of a social circle than that of one's family. This is why the relatively weak effect of subjective norms, as depicted by the low beta ($B = .132$), raised a question mark as to why might subjective norms have a smaller coefficient than both attitude and perceived behavioral control. Therefore, it was decided to resort to qualitative analysis, focus groups in particular. Three groups of seven members each were invited at separate occasions to meetings lasting about 90 min each. Focus group members comprised a convenience sample of MBA and senior students who provided valuable insight into our discussion.

The results of the focus group discussions pointed to the fact that though parents encourage family ties and familial bonding, they tend to discourage such bonding in business. Parents much prefer that their children go into partnership either alone or with nonfamily members because, if nonfamily partners were to act opportunistically, they could be sued and brought to justice, something which could not be done to the next of kin. In Middle Eastern culture, it is practically unheard of to sue a brother, a cousin, an uncle, or a nephew. Doing so is almost as unethical as the opportunistic deed itself. Therefore, though some parents may in fact encourage FET formation, other parents, in an effort to protect family members and resources, may secretly discourage children from forming FETs, thereby leading them to form negative perceptions about the norms surrounding FETs. This may offer some insight as to why subjective norms had such a low beta coefficient in our regression analysis. The parents were primarily motivated by a protectionist drive toward their entrepreneurial children in a social context that looks down on intrafamilial litigation just as much as it looks down on opportunistic behavior. The lack of a socially acceptable recourse against opportunistic behavior on the part of family members in business only strengthens the parents' protectionist drive, making it a significant cultural factor affecting FET formation.

Conclusions and Implications

The results of this study offer insight into the dynamics of FET formation, not only by confirming the influence of the dimensions of the theory of planned behavior, but also by shedding light on the influence of cultural variables which may potentially hinder FET formation.

Several implications can be concluded from this study. First, by confirming the influence of the positive attitude toward FETs, having a heightened perceived behavioral control, and positive subjective norms, policy makers can help a nation reap the benefits of FETs by promoting the formation of those teams in practical ways. Policy makers and relevant institutions could seek to integrate family entrepreneurship in primary and secondary education of the country's youth, thus building positive attitudes and subjective norms toward FETs, meanwhile strengthening the youth's perceived behavioral control. The practical approach suggests that young entrepreneurs be given multiple opportunities to form FETs under the supervision of instructors in schools as well as college, to help them experience the potential challenges and rewards of such undertakings.

Second, policy makers need to create socially acceptable means of recourse for family members who wish to pursue litigation but are hindered by social pressure. Examples of acceptable means of recourse might include conciliatory and mediation offices which are almost nonexistent in Middle Eastern countries, despite the fact that they may be perceived favorably due to their reconciliatory function. Such offices can offer effective means of conflict resolution between and among family business partners, in ways that do not approach formal litigation, thereby widening the comfort zone of entrepreneurs and their families regarding FETs.

Limitations and Future Research

Despite the insight that this study offers, it does have its limitations. One important limitation is that the study was conducted only in Lebanon, thus reflecting the Lebanese perspectives toward family, entrepreneurship, and attitudes toward them. It would be very useful to test the conclusions of this study in other contexts in the Middle East to see if those conclusions would hold. Another limitation is the convenience sampling technique and the sample size of 286 respondents. Though not much can be done about the sampling technique, given that there are no local databases or statistical records that can be accessed for research, the sample size could be augmented in future research in order to offer more reliable conclusions.

References

Ajzen, I. (1991). The theory of planned behavior. *Organizational Behavior and Human Decision Processes, 50*(2), 179–211.

Davidsson, P., & Wiklund, J. (2001). Levels of analysis in entrepreneurship research: Current research practice and suggestions for the future. *Entrepreneurship Theory and Practice, 25*(4), 81–100.

Discua Cruz, A., Howorth, C., & Hamilton, E. (2013). Intrafamily entrepreneurship: The formation and membership of family entrepreneurial teams. *Entrepreneurship Theory and Practice, 37*(1), 17–46.

Engle, R. L., Dimitriadi, N., Gavidia, J. V., Schlaegel, C., Delanoe, S., et al. (2010). Entrepreneurial intent: A twelve-country evaluation of Ajzen's model of planned behavior. *International Journal of Entrepreneurial Behavior & Research, 16*(1), 35–57.

Ensley, M. D., & Pearson, A. W. (2005). An exploratory comparison of the behavioral dynamics of top management teams in family and nonfamily new ventures: Cohesion, conflict, potency, and consensus. *Entrepreneurship Theory and Practice, 29*(3), 267–284.

Kristiansen, S., & Indarti, N. (2004). Entrepreneurial intention among Indonesian and Norwegian students. *Journal of Enterprising Culture, 12*(01), 55–78.

Krueger, N. F., Reilly, M. D., & Carsrud, A. L. (2000). Competing models of entrepreneurial intentions. *Journal of Business Venturing, 15*(5), 411–432.

Liñán, F., & Chen, Y. W. (2009). Development and cross-cultural application of a specific instrument to measure entrepreneurial intentions. *Entrepreneurship Theory and Practice, 33*(3), 593–617.

Nunnally, J. C. (1978). *Psychometric theory* (2nd ed.). New York: McGraw Hill.

Pearson, A. W., Carr, J. C., & Shaw, J. C. (2008). Toward a theory of familiness: A social capital perspective. *Entrepreneurship Theory and Practice, 32*(6), 949–969.

Schjoedt, L., Monsen, E., Pearson, A., Barnett, T., & Chrisman, J. J. (2013). New venture and family business teams: Understanding team formation, composition, behaviors, and performance. *Entrepreneurship Theory and Practice, 37*(1), 1–15.

Scott, M., & Rosa, P. (2002). Has firm level analysis reached its limits? Time for a rethink. *Entrepreneurship: Critical Perspectives on Business and Management, 3*(4), 29.

Ucbasaran, D., Lockett, A., Wright, M., & Westhead, P. (2003). Entrepreneurial founder teams: Factors associated with member entry and exit. *Entrepreneurship Theory and Practice, 28*(2), 107–128.

Chapter 49
The Government's Role in the Importance of Entrepreneurship Education Amongst University Students in Malaysia

Hanim Kamaruddin, Norasmah Othman, Rosilah Hassan, Wan Mimi Diyana Wan Zaki, and Sarmila Md Sum

Abstract The growth of entrepreneurship in Malaysia and the number of enterprises being created in the last decade are evidence of sheer amount and variety of supporting mechanisms and policies established by the government. These include funding, physical infrastructure, trade advisory and support, and entrepreneurship education to ensure that challenges in the national and global markets can be faced and abated with equipped knowledge and support. To nurture and sustain entrepreneurial education and related initiatives, the Malaysian Government has pushed forward the transformation of teaching and learning focusing on entrepreneurial skills in the National Higher Education Action Plan 2007–2010. Thus, the most significant endeavor is the emergence of a formal entrepreneurial education at the local higher education institutions (HEIs) in Malaysia. In the past 5 years, entrepreneurship education has grown dramatically in Malaysia resulting to 19 universities

H. Kamaruddin (✉)
Faculty of Law, Universiti Kebangsaan Malaysia (UKM), Bangi, 43600 Selangor, Malaysia
e-mail: hanim@ukm.edu.my

N. Othman
Faculty of Education, Universiti Kebangsaan Malaysia (UKM), Bangi,
43600 Selangor, Malaysia
e-mail: lin@ukm.edu.my

R. Hassan
Faculty of Information Science and Technology, Universiti Kebangsaan Malaysia (UKM),
Bangi, 43600 Selangor, Malaysia
e-mail: rosilah@ukm.edu.my

W.M.D.W. Zaki
Faculty of Engineering and Built Environment, Universiti Kebangsaan Malaysia (UKM),
Bangi, 43600 Selangor, Malaysia
e-mail: wmdiyana@ukm.edu.my

S. Md Sum
Faculty of Social Sciences and Humanities, Universiti Kebangsaan Malaysia (UKM),
Bangi, 43600 Selangor, Malaysia
e-mail: sarmila.mdsum@gmail.com

© Springer International Publishing Switzerland 2017
R. Benlamri, M. Sparer (eds.), *Leadership, Innovation and Entrepreneurship as Driving Forces of the Global Economy*, Springer Proceedings in Business and Economics, DOI 10.1007/978-3-319-43434-6_49

offering entrepreneurship education and training. Furthermore, in the Malaysia Education Blueprint 2015–2015, the government's aspiration is to instill an entrepreneurial mindset throughout Malaysia's higher education system. Such programs introduced at the tertiary level are to encourage the young generation to delve themselves into becoming "job creators" rather than "job seekers" by channeling and realizing their untapped potential to innovate creating economic and commercial value. Positive outcomes from entrepreneurial education would be perceived as a reduction in unemployment levels and job-seeking exercise by university graduates. However, there was a reported increase in the unemployment rate in 2015 of 3.1% amounting to 400,000 unemployed individuals who have completed their studies in the last 6 months despite being given entrepreneurship education. This chapter intends to discuss the government's role and initiatives in ensuring that the entrepreneurship education addresses the importance of self-reliance, willingness, and the level of interests of students at universities to embark on entrepreneurship venture upon graduating, thus reducing the dependency of graduates to be employed.

Keywords Entrepreneur • Education • Malaysia • University • Government

Introduction

The entrepreneurial education in Malaysia is incorporated into the National Higher Education Action Plan as an initiative to promote innovation and make change in the economy to create new wealth and generation of job opportunities. It is asserted that aspects of entrepreneurship can be learned (Timmon & Spinelli, 2004) whilst some argued to the contrary suggesting that some elements cannot be learned (Akola & Heinonen, 2006). However, despite this ongoing debate, there has been a great emergence in global education in entrepreneurship education prompted by key realization to enhance the economy through nurturing and supporting entrepreneurial ventures. Malaysia is no exception in promoting and encouraging entrepreneurship education programs in the development of entrepreneurship in Malaysia. The country has engaged itself in entrepreneurship since the British colonial rule and reinvented its economic considerations unique to Malaysian circumstances in the New Economic Policy (NEP) (1971–1990), National Development Policy (NDP) (1991–2000), and the New Economic Model (2010). The objectives of the NEP were to eradicate poverty and to disassociate a particular ethnic group with a specific economic activity or occupation. Furthermore, the policies embedded are focused on strengthening national entrepreneurship through nurturing interest in entrepreneurial education amongst the population. Thus, this particular sector in education has emerged to be one of the most popular research and learning domains in academic circles in Malaysia (Lee, Chang et al., 2005). It is suggested that entrepreneurship is viewed as the "panacea to the unemployment problem" (Ahmad, 2013) which professed itself to be a tool to overcome unemployment in a country. In Malaysia, the increase in unemployment rate is disconcerting where the rate has risen to 3.3%

recently (Department of Statistics, 2015). One of the reasons is due to the number of graduates that exceeds market demand which leads to an increase in the unemployment rate (Ariff, Ghada, Muslim, & Hamid, 2014). Fresh graduates are facing more difficulties to secure a job where the number of jobs is limited (Ismail, 2011; Keat, Selvarajah, & Meyer, 2011). The role of the government is therefore extremely important in fostering entrepreneurship education in Malaysia to ensure that unemployment rate is reduced by imparting relevant knowledge and skills that will discard the notion of being a job seeker to one who creates jobs. Hence, this chapter reviews existing policies and educational curriculum for entrepreneurial knowledge in Malaysia supported by the government and suggests further improvements to the role of the government to stress the importance of entrepreneurial education.

Policy Initiatives on Entrepreneurial Education

Entrepreneurial education and training can involve a range of public and private stakeholders including the government (Volkmann, 2009). A government's rationale for playing a role is related to its interest in addressing mindsets, knowledge-based skills, and cultural constraints to entrepreneurship. The role is shaped by the potential knowledge spillovers of entrepreneurial related knowledge and skills (across potential or practicing entrepreneurs in a certain area) as well as by evident market failures when individuals recognize the value of management expertise to their entrepreneurial outcomes (World Bank, 2012). Governments can serve as champions through establishment of national plans and agendas (Peña, Transue, & Riggieri, 2010) and can set policy frameworks that shape the context of entrepreneurial education within higher learning institutions (HEIs) (Pittaway & Cope, 2007). In this aspect, the Malaysian Government has been and continues to be supportive of entrepreneurial education. With the launch of the NEM in 2010 by the Prime Minister, the emphasis on creating new entrepreneurs was stressed to stimulate a competitive domestic economy and further led to the establishment of the Higher Education Entrepreneurship Development Policy in 2010. This particular policy gives importance to the inculcation of entrepreneurial values and cultures amongst students or graduates in the HEIs. The policy serves to enhance the development of entrepreneurial programs into a more defined, holistic, and well-organized curriculum aiming to produce graduates from institutions of higher learning with entrepreneurial attributes and thinking skills. In addition, the policy envisions to increase the number of entrepreneurs amongst the graduates with relevant skills and knowledge to stimulate economic transformation towards a high-income nation.

To realize these aims, the policy addresses six important thrusts (Kementerian Pengajian Tinggi Malaysia, 2013) that include the following:

1. To establish entrepreneurship institute in every HEI
2. To provide holistically and well-planned entrepreneurial education and programs

Table 49.1 List of higher
education institutions offering
entrepreneurial education

Universiti Kebangsaan Malaysia
Universiti Teknologi MARA
Universiti Putra Malaysia
Universiti Malaya
Universiti Islam Antarabangsa
Universiti Sains Islam Malaysia
Universiti Malaysia Sabah
Universiti Malaysia Sarawak
Universiti Malaysia Kelantan
Universiti Teknologi Malaysia
Universiti Teknologi Hussein Onn
Universiti Sains Malaysia
Universiti Malaysia Perlis
Universiti Malaysia Pahang
Universiti Utara Malaysia
Universiti Sultan Zainal Abidin
Universiti Perguruan Sultan Idris
Universiti Teknikal Melaka
Universiti Malaysia Terengganu

3. To empower the entrepreneurial development programs
4. To create and effective measuring mechanism
5. To provide a conducive and ecosystem for entrepreneurship development
6. To enhance competency of entrepreneurship trainers

The result of the implementation of the policy is truly encouraging with 19 HEIs
(Table 49.1) in Malaysia having introduced entrepreneurial education as a compulsory subject (Yusoff, Zainol, & Ibrahim, 2015).

Several issues were faced during the delivery of entrepreneurial education including the content and delivery method that seemed to emphasize more on theoretical knowledge than a practical approach of the subject. However, there are universities such as Universiti Kebangsaan Malaysia (UKM) that implement online business simulation (OBS) designed by Centre of Entrepreneurship and SMEs Development (CESMED) for students to experience practical aspect of entrepreneurial learning in the entrepreneurial course. Challenges linking to planning and execution of the entrepreneurial learning, lack of trained lecturers and teaching assistants, weakness or lack of technological support and infrastructure and funding, and lack of consistent reassurance to students to convince entrepreneurship as a career option are experienced during delivery of entrepreneurial curriculum. Hence, to move forward in achieving more graduates to become entrepreneurs upon graduation, the Strategic Plan on Higher Entrepreneurship Development in Higher Education was established in 2013. The purpose of this plan is to enhance the earlier 6 thrusts by introducing and implementing 15 core strategies (Table 49.2).

Table 49.2 Six thrusts and 15 proposed strategies on entrepreneurship education

2013 thrusts	Fifteen proposed strategies
• Empowering entrepreneurship institute in every HEIs	• Boost the function of the entrepreneurship institute in every HEIs
	• Improve the entrepreneurship institute planning and informing system
• Provide holistically and well-planned entrepreneurial education and programs	• Integrate entrepreneurial values and attributes in the teaching method across curriculum and faculty
	• Increase the practical element in entrepreneurship education
	• Increase the involvement of industrial workforce in the teaching and learning process
	• Increase active student involvement in entrepreneurship programs
• Empowering the entrepreneurial development programs	• Strengthen the support system for students' business
	• Offer high-impact interventional programs to the students who have higher tendency towards an entrepreneurship career
	• Encourage the development of entrepreneurship programs that are based on businesses, which are beneficial to the students, small- and medium-sized enterprises (SMEs), as well as the society
• Enhance the competency of HEI entrepreneurship trainers and facilitators	• Increase the number of trainers and facilitators that are competent and skillful
	• Bridge the gap of entrepreneurial theory and practical knowledge among HEI trainers
• Provide a conducive environment and ecosystem for entrepreneurship development	• Improve the skills and competencies of the entrepreneurship trainers and facilitators
	• Improve commitment of the higher management of HEIs
	• Improve commitment and involvement of every person in the HEIs
• Increase the effect of the implementation of HEI entrepreneurial education and development	• Establish a suitable instrument to measure the effect and impact of HEI entrepreneurship education and development programs

Source: Kementerian Pengajian Tinggi Malaysia (2013)

It was found that four out of six thrusts in the Strategic Plan on Entrepreneurship Development in Higher Education (2013–2015) have been successful (Shamsudin, Al Mamun, Binti Che Nawi, Md Nasir, & Zakaria, 2015). The successful thrusts are the first thrust which is to empower the entrepreneurship center in every HEI; the second thrust, which is to provide holistic and well-planned entrepreneurial education and programs; the fourth thrust, which is to enhance the competency of HEI's entrepreneurship trainers and facilitators; and finally the sixth thrust, which is to increase the effect of the implementation of HEI's entrepreneurial education and development. The less successful ones include the third thrust, which is to empower entrepreneurial development programs, and the fifth thrust, which is to provide a conducive environment and ecosystem for entrepreneurship development.

Entrepreneurship Educational Programs

Several entrepreneurship programs are introduced as a result of the policies to develop entrepreneurship in Malaysia. The main stakeholder that is tasked to enable these entrepreneurial programs is the Ministry of Education that began its efforts in the primary schools and later extended its reach to secondary schools (Othman et al., 2012). Entrepreneurial program at HEIs can be traced back to a pioneer program on entrepreneur in 1982 with KEMBARA Usahawan (KEMUSA) by Universiti Teknologi MARA (then Institut Teknologi MARA (ITM)) to create awareness on entrepreneurial opportunities amongst students (Rahim et al., 2015). This was followed by a fully developed course named Fundamentals of Entrepreneurship (ETR 300) for diploma students (Abdul Latif et al., 1996).

The National Entrepreneurship Institute (INSKEN) that was formed in 2005 has implemented some programs to stimulate entrepreneurial spirits and increase knowledge and skills such as the *Program Usahawan Bimbing Usahawan*. This particular program is set up by stakeholders in the industry and professionals through knowledge-sharing seminars, training and coaching segments such as the Business Design Workshop and Business Facilitator, Graduate Entrepreneur Scheme (SIS), *Program Galakan Perniagaan*, and *Program Pembudayaan Keusahawanan* (INSKEN, 2015).

It is noteworthy to state that there is a program that was introduced by the Malaysian Government to support entrepreneurial programs amongst students at the universities known as the 1Malaysia Entrepreneur (1MET) in 2013. The target audience that can participate in programs organized by 1MET is anyone between 18 and 40 years old especially school leavers and graduates who already have a job. The aim of 1MET is to transform Malaysia to become an entrepreneurial based nation by optimizing collaboration and usage of public and private resources in accordance with the ninth National Blue Ocean Strategy—NBOS.

On the day of the launch of 1MET, the Extreme Entrepreneurship World Tour was presented to spread the entrepreneurial mindset shared by some of the top global entrepreneurs through their stories inspiring young minds to venture in entrepreneurship. This extensive program by 1MET is designed in a form of a series of hands-on approach entrepreneurship boot camps such as the 1MET 3.0 2015 Bootcamp (Fig. 49.1) to provide basics of entrepreneurship to first-time entrepreneurs and also entrepreneurs already owning small businesses. Four areas are focused in this program including the stage of creating ideas (IDEATION), testing the idea (VALIDATION), building a prototype or drawing up concept (BUILDING), and finally pitching your ideas (PITCH). 1MET provides online resources for entrepreneurs of all the support programs available for them under various agencies including Malaysian Global Innovation and Creativity Center (MaGIC), MSC Malaysia, Meet Your Experts (ER360), *Majlis Amanah Rakyat*, Small Medium Enterprise (SME) Corp Malaysia, Ministry of Domestic Trade, Cooperatives and Consumerism (KDNKK), and Perbadanan Nasional Berhad (PNS). From all these agencies,

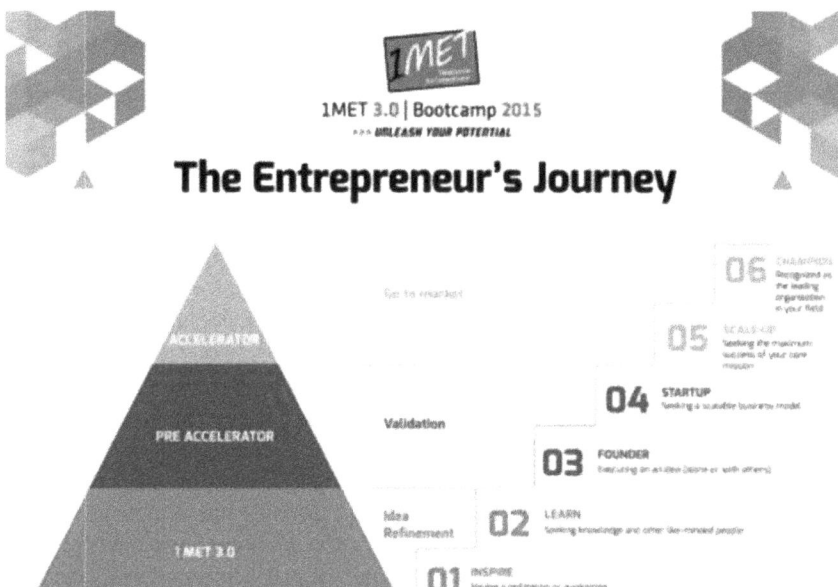

Fig. 49.1 1MET 3.0 Bootcamp 2015 (*Source*: 1MET)

MaGIC is the latest entrepreneurial entity formed by the Malaysian Government in 2014 to develop dynamic entrepreneurs with high endurance equipped to take up challenges and make impact at regional and global stage.

It is the leading agency that is significant to ensuring that Malaysia becomes the start-up capital in Asia based on three mandates that include supporting an entrepreneurial community, enhancing the start-up ecosystem, and exposing success stories and inspiring the *Rakyat* (public). Hence, MaGIC will support and foster strong communities where entrepreneurs are able to easily connect and share their ideas and solutions with each other, establish an academy for start-up education, seed accelerator programs, and provide qualified entrepreneurs with regional and global exposure and further intends to create a series of educational content about how start-ups are playing a significant role in solving real problems in the world, and reveal the entrepreneurs who are driving these innovations (MaGIC, 2015). It will also provide supporting infrastructure and services, access to start-up capital and investment, creative methodology, and training and collaboration with universities, research houses, and international organizations. Some of the programs and events organized by MaGIC to encourage students who are interested in entrepreneurship to attend include Pitching Karaoke Workshops, MaGIC Accelerator Programs, e@ Stanford Program, and Stanford Go2Market.

Conclusion

It is suffice to conclude, from this brief yet significant insight into the initiatives of the Malaysian Government to nurture entrepreneurial interest amongst the students at the universities, that continuous and rigorous efforts are developed and implemented at the HEIs and also by other supporting governmental agencies such as MaGIC. The entrepreneurial education at the HEIs must be frequently updated to ensure its effectiveness in resulting to creating interest and nurturing future entrepreneurs amongst university students. Only then the rate of unemployment in Malaysia can be decreased through the creation of job creators, thus reducing the amount of job seekers. In that aspect, the curriculum should further stress on transmitting specific mindsets and skills that include socio-emotional skills such as self-confidence, leadership values, motivation, resilience, and self-efficacy apart from the general business knowledge and skills needed for opening and managing a business.

The Malaysian Government recognizes the value of entrepreneurial related knowledge in education systems and institutions through the establishment of national policies and strategic plans. Furthermore, it demonstrated that creating entrepreneurial institutes or agencies and involving the private sector to support and collaborate on programs only suggest that the government encourages sharing and learning of good practices on entrepreneurship. These significant initiatives established by Malaysian Government throughout several decades rest upon its role to ensure that university students are exposed to entrepreneurial knowledge and skills to fulfill the vision of becoming a knowledgeable high-income country by 2020.

Acknowledgment The authors would like to thank Pusat Citra Universiti, Universiti Kebangsaan Malaysia, by giving the authors an opportunity to conduct this research. This research is funded by Institut Penyelidikan Pendidikan Tinggi Negara (IPPTN) (IPPTN/KPT/CLMV/2016/T05) (2), Research Project Code No: GG-2016-004, towards the writing of this chapter.

References

Abdul Latif, N. M. S., Jamaluddin, H., Jamil, M. Y., Nuruddin, N., Sarmidy, R., Buyong, S. Z., & Ahmad, Z. (1996). Kajian Kekesanan Ko-Kurikulum KEMUSA. Available at http://ir.uitm.edu.my/8363/1/LP_NIK%20MUSTAFFA%20SHAPRI%20HJ.%20ABDUL%20LATIF%2096_24.pdf. Date of accessed 21 November 2015.

Ahmad, S. Z. (2013). The need for inclusion of entrepreneurship education in Malaysia lower and higher learning institutions. *Education and Training, 55*(2), 191–203.

Akola, E., & Heinonen, J. (2006). *How to support learning of entrepreneurs? A study of training programmes for entrepreneurs in five European countries*. Paper presented at the RENT XX Conference, Research in Entrepreneurship and Small Business, Brussels, November 22–24.

Ariff, Z., Ghada, A., Muslim, H., & Hamid, Z. (2014). 'Legal Eagle' entrepreneurship education for law students: Special reference to international Islamic University Malaysia. *Social Sciences and Humanities, 22*, 83–98.

Department of Statistics. (2015). Retrieved February 26, 2016, from https://www.statistics.gov.my/#.

INSKEN, 2015. Available at www.insken.gov.my. Date of accessed 23 December 2015.

Ismail, N. A. (2011). Graduates characteristics and unemployment: A study among Malaysian graduates. *International Journal of Business and Social Science, 2*(16), 94–102.

Keat, O. Y., Selvarajah, C., & Meyer, D. (2011). Inclination towards entrepreneurship among university students: An empirical study of Malaysian university students. *International Journal of business and Social Science, 2*(4), 206–220.

Kementerian Pengajian Tinggi Malaysia. (2013). *Pelan Strategik Keusahawanan Institusi Pengajian Tinggi 2013–2015*, 5–7.

Lee, S. M., Chang, D., et al. (2005). Impact of entrepreneurship education: A comparative study of the US and Korea. *International Entrepreneurship and Management, 1*, 27–43.

MAGIC, 2015. Available at https://mymagic.my/en/. Date of accessed 15 December 2015.

Othman, N., Othman, N. H., & Ismail, R. (2012). Impact of Globalization on Trends in Entrepreneurship Education in Higher Education Institutions, International Journal of Trade, Economics and Finance, *3*(4):267–271.

Peña, V., Transue, M., & Riggieri, A. (2010). *A survey of entrepreneurship education initiatives.* Washington, DC: Institute for Defense Analyses, Science and Technology Policy Institute.

Pittaway, L., & Cope, J. (2007). Entrepreneurship education: A systematic review of the evidence. *International Small Business Journal, 25*, 479–510.

Rahim, H. L., Abdul Kadir, M. A. B., Abidin, Z. Z., Junid, J., Mohd Kamaruddin, L., Mohd Lajin, N. F., et al. (2015). Entrepreneurship education in Malaysia: A critical review. *Journal of Technology Management and Business, 2*(2), 1–11.

Shamsudin, S. F. F., Al Mamun, A., Binti Che Nawi, N., Md Nasir, N. A. B., & Zakaria, M. N. B. (2015). *Proceedings of the Asia Pacific Conference on Business and Social Sciences,* Kuala Lumpur.

Timmon, J. A., & Spinelli, S. (2004). *New venture creation: Entrepreneurship for the 21st century.* New York: McGraw-Hill.

Volkmann, C. (2009). Entrepreneurship in higher education. In C. Volkmann, K. E. Wilson, S. Mariotti, D. Rabuzzi, S. Vyakarnam, & A. Sepulveda (Eds.), *Educating the next wave of entrepreneurs: Unlocking entrepreneurial capabilities to meet the global challenges of the 21st century.* Cologny, Switzerland: World Economic Forum.

World Bank. (2012). *World development report 2013: Jobs.* Washington, DC: World Bank.

Yusoff, M. N. H. B., Zainol, F. A., & Ibrahim, M. D. B. (2015). Entrepreneurship education in Malaysia's public institutions of higher learning—A review of the current practices. *International Education Studies, 8*(1), 17–27.

Chapter 50
Motivation, Voices, and Visions of Women Entrepreneurs in the UAE

Norita Ahmad, Fatima Al-Mazrouee, and Mariela Ranova-Fredrick

Abstract The purpose of this study is to investigate the role of women entrepreneurs in the United Arab Emirates (UAE). This study examines similarities and differences among culturally diverse women entrepreneurs in the UAE. More specifically this chapter explores how motivation drivers change over time in reaction to market environment, as well as how social support interplays in combating the challenges women entrepreneurs face in this competitive marketplace. Furthermore, the study seeks to provide the foundation for further examination of women entrepreneurs because of their growing and forceful presence and influence in the UAE.

Keywords Women • Entrepreneurship • Motivation • Challenges • Social support • United Arab Emirates (UAE)

Introduction

The United Arab Emirates (UAE) has shown increased appreciation and understanding of the role women have not only in family and social life, but also as important contributors to the UAE's economic growth and development (King, 2015). Evidence streams from diverse areas such as the UAE's achievements in decreasing the gender gap in education, increasing the number of women entering the work force, as well as creating a marketplace in which women can play an important role in leadership and entrepreneurship. Female entrepreneurs have shown strong dedication to contributing to society and culture in the UAE. There is also strong evidence that women have strong self-fulfillment and achievement needs to contribute economically to their families (King, 2015). Thus, it makes sense that there is an increase in women entrepreneurship in the UAE, which is further evidenced by the growing research, which focuses on the challenges women face and the motivation drivers needed when starting a business. However, limited research

N. Ahmad (✉) • F. Al-Mazrouee • M. Ranova-Fredrick
American University of Sharjah, Sharjah, United Arab Emirates
e-mail: nahmad@aus.edu; g00020118@alumni.aus.edu; mariela.rfd@gmail.com

© Springer International Publishing Switzerland 2017   589
R. Benlamri, M. Sparer (eds.), *Leadership, Innovation and Entrepreneurship as Driving Forces of the Global Economy*, Springer Proceedings in Business and Economics, DOI 10.1007/978-3-319-43434-6_50

has been conducted on motivational changes and challenges women encounter after they establish their businesses. This research provides exploratory findings on these issues and establishes a strong foundation for further research.

Women Entrepreneurs

Recently, researchers have been investigating factors that affect women's motivation to become entrepreneurs (e.g., Jabeen, Katsioloudes, & Das, 2015; Ramadani, Hisrich, & Gërguri-Rashiti, 2015; Rey-Martí, Porcar, & Mas-Tur, 2015) and most of them divided the motives into the "push" and "pull" factor (e.g., Kargwell, 2012; Ramadani et al., 2015). Push factors (personal or external) usually have negative connotations because of the obvious roughness associated with pushing. However, push factors do account for women starting up a business (Kirkwood, 2009). Examples include economical reasons such as unemployment and recession, or personal motivators such as acquiring a better work-life balance. Pull factors, on the other hand, are related to a more inherently noble drive that individuals internally feel to start a business such as obtaining self-fulfillment, independence, or satisfaction from personal achievement (Kirkwood, 2009; Ramadani et al., 2015). Not surprisingly, most researchers have identified that pull factors are dominant and have a greater impact in entrepreneurship motivation. The reason is most likely linked to the power of racing after a dream rather than running away from a fear. But the key question for our research is whether or not these motivating impulses are gender specific.

The trend to investigate what motivates women entrepreneurs (especially women in developing and transitioning countries) has shown two positive results. First, there is a greater realization regarding women's desires to be self-employed. Second, there is a sharper understanding of unique challenges women face and, more practically, how to address and ultimately overcome them. Sarri and Trihopoulou (2005) indicated that women are motivated to become self-employed due to the need to express creativity, autonomy, and independence. To encourage women motivational factors, they pointed out that government policies should be addressed to stimulate pull, rather than push, factors.

An earlier study in Turkey, for example, indicated that the biggest motivation for women was also related to pull factors such as independence, personal achievement, and job satisfaction (Hisrich & Ayse Öztürk, 1999). This research also reveals the challenges that women faced related to obtaining capital, personnel problems, and management skill. Similar research, conducted in Nigeria, showed a common theme in women motivational characteristics and challenges. The researchers concluded that pull factors influence motivation and further confirmed that challenges are related to governmental policies, difficulties obtaining capital, lack of managerial skills, and proper support (Okafor & Amalu, 2010). In Malaysia, the situation showed the same theme. A research project concluded that women entrepreneurs are motivated by work-core and entrepreneurial-core motivational factors categorized as expressing job satisfaction, need to express creativity, and utilization of skills and independence (Raman, Anantharaman, & Jayasingam, 2008).

A survey done by the United Nation Conference of Trade and development (UNCTAD) highlighted the motivational factors influencing women across the globe. The survey concluded that women in Brazil, Jordan, Sweden, Switzerland, Uganda, and even in the USA are motivated to become entrepreneurs because of their desire to fulfill a dream, realize a passion, gain independence, and/or contribute to society and the community (UNCTAD, 2013). While the study found that inner desires of female entrepreneurs are the same, it also stated that many of the key challenges women face are also the same, and quite often external, such as access to finance, finding and keeping good personnel, lack of supportive resources (government policies and programs), and cultural constraints, such as the struggle to be taken seriously as a business owner based on perceptions of the inherent weakness in the gender (UNCTAD, 2013).

Despite the growing interest among researchers on female entrepreneurs, there is surprisingly limited study conducted in the UAE and the Middle East region. Research specifically focused on the UAE is almost "nonexistent" and few research projects are done with focus on female Emirati entrepreneurs (Jabeen et al., 2015; Kargwell, 2012; Naguib & Jamali, 2015). Like many other findings, they identified factors such as independence, contribution to society, and self-improvement as the driving motivational force of female Emiratis to become entrepreneurs. But one intriguing finding is that Emirati women are greatly encouraged by their family and as a possible consequence possess the self-motivation to pursue entrepreneurships. Family can be classified as an external factor of support, and, as indicated in earlier studies, lack of external support was one of the greatest challenges facing women entrepreneurs.

Overall a review of the literature shows that there are "macro-, micro-, and meso-level factors" that contribute to women's challenges in entrepreneurship such as limited access to network and capital, and cultural norms (Naguib & Jamali, 2015). However, it is worth emphasizing that the UAE is unique in that it has placed great initiatives and policies to stimulate an "entrepreneurial ecosystem" (Naguib & Jamali, 2015).

Research so far has focused mostly on the motivation and challenges faced by female Emirati entrepreneurs. What is greatly needed now is a new research to address how motivation changes over time in reaction to market environment, as well as how social support interplays in combating the challenges female entrepreneurs face.

Research Methodology

A qualitative research approach using in-depth semi-structured personal interviews was made due to the exploratory nature of this study. Strauss and Corbin (1991) claimed that interviews are an effective method to use in order to understand the underlying reasons behind the complexities of human decisions and behaviors. Furthermore, it enabled predetermined topics to be discussed and yet allowed unexpected responses to be explored in more detail as they arose (Anderson & Kanuka, 2003). It is also important to note that studies on this topic in the Middle Eastern region are not very abundant, which calls for an exploratory study that can be best achieved through interviews.

Data Collection

Data was collected using semi-structured in-depth interviews conducted with six women entrepreneurs from different nationalities who reside in and operate small business enterprises (SMEs) in the UAE market. Each in-depth interview was summarized and then evaluated for common patterns and the information was evaluated based on market and culture, means of social support, and inspiration-motivational changes.

Results and Analysis

The UAE market is seen as an attractive market to enter because of the ease in which one can open a new business as the UAE Government gives financial support and efficient programs to stimulate small businesses (Kargwell, 2012). Despite the ease, the UAE is still a highly competitive market for female entrepreneurs to start their businesses. As indicated by one of the entrepreneurs interviewed, the current market condition is tough, "the competition storms like ants." Furthermore, five out of six of the women explained that because of the high competition, in the long term businesses will struggle to stay strong and competitive in the market. Overall, all agreed that competition is one of their main challenges. Even though Naser, Wojoud, and Nuseibeh (2009) described that competition is not a barrier for women to become entrepreneurs in the UAE, our findings suggest that competition is actually a major concern once the company is established. This finding is consistent with Mutairi and Fayez (2015) who showed that competition is one of the main challenges female entrepreneurs face in Kuwait, Saudi Arabia, and Nigeria.

All of our respondents said that their struggles stem from their lack of skills and knowledge necessary to respond to challenges as well as to grab and exploit opportunities. It is interesting to note that these women have expressed motivation to gain more knowledge and education in order to develop their skills to be more competitive in the market. Previous studies have indicated that women face challenges in terms of lack of skills at the start of their businesses (Haan, 2004; Itani, Sidani, & Baalbaki, 2011; Okafor & Amalu, 2010). Our study not only supports those findings but also shows that women continue to struggle due to their lack of entrepreneurial capabilities, business experience, and support for training and development once the business is well under way.

The impact of culture on the market environment was also a large contributing factor to women entrepreneurs. Our study shows that women expatriate entrepreneurs have a harder time because they were not very familiar with the UAE culture. One of the interviewees expressed the expatriates' challenge this way:

> When I started my business I had a unique product to offer, but I did not know how to interact with the local clients at first. Once I understood the culture and what they would want from my products I was able to improve my product line into providing something suitable for all types of client, but most importantly to have a product for the locals that they would like to purchase because they would be my main clients.

Another woman entrepreneur who owns an *Abaya* fashion shop said:

One of my challenges is to satisfy the traditional UAE woman. As an owner you need to provide clients with a classy, high quality conservative style that is in with the fashion trends. For any business, this is challenging because UAE women have a wide range of tastes and you have to satisfy those tastes if you want your business to keep growing.

Expatriates and Emirati nationals both face challenges in terms of social attitudes and perceptions but there are some key differences. Women expatriate entrepreneurs entered into business to help their husband financially, while Emirati entrepreneurs chose business pursuits as a way to be productive. In other words, expatriate women might feel pressured to perform better in the market. This idea is supported by previous research that points out that expatriate women are motivated by push factors such as financial security and low income (Naguib & Jamali, 2015).

We identified that five out of six women entrepreneurs who receive social support find it relatively easy to find opportunities to grow and market their businesses. These women participate in networking and exhibitions and were able to create their own set of clients. For example, all of the women interviewed agreed that *word of mouth* (WOM) plays a very strong role in the UAE culture and usually brings in satisfactory results to the business. As explained by one of our interviewees:

… the word of mouth is very important for us, because if we have clients who are really happy with our products, they will definitely recommend our products to their friends and family, which would bring new traffic to the business.

Customers also provide another type of motivation factor for the business in the form of unique cultural feedback. Getting feedback, positive or negative, helps a business to grow over time. All six interviewees agreed that by receiving comments from their customers they were able to learn what customers liked and disliked about their product and services. Customer feedback is a very important factor because it helps the business to see itself from the customers' perspectives. Customers not only motivate the businesses by sending them a thank-you message, but also promote the business to their friends and families.

Our research discovered that all of the women entrepreneurs revealed a passion to create a business based on their personal interests. Even though each interviewee was in a different type of business, they all showed a passion for the products they offered and were inspired by their family or friends. Overall, a spark of inspiration, passion, and plan to fulfill dreams are the key motivational factors that led these women to start their businesses. In addition to these initial findings, we applied McClelland's motivation theory (Porter, Bigley, & Steers, 2003) to help us understand women entrepreneurs in the UAE market and to determine whether their behavior of motivation has changed from when they first started the business to where they are today (see Table 50.1).

What we see from Table 50.1 is that *affiliation* is considered as the least motivational factor when women started their business in the UAE. Even though positive family support and feedback are desired, the interviewees did not express strong need to be associated with a group and/or have a collaborative "fit" in such.

Table 50.1 Motivation drivers when starting up the business

Drivers	Person 1	Person 2	Person 3	Person 4	Person 5	Person 6
Achievement						
Have a strong need to set and accomplish goals	Strong	Strong	Medium	Strong	Medium	Strong
Take risks to achieve goals	Strong	Strong	Medium	Strong	Medium	Medium
Like to have feedback on progress and achievement	Strong	Strong	Strong	Strong	Strong	Medium
Like to work alone	Low	Low	Strong	Strong	Strong	Strong
Affiliation						
Want to be part of a group	Medium	Low	Low	Strong	Low	Low
Want to be liked and go along to whatever the rest of the group wants to do	Low	Medium	Strong	Medium	Low	Low
Favor collaboration over competition	Medium	Low	Low	Low	Low	Low
No to high risk and uncertainty	Medium	Strong	Medium	Medium	Medium	Low
Power						
Want to control and influence others	Low	Medium	Medium	Strong	Low	Low
Like to win arguments	Medium	Medium	Low	Strong	Low	Low
Enjoy competition and winning	Medium	Strong	Low	Medium	Medium	Strong
Enjoy status and recognition	Medium	Medium	Medium	Strong	Strong	Strong

This trait is consistent with Decker, Calo, and Weer (2012) findings that entrepreneurs have low need for emotional support, but prefer positive stimulation from their surrounding group.

Based on our interviews, we found that the motivation factors for women entrepreneurs changed over time due to the increasing number of competitors and cultural specificity in the market (see Table 50.2). One interviewee said,

> ... there is a large number of businesses currently in the UAE, but I can easily see every one or two weeks new businesses emerge in the market whether they are licensed or not. I have noticed that many of the businesses succeed here by having a strong reputation in the market and connections. So over time I had to change or improve the way I did my business in order to stay with the ones that are at the same level as I am.

This valuable insight highlights how female entrepreneurs must be flexible in order to stay competitive in the market. After some time in the business, women realize that they have kept their dominant motivator—*achievement*, but have, out of necessity, improved on *affiliation* and *power*. What is interesting is that they have shifted their motivator drives based on their business need in order to compete effectively in the market. Five out of six participants admitted that eventually they learned that a social fit and affiliation with groups in the industry are essential:

> ... in the UAE it is important to fit in with certain group because they provide you with the strong connections to enter into new opportunities which would be exhibitions or retail stores or even an increase in customer base.

Table 50.2 Motivation drivers on the current state of the business

Drivers	Person 1	Person 2	Person 3	Person 4	Person 5	Person 6
Achievement						
Have a strong need to set and accomplish goals	Strong	Strong	Strong	Strong	Strong	Strong
Take risks to achieve goals	Strong	Strong	Strong	Strong	Medium	Strong
Like to have feedback on progress and achievement	Strong	Strong	Strong	Strong	Strong	Strong
Like to work alone	Low	Low	Medium	Medium	Strong	Medium
Affiliation						
Want to be part of a group	Strong	Strong	Strong	Strong	Medium	Medium
Want to be liked and go along to whatever the rest of the group wants to do	Low	Medium	Low	Medium	Medium	Low
Favor collaboration over competition	Strong	Strong	Strong	Strong	Strong	Strong
No to high risk and uncertainty	Medium	Strong	Medium	Medium	Medium	Low
Power						
Want to control and influence others	Medium	Medium	Strong	Strong	Low	Low
Like to win arguments	Medium	Medium	Strong	Strong	Low	Strong
Enjoy competition and winning	Medium	Strong	Strong	Medium	Medium	Strong
Enjoy status and recognition	Medium	Medium	Strong	Strong	Strong	Strong

Thus, even though *affiliation* was low in the early stage of becoming entrepreneurs, women realize that *affiliation* is essential in order to increase their connection base. The contribution here cannot be underestimated as this insight can help governmental policies and programs to motivate and help women entrepreneurs with country-specific mentorship programs.

Another insight gained from the research is that some women entrepreneurs took full control and made the brand and the products (and themselves) rise to a strong reputation in the market. This approach stresses the shift in the necessity of power for women entrepreneurs. Having a strong reputation leads to loyal clients and growth opportunities, which, in turn, results in the women entrepreneur becoming the big powerhouse.

Discussion and Conclusion

The market in the UAE is very competitive and it affects the motivation drivers of any woman entrepreneur. Because of its rapid increase, competition has affected businesses in many ways and has led to some entrepreneurs changing their directions or motivation drivers, which led them into growing their business over time.

Key points of this research are, first, women face unique challenges in the UAE's competitive market. Second, women possess different kinds of motivations based on their nationality and cultural background. Third, motivation drivers change over time. The trend is to shift from passions and self-fulfillment and achievement to affiliation and power.

This is an exploratory study that provides a foundation for further research. This study provides an initial assessment of women entrepreneurs in the UAE in terms of market challenges they faced and their motivation factors. In addition, it provides insight into how women react, contend, and use these challenges to enhance their businesses. Given the small sample size of this study, future research could include a bigger sample size of female entrepreneurs in the UAE and classify the types of entrepreneurs to examine if motivational drivers vary among products and services.

References

Anderson, T., & Kanuka, H. (2003). *E-research: Methods, strategies, and issues*. Boston: Allyn and Bacon.

Decker, W. H., Calo, T. J., & Weer, C. H. (2012). Affiliation motivation and interest in entrepreneurial careers. *Journal of Managerial Psychology, 27*(3), 302–320. doi:10.1108/02683941211205835.

Haan, H. (2004). *Small enterprises: Women entrepreneurs in the UAE*. Labour Market Study No. 19. Centre for Labour Market Research & Information (CLMRI). The National Human Resource Development and Employment Authority (Tanmia), Dubai, UAE.

Hisrich, R. D., & Ayse Öztürk, S. (1999). Women entrepreneurs in a developing economy. *Journal of Management Development, 18*(2), 114–125.

Itani, H., Sidani, Y. M., & Baalbaki, I. (2011). United Arab Emirates female entrepreneurs: Motivations and frustrations. *Equality, Diversity and Inclusion: An International Journal, 30*(5), 409–424. doi:10.1108/02610151111150654.

Jabeen, F., Katsioloudes, M. I., & Das, S. S. (2015). Is family the key? Exploring the motivation and success factors of female Emirati entrepreneurs. *International Journal of Entrepreneurship and Small Business, 25*(4), 375–394.

Kargwell, S. A. (2012). Women entrepreneurs breaking through: Push and pull within UAE cultural context. *International Journal of Business and Social Science, 3*(17), 122–131.

King, N. (2015). Developing Dubai's female entrepreneurs. Retrieved November 2, 2015, from http://www.arabianbusiness.com/developing-dubai-s-female-entrepreneurs-594226.html.

Kirkwood, J. (2009). Motivational factors in a push-pull theory of entrepreneurship. *Gender in Management: An International Journal, 24*(5), 346–364. doi:10.1108/17542410910968805.

Mutairi, A. A., & Fayez, F. (2015). Factors motivating female entrepreneurs in Kuwait. *Journal of Applied Management and Entrepreneurship, 20*(1), 50.

Naguib, R., & Jamali, D. (2015). Female entrepreneurship in the UAE: A multi-level integrative lens. *Gender in Management, 30*(2), 135. Retrieved November 2, 2015, from http://ezproxy.aus.edu/login?url=http://search.proquest.com/docview/1668209439?accountid=16946.

Naser, K., Wojoud, R. M., & Nuseibeh, R. (2009). Factors that affect women entrepreneurs: Evidence from an emerging economy. *International Journal of Organizational Analysis, 17*(3), 225–247. doi:http://dx.doi.org/10.1108/19348830910974932.

Okafor, C., & Amalu, R. (2010). Entrepreneurial motivations as determinants of women entrepreneurship challenges. *Petroleum-Gas University of Ploiesti Bulletin: Economic Sciences Series, 62*(2), 67–77.

Porter, L. W., Bigley, G. A., & Steers, R. M. (2003). *Motivation and work behavior*. Boston: McGraw-Hill/Irwin.

Ramadani, V., Hisrich, R. D., & Gërguri-Rashiti, S. (2015). Female entrepreneurs in transition economies: Insights from Albania, Macedonia and Kosovo. *World Review of Entrepreneurship, Management and Sustainable Development, 11*(4), 391–413.

Raman, K., Anantharaman, R. N., & Jayasingam, S. (2008). Motivational factors affecting entrepreneurial decision: A comparison between Malaysian women entrepreneurs and women non entrepreneurs. *Communications of the IBIMA, 2*(12), 85–89.

Rey-Martí, A., Porcar, A. T., & Mas-Tur, A. (2015). Linking female entrepreneurs' motivation to business survival. *Journal of Business Research, 68*(4), 810–814.

Strauss, A., & Corbin, J. (1991). *Basics of qualitative research: Grounded theory procedures and techniques*. Newbury Park, CA: Sage.

Sarri, K., & Trihopoulou, A. (2005). Female entrepreneurs' personal characteristics and motivation: A review of the greek situation. *Women in Management Review, 20*(1), 24–36. doi:10.1108/09649420510579559.

UNCTAD. (2013). A Survey on women's entrepreneurship and innovation. Retrieved May 29, 2015, from http://www.empowerwomen.org/en/~/documents/2014/12/08/17/34/a-survey-on-womens-entrepreneurship-and-innovation.

Chapter 51
Weathering the Storm: Financial Variable as a Key Influence to Entrepreneurial Venture Survival Over Time in Canada

Said Baadel and Stefane Kabene

Abstract Each year numerous new small businesses confidently enter the marketplace but a vast majority of these firms will fail to survive beyond their tenth birthday. Past studies have focused on a variety of external factors such as geographic location and industry size. Despite the effects these variables play over time, a great amount of decisions are made internally and thus it is imperative to consider their impact on survival rates. Young firms with little experience can be heavily disadvantaged when attempting to gain funding within financial markets. Evidence indicates that a vast number of new small firms are forced to rely on equity financing, specifically in the form of internal resources. Beyond retained earnings, firms must rely on social networks in an attempt to solidify relationships with potential investors. Firms require capital to fund future growth but face barriers as turning a profit initially can be quite challenging. This chapter takes an in-depth look into one crucial internal variable, financing, and statistically analyzes its effect on the survival of small entrepreneurial ventures. The objective entails uncovering the causation for such internal downfall and providing such an insight may greatly assist small firms to compete and grow in their respected industries, therefore substantially increasing their chance of survival.

Keywords Financial survivability • SME entry and exit rates • Entrepreneurial venture survival • SME mortality rate

S. Baadel (✉)
Canadian University of Dubai, Dubai, United Arab Emirates

University of Huddersfield, Huddersfield, UK
e-mail: s.baadel@gmail.com

S. Kabene
Canadian University of Dubai, Dubai, United Arab Emirates
e-mail: s.baadel@gmail.com

© Springer International Publishing Switzerland 2017
R. Benlamri, M. Sparer (eds.), *Leadership, Innovation and Entrepreneurship as Driving Forces of the Global Economy*, Springer Proceedings in Business and Economics, DOI 10.1007/978-3-319-43434-6_51

Introduction

In today's economy, unfortunately, life is brief for a strong majority of new firms. With a steeply increasing mortality rate in the first 5 years, most entrants fail to survive their tenth birthday (Baldwin & Bian, 2000). While many entrepreneurs achieve success after an initial failed venture and receive valuable experience, the process of entry and failure is quite costly.

Entrepreneurial research has attempted to gain insight as to why certain firms succeed while others fail. A majority of the research concerning discontinuance has examined the patterns of entry and exit over time in combination with specific population dynamics (Thornhill & Amit, 2003). A great amount of research indicates that firms face the highest rate of fatality when they are young and inexperienced. However, if factors exist beyond age, then what are they and how can they be effectively avoided? This chapter seeks to contribute to our understanding of success and failure through the financial survivability analysis and its direct level of impact on the life span of a firm.

The small business sector provides the economy with a constant amount of input, similar to an efficient engine. Continual technological advancement leads to new products or enhanced services, which drives individuals to join the small school of fish within the overwhelming sea. The level of success achieved by a small firm is a direct result of the daily decisions of their management team within their respected marketplace. Through the analysis of specific internal variables influencing survival, small firms can improve their ability to understand their weaknesses and implement the proper solutions. Prior to analyzing the specific variables affecting the life span of such firms, it is important to gain insight into entrant and exit levels. For the remainder of this chapter, survival will be defined as the ability to remain solvent while maintaining adequate operations. In comparison, failure will be defined through forced closure due to an inability to meet financial obligations.

This chapter first provides clarification regarding the volume of entrants and exits annually of small and medium enterprises in Canada. Secondly, it discusses through statistical evidence how survival is directly influenced by a firm's ability to raise adequate financial capital. Thirdly, it discusses the link between financing and mortality of small businesses. Finally we conclude and provide a glimpse of future work.

Entrant and Exit Rates of SME in Canada

The negative effects of failure are not limited to the entrepreneur, as bankruptcy costs the Canadian economy billions of dollars annually. In 1993 alone, over 3700 incorporated businesses failed in Canada, with liabilities totaling roughly 4.1 billion dollars (Baldwin et al., 1997). As expected, a vast majority of this money was owed to Canadian banks, thus affecting their bottom lines while increasing the difficulty for young entrepreneurs to gain favorable credit terms. Further ripple effects are felt with a rise in unemployment rates, which in turn reduce consumer consumption and slow the economy. Small businesses have accounted for a disproportionately high share of employment growth over the past decade but with higher susceptibility to failure, jobs are far from secure. However, with risk comes reward and therefore by implementing an effective strategy one can highly increase one's opportunity for success.

These risky ventures and resources should not be regarded as a complete waste or liability to the economy. Failures should be seen as a direct investment that society makes in the dynamic competitive process. New firms provide a vital stimulus to the industrial population, and a certain number of small entrants evolve to be recognized business leaders. Others remain small but competitive through innovative strategies that allow them to secure a strong market niche through quality and flexible product offerings. Therefore the importance of the entry and exit process is evident as it provides the marketplace with important information regarding customer preferences (Baldwin et al., 1997). With so many household names fighting for limited market share what kind of contribution do these small firms provide within the overall economy? By taking a closer look at some industry data, we can draw a few conclusions.

Table 51.1 displays a 30-year perspective of the entry and exit rates for small businesses by sector between 1983 and 2012 (Macdonald, 2014). On average, new firms accounted for 15.2% of the overall business population, which is quite a substantial figure when considering the small size of a majority of new firms. The services industry slightly outpaced the manufacturing sector (16–14%) and one would expect this trend to continue as the focus and influence of the Canadian manufacturing sector decrease. The service industry showed positive signs in the professional, scientific, and technical services and business sectors with entrance rates of 16.8% and 16.88%,

Table 51.1 30-Year entry and exit rates by industry sector (Macdonald, 2014)

Goods-producing industries	Entry rate (%)	Exit rate (%)
Agriculture, forestry, fishing, and hunting	13.97	14.37
Mining, oil and gas extraction	15.40	12.86
Construction	16.08	14.41
Manufacturing	10.83	9.81
Wholesale	11.26	10.85
Retail	12.77	12.87
Transportation and warehousing	17.14	14.55
Information and cultural industries	16.98	15.04
Total (goods)	14.31	13.09
Service-providing industries		
Finance, insurance, real estate, and leasing	14.97	13.16
Professional, scientific, and technical services	16.80	12.83
Administrative and support	16.39	13.86
Arts, entertainment, and recreational	14.98	13.40
Accommodation and food services	16.38	15.14
Business sector	16.88	15.28
Other services (except public administration)	16.20	14.60
Total (services)	16.08	14.04
All industries (goods and services)	*15.20*	*13.57*

Table 51.2 Survival rates (Macdonald, 2012)

Duration (years)	Survival rate (%)	Hazardous rate (%)
1	80	23
2	65	22
3	56	18
4	48	16
5	43	14
6	38	13
7	35	12

respectively. These figures will likely grow due to technological advancements, which have allowed small firms to provide customized Web-based and E-commerce solutions for supply-chain management and enterprise resource planning. While these entry rates seem positive, only a small number of firms will actually succeed. Thus it is important to directly analyze the success and failure rates of firms over time.

Table 51.2 provides a better picture over 8-year duration. The present survival rates outline the probability that a new firm will live beyond a specific age. Interestingly, a new firm's chance of survival tends to decrease with age, which potentially reflects a lack of competitive advantage within the marketplace. Entrepreneurs face a positive rate of survival in year 1 of 80 % but this figure drops dramatically to 43 % in year 5 and a dismal 35 % by the seventh birthday. Comparatively, a hazard rate represents the chance of failure at a certain age— assuming that the risk of failure still exists. The hazardous rates above (Baldwin & Bian, 2000) correspond with the survival figures, with firms facing a 23 % probability of failure in year 1, a 14 % chance in year 5, and only a 12 % failure rate by year 7. These statistics allow for a better understanding of our annual entrance and exit rates, thus providing substance for further analysis regarding causation (Fig. 51.1).

Financial Survivability

A major challenge for small firms is the ability to gain access to financing. In comparison to large established firms, new ventures are widely described as constrained by the operations of debt and equity markets (Baldwin & Gellatly, 2006). Ironically though, access to debt and external equity is essential if small firms are to fund investments in new assets and enhance research and development. Therefore, does the ability to gain proper financing predict the life span of new entrepreneurial firms? Furthermore, is there a particular structure that surviving firms implement?

Within the increasingly competitive climate that firms operate in today, skilled labor has become an essential ingredient for the sustainability of firms' market position and has proven to be a substantial competitive advantage. Within smaller companies, this human capital becomes more vital as the amount of social loafing[1]

---

[1] Social loafing is defined as the reduction of effort that people often exhibit when working in a group where individual contributions are unidentifiable.

Fig. 51.1 Survival and hazardous rates

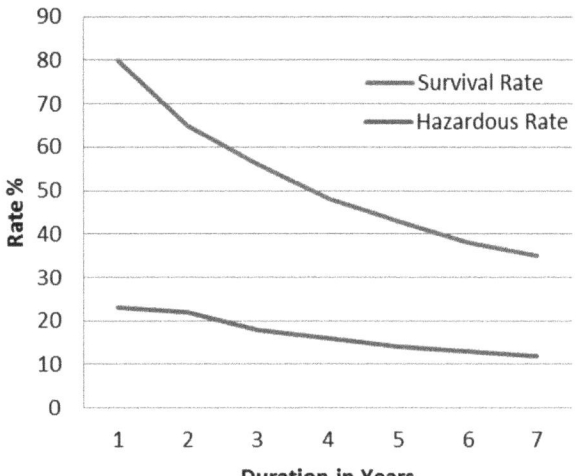

and other inefficient practices that are performed by employees have an increasingly negative impact. As a result the positive contributions such as a diverse skill set and a wide range of industry experience can prove to be invaluable. To what extent does the human capital of those engaged in a firm lead to its success? Moreover, is the correlation between the two strong enough to result in failure if adequate levels of human capital are not met?

Financing directly influences the annual research and development budgets of small firms. Historically, these functions have been the source of a majority of innovative solutions for numerous firms. Innovation allows small firms to gain sustainable competitive advantages within the economy, which can greatly increase their overall market share. However with evident constraints present, is the ability to remain innovative a strong sign of survival within the marketplace? Secondly, how do innovative firms compare to non-innovative firms?

There are many financial instruments that small enterprises utilize. Venture capital funding was less desirable when compared to private sources but several respondents even noted difficulties in gaining the support of venture firms. Other entrepreneurs managed to find success through alternative methods, specifically private equity, personal savings, personal loans, retained earnings, love money,[2] angel funding,[3] or sale of an existing technology (Bordt, Earl, Lonmo, & Joseph, 2004). This evidence indicates the high probability that small firms will be forced to utilize numerous alternatives when raising the necessary capital to remain afloat. Figure 51.2 highlights some of these percentages.

---

[2] Funds from friends, family, or relatives.

[3] Funds acquired through informal investors.

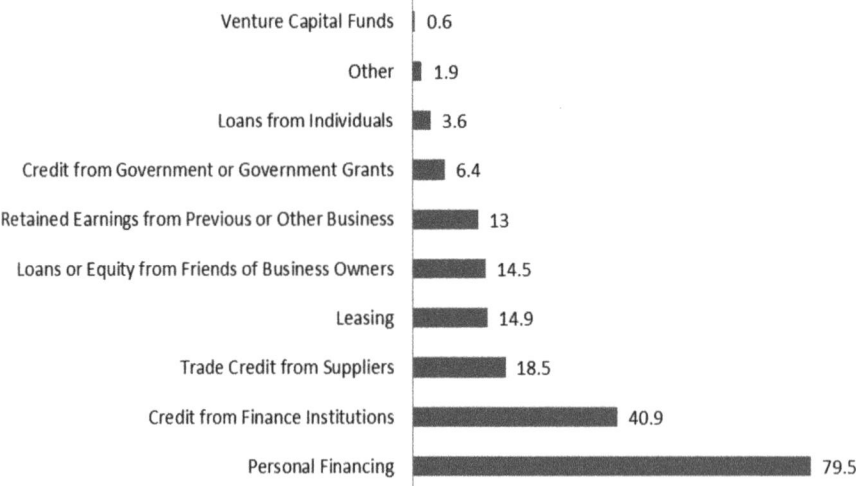

Fig. 51.2 Percentage of financial instruments for SMEs (*source*: Industry Canada, 2013)

Financing a firm's growth is essential to survival and thus calls for an adequate financial plan. The ability to innovate and grow can play quite an influential role regarding a firm's ability to survive. New firms survive due to their ability to remain unique by providing a service or product that clearly differentiates them from the competition. Companies that are constantly establishing state-of-the-art product offerings and services are in high demand and tend to become leaders within their respective sector, thus directly affecting their survival. Unfortunately, to maintain this advantage, firms are constantly required to invest in new assets or research and development in order to innovate. However, the capability to continually offer new innovative solutions requires a certain degree of funding and to be able to retain the best employees. This can sometimes prove to be overly challenging and is a major growth obstacles for small and medium enterprises as shown in a 2013 study by Statistics Canada below.

Baldwin and Gellatly (2006) attempted to gain an understanding of how firms are affected by different financing structures[4] and how these structures directly influence their decision making. Naturally, a number of these decisions will in turn predict their ability to survive within the marketplace. Table 51.3 provides further insight on numerous capital structures amongst a variety of small firms (Fig. 51.3).

---

[4]The proportional representation of different financial instruments within the capital mix.

Table 51.3 Percentage distribution of financing instruments amongst surviving firms (Baldwin & Gellatly, 2006)

Form of financing	All firms (%)	1–9 employees (%)	10–24 employees (%)	25+ employees (%)
Equity capital				
Retained earnings	38.8	38.8	38.6	39.0
Share capital	7.8	8.1	6.1	8.1
Long-term debt				
Secured	16.0	15.0	18.9	19.2
Unsecured	3.2	3.9	1.2	1.5
Short-term debt				
Secured	11.6	11.4	14.0	9.8
Unsecured	4.4	4.4	5.5	2.8
Other instruments				
Trade credit	10.8	10.9	8.1	14.5
Convertible debentures	0.2	0.2	0.0	0.1
Contract financing	2.4	2.8	1.5	1.3
Investment tax credits	0.3	0.2	0.5	0.5
Grants	0.2	0.2	0.2	0.7

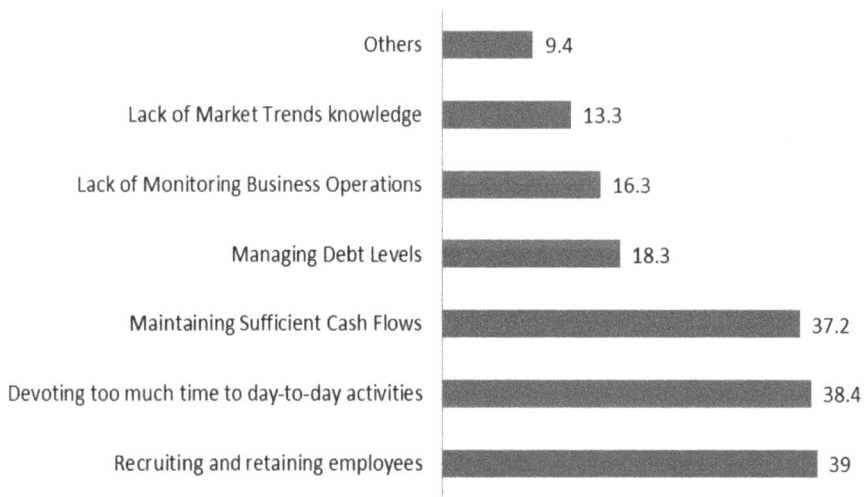

Fig. 51.3 Growth obstacles for SMEs (*source*: Industry Canada, 2013)

Analysis of the Link Between Financing and the Mortality of New Small and Medium Enterprises

After reviewing the chart, one can make a number of observations. Successful new firms rely heavily on equity financing as it makes up 46.6 % of their total capital structure. Retained earnings proved to be the single most important mode of financing for small firms, representing close to 40% on average (Baldwin & Gellatly, 2006). From a debt perspective, the financial structure contains 19.2% in long-term debt and an additional 16.0% in short-term obligations. Finally, of the other financing vehicles, only trade credit imposes a serious impact, comprising roughly 11% of capital structure. Their work resulted in equity rates of 36% with the percentage deriving from retained earnings declining as growth increased. Ironically, retained earnings account for only half of total equity within the corporate population but over 80% of equity in surviving entrants. When combined with the various trends within financial structures amongst surviving entrants, this self-dependence on retained earnings allows us to draw some interesting implications.

Debt markets are overly hesitant to fund new firms due to their inexperience and lack of track record. Table 51.3 further clarifies this theory and thus new firms within riskier industries are forced to rely on internal sources of funding as shown in Fig. 51.1.

However, with retained earnings providing such a substantial form of capital, failure seems that much more inevitable. Retained earnings require firms to turn a healthy annual profit, which will then allow them to reinvest in the corporation in order to support future growth. Historically though new firms are lucky to break even in their initial years of operation, thus making this alternative rather challenging. This provides us a critical insight as to why the survival rate drastically drops within the first few years of the birth of a small firm as indicated in Table 51.2.

Conclusion and Future Work

Small businesses play a very pivotal role within the economy by providing numerous employment opportunities and unique product offerings. Unfortunately, the average fatality rate drastically overshadows those that are destined for greatness. However, the causation attributed to this financial insolvency is not restricted to external factors. Internal elements have the ability to guide the firm through environmental instability but at the same time they can lead to the downfall of an organization.

Access to financial capital is critical for survival as it provides investment for long-term assets, research and development, as well as product innovation. Some of the major growth obstacles for small and medium enterprises include maintaining sufficient cash flows and to be able to recruit and retain employees. Without adequate financial backing and the hesitations from debt markets and investors to support small enterprises, new firms are forced to overly rely on personal and internal sources of funding. This form of financing is not sustainable in the long run and is a catalyst for a firm's mortality having a crucial influence on survivability of an entrepreneurial venture over time.

In future work, we will analyze other crucial internal factors such as human capital and the ability to offer innovative product solutions and how effective human resource strategies if properly implemented should greatly assist small firms to compete and grow in their respected industries, therefore substantially increasing their chance of survival.

References

Baldwin, J., & Bian, L. (2000). Failure rates for new Canadian firms: New perspectives on entry and exit. Statistics Canada. Catalogue no. 61-526-XPE.

Baldwin, J., & Gellatly, G. (2006). Innovation capabilities: The knowledge capital behind the survival and growth of firms. Statistics Canada. Catalogue no. 11-622-MIE, no. 013.

Baldwin, J., Gray, T., Johnson, J., Proctor, J., Rafiquzzaman, M., & Sabourin, D. (1997). Failing concerns: Business bankruptcy in Canada. Statistics Canada. Catalogue no. 61-525-XPE.

Bordt, M., Earl, L., Lonmo, C., & Joseph, R. (2004). Characteristics of firms that grow from small to medium size: Growth factors—Interviews and measurability. Statistics Canada: Science, Innovation and Electronic Information Division. Catalogue no. 88F0006XIE—No. 021.

Industry Canada. (2013). Financing statistics special edition: Key small business statistics. Statistics Canada, Small Business Branch. Catalogue no. Iu186-1/2013-3E-PDF.

Macdonald, R. (2012). Firm dynamics: The death of new Canadian firms: A survival analysis of the 2002 cohort of entrants to the business sector. Economic Analysis Division. Statistics Canada. Catalogue no. 11-622-M—No. 028.

Macdonald, R. (2014). Business dynamism in Canada: A 30-year perspective. Economic analysis division. Statistics Canada. Catalogue no. 11-626-x No. 038.

Thornhill, S., & Amit, P. (2003) Learning from failure: Organizational mortality and the resource-based view. Statistics Canada. Analytical Studies Branch research paper series. Micro-Economic Analysis Division. Catalogue no. 11F0019MIE—No. 202.

Chapter 52
Work Motivation in Temporary Organizations: A Review of Literature Grounded in Job Design Perspective

Ravikiran Dwivedula, Christophe N. Bredillet, and Ralf Müller

Abstract The purpose of this chapter is to propose an approach to structure literature review along robust theoretical lenses leading to conceptualization of work motivation in case of temporary organizations. The chapter is in response to studies calling for a "seamless" theory of work motivation spanning across different management disciplines, without being confined to a specific theoretical stance. We use job design perspective from industrial/organizational psychology literature as a point of departure. We present a comprehensive review of these theories highlighting their premises. Then we focus on the literature on work motivation in case of temporary organizations. We map this literature to the theories in order to consolidate the theoretical corpus underlying work motivation. Various facets of job design that constitute motivating nature of work are identified.

Keywords Work motivation • Temporary organizations • Project management • Job design

R. Dwivedula (✉)
Associate Professor, American College of Dubai, Al Garhoud, P.O. Box 12867, Dubai, UAE

Adjunct Professor, Université du Québec à Trois-Rivières, 3351 Boulevard des Forges, Troi-Rivières, QC, Canada G9A 5H7
e-mail: ravi.dwivedula@acd.ae

C.N. Bredillet
Université du Québec à Trois-Rivières, 3351 Boulevard des Forges, Troi-Rivières, QC, Canada G9A 5H7
e-mail: cnbredillet@hotmail.com

R. Müller
BI Norwegian Business School, Oslo 0422, Norway
e-mail: pmconcepts.ab@gmail.com

Introduction

Understanding the people management aspects and how they affect outcomes has been studied extensively in case of temporary organizations such as projects (c.f., Keegan, Huemann, & Turner, 2012). Variables such as leadership style, personality, and project workers' commitment for their effect on project success have been researched (Cohen, Ornoy, & Baruch, 2013; Müller & Turner, 2010). More notably, recent literature focused on understanding work motivation specifically in the context of temporary organizations (c.f., Sieler, Lent, Pinkowska, & Pinazza, 2012).

However, extant literature may have fallen short on consolidating the theories underlying work motivation in the case of temporary organizations. The theories on work motivation in case of industrial/organizational psychology are firmly established. However, such a comprehensive structure of theoretical corpus may not be available in the temporary organization literature. This limitation has led to a dialogue started by Locke and Latham (2004) who call for a seamless theory of work motivation that is able to integrate multiple theoretical lenses. This then calls for an approach where we do not demonstrate strong affiliation to any one specific theory to explain work motivation. Rather, we review a compendium of theories within the domain to explain the variable. However, we also need to balance our approach where our arguments are based on robust, established theoretical lenses which complement each other. Thus, the purpose of this study is to:

propose a comprehensive framework to structure work motivation literature in case of temporary organizations.

We have structured this chapter in the following way. The first section, Positioning the Research Study, justifies our approach to consider multiple theoretical lenses to explain work motivation in case of temporary organizations. We draw from the works of Sandberg and Alvesson (2011) who offer guidelines to develop a research problem for such studies. In the second section, Theory, we briefly introduce the theories of work motivation from I/O psychology literature. While work motivation has been explained from various points of view such as the need-based theories, and cognition-based theories, we have considered the job design perspective that explains work motivation as an outcome of specific job characteristics. The third section of the chapter, Work Motivation in Temporary Organizations, is where we present the literature review from the temporary organization domain. We structure the review around the theories of work motivation identified from the I/O psychology literature. This is followed by conclusion.

Positioning the Research Study: Application Spotting and "Moving" Between the "Boxes"

Sandberg and Alvesson (2011) examine the merits of two different approaches to formulate research questions which can be useful to state the research problem. At one end of the continuum is the "gap spotting" which can include incrementally extending an established theory or identifying significant gaps in the extant literature. Gap spotting may include confusion spotting (reconcile contradictions in the literature), neglect spotting (focusing on an underdeveloped area of research), and application spotting (identifying the shortcomings of a theory in a specific area and providing an alternative perspective to further our understanding of that theory). The purpose of such research is to reinforce or moderately revise the existing theories. On the other end of the continuum is "problematization." In this, the research questions are posed such that they challenge the underlying assumptions of existing theories in a significant way. It may include questioning minor assumptions pertaining to the theory to overtly question the assumptions of the entire field.

In a follow-up paper, Alvesson and Sandberg (2014) discuss the merits and demerits of research problems that have become extremely "contextualized," specific to (one) field without being relevant to other fields. Alvesson and Sandberg call such research studies as boxed-in research, where the research study can be limited or restricted by perspective (conforming and confining to specific theories/perspectives), domains (confining to specific topics without considering the cross-discipline influence on such topics), and methods (specific research methods being more prominently used than others to investigate research problems). Alvesson and Sandberg further present approaches to overcome these restrictions in three different ways—box changing, where the researcher has a primary point of reference (such as a theory) and the researcher considers new theories, ideas, or methods that significantly change the central elements in the existing thinking; box jumping—requires significant thematic, methodological, and theoretical considerations by embracing multiple theoretical, thematic, or methodological perspective by simultaneously working with two or more thematic or methodological perspectives; and box transcendence—working with very broad research questions that may not be confined to a particular field.

To explain the positioning of our research study, we consider these two criteria: (a) gap spotting versus problematization (which lie at the extreme ends of a continuum), and (b) box changing, box jumping, and box transcendence (which lie on a continuum).

The purpose of this research study is to demonstrate an approach to structure the literature on work motivation in temporary organizations by considering multiple theoretical perspectives. Our point of departure for this study is the lack of "consolidated" theoretical corpus. While we are not challenging the theoretical assumptions, we are extending the current theories on work motivation from I/O psychology literature to the realm of temporary organizations. This approach relates to "application spotting" as described by Sandberg and Alvesson (2011). In adopting this approach, it is obvious that we are considering multiple theoretical perspectives simultaneously while not confining the study to a particular research identity. This approach may connote to "box jumping" (as described by Alvesson and Sandberg (2014)).

The above discussion on the positioning of our research paper is summarized in Fig. 52.1.

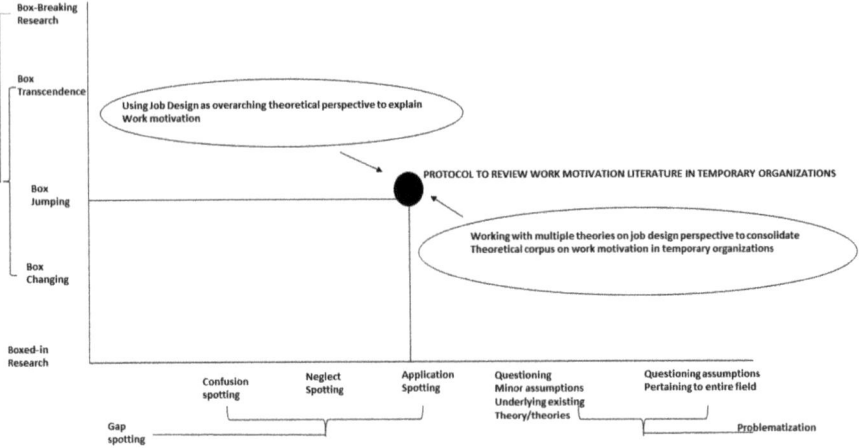

Fig. 52.1 Positioning the current research paper

Theory

There has been growing interest on what motivates project workers recently. Although the state of research is predominantly normative (connoting to practices), literature review reveals that these practices connote to major theories of work motivation. Various theoretical lenses such as socio-technical perspective (c.f., Schmidt & Adams, 2008), scientific management, job characteristic model (c.f., Beecham, Baddoo, Hall, Robinson, & Sharp, 2008; Björklund, 2010; Mahoney & Lederer, 2006), and intrinsic motivation perspective have been used to explain work motivation in temporary organizations. Table 52.1 summarizes the job design theories considered for the study and the corresponding basis for the work motivation item drawn from the theory.

Work Motivation in Temporary Organizations

We reiterate here that the focus of our chapter is to propose a theoretical framework to explain work motivation in temporary organizations. Therefore, specific characteristics of motivating nature of work are not discussed elaborately. However, we will present the major literature from temporary organizations that describe specific job characteristics which are motivating in the context of temporary organizations. We conducted an extensive literature review that is structured along the major theories of work motivation discussed above. We considered SCOPUS database to identify extant literature on work motivation in temporary organizations. In consonance with the purpose of this study, we restricted our review to scholarly articles that focused their discussion on the job design perspective to work motivation

Table 52.1 Job design theories of work motivation

Theory	Premise	Basis for work motivation item
Scientific management (Taylor, 1911)	Best way to perform each task in order to improve worker's productivity. This was done by emphasizing on employee supervision, and reward performance through financial incentives (piece-rate incentive system)	Financial incentives related to productivity (performance)
Tavistock studies on socio-technical systems approach (Trist & Bamforth, 1951; Cherns 1976)	Distinguishing the social and the technical subsystem of the organization and optimizing these subsystems to achieve individual and organizational objectives; job characteristics proposed for autonomous work groups	Principles of socio-technical systems—autonomy, task identity, meaningfulness of task, feedback on performance
Walker and Guest (1952)	Job redesign through job rotation and job enlargement	Employees required to undertake a variety of tasks through job rotation and job enlargement
Two-factor theory (Herzberg, Mausner, & Snyderman, 1959)	Determinants of employee satisfaction are intrinsic (called *motivation factors*) while those of dissatisfaction are extrinsic (called *hygiene factors*)	Nature of work itself as an intrinsic motivator for the employee; job security as an extrinsic motivator
Job enrichment (Paul Jr, Robertson, & Herzberg, 1969; Paul & Robertson, 1970)	Greater scope for personal achievement by providing more challenging and responsible work	Challenging nature of work, autonomy at work, and providing a sense of achievement to the employee
Job characteristic model (Hackman & Lawler, 1971; Hackman & Oldham, 1976)	Job characteristics leading to critical psychological states which in turn lead to individual and organizational outcomes; skill variety, task identity, and task significance lead to experienced meaningfulness at work; autonomy at work leads to greater experienced responsibility; feedback from work leads to more knowledge of the results	Five core job characteristics proposed—skill variety, task identity, task significance, autonomy, and feedback

(continued)

Table 52.1 (continued)

Theory	Premise	Basis for work motivation item
Redundancy of functions (Emery & Emery, 1976)	Proposed the idea of "industrial democracy" through creation of project groups (cutting across the organization's hierarchy), and suggested psychological requirements for the employees who are a part of such arrangement	Creation of groups within the organization is a precursor to project-based organizations
		Freedom to participate in decisions that affect their work activity. A chance to learn on the job and go on learning, optimal variety, mutual support, and respect of their work colleagues, a socially meaningful task
Demand control mode (Karasek, 1979)	Brings forward to main propositions related to autonomy and challenging work. High job demand and low job control lead to perceptions of the job being strenuous; jobs in which demand and control are high lead to perceptions of personal growth, learning, and well-being	Challenging nature of work, autonomy at work
Resource allocation perspective (Naylor, Pritchard, & Ilgen, 1980); distal motivation (Kanfer, 1990)	The choice to allocate resources to a particular task or a goal. This in turn depends on how valued are the outcomes to the individual and the benefits derived when compared to the efforts expended	Personal growth, and job enrichment (autonomy at work)
Job performance (Campbell, 1990)	Specific task and non-task behaviors at work that affect employee's performance; highlights the relation between job characteristics and performance	Communication and collegiality among group members are specific task behaviors that lead to performance
Extension to job characteristic model (Morgeson & Humphrey, 2006)	In addition to the five core job dimensions, three types of autonomy (work scheduling autonomy, work method autonomy, decision-making autonomy); knowledge motivation (job complexity, information processing, skill variety, and specialization); social work (social support, interdependence-initiated interaction, feedback from others); contextual characteristics (ergonomics, physical demands, work conditions, and use of equipment)	Autonomy at work
		Five core job dimensions
		Task variety, skill variety, feedback from others, feedback from work itself, access to work-specific information, informal communication

(in temporary organizations). The key strings used were "job design" and "project management"; "job design" and "temporary organization"; "job design" and "work motivation"; and "project management." Articles from peer-reviewed journals, articles in press, conference proceedings, and book chapters were considered.

The literature on work motivation in temporary organizations, though "sporadic" in terms of not being able to offer integrative underlying theoretical lenses to explain motivating job characteristics, has been fairly extensive. Various facets of job such as financial incentives linked to performance (c.f., Armstrong, 2003; Rose & Manley, 2010, grounded in scientific management studies (Taylor, 1911)), task identity, task meaningfulness, and feedback on performance (c.f., Andersen, 2010; Schmidt & Adams, 2008) drawn from Tavistock Studies on socio-technical systems perspective (Cherns, 1976; Trist & Bamforth, 1951; Walker & Guest, 1952), task variety (c.f., Hiemgartner, Tiede, & Windl, 2011; Sieler et al., 2012), grounded in socio-technical perspective (Walker & Guest, 1952), work as intrinsically motivating, and job security as extrinsic motivator (c.f., Mahoney & Lederer, 2006; Parker, Wall, & Cordery, 2001; Schmidt & Adams, 2008), drawn from Herzberg, Mausner, and Snyderman's two-factor theory (1959), task significance (c.f., Badir, Buechel, & Tucci, 2012; Procaccino, Verner, & Lorenzet, 2006; Schmidt & Adams, 2008) drawn from studies on job enrichment (Paul Jr et al., 1969; Paul & Robertson, 1970), skill variety, and task identity (Ling & Loo, 2015; Mahoney & Lederer, 2006), autonomy at work (c.f., Leung, Chan, & Dondyu, 2011), drawn from demand control model (Karasek, 1979; job characteristic model, Hackman & Oldham, 1976), personal growth and job enrichment (c.f., Li, Bingham, & Umphress, 2007, grounded in Naylor, Pritchard, and Ilgen's resource allocation perspective, 1980), communication and collegiality between the project actors (c.f., Beecham et al., 2008; Nesheim & Smith, 2015; Zika-Viktorsson, Sundtrsom, & Engwall, 2006), grounded in distal motivation theory (Campbell, 1990; Kanfer, 1990), and access to work-related information, and informal communication among project actors (c.f., Björklund, 2010; Ling & Loo, 2015; Turner & LloydWalker, 2008), drawn from Morgeson and Humphrey's extended job characteristic model (2006) (Fig. 52.2).

Future Direction

This chapter is a part of the larger research study that investigates the role of work motivation on project success. We hypothesize that a project worker's commitment to the organization and profession mediates the relationship between work motivation and project success. In line with this research which requires a "construction" of our reality of work motivation and how it affects the project outcomes, while at the same time acknowledging that a certain reality exists independent of our knowledge, we adopt realism as our epistemological stance. Thus, we use mixed research methods, employing qualitative research techniques such as focus group

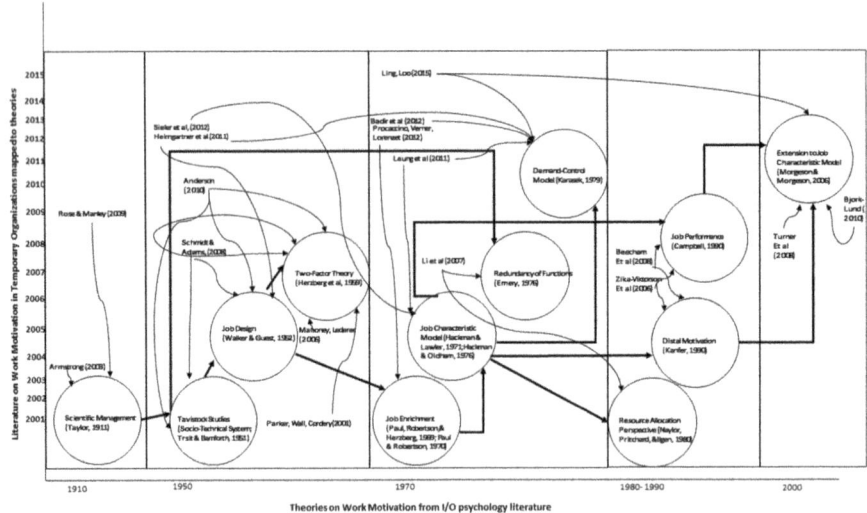

Fig. 52.2 Mapping literature to theories

interviews of project managers, and project management academicians to refine the operational definitions of our variables, and hypothesize the relationship between the variables. We use empirical approach, conducting a survey of project workers to test our hypotheses.

Conclusion

In this chapter, we build an interaction between established theories of work design from I/O psychology literature and those from the knowledge field of temporary organizations. It may be important to state that we are not merely "borrowing" literature from industrial/organization psychology and "domesticating" it to "fit" into the knowledge field of temporary organizations. Rather, we have genuinely attempted to build an interaction between the two domains of I/O psychology and temporary organizations by critically analyzing the theories and structuring the literature around these theories. It is expected that our work will lead to a comprehensive conceptualization of work motivation in temporary organizations that is grounded in multiple theoretical perspectives, and studies of similar nature will be undertaken in the future.

References

Alvesson, M., & Sandberg, J. (2014). Habitat and habitus: Boxed-in versus box-breaking research. *Organization Studies, 35*(7), 967–987.

Andersen, J. (2010). *An empirical study of design management practices in collaborative design and construction projects—The roles, activities, and conceptions of design management across project stages, and within the building.* Civil, and Process sectors of a construction company, PhD Thesis. School of Engineering, University of Queensland.

Armstrong, M. (2003). *A handbook of human resource management practice* (9th ed.). London: Kogan Page.

Badir, Y. F., Buechel, B., & Tucci, C. L. (2012). A conceptual framework of the impact of NPD project team and leader empowerment on communication and performance: An alliance context. *International Journal of Project Management, 30*(8), 914–926.

Beecham, S., Baddoo, N., Hall, T., Robinson, H., & Sharp, H. (2008). Motivation in software engineering: A systematic literature review. *Information and Software Technology, 50*(9), 860–878.

Björklund, T. A. (2010). Enhancing creative knowledgework: Challenges and points of leverage. *International Journal of Managing Projects in Business, 31*(3), 517–525.

Campbell, J. P. (1990). Modeling the performance prediction problem in industrial and organizational psychology. In M. D. Dunnette & L. M. Hough (Eds.), *Handbook of industrial and organizational psychology* (Vol. 1, pp. 687–732). Palo Alto, CA: Consulting Psychologists Press.

Cherns, A. B. (1976). The principles of organizational design. *Human Relations, 29*(8), 783–792.

Cohen, Y., Ornoy, H., & Baruch, K. (2013). MBTI personality types of project managers and their success: A field survey. *Project Management Journal, 44*(3), 78–87.

Emery, F. E., & Emery, M. (1976). A participative approach to democratization of work place, appendix. In F. E. Emery & E. Thorsud (Eds.), *Democracy at work.* Liden: Martinus Nijhoff.

Hackman, J. R., & Lawler, E. E. (1971). Employee reactions to job characteristics. *Journal of Applied Psychology Monograph, 55*, 259–286.

Hackman, J. R., & Oldham, G. R. (1976). Motivation through the design of work: Test of a theory. *Organization Behavior and Human Performance, 16*, 250–279.

Herzberg, F., Mausner, B., & Snyderman, B. B. (1959). *The motivation to work.* New York: Wiley.

Hiemgartner, R., Tiede, L.-W., & Windl, H. (2011). Empathy as a key factor for successful intercultural HCI design. In A. Marcus (Ed.), *Design, user experience, and usability. Theory, methods, tools and practice* (Lecture Notes in Computer Science, Vol. 6770, pp. 557–566). Berlin: Springer.

Kanfer, R. (1990). Motivational and individual differences in learning: An integration of developmental, differential, and cognitive perspectives. *Learning and Individual Differences, 2,* 219–237.

Karasek, R. A. (1979). Job demands, job decision latitude, and mental strain: Implications for job redesign. *Administrative Science Quarterly, 24*, 285–311.

Keegan, A., Huemann, M., & Turner, R. (2012). *Beyond the line: Exploring the HRM responsibilities of line managers, project managers, and the HRM department in four project-oriented companies in The Netherlands, Austria, the UK, and the USA.* London: Taylor & Francis.

Leung, M.-Y., Chan, I. Y. S., & Dondyu, C. (2011). Structural linear relationships between job stress, burnout, physiological stress, and performance of construction project managers. *Engineering, Construction and Architectural Management, 18*(3), 312–328.

Li, H., Bingham, J. B., & Umphress, E. E. (2007). Fairness from the top: Perceived procedural justice and collaborative problem solving in new product development. *Organization Science, 18*, 200–216.

Ling, F. Y., & Loo, C. M. (2015). Characteristics of jobs and jobholders that affect job satisfaction and work performance of project managers. *Journal of Management Engineering, 31*(3), 401–403.

Locke, E., & Latham, G. (2004). What should we do about motivation theory: Six recommendations for the twenty-first century. *Academy of Management Review, 29*(3), 388–403.

Mahoney, R. C., & Lederer, A. L. (2006). The effect of intrinsic and extrinsic rewards for developers on information systems project success. *Project Management Journal, 37*(4), 42–55.

Morgeson, F., & Humphrey, S. (2006). The work design questionnaire (WQQ): Developing and validating a comprehensive measure for assessing job design and the nature of work. *Journal of Applied Psychology, 91*, 1321–1399.

Müller, R., & Turner, R. (2010). Leadership competency profiles of successful project managers. *International Journal of Project Management, 28*, 437–448.

Naylor, J. C., Pritchard, R. D., & Ilgen, R. D. (1980). *A theory of behavior in organizations.* New York: Academic.

Nesheim, T., & Smith, J. (2015). Knowledge sharing in projects: Does employment arrangement matter? *Personnel Review, 44*(2), 255–269.

Parker, S. K., Wall, T. D., & Cordery, J. L. (2001). Future work design research and practice: Towards an elaborated model of work design. *Journal of Occupational and Organizational Psychology, 74*, 413–440.

Paul, W. J. Jr., Robertson, K. B., & Herzberg, F. (1969). Job enrichment pays off. *Harvard Business Review*, March–April 1969, 61–78.

Paul, W. J., & Robertson, K. B. (1970). *Job enrichment and employee motivation.* London: Gower.

Procaccino, J. D., Verner, J. M., & Lorenzet, S. J. (2006). Defining and contributing to software development success: Determining the process-related components affecting software developers' perception of project success. *Communications of the ACM, 49*(8), 79–83.

Rose, T. M., & Manley, K. (2010). Motivation toward financial incentive goals on construction projects. *Journal of Business Research, 64*(7), 765–773.

Sandberg, J., & Alvesson, M. (2011). Ways of constructing research questions: Gap spotting or problematization? *Organization, 18*(1), 23–44.

Schmidt, B., & Adams, J. (2008). Motivation in project management: The project manager's perspective. *Project Management Journal, 39*(2), 60–71.

Sieler, S., Lent, B., Pinkowska, M., & Pinazza, M. (2012). An integrated model of factors influencing project managers' motivation—Findings from a Swiss Survey. *International Journal of Project Management, 30*(1), 60–72.

Taylor, F. W. (1911). *The principles of scientific management.* New York: Harper.

Trist, E., & Bamforth, W. (1951). Some social and psychological consequences of the long wall method of coal getting. *Human Relations, 4*, 3–38.

Turner, R., & LloydWalker, B. (2008). Emotional Intelligence (EI) capabilities training: Can it develop EI in project teams? *International Journal of Managing Projects in Business, 1*(4), 512–534.

Walker, C. R., & Guest, H. (1952). *The man on the assembly line.* Cambridge, MA: Harvard University Press.

Zika-Viktorsson, A., Sundtrsom, P., & Engwall, M. (2006). Project overload: An exploratory study of work and management in multi project settings. *International Journal of Project Management, 24*(5), 385–394.

Chapter 53
Demand and Supply Firms' Interlock: A Youth-Based Entrepreneurial Initiative

Zaid O. Al Rayes and Hayaa M. Azzam Kayiaseh

Abstract This chapter presents an expanded structure for a conglomerate business setting. It considers the foundation of small entrepreneurship projects inspired by the need of creating sustainable businesses and managed by ambitious youth entrepreneurs. Conglomerates refer to the widely diversified companies operating in a number of distinct lines of businesses or classes of products and services, bonded financially, within the same overall firm. We design a revised conglomerate business structure in which supply and demand are interlocked by small entrepreneurship projects bonded financially in a three-structural-line setting within the same overall parent company. The project is based on hospitality as it became one of the most important business fields in today's businesses. Managing conglomerate bussiness is associated with many challenges that need more investigations and researches. Managing such diversified business group is one of the great challenges in this chapter. Also, it's usually costly to set up small entrepreneurship projects especially in Middle East and Gulf countries compared to other countries that encourage the establishments of youth entrepreneurship businesses.

Keywords Youth entrepreneurship • Conglomerates • Youth business challenges • Hospitality businesses

Introduction

Entrepreneurship relates to the actions of an entrepreneur, a creative "risk taker," into a new economic opportunity (new products/services, new production methods, new organizational schemes, or new product-market combinations) (Hébert & Link, 1989; Peneder, 2009). Entrepreneurship is highly emphasized in emerging countries, where micro, small, and medium projects account for around 45 % of employment and 33 % of GDP as compared to nearly 62 % and 64 %, respectively, in higher

Z.O. Al Rayes (✉) • H.M. Azzam Kayiaseh
American University of Sharjah, Sharjah, United Arab Emirates
e-mail: b00033833@aus.edu; g00033740@aus.edu

© Springer International Publishing Switzerland 2017
R. Benlamri, M. Sparer (eds.), *Leadership, Innovation and Entrepreneurship as Driving Forces of the Global Economy*, Springer Proceedings in Business and Economics, DOI 10.1007/978-3-319-43434-6_53

income countries, as reported by the World Bank unit of the International Finance Corporation (Gulf Business, Dec 2013). Developing countries, including the Middle East and Gulf, have not been yet associated with entrepreneurial endeavor. Probably, the cost of setting up an entrepreneurial project is too high in some countries, especially in the UAE, as reported by Philip Boigner (Gulf Business, Sept 2013). Entrepreneurship has been globally considered one of the effective means for addressing youth unemployment and ultimately enhancing economic independence among youth. Job unemployment stories experienced by educated youth as well as non-educated but skilled ones in developing countries have been pathetic (Awogbenle & Iwuamadi, 2010). That said, entrepreneurship and business planning are still half-through promoted in the region where governments are encouraged to support small, medium, and large enterprises so as to achieve a sustainable business environment and ultimately reduce youth unemployment rates within the region. Yasar Jarrar (Hedrick-Wong & Jarrar, 2015) has emphasized on entrepreneurship investment by all Middle East governments so that more job opportunities would be created and young talent could be fostered (Gulf Business, Aug 2015). On one side, youth entrepreneurship has been on the rise, creating job opportunities for self-employed youth and other young people they employ. On the other side, youth entrepreneurship promotes innovation and resilience in youth as well as economic growth sustainment and development (Schoof, 2006). In fact, job creation through entrepreneurship is considered as one of the main drivers for economic boost and sustainability. Ultimately, Middle East and Gulf region countries are highly encouraged to boost their entrepreneurial ecosystems to support a flourishing economy, where more job opportunities are created and unemployment is reduced substantially (Hedrick-Wong & Jarrar, 2015). By strengthening the country's entrepreneurial ecosystem, the dependence on scarce resources, mainly oil, can be reduced.

Theory and Prior Research

Conglomerates refer to the widely diversified companies operating in a number of distinct lines of businesses or classes of products and services, bonded financially, within the same overall firm (Bows, 1966; Ghemawat & Khanna, 1998). Conglomerates usually take the organizational business form of either the multidivisional diversified single firm or the diversified business group. In the diversified business group simple form, as in Fig. 53.1, the parent company effectively owns and controls its subsidiaries while it maintains accounting and legal freedom to a significant degree allowed by the parent company (Yoong-Deok & Young-Yong, 2004). Business diversification is crucial nowadays in reducing overall firm's risk and sustaining growth. Conglomerate business structure allows for a reduction in firm's cost by facilitating the sharing of common resources across related lines of businesses, such as customers, human resources, and technology. Indeed, related

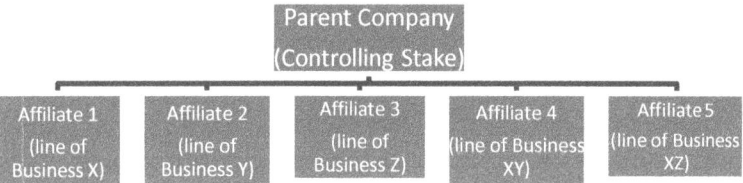

Fig. 53.1 Diversified business group model

business diversification boosts performance by allowing a preferential access to "strategic assets"—those that are uncommon, valuable, and very costly to imitate (Markides & Williamson, 1996). Conglomerates offer solutions as well to the problem of economic calculation in emerging economies where markets are characterized either as undeveloped or poorly developed ones. That said, conglomerates arise as a production structure to reduce market imperfections, thereby reducing economic calculation costs (Marshall, Yawitz, & Greenberg, 1984). Moreover, conglomerates participating in a number of different markets help in leveraging market power of those in individual markets (Ghemawat & Khanna, 1998). However, given the complexity of managing distinct lines of businesses, there come several challenges: agency costs, or "economic theory of agency" which refers to the relationship between an agent (manager) and a principal (owner), each working in alignment to their best interests (Hill & Hoskisson, 1987). Corporate control is yet another cost, which is reflected by the power of the mother company taking decisions in alignment with its set strategies. The challenge becomes in controlling all firm's affiliates and evaluating their performance, in alignment with the parent firm's strategy (Noble, 1969). We lastly present disclosure of segments as a crucial challenge in conglomerates. Given the various distinct lines of businesses and multiproduct/service industries, management of the parent company should be consistent in disclosing all financial information to stakeholders at the organization-wide level for sustaining transparency (Bows, 1966; Noble, 1969). The youth business conglomerate proposed in this chapter refers to social entrepreneurship which differs from economic entrepreneurship as it focuses on social value creation rather than primarily on wealth generation. Dees, Emerson, and Economy (2001) describe social entrepreneurship as a social related entrepreneurial mission where social value comes at first and later wealth creation. Ultimately, by social entrepreneurship, one can peruse both goals: financial self-sustainability and social value or the so-called social return on investment. That said, social entrepreneurship is not restricted to nonprofit business; it can also include profit organizations as long as their central direction is towards social value creation (Dees et al., 2001; Schoof, 2006).

Suggested Model: Al Rayes Group

The General Business Scheme

The general scheme of the suggested entrepreneurship project looks like a pyramid with four floors; we refer to them as "business lines." Each floor consists of specific number of apartments and each apartment consists of a number of rooms. Floors represent the degree of maturity and stability of the businesses included in the floor and the type of demand they deal with as shown in Fig. 53.2. Rooms represent different small businesses which are included into apartments based on both dependency on each other and related field. The top floor represents the mother company which can be defined as an investment company responsible for general management and cooperation between different business types, "floors." In general, Our model represents a group of small businesses that depend on each other to accomplish two main goals; the short-term goal relates to the survival in one of the most competitive markets in the world while the long-term goal is related to the expansion of each small business "floor."

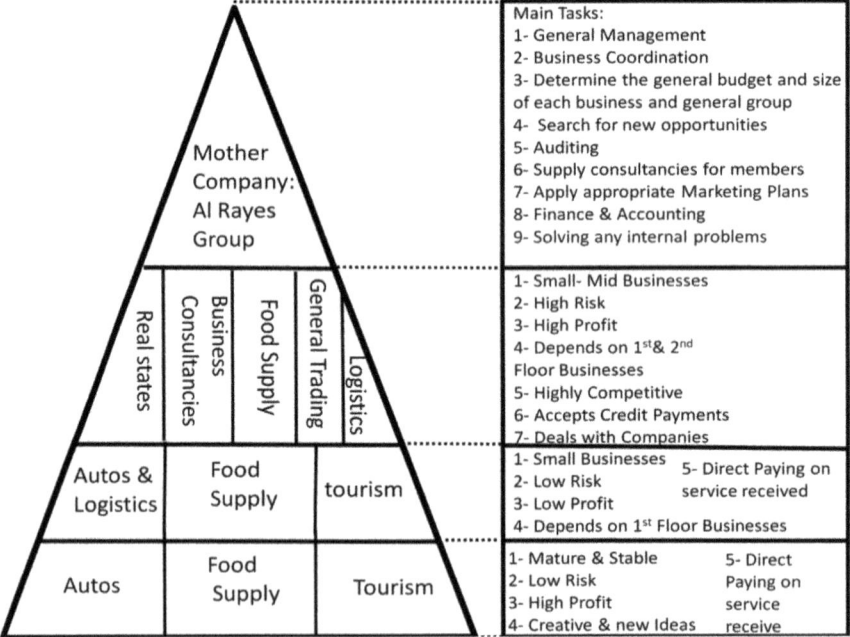

Fig. 53.2 Al Rayes group: (**a**) General structure. (**b**) Common factors in each floor business

First-Line "Floor" Businesses

The first floor represents a group of entrepreneurship projects that are mature enough, stable, and creative guarantying their business sustainability. This is because the entrepreneurship project chosen introduces demand services which satisfy daily necessary needs; hence, whatever the economic situation is, they will not go bankrupt. For example, a traditional restaurant in which services provided are considered as essentials or because the service provided is being supplied in a creative way in which the need is turned into an exciting activity such as the Engineering Café.

All these projects lie in the field of hospitality and tourism. The reason behind choosing this field is mainly because it's considered to be a low-risk field with good profit margin especially when we are talking about hospitality projects that are related to food services such as restaurants, coffee shops, and juice shops. Another reason is the good experience of authors in this field and the governmental vision of expanding this field. In addition, a lot of creative ideas can be fostered in such field. Finally, receivables in such field have low risk as the nature of such business, i.e., a restaurant, allows for instant payments as soon as provided service is received by the customer, i.e., food delivery. Table 53.1 includes a brief description of each business.

Let's take the idea of the Engineers Restaurant and apply it to our criteria of this business line. The general idea of the Engineers Restaurant and Café is that it supplies the meals to the customers using a new technological method that is not used

Table 53.1 First-line "floor" businesses

Entrepreneurship project	General description
Food supply	
Eastern restaurant	The restaurant supplies its food to university students
Engineering restaurant	Restaurant and café that supplies its services using new engineering technologies
Juice and ice cream shop	• Natural juices that are served in a creative way
	• Fresh ice cream being made on spot "fried ice cream"
Roastry and chocolate shop	Special designs and products supplied based on the client requirements
Candies shop	Includes crepe, waffles, and pancakes being made freshly
Tourism	
Van restaurant	Special van that supplies snacks and sandwiches to customers while they are having tours
Turkish path	Special Turkish path that is designed from the traditional ottoman paths
Desert resort	Supplies special sport activities being done in the desert
Autos	
Car garage	Gives special services to cars and directs youth who really like to make special designs and services to their cars

in any restaurant before. This restaurant and café include different engineering departments such as aerospace engineering section and civil engineering section. In the aerospace engineering section, meals are provided through special UAVs as well as in the civil engineering section meals are provided using a train. So the way of supplying the services is creative and simulates the engineering background of each engineering major. The decoration of the restaurant is made in a special engineering design. This idea is considered a creative and new idea that is expected to attract tourists who are visiting the city.

Second- and Third-Line "Floor" Businesses

Both second floor and third floor include entrepreneurship projects that depend on the first floor or first line of businesses. The projects chosen in the second and third lines of businesses introduce services that are of great interest to the first-line businesses. The second-line projects differ from the third-line projects in the degree of business risk and percentage of profit. This difference comes mainly from the fact that third-line projects deal with companies instead which means that less cash flow is available while in second-line projects we are dealing with cash payment only. Also, third-line projects have more market competitors and depend on the supply–demand balance in determining the prices and overall performance. As a result, the performance of the first-line businesses will have great effect on the performance of the third-line businesses. It can be seen from Fig. 53.3 that the second-line projects are smaller in size than the third-line projects. This is because the third-line businesses include projects that create and manufacture products from raw materials or import products from outside markets and sell to local market.

Entrepreneurship Project Real States	Entrepreneurship Project
Labor Residency Buildings	**Food Supply**
Real State Agency	Meat & Fish Shop
Stores	Fruit & Vegetable Shop
General Maintenance Company	
Business Consultancies	**Tourism**
General Business Consultancies Agency	Travel Agency
Special Gifts &Printing House	Laundry
Advertising & Publishing Agency	**Autos & Logistics**
Food Supply	Car Rental Agency
Central Kitchen	Internal Transportation Agency
General Trading & Logistics	
General Trading Company	
Import & Export Company	

Fig. 53.3 Dependent businesses: (**a**) Second-line "floor" businesses. (b) Third-line "floor"-dependent businesses

Mother Company

The mother company plays the major role in determining the general behavior and trend of all the businesses. It has the overall view that is not seen by the small businesses. As a result, the mother company is responsible for keeping all the small entrepreneurship projects that are under its management in the right track that serve well the entire group even if it comes at the cost of one or more of its members. As a result, all members should have the belief that decisions of the mother company are made for the entire group interest and profit because survival of the entire group will lead to survival of its members and vice versa. In addition, the mother company should guarantee that all small entrepreneurship projects are coordinating appropriately and satisfaction is found between both sides, supply and demand which are both members of the company. Further, the size of each project should be defined clearly. In fact, the appropriate sizing will guarantee the availability of appropriate amount of cash flow because the group has a part in which it supplies its services as credit. It also determines the degree of dependency of each project which reflects the ability of the project to sustain.

The mother company draws the general line of behavior of the entire company without intervention in the management of each business unless it detects a behavior or decision that is against the group vision. As a result, the group supplies small businesses of required consultancies and supports them financially against a profit margin taken from each entrepreneurship project.

Integrated Model: Al Rayes Group

Al Rayes Group works in five different business fields: hospitality, autos, logistics, real estates, and business consultancies as illustrated in Fig. 53.4. Our core business field that we rely on is the hospitality that can be divided into two main subgroups: food supply and tourism. Business cooperation includes the exchange of services and products of the different entrepreneurship businesses among each other to guarantee that the maximum amount of entrepreneurship business expenses are being recycled among the group. Table 53.2 illustrates the interaction of firm between the group divisions. Second-line and third-line businesses supply services and products to the first-line businesses and to each other. For instance, the printing house supplies services to businesses in both the first line and second line. On the other hand, the group deals with two different types of demand: end-user consumer and mid-user consumer. All the first-line businesses give services to the end-user consumer who pays cash and needs these services. The second-line businesses supply services to both types and this is the reason we mentioned that they have higher risk compared to the first-line businesses. Finally, the third-line businesses deal totally with mid-user consumer and can supply services as credit.

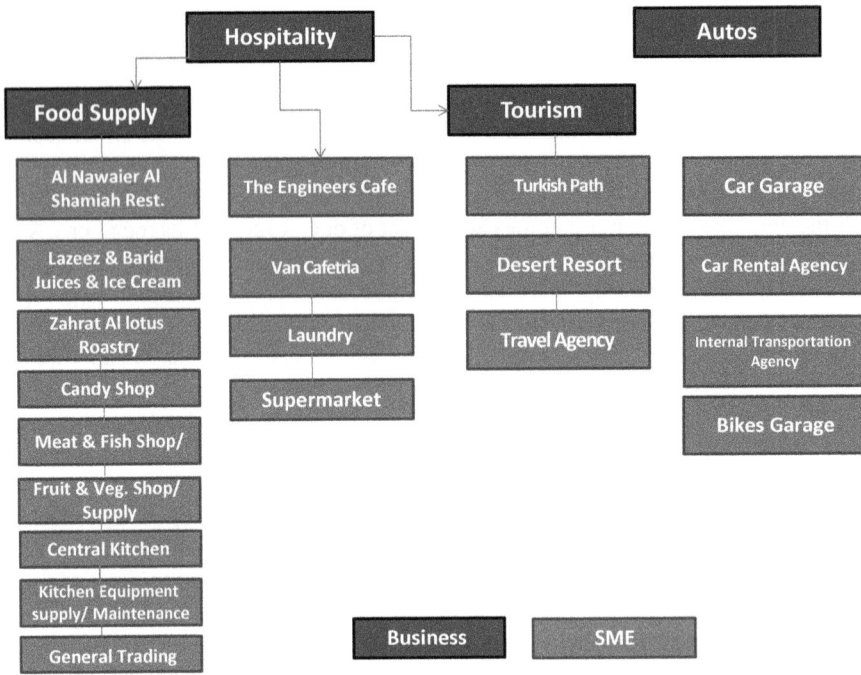

Fig. 53.4 Al Rayes organizational structure

Project Progress

The business point from where such large and complex project has started was Al Nawaier Al Shamiah Cafeteria. This small entrepreneurship project was launched in April 2013. Within 16 months, the cafeteria was able to expand to a restaurant with total number of 32 staff members. The profit then was used to open a new business which was a laundry. Its vision is always to work on a comparative advantage that introduces its services in new ways into the market. For example, the laundry introduced a postpaid membership electronic cards to its clients with a great package of services such as free delivery services and attractive cashback rates on the card. Within a period of 3 years, Al Rayes Group was able to have five entrepreneurship projects and it has a time plan to expand to 15 more entrepreneurship projects in the next 4 years. The project expands according to five phases that are beyond our research scope. The future plan was put based on the market requirements and status, financial resources, and each project significance to the entire group. The plan has a strategy to work in parallel with regard to the businesses included in the different three lines. The project is still in its first phase which is concentrating on the food supply division.

Table 53.2 Firms interlock within the revised conglomerate Al Rayes model

No.	Entrepreneurship project	Receive services from entrepreneurship project number
	Food supply (first line)	
1	Eastern restaurant	3, 4, 5, 6, 10, 11, 12, 13, 15, 17, 18, 19, 21, 24–32
2	Engineering restaurant	3–6, 12–15, 17, 18, 19, 21, 22, 24–32
3	Juice and ice cream shop	4–6, 11, 13, 15, 17, 18, 19, 21, 24–31
4	Roastry and chocolate shop	5, 6, 11, 13, 15, 17, 18, 19, 21, 24–31
5	Candies shop	4, 6, 10, 13, 15, 17, 18, 19, 21, 24–31
6	Supermarket	10, 15, 17–22, 24–33
	Tourism (first line)	
7	Van restaurant	4–6, 10, 12–15, 17–19, 21, 24–31
8	Turkish path	1, 4–6, 10, 13, 14, 15, 17–22, 24–33
9	Desert resort	1, 3–6, 10, 11, 13–33
	Autos (first line)	
10	Car garage	16–21, 24–29, 32, 33
11	Bike garage	16–21, 24–29, 32, 33
	Food supply (second line)	
12	Meat and fish shop	10, 15–21, 24–33
13	Fruit and vegetable shop	10, 15–21, 24–33
	Tourism (second line)	
14	Travel agency	16–19, 21–29
15	Laundry	17–21, 24–29, 32
	Autos and logistics (second line)	
16	Car rental agency	10, 17–22, 24–29
17	Internal transportation agency	10, 16, 18–22, 24–29
	Real estates (third line)	
18	Labor residency buildings	19, 21, 24, 27–29
19	Real estate agency	24–29
20	Stores	19, 21, 24, 27–29
21	General maintenance company	24–29, 32, 33
22	Office buildings	19, 21, 24, 27–29
23	Residential buildings	19, 21, 24, 27–29
	Business consultancies (third line)	
24	General business consultancy agency	10, 16–19, 22, 23, 27
25	Special gifts and printing house	10, 16–19, 22, 23, 27
26	Advertising and publishing agency	10, 16–19, 22, 23, 27
27	Internal audit agency	10, 16–19, 22, 23
28	Labor supply services/recruitment agency	10, 16–19, 22, 23, 27
29	External PRO/typing centre	10, 16–19, 22, 23, 27
	Food supply (third line)	
30	Central kitchen	24–29, 32, 33, 10, 15, 17–22
31	Kitchen equipment supply/ maintenance	10, 15, 17–22, 24–29, 32, 33
	General trading and logistics (third line)	
32	General trading company	17–29, 33
33	Import and export company	17–29

After 3 years of launching its first entrepreneurship project, this idea has been developed to be more practical so that it can meet the market requirements. The first group of projects are considered to be well developed and mature projects so that they can help the other dependent projects to sustain. There are certain number of challenges to reach to the ideal company divisions. These challenges are mainly within the bounds of the ability to manage and coordinate between other small businesses. In addition, the sizing of each small business should be determined in a way so that maximum utilization factor could be achieved for the company's resources.

Conclusion and Future Work

In conclusion, the project that has been introduced depends on the conglomerate business that defines certain number of small dependent entrepreneurship projects that help each other to sustain and expand. More researches should be done on resource allocation, as how to optimize the size of each project to get the maximum utilization factor of each available resource. Finally, the better the correlation between businesses, the higher the profit margin and overall stability.

References

Awogbenle, A. C., & Iwuamadi, K. C. (2010). Youth unemployment: Entrepreneurship development programme as an intervention mechanism. *African Journal of Business Management, 4*(6), 831.

Bows, A. J., Jr. (1966). *Problems in disclosure of segments of conglomerate companies*. New York: American Institute of Certified Public Accountants.

Dees, J. G., Emerson, J., & Economy, P. (2001). *Enterprising nonprofits: A toolkit for social entrepreneurs*. New York: Wiley.

Ghemawat, P., & Khanna, T. (1998). The nature of diversified business groups: A research design and two case studies. *The Journal of Industrial Economics, 46*(1), 35.

Hébert, R. F., & Link, A. N. (1989). In search of the meaning of entrepreneurship. *Small Business Economics, 1*(1), 39–49. doi: 10.1007/BF00389915

Encouraging entrepreneurship. 28 December 2013. Retrieved from www.gulfbusiness.com

Hill, C. W. L., & Hoskisson, R. E. (1987). Strategy and structure in the multiproduct firm. *Academy of Management Review, 12*(2), 331.

Markides, C. C., & Williamson, P. J. (1996). Corporate diversification and organizational structure: A resource-based view. *The Academy of Management Journal, 39*(2), 340–367.

Marshall, W. J., Yawitz, J. B., & Greenberg, E. (1984). Incentives for diversification and the structure of the conglomerate firm. *Southern Economic Journal, 51*(1), 1.

Noble, J. H. (1969). *Financial statement disclosure of conglomerate enterprises—The investors viewpoint*. Thesis Dissertation. Professional Papers. Page 2317.

Peneder, M. (2009). The meaning of entrepreneurship: A modular concept. *Journal of Industry, Competition and Trade, 9*(2), 77–99.

Third venture capital in the Middle East & North Africa Report. September 2013. Gulf Business, Retrieved from www.gulfbusiness.com.

UAE should foster entrepreneurship for sustainable growth. 29 August 2015. Gulf Business, Retrieved from www.gulfbusiness.com.

Schoof, U. (2006). *Stimulating youth entrepreneurship: Barriers and incentives to enterprise start-ups by young people* (Series on Youth and Entrepreneurship, SEED Working Paper No. 76). Bangkok: ILO Regional Office for Asia and the Pacific.

Yoong-Deok, J., & Young-Yong, K. (2004). Conglomerates and economic calculation. *Quarterly Journal of Austrian Economics, 7*(1), 53–64.

Hedrick-Wong, Y, & Jarrar, Y. Middle East and Africa inclusive growth report 2015. June 2015.

Chapter 54
A Web-Based Benchmarking Tool and Database for SMEs: Research in Progress

Norita Ahmad, Fariedah Maarof, Elgilani Eltahir Elshareif, and Jade Opulencia

Abstract This research focuses on developing a standard benchmarking tool and database that can be used by SMEs in the UAE to evaluate themselves against their competitors. The project presents an adaptation of an existing tool, QuickView, already in use in the USA. The short-term objectives of the project are to determine whether QuickView could be usable in the UAE, and to test whether SMEs in the UAE could be evaluated against the 4000 US SMEs on the QuickView database. Eventually, the goal is to help SMEs in the UAE improve bottom-line performance by transforming their practices for competitive advantage.

Keywords SMEs • Benchmarking tool • UAE • Performance measurement • Web-based

Introduction

In the midst of the current global economic downturn, the United Arab Emirates (UAE) is taking concrete steps to grow the economy, diversify from oil, and create quality employment for its citizens while moving towards a digitally enabled economy. In the UAE, it was estimated that small and medium enterprises (SMEs) contributed 60 % of gross domestic product (GDP) in 2015 (Faria, 2015). As such, the UAE Government recognizes the importance of SMEs as key to economic growth. SMEs are a dynamic sector of the economy that contribute significantly to the GDP and provide jobs for the majority of the private-sector employees. Given that the manufacturing sector has led the innovation and productivity growth over the past

N. Ahmad (✉)
American University of Sharjah, Sharjah, United Arab Emirates
e-mail: nahmad@aus.edu

F. Maarof • E.E. Elshareif • J. Opulencia
Canadian University of Dubai, PO Box 117781, Dubai, United Arab Emirates
e-mail: fariedah@cud.ac.ae; elgilani@cud.ac.ae; jade@cud.ac.ae

© Springer International Publishing Switzerland 2017   631
R. Benlamri, M. Sparer (eds.), *Leadership, Innovation and Entrepreneurship as Driving Forces of the Global Economy*, Springer Proceedings in Business and Economics, DOI 10.1007/978-3-319-43434-6_54

decade, strengthening the hands of SMEs becomes essential for the UAE to retain and improve its competitive edge in the dynamic global economies.

However, there lacks an applicable modeling methodology and tools to help SMEs to identify areas where changes would be needed in order for them to operate at a higher level of competence. This is critical, as SMEs typically have much limited resources. When facing massive uncertainty in today's dynamic and global economy, an SME's decisions on transforming their business operations are challenging and extremely risky. Therefore, a comprehensive investigation of SMEs' operation efficiencies is necessary, which aims to help them make assured and informed decisions to reposition themselves for competitive advantages.

This research focuses on developing a standard benchmarking tool and database that can be used by SMEs in the UAE to evaluate themselves against their competitors. The project presents an adaptation of an existing tool called QuickView, already in use in the USA. The short-term objectives of the project are twofold: (1) To determine whether QuickView, that is a primary assessment and business planning tool that was designed in the USA, could be usable in the UAE and (2) to test whether manufacturing SMEs in the UAE could be evaluated against the 4000 US SMEs on the QuickView database. The eventual goal of this research is to help SMEs in the UAE improve bottom-line performance by transforming their practices for competitive advantage. Specifically this research will

(1) Conduct a comprehensive study of variables that affect SMEs' performances in the global economy.
(2) Develop a generic, customizable, service-oriented, and adaptable business operations model to enable the quantitative analysis of a variety of strategic and operational challenges confronted by SMEs.
(3) Provide mechanisms to allow an individual SME to develop practical and prioritized.
(4) Countermeasures with greater certainty to transform its manufacturing business processes for a competitive advantage.

Research Background

The performance of an SME is affected by its business operational environment and adopted corresponding practice, which is quite often described if possible by using many quantifiable and nonquantifiable variables. Given the severely intensified competitive global market, how does an SME get better understanding of the problems and opportunities confronting its operations?

In this study, the development of a performance measurement model for SMEs is considered. The approach will be to take an existing benchmarking model, QuickView, which was developed by the Northeast Manufacturing Technology Center (NEMTC) located at Rensselaer Polytechnic Institute (RPI), one of the three original Manufacturing Extension Partnership Centers sponsored by the US Department of Commerce. NEMTC under grants from the National Institute of Standards and Technology (US Department of Commerce) and the New York State Department of Economic Development developed QuickView as an initial assessment and business-planning tool (Simons, Ron, & Michele, 1991). The idea behind QuickView development was to use the criteria that the large companies used to evaluate prospective suppliers and then use these criteria to measure the capability of the individual SME (Simons et al., 1991). QuickView is a simple but effective assessment tool to generate a performance report for an SME, which allows the SME to quickly identify how it performs when compared to its peers. QuickView questionnaire contained 229 questions, which were combined into 51 intermediate nodes called functional performance indicators. These 51 nodes were combined into 13 final factors called general performance indicators (e.g., grand total based on simple summation). The internal weighting system for the questions into nodes and the nodes into factors was determined empirically using focus groups of experienced extension agents and other manufacturing experts (Ahmad, 2005).

The questions are either quantifiable or nonquantifiable. When a question is nonquantifiable, it is answered with a number from a predefined scale-based group of numbers. These questions are widespread distributed in a variety of business aspects, stretching the following 12 critical operations:

1. Management practices (e.g., procedures, strategy, organizational structure)
2. Human resources (e.g., procedures, training)
3. Market management (e.g., customer service, trends)
4. Bidding/quoting (e.g., procedures, record keeping)
5. Purchasing (e.g., material management, supplier relations)
6. Engineering/design (e.g., procedures, technology)
7. Operations management (e.g., scheduling, delivery)
8. Manufacturing technology (e.g., equipment, tools, tolerances, maintenance procedures)
9. Maintenance (e.g., repairs, calibration checks)
10. Quality management (e.g., performance, procedures)
11. Pollution prevention and waste minimization (e.g., "green manufacturing," training)
12. Information management (e.g., how information is handled, technology support, and training)

Client's responses to this comprehensive questionnaire are plugged into QuickView, where a thorough analysis is done against over 4000 manufacturing companies' standards. The SME's performance profile is also compared to companies within their specific Standard Industrial Code (SIC) classification. A sophisticated expert-based benchmarking model is used to generate a report. The report is then used to help identify those operational areas that may need some attention, determine areas for capital and time investment, and highlight some of the nontechnical parts of the operation that may be delaying the company's growth and competitiveness. It is now in use in 38 states and has been so successful that the National Institute of Standards and Technology has designated it as a national model for SME assessments (CNYTDO, 2012).

As SMEs grow, they increasingly need connectivity to the world economy, knowledge about market opportunities, and a better understanding of their own operations. Apparently, there is a need for an applicable modeling methodology, which not only models the unique behaviors of an SME but also helps the SME optimize its priority of the countermeasures in a quantitative and assured fashion.

It is important to note that even though QuickView has been used for more than 20 years in the USA, it has two main limitations due to its large and fixed structure (Ahmad, 2005). First, it lacks an effective structure for formulating the selection problem and requires discrimination among large numbers of interacting, hard-to-evaluate qualitative and quantitative factors. Second, QuickView is also very limiting in its weighting and scoring aspects. In order to modify its weighting and scoring, the entire system must be recalculated. Therefore, the next step of the research is to update and modify the current structure of QuickView model to make it an open structure to allow for easy modification and update of specific industry and country. Ultimately, a Web-based version of the improved QuickView will be developed by utilizing a dedicated Web-based database server that collects, stores, manipulates, evaluates, and translates the acquired responses from participating SMEs.

The Assessment of SMEs in the UAE Using QuickView

This research seeks to expand upon previous research on performance measurement of SMEs (see Ahmad, 2005; Ahmad, Berg, & Simons, 2006; Ahmad & Piovoso, 2007; Ahmad, Piovoso, & Qiu, 2007; Ahmad & Qiu, 2006, 2009). As discussed above, this project will test the validity of QuickView by using it in a sample of SMEs in the UAE.

The research tasks can be summarized as follows:

(1) Phase 1: Conduct a survey sample of 20–30 SMEs.
(2) Phase 2: Based on the result of Phase 1, (a) if it was determined that the US QuickView model did not fit the SMEs in the UAE then a UAE-specific model and database will be created and (b) if it was determined that the US QuickView model did fit the SMEs in the UAE then an open-structure QuickView will be developed to allow it to be modified and updated for specific industry and country.
(3) Phase 3: Regardless of the result in Phase 1, a Web-based version of the improved QuickView will be developed. This can be accomplished by utilizing a dedicated Web-based database server that collects, stores, manipulates, evaluates, and translates the acquired responses from participating SMEs.

The first phase of the research was done at the beginning of 2015 and it took us more than 4 months to collect the data. At the end of the data collection period, we managed to collect 20 samples. The main objective of the first phase was to answer the question: "Should a non-US SME be compared to a US SMEs in the current database?" In order to help us answer the question, we looked at two different issues. The first issue was about the methodology itself—the questionnaires and the implementation of survey. The second issue was about the results of the survey—comparison between the data of the US database and the data of the UAE sample.

Methodology

The survey was conducted by visiting the companies that agreed to participate and this required a major commitment of time for each of them (phone calls, e-mails, and two to three visits of approximately 90 min each). Even though we believe that this process developed a much deeper knowledge of these companies as well as more reliable answers than a mail survey (Easterby-Smith, Thorpe, & Lowe, 1991), it was very time consuming for both the companies and the researchers.

Initial Findings

It is important to note that although the sample size was very small, we managed to draw some initial inferences and had a few interesting observation to share. The first observation was that the application of the survey was more difficult than antici-pated. The companies were somewhat reluctant to enter this process. We contacted about 100 companies and received responses from less than 20% of them. Even those who agreed to participate were not very happy with the total number of ques-tions that they had to answer. Most of them answered the vast majority of the questions but none of them completed the survey in its entirety.

Another observation was related to the fact that QuickView was developed more than 20 years ago when the requirements for manufacturing effectiveness/success were based on aspects that would be considered as "traditional" now, e.g., total quality management. In addition, given the fact that we are living in a golden age of technologies, we should also incorporate technology-related questions in our questionnaires.

On the positive side, several of the companies that participated in the survey saw the value in this kind of assessment and provided valuable feedback to us. For example, from the feedback, we realized that the approach to economic develop-ment needs a major strategic rethink. Current trends suggest that wealth generation will come from an integration or combination of production/operation activities, professional services, and information technology at the level of the individual SME. Specifically we should explore how the integration of different activities could be used to provide a basis for innovation and enterprise/entrepreneurial initia-tives that result in SMEs being able to provide value that makes their offerings attractive in international markets (differentiation), as well as internationally com-petitive. We should also explore on the importance of contributions by the private sector particularly in providing necessary services as well as the public sector in facilitating and encouraging linkages, and in providing programs to facilitate and help SMEs improve their international competitiveness.

These trends suggest that the scope and nature of the competitiveness of the firm could usefully be reviewed to suit the particular requirements and conditions of the businesses in the UAE in relation to international markets in a knowledge-intensive world. These trends also suggest that it is appropriate to start by analyzing the appropriateness of QuickView and developing a more appropriate benchmarking measure later.

A further benefit of this approach is that it would allow the researchers to arrive at a more parsimonious scale for benchmarking purposes. We would anticipate the following contributions to literatures:

1. Development of a tool for evaluating the requirements for success (or key innovation management capabilities) for SME businesses in the UAE in the new knowledge-intensive environment.
2. Identifying key dimensions influencing the performance of SME businesses in the UAE.
3. Comparison of the key dimensions influencing the performance of SME businesses in the UAE across industry sectors.
4. Comparison of the key dimensions of this benchmarking framework with those of a corresponding framework in a developed economy (with QuickView in the USA).

We would anticipate the following practical contributions:

1. A (hopefully parsimonious) tool for managers to benchmark the capabilities of their business and to identify areas for improvement that would be relevant to their situation in the UAE for competing in international markets.
2. A benchmarking tool that would allow comparison with requirements for similar businesses in the USA (using the QuickView database), that is, allow international benchmarking.
3. Findings that would allow the development of appropriate and relevant workshops for business managers to support the development of international competitiveness in their own businesses.

Discussion and Implications

In summary, we would expect that this project could contribute to a significant degree to both knowledge and practice in the field of business development, innovation management capability, and international competitiveness at the local and international levels.

The model will be structured for stepwise testing and validation. As new findings are found, they will be incorporated into the model. So the developed model can be refined and retuned and eventually be used as a standard Web-based benchmarking tool and database in the UAE.

The high complexity and need of full engagements from many participants (organizations and individuals) often prohibit companies from taking risk. This investigation provides an opportunity to investigate a potential reference model for further exploring competency model assisting manufacturers in improving their long-term competitiveness.

The managerial and research implication of this study is fourfold. First, this exploration targets hundreds of quantified variables affecting SME performance under the umbrella of the emerging global manufacturing and services. A comprehensive and better understanding of today's SME best practices in a quantitative manner will result. Second, the research will advance the knowledge basis of transforming current manufacturing enterprises into more coherent, integrated, and competitive service-oriented ones. Third, the proposed innovative methodology will solidify the foundation for further research in a variety of business process transformation services across manufacturing and other industries. Fourth, the emerging manufacturing competencies in developing countries have toughened the landscape and intensified the competition; therefore an applicable modeling methodology can be used to help an individual SME to develop practical and prioritized countermeasures with greater certainty to transform its manufacturing business processes for a competitive advantage.

References

Ahmad, N. (2005). *The design, development and analysis of a multi criteria decision support system model: Performance Benchmarking of small to medium-sized manufacturing enterprise (SME)*. Ph.D. Thesis. Rensselaer Polytechnic Institute, New York.

Ahmad, N., Berg, D., & Simons, G. R. (2006). The integration of analytical hierarchy process and data envelopment analysis in a multi-criteria decision-making problem. *International Journal of Information Technology & Decision Making, 5*(2), 263–276.

Ahmad, N., & Piovoso, M. (2007). Measuring efficiency of small and medium-sized manufacturing enterprises using partial least squares. *International Journal Services Operations and Informatics, 2*(1), 38–52.

Ahmad, N., Piovoso, M., & Qiu, R. (2007). Partial least squares (PLS) for SME's performance measurement. In: *Proceedings of the 17th International Conference on Flexible Automation and Intelligent Manufacturing*, June 18–20, 2007, Philadelphia, pp. 407–414.

Ahmad, N., & Qiu, R. (2006). Effectiveness evaluation services for small to medium-sized manufacturing enterprise. In: *2006 IEEE International Conference on Service Operations and Logistics, and Informatics*, Shanghai, China, June 21–23, 2006, pp. 1106–1112.

Ahmad, N., & Qiu, R. (2009). Integrated model of operations effectiveness of small to medium sized manufacturing enterprises. *Journal of Intelligent Manufacturing, 20*(1), 79–89.

Central New York Technology Development Organization. (2012). Retrieved November 12, 2015, from http://www.cnytdo.org/.

Easterby-Smith, M., Thorpe, R., & Lowe, A. (1991). *Management research: An introduction*. London: Sage.

Faria, W. (2015). SMEs vital to country's GDP growth. Retrieved November 24, 2015, from http://gulftoday.ae/portal/e290e5e6-a43f-4745-b484-cc54108d0d1d.aspx.

Simons, G. R., Ron, B., & Michele, C. (1991). Technology transfer in supplier development programs. *The Journal of Technology Transfer, 16*(4), 23–28.

Chapter 55
Analysis of Start-Up Ecosystems in Germany and in the USA

Richard C. Geibel and Meghana Manickam

Abstract The start-up ecosystems in Germany and in the USA are different in several dimensions and they have a huge impact on the success of start-ups. In this study the factors that affect the start-up ecosystems are compared. What start-ups consider as critical to their success and how this varies based on the location of the start-ups are analyzed. Using the developed scoring mechanism, the study compares the relative scores of various success factors between the German and American start-ups to identify areas for improvement. The findings suggest that Germany is successful in implementing co-working spaces and incubators but it lacks on accelerator programs. Further, it needs to develop a better support system for their start-ups while the German start-ups themselves need to focus on building a stronger internal team in order to boost the start-up ecosystem.

Keywords Success factors • Internal factors • External factors • Support from incubator/accelerator • American start-ups • German start-ups • Scoring mechanism • Start-up ecosystem • Areas for improvement • Start-up environment

Introduction

Entrepreneurship is a key factor that drives economic growth and innovation of a country and helps deliver new opportunities for all its citizens (Cordova et al., 2013). In order to compete in world markets, countries need to have the capacity and wherewithal to support the high rates of establishment and dissolution of start-ups (Bednarzik, 2000). Currently the USA ranks as the number one place, which

R.C. Geibel (✉)
Fresenius University of Applied Sciences, Cologne, Germany
e-mail: geibel@hs-fresenius.de

M. Manickam, M.Sc.
Department of Management Science and Engineering, Stanford University,
Stanford, CA, USA
e-mail: meghanam@stanford.edu

© Springer International Publishing Switzerland 2017   639
R. Benlamri, M. Sparer (eds.), *Leadership, Innovation and Entrepreneurship
as Driving Forces of the Global Economy*, Springer Proceedings in Business
and Economics, DOI 10.1007/978-3-319-43434-6_55

provides the most conducive environment for entrepreneurs while Germany lags behind (Nisen et al., 2013).

A report issued by the Global Entrepreneurship Monitor indicates that the percentage of adults involved in start-ups in the USA hit a record high of 13 % in 2013 while it was just 5 % in Germany (Ernesto & Bosma, 2013). Taking into account that a large percentage of start-ups fail, it becomes even more critical to ensure their success in countries like Germany to assure the positive development of the start-up ecosystem.

The success of a start-up depends on a plethora of factors. Given the rapidly growing popularity and importance of entrepreneurship around the world and the high risks associated with it, it is imperative to understand what the critical factors are for the success of a start-up. While existing literature focus on factors necessary for the success of a start-up in the pre-launch phase, there is a necessity to examine further how these factors vary across different geographical locations and culture.

This study focuses on a comprehensive understanding of what the critical success factors are for start-ups in different locations, specifically in the USA and Germany, and identifies key areas that the start-ups and incubators/accelerators need to focus their resources on in order to be successful. However, it is important to remember that this study is subjective despite efforts to be as objective as possible. The study develops a set of hypotheses based on surveys and expert interviews.

Success Factors

Critical success factor is defined as those characteristics, conditions, or variables that, when properly sustained, maintained, or managed, can have a significant impact on the success of a firm competing in a particular industry (Leidecker & Bruno, 1984). In order to determine what the critical success factors for start-ups are, we conducted an extensive literature review and developed a framework containing 25 important factors. These were analyzed to determine the top three critical success factors within each of the three categories, which is explained further in the next section.

Categorization of the Success Factors

The 25 success factors were grouped into three categories as "internal factors," "external factors," and "support from incubator/accelerator." Internal factors pertain to those variables that come from within the start-up and over which the founders have a great degree of control. External factors pertain to the external forces, which develop as a result of the environment in which the start-up is placed and over which the founders have little or no control (Feinleib, 2012). Finally, the last category refers to the factors, which are specific to the incubator/accelerator, if any, that the start-up is associated with.

Table 55.1 Categorization of the success factors

Internal factors (A)	External factors (B)	Support from incubator/accelerator (C)
1. Employees/team	1. Government policies	1. Mentorship
2. Work culture	2. Political stability	2. Expanding network connections
3. Co-founders	3. Location	3. Financial funding
4. Organization structure	4. Access to talent	4. Tax, legal, business, etc. support
5. Exit strategy	5. New market access	5. Infrastructure
6. Marketing strategy	6. Access to existing market	6. Workshops/events
7. Customer network	7. Competitors	
8. Product	8. Prior experience	
9. Ability to scale		
10. Company pitch		
11. Balancing work and family life		

This categorization allows for a clear understanding of what set of critical success factors play an important role in determining whether a start-up is successful or not. It also allows for easy comparison between start-ups across different geographical locations and identifications of areas of improvement. The list of the various success factors considered for our research can be found in Table 55.1.

Methodology

In order to determine what the success factors for a start-up were, this study was divided into two parts. The first part involved the identification and mapping of the various success factors into the three categories. The second part involved developing a scoring mechanism that would allow for easy comparison of the different success factors across different start-ups globally. Using this scoring mechanism, start-ups in the USA and in Germany were asked to score the different success factors and also identify how favorable or how well each of the success factors was satisfied. The average scores of the success factors in the USA and in Germany were then compared to identify areas of improvement. The scores by the start-ups in the USA were used as a benchmark in order to determine how the start-ups in Germany were currently performing.

Scoring Mechanism

Each success factor in the three categories is scored on a scale of 1–10 with 1 being the least critical and 10 being the most critical. Further, each start-up was also asked to score on a scale of 1–10 how well each factor was satisfied or was favorable to the start-up, 1 being 0 % satisfied/very unfavorable and 10 being 100 % satisfied/extremely favorable.

The scores for each success factor in each of the three categories are then averaged individually for all the start-ups in the USA to obtain a composite score for each success factor. The same is repeated for the start-ups in Germany. The top three critical success factors in each category were then further analyzed and used for developing recommendations.

Further, the composite scores of the different success factors within a category are averaged to give an overall score for each category for the USA and for Germany.

Selection of American Start-Ups

For the purpose of this study, we identified several successful start-ups from the USA, which were a part of top incubators/accelerators such as Techstars and Y-Combinator (Gruber, 2012). Data was collected from 17 successful start-ups located in the Silicon Valley, New York, Boston, Texas, and other upcoming start-up locations. Data was collected primarily through online surveys among others, which represented different geographical locations, industries, and size.

Selection of German Start-Ups

Similarly, successful start-ups in Germany were selected from the Cologne region due to its importance as an entrepreneurial hub alongside Berlin, London, Amsterdam, and other cities in Europe (Top 10 Most Vibrant Entrepreneurial Ecosystem Hubs in Europe, 2013) in view of its high GDP and rapidly developing start-up ecosystem for the first phase of the study. Further, its close proximity to our location made it possible to collect first-hand data through in-person interviews in addition to online surveys. As with the American start-ups, these start-ups in Cologne represented a diverse range of industries and size. Currently, more data from start-ups is being collected for the second phase of the study.

Results

The data from the survey showed that both the US and German start-ups place almost equal importance on each of the three categories, with German start-ups placing a much higher importance on the role incubator/accelerator play in their success. However, the German start-up ecosystem needs to further focus on improving how well they are able to achieve ideal levels of satisfaction of different factors within

Fig. 55.1 Overall score for perceived importance of different categories

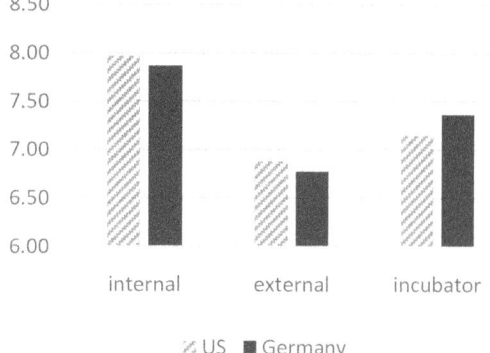

Fig. 55.2 Overall score for favorability/satisfaction of different categories

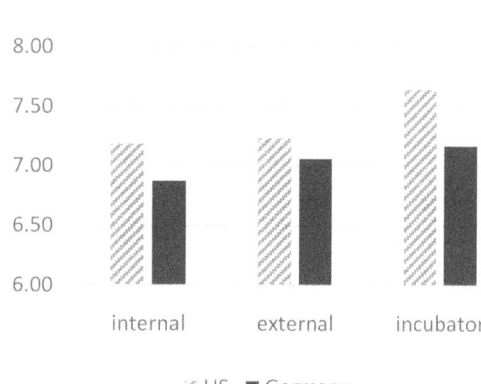

each category, particularly when it comes to support from incubator/accelerator. See Figs. 55.1 and 55.2 for the scores. The numbers by themselves mean nothing; it is the relative comparison of the scores that is of prime importance.

Internal Factors

From our research, it appears that the US start-ups place a high level of importance on the co-founders, work culture, and employees while the German start-ups place an inordinate amount of importance on their product, marketing strategy, and their ability to scale. The detailed scores of the different internal factors (A) are shown in Figs. 55.3 and 55.4.

Although these factors are just as important, we hypothesize that the US start-ups are very people oriented and first focus on the team and build a strong core foundation before developing their other capabilities. The German start-ups, on the other hand, focus more on the product/idea.

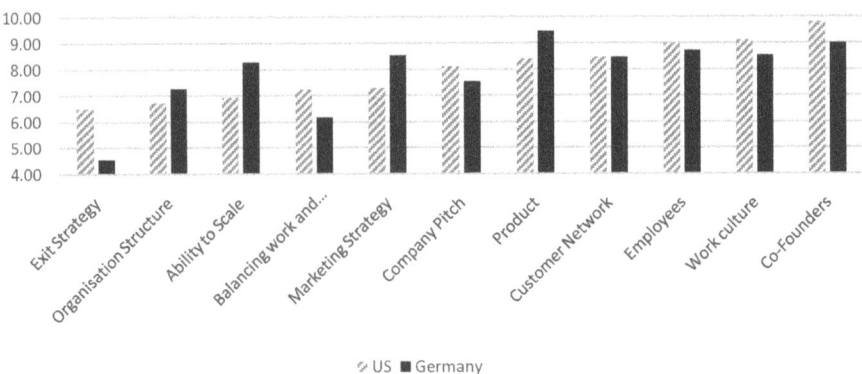

Fig. 55.3 Detailed score of importance of different internal factors

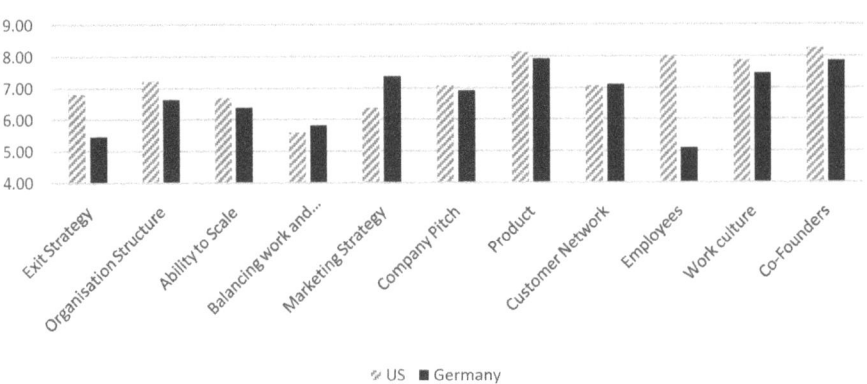

Fig. 55.4 Detailed score of favorability/satisfaction of different internal factors

Co-founders

Most founders in the USA feel strongly that it is important to have a co-founder with complementary skill sets with whom they have worked with in the past and who share a common vision for the company.

Employees

Finding the right people who share the company's vision and passion and who bring the right set of talents plays an important role in ensuring the start-up's success. Clearly Germany has yet to develop its talent pool to include a more internationally diverse population. Further, venture capitalists consider a good team to be one of the most important factors while making an investment (Harroch, 2013). Hence, to secure the required funding to market their product, the German start-ups first need to focus on building a stronger team.

Work Culture

The work culture sets the aims and aspirations for the current team and future hires. It has a direct impact on employee satisfaction, organization's ability to recruit, company image, and the product.

External Factors

Among the external factors, access to new and existing markets and access to talent are considered the top three success factors by both German and US start-ups. However, all three factors fall short of their US counterparts when it comes to how favorable each of these factors are. The detailed scores are shown in Figs. 55.5 and 55.6.

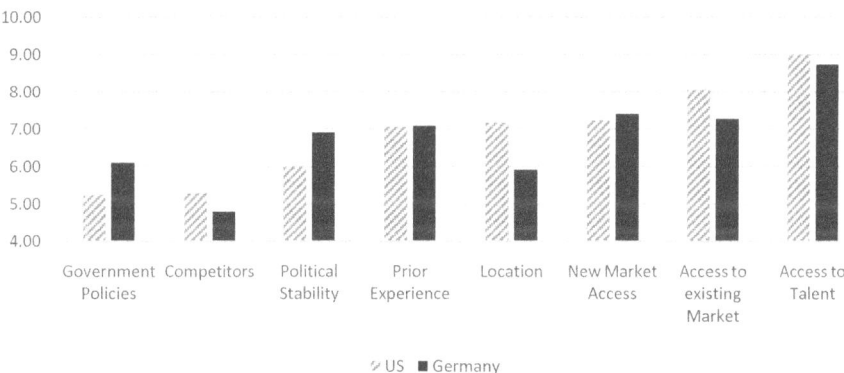

Fig. 55.5 Detailed score of importance of different external factors

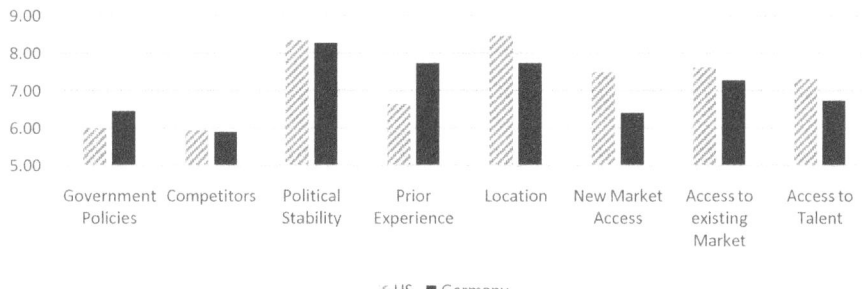

Fig. 55.6 Detailed score of favorability/satisfaction of different external factors

Access to Talent

Most of the successful start-up hubs in the USA are located in the Silicon Valley, New York, and Boston which have close ties with top universities such as Stanford University, MIT, Harvard, University of California, Berkeley, among others which boast a strong and talented international community of students. This makes it easier for start-ups to gain access to the top talent from across the world. The poor access to top talent in Germany also has a negative impact on how satisfied the entrepreneurs are with their employees. This is indicated by the poor employee score in the previous section.

Access to Existing Market and New Market

Majority of the Americans are the first among their peers to try out new gadgets and services (Soper, 2013). The USA has a higher concentration of early adopters making it an ideal hub for innovation and creativity. On the other hand, Germans are quite risk averse (Hedderich, 1999) making them a difficult customer segment to market new ideas since they focus on early and late majority. These factors combined together result in a higher favorability when it comes to location when compared to Germany.

Support from Incubator/Accelerator

While developing network connections, financial aid, and mentorship is considered to be critical by both start-ups in the USA and Germany, German incubators/accelerators appear to be more successful in providing workshops, infrastructure, and tax and legal support. The detailed scores of the different factors related to support from incubator/accelerator (C) are shown in Figs. 55.7 and 55.8.

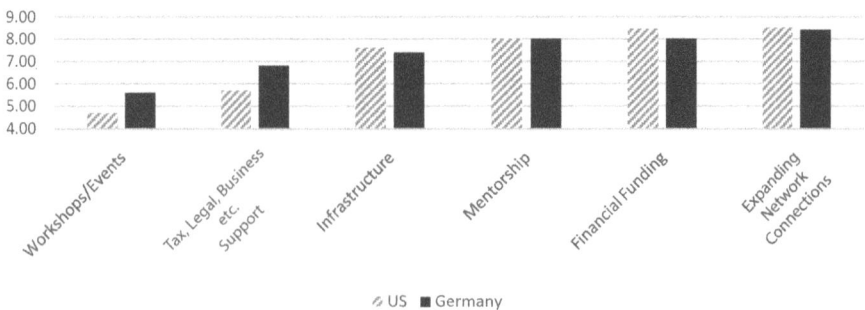

Fig. 55.7 Detailed score of importance of support from incubator/accelerator

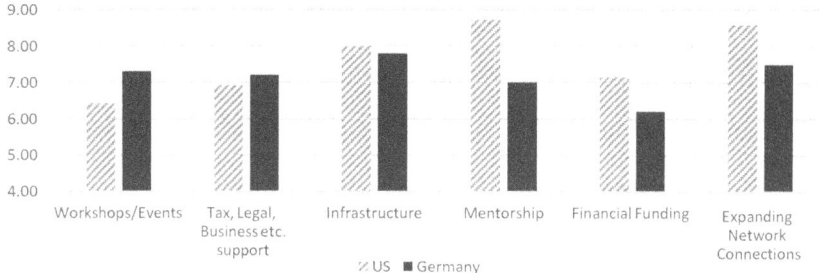

Fig. 55.8 Detailed score of favorability/satisfaction of support from incubator/accelerator

However, it is important to remember that German incubators tend to lean towards the model of a co-working space rather than the traditional American incubator/accelerator model, which is profit driven. That might explain the discrepancy in the scores. Therefore, considering that support from incubator/accelerator was rated the highest among the three categories, Germany needs to develop a system, which provides start-ups with better financial funding if they are to succeed.

Network Connection

This provides founders with potential new collaborators and customers, better insight into the industry and competitors, and knowledge of new technologies.

Financial Assistance

Initial funding in order to launch the idea and long-term funding from investors play an important role in ensuring that start-ups are able to successfully transform their ideas from the drawing board into real-life solutions. While most start-ups in the USA have access to a plethora of investors, the same is limited in Germany. This makes it difficult to raise pre-seed, first, and second round of capital and to scale the company quickly.

Mentorship

A good mentor will be able to help steer founders away from many mistakes that first-time entrepreneurs will likely make. By drawing knowledge from a plethora of experiences and other companies, founders can learn faster and avoid the same pitfalls while developing better strategies more efficiently.

However, this is slowly improving in Germany and entrepreneurs are gaining new insights through various business plan competitions and easier access to experienced entrepreneurs in their field.

Areas of Improvement for German Start-Ups

Based on our first phase of study, it is clear that the US start-up ecosystem has an intricate web of mentors, talent pool, easier access to markets and funding, strong founding teams, and more willing and curious customers to boost the start-up environment. When it comes to internal factors, German start-ups should focus on developing their internal team, particularly building a stronger employee base and work culture while also improving their exit strategies.

Regarding external factors, Germany needs to attract a more internationally diverse population to its universities which will act as a talent pool from which start-ups can draw new recruits with diverse skill sets. One of the biggest obstacles in this process is the widespread use of German as the prime language for teaching. This deters foreign students from studying in Germany. Encouraging teaching in English will act as a stimulus in attracting more international students.

Finally, while most incubators in Germany tend to provide facilities more aligned to a co-working space, they should also focus on connecting founders to more experienced mentors in the industry and venturing capitalists to secure funding. However, it is imperative to note that these recommendations are made based on a limited data set and a explorative analysis. A more in-depth and objective analysis will be performed in the second phase of the study when we have collected data from several more start-ups in other regions.

Future Work

The next step in this study is to collect data from emerging start-up hubs in Germany such as Berlin through a combination of online surveys and in-person interviews. This data will be used to revisit our scores for the different factors and refine our recommendations. We aim to further analyze how the success factors vary based on gender and industry sector and what can be done to encourage the growth of more female entrepreneurs. Further we aim to develop more objective results by back testing our hypothesis with the various levels of success of the different start-ups.

Conclusion

It can be concluded from this study that for the most part, the top success factors in the three different categories remain the same for both German and US start-ups despite the different locations. However, the main difference in start-up success arises primarily from how well founders are able to meet certain criteria and how favorable certain factors are to the start-up. While currently the USA has developed a very conducive environment for the start-up development, Germany needs to focus on developing better support systems to boost the start-up environment.

References

Bednarzik, R. W. (2000). Role of entrepreneurship in US and European job growth. *Monthly Labor Review, 123*, 3–16.

Cordova, D., et al. (2013). *Creating the environment for entrepreneurial success*. Center for International Private Enterprise. http://www.cipe.org/creating-environment-entrepreneurial-success.

Ernesto, J., & Bosma, N. (2013). Global entrepreneurship monitor 2012 global report. GEM.

Feinleib, D. (2012). Why startups fail. Forbes, 13 November 2012. http://www.forbes.com/sites/davefeinleib/2012/11/13/why-startups-fail-2/.

Gruber, F. (2012). Top 15 US startup accelerators ranked; Y combinator and techstars on top. Tech Cocktail, 22 August 2012. http://tech.co/top-startup-accelerators-ranked-2012-08.

Harroch, R. (2013). 65 questions venture capitalists will ask startups. Forbes, 10 June 2013. http://www.forbes.com/sites/allbusiness/2013/06/10/65-questions-venture-capitalists-will-ask-startups/.

Hedderich, N. (1999). When cultures clash: Views from the professions. *Die Unterrichtspraxis/Teaching German, 32*(2), 158–165.

Leidecker, J. K., & Bruno, A. V. (1984). Identifying and using critical success factors. *Long Range Planning, 17*(1), 23–32.

Nisen, M., et al. (2013). The US is by far the best place in the world to be an entrepreneur. Business Insider, 29 August 2013. http://www.businessinsider.com/best-country-to-be-an-entrepreneur-2013-8#!IJHsb.

Soper, T. (2013). Majority of U.S. adults call themselves early adopters of new technology. GeekWire, 22 January 2013. http://www.geekwire.com/2014/study-majority-americans-now-early-adopters-new-technology/.

Top 10 Most Vibrant Entrepreneurial Ecosystem Hubs in Europe. (2013). Foundum, 11 June 2013. http://blog.foundum.com/blog/2013/06/11/most-vibrant-entrepreneurial-ecosystem-hubs-in-europe/.

Chapter 56
Zero-Debt Start-Up in Capital-Intensive Solar Industry: A Case Study on Rays Experts

Nishtha Gupta, Monika Singla, and Udit Agrawal

Abstract The objective of this chapter is to present the case of a young entrepreneur from India. Rahul Gupta is the founder of Rays Experts, a solar energy entrepreneurial venture. The solar energy sector, according to a study by AT Kearney (Unni et al. Solar power and India's energy future (Publication). Retrieved December 31, 2015, from ATKearney website: http://www.atkearney.in/documents/10192/692844/ Solar Power in India—Preparing to Win.pdf/b6b34499-8285-4813-9d66-ecdc 293a8537, 2013), is slated to become worth billions of dollars over the next 8 years. It is a clean source of energy that provides not only a fillip to employment and economic growth but will also never run out. When only very few start-ups grow in the infrastructure sector in India, Rays Experts is giving large solar plant ventures a run for their money in just 2 years. Aspects related to the unique capital structure (it has no long-term debt on its balance sheet), financial management (playing with fixed costs), and unique business model are presented and analyzed in this case. Accounting ratio analysis has been used as a tool to understand company's financial strength. In a country like India that is still developing a successful entrepreneurial venture like Rays Experts, with no debt on its balance sheet, would provide very useful learning in terms of the methodology adopted for starting a successful venture with organic growth in the capital-intensive industry. It also sheds some light on the problems that a start-up can face in case of absence of external funding or debt.

Keywords Zero-debt start-up • Entrepreneurship • Indian solar start-up • Renewable energy • Capital structure

---

When everything seems to be going against you, remember that the airplane takes off against the wind, not with it.
Henry Ford, founder of Ford Motor Company.

N. Gupta (✉) • M. Singla • U. Agrawal
Indian Institute of Technology Delhi, Hauz Khas, New Delhi, India
e-mail: tt1120891@iitd.ac.in; smz138504@dms.iitd.ac.in; ch7120184@iitd.ac.in

© Springer International Publishing Switzerland 2017
R. Benlamri, M. Sparer (eds.), *Leadership, Innovation and Entrepreneurship as Driving Forces of the Global Economy*, Springer Proceedings in Business and Economics, DOI 10.1007/978-3-319-43434-6_56

Introduction and Case Methodology

Ever realized the importance of being at the right place, and at the right time? Then ask Rahul Gupta, founder and owner of Rays Experts, today India's third largest solar power firm, who instead of taking up a job from campus placements at IIT Roorkee, started his own company Rays Experts. He came across the idea of getting into this renewable energy business during his engineering graduation through a newspaper article and was quick enough to act within a year. He started this company in 2010 with a capital of INR 0.01 crores which he had earned through his independent consultancy projects in college. As reported by India Today (2009), solar was just being introduced in the country then and the first commercial solar power plant was just being set up in the state of Punjab (Chhabra, "India's first solar power plant opens in Punjab," 2009). He and his sister, Nidhi Gupta, are the only shareholders of this private limited company. This is the story of very-down-to-earth small-town guy, Rahul Gupta, who was told at his placement that he needs to go through his entire curriculum of engineering again just to be anywhere. His power to struggle probably had other plans for him.

The portfolio of around 15 top Indian companies working in the solar sector was studied, and one of them, a conglomerate, big by name, popularity, and work, Tata Solar Power, was chosen for benchmarking. Relevant global comparison is also brought out.

Different financial records of Ray Experts for the past 5 years were minutely studied and were compared with Tata Power Solar and the power generation and supply industry. The data for the latter two was obtained from *Capitaline database*, last assessed on 21 April 2015. The power generation and supply industry consist of all sources of power, including thermal, hydro, and wind as well. Data of Rays Experts for the year 2015–2016, wherever present, is projected data.

Formal and informal meetings and telephonic conversations with the director and financial head of the company were held and recorded for getting their quotes and experiences. The staff was contacted for collecting the relevant data. Some inferences and suggestions have been made based on these talks and the data available in the public domain.

Company Profile

Solar sector in India has four segments: basic raw material manufacturers, module manufacturers, EPC, and IPPs. Basic raw materials come from mainly Taiwan and China. Module manufacturers in India include TATA, Moser Baer, Waaree, Vikram Solar, and other small players with small capacities. IPPs or developers, like SunEdison, Azure, and ACME, own the solar power plants and give out tenders to EPCs like Rays Experts, Sterling and Wilson Solar, TATA, Mahindra, and LnT to install the solar power plants.

Table 56.1 Relative costs for installing small- and large-scale power plants

Capacity (MW)	Overnight capital costs (US$/kWh)	Fixed operation and maintenance cost (US$/ kW-year)	Variable O&M cost (US$/MWh)
20	4183	27.75	0.00
150	3873	24.69	0.00

Rays Experts is an engineering, procurement, and construction (EPC) company in this sector, but still is a lot different from its competitors. Normal EPC companies in this sector simply take solar power plant installation projects, say for 5 MW, and buy the materials needed and install it at the site. On the other hand, Rays holds the ideology that everyone should have access to renewable energy irrespective of their financial capacity. It creates a large infrastructure base at one place of capacity, say 50 MW. The company then takes turnkey projects for setting up the solar power plants and provides end-to-end services. It takes care of all the issues like land acquisition, clearances, permits, local issues, inspection, generation guarantees, performance, and generation losses, and connects the electricity produced to the main grid. Hence, it is able to cater to ten projects demanding 5 MW capacity at much cheaper rates. It uses the principle of dividing the fixed costs, as they increase slowly in comparison to the capacity increment (Table 56.1). It also takes the responsibility of the operation and maintenance of the power plant. Just investing the money and doing no other hard work, as Rays takes care of every step involved, and obtaining renewable energy at much cheaper rates is what makes Rays lucrative to clients. The company targets to win the EPC projects from independent power producer (IPP) giants.

The majority of Rays' revenue comes from EPC projects and some part of it from operations and maintenance and other after installation tasks. From this year onwards O&M will be earning a revenue of around Rs 7 crores as the company plans to do away with initial discounts and schemes.

Within a span of less than 5 years, the company has grown to boast of an experience of 232 MW of solar power production, out of which 182 MW projects are successfully commissioned and already performing. It presently has the market share of 3.4 % of the total installed capacity of India. As of FY-14, the company's installed capacity was 137 MW against total installed capacity of India being 4000 MW.

This feat may not appear as impressive without the fact that it is a 100 % debt-free company and had the annual turnover of INR 280 crores in the FY 2013–2014 and turnover of INR 350 crores in FY 2014–2015. It today boasts of being in top three portfolio holders in India in MW-size project development companies and has had an excellent track record of commissioning all projects before deadline.

On being asked the USP, Rahul Gupta believes that the company's use of supervisory control and data acquisition (SCADA) is what differentiates Rays from its competitors. In simple terms, SCADA is a data acquisition system which helps in real-time data transfer and analysis, helping the company to monitor the solar panels from anywhere in the world. The supervisors are able to monitor the plants even from their homes. No competitor in India is using this technology currently. Fun fact about this system is that this program was built by an undergraduate summer intern!

Solar Parks: Playing Around with the Fixed Costs

The solar power sector is a capital-intensive sector with large investments required in the fixed capital or infrastructure. There are virtually negligible operating costs involved. Rahul Gupta changed the common players' business model to optimize these fixed costs so that the break-even point and payback period are reduced.

The large capital costs become a problem with the customers who want to have smaller capacity installed. The capital costs per unit of electricity produced shoot up by nearly 8% when we scale down the plant from 150 to 20 MW. One has to keep in mind that this may be dependent on a number of factors like location, labor availability, regulations, and degree of scale down but about 8–10% as shown above can be taken as an estimate for increase in the capital cost/(unit of electricity produced) for the scale-down of medium-scale power plant (about 150–200 MW) to small scale (about 10–20 MW). Thus, as we increase the capacity of solar parks to an optimal limit, the payback period is greatly reduced, since the fixed cost, which makes up more than 90% of the costs in this industry, remains constant for a range. This effect is much more visible if the scale-down is from 20 MW to say 1–2 MW. Now, for an investor with limited amounts of funds available, this scenario presents a major problem since he or she will not be able to invest in a project with an ability to generate adequate cash flows.

Rays Experts addresses this problem through the concept of *solar parks*. This can be understood in the following way. Let us assume that some investors like to invest in the solar power because of the high rates of return in this industry (approximately 100%). The company gives the investors the freedom to invest an amount as low as 1 crore. Now had these small-scale investors directly invested in an individual solar power plant, it would have been a 1–2 MW plant and would not have been able to generate enough returns. This would have made this sector less attractive to the investors. Now, with the present model, even if the investor is investing a comparatively smaller amount (INR 1 crore), his or her investment is getting connected to a park of say 50 MW capacity. This, because of the economies of scale, is able to provide higher returns and have a lower payback period and thus becomes an attractive investment option. Thus, the present model is attracting the investors from other sectors into the solar power generation sector by increasing the returns and having a lesser payback period.

But, again, how it manages the funds, and most importantly the land?

Land

The company requires a huge amount of investment to acquire land on which it can install solar parks. Rahul devised a novel method for acquiring this land.

The market value of real estate in India is very high and always on a growth trend. For a company that is entirely surviving on internal cash flows and has no source of funding from outside, it becomes very hard to acquire land to install a solar park. Since this investment has to be made at the very inception of the project, there has to be a source of funding that is able to cater to this huge requirement of capital at the very start of the project.

Now, Rays looks out for some investors and asks them to just invest the money into the land which will be used for solar parks and assures them fixed returns regardless of the success or failure of the project. The entire risk of the project is borne by the company. The company keeps giving them the assured returns for a predefined specified period of time. After the project shifts into the later phase of the development, the IPP players, who had asked for the installment of power generation capacity, begin paying their dues. From this payment, the company buys back the land from the investors as predefined in the contract.

This methodology has its own risks. The company cannot take debt as it doesn't have the leveraging capacity. There can be cash gaps if the project or the payment is delayed. How does the company manage these cash gaps? That is, without having any leveraging capacity, having zero debt-equity ratios, how does the company deal with the shortage of funds in fulfilling the orders when the advance given is not enough to complete the project?

Cash Gap Management

It does so by cleverly and analytically rotating the advance received by the company from multiple simultaneous projects running. Say, a project worth Rs 7 crore has Rs 6.5 crore manufacturing cost and Rs 50 lakh profit, and the company receives an advance of only Rs 70 lakhs whereas Rs 3 crores are required for the next step of the project. The company faces a cash gap in this situation. Years-old and an established company with vintage can use working capital investment provided by banks. But Rays can't do that because of not having a long history and collateral. Moreover, to be able to bid for a project a huge amount of money is required to be deposited in fixed deposit as bank guarantee. In this situation, it uses the advances received from the other projects to fund the next step of the current project. After the completion of the current project, when the full amount by the IPP is received, it obtains flowing cash to fund its other projects. This scheme works as long as they win projects continuously.

Now let us look at the amazing financial numbers of the company, and just gaze bewildered, how with zero debt, the various ratio run amok.

Table 56.2 Rays Experts' revenue and profit trends

Financial year	Revenues (in INR crore)	Profit (In INR crore)
2011–2012	1.57	0.13
2012–2013	38.89	1.355
2013–2014	227.3	8.9445
2014–2015	350.0	14.39
2015–2016	600.0	

Revenue and Profit Trends

The company grows organically. The above data shows the growth rate of **311 %** from the FY 2012–2013 to FY 2013–2014.

Rays, just a 5-year-old start-up, has already beaten Tata Solar Power in terms of total business done. Rays' profitability is almost twice that of Tata's.

In terms of profit trends, the last year was a sad FY for all the companies operating in this sector, except Rays. Not just its revenues but also PATs have been growing tremendously in an industry that has remained more or less stagnant, or floundered in losses. As it is "cheaper" than its competitors and better in service, it is able to win projects even in a weak FY for renewable energy. Rays Experts has grown exponentially since the inception of the company. The trends of the key financial parameters have been analyzed in Table 56.2.

Comparison of Key Financial Ratios with Industry and Its Peers

The likes of EPC giants SunEdison, ACME, and Madhav sat in the same space as Rays to bid for the prestigious 7 MW DMRC (Delhi Metro Rail Corporation) solar rooftop project. As an aberration to the well-known names, the project was won by Rays. Rays Experts will pay for the capital investment involved with the project and DMRC will pay for the units generated by the plant. As Rays is producing power at a consistent and low tariff of Rs 6.248, it got an edge over its competitors (DMRC, "First Module of DMRC's Roof Top Solar Power Plant Inaugurated at dwarka sector 21") and (IANS, "Rays Power to make 7 MW solar rooftop project," 2015).

Initiative to build up solar energy plants has faced a lot of financing troubles. Bank debts and complex tax equity debts are expensive and cheaper forms of debt aren't easily available due to the understanding of solar energy as less reliable and less predictable form of energy, added to the scarcity of past data and trends on the success of the same.

Yield co is a common financial model adopted by some renewable energy companies operating in the IPP sector. Forbes (2014) explains it as a financial model usually followed by a spin-off company which raises its IPOs independently. It follows dividend distribution policy (Trefis Team, "Understanding Solar Yieldcos," 2014).

It bundles renewable energy-producing assets that ensure secure cash flow returns. Every quarter, a cash allocation is made for dividend distribution, and in this manner yield cos are able to finance their projects much cheaper. It is one of the cheapest equity funding sources. This can be due to multiple reasons. One that a large amount of cash flow is generated by selling renewable energy that is given out as quarterly dividends. Yield co-investments are relatively liquid. Moreover, tax advantage can be obtained. SunEdsion operates via this model in its IPP segment (Urdanick, "A Deeper Look into Yieldco Structuring," 2014) and ("Solar company spinoffs lure investors with dividends," 2014).

The competitor, ReNew Power of Sumant Sinha, obtained its equity from Goldman Sachs. Sumant Sinha (Wikipedia, "Renew Power," (n.d.)) leveraged his reputation of experience, intelligence, skill, and credibility to obtain such large amount of funds. According to the founder of the company and a report by Reuters (2014), the investors are lured towards such companies and Rays Experts further faces a huge competition in acing the listed market.

The German Solar Park building company Juwi is firming its grips in India, and rather than being seen as a competitor, it is seen as a benchmark by Rays Experts.

The ratios for the industry as a whole and Tata calculated from the data taken from Capitaline database are given in Table 56.3 and comparison performed:

- Rays' current ratio is 1.2, lesser than its competitor and the industry average. Also, the lack of collateral rules out the possibility of overdraft. Rays' current liabilities are just a little less than its current assets. It is because a large part of its financing is done by current liabilities. The company direly feels the need of leverage. The company is still managing without debt by intelligent and well-planned use of advances, and longer creditors' turnover period. The current ratio has been increasing over the years which indicates improvement in company's financial management, as proven by other ratios too.

- Its creditors turnover ratio hasn't shown a trend and varies from very high to very low. Rays needs to streamline this, all the while maintaining good relations with its suppliers. Rays needs to focus more on increasing the predictability of its supply chain.

- Contrary to expectations, the returns on shareholders' equity of Rays is much more than its competitors following debt funding model. If it had more debt financing, it could have had even higher returns on equity.

- The return on assets of Rays Experts is much more than the industry average figure. Rahul emphasized that you might even consider investing in this sector after going through Rays' accounts! Solar industry like the thermal power industry needs a large capital investment but on contrary to it doesn't need regular coal input or high maintenance and operational costs. This is the reason why Ratul Puri, chairman of Hindustan Power Projects; Tarun Singh—an electrical engineer working in the USA for 8 years, founder of Veddis Solar; Shubham Sandeep, an alumnus of IIT Delhi, founder of Aeon Solaris; Ajay Goyal, CEO of Tata Power Solar; Sumant Sinha, the owner of Renew Power, and most popularly Harish Hande of SELCO left their lucrative jobs and explored this no-brainer.

Table 56.3 Comparison of key financial ratios of Rays with its competitors and the solar power industry

Company (financial year)	Rays (13–14)	Tata Power (13–14)	Industry (13–14)	Rays (12–13)	Tata Power (12–13)	Industry (12–13)	Rays (11–12)	Tata Power (11–12)	Industry (11–12)
Current ratio	1.11	1.48	1.78	1.04	1.33	1.78	0.93	1.256	1.80
Return on shareholders equity (%)	85.71	−63.43	4.85	89.93	−23.17	−2.03	85.61	−4.54	2.67
Return on assets (%)	18.31	−27.71	2.08	6.93	−15.79	−0.77	3.67	−1.96	1.08
Interest coverage ratio	930.36	−3.21	2.82	313.92	−3.36	1.15	43.57	−0.09	2.01
Total debt to total assets	0.78	1.06	0.51	0.94	0.88	0.55	0.96	0.51	0.52
Working capital turnover ratio	56.65	5.9	3.56	94.95	5.24	3.68	−7.06	8.69	3.58
Fixed assets turnover ratio	32.41	−9.52	0.43	99.15	6.12	0.56	3.69	2.22	0.57
Short-term debts to total assets ratio	0.77	NA	−0.05	0.92	NA	0.03	0.94	NA	0.02
Creditors turnover ratio	5.74	NA	NA	4.87	NA	NA	0.15	NA	NA

- Interest Coverage ratio of Rays is 500 times more than competitors and has been increasing over the years. This means that the company is playing "too safe," where it could have easily boosted its earnings by taking debt. It hasn't been able to attract meaningful investors and debt providers due to lack of collateral and agreements.
- Even with negligible long-term debts, the company has significant total debt to total assets ratio as the company finances its operations primarily by current liabilities. The company isn't safe from this point of view but its situation has been improving over the years and in coherence with other ratios, it is expected to improve further.
- Rays' working capital turnover ratio is much higher than its competitors and industry as a large portion of its financing is by current debts, which is very close to value of current assets. This makes the need of working capital too less. A working capital turnover that is too high can be misleading. On the surface, it appears that you are operating at a very high efficiency, but in reality, your working capital level might be dangerously low. Very low working capital can possibly cause the company to run out of money to fund the business.
- As seen by the trends in fixed assets turnover ratio, Rays has been more effective in using the investment in fixed assets to generate revenues. This ratio is much better because Rays is a start-up and hence lesser fixed assets, whereas a turnover of nearly as much as the years-old giants.
- The short-term debts/total assets ratio is found out to prove that Rays Experts' majority financing is by short-term debts whereas the traditional power industry only negligibly operates on short-term debts. The company is using short-term debt to not just pay its current liabilities, but also finance its long-term assets. This lends the company into a very risky position and the earlier this situation changes, the better it is.

The Way Ahead: Requirement of a Long-Term Debt

As the trend of revenue and profit figures of Rays proves, the company has immense growth potential. Rahul Gupta says that his company's standard projected growth with the present financial model is 10–20 % only. To keep pace in the next 5 years and achieve greater growth rates, as high as 50 %, the company needs debt. In the present financial model he reinvests a part of the earned money. His company relies highly on retained earnings. But to achieve such a high growth rate for the next 5 years, all earned money can't be reinvested. It always helps to have debt. But the company doesn't have any vintage to create leverage. It is helpful in one sense as Rahul Gupta can sleep peacefully without any pressure of interest, or fear of the company getting killed by unpaid debts, but on the other hand, debt would help the company to increase its ROE.

The advantages of debt are well known. Debt has lower financing cost and hence companies often reduce the overall cost of capital, by financing from mixed sources. Debt is a cheaper form of financing because it requires periodical interest payment, and principal payment at maturity to debt holders. At the time of dissolution of company the debt holders have primary rights for getting paid. This puts debt holders at safer positions than investors. They bear lesser risk. Investors might not earn anything if the company fails, but the people who have invested in debt surely earn.

Debt also allows the company to remain a privately managed company if it doesn't want interference in management decisions by a large number of shareholders. Moreover, the company can retain profits rather than giving out to equity holders. The more is the financing from equity, the more dividends have to be rolled out. A company's aim is to increase the wealth of the shareholders; hence holding debt also helps to have high return on equity. As interest is a tax-deductible expense, company pays lesser due to tax savings, whereas distributing dividends is from after tax income, and might incur additional taxes.

But alas! Having debt isn't so easy. Neither is having investor. Once a renowned dealer offered to invest a good sum of money in Rays, and it took a lot of courage for the two shareholders to say NO to him, as the money was a huge amount for the investor but still an insignificant fund for Rays' operations.

Global Solar Scenario and China's Rise in the Solar Industry

The solar industry has grown rapidly in the last decades. From a German-centered industry, it has widened its horizon to many other countries in the world, developed and developing alike. By the end of 2011, the global solar capacity had already exceeded 65 GW. Along with government's incentives, capacity addition by the new players in the field has been a major reason for this kind of response. In the EPC business, the big players have been mainly concentrated from the USA and China. Also, it is seen that the Chinese EPC companies have made faster progress in the recent years. These statistics are in the terms of installed capacities of solar power. First Solar from the USA is the largest EPC company worldwide and it installed projects with an output of more than 1.1 GW in 2013. Coming to the Chinese EPC players, three companies, Shanghai Solar Energy, Zhongli Talesun Solar, and Astronergy, made the EPC top ten chart for the first time in 2013. TBEA Sun Oasis, again a Chinese EPC company, quadrupled its installation capacity to 1 GW in 1 year. European companies, on the other hand, have begun to lose considerable grounds.

The possible reasons for China's rise to power in this industry and steps that Indian Government can take to further strengthen this industry in India can be attributed as follows. In China, majority of companies in solar EPC business have their in-house manufacturing and R&D department. Also, many of such companies are subsidiaries of huge corporates and thus have large amounts of capital available to them. Also, being a subsidiary of bigger companies, they have better leverage in securing large-scale and profitable projects, including global projects. Now, China's rise in its manufacturing power in the recent years is playing in its advantage for these companies. Their cost of project materials reduces because of the in-house production. The cost of manufacturing in China is relatively low in comparison to other countries and the domestic consumption of solar power in China is increasing constantly. Government provides subsidies for the renewable energy sector. Also, the corporate tax rate of China is 25% against around 33% in India. The cost of doing business in India is much higher than in China.

The cost of manufacturing in India too is low, so playing onto its advantage EPC players of India can be made global players. According to Mr. Gupta, his company would have been in much better position if easy debt was available to him back then. Thus, incentivized debt schemes for renewable energy sector can be put in place under presently ongoing "Make in India" campaign. There are many schemes run by the Government of India and other state governments for increasing the use of solar energy but about all of them are directed towards the consumer segment. No direct incentives are there for the companies in business.

Conclusion

The secret behind the company's success is the founder's entrepreneurial mindset and presence at the right place at the right time. His new ways of thinking, unique business model, intelligent use of limited resources, and a continuous urge to find the best process in least funds allowed the company to start and take-off. It has been able to grow steeply even with zero debt-equity ratio by innovatively managing its current liabilities. The company is ahead of its competitors as it provides end-to-end services and at much cheaper rates. Its growth rate has been much more tremendous than the years-old giants and rich conglomerates of the industry. But to increase it even further, debt is becoming a necessity for Rays Experts at this stage. The company is able to fund its operations only till the projects keep coming, which lends it into a very risky position. The company should increase its efforts to raise debt if it wants greater returns on the two shareholders' money. The government should devise methods like China to encourage the much-needed exploration of renewable energy in India. With the depletion of natural resources and increase in pollution, the importance of this sector is expected to grow exponentially in the coming years, and more opportunities will come the company's way.

So, the take-away lesson is to be aware and decisive enough to act when required.

References

Chhabra, A. (2009, December 15). *India's first solar power plant opens in Punjab*. Retrieved December 31, 2015, from http://indiatoday.intoday.in/story/India's first solar power plant opens in Punjab/1/75126.html.

First Module of DMRC's Roof Top Solar Power Plant Inaugurated at dwarka sector 21; Expected to Start Productions Next month. (n.d.). Retrieved December 31, 2015, from http://www.delhi-metrorail.com/press_reldetails.aspx?id=DYXhbh1IRv8lld.

IANS. (2015, April 1). *Rays Power to make 7 MW solar rooftop project for Delhi Metro*. Retrieved December 31, 2015, from http://www.business-standard.com/article/news-ians/rays-power-to-make-7-mw-solar-rooftop-project-for-delhi-metro-115040101540_1.html.

ReNew Power, Wikipedia, the Free Encyclopedia. (n.d.). Retrieved December 31, 2015, from https://en.wikipedia.org/wiki/ReNew_Power.

Reuters. (2014, January 16). *Solar company spinoffs lure investors with dividends*. Retrieved December 31, 2015, from http://www.reuters.com/article/2014/01/16/solar-yield-idUSL4N0JE2NU20140116.

Trefis Team. (2014, June 17). *Understanding Solar Yieldcos*. Retrieved December 31, 2015, from http://www.forbes.com/sites/greatspeculations/2014/06/17/understanding-solar-yieldcos/#a0df98264f53.

Urdanick, M. (2014, March 09). *A deeper look into Yieldco structuring*. Retrieved December 31, 2015, from https://financere.nrel.gov/finance/content/deeper-look-yieldco-structuring.

Chapter 57
Personality Trait and Innovation Performance of Micro and Small Enterprises

Shukurat Moronke Bello

Abstract Micro and small enterprises have gained increasing attention in the innovation literature. However, empirical studies on the factors that influence the innovative performance of these enterprises are still at infancy. Exceptional innovative performance of MSEs may be determined by the personality trait of the business owner/manager. This study is a pilot survey conducted on a few numbers ($N = 38$) of micro and small manufacturing, service and retail enterprises in Kano, Nigeria. A questionnaire was distributed to explore the potential influence of personality trait on micro and small enterprise innovation performance. Cronbach's alpha test is employed to measure the internal consistency of the instrument. The findings of this study encourage further testing and conclude that most measures have high reliability scores ranging from .63 to .89. This suggests the possibility of applying the instrument among MSEs in Kano, Nigeria.

Keywords Innovation performance • Personality • Pilot survey

Introduction

In the current business environment characterised by competition and economic crisis, innovation plays an important role. Small and Medium Enterprise Development Agency of Nigeria (SMEDAN) in 2008 reported that most small- and medium-scale businesses in Nigeria die before their fifth anniversary. However, researchers are continuing to explore the factors that cause entrepreneurial failure. Ashibogwu (2008) noted that one of the reasons for the high failure of micro, small and medium enterprises is the lack of market research to confirm demand and assess suitability of the proposed offering. Thus, individual differences such as personality might influence owners'/managers' ability to generate, promote and realise new ideas that are useful to organisational success. As noted by Lobacz and Glodek

S.M. Bello (✉)
Department of Business Administration and Entrepreneurship, Bayero University Kano, Kano, Nigeria
e-mail: smbello.bus@buk.edu.ng

© Springer International Publishing Switzerland 2017   663
R. Benlamri, M. Sparer (eds.), *Leadership, Innovation and Entrepreneurship as Driving Forces of the Global Economy*, Springer Proceedings in Business and Economics, DOI 10.1007/978-3-319-43434-6_57

(2015), small, innovative enterprises are regarded as (fast) growing enterprises managed by the owners (entrepreneurs). Those are enterprises which are proactively seeking for new solutions in order to provide better market offers to its (potential) customers (Lobacz & Glodek, 2015).

Despite the increasing academics and business interest on personality trait as a key indicator of business success (Brandstätter, 2010; Leutner, Ahmetoglu, Akhtar, & Chamorro-Premuzic, 2014), little research has explored the relationship between personality traits and innovation performance. This study complements the existing knowledge in innovation of micro and small enterprises; it seeks to determine the reliability of the scales ('Big Five Inventory Scale' and 'Measure of Entrepreneurial Tendencies and Abilities Scale') to be used on a larger sample in relation to owners'/managers' personality trait in Nigerian organisations.

Pilot test is useful for the appropriateness or the suitability of the research sample. However, several studies, mostly in developed countries, have confirmed the reliability of the measurement scales. The fact that the instrument will be used on a new population and a new location (Kano, Nigeria) deems it necessary to conduct a pilot study. As Portney and Watkins (2009) opined a tested questionnaire on reliability does not guarantee the same degree of reliability in every situation. The validity of the measuring instrument is the extent to which the instrument is measuring what it is supposed to measure and not something else, whereas the reliability indicates the extent to which an instrument is error free, and, thus, consistent and stable across time and also across the various items in the scale (Sekaran & Bougie, 2010).

Hence, the objective of this study is to determine the reliability of the research instrument to the selected sample frame. In doing this, the remainder of this chapter is structured into four sections. Section "A Brief Literature Review" presents a brief of MSEs in Nigeria and reviews the concept of innovation performance and personality trait, the methodology used for the research is detailed in the third section, the fourth section presents the result of the pilot study and the final part concludes the chapter.

A Brief Literature Review

Micro and Small Enterprises in Nigeria: There is no generally accepted classification of MSEs; the classification/definition depends on the country, the agency or the institution and varies over time. Usually, the definition of MSEs is derived from countries based on the role of MSEs in the economy, policies and programmes designed by particular agencies or institutions. For instance, in Nigeria, the National Policy on Micro, Small and Medium Enterprises (2015) defined MSEs on a dual criteria: assets worth (excluding land and buildings) and number of employees. Micro enterprises are businesses whose total assets (excluding land and buildings) are less than ten million Naira with a workforce not exceeding ten employees. Small enterprises are those businesses whose total assets (excluding land and building) are above ten million Naira but not exceeding 100 million Naira with a total workforce of above 10, but not exceeding 49 employees.

According to SMEDAN (2015), micro enterprises in Nigeria are mainly operated by a sole proprietor/manager, aided by unpaid family workers and occasional paid employee and apprentice. These enterprises are characterised by low output level, low level of technology and low skill (SMEDAN, 2015). In 2013, the number of small enterprises in Nigeria was 68,168 with a large reservoir of educated manpower and technical skills and has the potential of growth through nurturing, capacity building and support (SMEDAN, 2015).

The Concept of Innovation Performance: Schumpeter (1934) referred to the term 'innovation' as anything that was carried out through new combinations and manifestation of (1) the introduction of a new (or improved) good, (2) the introduction of new methods of production, (3) the opening of a new market, (4) the exploitation of a new source of supply and (5) the re-engineering/organisation of business management processes. Therefore, innovativeness is described as the organisational wide acceptance of novel creation and new products, services, processes, administrative systems or any combinations of these that influence the overall firm performance (Bulut & Yilmaz, 2008). Innovation performance is defined as the propensity of a firm to actively support new ideas, novelty, experimentation and creative solution (Wang & Ahmed, 2004). Innovation performance includes the creation of new ideas for difficult issues, searching out new working methods, techniques, technologies or instruments; identifying performance gaps; mobilising support for innovative ideas and the transformation of innovative ideas into useful applications (De Jong & Den Hartog, 2007; Janssen, 2000; Kheng & Mahmood, 2013).

Ahmetoglu (2015) proposed the Measure of Entrepreneurial Tendencies and Abilities (META) to assess the extent to which individuals differ in their inclination to engage in innovative entrepreneurial behaviours (proactivity, creativity, opportunism and vision). These entrepreneurial innovation behaviours are based on the notion that entrepreneurship comprises a set of behaviours and the tendency to engage in such behaviour depends on the personality traits of individuals (Leutner et al., 2014).

The Concept of Personality Trait: Personality is defined as the relatively enduring pattern of thoughts, emotions and behaviours that characterise a person, along with the psychological processes behind those characteristics (McShane & Von Glinow, 2010). The basic principle of personality is that people have inherent traits that can be identified by the consistency or stability of their behaviour across time and situations. In a general sense, personality traits comprise abilities, motives, attitudes and characteristics of temperament as overarching style of a person's experience and actions (Brandstätter, 2010). Several models (e.g. Eysenck's three-factor model, the five-factor model of personality traits (Big Five), the Myers-Briggs Type Indicator and HEXACO model) have been conceptualised by researchers on personality traits. McShane and Von Glinow (2010) opined that the most widely respected and supported model personality in research is the Big Five Model.

The concept of the Big Five Personality trait from personality literature is openness to experience, conscientiousness, extraversion, agreeableness and neuroticism. Brandstätter (2010) described openness to experience as the breadth, depth, originality and complexity of an individual's mental and experiential life. Conscientiousness is described as a socially prescribed impulse control that facilitates task- and goal-directed behaviour, such as thinking before acting, delaying gratification, following norms and rules and planning, organising and prioritising tasks. According to Zhao, Seibert and Lumpkin (2010), conscientiousness as a global trait (without distinction of facets) has a positive correlation with both intention to become an entrepreneur and entrepreneurial performance. Extraversion implies an energetic approach toward the social and material world and includes traits such as sociability, activity, assertiveness and positive emotionality (Brandstätter, 2010). Neuroticism contrasts emotional stability and even-temperedness with negative emotionality, such as feeling anxious, nervous, sad and tense. Hence, entrepreneurial behaviour is any act involving the recognition and exploitation of opportunities, or innovation, and results in the creation of economic and social value (Ahmetoglu, 2015).

Methods

In a cross-sectional survey, convenience sample of 40 MSE owners/managers in manufacturing, personal service and retail business operating in Kano participated in the pilot study. The majority of them had first degree (71%) and four were women. Table 57.1 shows the descriptive statistics on the demographic characteristics of respondents.

Table 57.1 Results of descriptive statistics

Variable	Item	Frequency	Percentage
Gender	Male	34	89.5
	Female	4	10.5
Age of owner/manager	20 years or below	9	27.3
	21–30 years	10	26.3
	31–40 years	13	34.2
	41–50 years	6	15.8
Educational qualification	ND/NCE	11	28.9
	B.Sc./B.A.	27	71.1
Marital status	Single	19	50
	Married	19	50
Type of industry	Retail	8	21.1
	Service	25	65.8
	Manufacturing	5	13.2
Number of employees	1–9	35	92.1
	10–99	3	7.9
Business age	Less than 1 year	6	15.8
	1–5 years	28	73.7
	6–10 years	4	10.5

The questionnaire for this study is developed by using scales of prior studies. All constructs are measured using a five-point Likert scale (from strongly disagree = 1 to strongly agree = 5). For the personality trait, a 44-item scale by John and Srivastava (1999), the Big Five Inventory (BFI), consists of five personality trait dimensions: extraversion, openness to new experience, agreeableness, neuroticism and conscientiousness were adopted for this study. The innovation performance measure consists of Measure of Entrepreneurial Tendencies and Abilities (META), a 44-item four-dimension scale by Ahmetoglu (2015). The META dimensions are entrepreneurial proactivity, entrepreneurial creativity, entrepreneurial opportunism and entrepreneurial vision.

The Pilot Study: A total of 40 copies of the questionnaire were distributed and 38 were returned. This high response rate of about 95 % was achieved probably due to personal distribution and retrieval of the questionnaire copies by the researcher. This process was completed within 2 weeks in the month of September 2015. A reliability test of the instrument was performed by adopting internal consistency method. According to Sekaran and Bougie (2010) the most popular test of inter-item consistency reliability is Cronbach's alpha coefficient. Hence, the Cronbach's alpha test is employed in this study to measure the internal consistency of the instrument.

Cronbach's alpha reliability can be judged by some rule-of-thumb criteria: an alpha coefficient of 0.70 has been accepted as the minimum threshold for assessing reliability/internal consistency (Nunnally & Bernstein, 1994).

Discussion of Findings

The results from the pilot study show that most dimensions possess high reliability standard ranging from .63 to .89. The summary of results of the reliability test is shown in Table 57.2.

Table 57.2 Results of reliability test

Variable	Dimension	Alpha's coefficient	No. of items
Personality trait	Extraversion	.76	8
	Openness	.89	10
	Agreeableness	.64	9
	Neuroticism	.86	8
	Conscientiousness	.74	9
Innovation performance	Entrepreneurial proactivity	.85	11
	Entrepreneurial creativity	.70	11
	Entrepreneurial opportunism	.69	11
	Entrepreneurial vision	.63	11

In the reliability analysis for the Big Five Inventory, only the agreeableness dimension possessed a value below minimum threshold ($\alpha=0.64$). The agreeableness alpha coefficient is similar to the one obtained in the study of Zomorano, Carrillo, Silva, Sandoval and Pastrana (2014) and Rodríguez and Church (2003). Furthermore, prior research (Leutner et al., 2014) on META revealed higher alpha reliability coefficient than the present study. The differences in the results may be attributed to the fact that this is a pilot survey, and such coefficient was obtained from a larger sample.

Another important finding of this pilot survey is the time used to complete the questionnaire. Contrary to the 15 min estimated for the completion of the questionnaire, it was found out that the majority of the respondents completed the questions within 25–30 min. Only 25 % of the respondents completed it within the estimated time of 15 min.

Conclusion

This study analysed the reliability/internal consistency of the instrument to be used on the main survey on personality trait and innovation performance of micro and small enterprises in Kano, Nigeria. The results of the Cronbach's alpha show that the Big Five Inventory scale and the META scale have high reliability coefficient for most of the constructs. Therefore, instrument is suitable on the sample frame.

Limitations and Future Research: There are some limitations to this study. The present study was conducted using non-probability sample technique. Specifically convenience sampling was used to select the respondents. In addition, this research is a pilot survey; more valid conclusion can be made about the reliability of the instrument on a larger sample.

Therefore, future studies can use other probability sample techniques for selecting respondents. To further establish the reliability of the instrument, future research can examine the influence of personality trait on innovation performance of employees in corporate organisations.

References

Ahmetoglu, G. (2015). The entrepreneurial personality: A new framework and construct for entrepreneurship research and practice. Doctoral thesis, Goldsmiths, University of London. [Thesis]: Goldsmiths Research Online.

Ashibogwu, M. (2008). Common failures of family business. *Business Day, Nigeria. Monday, May, 18.*

Brandstätter, H. (2010). Personality aspects of entrepreneurship: A look at five meta-analyses. *Personality and Individual Differences, 51,* 222–230.

Bulut, C., & Yilmaz, C. (2008) Innovative performance impacts of corporate entrepreneurship: An empirical research in Turkey. In: *Proceedings of Academy of Innovation and Entrepreneurship Conference*, Beijing, China, pp. 414–417.

De Jong, J. P. J., & Den Hartog, D. N. (2007). How leaders influence employees' innovative behaviour. *European Journal of Innovation Management, 10*(1), 41–64.

Janssen, O. (2000). Job demands, perceptions of effort-reward fairness and innovative work behaviour. *Journal of Occupational and Organizational Psychology, 73*(3), 287–302.

John, O. P., & Srivastava, S. (1999). The Big Five trait taxonomy: History, measurement and theoretical perspectives. In L. A. Pervin & O. P. John (Eds.), *Handbook of personality: Theory and research* (Vol. 2, pp. 102–138). New York: Guilford Press.

Kheng, Y. K., & Mahmood, R. (2013). The relationship between pro-innovation organizational climate, leader-member exchange, and innovative work behaviour: A study among the knowledge workers of the knowledge intensive business services in Malaysia. *Business Management Dynamics, 2*(8), 15–30.

Leutner, F., Ahmetoglu, G., Akhtar, R., & Chamorro-Premuzic, T. (2014). The relationship between the entrepreneurial personality and the big five personality traits. *Personality and Individual Differences, 63*, 58–63.

Lobacz, K., & Glodek, P. (2015). Development of competitive advantage of small innovative firm—How to model business advice influence within the process. *Procedia Economic and Finance, 23*, 487–494.

McShane, S. L., & Von Glinow, M. (2010). *Organizational behaviour: Emerging knowledge and practice for the real world* (5th ed.). New York: McGraw-Hill/Irwin.

Nunnally, J. C., & Bernstein, I. H. (1994). *Psychometric theory* (3rd ed.). New-York: McGraw-Hill.

Portney, L. G., & Watkins, M. P. (2009). *Foundation of clinical research. Application to practice* (3rd ed.). Englewood Cliffs: Pearson Prentice Hall.

Rodríguez, C., & Church, A. T. (2003). The structure and personality correlates of affect in Mexico: Evidence of cross-cultural comparability using Spanish Language. *Journal of Cross Cultural Psychology, 34*(2), 211–230.

Schumpeter, J. A. (1934). The theory of economic development: An inquiry into profit, capital, credit, interest and the business cycle. *Harvard Economic Studies, 46*, Harvard College, Cambridge, MA.

Sekaran, U., & Bougie, R. (2010). *Research methods for business: A skill building approach* (5th ed.). Chichester: Wiley.

Small and Medium Enterprise Development Agency of Nigeria (SMEDAN). (2008). National policy on micro, small and medium enterprises. A publication of Federal Republic of Nigeria.

Small and Medium Enterprise Development Agency of Nigeria (SMEDAN). (2015). National policy on micro, small and medium enterprises. A publication of Federal Republic of Nigeria. Retrieved October 5, 2015, from http://www.smedan.gov.ng.

Wang, C. L., & Ahmed, P. K. (2004). The development and validation of the organizational innovativeness construct using confirmatory factor analysis. *European Journal of Innovation Management, 7*, 303–313.

Zhao, H., Seibert, S. E., & Lumpkin, G. T. (2010). The relationship of personality to entrepreneurial intentions and performance: A meta-analytic review. *Journal of Management, 36*(2), 381–404.

Zomorano, E. R., Carrillo, C. A., Silva, A. P., Sandoval, A. M., & Pastrana, I. M. R. (2014). Psychometric properties of the big five inventory in Mexican sample. *Salud Mental, 37*, 491–497.

Chapter 58
Development Prospects for Franchising in Southeast Asia: A Review and Outlook

Marko Grünhagen and Andrew Terry

Abstract Academic studies on global franchising had focused initially, from the late 1970s to the 1990s, on developed economies, including North America, Western Europe, and Australia, while over the last decade the research focus has moved to include transitional and emerging markets, such as the Asian economies of China and India. Only recently has academic research on franchising shifted towards developing Southeast Asian markets (Dant and Grünhagen, J Market Channels 21(3):124–132, 2014). The literature on scholarly research into franchise activities in the developing markets of Southeast Asia remains in its infancy (for notable exceptions see Binh and Terry, J Market Channels 18(2):147–163, 2011; Binh & Terry, 2014; Grünhagen, Le, & Ho, 2014).

Keywords Franchising • Developing economies • Southeast Asia

Franchising has been shown to be a significant contributor to the economic development of entire economies (e.g., Grünhagen & Witte, 2005; Michael, 2014). In recent years a renewed focus of the franchise industry has shifted to the developing markets of Southeast Asia, such as Cambodia, Myanmar, and Vietnam, with their exceedingly young labor markets, rapidly growing middle classes, and low-wage structures.

The franchising industry has been charged with fostering homogeneity and reducing local cultural diversity around the globe, a claim that resonates particularly in Asia where McDonald's and other fast-food chains have been blamed with the proliferation of American cultural imperialism (Luxenberg, 1985). At the same time, brands like McDonald's are getting assimilated rapidly in traditional societies like China (Grünhagen, Dant, & Zhu, 2012; Watson, 1997).

M. Grünhagen (✉)
Eastern Illinois University, Charleston, IL, USA
e-mail: mgrunhagen@eiu.edu

A. Terry
University of Sydney, Sydney, NSW, Australia

© Springer International Publishing Switzerland 2017   671
R. Benlamri, M. Sparer (eds.), *Leadership, Innovation and Entrepreneurship as Driving Forces of the Global Economy*, Springer Proceedings in Business and Economics, DOI 10.1007/978-3-319-43434-6_58

Academic studies on global franchising had focused initially, from the late 1970s to the 1990s, on developed economies, including North America, Western Europe, and Australia, while over the last decade the research focus has moved to include transitional and emerging markets, such as the Asian economies of China and India. Only recently has academic research on franchising shifted towards developing Southeast Asian markets (Dant & Grünhagen, 2014). The literature on scholarly research into franchise activities in the developing markets of Southeast Asia remains in its infancy (for notable exceptions see Binh & Terry, 2011, 2014; Grünhagen, Le, & Ho, 2015).

Western franchised brands have been present in many parts of East and Southeast Asia for several decades. For consumers younger than 30 years of age their presence is as commonplace as it is for consumers in the West. The widespread availability of such offerings has democratized the local marketplace, as access to Western products is not merely a privilege of the wealthy any longer.

In the developing markets of Southeast Asia specifically, Western franchise systems have been present since the 1990s; yet their expansion into these developing markets has been rather tentative, given the hitherto greater opportunities in Asia's emerging and developed markets, such as China, India, Malaysia, and Singapore. However, spurred by the advent of Western franchisors, a very dynamic local franchise industry has developed over the last two decades. Franchise systems indigenous to developing Southeast Asian markets have become quite sophisticated through expatriate executives, franchisees who have travelled to the West, and the like. The persistent notion of the past that local franchise systems may not be as savvy or refined as "global" players in the industry has markedly changed (Grünhagen, Le, & Ho, 2015).

Only in recent years (essentially since the mid-2000s) have Western systems paid renewed attention to the developing markets of Southeast Asia. This development has been largely driven by a slowdown of the Chinese economy, paired with rising incomes, growing populations, and steadily enhanced infrastructure developments in the region's developing economies, such as Vietnam, Cambodia, Myanmar, and Laos.

A brief summary of the political, economic, regulatory, and institutional requirements for the success of franchise systems in the developing markets of Southeast Asia is provided. In essence, without government backing, a functioning private sector, a supportive regulatory framework, and a network of local and regional institutions that encourage the franchise business model, a strong domestic franchise sector is unlikely to flourish.

A major challenge common to most countries throughout Southeast Asia is, first and foremost, a lack of a developed infrastructure. Further, significant hopes are associated with the recently ratified Trans-Pacific Partnership (TPP), a trade agreement around the Pacific Rim signed by, among others, the USA, Australia, and New Zealand, as well as Vietnam, Malaysia, Brunei, and Singapore in Southeast Asia. Indonesia, Thailand, and the Philippines have declared their interest to join in the future. Positive prospects include the opening of markets and reduction of tariffs for Western imports, from which large Western franchisors expect to benefit in their efforts to expand into the developing markets of Southeast Asia.

Similarly, APEC (Asia Pacific Economic Cooperation) as well as the recently enhanced collaboration among the countries of ASEAN (Association of Southeast Asian Nations) towards the creation of a "common market" (ASEAN Economic Community — AEC) have garnered the hopes of the developing markets in the region. The single AEC market will provide opportunities as well as challenges for ASEAN franchise systems. It will facilitate the expansion of local franchise systems, but will also expose domestic franchise sectors to increasing competitive pressures. Those franchisors who have built strong and viable systems will be much better positioned, but those lacking system consistency will be increasingly vulnerable.

References

Binh, N. B., & Terry, A. (2011). Good Morning, Vietnam! Opportunities and challenges in a developing franchise sector. *Journal of Marketing Channels, 18*(2), 147–163.

Binh, N. B., & Terry, A. (2014). Meeting the challenges for franchising in developing countries: The Vietnamese experience. *Journal of Marketing Channels, 21*(3), 210–221.

Dant, R. P., & Grünhagen, M. (2014). International franchising research: Some thoughts on the what, where, when, and how. *Journal of Marketing Channels, 21*(3), 124–132.

Grünhagen, M., & Witte, C. L. (2005). The Role of Franchising as a Driver of Economic Development for Emerging Economies. *Journal of Business, Industry and Economics, 5 (Spring)*, 27–45.

Grünhagen, M., Dant, R. P., Zhu, M., Le, T. P., Ho, C., & Witte, C. L. (2005). The role of franchising as a driver of economic development for emerging economies. *Journal of Business, Industry and Economics, 5*, 27–45.

Grünhagen, M., Dant, R. P., & Zhu, M. (2012). Emerging consumer perspectives on American franchise offerings: Variety seeking behavior in China. *Journal of Small Business Management, 50*(4), 596–620.

Grünhagen, M., Le, T. P., & Ho, C. (2015). HR and franchising in an emerging economy: Preliminary insights from an interview study in Vietnam. *International Conference on Global Business, Economics, Finance and Social Sciences*, Bangkok, Thailand.

Luxenberg, S. (1985). Roadside empires: How the chains franchised America, New York, NY: Viking.

Michael, S. C. (2014). Can franchising be an economic development strategy? An empirical investigation. *Small Business Economics, 42*, 611–620.

Watson, J. L. (Ed.). (1997). *Golden arches east: McDonald's in East Asia*. Stanford, CA: Stanford University Press.

Chapter 59
Entrepreneurship Education in UKM: Essential Skills for First-Year Students

Rosilah Hassan, Wan Mimi Diyana Wan Zaki, Hanim Kamaruddin, Norasmah Othman, Sarmila Md Sum, and Zulkifli Mohamad

Abstract Most universities have developed entrepreneurial learning known as academic entrepreneurship (AE) by introducing entrepreneur-related courses for cross-discipline students. In order to increase student's opportunities in developing business skills, Institute of Higher Education (IPT) in Malaysia encourages entrepreneurial program in higher academic institutions. The government supports the effort to reach the vision of Malaysia's Economic Transformation Program (ETP) by 2020 in enhancing entrepreneurship abilities. Moreover, academic entrepreneurship has rooted in many global universities whereby the entrepreneurship subjects are introduced across the board regardless of faculties in order to provide basic entrepreneurial knowledge using adaptable learning pattern. The faculty entrepreneurship concept is applied in the teaching and learning process at Universiti

R. Hassan (✉)
Faculty of Information Science and Technology,
Universiti Kebangsaan Malaysia (UKM), Bangi, 43600 Selangor, Malaysia
e-mail: rosilah@ukm.edu.my

W.M.D.W. Zaki
Faculty of Engineering and Built Environment, Universiti Kebangsaan Malaysia (UKM),
Bangi, 43600 Selangor, Malaysia
e-mail: wmdiyana@ukm.edu.my

H. Kamaruddin
Faculty of Law, Universiti Kebangsaan Malaysia (UKM), Bangi, 43600 Selangor, Malaysia
e-mail: hanim@ukm.edu.my

N. Othman
Faculty of Education, Universiti Kebangsaan Malaysia (UKM), Bangi,
43600 Selangor, Malaysia
e-mail: lin@ukm.edu.my

S. Md Sum
Faculty of Social Sciences and Humanities, Universiti Kebangsaan Malaysia (UKM),
Bangi, 43600 Selangor, Malaysia
e-mail: sarmila@ukm.edu.my

Z. Mohamad
Pusat Citra Universiti, Universiti Kebangsaan Malaysia (UKM), Bangi,
43600 Selangor, Malaysia

© Springer International Publishing Switzerland 2017
R. Benlamri, M. Sparer (eds.), *Leadership, Innovation and Entrepreneurship as Driving Forces of the Global Economy*, Springer Proceedings in Business and Economics, DOI 10.1007/978-3-319-43434-6_59

675

Kebangsaan Malaysia (UKM) by providing entrepreneurial courses for first-year students from all faculties. The course comprises Fundamentals of Entrepreneurship and Innovation and was initiated 5 years ago involving 12 faculties in UKM. These papers introduce basic elements of entrepreneurship and related skills to students in different disciplines. Its main objective is to promote and generate business interests and ideas among students by providing fundamental knowledge of entrepreneurship so that a career in entrepreneurship is deemed as a feasible career option. Changing mind sets of students to be a job creator rather than a job seeker is today's challenge that can be overcome by dissemination of invaluable business tools and materials which is the core aspect of this course. Concepts and theories of entrepreneurship including team building, teaming and leadership, strategy and management aptitudes, marketing and market research, financial and legal principles, manufacturing or production processes, and oral presentation skills will be taught. The link between various components of a business will be demonstrated and identified through business simulation games performed by students themselves. Series of periodic seminars and recorded videos displaying experiences of local successful entrepreneurs are presented to inspire students to embrace values and challenges of an entrepreneur. A business pitching and business concept poster competitions are held to assess students' understanding and reflection of the course content translated into these forms of "hands-on" activities.

Keywords Entrepreneurial learning • Academic entrepreneur (AE) • Universiti Kebangsaan Malaysia (UKM) • Teaching and learning • Entrepreneur

Introduction

Entrepreneurship (Rahim & Chik, 2014; Zakaria, Yusoff, & Madun, 2011) is a process to develop, organize, and manage a business venture and associated risks coupled with a responsibility to strive for success or coping with failure. The term "entrepreneur" (Uzunidis, Boutillier, Laperche 2014) can be applied to anyone who organizes a new project or opportunity and most often is used in a business context. Entrepreneurs need to be equipped with the right skills in running a business. An "innovation" (Bessant & Tidd, 2011; Brennan & McGowan, 2006; Brennan, Wall, & McGowan, 2005) is a specific mechanism by which entrepreneurs exploit changes and convert it to be an opportunity for different businesses or services. With that concept in mind, UKM has come up with a course that serves as an introduction course to entrepreneurship (Hassan et al., 2015) which is known as LMCW1022 (Basic Entrepreneurship and Innovation). This course is known as academic entrepreneurship (AE) (Hassan, Mohd Tawil, Hanafiah, & Wan Zaki, 2016), carried out throughout a university semester involving normal lectures, public lectures (visiting entrepreneur), business idea presentation day, and simulation online games assisted by lecturers and teaching assistants. A business concept presentation and poster competition will be held after lectures and seminars with an aim of assessing the students' comprehension and understanding of what was communicated to them during lectures and seminars. Online quizzes are also set at every 3-week interval to evaluate students' progress and grasp of the course project. An online business simulation (OBS) (www.obs.ukm.my) game is organized where a student will be able to engage in a mockup business model and this activity will finally engage students to form a company and participate in the same exercise as a team. In the process of implementing the course, we have used four different versions and updated books.

Objectives

The objectives of these courses are primarily aimed at understanding basic concepts in entrepreneurship in its process to develop, organize, and manage a business enterprise. It is designed to equip the students with business knowledge and responsibilities that are attached to building and creating a physical business. The demand for entrepreneurial learning has been and is still steadily increasing (Brussels, 2012). The course further aims at describing relationship between the various components needed in any entrepreneurship through the medium of OBS games. It is hoped that the students are able to apply the given knowledge or skills in a made-up online business resulting in positive (or negative) outcome according to the decisions undertaken by them. Another purpose of these course is also aimed at honing or refining a business idea presentation through business pitch activity in which students will undertake a task to create, develop, and convey a business idea to an audience. In relation to this, a poster representing their business idea or product shall be displayed incorporating many elements of a business peculiar to their merchandise or invention. More importantly, this course gives opportunity for students to innovate original creations that may fulfill the wants or needs of an individual or the community at large.

Course Overview

Firstly initiated by a teaching module from Steven Institute of Technology (SIT), New York, in 2012 and 2013. In 2014, the group of lecturers combined their ideas to publish the first basic entrepreneurial book from UKM named as Fundamental of Entrepreneurship and Innovation. It was a result of written contributions by 30 lecturers from different faculties. This book contains 12 chapters: Entrepreneurship Introductory, Generating Business Ideas, Recognizing Opportunity, Developing Entrepreneurship Team and Organization, Operational Management, Strategizing Marketing, Financing Aspects in a Small Business, Business Model Canvas, Legal Issues in Entrepreneurship, Business Ethics in Entrepreneurship, Entrepreneurship Presentation, and Integrating Gamification into Business Development. All chapters are well organized to help the entrepreneurs in understanding the requirements in opening up a business. The book was revised in 2016 (Hassan et al., 2016),

Year 2013	Year 2014	Year 2015	Year 2016
Teaching Module	Text Book	Text Book	Text Book
CMIE1012	CMIE1012	LMCW1022	LMCW1022

Fig. 59.1 The collection of the book

incorporating new materials, and it underwent an evaluation by experts from the business industries and the academia. Figure 59.1 shows the collection of the books which have been used until today.

Approach

The approach of the courses centers on several compositions in which it is hoped that the students are able to follow the course clearly and effectively. These include the following:

- A class of 100 students will have two lecturers to teach and assist in lectures and seminars.
- An introductory class is held at each faculty at the beginning of the course as a starter to "kick boost" entrepreneurial spirit among students.
- Business concept presentation will take place in each class and finally the best team of students will compete at the faculty or university level.
- Three big events that are held include Public Lecture 1 (Fig. 59.2), Public Lecture 2 (Fig. 59.3), and the UKM Entrepreneur Day (Fig. 59.4).
- All the logistics will be arranged by all lecturers and teaching assistants to accommodate more than 4000 people in attendance including students, academic staffs, and visitors.
- Entry survey and exit survey for students to receive feedback on the success of achieving objectives of the course (Fig. 59.5).

During a Public Lecture, the organizer invites at least two successful young entrepreneurs as the motivational speakers. The session usually lasts for 2 h and

Fig. 59.2 Public Lecture 1

Fig. 59.3 Public Lecture 2

there is a question-and-answer session. Both speakers normally share their experiences and give valuable tips to students on opening a start-up business. Figures 59.2 and 59.3 show the event of the day.

During UKM Entrepreneur Day, awarding ceremony will be held for the winners throughout entrepreneurship activities accomplished in UKM. Among the awards presented were the best group poster, best individual pitching, and the overall awards for the best faculty in entrepreneurship which includes most involvement in entrepreneurial activities organized. Figure 59.4 shows the event of the day.

The online entry survey is conducted during the entrance of this course (first week of the semester) to determine students' needs in learning while the online exit survey is prepared at the end of the semester (week 14) after completing the course. The questions conveyed are intended to analyze students' understanding throughout the learning. Figure 59.5 shows the preface of the entry and exit survey.

Before the semester begins, Pitching Day is organized for students who have been given an exemption on the basis of credit transfer. In each student's presentation session, a panel of three assessors will judge the student's pitching performance. Figure 59.6 illustrates the activity during Pitching Day.

The course will be concluded with an entrepreneurial day participated by students from all faculties in UKM. Business concept presentation will be held during

Fig. 59.4 Activities during UKM Entrepreneur Day

that event and an award ceremony is held for overall winners for entrepreneurship activities implemented in UKM. Among the awards presented include best poster, best individual pitching, best group pitching, and the overall awards for the best faculty. Many notable people from the business industry are appointed judges for the competition.

Assessment Tool

Malaysia has become one of the countries which rapidly developed in terms of information and communication technology (ICT) for the past few years. Therefore, the user of communication tools such as social networking has become a medium of

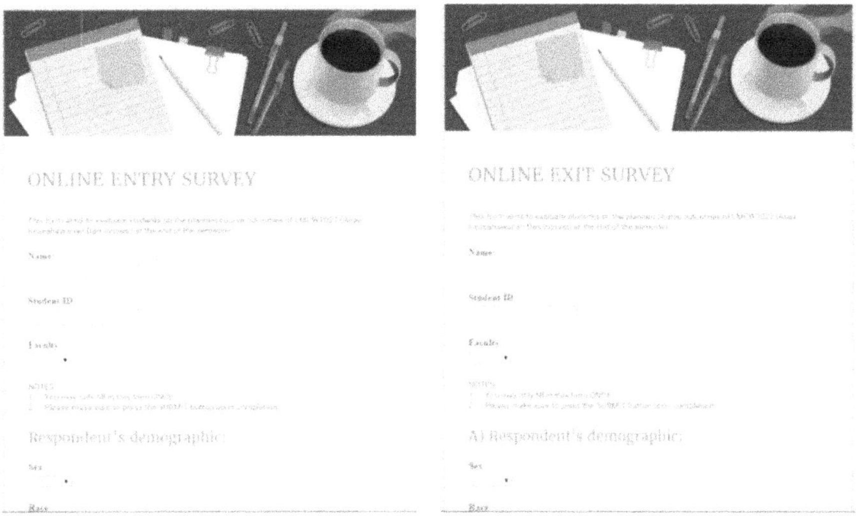

Fig. 59.5 Entry and exit survey

Fig. 59.6 Pitching Day

information and communication in many ways such as the i-Folio. I-Folio is the acronym for Integrated Portfolio Management System by UKM consisting of course portfolio and learning portfolio to assist lecturers and students to update course information as well as uploading and downloading course materials and discussion using the preface shown in Fig. 59.7. 50 % of all courses offered by higher education institutions have to be conducted using the blended learning mode due to the requirements outlined by MOE's National e-Learning Policy. Blended learning includes at least 30 % of online contents and/or activities.

i-Folio   Facebook

Fig. 59.7 Communication tools through i-Folio and Facebook

(a)   (b)

Fig. 59.8 Online tools: (**a**) Quiz online, and (**b**) OBS

The four components of the assessment and marks have been set as below:

- Online quiz module: 20–30 %
- Oral presentations: 20–30 %
- OBS: 30–40 %
- Attendance to public lecture: 5–10 %

The system for LMCW1022 course is leased from Scriptopro (www.scriptopro.com/) online quiz creation tool available through www.scriptopro.com as shown in Fig. 59.8a. All students are required to take the quizzes as part of the component for assessment in which random questions are set based on the 11 chapters of the current textbook.

The OBS (Rosilah, Norngainy, & Norizan, 2014), as shown in Fig. 59.8b, is a simulation program used for business training and analysis. It offers individuals an opportunity to make necessary decisions in managing a company. In fact, OBS also enforces the individual to work in a team and stimulates the team members to think critically and strategically in obtaining business analysis in three major sections, namely, operation, marketing, and financial other than enhancing leadership skills.

Thus, it allows the team members to experience the concepts in business and entre-preneurship. It also provides understanding of business concepts in a competitive but safe environment. Even though the online modules such as online quizzes and OBS have become a trend in teaching, a lecture delivery in a classroom remains to be the best platform for knowledge transfer from the lecturers to the students. The students from each faculty will be divided into smaller groups, i.e., 100 students in a class, and they are supervised by two lecturers from the respective faculties so that the knowledge can be effectively delivered to the students. In addition, the students who enrolled for this course are able to learn through engagement, real entrepre-neurship lessons, and experiences from invited entrepreneurs via the Public Lecture 1 and Public Lecture 2. These activities have created a good platform for the students to know and communicate with the local successful entrepreneurs. The students are also encouraged to socialize with community around the campus in order to gener-ate and propose innovative business ideas for their business concept presentation and poster competition. They are encouraged to communicate with the community members and conduct brief surveys about their ideas. These activities may help the institution to produce better graduates with resilience.

Findings

From a statistical data collected in 2015 (entry survey and exit survey), it is shown that this project makes a difference in relation to students' awareness and intentions towards entrepreneurship. Through the two series of public lectures, business con-cept presentation and entrepreneurial activities conducted in classes, and during UKM Entrepreneur Day, all first-year students who are from different fields of study such as medical, pharmacy, dentistry, and engineering have opportunities to partici-pate in business plan preparation and presentation. In addition, the students who go through this course will have basic experience in managing and developing entrepreneurship processes including finance and marketing using the OBS games. Thus, they have learnt to analyze all operations by strategic thinking, solving prob-lem, and decision-making exercise. As a result, the students have portrayed more positive entrepreneurial attitudes and intentions as well as innovative characteris-tics. Furthermore, the project has taught the students to be effective leaders, manag-ers, and team players which later may help them to be graduates and improve their employability.

Conclusion

By looking at the increasing number of students for the Fundamental of Entrepreneurship and Innovation course since early 2010, it is vital that improve-ments in the delivery and content of the course to be made and endorsed by relevant agencies. As a way forward, research as to the achievements of the learning outcomes among students must be addressed. This exercise will reveal if the acculturation of entrepreneurship has actually taken place among both students and academics. As the teaching of entrepreneurship in the institutions is new, it is also important to see the extent of acceptance of the course and its aims in the academic fraternity. The biggest challenge in conducting academic entrepreneurship is implementing these courses for lecturers and students from various academic backgrounds. Therefore, every faculty in UKM has a coordinator of entrepreneurship and innovation, which will oversee the course and the entrepreneurial activities conducted in their respective faculties. Lecturers will be given training in entrepreneurship course through workshops named "Training of Trainers" (ToT) to equip them in conducting the course to the students. More number of lecturers will be involved based on the number of students at their faculty. Certainly there is a big difference between "teachers" who teach with great interest, passion, and commitment and those who teach only for the sake of fulfilling their academic duties. Furthermore, consideration needs to be given when dealing with generation Y students (those born in the late 1980s or afterwards); these groups are called as Internet generation. Therefore, the practices of social networking tools as a communication medium such as Facebook and Instagram are necessary requirements for the lecturers as well.

Acknowledgment The authors would like to thank Pusat Citra Universiti, Universiti Kebangsaan Malaysia, for giving the authors an opportunity to conduct this research. This research is funded by Institut Penyelidikan Pendidikan Tinggi Negara (IPPTN) (IPPTN/KPT/CLMV/2016/T05) (2), Research Project Code No: GG-2016-004 towards the writing of this chapter.

References

Bessant, J., & Tidd, J. (2011). *Innovation and entrepreneurship* (2nd ed.). Chichester: Wiley.

Brennan, M. C., & McGowan, P. (2006). Academic entrepreneurship: An exploratory case study. *International Journal of Entrepreneurial Behavior & Research, 12*(3), 144–164.

Brennan, M. C., Wall, A. P., & McGowan, P. (2005). Academic entrepreneurship: Assessing preferences in nascent entrepreneurs. *Journal of Small Business and Enterprise Development, 12*(3), 307–322.

Brussels. (2012). Effects and impact of entrepreneurship programmes in higher education. Report was prepared in 2012 for the European Commission, DG Enterprise and Industry. file:///C:/Users/Rosilah/Downloads/effects_impact_high_edu_final_report_en_7428.pdf.

Hassan, R., Mohd Tawil, N., Hanafiah, M. H., & Wan Zaki, W. M. D. (2016). Principles of entrepreneurship and innovation, Bangi. ISBN 9789839122275. Pusat Citra Universiti, UKM.

Hassan, R., Mohd Tawil, N., Ramlee, S., Ismail, K., & Wahi, W. (2015). Exploring academic entrepreneurship: A case study at Universiti Kebangsaan Malaysia, 10th European Conference on Innovation and Entrepreneurship, University of Genoa, Italy, September 17–18, 2015.

OBS website, www.obs.ukm.my.

Rahim, H. L., & Chik, R. (2014). Graduate entrepreneurs creation: A case of Universiti Teknologi MARA, Malaysia. *Australian Journal of Basic and Applied Sciences, 8*(23), 15–20.

Rosilah, H., Norngainy, M. T., & Norizan, A. R. (2014, August). An overview of business simulation system for Malaysian entrepreneur. IEEE ICE2T — 2014 4th International Conference on Engineering Technology and Technopreneurship (ICE2T), pp. 15–18.

Scriptopro website, www.scriptopro.com/.

Uzunidis, D., Boutillier, S., & Laperche, B. (2014). Entrepreneurs 'resource potential' and the organic square of entrepreneurship: Definition and application to the French case. *Journal of Innovation and Entrepreneurship, 3*(1), 1–17.

Zakaria, S., Yusoff, W. F. W., & Madun, R. H. R. (2011). Entrepreneurship education in Malaysia: Nurturing entrepreneurial interest amongst students. *Journal of Modern Accounting and Auditing, 7*(6), 615–620.

Chapter 60
The Relationship Between Conflict Management and Job Performance

Mohd Yunus Majid and Fariedah Maarof

Abstract The aim of this study is to examine the relationship between conflict management (CM) and job performance (JP). There are five styles of conflict management which are integrating, dominating, obliging, avoiding, and compromising. However, in this research the author only focuses on integrating, obliging, and compromising styles which are considered as our independent variables and job performance as our dependent variable. Accordingly, dominating (high concern for self and low concern for others) and avoiding (low concern for self and others) styles do not fit Malaysian culture. Data consists of respondents in the banking sector. Correlation analysis was used to support the findings. It was found out that obliging and compromising have a significant relationship with job performance while no relationship exists between integrating and job performance. It appears that the reserved and soft-spoken Malaysian would opt to sacrifice their goals (obliging) and can easily agree with the outcomes of the conflict management (compromise), as supported by research findings by Wang et al. (Manag Int Rev 45:3–21, 2005). The individualistic-collectivist culture characteristics indicate different approaches between Western and Asian managers in handling conflict management, Wang et al. (Manag Int Rev 45:3–21, 2005).

Keywords Conflict management • Job satisfaction • Integrating • Obliging • Compromising

Introduction

Conflict is unavoidable and professionals spend great amount of their time dealing with it. Studies have shown that conflict embraces all levels and aspects of organizations and hence conflict management is crucial because, when managed

M.Y. Majid (✉)
Universiti Tenaga Nasional, Bangi, Malaysia
e-mail: yunus@uniten.edu.my

F. Maarof
Canadian University of Dubai, Dubai, United Arab Emirates
e-mail: fariedah@cud.ac.ae

© Springer International Publishing Switzerland 2017   687
R. Benlamri, M. Sparer (eds.), *Leadership, Innovation and Entrepreneurship as Driving Forces of the Global Economy*, Springer Proceedings in Business and Economics, DOI 10.1007/978-3-319-43434-6_60

properly, it will resolve a lot of misunderstanding, eliminate miscommunication, clear up unsolved issues, and improve leadership effectiveness, Tjosvold (2008), Korbanik, Baril, and Watson (1993), Darling and Fogliasso (1990). Customarily organizations often view conflict as undesirable and unproductive, rather than as a way to sort out things, Boonsathorn (2007). Conversely, in an organizational context, conflicts are common, yet most of the time meaningful, and eventually promote better working environment. Avoiding conflict has been proved ineffectual while wishing for a conflict-free work environment is unrealistic, Tjosvold (2002). As professionals interact in organizations, diverse cultural backgrounds, beliefs, gender, education experience, values, and situations may spawn tension and conflict. When conflict is recognized, acknowledged, and managed in a proper manner, personal and organizational benefits will result that will encourage creativity and growth (Silverthorne, 2005). Accordingly, productively managed conflict can strengthen trust between team members and thereby improved team performance (Kozlowski & Klein, 2000). It turns out that, today, to be an effective manager, they seek not to avoid but to manage conflict within the organization (Rahim, Antonioni, & Psenicka, 2001).

Purpose of Study

The purpose of this study is to examine the relationship between conflict management and job performance of executives in Malaysian banking sectors. Besides this, only three out of five conflict management styles were zoomed in, i.e., integrating, obliging, and compromising.

Literature Review

Conflicts exist when the goals of at least two competing parties are not compatible to each other due to competing scarce resources and conflict management refers to responses or behavior that people use in the conflict (Wilmot & Hocker, 2001). Job performance is about adhering to established standards when doing one's job. It involves actions and activities that can be monitored and measured, Mrayyan and Al-Fouri (2008). Over the last four decades, as job performance phenomenon increasingly becomes more complex, management and researches have shifted their perspectives on how they look at job performance; Arvey and Murphy (1998); Barbuto, Phipps, and Xu (2009); Blickle et al. (2010); Griffin et al. (2007); Griffin, Neal, and Parker (2007); and Mrayyan and Al-Fouri (2008) argued that the shift was from narrow focus of fixed tasks to wider span of work roles.

Conflict Management and Job Performance

The approach towards conflict management has been continuously studied and researchers have categorized them through a variety of classifications. Follett (1940) first conceptualized the first five-style classification of behavioral conflict handling—domination, compromise, integration, avoidance, and suppression. Deutsch (1949) explores another conceptuality involving either cooperation or competition. It is argued that conflict management styles were related to attaining goals based on high/low concern for production and high/low concern for people. Five styles, i.e., withdrawing, smoothing, forcing, problem solving, and compromising, were proposed. Later, other researchers like Rahim and Bonoma (1979) extended this model by focusing on the desire to satisfy your own concerns and the desire to satisfy the other's concerns and this has ensued the five different styles of conflict management—integrating, obliging, dominating, avoiding, and compromising.

Rahim (2002) posited that organizational learning and effectiveness can be enhanced through a correct diagnosis of organizational conflict and involvement of structural interventions in the conflict. However, further inspection in related literature exposed that there have been mixed preferences regarding the practice of conflict management. Boonsathorn (2007) indicated that Thai executives were more inclined towards avoiding and obliging styles of conflict management than the American executives. However, from the study, staying longer in other cultures would change their approach, the more they seem to using a dominating style, and the less relying on avoiding and obliging styles (Boonsathorn, 2007). Elsayed-Ekhouly and Buda (1996) learned that Middle East executives revealed more integrating and avoiding styles, while American executives unveiled more obliging, dominating, and compromising styles.

Kozan (1989) claimed that the Turkish approach of conflict management was very much influenced by hierarchy levels. The respect for higher authority compels subordinates to resort to a more accommodative approach, while suppressing/and or avoiding competition between peers (focus on collectivism and group harmony), and imposing solutions on subordinates (analogous to a parent–child relationship). In situation where group consists of different cultures, commonly, a third party would be used in resolving conflicts to maintain harmony in organizations. Ergin and Kozan (1999) and Kozan, Ergin, and Varoğlu (2007) confirmed that more than 65 % of conflicts in Turkish organizations resort to third parties.

Integrating and Job Performance

Integrating style has been characterized as someone who has high concern for themselves and for others, Gross and Guerrero (2000), Kim, Wang, Kondo, and Kim (2006), Ozkalp, Sungur, and Ozdemir (2008), Rahim (1992), and Shih and Susanto (2008), and the goal of this style is to reduce organizational conflict, Barbuto et al. (2009). This approach is considered as one of the most effective conflict management strategies, Gross and Guerrero (2000), and MacIntosh and Steven (2008), as it reduces not only conflict, but also stress, Barbuto et al. (2009). Common approach to this style includes openness, information sharing, cooperation, and finding alternative solutions to maximize outcome, Daly, Lee, Soutar, and Rasmi (2009); and Rahim (2002). Furthermore, it is reiterated that this style is also suitable when fusion of ideas is desirable to solving a complex problem where different set of skills and resources must be integrated. It was also found that this style improves job performance, De Dreu and Beersma (2005).

Obliging and Job Performance

This lose-win approach is about sacrificing oneself for the sake of others. The concern to preserve relationship is more important than achieving their own goals or outcomes, Rahim (2000). However, it is posited that this style was generally neutral and at times can be neither effective nor highly appropriate, Gross and Guerrero (2000). This style may be appropriate when a group or team is not familiar with the subject matter involved in a conflict or the goals of the other group much more important than their goals. This style may be appropriate when a party is dealing from a position of weakness or believes that preserving relationship is important, Rahim (2002).

Compromising and Job Performance

This give-and-take approach focuses on mutually acceptable outcomes or goals by both parties, Kim et al. (2006), and minimizing loss on both sides, Shih and Susanto (2008). This style is useful when the goals of the conflicting parties are mutually exclusive or when both parties are equally compelling, and because of that they fail to reach a consensus, Rahim (2002). Conversely, this style is also not appropriate when one party is more powerful than the other while believing that its position is right. Apparently, according to Daly et al. (2009), Shih and Susanto (2008), and Trubisky, Ting-Toomey, and Lin (1991), this style along with the integrating style is the most preferred style by some professionals when faced with organizational conflict.

Research Methodology

Hypothesis

Since our goal is to find the relationship between conflict management and job performance, we develop four hypotheses, one relating to the overall relationship while three others relating to the conflict approach. Our hypotheses are as follows:

H1: There is a significant relationship between conflict management and job performance.
H2: There is a significant relationship between integrating approach and job performance.
H3: There is a significant relationship between obliging approach and job performance.
H4: There is a significant relationship between compromising approach and job performance.

Research Framework

Figure 60.1 shows the relationship between the independent variables, i.e., conflict management, and dependent variable, i.e., job performance. Constructs for the independent variables are integrating, obliging, and compromising approach.

Data Collection

Due to time and financial constraints, sample data consisting of 250 questionnaires were sent to executives in the banking sector. However, only 164 (65.6%) were returned and used for the analysis. Questionnaires were sent at random.

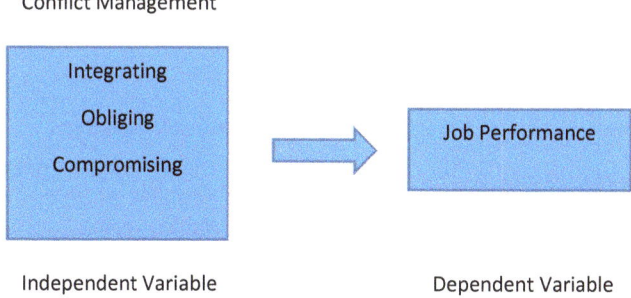

Fig. 60.1 Variables showing the relationship between conflict management and job performance

Finding and Analysis

Data were analyzed using SPSS V21.

Validity and Reliability Analysis

Table 60.1 summarizes the reliability analysis for all the independent variables, including the three constructs and the dependent variable.

It can be concluded that all the variables and constructs are reliable as the Cronbach's alpha coefficient shows a relatively high consistency.

Testing of Hypothesis

H1: There is a significant relationship between conflict management and job performance.

Based on the correlation result given in Table 60.2, there is a significant relationship between conflict management and job performance, with $r=0.237$, $N=164$, and $p<0.01$. Managing conflict is important to improve job performance. Proper management of conflict would improve job performance. The result shows consistency with that of Rahim (2002). He continued emphasizing that certain type of conflicts relating to tasks, policies, and other organizational issues have been proved to promote positive effect on individual and group performance.

H2: There is a significant relationship between integrating approach and job performance.

Hypothesis 2 is rejected as the result shows that $r=0.142$, $N=164$, and $p>0.05$, confirming that the relationship is not significant. Interestingly, although this approach is considered as one of the most effective conflict management strategies, as mentioned by Gross and Guerrero (2000), and MacIntosh and Steven (2008), where openness, information sharing, and cooperation are required towards problem solving and minimizing of organizational conflict; it seemed that, in our case,

Table 60.1 Reliability statistics

Cronbach's alpha	No. of items	Variables/constructs
0.713	9	Conflict management (independent)
0.873	5	Integrating approach
0.893	4	Obliging approach
0.820	6	Compromising approach
0.814	12	Job performance (dependent)

Table 60.2 Correlation value for all the variables

	CM	IA	OA	CA	JP
CM Pearson	1	.645**	.567**	.533**	.237**
Correlation	164	.000	.000	.000	.002
Sig. (2-tailed)		164	164	164	164
N					
IA Pearson		1	.279**	.258**	.142
Correlation		164	.000	.001	.000
Sig. (2-tailed)			164	164	164
N					
OA Pearson			1	.236**	.421**
Correlation			164	.002	.000
Sig. (2-tailed)				164	164
N					
CA Pearson				1	.188*
Correlation				164	.016
Sig. (2-tailed)					164
N					
JP Pearson					1
Correlation					164
Sig. (2-tailed)					
N					

**Correlation is significant at the 0.01 level (2-tailed)
*Correlation is significant at the 0.05 level (2-tailed)

the Malaysian executives are not ready for that. This shows that executives do not give high concern for themselves and the other parties in order to cooperate or manage the conflict among them. They may also do not give positive reaction, opinion, and judgment regarding the conflict. Malaysian culture slightly differs from the Western culture in such a way that the Malaysians are more reserved and tolerant and easy to concede to other opinions or ideas even though their opinions or ideas are more superior.

H3: There is a significant relationship between obliging approach and job performance.

With $r = 0.421$, $N = 164$, and $p < 0.01$, it can be summarized that there is a significant relationship between obliging approach and job performance. Obliging approach is also a common approach used by executive to manage conflict and improve job performance. This lose-win approach is very common for Malaysian executives. Probable reason would be because Malaysians don't like to argue, are more reserved, and prefer to preserve relationship among peers rather than going for open confrontation.

H4: There is a significant relationship between compromising approach and job performance.

Hypothesis 4 is also accepted based on the statistics $r=0.188$, $N=164$, and $p<0.05$. This tells us that executives use compromising style to overcome conflict in order to improve job performance. This give-and-take approach is also quite common for the Malaysian executives. This finding is also supported by Wang, Lin, Chan, and Shi (2005).

Conclusion

We mentioned earlier that previous results regarding conflict management are mixed. Cultural differences and hierarchical levels have contributed towards the mixed results, Boonsathorn (2007), Elsayed-Ekhouly and Buda (1996), and Kozan (1989, 2002). For a more complex situation, the involvement of third party would be a better approach, Kozan et al. (2007). Further researches could reveal other factors that may possibly have significant influence over conflict management. Our results also concur with the previous findings, showing that preferences for conflict management in the banking sector are also mixed.

References

Arvey, R. D., & Murphy, K. R. (1998). Performance valuation in work settings. *Annual Review of Psychology, 49*, 141–168.

Barbuto, J. E., Jr., Phipps, K. A., & Xu, Y. (2009). Testing relationship between personality, conflict styles, and effectiveness. *International Journal of Conflict Management, 21*(4), 1044–1068.

Blickle, G., Frohlich, J. K., Ehlert, S., Pirner, K., Dietl, E., Hanes, T. J., et al. (2010). Socioanalytic theory and work behavior: Roles of work values and political skill in job performance and promotability assessment. *Journal of Vocational Behavior, 78*, 136–148.

Boonsathorn, W. (2007). Understanding conflict management styles of Thais and Americans in multinational corporations in Thailand. *International Journal of Conflict Management, 18*(3), 196–221.

Daly, T. M., Lee, J. A., Soutar, G. N., & Rasmi, S. (2009). Conflict-handling style measurement: A best-worst scaling application. *International Journal of Conflict Management, 21*(3), 281–308.

Darling, J. R., & Fogliasso, C. E. (1990). Conflict management across cultural boundaries: A case analysis from a multinational bank. *European Business Review, 99*(6), 383–396.

De Dreu, C. K., & Beersma, B. (2005). Conflict in organizations: Beyond effectiveness and performance. *European Journal of Work and Organizational Psychology, 14*, 105–117.

Deutsch, M. (1949). A theory of cooperation and competition. *Human Relations, 2*, 129–151.

Elsayed-Ekhouly, S. M., & Buda, R. (1996). Organizational conflict: A comparative analysis of conflict styles across cultures. *International Journal of Conflict Management, 7*(1), 71–81.

Ergin, C., & Kozan, M. K. (1999). The influence of intra-cultural value differences on conflict management practices. *International Journal of Conflict Management, 10*(3), 249–267.

Follett, M. (1940). Constructive conflict. In H. C. Metcalf & L. Urwick (Eds.), *Dynamic administration: The collective papers of Mary Parker Follett* (pp. 30–49). New York: Harper & Row.

Griffin, M. A., Neal, A., & Parker, S. K. (2007). A new model of work role performance: Positive behavior in uncertain and interdependent contexts. *Academy of Management Journal, 50*(2), 327–347.

Gross, M. A., & Guerrero, L. K. (2000). Managing conflict appropriately and effectively: An application of the competence model to Rahim's organizational conflict styles. *International Journal of Conflict Management, 11*(3), 200–226.

Kim, T., Wang, C., Kondo, M., & Kim, T. (2006). Conflict management styles: The differences among the Chinese, Japanese and Koreans. *International Journal of Conflict Management, 18*(1), 96–104.

Korbanik, K., Baril, G., & Watson, C. (1993). Managers' conflict management style and leadership effectiveness: The moderating effects of gender. *Sex Roles, 29*, 405–420.

Kozan, M. K. (1989). Cultural influences on styles of handling interpersonal conflicts: Comparisons among Jordanian, Turkish, and US managers. *Human Relations, 42*, 782–799.

Kozan, M. K., Ergin, C., & Varoğlu, D. (2007). Third party intervention strategies of managers in subordinates' conflicts in Turkey. *International Journal of Conflict Management, 18*(2), 128–147.

Kozlowski, S. W. J., & Klein, K. J. (2000). A multilevel approach to theory and research in organizations: Contextual, temporal, and emergent process. In K. J. Klein & S. W. J. Kozlowski (Eds.), *Multilevel theory, research, and methods in organizations* (pp. 3–90). San Francisco: Jossey-Bass.

MacIntosh, G., & Steven, C. (2008). Personality, motives and conflict strategies in everyday service encounters. *International Journal of Conflict Management, 19*(2), 112–131.

Mrayyan, M. T., & Al-Fouri, I. (2008). Career Commitment and Job Performance of Jordanian Nurses. *Nurse Forum, 43*(1), 24–37.

Ozkalp, E., Sungur, Z., & Ozdemir, A. A. (2008). Conflict management styles of Turkish Managers. *Journal of European Industrial Training, 33*(5), 419–438.

Rahim, M. A. (1992). *Managing conflict in organizations* (2nd ed.). New York: Praeger.

Rahim, M. A. (2000). Empirical studies on conflict management. *International Journal of Conflict Management, 11*(1), 5–8.

Rahim, M. A. (2002). Toward a theory of managing organizational conflict. *International Journal of Conflict Management, 13*(3), 206–235.

Rahim, M. A., Antonioni, D., & Psenicka, C. (2001). A structural equations model of leader power, subordinates' styles of handling conflict, and job performance. *International Journal of Conflict Management, 12*(3), 191–211.

Rahim, M. A., & Bonoma, V. T. (1979). Managing organizational conflict: A model for diagnosis and intervention. *Psychological Reports, 44*, 1323–44.

Shih, H., & Susanto, E. (2008). Conflict management styles, emotional intelligence, and job performance in public organization. *International Journal of Conflict Management, 21*(2), 147–168.

Silverthorne, C. P. (2005). *Organizational psychology in cross-cultural perspective*. New York: New York University Press.

Tjosvold, D. (2002). Managing anger for teamwork in Hong Kong: Goal interdependence and open-mindedness. *Asian Journal Social Psychology, 5*, 107–123.

Tjosvold, D. (2008). The conflict-positive organization: It depends upon us. *Journal of Organizational Behavior, 29*, 19–28.

Trubisky, P., Ting-Toomey, S., & Lin, S. L. (1991). The influence of individualism-collectivism and self-monitoring on conflict styles. *International Journal of Intercultural Relations, 15*(1), 65–84.

Wang, C. L., Lin, X., Chan, A. K. K., & Shi, Y. (2005). Conflict handling styles in international joint ventures: A cross-cultural and cross-national comparison. *Management International Review, 45*(1), 3–21.

Wilmot, W. W., & Hocker, J. L. (2001). *Interpersonal conflict*. New York: McGraw-Hill.

Part IV
New Trends in Global Economics, Finance, and Management

Chapter 61
Volatility Persistence and Shock Absorption Capacity of the Malaysian Stock Market

Elgilani Eltahir Elshareif and Muhammed Kabir

Abstract Estimation of the extent of volatility in stock markets induced by external shocks and the persistence of it is very important and has policy significance for the macroeconomic policy makers, central bankers, and the financial market participants. In the current study, we examine the overestimation bias of volatility and its persistence using EGARCH-M models for the Malaysian stock market composite index (KLCI), as well as three sub-sectoral indices. The empirical evidence shows that there are asymmetric responses by the stock indices whereby volatility originating from ascending versus descending stock market has different impacts. In addition, we have found that the volatility is highly persistent and the shock absorption capacity of the stock market has been underestimated. However, this finding suggests that there might have been some estimation bias due to misspecification of the model. This implies that the policy makers and market participants must exercise caution in drawing conclusions from this class of models.

Keywords Volatility persistence • Malaysian stock market • Shock absorption capacity • EGARCH-M

Introduction

The impact of external stocks to the domestic stock markets in the Asian region has led to volatility shifts during the last three decades. All the stock markets in the region have experienced significant shifts in the financial volatility, and Malaysian market is no exception. During periods of external shocks, the volatility of the Kuala Lumpur Stock Exchange (KLSE) increased quite a bit which affected the

E.E. Elshareif (✉)
Canadian University of Dubai, PO Box 117781, Dubai, United Arab Emirates
e-mail: elgilani@cud.ac.ae

M. Kabir
Canadian University of Dubai, PO Box 117781, Dubai, United Arab Emirates

University of New Brunswick, Saint John, NB, Canada
e-mail: kabir@cud.ac.ae

© Springer International Publishing Switzerland 2017
R. Benlamri, M. Sparer (eds.), *Leadership, Innovation and Entrepreneurship as Driving Forces of the Global Economy*, Springer Proceedings in Business and Economics, DOI 10.1007/978-3-319-43434-6_61

confidence level of investors. This impact of the heightened volatility was reflected in a substantial decline in the key benchmark Kuala Lumpur Composite Index (KLCI). The high volatility shift in the Malaysian stock market received a great deal of attention from researchers, policy makers, and market participants, including investors, brokers, dealers, and regulators. As it is expected, a high level of uncertainty reduced investors' confidence and who then postponed their decision to investment which then impacted economic growth.

It is important to both policy makers and market practitioners to understand the behavior of stock market volatility. Policy makers are, by and large, interested in the main determinants of volatility, its impact on real economic activity, and evaluating regulatory framework to optimally manage international capital flows. On the other hand, market participants are primarily concerned in the direct effects the time-varying volatility wields on the pricing of financial assets and the concomitant hedging strategies to manage risks.

It is now widely accepted that the assumption of constant variances over time is no longer valid, and hence it cannot be measured using the conventional measures of variances and covariance. Instead, one has to use the generalized autoregressive conditional heteroskedasticity (GARCH) model which can capture the time-varying properties of the stochastic shocks in the system. This class of models have been developed by a number of authors and now are being used in financial econometric research (see Bollerslev, 1986; Bollerslev, Chou, & Kroner, 1992; Engle & Ng, 1993).

Volatility is considered highly persistent if a shock to a given system is permanent, and the past volatility can be used in constructing forecasts of future volatility. However, quiet periods where prices are somewhat stable could be followed by comparatively high-volatility periods. A survey of the literature reveals that although numerous studies were carried out to study the impact of the 1997 Asian financial crisis and 2007 global financial crisis on the regional stock markets, studies dealing with the effects of sudden changes in volatility on stock markets using a decomposition approach during these two periods were few and far between.

In the current study, the overestimation bias of volatility and its persistence in the Malaysian stock market have been examined, and unlike the previous studies, in this study the market has been disaggregated which has enabled us to make a comparative study of the differential impact of volatility on the composite market and also the subsectors of the market during the period 1990–2011. Therefore, the research question to be addressed is the following:

Is there an overestimation bias of volatility and its persistence in the Malaysian stock market?

This question is important for policy makers, portfolio managers, and investors who are managing funds to optimize risk-adjusted returns.

The remainder of this chapter is organized as follows. Section "Methodology" presents the methodology. Section "Data and Descriptive Statistics" describes the data and descriptive statistics. Section "Empirical Results" reports the empirical results and final section presents the concluding remarks.

Methodology

It is well recognized that the GARCH models are widely used for stock market volatility analyses. Since the introduction of the autoregressive conditional hetero-skedasticity (ARCH) model by Engle (1982) to explain the volatility of inflation rates, many researchers have employed ARCH with some modifications to different types of financial time series. One of the model modifications is the GARCH model developed by Bollerslev (1986). However, the GARCH model cannot capture the leverage or asymmetric effect found by, among others, Black (1976), and confirmed by the findings of Campbell and Hentschel (1992), French, Schwert, and Stambaugh (1987), Ghassan and AlHajhoj (2016), Glosten, Jagannathan, and Runkle (1993), Nelson (1991) and Schwert (1990). It has been found that the degree of volatility has been asymmetric in response to negative versus positive shocks. One method that captures such asymmetric responses is Nelson's (1991) exponential GARCH or EGARCH model. In addition, EGARCH model can be enhanced further to incorporate the interdependence between risk and returns. These enhanced models are called EGARCH-M. The EGARCH-M model for the weekly stock market returns can be represented by the following system of equations:

$$r_t = \pi_0 + \sum_{i=1}^{p} \pi_i r_{t-i} + \varepsilon_t + \sum_{j=1}^{q} \theta \varepsilon_{t-j} + \varphi \sqrt{h_t} \tag{61.1}$$

$$\varepsilon_t \left| \phi_{t-1} \right. \sim GED \tag{61.2}$$

$$\log(h_t) = \omega + \sum_{i=1}^{p} \alpha_i \left| \frac{\varepsilon_{t-i}}{h_{t-i}} \right| + \sum_{k=1}^{r} \gamma_k \frac{\varepsilon_{t-k}}{h_{t-k}} + \sum_{j=1}^{q} \beta_j \log(h_{t-j}) \tag{61.3}$$

where r_t represents respective weekly stock return; ε_t is the market innovation or residuals; h_t is the respective conditional variance of the returns process based on the information set (ϕ_{t-1}) of relevant and available past data; and ω, β, γ, and α are parameters to be estimated. The conditional variance is asymmetrical, if the estimated leverage-effect term, γ, is significantly different from zero ($\gamma \neq 0$). Parameters in the variance equation (Eq. 61.3) are obtained through the maximum likelihood estimation, namely the Marquardt method with robust standard errors.

The robustness of the EGARCH-M models was examined by using three standard diagnostic tests, namely the Ljung Box Q-statistic for autocorrelation, Jarque-Bera statistic for non-normality of the standardized residuals, and the ARCH LM test for conditional heteroskedasticity (ARCH) effect.

Data and Descriptive Statistics

The data used in this study consist of the weekly closing stock price index of Kuala Lumpur Composite Index (KLCI), and three of its sub-indices which are plantation (PLT), industrial (IND), and finance (FIN). Weekly rather than daily data were

Table 61.1 Descriptive statistics for the Malaysian stock market indices

	KLCI	Industrial	Finance	Plantation
Mean	0.0012	0.0013	0.0016	0.0016
Std. Dev.	0.0129	0.0126	0.0147	0.0138
Skewness	2.1998	3.4857	2.3142	1.1366
Kurtosis	30.4179	45.8603	30.1676	24.4249
Jarque-Bera	34346.01	83988.27	33829.48	20676.11
(P-value)	0.0000	0.0000	0.0000	0.0000
Observations	1069	1069	1069	1069

Notes: Skewness measures the asymmetry of the distribution of the series around its mean. The skewness of a normal distribution is zero. Kurtosis measures the peakness or flatness of the distribution of the series. The kurtosis of the normal distribution is 3. If the kurtosis exceeds 3, the distribution is leptokurtic, and if less than 3 platykurtic relative to the normal distribution

chosen to avoid the potential biases associated with microstructural issues, non-trading, the bid-ask spread effect in daily data, and problems of thin trading which were often associated with most emerging markets. All stock price series were collected from DataStream and spanned from June 1990 to June 2011. The stock market returns were calculated according to the following expression:

$$r_t = \left(\log S_t - \log S_{t-1} \right) \times 100 \tag{61.4}$$

where $\log S_t$ was the natural logarithm of the index at week t. Dividends were assumed away (see Campbell, Lo, & Mackinlay, 1997).

Table 61.1 reports the descriptive statistics for the four indices and a number of observations can be made from these data. First, during our sample period from June 1990 to June 2011, all the Malaysian stock prices has a positive mean return, with the finance and plantation indices demonstrating a higher return than others. Secondly, the standard deviation, which measures stock return volatility, indicated that the finance and plantation indices have the highest standard deviation. Thirdly, returns from KLCI and all the other sub-indices displayed positive skewness and these are not normally distributed. Fourthly, the kurtosis values for all the four indices exceeded 3, indicating a leptokurtic distribution. Finally, the Jarque-Bera (JB) statistic reported in the fifth column of Table 61.1 confirmed the significant departure of these stock returns from normal distribution, which was similar to the findings of Kang, Cho, and Yoon (2009) and Wang and Moore (2009), even though these previous analyses were done on other markets.

Empirical Results

We estimated the extent of volatility and its persistence in the Malaysian stock market induced by external shocks. The results from the EGARCH-M models in Table 61.2 show that all the parameters are highly significant. The persistence of

Table 61.2 EGARCH-M parameters

EGARCH-M							
Indices	α	β	$\alpha + \beta$	γ	Log-likelihood	LM ARCH (20)	Q (20)
KLCI	0.245 (0.000)	0.968 (0.000)	1.213	−0.05807 (0.070)	2489.89	0.1467 (0.99)	17.32 (0.501)
Industrial	0.288 (0.000)	0.950 (0.000)	1.238	−0.10647 (0.005)	2341.08	0.5019 (0.88)	16.49 (0.734)
Finance	0.341 (0.000)	0.892 (0.000)	1.233	−0.08016 (0.024)	2508.83	0.2291 (0.99)	14.92 (0.667)
Plantation	0.608 (0.000)	0.624 (0.000)	1.232	−0.16508 (0.035)	2843.43	1.11 (0.32)	28.28 (0.029)

Notes: *p*-Values were reported in the parenthesis. Q (20) were the Ljung-Box Q statistics for 20th order in standardized residuals. An ARCH LM (20) test statistic checks for autoregressive conditional heteroskedasticity up to order 20 (the optimal structure of ARCH LM test was detected at lag 20)

shocks as measured by the sum $(\alpha + \beta)$ appears to be very high indicating that shocks may have a permanent effect on the variance of returns and the shock absorption capacity of the stock market may have been underestimated. This result makes it pertinent to reexamine the model specification to ascertain that the high-volatility persistence is not spurious.

The estimated γ coefficient reveals that the response of the stock indices has been asymmetric. All the γ coefficients are statistically significant indicating that asymmetries are present in the Malaysian stock market and negative shocks lead to higher volatility in stock return compared with positive shocks. Our overall results are consistent with Law (2006).

The estimated model was subjected to a battery of statistical tests to evaluate the robustness of the model. The Ljung-Box Q statistics were calculated to test for serial correlation in standardized residuals and all the series were found to be free of serial correlation. The ARCH-LM test suggested the absence of heteroskedasticity in the residuals. In addition, the estimated residuals from models with sudden shifts in volatility show higher log-likelihood values and smaller values of skewness and kurtosis in comparison to the estimated residuals from the original models.

Conclusions

In the current study, we have examined the overestimation bias of volatility and its persistence using EGARCH-M models for the Malaysian stock market composite index (KLCI), as well as three sub-sectoral indices, namely industrial (IND), finance (FIN), and plantation (PLT). The empirical evidence shows that there are asymmetric responses by the stock indices whereby volatility originating from ascending versus descending stock market has different impacts. In addition, we have found that the volatility is highly persistent and the shock absorption capacity of the stock market has been underestimated. However, this finding suggests that there might have been some estimation bias due to misspecification of the model.

The results have significance for policy makers, portfolio managers, and investors who are managing funds to optimize risk-adjusted returns. However, in view of the overestimation of the volatility persistence, the policy makers and market participants must exercise caution before drawing conclusions one way or another.

It must be mentioned here that the EGARCH-M models can play an important role in identifying the relationship between volatility and returns using γ parameter. It is not always appreciated by researchers why the downward volatility is normally more pronounced compared with upward volatility. Downward movement in stock prices besides being a negative factor for portfolio managers also triggers margin calls that only accentuate the extent of volatility. The estimated γ helps draw attention to these facts.

References

Black, F. (1976). Studies in stock price volatility changes. In *Proceedings of the 1976 business meeting of the business and economics statistics section* (pp. 177–181). American Statistical Association.

Bollerslev, T. (1986). Generalized autoregressive conditional heteroskedasticity. *Journal of Econometrics, 31*, 307–327.

Bollerslev, T., Chou, R. Y., & Kroner, K. F. (1992). ARCH modeling in finance: A review of the theory and empirical evidence. *Journal of Econometrics, 52*, 5–59.

Campbell, J. Y., & Hentschel, L. (1992). No news is good news: An asymmetric model of changing volatility in stock returns. *Journal of Financial Economics, 31*, 281–318.

Campbell, J., Lo, A., & Mackinlay, A. (1997). *The econometrics of financial markets*. Princeton, NJ: Princeton University Press.

Engle, R. (1982). Autoregressive conditional heteroskedasticity with estimates of the variance of U.K. Inflation. *Econometrica, 50*, 987–1008.

Engle, R., & Ng, V. (1993). Measuring and testing the impact of news on volatility. *Journal of Finance, 48*, 49–78.

French, K., Schwert, G. W., & Stambaugh, R. (1987). Expected stock returns and volatility. *Journal of Political Economy, 99*, 385–415.

Ghassan, H. B., & AlHajhoj, H. R. (2016). Long run dynamic volatilities between OPEC and non-OPEC crude oil price. *Journal of Applied Energy, 169*, 384–394.

Glosten, L. R., Jagannathan, R., & Runkle, D. E. (1993). On the relation between the expected value and the volatility of the nominal excess return on stocks. *Journal of Finance, 48*, 1779–1801.

Kang, S. H., Cho, H. G., & Yoon, S. M. (2009). Modeling sudden volatility changes: Evidence from Japanese and Korean stock markets. *Physica, A388*, 3543–3550.

Law, S. H. (2006). Has stock market volatility in the Kuala Lumpur stock exchange returned to pre-Asian financial crisis levels? *ASEAN Economic Bulletin, 23*, 212–219.

Nelson, D. (1991). Conditional heteroskedasticity in asset returns: A new approach. *Econometrica, 59*, 347–370.

Schwert, G. W. (1990). Stock volatility and the crash of '87'. *Journal of Finance, 45*, 1129–1155.

Wang, P., & Moore, T. (2009). Sudden changes in volatility: The case of five central European stock markets. *Journal of International Financial Markets, Institutions & Money, 19*, 33–46.

Chapter 62
Augmented Reality: Uses and Future Considerations in Marketing

Saifeddin Alimamy, Kenneth R. Deans, and Juergen Gnoth

Abstract Technology has changed the way marketers interact and engage with customers and data. New and exciting technologies are emerging but there is little consensus about their relative importance beyond the initial hype. Augmented reality (AR) is one such technology that has the potential to facilitate dialogue and interaction between physical and digital worlds potentially leading to the creation of value for both customers and organizations. In this chapter we propose that AR can also aid the research process and generate deeper and more meaningful customer insights which will aid the reduction of customer-perceived risks. This chapter emphasizes the importance of AR in marketing and seeks to encourage discussion of the potential uses for AR in overcoming traditional limitations in marketing and customer research.

Keywords Augmented reality • Marketing • Technology • Experiential marketing • Mixed methods • Research methods • Simulation • Perceived risk • Innovation

Background

The most widely used definition of marketing involves the "creation" and "capturing" of value (Kotler & Armstrong, 2010). The concept of value has been discussed numerous times and more recently there has been a growing emphasis on customer and organizational interactions which pave the way for a mutual value-creation relationship to be created (Grönroos, 2006, 2008; Vargo & Lusch, 2004). Thus, adding elements of interactivity allows for deeper customer engagement and higher customer satisfaction (Ballantyne and Varey, 2006; Ballantine, 2005; Dholakia & Zhao, 2009). One particular type of interactivity that has been growing in popularity is

S. Alimamy (✉) • J. Gnoth
University of Otago, Dunedin, New Zealand
e-mail: alisa987@student.otago.ac.nz; juergen.gnoth@otago.ac.nz

K.R. Deans
La Rochelle Business School, La Rochelle, France
e-mail: deansk@esc-larochelle.fr

© Springer International Publishing Switzerland 2017   705
R. Benlamri, M. Sparer (eds.), *Leadership, Innovation and Entrepreneurship as Driving Forces of the Global Economy*, Springer Proceedings in Business and Economics, DOI 10.1007/978-3-319-43434-6_62

Fig. 62.1 Tourist location enhanced by AR

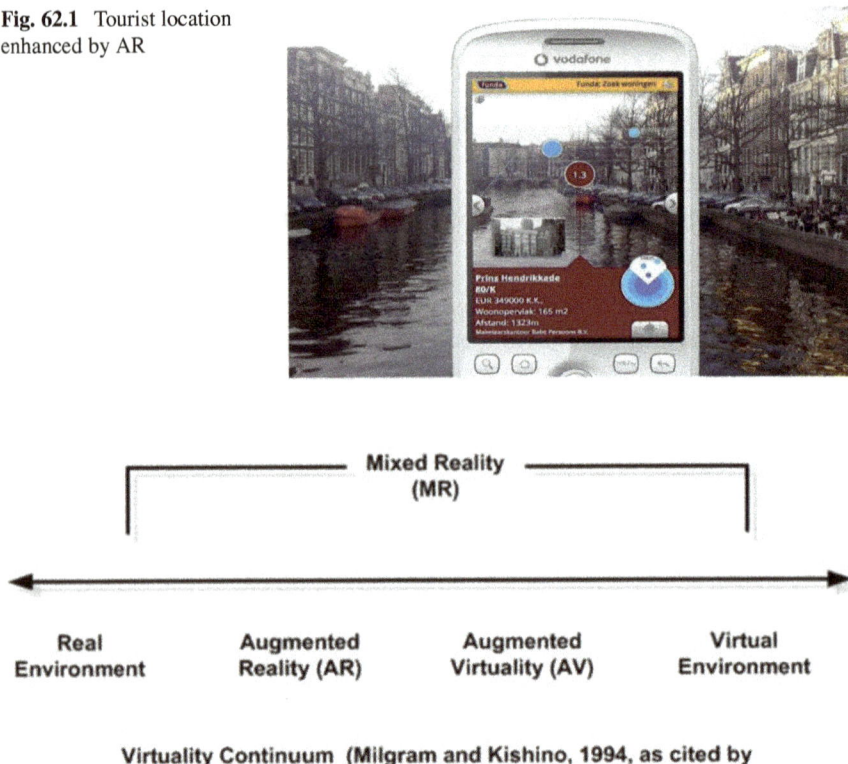

Virtuality Continuum (Milgram and Kishino, 1994, as cited by Christian, 2006, p. 2)

Fig. 62.2 Virtuality continuum (Milgram and Kishino 1994)

AR. AR is the incorporation of digital elements into the physical world through technology. It enhances the physical world by adding elements such as textual content, URL links, video, and audio into previously static objects (Vaughan-Nichols, 2009). Users of AR point a device with a camera, e.g., smartphone or tablet, at a particular graphic, barcode, product, or other physical "trigger" to augment that 3D space and add additional elements or information that are overlaid in a video stream on top of the physical product Clawson (2009). Figure 62.1 shows how information can be overlaid on a device:

Thus it can be seen that AR adds elements that the user can interact with while they view something of interest. The difference between AR and virtual reality (VR) is that VR fully replaces the physical world with another world whereas AR retains the existing world but with additional information (Figs. 62.2 and 62.3).

Historically, AR was only used in specific industries and applications such as a pilots' heads up display (HUD) units and flight/military simulations. In other words, it was used in situations with a high risk when something went wrong and so it was essential to test products and services so that they were ready when the situation demanded.

AR and Perceived Risk

One of the main goals for marketers is to increase customers' likelihood of purchasing products. Two major theories underpinning customers' willing to purchase have been developed (Agarwal & Teas, 2001). One stream of research states that customers will choose products that offer them the greatest perceived value (Zeithaml, 1988). The second stream of research states that customers will choose the products that have the least perceived risk (Bauer, 1960). Bauer proposed that risk is integrated in consumer behavior because purchasing "produce consequences which he [the customer] cannot anticipate with anything approximating certainty, and some of which at least are likely to be unpleasant" (Bauer, 1960, p. 24). Since the entry of risk in the consumer behavior field, research has tested and proved the premise (Cox, 1967; Cox & Rich, 1964; Dowling & Staelin, 1994; Verhage, Yavas, & Green, 1990).

Perceived risk is the uncertainty that customers face as well as the potential negative consequences that will result from the purchase of a product (Dowling & Staelin, 1994; Taylor, 1974). Thus, the more risk that customers perceive, the less likely they will make a purchase. In order to reduce the risks, organizations and customers have adopted "risk relievers" (Ross, 1975; Zuckerman & Kuhlman, 1978) that aid in the reduction of risk. A risk reliever is any type of action, e.g., information acquisition that a buyer or seller uses as a strategy to reduce risk (Roselius, 1971). We propose that AR will reduce perceived risk dimensions associated with a purchase. The following model sums up the scope of the proposed research:

Social Risk

One of the dimensions of risk is social risk (Kaplan et al., 1974) which is defined as "to what extent does the person [customer] think that other people judge him by his brand decision" (Brody & Cunningham, 1968, p. 51); a customer usually seeks social reassurances and "social approval" (Newton & Cox, 1967) from other people who they value, such as friends and family.

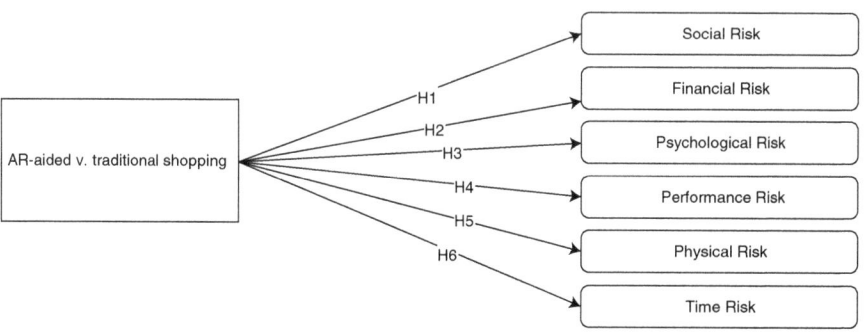

Fig. 62.3 Proposed conceptual model

Social risk is also attributed to the "tendency to engage in word of mouth" (Perry & Hamm, 1969; Roselius, 1971). When a customer perceives the social risk to be high, they will usually turn towards communication with their friends and family to seek approval (Newton & Cox, 1967).

Previous research found that performance risk is generally rated higher than social risk (Lutz & Reilly, 1973) when assessing a variety of different consumer products. Other researches have also stated that social risk, although a significant dimension, does not generally rank the highest compared to other dimensions (Kaplan et al., 1974). This is true for most types of products, as can be determined through previous research (Kaplan et al., 1974).

It is assumed that AR-aided shopping allows for customers to connect with others (Bodhani, 2012; Bulearca and Tamarjan, 2010; Chevalier and Mayzlin, 2006) such as family and friends, to ask for their opinion and show the products before they purchase them. This reduces the social risk, regardless if the product is of high or low involvement. Therefore, it is hypothesized that:

H1 Shopping with AR has a lower perceived social risk than shopping without AR.

Financial Risk

Financial risk (FIR) is the risk of loss of monetary resources, i.e., money for the customer (Derbaix, 1983; Horton, 1976; Sweeney et al., 1999). The more a consumer pays for a product, i.e., the price, the higher the potential of loss.

Although the risk dimension rankings are not universal, research identifies financial risk as one of the most significant components of total overall risk (see, e.g., Kaplan et al., 1974; Stone & Grønhaug, 1993). This research attempts to test similarly to previous research, except with the addition of AR-aided technology.

Within the context of AR, it is expected that allowing customers access to more information of prices and giving them warantee information and the ability to interact with other customers reduce the perceived financial risk of purchasing a product Shimp and Bearden (1982). Therefore, it is hypothesized that:

H2 Shopping with AR has a lower perceived financial risk than shopping without AR.

Psychological Risk

Psychological risk (PSR) is conceptualized as the risk of discomfort that may arise due to anticipated post-purchase regret or worry (Perugini & Bagozzi, 2001) from the purchase and consumption of the product (Dholakia, 2001). Furthermore, psychological risk is also defined as "the loss incurred when the product chosen does not fulfill the consumer's self-image or perceptions of self" (Chu & Li, 2008). This is in line with cognitive dissonance theory which states that there is a "dissonance," or gap between two types of knowledge. In this case, the dissonance is between how the customer expects the product to be and the reality of the product and how it actually makes the customer feel. The risk of cognitive dissonance can therefore be considered as psychological risk.

It is assumed that AR-aided shopping will reduce the PSR through a combination of risk-reducing strategies that are activated through the AR application. Some of the proposed risk-reducing functions of the AR application include price comparisons, warrantee information, and ability to discuss products with a salesperson to ensure that they are getting a product that fits within their self-identity. Additional features include customer reviews that affirm the product design and performance matches their psychological self (Duan et al. 2008; Godes and Mayzlin 2004).

By using AR to purchase products, customers may feel that the psychological risk of purchase is lower than without. Therefore, it is proposed that:

H3 Shopping with AR has a lower perceived psychological risk than shopping without AR.

Performance Risk

Performance risk (PER), also called product or functional risk (Sääksjärvi & Lampinen, 2005), is one of the introductory risk factors that was discussed originally in Bauer's research (Bauer, 1960). Furthermore, it was also researched that performance risk correlated the highest than any other risk factors for 8 out of the 12 products that were tested in the original Jacoby and Kaplan research (Jacoby & Kaplan, 1972).

Perceived performance risk is the perceived loss experienced if a product does not perform according to expectations (Horton, 1976). In previous research, when the perceived performance risk was low to medium, customers bought the product without researching much and would essentially "trial" the product (Lutz & Reilly, 1973) but if they perceived the product to have high performance risk, they preferred to observe and experience the product before purchase (Lutz & Reilly, 1973). Analyzing the results, it is observed in this experiment that if performance risk is reduced, overall perceived risk will decrease and purchase intent will therefore increase. Since AR-aided technology adds elements of experiences, dialogue, and additional information about products, it is hypothesized that:

H4 Shopping with AR has a lower perceived performance risk than shopping without AR.

Physical Risk

Perceived physical risk (PYR) is the lowest risk dimension that is correlated with OPR (Jacoby & Kaplan, 1972). PYR is defined as the chance of a purchase to cause physical harm. Relative to the product category, it is assumed that PYR will be more important for potentially harmful products and less relevant for normal day-to-day products. Further, it is proposed that PYR might be more relevant for food-based products due to the consumption nature of the product. Having additional information, e.g., nutritional information and dialogue, is assumed to reduce the physical risk. It is therefore assumed that:

H5 Shopping with AR has a lower perceived physical risk than shopping without AR.

Time Risk

Perceived time risk (PTR) is another dimension that researchers have considered as significant (Brooker, 1984; Roselius, 1971). Time risk is defined as the potential loss incurred from the time and energy used to purchase the wrong product (Roselius, 1971).

Roselius (1971) examined the ten risk reduction strategies in respect to the dimensions of risk and concluded that there is no consensus as to which reliever is better than others but that sellers should "first determine the kind of risk perceived by his customers and then create a mix of risk relievers suited for his combinations of buyer types and loss type" (Roselius, 1971, p. 61). Additional experiments revealed that time risk was ranked relatively low compared to other dimensions of risk when it comes to selection of automobiles (Peter & Tarpey, 1975).

In this chapter thesis, time risk will be considered as one of the dimensions to be tested. It is assumed that the additional information from AR application will serve as a risk-reduction strategy. It is therefore proposed that:

H6 Shopping with AR has a lower perceived time risk than shopping without AR.

Conclusion and Implications

AR technology is becoming widespread in the fields of marketing and research. With that diffusion, it is important for academics and marketers to look at the benefits of this technology. In this chapter, we propose that one of the main advantages of AR is to reduce the perceived risks associated with making a purchase decision and future work aims to support these theoretical claims with empirical evidence. Furthermore, we outline the importance of interactions in marketing and how using technology like AR can aid in the creation of experiences.

References

Agarwal, S., & Teas, R. K. (2001). Perceived value: Mediating role of perceived risk. *Journal of Marketing Theory and Practice, 9*(4), 1–14.

Ballantine, P. W. (2005). Effects of interactivity and product information on consumer satisfaction in an online retail setting. *International Journal of Retail & Distribution Management, 33*(6), 461–471.

Ballantyne, D., & Varey, R. J. (2006). Creating value-in-use through marketing interaction: The exchange logic of relating, communicating and knowing. *Marketing Theory, 6*(3), 335–348.

Bauer, R. A. (1960). Consumer behavior as risk taking. In R. S. Hancock (Ed.), *Dynamic marketing for a changing world* (pp. 389–398). Chicago: American Marketing Association.

Bodhani, A. (2012). Shops offer the e-tail experience. *Engineering & Technology, 7*(5), 46–49.

Brody, R. P., & Cunningham, S. M. (1968). Personality variables and the consumer decision process. *Journal of Marketing Research, 5*, 50–57.

Brooker, G. (1984). An assessment of an expanded measure of perceived risk. *Advances in Consumer Research, 11*(1), 439–441.

Bulearca, M., & Tamarjan, D. (2010). Augmented reality: A sustainable marketing tool? *Global Business & Management Research, 2*(2), 237–252.

Chevalier, J. A., & Mayzlin, D. (2006). The effect of word of mouth on sales: Online book reviews. *Journal of Marketing Research, 43*(3), 345–354.

Chu, K.-K., & C.-H. Li (2008). A Study of the Effect of Risk-reduction Strategies on Purchase Intentions in Online Shopping. *IJEBM, 6*(4), 213–226.

Clawson, T. (2009, December). Augmented reality—Don't believe the hype. *Revolution Magazine.*

Cox, D. F. (1967). *Risk taking and information handling in consumer behavior.* Boston: Harvard University Press.

Cox, D. F., & Rich, S. U. (1964). Perceived risk and consumer decision-making: The case of telephone shopping. *Journal of Marketing Research, 1*(4), 32–39.

Derbaix, C. (1983). Perceived risk and risk relievers: An empirical investigation. *Journal of Economic Psychology, 3*(1), 19–38.

Dholakia, U. M. (2001). A motivational process model of product involvement and consumer risk perception. *European Journal of Marketing, 35*(11/12), 1340–1362.

Dholakia, R. R., & Zhao, M. (2009). Retail web site interactivity: How does it influence customer satisfaction and behavioral intentions? *International Journal of Retail & Distribution Management, 37*(10), 821–838.

Dowling, G. R., & Staelin, R. (1994). A model of perceived risk and intended risk-handling activity. *Journal of Consumer Research, 21*(1), 119–134.

Duan, W., Gu, B., & Whinston, A. B. (2008). Do online reviews matter?—An empirical investigation of panel data. *Decision Support Systems, 45*(4), 1007–1016.

Godes, D., & Mayzlin, D. (2004). Using online conversations to study word-of-mouth communication. *Marketing Science, 23*(4), 545–560.

Grönroos, C. (2006). Adopting a service logic for marketing. *Marketing Theory, 6*(3), 317–333.

Grönroos, C. (2008). Service logic revisited: Who creates value? And who co-creates? *European Business Review, 20*(4), 298–314.

Horton, R. L. (1976). The structure of perceived risk: Some further progress. *Journal of the Academy of Marketing Science, 4*(4), 694–706.

Jacoby, J., & Kaplan, L. B. (1972). The components of perceived risk. *Advances in Consumer Research, 3*(3), 382–383.

Kaplan, L. B., et al. (1974). Components of perceived risk in product purchase: A cross-validation. *Journal of Applied Psychology, 59*(3), 287.

Kotler, P., & Armstrong, G. (2010). *Principles of marketing.* Upper Saddle River, NJ: Pearson Education.

Lutz, R. J., & Reilly, P. J. (1973). An exploration of the effects of perceived social and performance risk on consumer information acquisition. *Advances in Consumer Research, 1*(4), 393–405.

Milgram, P., & Kishino, F. (1994). A taxonomy of mixed reality visual displays. *IEICE Transactions on Information and Systems, 77*(12), 1321–1329.

Newton, D. A. (1967). A marketing communications model for sales management. In D. F. Cox (Ed.), *Risk-taking and information-handling in consumer behavior* (pp. 579–602). Boston: Harvard University Press.

Perry, M., & Hamm, B. C. (1969). Canonical analysis of relations between socioeconomic risk and personal influence in purchase decisions. *Journal of Marketing Research, 6*, 351–354.

Perugini, M., & Bagozzi, R. P. (2001). The role of desires and anticipated emotions in goal-directed behaviours: Broadening and deepening the theory of planned behaviour. *British Journal of Social Psychology, 40*(1), 79–98.

Peter, J. P., & Tarpey, L. X., Sr. (1975). A comparative analysis of three consumer decision strategies. *Journal of Consumer Research, 2*, 29–37.

Roselius, T. (1971). Consumer rankings of risk reduction methods. *The Journal of Marketing, 35*(1), 56–61.

Ross, I. (1975). Perceived risk and consumer behavior: A critical review. *Advances in Consumer Research, 2*(1), 1–19.

Sääksjärvi, M., & Lampinen, M. (2005). Consumer perceived risk in successive product generations. *European Journal of Innovation Management, 8*(2), 145–156.

Shimp, T. A., & Bearden, W. O. (1982). Warranty and other extrinsic cue effects on consumers' risk perceptions. *Journal of Consumer Research, 9*(1), 38–46.

Stone, R. N., & Grønhaug, K. (1993). Perceived risk: Further considerations for the marketing discipline. *European Journal of Marketing, 27*(3), 39–50.

Sweeney, J. C., et al. (1999). The role of perceived risk in the quality-value relationship: A study in a retail environment. *Journal of Retailing, 75*(1), 77–105.

Taylor, J. W. (1974). The role of risk in consumer behavior. *The Journal of Marketing, 38*(2), 54–60.

Vargo, S. L., & Lusch, R. F. (2004). Evolving to a new dominant logic for marketing. *Journal of Marketing, 68*(1), 1–17.

Vaughan-Nichols, S. J. (2009). Augmented reality: No longer a novelty? *Computer (Long Beach, CA), 42*(12), 19–22. doi:10.1109/MC.2009.380.

Verhage, B. J., Yavas, U., & Green, R. T. (1990). Perceived risk: A cross-cultural phenomenon? *International Journal of Research in Marketing, 7*(4), 297–303.

Zeithaml, V. A. (1988). Consumer perceptions of price, quality, and value: A means-end model and synthesis of evidence. *The Journal of Marketing, 52*(3), 2–22.

Zuckerman, M., & Kuhlman, D. (1978, August). *Sensation seeking and risk taking in response to hypothetical situations*. Paper presented at the meeting of the International Association of Applied Psychology, Munich, Germany.

Chapter 63
Business Cycle Forecasts and Futures Volatility

Hanene Belhaj and Dorra Larbi

Abstract This chapter assesses the extent to which the US business cycle is affected by fluctuations in futures price while controlling for other macroeconomic and financial variables. We examine the usefulness of futures volatility to predict whether or not the US economy will be in a recession.

Our study builds on two research veins. The first is comprised of many studies that attempt to predict business cycles by using a range of economic variables. Many of these studies emphasize the role of financial variables in macroeconomic forecasts (Estrella and Mishkin, Review of Economics and Statistics, 80(1):45–61, 1998). This role has been certainly exacerbated during the recent financial crisis of 2007–2009.

The second vein originates within the literature which widely recognizes the role of financial variables such as prices of financial instruments as leading indicators (Estrella and Mishkin, Review of Economics and Statistics, 80(1):45–61, 1998). In US data for example, equity returns and the short-term interest lead GDP growth by one or two quarters (Backus et al., Asset prices in business cycle analysis (manuscript), 2007). Commodities, combined with stocks, are one of these financial instruments that were involved in the macroeconomic forecasts.

Our study examines futures volatility as predictors of US recessions. The volatility of this instrument could be an indicator of the economic situation. This study aims at either confirming or invalidating that periods of economic downturns are characterized by a high volatility in the index futures market.

Keywords Business cycle • Macroeconomic forecasts • Index futures volatility

H. Belhaj (✉)
Department of Economics and Finance, School of Business Administration,
Canadian University in Dubai, P.O. Box 117781, Dubai, UAE
e-mail: hanan@cud.ac.ae

D. Larbi
University of Picardie Jules Verne, Amiens, France
e-mail: dorra.laribi@gmail.com

© Springer International Publishing Switzerland 2017   713
R. Benlamri, M. Sparer (eds.), *Leadership, Innovation and Entrepreneurship as Driving Forces of the Global Economy*, Springer Proceedings in Business and Economics, DOI 10.1007/978-3-319-43434-6_63

Introduction

The global financial crisis (GFC) in the world economies has contributed to the consideration of the connection between financial variables and the business cycle, particularly the US economy.

This chapter primarily focuses on determining the factors that can influence the business cycle in the US economy. It discusses the changes in the futures prices and the effects that they have on the business cycle of the US economy under controlled financial and macroeconomic financial variables (Bregendahl, Michael, John Madsen, & Mortensen, 2010). It also establishes the importance of different futures volatility to forecast whether the US economy will face a recession in the coming years.

It lies on two research approaches. The first looks into the various studies that predict the business cycles based on different economic variables. It emphasizes the functions of financial variables in macroeconomic forecasts. The second approach focuses on the asset prices as the lead indicators of the business cycle. According to a study conducted by Bansal and Aaron (2004), the returns on equity and short-term interest contribute to the growth in GDP by one or two quarters. This second approach recognizes the role played by financial variables including prices of financial instruments as leading indicators.

The chapter assesses the extent to which the US business cycle is affected by fluctuations in futures price while controlling other macroeconomic and financial variables. It examines how far futures volatility helps to predict whether or not the US economy will be in a recession.

Business Cycle and Financial Variables

Many studies have underlined the role of the financial variables in the macroeconomic forecasts of the business cycle concept.

Literature on business cycle is abundant. According to Mitchel (1927) business cycle is characterized by a "sequence of expansions and contractions particularly emphasizing turning points and phases of the cycle." Lucas (1977) as contained in Kydland and Prescott (1990:2) defined business cycle as the statistical properties of the co-movements of deviations from the trend of various economic aggregates with those of real output. Kydland and Prescott (1982) described business cycles as recurrent nature of events. Another definition is due to Lucas (1980) in which business cycle is viewed as "the recurrent fluctuations of output about trend and the co-movements among other aggregate time series."

In more recent literature, the business cycle is majorly tracked and determined in terms of unemployment and GDP. It is the skyward and plunging movements of the GDP coupled with different occasions of growth and reduction in the patterns of the long-term growth. The typical cycles are accompanied by shifts, between periods of relative economic growth and decline. The business cycle, therefore, is seen as a series in a pattern of four periods. The periods are trough, expansion, contraction, and peak. The expansion period represents the prosperity phase where there are boom and upward movement in the economy.

The theoretical and empirical frameworks in the literature concentrated in examining the relationship between the macroeconomic and the financial variables. Other papers focus on the stock market forecasting power for future real growth in the economy (Fama & French, 1996; Vassalou, 2000). From an international point of view, Nasseh and Strauss (2000) demonstrated the existence of a significant long-run relationship between stock prices and domestic and international economic activity in European countries.

Andreou, Osborn, and Sensier (2000) examined a set of financial variables (interest rates, stock market price indices, dividend yield, and monetary aggregates) and heir influence on economic activity and business cycle. The most reliable leading indicator would seem to have been the interest rate term structure. In addition, the chapter assesses that the volatility of financial variables may also contain predictive information for growth and production volatility.

A recent paper on our subject is written by Stock and Watson (2002) who thoroughly demonstrated the predictive power of asset prices on inflation and real output. According to their findings "some asset prices predict either inflation or output growth sin some countries in some periods, but which predicts what, when and where is itself difficult to predict." However, they pointed out that forecast produced by combining these individual forecasts seems to improve when compared to forecast from benchmark univariate models.

As another paper connected to the framework in our study, Estrella and Mishkin (1998) examine various financial variables as predictors of US recessions. Results show that stock prices are useful with one to three quarter horizons. The results obtained using the yield curve suggest that these measures can play a useful role in macroeconomic models.

In conclusion, many papers studied and demonstrated that some financial and macroeconomic series have significant predictive power for future economic activity across a number of countries (Estrella & Hardouvelis, 1991). The early literature is summarized in the comprehensive literature review of Stock and Watson (2003) and the more recent literature focusing on the yield curve is summarized by Wheelock and Wohar (2009).

Business Cycle and Forecasting Models

Different business cycle forecasting methods exist. In the 1970s, many large macro models had poor forecasting performance and led first to the use of vector autoregressions (VAR) and then to estimated DSGE models. Other structural models based on microeconomic foundations appeared as a response to this poor performance. Kydland and Prescott (1982) propose the real business cycle (RBC) model based on principles of neoclassical growth models, in which real shocks are sources of economic fluctuations under flexible prices.

Rotemberg and Woodford (1998) propose the New Keynesian DSGE model using a similar framework. The findings from this literature are that DSGE forecasts are slightly comparable to those from VARs and BVAR (Chauvet & Potter, 2012). Wieland and Wolters (2010) find that structural models fail to forecast turning points, large recession, and booms but have a similar accuracy to BVAR forecasts.

In brief, the findings in the literature support the evidence of Nelson (1972) that forecast from simple autoregressive models has a better performance than large-scale macroeconomic models. The best models for tracking future GDP growth during expansions are the AR(2) and the univariate Markov switching model, and the VAR model that includes the term spread. The latter and the BVAR do better than the DSGE model during expansions, but the gains are offset by their poor performance during recessions (Chauvet & Potter, 2012).

Data Description

In this chapter, we adopt the use of the leading indicators developed by the Conference Board. The leading economic indicators (LEI) represent one way of forecasting the shifts in the business cycle patterns. The economic variables integrated within the structure of the leading economic variables are chosen based on their proven economic consistency, significance, timeliness, and uniformity to the ancient business cycles Liew and Vassalou (2000).

The leading indicators used are the following (monthly data from 1998 to 2014):

1. Value of manufacturers' new orders for consumer goods
2. Value of manufacturers' new orders for construction materials and supplies industries
3. Value of manufacturers' new orders for capital goods: nondefense capital goods industries
4. Average weekly hours of production and nonsupervisory employees
5. Manufacturers' new orders: durable goods
6. M2 money stock
7. New private housing units authorized by building permits
8. Consumer sentiment

Regarding futures, we used S&P500 Index Futures, monthly data, from January 1999 till December 2014.

For the volatility measures, we adopt implied volatility measured by the VIX and Economic Policy Uncertainty Index (constructed using three underlying components: newspapers, tax-code expiration date, professional forecasters' survey).

Methodology

Based on the literature, we use a linear model combined with GARCH to consider the dynamic aspect of that volatility (Bollerslev, 1986). Futures volatility and economic uncertainty proxies are examined as predictors of US economic activity. The aim is either confirming or invalidating that periods of economic downturns are preceded by a high volatility and uncertainty.

Our study consists of the following steps:

Step 1: We estimate the conditional volatility using GARCH model of the index futures returns.

Step 2: Estimate each of the leading indicators as a function of lagged historical volatility, conditional volatility, and implied volatility. Where i changes with the leading indicator (we made 8 regressions per volatility measure), we applied an autoregressive model:

$$Y_t^i = \alpha_{i,j} + \beta_{i,j} Y_{t-1}^i + \gamma_{i,j} V_{t-1}^j + \varepsilon_t^{i,j}$$

where

$-i =$ ACDGNA, ACMSNO, ANDENO, AWHMAN, DGORDER, M2SL, PERMIT, UMCSENT.

$-V_{t-1}^j$ is the lagged volatility proxy (j: historical volatility, conditional volatility, and implied volatility).

Step 3: For each of the volatility proxy we do the following regressions using the leading index as dependent variable:

$$LI_t = \alpha_j + \beta_j LI_{t-1} + \gamma_j V_{t-1}^j + \varepsilon_t^j$$

Empirical Results

Table 63.1 reports summary statistics for Leading indicators and futures return.

In **steps 1 and 2**, we generate historical and conditional volatility.

Futures conditional volatility will be used as an explanatory variable in the coming steps.

Step 3: For each of the leading indicators we do the linear AR(1) model using the three volatility proxies as explanatory variables.

Table 63.1 Descriptive statistics

	Mean	Std. deviation	Minimum	Maximum
Leading index	60.1669	66.1818	−202.8	145.8
Futures return	0.11%	0.0461	−18.88	13.98

Table 63.2 Empirical results

	Volatility measure	Coefficient	t-Statistic
ACDGNA		1.201	14.399***
		4.146	13.609***
	VIX_{t-1}	1.286	29.830***
ACMSNO		1.483	14.702***
		5.166	14.014***
	VIX_{t-1}	1.587	31.155***
ANDENO		2.479	14.422***
		8.425	13.195***
	VIX_{t-1}	2.628	28.273***
AWHMAN		1.566	15.680***
		5.579	15.843***
	VIX_{t-1}	1.664	36.455***
DGORDER		7.378	14.528***
		2.543	13.560***
	VIX_{t-1}	7.872	29.836***
M2SL		2.685	13.677***
		9.597	13.627***
	VIX_{t-1}	2.864	25.725***
PERMIT		4.890	12.138***
		1.655	11.230***
	VIX_{t-1}	5.256	21.345***
UMCSENT		3.214	14.918***
		1.124	14.692***
	VIX_{t-1}	3.402	30.629***

*** $t < 0.001$

The empirical results from the AR(1) regressions cited in step 3 show that for all the 24 regressions estimated, lagged volatility measure is positively correlated to all leading indicators with significant coefficient (Table 63.2).

These findings confirm the idea that the index futures historical volatility, conditional volatility, and implied volatility have a predictive component for the business cycle. The co-movement among the leading indicators of the business cycle and the lagged volatility proxies seems confirming the assumption of this chapter. Thus, volatility measures precede by 1 month the leading indicators in predicting the business cycle.

Step 4: When we are using lagged volatility measures and economic uncertainty as explanatory variables of the leading index, results confirm the findings of the previous step.

All lagged volatility measures are positively correlated to the index. This empirical outcome strengthens the conclusion declaring that volatility proxies have a predictive power in leading the business cycle.

The results are identical for the economic uncertainty, demonstrating that this measure is positively correlated to the leading index (with a significant coefficient) confirming the idea that the economic uncertainty is predicting the business cycle.

Stock market historical returns are also positively correlated to the leading index. As widely studied in previous literature, this financial measure is a good predictor of the economic situation.

Conclusion

Forecasting of the business cycles implies predicting the occurrence of a given state of the economy. Several variable indicators exist that explain the influence behind different business cycles.

This chapter assesses how index futures historical volatility, conditional volatility, and implied volatility have a predictive component of the business cycle. The movement among the leading indicators of the business cycle and the lagged volatility proxies seems confirming the assumption of this chapter. All lagged volatility measures have positive impact on the leading index. This empirical outcome strengthens the conclusion declaring that volatility proxies have a predictive power in leading the business cycle. The results state also that economic uncertainty helps forecasting the business cycle.

Further research on time lags, using other methodologies (regime switching models for example), could enhance our empirical findings.

References

Andreou, E., Osborn, D., & Sensier, M. (2000). A comparison of the statistical properties of financial variables in the USA, UK and Germany over the business cycle. *The Manchester School, 68*(3), 396–418.

Bansal, R., & Aaron, Y. (2004). Risks for the long run: A potential resolution of asset pricing puzzles. *The Journal of Finance, 59*(4), 1481–1509 (print).

Bollerslev, T. (1986). Generalized autoregressive conditional heteroscedasticity. *Journal of Econometrics, 31*(3), 307–327.

Bregendahl, M., Michael, H., John Madsen, H., & Mortensen, R. (2010). Afsætning 1. Copenhagen: Systime.

Chauvet, M., & Potter, S. (2012). *Forecasting output during the great recession*. Working Paper, University of California Riverside.

Estrella, A., & Hardouvelis, G. A. (1991). The term structure as a predictor of real economic activity. *Journal of Finance, 46*(2), 555–576.

Estrella, A., & Mishkin, F. S. (1998). Predicting U.S. recessions: Financial variables as leading indicators. *Review of Economics and Statistics, 80*(1), 45–61.

Fama, E. F., & French, K. R. (1996). Multifactor explanations of asset pricing anomalies. *The Journal of Finance, 51*, 55–184.

Kydland, F. E., & Prescott, E. C. (1982). Time to build and aggregate fluctuations. *Econometrica, 50*, 1345–1370.

Kydland, F. E., & Prescott, E. C. (1990). Business cycles: Real facts and a monetary myth. *Federal Reserve Bank of Minneapolis Quarterly Review, 14*(2), 3–18.

Liew, J., & Vassalou, M. (2000). Can book-to-market, size and momentum be risk factors that predict economic growth? *Journal of Financial Economics, 57*, 221–245.

Lucas, R. E., Jr. (1977). Understanding business cycles. In K. Brunner & A. H. Meltzer (Eds.), *Stabilization of the domestic and international economy*. New York: North-Holland.

Lucas, R. E., Jr. (1980). Methods and problems in business cycle theory. *Journal of Money, Credit and Banking, 12*, 696–715.

Mitchel, W. (1927). *Business cycles: The problem and its setting*. NBER, Volume ISBN: 0-870-14084-1.

Nasseh, A., & Strauss, J. (2000). Stock prices and domestic and international macroeconomic activity: A cointegration approach. *The Quarterly Review of Economics and Finance, 40*, 229–245.

Nelson, C. R. (1972). The prediction performance of the FRB-MIT-PENN Model of the U.S. Economy. *American Economic Review, 62*, 902–917.

Rotemberg, I., & Woodford, M. (1998). *An optimization-based econometric framework for the evaluation of monetary policy: Expanded version*. NBER Technical Working Papers 0233, National Bureau of Economic Research, Inc.

Stock, J., & Watson, M. (2002). Macroeconomic forecasting using diffusion indexes. *Journal of Business and Economic Statistics, 20*, 147–162.

Stock, J. H., & Watson, M. W. (2003). Forecasting output and inflation: The role of asset prices. *Journal of Economic Literature, 41*(3), 788–829.

Vassalou, M. (2000, March). *New related to future GDP growth as risk factors in equity returns*. Working paper, Columbia University and CEPR.

Wheelock, D., & Wohar, M. (2009). Can the term spread predict output growth a recessions? A survey of the literature. *Federal Reserve Bank of St. Louis Review, 91*(5, Part 1), 419–440.

Wieland, V., & Wolters, M. H. (2010). *The diversity of forecasts from macroeconomic models of the U.S. Economy*. Working paper, Goethe University.

Chapter 64
Relationship Between Working Capital Management and Profitability: A Case of Tabreed (National Central Cooling Company PJSC)

R. Venkatachalam

Abstract Working capital management is a function of management to decide the optimum level of the various items of working capital. Though the current assets do not help increasing productivity, they are very much important in carrying a successful business. Too much of working capital may lead to idle current assets and increase carrying cost of current assets and it reduces the profit. On the other hand, if too low working capital is maintained the business faces liquidity risk and may lead to bankruptcy. This study aims to investigate the relationship between profitability and the various components of current assets of Tabreed. Pearson simple correlation technique and multiple regression analysis were employed. The study showed that working capital turnover ratio, cash turnover ratio and debtors turnover ratio have positive association with return on investment and other ratios such as current ratio, quick ratio, current assets-to-total assets ratio, current assets-to-sales ratio, and inventory turnover ratio have negative association with profitability.

Keywords Capital working management • Profitability • Multiple regression Analysis • Liquidity risk

Introduction

Working capital management is an important aspect in financial management. Investment in current assets represents a major portion of total assets. While sales are increasing in business, to support the sales current assets such as inventories and receivables would be increasing simultaneously. Along with current assets, current liabilities would also increase. It should be understood whether the current assets and the current liabilities are to be managed at optimum level in order to enhance

R. Venkatachalam (✉)
Canadian University of Dubai, Dubai, United Arab Emirates
e-mail: venkat@cud.ac.ae

© Springer International Publishing Switzerland 2017
R. Benlamri, M. Sparer (eds.), *Leadership, Innovation and Entrepreneurship as Driving Forces of the Global Economy*, Springer Proceedings in Business and Economics, DOI 10.1007/978-3-319-43434-6_64

profitability. Permanent assets such as plant, property, and equipment would increase productivity in a business. Growth in current assets should be parallel to growth in sales. If current assets increase more than the sales growth, the situation may lead to idle current assets. Though the current assets help improving sales and thus profitability, it should be remembered that there is cost involved in carrying such current assets. The working capital policy of a business plays an important role in determining the optimum level of current assets and thus optimum working capital.

Adequate current assets would support the sales of a business. Inadequate inventory, an important component of current assets, would lead to stockout problems which would decrease the sales. If payment terms of sales are not in line with competition in the market, the business entity may lose its market share and it may lead to low profitability. On the other hand, more than required inventory or very slow collection of receivables would block capital of business entity which has carrying cost and this would lead to low profitability.

The short life span of working capital components and their swift transformation from one form to another form require the business to take decisions frequently. Various factors such as nature of business, seasonality of operations, production policy, market conditions and terms, and conditions of suppliers affect the working capital requirements.

Ineffective management of working capital directly affects liquidity and profitability of the business. During recession, the business gives more attention for working capital management since liquidity in the market is very tight.

An appropriate working capital management policy sets minimum and maximum level of inventory, cash. It dictates the terms of credit sale. An efficient working capital management sets limits for various working capital components, continuously monitors the variances, and takes corrective actions for reaching their goals.

It is necessary for an organization to find out the optimum level of working capital in order to survive during recessionary periods. Optimum level of working capital helps to achieve optimum profit and thus to enhance the wealth of shareholders. This study aims to probe into the drivers of working capital and their impact on profitability of Annual report of Tabreed (Tabreed, 2015).

Profile of Tabreed

Tabreed is a district cooling company incorporated in Dubai, UAE. Though the company is popularly known as Tabreed in the market the company is legally incorporated in the name of National Central Cooling Company PJSC. District cooling is a superior alternative to conventional air conditioning since it helps reducing energy consumption and also protecting the environment. The company has been providing innovative cooling techniques to government, commercial, and private organization in Gulf countries since 1998. The principal activities of the company include supply of chilled water, and operation and maintenance of cooling plants.

For the year ended 31 December 2015, the company earned revenue of AED 1.17 billion and net profit of AED 348 million. As of 31 December 2015, they employed total assets of AED 8.2 billion.

Need for the Study

There have been numerous studies on working capital management in companies engaged in manufacturing and trading sector situated in various countries. Very few research studies are available on companies operating in Middle East region. As far as UAE is concerned, no research has been done in this area in respect of service-providing companies. Inventory, the major component of current assets, is negligible in service-providing industry. This chapter is the first attempt to study the relationship between working capital management and firm's profitability in a service industry.

Objectives of the Study

The study has the following four objectives:

- To study the relationship between working capital management and profitability
- To establish the nexus between the liquidity and profitability of Tabreed
- To identify the effects of various components of working capital on profitability of the company
- To draw conclusion on the impact of working capital management over profitability of Tabreed

Literature Review

Soenen (Soenen, 1993) analyzed the relationship between the working capital cycle and profitability in the US firms. The research exposed a negative relationship between the working capital cycle's length and firm's profitability. Moreover, it was established that the inverse relationship is different among various industries.

Khatic and Varghese (2015) observed that even though the profitability position was strong, the liquidity position of firm was not at acceptable level.

Nazir and Afza (2009) investigated the relationship between the aggressive/conservative working capital asset management and financing policies. The study revealed a negative relationship between the profitability of firms and degree of aggressiveness of the working capital policy.

The studies of Charitou, Lois, and Santoso (2012) stressed that the efficient utilization of firm's resources would lead to increase in shareholders' wealth.

Bagchi, Chakrabarti, and Roy (2012) studied the influence of working capital management on profitability and found a negative association between working capital management and firm's profitability.

Hsieh and Wu (2013) examined the working capital management and profitability. They found a significant negative relationship between the gross operating income and the accounts receivable collection period, inventory turnover period, accounts payable period, and working capital cycle among publicly traded Chinese companies.

Sharma and Kumar (2011) did research regarding the effect of working capital on profitability of Indian companies. They took a sample of 263 nonfinancial Bombay Stock Exchange firms from 2000 to 2008 and employed OLS multiple regression. Data revealed that working capital management and profitability are positively correlated in Indian communities. There was a negative correlation between inventory days and receivable days with company's profitability, whereas account receivable days and working capital cycle had a positive correlation with profitability.

Shin and Soenen (2000) examined the relationship between net trade cycle and profitability. They concluded that there was a strong negative association between the firm's NTC and its profitability.

Hypotheses of the Study

The following hypotheses are set for the purpose of the study.

H0 There is no significant difference between liquidity and profitability of Tabreed during the period of study.

H1 There is significant difference between liquidity and profitability of Tabreed during the period of study.

Data and Methodology

The annual reports of Tabreed for the accounting years from 2011 to 2015 were the source of data. The data for the study were taken from audited balance sheet and income statement. The annual reports were downloaded from the official website of Tabreed. Various relevant ratios regarding working capital management have been selected for processing data. The ratios which are affecting working capital and profitability have been selected.

In order to measure the efficiency of working capital management, the following ratios have been calculated on the data available related to the company: return on investment (ROI), current ratio (CR), quick ratio (QR), current assets-to-total assets ratio (CATAR), current assets-to-sales ratio (CASR), working capital turnover ratio (WCTR), inventory turnover ratio (ITR), cash turnover ratio (CTR), and debtors turnover ratio (DTR).

ROI is the good measure of profitability and therefore it is selected as the dependent variable. ROI is depending upon the size of current assets and turnover. Hence eight working capital ratios have been identified as independent variables.

Pearson's simple correlation coefficient technique has been employed to establish the degree of association between the working capital management and profitability. For analyzing the behavior of these ratios student-t test has been used.

In order to derive an equation which provides estimates of the dependent variable (i.e., ROI) from values of two independent variables, multiple regression analysis has been employed.

Results and Discussions

The relationship between working capital components and profitability is established by calculating Karl Pearson's correlation coefficient between ROI of Tabreed and the various ratios regarding working management (Table 64.1).

The study shows the following:

- There is positive association between ROI and working capital turnover ratio, CTR, and DTR. Other ratios such as current ratio, quick ratio, current assets-to-total assets ratio, current assets-to-sales ratios, and inventory ratios do have negative relationship with ROI.

Table 64.1 Simple correlation analysis between selected ratios relating to working capital management and return on investment of Tabreed

Particulars	2011	2012	2013	2014	2015	Correlation coefficient
Current ratio (CR)	1.338	1.380	1.473	1.381	1.089	−0.390
Quick ratio (QR)	1.309	1.344	1.433	1.333	1.045	−0.431
Working capital turnover ratio (WCTR)	2.767	3.093	2.540	3.448	15.221	0.591
Current assets-to-total assets ratio (CATAR)	0.183	0.156	0.160	0.143	0.114	−0.928
Current assets-to-sales ratio (CASR)	1.431	1.174	1.225	1.050	0.804	−0.934
Cash turnover ratio (CTR)	2.178	2.016	1.639	2.706	6.621	0.589
Inventory turnover ratio (ITR)	32.794	33.206	29.730	26.929	30.842	−0.544
Debtors turnover ratio (DTR)	2.667	2.740	4.783	4.470	4.924	0.753
Return on investment (ROI) %	3.4	4.2	4.2	4.5	4.7	

- The coefficient correlation between ROI and CATAR is −0.928 and the correlation between ROI and CASR is −0.934. This implies that increase in share of current assets either on total assets or sales will have strong negative impact on ROI. Further, it is evidenced that CATAR and CASR do have perfect positive relationship (0.999). It is logical that the ratio of current asset share increases the cost of carrying such current assets and reduces the profit.
- The correlation coefficient between ROI and WCTR is 0.591. It shows that there is a positive relationship between profitability and WCTR. It is clear from these results that the higher the WCTR, the greater the profitability of the company.
- The correlation coefficient between ROI and CTR is 0.589. This also shows that there is positive relationship between ROI and CTR. If CTR increases, then it pushes the profitability up.
- As far as current ratios (CR) and quick ratios (QR) are concerned, both have negative relationship with ROI. The correlation coefficient between ROI and CR is −0.390 and with QR is −0.431. It implies that fat current ratios are quick ratios that would bring down the ROI. Conversely, the slim CR and QR will enhance the ROI. This is further evidenced that the relationship between CR and QR is perfectly positive.
- The correlation coefficient between ROI and inventory turnover ratio (ITR) is negative (−0.544). This shows that the higher the ITR, the lower the profitability. However, inventory is very much insignificant in Tabreed since the company is a service provider. Looking at the financial statements, inventory forms 2–4 % of the total current assets.

Table 64.2 Other statistical values of variables

	CR	QR	WCTR	CATAR	CASR	CTR	ITR	DTR	ROI
Mean	1.3322	1.2928	5.4128	0.1512	1.1368	3.0320	30.7002	3.9168	4.2000
Median	1.3800	1.3330	3.0930	0.1560	1.1740	2.1780	30.8420	4.4700	4.2000
Standard error	0.0646	0.0653	2.4565	0.0113	0.1034	0.9134	1.1367	0.5008	0.2213

Table 64.3 Correlation matrix of Tabreed for the period 2011–2015

Ratio	ROI	CR	QR	WCTR	CATAR	CASR	CTR	ITR	DTR
ROI	1.000								
CR	−0.390	1.000							
QR	−0.431	0.999	1.000						
WCTR	0.591	−0.948	−0.957	1.000					
CATAR	−0.928	0.703	0.734	−0.842	1.000				
CASR	−0.934	0.692	0.725	−0.829	0.999	1.000			
CTR	0.589	−0.963	−0.974	0.991	−0.846	−0.835	1.000		
ITR	−0.544	−0.152	−0.108	0.017	0.380	0.384	−0.060	1.000	
DTR	0.753	−0.246	−0.285	0.502	−0.706	−0.693	0.491	−0.733	1.000

Table 64.4 t-Values of independent variables and conclusion

Independent variable	t-Value	Critical value	Comments
CR	12.4366	2.306	Means are significantly different
QR	12.5937	2.306	Means are significantly different
WCTR	3.4611	2.306	Means are significantly different
CATAR	18.2645	2.306	Means are significantly different
CASR	11.5379	2.306	Means are significantly different
CTR	1.2426	2.306	Means are not significantly different
ITR	−22.8814	2.306	Means are not significantly different
DTR	0.5171	2.306	Means are not significantly different

- The correlation coefficient between ROI and DTR is positive (0.753). This is in line with logical result. When there is high DTR, either sales are high or the receivables are slim or both; when there is slim receivable the investment in the receivable is slow and thereby low cost, which leads to high profitability.
- The CTR has perfectly positive correlation with WCTR and it is highly logical that cash is a part of working capital. However, CTR has negative relationship with CR, QR, CATAR, and CASR (Tables 64.2, 64.3, and 64.4).

Analysis of Multiple Regression

In order to determine an equation which provides estimates of a dependent variable from values of the two or more independent variables, multiple regression analysis is employed.

To fit the regression line, ROI has been taken as the dependent variable.

(A) Since CATAR has perfect negative correlation with ROI and DTR has significant positive correlation with ROI, both the variables have been selected as independent or explanatory variables.

The following regression equation is obtained:
ROI = −0.0032 + 0.36154CATAR − 0.0024DTR
From the above equation, it is easily understood that DTR impact on ROI is insignificant and the major determinant of ROI is CATAR.

Next it is considered that CR and WCTR are influential on ROI.

(B) It is very much crucial to maintain current ratio and working capital at a certain minimum level irrespective of the related cost of maintaining working capital. Therefore, both the variables have been selected as independent variables.

The regression equation is as follows:

$ROI = -0.0708 + 0.075\ CR + .002\ WCTR$

Compared to CR, WCTR is insignificant. CR is the deciding factor for ROI. In order to break even, CR should be 0.944. According to principles of financial management, CR should be at least 1.5. If so, ignoring WCTR, ROI would be around 4.2%. Every one unit of CR, ROI is increased by 7.5%.

Student t-Values

The relationship between the dependent variable (ROI) and other independent variables is as follows:

As far as CR, QR, WCTR, CATAR, and CASR are concerned since the t value is greater than the critical value, the hypothesis (H0) is not accepted. Therefore, there is relationship between working capital management and profitability of the firm.

However, in respect of CTR, ITR, and DTR, since the t-value is less than the critical value, the hypothesis (H0) is accepted. Therefore, there is no relationship between the turnover ratios and profitability of the firm.

It is interesting to note that the turnover ratios do not have relationship with profitability and the exception is WCTR.

Conclusion

Studying the eight ratios regarding working capital management, five ratios, CR, QR, CASR, CATAR, and ITR, have negative relationship with ROI. Among these, ITR has insignificant role to play in this study since the firm has negligible inventory compared to its total assets. The ratio of inventory to total assets does not exceed 4%.

For the rest four ratios, the main driver is current assets. Since inventory level is very low in the current study, current assets are almost equal to quick assets. This is also further evidenced by correlation coefficient of 0.999 between CR and QR.

The other ratios WCTR, CTR, and DTR have positive relationship with ROI. Logically the ratios would increase when turnover of the company goes up or working capital/cash/debtor level goes down. This change would either increase revenue or reduce cost or both.

Therefore in order to increase ROI, the company should adopt any or all of the following:

- The level of current assets should not be allowed to go beyond a range of reasonable level.
- Idle current assets are to be identified and the firm should reduce the level of current assets to total assets.
- The level of receivables and cash is to be maintained at optimum level and should be monitored continuously.
- Cash and cash equivalents were considered too high during the period from 2011 till 2013 (around 60% of sales). In 2015, it was drastically reduced to 15% of turnover. This was the major reason for hike in ROI from 3.4 to 4.7%.
- Current ratio has been declining from 2013 and the ratio was 1.09 in 2015 which is very low. The company should consider strengthening working capital in order to manage liquidity risk.

References

Tabreed (2015). Annual report of Tabreed 2011–2015, https://www.tabreed.ae/en/investor-relations/reports-and-presentations.aspx.

Bagchi, B., Chakrabarti, J., & Roy, P. B. (2012). Importance of working capital management on profitability: A study on Indian FMCG companies. *International Journal of Business Management, 7*(22), 1–10.

Charitou, M., Lois, P., & Santoso, H. B. (2012). The relationship between working capital management and firm's profitability: An empirical investigation for an emerging Asian country. *International Business and Economic Research Journal, 11*(8), 839.

Hsieh, C., & Wu, C. Y. (2013). Working capital management and profitability of publicly traded Chinese companies. *The Asia Pacific Journal of Economics and Business, 17*(1/2), 1–11.

Khatic, S. K., & Varghese, T. (2015). Impact of working capital management on firm's profitability: An empirical study of ITC limited. *International Journal of Information, Business and Management, 7*(4), 284–305.

Nazir, M. S., & Afza, T. (2009). Impact of aggressive working capital management policy on firm's profitability. *IUP Journal of Applied Finance, 15*(8), 19–30.

Sharma, A. K., & Kumar, S. (2011). Effect of working capital management on firm profitability—Empirical evidence from India. *Global Business Review, 1291*, 159–173.

Shin, H. H., & Soenen, L. (1998). Efficiency of working capital management and corporate profitability. *Financial Practice and Education, 8*(2), 37–45.

Shin, H.-H., & Soenen, L. A. (2000). Liquidity management or profitability—Is there room for both? *AFB Exchange, 20*(2), 46–49.

Soenen, L. A. (1993). Cash conversion cycle and corporate profitability. *Journal of Cash Management, 13*, 53–57.

Chapter 65
Information Systems Strategies to Reduce Financial Corruption

Ali Abdulbaqi Ameen and Kamsuriah Ahmad

Abstract Small and large organizations use available technologies to manage business activities and assist in decision making. Most organizations operate their business activities efficiently using various information systems (IS). These systems are
used to collect data and process it according to the analyst, manager, or business
owners' needs. Among the existing systems, the organization normally used financial information systems (FISs) to accumulate and analyze financial data for optimal financial planning and forecasting decisions and outcomes. FIS closely linked
with all aspects of administrative in the organizations. This system is an integral part
of business and is fundamental for stability, sustainability, and growth of an organization. In recognition of the importance of FIS, various countries and international
organizations started to invest in such systems. This system is increasingly being
used to improve transparency in the organizations and as a result FIS can play an
important role in fighting corruption in public finance systems. This chapter aims to
investigate and to identify the existing IS strategies that are used in fighting financial
corruption. The finding reveals that there are a number of IS strategies to combat
corruption but among those FISs possess the ability to contribute effectively towards
anticorruption efforts. At the end, this chapter identifies five factors of FIS that contribute to anticorruption strategies. This study could play a significant role in
explaining the complex relationship between the related factors and the quality of
FISs to facilitate the anticorruption process.

Keywords Information systems • Financial information system • Reduce financial
corruption • Anticorruption strategies

A.A. Ameen (✉) • K. Ahmad
Faculty of Information Science and Technology, Universiti Kebangsaan Malaysia,
Bangi, Selangor, Malaysia
e-mail: ali71@siswa.ukm.edu.my; kamsuriah@ukm.edu.my

© Springer International Publishing Switzerland 2017   731
R. Benlamri, M. Sparer (eds.), *Leadership, Innovation and Entrepreneurship
as Driving Forces of the Global Economy*, Springer Proceedings in Business
and Economics, DOI 10.1007/978-3-319-43434-6_65

Introduction

The World Bank estimated that each year between US$1 trillion and US$1.6 trillion is lost to corruption. The lost includes tax evasion, bribes, inflated budgets, and illegal expenditures (Otusanya, Lauwo, & Adeyeye, 2012). This estimate does not include embezzlement of public funds or theft of public assets, which are extremely difficult to estimate. Corruption is a form of dishonest or unethical conduct by a person entrusted with a position of authority, often to acquire personal benefit. Corruption can take many forms that vary in degree from the minor use of influence to institutionalized bribery. Transparency International's definition of corruption is "the abuse of entrusted power for private gain." This definition is also used in this study. Corruption typically occurs when there is an opportunity for an exchange of resources and services that can be kept covert. It occurs in the context of systems that create opportunities for corrupt behavior. Therefore, when searching for the sources of corruption it is necessary to focus not on corrupt individuals, but on corrupt systems. Corruption brings substantial economic, social, and moral costs to the society affected by it. Essentially, the costs caused by corruption are the reason why the fight against corruption should be taken seriously. Given the problems presented by corruption, searching for solutions is necessary. It's important to determine the key influencing factors on IS as an anticorruption strategy (ACS). The review indicates that most studies on IS as an ACS appear to be extremely diverse and complex. The research aims to identify the main IS strategies that exist in the literature that were used to reduce financial corruption.

Background

This chapter attempts to provide better understanding for the FISs and their role in reducing corruption. It also focuses on exploring the relationship between IS, systems software applications, and anticorruption strategies. In particular, it explores (1) the relationship between the uses of IS and anticorruption strategies, and (2) the key factors that influence the ability of the FIS to reduce corruption. The study used an iterative design approach, which consists of three investigated techniques such as conducting a literature review, content analysis, and website analysis. The findings indicate that most of the studies conducted on IS as an ACS are extremely diverse, which indicates that FIS has been used as a mechanism to reduce corruption. Table 65.1 describes various studies on IS strategies to reduce corruption found in the literature from the year 2003 to 2012. The number of occurrences of research in this area is compiled and recorded.

The table shows the most frequent IS strategies that are used as an ACS found in the literature. The findings show that most scholars have focused on utilizing e-government, ICT applications, social media, and Web applications as tools in corruption reduction strategies. Only a few studies have focused on the role of FIS in reducing corruption. The table statistically highlights the most important studies

Table 65.1 IS strategies to reduce corruption

No.	Key electronic ACS	Frequency	%
1	E-government	56	65
2	ICT applications	50	58
3	Social media	48	56
4	Web applications	39	45
5	Procurement systems	36	42
6	Tax and customs system	34	40
7	Mobile technology	27	31
8	Financial information systems	12	14

that left a significant effect on controlling corruption from the perspective of relevant scholars and specialists. Most scholars have focused on utilizing e-government as tools in corruption reduction strategies; however the research using FIS as an ACS received the least, with only 14 %. Therefore the interest of this study is to explore further the significance of FIS as an anticorruption strategy.

Information Systems and Anticorruption Strategies

Numerous studies have concentrated on efforts to employ ICT component as an important means in the corruption reduction strategies. These studies have concentrated on using information systems to improve e-government innovations, to harness ICT application, to adapt various Internet applications, and to use social media. Literature has revealed that the main attempt to employ ICTs as part of ACS is to prevent corruption electronically. In the public financial sector, the information systems play a significant role in reducing revenues and expenditure corruption. Figure 65.1 summarizes the findings that show the electronic anticorruption tools and strategies. The strategies that can be used to reduce corruption are discussed in the next subtopic.

E-Government Strategy

A wide range of studies have been conducted that focused on the importance of improving e-government to reduce corruption (Andersen, 2009; Bertot et al., 2010). The success of harnessing the e-government initiative depends on the citizen education, culture, and their acceptance of ICT technology. Governments strongly prefer delivering services through the Internet to boost cost efficiency. Andersen (2009) determined that e-government has a significant control of corruption and exhibits a positive and economically promising effect. E-government has received increasing attention from the academic and particular community. This strategy comprises a main part of e-services that involves in providing the governmental services and processes online.

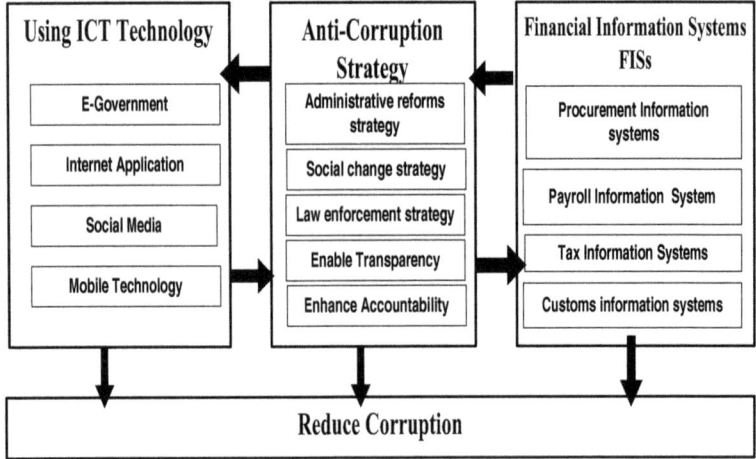

Fig. 65.1 IS anticorruption tools and strategies

Web Application Strategy

Web-based technology is another popular strategy to reduce corruption (Zhang & Zhang, 2009). This technology allows the public to monitor corruption-prone activities, such as permit applications or approvals, and to raise questions in case of irregularities. Widespread use of centralized and high-speed countrywide networks has significantly contributed to their performance (Rodríguez, Caba Pérez, & López Hernández, 2007). Web-based financial services use the Internet as a communication standard by combining a web browser, a display standard, and a web server as an access point to back-end stand-alone systems. Numerous researchers have suggested the blackguard stand-alone possibility of adapting an Internet application to reduce corruption (Hui, 2008; Pathak, Naz, Rahman, Smith, & Agarwal, 2009). Many tools have been developed to stop corruption; considerable focus has been given lately on e-government, particularly using communication technologies, such as the Internet and mobile phones. The intention of these tools is to open government processes publicly and allow citizens to access information (Zhang & Zhang, 2009). Internet can also probably act as a corruption suppressor because of its positive effect on spreading information about official misconduct, which inevitably increases detection of corrupt behaviors of politicians and public servants, and, thus, reduces them (Andersen, Bentzen, Dalgaard, & Selaya, 2011).

Social Media Strategy

Social media can refer as an enabling technology and the contents they generated through three kinds of instruments, namely social networking sites such as Facebook, micro blogging services like Twitter, and multimedia sharing services such as

Flicker and YouTube. Social media is utilized as an anticorruption instrument to create attitudes and culture of transparency and establishes new avenues for openness. Bertot et al. (2010) reviewed literatures and found evidence for the potential of using social media to reduce corruption. Using social media is a central part of transparency and more recent anticorruption initiatives. It has transformed the manner in which people are able to interact with one another and the means in which governments can promote transparency and reduce corruption (Bertot et al., 2010). It has promoted transparency by empowering citizens to monitor the activities of the governments collectively (Arpit, 2012). This strategy has enabled users to access content easily and to interact with others via highly accessible Web-based technologies. Citizen participation, collaboration, empowerment, and time exploiting are the main potential strengths to reduce corruption. It facilitates citizen journalism, which improves transparency and enables users to interact with other parties to socialize, share information, or achieve a common goal or interest.

Mobile Technology Strategy

Using mobile technology as part of ACS is among the recent approach in corruption reduction (Bhuiyan, 2011; Hellstrom, 2010). At present, mobile technology has a significant role in our lives. Substantial growth in adopting these technologies, including nations with low landline and Internet penetration, has been observed. Mobile technology can have a significant role in promoting good governance, increasing accountability, and reducing corruption. In most countries, mobile technology adoption is high and has considerably outpaced computer and Internet adoptions (Bertot, Jaeger & Grimes, 2010). This technology can be effectively deployed to disseminate news on corrupt practices. In fact, some mobile technologies, such as iPhone, are completely accessible to people with visual impairments because of the presence of a touch screen and the absence of a tactile keyboard. Mobilizing users and the community to report corruption cases will make it easier to impose corrective actions on involved individuals as well as to organize systems to avoid a corrupt attitude (Ameen & Ahmad, 2014). Thus, supporting the emerging nature of e-government and mobile government that holds considerable promise for deploying transparency initiatives is vital.

Using FIS in Corruption Reduction Strategies

Public finance can increase economic growth, and consequently helps in reducing poverty. However, corruption reduces revenues and increases illegal public expenditure. Based on the literature analysis, only a few studies have focused on the role of FIS in reducing corruption. That means more research on this strategy is needed. Most countries have focused on using ICT in their activities to strengthen the reformation process as the necessary ingredient to a good financial governance transparency (Ameen & Ahmad, 2014). ICT offers nations a modern approach to create

Fig. 65.2 Using FIS to reduce corruption

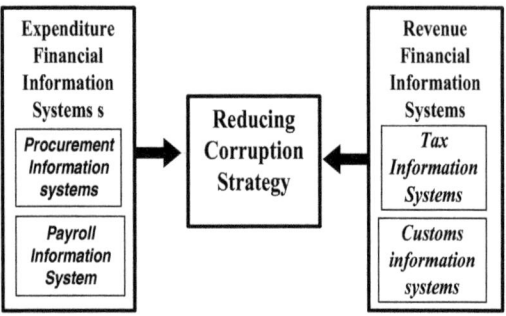

transparency and promote anticorruption practices. Most countries intend to introduce FIS in financial procedures, revenues, and expenditure systems (Bertot et al., 2010). Figure 65.2 illustrates several information systems that can be used to reduce corruption in the financial sector, in both expenditures and revenues. Procurement and payroll information systems were assisting in reducing the expenditure corruption, whereas tax and custom information systems have the same role in reducing revenue corruption (Ameen & Ahmad, 2014).

Procurement Information Systems

Procurement information systems have been established as a response to the requirement to computerize purchases and contracts. This requirement arises from the lack of standards, which makes it difficult to determine the extent of corruption effect in terms of expenditures, particularly for public goods. However, the public and private sectors have different practices with regard to procurement and contract specifications. Researchers frequently rely on untrustworthy accounts because of lack of detailed information on behavioral responses. Without computerized information systems, such situations do not facilitate the construction of an analytical framework to explain corruption and develop ways to control it (Chand & Moene, 1999). Nevertheless, using decision support systems in public procurements limits the possible damaging effects of corruption (Csáki & Gelléri, 2005). In many nations, the public procurement information system is one kind of FIS that has been regarded as a successful solution to corruption problems. Literature has clarified several examples from different countries such as the Czech Republic, Malaysia, the Philippines, and Russia (Andersen, 2009).

Tax and Information System Strategy

Tax information systems are not involved in the actual delivery of services such as filing a tax or renewing a license. This situation has a huge effect in terms of transparency and anticorruption (Bhatnagar, 2003). These systems play an important role in preventing corruption by improving transparency, which enables extensive cross-checking of information. It provides an opportunity to utilize a computerized selection of taxpayers for auditing and monitoring practices, and enabling a timely response to taxpayers who are requesting information and assistance. Computerization, as a corruption reduction strategy, dramatically enhances the efficiency of most functions in tax administration by providing tamper-proof and paper-free information based on the identity of potential taxpayers, third-party information, accounts, and transactions. The tax information system facilitates cross-matching among various sources of information, which helps verifies returns filed and provides accuracy in tax collection and recovery operations. Tax computerization assists in selecting audits and enhances taxpayer information and assistance (Vishwanath & Kaufmann, 1999). According to Seongcheol, Hyun Jeong, and Heejin (2009), tax information systems assist in preventing corruption in some countries, such as Korea, Mexico, and the Philippines. These FISs provide administrative services to many civil affairs committees and reduce contact between tax collectors and taxpayers, and consequently reduce opportunities for corruption (Andersen, 2009). The successful implementation of information systems in tax administration has yielded impressive results (Hui, 2008).

Customs Information System

As illustrated in Fig. 65.2, customs information system is one of the most important means to reduce corruption, and customs automation is one of the major cost elements of investment toward customs improvements (Milner, Morrissey, & Zgovu, 2008). ICTs can improve the efficiency of customs authority through public financial processes by reducing corruption opportunities. Recently, the ASYCUDA, which was developed by UNCTAD, is used by over 70 developing countries to manage tariff collection and reduce border-line corruption. The system accelerates the movement of goods and reduces transport expenses (Wakelin & Shadrach, 2001). Furthermore, it helps increase government revenues by reducing corruption. A customs information system has a significant role in tariff collection and has increased direct and transit trades (Wijayasiri & Jayaratne, 2010). ASYCUDA uses international codes and standards developed by the International Organization for Standardization, the World Customs Organization, and the United Nations. The system can be adopted to suit the customs characteristics of any country. The system allows electronic data interchange between traders and customs administrations, during which data are exchanged with external systems such as banks or carriers. The system applies the rule of electronic data interchange for administration, commerce, and transport (Wijayasiri & Jayaratne, 2010). The latest edition, which is known as ASYCUDA World, is an e-customs version that is compatible with major database management and operating systems such as Oracle, DB2, Sybase, Microsoft Windows, Linux, and HP-UX.

Discussion

This research utilized an analysis on the existing researches to indicate the most strategies that harness IS as an ACS. Related concepts were discussed focusing on the information systems strategies to reduce corruption. As shown in Table 65.1, among the information systems strategies used to reduce corruption, only a few studies have focused on the ability of FIS to contribute towards these efforts. In order to analyze the ability of FIS to reduce corruption, an analysis is conducted. FISs are system software that accumulates and analyzes financial data in order to make good financial management decisions. The use of FIS allows governments to link databases in different departments to streamline the backend of public administration processes. In addition, an FIS could also increase tracking of accounting events in conjunction with IT resources and the interface through which governments interact with citizens. This system assists in evaluating and controlling within an entity and to assures appropriate usage and accountability for their resources. It associates in management decision making, inventing planning, and performance management systems and provides proficiency in financial reporting and control to facilitate administration in the formulation and implementation of an organization's strategy. These financial reports are prepared for non-management groups such as shareholders, regulatory, creditor, agencies, and tax authorities. The reports could be used as indicators for corrupt transactions. In the context of public finance, several factors indicate that FIS could reduce corruption by promoting good governance, strengthening reform-oriented initiatives, reducing potential for corrupt behavior, enhancing relationships between government employees and citizens, allowing for citizen tracking of activities, and monitoring and controlling the behavior of government employees. By producing such reports, FIS can bring more transparency, auditing, and controlling into public financial administration. Thus, FIS can become one of the key components of an ACS. There are five factors that can contribute when using FIS as an anticorruption strategy. These factors are system quality, information quality and service quality of the system, FIS characteristics, and anticorruption factors. FIS must be quality systems, which means that the information system processing which includes the software and data components must be technically sound. The output of the information system which can be in the form of reports or online screens should produce quality information. FIS must be able to provide quality service to other authorities and have the ability to monitor, control, and track transactions. These factors have significant effect on FIS as an anticorruption strategy.

Conclusion and Future Work

FISs play significant role in financial management, which are the important parts of huge institutional management. Therefore FISs have the potential to become a significant key component of a broader anticorruption strategy. The chapter reviews various strategies on exploiting ICTs to reduce corruption. These strategies include adapting Internet application, improving e-government, and harnessing social media. Therefore in order to reduce corruption effectively, FISs should be used in the fields of procurement, tax, customs, and the debt management. This study also discusses some important factors in the field of information system and anticorruption that contribute in reducing corruption. As a future research, the study plans to investigate the role of individual FISs in reducing corruption. In the financial reform strategy which is constructed by revolutionary changes in science and technology, the employment of FISs in the strategy will facilitate transparency in the public financial administration process.

Acknowledgment The authors would like to thank the Faculty of Information Science and Technology, Universiti Kebangsaan Malaysia, for giving the authors an opportunity to conduct this research. This research is funded by Universiti Kebangsaan Malaysia under Exploratory Research Grant Scheme FRGS/1/2014/ICT07/UKM/02/3 and DPP-2015-019.

References

Ameen, A., & Ahmad, K. (2014). A systematic strategy for harnessing financial information systems in fighting corruption electronically. In *Proceedings of knowledge management international conference*.

Andersen, T. B. (2009). E-Government as an anti-corruption strategy. *Information Economics and Policy, 21*(3), 201–210.

Andersen, T. B., Bentzen, J., Dalgaard, C. J., & Selaya, P. (2011). Does the internet reduce corruption? Evidence from US states and across countries. *The World Bank Economic Review, 25*(3), 387–417.

Arpit, B. (2012). E-government and social media as openness and anti-corruption strategy. *Research Journal of Management Sciences, 1*(1), 5.

Bertot, J.C., Jaeger, P.T. and Grimes, J.M., (2010). Using ICTs to create a culture of transparency: E-government and social media as openness and anti-corruption tools for societies, Government information quarterly, 27 (3), 264-271..

Bhatnagar, S. (2003). E-government and access to information. *Global Corruption Report, 1*, 24–32 (Transparency International).

Bhuiyan, S. H. (2011). Modernizing Bangladesh public administration through e-governance: Benefits and challenges. *Government Information Quarterly, 28*(1), 54–65.

Chand, S. K., & Moene, K. O. (1999). Controlling fiscal corruption. *World Development, 27*(7), 1129–1140.

Csáki, C., & Gelléri, P. (2005). Conditions and benefits of applying decision technological solutions as a tool to curb corruption within the procurement process: The case of Hungary. *Journal of Purchasing and Supply Management, 11*(5–6), 252–259.

Hellstrom, J. (2010). Mobile technology as a means to fight corruption in East Africa. *SPIDER ICT4D, 1*(3), 47–69.

Hui, L. (2008, October). E-Government to combat corruption in the Asia Pacific Region. In *Conference on wireless communications, networking and mobile computing, 2008*.

Milner, C., Morrissey, O., & Zgovu, E. (2008). Trade facilitation in developing countries. *CREDIT Research Paper, 8*(05), 209–231.

Otusanya, J., Lauwo, S., & Adeyeye, G. B. (2012). A critical examination of the multinational companies: Anti-corruption Policy in Nigeria. *Accountancy Business and the Public Interest, 11*, 1–49.

Pathak, R. D., Naz, R., Rahman, M. H., Smith, R. F. I., & Agarwal, K. N. (2009). E-governance to cut corruption in public service delivery: A case study of Fiji. *International Journal of Public Administration, 32*(5), 415–437.

Rodríguez, M. P., Caba Pérez, C., & López Hernández, A. M. (2007). E-government and public financial reporting: The case of Spanish regional governments. *The American Review of Public Administration, 37*(2), 142–177. doi:10.1177/0275074006293193.

Seongcheol, K., Hyun Jeong, K., & Heejin, L. (2009). An institutional analysis of an e-government system for anti-corruption: The case of OPEN. *Government Information Quarterly, 26*(1), 42–50.

Vishwanath, T., & Kaufmann, D. (1999). Towards transparency in finance and governance. *SSRN eLibrary*. doi: 10.2139/ssrn.258978.

Wakelin, O., & Shadrach, B. (2001). Impact assessment of appropriate and innovative technologies in enterprise development. *Manchester: EDIAIS. Manchester, 1*(1), 1–36.

Wijayasiri, J., & Jayaratne, S. (2010). The impact of information technology in trade facilitation on small and medium-sized enterprises in Sri Lanka. *Studies in Trade and Investment, 69*(1), 177–214.

Zhang, J., & Zhang, Z. (2009). Applying e-government information system for anti-corruption strategy. In *ICMeCG 2009, Nanchang, China.*

Chapter 66
Cross-Market Price Mechanism Between the US Copper Futures Market and a Newly Proposed Chinese Dollar Index

Ikhlaas Gurrib

Abstract Recent changes in China's copper demand have lately received much attention due to its close relationship to the country's economic activity. Although an emerging market, China accounts for around 40 % of the world's copper demand and the USA is the third biggest market for exports, making it imperative to assess the relationship between copper futures prices and a newly proposed Chinese dollar index. The purpose of this study is to analyse if changes in the copper futures prices can be used as a market timing tool to predict movements in the Chinese dollar index, and vice versa. To enhance the predictive market timing ability, an adaptive relative strength index model is used to track changes in market conditions better. The analysis is conducted using both daily and weekly data over the June 2007–December 2015 period. Findings will suggest if the technical analysis tool can be used to forecast copper prices based on changes in the Chinese dollar index, or if accurate forecasts can be made on the Chinese dollar index based on movements in copper's prices, over different frequency intervals. More importantly, this would have policy implications in that it would reveal whether global copper prices can be affected by Chinese Yuan's movements against other major global currencies, suggesting a need for regulatory bodies to relook at the effect of non-fundamental factors on commodity and currency markets.

Keywords Copper futures prices • Chinese Yuan • Adaptive relative strength index

Introduction

According to BIS (2015), in their quest of reassessing continually global economic outlook, investors are gradually more focused on the activities of emerging market economies such as China. For instance, Klotz, Lin, and Hsu (2014) found that

I. Gurrib (✉)
Canadian University of Dubai, School of Graduate Studies, Dubai, United Arab Emirates
e-mail: ikhlaas@cud.ac.ae

© Springer International Publishing Switzerland 2017   741
R. Benlamri, M. Sparer (eds.), *Leadership, Innovation and Entrepreneurship as Driving Forces of the Global Economy*, Springer Proceedings in Business and Economics, DOI 10.1007/978-3-319-43434-6_66

China's economic activity played an important role in global commodity price dynamics over the period 1998–2012. More recently, although the depreciation of the renminbi allowed for cheaper exports, the fastest drop in the Purchasing Managers' Index (PMI) over the last 6 years led investors to be more concerned with the growth prospects of China, emerging market economies (EME) and eventually the global economy. The Chinese equities and world equity markets have since then fallen, accompanied with a volatile downward trend in commodity prices. More importantly, the implied volatility of at-the-money options on long-term bond futures of Germany, Japan, the UK and the USA showed an opposite trend with the implied volatility of at-the-money options on commodity futures contracts on oil, gold and copper as per BIS (2015), suggesting a negative relationship between commodity prices and the equity stock prices. This was supported by the increased S&P 500 market volatility index (VIX) and the increased volatility of the emerging market exchange-traded-fund volatility index (VXEEM) of the Chicago Board Options Exchange (CBOE) since August 2015. This is also evidenced through the copper spot prices which have dropped nearly 15 % over the period of 29th May to 2nd September 2015 (ICSG, 2015a). Over the period January 2001–July 2015, copper prices have fluctuated from 80 (US cents/pounds of copper) in the early 2001, peaked at $4.50 per pound in January 2011 and dropped since then to be around $2.40 per pound in July 2015. As per the International Copper Study Group, the demand of copper from emerging markets remains significant, where, after having more than tripled since 2004, China alone currently represents 45 % of world demand (ICSG, 2015b).

As observed in Fig. 66.1, which shows the performance of copper futures prices and the S&P 500 market index over the last 10 years, the relationship between the two has changed significantly after copper prices have peaked in 2011, where the latter has lost nearly 19 % of its value since 2006, while the S&P 500 had performed relatively better with a positive gain of 60 % since 2006. In support of the importance of information flows among markets like the commodity and equity markets, Nijs (2014) asserts that cross-market correlations with commodity markets have increased in recent years,

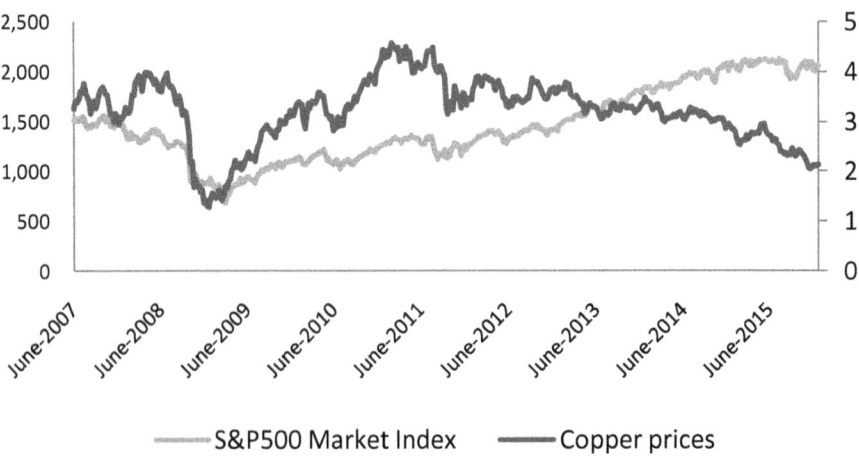

Fig. 66.1 Performance of S&P 500 market index and copper prices (June 2007–December 2015)

such that factors other than fundamentals are driving commodity prices. While a study of the relationship between US market-based indices and copper prices might be of value, particularly for regulatory bodies such as the Commodity Futures Trades Commission (CFTC) and the Securities Exchange Commission (SEC), the importance of the Chinese market players in the copper market cannot be left subdued.

To this end, the purpose of this study is to analyse if changes in the copper futures prices can be used as a market timing tool to predict movements in a newly proposed Chinese dollar index, and if movements in the Chinese dollar index can be used to predict changes in copper prices. This is the first study to adopt an adaptive relative strength index model, which is under the umbrella of technical analysis tools. Findings from the use of different frequency intervals would suggest if the use of a particular data frequency would refine the market timing opportunities in a market where fundamentals are meant to guide the movements of its prices as laid out by the efficient market hypothesis. By defragmenting the analysis over the pre-2011 and post-2011 period, this is the first study to shed further light in the reversal of previously held cross-market correlations between commodity markets such as copper and currency markets such as the Chinese Yuan. This study would also have policy implications in that it would reveal whether global copper prices can be affected or are affected by the strength or weakness of the Chinese Yuan relative to other major currencies such as the US dollar, Canadian dollar, Australian dollar, among others. This would suggest a need for regulatory bodies to relook at the effect of non-fundamental factors in forecasting future commodity and currency markets which, by nature, are the most volatile markets. The rest of the chapter provides some recent literature reviews on the commodity markets, with specific reference to the copper futures market, before laying down the data and methodology, which focus on the use of the adaptive relative strength index. The final part of the study provides the conclusive remarks with a focus on the policy implications for regulatory bodies.

Literature Review

While literature reviews on commodity markets are abundant, recent work on specific commodity markets such as the gold, crude oil and copper markets has gained more momentum lately. Findings with respect to the copper market are more relevant to our study, where the Shanghai Futures Exchange (SFE) has become the second largest copper market as per Fung, Liu, and Tse (2010). Ruthledge, Karim, and Wang (2013), using vector error correction models, found 5-year daily prices of copper from the London Metals Exchange (LME), SFE and the New York Mercantile Exchange's Commodity Exchange division (COMEX) to be strongly correlated, suggesting cross-exchange correlations among the different exchanges, and that the three primary copper markets can be regarded as one market where the transmission mechanism is efficient. Similarly, Yin and Han (2013) studied the mean and volatility across major global futures markets before and after the global financial crisis, and found the spillover effect to be stronger following the crisis. Lien and Yang (2009) studied the short-run return and volatility spillovers across three major international copper futures markets, and found the return and volatility spillovers between the two developed markets to be bidirectional and significant. Fung, Leung, and Xu (2003) examined patterns of information flows for copper futures traded in both the developed US market and the emerging Chinese market using a bivariate GARCH model and found that the US copper futures market plays a leading role in transmitting information to the Chinese copper futures market. Hua and Chen (2004) and Gao and Liu (2007) show that there are significant co-integration relationships and bidirectional lead-lag relationships between the SHFE and the LME copper futures markets.

More recently, Grieb (2015) analysed information transmissions from the dollar index and the S&P 500 to nine commodity futures markets and found strong patterns of spillovers among the markets. This is in line with earlier studies like King and Wadhwani (1990) and Driesprong, Jacobsen, and Maat (2008) which support the contagion theory that investors respond directly to publicly available information and rely on price information not available in their local market as a proxy for information for their respective markets. Existing literature from Stoll and Whaley (2010), Masters (2008) and Kennedy (2012) also support the presence of more financial institutions in the form of index investors in commodity futures markets, driving up futures prices since 2004. Contrary to the support of a possible commodity financialisation hypothesis, where evidence of herd behaviour exists among markets, Demirer, Lee, and Lien (2015) found no significant effect of the stock market on herd behaviour in the commodity futures markets. This was also supported by Hamilton and Wu (2015) who found little support of commodity index positions in predicting returns in those futures markets. While previous studies provided a good background to the possible existence of cross-market interdependence or the possible influence of index investors on commodity markets' prices, the use of market timing strategies based on market indices' over- or undershooting, in volatile commodity markets such as the copper futures, is non-existent. This study closes the gap by introducing the use of an adaptive relative strength index model to analyse the possible market timing ability of the proposed Chinese dollar index to predict copper futures prices, and the possible market timing ability of the copper futures prices to predict movements in the Chinese dollar index, where the Chinese Yuan's strength or weakness is measured against other major global foreign currencies.

Research Methodology and Data

Proposed by Wilder (1978), the relative strength index (RSI) added a new dimension to technical analysis, by integrating tops and bottoms, support and resistance levels, and providing impending market turning points. The model is structured as follows:

$$RSI_t = 100 - \left[\frac{100}{1 + RS} \right] \tag{66.1}$$

where $RS = \dfrac{Average\ of\ 14\ days\ with\ an\ Up\ close}{Average\ of\ 14\ days\ with\ a\ Down\ close}$. While the initial RSI is based on an average of the previous 14-day close prices, for subsequent RSI values, the average of up-close and down-close is calculated as follows, thereby smoothing out the RSI data:

$$\frac{Average\ of\ 14\ days\ with\ an\ Up\ close}{Average\ of\ 14\ days\ with\ a\ Down\ close} = \frac{\left(Previous\ average\ Up\ close * 13\right) + Today's\ Up\ close}{\left(Previous\ average\ Down\ close * 13\right) + Today's\ Down\ close}$$

The RSI provides top and bottom levels when the index goes above 70 and below 30, where the index will usually bottom or top out before the actual commodity market bottoms or tops out, suggesting the possibility of a reversal in the commodity prices. The RSI values also provide information about failure swings, which provide strong indications of market reversals. Further, support and resistance levels usually based on RSI values occur well before support and resistance levels on prices. Finally, but not least, the RSI tool provides information about divergence, where divergence between price movements and RSI suggests a significant market turning point. While the RSI can provide important layers of information, it is however constrained with a 14-day period adjustment. The adaptive RSI introduces a smoothing factor which allows for the look-back period to be adjusted dynamically as follows:

$$Adaptive\,RSI_t = Adaptive\,RSI_{t-1} + \delta\left(Close - Adaptive\,RSI_{t-1}\right) \qquad (66.2)$$

where the smoothing factor $\delta = 2\left|\dfrac{RSI_t}{100} - 0.5\right|$. The data used for the study is based on copper futures prices as provided by the Chicago Mercantile Exchange (CME). The analysis would be conducted using both daily and weekly data over the June 2007–December 2015 period. The use of the different data frequency would allow the comparison between an investor relying on a smoother data (weekly data) as opposed to a more volatile one in predicting the direction of copper futures prices. As for the S&P 500 market index data, it would be accessed from the New York Stock Exchange (NYSE). The study is further strengthened by defragmenting the model into a pre-2011 and post-2011 period, to test for the break into the possible cross-market correlations between copper market and the market index. Due to the scope of this study, and in line with Wilder (1978), the overbought/oversold threshold levels are kept at 70/30. This assumption can be relaxed in future research. In line with Gurrib and Elshareif (2016), who constructed an index based on an arithmetic variation in each currency pair, a Chinese dollar index is proposed to capture the strength of the Chinese Yuan against a basket of major currencies, namely the Euro, Japanese Yen, British Pound, Hong Kong dollar, Australian Dollar and US dollar. This is in line with the China Foreign Exchange Trade System (CFETS), which has introduced a CFETS RMB index in December 2015 where the Yuan is paired with 13 other currencies, where the 6 countries represent a cumulative weight of more than 75 % in the CFETS index.

Policy Implications and Conclusion

The study has important implications ranging from the investor's market timing ability to financial regulation. The use of different data frequencies such as daily or weekly data would suggest whether a smoother data frequency based on weekly data would result in more accurate forecasting abilities in predicting the movements of the Chinese dollar index and copper futures prices. A more accurate forecasting ability for an RSI based on a period other than 14 would suggest that commodity prices such as copper and indices such as the Chinese Yuan index tend to be better fitted in models with dynamic look-back periods. Pre- and post-2011 findings would also suggest whether there has been a change in the previously held cross-market correlations between copper and the strength or weakness of the Chinese currency against other major currencies such as the US dollar and Euro. This is important for regulatory bodies such as the Commodity Futures Trading Commission (CFTC), as part of their mandate to maintain price stability in the commodity futures markets, to be able to further avoid potentially contagion effects flowing among markets. Due to the fact that any overbought or oversold levels are based on the relative strength indices, and not specific net positions of hedgers or speculators in the copper markets, the findings would support the non-destabilising effect that specific types of traders have on copper prices as held previously in literature on studies which focused on specific types of traders such as speculators. The reliance of information from markets like copper on the Chinese dollar index in determining future prices or indices' movements would support the hypothesis that, despite a break in the movement of copper price or the S&P 500 market index relationship since 2011, non-fundamental factors can potentially affect the predictive ability, not only of copper prices, but also in regard to the predictive strength or weakness of the Chinese Yuan relative to other currencies such as the US dollar. Lastly, but not least, the adoption of a Chinese dollar index not only complements existing international practices of a country's regulatory body to maintain its own currency index, but also provides timely information to market participants about the strength of the Chinese Yuan relative to other major currencies, and not only relative to the US dollar as recently observed in the headlines. While this study sets the framework required to analyse the cross-market price mechanism between the US copper futures markets and a newly proposed Chinese index, important avenues of future research include the assessment of a long-run relationship between the US copper futures prices and the Chinese dollar index using a co-integration approach. This study can also be enriched by assessing short-term dynamics through vector error correction models, and robust tested by appropriate Granger causality testing to determine significant lead and lag relationships between the US copper futures prices and the Chinese dollar index.

References

BIS. (2015). Bank of International Settlements: International banking and financial market developments. *BIS Quarterly Review*. Retrieved from January 20, 2016, http://www.bis.org/publ/qtrpdf/r_qt1509.pdf.

Demirer, R., Lee, H. T., & Lien, D. (2015). Does the stock market drive herd behaviour in the commodity futures markets? *International Review of Financial Analysis, 39*, 32–44.

Driesprong, G., Jacobsen, B., & Maat, B. (2008). Striking oil: Another puzzle? *Journal of Financial Economics, 89*(2), 307–327.

Fung, H. G., Leung, W. K., & Xu, X. E. (2003). Information flows between the US and China commodity futures trading. *Review of Quantitative Finance and Accounting, 21*, 267–285.

Fung, H., Liu, Q. F., & Tse, Y. (2010). The information flow and market efficiency between the U.S. and Chinese aluminum and copper futures markets. *Journal of Futures Markets, 30*(12), 1192–1209.

Gao, J., & Liu, Q. (2007). The information transmission between LME and SHFE in copper future markets. *The Journal of Financial Studies, 2*, 63–73.

Grieb, T. (2015). Mean and volatility transmission for commodity futures. *Journal of Economics and Finance, 39*, 100–118.

Gurrib, I., & Elshareif, E. (2016). Optimizing the performance of the fractal adaptive moving average strategy: The case of EUR/USD. *International Journal of Economics and Finance, 8*(2), 171–178.

Hamilton, J. D., & Wu, J. C. (2015). Effects of index-fund investing on commodity futures prices. *International Economic Review, 56*(1), 187–205.

Hua, R., & Chen, B. (2004). International linkages between Chinese and overseas futures markets. *China Economic Quarterly, 3*, 727–742.

ICSG. (2015a). *International copper study group: Refined usage data*. Retrieved from February 20, 2016, http://www.icsg.org/index.php/component/jdownloads/finish/165/872.

ICSG. (2015b). *International copper study group: Release of ICSG 2015 statistical yearbook*. Retrieved from 2016, http://www.icsg.org/index.php/press-releases/finish/170-publications-press-releases/2111-2015-11-30-press-release-yearbook-2015.

Kennedy, J. P. (2012, April). The high cost of gambling on oil. *New York Times*.

King, M. A., & Wadhwani, S. (1990). Transmission of Volatility between Stock Markets. *Review of Financial Studies, 3*(1), 5–33. doi:10.1093/rfs/3.1.5

Klotz, P., Lin, T. C., & Hsu, S. (2014). Global commodity prices, economic activity and monetary policy: The relevance of China. *Resources Policy, 42*, 1–9.

Lien, D., & Yang, L. (2009). Intraday return and volatility spill-over across international copper futures markets. *International Journal of Managerial Finance, 5*, 135–149.

Masters, M. W. (2008). *Testimony before committee on homeland security and governmental affairs of the United States Senate* (2008) (testimony of Masters, M. W.).

Nijs, L. (2014). *The handbook of global agricultural markets: The business and finance of land, water, and soft commodities*. UK: Palgrave Macmillan.

Ruthledge, R., Karim, K., & Wang, R. (2013). International copper futures market price linkage and information transmission: Empirical evidence from the primary world copper markets. *Journal of International Business Research, 12*(1), 113–131.

Stoll, H. R., & Whaley, R. E. (2010). Commodity index investing and commodity futures prices. *Journal of Applied Finance, 20*, 7–46.

Wilder, J. W. (1978, June). *New concepts in technical trading systems*. Trend Research.

Yin, L., & Han, L. (2013). Exogenous shocks and information transmission in global copper futures markets. *Journal of Futures Markets, 33*(8), 724–751.

Chapter 67
The Assessment of the Global Financial Crisis on Dubai Financial Market Performance

Ahmed K. Al Jarouf, Mohammed Al Mansoori, Suzan Nooraddin, and Elgilani Eltahir Elshareif

Abstract The United Arab Emirates (UAE) has implemented its long-term vision 2021. The main goal of this vision is to diversify the economic activity to edge up on the back of non-oil sector, despite the fact that UAE's economy is considered one of the most diversified economies across the region. The significant drop in oil prices in addition to performances of other global markets represents a challenge for Dubai stock market. This may have an important effect on the share prices of Dubai stock market and its performance. In this chapter, we collect market data for oil prices, US NASDAQ Composite, and DFM from the official website of Dubai Financial Market (www.dfm.ae) and (www.nasdaq.com) to explore the patterns of pre-after the global financial crisis performance and to observe the performance of the Dubai financial market in comparison to NASDAQ. We also look at the impact of drop in oil price on the performance of DFM. Our results support that the DFM performed well after the crisis. However, the lower oil prices have reversed this situation.

Keywords DFM's performance • US NASDAQ • Oil price • Global financial crisis

Introduction

The Dubai financial market (DFM) was established in March 2000. It was found as a secondary market for securities trading for local public joint stock companies (PJSC). Like any financial market globally, DFM plays a significant role in the economy of the country and attracts a variety of investors, who are looking for an opportunity to seize. Dubai and the region in general have been going through a lot of events that played a major role in shaping the performance of the market in discussion.

A.K. Al Jarouf (✉) • M. Al Mansoori • S. Nooraddin • E.E. Elshareif
Canadian University of Dubai, PO Box 117781, Dubai, United Arab Emirates
e-mail: ahmed.khaldoun@hotmail.com; elgilani@cud.ac.ae

© Springer International Publishing Switzerland 2017   749
R. Benlamri, M. Sparer (eds.), *Leadership, Innovation and Entrepreneurship as Driving Forces of the Global Economy*, Springer Proceedings in Business and Economics, DOI 10.1007/978-3-319-43434-6_67

There are 65 companies currently listed in DFM, which are mainly local or regional. There is another stock exchange market in Dubai, which is NASDAQ Dubai. NASDAQ was founded in 2005 to enable the exchange of regional and international shares of international companies in the Middle East. NASDAQ Dubai is 66 % owned by DFM and Borse Dubai owns the remaining 33 %.

The remainder of this chapter is organized as follows. Section "Literature Review" presents the impact of global financial crisis on DFM performance. Section "The impact of Global Financial Crisis on Dubai Financial Market Performance" assesses the impact of the lower oil price on DFM performance. Section "Results and Discussion" presents the concluding remarks and future work.

Literature Review

Onour (2007) As GCC countries are major suppliers of oil the study reasons that the GCC stock markets would therefore be susceptible to change in oil prices. The methods selected to aid in clarifying the relationship between the two variables are both short- and long-term determinants of GCC stock markets' volatility. The paper concludes that the influence of oil price change on GCC stock market returns is observed in the long term influencing major macroeconomic indicators that influence profitability of firms traded in GCC stock markets.

The study of seeks to contradict the findings of earlier studies that state that there exists no linkage between oil prices and GCC stock markets, attributing the results to employing weak or wrong methods and models to investigate the relation between the stock market and oil prices. Because previous works have depended heavily on using only linear linkages, the researchers chose to use a newly developed method named Breitung method for nonlinear cointegration analysis stating that the method detects cointegration when the error-correction mechanism is nonlinear. The study concludes with that there exists a relationship between oil prices and the GCC stock market in a nonlinear manner.

The paper of Arouril and Fouquau (2009) proposes that since the GCC countries are dependent on their oil industry there should exist a relationship between oil prices and the stock market and seeks to investigate how GCC stock markets are impacted by oil price shocks. They build on previous studies that have stated that there exists a nonlinear relationship between stock markets and oil prices. The study focuses on studying both linear and nonlinear relationships. They found that the relationship is significant in only a part of the GCC including the countries UAE, Qatar, and Oman as the stock markets here react positively to oil price increases while in the remaining GCC countries Bahrain, Kuwait, and Saudi Arabia the study revealed that oil changes had no effect on stock market returns.

Another paper done by Kang, Ratti, and Yoon (2015) investigates the connection of oil prices on the US stock market return and volatility. The mathematical model they utilized was constructed from daily data on return and volatility to covariance of return and volatility at a monthly frequency. "The measures of daily volatility are realized-volatility at high frequency (normalized squared return), conditional-volatility recovered from a stochastic volatility model, and implied-volatility deduced from options prices." Positive shocks to aggregate demand and to oil-market-specific demand are associated with negative effects on the covariance of return and volatility.

The comparative study between oil prices and its influence on the stock market was the issue raised in this research by Filis, Degiannakis, and Floros (2011). A dynamic conditional correlation model was used to investigate the time-varying correlation between stock market prices and oil prices for six countries; the countries were divided into oil-importing and oil-exporting countries (Canada, Mexico, and Brazil for oil exporting and the USA, Germany, and the Netherlands for oil importing). Their findings demonstrate that a negative relationship exists between the two variables with the relationship turning positive when the global financial crisis hit in 2008.

The Impact of Global Financial Crisis on Dubai Financial Market Performance

In this chapter, we are going to explore the patterns of performance in the market. We have gathered historical market data to help in the analysis. The data is taken from December 2005 until February 2016, as monthly Market General Index. After obtaining the data, we have graphed the indices against time, to get the following graph (Fig. 67.1).

Fig. 67.1 DFM—NASDAQ—OIL

DFM Pitfalls (2004–2005)

The first drop occurred at the end of 2005 through July 2006. There were no explicit reasons to such a drop, as stated by Dubai Chamber of Commerce (DCC) (2006). There were speculations about the reason of that event, since the economic growth was showing a promising future, and by analyzing the GDP and investment data, there was a conclusion that supports a very strong economic growth. This event brings us back to the term structure of securities and its relationship to the expectations of the investors. The expectations theory suggests that the interest rates in the future (long term) would be the sum of the current and expected future rates by investors. We can relate to that by studying the mental status of those investors in 2005. The market showed incomparable growth over a very short period, as shown in Fig. 67.2.

This will lead to speculations and pessimism in analyzing the market for the future years. That said, the market share prices were noticed to be falling dramatically through the period mentioned above.

The other reason according to DCC is the lack of trust from the investors' side towards the companies and their financial reports.

The above two mentioned reasons lead to the sudden and harsh drop in the share prices. There is no solid reason for that event, but a clear observation would lead to the conclusion that the drop was due to the behavior of the investors.

Market Pitfalls (July to November—2008)

The year 2008 came with many undesirable changes to the global market in general and the local financial market precisely.

After the event that occurred in 2005 in the DFM, the market performance started recovering and stabilizing to a curtain point. The relative stability remained in the market, where the market exchange matured after the great hit in terms of investors being more cautious. Figure 67.3 illustrates the mentioned earlier.

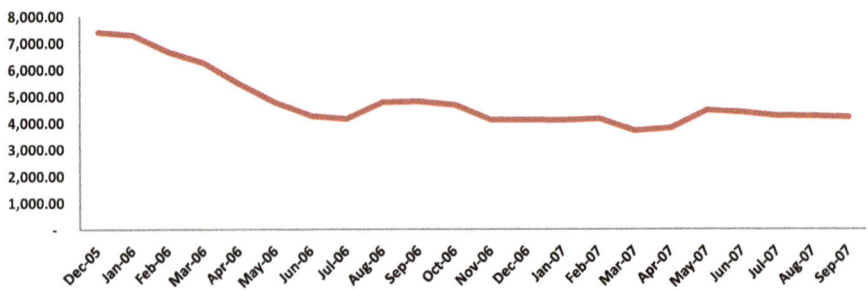

Fig. 67.2 DFM General Index 2006–2007

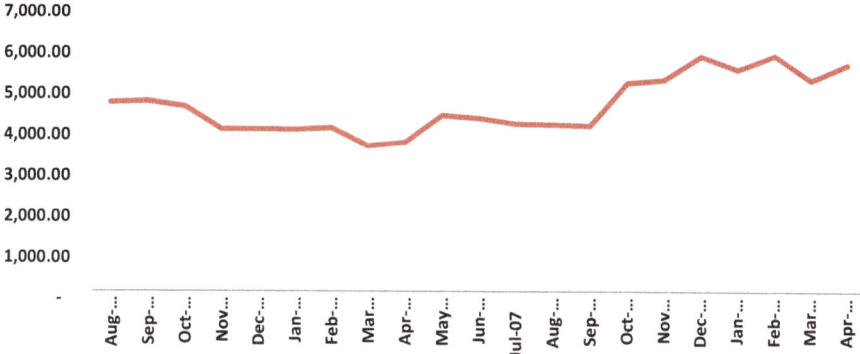

Fig. 67.3 DFM General Index 2006–2008

Fig. 67.4 DFM General Index 2008

That stability was bound to be disrupted by the global financial crisis that occurred in the early 2008 and extended for years later. The market index has dropped dramatically from 6000 points to a 1000 points index in a single year. The steepest drop that occurred in the market so far took place between September and November of 2008. The drop scored a change in the index equal to 1185.59 in October, followed by 977.37 in November (Fig. 67.4).

The Global Financial Crisis (2008)

The global financial crisis had its effect upon Dubai's market like any other market in the region or the world in general. Given that the market was still in its eighth year of performance, the effect of the crisis was dramatic, as shown earlier.

The reason behind the crisis does not concern us in this chapter. We will be looking at the effects it had in the global financial market and the local financial market in details.

The sector that got affected the most during the financial crisis was the real estate and construction sector, according to Al Malkawi and Pillai (2013). The real estate and construction sector played the main role in the dramatic drop in the market. One of the main impacts the crisis had on these sectors was the shying away of creditors on issuing loans or other financing facilities to companies in the industry, hence the use of capital or retained earnings by these companies. The earlier resulted in losing value of shares.

Post-Crisis and DFM Maturity

We have been looking at different events related to the unexpected turn in the stock market. One of the positive outcomes that we see post-crisis is the maturity in DFM and the higher stability during this period. Although we can still notice some spikes in the overall performance, it is still controllable and acceptable in comparison to the pre-crisis era (Fig. 67.5).

Methods

The data of the financial markets was gathered through different sources: Dubai financial market, Abu Dhabi Securities, and NASDAQ Composite. In addition to crude oil prices from the global trading market.

In general, the data was collected for a time span from January of 2006 until February of 2016. Index data was obtained on the first day of each month with a monthly gap between each index. The same time span applies for the crude oil prices.

Afterwards, the data was analyzed through Pearson's correlation and Spearman's correlation, respectively.

The comparison was done to Dubai financial market, Abu Dhabi's Securities, NASDAQ Composite, and crude oil prices for the given time span.

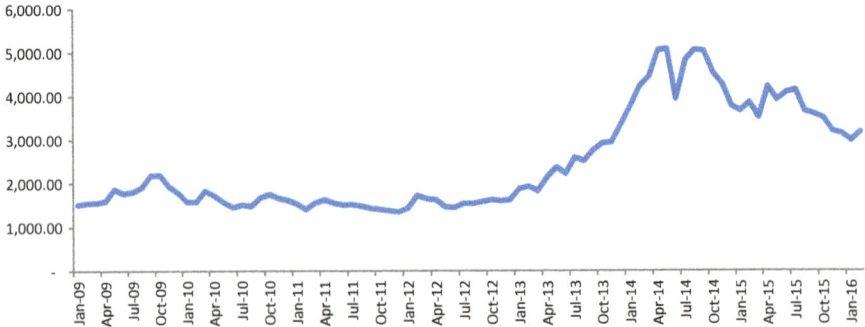

Fig. 67.5 DFM General Index 09 to 16

Results and Discussion

Analysis and Comparison to NASDAQ USA

In this section, we will be looking at both markets during three different periods:

1. The entire period: 2006–2016
2. The pre-crisis: 2006–2008
3. The post-crisis: 2009–2016

We will start off by presenting the entire period that we have studied, which is from December 2005 until February 2016, to get a general idea of how both markets have been performing. Then, we will look at the pre-crisis period, which is from December 2005 until February 2016, to detail the performance of the young DFM to the mature NASDAQ. In the end, we will detail the post-crisis period, which is from January 2009 until February 2016, to grasp the change that occurred in the DFM and how the crisis affected both markets.

The Entire Period: 2006–2016

Figure 67.6 shows the stability in performance of NASDAQ in comparison to DFM. The spikes in DFM are obvious and affect the market dramatically, while there are hardly any spikes in NASDAQ. The reason may be the maturity of the market, which is related to how investors would react to changes or news.

We have analyzed 105 entries of index in total for both markets. The values we obtained were on a monthly basis during the end of each month. As shown below:

Table 67.1 shows that the correlation between the indices for both markets is 9 %, which is a negligible value that means that there is no significant effect for the

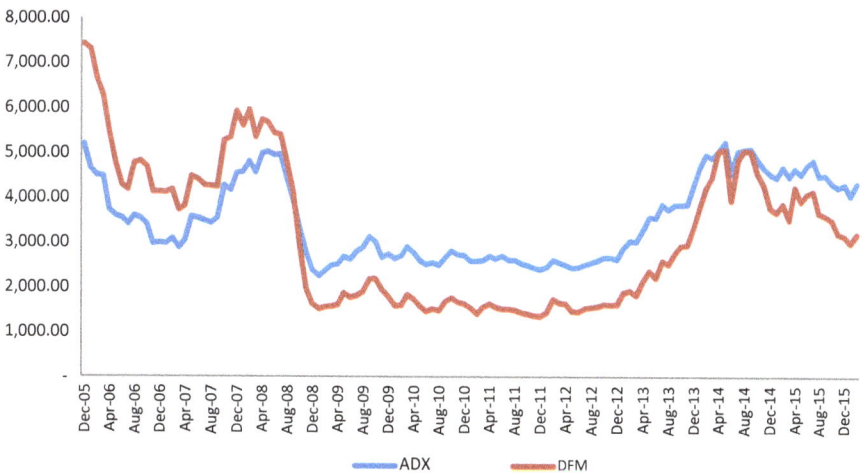

Fig. 67.6 DFM and NASDAQ USA

Table 67.1 Entire period

Entire duration	
Total entries	122
Different direction	51
Same direction	71
Correlation	18%
Period	2006–2016

Table 67.2 DFM statistics

DFM (index)	
Avg.	3169.99
Median	2945.91
Std. dev.	1583.10
Min	1353.39
Max	7426.37

Table 67.3 NASDAQ statistics

NASDAQ Composite (index)	
Avg.	3001.31
Median	1365.62
Std. dev.	1003.94
Min.	1377.84
Max	5128.30

changes in the US stock market on DFM. This is due to the fact that the indices of DFM had higher values during the pre-crisis period and the construction boom era, as discussed earlier.

We have found statistical values to support the argument stated above, in Tables 67.2 and 67.3.

As seen from the above data, the standard deviation of DFM is more than double the standard deviation of NASDAQ. This indicates that the separation between the indices is higher, hence the difference in change between both markets. That said, we conclude that the lack of correlation is due to the high index values that DFM scored during the construction boom, as we shall represent later.

On the other hand, we have noticed that 63% of the indices in both markets moved in the same direction (either increasing or decreasing). This is an interesting observation, since the correlation between the indices is negligible. Could there be a relationship between both market behaviors?

The Pre-crisis: 2006–2008

Referring to Fig. 67.5, we can see the big gap between the indices of both markets. The large values of indices are related to the boom in construction and real estate market in the Gulf region in general and the UAE precisely, according to Renaud (2012).

Table 67.4 Pre-crisis

Pre-crisis	
Total entries	25
Different direction	11
Same direction	14
Correlation	−19%
Period	2006–2008

Table 67.5 Post-crisis

Post-crisis	
Total entries	86
Different direction	22
Same direction	64
Correlation	83%
Period	2009–2016

The analysis that was done on the data would show the following (Table 67.4):

From the results above, it is noticeable that there was no correlation in the data it the given period.

The Post-crisis: 2009–2016

Referring to Fig. 67.5 again, DFM started slowly picking up pace and recovering from the crisis. It is clear that the market is not performing as well as it used to before the crisis. Certainly, the pre-crisis period was an abnormal period in the market, as it was booming, but the market performance indicators show that the market is going back to its shape before the crisis. The DFM index has reached an index of 3770 points for the first time in 6 years.

After analyzing the indices from both markets during the post-crisis period, we found out the following (Table 67.5):

The correlation in both markets during this period has increased in a significant way in comparison to the pre-crisis period.

The significant correlation value we obtained can be due to a lot of reasons such as:

1- The mentality of the investors and gaining more knowledge and experience about the significance of the events taking place in the international market
2- Constant increase in the crude oil prices worldwide, as shown earlier
3- The fact that the UAE started exploring other sources of income, aside from oil: an example would be tourism

The Impact of Lower Oil Price on Dubai Financial Market Performance

Crude oil prices have been plunging since late 2014, and it has affected global trade markets in general. The recent oil price drops have affected DFM performance in a noticeable way. Since the drop in prices started, the DFM Index has been dropping in a similar manner. To illustrate this, Fig. 67.7 shows a comparison between crude oil prices and DFM index from the period of June 2014 until February 2016.

The UAE is an oil-dependant country in general, but Dubai has been trying to diversify its sources of income throughout the past decade. We do not believe that the drop in the market was due to the oil trade of the country, as much as it has to do with foreign investments and the attitude of investors towards such a drop in oil prices.

Through Spearman's correlation, the results obtained show a negative correlation of −0.79 between DFM market indexes and crude oil prices for the period between 2006 and 2016. In comparison to other studies done to analyze the relationship between crude oil prices and international stock markets. The findings support our calculations of a negative correlation between Dubai financial market and the stock market. According to the publication of Isaac J. M. and Ronald A. R., an analysis was done on a long-run relationship between the world price of crude oil and international stock market 1971–2008 using a cointegrated vector error correction model with additional regressors. A second publication by George F., Stavros D., and Christos F. based on data from six countries investigates the correlation between stock market prices and oil prices for both oil-exporting and oil-importing countries. The results show that oil prices exercise a negative effect in all stock markets, regardless the origin of the oil price shock. The only exception is the 2008 global financial crisis where the lagged oil prices exhibited a positive correlation with stock markets.

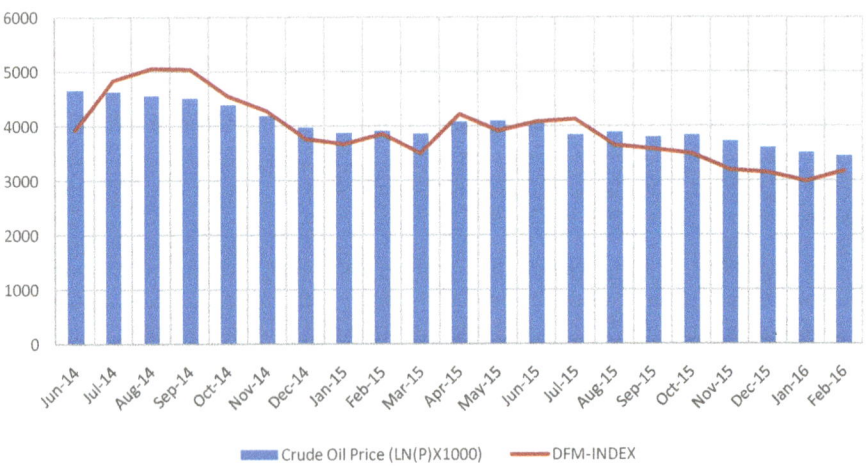

Fig. 67.7 Crude oil and DFM

Concluding Remarks and Future Work

Overall, DFM has been growing and gaining experience over time. The fact that the market has gained momentum and constant growth after the crisis proves that the market is moving in the right direction.

In addition, we were not able to notice any correlation between DFM and NASDAQ due to the instability and the boom in DFM prior to the crisis. After the crisis, the market stabilized and became more mature and aware of global events and its importance on stock exchange, hence the higher correlation between DFM and NASDAQ.

Furthermore, crude oil is a major player in the stock exchange and the status of the financial market in Dubai, as seen in the analysis. The UAE is trying to avoid these effects by exploring different sectors and sources of income.

On the other hand, we have faced difficulties in obtaining the data about DFM, which added limitations to our overall analysis, as we were not able to gather daily index values. NASDAQ information and data were easily obtained through their official website, which was very helpful in the analysis.

In the future, we would like to obtain more detailed data about DFM and analyze it using more sophisticated methods and calculations to obtain more reliable results and a better understanding of how the market performance in Dubai has changed over the last 10 years. In addition, we would like to use sophisticated techniques to find a relationship between oil prices and market performance.

References

Al Malkawi, H. N., & Pillai, R. (2013). The impact of financial crisis on UAE real estate and construction sector: Analysis and implications. *Humanoconomies, 29*(2), 115–135.

Arouril E. M. & Fouquau J. (2009). *Oil prices and stock markets in GCC countries: New evidence from nonlinear cointegration analysis*. Retrieved from doi: 10.1108/03074350710753735.

Dubai Chamber of Commerce. (2006). Structure and performance of Dubai financial market. *The Economic Bulletin, 3*(29).

Filis, G., Degiannakis, S., & Floros, C. (2011). Dynamic correlation between stock market and oil prices: The case of oil-importing and oil-exporting countries. *International Review of Financial Analysis, 20*(3), 152–164.

Kang, W., Ratti, A. R., & Yoon, H. K. (2015). The impact of oil price shocks on the stock market return and volatility relationship. *Journal of International Financial Markets, Institutions and Money, 34*, 41–54.

Onour, A. I. (2007, September). *Impact of oil price volatility on Gulf Cooperation Council stock markets' return*. Organization of the Petroleum Exporting Countries.

Renaud, B. (2012). Real estate bubble and financial crisis in Dubai: Dynamics and policy response. *Journal of Real Estate Literature, 20*(1), 51–77.

Chapter 68
Internal Rate of Return (IRR): A New Proposed Approach

Murad Mohammed Mujahed and Elgilani Eltahir Elshareif

Abstract This study tries to develop a new internal rate of return (IRR) approach assuming constant and positive cash flows. The traditional IRR method is implicitly based on trial and error that needs two initial guesses and slowly converges to the solution. The development so far was based on Newton–Raphson methods that reduce the two guesses to only one guess with quadratic convergence. However, this development has many limitations such as divergence at inflection points and pitfalls like division by zero. The progress of our study so far is to eliminate the initial guess with assumption of equal series of positive cash flows. Further, the expected finding of the new approach will assist practitioners and academics to compute the IRR accurately as the rate of return on the declining balance of the investment, analogous to the YTM on a premium bond and the contract rate on a fully amortized loan.

Keywords Bisection • Newton–Raphson • IRR

Introduction

The internal rate of return (IRR) is the interest rate at which the net present value (NPV) of all the cash flows (both positive and negative) from a project or investment equals to zero. The IRR is massively used as a primary and important tool in capital budgeting decisions by scholars, practitioners, analysts, and CEOs. It is used in capital budgeting to measure the profitability of an investment by comparing it with the company's required rate of return. If the IRR exceeds the company's required rate of return then it is accepted. But if it falls below the company's required rate of return then it should be rejected. The IRR method is the most common used; about 75 % of the CEOs always use it in their capital budget decisions. To find the IRR

M.M. Mujahed (✉) • E.E. Elshareif
Canadian University of Dubai, PO Box 117781, Dubai, United Arab Emirates
e-mail: moraddns@hotmail.com; Elgilani@cud.ac.ae

© Springer International Publishing Switzerland 2017   761
R. Benlamri, M. Sparer (eds.), *Leadership, Innovation and Entrepreneurship as Driving Forces of the Global Economy*, Springer Proceedings in Business and Economics, DOI 10.1007/978-3-319-43434-6_68

mathematically, we have to find the discount rate that will make the summation of the present value of all the cash flows to be zero, as shown in the equation below:

$$NPV = CF_0 + \frac{CF_1}{(1+IRR)} + \frac{CF_2}{(1+IRR)^2} + \frac{CF_3}{(1+IRR)^3} + \cdots\cdots + \frac{CF_N}{(1+IRR)^N}$$

Such that

NPV is the net present value that should be zero.
CF_0 is the initial investment.
$CF_1, CF_2, \ldots\ldots CF_N$ are the cash flows in the years 1, 2, ... N.

$$CF_0 + \frac{CF_1}{(1+IRR)} + \frac{CF_2}{(1+IRR)^2} + \frac{CF_3}{(1+IRR)^3} + \cdots\cdots + \frac{CF_N}{(1+IRR)^N} = 0$$

Mathematically speaking, the above equation does not have a direct and clear method to solve it; instead the method used so far depends on trial and error, in which we need to start by an initial guess of a point or two points. And this guessing if not chosen carefully may lead to serious problems and limitations as we will mention later. From here we start our research question which is

RQ: Can we develop an approach to find a proper solution to the IRR, other than the existing methods that need an initial guessing?

This question is important for the following reasons: first, because if the initial guess is not close enough to the true root, then it may not converge and this we will discuss it later. Second, the proposed approach will give us an accurate solution, save time, and result in better decision making.

In Section "Literature Review" of this chapter a review of the literature is given. Section "New proposed Approach" details the new proposed approach, and Section "Concluding Remarks" is the conclusion.

Literature Review

In this section, we will review literature related to bisection method as well as Newton–Raphson method.

Bisection Method

$$CF_0 + \frac{CF_1}{(1+IRR)} + \frac{CF_2}{(1+IRR)^2} + \frac{CF_3}{(1+IRR)^3} + \cdots\cdots + \frac{CF_N}{(1+IRR)^N} = 0$$

The equation above can be solved using trial and error; generally speaking two main techniques are used: either the closed (bracketed) techniques or the open techniques. From the closed techniques we will select the bisection method.

The historical development of root-finding techniques of different types of equations using the bisection method started after the intermediate value theorem was first proven in 1817 by Edwards (1979) with the bisection theorem; the disadvantage of this technique was the slow convergence.

This method can be applied to solve $f(x) = 0$, by using the intermediate value theorem that says "If $f(x)$ is a continuous and differentiable function on some interval (a, b) such that it satisfies the following conditions f(a)>0, f(b)<0 (they must have opposite signs). In this case, $f(x)$ must have at least one solution c, where $c \in (a,b)$." In our case we don't have an interval (a, b), so basically we need to guess two points a and b that satisfy the conditions; then the first iteration will be a point that bisects the interval (a, b), say c, so the first iteration will be $c = \dfrac{a+b}{2}$; then if $f(c) = 0$, then c is the solution and the process stops; if not then $f(c)$ is either positive or negative, and again we will have two points with opposite signs, say c and b. The second iteration is $d = \dfrac{c+b}{2}$. And the process continues until we find the zero of the function exactly or an approximation for it; usually we stop until we reach a specific tolerance of error $\dfrac{|b-a|}{2^n} \leq error_{tol}$, where n is the number of iterations. One of the advantages of the bisection method is that it never diverges; moreover it guarantees the convergence of a root if one exists within the interval (a, b). On the other hand one of the disadvantages is that it converges slowly, so we need a lot of iterations. Moreover, we need two initial guesses to start.

Newton–Raphson Method

Newton started to investigate in the root-finding techniques using the derivative in the first decades of the sixteenth century, but he didn't publish anything that time. Then came Raphson in 1690 and developed Newton's method. Later on Fourier (1890) analyzed the convergence of Newton–Raphson method and showed that it has a quadratic convergence (Srivastava & Srivastava, 2011); he calculated the average numerical rate of convergence in calculating the cube root of numbers from 1 to 25 for both the bisection method and the Newton–Raphson method and found using a computer program in C language that the average numerical rate of Newton–Raphson method is eight times faster than the bisection method.

Yamamoto (2000) said that although the convergence is very fast and the number of the digits will double in every iteration, which helps us in reaching our tolerance of errors quickly, the guarantee of convergence is still ambiguous and it is a very big disadvantage of Newton–Raphson method, and suggested that the initial guess x_0 must be chosen very close to the true root. Qi and Chen (1995) suggested that effective and globally convergent algorithm must be available to guarantee the convergence, and if this algorithm can be found then it will solve the problem.

In the beginning of the 1980s, Adomian developed a numerical technique for solving the functional equations known as the Adomian decomposition method (Adomian, 1988). Then Abbasbandy (2003) and Babolian and Biazar (2002) presented an efficient numerical algorithm for solving nonlinear equations based on Adomian decomposition method. Chun (2005) showed in his paper that the order of convergence of the iterative methods constructed based on the Adomian decomposition method increases as it progresses. Basto, Semiao, and Calheiros (2006) developed a new iterative method and compared it with Newton–Raphson, Abbasbandy, Adomian, and Babolian show that it performs the same or better in some examples where the Adomian decomposition method should be slightly modified.

Newton–Raphson method is a better method because it converges quickly to the root (if exists). The algorithm of Newton–Raphson method is to find an initial estimation which we call it a "guess" say x_0 that is close to the true root say r, and it is not guaranteed to be close because we already don't know what the real root is. Or it can be done using the bisection method by finding two numbers, say a and b, such that their values have opposite signs; then we guarantee that there is a root for the equation within (a, b). Then r can be written as $r = x_0 + h$ and then

$$0 = f(r) = f(x_0 + h) \approx f(x_0) + hf'(x_0)$$

Then

$$h \approx \frac{f(x_0)}{f'(x_0)}$$

And since $r = x_0 + h$, $r = x_0 + \dfrac{f(x_0)}{f'(x_0)}$, by letting $r = x_1$, so the first iteration is

$$x_1 = x_0 + \frac{f(x_0)}{f'(x_0)}$$

The next iteration is obtained in the same way as the first one:

$$x_2 = x_1 + \frac{f(x_1)}{f'(x_1)}$$

And by repeating the process, the general form can be given by

$$x_{n+1} = x_n + \frac{f(x_n)}{f'(x_n)} \tag{68.1}$$

And the process continues until it converges to a zero, and if it does converge it will approximate the root quickly because Newton–Raphson method has a quadratic convergence; in other words, the accuracy of the digits will double in every iteration.

As we notice in Eq. (68.1), we need to get the derivative of $f(x)$ in every iteration, so one of the pitfalls is to have $f'(x_n) = 0$ for some n; then the method fails because it's an inflection point; this can be illustrated graphically and numerically in the following example; let $f(x) = (x-1)^3 + 0.512$ and the Newton–Raphson method can be reduced to $x_{n+1} = x_n + \dfrac{(x_n - 1)^3 + 0.512}{3(x_n - 1)^2}$; we can see that $x = 1$ is an inflection point where the Newton method diverges at the 6th iteration; then it converges back at the 18th iteration to the exact root which is $x = 0.2$.

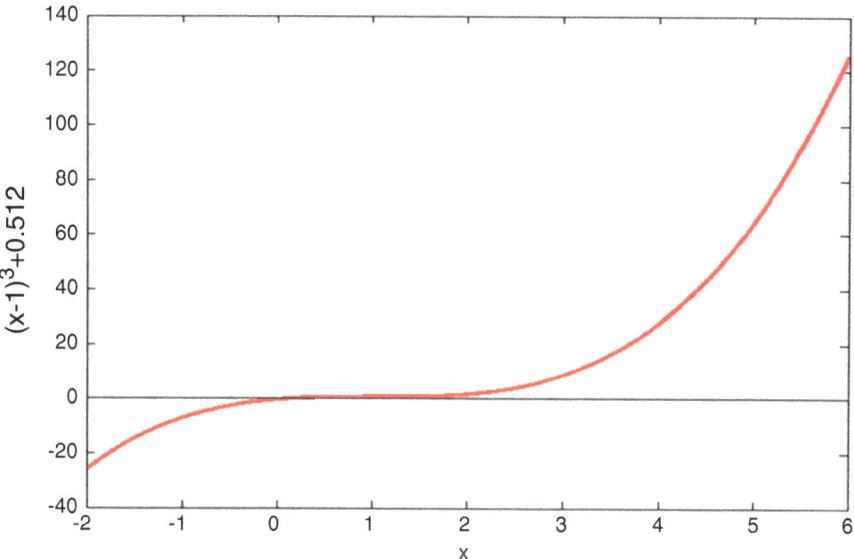

Also other disadvantage is that the results obtained from the Newton–Raphson method may oscillate about the local maximum or minimum values without converging on a root but converging on the local maximum or minimum. And the first few x_n may refuse to settle down eventually; it may lead to division by a number close to zero and may diverge. That's why we have to choose the initial guess with care and in a proper way to guarantee the convergence.

New Proposed Approach

In a new attempt to eliminate the disadvantages of Newton–Raphson method which is the initial guess that may create many pitfalls like divergence at the inflection points, the division by zero, the oscillations near the maximum and minimum points, and the root jumping we introduce a new proposed approach with some assumptions that simplify our problem.

Our objective is to solve the following equation for IRR:

$$CF_0 + \frac{CF_1}{(1+IRR)} + \frac{CF_2}{(1+IRR)^2} + \frac{CF_3}{(1+IRR)^3} + \ldots\ldots\ldots + \frac{CF_N}{(1+IRR)^N} = 0 \qquad (68.2)$$

For simplicity we will assume that all the free cash flows are equal and positive; then our equation will be

$$CF_0 + \frac{CF}{(1+IRR)} + \frac{CF}{(1+IRR)^2} + \frac{CF}{(1+IRR)^3} + \ldots\ldots\ldots + \frac{CF}{(1+IRR)^N} = 0$$

By replacing $CF_0 = \alpha CF$, we have

$$\alpha CF + \frac{CF}{(1+IRR)} + \frac{CF}{(1+IRR)^2} + \frac{CF}{(1+IRR)^3} + \ldots\ldots\ldots + \frac{CF}{(1+IRR)^N} = 0$$

$$CF\left(\alpha + \frac{1}{(1+IRR)} + \frac{1}{(1+IRR)^2} + \frac{1}{(1+IRR)^3} + \ldots\ldots\ldots + \frac{1}{(1+IRR)^N} \right) = 0$$

$$CF\left(\alpha + \frac{1}{(1+IRR)}\left(1 + \frac{1}{(1+IRR)^1} + \frac{1}{(1+IRR)^2} + \ldots\ldots\ldots + \frac{1}{(1+IRR)^{N-1}} \right) \right) = 0$$

$$CF\left(\alpha + \frac{1}{(1+IRR)}\left(\sum_{k=0}^{N-1}\left(\frac{1}{1+IRR} \right)^K \right) \right) = 0$$

$$CF\left(\alpha + \frac{1}{(1+IRR)}\left(\frac{1-(1+IRR)^{-N}}{IRR}(1+IRR) \right) \right) = 0$$

Dividing both sides by CF and canceling the term $(1+IRR)$ we get

$$\left(\alpha + \left(\frac{1-(1+IRR)^{-N}}{IRR} \right) \right) = 0$$

$$(1+IRR)^{-N} - \alpha IRR + 1 = 0 \qquad (68.3)$$

This last equation is a more simplified form of the first equation, which makes it easier to find a solution and get the IRR without a financial calculator.

Concluding Remarks

In solving the IRR, practitioners usually use the bisection method with two initial guesses or Newton–Raphson method with one initial guess. Sometimes they use both of them by guessing two points a and b which their values have opposite signs so as to guarantee the existence of the root inside this interval (a, b), and reduce the probability of divergence from the true root, and then use the Newton–Raphson algorithm by guessing an initial estimate within (a, b).

In our proposed approach that assumes equal positive cash flows we eliminate the initial guess and simplify our main equation below:

$$NPV = CF_0 + \frac{CF_1}{(1+IRR)} + \frac{CF_2}{(1+IRR)^2} + \frac{CF_3}{(1+IRR)^3} + \ldots\ldots\ldots + \frac{CF_N}{(1+IRR)^N} = 0$$

to a simpler form

$$(1+IRR)^{-N} - \alpha IRR + 1 = 0, \text{ where } \alpha = \frac{CF_0}{CF}.$$

The latest equation is easier to deal with, hoping that we or other practitioners and academics will be able to find a solution to this equation in the near future.

References

Abbasbandy, S. (2003). Improving Newton–Raphson method for nonlinear equations by modified Adomian decomposition method. *Applied Mathematics and Computation, 145*, 887–893.

Adomian, G. (1988). A review of the decomposition method in applied mathematics. *Journal of Mathematical Analytical Applications, 135*, 501–544.

Babolian, E., & Biazar, J. (2002). Solution of nonlinear equations by modified Adomian decomposition method. *Applied Mathematics & Computations, 132*, 162–172.

Basto, M., Semiao, V., & Calheiros, F. L. (2006). A new iterative method to compute nonlinear equations. *Applied Mathematics and Computation, 173*, 468–483.

Chun, C. (2005). Iterative methods improving Newton's method by the decomposition method. *Computers and Mathematics with Applications, 50*, 1559–1568.

Edwards, C. H. (1979). *Bolzano, Cauchy and continuity. The Historical Development of Calculus* (pp. 308, 309). New York, NY: Springer New York.

Fourier J. B. J. (1890). Question d'analyse algebrique, *Oeuvres Completes (II), Gauthier-Villars*, Paris (pp. 243–253).

Qi, L., & Chen, X. (1995). A globally convergent successive approximation method for severely non smooth equations. *SIAM Journal of Control, 33*, 402–410.

Srivastava, R. B., & Srivastava, S. (2011). Comparison of Numerical rate of convergence of bisection, Newton–Raphson's, and secant methods. *Journal of Chemical, Biological and Physical Sciences, 2*(1), 472–479.

Yamamoto, T. (2000). Historical developments in convergence analysis for Newton's and Newton-like methods. *Journal of Computational and Applied Mathematics, 124*(1–2), 1–23.

Chapter 69
Quantitative Risk Analysis for International Project Management and Programs in an Emerging Economy

Chris I. Enyinda

Abstract Historically, international projects are prone to both endogenous and exogenous risks. And the World Bank international projects and programs are not immune to similar risks. What is important though is the ability of project managers to identify the sources of endogenous and exogenous risks and how to leverage proactive or predictive project risk management strategies. Arguably, predictive project risk management is the lifeline for successful projects and programs. Managing portfolio of risks in international projects is imperative for the World Bank's mission of economic development and poverty eradication in developing countries. Inability to identify sources of risks attached to projects and programs can contribute to missed opportunities. It can also discourage the World Bank and other international agencies from approving or awarding future development projects and programs. Although in spite of the growing menace of risks in development projects and programs, project managers have little or no knowledge of project risk management. This chapter proposes a multi-attribute decision support approach to model and analyze the risk for the World Bank projects and programs in Nigeria.

Keywords The World Bank • International Project Management • Risk analysis • Nigeria • The AHP

Introduction

The World Bank projects in Africa are worth multimillions of dollars. A successful completion and delivering of these projects relies on efficient and effective operations and supply-chain management (Enyinda & Obuah, 2015). Hillson (2003, p. 3) states that "the purpose of project management is to act as a change agent, delivering

C.I. Enyinda (✉)
Department of Marketing and International Business, School of Business Administration, Canadian University Dubai, Dubai, UAE
e-mail: christian@cud.ac.ae

© Springer International Publishing Switzerland 2017
R. Benlamri, M. Sparer (eds.), *Leadership, Innovation and Entrepreneurship as Driving Forces of the Global Economy*, Springer Proceedings in Business and Economics, DOI 10.1007/978-3-319-43434-6_69

a change to the status quo, and achieving this in a controlled and managed way." Predictive project risk management is the lifeline for international development project and program objectives, particularly economic development and poverty alleviation in the developing countries. Indeed, projects and programs serve the needs of the society. Asbjørnslett (2002, p. 93) asserts "project supply chain management seeks value enhancement in projects through ... through the characteristics of logistics throughout the project life cycle with an agile approach to demand chain management in the development phase and a lean approach to supply chain management in the operations phase." Vrijhoef and Koskela (2000) contend that supply-chain management in construction project helps to reduce cost and duration of project-site activities, ensure dependable material and labor flows to the site to avoid disruption to the workflow, focusing on the relationship between the site and direct suppliers, and move activities from the protect sites to the earlier stages of the supply chain.

The spate of global disruptive influences ranging from natural disaster (e.g., earthquake, flooding, drought) and pandemic (e.g., Ebola to Zika virus) to man-made (e.g., security, political, bribery, and corruption) are in no small measure affecting all aspects of life endeavors. The globalization of business cum the wide spread of project supply-chain actors and stakeholders often lead to a geographically dispersed supply network involved in a project, supplying for and to the project object (Asbjørnslett, 2002). Bribery and corruption risk in developing countries often hamper successful completion of development projects. According to Pop (n.d.), "the size and scope of development projects, often with intricate supply chains, numerous contractors and project phases, and significant government involvement, increase the risk of bribery, corruption and fraud." In developing nations these risks tend to escalate because of underdeveloped nature of regulatory capacity and where social customs are not aligned with international norms of ethical business conduct (Pop, n.d.). In addition, because operations of projects are often carried out by way of joint ventures or subsidiaries and with the aid of local agents, it tends to make bribery and corruption easier to hide from the head contractor and legal authorities (Lurie & Burkil, 2013; Pop, n.d.). Recently, risk and risk management have been the subject of discussion at the World Bank because of time, budget overrun, and rampant corruption linked to the development projects and programs. As a result, a significant number of projects were abjectly delayed or terminated. It has become a vexing concern to the World Bank because the inability to proactively manage the prevalence of project and program risks can result in "significant obstacles to attaining the World Bank Group's two main goals: ending extreme poverty by year 2030 and boosting shared prosperity of the bottom 40% of the population in the developing countries" (Loayza, N. V., & Otker-Robe, 2013). Therefore, managing risk effectively is exceedingly paramount as it can be a powerful instrument for economic development and poverty alleviation (Loayza, N. V., & Otker-Robe, 2013). Thus, risk management is highly crucial for the bank's development projects and programs in developing countries, Nigeria in particular (WSDOT, 2014): it (1) recognizes risk and uncertainty and provides forecasts of possible outcomes or consequences; (2) produces tangible project outcomes via better informed decision making; (3) has a positive impact on creative thinking and innovation; (4) generates much better project control in terms of reducing overhead and time, and improvement on benefits to stakeholders; and (5) contributes to project objectives and success.

Saaty's (1980) analytic hierarchy process (AHP) is leveraged in modeling risk management in project procurement and supply-chain operations in which the goal to achieve has multiple and conflicting criteria. Project procurement and supply-chain operation risk factors are both qualitative and quantitative in nature, and selecting the alternative risk mitigation strategies is equally conflicting. As a multi-criteria decision-making process, the AHP enables decision makers or a group of decision makers to set priorities and deliver the best decision where both quantitative and qualitative aspects of a decision must be considered. The advantages associated with AHP include its reliance on easily derived expert opinion data, ability to reconcile differences (inconsistencies) in expert judgments and perceptions, and the existence of Expert Choice Software that implements the AHP. Although in spite of its criticism associated with rank reversal when an alternative is expunged, its use in many studies including management, marketing, economics, international business, project management, operations and supply-chain management, pharmaceutical, among many others continues to grow exponentially.

The purpose of this chapter is to identify the sources of endogenous and exogenous risks attached to the World Bank projects and programs in Nigeria and to identify areas in which risk management can be focused on. The remainder of this chapter is organized as follows. Section "Literature Review" presents literature review on project management, risks and project risk sources, risk management, and project risk management strategies. Section "Methodology" briefly discusses the research methodology, data collection, and analysis. Results and discussion are provided in Section "Data Source and Discussion." Finally, Section "Data Analysis, Results, and Discussions" presents the conclusions and implications.

Literature Review

The theoretical framework of this section will cover briefly three streams of studies including risk and sources of project risk, risk management, and project risk management.

Risk and Sources of International Project Risk

Risk has been defined in a variety of ways. The PMBOK (2004) view risk as an uncertain event or condition that, if it happens, has a positive or negative impact on a project's objectives. Risk is an exposure or a probability of loss (gain)/ruin or a barrier to achieving success (Hertz & Thomas, 1994; Jaafari, 2001; Mullins, Forlani, & Walker, 1999; Miles & Wilson, 1998). Risks can potentially disrupt the ability of project managers meeting or fulfilling the project objectives and tasks may be prolonged more than planned with more negative consequences (Kutsch, 2010; PMBOK, 2004). Given the disruptive nature of unidentified risks to project objectives (PMBOK, 2004) declared risk management as one of its nine key knowledge areas in project management. Flyvbjerg, Bruzelius, and Rothengatter (2003) note that mega projects often lead to cost overrun, schedule delays, and worst project terminations because risks are not properly identified. PMBOK (2013) attests that project risk is composed of threats to the project's objectives (negative outcomes) and opportunities to improve on those objectives (positive outcomes). Risk factors attached to projects influence the time, budget, and quality performance of the project (Akintoye & Macleod, 1997). Risk identification entails determining which risks will likely affect the project and then documenting their characteristics (WSDOT, 2014). Risk exists in every project and the sources must be identified and evaluated frequently throughout the life cycle of the project (PMBOK, 2013). For uncertainty that confronts a project, PMBOK (2013) describes it as an uncommon state of nature that is characterized by absence of information associated with a desired outcome. For internal sources of risk and uncertainties, Hillson (2003) suggests that they can emanate from the changing requirements on the project to be done or scope of work, people involved in the work, productivity rates, supply-chain members' performance, and use of new technology or novel approaches and methods.

For the external sources, they include the environment in which the project is undertaken, market conditions, competitors' actions, changing exchange rates or inflation rates, weather conditions, or other stakeholders in the project who are able to influence the performance (Hillson, 2003) negatively or positively. Project risk denotes any uncertainty that affects one or more project objectives (WSDOT, 2014). Projects by nature face a number of risks. "Risk as a quintessential part of international development projects and/or programs is uncertain and multidimensional" (Enyinda, Vladica, & Backhar, 2013, pp. 372–379). Hillson (2003) asserts "like everything else in life, all projects are inevitably subject to uncertainty" and risk. Thus, projects are not immune from risk. Identifying and understanding the sources of project risks enable project managers to meet or satisfy end users or society service expectations. Hillson (2003) notes the following project risks: natural environment (e.g., physical environment, facilities/sites, local services); cultural (political, legal/regulatory, interest groups); economics (labor market, labor conditions, financial market); and technology requirements (e.g., scope uncertainty, complexity, conditions of use). A common source of uncertainty is engineering decisions taken early and leading to changes that again may result to alterations in the project supply chains such as termination of one supply chain in lieu of another (Asbjørnslett, 2002). Tah and Carr (2001) contend that for project managers to ensure delivery of projects to cost, schedule, and performance requirements, they must endeavor to identify and manage risks to projects at all project phases from the initial assessment of strategic options through the procurement, fabrication, construction, and commissioning phases while assuming due account of subsequent operation and maintenance. PMBOK (2008) classified risks into technical, external, organizational, environmental, or project management.

Some of the risk sources associated with construction project activities that are capable of impacting project performance by way of time, budget, and quality include acts of God, physical, environmental, design, job site-related, logistics, economic and financial, legal, political and environmental, construction, and operation risks (Mustafa & Al-Bahar, 1991; Perry & Hayes, 1985). Kwak (2002) identified risk factors in international development projects, including political, legal, cultural, technical, managerial, economic, environmental, social, corruption, and physical aspects. Kwak and Smith (2009) examined budget and schedule risks attached to mega defense acquisition projects. Environmental factors affecting international projects are economic, legal and political, security, infrastructure, culture, and geography (Gray & Larson, 2008). Viswanathan (2015) categorized scope, scheduling, technology, and resources as project risks.

Risk Management

Risk analysis is about assessing risks, while risk management deploys risk analysis to develop management strategies to mitigate risk (Galway, 2004). Risk management entails "the process of identifying, analyzing and responding to risk-maximizing positive events and minimizing consequences of negative events" (PMBOK, 2013). Kutsch (2010) argues that although just about every risk may be of interest to project managers, the management of risk requires information about threat, probability, and response. Effective project operations and supply-chain risk management are at the heart of successful projects. Primo and Filho attest that risk management has a direct impact on project success. Risk management is important to project activities in reducing losses, profitability (Akintoye & Macleod, 1997), and other benefits to the society at large. Hillson (2003) contends that "the most common application of risk management is in projects, where project risks are defined as those uncertainties that could affect project objectives, including time, cost, quality, scope, and performance." A lack of comprehensive risk management strategies in the planning phases of projects and programs has often resulted in significant scope increases that can result in schedule delays, and increasing cost estimates (Kwak & Smith, 2009). Proper risk management can assist the project manager to mitigate risks that can potentially impact projects (Khalili & Maleki, 2011). Therefore, those organizations that neglect to perform deliberate risk management will face the consequence of not meeting the project objectives.

Project Risk Management Strategies

Predictive project risk management is an important aspect of project management. A number of authors have examined and recommended a number of ways to manage risks in projects (e.g., Baldry, 1998; Barber, 2005; Baccarini & Archer, 2001; Chapman, 1997, 2006; Chapman & Ward, 2004; Dvir, Raz, & Shenhar, 2003; Hillson, 2002; Klein & Cork, 1998; Olsson, 2007; Perminova, Gustanfsson, & Wikstrom, 2008; Raz & Michael, 2001; Ward, 1999; Ward & Chapman, 2003; Williams, 1994). PMBOK (2013, p. 309) defines project risk management as "the processes of conducting risk planning, identification, analysis, response planning, and monitoring and control on a project." Predictive project risk management can lead to a successful project management that can "... deliver value to project parties (clients, consultants, contractors, subcontractors, etc.) and other stakeholders (users, investors, communities affected by the project ..." (Primo & Filho, 2012). WSDOT (2014) claims that risk response involves the process of developing options and determining course of actions to improve opportunities and reduce risks impacting the project's objectives. WSDOT (2014) further contends that a "balanced project risk management is characterized by efficient processes that match the organization's tolerance for risk, a proactive approach to management of projects and risks, effective allocation of resources for risk management, well-managed projects with few surprises, taking advantage of opportunities, and dealing with threats effectively." Project risk management strategies recommended by PMBOK (2013) include mitigation/reduction, transfer/share, avoid, and accept/retain. They have been used in a number of empirical studies (e.g., Enyinda & Backhar, 2013; Enyinda & Obuah, 2015; Hillson, 2013).

Methodology

The AHP is a multi-criteria decision-making method that supports decision makers confronted with a complex problem with multiple conflicting and subjective criteria. International projects are typical multi-criteria decision-making problem that involves multiple criteria that can be both qualitative and quantitative. Thus, a multi-criteria approach proposed for this study is AHP. AHP allows decision makers to model a complex problem in a hierarchical structure, showing the relationships of the overall goal, criteria (objectives), sub-criteria, and alternatives. There are four steps required in AHP development, including problem modeling, weight valuation, weights aggregation, and sensitivity analysis.

Application of AHP to International Project Risk Management

A typical AHP is composed of the following four phases. (1) Construct a hierarchy that describes the problem. The overall goal is at the top of the structure, with the main attributes on a level below. (2) Derive weights for the lowest level attributes by conducting a series of pair-wise comparisons in which each attribute on each level is compared with its family members in relation to their significance to the parent. However, to compute the overall weights of the lowest level, matrix arithmetic is required. (3) The options available to a decision maker or a group of decision makers are scored with respect to the lowest level attributes. Similarly, the pair-wise comparison approach is used. (4) Adjusting the options' scores to reflect the weights given to the attributes, and adding the adjusted scores to produce a final score for each optimum. According to Simon (1960), the methodology of decision-making process encompasses identifying the problem, generating and evaluating alternatives, designing, and obtaining actionable intelligence. Figure 69.1 depicts the hierarchical structure of the international project risks. The overall goal is depicted in the first level of the hierarchy. Second, build the hierarchy from the top through the

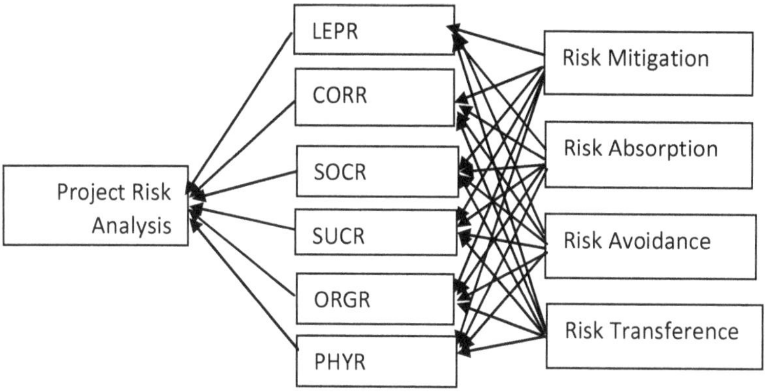

Fig. 69.1 Project risk analysis

intermediate levels (criteria on which subsequent levels depend on) to the lowest level, which usually contains the list of alternatives. The major criteria or attributes identified include legal and political risk (LEPR), corruption risk (CORR), social-cultural risk (SOCR), supply-chain risk (SUCR), organizational risk (ORGR), and physical risk (PHYR). The risk management alternatives include risk reduction/mitigation, risk absorption, risk avoidance, and risk transference. Third, construct a set of pair-wise comparison matrices for each of the lower levels. The pair-wise comparison is made such that the attribute in row i ($i = 1, 2, 3, 4...n$) is ranked relative to each of the attributes represented by n columns. The pair-wise comparisons are done in terms of which element dominates another. These judgments are then expressed as integer values 1–9 (e.g., $a_{ij} = 1$ means that i and j are equally important and $a_{ij} = 9$ signifies that i is extremely more important than j).

Establishment of Pair-Wise Comparison Matrix A

The pair-wise comparisons are accomplished in terms of which element dominates or influences the order. We used the AHP to quantify experts' opinions depicted as an n-by-n matrix as follows:

$$
A = \begin{bmatrix} a_{ij} \end{bmatrix} = w_i / w_j = \begin{bmatrix} w_1/w_2 & w_1/w_2 & \cdots & w_1/w_n \\ w_2/w_1 & w_2/w_2 & \cdots & w_2/w_n \\ \cdot & \cdot & \cdot & \cdot \\ \cdot & \cdot & \cdot & \cdot \\ \cdot & \cdot & \cdot & \cdot \\ w_n/w_1 & w_n/w_2 & \cdots & w_n/w_n \end{bmatrix} = \begin{bmatrix} 1 & a_{12} & \cdots & a_{in} \\ 1/a_{12} & 1 & \cdots & a_{2n} \\ \cdot & \cdot & \cdot & \cdot \\ \cdot & \cdot & \cdot & \cdot \\ \cdot & \cdot & \cdot & \cdot \\ 1/a_{1n} & 1/a_{2n} & \cdots & 1 \end{bmatrix}
$$

If c_i is judged to be of equal importance as c_j, then $(a_{ij}) = 1$. If c_i is judged to be more important than c_j, then $(a_{ij}) > 1$. If c_i is judged to be less important than c_j, then $(a_{ij}) < 1$; $(a_{ij}) = 1/a_{ji}$, $(i, j = 1, 2, 3, \ldots, n)$, $a_{ij} \neq 0$.

Data Source and Discussion

Questionnaire Design and Data Collection

Data were collected from April 14 to 18, 2013, during an executive training of a group of 25 managers on result-based approach to project operations and supply-chain risk assessment in Dubai, UAE. The managers were charged with managing wide range of the World Bank international development projects and programs in Nigeria. A combination of questionnaire survey and brainstorming technique was used to obtain participants' expert opinions on the sources of project procurement and supply-chain operation risks prevalent in development projects in Nigeria. Brainstorming is one of the techniques often used in identifying sources of risks in project management. Brainstorming techniques entail getting subject matter experts, project team members, risk management team members, and other stakeholders participate in identifying potential risks. Heldman contends that the existence risk can disrupt project completion or meeting project goals and objectives. The risks attached to project operations and supply chain identified during the brainstorming session were corruption, political, social, legal, cultural, design, technical, organizational, economic, environmental, physical, external, institutional, funding, infrastructure, project management, procurement, security, project site related, and act of nature. Respondents believed that the identified risk events used in the study are responsible for poor quality of work, delays, and associated losses. Essentially, the risks are the culprits for not often fulfilling or meeting project objectives. Based on the thorough review of literature and the expert opinions of the project managers, we developed a questionnaire based on Saaty's (2008) AHP. They provided response to several pair-wise comparisons, where two categories at a time were compared with

Table 69.1 Matrix risk attribute comparison

	LEPR	CORR	SOCR	SUCR	ORGR	PHYR
LEPR	1	1	1	5	5	1
CORR	1	1	3	9	9	3
SOCR	1	1/3	1	3	5	1
SUCR	1/5	1/9	1/3	1	1	1/7
ORGR	1/5	1/9	1/5	1	1	1/7
PHYR	1	1/3	1	7	7	1
Sum	5	2.89	6.53	26	28	6.29

respect to the goal. Results of the questionnaire survey are used as input for the AHP. It took a total of 15 judgments (i.e., $6(6-1)/2$) to complete the pair-wise comparisons of the major objectives or major risk criteria shown in Table 69.1. To derive estimates of the criteria priorities, the data reported in the matrix is used. The priorities provide a measure of the relative importance of each criterion. The AHP Expert Choice Software is used to analyze the data reported in Table 69.1.

Data Analysis, Results, and Discussions

The priorities reported in Table 69.2 for legal and political, corruption, social-cultural, organizational, supply chain, and physical risk criteria are obtained using the AHP Expert Choice Software. The inconsistency reported by the Expert Choice Software, $CR = 0.03 < 0.10$. This implies that the project and program managers/subject matter experts' evaluation are consistent. For the major risk criteria, corruption risk (0.36291) is the important risk, followed by legal and political risk (0.20941), among others. Essentially, corruption > legal and political risk > physical risk > social cultural risk > supply-chain risk > organizational risk.

Table 69.2 Matrix of risk attribute comparison

	LEPR	CORR	SOCR	SUCR	ORGR	PHYR	**Priority**
LEPR	0.227	0.346	0.153	0.192	0.179	0.159	**0.209**
CORR	0.227	0.346	0.459	0.346	0.321	0.477	**0.363**
SOCR	0.227	0.115	0.153	0.115	0.179	0.159	**0.158**
SUCR	0.045	0.038	0.051	0.038	0.036	0.023	**0.039**
ORGR	0.045	0.038	0.031	0.038	0.036	0.023	**0.035**
PHYR	0.227	0.115	0.153	0.269	0.250	0.159	**0.196**
$CR \leq .10$	0.03						

Table 69.3 Composite risk management options

	LEPR	CORR	SOCR	SUCR	ORGR	PHYR	**Priority**	Rank
	0.209	0.363	0.158	0.039	0.035	0.196		
Risk avoidance	0.360	0.473	0.314	0.390	0.447	0.412	**0.408**	1
Risk absorption	0.197	0.085	0.104	0.072	0.074	0.092	**0.115**	3
Risk mitigation	0.350	0.366	0.507	0.438	0.425	0.389	**0.391**	2
Risk transfer	0.093	0.075	0.075	0.099	0.054	0.107	**0.068**	4
$CR \leq .10$	0.03	0.06	0.06	0.04	0.06	0.04		

Determination of Composite Score (Overall Priority)

The final phase of the AHP-based risk analysis is summarized in Table 69.3. The six major risk priorities are multiplied by each row of the risk management response priorities to determine the composite or the overall risk management priority score. With respect to the overall priority scores of risk management response options, risk avoidance (0.408) is the most preferred risk management option, followed by risk mitigation/reduction (0.391), among others. Specifically, risk avoidance > risk mitigation/reduction risk > risk absorption/retention > risk transfer. Thus, risk avoidance is judged to be the overall best risk mitigation option. And the consistency ration is .10.

Conclusions and Implications

Risk management objectives are to reduce the number of surprise events, minimize consequences of adverse events, and maximize the results of positive events. Project risk management offers a number of values to projects: it (1) recognizes risk and uncertainty and provides forecasts of possible outcomes or consequences; (2) produces tangible project outcomes via better informed decision making; (3) has a positive impact on creative thinking and innovation; (4) generates much better project control in terms of reducing overhead and time, and improvement on benefits to stakeholders; and (5) contributes to project objectives and success (WSDOT, 2014). The value in project risk analysis includes real-time availability of information during project and program planning and decision making, verification of project objectives, effective risk communications, and increased chance of project and program success. International project managers that manage risk proactively will reduce cost overrun, improve quality and performance, and meet the World Bank mission. In this chapter, the identification and quantitative analysis of project and program risk provide the possibility to manage risks leveraging the AHP model. This research will contribute and offer insights towards improved and more effective performance in the World Bank international development projects and programs. In addition, it will offer valuable insights and guidelines for project managers handling the bank's sponsored projects and programs. Indeed, this research hopefully will provide project and program managers with a predictive methodology to evaluate and quantify risks that can disrupt project objectives.

References

Akintoye, A. S., & Macleod, M. J. (1997). Risk analysis and management in construction. *International Journal of Project Management, 5*(1), 31–38.

Asbjørnslett, B. E. (2002). *Project supply chain management: From agile to lean.* Ph.D. thesis, Norwegian University of Science and Technology. Retrieved from February 10, 2016, http://www.diva-portal.org/smash/get/diva2:125021/FULLTEXT01.pdf.

Baccarini, D., & Archer, R. (2001). The risk ranking of projects: A methodology. *International Journal of Project Management, 19,* 139–145.

Baldry, D. (1998). The evaluation of risk management in public sector capital projects. *International Journal of Project Management, 16*(1), 35–41.

Barber, R. B. (2005). Understanding internally generated risks in projects. *International Journal of Project Management, 23,* 584–590.

Chapman, C. (1997). Project risk analysis and management—PRAM the generic process. *International Journal of Project Management, 15*(5), 273–281.

Chapman, C. (2006). Key points of contention in framing assumptions for risk and uncertainty management. *International Journal of Project Management, 24,* 3–13.

Chapman, C., & Ward, S. (2004). Why risk efficiency is a key aspect of best practice projects. *International Journal of Project Management, 22,* 619–632.

Dvir, D., Raz, T., & Shenhar, A. J. (2003). An empirical analysis of the relationships between project planning and project success. *International Journal of Project Management, 21,* 89–95.

Enyinda, C. I., & Obuah, E. (2015). Modeling risk management in project procurement and supply chain operations: Evidence from development projects in Nigeria. In *Peer—Reviewed proceedings of the 16th annual conference of IAABD* (pp. 228–237), ISBN: 970-0-620-65831-7.

Enyinda, C. I., Vladica, F., & Backhar, K. (2013). An assessment of fiduciary risk in project management in Nigeria: Implications for project and program C-Level Executives. In *Peer-Reviewed Proceedings of the 14th Annual Conference of IAABD* (pp. 372–379). ISBN 0-9765288-8-6.

Flyvbjerg, B., Bruzelius, N., & Rothengatter, W. (2003). *Megaprojects and risk—An anatomy of ambition.* Cambridge: Cambridge University Press.

Galway, L. (2004). *Quantitative risk analysis for project management: A critical review.* Rand, Santa Monica, CA, WR-112-RC.

Gray, C. F., & Larson, E. W. (2008). *Project management: The managerial process,* 4th ed. The McGraw-Hill Companies.

Hertz, D. B., & Thomas, H. (1994). *Risk analysis and its applications.* Detroit, MI: John Wiley & Sons.

Hillson, D. (2002). Extending the risk process to manage opportunities. *International Journal of Project Management, 20,* 235–240.

Hillson, D. (2013). *Effective opportunity management for projects: Exploiting positive risk project.*

Jaafari, A. (2001). Management of risks, uncertainties and opportunities on projects: Time for a fundamental shift. *International Journal of Project Management, 19,* 89–101.

Khalili, H. A., & Maleki, A. (2011). Project risk management techniques in resource allocation, scheduling and planning. *World Academy of Science, Engineering and Technology, 59.*

Klein, J. H., & Cork, R. B. (1998). An approach to technical risk assessment. *International Journal of Project Management, 16*(6), 345–351.

Kutsch, E. (2010). Deliberate ignorance in project risk management. *International Journal of Project Management, 28*(3), 245–255.

Kwak, Y. H. (2002). Critical success factors in international development project management. In *CIB 10th International symposium construction innovation & global competitiveness, Cincinnati, Ohio, September 9–13.*

Kwak, Y. H., & Smith, B. M. (2009). Managing risks in mega defense acquisition projects: Performance, policy, and opportunities. *International Journal of Project Management, 27,* 812–820.

Loayza, N. V., & Otker-Robe, I. (2013). *World development report 2014: Risk and opportunity— Managing risk for development* (pp. 1–49). World Development Report. Washington DC: World Bank.

Lurie, J., & Burkil, N. (2013). *Bribery and construction in the construction industry: Challenges for international construction and engineering projects.* Retrieved from February 15, 2016, https://www.dorsey.com/newsresources/publications/2013/02/bribery-and-corruption-in-the-construction-indu2__.

Miles, F. M., & Wilson, T. G. (1998). Managing project risk and the performance envelope. In *Proceedings of the 13th annual applied power electronics conference and exposition, February 15–19*. Singapore: APEC.

Mullins, J. W., Forlani, D., & Walker, O. C. (1999). Effects of organizational and decision-maker factors on new product risk taking. *Journal of Product Innovation Management, 16*, 282–294.

Mustafa, M. A., & AI-Bahar, J. F. (1991). Project risk assessment using the analytic hierarchy process. *IEE Transactions of Engineering Management, 38*, 46–52.

Olsson, R. (2007). In search of opportunity management: Is the risk management process enough. *International Journal of Project Management, 25*, 745–752.

Perminova, O., Gustanfsson, M., & Wikstrom, K. (2008). Defining uncertainty in projects—A new perspectives. *International Journal of Project Management, 26*, 73–79.

Perry, J. G., & Hayes, R. W. (1985). Risk and its management in construction projects'. *Proceedings of Institution of Civil Engineers, Part 1, 78*, 499–521.

PMBOK. (2004). *A guide to the project management body of knowledge*. Newtown Square, PA: Project Management Institute.

PMBOK. (2008). *Guide to the project management body of knowledge* (4th ed.). Newtown Square: Project Management Institute.

PMBOK. (2013). *A guide to the project management body of knowledge* (5th ed.). Newtown Square, PA: Project Management Institute.

Pop, D. M. (n.d.). *Tackling corruption in development projects: World Bank Sanctions and Corporate*. Retrieved from Febraury 15, 2016, http://www.sustainalytics.com/tackling-corruption-development-projects-world-bank-sanctions-and-corporate-risks.

Primo, M. A. M., & Filho, J. F. R. (2012). The role of procurement and supply chain in the success of large projects. In G. Lim, & J. W. Herrmann (Eds.), *Proceedings of the industrial and systems engineering research conference*.

Raz, T., & Michael, E. (2001). Use and benefits of tools for project risk management. *International Journal of Project Management, 19*, 9–17.

Simon, H. A. (1965). *The shape of automation for men and management*. New York: Harper and Row. Reprint of Simon, H. A. (1960). *The new science of management decision*. New York: New York University.

Tah, J. H. M., & Carr, V. (2001). Towards a framework for project risk knowledge management in the construction supply chain. *Advances in Engineering Software, 32*, 835–846.

Viswanathan, B. (2015). *Understanding the 4 types of risks involved in project management*. Retrieved from February 13, 2016, http://project-management.com/understanding-the-4-types-of-risks-involved-in-project-management/.

Vrijhoef, R., & Koskela, L. (2000). The four roles of supply chain management in construction. *European Journal of Purchasing & Supply Management, 6*, 169–178.

Ward, S. C. (1999). Assessing and managing important risks. *International Journal of Project Management, 17*(6), 331–336.

Ward, S., & Chapman, C. (2003). Transforming project risk management into project uncertainty management. *International Journal of Project Management, 21*, 97–105.

Williams, T. M. (1994). Using a risk register to integrate risk management in project definition. *International Journal of Project Management, 12*(11), 17–22.

WSDOT. (2014). *Project risk management guide*. Washington State Department of Transportation.

Part V
Islamic Banking and Finance

Chapter 70
Musharakah Financing as Addressed in IFSB Standard: A Regulatory Perspective

Abdussalam Ismail Onagun

Abstract Islamic finance has continued to expand and demonstrate its resilience in the current more challenging international financial environment. However, this expansion has been confined in terms of debt-based contracts, rather than employing equity-based contracts such as a Musharakah contract. Principally Islamic finance promotes transactions that are based on profit and risk sharing through Mudarabah (partnership of work and capital) and Musharakah (joint venture) contracts, thus encouraging participatory finance and promoting participation in the risk-reward and financial results. However, statistics suggests that the industry has put more weight on the debt-financing instruments. There are several reasons and rationales put forward by the Islamic banks for the non-existence of the Musharakah contract. The majority of Islamic banks have limited themselves to low-risky trade-financing assets. This research paper analyse the Musharakah financing and reasons why Islamic banks tend to avoid such financing models from mainly two facets: Shari'ah perspective and regulatory perspective. Shari'ah perspective will highlight the main Shari'ah issues and minimum Shari'ah requirements that need to be observed while employing Musharakah contract in Islamic banks, while the regulatory perspective will underscore the significance of risk management dimension, minimum capital adequacy and Shari'ah-compliant securitisation related to Musharakah exposures. Finally the chapter concludes on the role of implementing IFSB standard in solving the risk exposure in Musharakah financing and the role of regulatory authority in implementing equity-based contract (Musharakah financing).

Keywords Regulatory authority • Trade-financing • Islamic banks • Musharakah financing • Securitisation

A.I. Onagun (✉)
University of Modern Sciences, Dubai, UAE
e-mail: i.abdussalam@ums.ae; abdussalam3@yahoo.com

© Springer International Publishing Switzerland 2017   783
R. Benlamri, M. Sparer (eds.), *Leadership, Innovation and Entrepreneurship as Driving Forces of the Global Economy*, Springer Proceedings in Business and Economics, DOI 10.1007/978-3-319-43434-6_70

Introduction

Musharakah contract is the second form of equity-based financing. Unlike Mudarabah, Musharakah requires the contribution of funds of all parties involved in the business. In modern Islamic banking practices, Musharakah is used as a mode of financing. When a client requests financing from an Islamic bank for a particular project, the bank signs a Musharakah contract with the client after studying the project. By this way, the bank becomes a partner with the client and they share the profits or losses occurred by the project. The aims and objectives of this research paper are to address the reasons why Islamic financial institutions tend to avoid profit- and loss-sharing products (*Musharakah* financing) and how the implementation of equity-based contract (*Musharakah* financing) by regulatory authority can offer solutions for this problem.

Literature Review

Definition of Musharakah

Musharakah financing which is equity-based participation is executed by Islamic banks to their clients in the form of partnership contracts where both parties share profits and losses in comparison with the conventional banks' system which are interest-based banking. Musharakah literally means sharing which is originated from an Arabic word "shirkah".

However, it technically means a form of partnership agreement between two or more parties which are the Islamic bank and its clients where they contribute their capital to a specific venture in which the profits generated are shared based on the pre-agreed terms in the Musharakah contract while the losses are shared in regard to the capital contribution ratio of each party.

The ventures that the parties contribute their capital in must be Shari'ah compliant such as trading, investments and construction. In addition, "Islamic banks use this contract on the liability side to attract deposits through investment accounts" (Ibrahim, 2012). Furthermore, the below diagram explains the process of a *Musharakah* financing in Islamic financial institutions (Tahani, 2014).

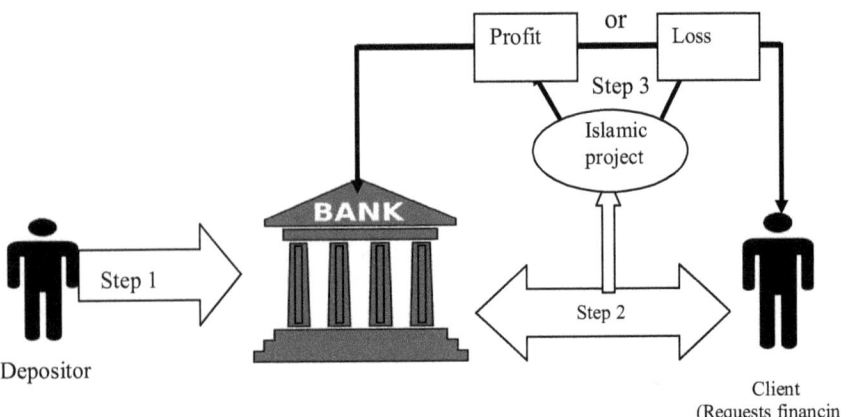

Step 1: Depositors deposit funds in the bank.

Step 2: By using Musharakah contract, the Islamic bank and its client, who requested financing for an Islamic project, mix their funds together in order to finance an agreed-upon Islamic project for a certain period of time. Both of them have the right to contribute to the management of the project.

Step 3: The Musharakah project might generate profit or suffer loss. If it generates profit, then it will belong to both parties according to the agreed-upon ratio in the Musharakah contract. But, if it suffers a loss, it will be shared in proportion to the capital contribution of each party (Tahani, 2014).

Legality of Musharakah Financing

The legality of Musharakah contract is based on Quran, Sunnah and consensus by Muslim jurists. As for the Quran, several verses indicate the legitimacy of Musharakah contract such as in (Surat Al-Nisa':12): "but if more than two, they share in a third".

The legality of Musharakah financing in the Sunnah is based on several narrations such as the narration by Abu Hurayrah that the Prophet SAW said: "I am the third (partner) of the two partners as long as they do not betray each other. When one of them betrays the other, I depart from them" (Bukhari, 1989). This Hadith is an evidence of avoiding betrayal in Musharakah financing among the partners.

Concerning the consensus of Muslim jurists, the consensus of the legality of Musharakah contract is mentioned by one of the Muslim jurists Imam Ibn al-Munzir in his book which is "And they (Muslim jurists) agree on the validity of partnership where each of the two partners contributes capital in dinar or dirham, and co-mingles the two capitals to form a single property which is indistinguishable, and they would sell and buy what they see as (beneficial) for the business, and the surplus will be distributed between them whilst the deficit will be borne together by them, and when they really carry out [as prescribed], the partnership is valid" (Tahani, 2014).

Types of Musharakah

For the purpose of determining the minimum capital adequacy requirement, IFSB-2 makes distinctions between the three main categories of *Musharakah* and provides guidance for how to apply appropriate risk weight for such investments to calculate minimum capital requirements for *Musharakah* exposure under three categories (IFSB, 2005a, 2005b) explained below:

(a) Private commercial enterprise to undertake trading activities in foreign exchange, shares and/or commodities. This type of *Musharakah* exposes the Islamic banks to the risk of underlying activities, namely foreign exchange, equities or commodities.

(b) Private commercial enterprise to undertake a business venture. This type of *Musharakah* exposes the Islamic banks to the risk as an equity holder, which is similar to the risk assumed by a partner in venture capital or a joint venture, but not to market risk. As an equity investor, the Islamic bank serves as the first loss position and its rights and entitlements are subordinated to the claims of secured and unsecured creditors.

(c) Joint ownership of real estate or movable assets (such as cars) is divided into two subcategories.

- *Musharakah* with *Ijārah* sub-contract: Ownership of such assets can produce rental income for the partnership, through leasing the assets to third parties by means of *Ijārah* contracts. In this case, the risk of the *Musharakah* investment is essentially that of the underlying *Ijārah* contracts, i.e. credit risk mitigated by the collateral represented by the leased assets. However, in some cases the lessee is not a third party but the IIFS's partner as customer. The existence of such an *Ijārah* sub-contract in addition to a *Musharakah* exposes the IIFS to credit risk in respect of the partner's obligation to service the lease rentals.
- *Musharakah* with *Murābahah* sub-contract: The Islamic bank is entitled to its share of revenue generated from selling the assets to third parties by means of *Murābahah* contracts that expose the Islamic banks to credit risk in respect of the *Murābahah* receivables from the buyer/counterparty.

Discussion and Analysis

Shari'ah *Requirements of Musharakah Financing*

The details below are the *Shari'ah* requirements in the implementation of *Musharakah* investment/financing which include but not limited to the following list:

(a) **Capital contribution in *Musharakah* contract**

- All forms of debts shall not qualify as *Musharakah* capital. All account receivables and payment due from other partner or third parties are considered as debt.
- A non-monetary asset with an integral debt component to the asset may be contributed as a *Musharakah* capital provided that the integral debt is less than 50 % of the asset value.
- The issue of funds placed with the Islamic financial institutions in the form of deposits may be invested as capital in a *Musharakah* contract.
- The rights, obligation and liabilities of all assets contributed to the Musharakah venture shall be jointly and severally assumed by partners.
- The issue of any loss of capital in the course of the venture shall be recognised as capital impairment.
- The capital of the IIFS is to be invested in *Shari'ah*-compliant investments or business activities.

(b) **Profit sharing in *Musharakah***

- Priority of profit distribution in *Musharakah* contract that stipulates a prede-termined fixed amount of profit to one partner which deprives the profit share of the other partner.
- The profit-sharing ratio may be revised either subject to the mutual consent of the partners or subject to a certain benchmark agreed upon by the partners as the case may be. The profit expressed in the form of a certain percentage should not be linked to the capital amount.
- A profit-sharing ratio may be ultimately translated into a fixed percentage based on the capital investment amount once profit is realised. A partner who has agreed to a certain profit-sharing ratio may waive the rights to profits to be given to another partner on the basis of principle of Mubarahat (waiver) at the time of profit realisation and distribution as well as at the time of the contract.
- The mechanism for estimating profit on Musharakah capital employed may be benchmarked to conventional benchmarks, such as but not limited to base lending rate (BLR), in order to determine the indicative profit rate. Profit may be distributed from actual or realised profits through the sale of assets of the Musharakah partnership (al-tandhid alhaqiqi or al-fi'li). Profit distribution may also be on the basis of constructive valuation (al-tandhid al-hukmi) of the assets including accounts receivables.

(c) **Guarantee in Musharakah contract**

- All partners in a Musharakah contract maintain the assets on a trust basis. Therefore, in the case of misconduct, negligence or breach of contract of managing partner, is it acceptable to impose capital charge on him or her if he or she can't provide any evidence:

Shari'ah issues

- The issue of the managing partner to bear direct/indirect expenses and expenditures of the asset with the increase in his or her profit, in order to facilitate the accounting procedure
- The issue of permissibility for a partner in *Musharakah* contract to stipulate that another partner provides a personal guarantee to cover cases of misconduct, negligence or beach of contract
- The extending of guarantee in the cases of misconduct, negligence or beach of contract to the expected profits, supported by the feasibility study, and not confined to the guarantee of losses
- Mechanisms and practical applications for the use of *Musharakah* contract as alternative to overdrafts

---

(d) **Diminishing Musharakah (also known as *Musharakah Mutanaqisah*)**

- The issue of permissibility for partners in diminishing Musharakah to give a binding promise that entitles the other partner to acquire, on the basis of a sale contract, his or her equity share gradually, according to the market value/face value or a price agreed at the time of acquisition.
- The issue of permissibility for a partner in diminishing Musharakah to rent or lease the share of the other partner for a specified amount and for whatever dura-tion and responsibility of periodical maintenance of this share. (Dr Abdussalam: Do you think I have addressed these two issues in the table below?)

Shari'ah issues

Item	*Shari'ah* requirement	Observation
Two agreements in one	Shari'ah prohibits the combination of two agreements in one transaction that are made conditional upon each other	It is still permissible for the contracting parties to combine the two contracts of Musharakah and ijara into one document as long as both were concluded separately and do not overlap
Refinancing	The transaction may be seen as two contracts (old and new contract) in one	It is akin to having a new partner in a new partnership in the same venture/asset, albeit with different value. The first Musharakah financing must be terminated for the new Musharakah to take place
Ownership	As a partner in the ownership of the property, the financier shares the responsibility and risks arising from the said property. In an ijara relationship, the owner (lessor) has to bear the cost of basic and structural maintenance while the occupying party (customer/lessee) shall bear the routine and operational maintenance of the property	Since the customers' ultimate objective of engaging in the transactions is to own an asset, and not merely to rent it for a certain period of time, it has been arguably accepted that the customer should bear all the costs, particularly when the customer is acknowledged as the sole legal owner in the document of title
	The general principle expounds that takaful of an asset is the responsibility of the owner; however some stress that it should be at the expense of the hirer	Some Shari'ah legal opinions affirmed that it is lawful to make the hirer responsible for a known amount of insurance as it may then become part of the lease payment
Wa'ad (unilateral promise)	By virtue of the wa'ad, the customer shall be obliged to acquire the bank's ownership share in the property at the buyout amount when there are changes in circumstances resulting in illegality, even if it is not caused by the customer	In contemporary juristic opinions, wa'ad becomes legally binding if it is made conditional upon the fulfilment of an obligation and the promisee has already incurred expense on the basis of such a promise
Compensation	Some view penalties for late payment of rentals as not permissible	The AAOIFI Shari'ah Rules for ijara and ijara muntahiya bittamlik provided that the lessee shall undertake to donate a certain amount or percentage of rental due in the case where there is no good reason for late payment
		There are slight divergences in the legal documentations, while a legal documentation explicitly requires such compensation to be donated to any registered charitable organisation or utilised for any charitable purpose; the other documentation is silent in this regard

(continued)

Sale of share in the case of non-indebtedness	The bank may exercise its rights as trustee to sell off the property and the proceeds/loss should be shared between the partners according to stated ratios	As redemption and failure to redeem are always the two common scenarios, the partners will be stuck with the business in the event that the redeeming party fails to do so. This explains why agreements are slanted in favour of banks over the redeeming party
	As a Shari'ah requirement, the redemption sum or formula has to be certain and fixed in advance. Hence, any reference to the market price at the point of redemption may trigger issues of riba	
Event of loss on property	The loss will be shared by the bank and customer according to the last ownership ratio if there is shortfall in the recovery of payment	The customer usually pays to the bank the difference between the amount due to the bank and the amount so realised
		Until payment of such differential amount, the customer shall pay late payment compensation charges on the differential sum until the date of actual payment made
Event of default (in the case of developer's winding up or property abandoned)		The customer shall be obligated to acquire the bank's ownership share in the property at the buyout amount for matters such as "developer's winding up" and "property abandoned", which are not the fault of the customer
		This resembles a conventional loan whereby the customer will continue to make payments if the property is destroyed until the insurance proceeds are received

Regulatory Requirements of Musharakah Financing

Risk Management

The distinct risk profile of *Musharakah* contract, which is a form of equity participation, exposes the IIFS to various types of risks, such as counterparty credit risk, market risk, liquidity risk and reputational risk. An IIFS acts as a partner in a *Musharakah* contract and is exposed to the risk of losing its capital upon making payment of its share of capital in a *Musharakah* contract. A *Musharakah* can expose the IIFS either to capital impairment risk or to "credit risk", depending on the structure and purpose of the *Musharakah* and the types of asset in which the funds are invested (IFSB-2, 2005).

In addition, when IIFS employs different financing instruments (where one of which includes *Musharakah*) at different contract stages, as different stages may give rise to different risks, in all cases, IIFS should give considerations as to the quality of the partner (i.e. the risk profiles of potential partners: *Muārib* and/or *Musharakah* partner), underlying business activities and ongoing operational matters.

IFSB has recognised the significance of this contract and the Guiding Principles of Risk Management (IFSB-1, 2005) provide a set of guidelines of best practices for establishing and implementing effective risk management in IIFS including *Musharakah*, which give practical effect to managing the risks underlying the business objectives that IIFS may adopt.

The capital invested through *Musharakah* may be used: (1) to purchase shares in a publicly traded company or privately held equity, or (2) invested in a specific project, portfolio or through a pooled investment vehicle. In the case of a specific project, IIFS may invest at different investment stages.

In short, a number of operational challenges will be faced by the IIFS when employing *Musharakah* contract, among other things:

1. **Identifying and monitoring the transformation** of risks at various stages of *Musharakah* investment life cycles
2. Lack of due diligence because of **lack of reliable information** on which to base their investment appraisals. Such due diligence is essential to the fulfillment of IIFS's fiduciary responsibilities as an investor of IAH funds on a *Musharakah* basis;
3. *Shari'ah*-**compliant risk-mitigating techniques** (e.g. quality of the *Takaful* or insurance coverage), which reduce the impact of possible capital impairment of an investment
4. **Potential manipulation of reported** results leading to overstatements or understatements of partnership earnings
5. **Inappropriate and inconsistent valuation** methodologies
6. Lack of **stress analysis and cash flow predictability** in *Musharakah* exposures
7. **Strength of the *Musharakah* partner** (i.e. ineffective management and substandard partners' quality; management and partner difficulties have contributed to difficulties in managing properties)
8. **Divestment and liquidation** (i.e. criteria for exit strategies, including the redemption of equity investments and the divestiture of underperforming investments)
9. **Political, legal and regulatory environment** (i.e. government support and project/business venture's importance for the country, favourable and stable regulatory environment, well-defined property rights to function efficiently, unfair treatment in taxation is also considered to be a major obstacle, secondary markets for trading in Islamic financial instruments, particularly Musharakah, are non-existent, and enforceability of contracts).

Capital Adequacy Requirements

The IIFS that is exposed to the risks inherent in *Musharakah* activities is required to hold sufficient capital. The Capital Adequacy Standard (IFSB-2), which complements Pillar I in Basel II, provides guidelines on minimum capital requirements for exposures in various contracts including *Musharakah* that enable an IIFS to measure the extent to which its capital position is commensurate with its overall risk profile and business strategy, thereby assessing its ability to absorb a reasonable level of unexpected losses before becoming insolvent.

These requirements cover the risk of losing invested capital arising from entering into contracts or transactions that are based on the *Musharakah* and diminishing *Musharakah* where the IIFS and their customers/partner(s) contribute to the capital of the partnership and share its profit or loss.

For the purpose of determining the minimum capital adequacy requirement, IFSB-2 makes distinctions between the three main categories of *Musharakah* and provides guidance for how to apply appropriate risk weight for such investments to calculate minimum capital requirements for *Musharakah* exposure under three types of *Musharakah* financing explained in the types of *Musharakah*:

In addition to applying simple risk weight method (i.e. 400%) as stated in the IFSB-2, in appropriate cases, the supervisor may permit an IIFS to employ an alternative approach, namely **the supervisory slotting criteria approach**. Under this method, an IIFS is required to map its internal risk grades into four (i.e. between 90 and 270% RW) supervisory categories for specialised financing as set out in Appendices of the IFSB-2, and each of these categories will be associated with a specific risk weight.

Regulatory Issues
Some regulatory authorities view that the 300–400% RW is too high.

Shari'ah-Compliant Securitisation of Musharakah-Related Exposures

Apparently *Musharakah*-based contracts demand higher capital adequacy requirements, but IIFS can also benefit from taking exposures in *Musharakah* in terms of capital relief through *Shari'ah*-compliant securitisation. The IFSB has recognised this under IFSB-7 (2009), where business ventures organised as *Musharakah* partnerships by IIFS can be securitised, and the resultant *sukuk* are tradable. This is for relief from higher capital requirements on these exposures; however, an originating IIFS may exclude securitised exposures from the calculation of its risk-weighted assets only if all of the conditions have been met as set under asset derecognition criteria in IFSB-7 (2009).

Role of the Regulatory Authority

The role of regulatory authority is also important to be underlined. The regulatory authority should satisfy itself that adequate policies and procedures are in place for *Musharakah* exposure risk management, taking into account the IIFS's appetite and tolerance for risk. In addition, the regulatory authority should also ensure that IIFS has sufficient capital when engaging in equity investment activities. In regard to calculating minimum capital requirements for *Musharakah* exposures, regulatory should provide adequate guidance to IIFS, who wishes to employ regulatory slotting criteria approach as stated in IFSB-2 (2005).

Conclusion

In concluding remarks, there is compelling need to diversify the IIFS's portfolio with right mix of debt and equity contracts. This diversification can be achieved by following IFSB guidelines. However, IIFS should be familiar and competent, to offer development finance products based on *Mudarabah* and *Musharakah* principles, which supposedly would open the access to capital for entrepreneurs who are committed towards their business but are hampered by their lack of asset collaterals. The existences of Musharakah instrument in IIFS will be in compliant not only with the profit motive of the IIFS but also with socio-economic objectives.

The regulatory authority should be open to providing adequate incentives for risk and profit sharing (Musharakah financing) and the Islamic finance industry needs to adopt more conformed standards to enhance system predictability and stability while promoting greater awareness among fund suppliers about the terms and conditions of profit sharing under different contractual arrangements. For instance as illustrated and well articulated in one of the papers of Sundararajan (2007): for an IAH who largely provides funds on a Mudarabah basis and the Islamic financial institution which invests these funds (often commingled with shareholders' and other funds) in various Islamic financial contracts (like salam, istisna', Musharakah) the risk is the expected variance in the measure of profit distribution between investment account holder (IAH) and bank. IFIs have to recognise that this uncertainty or Mudarabah risk can arise from a variety of factors both systemic and bank specific. Risk mitigation for IAH can be achieved through use of profit equalisation reserves (PER), investment risk reserves (IRR) and variation in mudarib's share.

In this regard, IFSB has provided guidelines for Musharakah financing and IFSB Guiding Principles on Risk Management have served a good purpose. They provide guidance for different risks to which Islamic finance industry is exposed and offer guidance on the methodology for credit risk, market risk, liquidity risk, operational risk, equity investment risk and rate of return risk for different types of financial transactions.

References

IFSB. (2005). *IFSB-2: Capital adequacy standard for institutions (other than insurance institutions) offering only Islamic financial services*.

IFSB. (2005). *IFSB-1: Guiding principles on risk management for institutions (other than insurance institutions) offering only Islamic financial services (IIFS)*.

IFSB. (2009). *IFSB-10 Guiding principles on Shari'ah governance for institutions offering Islamic financial services, 2009*.

Sundararajan, V. (2007). Risk characteristics of Islamic products: Implications for risk measurement and supervision. In S. Archer & R. A. A. Karim (Eds.), *Islamic finance: Regulatory challenge*. Singapore: Wiley.

Tahani, N. (2014). *Equity based financing in Islamic banks*. Case study of Dubai Islamic Bank.

Chapter 71
Performance Measurement of KMI 30 and KSE 30 Index in Karachi Stock Exchange

Ali Salman

Abstract There is a dramatic shift in the investment preference of investors from conventional to Shariah-complaint companies in the last decade. This study provides evidence on the performance measurement of Karachi Meezan Index which represents Shariah-complaint stocks in comparison to KSE 30 which represents conventional stocks registered under Pakistan Stock Exchange formerly known as Karachi Stock Exchange. Daily index prices are incorporated in the analysis from 21 March 2012 to 7 September 2015. Independent sample t-test model is employed to measure the difference in the risk and return of each index. Regression analysis is used to study the relationship between stock return and financial ratios. Results showed that KMI stocks generate higher average return and lower risk as compared to KSE 100 index. Moreover, KMI 30 index shows higher risk-adjusted return of Treynor ratio as compared to conventional counterpart. In regression analysis, net income margin shows a significant negative relationship with KSE 30 index return. However, DER shows negative relationship with KMI 30 index but not significant.

Keywords KMI 30 index • KSE 30 index • Risk and return • Risk-adjusted return • Financial ratios

Introduction

A general opinion exists among investors that ethical stocks underperform as conventional counterparts. It is argued that ethical investors likely to earn less than the market portfolio due to lack of diversification (Bauer, Otten, & Rad, 2006). Over the past years, it is observed that the demand for Islamic financial securities has improved immensely as compared to conventional securities. The three major reasons highlighted by Davies and Reuters (2012) for shift in the investment trend from conventional to Syariah-based financial products: Firstly, increase in the demand for

A. Salman (✉)
Lecturer at University of South Asia, Lahore, Pakistan
e-mail: ali.salman@usa.edu.pk; salmankhawaja1@gmail.com

© Springer International Publishing Switzerland 2017
R. Benlamri, M. Sparer (eds.), *Leadership, Innovation and Entrepreneurship as Driving Forces of the Global Economy*, Springer Proceedings in Business and Economics, DOI 10.1007/978-3-319-43434-6_71

Syariah-complaint financial products in Muslim-majority countries all over the world. Secondly, most studies show that Islam is the fastest growing religion in the West irrespective of negative propaganda carried by the Western social media (Foreign Policy-2015, n.d.). Third, change in the preference attitude of Gulf oil-producing country investors for investment in Syariah-compliant companies.

Syariah-complaint financial products are described by conventional finance scholar as ethical based company but there is a difference between both of the terms. Syariah-complaint investment is not only subject to ethical principles but also to rules of Maqasid al Shariah. Islamic-compliant companies are not only based on the legal maxim of "*permissibility*" on the matter of Mu'amalat except what is clearly prohibited under primary sources of Syariah. According to Maqasid al Shariah, it is clearly stated to protect faith, life, wealth, linage, and intellect through abstaining from haram activities such as pork, liquor, gambling, or any other activity which is strictly forbidden in Islam. In relation to Riba (interest) in Quran Allah says

> "*O ye who believe! Fear Allah and give up what remains of interest, if you are truly believers. But if you do it not, then beware of war from Allah and His Messenger; and if you repent, then you shall have your principal; thus you shall not wrong nor shall you be wronged*". Chapter 2, Al Baqara, Verses 278–279

Gharar is defined by different scholars in two major ways: First it implies "uncertainty." Second, it implies "fraud or deceit." From Quran verses it proves that uncertainty is strictly prohibited. Maisir is defined as a contract between two parties where the ownership of an asset depends on a game of chance which depends on future uncertain outcome, for example Casino games, animals' games, or lottery. Maisir is defined as gambling or game of chance. According to Muhammad Ayub, Maisir is defined as wishing for something valuable without undertaking any liability against it or without paying anything in return as compensation for it or working for it. In Quran Misir is referred to as "game of arrows."

> They ask you about wine and gambling. Say: 'In them both lies grave sin, though some benefit, to mankind. But their sin is more grave than their benefit.' Qur'an, 2:219 (al-Baqara)

Qimar is a subset of maysir. Qimar is defined as wagering or betting. In simple terms it is related to zero sum of game theory where one person wins and other looses from a bet.

For registering as Syariah-compliant stock in KSE, the company must comply with the following conditions. Firstly, the company must not be involved in haram activities such as local selling, casino business, and gambling and pornography business. Secondly, interest-bearing debt which includes bank loans and finance lease must be less than 37% of total assets. Thirdly, non-Shariah investment such as investment in conventional bonds, T-bills, money market instrument like certificate of deposit, call deposit, floating rate notes, and Pakistan investment Bonds (PIB) must be less than 33% of total assets. Fourthly, ratio of illiquid assets to total assets should be greater than equal to 25%. Fifthly, the company's income from non-Shariah activities must not exceed 5% of its total revenue. Lastly, market price per share must be greater than net liquid assets per share.

Income from investment which incorporates an element of Riba is strictly prohibited under Islam rules of Muamalat because it causes unfair treatment with the borrowers through compelling them to pay un-justifying incremental cash flow over a period of time. Similarly, it also increases the level of uncertainty in the collection of payment. Conventional contracts such as forward contracts, SWAPS, and options are forbidden due to persistence of high level of uncertainty under them.

Pakistan Stock Exchange

Karachi Stock Exchange took birth on September 18, 1947. Recently, under new capital market reforms by the PML N government, a legislation is passed through which all three major stock markets of Pakistan like Islamabad, Karachi, and Lahore are merged into single entity named as Pakistan Stock Exchange on 16 January 2016. Initially, ex-Pakistan Stock Exchange commenced its operation along with five companies with the total paid-up capital of 47 million Rupees. However, with the passage of time, the trading activities took its momentum and until December 2015, there were 555 registered companies with the total market capitalization of $67 billion . There are total 883 local and 1886 foreign institution investors. Along with it, there are 400 brokerage houses and 21 asset management companies operating under the umbrella of PSE. There are 16 companies of PSE which are being traded in MSCI frontier market index. With the growing capacity of Pakistan Stock Exchange, Karachi automated trading system (KATS) was introduced in 2002 which had the initial capacity of 1 million share trade per day. Currently, there are five indices registered in PSE with the name of KSE 100 index, all share index, KSE 30 index, KMI 30 index, and all share Islamic index.

KMI 30 index was introduced in 2009 with joint collaboration of Pakistan Stock Exchange and Meezan Investment Firm to promote Islamic financial activities in Pakistan. KMI index represents a list of 30 companies which had cleared Syariah screen process and then been allowed to trade under the umbrella of Shariah compliant index (KMI 30). According to Al Meezan Investment Management Ltd. (n.d.), there are total 125 Shariah-compliant stocks registered in KSE for the year ended December 2014. KSE 30 and KMI 30 are calculated through the method of free float market capitalization.

This chapter examines the performance of KSE 30 Index which represents the average prices of 30 Syariah-complaint stocks. However, KSE 30 index represents average prices of all 30 stocks registered under KSE 30 index (Fig. 71.1).

Research Objectives

The main objectives of this chapter are:

1. To make comparison of the risk and return of Syariah-complaint stocks through KMI 30 index and conventional stocks through KSE 30 index

	KMI 30 Index	KSE 30 Index
Fixed Line Telecommunication	1	1
Oil and Gas	8	7
Construction and Material (Cement)	8	4
Chemicals	2	4
Electricity	2	3
Personal Good(Textile)	2	2
Pharma and Bio Tech	3	
Food Producers	1	1
General Industrials	1	
Engineering	1	
Commercial banks	1	7
Non-life insurance		1
Total	**30**	**30**

Fig. 71.1 OLY—Pakistan's pioneer think tank (2015)

2. To investigate relationship between financial ratios of Syariah-compliant companies registered under KMI 30 index and companies registered under KSE 30 index with their respective index returns

Hypothesis

Ho1 There is no significant difference between the average return of KSE 30 index and KMI 30 index.

Ho2 There is no significant difference in the level of risk between KSE30 and KMI 30 index.

Ho3 There is no significant relationship between the index returns and internal liquidity ratio (quick ratio) and operating efficiency ratio (total assets-to-turnover ratio) and operating profitability ratio (net income margin) and financial leverage ratio (total debt-to-total equity ratio).

Literature Review

Despite an increase in the popularity of Islamic finance in Muslim-majority countries still there is a deficiency of empirical research on the performance of Islamic and conventional stocks in Pakistan Stock Exchange. Malaysia and Indonesia are the pioneer countries which have worked on evaluating the performance of Islamic finance versus conventional finance through producing lot of literature over the last 10 years.

Researches on ethical grounds have faced lot of criticism from most of the academic scholars and practitioners over their contradiction on the principle of traditional portfolio theories such as modern portfolio theory of Markowitz (1952).

The performance of investment portfolio of Syariah and conventional stocks in Kuala Lumpur Composite Index was inspected by Ahmad and Ibrahim (2002) for the duration of 1999–2000. The research time period of the sample was divided into three categories: downward performance period, normal period, and growing period. Stock performance was evaluated with the help of relative rate of return, and risk was calculated with the help of standard deviation. The results showed that KLSI outperformed during growing period and underperformed during downward period and normal period. Overall, there is no significant difference found in all three periods.

Omran and Hussein (2005) examined the performance of Islamic stock index against the Dow Jones World Index on monthly data basis from the period of 1995 to 2003. The sample time duration was divided into three subcategories: bull period, entire period, and bear period. The return on indexes was calculated by using CAPM model, Treynor ratio, and Sharpe ratio. Islamic index showed positive abnormal returns in the bull time period and entire time period whereas they underperformed against their Dow Jones World Index in bear market time period.

Albaity and Ahmad (2008) studied the performance of Syariah index in comparison to non-Syariah composite index registered in Kuala Lumpur Stock Exchange from the time period of 1999 to 2005. They studied causality and Johansen cointegration test and risk-adjusted performance measurement techniques. The risk and return are explained with the help of statistical measures of mean and standard deviation. The results showed no significant difference in the returns of both indices and in long run both indices' returns showed opposite directions.

Ahmad and Albaity (2011) explored the difference in return between Syariah and conventional stock returns of companies registered in Malaysian Stock Exchange from the period of 2000 to 2006. Market capitalization, market-to-book ratio, price-to-earnings ratio, and debt-to-equity ratio were used to determine the stock returns. There were no significant difference between Syariah and conventional stock return. Market-to-book ratio and size were found to be the most significant variables in affecting the stock returns of Syariah stocks. However, market-to-book ratio and market risk were found to be significant variables to affect the return of non-Syariah stocks.

Financial ratios played a very critical role in evaluating the stock performance. Therefore, Manao and Deswin (2001) evaluated the relationship between the stock return and the financial ratios during the financial crisis in Indonesia by adding firm size as the variable. Seven financial ratios were used in the study: quick ratio (QR), earning per share (EPS), total assets turnover ratio (TATO), current liabilities to total assets (CLTA), price to book value (PBV), gross profit margin (GPM), and return on equity (ROE). Sample size of 120 manufacturing companies registered in Jakarta Stock Exchange were chosen for statistical testing. The selected companies were distributed into three categories of small size, medium size, and big size. In the results, PBV and earning per share showed significant stimulus on the above model.

The relationship between the stock returns and the variables such as firm size, cash flow from operating activities, and financial ratios were investigated by Martani et al. (2009) by using the sample of manufacturing companies listed in Indonesian Stock Exchange. The results showed that net profit margin (NPM), PBV, ROE, and TATO during the period of 2003 to 2006 had shown a significant effect on stock-adjusted return and abnormal return.

Natarajan and Dharani (2012) in their study examined the risk and return of Nifty Index and Nifty Syariah index during the time period of January 2011 to 31 December 2010. The sample time duration was divided into bull and bear market period from January 2011 to 31 December 2010. The objectives of the research were to investigate the risk and return of both indexes and test the presence of any significant difference between both indices in India. The return of both indexes was calculated by using Sharpe ratio, Treynor ratio, and Jensen's alpha ratio. Simple *t*-test was used to measure the difference in mean return of both indices. The results showed that both indices performed in the same style.

In this chapter, I have examined the relation between the stock index returns of KMI 30 and KSE 30 index to financial ratios which includes the internal liquidity ratio, operating efficiency ratios, operating profitability ratios, and financial risk (leverage ratios) of all the companies registered. Internal liquidity ratios include current ratio, quick ratio, and cash conversion cycle.

Operating efficiency ratios include TATO and net fixed assets turnover ratio. Operating probability ratios include gross profit-to-sales ratio, total debt-to-total investment capital ratio, and total debt-to-total assets ratio.

Methodology

This study is based on secondary data collected from Pakistan Stock Exchange on daily indices prices of KMI 30 and KSE 30 which were collected from 21 March 2012 to 7 September 2015. The reason for selection of this time period is the non-availability of data of daily index prices of KMI 30 index since January 2009. For the purpose of good performance evaluation, standardization is achieved through taking same time period for both indices in the calculation. KSE 30 index represents the characteristic and performance of all conventional stocks whereas KMI 30 index symbolizes the characteristics and performance of Syariah-compliant stocks.

Return on financial instrument depends on two components. Firstly the capital gain which is derived through calculating the change in market prices called capital gain or loss. Secondly the dividend on holding the stock which can be on quarter, semiannual, or annual basis solely depends on the companies' policies. In this research, daily returns on stocks are computed without adjusting the dividend impact with the help of the following formula (Fig. 71.2):

$$Rt = Ln\left(Pt \, / \, Pt - 1\right)$$

Rt is the daily return on index.

	KMI 30 Index	KSE 30 Index	KSE 100 Index
Mean	10.5786	9.7533	10.0556
Standard Deviation	.28223	.20621	.30983
Skewness	-.402	-.494	-.343
Kurtosis	-1.136	-1.269	-1.290
Beta	0.91	0.66	1
Minimum	10.03	9.35	9.49
Maximum	11.01	10.03	10.50

Fig. 71.2 Brigham & Ehrhardt, Financial Management, 11 Edition, Chapter 4, pg.148

Pt is the daily price of time period of t.
Pt − 1 is the daily price of prior period of t.

Variability on the investment return is measured with the help of standard deviation in the average returns of a portfolio and beta which denotes systematic risk (it shows the volatility of individual stock or portfolio return to market portfolio return). Beta coefficient of both indices is calculated by using the following formula:

$$\beta_p = \frac{Cov\left(r_p - r_b\right)}{Var\left(r_b\right)}$$

BP is the beta which represents the portfolio of KSE 30 index and KMI 30.
Rp shows average return of individual index.
Rp (KMI) represents KMI 30 index (Syariah-compliant stock return — Karachi Meezan Index).
Rp (KSE) represents KSE 30 index (non-Syariah-compliant stock return — Karachi Stock Index).
Rb represents the average return of market portfolio which is denoted by KSE 100 index.
Var (Rb) is variance in return of market portfolio represented as KSE 100 index.
RF (risk-free rate) is being represented by (KIBOR) Karachi interbank offer rate over 12 month period since year 2012 to 2015.

Risk-Adjusted Return Performance Measurement

There is positive relationship between risk and return. The higher the risk, the higher the return and vice versa. Therefore, risk-adjusted measurement is necessary in evaluating the performance of an investment. There are several performance measurement techniques in capital market theory which helps in measuring the performance of portfolio of assets by incorporating the risk factor. Three famous risk-adjusted measurement techniques are Jensen's ratio, Treynor ratio, and Sharpe ratio. All these are employed in this research.

Year	Shape Ratio		Treynor Ratio		Jensen's Alpha	
	KMI 30	**KSE 30**	**KMI 30**	**KSE 30**	**KMI 30**	**KSE 30**
2012	-28.321	-62.34	89.149	9070.801	-0.051	-0.001
2013	6.255	-0.312	9.286	-0.284	-0.062	0.004
2014	6.335	-18.613	-23.610	148.87	0.004	-0.002
2015	24.062	6.22	10.809	-743758.6	-0.128	0.000
Average	**2.08275**	**-18.761**	**21.4085**	**-183635**	**-0.0593**	**0.00025**

Fig. 71.3 Google.com, 2015

Sharpe ratio measures the reward-to-variability ratio, in other words excessive average return over the risk-free rate per unit of total risk of the portfolio. Excessive return is the difference between return on individual stock or portfolio minus risk-free rate which is KIBOR in this case. This model was developed by Nobel Laureate William F. Sharpe. The assumption in this research is that all three indices consist of well-diversified portfolio of assets which means that there is negative correlation among stocks in all three respective portfolio of stocks. Secondly, we assume that data is normally distributed. Generally, the higher the value, the better the performance and vice versa (Fig. 71.3):

$$S_p = \frac{\bar{r}_p - \bar{r}_f}{\sigma_p}$$

Ri is the return of stock market index (KSE 30/KMI 100).
Rf is the risk-free rate of return (KIBOR rate).
σi is the standard deviation of stock market index (KSE 30/KMI 30).

Second performance measurement technique is Treynor ratio. It is defined as the excess return on investment over the riskless investment over per unit of systematic risk called market risk:

$$TI = \frac{Ri - Rf}{Bi}$$

Ri is the return of stock market index (KSE 30/KMI 100).
Rf is the risk-free rate of return (KIBOR rate).
Bi is the market risk of respective index (KSE 30 index and KSE 100 index return).
Ri is the return of stock market index (KSE 30/KMI 100).
R*m* is the market benchmark return which is KSE 100 index.
Bi is the market risk of respective index (KSE 30 and KMI 30).

Financial Ratio Analysis

Regression analysis is used to evaluate the relationship between the stock return of both respective indices of Shariah- and non-Shariah-compliant stocks in relation to their respective financial performance. Financial ratios are categorized into four categories: liquidity ratio which explains the ability of a company to pay back short-term obligation. Therefore, quick ratio is used to measure the solvency position of companies as compared to current ratio because closing stock is less liquid asset; hence, it is deducted from current assets in quick ratio calculation. Operating efficiency is measured with the help of TATO. Profitability is calculated with the help of net income margin.

Independent Variable

Liquidity performance:	*Quick ratio (QR) = (Current assets- closing stock)/current liability*
Operating efficiency:	*Total assets turnover (TATO) = (Sales/closing total assets)*
Profitability ratio:	*Net income margin (NIM) = (Net income/sales)*
Financial leverage:	*Debt-to-equity ratio (D/E) = Total liabilities/total assets-total liabilities*

Dependent Variable

Stock return *(Rt)*:	*Average of daily stock returns* of
KMI 30 index *(Rt (KMI)*:	*Shariah-compliant stock return index*
KSE 30 index *(Rt (KSE)*:	*Conventional stock return index*

Hypothesis

There is no relationship between the financial ratios of stock return of both Shariah- and non-Shariah-compliant stocks in relation to their liquidity ratio, operating efficiency ratio, profitability ratio, and financial leverage ratio.

Results and Finding

The main purpose of this research is to exam the financial performance of Shariah-complaint stock index in comparison to conventional stock index registered in Pakistan Stock Exchange through comparing the risk and return of each respective index. SPSS descriptive statistics analysis is run to measure the difference in the risk and return of each index. The collected data is nonparametric because data do not follow the conditions of normal distribution; therefore, independent sample *t*-test is applied. As shown in Table 71.1, KMI 30 index has high mean value as compared to KSE 30 index and KSE 100 index. However, it confirms that Shariah index provides higher average return of 10.59 as compared to conventional stock indices of KSE 30 and 100 index of 9.753 and 10.0556, respectively.

Table 71.1 Index risk and return

	KMI 30 index	KSE 30 index	KSE 100 index
Mean	10.5786	9.7533	10.0556
Standard deviation	.28223	.20621	.30983
Skewness	−.402	−.494	−.343
Kurtosis	−1.136	−1.269	−1.290
Beta	0.91	0.66	1
Minimum	10.03	9.35	9.49
Maximum	11.01	10.03	10.50

Table 71.2 Risk-adjusted return performance measurement of KMI 30 index AND KSE 30 index

Year	Sharpe ratio		Treynor ratio		Jensen's alpha	
	KMI 30	KSE 30	KMI 30	KSE 30	KMI 30	KSE 30
2012	−28.321	−62.34	89.149	9070.801	−0.051	−0.001
2013	6.255	−0.312	9.286	−0.284	−0.062	0.004
2014	6.335	−18.613	−23.610	148.87	0.004	−0.002
2015	24.062	6.22	10.809	−743,758.6	−0.128	0.000
Average	**2.08275**	**−18.761**	**21.4085**	**−183,635**	**−0.0593**	**0.00025**

Standard deviation is used as proxy to measure the risk of deviation from the average mean return for each index. The result shows that KMI 30 index has a higher risk of 28.2% as compared to 20.62% of KSE 30 index. KSE 100 index depicts lower mean return of 10.0556 as compared to KMI 30 index return which is 10.5786. However, the KSE 100 has higher risk as compared to KMI30 index. The reason may be that Syariah stocks are more frequently traded as compared to conventional stocks in KSE whereas in IDX (Indonesian Stock Exchange) results show an opposite result in the research conducted by Setiawan and Oktariza (2013). Beta measures the sensitivity of individual stock or index return to market return; the results show that both Shariah and conventional indices have lower sensitivity as compared to market by 0.91 and 0.66. KMI 30 shows the maximum average return of 11.01 and KSE 30 index shows minimum average return of 9.35.

Risk performance measures are also engaged in this return to perform a better evaluation of each Shariah and conventional indices.

As shown in Table 71.2, according to Sharpe ratio, KMI 30 has a better higher average risk-adjusted return of 2.08 as compared to −18.76 of KSE 30 index return for the years 2012–2015. However, according to Treynor ratio measures reward to volatality ratio. it is calculated as return on individual portfolio less return on risk free asset divide by market beta which is defined as systematic risk. Hence, KMI 30 index shows positive higher return of 21.40 among all three techniques of performance measurement. KSE 30 index shows positive return only under Jensen's alpha in the last 3 years.

Regression analysis is employed to measure the relationship between the financial ratios of Shariah and conventional indices with their respective return over the

Stocks Variable	Conventional		Shariah	
	t-statistics	Prob	t-statistics	Prob
C	1773.991	.000	1888.070	.000
Quick ratio (QR)	.989	.326	.983	.328
Total assets turnover ratio (TATO)	1.090	.279	.831	.408
Net income margin(NIM)	-3.650	.000	.515	.608
Debt to equity ratio(DER)	.140	.889	-.350	.727

Fig. 71.4 Ratio analysis of conventional and Shariah stocks (*conventional*: R-square $= .174$, adjusted R square $= .129$; *Shariah*: R-square $= .019$, adjusted R square $= .021$)

last 3 years from 2011 to 2014. The reason for an exemption of year 2015 is that the audited financial statements of most of the listed companies are not published yet. Ordinary least square method is used to find the relationship between the dependent variables which are KMI 30 and KSE 30 index return and independent variables are quick ratio QR, TATO, net income margin (NIM), debt-to-equity ratio (DER) (Fig. 71.4).

The results in Fig. 71.4 show the relationship between conventional stock index return with the financial ratios. The variables like QR, TATO, and DER show a positive relationship with KSE 30 index but these independent variables do not have significant influence on conventional stock index return. However, NIM shows a significant negative relationship at 5 % level of significance with the KSE 30 index return. It means that there is an inverse relationship between net profit margin and stock return. As profitability of conventional stocks increases, return on conventional stocks falls. R square values explain the proportion of variation in the dependent variable explained by the independent variable value. Hence, in the above model R square shows regression square value as 17.4 % variation which means that change in return on conventional stock index return is not properly being explained by the given dependent variables.

The results in Fig. 71.4 explain the relationship between Shariah index return with the respective companies' financial ratios. The result shows a positive relationship between Shariah index return with their counter index but it does not show a significant relationship between the variables.

R square value is approximately 2 % in Shariah and 17.4 % in conventional stock index return. It explains that only 2 % and 17.4 % variation in dependent variables are being explained by the above model; however, there are 98 % and 82.6 % other variables which are not incorporated in the above regression model such as price to earnings, earning per share, and return on equity.

Conclusion

This chapter has empirically focused on measuring the performance of Shariah and conventional index registered under Pakistan Stock Exchange from March 2012 to November 2015. The risk and return between both indices are calculated with the help of SPSS, independent sample *t*-test, and relationship between financial ratios and stock returns is measured by ordinary least square technique.

The results show that there is significant difference in the return between Shariah-compliant stocks represented by KMI 30 index which follows the Shariah rules and principles and conventional stock return represented by KSE 30 index. In Pakistan Stock Exchange KMI 30 shows higher average return against KSE 30 index and KSE 100 index. On the other side, KMI index shows lower risk of 28.22 % than 30.98 % of KSE 100 index.

Furthermore, modern risk-adjusted return techniques of Sharpe ratio, Treynor ratio, and Jensen's alpha ratio are employed in this chapter and results show that KMI 30 has a better higher average risk-adjusted return of 2.08 as compared to −18.76 of KSE 30 index return. However Treynor ratio return of KMI 30 index is 21.40 which is higher among all other remaining techniques of performance measurement.

Furthermore, the results of regression analysis show that NPM has a significant negative relation with conventional index return whereas QR, TATO, and DER do not have any significant relationship with the stock returns of Shariah and conventional stocks.

According to Martani, Mulyono, and Khairurizka (2009) and Purnomo (1998), regression model is more feasible for explaining the relationship between the non-financial and independent variables like political condition, unemployment, investor's preference, and attitude or government policies whereas dependent variable can be used as stock prices of a company. Overall, it can be concluded that in Pakistan stock market general investors' decision for investment in the type of stock is merely based on personal prejudice and word of mouth rather than objectivity yield from the financial performance analysis of their annual.

References

Ahmad, Z., & Ibrahim, H. (2002). A study of the performance of the KLSE Syariah index. *Malaysian Management Journal, 6*(1), 25–34.

Al Meezan Investment Management Ltd. (n.d.). *Knowledge Centre Shariah Screening Criteria*. Al Meezan Investment Management Ltd., Web. July 3, 2015.

Albaity, M., & Ahmad, R. (2008). Performance of Syariah and composite indices: Evidence from Bursa Malaysia. *Asian Academy of Management Journal of Accounting and Finance, 4*(1), 23–43.

Albaity, M., & Ahmad, R. (2011). A comparative analysis of the firm specific determinants of Syariah compliant versus on-Syariah compliant firms in Bursa Malaysia. *Asian Journal of Business and Accounting, 4*(1), 59–84.

Bauer, R., Otten, R., & Rad, A. (2006). Ethical investing in Australia: Is there a financial penalty?. *Pacific-Basin Finance Journal, 14*(1), 33–48. http://dx.doi.org/10.1016/j.pacfin.2004.12.004

Davies, A (2012) Global Islamic finance assets hit $1.3 trillion, Reuters, viewed December 2012, http://www.reuters.com/article/2012/03/29/islamic-financegrowth-idUSL6E8ET3KE20120329.

Foreign Policy-2015. (n.d.). *The list: The world's fastest growing religions comments*. Web. June 27, 2015.

Google.com. (2015). *Sharpe ratio formula—Google Search*. Retrieved October 25, 2015, from https://www.google.com/search?q=sharpe+ratio+formula&source=lnms&tbm=isch&sa=X&v ed=0CAcQ_AUoAWoVChMImuiw3vjdyAIVgeimCh36vg35&biw=1242&bih=566#imgrc= VNm06TQ4KbL8uM%3A.

Hussein, K., & Omran, M. (2005). Ethical investment revisited: Evidence from Dow Jones, Islamic indexes. *Journal of Investing, 14*(3), 105–124.

Manao, H., & Deswin, N. (2001). Asosiasi Rasio Keuangan dengan Return Saham: Pertimbangan Ukuran Perusahaan serta Pengaruh Krisis Ekonomi di Indonesia.

Markowitz, H. (1952). Portfolio selection. *Journal of Finance, 7*(1), 77–91.

Martani, D., Mulyono, & Khairurizka, R. (2009). The effect of financial ratios, firm size, and cash flow from operating activities in the interim report to the stock return. *Chinese Business Review, 8*(6), 44–55 (ISSN: 1537–1506).

Natarajan, P., & Dharani, M. (2012). Shariah Compliant Stocks in India - a Viable and Ethical Investment Vehicle. *Arabian Journal of Business and Management Review, 1*(6), 50–62.

OLY—Pakistan's Pioneer Think Tank (2015). KMI 30 index composition. Retrieved November 2, 2015, from http://oly.com.pk/KMI-30-index-composition/.

Purnomo, Y. (1998). Keterkaitan Kinerja Keuangan dengan Harga Saham. *Usahawan, 27*(12).

Setiawan, C., & Oktariza, H. (2013). Syariah and conventional stocks performance of public companies listed on Indonesia Stock Exchange. *Journal of Accounting, Finance and Economics, 3*(1), 51–64.

Chapter 72
The Challenges and Opportunities of Islamic Banking in Lebanon

Jamil Hammoud

Abstract This chapter presents the results of phase one of a two-phase research work about the opportunities and challenges of Islamic banking in Lebanon. It is motivated by the fact that in 12 years, only four Islamic banks are operating in the country with less than 1 % market share.

Phase one is an open-ended exploration using interviews with ten key informants and industry experts in a qualitative approach. In phase two (in process), the panel of key informants will be expanded and the interviews will be structured and semi-structured.

It is hoped that this research will contribute toward better development of the Islamic banking industry in the country.

Keywords Islamic banking • Islamic finance • Banking • Lebanon • Islamic economics

Introduction

Islamic banking and finance have gained significant importance throughout the last three decades, not only in Arab and Islamic countries, but also in other areas of the world, especially Europe, North America, and Australia.

Islam prohibits the charging and payment of interest in financial transactions, and advocates risk sharing and investments in productive business activities deemed in line with the religion's system of morals and values. Consequently, Islamic banking refers to a system of banking that complies with Islamic law, known as "Shari'ah" law, the underlying principles of which are mutual risk and profit sharing between parties, assurance of fairness and transparency for all stakeholders, and prohibition of speculation.

In spite of wide appreciation in a number of Islamic communities for such products as "Mudarbah" and "Murabahah," the absence of Shariah-compliant legal framework, needed to make interest-free banking acceptable, remains the major

J. Hammoud (✉)
Rafic Hariri University, Mechref, Lebanon
e-mail: hammoudja@rhu.edu.lb

© Springer International Publishing Switzerland 2017   809
R. Benlamri, M. Sparer (eds.), *Leadership, Innovation and Entrepreneurship as Driving Forces of the Global Economy*, Springer Proceedings in Business and Economics, DOI 10.1007/978-3-319-43434-6_72

snag behind the relatively low penetration of Islamic banking transactions in financial markets. This is of course in addition to traditional, cultural, and social challenges in accepting the idea of Islamic finance and banking.

Whereas the challenge of the legal framework could be tackled by governmental legislative and legal institutions, the sociocultural challenge has thus far proven to be difficult, especially in countries dominated by alternative religious value systems. Moreover, pluralistic society countries such as Lebanon seem yet to have their own distinctive sets of challenges.

Need for the Study

BLOM Development Bank's General Manager Moataz Natafji recently told Global Finance that (June 12, 2015) deposits in the entire Lebanese banking system amount to $152 billion. About $1 billion of that is the share of the country's four Islamic banks, which constitutes less than 1 %. Yet 12 years have passed since the central bank first authorized Islamic banking (Law 525).

Obviously, the level of Islamic banking activity in the country throughout the past 12 years has been insignificant, and questions arise as to why this industry has failed thus far to do better.

Research Issue and Methodology

In light of the need for the study clarified above, and in comparison with significant growth figures reported for the Islamic banking industry worldwide, the author of this chapter poses the following research question: What are the opportunities and challenges facing Islamic banking in Lebanon?

With little research conducted about the Lebanese Islamic banking industry, as shown in the literature review below, our research in this chapter is exploratory and qualitative. It consists of semi-structured interviews conducted in a two-stage process.

In the first stage, interviews are conducted with ten key informants, selected for their hands-on knowledge about and expertise in the industry. Diligence was given to making sure that they are representatives of various sides of the industry who are able to provide perspectives on identification of the main issues with an approach of open-ended exploration. Consequently, five of the ten are experts from three of the four Islamic banks of the country, ranging in positions from Branch Manager to General Manager. In addition, two of the ten are experts from two conventional banks. While two more are religious clerics with direct experience in Islamic banking Shari'ah committees, one is an academic specialized in Islamic finance and banking.

The second stage of the research process, which is currently in progress, is designed to reduce open-ended exploration by addressing specific issues identified in the first stage. It is also designed to expand and diversify further the panel of experts interviewed, hopefully to solidify the results.

Literature Review

Studies on the opportunities and challenges of Islamic banking in general are numerous. For purposes of a better understanding, we are able to broadly classify them into three types: general systemic studies (Ahmad, Masood, & Khan, 2010; Amin, 2008; Ariss & Sarieddine, 2007; Dusuki & Aboizaid, 2007; Iqbal, 2001; Iqbal, Ahmad, & Khan, 1998), country-specific studies Akram, Rafique, & Alam, 2011; Butt et al., 2011; Jabr, 2003; Njamike, 2010; Sanusi, 2011), and Lebanon-specific studies (Bizri, 2014; Saleh & Zeitun, 2005).

General Systemic Studies

General systemic studies treat various aspects related to the viability of the Islamic banking system as a whole. Ahmad et al. (2010) treated the use of *Takaful* and its popularity in the global insurance sector. They conclude that this instrument faces a number of challenges including inadequate qualified staff in both conventional insurance and *Shari'ah* finance, lack of awareness, lack of financial innovations, inadequate interpretation of what constitutes *Takaful*, lack of regulatory frameworks, and disparity in accounting practices.

Ariss and Sarieddine (2007) investigate guidelines for risk management and capita adequacy in Islamic banking. They cite challenges of Islamic banking as liquidity risk, lack of a wide range of derivative instruments, and complications in measurement of *Shari'ah* compliant.

In his study, Iqbal (2001) identifies a number of challenges which face Islamic banking and he names limited set of short-term financial instruments and inadequate medium- to long-term financial instruments, limited coverage of Islamic finance, concentration of Islamic banking, poor risk management and governance framework, and difference between Islamic finance in theory and in practice.

These three studies and others seem to converge around the challenges of the legal and regulatory framework, the interpretation of Shari'ah principles and compliance, the availability of intermediate- and long-term financing instruments, divergence in accounting standards, and lack of awareness.

Review of Country-Specific Studies

Country-specific studies examine the conditions particular to the context of the country in question. For instance, Ahmad et al. (2010) examine the growth and development as well as the prospects of the Pakistani Islamic banking system. The authors track significant growth and expect Islamic banking branches to expand in the future. However, they cite competition and cultural differences as major challenges facing the industry.

Jabr (2003) concludes that the challenges and opportunities of Islamic banks in the Palestinian territories are as follows: lack of adequate banking law for Islamic banking; lack of awareness; lack of operational differences between Islamic and conventional banks; lack of experience in Islamic *Shari'ah*; excessive short-term financial instrument; inability to make use of *Mudaraba* and *Musharaka*; inferior technical resources and technology; and inability to differentiate ownership from management.

Njamike (2010) uses descriptive analysis to explore the issues and challenges that would be faced by Islamic banks in Zimbabwe. The analysis shows that the major problems and challenges in introducing Islamic banking in Zimbabwe are political intervention in the selection of borrowers, financial instability, inability of the government to restore law and order in the country, resistance from the banking community, inadequate infrastructure for information dissemination, inconsistency in policy making and implementation of the fiscal and monetary authorities, Central bank control and supervision of Islamic banking with unqualified persons in Islamic finance, absence of Islamic interbank, misperception, current political and economic situation, and default culture.

Finally, Sanusi (2011) explores the issues and challenges of Islamic banking in Nigeria. The study finds that the challenges of Islamic banking in Nigeria are inadequate manpower; lack of *Shari'ah*-compliant liquidity management instruments; lack of Islamic insurance (*Takaful*); lack of knowledge of accounting and auditing standard require by Islamic financial institutions; inadequate legal framework; lack of *Shari'ah* scholars knowledgeable in conventional economics, law, accounting, banking, and finance; problem of multiple taxation; lack of tax relief on Islamic banking profits; and misperception of Islamic banking in Nigeria.

The studies cited above and others similar to them do not differ greatly in their results from systemic studies. However, issues of cultural differences and the running of conventional banking alongside Islamic banking become more evident and worrisome in the contexts of specific countries.

Lebanon-Specific Studies

Aside from numerous journalistic articles, we could not find more than a few scholarly studies addressing Lebanese Islamic banking and finance.

Bizri (2014) investigates the status of Islamic banking in Lebanon by addressing the perceptions of existing and potential clients. She finds "that clients consider five variables in deciding whether or not to patronize Islamic banks. These variables are trust in Islamic banks and their true compliance with Shari'ah, customers' familiarity with Islamic modes of finance, cost of financing and other transactions, accessibility of Islamic banks, and the quality of service offered by those banks." In his thesis, Chammas (2006) conducts a market analysis of Islamic finance in Lebanon with focus on needed modifications to the legal framework and suggestion of Islamic banking instruments appropriate for Lebanon.

Saleh and Zeitun (2005) adopt ratio analysis to examine the Lebanese experience with Islamic banking since the foundation of the first Islamic bank. They find that lack of public awareness and acceptance, lack of research and development institutions, inadequate manpower, and high competition from conventional banks offering Islamic windows are the major challenges of Islamic banking in Lebanon. They were however optimistic that Islamic banking in Lebanon will prosper because of its ability to attract more investment and capital into the country, the vital role it plays in financing and developing telecommunications, agriculture, industry sectors in the Lebanese economy, its long-term strategy to increase its customer base, and its current support from the general public as well as private business.

Data and Interpretations

Since the purpose of phase one of the research was open-ended exploration, interviewees were asked to answer mostly open-ended and unstructured questions. Only a few structured and common questions were asked. Open-ended exploration has the advantage of allowing interviewees to discuss whatever they want. Meanwhile, it allows for significant variations in issues raised, and concentration on issues deemed important by each interviewee from his/her angle of interest and expertise.

To interpret the data, the researcher utilized qualitative analytical tools such as identification of commonality, categorization, exclusion of irrelevant information such as personal experiences, reorganization, and synthesis.

Our analysis and interpretation of the data allowed us to categorize opportunities as market share potential and possible expansion into capital markets. Meanwhile, we were able to categorize challenges as legal and regulatory, social and cultural, and Shari'ah compliance.

Opportunities

With Islamic banking claiming less than 1% of deposits and assets, and an estimated Muslim population of more than 60%, all interviewees are convinced that Islamic banking has great potential to grow its market share. Islamic bankers suggest that one sure way to grow and claim bigger market share lies in the ability to diversify product and instrument offerings to satisfy customer's varied needs.

The second important opportunity identified was possible expansion into capital markets. One possibility in this regard that was talked about a lot was the issuance of Sukuk which would require the establishment of a secondary market and the development of trading mechanisms.

Challenges

All interviewees agreed that the inadequacy of the present legal and regulatory framework is a serious challenge. For instance, the Central Bank treats Islamic banks as traders, unlike conventional banks. This treatment implies double taxation, an issue that is yet to be resolved by the Ministry of Finance. Moreover, Islamic banks face risk-increasing restrictions in granting long-term housing loans. Regulatory restrictions have also limited the banks' ability to diversify their product and instrument offerings.

Social and cultural challenges stem from the label of "Islamic" in a pluralistic society with heightened confessional tensions. For non-Muslims, doing business with an Islamic bank is a compromise of one's own religious beliefs. As for Muslims, divisions between Shiite and Sunni seem to also impact the customer's choice of a bank. Yet all interviewees pointed their fingers at what they considered significant lack of awareness about and knowledge of Islamic banking.

Shari'ah compliance is also a challenge that has been complicating the work of Islamic banks. For one thing, interpretation of Shari'ah requirements is not always easy. A number of interviewees cited lack of agreement on how to price Mourabahah fees as an example. For another thing, bankers complain that subjecting products to Shari'ah requirements in many cases makes them lose their competitiveness.

Conclusions

This chapter reports the results of phase one of a two-phase research that is in progress.

Twelve years after the passage of the Islamic Banking Law in Lebanon, the industry is still in its start-up and early development stage. While the promise and the potential are still there to exploit, a number of serious challenges continue to face Lebanese Islamic banking.

Opportunities include potential market share and expansion into capital markets. Meanwhile challenges are categorized as legal and regulatory, social and cultural, and Shari'ah compliance. It should be kept in mind here that detailed elaboration of opportunities and challenges will constitute a part of phase two of the research. Meanwhile, phase two may still reveal additional issues.

References

Ahmad, M. I., Masood, T., & Khan, M. S. (2010). *Problems and prospects of Islamic banking: A case study of Takaful*. MPRA Paper No. 22232, Posted April 20, 2010/16:55.

Akram, M., Rafique, M., & Alam, H. M. (2011). Prospects of Islamic banking: Reflection from Pakistan. *Australian Journal of Business and Management Research, 1*(2), 125.

Amin, H. (2008). E-Business from Islamic perspectives: Prospects and challenges. *Journal of Internet Banking and Commerce, 13*(3), 1–4.

Ariss, R. T., & Sarieddine, Y. (2007). Challenges in implementing capital adequacy guidelines to Islamic banks. *Journal of Banking Regulation, 9*(1), 46–59.

Bizri, R. (2014). A study of Islamic banks in the non-GCC MENA region: Evidence from Lebanon. *The International Journal of Bank Marketing, 32*(2), 130–149.

Butt, I., Saleem, N., Hassan, A., Altaf, M., Jaffer, K., & Mahmood, J. (2011). Barriers to adoption of Islamic banking in Pakistan. *Journal of Islamic Marketing, 2*(3), 259–273. doi:10.1108/17590831111164787.

Chammas, G. (2006). *Islamic finance industry in Lebanon: Horizons, enhancements and projections.* Thesis at ESA, Beirut, Lebanon. Retrieved January 11, 2016, from https://ribh.files.wordpress.com/2007/09/islamic-finance-industry-in-lebanon-ghassan-chammas-esa-beirut.pdf.

Dusuki, A. W., & Aboizaid, A. (2007). A critical appraisal on the challenges of realising maqasid Al-Shari'ah in Islamic banking and finance. *IIUM Journal of Economics and Management, 15*(2), 143–165.

Iqbal, Z. (2001). Challenges facing Islamic financial industry. *Journal of Islamic Economics, Banking and Finance.*

Iqbal, M., Ahmad, A., & Khan, T. (1998). *Challenges facing Islamic banking.* Islamic Development Bank, and Islamic Research and Training Institute Occasional Paper No. 1.

Jabr, H. (2003). Islamic banking in Palestine challenges and prospects. *An-Najah Univ. J. Res. (H.Sc), 17*(1).

Njamike, K. (2010). Introduction of Islamic banking in Zimbabwe: Problems and challenges. *Journal of Sustainable Development in Africa, 12*(8), 70–78.

Saleh, A. S., & Zeitun, R. (2005). The development of Islamic banking in Lebanon: Prospects and future challenges. *Review of Islamic Economics, 9*(2), 77–91.

Sanusi, L. S. (2011). *Islamic finance in Nigeria: Issues and challenges.* Lecture delivered at Markfield Institute of Higher Education (MIHE), Leicester, UK, June 17, 2011.

Lightning Source UK Ltd.
Milton Keynes UK
UKHW021132211218
334386UK00002B/8/P